The

Works of Plato

IN FIVE VOLUMES

Volume IV

Translated by

Thomas Taylor

and

Floyer Sydenham

Published by

The Prometheus Trust

Volume XII
of
The Thomas Taylor Series

The Prometheus Trust

28 Petticoat Lane, Dilton Marsh,
Westbury, Wiltshire,
BA13 4DG, UK

A registered charity,
number 299648.

The Works of Plato, volume IV

This Edition published in 1996.
Reprinted 2008

ISBN 1 898910 11 1
and 978 1 898910 11 4

First Edition published in 1804.

British Library Cataloguing-in-Publication Data.
A catalogue record for this book is
available from the British Library.

Printed in England by Antony Rowe, Chippenham, Wiltshire.

CONTENTS

The Five Volumes of the Works of Plato

Volume I

General Introduction

The First Alcibiades

The Life of Plato

The Republic

Volume II

The Laws

The Timæus

The Epinomis, or *The Philosopher*

The Critias, or *Atlanticus*

Volume III

The Parmenides

The Phædrus

The Banquet

The Sophista

The Greater Hippias

Volume IV

The Theætetus

The Minos

The Crito

The Gorgias

The Second Alcibiades

The Politicus

The Apology of Socrates

The Phædo

The Philebus

Volume V

The Euthyphro

The Protagoras

The Laches

The Charmides

The Euthydemus

The Rivals

The Clitopho

The Cratylus

The Meno

The Theages

The Lysis

The Lesser Hippias

The Hipparchus

The Menexenus

The Io

The Twelve Epistles

Changes to the original text

i.   Where Taylor had *the one, the one itself, the good* or *the good itself* this edition gives these names capital initials; this to distinguish them as the highest names the Platonists gave to God. Other principles have been left in lower case.

ii.   A few very obvious grammatical errors and archaic spellings have been corrected; wherever there is any doubt as to the validity of possible errors the original has been followed.

iii.   We have followed Taylor's explicit method of printing Greek characters without accents or breathings (see his defence of his Greek at the end of his *The Fable of Cupid and Psyche* and also his reference to this in the Introduction of *Proclus' Commentary on Euclid*).

iv.   Many references to works quoted are added, and some original references are given more precise indicators.

v.   Stephanus line numbers have been added to the dialogues throughout. The ancient commentaries are also line numbered where possible: in this volume the numbering for Damascius' Commentary (in Taylor's time considered to be Olympiodorus' Commentary) on the *Philebus* is given and follows L G Westerink's *Damascius, Lectures on the Philebus* (North Holland Publishing Co., 1959), and also that on Olympiodorus' Commentary on the *Phædo*, which follows the same translator's *The Greek Commentaries on Plato's Phædo* (North Holland, 1976). It should be noted in the latter Commentary, that although Taylor refers throughout to Olympiodorus, modern scholarship also attributes the second book of this two book commentary to Damascius: the numbering of these books differ and can be distinguished by the fact that the first book's numbering has two sets of numbers (*eg*. 13.4), while the second book has only one (*eg*. .345). Greek text, where given, has the textual pagination.

vi.   Page numbers in references to works translated or written by Thomas Taylor refer to the Thomas Taylor Series, not original editions.

vii.   Some notes have been rearranged: a few short notes which were included in the Additional Notes have been inserted as footnotes, while several long footnotes are now to be found in the Additional Notes.

The Thomas Taylor Series

Volume I - *Proclus' Elements of Theology*

Volume II - *Select Works of Porphyry*
Abstinence from Animal Food; Auxiliaries to the Perception of Intelligibles; Concerning Homer's Cave of the Nymphs; The Wanderings of Ulysses -. Taylor

Volume III - *Collected Writings of Plotinus*
Twenty-seven treatises being all the writings of Plotinus translated by Taylor.

Volume IV - *Collected Writings on the Gods & the World*
Sallust On the Gods and the World; The Sentences of Demophilus; Ocellus on the Nature of the Universe; Taurus and Proclus on the Eternity of the World; Maternus on the Thema Mundi; The Emperor Julian's Orations to the Mother of Gods and to the Sovereign Sun; Synesius on Providence; Taylor's essays on the Mythology and the Theology of the Greeks.

Volume V - *Hymns and Initiations*
The Hymns of Orpheus together with all the published hymns translated or written by Taylor; Taylor's essay on Orpheus.

Volume VI - *The Dissertations of Maximus Tyrius*
Forty-one treatises from the middle Platonist, and an essay from Taylor - The Triumph of the Wise Man over Fortune.

Volume VII - *Oracles and Mysteries*
A Collection of Chaldean Oracles; Essays on the Eleusinian and Bacchic Mysteries; The History of the Restoration of the Platonic Theology; An essay on A Platonic Demonstration of the Immortality of the Soul.

Volume VIII - *The Theology of Plato*
The six books of Proclus on the Theology of Plato; to which is added a further book (by Taylor), replacing the original seventh book by Proclus, now lost. Extensive introduction and notes are also added.

Volume IX - *The Works of Plato I*
General Introduction, Life of Plato, First Alcibiades, Republic

Volume X - *The Works of Plato II*
Laws, Epinomis, Timæus, Critias.

Volume XI - *The Works of Plato III*

Parmenides, Sophista, Phædrus, Greater Hippias, Banquet.

Volume XII - *The Works of Plato IV*

Theætetus, Politicus, Minos, Apology of Socrates, Crito, Phædo, Gorgias, Philebus, Second Alcibiades.

Volume XIII - *The Works of Plato V*

Euthyphro, Meno, Protagoras, Theages, Laches, Lysis, Charmides, Lesser Hippias, Euthydemus, Hipparchus, Rivals, Menexenus, Clitopho, Io, Cratylus, Epistles.

Volume XIV - *Apuleius' Golden Ass & Other Philosophical Writings*

The Golden Ass (or Metamorphosis), On the Dæmon of Socrates, On the Philosophy of Plato.

Volumes XV & XVI - *Proclus' Commentary on the Timæus of Plato*

The Five Books of this Commentary, with additional notes and short index.

Volume XVII - *Iamblichus on the Mysteries and Life of Pythagoras*

Iamblichus On the Mysteries of the Egyptians, Chaldeans, and Assyrians; Iamblichus' Life of Pythagoras; Fragments of the Ethical Writings of Certain Pythagoreans; Political Fragments of Archytas, Charondas, Zaleucus, and other Ancient Pythagoreans.

Volume XVIII - *Essays and Fragments of Proclus*

Providence, Fate and That Which is Within our Power; Ten Doubts concerning Providence; The Subsistence of Evil; The Life of Proclus; The Fragments of the Lost Writings of Proclus.

Volume XIX - *The Works of Aristotle I*

The Physics, together with much of Simplicius' Commentary.

Volume XX - *The Works of Aristotle II*

The Organon: The Categories (& Porphyry's Introduction); On Interpretation; Prior and Posterior Analytics; The Topics; The Sophistical Elenchus.

Volume XXI - *The Works of Aristotle III*

The Great Ethics; The Eudemian Ethics; The Politics; The Economics.

Volume XXXI & XXXII - *Pausanias' Guide to Greece*

Pausanias' Guide to Greece: in ten books, with copious notes and an extensive index.

Volume XXXIII - *Against the Christians and Other Writings*

Celsus, Porphyry and Julian's writings against the Christians (extant fragments); Julian's Arguments Against the Christians; Thomas Taylor's miscellaneous verses, letters, articles, etc. drawn from his *Collectanea*, his *Miscellanies in Prose and Verse*, and his contributions to the *Classical Journal*; also includes his Rights of Brutes; his Reply to the Supplement of Dr Gillies; his appendix On Critics; his Panegyric on the Philosophers of Antiquity; and a bibliography.

THE

THEÆTETUS

A DIALOGUE

ON SCIENCE

INTRODUCTION

The following very learned and admirable dialogue is on a subject which, to a rational being, is obviously of the utmost importance. For what can be more important to such a being than an accurate knowledge of things human and divine, practical and theoretic? And as such a knowledge cannot be obtained without science, the inquiry what science is, must consequently rank among those investigations that are the most useful and necessary to man.

As this dialogue is wholly of the maieutic kind, Socrates, with admirable skill, acts the part of a midwife towards Theætetus, one of the principal persons of the dialogue, in leading forth his conceptions concerning science into light. For this purpose, he, in the first place, asks him what science is? And Theætetus replies, that science is geometry and arithmetic, together with other disciplines of this kind, and the several arts. This answer is however rejected by Socrates, as by no means according with the question; because, when asked what science is, he replies by enumerating how many sciences there are, and on what subjects they are employed. In the next place, Socrates introduces the definition of Protagoras, that science is sense. For Protagoras asserted, that man is the measure of all things, and that every thing was to every man such as it appeared to him. This doctrine was, indeed, founded in the philosophy of Heraclitus, of which the principal dogma was this, that nothing is permanent, but that all things are in a continual flux. Socrates, however, confutes this opinion, because, if it were admitted, the perceptions of the intoxicated and insane, of those who dream, and of those whose senses are vitiated by disease, would be true, because they appear to be so, though at the same time they are evidently false. From this hypothesis also, all men would be similarly wise, the opinions of the most illiterate in geometry would be as true as any geometrical theorems; and in the actions of human life the means of accomplishing any end would be indifferent, and consequently all deliberation and consultation would be vain.†

In order to demonstrate that science is not sense, Socrates, in the first place, obtains this from Theætetus, that sense arises from the soul

† This absurd opinion is very subtilely opposed by Sextus Empiricus. If, says he, every imagination be true, then the imagination that not every imagination is true will also be true, and so the assertion that every imagination is true will be false. Ει πασα φαντασια εστιν αληθης, και το μη πασαν φαντασιαν ειναι αληθη, κατα φαντασιαν υφισταμενον εσται αληθες· και ουτω το πασαν φαντασιαν ειναι αληθη γενησεται ψευδος.

perceiving corporeal things externally situated, through several organs of the body. And secondly, that one sense, or organical perception, cannot take cognizance of the object of another; as sight cannot see sounds, nor the hearing hear light and colours. Hence he infers, that when we compare the objects of several senses together, and consider certain things which are common to them all, this cannot be sense, or organical perception, because one sense cannot consider the object of another. And if there is any thing common to both, it cannot perceive it by either organ. Thus, for instance, when we consider sound and colour together, and attribute several things to them in common, as, in the first place, essence, and in the next place, sameness in each with itself, and difference from the other; when we also consider that both of them are two, and each of them one, by what sense or organ does the soul perceive all these things which are common both to sound and colour? It cannot be by the senses of sight or hearing, because these cannot consider each other's objects; nor can any other corporeal organ be found by which the soul may passively perceive all these, and consider the objects of both those senses of sight and hearing. Hence, Theætetus is made to confess that the soul does not organically perceive these things by any sense, but by itself alone without any corporeal organ.

Theætetus, therefore, being convinced that science is not sense, in the next place defines it to be true opinion. This, however, is confuted by Socrates, because rhetoric also produces true opinion when its assertions are true, but yet cannot produce science. For there never can be any science of things which are perpetually in motion, and which subsist differently at different times. Such, however, are human affairs with which orators are conversant, especially when they induce their hearers to believe that of which they are themselves doubtful. After this, Theætetus adds the definition of Leucippus and Theodorus the Cyrenæan, that science is true opinion in conjunction with reason; and hence, that things which possess reason can be known, but by no means those which are deprived of it. This, however, is also confuted by Socrates, who shows, that whether reason (logos) signifies external speech, or a procession through the elements of a thing, or definition, science cannot be true opinion in conjunction with reason.

Though Socrates, therefore, confutes all these definitions of science, as being erroneous, yet he does not inform us what science is; for this would have been contrary to the character of the dialogue, which, as we have already observed, is entirely maieutic, and consequently can do no more than present us with the conceptions of Theætetus fairly unfolded into light. As all these conceptions, therefore, are found to be false, we must search elsewhere for an accurate definition of science.

What then shall we say science is, according to Plato? We reply, that considered according to its first subsistence, which is in intellect, it is *the eternal and uniform intelligence of eternal entities;* but in partial souls, such as ours, it is *a dianoëtic perception of eternal beings;* and is, consequently, a perception neither eternal nor uniform, because it is transitive, and accompanied with the intervention of oblivion.

THE

THEÆTETUS

PERSONS OF THE DIALOGUE

EUCLID[†]   SOCRATES
TERPSIO   THEODORUS
AND THEÆTETUS[‡]

142a   EUC. Are you just now come, O Terpsio, or is it some time since you came from the country?

TER. I have left the country for a considerable time, and have been seeking for you about the forum, and wondered that I could not find you.

EUC. I was not in the city.

TER. Where then was you?

EUC. As I was going down to the port, I met with Theætetus, who was carried along from the camp at Corinth to Athens.

TER. Was he alive or dead?

b   EUC. He was living, but could hardly be said to be so: for he was in a very dangerous condition, through certain wounds: and, what is worse, he was afflicted with a disease while in the camp.

TER. Was it a dysentery?

EUC. It was.

---

† This Euclid was a celebrated philosopher and logician of Megara. The Athenians having prohibited the Megarians from entering their city on pain of death, this philosopher disguised himself in woman's clothes that he might attend the lectures of Socrates. After the death of Socrates, Plato and other philosophers went to Euclid at Megara to shelter themselves from the tyrants who governed Athens.

‡ This Theætetus is mentioned by Proclus on Euclid [II, 66, see TTS vol. XXIX, p. 145], where he gives a short history of geometry prior to Euclid, and is ranked by him among those contemporary with Plato, by whom geometrical theorems were increased, and rendered more scientific.

TER. What a man do you speak of as in a dangerous condition!

EUC. A worthy and good man, O Terpsio: for I just now heard certain persons paying him very great encomiums for his military conduct.

TER. Nor is this wonderful: but it would be much more wonderful if this had not been the case. But why was he not carried to Megara?

c   EUC. He hastened home; for I both entreated and advised him to do so: but it was against his will. And besides this, attending him in his journey, when I again left him, I recollected, and was filled with admiration of Socrates, who often spoke in a prophetic manner about other things, and likewise about this. For a little before his death, if I am not mistaken, meeting with Theætetus, who was then a young man, and discoursing with him, he very much admired his disposition. Besides this, when I came to Athens, he related to me his discourses

d   with Theætetus, which very much deserve to be heard; and observed, that he would necessarily be renowned, if he lived to be a man. And it appears indeed that he spoke the truth.

TER. But can you relate what those discourses were?

143a   EUC. Not verbally, by Jupiter: but as soon as I returned home, I committed the substance of them to writing, and afterwards at my leisure wrote nearly the whole of them, through the assistance of memory. As often too as I came to Athens, I asked Socrates about such particulars as I could not remember, and, on my return hither, made such emendations as were necessary; so that I have nearly written the whole discourse.

TER. True. For I have heard you assert the same thing before: and in consequence of always desiring to urge you to relate this discourse I am come hither. But what should hinder this from taking place at present? For I am perfectly in need of rest, as coming from the country.

b   EUC. I likewise accompanied Theætetus as far as Erineus; so that rest will not be unpleasant to me. Let us go, therefore, and while we rest a boy shall read to us.

TER. You speak well.

EUC. This then is the book, O Terpsio. But it was not composed by me, as if Socrates related it to me, as in reality he did, but as if he was discoursing with the persons with whom he said he discoursed. But he said that these were, the geometrician Theodorus, and Theætetus. That

c   we may not, therefore, in the course of the writing, be troubled with the frequent repetition of I say, and He said, He assented, or He denied, I have introduced Socrates himself discoursing with them.

TER. And this is not at all improper, O Euclid.

EUC. Here, boy, then, take the book and read.

d SOC. If, O Theodorus, I was more attentive to those in Cyrene than to any others, I should inquire of you respecting them, if any young men there applied themselves to geometry, or any other philosophic study. But now, as I love those less than these, I am more desirous to know which of our young men are likely to become worthy characters. For such as these I explore myself as far as I am able, and inquire after them of others, with whom I see young men associating. But you have by no means a few followers: and this very justly. For you deserve to

e be followed, both for other things, and for the sake of geometry. If, therefore, you have met with any young man who deserves to be mentioned, it would give me pleasure to hear some particulars respecting him.

THEO. Indeed, Socrates, it is in every respect fit both that I should relate, and that you should hear, what a youth I have met with from among your citizens. And if he were beautiful, I should be very much afraid to mention him, lest I should appear to be enamoured with him. But, now, (do not be indignant with me,) he is not handsome. For he resembles you, having a flat nose, and prominent eyes: but he has these in a less degree than you. You see I speak freely to you. Know then, that I have never yet met with any young man (though I have associated with many) who naturally possess a good disposition in such a wonderful degree. For it is difficult to find one who is docile, remarkably mild, and who besides this may compare with any one for fortitude. Indeed, I do not think there ever were any, nor do I see any

144a with these qualifications. For some are acute indeed, as this one, sagacious, and of a good memory; but they are for the most part prone to anger, and are hurried along precipitately like ships without their ballast, and are rather naturally furious than brave. And again, those

b whose manners are more sedate are in a certain respect sluggish and full of oblivion, when they apply themselves to disciplines. But the young man I am speaking of applies himself to disciplines and investigations in so easy, blameless, and ready a manner, that it may be compared to the silent flux of oil; so that it is wonderful that such a great genius should accomplish these things in such a manner.

SOC. You announce well. But of which of our citizens is he the son?

c THEO. I have heard the name, but I do not remember it. But he is in the middle of those who are now approaching to us. For both he, and these who are his companions, were just now anointed beyond the stadium; but now they appear to me, in consequence of having been anointed, to come hither. Consider, however, if you know him.

Soc. I do know him. He is the son of Euphronius the Suniensian, who was entirely such a man as you have just related the son to be; and who, besides being a worthy character, left behind him a very large estate.

d   Theo. His name, O Socrates, is Theætetus. But certain of his guardians appear to me to have dissipated his estate. However, notwithstanding this, he is wonderfully liberal with respect to money, Socrates.

Soc. You speak of a generous man: Order him to come to me, and sit with us.

Theo. I will. - Theætetus, come hither to Socrates.

Soc. By all means come, Theætetus, that I may behold myself, and see what sort of a face I have. For Theodorus says it resembles yours. But

e   if we had each of us a lyre, and he should say that they were similarly harmonized, ought we immediately to believe him, or should we consider whether he says this as being a musician?

Theæ. We should consider this.

Soc. On finding, therefore, this to be the case, should we not be persuaded by him? but, if he was ignorant of music, should we not disbelieve him?

Theæ. True.

145a   Soc. Now, therefore, I think, if we are at all careful respecting the similitude of our faces, that we should consider if he speaks as being a painter, or not.

Theæ. So it appears to me.

Soc. Is, therefore, Theodorus a painter?

Theæ. Not that I know of.

Soc. Nor is he a geometrician?

Theæ. He is perfectly so, Socrates.

Soc. Is he also skilled in astronomy, logistic, music, and such other disciplines as follow these?

Theæ. He appears to be so to me.

Soc. If, therefore, he says that we resemble each other in a certain part of our body, at the same time praising or blaming this resemblance, it is not altogether worth while to pay much attention to him.

Theæ. Entirely so, Socrates.

b   Soc. Take notice, therefore, O friend Theætetus, it is your business to evince, and mine to consider. For know, that Theodorus having praised in my hearing many strangers and citizens, has not praised any one of them so much as just now he did you.

c   THEÆ. It is well, Socrates; but consider whether he did not speak jocosely.

SOC. It is not usual for Theodorus to do so. But do not reject what is granted, in consequence of believing that he spoke this in jest, lest he should be compelled to bear witness. For no one can object to what he said. Persist, therefore, confidently in what is granted.

THEÆ. It is proper, indeed, to do so, if it seems fit to you.

SOC. Tell me, then, - Do you learn any geometry of Theodorus?

THEÆ. I do.

d   SOC. Do you, likewise, learn things pertaining to astronomy, harmony, and computation?

THEÆ. I endeavour to do so.

SOC. For I also, O boy, both from this man, and from others who appear to me to understand any thing of these particulars, endeavour to learn them; but, at the same time, I am but moderately skilled in them. There is, however, a certain trifling thing of which I am in doubt, and which I wish to consider along with you, and these that are present. Tell me, therefore, whether to learn is not to become wiser in that which any one learns?

THEÆ. Undoubtedly.

SOC. But I think that the wise are wise by wisdom.

THEÆ. Certainly.

e   SOC. But does this in any respect differ from science?

THEÆ. What?

SOC. Wisdom. Or are not those who have a scientific knowledge of any thing, also wise in this thing?

THEÆ. Undoubtedly.

SOC. Is, therefore, science the same as wisdom?

THEÆ. Yes.

SOC. This, therefore, is that which I doubt; and I am not able sufficiently to determine by myself what science is. Have we then any 146a thing to say to this? What do you say it is? And which of us can first give this information? But he who errs, and is perpetually detected in an error, shall sit as an ass, as the boys say when they play at ball. But he who shall be found to speak without error shall be our king, and shall order whatever he wishes us to answer. Why are you silent? Have I, O Theodorus, behaved in a rustic manner, through my love of conversation, and through my desire to make you discourse and become friends with each other?

b   THEO. A thing of this kind, O Socrates, is by no means rustic. But order some one of these young men to answer you. For I am unaccustomed to this mode of discourse; and my age does not permit me to become accustomed to it now. But a thing of this kind is adapted to these young men, and they will be greatly improved by it. For, in reality, youth is adapted to every kind of improvement. But, as you began with, do not dismiss Theætetus, but interrogate him.

SOC. Do you hear, Theætetus, what Theodorus says? whom I am of opinion you will not disobey. For you would neither be willing to do so, nor is it lawful for a young man to be unpersuaded by a wise man, when he commands in things of this kind. Tell me, therefore, in a proper and ingenuous manner, what science appears to you to be?

THEÆ. It is fit to comply, Socrates, since you command me. And if I in any respect err, do you correct me.

SOC. We shall by all means do so, if we are able.

THEÆ. It appears to me, then, that sciences are such things as any one may learn of Theodorus, such as geometry, and the other particulars which you just now enumerated. And besides these, the shoemaker's art, and the arts of other workmen; and that all and each of these are no other than science.

SOC. Generously and munificently, O friend, when asked by me concerning one thing, have you given many, and things various, instead of that which is simple.

THEÆ. How so? Why do you say this, Socrates?

SOC. Perhaps what I say is nothing: but I will tell you what I think. When you speak of the shoemaker's art, do you speak of any thing else than the science of making shoes?

THEÆ. Of nothing else.

SOC. But what when you speak of the carpenter's art? Do you speak of any thing else than the science of operations in wood?

THEÆ. Of nothing else than this.

SOC. In both therefore you define that of which each is the science.

THEÆ. I do.

SOC. But that which we asked, O Theætetus, was not this, of what things there is science, nor how many sciences there are; for we did not inquire, wishing to enumerate them, but in order to know what science itself is. Or do I say nothing?

THEÆ. You speak with perfect rectitude.

SOC. But consider also this. If any one should interrogate us respecting any vile and obvious thing, as, for instance, clay, what it is, if we should answer him, that clay is that from which pans, puppets and tiles are made, or certain other artificial substances, should we not be ridiculous?

THEÆ. Perhaps so.

Soc. In the first place, indeed, what can we think he who asks this question can understand from our answer, when we say that clay is that from which pans, puppets and tiles, or certain other artificial substances are made? Or do you think that any one can understand the name of a thing, when he does not know what that thing is?

THEÆ. By no means.

Soc. Neither, therefore, will he understand the science of shoes who does not know what science is.

THEÆ. Certainly not.

Soc. Nor, again, will he understand the currier's art, nor any other art, who is ignorant of science.

THEÆ. It is so.

Soc. The answer, therefore, is ridiculous, when any one, being asked what science is, gives for an answer the name of any art. For answers, that there is a science of a certain thing, when this is not what he was asked.

THEÆ. It seems so.

Soc. And, in the next place, when he might have given a short and simple answer, he wanders immensely. As in the question concerning clay, a short and simple answer might have been given, that clay is earth mingled with moisture. At the same time, dismissing the consideration of that which is composed of clay.

THEÆ. Now, indeed, Socrates, it thus appears to me to be easy. For you seem to ask that which lately came into my mind as I was discoursing with your namesake here, Socrates.

Soc. What was that, Theætetus?

THEÆ. Theodorus here has written a treatise on powers, concerning magnitudes of three and five feet, evincing that they are not commensurable in length† to a magnitude of one foot: and thus proceeding through every number as far as to a magnitude of seventeen feet, in this he stops his investigation. A thing of this kind, therefore, occurred to me, since there appear to be an infinite multitude of powers, we should endeavour to comprehend them in one thing, by which we may denominate all these powers.

Soc. Is a thing of this kind discovered?

THEÆ. It appears so to me. But do you also consider.

---

† Magnitudes commensurable in length are such as have the proportion to each other of number to number. As the square roots, therefore, of 3 and 5 feet cannot be obtained, those roots are incommensurable in length with the square root of one foot.

SOC. Speak then.

THEÆ. We give to the whole of number a twofold division: one, that which may become equally equal, and which we assimilate among figures to a square, calling it quadrangular and equilateral.

SOC. And very properly.

148a   THEÆ. But that number which subsists between this,† such as three and five, and every number which is incapable of becoming evenly even, but which is either more less, or less more, and always contains a greater and a lesser side, we assimilate to an oblong figure, and call it an oblong number.

SOC. Most excellent. But what follows?

THEÆ. Such lines as square an equilateral and plane number, we define
b   to be length; but such as square an oblong number, powers; as not being commensurate‡ to them in length, but to planes, which are capable of being commensurable. And about solids there is another thing of this kind.

SOC. Best of men, O boys: so that Theodorus cannot, as it appears to me, be accused of giving a false account.

THEÆ. But, indeed, Socrates, I am not able to answer you concerning science as I am concerning length and power; though you appear to me to inquire after a thing of this kind. So that again Theodorus appears to be false.

c   SOC. But what? if, praising you for running, he should say that he never met with any youth who ran so swift, and afterwards you should be vanquished in running by some adult who is a very rapid runner, do you think he would have less truly praised you?

THEÆ. I do not.

SOC. But with respect to science, (as I just now said,) do you think it is a trifling thing to find out what it is, and not in every respect arduous?

THEÆ. By Jupiter, I think it is arduous in the extreme.

d   SOC. Confide, therefore, in yourself, and think what Theodorus said. Endeavour, too, by all possible means to obtain a reason both of other things, and likewise of science, so as to know what it is.

THEÆ. It appears we should do so, O Socrates, for the sake of alacrity.

---

† Equally equal, or square numbers, are such as 4, 9, 16, 25, &c. and the numbers which subsist between these, and which Plato calls oblong, are 3, 5, 6, 7, 8, 10, 11, 12, &c.

‡ That is to say, the sides or roots of oblong numbers, such as the above, are incommensurable in length, or are surds.

SOC. Come then: for you explained just now in a beautiful manner. Endeavour, imitating your answer respecting powers, that just as you comprehended these, which are many, in one species, so you may comprehend many sciences in one reason or definition.

e THEÆ. But know, O Socrates, that I have often endeavoured to accomplish this, on hearing the questions which are discussed by you. But I can neither persuade myself that I can say any thing sufficient on this occasion, nor that I can hear any one discoursing as you advise; nor yet am I able to desist from investigation.

SOC. You are tormented with the pangs of labour, friend Theætetus, not because you are empty, but because you are full.

THEÆ. I do not know, Socrates: but I tell you what I suffer.

149a SOC. O ridiculous youth, have you not heard that I am the son of the generous, and at the same time severe, midwife Phænarete?

THEÆ. I have heard this.

SOC. And have you also heard that I study the same art?

THEÆ. By no means.

SOC. Know, however, that it is so; but do not betray me to others. For they are ignorant, my friend, that I possess this art; and in consequence of being ignorant of this, they do not assert this respecting me, but they say that I am a most absurd man, and that I cause men to doubt. Or have you not hear this?

b THEÆ. I have.

SOC. Shall I tell you the reason of this?

THEÆ. By all means.

SOC. Conceive every thing pertaining to midwives, and you will easily understand what I mean. For you know, that none of them deliver others, while they yet conceive and bring forth themselves, but when they are no longer capable of conceiving.

THEÆ. Entirely so.

SOC. But they say that Diana is the cause of this; who being herself

c a virgin takes care of births. She does not, therefore, permit those that are barren to be midwives, because human nature is too imbecil to undertake an art in which it is unexperienced: but she orders those to exercise this profession, who from their age are incapable of bearing children; by this honouring the similitude of herself.

THEÆ. It is likely.

SOC. And is not this also probable and necessary, that those who are pregnant, or not, should be more known by midwives than by others?

d THEÆ. Entirely so.

SOC. Midwives, likewise, by medicaments and enchantments, are able to excite and alleviate the pangs of parturition, to deliver those that bring forth with difficulty, and procure a miscarriage when the child appears to be abortive.

THEÆ. It is so.

SOC. Have you not also heard this concerning them, that they are most skilful bride-maids, as being perfectly wise, with respect to knowing what kind of man and woman ought to be united together, in order to produce the most excellent children?

THEÆ. I did not altogether know this.

e SOC. But you know that they glory in this more than in cutting the navel. For do you think it belongs to the same, or to a different art, to take care of and collect the fruits of the earth, and again, to know in what ground any plant or seed ought to be sown?

THEÆ. To the same art.

SOC. But in women, my friend, do you think the art pertaining to the care of offspring differs from that of collecting them?

THEÆ. It is not likely that it does.

150a SOC. It is not. But through the unjust and absurd conjunction of man and woman, which is called bawdry, midwives as being chaste avoid acting in the capacity of bride-maids, fearing lest by this mean they should be branded with the appellation of bawds, since it alone belongs to legitimate midwives to act as bride-maids with rectitude.

THEÆ. It appears so.

SOC. Such then is the office of midwives; but it is less arduous than the part which I have to act. For it does not happen to women, that b they sometimes bring forth images, and sometimes realities. But this is a thing not easy to discriminate. For, if it did happen, to distinguish what was true from what was false would be to midwives the greatest and the most beautiful of all works. Or do you not think it would?

THEÆ. I do.

SOC. But to my art other things belong which pertain to delivery; but it differs in this, that it delivers men and not women, and that it considers their souls as parturient, and not their bodies. But this is the c greatest thing in our art, that it is able to explore in every possible way, whether the dianoëtic part of a young man brings forth an image, and that which is false, or something prolific and true. For that which happens to midwives happens also to me: for I am barren of wisdom. And that for which I am reproached by many, that I interrogate others, but that I do not give an answer to any thing, is truly objected to me, owing to my possessing nothing of wisdom. But the cause of this is as follows: Divinity compels me to act as a midwife, but forbids me to generate. I am not, therefore, myself in any respect wise; nor is there any invention of mine of such a kind as to be the offspring of my soul. But of those who converse with me, some at first appear to be entirely void of discipline, but all to whom Divinity is propitious, during the course of the conversation, make a wonderful proficiency, as is evident both to themselves and others. This likewise is clear, that they do not learn any thing from me, but that they possess and discover many beautiful things in themselves: Divinity indeed, and I being the cause of the midwife's office. But this is evident from hence: Many, in consequence of not knowing this, but believing themselves to be the cause, and despising me, perhaps through the persuasions of others, have left me sooner than was proper; and after they have left me through associating with depraved characters, have become as to what remains abortive. Likewise, through badly nourishing what they have brought forth through my assistance they have destroyed it, in consequence of preferring things false and images to that which is true. Lastly, they have appeared both to themselves and others to be unlearned. One of these was Aristides the son of Lysimachus, and many others; who when they again came to me, in consequence of wanting my conversation, and being affected in a wonderful manner, some of them my dæmoniacal power restrained me from conversing with, but with others he permitted me to converse, who at length made a considerable proficiency. For those that associate with me suffer this in common with the parturient; they are tormented, and filled with doubt and anxiety, and this in a far greater degree than the parturient. This torment my art is able both to excite and appease. And such is the manner in which they are affected. But sometimes, O Theætetus, I very benignantly unite in marriage with others those who do not appear to me to be pregnant, as I know that they do not require my assistance; and (as I may say in conjunction with Divinity) I very sufficiently conjecture with whom it will be advantageous to them to be united. And many of these indeed I have delivered to Prodicus, and many others to wise and divine men. For the sake of this, O most excellent youth, I have been thus prolix in relating these things to you. For I suspect, as you also think, that you are tormented in consequence of being pregnant with something internally. Commit yourself therefore to me as being the son of a midwife, and as being myself skilled in what pertains to parturition. Endeavour, too, cheerfully to answer me what I shall ask you, and to the best of your ability. And if in consequence of considering what you say, it shall appear to me that you have conceived an image, and not that which is true, do not be angry with me, like women who are delivered of their first child, if I privately remove and throw it away. For many, O wonderful young man, are so affected towards me, that they are actually ready to bite me, when I throw aside any trifle of theirs, not thinking that I do this with a benevolent design; since they are very far from

d knowing that no divinity is malevolent to men, and that I do not perform any thing of this kind through malevolence. But it is by no means lawful for me to admit that which is false, and destroy that which is true. Again, therefore, from the beginning, O Theætetus, endeavour to inform me what science is; but by no means endeavour to speak beyond your ability. For if Divinity is willing and affords you strength, you will be able.

THEÆ. Indeed, Socrates, since you thus urge me, it would be base for any one not to offer what he has to say, with the greatest alacrity. It

e appears then to me that he who has a scientific knowledge of any thing, perceives that which he thus knows; and, as it now seems, science is nothing else than sense.

SOC. Well and generously answered, O boy: for it is requisite thus to speak what appears to be the case. But come, let us consider this in common, whether this offspring is any thing solid or vain. Do you say that science is sense?

THEÆ. I do.

152a SOC. You appear, indeed, to have given no despicable definition of science, but that which Protagoras[†] has given: though he has said the same thing, in a somewhat different manner. For he says that man is the measure of all things; of beings so far as they have a being, and of non-beings so far as they are not. Have you ever read this?

THEÆ. I have read it often.

SOC. Does he not, therefore, speak thus: such as particulars appear to me, such are they to me; and such as they appear to you, such are they to you: but you and I are men?

THEÆ. He does speak in this manner.

b SOC. But do you not think it probable that a wise man will not trifle, nor speak like one delirious? Let us, therefore, follow him thus: When the same wind blows, is not sometimes one of us stiff with cold, and another not? And one in a small degree, but another extremely cold?

THEÆ. This is very much the case.

---

† This sophist was of Abdera in Thrace. He was the disciple of Democritus, and an atheist. This his absurd opinion that science is sense, may however be considered as the fountain of experimental philosophy.

SOC. Whether, therefore, shall we say, that the wind at that time is in itself cold or not cold? Or shall we be persuaded by Protagoras, that to him who is stiff with cold, the wind is cold; but to him who is not, that it is not cold?

THEÆ. It appears so.

SOC. Does it, therefore, appear so to each?

THEÆ. Yes.

SOC. But for a thing to appear, is it the same as to be perceived?

THEÆ. It is.

c   SOC. Phantasy, therefore, and sense are the same in things hot, and every thing else of this kind. For such as every one perceives things to be, such they are and appear to be to every one.

THEÆ. So it seems.

SOC. Sense, therefore, is always of that which has a being, and is without falsehood, as being science.

THEÆ. It appears so.

SOC. Whether or no, therefore, by the Graces, was Protagoras a man perfectly wise; and did he obscurely signify this to us who rank among the vulgar, but speak the truth to his disciples in secret?

d   THEÆ. Why, Socrates, do you say this?

SOC. I will tell you, and it is by no means a despicable assertion. There is not anything which is itself essentially one thing;[1] nor can you properly denominate any thing, as endued with some particular quality. But if you denominate it as great, it will appear to be small; and if heavy, light. And all things subsist in such a manner, as if nothing was one thing, or any thing particular, or endued with a certain quality. But

e   from their lation, motion, and mixture with each other, all things become that which we said they were, and are not rightly denominated by us. For there is not any thing, which at any time *is,* but it is always in generation, or *becoming to be.* And in this all the wise in succession consent, except Parmenides;[†] *viz.* Protagoras, Heraclitus, and Empedocles: and of the poets, those who rank the highest in each kind of poetry, in comedy, indeed, Epicharmus, and in tragedy, Homer. For when this latter calls Ocean[2] and mother Tethys the origin of the gods, he asserts that all things are the progeny of flux and motion. Or does he not appear to say this?

THEÆ. To me he does.

153a   SOC. Who then can contend against such an army, and which has Homer for its leader, without being ridiculous?

---

† See the *Sophista* and *Parmenides* [TTS vol. XI].

THEÆ. It is not easy, O Socrates.

SOC. It is not indeed, Theætetus. Since this may be a sufficient argument in favour of their assertion, that motion imparts to things the appearance of being, and of becoming to be; but rest of non-being, and perishing. For heat and fire, which generate and govern other things, are themselves generated from lation and friction. But these are motions. Or are not these the origin of fire?

b   THEÆ. They are.

SOC. And besides this, the genus of animals originates from the same things.

THEÆ. Undoubtedly.

SOC. But what? Is not the habit of the body corrupted by rest and indolence, but for the most part preserved by exercise and motion?

THEÆ. It is.

SOC. But does not habit in the soul possess disciplines through learning and meditation, which are motions; and is it not thus preserved

c   and made better? But through rest, which is negligence and a privation of discipline, it does not learn any thing, or if it does, it forgets it. Is not this the case?

THEÆ. Very much so.

SOC. Motion, therefore, is good, both with respect to soul and body; but rest is the very contrary.

THEÆ. It appears so.

SOC. I add further, with respect to times of serenity and tranquillity, and all such as these, that rest putrifies and destroys, but that other things preserve. And besides this, I will bring the affair to a conclusion

d   by forcing the golden chain into my service. For Homer intended by this to signify nothing else than the sun;† because, as long as the sun and its circulation are moved, all things will be, and will be preserved, both among Gods and men. But if this should stand still, as if it were bound, all things would be dissolved, and that which is proverbially said would take place, *viz.* all things would be upwards and downwards.

THEÆ. But Homer appears to me also, O Socrates, to signify that which you say.

---

† Agreeably to this explanation of Homer's golden chain, Plato, in the sixth book of his *Republic*,[508a] calls the light of the sun "a bond the most honourable of all bonds." Hence, according to Plato, the circulation of the sun connects and preserves all mundane natures, as well as its light; and as the sun has a supermundane as well as a mundane subsistence, as we shall show in the notes on the *Cratylus*, it must also be the source of connection to those Gods that are denominated supermundane.

SOC. In the first place, therefore, O best of young men, conceive thus respecting the eyes: that which you call a white colour is not any thing else external to your eyes, nor yet in your eyes; nor can you assign any place to it. For, if you could, it would now have an orderly position, and would abide, and be no longer in generation.

THEÆ. But how?

SOC. Let us follow what we just now said, establishing nothing as essentially one thing; and thus black and white, and any other colour, will appear to us to be generated from the darting forth of the eyes to a convenient lation. And every thing which we denominate a colour, will neither be that which darts forth, nor that which is darted forth, but something between these, which becomes peculiar to every thing. Or do you strenuously contend, that such as every colour appears to you, such also it appears to a dog, and every other animal?

THEÆ. Not I, by Jupiter.

SOC. But what with respect to another man? Will you contend that any thing appears to him in a similar manner as to you? Or rather, that a thing does not appear the same to you, because you are never similar to yourself?

THEÆ. This appears to me to the case rather than that.

SOC. If, therefore, that which we measure, or that which we touch, was great, or white, or hot, it would never, by falling upon any thing else, become a different thing, because it would not be in any respect changed. But if that which is measured or touched by us, was either great, or white, or hot, it would not, in consequence of something else approaching to it, or becoming passive, become itself any thing else, as it would not suffer any thing. Since now, my friend, we are in a certain respect easily compelled to assert things wonderful and ridiculous, as Protagoras himself would acknowledge, and every once who assents to his doctrines.

THEÆ. How is this, and what things do you speak of?

SOC. Take a small example, and you will understand all that I wish. If we compare four to six dice, we say that the six are more than four, and that the two are to each other in a sesquialter ratio: but if we compare twelve to the six, we say that the six are less than, and are the half of, twelve. Nor is it possible to say otherwise. Or can you endure to say otherwise?

THEÆ. Not I, indeed.

SOC. What then? If Protagoras, or any other, should say to you, O Theætetus, can any thing become greater or more in any other way than by being increased? What would you answer?

d THEÆ. If, O Socrates, I should answer to the present question, what appears to me to be the case, I should say that it cannot; but if I should reply to the former question, in order that I might not contradict myself, I should say that it might.

SOC. Well and divinely said, by Juno, my friend. But, (as it appears) if you should answer that it is so, that saying of Euripides[†] might be adopted: for the tongue would be irreprehensible for us, but not the mind.

THEÆ. True.

SOC. If, therefore, I and you were skilful and wise, after we had examined every thing belonging to our minds, we should then make
e trial of each other from our abundance, and sophistically approaching to this contest, should make our arguments strike against each other. But now, as being rude and unskilful, we wish, in the first place, to contemplate the things themselves in themselves, that we may know what it is which we dianoëtically perceive, and whether we accord with each other, or not.

THEÆ. I wish this to be the case by all means.

155a SOC. And so do I. But since we are thus disposed, let us in a quiet manner, as being abundantly at leisure, again consider, not morosely, but examining ourselves in reality, what the nature is of these appearances within us. And, on the first consideration of these, we shall say (as I think) that nothing at any time ever becomes greater or lesser, neither in bulk, nor in number, as long as it is equal to itself. Is it not so?

THEÆ. It is.

SOC. And, in the second place, that to which nothing is either added or taken away, will neither at any time ever be increased, or corrupted, but will always be equal.

THEÆ. And, indeed, very much so.

b SOC. And shall we not also say, in the third place, that a thing which was not formerly, but subsists afterwards, cannot exist without making and being made?

THEÆ. So, indeed, it seems.

SOC. These three things, then, which are acknowledged by us, oppose each other in a hostile manner in our soul, when we speak about dice, as above, or when we say that I, who am so old, am neither increased, nor suffer a contrary passion in myself; while you, who are a young man, are now greater, and afterwards less, since nothing is taken away
c from my bulk, but yours is increased. For, through a length of time, I

† Eur. Hippol. 1, 612.

am what I was not formerly, being no longer in a state of progressive
increase: for without making, it is impossible that a thing can be made.
But losing nothing of my bulk, I do not at any time become less. And
there are ten thousand other things of this kind, which happen to ten
thousand other persons, if we admit these things. Speak, Theætetus: for
you appear to me not to be unskilled in things of this kind.

THEÆ. By the Gods, Socrates, I wonder in a transcendent manner
what these things are: and, truly, sometimes looking at them, I labour
under a dark vertigo.

d   SOC. Theodorus, my friend, appears not to have badly conjectured
concerning your disposition; since to wonder is very much the passion
of a philosopher. For there is no other beginning of philosophy than
this. And he who said[†] that Iris is the daughter of Thaumas,[‡] did not
genealogize badly. But whether do you understand on what account
these things, from which we say Protagoras speaks, are such as they are,
or not?

THEÆ. I do not yet appear to myself to understand.

e   SOC. Will you not, therefore, thank me, if I unfold to you the
concealed truth of the conceptions of this man, or rather, of celebrated
men?

THEÆ. How is it possible I should not? Indeed, I should thank you
exceedingly.

SOC. Looking, round, therefore, now see that no profane person hears
us. But *those are profane who think there is nothing else than that which
they are able to grasp with their hands; but do not admit that actions, and
generations, and every thing which is invisible, are to be considered as
belonging to a part of essence.*

156a   THEÆ. You speak, Socrates, of hard and refractory men.

SOC. They are indeed, O boy, very much destitute of the Muses: but
there are many others more elegant than these, whose mysteries I am
about to relate to you. But the principle of these men, from which all
that we have just now said is suspended, is this: - That this universe is
motion,[3] and that besides motion there is nothing. Likewise, that of
motion there are two species; each of which is infinite in multitude, but
that one species has the power of acting, and the other of suffering.

b   From the congress and mutual friction of these a progeny is produced,

† *i.e.* Hesiod, in Theog. v. 780.

‡ *i.e.* Of *wonder.* Iris, therefore, being the daughter of Wonder, is the exciting cause
of this passion in souls.

infinite in multitude, but twofold in species: one, indeed, being that which is sensible, but the other sense, which always concurs and subsists together with sensible. And the senses, indeed, are denominated by us as follows, seeing, hearing, smelling, tasting, and the touching things hot and cold. Pleasures and pains, desires and fears, innumerable other passions without a name, and an all-various multitude which are denominated, follow these. But to each of these the sensible genus is allied, *viz.* all-various colours to all-various sights; and in a similar manner, voices to hearings, and other sensibles are allied to other senses. What then is the intention of this discourse, O Theætetus, with reference to the former? Do you understand what it is?

THEÆ. Not very much, Socrates.

SOC. But see whether it can in a certain respect be finished. For it wishes to assert that all these things are, as we have said, moved, and that there is swiftness and slowness in their motions. So far, therefore, as their motions are slow, they possess motion in the same, and towards things near, and thus generate. But things thus generated are more slow. And again, so far as their motions are swift, they possess a motion towards things at a distance, and thus generate: but the things thus generated are more swift. For they are borne along, and their motion naturally subsists in lation. When, therefore, the eye and any thing commensurate to this generate by approximation, whiteness, and the sense connate to this, which would never have been produced if each of these had been directed to something else, then, in the interim, sight tending to the eyes, and whiteness to that which together with it generates colour, the eye becomes filled with vision, and then sees, and becomes not sight, but an eye seeing. But that which in conjunction with it generates colour becomes filled with whiteness, and is made not whiteness, but a thing white; whether it is wood or stone, or any thing else which may happen to be coloured with a colour of this kind. And in a similar manner with respect to other things, such as the hot and the hard, &c. we must conceive that no one of these is essentially any thing; but, as we have already observed, that all things, and of all-various kinds, are generated in their congress with each other, from motion. Since, as they say, there is no stability in conceiving, that either that which acts, or that which suffers, is any one thing. For neither is that which acts any thing till it meets with that which is passive, nor that which is passive till it meets with that which acts. For that which meets with and produces any thing, when it falls upon another, then renders that which is passive apparent. So that from all this, that which we said in the beginning follows, that there is not any thing which is essentially one thing, but that it is always becoming to be something to some particular thing, but is itself entirely exempt from being. Indeed, just now we frequently used the tern *being,* compelled to this by custom and ignorance; but, according to the assertions of the wise, we ought not to predicate any thing, either of any other, or of myself, or of this, or that, or call it by any other name which signifies permanency but we should affirm according to nature, that they are generated and made, corrupted and changed. For, if any one asserts that they stand still, he may easily be confuted. But it is requisite thus to speak of things separately, and of many things collected together; in which collection, man, a stone, every animal, and species are placed. Do not these things, O Theætetus, appear to you to be pleasant; and are they not agreeable to your taste?

THEÆ. I do not know, Socrates: for I cannot understand respecting yourself, whether you assert these things as appearing to be so to you, or in order to try me.

SOC. Do you not remember, my friend, that I neither know any of these particulars, nor make any of them my own, but that I am barren of them? Likewise, that I act the part of a midwife towards you, and that for the sake of this I enchant you, and place before you the doctrines of each of the wise, that you may taste them, till I lead forth your dogma into light? But when I have led it forth, I then examine whether it appears to be vain and empty, or prolific. But boldly and strenuously, in a becoming and manly manner, answer what appears to you to be the truth respecting the things I shall ask you.

THEÆ. Ask then.

SOC. Tell me then again, whether it is your opinion that nothing has a being, but that the good, and the beautiful, and everything which we just now enumerated, always subsist in becoming to be?

THEÆ. When I hear you discoursing in this manner, the assertion appears to be wonderful, and it seems that what you discuss should be admitted.

SOC. Let us, therefore, not omit what remains. But it remains that we should speak concerning dreams, diseases, and, besides other things, of insanity; likewise, concerning whatever is seen or heard, or in any other way perceived perversely. For you know that in all these the doctrine which we just now related, will appear without any dispute to be confuted; since the senses in these are more deceived than in any thing else: and so far is it from being the case that things are such as they appear to every one, that, on the contrary, no one of those things which appear to have a being can in reality be said to be.

THEÆ. You speak with the greatest truth, Socrates.

SOC. What then, O boy, can remain for him to say, who asserts that sense is science, and that things which appear to every one are to that individual what they appear to be?

THEÆ. I am averse to reply, Socrates, since I know not what to say; because just now when I was speaking you terrified me. For, in reality, I cannot hesitate to grant, that those who are insane, or dreaming, think falsely, since some among the former of these consider themselves as Gods, and those that dream think they fly like birds.

SOC. Whether or no, therefore, are you aware of this dubious question concerning these particulars, and especially concerning perceptions in sleep, and when we are awake?

THEÆ. What question is this?

SOC. That which I think you have often heard, when it is asked, as at present, by what arguments any one can evince, whether we are asleep, and all our thoughts are dreams, or whether we are in a vigilant[†] state, and in reality discourse with each other.

THEÆ. And indeed, Socrates, it is dubious by what arguments any one can evince this. For all things follow, as it were, reciprocally the same things. For, with respect to our present discourse, nothing hinders but that our appearing to converse with each other may be in a dream: and when in sleep we appear to relate our dreams, there is a wonderful similitude in this case to our conversation when awake.

SOC. You see, then, it is not difficult to doubt, since it is dubious whether things are dreams or vigilant perceptions; and especially since the time which we devote to sleep is equal to that which we devote to vigilance: and in each of these our soul anxiously contends, that the present dogmas are the most true. So that in an equal time we say that these things and those are true; and in a similar manner we strenuously contend for their reality in each.

THEÆ. Entirely so.

SOC. The same may be said, therefore, respecting disease and insanity, except that in these the time is not equal.

THEÆ. Right.

SOC. What then? Shall truth be defined by the multitude and paucity of time?

THEÆ. But this, indeed, would be very ridiculous.

---

† Sense is nothing more than a dreaming perception of reality; for sensibles are merely the images of true beings.

SOC. Have you any thing else by which you can clearly show which of these opinions are true?

THEÆ. It does not appear to me that I have.

SOC. Hear, therefore, from me, what they will say who define appearances to be always true to those to whom they appear. For I think they will say, interrogating you in this manner: O Theætetus, does that which is in every respect different, possess a certain power which is the same with another thing? And must we not admit, that a thing in every respect different is not partly the same, and partly different, but that it is wholly different?

159a THEÆ. It is impossible, therefore, that it should possess any thing the same, either in power, or in any thing else, since it is altogether different.

SOC. Must we not, therefore, necessarily confess, that a thing of this kind is dissimilar?

THEÆ. It appears so to me.

SOC. If, therefore, any thing happens to become similar or dissimilar to any thing, whether to itself or to another, so far as it is similar must we not say it becomes same, but, so far as dissimilar, different?

THEÆ. It is necessary.

SOC. Have we not said before, that there are many, and indeed an infinite number of things which act, and in a similar manner of things which suffer?

THEÆ. Yes.

SOC. And besides this, that when one thing is mingled with another and another, it does not generate things which are the same, but such as are different?

b THEÆ. Entirely so.

SOC. Shall we speak of me and you, and other things after the same manner? As, for instance, shall we say that Socrates when well is similar to Socrates when ill, or dissimilar?

THEÆ. Do you mean to ask whether the whole of Socrates when ill is similar or dissimilar to the whole of Socrates when well?

SOC. You understand me perfectly well. This is what I mean.

THEÆ. I answer, then, that it is dissimilar and different.

SOC. Whether, therefore, is it so, considered as dissimilar?

THEÆ. It is necessary.

c SOC. And would you speak in a similar manner respecting those that are asleep, and all such particulars as we just now discussed?

THEÆ. I should.

SOC. But does not each of those things which are naturally capable of effecting any thing, when it receives Socrates as well, use me as a different man from what it does when it receives me as ill?

THEÆ. Is it possible it should not?

SOC. And do we not generate from each things that are different, I being the patient, and that thing the agent?

THEÆ. Undoubtedly.

SOC. But when I drink wine, being well, it appears to me to be pleasant and sweet.

d   THEÆ. Certainly.

SOC. But, from what has been granted, an agent and a patient generate sweetness and sense, both being borne along together. And sense, indeed, existing from the patient, causes the tongue to perceive; but sweetness, from the wine being borne along about it, causes the wise both to be and to appear sweet to a healthy tongue.

THEÆ. The former particulars were entirely allowed by us to subsist in this manner.

SOC. But when I drink wine, being diseased, my tongue does not in reality receive it the same as before: for it now approaches to that which is dissimilar.

THEÆ. It does.

e   SOC. But Socrates thus affected, and the drinking the wine again generate other things; about the tongue a sensation of bitterness; but about the wine, bitterness generated and borne along. And the wine, indeed, is not bitterness, but bitter; and I am not sense, but that which is sentient.

THEÆ. Entirely so.

SOC. I therefore, thus perceiving, do not ever become any thing else.
160a   For of a different thing there is a different sense, which renders the perceiver various and different. Nor does that which thus affects me become a thing of this kind, by concurring with another thing, and generating the same. For, generating another thing from another, it would become itself various.

THEÆ. These things are so.

SOC. Nor, indeed, am I such to myself, nor is that thing generated such to itself.

THEÆ. Certainly not.

b   SOC. But it is necessary that I should become sentient of something, when I become sentient: for it is impossible that I should be sentient, and yet sentient of nothing. And it is likewise necessary that that thing should become something to some one, when it becomes sweet or bitter, or any thing of this kind. For it is impossible that a thing can be sweet, and yet sweet to no one.

THEÆ. Entirely so.

SOC. It remains then, I think, that we should mutually be, if we are; and if we are becoming to be, that we should be mutually in generation; since necessity binds our essence. But it does not bind it to any other thing, nor yet to ourselves. It remains, therefore, that we are bound to each other. So that, if any one says a certain thing is, or is becoming to be, it must be understood that it is, or is becoming to be something, or of something, or to something. But it must not be said that it is in itself either that which is, or which is becoming to be. Nor must we suffer this to be said, either by the thing itself, or by any other, as the discourse we have already discussed evinces.

c   THEÆ. Entirely so, Socrates.

SOC. Since that which affects me, belongs to me and not to another, do not I also perceive it, and not another?

THEÆ. Undoubtedly.

SOC. My sense, therefore, is true to me. For it always belongs to my essence. And I, according to Protagoras, am a judge of things which have a being pertaining to myself, that they are, and of non-beings, that they are not.

THEÆ. It appears to.

d   SOC. How then is possible, since I am not deceived, and do not stagger in my dianoëtic part, either about things which are, or things in generation, that I should not possess scientific knowledge of things which I perceive?

THEÆ. There is no reason why you should not.

SOC. It was beautifully, therefore, said by you, that science is nothing else than sense. And the doctrine of Homer and Heraclitus, and all of this tribe, that all things are moved like streams, accords with that of the most wise Protagoras, that man is the measure of all things; and with

e   that of Theætetus, that, things subsisting in this manner, sense is science. For do we not, O Theætetus, say, that this is as it were your offspring recently born, but delivered by me by the midwife's art? Or how do you say?

THEÆ. It is necessary to say so, Socrates.

SOC. But this, as it appears, we have scarcely been able to generate, whatever it may be. Since however it is delivered, celebrating the usual solemnities on the fifth day after the nativity, let us run through a circle of disputations, considering whether it does not deceive us, and is not

161a worthy of being educated, but is vain and false. Or do you think that you ought by all means to nourish your offspring, and not abandon it? Or could you endure to see it reprobated, and not be very much offended if any one should take it away from you, as being your first born?

THEO. Theætetus, Socrates, could endure this. For he is not morose. But by the Gods tell me, if this is not the case.

SOC. You are sincerely a philologist, and a good man, Theodorus: for you think I am a sack of discourse, out of which I can easily take words, and say that these things are not so. But you do not understand the truth of the case, that no assertions proceed from me, but always from him who discourses with me. Indeed I know nothing, except a small matter, *viz.* how to receive a reason from another wise man, and apprehend it sufficiently. And now I endeavour to determine this question, by means of Theætetus, and not from myself.

THEO. You speak well, Socrates; and, therefore, do as you say.

SOC. Do you know, Theodorus, what it is I admire in your associate Protagoras?

THEO. What is it?

SOC. In other respects his assertion, that a thing is that which it appears to any one, is, I think, a very pleasant one; but I wonder that at the beginning of his discourse, when he speaks of truth, he did not say, that a swine or a cynocephalus,[†] or any other more unusual thing endued with sense, is the measure of all things, that he might begin to speak to us magnificently, and in a manner perfectly contemptuous; evincing that we should admire him for his wisdom as if he were a God, when at the same time with respect to understanding, he is not at all superior to a little frog, much less to any other man. Or how shall we say, Theodorus? For if that of which each person forms an opinion through sense is true to each, and no other *passion*[‡] of any one judges better than this, and one person is not better qualified to judge whether an opinion is true or false than another, but, as we have often said, every one is alone able to form an opinion of things pertaining to himself, and all these are right and true, - then why, my friend, is Protagoras so wise, that he is thought to be justly worthy of instructing others, and receiving a mighty reward for so doing, while we are considered as more unlearned, and are advised to become his disciples,

---

† An animal which has nothing pertaining to a dog except the head.

‡ Socrates here very properly calls sense a *passion;* for it is a passive perception of things.

though each person is the measure of his own wisdom? Or how is it possible not to say that Protagoras asserts these things in order to seduce the people? I pass over in silence, what laughter both myself and my obstetric art must excite; and besides this, as I think, the whole business of discourse. For will not the consideration and endeavour to confute the phantasies and opinions of others, since each is true, be nothing
162a more than long and mighty trifles, if the truth[†] of Protagoras is true, and he does not in sport speak from the adytum of his book?

THEO. As I am a friend, Socrates, to Protagoras, as you just now said, I cannot suffer with my consent that he should be confuted, nor yet am I willing to oppose your opinion. Again, therefore, take to yourself Theætetus; for he appears to have attended to you in a very becoming manner.

b   SOC. If then, Theodorus, you should go to the palæstræ at Lacedæmon, and should see among those that are naked some of a base form, would you not think it worth while to exhibit your own naked figure?

THEO. But what do you think, if, complying with my request, they should permit me, as I hope you will at present, to be a spectator without being drawn to the gymnasium, my limbs being now stiff, and engaging in wrestling with one who is younger, and whose joints are more supple than mine?

SOC. But if this be the case, Theodorus, and it is friendly to you,
c   then, according to the proverb, it is not hostile to me. Let us, therefore, again go to the wise Theætetus. But answer me, in the first place, Theætetus, to what we just now discussed, Would you not wonder, if on a sudden you should appear to be not inferior in wisdom, either to any man or God? Or do you think that the Protagorean measure pertains less to Gods than to men?

d   THEÆ. I do not by Jupiter. And I very much wonder at your question. For when we discussed in what manner it might be said, that what appears to any one is true to any one, it appeared to me to be perfectly well said, but now the very contrary has rapidly taken place.

SOC. My dear boy, you are as yet a youth, and are therefore easily obedient to and persuaded by conversation. For to these things Protagoras or any one of his sect would say: O generous boys, and aged
e   men, you here sit together, conversing and calling on the Gods, concerning whom, whether they are or are not, I do not think it proper either to speak or write. Likewise hearing the things which the

---

† Socrates says this in derision of what Protagoras calls the truth.

multitude admit, these you assert: and among others, that it would be a dire thing if every man did not far surpass every brute in wisdom; but you do not adduce any demonstration, or necessity, that it should be so, but only employ probability. Which if Theodorus, or any other geometrician, should employ when geometrizing, he would be considered as undeserving of notice. Do you, therefore, and Theodorus consider, whether you should admit persuasion and probable arguments, when discoursing about things of such great consequence.

163a

THEÆ. But, Socrates, both you and we should say that this would not be just.

SOC. Now, however, as it appears from your discourse, and that of Theodorus, another thing is to be considered.

THEÆ. Entirely another thing.

SOC. Let us, therefore, consider this, whether science is the same with sense, or different from it? For to this in a certain respect the whole of our discourse tends: and for the sake of this we have agitated these particulars, which are both numerous and wonderful. Is it not so?

THEÆ. Entirely so.

b

SOC. Do we then acknowledge that all such things as we perceive by seeing and hearing, we at the same time scientifically know? So that for instance, shall we say, that we do not hear the Barbarians, when they speak, before we have learned their language or that, without this, we both hear them and at the same time know what they say? And again, whether when ignorant of letters, but looking at them, we do not see them, or shall we strenuously contend that we know, if we see them?

THEÆ. We should say this, Socrates, that, if we see and hear things, we know them scientifically; and that in the latter of these instances, on perceiving the figure and colour we scientifically know the letters; and that in the former instance, we at the same time both hear and know

c

the sharpness and flatness of the sounds: but that what grammarians and interpreters teach respecting these things, we neither perceive nor scientifically know by seeing or hearing.

SOC. Most excellently said, Theætetus. Nor is it worth while to oppose you in these things, that you may thence make a greater proficiency. But consider also this other thing which will take place, and see how it may be repelled.

THEÆ. What is that?

d

SOC. It is this: If any one should ask whether it is possible that a person can be ignorant of that which he has a scientific knowledge of, while he yet remembers it, and preserves it, then when he remembers it.

But I shall be prolix, as it appears, through desiring to inquire whether any one does not know that which he has learnt and remembers.

THEÆ. But how is it possible he should not, Socrates? For, otherwise, what you say would be a prodigy.

SOC. Do I, therefore, rave or not? Consider. Do you not then say that to see is to perceive, and that sight is sense?

THEÆ. I do.

e SOC. Has not, therefore, he who sees any thing a scientific knowledge of that which he sees, according to the present discourse?

THEÆ. He has.

SOC. But what, do you not say that memory is something?

THEÆ. Yes.

SOC. But whether is it of nothing or something?

THEÆ. O something, doubtless.

SOC. Is it not, therefore, of those things which he learns and perceives?

THEÆ. It is of such things as these.

SOC. But what, does any one ever remember that which he sees?

THEÆ. He does remember it.

SOC. Does he likewise when he shuts his eyes? or, when he does this, does he forget?

THEÆ. But this, Socrates, would be a dire thing to say.

164a SOC. And yet it is necessary to say so, if we would preserve the former discourse: but if not, it must perish.

THEÆ. And I indeed by Jupiter suspect so, though I do not sufficiently understand: but tell me in what respect it must be so.

SOC. In this. We say that he who sees any thing has a scientific knowledge of that which he sees: for it is confessed by us that sight and sense, and science are the same.

THEÆ. Entirely so.

SOC. But he who sees, and has a scientific knowledge of that which he sees, if he shuts his eyes, he remembers indeed that thing, but does not see it. Is it not so?

THEÆ. It is.

b SOC. But not to see is not to know scientifically; since to see is to have a scientific knowledge.

THEÆ. True.

SOC. It happens, therefore, that when any one has a scientific knowledge of any thing, and still remembers it, he does not know it scientifically, since he does not see it; which we say would be monstrous, if it should take place.

THEÆ. You speak most true.

SOC. But it appears that something impossible would happen, if any one should say that science and sense are the same.

THEÆ. It appears so.

SOC. Each, therefore, must be confessed to be different.

THEÆ. So it seems.

c   SOC. As it appears then, we must again say from the beginning what science is. Though what shall we do, Theætetus?

THEÆ. About what?

SOC. We appear to me, like dunghill cocks, to leap from our disputation, before we have gained the victory, and begin to crow.

THEÆ. How so?

SOC. Though we have assented to the established meaning of names, yet we appear to have contradicted this meaning, and to have been delighted in so doing, in our discourse: and though we have confessed ourselves not to be contentious but wise, yet we are ignorant that we do the same as those skilful men.

d   THEÆ. I do not yet understand what you say.

SOC. But I will endeavour to explain what I understand about these things. For we inquired whether any one who has learnt and remembers a thing, has not a scientific knowledge of that thing: and we evinced that he who knows a thing, and with his eyes shut remembers it, but does not see it, at the same time is ignorant of and remembers it. But that this is impossible. And so the Protagorean fable is destroyed, and at the same time yours, which asserts that science and sense are the same.

e   THEÆ. It appears so.

SOC. But this I think, my friend, would not be the case if the father of the other fable were alive, but he would very much defend it. But now, being an orphan, we reproachfully deride it. For the guardians which Protagoras left, and of which Theodorus is one, are unwilling to assist it. But we, for the sake of justice, should venture to give it assistance.

165a   THEO. Indeed, Socrates, I am not one of the guardians of the doctrine of Protagoras, but this ought rather to be said of Callias the son of Hipponicus. For we very rapidly betook ourselves from mere words to geometry. Nevertheless, we shall thank you if you assist this doctrine.

SOC. You speak well, Theodorus. Consider, therefore, the assistance which I shall give. For he who does not attend to the power of words, by which, for the most part, we are accustomed to affirm or deny any thing, must assent to things more dire than those we have just mentioned. Shall I tell you in what respect, Theætetus?

b THEO. Tell us in common, therefore: but let the younger answer. For, if he errs, it will be less disgraceful.

SOC. But I speak of a most dire question; and I think it is this. Is it possible that he who knows any thing can be ignorant of this thing which he knows?

THEO. What shall we answer, Theætetus?

THEÆ. I think it is not possible.

SOC. But this is not the case, if you admit that to see is to know scientifically. For what ought you to reply to that inevitable question, which, as it is said, is shut up in a well, if any one should ask you, O

c intrepid man, whether, on covering one of your eyes with your hand, you can see your garment with the covered eye?

THEÆ. I think I should say, Not with this, but with the other eye.

SOC. Would you not, therefore, see, and at the same time not see, the same thing?

THEÆ. I should in a certain respect.

SOC. But he will say, I neither ordered you to answer thus, nor did I ask in what respect you might be said to see, but whether, if knowing a thing scientifically, you also did not scientifically know it. But now you confess that not seeing, you see: and prior to this you acknowledged, that to see was to have a scientific knowledge, and that not to see, was not to know scientifically. Think what will happen to you from these things.

d THEÆ. I think the very contrary to what we admitted will take place.

SOC. But, perhaps, O wonderful youth, you will suffer many things of this kind, if any one should ask you whether it is possible to know scientifically, in an acute and dull manner, and near, but not at a distance; vehemently and with remission, and in ten thousand other ways. For an insidious man, armed with a shield, and led to discussion by hire, when you admit science and sense to be the same, will drive you to hearing, smelling, and such like senses, and there detaining, will confute you, and will not dismiss you, till having admired his exquisite wisdom you are bound by him. And being thus brought into captivity

e and bound, you will be obliged to redeem yourself for a sum of money which is agreed upon by him and you. But you will perhaps say, after what manner can Protagoras defend his opinions? Shall we endeavour to say something else?

THEÆ. By all means.

SOC. But all this which we have said in defence of him, will, I think,
166a be ineffectual. For, despising us, he will say: That good man, Socrates,
when he was asked by a boy, whether any one could at the same time
remember a thing, and be ignorant of it, was frightened, and in his fear
denied that any one could; and, through being unable to look straight
forward, made me appear ridiculous in his discourses. But, most
sluggish Socrates, the thing is thus: When by inquiry you consider any
one of my assertions, if he whom you interrogate answers in the same
manner as I should answer, and is deceived, in this case I am confuted.
b But if he answers in a different manner, he alone whom you interrogate
is deceived. For, in the first place, do you think that any one would
grant you, that memory can be present to him who no longer suffers a
passion of such a kind as he once suffered? It is far from being the case.
Or do you think he would hesitate to acknowledge, that the same thing
may at the same time be both known and not known? Or, if he should
fear to assert this, do you think he would admit that any one thing is
dissimilar to another, before it is itself made dissimilar to that which has
a being? Or rather, that this is something, and not those; and that those
c will become infinite in dissimilitude has a subsistence; admitting that it
is requisite to avoid the mutual hunting of words. But, (he will say) O
blessed man, approach in a still more generous manner to what I say,
and confute, if you are able, my assertion, that peculiar senses do not
belong to each of us; or that, if they are peculiar, that which appears
will not any thing the more belong only to one individual. Or, if it is
necessary it should exist, it may be denominated by him to whom it
appears. But when you speak of swine and cynocephali, you not only
d grunt yourself, but you persuade those that hear you to do this at my
writings; and in this respect do not act well. For I say, that the truth
subsists, as I have written: for each of us is the measure both of beings
and non-beings. But one thing differs widely from another, because they
appear to one person different from what they do to another. I am
likewise far from asserting, that there is any such thing as wisdom, or a
wise man. But I call him a wise man who, changing the condition of
him to whom things appear and are evil, causes them to appear and to
e be good to such a one. Do not, therefore, pursue my discourse in words
only, but still in a clearer manner thus learn what I say. And in order
to this, recollect what was said before, that to a sick man the things
which he tastes appear and are bitter; but that to him who is well they
167a are and appear to be the contrary. But it is not proper to make either
of these the wiser on this account: (for this is impossible) nor must it be
asserted, that he who is sick is an ignorant person, because he entertains

such opinions, and that he who is well is wise, because he thinks differently; but that he is changed into a different habit. For one habit is better than another. In a similar manner, too, in erudition, there is a mutation from one habit to a better. But the physician effects a mutation by medicines, and the sophist by discourses. For no one can cause him who thinks falsely to think afterwards truly. For it is not possible for any one to have an opinion of things which are not, or of
b things different from what he suffers. But the things which he suffers are always true. And I think that he, who, through a depraved habit of soul, forms opinions of things allied to himself, may, through a good habit, be made to entertain opinions of different things, which some, through ignorance, denominate true phantasms. But I say that some things are better than others, but that they are by no means more true. Likewise, friend Socrates, I am far from calling the wise frogs. But I call those that are wise in things pertaining to bodies, physicians; and in things pertaining to plants, husbandmen. For I say that these men insert
c in their plants, when any one of them is diseased, useful, healthy, and true senses, instead of such as are depraved: but that wise men and good rhetoricians cause things that are good to appear just to cities, instead of such as are base. For such things as appear to each city to be just and beautiful, these are to that city such as it thinks them to be. But a wise man, instead of such particulars as are noxious to cities, causes them to become and to appear to be advantageous. After the same manner a sophist, when he is thus able to discipline those that are instructed, is a
d wise man, and deserves a great reward from those he instructs. And thus some are more wise than others, and yet no one entertains false opinions. And this must be admitted by you, whether you are willing or not, since you are the measure of things. For this assertion is preserved in these; against which, if you have any thing else which you can urge from the beginning, urge it, by adducing opposing arguments. But if you are willing to do this by interrogations, begin to interrogate. For neither is this to be avoided, but is to be pursued the most of all things, by him who is endued with intellect. Act, therefore, in this manner, lest you should be injurious in interrogating. For it is very
e absurd, that he, who, by his own confession, applies himself to the study of virtue, should in discourse accomplish nothing else than injustice. But he acts unjustly in a thing of this kind, who does not exercise himself separately in contending, and separately in discoursing: and who in the former jests and deceives as far as he is able, but in the latter acts seriously, and corrects him with whom he discourses; alone pointing out
168a to him those errors by which he was deceived, both by himself and the

former discussions. If, therefore, you act in this manner, those who discourse with you will accuse themselves of their own perturbation and perplexity, but not you. They will likewise follow and love you, but hate themselves, and will fly from themselves to philosophy; that, becoming different from what they were, they may liberate themselves from their former habits. But if you act in a manner contrary to this, as is the case with the multitude, the very contrary will happen to you;

b   and you will cause those that associate with you, when they become elderly, to hate this pursuit, instead of being philosophers. If, therefore, you will be persuaded by me, then, as was said before, bringing with you a mind neither morose nor hostile, but propitious and mild, you will truly consider our assertion, that all things are moved, and that whatever appears to any one, whether to an individual or a city, is that very thing which it appears to be. And from hence you will consider, whether science and sense are the same with, or different from, each

c   other; nor will you, as was the case just now, discourse from the established custom of words and names, which drawing the multitude in a casual manner, mutually involve them in all-various doubts. Such, O Theodorus, is the assistance, which to the utmost of my power I have endeavoured to give to your associate. These are small things, indeed, from the small. But, if he were alive, he would more magnificently defend his own doctrines.

THEO. You jest, Socrates: for you have very strenuously assisted the man.

d   SOC. You speak well, my friend. But tell me: Do you take notice that Protagoras just now, when he was speaking, reproached us, that when we were discoursing with a boy, we opposed his doctrines with a puerile fear; and besides this, that forbidding us to jest, and venerating moderation in all things, he exhorted us to discuss his doctrines seriously?

THEO. How is it possible, Socrates, I should not take notice of this?

SOC. What then? Do you order us to obey him?

THEO. Very much.

e   SOC. Do you see, therefore, that all these, except you, are boys? If then we are persuaded by him, it is requisite that you and I, interrogating and answering each other, should seriously examine his doctrine, that he may not have to accuse us that we have again considered his assertion, jesting, as it were, with young men.

THEO. But what? Will not Theætetus much better follow you in your investigation than many that have long beards?

SOC. But not better than you, Theodorus. Do not, therefore, think that I ought by all possible means to assist your deceased associate, but 169a not afford you any assistance. But come, best of men, follow me a little, till we see this, whether you ought to be the measure of diagrams, or whether all men are, like you, sufficient with respect to astronomy, and other things in which you deservedly appear to excel.

THEO. It is not easy for him, O Socrates, who sits with you, to refuse an answer to your questions. But I just now spoke like one delirious, when I said that you would permit me not to divest myself of my garments, and that you would not compel me like the Lacedæmononians. But you appear to me rather to tend to the manners of Sciron.[†] For the Lacedæmonians order us either to strip or depart: b but you seem to me rather to act like Antæus. For you do not dismiss him who engages with you, till you have compelled him to wrestle with you in arguments, naked.

SOC. You have most excellently, Theodorus, found out a resemblance of my disease. But I am, indeed, more robust than these. For an innumerable multitude of Herculeses and Theseuses, who were very powerful in discourse, have contended with me, and have been very much wearied: but, notwithstanding this, I have not in the least desisted; c with so dire a love of this exercise am I seized. Do not, therefore, through envy, refrain from exercising yourself with me, and benefiting at the same time both me and yourself.

THEO. I shall no longer oppose you. Lead me, therefore, wherever you please. For it is perfectly necessary that he who is confuted should endure this fatal destiny which you have knit; yet I shall not attempt to exert myself beyond what I promised you.

SOC. This will be sufficient. But diligently observe this with respect to me, that I do not, through forgetfulness, adopt a puerile mode of discourse, so as that we may again be exposed to censure.

d THEO. I will endeavour to do this, as far as I am able.

SOC. Let us, therefore, again resume this in the first place, which we discussed before, and see whether we properly or improperly reprobate the assertion of Protagoras, that every one is sufficient to himself with respect to wisdom. For Protagoras has granted us, that even some among the wise differ with respect to better and worse. Has he not?

---

† This was a celebrated thief in Attica, who plundered the inhabitants of the country, and hurled them from the highest rocks into the sea, after he had obliged them to wait upon him, and to wash his feet. Theseus attacked him, and treated him as he had treated travellers.

THEO. Yes.

e   SOC. If, therefore, he being himself present acknowledges this, and we do not admit it through his assistance, there is no occasion to establish it by resuming the arguments in its favour. But now, since some one may consider us as not sufficient assertors of his doctrine, it will be better, as the case is, to assent to this position in a still clearer manner. For it is of no small consequence whether this takes place or not.

THEO. It is true.

SOC. Not from other things, therefore, but from his own assertions, we acquire our mutual assent in the shortest manner possible.

170a   THEO. How so?

SOC. Thus. Does he not say that what appears to any one is that very thing to him to whom it appears?

THEO. He does say so.

SOC. Therefore, O Protagoras, we speak the opinions of a man, or rather of all men, and we say, that no one can partly think himself wiser than others, and others partly wiser than himself. But in the greatest dangers, when in armies, or in diseases, or in tempests at sea, do not

b   men look to the governors in each of these as Gods, and consider them as their saviours; these governors at the same time being superior in nothing else than in knowledge? And in all human affairs, do not men seek after such teachers and governors, both of themselves and other animals, as are thought to be sufficient to all the purposes of teaching and governing? And in all these, what else shall we say, than that men are of opinion that there is wisdom and ignorance among themselves?

THEO. Nothing else.

SOC. Do they not, therefore, think that wisdom is true dianoëtic energy, but ignorance false opinion?

c   THEO. Undoubtedly.

SOC. What then, O Protagoras, shall we assert? Shall we say that men always form true opinions; or that their opinions are sometimes true and sometimes false? For, from both these assertions, it will happen that they do not always form true opinions, but both true and false. For consider, Theodorus, whether any one of the followers of Protagoras, or you yourself, will contend, that there is no one who thinks that there is not some one who is unlearned, and forms false opinions.

THEO. But this is incredible, Socrates.

d   SOC. But the assertion, that man is the measure of all things, necessarily leads to this.

THEO. How so?

SOC. When you judge any thing from yourself, and afterwards declare your opinion of that thing to me, then, according to the doctrine of Protagoras, your opinion is true to you; but, with respect to us, may we not become judges of your judgment? Or shall we judge that you always form true opinions? Or shall we not say that an innumerable multitude of men will continually oppose your opinions, and think that you judge and opine falsely?

e THEO. By Jupiter, Socrates, there is, as Homer says, a very innumerable multitude who will afford me sufficient employment from human affairs.

SOC. But what? Are you willing to admit we should say, that you then form true opinions to yourself, but such as are false to an innumerable multitude of mankind?

THEO. This appears to be necessary, from the assertion of Protagoras.

SOC. But what with respect to Protagoras himself? Is it not necessary, that if neither he should think that man is the measure of all things, nor the multitude, (as, indeed, they do not think this,) that this truth which he has written should not be possessed by any one? But if he thinks

171a that man is the measure, but the multitude do not accord with him in opinion, do you not know, in the first place, that by how much greater the multitude is to whom this does not appear to be the case, than to whom it does, by so much the more it is not than it is?

THEO. It is necessary; since, according to each opinion, it will be and will not be.

SOC. In the next place, this thing will subsist in the most elegant manner. For he, with respect to his own opinion, will admit, that the opinion of those that dissent from him, and by which they think that he is deceived, is in a certain degree true, while he acknowledges that all men form true opinions.

THEO. Entirely so.

b SOC. Will he not, therefore, admit that his own opinion is false, if he allows that the judgment of those who think he errs is true?

THEO. It is necessary.

SOC. But others will never allow themselves to be deceived; or do you think they will?

THEO. They will not.

SOC. Protagoras, however, from what he has written, will acknowledge that this opinion is true.

THEO. It appears so.

c SOC. From all, therefore, that Protagoras has asserted, it may be doubted, or rather will be granted by him, that when he admits that he who contradicts him forms a true opinion, neither a dog, nor any man, is the measure of all things, or of any one thing, which he has not learned. Is it not so?

THEO. It is.

SOC. Since, therefore, this is doubted by all men, the truth of Protagoras will not be true to any one, neither to any other, nor to himself.

THEO. We attack my associate, Socrates, in a very violent manner.

SOC. But it is immanifest, my friend, whether or not we are carried beyond rectitude. For it is likely that he, as being our elder, is wiser

d   than we are. And if suddenly leaping forth he should seize me by the shoulders, it is probable that he would prove me to be delirious in many things, as likewise you who assent to me, and that afterwards he would immediately vanish. But I think it is necessary that we should make use of ourselves such as we are, and always speak what appears to us to be the truth. And now then shall we say that any one will grant us another thing, that one man is wiser or more ignorant than another?

THEO. It appears so to me.

e   SOC. Shall we say that our discourse ought especially to persist in this to which we have subscribed, in order to assist Protagoras, - I mean, that many things which are apparent are such as they appear to every one, viz. things hot, dry, sweet, and all of this kind? And if in some things it should be granted that one person dissents from another, as about things salubrious and noxious, Protagoras would assert, that not every woman, boy, and brute, is sufficient to cure itself by knowing what is salubrious, but that in this case, if in any, one differs from another.

THEO. So it appears to me.

172a SOC. With respect to political concerns, therefore, such as things beautiful and base, just and unjust, holy and unholy, are such opinions respecting these, as each city legally establishes for itself, true opinions to each? And in these, is neither one individual, nor one city wiser than another? But in the establishment of what is advantageous, or the contrary, to a city, Protagoras would doubtless grant that one counsellor

b   is better than another, and that the opinion of one city is more true than that of another. Nor will he by any means dare to say, that what a city establishes in consequence of thinking that it is advantageous to itself, is to be preferred before every thing. But cities, with respect to what is just and unjust, holy and unholy, are willing strenuously to contend, that none of these have naturally any essence of their own, but that what appears to be true in common is then true when it appears, and as long as it appears. And those who do not altogether speak the doctrine of Protagoras, after this manner lead forth their wisdom. But with respect to us, Theodorus, one discourse employs us emerging from another, a greater from a less.

c THEO. We are not, therefore, idle, Socrates.

SOC. We do not appear to be so. And indeed, O blessed man, I have often as well as now taken notice, that those who have for a long time been conversant with philosophy, when they go to courts of justice deservedly appear to be ridiculous rhetoricians.

THEO. Why do you assert this?

SOC. Those who from their youth have been rolled like cylinders in courts of justice, and places of this kind, appear, when compared to those who have been nourished in philosophy and such-like pursuits, as slaves educated among the free-born.

d

THEO. In what respect?

SOC. In this, that these latter, always, as you say, abound in leisure, and at leisure peaceably discourse, just as we at present engage in a digressive conversation for the third time. In like manner, they, if any question occurs more pleasing to them than the proposed subject of discussion, are not at all concerned whether they speak with brevity, or prolixity, if they can but be partakers of reality. But the others when they speak are always busily engaged; (for defluent water urges) nor is it permitted them to discourse about that which is the object of their desire; but their opponent places before them necessity, and the formula of a book, without which nothing is to be said, which they call an oath respecting calumny, on the part of the plaintiff and defendant. Their discourses too are always concerning a fellow slave, against the master, who sits holding the action in his hand. Their contests likewise never vary, but are always about the same thing: and their course is often respecting life itself. So that, from all these circumstances, they become vehement and sharp, knowing that the master may be flattered by words, and that they shall be rewarded for it in reality; and this because their souls are little and distorted. For slavery from childhood prevents the soul from increasing, and deprives it of rectitude and liberty; compelling it to act in a distorted manner, and hurls into tender souls mighty dangers and fears; which not being able to endure with justice and truth, they immediately betake themselves to falsehood and mutual injuries, and become much bent and twisted. So that, their dianoëtic part being in a diseased condition, they pass from youth to manhood, having rendered themselves as they think skilful and wise. And such are men of this description, O Theodorus. But are you willing that I should give you an account of men belonging to our choir, or that, dismissing

e

173a

b

them, we should again return to our proposed investigation; lest, as we just now said, we should too much digress?

THEO. By no means, Socrates. For you very properly observed, that we, as being in the choir of philosophers, were not subservient to discourse, but discourse to us, and that it should attend our pleasure for its completion. For neither a judge nor a spectator, who reproves and governs, presides over us, as is the case with the poets.

SOC. Let us speak then, since it is agreeable to you, about the Coryphæi.[4] For why should any one speak of those that are conversant with philosophy in a depraved manner? In the first place then, the Coryphæi, from their youth, neither know the way to the forum, nor where the court of justice or senate house is situated, or any other common place of assembly belonging to the city. They likewise neither hear nor see laws nor decrees, whether promulgated or written. And as to the ardent endeavours of their companions to obtain magistracies, the associations of these, their banquets, and wanton feastings accompanied with pipers, these they do not even dream of accomplishing. But whether any thing in the city has happened well or ill, or what evil has befallen any one from his progenitors, whether male or female, these are more concealed from such a one than, as it is said, how many measures called choes the sea contains. And besides this, he is even ignorant that he is ignorant[†] of all these particulars. For he does not abstain from them for the sake of renown, but in reality his body only dwells and is conversant in the city; but his dianoëtic part considering all these as trifling, and of no value, he is borne away, according to Pindar, on all sides, geometrizing about things beneath, and upon the earth, astronomizing above the heavens, and perfectly investigating all the nature of the beings which every whole contains, but by no means applying himself to any thing which is near.

THEO. How is this, Socrates?

SOC. Just, O Theodorus, as a certain elegant and graceful Thracian maid-servant, is reported to have said to Thales, when while astronomizing he fell into a well, that he was very desirous of knowing what the heavens contained, but that he was ignorant of what was before him, and close to his feet. In the same manner all such as are

---

† The multitude, as I have elsewhere observed, are ignorant that they are ignorant with respect to objects of all others the most splendid and real; but the Coryphæan philosopher is ignorant that he is ignorant, with respect to objects most unsubstantial and obscure. The former ignorance is the consequence of a defect, but the latter of a transcendency of gnostic energy.

conversant in philosophy may be derided. For, in reality, a character of
this kind is not only ignorant of what his neighbour does, but he
scarcely knows whether he is a man or some other animal. But what
man is, and what a nature of this kind ought principally to do or suffer,
this he makes the object of his inquiry, and earnestly investigates. Do
you understand, Theodorus, or not?

THEO. I do; and you speak the truth.

SOC. For in reality, my friend, when a man of this kind is compelled
to speak (as I said before) either privately with any one, or publicly in
a court of justice, or any where else, about things before his feet, and in
his view, he excites laughter not only in Thracian maid-servants, but in
the other vulgar, since through his unskilfulness he falls into wells and
every kind of ambiguity. Dire deformity, too, causes him to be
considered as a rustic. For when he is in the company of slanderers he
has nothing to say reproachful, as he does not know any evil of any one,
because he has not made individuals the objects of his attention.
Hence, not having any thing to say, he appears to be ridiculous. But
when he is in company with those that praise and boast of others, as he
is not only silent, but openly laughs, he is considered as delirious. For,
when he hears encomiums given to a tyrant, or a king, he thinks he
hears some swineherd, or shepherd, or herdsman proclaimed as happy,
because he milks abundantly; at the same time, he thinks that they feed
and milk the animal under their command in a more morose and
insidious manner. And that it is necessary a character of this kind
should be no less rustic and undisciplined through his occupation, than
shepherds; the one being enclosed in walls, and the other by a sheepcot
on a mountain. But when he hears any one proclaiming that he
possesses ten thousand acres of land, or a still greater number, as if he
possessed things wonderful in multitude, it appears to him that he hears
of a very trifling thing, in consequence of being accustomed to survey
the whole earth. As often, too, as any one celebrates the nobility of his
family, evincing that he has seven wealthy grandfathers, he thinks that
this is entirely the praise of a dull mind, and which surveys a thing of
a trifling nature; through want of discipline being incapable of always
looking to the universe, and of inferring by a reasoning process, that
every man has had innumerable myriads of grandfathers and progenitors,
among which there has often been an innumerable multitude of rich and
poor, kings and slaves, barbarians and Grecians. But when any one
celebrating his progenitors enumerates five-and-twenty of them, and
refers their origin to Hercules the son of Amphitryon, it appears to him
a thing unworthy to be mentioned. For, as it is entirely owing to

b fortune that any one is able to enumerate five-and-twenty progenitors from Hercules, he would laugh even if any one could enumerate fifty from the same origin; considering such as unable to reason, and liberate themselves from the arrogance of an insane soul. But, in every thing of this kind, the coryphæus we are describing will be ridiculed by the vulgar, partly because he will be considered by them as arrogant, and partly because he is ignorant of and dubious about things before his feet.

THEO. You entirely, Socrates, speak of things which take place.

c SOC. But when any one, my friend, draws him on high, and is willing that he should abandon the consideration of whether I injure you, or you me, for the speculation of justice and injustice, what each of them is, and in what they differ from all other things, or from each other; or that, dismissing the inquiry whether a king is happy who possesses abundance of gold, he should ascend to the contemplation of a kingdom, and universally of human felicity and misery, of what kind they are to any one, and after what manner it is proper to human nature to acquire

d this thing and fly from that; - about all these particulars, when that little sharp soul so conversant with law is required to give a reason, then he in his turn is affected worse than the coryphæus. For he becomes giddy, through being suspended from a lofty place of survey, and being unaccustomed to look so high. He is also terrified, filled with uncertainty, and speaks in a barbaric manner; so that he does not, indeed, excite laughter in the Thracian vulgar, nor in any other undisciplined person (for they do not perceive his condition), but in all

e those whose education has been contrary to that of *slaves*. And such, O Theodorus, is the condition of each; the one whom we call a philosopher, being in reality nourished in liberty and leisure; and who, though he ought not to be blamed, yet appears to be stupid and of no value, when he engages in servile offices, since he neither knows how to bind together bundles of cover-lids, nor to make sauce for banquets, nor compose flattering speeches. But the other of these characters is able to accomplish all these servile offices with celerity and ease, but knows not how to clothe himself dexterously in a liberal manner; nor how in harmonious language properly to celebrate the true life of the Gods and blessed men.

176a THEO. If, O Socrates, you could persuade all men to assent to what you say, as you have persuaded me, there would be more peace and less evil among men.

SOC. But it is impossible, Theodorus, that evils should be destroyed; (for it is necessary that there should be always something contrary to good) nor yet can they be established in the Gods; but they necessarily revolve about a mortal nature, and this place of our abode. On this account we ought to endeavour to fly from hence thither, with the utmost celerity. But this flight consists in becoming as much as possible similar to divinity. And this similitude is acquired by becoming just and holy, in conjunction with prudence. But, O best of men, it is not altogether easy to procure persuasion, that vice is not to be avoided, and virtue pursued, for the sake of those things which the vulgar adopt, *viz.* that we may not seem to be vicious, but may seem to be good: for these are, as it is said, the nugacities of old women, as it appears to me. The truth however is as follows: Divinity is never in any respect unjust, but is most just. And there is not any thing more similar to him, than a man when he becomes most just. About this, the true skill of a man, his nothingness and sloth are conversant. For the knowledge of this is wisdom and true virtue; but the ignorance of it, a privation of discipline, and manifest improbity. Every thing else which appears to be skill and wisdom, when it takes place in political dynasties, is troublesome, but when in arts illiberal. It will be by far the best, therefore, not to permit him who acts unjustly, and who speaks or acts impiously, to be skilled in any art, on account of his cunning. For a character of this kind will exult in his disgrace, and will not think that he is a mere trifle, and the burthen of the earth, but he will consider himself to be such a man as ought to be preserved in a city. The truth, therefore, must be spoken, that such men as these are by so much the more that which they think they are not, from their not thinking the truth respecting themselves. For they are ignorant of the punishment of injustice, of which they ought by no means to be ignorant. For this punishment does not consist, as it appears to me, in stripes and death (which those who do not act unjustly sometimes suffer), but in that which it is impossible to avoid.

THEO. What do you mean?

SOC. Since, my friend, there are two paradigms in the order of things, one of a divine nature, which is most happy, the other of that which is destitute of divinity, and which is most miserable, these men, not perceiving that this is the case, through folly and extreme insanity, secretly become similar to one of these paradigms, through unjust actions, and dissimilar to the other. But for such conduct they are punished, while they lead a life correspondent to that to which they are assimilated. If, likewise, we should say that these men, unless they are liberated from their dire conduct, will not, when they die, be received into that place which is pure from evil, but that after death they will always retain the similitude of the life they have lived upon earth, the

evil associating with the evil, - if we should thus speak, these dire and
crafty men would say that they were hearing nothing but jargon and
reverie.

THEO. And very much so, Socrates.

b   SOC. I know they would speak in this manner, my friend. But this
one thing happens to them, that if at any time it is requisite for them to
give a reason privately respecting the things which they blame; and if
they are willing to continue disputing in a manly manner for a long
time, without cowardly flying from the subject, then at length, O
blessed man, this absurdity ensues, that they are not themselves pleased
with their own assertions, and their rhetoric so entirely fails them, that
they appear to differ in no respect from boys. Respecting men of this
kind, therefore, let thus much suffice, since our discourse for some time
has been entirely a digression. For, if we do not stop here, in
consequence of more matter always flowing in, the subject which we
c   proposed from the first to discuss will be overwhelmed. Let us,
therefore, return to our former inquiry, if it is agreeable to you.

THEO. Things of this kind, Socrates, are not unpleasant to me to hear.
For, in consequence of my age, I can easily follow you. But let us, if
you please, resume our inquiry.

SOC. We were, therefore, arrived at that part of our discourse in
which we said, that those who considered essence as subsisting in lation,
and that a thing which appeared to any one is always what it appears to
be, to him to whom it appears, were willing strenuously to assert this
in other things, and not less so respecting what is just; as that what any
d   city establishes as appearing just to itself, this more than any thing is
just, so far as it continues to be established. But, with respect to good,
no one is so bold as to contend, that whatever a city establishes, through
an opinion of its being useful to itself, will be useful to it as long as it
is established, unless any one should assert this of a mere name. But this
would be a scoff with respect to what we are saying. Or would it not?

THEO. Entirely so.

e   SOC. But does not a city consider the thing named, and not merely
the name?

THEO. Undoubtedly.

SOC. But that which it denominates, that it doubtless regards in the
business of legislation, and establishes all the laws, so far as it is able,
most useful to itself. Or does it establish laws, looking to any thing
else?

178a   THEO. By no means.

Soc. Does it, therefore, always accomplish its purpose, or is it often deceived in its opinion?

Theo. I think it is often deceived.

Soc. If any one, however, should inquire respecting every species, in what the useful consists, he would still more readily acknowledge this. But the useful in the business of legislation is in a certain respect concerning the future time. For, when we establish laws, we establish them that they may be useful in futurity.

b Theo. Entirely so.

Soc. Let us, therefore, thus interrogate Protagoras, or any one of his votaries. Man, as you say, O Protagoras, is the measure of all things, of things white, heavy, light, and the like. For, as he contains a criterion in himself, and thinks conformably to the manner in which he is acted upon, he forms an opinion of things true to himself, and which are true in reality. Is it not so?

Theo. It is.

c Soc. Shall we also say, O Protagoras, that he contains in himself a criterion of things future; and that such things as he thinks will happen, such things do happen to him thinking so? So that, for instance, when any idiot thinks that he shall be attacked with a fever, and that a heat of this kind will take place, but a physician is of a different opinion, which of these opinions shall we say will be verified in futurity? Or shall we say that both will be verified? and that the physician will not be affected either with heat or fever, but that the idiot will suffer both?

Theo. This, indeed, would be ridiculous.

d Soc. But I think, likewise, that the opinion of the husbandman, and not of the harper, would prevail, respecting the future sweetness or roughness of wine.

Theo. Undoubtedly.

Soc. Nor would a master of the gymnasium think better respecting that consonance, or dissonance, which would in future appear to him to be consonant or dissonant, than a musician.

Theo. By no means.

Soc. And when a banquet is to be prepared, will not the opinion of a cook respecting its future agreeableness be preferred to that of any other person who is unskilled in seasoning? For we do not oppose the assertion respecting that which is, or was, agreeable; but, respecting that

e which in future will appear, and will be agreeable to any one, whether is every one to himself the best judge, or whether are you, O Protagoras, better able to foresee what will probably take place in doubtful affairs than an idiot?

THEO. I think, Socrates, that Protagoras professes in these greatly to excel all men.

179a   SOC. O miserable man! no one, by Jupiter, would have followed him, and given him a considerable sum of money, if he had not persuaded his disciples that in future it would happen, and would appear to be the case, that neither any diviner, nor other person, would judge better than himself.

THEO. Most true.

SOC. But does not the establishment of laws, and the useful, regard futurity? And does not every one acknowledge, that a city, though governed by laws, often necessarily wanders from that which is most useful?

THEO. Very much so.

b   SOC. We have, therefore, sufficiently urged against your preceptor, that he must necessarily confess, that one man is wiser than another, and that such a one is a measure; but that there is no necessity that I, who am void of science, should become a measure, as his discourse just now compelled me to be, since, whether I am willing or not, I am so.

THEO. From that, Socrates, it appears to me, that his doctrine is particularly convincing, and from this also, that it makes the opinions of others valid. But cities reprobate his assertions, and by no means think them to be true.

c   SOC. In many other things, Theodorus, it may be inferred, that not every opinion of every one is true. But, with respect to the passion present to every one, from which the senses and opinions according to these are produced, it is more difficult to apprehend that they are not true. But, perhaps, I say nothing to the purpose. For, when they occur, they cannot be confuted: and those who say that they are clear and

d   sciences, perhaps say the truth. And Theætetus here did not assert foreign from the purpose, that sense and science are the same. Let us, therefore, approach nearer, as the doctrine of Protagoras orders us, and consider whether this essence, which is thus borne along, emits an entire or a broken sound. For the contention about it is neither mean nor among a few.

THEO. It is very far, indeed, from being mean, but it is very much circulated about Ionia. For the followers of Heraclitus discourse about it very strenuously.

SOC. On this account, friend Theodorus, we should rather consider this affair from the beginning, in the same manner as it is discussed by them.

e   THEO. By all means, therefore. For, with respect to these Heraclitics, Socrates, or as you say, Homerics, and such as are still more ancient than these, about Ephesus, and who wish to be considered as skilful persons, it is no more possible to discourse with them than with men raging᾿ mad. For their writings are indeed borne along. But as to

180a waiting patiently in discourse and inquiry, and continuing quiet during questioning and answering, this is present with them less than nothing; or rather, these men are so far from possessing any rest, that their privation of it even transcends that which is less than nothing. But if any one asks them a question, they immediately draw, as from a quiver, certain dark enigmatical words, and dart them at you. And if you ask the reason of this, they will again strike you with another dark shower of words, but with the names changed. But you will never bring any thing to a conclusion with them, nor do they ever conclude any thing among themselves. Indeed, they take very good care that there shall not

b   be any thing stable, either in their discourse, or in their souls; thinking, as it appears to me, that this very thing itself is stable. But these are the weapons with which they strenuously fight, and which, as far as they are able, they on all sides hurl forth.

SOC. Perhaps, Theodorus, you have seen these men fighting, but have never seen them when peaceably disposed. For they are not your associates. But I think they speak such things as these, when at leisure, to their disciples, whom they wish to render similar to themselves.

c   THEO. What disciples, blessed man? For, among men of this kind, one is not the disciple of another, but they spring up spontaneously, wherever each of them happens to be seized with a fanatic fury; and at the same time each thinks that the other knows nothing. From these, therefore, as I just now said, neither willingly nor unwillingly will you ever receive a reason. But it is necessary that we should consider the affair as if it was a problem.

d   SOC. You speak to the purpose. But, with respect to the problem, we receive one thing from the ancients, (who concealed in verse their meaning from the multitude,) that Ocean and Tethys are the generation of all other things, that all things are streams, and that nothing abides. But from the moderns, as being more wise, the thing is so clearly demonstrated, that even curriers, on hearing them, are able to learn their wisdom, and lay aside their foolish opinion, that some things stand still, and others are moved. And learning that all things are moved, they venerate the authors of this doctrine. But we have almost forgotten, Theodorus, that others evince the very contrary to this opinion; I mean,

e   that the proper name of the universe is the immovable, and such other assertions as the Melisseans and Parmenideans, opposing all these, strenuously defend - as, that all things are one, and that this one abides in itself, not having a place in which it can be moved. What then shall we say to all these, my friend? For, proceeding by small advances, we 181a have secretly fallen into the midst of both of them. And if we fly, without in any respect resisting, we shall be punished like those in the palæstræ playing in a line, who, when they are caught on both sides, are drawn in contrary directions. It appears therefore to me, that we should first of all consider those with whom we began - I mean the flowing philosophers - and, if they appear to say any thing to the purpose, that we should draw ourselves together with them, and endeavour to fly from the others. But if those who consider the universe as stable shall appear to have more truth on their side, we should fly to them from b those who move even things immovable. And if it shall appear that neither of them assert any thing sufficient, we shall become ridiculous, in consequence of thinking that we, who are men of no importance, can say any thing to the purpose, when we only reprobate men very ancient and perfectly wise. Consider therefore, Theodorus, whether it is expedient to proceed into such a mighty danger.

THEO. Nothing ought to prevent us, Socrates, from considering what each of these men say.

c   SOC. Let us consider their assertions then, since you so earnestly desire it. It appears, therefore, to me, that this speculation should commence from motion, - I mean, what that motion is by which they say all things are moved. But what I wish to say is this: whether they say there is one species of motion, or, as it appears to me, two. Nor do I alone wish to know this myself, but that you also may partake, together with me, of this information, that we may in common be affected in such a manner as is proper. Tell me, therefore, do you say a thing is moved when it changes one place for another, or is turned round in the same place?

THEO. I do.

SOC. Let this, therefore, be one species. But when any thing abiding d in the same place becomes old, or, from being white, becomes black, or, from being soft, hard, or is changed by any other internal change, may not this be deservedly called another species of motion?

THEO. It appears so to me.

SOC. It is necessary, therefore, that there should be these two species of motion, *viz.* alliation, or internal change, and lation.

THEO. Rightly said.

SOC. Having, therefore, made this division, let us now discourse with those who assert that all things are moved, and thus interrogate them: Whether do you say that every thing is moved both ways, *viz.* according to lation and alliation, or that one thing is moved both ways, and another only in one way?

THEO. By Jupiter, I know not what to say, but I think they would reply, that every thing is moved both ways.

SOC. Otherwise, my friend, things would appear to them to be both moved and stand still, and it would not be in any respect more proper to assert that all things are moved, than that they stand still.

THEO. Most true.

SOC. Since, therefore, it is necessary they should be moved, and that no one thing should not be moved, all things will always be moved with every kind of motion.

THEO. It is necessary.

SOC. Consider, likewise, this respecting their assertions, - I mean concerning the generation of heat, or whiteness, or any thing else. Do we not say that they assert, that each of these is borne along, together with sense, between the agent and the patient? And that the patient, indeed, is sensible, but not yet become sense: but that the agent is that which effects something, but is not quality? Perhaps, therefore, quality may appear to you to be an unusual name, and you do not understand me thus speaking collectively. Hear me, then, according to parts. For the agent is neither heat nor whiteness, but becomes hot and white; and so with respect to other things. For do you not recollect that we have observed before, that nothing is any one thing essentially, neither that which is an agent, nor that which is a patient, but that from the concourse of both with each other, sense, and things sensible, being generated, some things became certain qualities, but others sentient?

THEO. I recollect. For how is it possible I should not?

SOC. As to other things, therefore, we shall omit the consideration, whether they speak in this manner concerning them, or not. But let us alone attend to this thing, for the sake of which we are now discoursing; and let us ask them, are all things moved, and do they flow as you say? For is not this what they say?

THEO. Yes.

SOC. Are they not, therefore, moved with both those motions which we enumerated, *viz.* lation and alliation?

THEO. Undoubtedly; since it is necessary that they should be perfectly moved.

SOC. If, therefore, they were only borne along, but were not internally changed, we might be able to say what kind of things flow that are borne along. Or how shall we say?

THEO. Thus.

d SOC. But since neither a flowing white thing permanently continues to flow, but is changed, so that there is even a flux of its whiteness, and a transition into another colour, and we are not able to discover that it abides in this, can we with rectitude pronounce it to be any particular colour?

THEO. But how is it possible, Socrates, that we can pronounce this of a thing white, or of any thing else of a similar kind, since, while we speak about it, it is always privately departing, because continually flowing?

e SOC. But what shall we say of any one of the senses, as of seeing or hearing? Does any thing in seeing or hearing ever abide?

THEO. This ought not to be the case, since all things are moved.

SOC. We must say, therefore, that neither does any one see more than not see, or use any other of the senses more than not use them, since all things are in every respect moved.

THEO. We must say so.

SOC. But sense is science, as we say, I and Theætetus

THEO. You do say so.

SOC. On being asked, therefore, what science is, we must answer, that it is not more science than not science.

183a THEO. So it appears.

SOC. An emendation, therefore, of the answer will very opportunely present itself to us, when we desire to evince that all things are moved, in order that the answer may appear to be right. But this it seems will appear, that if all things are moved, every answer to every question will be similarly right which says, that a thing subsists and yet does not subsist in a certain particular manner, or, if you will, that it is in generation, that we may not stop them by our discourse.

THEO. Right.

b SOC. Except in this, Theodorus, that we should say it is so, and yet is not so. But it is requisite not even to speak in this manner, (for neither will it be any longer moved thus, nor yet not thus,) but another word must be employed by those that speak in this manner, because they have no words by which they can denominate things according to their hypothesis, unless, perhaps, they use the expression *not in any particular manner.* But this will be particularly adapted to them, when spoken an infinite number of times.

THEO. It will thus, indeed, be accommodated to them in the highest degree.

c SOC. We have therefore, Theodorus, done with your friend, nor can we grant him, that every man is the measure of all things, or any man, unless he is endued with wisdom. Nor must we admit that science is sense, according to the doctrine that all things are moved; unless Theætetus here says otherwise.

THEO. You speak most excellently, Socrates. For, these things being brought to a conclusion, it is proper that I also should have done with Protagoras, according to our compact.

d THEÆ. But not so, Theodorus, till you and Socrates have discussed the doctrine of those who assert that the universe is immovable, as you just now mentioned.

THEO. As you are a young man, Theætetus, you teach those that are advanced in years to act unjustly, by transgressing compacts. But prepare yourself to answer Socrates in the remaining part of this inquiry.

THEÆ. Doubtless I shall, if he wishes it: yet it would give me great pleasure to hear what I mentioned.

THEO. You incite horses to the plain when you incite Socrates to discourse. Ask, therefore, and hear.

e SOC. But, O Theodorus, I appear to myself as if I should not comply with Theætetus in his request.

THEO. But why should you not comply?

SOC. Though I should be ashamed to speak concerning Melissus and others, who assert that the universe is one and immovable, lest I should appear to revile them in an insolent manner, yet I should be less ashamed with respect to them than with respect to Parmenides. For, that I may use the words of Homer, Parmenides appears to me to be both venerable and skilful. For I was acquainted with him when I was

184a very young and he was very much advanced in years, and he appeared to me to possess a certain profundity perfectly generous. I am afraid, therefore, lest we should neither understand the meaning of his words, and much more, lest we should be deficient in apprehending the conceptions contained in his writings: and what is greatest of all, lest with respect to the subject of our present inquiry, what science is, we should leave the consideration of it unfinished, through employing contumelious language. Besides, the question which we have now excited, and which contains in itself an ineffable multitude of particulars, would be unworthily treated, if discussed in a careless manner; and on the other hand, if it is extended to too great a length, it will prevent the discovery of science. But it is proper that neither of these should take b place, but that we should endeavour, by the obstetric art, to free from confinement the fœtus of Theætetus respecting science.

THEÆ. It is proper indeed to do so, if it seems requisite to you.

SOC. Again, therefore, Theætetus, in addition to what has been said above, consider this. Do you say that science is sense or not?

THEÆ. I do.

SOC. If then any one should ask you, by what it is that a man sees things white and black, and hears sounds flat and sharp, you would answer, I think, that it is by the eyes and ears.

THEÆ. I should.

c SOC. But to use nouns and verbs with facility, without entering into an accurate investigation of them, is for the most part a thing not ignoble; but rather the contrary to this is servile. Sometimes, however, this is necessary: as in the present case we are compelled to examine whether your answer is right or not. For, consider whether the answer is more right, that we see by, or that we see through, the eyes; and that we hear by, or that we hear through, the ears?

THEÆ. It appears to me, Socrates, that it is more proper to consider the eyes and ears as things through which, rather than as things by which, we perceive.

d SOC. For it would be a dire thing, O boy, if many senses were seated in us, as in wooden horses, and did not all of them tend to one certain idea, whether this is soul, or whatever else it may be proper to call it; and by which, through the senses as organs, we perceive sensible objects.

THEÆ. This appears to me to be the case, rather than that.

SOC. On this account I diligently investigate these things with you, that we may discover whether by one certain thing belonging to us we perceive things black and white, through the eyes, but certain other particulars through the other organs of sense; and whether, when interrogated, you are able to refer all such things as these to the body.

e But perhaps it will be better that you should answer to these inquiries, than that I should be entangled with a multiplicity of questions from you. Tell me, therefore: Do you admit that the things through which you perceive the hot and the dry, the light and the sweet, belong each of them to the body, or to any thing else?

THEÆ. To nothing else.

185a SOC. Are you also willing to acknowledge that such things as you perceive through one power it is impossible to perceive through another? As, that what you perceive through hearing you cannot perceive through seeing, and that what you perceive through seeing you cannot perceive through hearing?

THEÆ. How is it possible I should not be willing?

Soc. If, therefore, you dianoëtically perceive any thing about both these, you do not accomplish this through any other organ,[†] nor yet through any other do you perceive respecting both of them.

THEÆ. Undoubtedly not.

Soc. But, with respect to sound and colour, do you not, in the first place, dianoëtically conceive this concerning both of them, that both have a subsistence?

THEÆ. I do.

Soc. And, therefore, that the one is different from the other, and the same with itself?

b THEÆ. Undoubtedly.

Soc. And again that both are two, and each one?

THEÆ. And this also.

Soc. Are you also able to consider whether they are similar or dissimilar to each other?

THEÆ. Perhaps so.

Soc. But through what is it that you dianoëtically conceive all these things about them? For you can neither apprehend any thing common respecting them, through the hearing, nor the sight. Further still, this also is an instance of what we say. For, if it were possible to consider

c this of both, whether or not they are salt, you know you would be able to assign that by which you considered this; and this would appear to be neither sight nor hearing, but something else.

THEÆ. But what should hinder this power from operating through the tongue?

Soc. You speak well. But with respect to that power which through a certain thing shows you that which is common to all things, and that which is common to these, and through which you denominate a thing to be, or not to be, through what instruments does it perceive the several particulars about which we were just now inquiring?

d THEÆ. You speak of essence and non-being, similitude and dissimilitude, same and different, and the two species of numbers. For it is evident that you inquire through what instrument of the body we perceive by the soul, the even and the odd, and such other things as are consequent to these.

Soc. You follow, Theætetus, surpassingly well; for these are the very things about which I interrogate.

---

† That is, this is not accomplished through any other organ than the dianoëtic power. Plato very properly here uses the word διανοῇ, because he is *scientifically* considering what *science* is.

THEÆ. But by Jupiter, Socrates, I know not what to say, except that which appeared to me at first, that there is not any peculiar organ to these as there is to sensible particulars, but it appears to me that the soul itself considers by itself such things as are common in all things.

SOC. You are beautiful, Theætetus, and not, as Theodorus said, deformed. For he who speaks beautifully is beautiful and good. But, besides being beautiful, you have done well with respect to me. For you have liberated me from a very copious discourse, since it appears to you that the soul considers some things by itself, and others through the powers of the body. For this was what appeared to me to be the case, and which I wished might likewise appear so to you.

186a   THEÆ. It certainly does appear so to me.

SOC. Among what things, therefore, do you place essence? For this especially follows in all things.

THEÆ. I place it among those things which the soul itself by itself aspires after.

SOC. Do you say the same of the similar and the dissimilar, of same and different?

THEÆ. I do.

SOC. But what of the beautiful and the base, good and evil?

b   THEÆ. It appears to me that the soul principally considers the essence of these in mutually comparing them with each other, and considering in itself things past and present with reference to such as are future.

SOC. Take notice also of this: the soul perceives the hardness of a thing hard, through the touch, and in a similar manner the softness of a thing soft; or does it not?

THEÆ. It does.

SOC. But the essence of these, what they are, their mutual contrariety, and the essence of this contrariety, the soul endeavours to discriminate by retiring into herself, and comparing them with each other.

THEÆ. Entirely so.

c   SOC. But is not a power of perceiving such passions as extend to the soul through the body naturally present both with men and brutes, as soon as they are born? And is not reasoning about the essence and utility of these, generated in those in whom it is generated, with difficulty, in a long course of time, through a variety of particulars, and through discipline?

THEÆ. Entirely so.

SOC. Can we, therefore, apprehend the truth by that by which we cannot apprehend essence?

THEÆ. Impossible.

SOC. But can any one possess science of a thing, when at the same time he does not apprehend the truth of that thing?

d THEÆ. But how can he, Socrates?

SOC. Science, therefore, is not inherent in passions, but is inherent in a reasoning process about them. For by this, as it appears, we may be able to touch upon essence and truth? But this cannot be effected by passions.

THEÆ. It appears to.

SOC. Can you, therefore, call passion and science the same thing, when there is such a great difference between them?

THEÆ. It would not be just to do so.

SOC. But what name do you give to seeing, hearing, smelling, tasting, becoming hot, and becoming cold?

e THEÆ. I should give to all these the name of perception. For what other name can be given to them?

SOC. Do you, therefore, call the whole of this sense?

THEÆ. Necessarily so.

SOC. But we said that this was not capable of touching upon truth, because it could not apprehend the essence of a thing.

THEÆ. It certainly cannot.

SOC. Neither, therefore, can it touch upon science.

THEÆ. It cannot.

SOC. Science, therefore, and sense, Theætetus, can never be the same.

THEÆ. It appears, Socrates, they cannot.

187a SOC. And now it becomes most eminently apparent, that science is something different from sense. But we did not begin this conversation for the sake of finding out what science is not, but that we might discover what it is. At the same time, we have advanced thus far, as to be convinced that we must not at all seek for it in sense, but in that name which the soul then possesses when it is conversant with beings, itself by itself.

THEÆ. But this, Socrates, is I think called *to opine*.

SOC. You suspect† rightly, my friend. And now again consider from
b the beginning, obliterating all that has been already said, whether you

---

† Socrates, in saying that Theætetus *suspects rightly*, indicates that he has not a dianoëtic and scientific conception of the name in which science is to be found. For this name is *dianoia*, or the dianoëtic power of the soul, whose very essence, as we have elsewhere observed, consists in reasoning scientifically. Hence he very properly says ορθως γαρ οιει, You suspect rightly. For his conception was nothing more than a vague conjecture or suspicion; at the same time that it was as *accurate* as could be obtained by mere suspicion.

can see more clearly, since we have proceeded thus far. And again tell me what science is.

THEÆ. It is impossible, Socrates, to say that every opinion is science, because there are false opinions. But it appears that true opinion is science. And this is my answer. But if in the course of the inquiry it shall not appear to be so, as it does at present, I shall endeavour to say something else.

SOC. In this manner, Theætetus, it is proper to act - I mean, to speak with alacrity, and not, as you were at first, be averse to answer. For, if we thus conduct ourselves, we shall either find that which is the object of our search, or we shall in a less degree think that we know that which we do not by any means know. Nor will a thing of this kind be a despicable gain. And now then what do you say? Since there are two species of opinion, one true, and the other false, do you define science to be true opinion?

THEÆ. I do. For this now appears to me to be the case.

SOC. Is it, therefore, worth while again to resume the discourse about opinion?

THEÆ. What do you mean?

SOC. I am now disturbed, and often have been, so that I am involved in much doubt, both with respect to myself and others, as I am not able to say what this passion in us is, and after what manner it is generated in the soul.

THEÆ. How is this?

SOC. I am now speaking of false opinion; and am considering whether we shall omit the discussion of it, or speculate about it in a different manner from what we did a little before.

THEÆ. But why should you be dubious in this affair, Socrates, if you see the manner in which it is proper to act? For you and Theodorus said just now not badly, respecting leisure, that nothing urges in inquiries of this kind.

SOC. You very properly remind me. For perhaps it will not be foreign from the purpose again to tread in the same steps. For it is better to finish a little well, than much insufficiently.

THEÆ. Undoubtedly.

SOC. What then shall we say? Shall we say that every opinion is false? or that some of us entertain false opinions, and others true - as if this was naturally the case with respect to opinions?

THEÆ. We should doubtless speak in this manner.

SOC. Does not this happen to us, as well about all things, as about each thing, that we either know or do not know? For at present I omit to speak of learning and forgetting, as subsisting between these, because it contributes nothing to our design.

THEÆ. But, Socrates, nothing else remains respecting every particular, except knowing or not knowing it.

SOC. Is it not therefore necessary, that he who forms an opinion should either form an opinion of things of which he knows something, or of things of which he knows nothing?

THEÆ. It is necessary.

b SOC. Is it not likewise impossible, that he who knows a thing should not know it, or that he who does not know it should know it?

THEÆ. Undoubtedly.

SOC. Does, therefore, he who opines falsely respecting the things which he knows, opine that these are not the things which he knows, but different from them, but of which he has at the same time a knowledge? And though he knows both, is he ignorant of both?

THEÆ. But this, Socrates, is impossible.

SOC. Does he, therefore, think that the things of which he is ignorant are certain other things of which likewise he is ignorant? And can he who neither knows Theætetus nor Socrates ever be induced to think that Socrates is Theætetus, or Theætetus Socrates?

c THEÆ. How is it possible he can?

SOC. Nor, again, can any one think that the things which he knows are the same as those of which he is ignorant; or that the things of which he is ignorant are the same as those which he knows.

THEÆ. For this would be monstrous.

SOC. How then can any one entertain false opinions? For it is impossible to opine in ways different from these; since we either know or do not know all things. But in these it by no means appears possible to opine falsely.

THEÆ. Most true.

d SOC. Whether, therefore, ought we to consider the object of our inquiry, not by proceeding according to knowing and not knowing, but according to being and non-being?

THEÆ. How do you say?

SOC. It is not a simple thing; because he who, with respect to any thing, opines things which are not, must unavoidably opine falsely, in whatever manner the particulars pertaining to his dianoëtic part may subsist.

THEÆ. It is proper it should be so, Socrates.

SOC. How then shall we answer, Theætetus, if any one should ask us (but it is possible that what I say may take place), What man can opine that which is not, whether respecting beings themselves, or whether considered itself by itself? To this, as it appears, we should reply, that he can then opine about that which is not, when opining he does not opine the truth. Or how shall we say?

THEÆ. In this manner.

SOC. Does a thing of this kind, therefore, take place elsewhere?

THEÆ. Of what kind?

SOC. That some one sees something, and yet sees nothing.

THEÆ. But how can he?

SOC. But if he sees one certain thing, he sees something which ranks among beings. Or do you think that *the one* does not rank among beings?

THEÆ. I do not.

SOC. He, therefore, who sees one certain thing sees a certain being.

THEÆ. It appears so.

SOC. And, therefore, he who hears a certain thing hears one certain thing, and a certain being.

THEÆ. He does so.

SOC. And does not he also who touches a certain thing touch one certain thing, and that which has a being, since it is one thing?

THEÆ. And this also.

SOC. And does not he who opines opine one certain thing?

THEÆ. I grant it.

SOC. He, therefore, who opines that which has no being opines nothing.

THEÆ. So it appears.

SOC. But he who opines nothing does not opine in any respect.

THEÆ. It is evident, as it appears.

SOC. It is impossible, therefore, to opine that which is not, either about beings, or itself by itself.

THEÆ. So it appears.

SOC. To opine falsely, therefore, differs from opining things which are not.

THEÆ. It appears that it differs.

SOC. For neither is false opinion inherent in us in this manner, nor in the manner which we considered a little before.

THEÆ. It is not.

SOC. Perhaps, therefore, we may denominate this as follows.

THEÆ. How?

SOC. We say that a certain foreign opinion is a false opinion, when some one, by an alteration in his dianoëtic energy, says that a certain thing is a different thing. For thus he always opines that which has a being, but he opines one thing instead of another; and, in consequence of erring in that which he considers, he may be justly said to opine falsely.

THEÆ. You now appear to me to have spoken with the greatest rectitude. For, when any one opines that which is deformed instead of that which is beautiful, or that which is beautiful instead of that which is deformed, then he truly opines falsely.

SOC. It is evident, Theætetus, that you despise, and do not reverence me.

THEÆ. In what respect?

d SOC. I do not think I appear to you to have apprehended that which is truly false, when asked whether the swift and the slow, the light and the heavy, or any other contraries, do not become contrary to themselves, according to their own nature, but according to the nature of thing which are contrary to them. This, therefore, I dismiss, lest you should be confident in vain. But is it agreeable to you, as you say, that to opine falsely is the same as to opine foreign to the purpose?

THEÆ. It is.

SOC. It is possible, therefore, according to your opinion, to establish by the dianoëtic power one thing as another, and not as that thing which it is.[†]

THEÆ. It is possible.

e SOC. When, therefore, the dianoëtic power does this, is it not necessary that it should either cogitate about both these, or about one of them?

THEÆ. It is necessary.

SOC. And, therefore, it must either cogitate about them both together, or separately.

THEÆ. Most excellent.

SOC. But do you call dianoëtic energy the same as I do?

THEÆ. What do you call it?

SOC. The discourse which the soul itself evolves in itself about the objects of its consideration. I explain the thing to you like an unskilful person. For the soul, when it energizes dianoëtically, appears to me to

---

† This is effected when the dianoëtic power converts itself to imagination, and in consequence of this produces false reasoning.

190a do nothing else than discourse with itself,[†] by interrogating and answering, affirming and denying. But when, having defined it asserts without opposition, whether more slowly or more rapidly, then I call this opinion.[‡] So that I denominate to opine, to speak, and opinion, a discourse not directed to any other, nor accompanied with voice, but directed to itself. But what do you call it?

THEÆ. The same.

SOC. When any one, therefore, opines that one thing is another, he says to himself, as it appears, that one thing is another.

b THEÆ. Undoubtedly.

SOC. Recollect, whether if at any time you say to yourself, that the beautiful is more than any thing base, or that the unjust is just, or, which is the summit of all, whether you ever attempt to persuade yourself, that that which is one thing is more than any thing another thing. Or, on the contrary, have you never dared even in sleep to say to yourself, that things even are entirely odd, or any thing else of this kind?

THEÆ. Certainly never.

c SOC. Do you think, then, that any other person, whether he is in a sane or an insane condition, will seriously dare to say to himself, and this accompanied with persuasion, that a horse is necessarily an ox, or two things one thing?

THEÆ. By Jupiter, I do not.

SOC. If, therefore, to opine is for a man to speak to himself, no one, while he says and opines both these, and touches upon both with his soul, will say and opine that one of those is the other. But we will dismiss, if you please, this word *the other.* For my meaning is this: that no one will opine that the base is the beautiful, or any thing else of this kind.

d THEÆ. You have my permission, Socrates, to dismiss this word; and the case appears to me to be as you say.

SOC. He, therefore, who opines both these cannot opine that one of them is the other.

THEÆ. So it appears.

---

† As the dianoëtic is accurately considered a scientific energy, it is very properly defined by Socrates to be a discourse of the soul with itself. Or, in other words, it is an energy of the rational soul, directed to itself, and not converted to the phantasy.

‡ Opinion is the conclusion of the dianoëtic energy. See the *Sophista.*

SOC. And again, he who only opines one of these, but by no means the other, can never opine that one of them is the other.

THEÆ. True. For he would be compelled to touch upon that about which he does not opine.

e SOC. Neither, therefore, can he who opines both, nor he who only opines one of them, opine foreign to the purpose. So that he will say nothing, who defines false opinion to be heterodoxy. For neither will false opinion appear to reside in us in this manner, nor in that which we have already mentioned.

THEÆ. It does not appear that it will.

SOC. But, Theætetus, if this should not appear to be the case, we should be compelled to confess many things, and of an absurd nature.

THEÆ. What are these?

SOC. I will not tell you, till I have endeavoured to consider the affair in every possible way. For I should be ashamed, with respect to that of
191a which we are in doubt, if we were compelled to confess what I now say. But if we shall discover the object of our search, and become free, then we may speak concerning others, as suffering these things, while we shall be raised beyond the reach of ridicule. But if we should be involved in inextricable doubts, and thus become abject, and filled with nausea, then, I think, we should permit our discourse to trample on us, and use us as it pleases. Hear, then, whether I have found out any passage to the object of our inquiry.

THEÆ. Only speak.

SOC. I shall not say that we rightly consented, when we acknowledged that it was impossible any one could opine that the things which he knows are things which he does not know, and thus be deceived: but I say that this is in a certain respect possible.

b THEÆ. Do you say that which I suspected might be the case when we made this assertion, as that I knowing Socrates, and seeing another person at a distance whom I do not know, might think it was Socrates, whom I do know? For that which you say takes place in a thing of this kind.

SOC. Are we not, therefore, driven from the hypothesis which caused us to acknowledge, that, with respect to things which we know, we are ignorant of them, at the same time that we know them?

THEÆ. Entirely so.

c SOC. We must not, therefore, establish this hypothesis, but the following: and perhaps some one will in a certain respect assent to us, or perhaps will oppose us. But we are now in that situation in which it is necessary to examine the discourse which perverts all things.

Consider, therefore, whether I say any thing to the purpose. Is it then possible for any one who formerly was ignorant of something, afterwards to learn that thing?

THEÆ. It certainly is possible.

SOC. And can he not also learn another and another thing?

THEÆ. Why should he not?

SOC. Place for me, for the sake of an example, one waxen image[†] in our souls: in this soul a greater image, and in that a lesser: and in this of purer, but in that of impurer and harder wax: and in some again of a moister kind, but in others sufficiently tempered.

THEÆ. I place it.

SOC. We must say, then, that this is a gift of Mnemosyne the mother of the Muses; and that in this, whatever we wish to remember of things which we have seen, or heard, or understood, is impressed like images made by a seal, by insinuating itself into our senses and conceptions. And further, that we remember and know that which is impressed in this waxen image, as long as the impressed figure remains; but when it is destroyed, or can be no longer impressed, we forget and cease to know.

THEÆ. Be it so.

SOC. Consider, therefore, whether he who knows these impressions, and attends to what he either sees or hears, can after this manner opine falsely?

THEÆ. After what manner?

TER. With respect to what he knows, at one time opining that he knows, and at another time that he does not know. For we improperly granted above, that it was impossible for this to happen.

THEÆ. But how do you now say?

SOC. It is requisite thus to speak about these things, defining them from the beginning: That it is impossible that he who knows any thing, and has a monument of it in his soul, but does not perceive it, can opine that it is something else which he knows, and the image of which he possesses, but does not perceive. And again, it is impossible that any one can opine that what he knows is that which he does not know, and of which he does not possess the image: or that what he does not know

---

† What is here said must not be understood literally; for Plato was by no means of opinion that images are fashioned by external objects in the soul. But nothing more is here meant, than either that the soul naturally possesses these images, or that, taking occasion from external motions, and the passions of body, she conceives forms in herself by her own native power.

is that which he knows. It is likewise impossible for any one to opine that what he perceives is some other sensible object different from what he perceives: or that what he perceives is something which he does not perceive: or that what he does not perceive is something else which he does not perceive: or that what he does not perceive is something which he does perceive. Nor, again, can any one opine that what he knows and perceives, and of which he has a sensible image, is something else which he knows and perceives, and of which he in like manner possesses a sensible image: or that what he knows and perceives, and of which he possesses an image in a proper manner, is the same as that which he simply knows: or that what he knows and perceives, and similarly retains, is that which he perceives: or again, that what he neither knows nor perceives is the same as that which he simply does not know: or that what he neither knows nor perceives is the same as that which he does not perceive. For in all these it is impossible to opine falsely. It remains, therefore, that false opinion must take place in some things of this kind, if it has any subsistence.

THEÆ. In what things, therefore? that I may see whether I can learn better from these. For at present I do not follow you.

SOC. In those things which any one knowing, opines that they are certain other things which he knows and perceives; or which he does not know, but perceives; or which both knowing and perceiving, he opines that he knows and perceives.

THEÆ. I now leave you behind, at a greater distance than before.

SOC. Hear then again as follows: I knowing Theodorus, and remembering in myself what kind of man he is, and in like manner Theætetus, sometimes I see them, and sometimes I do not: and sometimes I touch them, and sometimes not; and hear or perceive them with some other sense: but sometimes I do not apprehend any thing respecting you by any sense, yet nevertheless I remember you, and know you in myself.

THEÆ. Entirely so.

SOC. Learn this, therefore, the first of the things which I wish to evince to you, that it is possible for a man not to perceive that which he knows, and that it is likewise possible for him to perceive it.

THEÆ. True.

SOC. Does it not often happen that a man does not perceive that which he does not know, and likewise often happen that he perceives it only?

THEÆ. This also is true.

193a   SOC. See, then, if you can now follow me better. Socrates knows
Theodorus and Theætetus, but sees neither of them, nor is any other
sense present with him respecting them. Can he ever in this case opine
in himself, that Theætetus is Theodorus? Do I say any thing, or
nothing?

THEÆ. You speak pertinently; for he cannot thus opine.

SOC. This then was the first of those things which I said.

THEÆ. It was.

SOC. But the second was this, that while I know one of you, but do
not know the other, and perceive neither of you, I can never opine that
he whom I know is the man whom I do not know.

THEÆ. Right.

b   SOC. But the third was this, that while I neither know nor perceive
either of them, I can never opine that he whom I do not know is some
other person whom I do not know: and in a similar manner think that
you again hear all that was said above, in which I can never opine falsely
respecting you and Theodorus, neither while knowing nor while
ignorant of both; nor while knowing one, and not knowing the other.
And the same may be said respecting the senses, if you apprehend me.

THEÆ. I do apprehend you.

c   SOC. It remains, therefore, that I must then opine falsely, when
knowing you and Theodorus, and preserving in that waxen image, as in
a seal ring, the impression of both of you for a long time, and not
sufficiently seeing both of you, I endeavour, by attributing the proper
impression of each to my particular sight, so to harmonize this
impression to the vestige of sight, that a recognizance may take place:
but afterwards failing in the attempt, and changing like those that
change their shoes, I transfer the vision of each to a foreign impression,
and err by being similarly affected to the passions of sight in mirrors,
d   where things on the right hand flow back to those on the left hand. For
then heterodoxy takes place, and I opine falsely.

THEÆ. It appears, Socrates, that the passion of opinion is such as in
a wonderful manner you have represented it to be.

SOC. Still further, when knowing both of you, I besides this perceive
one of you, and not the other, then I have a knowledge of him whom
I do not perceive, but not according to sense; which is what I said
before, but you did not then understand me.

THEÆ. I did not.

SOC. This however I said, that he who knows and perceives one of
e   you, and has a knowledge of you according to sense, will never opine
that this object of his knowledge and perception is some other person

whom he knows and perceives, and of whom he has a knowledge according to sense. Was not this what I said?

THEÆ. It was.

SOC. But in a certain respect that which I just now said is omitted, - I mean, that false opinion then takes place, when any one knowing and seeing both of you, or possessing any other sense of both of you, and likewise retaining your images in his soul, has not a proper perception of either of you, but, like an unskilful archer, wanders from and misses the mark, which is therefore denominated a falsehood.

THEÆ. And very properly so.

SOC. When, therefore, sense is present to one of the impressions, and not to the other, and that which belongs to the absent sense is adapted to the sense then present, in this case the dianoëtic part is entirely deceived. And, in one word, it is not possible, as it appears, either to be deceived, or to have a false opinion, respecting things which a man has neither ever known or perceived, if we now say any thing to the purpose. But respecting things which we know and perceive, in these opinion is rolled about and evolved, becoming both true and false. And when it collects and marks its proper resemblances in an opposite and straight forward direction, then it is true, but when in a transverse and oblique direction, false.

THEÆ. These things, therefore, Socrates, are beautifully said.

SOC. And you will much more say so, when you hear what follows. For to opine the truth is beautiful, but to lie is base.

THEÆ. Undoubtedly.

SOC. They say, therefore, that hence the following particulars take place. When that waxen image in the soul is profound, abundant, smooth, and sufficiently perfect, then the several particulars which proceed through the senses, being impressed in this heart† of the soul, (as Homer calls it, obscurely signifying its similitude to wax,) so as to become pure signatures, and of sufficient profundity, - in this case they become lasting. And, in the first place, men with such impressions as these are docile: in the next place, they are endued with a good memory: and, in the third place, they do not change the impressions of the senses, but opine the truth. For, as these impressions are clear, and situated in an ample region, they swiftly distribute sensible particulars to their proper resemblances, which are called beings; and such men are denominated wise. Or does it not appear so to you?

THEÆ. It does in a transcendent degree.

---

† For κηρ or κεαρ is the *heart*, and κηρος is *wax*.

e   SOC. When, therefore, any one's heart is hairy (which the perfectly
wise poet has celebrated), or when it is of a muddy nature, and not of
pure wax, or when it is very moist, or hard, then it is in a bad
condition. For those in whom it is moist are indeed docile, but become
oblivious; and those in whom it is hard are affected in a contrary
manner. But men in whom it is hairy and rough, in consequence of its
possessing something of a stony nature, mingled with earth or clay, these
contain obscure resemblances. The resemblances too are obscure in
those in whom this heart is hard: for in this case it has no profundity.
195a   This likewise happens to those in whom it is moist: for, in consequence
of the impressions being confounded, they swiftly become obscure. But
if, besides all this, they fall on each other, through the narrowness of
their receptacle, since it belongs to a little soul, then the resemblances
become still more obscure. All such as these, therefore, opine falsely.
For when they see, or hear, or think about any thing, as they are unable
swiftly to attribute things to their resemblances, they judge erroneously;
because they see, hear, and understand for the most part perversely.
And such as these are called deceivers, and are said to be ignorant of
things.
b   THEÆ. You speak with the greatest rectitude of all men, Socrates.
       SOC. Shall we say, then, that false opinions reside in us?
       THEÆ. Very much so.
       SOC. And true opinions likewise?
       THEÆ. And true opinions.
       SOC. Socrates, I think, therefore, it has been sufficiently acknowledged
by us, that these two opinions have a subsistence more than any thing.
       THEÆ. It has in a transcendent degree.
       SOC. A loquacious man, Theætetus, appears in reality to be a dire and
unpleasant man.
       THEÆ. With reference to what do you speak in this manner?
c   SOC. With reference to my own indocility, and real loquacity, at
which I am indignant. For what else than a loquacious man can he be
called, who through his stupidity draws discourse upwards and
downwards, not being able to procure persuasion, and who with
difficulty abandons an assertion?
       THEÆ. But why are you indignant?
       SOC. I am not only indignant, but I am fearful what I should answer,
if any one should ask me, O Socrates, have you found that false opinion
is neither in the mutual energies of the senses, nor in dianoëtic energies,
d   but in the conjunction of sense with the dianoëtic energy? But I think

I should say, boasting, as if we had discovered something beautiful, that we had found it to be so.

THEÆ. What has been just now evinced appears to me, Socrates, to be no despicable thing.

SOC. Do you, therefore, he will say, assert that we can never opine, that a man whom we alone dianoëtically conceive, but do not see, is a horse which we neither at present see, nor touch, nor perceive by any other sense, but only dianoëtically conceive? I think I should say that I do assert these things.

THEÆ. And very properly.

e   SOC. Will it not, therefore, follow, he will say, according to this reason, that no one will ever think eleven, which he only dianoëtically perceives, to be twelve, which he only dianoëtically perceives? What answer would you give?

THEÆ. I should answer, that some one seeing or touching eleven things, might opine them to be twelve; but that he would never opine in this manner respecting the numbers which he possesses in his dianoëtic part.

196a   SOC. But what, he will say, do you think that any one can speculate about five and seven - I do not mean five and seven men, or any thing else of this kind, but five and seven themselves, which we said were in his soul like impressions in wax - so as never to opine falsely respecting them? Or will not some men, when they consider these things by themselves, and inquire about their amount, opine that they are eleven, and others that they are twelve? Or will all men say and opine that they are twelve?

b   THEÆ. By Jupiter they will not; but the greater part will opine that they are eleven. And if any one should ask them the amount of more numbers, their answer would be still more erroneous. For I think that you rather speak about every number.

SOC. You think rightly. Consider, therefore, whether this ever happens, that any one opines that the twelve which are impressed in his soul are eleven?

THEÆ. It seems this does happen.

SOC. Does not this then revolve to the former assertions? For he who suffers that which he knows, opines that it is some other thing which he also knows, which we said was impossible: and from this very circumstance we are compelled to confess, that there is no such thing as

c   false opinion, lest the same person should be forced to know and at the same time not to know the same things.

THEÆ. Most true.

SOC. Hence it appears that false opinion must be otherwise defined than a mutation of the dianoëtic energy with respect to sense. For, if this was a true definition, we should never be deceived in dianoëtic conceptions themselves. But now there is either no such thing as false opinion, or, if there is, a man may be ignorant of that which at the same time he knows. And which of these will you choose?

THEÆ. You have proposed an ambiguous choice, Socrates.

SOC. But it appears that reason will not permit both these to take
d   place. At the same time, however, (for all things must be attempted), what if we should endeavour to divest ourselves of shame?

THEÆ. How?

SOC. By being willing to say what it is to have a scientific knowledge of a thing.

THEÆ. But why would this be impudent?

SOC. You do not appear to understand that the whole of our discourse from the beginning is an investigation of science, as if we did not know what it is.

THEÆ. I understand you.

SOC. But does it not appear to be the part of impudent persons, to show what it is to have a scientific knowledge, at the same time that
e   they are ignorant what science is? But, Theætetus, it is now some time since we have not spoken with purity. For we have ten thousand times employed the terms, We know, and We do not know, We have a scientific knowledge, and We have not a scientific knowledge, as if we mutually understood something, in which at the same time we are ignorant what science is. But at present, if you are willing, we will use the terms, to be ignorant, and to understand, in such a manner as it is proper to use them, since we are destitute of science.

THEÆ. But how in this case, Socrates, shall we be able to discourse?
197a SOC. Not at all while I remain as I am. But I might be able, if I was contentious: and now, if any contentious person was present, he would say that he abstained from such terms, and would very much deter us from what I say. But, as we are bad, man, are you willing I should dare to say what it is to know scientifically? For it appears to me to be worth while.

THEÆ. Dare then, by Jupiter. For you will greatly deserve to be pardoned for the attempt.

SOC. Have you heard what at present they say it is to know scientifically?

THEÆ. Perhaps so; but at present I do not remember.
b   SOC. They say that it is the habit of science.

THEÆ. True.

SOC. We, therefore, shall make a trifling alteration, and say that it is the possession of science.

THEÆ. But in what do you say this differs from that

SOC. Perhaps in nothing. But when you have heard that which appears to me to be the case, examine it together with me.

THEÆ. I will, if I can.

SOC. To *possess*, therefore, does not appear to me to be the same as to *have* a thing. Thus, if any one buys a garment, and, having the power of using it when he pleases, does not wear it, we should not say that he *has* the garment, but that he *possesses* it.

THEÆ. And very properly.

c   SOC. See then whether it is possible to possess science in this manner, without having it: just as if some one having caught certain wild doves,[†] or other wild birds, and having constructed an aviary for them at home, should feed and nourish them. For in a certain respect we should say that he always *has*, because he *possesses* them. Should we not?

THEÆ. We should.

SOC. But in another respect we should say that he by no means *has* them, but that he has a power, since he has shut them up for his own

d   use, in an inclosure of his own, of taking and having them when he pleases, and of again dismissing them: and that he can do this as often as it is agreeable to him.

THEÆ. Exactly so.

SOC. Again, as before we devised I know not what waxen figment in the soul, so now let us place a certain aviary containing all sorts of birds in the soul, some of which fly in flocks, apart from others; but others again fly in small companies; and some fly alone, wherever they may happen to find a passage.

e   THEÆ. Let it be so: but what follows?

SOC. It is requisite to say, that this receptacle is empty in children: but in the place of birds we must understand sciences, and say, that he who possesses science, and confines it in this inclosure, learns or discovers

---

† It is justly observed by Proclus, in his admirable Commentary on the first book of Euclid's *Elements* [I, 10, see TTS vol. XXIX, p.105], that Socrates here, mingling the jocose with the serious, assimilates the sciences which are in us to doves. He also says that they fly away, some in flocks, and others separate from the rest. For the sciences that are more common contain in themselves many that are more partial; and those that are distributed according to species, touching on the objects of their knowledge, are separated from, and unconjoined with, each other, in consequence of originating from different primary principles.

that thing of which he possesses the science; and that this is to have a
scientific knowledge.

THEÆ. Be it so.

198a SOC. But again, consider, when any one is willing to investigate
sciences, and receiving to *have* them, and afterwards dismiss them, by
what names all these particulars ought to be expressed. Shall we say by
the same names as at first, when sciences were *possessed*, or by other
names? But from what follows you will more clearly understand what
I say. Do you not call arithmetic an art?

THEÆ. I do.

SOC. Suppose this to be the hunting of the sciences of all the even and
odd.

THEÆ. I suppose it.

b SOC. But I think by this art the arithmetician has the sciences of
numbers in his power, and delivers them to others.

THEÆ. He does so.

SOC. And we say that he who delivers these sciences teaches, but that
he who receives them learns; and that he who *has* them, in consequence
of possessing them in that inclosure which we mentioned, knows
scientifically.

THEÆ. Entirely so.

SOC. But attend to what follows. Does not he who is a perfect
arithmetician know scientifically all numbers? For the sciences of all
numbers are in his soul.

THEÆ. Undoubtedly.

c SOC. Does not a man of this kind sometimes enumerate with himself
internally, and sometimes externally, such things as have number?

THEÆ. Certainly.

SOC. But to number is considered by us as nothing else than the
speculation of the quantity of any number.

THEÆ. It is so.

SOC. He, therefore, who has a scientific knowledge, by thus
speculating, appears not to know, though we have confessed that he
knows every number. Do you hear these ambiguities?

THEÆ. I do.

d SOC. When, therefore, we assimilated sciences to the possession and
fowling of doves, we said that fowling was twofold; one kind being prior
to acquisition, and subsisting for the sake of possession, and subsisting
for the sake of receiving and having in the hands things which were
formerly possessed. So these sciences, which any one had formerly been
endued with by learning, and which he had known before, may again

be learnt, by resuming and retaining the science of every particular which he formerly possessed, but which he has not at hand in his dianoëtic part.

THEÆ. True.

SOC. On this account, I just now inquired how names respecting these things were to be used, as when an arithmetician numbers, or a grammarian reads. For, in either case, he who knows again applies himself to know by himself what he already knows.

THEÆ. But this is absurd, Socrates.

SOC. Shall we therefore say, that the grammarian reads, or the arithmetician numbers, things of which he is ignorant, though we have granted that the one knows all letters, and the other every number?

THEÆ. But this also is irrational.

SOC. Are you, therefore, willing we should say, that we are not at all concerned how any one may employ the names of knowing and learning? But since we have determined that it is one thing to *possess*, and another to *have*, science, we must say that it is impossible for any one not to possess that which he does possess. So that it will never happen that any one does not know that which he does know; though about this very thing false opinion may be received. For it may happen that we may take the science of one thing for the science of another, when, hunting after some one of our inward sciences, we erroneously receive instead of it some other that flies away. As when any one opines that eleven things are twelve: for then, receiving the science of eleven things instead of twelve, he takes out of his aviary a pigeon instead of a dove.

THEÆ. It is reasonable to suppose so.

SOC. But when he receives that which he endeavours to receive, then he is free from falsehood, and opines things which are. And after this manner false and true opinion subsist: and thus none of the particulars which disturbed us before will be any longer an impediment to us. Perhaps, therefore, you assent to me: or how will you do?

THEÆ. Assent to you.

TER. We are then now freed from the dilemma respecting a man knowing and at the same time not knowing a thing. For it will no longer happen that we shall not possess that which we do possess, whether we judge falsely or not. However, a more dire passion than this appears to me to present itself to the view.

THEÆ. What is that?

TER. If the permutation of sciences should ever become false opinion.

THEÆ. But how?

d   SOC. In the first place, is it not absurd, that he who has the science of
any thing should be ignorant of that thing, not through ignorance, but
through the science of the thing? And in the next place, that he should
opine this thing to be that, and that thing this? And is it not very
irrational to suppose, that when science is present the soul should know
nothing, but should be ignorant of all things? For, from this assertion,
nothing hinders but that ignorance when present may enable a man to
know something, and cause blindness to see, if science ever makes a man
to be ignorant of any thing.

e   THEÆ. Perhaps, Socrates, we have not properly introduced birds, as
we alone placed sciences in the soul, but we ought at the same time to
have placed the various kinds of ignorance flying in companies; and a
man employed in fowling, at one time receiving science, and at another
time ignorance, about the same thing: through ignorance opining what
is false, but through science the truth.

       SOC. It is by no means easy Theætetus, not to praise you. However,
again consider what you have said. For let it be as you say. But he who
receives ignorance, you will say, opines things false. Is it not so?

200a   THEÆ. It is.

       SOC. But yet he will not think that he opines falsely.

       THEÆ. He will not.

       SOC. But that he opines truly. And he will be affected with respect
to those things in which he errs, like one endued with knowledge.

       THEÆ. Undoubtedly.

       SOC. He will therefore opine that he has by fowling obtained science,
and not ignorance.

       THEÆ. It is evident.

       SOC. Hence, after having made a long circuit, we have again fallen
into the first doubt. For that reprover whom we mentioned before will

b   laughing say to us, O best of men, whether can he who knows both
science and ignorance opine that what he knows is some other thing
which he also knows? or, knowing neither of these, can he opine that
a thing which he does not know is some other things which he does not
know? or, knowing one of these, and not the other, can he opine that
what he knows is that which he does not know? or that what he does
not know is that which he does know? Or, again, tell me whether there
are sciences of sciences, and of the various kinds of ignorance, which he

c   who possesses, and incloses in other certain ridiculous aviaries, or waxen
figments, knows so far as he possesses them, though he has them not at
hand in his soul? And thus you will be compelled to revolve infinitely

about the same thing, without making any proficiency. What shall we reply to these things, Theætetus?

THEÆ. By Jupiter, Socrates, I do not know what ought to be said.

SOC. Does not, therefore, O boy, the discourse of this man very properly reprove us, and evince that we have not done right in investigating false opinion prior to science, and leaving science undiscussed? But it is impossible to know this till we have sufficiently determined what science is.

THEÆ. It is necessary, Socrates, to suspect at present, as you say.

SOC. What then can any one again say from the beginning respecting science? For we are not yet weary of speaking.

THEÆ. Not in the least, if you do not forbid it.

SOC. Tell me, then, in what manner we can so speak concerning science as not to contradict ourselves.

THEÆ. In the same manner as we attempted before, Socrates; for I have not any thing else to offer.

SOC. In what manner do you mean?

THEÆ. That true opinion is science. For to opine truly is without error; and every thing that proceeds from it is beautiful and good.

SOC. He who in fording a river, Theætetus, is the leader of others, if interrogated respecting the depth of the water, will answer that the water will show its own depth. In like manner, if, entering into the present subject, we inquire, the impediment to our passage will, perhaps, present to us the object of our search: but, if we remain where we are, nothing will become manifest.

THEÆ. You speak well: but let us proceed and consider.

SOC. Is not this, therefore, a thing of brief consideration? For the whole of art, and its professors, evince that art is not science.

THEÆ. How so? And who are these professors?

SOC. Those that excel all others in wisdom, and who are called orators and lawyers. For these persuade, but do not teach by their art, and cause their hearers to opine whatever they please. Or do you think there are any teachers so skilful, as to be able in cases of robbery, and other violences, to evince sufficiently the truth of the transactions by means of a little water?

THEÆ. I by no means think there are: but these men persuade.

SOC. But do you not say that to effect persuasion is the same thing as to produce opinion?

THEÆ. Undoubtedly.

SOC. When, therefore, judges are justly persuaded respecting things which he who sees can alone know, but by no means otherwise, is it c possible that thus judging by report, and receiving true opinion without science, they can judge rightly respecting things of which they are persuaded, if we admit that they judge well?

THEÆ. I entirely think they can.

SOC. But, my friend, if true opinion, judgment, and science are the same, that consummate judge can never opine with rectitude without science: but now each appears to be something different.

THEÆ. I had forgotten, Socrates, what I heard a certain person say concerning science, but I now remember. But he said that true opinion
d in conjunction with reason is science, but that without reason it is void of science; and that things cannot be known scientifically of which there is no reason, but that things may be thus known which have a reason.

SOC. How well you speak! But tell me how he divided things which may be scientifically known, and which cannot be so known, that we may see whether you and I similarly understand them.

THEÆ. I do not know that I can discover how he divided these; but I can follow another person discoursing.

SOC. Hear, then, a dream for a dream. For I also appear to have
e heard from certain persons that the first elements,† as it were, from which we and other things are composed cannot be rationally described. For they say that each of these can alone be denominated by itself, but
202a cannot be called any thing else, neither as that which is nor as that which is not; because essence, or non-essence, would thus be assigned to it. But it is requisite to add nothing, if any one speaks of a thing itself alone. For neither the term this, nor that, nor each, nor alone, nor any other such appellations, should be employed, because these are applied to things in a circular progression, and are different from the things to which they are added. But it is necessary, if possible, to speak of the thing itself, and, if it has a proper definition, to assert something respecting it, without the addition of any thing else. Now, however, no
b one of things first can be made the subject of discourse; for it does not admit of any thing else than a denomination. But the things composed from these, as they are themselves woven together, so from the weaving together of their names discourse is produced. For the connection of names is the essence of discourse. Hence, the elements themselves are ineffable and unknown, but at the same time are objects of sense: but syllables are known and effable, and may be apprehended by true

---

† Prodicus the Chian, imitating Leucippus, asserted that the elements of things, because they are simple, and therefore without definition, are unknown; but that composites, since they can be defined, may be known.

c   opinion. When, therefore, any one receives a true opinion of any thing, without reason, then his soul perceives the truth respecting it, but he does not know the thing; because he who is incapable of giving and receiving a reason concerning a thing must be destitute of science respecting it. But when he receives a reason, then he may be able to know all these, and acquire science in perfection. Have you not, therefore, heard a dream, or is it any thing else?

THEÆ. It is nothing else.

SOC. Is it, therefore, agreeable to you that we should establish science to be true opinion in conjunction with reason?

THEÆ. Very much so.

d   SOC. Have we, therefore, Theætetus, this very day detected that which formerly many wise men investigating grew old before they discovered?

THEÆ. To me, Socrates, what was just now said appears to be well said.

SOC. And it is very fit it should: for what science can there be without reason and right opinion? But one of the assertions does not please me.

THEÆ. What is that?

SOC. That which appears to be very elegantly said; that the elements of speech are unknown, but the genus of syllables known.

e   THEÆ. Is not this right?

SOC. Take notice. For we have as hostages of discourse those very paradigms, which he employing said all that I have related.

THEÆ. What are these paradigms?

SOC. The things pertaining to letters, *viz.* elements and syllables. Or do you think that he who said what we have related spoke in this manner looking to any thing else than these?

THEÆ. To nothing else than these.

203a   SOC. Let us, therefore, receiving these, examine them, or rather ourselves, whether we learn letters in this manner, or not. In the first place, then, have syllables a definition, but not the elements?

THEÆ. Perhaps so.

SOC. To me, also, it very much appears to be so. if, therefore, any one should thus ask respecting the first syllable of the word Socrates, O Theætetus, *viz.* what is *So?* what would you answer?

THEÆ. That it is *S* and *o.*

SOC. You have, therefore, this definition of the syllable.

THEÆ. I have.

b   SOC. But come, in a similar manner give me a definition of the letter
S.

THEÆ. But how can any one speak of the elements of an element?
For S, Socrates, is only a certain sound of mute letters, the tongue, as it
were, hissing: but of the letter B there is neither voice nor sound, nor of
most of the elements. So that it is very well said that they are ineffable,
among which the well-known seven vowels are alone vocal, but have not
any reason or definition.

SOC. This therefore, my friend, we have rightly asserted respecting
science.

THEÆ. So it appears.

c   SOC. But have we rightly shown that a syllable is known, but not an
element?

THEÆ. It is likely.

SOC. But with respect to this syllable, whether shall we say that it is
both the elements; and, if there are more than two, that it is all those
elements? Or shall we say that it is one certain idea produced from the
composition of the elements?

THEÆ. It appears to me that we should say it is all the elements.

SOC. See, then, with respect to the two letters S and o, which form
the first syllable of my name, whether he who knows this syllable
knows both these letters?

d   THEÆ. Undoubtedly.

SOC. He knows, therefore, S and o.

THEÆ. Yes.

SOC. But what, if he knows each, and, knowing neither, knows both?

THEÆ. But this would be dire and absurd, Socrates.

SOC. But if it is necessary to know each, if any one knows both, it is
necessary that he who in any future time knows a syllable should
previously know all the elements: and so that beautiful assertion escaping
from us will disappear.

e   THEÆ. And very suddenly too.

SOC. For we did not well secure it. For, perhaps, a syllable ought to
have been adopted, and not the elements; but one certain species
produced from them, and which is different from the elements.

THEÆ. Entirely so: and perhaps the thing takes place in this manner
rather than in that.

SOC. We should consider, therefore, and not in so effeminate a
manner betray a great and venerable assertion.

THEÆ. We ought not, indeed.

204a SOC. Let a syllable then, as we just now said, be one idea produced from several according elements, as well in letters as in all other things.

THEÆ. Entirely so.

SOC. It ought not, therefore, to have any parts.

THEÆ. Why not?

SOC. Because the whole of that which has parts must necessarily be all the parts. Or do you say that a whole which is produced from parts is one certain species different from all the parts?

THEÆ. I do.

b SOC. But with respect to the all, and the whole, whether do you call each of these the same, or different?

THEÆ. I have not any thing clear to say; yet since you order me to answer with alacrity, I will venture to say that each of these is different.

SOC. Your alacrity, Theætetus, is right; but whether your answer is so, we must consider.

THEÆ. It is necessary.

SOC. Does not the whole, therefore, differ from the all, according to your present assertion?

THEÆ. It does.

c SOC. But do all things and the all differ in any respect? As when we say one, two, three, four, five, six: or twice three, or thrice two, or four and two, or three and two and one, or five and one; - whether in all these do we say the same thing, or that which is different?

THEÆ. The same thing.

SOC. Do we say any thing else than six?

THEÆ. Nothing else.

SOC. According to each mode of speaking, therefore, we find that all are six.

THEÆ. We do.

SOC. Again, therefore, we do not say any one thing when we say all things.

THEÆ. It is necessary.

SOC. Do we say any thing else than six things?

THEÆ. Nothing else.

d SOC. In things, therefore, which consist from number, we say that the all is the same with all things.

THEÆ. So it appears.

SOC. Should we not, therefore, say respecting them, that the number of an acre is the same as an acre?

THEÆ. We should.

Soc. And in a similar manner that the number of a stadium is a stadium?

Theæ. Yes.

Soc. And so respecting the number of an army, and an army itself, and all other such like particulars? For every number, being an all, is each of these particulars.

Theæ. It is.

e Soc. But is the number of each of these any thing else than parts?

Theæ. Nothing else.

Soc. Such things, therefore, as have parts consist of parts.

Theæ. It appears so.

Soc. But it is acknowledged that all the parts are the all, since every number is the all.

Theæ. It is so.

Soc. The whole, therefore, is not from parts: for it would be the all, in consequence of being all the parts.

Theæ. It does not appear that it is.

Soc. But does a part belong to any thing else than to a whole?

Theæ. It belongs to the all.

205a Soc. You fight strenuously, Theætetus. But is not the all, then this very thing the all, when nothing is wanting to it?

Theæ. it is necessary.

Soc. And is not, after the same manner, the whole that which it is, when nothing is wanting to it? And is it not true, that that which is in want of any thing, in consequence of this deficiency, is neither the whole, nor the all?

Theæ. It now appears to me, that the whole and the all in no respect differ from each other.

Soc. Do we not say that the whole and the all are all the parts of that of which they are the parts?

Theæ. Entirely so.

b Soc. Again, therefore, that we may resume what we attempted before, if a syllable is not elements, must it not necessarily follow that it has not elements as parts of itself? or that, if it is the same with them, it must with them be similarly known?

Theæ. It must.

Soc. Lest, therefore, this should take place, we must establish the one to be different from the other.

Theæ. We must.

SOC. But if elements are not parts of a syllable, can you assign any other things which are parts of a syllable, and yet are not the elements of it?

THEÆ. I should by no means grant, Socrates, that things which are not the elements can be the parts of a syllable. For it is ridiculous, neglecting the elements, to proceed in search of other things.

c   SOC. According to the present reasoning, therefore, Theætetus, a syllable will be in every respect one particular impartible idea.

THEÆ. It appears so.

SOC. Do you remember, therefore, my friend, that we admitted a little before, and thought it was well said, that there could be no reason or definition of things first, from which other things are composed, because each thing considered itself by itself is not a composite; and that neither the term 'to be' can with propriety be accommodated to it, nor the term 'this', because these are asserted as things different and foreign; and that this very circumstance causes a thing to be ineffable and unknown?

THEÆ. I do remember.

d   SOC. Is any thing else, therefore, than this the cause of any thing being uniform and impartible? For I see no other cause.

THEÆ. It does not appear that there is any other.

SOC. Will not a syllable, therefore, be a species of this kind, since it has no parts, and is one idea?

THEÆ. Entirely so.

SOC. If, therefore, a syllable is many elements, and a certain whole, and these elements are its parts, syllables and elements may be similarly known, and are similarly effable, since all the parts appear to be the same with the whole.

e   THEÆ. And very much so.

SOC. But if a syllable is one impartible thing, a syllable and an element are equally ineffable and unknown. For the same cause renders them such.

THEÆ. I cannot say otherwise.

SOC. We must not, therefore, admit the assertion, that a syllable is a thing known and effable, but an element the contrary.

THEÆ. We must not, if we are persuaded by this reasoning.

206a   SOC. But what again, if any one should assert the contrary, would you not rather admit it from those things of which you were conscious when you learnt your letters?

THEÆ. What things are those?

SOC. As that you endeavoured to learn nothing else than how to know the elements by your eyes and ears, each itself by itself, that the position of them, when they were pronounced or written, might not disturb you.

THEÆ. You speak most true.

SOC. But is the learning to play on the harp in perfection any thing else than the ability of knowing what sound belongs to every chord? For this every one agrees should be called the elements of music.

THEÆ. It is nothing else.

SOC. As, therefore, we are skilled in elements and syllables, if it was requisite to conjecture from these respecting other things, we should say that the genus of the elements possessed a much clearer and more principal knowledge than that of syllables, with respect to receiving each discipline in perfection. And if any one should say that a syllable is a thing known, but that an element is naturally unknown, we should think that he jested either voluntarily or involuntarily.

THEÆ. And very much so.

SOC. But, as it appears to me, there are yet other demonstrations of this thing. We must not, however, on account of these particulars, forget the thing proposed by us, *viz.* to investigate the assertion, that reason united with true opinion becomes most perfect science.

THEÆ. It is proper, therefore, to consider this.

SOC. Come then, inform me what is the signification of the word *logos:* for it appears to me to signify one of three things.

THEÆ. What are they?

SOC. The first will be to make its own dianoëtic conception apparent, through voice, in conjunction with verbs and nouns; thus impressing opinion in the flux through the mouth, as in a mirror, or in water. Or does not logos appear to you to be a thing of this kind?

THEÆ. It does: and we say that he who does this speaks.

SOC. Cannot, therefore, every one do this - I mean, point out with more or less swiftness what appears to him respecting particulars - unless he is either naturally deaf or dumb? And thus it will follow, that whoever opines any thing rightly will appear to opine in conjunction with logos; and true opinion will never subsist without science.

THEÆ. True.

SOC. We must not, therefore, easily condemn him who asserts science to be that which we just now mentioned, as if he said nothing. For perhaps this was not his meaning; but, being asked what each particular is, he might be able to answer the interrogator, through the elements.

THEÆ. How to you mean, Socrates?

SOC. The same as Hesiod,[†] when he speaks of a chariot as composed of a hundred pieces of wood; which I am not able to say, nor do I think you are. But we should be contented, if, when asked what a chariot is, we were able to say that it is wheels, an axis, plankings, arches, and a yoke.

THEÆ. Entirely so.

SOC. But he perhaps would think we are ridiculous, just as if we were asked concerning your name, and should answer by a syllable; considering us indeed in what we say as thinking and speaking properly,

b but that we are grammarians, and that we possessed and spoke grammatically the definition of the name of Theætetus. He would likewise say, that no one can speak scientifically about any thing, till he has brought it to a conclusion through the elements, in conjunction with true opinion, as we observed before.

THEÆ. We did so.

SOC. After this manner, therefore, he would think we may possess

c true opinion respecting the chariot; but that he who is able to pervade its essence through those hundred pieces of wood, can also comprehend its logos or definition, in conjunction with true opinion; and, instead of being one that opines, will thus possess art and science, respecting the essence of the chariot, determining the whole of it, through its elements.

THEÆ. Does not this appear to you, Socrates, to be well said?

SOC. If it appears so to you, my friend, and if you admit that this discursive process through an element respecting every thing is logos, or reason, and that this is the case with the process through syllables, or

d that it is something still greater, void of reason. Tell me what you think, that we may consider it.

THEÆ. But I very much admit this.

SOC. But do you admit it in such a manner as to think that any one has a scientific knowledge of any thing, when the same thing appears to him at a different times to belong to different things; or when he opines different things at different times of the same thing?

THEO. Not I, by Jupiter.

SOC. Have you forgotten that both you and others thought in this manner, when you first learnt your letters?

---

† The future editors of Hesiod may increase the fragments of that poet with this part of a verse,

. . . . εκατον δε τε δουραθ' αμαξης.

[*Works and Days*, 455.]

THEÆ. Do you mean to say, that we thought that at one time one letter, and at another time another, belonged to the same syllable; and that the same letter was at one time to be referred to its proper syllable, and at another time to a different syllable?

Soc. This is what I mean.

THEÆ. By Jupiter, I do not forget; nor do I think that those who are thus affected possess a scientific knowledge.

Soc. What then, when any one at that time writing the word Theætetus, opines that he ought to write *Th* and *e*, and accordingly writes these letters; and again attempting to write Theodorus, opines that he ought to write *Th* and *e*, and writes these letters, shall we say that he knows scientifically the first syllable of your names?

THEÆ. But we just now acknowledged, that he who is affected in this manner does not yet know.

Soc. Does any thing, therefore, hinder the same person from being affected in the same manner respecting the second, third, and fourth syllable?

THEÆ. Nothing hinders.

Soc. Will not such a one, therefore, in consequence of his discursive process through an element, write Theætetus with true opinion when he writes it in its proper order?

THEÆ. It is evident he will.

Soc. Will he not, therefore, be still void of science, but opine rightly, as we said?

THEÆ. Yes.

Soc. And will he not possess reason in conjunction with right opinion? For he wrote making a discursive process through an element, which we acknowledge is logos or reason.

THEÆ. True.

Soc. There is, therefore, my friend, such a thing as right opinion in conjunction with reason, which it is not yet proper to call science.

THEÆ. It appears so.

Soc. We are enriched then, as it appears, with a dream, while we opine that we possess a most true definition of science.

THEÆ. Or we ought not yet to blame. For perhaps some one may not define *logos* in this manner, but may choose the remaining species of the three, one of which we said would be adopted by him who defined science to be right opinion in conjunction with reason.

Soc. You have very properly reminded me: for one species still remains. For the first species was an image as it were of dianoëtic conception in voice; and the second, that which we just now mentioned, a procession to the whole through an element.

THEÆ. But what do you say the third is?

SOC. That which the multitude would say it is, to be able to assign a certain mark by which the object of inquiry differs from all other things.

THEÆ. Can you give me as an instance a certain logos of this kind respecting any thing?

d SOC. If you are willing, I think it will be sufficient for you to admit respecting the sun, that it is the most splendid of all the natures that revolve in the heavens round the earth.

THEÆ. Entirely so.

SOC. Take then that for the sake of which this was said. But it is that which we just now mentioned: that when you receive the difference of any thing, by which it differs from other things, you will receive, as some say, the logos or definition: but as long as you touch upon any thing common, you will have the definition of those things to which this something common belongs.

e THEÆ. I understand you: and it appears to me very proper to call a thing of this kind logos.

SOC. But he who, in conjunction with right opinion, receives the difference by which any thing whatever is distinguished from other things, will be endued with science respecting that of which he formerly possessed opinion.

THEÆ. We say it is so.

SOC. Now therefore, Theætetus, in consequence of approaching nearer to what is said, as to a certain adumbration, I find I do not in the least understand it; but, while I beheld it at a distance, it appeared to me that something was spoken to the purpose.

THEÆ. But how is this?

209a SOC. I will tell you, if I can. When I have a right opinion respecting you, if I likewise receive your definition, then I know you; but if not, then I only opine. Is it not so?

THEÆ. It is.

SOC. But logos, or definition, was an interpretation of your difference.

THEÆ. It was.

SOC. When, therefore, I only opine, I do not perceive by the dianoëtic energy any one of those things by which you differ from others.

THEÆ. You do not, as it appears.

SOC. I, therefore, only dianoëtically perceive something common, which you possess no less than another.

b THEÆ. It is necessary.

SOC. By Jupiter, then, inform me how, in a thing of this kind, I rather opine you than any other? For, suppose me thus dianoëtically considering: This is Theætetus, who is a man, and has nostrils, eyes, and a mouth, and in like manner each of the other members. Does this dianoëtic conception cause

me to perceive Theætetus more than Theodorus? or, as it is said, more than the last of the Mysians?

THEÆ. How should it?

SOC. But if I not only dianoëtically consider that he has nostrils and
c   eyes but likewise that he has a flat nose and prominent eyes, shall I opine you more than myself, or any other such person?

THEÆ. You will not.

SOC. But I think I shall not opine in myself, Theætetus, till a certain monument of his flat nose, exhibiting its difference from other flat noses which I perceive, is impressed in me, and in like manner other particulars from which you are composed; which, if I had met with you yesterday, would remind me, and cause me to form a right opinion respecting you.

THEÆ. Most true.

d   SOC. Right opinion, therefore, respecting every thing will be conversant with difference.

THEÆ. It appears so.

SOC. What then will be the consequence if reason is assumed together with right opinion? For it would be ridiculous if any one should order us to opine in what it is that any thing differs from other things.

THEÆ. How so?

SOC. For, respecting things of which we have a right opinion, so far as they differ from others, he would order us to assume a right opinion of them, so far as they differ from others. And thus, like the circumvolution of a whip, or a pestle, or the like, from this mandate
e   nothing would be said. For it might more justly be called the mandate of one blind; since it would order us to receive things which we possess, that we might learn things which we opine; and thus would be perfectly similar to the mandate of one deprived of sight.

THEÆ. Tell me what it is you just now asked.

SOC. If some one, O boy, ordering us to receive reason, should at the same time order us to know, but not opine difference, reason would be
210a a pleasant thing, and the most beautiful of all things pertaining to science. For to know is in a certain respect to receive science. Is it not?

THEÆ. It is.

Soc. When asked, therefore, as it appears, what science is, he would answer, that it is right opinion with the science of difference. For, according to him, this will be the assumption of reason.

Theæ. It appears so.

Soc. But it is in every respect foolish for us, who are investigating science, to say that it is right opinion with science, either of difference or of any thing else. Neither sense therefore, Theætetus, nor true opinion, nor reason in conjunction with true opinion, will be science.

b　Theæ. It does not appear that they will.

Soc. Are we, therefore, pregnant and parturient, my friend, with any thing further respecting science, or have we brought forth every thing?

Theæ. By Jupiter, through you I have already said more than I had in myself.

Soc. Does not, therefore, all this show that the obstetric art has brought for us that which is vain, and which does not deserve to be nourished?

Theæ. Entirely so.

c　Soc. If, therefore, after this you should endeavour to become pregnant with other things, and your endeavour should be successful, you will, through the present discussion, be full of better things. But if you should be empty, you will be less troublesome to your companions, and more moderate and mild; in consequence of not thinking that you know things which you do not know. For thus much my art is able to accomplish, but nothing more. Nor do I know any thing of those particulars which are and have been known to great and wonderful men. But this obstetric art I and my mother are allotted from divinity; she

d　about women, and I about ingenuous and beautiful youths. Now, therefore, I must go to the porch of the king, to answer to the accusation of Melitus. But to-morrow, Theodorus, we will again return hither.

Additional Notes

on the

THEÆTETUS

1 (See page 19, line 152d) This is true only of the sensible world; nor does Socrates make this assertion with a view to any thing else than the flowing and unreal condition of matter and its inherent forms. For the sensible world, as I have before observed in a note on the Orphic hymn to Nature [TTS vol. V, p. 46, n. 3], from its material imperfection, cannot receive the whole of divine infinity at once; but can only partake of it gradually and partially, as it were by drops in a momentary succession. Hence it is in a continual state of flowing and formation, but never possesses real being; and is like the image of a lofty tree seen in a rapid torrent, which has the appearance of a tree without the reality; and which seems to endure perpetually the same, yet is continually renewed by the continual renovation of the stream.

2 (See page 19, line 152e) Ocean, considered according to its first subsistence, as a deity, belongs, according to the Grecian theology, to that order of Gods which is called intellectual, and of which Saturn is the summit. This deity also is called a fontal God, $\pi\eta\gamma\alpha\iota\sigma\varsigma\ \theta\epsilon\sigma\varsigma$, and is said by Homer to be the origin of the Gods, because he gives birth to their procession into the sensible universe. In short he is the cause to all secondary natures of every kind of motion, whether intellectual, psychical, or natural, but Tethys is the cause of all the separation of the streams proceeding from Ocean, conferring on each a proper purity of natural motion. See more concerning these deities in the Notes on the *Cratylus*. [See also Homer's *Iliad* 14, 201 and 302.]

3 (See page 23, line 156a) Plato here presents us with the substance of the atomical or mechanical philosophy, which asserted that the universe was produced by nothing else but the motion of indivisible particles, by means of which all things are generated and corrupted. It likewise asserted that all these sensible qualities which are noticed by the several senses, such as colours, sounds, savours, odours, and the like, are not things really existing external to us, but passions or sensations in us, caused by local motions on the organs of sense. This atomical philosophy, according to Possidonius the Stoic, as we are

informed by Strabo,[†] is more ancient than the times of the Trojan war, and was first invented by one Moschus a Siconian, or rather, if we prefer the testimony of Sextus Empiricus,[‡] a Phœnician. This Moschus is doubtless the same person with that Moschus the physiologist, mentioned by Iamblichus[§] in his Life of Pythagoras. For he there informs us that Pythagoras, during his residence at Sidon in Phœnicia, conversed with the prophets that were the successors of Moschus the physiologist, and was instructed by them. Hence it appears that this physiology was not invented either by Epicurus or Democritus.

Plato, as may be collected from his *Timæus*, adopted this physiology: for he there resolves the differences of the four elements into the different geometrical figures of their insensible parts; and in so doing he likewise followed the Pythagoreans. However, he differed from the atomists in this, as I have observed in the Introduction to the *Timæus*, that he assigned commensuration and active fabricative powers to these insensible figures, which they did not; and he likewise differed from them in his arrangement of earth.

4 (See page 44, line 173c) The virtues are either physical, which are mingled with the temperaments, and are common both to men and brutes; or they are ethical, which are produced from custom and right opinion, and are the virtues of well-educated children; or they are political, which are the virtues of reason adorning the rational part as its instrument; or they are cathartic, by which the soul is enabled to withdraw from other things to itself, and to free itself, as much as the condition of human nature permits, from the bonds of generation; or they are theoretic, through which the soul, by giving itself wholly to intellectual energy, hastens to become as it were intellect instead of soul. This last order of the virtues is that by which Plato now characterizes the Coryphæan philosophers. The other virtues are also mentioned by him in other dialogues, as we shall show in our notes on the *Phædo* [p. 309].

---

† Ει δει πιστευσαι τῳ Ποσιδονῳ το περι των ατομων δογμα παλαιον εστιν, ανδρος Σιδονιου Μοσχου προ των Τροϊκων χρονων γεγονοτος. Lib. xvi.

‡ Advers. Mathemat. p. 367.

§ Τοις τε Μοσχου του φυσιολογου προφηταις απογονοις και τοις αλλοις, και Φοινικιοις ιεροφανταις.

THE

POLITICUS

A DIALOGUE

CONCERNING

A KINGDOM

INTRODUCTION

As there is one end for which nature, or rather the author of nature, produced the parts of the human body, and another for which he formed the whole man, so likewise he directed an individual of the human species to one end, a family to another, and again a city and kingdom to another. And lastly, that is to be considered as the best end, for the sake of which he produced the whole human race. Let no one however think, that though there is a certain end of every partial association among mankind, yet there is none of the whole; and that though there is order in the parts of human life, yet there is confusion in the whole; or, in short, that though the parts possess union from being directed to one end, yet the whole is dispersed and unconnected: for, if this were admitted, parts would be more honourable than the whole; though the former subsist for the sake of the latter, and not the latter for the sake of the former. Hence it is necessary that there should be a certain end of the human race, and that it should consist in whose energies through which it may imitate as much as possible things supernal; by science speculating things natural, human and divine; by prudence properly managing human affairs; and by piety cultivating and venerating divinity. An end, therefore, of this kind requires a twofold life, consisting both in action and contemplation, yet so constituted as that action may subsist for the sake of contemplation, as that which is more excellent and divine.

Plato in this dialogue demonstrates that this end can alone be obtained by the human race, under the government of a king who possesses consummate probity and science. Hence employing a most accurate division which is essentially necessary to definition and science, and in which Plato and his genuine disciples excelled in a transcendent degree, he Homerically denominates a king the shepherd and curator of the human race.[268c] This king, too, he compares to a physician; since such a one, by imposing laws both on the willing and the unwilling, procures salutary remedies for his subjects. But he more frequently calls a governor and curator of his kind, a politician than a king, signifying by this that he will be so humane and mild, that among the citizens he will appear to be a fellow-citizen, and will evince that he is rather superior to them in justice, prudence and science, than in any other endowments. He likewise asserts[259b], that the man who far surpasses all others in justice and prudence is born a king, though he should live the life of a private individual: and it may be collected from his other dialogues as his opinion, that royal authority should be given to the older and more worthy, a senate of whom should be the colleagues of the king, forming, as it were, a certain aristocracy, or government of the most excellent men. As he proves too in this dialogue that a royal surpasses every other form of government, he likewise shows that a tyranny is the worst kind of dominion, since it governs neither by law nor intellect, but by unrestrained impulse and arbitrary will. As the next in excellence to a royal government, he praises an aristocracy, but reprobates an oligarchy, or the government of a few: and he considers a popular government as deserving praise in the third degree, if it governs according to law. After this he discusses the duty of a king, and shows that it consists in providing such things as are necessary for the human race, and especially such as contribute to its felicity, in prudently judging what arts are subservient to this end in peace and war, in public and private conduct; and in exercising sovereign authority in conjunction with the senate.

With respect to what he says of the motion of the spheres and the kingdoms of Saturn and Jupiter, the mystic meaning of this fabulous narration will be unfolded in the notes on this dialogue.

THE

POLITICUS

PERSONS OF THE DIALOGUE

SOCRATES,   A GUEST
THEODORUS,   AND SOCRATES JUN

257a   SOC. I am greatly indebted to you, Theodorus, for making me acquainted with Theætetus and this guest.

THEO. Perhaps, Socrates, you will be indebted to me the triple of this, after these men have made you a politician and a philosopher.

SOC. Be it so. But shall we say we have heard this of you, who are most skilful in reasoning, and in things pertaining to geometry?

b   THEO. What is that, Socrates?

SOC. That we should consider each of these men as of equal worth, though they are more remote from each other in honour than accords with the analogy of your art.

THEO. By our God Ammon, Socrates, you have properly, justly, and promptly reproved me for my error in computation! But I shall speak with you about this at some other time. But do not you, O guest, in any respect be weary in gratifying us, but discuss for us, in order, either a politician first, or, if it is more agreeable to you, a philosopher.

c   GUEST. We shall do so, Theodorus, as soon as we attempt this discussion, nor shall we desist till we arrive at the end of it. But what ought I to do respecting Theætetus here?

THEO. About what?

GUEST. Shall we suffer him to rest, and take in his stead Socrates here, as our associate in the discussion? Or how do you advise?

THEO. As you say, take Socrates in his stead: for, both being young men, they will easily by resting be able to endure every kind of labour.

d   SOC. And indeed, O guest, both of them appear to be allied to me in a certain respect. For you say that one of them (Theætetus) appears to

258a   resemble me in the formation of his face; and the other possesses a certain alliance, through having the same name as myself. But it is requisite that we who are allied should always readily recognize this

alliance by discourse. With Theætetus, therefore, I yesterday joined in
discourse, and to-day I have heard him answering this guest: but neither
of them has yet discourse with Socrates here. It is, however, proper that
he should be considered. Let him then answer me some other time, but
at present let him answer you.

GUEST. Let it be so, Socrates. Do you hear this, Socrates junior?

SOC. JUN. I do.

GUEST. Do you, therefore, assent to what he says?

SOC. JUN. Entirely so.

b   GUEST. It appears, therefore, that you will be no impediment to our
discussion; and perhaps it is requisite that much less should I be an
impediment. But after a sophist, it is necessary, as it appears to me, that
we should investigate a politician. Tell me, therefore, whether this
character should be placed among the number of those that possess a
scientific knowledge. Or how shall we say?

SOC. JUN. That it ought.

GUEST. We must, therefore, make a division of the sciences, just as we
made a division in our investigation of the sophist.

SOC. JUN. Perhaps so.

GUEST. But yet it appears to me, Socrates, that we should not divide
in the same manner.

SOC. JUN. Undoubtedly not.

c   GUEST. But after another manner.

SOC. JUN. It appears so.

GUEST. Who then can find the political path? For it is requisite to
find it, and, separating it from other things, to impress it with one idea,
and, marking the other deflections, with another species, to make our
soul conceive that all the sciences are comprehended in two species.

SOC. JUN. I think, O guest, that this is your business, and not mine.

d   GUEST. But indeed, Socrates, it is also requisite that it should be your
when it becomes apparent to us.

SOC. JUN. You speak well.

GUEST. Are not, therefore, the arithmetic, and certain other arts allied
to this, divested of action, and do they not afford knowledge alone?

SOC. JUN. Yes.

GUEST. But those arts which pertain to architecture, and the whole
e   of manual operation, possess, as it were, science connate with actions,
and at the same time give completion to bodies produced by them,
which before this had not a being.

SOC. JUN. Undoubtedly.

GUEST. After this manner, therefore, divide all sciences, calling one practic, and the other gnostic alone.

SOC. JUN. Let there be, therefore, one whole science, and two species of it.

GUEST. Whether, therefore, shall we consider and denominate a politician, a king, a despot, and the governor of a family, as one and the same thing? Or shall we say there are as many arts pertaining to these as there are names? Or rather follow me hither.

259a SOC. JUN. Whither?

GUEST. To the consideration of this. If any private person is able to advise sufficiently a public physician, is it not necessary to call him by the name of that art which he who is advised professes?

SOC. JUN. Yes.

GUEST. And if any private person is able to give advice to a king, shall we not say that such a one possesses that science which the king himself ought to possess?

SOC. JUN. We shall.

b GUEST. But is not the science of a true king royal?

SOC. JUN. Yes.

GUEST. And may not he who possesses this science, whether he is a private man, or a ruler, be in every respect rightly called, according to this art, royal?

SOC. JUN. He may, justly.

GUEST. And are not the governor of a family and a despot the same?

SOC. JUN. Undoubtedly.

GUEST. But what? Is it of any consequence, with respect to empire, whether the city is of a small or of an ample size?

SOC. JUN. It is of no consequence.

c GUEST. It is evident, therefore (which is the thing we were just now inquiring), that there is one science respecting all these. But we do not think it is of any consequence whether any one denominates this science royal, or political, or economic.

SOC. JUN. For of what consequence can it be?

GUEST. This too is evident, that every king is able to do but a little with his hands, and the whole of his body, towards the possession of empire, but much by the wisdom and strength of his soul.

SOC. JUN. It is evident.

d GUEST. Are you willing, therefore, we should say that a king is more allied to the gnostic than to the manual, and, in short, to the practic science?

SOC. JUN. Undoubtedly.

GUEST. We must, therefore, combine into the same the political science and a politician, the royal science and a royal man, as all these are one thing.

SOC. JUN. It is evident.

GUEST. Let us, therefore, proceed in an orderly manner, and after this divide the gnostic science.

SOC. JUN. Entirely so.

GUEST. Attend, then, and inform me whether we can apprehend any way of escape in this.

SOC. JUN. Tell me of what kind.

e   GUEST. Of this kind. There is a certain logistic art.

SOC. JUN. There is.

GUEST. And this I think entirely belongs to the gnostic arts.

SOC. Undoubtedly.

GUEST. But the logistic art knows the difference in numbers. shall we, therefore, attribute to it any further employment than that of distinguishing and judging about things known?

SOC. JUN. Why?

GUEST. For no architect works himself, but rules over workmen.

SOC. JUN. It is so.

GUEST. And he imparts indeed knowledge, but not manual operation.

SOC. JUN. He does.

260a   GUEST. He may justly, therefore, be said to participate of the gnostic science.

SOC. JUN. Entirely so.

GUEST. But I think this belongs to the office of a judge, not to possess the end, nor to be liberated, in the same manner as the reckoner is liberated, but to order every manual operator that portion of work which is adapted to him, till that which they are commanded to do receives its completion.

SOC. JUN. Right.

b   GUEST. Are not, therefore, all such things as these gnostic, and likewise such as are consequent to the logistic art? And do not these two genera differ from each other in judgment and mandate?

SOC. JUN. They appear to do so.

GUEST. If, therefore, we should divide the whole of the gnostic science into two parts, denominating the one mandatory, and the other judicial, may we not say that we have made an elegant division?

SOC. JUN. Yes, according to my opinion.

GUEST. But those that do any thing in common are delighted when they accord with each other.

SOC. JUN. Undoubtedly.

GUEST. As far, therefore, as we accord in this particular we shall bid farewell to the opinions of others.

SOC. JUN. Entirely so.

c GUEST. Come, then, inform me in which of these arts we must place a royal character. Must we place him in the judicial art, as a certain spectator? Or rather, shall we place him in the commanding art, acting as a despot?

SOC. JUN. Undoubtedly, rather in this.

GUEST. Let us again consider whether the commanding art admits of distinction. For it appears to me, that as the art of a huckster differs from his art who sells his own goods, so the royal genus from the genus of public criers.

d SOC. JUN. How so?

GUEST. Hucksters, first receiving the saleable works of others, afterwards sell them again themselves.

SOC. JUN. Entirely so.

GUEST. In like manner, the tribe of criers, receiving the mandates of others, again imparts them to others.

SOC. JUN. Most true.

e GUEST. What then? Shall we mingle the royal into the same with the interpretative, commanding, prophetic, and præconic† genus, and with many other arts allied to these, all which have this in common that they command? Or are you willing that, as we just now assimilated, we should at present assimilate a name? since this genus of those who command their own concerns is nearly without a name. And thus we shall so divide these as to place the royal genus among the number of those that command their own concerns, neglecting every other particular, which any one may denominate as he pleases. For our method was adopted for the sake of a ruler, and not for the sake of the contrary.

SOC. JUN. Entirely so.

261a GUEST. Since, therefore, this is sufficiently separated from those, and is brought by division from that which is foreign to that which is domestic, it is necessary that this again should be divided, if we have yet any compliant section in this.

SOC. JUN. Entirely so.

GUEST. And, indeed, it appears that we have. But follow me in dividing.

---

† Pertaining to criers.

Soc. Jun. Whither?

Guest. Do we not find that all such as rule by command issue out their commands for the sake of the generation of something?

b   Soc. Jun. Undoubtedly.

Guest. And, indeed, it is not in every respect difficult to give a twofold division to all generated natures.

Soc. Jun. After what manner?

Guest. Some among all of them are animated, and others are inanimate.

Soc. Jun. They are so.

Guest. If we wish to cut the commanding division into these parts of the gnostic science, we should accordingly cut them.

Soc. Jun. According to what?

c   Guest. One part of it should be assigned to the genera of inanimate natures, and the other to the genera of such as are animated. And thus the whole will receive a twofold division.

Soc. Jun. Entirely so.

Guest. One part, therefore, we must omit, and resume the other; the whole of which we must again divide into two parts.

Soc. Jun. But inform me which of these is to be resumed.

Guest. By all means, that which rules over animals. For it is not the province of the royal science to command things inanimate, like the architectonic science; but, being of a more generous nature, it always possesses its power in animals, and about things pertaining to them.

d   Soc. Jun. Right.

Guest. With respect to the generation and nurture of animals, attention to the latter is confined to one animal, but the care belonging to the former extends in common to the whole herd.

Soc. Jun. Right.

Guest. But we do not find that the attention of the politic science is of a private nature, like that of an ox-driver, or an equerry; but it is rather similar to the attention paid by him who feeds horses and oxen.

Soc. Jun. This appears to be the case.

e   Guest. Whether, therefore, with respect to the nurture of animals, shall we denominate the nurture of a flock the common nurture of many, or a certain common nutrition?

Soc. Jun. Both may be adopted in discourse.

Guest. You have answered well, Socrates. And if you avoid paying serious attention to names, you will appear in old age to be more rich in intellectual prudence. Let us, therefore, now do as you advise. But

262a   do you understand how some one, by showing that the nurture of a herd is twofold, will render that which is now investigated in things double, to be sought after in halves?

SOC. JUN. I endeavour to do so: and it appears to me that there is one kind of nurture of men, and another of brutes.

GUEST. You have divided in every respect promptly and valiantly. We must however to the utmost of our power be careful that we may not suffer this again.

SOC. JUN. What?

b GUEST. That we do not take away one small part in opposition to many and great parts, nor yet take it away without species, but always in conjunction with species. For it is most beautiful to separate immediately the object of inquiry from other things, if the separation is rightly made; just as you a little before hastily thought respecting division, in consequence of perceiving the discourse tending to mankind. Though indeed, my friend, it is not safe to divide with subtilty: but it is more safe to proceed dividing through media; for thus we shall more readily meet with ideas. But the whole of this confers to the objects of our investigation.

c SOC. JUN. How do you mean, O guest?

GUEST. I will endeavour to speak yet more clearly, on account of the benevolence of your nature, Socrates. It is impossible, therefore, to evince the things now proposed in such a manner that nothing shall be wanting: but yet we must endeavour to rise a little higher in our speculation, for the sake of perspicuity.

SOC. JUN. In what respect then do you say we have not just now rightly divided?

d GUEST. In this respect, that if any one should attempt to give a twofold division to the human genus, he would divide just as many of the present day divide. For these separate the Grecian genus apart from all others, as one thing; and denominate all other kinds of men, which are innumerable, unmixt, and discordant with each other, by one appellation, that of Barbarians; and through this one appellation, the genus itself appears to them to be one. But this is just as if some one, thinking that number should be divided into two species, should cut off ten thousand from all numbers, as one species, and, giving one name to all the rest, should think that this genus will become separate and different from the other through the appellation. He however will e divide in a more beautiful manner, and more according to species, and a two-fold division, who cuts number into the even and odd, and the human species into male and female; and who then separates the Lydians or Phrygians, or certain other nations, from all others, when he is incapable of finding the genus and at the same time part of each of the divided members.

263a　　SOC. JUN. Most right. But inform me, O guest, how any one may more clearly know that genus and part are not the same, but different from each other.

GUEST. O Socrates, best of men, you enjoin me no trifling thing. And, indeed, we have now wandered further from our proposed discourse than is fit; and yet you order us to wander still more. Now, therefore, let us again return thither, whence we have digressed, as it is

b　fit we should; and hereafter we will at leisure investigate the question proposed by you. However, do not by any means think that you have heard this clearly determined from me.

SOC. JUN. What?

GUEST. That species and part are different from each other.

SOC. JUN. Why so?

GUEST. When any thing is a species of something, it is also necessary that it should be a part of the thing of which it is said to be the species: but it is by no means necessary that a part should be a species. Always consider me, therefore, Socrates, as asserting this rather than that.

SOC. JUN. Be it so.

c　GUEST. But inform me after this.

SOC. JUN. What?

GUEST. Respecting that whence we have digressed hither. For I think that we principally digressed in consequence of your being asked how the nurture of a herd should be divided, and very readily answering that there were two kinds of animals, the one human, and the other comprehending the whole of the brutal species.

SOC. JUN. True.

GUEST. And you then appeared to me, having taken away a part, to have thought that the remainder should be left as one genus of all brutes, because you could call all of them by the same name, *viz.* brutes.

d　SOC. JUN. These things were so.

GUEST. But this, O most valiant of men, is just as if some other prudent animal, as for instance a crane, should after your manner call cranes rational, thus exalting himself, and consider them as forming one genus among other animals, but, comprehending all the rest together

e　with men, should perhaps denominate them nothing else than brutes. We should endeavour, therefore, to avoid every thing of this kind.

SOC. JUN. How?

GUEST. By not dividing every genus of animals, that we may be less exposed to this mistake.

SOC. JUN. For there is no occasion.

GUEST. We, therefore, then erred in this respect.

SOC. JUN. In what respect?

GUEST. That part of the gnostic science which is commanding was determined by us to be of that kind which is employed in the nurture of animals, *viz.* of gregarious animals. Was it not?

SOC. JUN. It was.

264a GUEST. The whole animal genus, therefore, was then divided into the tame and wild. For those animals that are naturally capable of being rendered gentle are called tame; but those that are not are denominated wild.

SOC. JUN. Well said.

GUEST. But the science which we are in search of, was and is in tame animals, and is to be investigated among such of these as are gregarious. Is it not so?

SOC. JUN. Yes.

GUEST. We must not, therefore, divide as then, looking to all animals, nor must we divide hastily, in order that we may rapidly comprehend the politic science. For this would cause us to suffer that which the proverb speaks of.

b SOC. JUN. What is that?

GUEST. By dividing too hastily, we shall finish more slowly.

SOC. JUN. And it would very properly cause us to suffer, O guest.

GUEST. Be it so then. But let us again from the beginning endeavour to divide the common nurture of animals. For perhaps the discourse itself being brought to a conclusion will more clearly unfold that which you desire. But tell me this.

SOC. JUN. What?

c GUEST. What perhaps you have often heard from certain persons. For I do not think you have met with those who tame fish about the Nile, or the royal lakes. But perhaps you have been a spectator of the taming of these in fountains.

SOC. JUN. I have been a spectator of this, and I have heard of the former from many.

GUEST. You have likewise heard and believe that geese and cranes are fed by certain persons, though you have never wandered about the Thessalian plains.

SOC. JUN. Undoubtedly.

d GUEST. I have asked you all these questions, because the nurture of herds of animals is partly aquatic, and partly terrestrial.

SOC. JUN. It is so.

GUEST. Does it not, therefore, appear to you, as well as to me, that the science respecting the common nurture of animals should receive a twofold division, and that one part should be denominated that which nourishes in moisture, and the other that which nourishes in dryness?

SOC. JUN. It does appear to me.

GUEST. But we do not in the same manner inquire to which of these arts the royal science belongs. For it is evident to every one.

e   SOC. JUN. Undoubtedly.

GUEST. For every one can divide the nurture of herds in dryness.

SOC. JUN. How?

GUEST. Into the volant and gradient.

SOC. JUN. Most true.

GUEST. That the political science, however, is to be investigated among gradient animals, is, as I may say, obvious to the most stupid. Or do you not think it is?

SOC. JUN. I do.

GUEST. But it is requisite that, dividing the art of feeding animals, like an even number, we should show that it is twofold.

SOC. JUN. This is evident.

265a   GUEST. Moreover, the part to which our discourse impels us appears to extend itself in two certain paths; the one being short, in consequence of separating a small from a large part; but the other long, from preserving that precept which we mentioned before, that we ought to divide through media, as this is the most ample division. It is permitted us, therefore, to proceed in either of these paths, as is most agreeable to us.

SOC. JUN. Is it then impossible to proceed in both?

GUEST. Not in both at once, O wonderful youth! But it is evident that it is possible to proceed in them separately.

b   SOC. JUN. I will choose, therefore, to proceed in each apart from the other.

GUEST. It is easy so to do, since what remains is but short. In the beginning, indeed, and middle of our journey we should have found it difficult to comply with this mandate. But now, since it appears to be best, let us first proceed in the longer road. For, as we have but recently engaged in this affair, we shall more easily journey through it. But look to the division.

SOC. JUN. Say what it is.

GUEST. The pedestrian genus of such tame animals as are gregarious must be divided by us according to nature.

SOC. JUN. Why?

GUEST. Because they must be divided into such as are without horns, and into such as are horned.

c   SOC. JUN. It appears so.

GUEST. Dividing then the art of feeding pedestrian animals, describe the condition of each part. For, if you should be willing to name them, you would be involved in difficulties more than is becoming.

SOC. JUN. How then is it proper to speak of them?

GUEST. Thus. Since the science of feeding animals receives a twofold division, one member of it consists in the horned part of the flock, but the other in that part which is without horns.

d   SOC. JUN. Let these things be so said: for they are sufficiently shown to be so.

GUEST. Again, therefore, it will appear to us, that a king feeds a certain herd of mutilated hornless animals.

SOC. JUN. For how is it possible this should not be evident?

GUEST. Breaking this, therefore, in pieces, we will endeavour to exhibit that which is transacted by a king.

SOC. JUN. Entirely so.

GUEST. Whether, therefore, are you willing we should divide this herd into what is called the fissured and the solid hoof? Or shall we divide it into common and private generation? For you understand me.

SOC. JUN. What kind of generation do you mean?

e   GUEST. That of horses and asses, which naturally generate from each other.

SOC. JUN. They do.

GUEST. But the remaining species, belonging to the one herd of tame animals, do not promiscuously mingle with each other, but those only of the same kind copulate together.

SOC. JUN. Undoubtedly.

GUEST. But whether does the political science appear to take care of the common, or of the private generation of animals?

SOC. JUN. It is evident that it takes care of the unmingled generation of animals.

GUEST. It is evident, then, as it seems, that we should give a twofold division to this, as we did to the preceding particulars.

SOC. JUN. It is indeed necessary.

266a   GUEST. But we have already nearly separated into minute parts every tame and gregarious animal, except two genera. For it is not fit to rank the genus of dogs among gregarious cattle.

SOC. JUN. It is not. But how shall we divide these two?

GUEST. After that manner, which it is just you and Theætetus should adopt in distributing, since you have touched on geometry.

SOC. JUN. What manner is that?

GUEST. By the diameter, and again by the diameter of the diameter.

SOC. JUN. How do you say?

b　　GUEST. Is the condition of the human genus in any other way naturally adapted to progression than as a diameter, in power a biped?

SOC. JUN. In no other way.

GUEST. But again, the condition of the remaining genus is, according to the power of our power, a diameter, since it naturally consists of twice two feet.

SOC. JUN. Undoubtedly. And now I nearly understand what you wish to evince.

c　　GUEST. But besides these things, do we perceive, Socrates, a circumstance worthy of laughter, which happened to us in making the former division?

SOC. JUN. What is that?

GUEST. The human genus, mingled and concurring with a genus the most generous and tractable of all others.

SOC. JUN. I perceive it, and likewise that it is a very absurd circumstance.

GUEST. Is it not fit that the slowest things should arrive last of all?

SOC. JUN. It is.

GUEST. But we do not perceive this, that a king appears still more ridiculous when running together with the herd, and performing his

d　　course in conjunction with him who is exercised in the best manner with respect to a tractable life.

SOC. JUN. Entirely so.

GUEST. For now, Socrates, that is more apparent which was said by us in our investigation of a sophist.

SOC. JUN. What is that?

GUEST. That, in such a method of discourse as this, he neither pays more attention to what is venerable than what is not, nor does he prefer the small to the great, but always accomplishes that which is most true.

SOC. JUN. It appears so.

e　　GUEST. After this, that you may not accuse me, as you have inquired what is the shorter way to the definition of a king, I will, in the first place, consider this.

SOC. JUN. By all means, do so.

GUEST. But I say that a gradient animal ought to have been divided by us above into the biped and quadruped genus; and perceiving that man then alone remained in conjunction with the volant genus, the biped herd should again have been divided into the winged and without wings. But this division being made, and being evinced by that art which is the nurse of men, a political and royal character should be placed over it, like a charioteer, and the reins of the city should be given to him, in consequence of this science being adapted to him.

267a SOC. JUN. You have answered me beautifully, and as if you had been discharging a debt; and you have added a digression, by way of interest, and as the completion of your discourse.

GUEST. Come, then, let us conject, by recurring from the beginning to the end, the discourse concerning the name of the politic art.

SOC. JUN. By all means.

GUEST. One part, therefore, of the gnostic science was asserted by us in the beginning to be of a commanding nature; and we said that the part of this science which commands from itself was assimilated to this.

b Again, we asserted that the nurture of animals was apart of the self-commanding science, and that this was not the smallest part. Likewise, that the nurture of herds was a species of the nurture of animals; and that the art which is nutritive of animals without horns, especially belongs to the art of feeding pedestrian animals. Again, it is necessary to connect not less than the triple of this part, if any one is desirous of comprehending it in one name, *viz.* the science of an unmingled genus

c of feeding. But a section from this, which alone remains, and which feeds men, as ranking among bipeds, is the part which we are now exploring, and which we denominate royal, and at the same time political.

SOC. JUN. Entirely so.

GUEST. Do you therefore think, Socrates, that we have really done well, as you say?

SOC. JUN. In what?

d GUEST. I mean that the thing proposed by us has been in every respect and sufficiently discussed. Or has our investigation been particularly deficient in this, that it has given, indeed, a description of the thing, but such a one as is not perfectly finished?

SOC. JUN. How do you say?

GUEST. I will endeavour to explain my meaning more clearly.

SOC. JUN. Do so.

GUEST. Since, therefore, it has appeared that there are many pastoral arts, the politic science is one of these, and is the curator of one certain herd.

SOC. JUN. It is.

GUEST. Our discourse defined this to be neither the nurse of horses, nor of any other brutes, but to be the common nutritive science of men.

SOC. JUN. It did so.

e   GUEST. But let us contemplate the difference of all shepherds and kings.

SOC. JUN. What is the difference?

GUEST. If any one possessing the name of another art should assert and vindicate to himself the nutrition in common of the human herd, what should we say?

SOC. JUN. How is this?

GUEST. Just as if all merchants, husbandmen, and cooks, and besides these the professors of gymnastic, and the genus of physicians, should verbally oppose the shepherds of the human race, whom we have called politicians, and should assert that the care of nurturing men belonged to
268a them, and that they were not only shepherds of the herds of men, but even of rulers themselves.

SOC. JUN. And would not their assertion be right?

GUEST. Perhaps so. And let us also consider this. For we know that no one would contend with a herdsman about things of this kind; since he is, doubtless, the nurse, the physician, and as it were brideman of a
b   herd, and is alone skilled in the obstetric art respecting parturition and offspring. No one, besides, is better calculated, by such sport and music as the nature of cattle is capable of receiving, of consoling, and by alluring arts mitigating, with instruments, or the mere mouth, the herd committed to his care. And the same may be said of other shepherds. Or may it not?

SOC. JUN. Most right.

c   GUEST. How, then, will our discourse respecting a king appear to be right and entire, since we assert that he alone is the shepherd and nurse of the human herd, when at the same time ten thousand others contend for the same office?

SOC. JUN. By no means.

GUEST. Did we not, therefore, a little before very properly fear, when we suspected lest we should only introduce a certain royal figure, and should not perfectly define a political character, unless we comprehended those that are connected with this character, and who profess themselves to be equally shepherds; and, separating a king from them, alone exhibited him pure?

d   SOC. JUN. Our fear, indeed, was most right.

GUEST. This therefore, Socrates, must be done by us, unless we intend to disgrace our discourse at the end.

SOC. JUN. But this must by no means take place.

GUEST. Again, therefore, we must proceed in another way from another beginning.

SOC. JUN. In what way?

GUEST. By nearly inserting a jest. For it is requisite to employ a copious part of a long fable,[1] and to act in the same manner with what remains of our discussion, as we did above, *viz.* always to take away a part from a part, till we arrive at the summit of our inquiry. Is it not proper to act in this manner?

SOC. JUN. Entirely so.

GUEST. Give me then, after the manner of boys, all your attention to the fable: for you are not very much removed from puerile years.

SOC. JUN. Only relate it.

GUEST. There were then, and still will be, many memorials of ancient affairs; and among others, there is one prodigious relation respecting the contention of Atreus and Thyestes. For you have heard and remember what is then said to have happened.

SOC. JUN. Perhaps you speak of the prodigy respecting the golden ram.

GUEST. By no means: but respecting the mutation of the rising and setting of the sun, and the other stars. For whence they now rise they did then set: and their rising was from a contrary place. Divinity, therefore, then giving a testimony to Atreus, changed the heavens into the present figure.

SOC. JUN. This also is reported.

GUEST. We have likewise heard from many respecting the kingdom of which Saturn was the founder.

SOC. JUN. We have from very many.

GUEST. And were not those ancient men born from the earth, and not generated from each other?

SOC. JUN. This also is one of the things which are said to have happened formerly.

GUEST. All these things, therefore, proceed from the same circumstance, and ten thousand others besides these, and which are still more wonderful. But, through length of time, some of them have become extinct, and others are related in a dispersed manner, separate from each other. But that circumstance which is the cause of this taking place has not been mentioned by any one. It must, however, now be related: for the relation will contribute to the demonstration of the nature of a king.

SOC. JUN. You speak most beautifully. Speak, therefore, and do not omit any thing.

GUEST. Hear, then. Divinity himself sometimes conducts this universe in its progression, and convolves it: but at another time he remits the reins of his government, when the periods of the universe have received a convenient measure of time. But the world is again spontaneously led round to things contrary, since it is an animal, and is allotted wisdom from him who cooperated with it from the first in harmonizing all its parts with the whole. This progression, however, to

d things contrary is naturally implanted in it through the following cause.

SOC. JUN. Through what cause?

GUEST. To subsist always according to the same, and in a similar manner, and to be the same, alone belongs to the most divine of all things: but the nature of body is not of this order. But that which we call heaven and the world, receives many and blessed gifts from its

e producing cause. However, as it participates of body, it cannot be entirely void of mutation: nevertheless, as far as it is able, it is moved in the same, and according to the same, with one lation. Hence it is allotted a circular motion, because there is the smallest mutation of its motion. But nearly nothing is able to revolve itself, except that which is the leader of all things that are moved. And it is not lawful that this should at one time move in one way, and at another time in a different way. From all this, therefore, it must be said, that the world neither always revolves itself, nor that the whole of it is always convolved by Divinity with twofold and contrary convolutions: nor, again, that two

270a certain Gods convolve it, whose decisions are contrary to each other. But that must be asserted which we just now said, and which alone remains, that at one time it is conducted by another divine cause, receiving again an externally acquired life, and a renewed immortality from the demiurgus; but that at another time, when he remits the reins of government, it proceeds by itself, and, being thus left for a time, performs many myriads of retrograde revolutions, because it is most great, and most equally balanced, and accomplishes its progressions with the smallest foot.

b SOC. JUN. All that you have said appears to be very probable.

GUEST. From what has been said, therefore, we may now, by a reasoning process, apprehend that circumstance which we said was the cause of all wonderful things. For it is this very thing.

SOC. JUN. What?

GUEST. That the circular motion of the universe is at one time accomplished as at present, and at another time in a contrary manner.

SOC. JUN. But how is this the cause of all wonderful things?

c GUEST. It is requisite to think that this mutation is the greatest and most perfect of all the celestial conversions.

SOC. JUN. It is likely.

GUEST. It is proper, therefore, to think that the greatest mutations then happen to us who are the inhabitants of the world.

SOC. JUN. And this also is likely.

GUEST. But do we not know that the nature of animals sustains with difficulty great, numerous, and all-various mutations?

SOC. JUN. Undoubtedly.

d GUEST. Hence, the greatest corruptions of other animals then necessarily take place, and very few of the human race remain. And to these many other wonderful and novel circumstances at the same time happen; but this is the greatest, and follows that revolution of the universe in which a conversion is effected contrary to the present.

SOC. JUN. What circumstance do you mean?

GUEST. That which takes place the first of all, when, in whatever age a mortal animal is constituted, he is no longer seen advancing to old age,

e but is again changed to the contrary, and naturally becomes, as it were, younger and more delicate. The white hairs, too, of those more advanced in years then became black,[†] and the cheeks of those that had beards became smooth; and thus each was restored to the past flower of his age. The bodies, likewise, of such as were in the bloom of youth, becoming smoother and smaller every day and night, again returned to the nature of a child recently born: and such were assimilated to this nature, both in soul and body. And at length their bodies, rapidly wasting away, perished. But the dead bodies of those who at that time died through violence were in like manner immanifestly, and in a few days, corrupted.

271a SOC. JUN. But what was then, O guest, the generation of animals, and after what manner were they produced from each other?

GUEST. It is evident, Socrates, that at that time there was no generation of one thing from another. But, as it is said that there was once an earth-born race, this race was at that period restored back again

b from the earth. This information, too, was delivered to us by those our first progenitors, who lived immediately after the close of the last

---

† Plato, in what he here asserts of the Saturnian age, wonderfully accords with Orpheus, who, as we are informed by Proclus in Plat. Theol. X, 10, [TTS vol. VIII, p. 320], mystically says, "that the hairs of the face of Saturn are always black, and never become hoary."

revolution. For they were public witnesses of the truth of our assertions, which at present are disbelieved, though improperly, by the multitude. For I think this particular ought to be attended to, as consequent to a part of the narration. For, if old men tended to the nature of boys, it follows, that such as were dead, but laid in the earth, must be again restored from thence, revive again, and follow that revolution of the universe, in which generation is convolved in a contrary order; and that the earth-born race, which according to this reason is necessarily produced, should thus be denominated and defined, *viz.* such of them as Divinity has transferred into another destiny.

SOC. JUN. This very much follows from what has been said above. But with respect to the life which you say was under the power of Saturn, did it subsist in those revolutions, or in these? For it is evident that the mutation of the stars and the sun happens in both these revolutions.

GUEST. You follow the discourse well. But, in answer to your question respecting all things being produced spontaneously for mankind, this by no means is the case in the present, but happened in the former revolution. For then divinity was first the ruler and curator of the whole circulation; just as now the several parts of the world are locally distributed by ruling Gods. Divine dæmons, too, were allotted, after the manner of shepherds, animals according to genera and herds; each being sufficient for all things pertaining to the several particulars over which he presided. So that there was nothing rustic, no mutual rapine, no war, nor sedition of any kind; and ten thousand other things took place, which are the consequences of such a period. But what is said respecting the spontaneous life of these men is asserted because Divinity himself fed them, and was their curator; just as men who are of a more divine, are the shepherds of brutes, who are of a baser, nature. In consequence, too, of men being fed by Divinity, there were no polities, nor possessions of women and children. For all these were restored to life from the earth, and without having any recollection of former events. But all such things as these were absent. The inhabitants, too, had fruits in abundance from oaks, and many other trees, which did not grow through the assistance of agriculture, but were spontaneously given by the earth. And for the most part they were naked, slept without coverlids, and were fed in the open air. For the temperament of the seasons was innoxious to them. They had soft beds, too, from grass, which germinated in unenvying abundance from the earth. And thus, Socrates, you have heard what was the life of men under the reign of Saturn: but you yourself have seen what the condition of the present life is, which is said to be under Jupiter. But are you able, and likewise willing, to judge which of these is the more happy?

SOC. JUN. By no means.

GUEST. Are you willing, therefore, that I should after a manner judge for you?

SOC. JUN. Entirely so.

GUEST. If, therefore, those that were nurtured by Saturn in so much
c leisure, and with the power not only of conversing with men, but with brutes, used all the above-mentioned particulars for the purpose of philosophy, associating with brutes and with each other, and inquiring of every nature which had a perceptive power of its own, in what respect it differed from others as to the common possession of prudence; from all this it may be easily inferred, that the men of those times were incomparably more happy than those that exist at present. But if, being abundantly filled with meats and drinks, their discourses with each other, and with brutes, were such as at present they are related to have been, from this also, in my opinion, their superior felicity may be very
d easily inferred. At the same time, however, we shall dismiss these particulars till some sufficient judge of them shall arise, who will unfold to us whether the men of that period were inclined to sciences and discourse. But let us now relate on what account we introduced the fable, that we may after this bring to a conclusion what remains. For, after the time of all these was consummated, and it was requisite that a mutation should take place, and besides this, the whole terrestrial genus being consumed, as all the generations of every soul had received their completion, and as many seeds having fallen on the earth as were
e destined to each soul, - then the governor of the universe, laying aside as it were the handle of his rudder, departed to that place of survey whence he contemplates himself. But then fate and connate desire again convolved the world. All those Gods, therefore, who govern locally, in conjunction with the greatest dæmon, knowing what had now happened, again deprived the parts of the world of their providential
273a care. But the world becoming inverted, conflicting with itself, and being agitated by an impulse contrary to its beginning and end, and likewise making an abundant concussion in itself, produced again another corruption of all-various animals. After these things, however, and the expiration of a sufficient length of time, the tumult, confusion, and concussions ceased, and the world, becoming tranquil and adorned, again proceeded in its usual course, possessing a providential care and dominion, both over itself and the natures which it contains;

remembering to the utmost of its power, the instructions of the
demiurgus and father.† At the beginning, therefore, it accomplished this
more perfectly, but at the end more remissly. But the cause of this is
the corporeal form of the temperature, and which was nursed together
with an ancient nature. For it was a participant of much disorder before
it arrived at the present ornament. For, from its composing artificer,
indeed, it possesses every good; but, from its former habit, all that
atrocity and injustice which subsist within the heavens. And these the
world both possesses from that former habit, and inserts in animated
natures. The world, therefore, when nourishing the animals which it
contains, in conjunction with the governor, brings forth small evils, and
mighty goods: but when it is separated from him, during the nearest
time of its departure, it conducts all things beautifully. At a more
distant period, however, and from oblivion being generated in it, the
property of its former dissonance rules with greater force. And at the
last period of time it becomes deflorescent; and producing small goods,
but mingling much of the temperament of things contrary to good, it
arrives at the danger of both itself, and the natures which it contains,
being dissolved. Hence that God who adorned the world, then
perceiving the difficulties under which it labours, and anxious lest, being
thus tempestuously agitated, it should be dissolved by the tumult, and
be plunged into the infinite sea of dissimilitude, again resumes the helm,
and adorns and corrects whatever is diseased and dissolved through the
inordinate motion of the former period, and renders the world immortal
and unconscious of age. This, therefore, is the end of the whole
narration. But this is sufficient to show the nature of a king to such as
attend to what has been already said. For, the world being again
converted to the present path of generation, the progression of its age
again stopped, and it imparted novel things, the very contraries to what
it then imparted. For animals proximate to death, on account of their
smallness, are increased. But bodies recently born from the earth, hoary,
again dying, descend into the earth; and all other things are transmuted,
imitating and following the condition of the universe. The imitation,
likewise, of motion, generation, and nutriment, follows all things from
necessity. For it is no longer possible for an animal to be produced in
the earth, through other things mutually composing it; but, as the world
was destined to be the absolute ruler of its own progression, after the
same manner its parts also were destined by a similar guidance to spring
forth, generate, and nourish, as far as they are able. But we have now

---

† *i.e.* Jupiter. See the *Timæus*.

b arrived at that for the sake of which the whole of our discourse was undertaken. For, with respect to other animals, many particulars, and of a prolix nature, might be discussed; such as, from what things they are severally composed, and through what causes they were changed: but the particulars respecting men are shorter, and more to our purpose. For, mankind being destitute of the guardian care of the dæmon whose possession we are, and who is the shepherd of our race, and as many animals who are naturally cruel became transported with rage, hence men, now imbecil, and without a guard, were torn in pieces by such

c animals. And besides this, men in those first times were unskilful, and had no knowledge of the arts, because the earth spontaneously afforded them nutriment: but they did not know how to procure it, because they were not compelled by any previous necessity. From all these causes they were involved in the greatest difficulties. Hence, those gifts which are said to have been formerly imparted to us by the Gods were imparted with necessary instruction and erudition: fire, indeed, from Prometheus,† but the arts from Vulcan and Minerva. Again, seeds and

d plants were imparted by other divinities; and, in short, all such things as are the support of human life. For men, as we have said, were not left destitute of the guardian care of the Gods; and it became requisite that they also should pay attention to the concerns of life, in the same manner as the whole world; in the imitating and following which, through all the revolutions of time, we live and are born in a different manner at different periods. And let this be the end of the fable. But

e we shall make it useful to discover how far we have erred in the above definition of a royal and political character.

SOC. JUN. In what respect, and how far, do you say we have erred?

GUEST. Partly less, and in a more generous manner, and partly in a greater degree, and more abundantly.

SOC. JUN. How?

275a GUEST. Because, while we were asked respecting a king and politician belonging to the present circulation and generation, we adduced a shepherd of a herd of men belonging to the contrary period; and in consequence of this shepherd being a God, and not a man, we transgressed abundantly: but again, because we evinced that this shepherd was the governor of the whole city, but yet did not say after what manner, in this respect we asserted what is true, but were deficient as to

---

† Prometheus is the inspective guardian of the descent of rational souls; and the fire which he imparted to mortals is the rational soul itself, because this like fire naturally tends upwards, or, in other words, aspires after incorporeal natures.

the whole and the perspicuous; and on this account we erred less in this latter case than in the former.

SOC. JUN. True.

GUEST. We ought, therefore, as it seems, to think that we shall then have perfectly described a political character when we have defined the mode of governing a city.

SOC. JUN. Beautifully said.

b   GUEST. On this account we related that fable, not only that those might be pointed out who oppose the royal character we are now investigating with respect to the nurture of a herd, but that we might more clearly perceive him who alone ought to be called a pastor, since after the manner of a shepherd and herdsman he takes care of the nurture of the human race.

SOC. JUN. Right.

c   GUEST. But I think, Socrates, that this figure of a divine shepherd is still greater than that which belongs to a king; and that the politicians of the present day are naturally much more similar to subjects than governors, and in a manner more allied to these participate of discipline and nurture.

SOC. JUN. Entirely so.

GUEST. But we must not inquire whether they have been more or less so, and whether they are naturally so or not.

SOC. JUN. Undoubtedly not.

d   GUEST. Again, therefore, let us thus resume our inquiry. We said, then, that there was a self-commanding art respecting animals, which took care of them, not privately, but in common; and this art we then directly called the herd-nourishing art. Do you recollect?

SOC. JUN. Yes.

GUEST. In this, therefore, we erred. For we have not by any means comprehended in a definition the political character, nor given it a name; but its name as yet flies from us.

SOC. JUN. How so?

GUEST. To nourish the several herds of animals belongs to all other shepherds; but we have not given a fit name to the political character, which requires the application of something common.

e   SOC. JUN. You speak the truth, if this common something can be obtained.

GUEST. But is it not possible to apply healing, as that which is common to all things, without either defining nutriment, or any other thing? and to introduce another certain art, either pertaining to the nurture of herds, or therapeutic, or adapted to take care of something;

and thus to comprehend the political character together with others, since reason signifies that this ought to be done?

276a   SOC. JUN. Right. But after this, in what manner must the division be made?

GUEST. As before we divided the herd-nourishing art into the gradient and winged tribes, and into the horned and without horns, in the same manner we should divide the art pertaining to the care of herds, which will thus be similarly comprehended in our discourse, together with the kingdom of Saturn.

SOC. JUN. It appears so. But go on with your inquiries.

b   GUEST. If, then, the name of the art pertaining to the care of herds had been thus adopted, no one would have opposed us, as if there were no careful attention whatever; just as then it was justly contended, that there is no art in us which deserves the appellation of nutritive; and that, if there were any such art, it belongs to many things prior to, and preferable to, any thing pertaining to kings.

SOC. JUN. Right.

c   GUEST. But no other art endeavours to accomplish this more, and in a milder manner, as if it paid a careful attention to the whole of human communion, than the royal art.

SOC. JUN. Right.

GUEST. But after these things, Socrates, do you perceive how very much we have erred about the end?

SOC. JUN. What kind of error have we committed?

GUEST. We have erred in this, that though we have conceived that there is a certain nutritive art of a biped herd, yet we ought not immediately to have called it royal and politic, as if entirely complete.

SOC. JUN. Why not?

d   GUEST. In the first place, as we have said, the name ought to be accommodated more to attentive care than to nutriment: and in the next place, this attentive care ought to be divided. For it will receive no small sections.

SOC. JUN. Of what kind?

GUEST. The sections will be a divine shepherd, and a human curator.

SOC. JUN. Right.

GUEST. And again, it is necessary to give a twofold distribution to human care.

SOC. JUN. What are the two parts?

GUEST. The violent and the voluntary.

SOC. JUN. What then?

e   GUEST. And erring in this, with greater ineptitude than is becoming,
we considered a king and a tyrant as the same, though they are most
dissimilar both in themselves and in their mode of government.

SOC. JUN. True.

GUEST. Now, therefore, again correcting ourselves (as I have already
said), we shall divide human care into the violent and the voluntary.

SOC. JUN. Entirely so.

GUEST. And the violent we shall call tyrannic: but the voluntary, and
the attention paid to the herds of voluntary biped animals, we shall
denominate politic. We shall therefore evince, that he who possesses this
art and care is truly a king and a politician.

277a   SOC. JUN. And thus the demonstration, O guest, respecting political
affairs will, as it appears, be perfect.

GUEST. It will be well for us, Socrates, if this is the case. But it is
requisite that these things should not only be apparent to you, but
likewise to me, in common with you. But at present a king appears to
me not to possess as yet a perfect figure: but just as statuaries, who by
hastening their work sometimes unseasonably, and adding more and
larger things than are fit, finish it more slowly; so we at present have

b   not only rapidly and magnificently evinced that we erred in the former
part of our discussion, in consequence of thinking that great paradigms
should be employed about a king, but we reviled the wonderful bulk of
the fable, and were compelled to use a greater part of it than was proper.
On this account, we have made a more prolix demonstration, and have
not entirely finished the fable. But, indeed, our discourse, like an
animal, appears to have its exterior delineation sufficiently perfect, but

c   is not yet perspicuous, through paint, and the mixture of colours. But
it is more becoming to exhibit every animal by words and discourse, to
such as are able to follow the disquisition, than by painting, and the
whole of manual operation; but other things are to be exhibited through
the operations of the hand.

SOC. JUN. This, indeed, is rightly said: but show me why you say you
have not yet spoken sufficiently.

d   GUEST. It is difficult, O divine youth, to exhibit great things
perspicuously, without examples. For each of us appears to know all

things as in a dream,† and again to be ignorant of all things according to a wakeful perception.

SOC. JUN. How do you say this?

GUEST. We appear at present to have moved very absurdly the passion respecting science which is in us.

SOC. JUN. In what respect?

GUEST. The example, O blessed youth, which I have adduced will again require an example.

e SOC. JUN. Why? Tell me, and do not in any respect be remiss on my account.

GUEST. I will, since you are prepared to follow me. For we know what boys do as soon as they have acquired a knowledge of their letters.

SOC. JUN. What is that?

278a GUEST. They sufficiently perceive each of the elements in the shortest and easiest syllables, and are able to speak the truth concerning them.

SOC. JUN. Undoubtedly.

GUEST. But, being again dubious about these in other syllables, they are deceived in opinion and discourse.

SOC. JUN. Entirely so.

GUEST. May they not, therefore, thus be easily, and in the most beautiful manner, led to things which they do not yet know?

SOC. JUN. How?

b GUEST. By leading them first to those syllables in which they have had right opinions respecting these very same things; but, when we have thus led them, to place before them things which they do not yet know; and, by comparing them together, to show them that there is the same similitude and nature in both the complications, till the things conceived by true opinion are presented to the view compared with all the unknown particulars. But these being presented to the view, and examples of them produced, it will cause them to denominate that which is different in all the elements of every syllable as different from other things; but that which is the same, as always the same, according to things the same with itself.

c SOC. JUN. Entirely so.

GUEST. This, therefore, we sufficiently comprehend, viz. that the generation of a paradigm then takes place, when that which is the same

---

† The soul possesses a twofold knowledge, one indistinct, but the other distinct, scientific, and without ambiguity. For we essentially contain the reasons of things, and breathe, as it were, the knowledge of them; but we do not always possess them in energy.

in another divulsed particular being rightly conceived by opinion, and accommodated to each, produces one true opinion of both.

Soc. JUN. It appears so.

d   GUEST. Shall we therefore wonder, if our soul, suffering the same thing naturally about the elements of all things, at one time is established in certain particulars by truth itself about each individual thing, and at another time fluctuates in other particulars, about all things? And that when, in certain commixtions, it thinks rightly, it should again be ignorant of these very same things, when it is transferred to long and difficult syllables of things?

Soc. JUN. There is nothing wonderful in this.

GUEST. For how, my friend, can any one, beginning from false opinion, arrive at any, even the smallest part of truth, and thus acquire wisdom?

e   Soc. JUN. Nearly no one.

GUEST. If, therefore, these things naturally subsist in this manner, you and I shall not in any respect err, if we first of all endeavour to perceive the nature of the whole paradigm in another small and partial paradigm; and after this, betaking ourselves to the paradigm of a king, which is the greatest of all paradigms, and deriving it from lesser things, endeavour again, through a paradigm, to know by art the remedy of political affairs, that we may be partakers of wakeful perceptions instead of a dream.

Soc. JUN. Perfectly right.

279a   GUEST. Again, therefore, let us resume the former part of our discourse, *viz.* that since an innumerable multitude, together with the royal genus, doubt respecting the government of a city, it is requisite to separate all these from the royal genus, and to leave it by itself. And for this purpose we said it was requisite that we should have a certain paradigm.

Soc. JUN. And very much so.

GUEST. But what paradigm can any one adduce which both contains political concerns, and is the smallest possible, so that he may sufficiently find the object of his investigation? Are you willing, by

b   Jupiter, unless we have something else at hand, that we choose the weaving art? Not the whole, indeed, if it is agreeable to you: for, perhaps, the weaving of wool will be sufficient. For it may happen that this part being chosen may testify that which we wish to evince.

Soc. JUN. For why should it not?

GUEST. Shall we therefore now, with respect to this part of the weaving art, act in the same manner as we did above, *viz.* divide every particular by cutting the parts of parts? and, passing over all things in the shortest manner possible, return to that which is useful to our present purpose?

SOC. JUN. How do you say?

GUEST. My answer to you shall be an explanation of the thing.

SOC. JUN. You speak most excellently.

GUEST. Of all the things which we fabricate and possess, some are for the sake of doing something, and others are auxiliaries against any inconvenience we may suffer. And of auxiliaries, some are alexipharmic,[†] as well divine as human; but others are subservient to defence. And of things subservient to defence, some consist of warlike apparatus, and others are inclusures. And of inclusures, some are veils, and others are defences against heat and cold. But of defences, some are coverings, and others are apparel. And of apparel, one part is an under veil, and another a surrounding covering. And of surrounding coverings, some are simple, and others composite. But of the composite, some are perforated, but others are connected together without perforation. And of those that are without perforation, some are composed from the nerves of things growing out of the earth, but others are hairy. And of the hairy, some are conglutinated by water and earth, but others are themselves connected together with themselves. To these auxiliaries and coverings, which are wrought from the same things being bound together, we give the name of garments. But we call that art which is especially conversant with garments, vestific, from the thing itself, in the same manner as above we called the art respecting a city politic. We likewise say that the weaving art, so far as for the most part it weaves garments, differs in nothing but the name from the vestific art; just in the same manner as we formerly observed that a royal differed only nominally from a political character.

SOC. JUN. Most right.

GUEST. But after this we should thus reason: that some one may, perhaps, think it has been sufficiently shown that the weaving art is conversant with garments, but may not be able to perceive, that though it is not yet distinguished from things which cooperate near together, it is separated from many other things of a kindred nature.

SOC. JUN. Tell me what things of a kindred nature.

GUEST. You do not understand what has been said, as it seems. It appears, therefore, that we should return from the end to the beginning. For, if you understand propinquity, we have now separated this from

---

† *i.e.* Remedies of evils.

the weaving art, by distributing the composition of coverings into things put under, and things surrounding us.

SOC. JUN. I understand you.

c GUEST. We have likewise separated every kind of fabrication from thread and broom, and all such plantal productions as we just now called nerves. We also defined the compressive art, and the composition which employs perforation and sewing, which for the most part pertains to the currier's art.

SOC. JUN. Entirely so.

GUEST. We also separated the fabrication of simple coverings from skins, and of such coverings as are employed in building, and in the whole of the tectonic, and in all other arts which are employed in stopping the effluxions of water. Also such arts as procure restraints in

d joining, and violent actions, and which are employed about the construction of doors, and distribute the parts of the cementing art. We have likewise divided the armour-making art, which is a section of the great and all-various power effective of defence. We also defined, in the

e very beginning, the whole art of cooking, which is conversant with alexipharmics; and we left a certain art, which appears to be that we are in pursuit of, *viz.* which defends against cold, produces woollen vestments, and is called the art of weaving.

SOC. JUN. It seems so.

GUEST. But we have not yet, O boy, perfectly discussed this matter.

281a For he who is first engaged in the making of garments appears to act in a manner directly contrary to the weaver.

SOC. JUN. How so?

GUEST. For the work of the weaver is a certain knitting together.

SOC. JUN. It is.

GUEST. But the work of him who first engages in the making of garments consists in dissolving things joined together.

SOC. JUN. What kind of work is this?

GUEST. The work of the art of carding wool. Or shall we dare to call the art of carding wool the weaving art, and a wool-carder a weaver?

SOC. JUN. By no means.

b GUEST. But if any one should call the art effective of the thread and woof in a loom the weaving art, he would assert a paradox, and give it a false name.

SOC. JUN. Undoubtedly.

GUEST. But whether shall we say that the whole attention and care of the fuller and the mender contribute nothing to the making of garments? Or shall we also call these weaving arts?

SOC. JUN. By no means.

GUEST. But all these contend with the power of the weaving art, respecting the care and the making of garments; attributing, indeed, to it the greatest part, but likewise assigning to themselves great portions of the same art.

c   SOC. JUN. Entirely so.

GUEST. Besides these, it further appears requisite, that the arts effective of the instruments through which the weaver accomplishes his work, should be considered as concauses of every work accomplished by weaving.

SOC. JUN. Most right.

GUEST. Whether, therefore, will our discourse about the weaving art, a part of which we have chosen, be sufficiently defined, if we assert that it is the most beautiful and the greatest of all the arts which are

d   employed about woollen garments? Or shall we thus, indeed, speak something of the truth, but yet neither clearly nor perfectly till we have separated all these arts from it?

SOC. JUN. This will be the case.

GUEST. Must we not, therefore, in the next place act in this manner, that our discourse may proceed in an orderly series?

SOC. JUN. Undoubtedly.

GUEST. In the first place, therefore, let us consider two arts which subsist about all things.

SOC. JUN. What are they?

GUEST. One is the concause of generation, and the other is the cause itself.

SOC. JUN. How?

e   GUEST. Such arts as do not fabricate the thing itself, but prepare instruments for the fabricators, without which instruments the proposed work cannot be effected, - these are concauses: but those which fabricate the thing itself are causes.

SOC. JUN. This distinction is reasonable.

GUEST. In the next place, those arts which produce the distaff, and the shuttle, and such other instruments as contribute to the making of garments, - all these I call concauses: but those which pay attention to and fabricate garments I call causes.

SOC. JUN. Most right.

282a   GUEST. But, of causes, it will be proper especially to collect that which pertains to the washing of garments, and that which is skilled in mending, and all the therapeutic care about these, since the cosmetic art is abundant, and to denominate the whole the fuller's art.

SOC. JUN. It will so.

b   GUEST. But there is one art comprehending that part which cards wool and spins, and likewise every thing pertaining to the making of garments, and which is called by all men the wool-working art.

SOC. JUN. How so?

GUEST. The art of carding wool, and the half of that art which uses the shuttle, and that art which separates from each other things joined together, - all these, in short, form a part of the wool-working art, of which there are two great parts, one collective, and the other separative.

SOC. JUN. There are so.

GUEST. The art of carding wool, therefore, and all those other arts
c   which we just now mentioned, belong to the separative part. For that art which divides in wool and thread, after one manner with the shuttle, and after another with the hands, has all the names which we have just now mentioned.

SOC. JUN. Entirely so.

GUEST. Again, we must take a part of the collective part, and of the wool-working art contained in it; but we must pass by all such things of a separating nature as we happen to find there, and bisect the wool-working art, together with the collective and separative section.

SOC. JUN. Let us divide them.

d   GUEST. It will be proper for you, therefore, Socrates, to divide the collective, together with the wool-working part, if we wish to apprehend sufficiently the proposed weaving art.

SOC. JUN. It will be requisite.

GUEST. It will indeed: and we say, therefore, that one part of it is streptic, or conversant with rolling, and the other symplectic, or complicative.

SOC. JUN. Do I then understand you? For you appear to me to say that the elaboration of the thread is streptic.

GUEST. Not the elaboration of this only, but likewise of the woof. Or can we find any generation of it which is not streptic?

SOC. JUN. By no means.

e   GUEST. Define also each of these: for perhaps you will find the definition seasonable.

SOC. JUN. In what respect?

GUEST. In this. We say that the work of the wool-carder, when it is drawn out into length and breadth, is a certain fracture.

SOC. JUN. We do.

GUEST. This, when it is turned by the distaff, and becomes a solid thread, is called stamen: but they say that the art which directs this is stemonic, or conversant with stuff to be woven.

SOC. JUN. Right.

283a GUEST. But such things as receive a loose contortion, and by the implication of the thread with the attraction of the polish acquire a measured softness, - of these we call what is spun the woof, but the art itself which presides over these, woof-spinning.

SOC. JUN. Most right.

b GUEST. And now that part of the weaving art which we proposed is obvious to every one. For, with respect to a part of the collective art in the working of wool, when it accomplishes that which is woven by a fit knitting together of the woof and the thread, then the whole of the thing woven is called a woollen garment, but the art presiding over this, textorian.

SOC. JUN. Most right.

GUEST. Be it so. But why then did we not immediately answer, that the plectic art is that which weaves together the woof and the thread, instead of proceeding in a circle, and defining many things in vain?

SOC. JUN. It does not appear to me, O guest, that we have said any thing in vain.

GUEST. This is not at all wonderful. But perhaps, O blessed youth, it will be seen that you will often hereafter fall into this disease. Nor c is it wonderful. But hear a certain discourse, which is proper to be delivered respecting all such particulars as these.

SOC. JUN. Only relate it.

GUEST. Let us, therefore, in the first place, behold the whole of excess and deficiency, that we may praise and blame according to reason whatever is said with more prolixity or brevity than is becoming in disputations of this kind.

SOC. JUN. It will be proper so to do.

GUEST. But I think we shall do right by discoursing about these things.

SOC. JUN. About what things?

d GUEST. About prolixity and brevity, and the whole of excess and deficiency. For the art of measuring is conversant with all these.

SOC. JUN. It is.

GUEST. We will divide it, therefore, into two parts. For it is requisite to that after which we are hastening.

SOC. JUN. Inform me how this division is to be made.

GUEST. Thus. One part according to the communion of magnitude and parvitude with each other; but the other part according to the necessary essence of generation.

SOC. JUN. How do you say?

GUEST. Does it not appear to you to be natural, that the greater ought to be called greater than nothing else than the lesser? and again, that the lesser should not be lesser than any thing than the greater?

e   SOC. JUN. To me it does.

GUEST. But what? Must we not say that what surpasses the nature of mediocrity, and is surpassed by it, whether in words or actions, is that by which especially good and bad men differ from each other?

SOC. JUN. It appears so.

GUEST. These twofold essences, therefore, and judgments of the great and the small must be established; but not, as we just now said, with reference to each other only. But, as we now say, they are rather partly to be referred to each other, and partly to mediocrity. Are we however willing to learn on what account this is requisite?

SOC. JUN. Undoubtedly.

284a   GUEST. If some one refers the nature of the greater to nothing else than the nature of the lesser, he will not refer it to mediocrity. Or will he?

SOC. JUN. He will not.

GUEST. May we not, therefore, divide the arts themselves, and all their works, according to this reasoning? And shall we not entirely take away the political science which we are now investigating, and that which is called the weaving art? For all such things as these guard against that which is more or less than mediocrity, not as if it had no subsistence, but as a thing of a difficult nature in actions. And after this manner preserving mediocrity, they effect every thing beautiful and good.

b   SOC. JUN. Undoubtedly.

GUEST. If, therefore, we take away the politic science, will not our investigation after this of the royal science be dubious?

SOC. JUN. Very much so.

GUEST. Whether, therefore, as in our investigation of a sophist, we compelled non-being to be, after discourse about it fled from us, so now shall we compel the more and the less to become measured, not only c   with reference to each other, but likewise to the generation of mediocrity? For no one can indubitably become a politician, or knowing in any thing else pertaining to actions, unless he assents to this.

SOC. JUN. We ought, therefore, especially to do this now.

GUEST. This, Socrates, is a still greater work than that; though, as we may remember, that was very prolix. But a thing of this kind may be supposed respecting them, and very justly.

SOC. JUN. Of what kind?

d GUEST. That there is occasion for what we are now speaking of, in order to evince what is accurate respecting this thing. Further still, with respect to the present particulars, it appears to me to have been shown sufficiently, that this discourse will afford us magnificent assistance, as leading us to think that all arts are to be similarly measured according to the more and the less, not only among themselves, but likewise with reference to the generation of mediocrity. For, this having a subsistence, they also are: and, these subsisting, this also is. And either of these being taken away, neither of them will subsist.

e SOC. JUN. This indeed is right. But what follows?

GUEST. We should evidently divide the art of measuring (as we have said) into two parts; placing as one of its parts all those arts which measure number, length, breadth, depth, and velocity, with reference to the contrary; but placing as its other part, such arts as regard the moderate and the becoming, the seasonable and the fit, and all such as fly from the extremes to the middle.

SOC. JUN. Each of these sections is great, and they differ much from each other.

285a GUEST. That, Socrates, which is sometimes asserted by many of those elegant men, who think they assert something wise, when they say that the art of measuring is conversant with all generated natures, is now asserted by us. For all artificial things after a certain manner participate of measure; but, in consequence of not being accustomed to divide according to species, these men immediately collect into the same these things which so widely differ from each other, and consider them as similar. And, again, they do the very contrary to this: for things which b are different they do not divide according to parts, though it is requisite that, when any one first perceives the communion of many things, he should not desist till he perceives all the differences in it which are placed in species: and again, when he perceives all-various dissimilitudes in multitudes, he cannot desist from this difficult perception, till, having inclosed all such things as are allied in one similitude, he comprehends them in the essence of a certain genus. And thus much may suffice respecting these particulars, and concerning defect and excess. This only must be carefully observed, that two genera of measures about these particulars have been invented, and that we should remember what they are.

c SOC. JUN. We will remember.

GUEST. But, after this discussion, let us assume another respecting the objects of our investigation, and the whole purport of this discourse.

SOC. JUN. What is it?

GUEST. If any one should ask us respecting the custom of those that learn their letters, when they are asked from what letters a word is composed, shall we say that the inquiry is then made for the sake of one

d word only, or that they may become more skilful in every thing pertaining to grammar?

SOC. JUN. Evidently that they may become more skilful in the whole of grammar.

GUEST. But what again? Is our inquiry respecting a politician undertaken by us more for the sake of the politician, than that we may become more skilful in every discussion?

SOC. JUN. This also is evident, that it is undertaken on this latter account.

e GUEST. No one indeed endued with intellect would be willing to investigate the art of weaving, for its own sake alone: but I think most men are ignorant, that there are certain sensible similitudes of things which are naturally capable of being easily learnt, and that there is no difficulty in making these manifest, when any one wishes to point them out to some one inquiring a reason respecting them, not in conjunction with things, but with facility, without assigning a reason. But of things

286a the greatest and the most honourable, there is not any image clearly fabricated for men, which being exhibited by him who wishes to fill the soul of the inquirer, can, by being harmonized to some one of the senses, sufficiently fill the soul. Hence it is requisite to meditate how we may be able to give and receive a reason for every thing. For incorporeal natures, as they are the most beautiful and the greatest of all things, can alone be clearly pointed out by reason, but by nothing else.

b And all we have said at present is asserted for the sake of these things. But the consideration of every particular is more easily effected in small things than in such as are great.

SOC. JUN. You speak most beautifully.

GUEST. Do we, therefore, remember on what account all these things have been said by us?

SOC. JUN. On what account?

GUEST. Principally on account of the difficulty in which we were involved, through the prolix discourse about the weaving art, and the revolution of the universe. We likewise considered the discourse of the sophist about the essence of non-being, as full of prolixity. And on all these accounts we terrified ourselves, fearing lest we should speak superfluously in conjunction with prolixity. Consider, therefore, all

c   these things as said by us, in order that we may not suffer any thing of this kind again.

SOC. JUN. Be it so. Only discuss what remains.

GUEST. I say, therefore, it is requisite that both you and I should be mindful of what we have now said, as often as brevity or prolixity of

d   discourse is blamed, not judging the prolixities by one another, but according to that part of the measuring art, which we said above ought to be remembered with a view to the becoming.

SOC. JUN. Right.

GUEST. But yet all things are not referred to this. For we do not require in order to obtain pleasure a prolixity which harmonizes with nothing, unless as a certain appendix. Nor is it proper to make the easy and rapid discovery of the object of our investigation our principal intention; but this ought to be considered by us as a secondary thing. But we should by far most especially, and in the first place, honour the method which is able to divide according to species. We should likewise by no means be indignant with a discourse, however extended, which

e   renders the hearer more inventive; and the same must be said of a discourse however short. Further still, it becomes him who blames long discourses in disquisitions such as these, and who does not admit circular

287a   periods, not to condemn them altogether rapidly, and immediately, but to show first that we shall be more fit for discussion, and more capable of discovering things by reason, by shorter discourses: but we should neither pay any attention to, nor even seem to hear any other praise or blame. And thus much may suffice for these things, if it also seems so

b   to you. Let us, therefore, again return to the political character, introducing the before-mentioned paradigm of the weaving art.

SOC. JUN. You speak well: and let us do as you say.

GUEST. Is not, therefore, the office of a king to be separated from that of many shepherds, or rather from that of all those who have the charge of herds?

SOC. JUN. Yes.

GUEST. But we say that the consideration of causes and concauses respecting a city remains, which are first to be divided from each other.

c   SOC. JUN. Right.

GUEST. You know, therefore, that it is difficult to bisect these. But the cause of this will, I think, in the course of our inquiry be not less apparent.

SOC. JUN. It will be proper, therefore, so to do.

GUEST. Let us, then, divide them into parts, like victims, since we cannot bisect them: for it is always requisite to cut into the nearest number possible.

SOC. JUN. How, therefore, shall we do at present?

GUEST. Just as we did above: for we placed all such instruments as are subservient to weaving, as concauses.

SOC. JUN. We did.

d   GUEST. The same thing, therefore, must be done by us now, and it is still more necessary than it was then. For such things as fabricate in a city either a small or a large instrument are all of them to be considered as concauses; since without these a city could never subsist, nor yet the politic science. But yet again we do not establish any one of these as the business of the royal science.

SOC. JUN. We do not.

GUEST. We likewise attempt to accomplish a difficult thing, in separating this genus from others. For he who says that it is an instrument of some particular being, appears to speak probably: but at

e   the same time we must say that this is different from the possessions belonging to a city.

SOC. JUN. In what respect?

GUEST. Because it has not this power. For causes do not adhere to generation as an instrument, but on account of the safety of that which is fabricated.

SOC. JUN. What kind of thing do you mean?

GUEST. An all-various species produced from things dry and moist, fiery and without fire, and which we call by one appellation, a vessel, though it is an abundant species: but I think this does not at all belong

288a   to the science we are investigating.

SOC. JUN. Undoubtedly not.

GUEST. But the third species, or that of possessions, appears to be multiform, consisting of the terrestrial and aquatic, the much-wandering and the inerratic, the honourable and the ignoble; and it has one name, because the whole of it subsists for the sake of a certain fitting, as it always becomes a seat to something.

SOC. JUN. What kind of thing is it?

GUEST. It is that which is called a vehicle, a thing which is not entirely the work of the politic science, but rather of the tectonic, ceramic,[†] and calcotypic.[‡]

---

† *i.e.* Pertaining to the potter's art.

‡ *i.e.* Pertaining to the brazier's art.

SOC. JUN. I understand you.

b GUEST. Must we then mention a fourth species of these, in which most of the things formerly spoken of by us are contained? *viz.* every kind of garment, many arms, walls, all inclusures, consisting either of earth or stone, and ten thousand other things. And since all these are constructed for the sake of defence, the whole may most justly be called a fortification; and, for the most part, may more properly be considered as much more the work of the architect and weaver than of the politician.

SOC. JUN. Entirely so.

c GUEST. Are we, therefore, willing to rank in the fifth place the arts of adorning, painting, and music, together with such arts as use these; from which certain imitations are devised for the sake of procuring us pleasure, and which may be justly comprehended in one name?

SOC. JUN. In what name?

GUEST. They may be denominated sportive.

SOC. JUN. Undoubtedly.

GUEST. This one name, therefore, accords with all these: for no one of them does any thing seriously, but all their operations are for the sake of sport.

d SOC. JUN. This also I nearly understand.

GUEST. But ought we not to place as a sixth all-various species, and, which is the offspring of many other arts, that art which prepares bodies for all the above-mentioned particulars?

SOC. JUN. Of what art are you speaking?

GUEST. That art which digs gold and silver, and other metals, out of

e the bowels of the earth; likewise that which cuts down trees, that which constructs something by shaving off the hair, the knitting art, that which cuts off the barks of trees, and the skins of animals, and all such arts as are conversant with things of this kind. Also, such arts as procure cork, books, and bonds, fabricating composite species from genera which are not composite. The whole of this we call the first-born possession of mankind, simple, and by no means the work of the royal science.

SOC. JUN. Right.

GUEST. The possession of nutriment, and such things as when mingled with the body can, by their parts, administer to its wants, must

289a be ranked in the seventh place. And the whole of this must be denominated by us nutriment, unless we have any thing better to adopt instead of it. However, we may place the whole of this under

agriculture, hunting, gymnastic, medicine, and cooking, and attribute it
to these more properly than to the politic science.

Soc. Jun. Undoubtedly.

Guest. Nearly, therefore, all possessions, except those of tame
animals, may I think be found in these seven genera. But consider: for
b   it was most just that the species which we call first-born should be
introduced first; and after this, instrument, vessel, vehicle, fortification,
that which is sportive, and cattle. But if any thing of no great
consequence is latent, which may be accommodated to some one of
these, we omit it; such as the idea of coin, of seals, and of every thing
impressed or carved. For these things are not very much allied to the
genus; but some accord with it, for the purpose of ornament, others as
subservient to instruments, violently, indeed, but at the same time they
c   may be drawn to this end. But the nurture of herds which we before
distributed, seems to comprehend the whole possession of tame animals,
slaves being excepted.

Soc. Jun. Entirely so.

Guest. The genus of slaves, and of all servants, remains, in which I
prophesy, that those who contend with a king respecting the thing
woven will become apparent, in the same manner as above, those that
knit, and those that comb wool, and such others as were then
mentioned by us, contended with the weavers. But all the others who
d   were called by us concauses, together with the works just now
mentioned, are set aside, and are separated from royal and political
action.

Soc. Jun. It appears so.

Guest. Let us then, approaching nearer, consider the rest, that we
may more firmly perceive them.

Soc. Jun. It is, therefore, requisite to do so.

Guest. We shall find, then, that the greatest servants, so far as we can
see in this affair, are engaged in a pursuit, and possess a property the
very contrary to what we have expected.

Soc. Jun. What are these?

e   Guest. Men acquired by purchase; whom, beyond all controversy, we
ought to call slaves, and of whom we should assert, that they by no
means vindicate to themselves the royal art.

Soc. Jun. Undoubtedly.

Guest. But what shall we say of those free-born men who voluntarily
engage in the servile employments mentioned by us above, *viz.* who
transmit the works of husbandry, and of the other arts, to each other,

290a and who are engaged in mutual traffic, domestic or foreign, whether they change money for other things, or like for like, (whom we denominate money-changers, pilots, and hucksters,) shall we say that these will contend for any part of the politic science?

SOC. JUN. Perhaps merchants will.

GUEST. But yet we never find that those mercenaries who readily offer their services to every one vindicate to themselves the royal science.

SOC. JUN. For how can they?

GUEST. What then shall we say of those that act in this servile capacity every where?

SOC. JUN. Of whom are you speaking? and of what kind of servile offices?

b GUEST. I speak of the tribe of criers, and of those who become wise respecting letters,[†] and often act in the capacity of servants, together with certain other persons who are very skilful in the labours pertaining to government. What again shall we say of these?

SOC. JUN. That which you just now said, that they are servants, but no rulers in cities.

GUEST. I do not think, therefore, I was looking at a dream, when I said that many on this account would be seen strenuously contending for the royal science, though it may appear to be very absurd to seek after these in any servile portion.

c SOC. JUN. Very much so, indeed.

GUEST. Let us, besides, approach still nearer to those whom we have not yet examined. But these are such as possess a certain portion of ministrant science about divination. For they are considered as interpreting to men things proceeding from the Gods.

SOC. JUN. They are.

GUEST. The genus too of priests, as established by law, knows in what manner we should offer gifts, through sacrifices, to the Gods, so as to render the divinities propitious to us; and likewise, after what manner we should request of them, by prayer, the possession of good things. But both these are parts of the ministrant art.

SOC. JUN. So it appears.

GUEST. Now, therefore, we appear to me to touch, as it were, upon a certain vestige of the object of our search. For the figure of priests and prophets is very replete with prudence, and receives a venerable opinion through the magnitude of the undertakings. Hence, among the

† *Viz.* grammarians.

Egyptians, a king is not allowed to govern without the sacerdotal
e   science; so that, if any one belonging to another genus of men usurps the
kingdom, he is afterwards compelled to be initiated in their mysteries,
that he may be skilled in the sacerdotal science. Further still, in many
places belonging to the Greeks, we shall find that the greatest sacrifices
of this kind are under the direction of the greatest magistrates; and the
truth of what I assert is particularly evinced among you. For, when a
king is elected, they say that the most venerable of all the ancient
sacrifices, and such as are most peculiar to the country, are to be
consigned to the care of the new king.

SOC. JUN. Entirely so.

291a GUEST. We should, therefore, consider these kings chosen by lot,
together with the priests, their servants, and a certain other numerous
crowd, which just now became manifest to us, apart from our former
assertions.

SOC. JUN. Of whom are you speaking?

GUEST. Of certain very wonderful persons.

SOC. JUN. Why so?

b   GUEST. As I was just now speculating, the genus of them appeared to
me to be all-various. For many men resemble lions and centaurs, and
other things of this kind; and very many are similar to satyrs, and to
imbecil and multiform wild beasts. They likewise rapidly change their
ideas and their power into each other. And indeed, Socrates, I appear
to myself to have just now perceived these men for the first time.

SOC. JUN. Speak: for you seem to behold something unusual.

GUEST. I do: for the unusual or wonderful happens to all men from
ignorance. And I myself just now suffered the very same thing: for I
was suddenly involved in doubt on perceiving the choir of civil
concerns.

c   SOC. JUN. What choir?

GUEST. The greatest enchanter of all sophists, and the most skilled in
this art, who must be separated from truly political and royal characters,
though this is difficult in the extreme, if we intend to see clearly the
object of our investigation.

SOC. JUN. We must by no means omit to do this.

GUEST. We must not, indeed, according to my opinion: but tell me
this.

SOC. JUN. What?

d   GUEST. Is not a monarchy one of our political governments?

SOC. JUN. It is.

GUEST. And after a monarchy I think an oligarchy may be placed.

SOC. JUN. Undoubtedly.

GUEST. But is not the third scheme of a polity the government of the multitude, and which is called a democracy?

SOC. JUN. Entirely so.

GUEST. May not these three become after a manner five, since they produce two other names from themselves?

SOC. JUN. What are these two?

e GUEST. Those who now look to the violent and the voluntary, to poverty and riches, law and the transgression of law, which take place in these governments, and who give a twofold division to each of the two, and call monarchy by two names, as affording two species, *viz.* tyrannic and royal.

SOC. JUN. Undoubtedly.

GUEST. But they denominate a city which is governed by a few an aristocracy and an oligarchy.

SOC. JUN. Entirely so.

292a GUEST. But no one is ever accustomed to change the name of a democracy, whether the people govern the rich violently, or with their consent, and whether they accurately defend the laws or not.

SOC. JUN. True.

GUEST. What then? Shall we think that any one of these polities is right, thus bounded by these definitions, *viz.* by one, and a few, and a many, by riches and poverty, by the violent and the voluntary, by written laws, and the privation of laws?

SOC. JUN. What should hinder?

b GUEST. Consider more attentively, following me hither.

SOC. JUN. Whither?

GUEST. Shall we abide by that which was asserted by us at first, or shall we dissent from it?

SOC. JUN. Of what assertion are you speaking?

GUEST. I think we said that a royal government was one of the sciences.

SOC. JUN. We did.

GUEST. Yet we did not consider it as any one science indiscriminately; but we selected it from the other sciences, as something judicial and presiding.

SOC. JUN. We did.

GUEST. And of the presiding science, dividing one part, as belonging c to inanimate works, and the other as belonging to animals, we have proceeded thus far, not forgetting that we were scientifically employed;

but we have not yet been able to determine with sufficient accuracy
what this science is.

SOC. JUN. Right.

GUEST. Do we, therefore, understand this, that the definition must
not be made by the few, nor by the many, nor yet by the voluntary or
involuntary, nor by poverty or riches, but according to a certain science,
if we follow what has been formerly delivered?

d   SOC. JUN. But, indeed, it is impossible that this should not be done.

GUEST. From necessity, therefore, we must now consider in which of
these the science respecting the government of men happens to subsist;
this government being nearly the greatest of all others, and the most
difficult to obtain. For it is requisite to inspect it, that we may perceive
what are the things which must be taken away from a prudent king, and
who those are that pretend to be, and persuade the multitude that they
are, politicians, but who are by no means so.

SOC. JUN. Our former reasoning evinces that it is requisite to act in
this manner.

e   GUEST. Does it then appear to you that the multitude in a city is able
to acquire this science?

SOC. JUN. How can they?

GUEST. In a city, therefore, consisting of a thousand men, is it
possible that a hundred or five hundred of the inhabitants can
sufficiently acquire this science?

SOC. JUN. If this were the case, it would be the most easy of all arts.
For we know that among a thousand men there cannot be found so
great a number of those that excel the other Greeks in the game of
chess, much less can there be found as many kings. But, according to
our former reasoning, it is requisite to call him royal who possesses the
royal science, whether he governs or not.

293a   GUEST. You very properly remind me: but I think it follows from
this, that a right government, when it subsists rightly, ought to be
investigated about one person, or two, or altogether about a few.

SOC. JUN. Undoubtedly.

b   GUEST. And, as we now think, those that govern according to a
certain art are to be considered as political and regal characters, whether
they govern the willing or the refractory, whether according to or
without written laws, and whether they are rich or poor. For we call
those who heal the maladies of the body, no less physicians, whether
they cure by cutting, or burning, or any other painful application, the
voluntary or the refractory; and whether from writings or without
writings; and whether they are poor or rich. In all these cases we say

that they are no less physicians, so long as they proceed according to art, in purging or some other way attenuating the body, or in causing it to increase; and so long as, alone regarding the good of the body, they restore it from a worse to a better habit, and preserve it when thus restored. After this manner alone, as I think, we must say that the definition of the medicinal or any other government is rightly made.

SOC. JUN. And very much so.

GUEST. It is necessary, therefore, as it seems, that that polity alone must in the highest degree be rightly established, in which the governors are found to be truly, and not in appearance only, scientific; whether they govern according to laws, or without laws; whether they rule over the obedient, or the refractory; and whether they are rich or poor. For no one of these is of any consequence with respect to rectitude of government.

SOC. JUN. Beautifully said.

GUEST. Nor yet is it of any consequence, whether they purge the city with a view to its good, by putting to death or banishing certain persons; or whether they send out colonies, like a swarm of bees, and thus diminish the people; or whether, introducing certain foreigners, they make citizens of them, and thus increase the city. For, so long as, employing science and justice, they cause the city, to the utmost of their power, to pass from a worse to a better condition, and preserve it in this state, - so far, and according to such definitions, we say that a polity is alone rightly established; but that such others, as we have mentioned, are neither genuinely nor truly polities. We must likewise willingly say that such polities as imitate this are consonant to reason, and tend to things more beautiful, but that such as do not, tend to deformity by an imitation of things evil.

SOC. JUN. Other things indeed, O guest, appear to have been discussed sufficiently: but it is not easy to admit your assertion, that it is requisite to govern without laws.

GUEST. You have got before me a little, Socrates, by your question. For I was going to ask you, whether you admit all these things, or whether you find any difficulty in anything that has been said. It is however evident, that we now wish to inquire concerning the rectitude of those that govern without laws.

SOC. JUN. Undoubtedly.

GUEST. After a certain manner it is evident that legislation pertains to the royal science: but it is best, not for the laws to prevail, but a man who is royal in conjunction with prudence. Do you know why?

SOC. JUN. Inform me.

GUEST. Because law cannot, by comprehending that which is most excellent, and at the same time most accurately just, for all men, always
b   enjoin that which is best. For the dissimilitudes of men and actions, and the unceasing restlessness, as I may say, of human affairs, do not permit any art whatever to be exhibited respecting all things, and through every time. Shall we admit these assertions?

SOC. JUN. Undoubtedly.

GUEST. But we see that law nearly endeavours to accomplish this very
c   thing, like a certain arrogant and ignorant man, who does not suffer any thing to be done contrary to his own orders, nor any one to ask whether it would not be better to make some new regulation, contrary to what he has ordained.

SOC. JUN. True. For the law does as you say.

GUEST. But it is impossible that a thing which is simple should prevail in things which are never at any time simple.

SOC. JUN. It appears so.

GUEST. The cause, therefore, must be found out why it is necessary
d   to establish laws, since law does not possess the greatest rectitude.

SOC. JUN. Undoubtedly.

GUEST. Are there not, therefore, among us, as also in other cities, certain exercises of men collected together, whether belonging to the course, or to any thing else which is undertaken for the sake of contention?

SOC. JUN. There are very many such exercises.

GUEST. Come then, let us again recall to our memory the mandates of those who preside over gymnastic exercises according to art.

SOC. JUN. What are their mandates?

GUEST. They do not think that a subtle division should be made, according to each individual, so as to enjoin that which is adapted to the
e   body of each; but that attention should be paid to what is more common, and which is advantageous for the most part, and to a many.

SOC. JUN. Excellent.

GUEST. Hence at present assigning equal labours to collected bodies of men, they at the same time impel them to begin the contest together, and to rest from the race, from wrestling, and from all the labours of the body, at one and the same time.

SOC. JUN. They do so.

295a GUEST. We, therefore, think that the legislator who presides over the herds of men, and enjoins them what is just respecting their compacts with each other, cannot, while he gives laws to them collectively, accurately assign what is fit to each individual.

SOC. JUN. This is likely to be the case.

GUEST. But I think that in a less subtle way he will establish laws for the multitude, and for the most part, both written and unwritten, and such as are agreeable to the manners of the country.

SOC. JUN. Right.

b   GUEST. Right indeed. For how, Socrates, can any one attend sufficiently to individuals through the whole of life, and accurately enjoin what is adapted to each? For, though he who possesses the royal science could, I think, do this, he would scarcely prescribe for himself those impediments which are called laws.

SOC. JUN. It appears so, O guest, from what has been now said.

GUEST. Rather, O most excellent youth, from what will be said.

SOC. JUN. What is that?

c   GUEST. This. For we thus say to ourselves: If a physician, or master of gymnastic, intending to travel, and to be absent from those under his care for a long time, should think that those who are exercised, or those who are sick, would not remember his precepts, he will wish to write commentaries for them. Or how shall we say?

SOC. JUN. That he will wish to do so.

GUEST. But what? If the physician should return sooner than he thought, will he venture to order them certain other things besides those contained in his writings, if any thing better should occur for the sick,

d   through winds, or any thing else, which is wont to take place through Jupiter, contrary to expectation? Will he think that he ought strenuously to persevere in his former injunctions, neither himself ordering any thing else, nor the sick man daring to do any thing different from his written prescriptions; these being medicinal and salubrious, but things of a different nature, noxious, and contrary to art? Or rather, every thing of this kind happening about all things according to science and true art, will not his edicts become the most ridiculous of all others?

e   SOC. JUN. Entirely so.

GUEST. But shall not he who writes things just and unjust, beautiful and base, good and evil, and who establishes unwritten laws for the herds of mankind, who live in cities according to written laws, - shall not he, I say, who has written laws according to art, or any other who resembles him, be permitted on his return to enjoin things different

296a   from these? Or, rather, would not this interdiction appear in reality to be no less ridiculous than the former?

SOC. JUN. Undoubtedly.

GUEST. Do you know, therefore, what the multitude say respecting a thing of this kind?

SOC. JUN. I do not at present remember.

GUEST. But it is very specious. For they say, if any one has found out laws better than those that are already established, and can persuade his citizens that they are better, he should establish them; otherwise not.

SOC. JUN. Do they not, therefore, say rightly?

b   GUEST. Perhaps so. But if some one should introduce that which is best, not by persuasion, but by force, what name must be given to this violence? Or, rather, first answer me respecting the former particulars.

SOC. JUN. Of what particulars are you speaking?

GUEST. If any one who is properly skilled in the medical art should not persuade but compel a boy, or a man, or a woman, to do that which is better, but at the same time contrary to written prescriptions, what will be the name of this violence? Ought it not to be called rather any

c   thing than a transgression of art, or a noxious error? And should we not say that every thing will happen to the compelled person, rather than any thing noxious and contrary to art from the compelling physicians?

SOC. JUN. You speak most true.

GUEST. But what is that error to be called which is contrary to the political art? Must it not be denominated base, evil, and unjust?

SOC. JUN. Entirely so.

GUEST. But come, will not he be the most ridiculous of all men, who should blame the violence of those that force men to act more justly, better, and more beautifully than before, contrary to written precepts,

d   and the laws of their country? And ought not every thing rather to be asserted of those that are thus compelled, than that they suffer things base, unjust, and evil?

SOC. JUN. Your assertion is most true.

GUEST. But if he who compels is rich, will his compulsions be just, - but, if he is poor, unjust? Or shall we not rather say, that he who effects what is advantageous, whether he persuades or does not persuade, whether he is rich or poor, and whether he acts according or contrary

e   to written injunctions, will act conformably to the most true definition of the right government of a city? For a wise and good man will always govern in this manner, always attending to the advantage of his subjects, in the same manner as a pilot is watchful for the safety of the ship and

297a   the sailors. And as the pilot preserves the sailors, not by written mandates but by exhibiting to them laws according to art, after the same manner an upright polity will be produced by those who are thus able to govern, by exhibiting a strength of art better than the laws. And, in short, prudent governors never err in any part of their conduct, as long as they observe this one thing, *viz.* by always distributing that which is

b   most just to the citizens, in conjunction with intellect and art, to preserve them, and, from being worse, render them better to the utmost of their power.

SOC. JUN. These assertions cannot be contradicted.

GUEST. Nor yet those.

SOC. JUN. What assertions do you mean?

GUEST. That no multitude whatever can receive that science, by which a city is governed according to intellect, but that an upright

c   polity must be investigated about a small number, and a few, and one person; and that other polities are to be considered as imitations, as we observed a little before, some resembling this in a more beautiful, and others in a more deformed manner.

SOC. JUN. How do you say this? For I do not understand what you just now said respecting imitations.

d   GUEST. He would not act badly, who, after introducing a discourse of this kind, should desist before he had shown the error which is at present committed.

SOC. JUN. What error do you mean?

GUEST. It is requisite to investigate a thing of that kind, which is not altogether usual, nor yet easy to perceive; but at the same time we must endeavour to apprehend it. For, since an upright polity is that alone of which we have spoken, do you not know that other polities ought to be preserved, while they use the institutions of this, and do that which we just now praised, though it is not most right?

SOC. JUN. What is that?

e   GUEST. That no citizen shall dare to act in any respect contrary to the laws, and that he who dares to do so shall be punished with death, and shall suffer all extreme punishments. This is most right and beautiful in the second place; for that which was just now mentioned must be ranked in the first place. But we should unfold the manner in which that which we call secondary subsists. Or should we not?

SOC. JUN. Undoubtedly.

GUEST. But let us again return to images, to which it is always necessary to assimilate royal governors.

SOC. JUN. What kind of images?

GUEST. The generous pilot, and, as Homer says, the physician, who is of equal worth with many others. Let us consider the affair by devising a certain figure in these things.

SOC. JUN. Of what kind?

298a   GUEST. Such a one, as if we all conceived that we suffered the most
dire things from these persons. For such of us as they wish to save, they
do save; and such as they wish to injure, they injure by cutting and
burning; at the same time ordering money to be given them as a reward
for this, not spending any thing themselves on the sick, but they and
b   their familiars making use of others. And lastly, receiving money either
from the kindred or from certain enemies of the sick man, they cause
him to die. Pilots too effect ten thousand other things of this kind. For
they designedly leave men by themselves in certain recesses, and,
committing an error in navigation, hurl them into the sea, and injure
them in other respects. In consequence of considering these things, let
us suppose that we consult how we may deprive these arts of their
independent authority, so that they may no longer possess absolute
c   power, either over slaves or the free-born. Hence, we assemble together
for this purpose, and convene either all the people, or the rich only. In
this assembly, obscure individuals and mechanics give their opinion
respecting the ship and diseases; *viz.* after what manner medicines, and
d   medical instruments, should be employed about the diseased; and
likewise ships and nautical instruments in navigation, in the dangers to
which ships are subject, through the winds, the sea, and pirates, and
when there is occasion to fight with long ships against others of the like
kind. Let us likewise suppose that the opinions, either of certain
physicians and pilots, or of other private persons, given in this assembly,
are inscribed in triangular tables and pillars, and that certain unwritten
e   customs of the country are established, according to which in all future
times navigation is to be conducted, and remedies for the sick
administered.

SOC. JUN. You have spoken of very absurd things.

GUEST. Let us likewise suppose that yearly governors of the multitude
are established, whether chosen by lot from the rich, or from all the
people; and let them govern both ships and the diseased, according to
those written institutions.

SOC. JUN. These things appear still more difficult.

GUEST. Let us likewise see what is consequent to these things. For
299a   when the year of each governor is expired, it will be necessary that
courts of justice should be established, which are composed either of
chosen rich men, or from all the people, for the purpose of calling the
governors to account, and reproving them when requisite. Let every one
likewise who is willing be permitted to accuse the governors, as neither
governing the ships, during the year, according to the written

injunctions, nor according to the ancient manners of their ancestors. And let the same things be permitted to take place respecting those that cure the diseased. But let those that are convicted be punished in whatever manner the judges shall think fit.

SOC. JUN. He, therefore, who voluntarily governs these men will most justly suffer from them, and receive whatever punishment they please.

GUEST. Further still, it will be requisite that a law should be established for all these, that if any one introduces a mode of piloting different from the written institutions, or shall be found investigating the salubrious, and the truth of the medicinal art, contrary to the writings, about winds, heat and cold, or devising any thing whatever, about affairs of this kind; - in the first place, he shall neither be called a pilot nor a physician, but a certain boastful and garrulous sophist; and, in the next place, he shall be brought before a court of justice, by any person who is willing, as one who corrupts other young men, and persuades them that every one should be permitted to pilot ships, and cure the diseased, not according to the laws, but according to his own will. And if any one shall be found persuading either young or old men, contrary to the laws, and the written mandates, he shall be punished in the extreme. For nothing ought to be wiser than the laws. Besides, no one should be ignorant of the medicinal and the salubrious, nor of nautical affairs. For every one who is willing is permitted to learn the written mandates, and the customs of his country. If these particulars, Socrates, should take place about these sciences, *viz.* about military concerns, the whole of hunting, and painting, imitation, and architecture, the formation of instruments of every kind, agriculture, botany; or, again, about the care pertaining to horses, and herds of cattle of every kind, prophecy, the whole of servile offices, the game of chess, the whole of arithmetic in its simple state, whether it is conversant with planes or depths, or swiftness and slowness; - if these particulars, I say, should take place about these sciences, so as to cause them to be effected according to the written mandates, and not according to art, what shall we say?

SOC. JUN. It is evident that all arts must be entirely subverted, without ever being restored, in consequence of the law which forbids investigation. So that life, which is at present difficult, would then be perfectly intolerable.

GUEST. But what will you say to this? If we should compel each of the above-mentioned particulars to take place according to written injunctions, and should appoint as the guardian of these writings a man either chosen by suffrage, or chance, but who paying no attention to them, either for the sake of a certain gain, or private pleasure, should endeavour, though ignorant of every thing, to act contrary to these mandates; would not this be a greater evil than the former?

SOC. JUN. It most truly would.

b   GUEST. For he who should dare to act contrary to those laws which have been established from long experience by those who, consulting how to gratify the people, have persuaded them to adopt them, will commit an error of a very extended nature, and subvert every action in a much greater degree than written mandates are capable of effecting.

SOC. JUN. How is it possible he should not?

c   GUEST. Hence, as it is said, there is a second navigation for those that establish laws and written mandates respecting any thing whatever, *viz.* that neither one person, nor the multitude, should ever be suffered to do any thing at any time contrary to them.

SOC. JUN. Right.

GUEST. Will not these writings, therefore, be certain imitations of truth, composed by intelligent men, in the greatest perfection of which they are capable?

SOC. JUN. Undoubtedly.

GUEST. But, if we remember, we have said, that a man truly knowing in political concerns will do many things from art, without paying any attention to written mandates, when any thing occurs to him better than

d   what he has left behind him in writing.

SOC. JUN. We did say so.

GUEST. And if any thing better than what is established by law should occur either to an individual, or to the people at large, will they not in this case, to the utmost of their power, act in the same manner as the true politician?

SOC. JUN. Entirely so.

GUEST. If, therefore, they should act in this manner, without possessing science, they would attempt to imitate that which is true, but

e   the whole of their imitation would be vicious; but if their conduct is the effect of art, this is no longer an imitation, but is a thing itself most true.

SOC. JUN. It is so in every respect.

GUEST. It was likewise acknowledged by us above, that the multitude is incapable of receiving any art whatever.

SOC. JUN. It was.

GUEST. If, therefore, there is a certain royal art, the multitude of the rich, and the whole of the people, can never receive this politic science.

SOC. JUN. For how can they?

301a GUEST. It is requisite then (as it seems) that such-like polities, if they intend to imitate as much as possible that true polity which is governed according to art by one man, must never do any thing contrary to their written laws, and the customs of their country.

SOC. JUN. You speak most beautifully.

GUEST. When, therefore, the rich imitate this polity, we then denominate such a polity an aristocracy: but when they pay no attention to the laws, an oligarchy.

SOC. JUN. So it appears.

b GUEST. And again, when one man governs according to the laws, imitating him who is endued with science, then we call such a one a king, not distinguishing by name him who governs with science from the monarch who governs with opinion according to the laws.

SOC. JUN. We appear to do so.

GUEST. If, therefore, one man governs, who truly possesses a scientific knowledge of government, he is entirely called by this name a king, and by no other: for this alone, of the five names of the polities just now mentioned, belongs to him.

SOC. JUN. So it appears.

c GUEST. But when one man governs neither according to the laws, nor according to the customs of the country, but at the same time pretends that he possesses a scientific knowledge, and that it is best to act in this manner, contrary to the written mandates, though a certain intemperate desire and ignorance are the leaders of this imitation, must not a man of this kind be called a tyrant?

SOC. JUN. Undoubtedly.

GUEST. Thus, then, we say, a tyrant, a king, an oligarchy, an aristocracy, and a democracy, will be produced; mankind indignantly

d bearing the authority of a monarch, and not believing that any man will ever be found worthy of such a government, so as to be both willing and able to govern with virtue and science, and properly distribute to all men things just and holy. They are likewise fearful, that one man endued with absolute power will injure, oppress, and slay whomsoever he pleases: though, if such a character should arise, as we have mentioned, he would be beloved, and his administration, on account of its accurate rectitude, would alone render a polity happy.

SOC. JUN. Undoubtedly.

e GUEST. But now, since no such king is to be found in cities, who, as if produced in a swarm of bees, excels from the very beginning both in body and soul, it is requisite, as it seems, that men assembling together should compose written institutions, treading in the footsteps of the most true polity.

Soc. Jun. It appears so.

Guest. And shall we wonder, Socrates, that in such-like polities those evils should take place which we behold at present, and which will subsist in future, when they rest on the foundation of written mandates and long established customs, and not on the firm basis of science? Or ought we not rather to admire how strong a thing a city naturally is? For, though cities have subsisted for an immense length of time in this condition, yet some of them have continued stable, and have not been subverted; at the same time many of them, like vessels merged in the sea, have perished, do perish, and will perish, through the depravity of the pilots and sailors, who are involved in the *greatest* ignorance respecting the greatest concerns; for though they know nothing about political affairs, yet they think their knowledge of the political science is the most clear of all scientific knowledge.

Soc. Jun. Most true.

Guest. As, therefore, all these erroneous polities are full of difficulties, we should consider in which it is the least difficult and burthensome to live; for, though this is superfluous with respect to our present inquiry, yet, perhaps, universally we all of us do all things for the sake of this.

Soc. Jun. It is impossible it should not be requisite to consider this.

Guest. Of three things, therefore, they say that one is remarkably difficult, and at the same time easy.

Soc. Jun. How do you say?

Guest. No otherwise than as I said before, that there are three polities, a monarchy, the government of a few, and the government of a many, which three polities were at first mentioned by us in a confused manner.

Soc. Jun. There were.

Guest. Bisecting, therefore, each of these, we shall produce six, separating from these the upright polity, as a seventh.

Soc. Jun. How so?

Guest. We must distribute monarchy into the royal and the tyrannic; but the polity which is not composed from a multitude, into an aristocracy and oligarchy, which form an illustrious division. Again, we formerly considered the polity which is composed from a multitude as simple, and called it a democracy, but we must now establish this as twofold.

SOC. JUN. How so? And after what manner do we make this division?

e   GUEST. Not at all different from the others, though the name of this is now twofold. But to govern according to the laws, and to transgress the laws, is common both to this and the other polities.

SOC. JUN. It is so.

GUEST. Then, indeed, when we were investigating an upright polity, this section was of no use, as we have shown above: but since we have separated it from the others, and have considered the others as necessary, in these we divide each according to the legal, and the transgression of law.

SOC. JUN. It appears so from what has now been said.

GUEST. A monarchy, therefore, when conjoined with good written institutions, which we call laws, is the best of all the six polities; but when subsisting without law is grievous, and most burthensome to live under.

SOC. JUN. I appears so.

303a   GUEST. But the polity which is composed of not many, ought to be considered by us as a medium, in the same manner as a few is a medium between one and many. But again, we should consider the polity which is composed of many as in all things imbecil, and as incapable, when compared with the others, of accomplishing either any great good or great evil; in consequence of authority in this polity being divided according to small parts among many. Hence, this is the worst of all these legal polities, but the best of all such as are illegal. And where all are intemperate, it is best to live in a democracy; but where all are temperate, this polity is the worst to live in. The first and best condition of life is in the first polity, the seventh being excepted. For this must be separated from all the other polities, in the same manner as divinity from men.

SOC. JUN. These things appear thus to subsist and happen; and that must be done which you mention.

c   GUEST. Ought not, therefore, the governors of all these polities (the governor of the scientific polity being excepted) to be withdrawn, as not being truly political but seditious characters; and as presiding over the greatest images, and being such themselves? And as they are the greatest imitators and enchanters, are they not the greatest sophists of sophists?

SOC. JUN. This appellation seems to pertain, with the greatest rectitude, to those that are called politicians.

GUEST. Be it so. This, indeed, is as a drama for us; just as we lately said that we saw a certain Centauric and Satyric Bacchic choir, which was to be separated from the politic art, and now this has scarcely been separated by us.

d   SOC. JUN. So it appears.

GUEST. But another thing still more difficult than this remains, which is more allied to the royal genus, and which at the same time it is more difficult to understand. And we appear to me to be affected in a manner similar to those that purify gold.

SOC. JUN. How so?

e   GUEST. Those workmen first of all separate earth, stones, and many other things; but, after this, such things as are allied to gold remain, which are honourable, and alone to be separated by fire, - I mean brass and silver, and sometimes diamonds. These being with difficulty separated by fusion, scarcely suffer us to see that which is called perfectly pure gold.

SOC. JUN. So it is said respecting these things.

GUEST. After the same manner, we also appear now to have separated from the politic science things different, and such as are foreign and not friendly, and to have left such as are honourable and allied to it. But among the number of these, the military and judicial arts, and that

304a   rhetoric which communicates with the royal science, persuading men to act justly, and which, together with that science, governs the affairs of cities, may be ranked. These if some one should after a certain manner separate with facility, he will show naked and alone by himself that character which we are investigating.

SOC. JUN. It is evident that we should endeavour to do this.

GUEST. For the sake of an experiment, therefore, it will be evident: but we should endeavour to render it apparent through music. Inform me, therefore.

SOC. JUN. What?

b   GUEST. Have we any discipline of music, and universally of the sciences, concerning manual operations?

SOC. JUN. We have.

GUEST. But what? Shall we say that any one among these is a certain science which teaches us what we ought to learn respecting these things, and what we ought not? Or how shall we say?

SOC. JUN. We must say that there is.

GUEST. Shall we not, therefore, confess that this is different from the others?

SOC. JUN. Yes.

c GUEST. But whether must we say that no one of them rules over the other? or that the others rule over this? or that this, as a guardian ought to rule over all the others?

SOC. JUN. That this science ought to rule over the others, which teaches us, whether it is requisite to learn any one of them, or not.

GUEST. You assert, therefore, that it ought to rule over both the teacher and the learner.

SOC. JUN. Very much so.

GUEST. And do you likewise assert, that the science which judges whether it is requisite to persuade or not, should rule over him who is able to persuade?

SOC. JUN. Undoubtedly.

d GUEST. To what science, therefore, shall we attribute that which persuades the multitude and the crowd, through mythology, but not through doctrine?

SOC. JUN. I think it is evident that this is to be attributed to the rhetoric science.

GUEST. But again, to what science shall we attribute the power of judging, whether we should act towards certain persons through persuasion, or through a certain violence; or, universally, whether we ought ever to employ either persuasion or violence?

SOC. JUN. To that which rules over the arts of persuasion and discourse.

GUEST. But this, as I think, will not be any other than the power of the politician.

SOC. JUN. You speak most beautifully.

e GUEST. Thus, therefore, the rhetoric appears to have been very rapidly separated from the politic science, as being another species, but subservient to this science.

SOC. JUN. Certainly.

GUEST. But again, what must we conceive respecting this power?

SOC. JUN. What power?

GUEST. That by which we war upon those against whom we have declared war. Whether shall we say that this is endued with, or deprived of, art?

SOC. JUN. How can we conceive that power to be deprived of art which the commanding art and all warlike actions employ?

GUEST. But shall we consider that power which is able to consult scientifically, whether it is proper to engage in war, or make peace, as different from this, or the same with it?

Soc. Jun. From what has been before established, it necessarily follows that it must be different.

305a   Guest. Must not, therefore, the military science have dominion over the warrior, if we in a similar manner follow what has been before advanced?

Soc. Jun. It must.

Guest. What science then shall we endeavour to evince as the despot of the whole of the military art, which is thus skilful and mighty, except the truly royal science?

Soc. Jun. No other whatever.

Guest. We must not, therefore, consider the science of military commanders as the same with the political, to which it is subservient.

Soc. Jun. It is not proper we should.

b   Guest. But come, let us contemplate the power of judges who judge rightly.

Soc. Jun. By all means.

Guest. Is it not, therefore, capable of doing more than merely judging what is just or unjust, respecting such compacts as are legal, and which have been established by royal authority; employing for this purpose its own proper virtue, so as never to wish to dissolve mutual accusations, either through the influence of certain gifts, or fear, or pity,

c   or hatred, or love, contrary to the order of the legislator?

Soc. Jun. It will never wish to act in this manner; but that which you have mentioned is nearly the employment of this power.

Guest. We find, therefore, that the strength of judges is not royal, but is the guardian of the laws, and subservient to the royal science.

Soc. Jun. It appears so.

Guest. This also must be observed, that no one of the above mentioned sciences will appear to be the politic science to him who perceives all of them. For the province of the truly royal science is not

d   to act itself, but to rule over those that are able to act, since it knows the dominion and impulse of those that are the greatest in the city, respecting what is opportune and the contrary: but it is the province of the other sciences to do as they are ordered.

Soc. Jun. Right.

Guest. Hence, since the sciences which we have just now discussed neither rule over each other nor themselves, but each is conversant with a certain proper employment of its own, they are justly denominated according to the peculiarity of their actions.

e   Soc. Jun. It appears so.

GUEST. But rightly comprehending by a common appellation the power of that science which rules over all these, and takes care of the laws, and of every thing in the city, we may most justly, as it seems, call it the politic science.

SOC. JUN. Entirely so.

GUEST. Shall we not, therefore, discuss this science at present, according to the paradigm of the weaving art, since all the genera pertaining to a city have become manifest to us?

SOC. JUN. And very much so.

GUEST. We must therefore, as it seems, relate what the royal connection is, after what manner it weaves together, and what kind of web it produces for us.

306a SOC. JUN. It is evident.

GUEST. It is, indeed, a thing difficult to be evinced; but, as it appears, it is necessary it should be unfolded.

SOC. JUN. It must, by all means.

GUEST. For, that a part of virtue differs from the species of virtue, may be easily proved from the opinion of the multitude, in opposition to the contentious.

b SOC. JUN. I do not understand you.

GUEST. But again, thus consider. For I think that you consider fortitude as one part of virtue.

SOC. JUN. Entirely so.

GUEST. And likewise, that temperance is different from fortitude, but that the former is a part of the same thing as the latter.

SOC. JUN. Yes.

GUEST. We must dare to unfold a certain wonderful discourse respecting these things.

SOC. JUN. Of what kind?

c GUEST. That after a certain manner they are in many things very adverse and contrary to each other.

SOC. JUN. How do you say?

GUEST. My assertion is by no means usual. For all the parts of virtue are said to be friendly to each other.

SOC. JUN. It is so said.

GUEST. Let us consider, therefore, with the greatest attention, whether this is so simple, or differs more than any thing from these, in things of a kindred nature.

SOC. JUN. Inform me how we are to consider.

GUEST. In all such things as we call beautiful it is proper to investigate, and refer them to two species contrary to each other.

SOC. JUN. You speak most clearly.

d   GUEST. Have you ever then either praised yourself, or heard some other person praising sharpness and swiftness, either in bodies or souls, or the motion of voice, or in such imitations of these as musical and graphical imitations exhibit?

SOC. JUN. Undoubtedly I have.

GUEST. Do you likewise remember after what manner praise is bestowed in each of these?

SOC. JUN. By no means.

GUEST. Shall we, therefore, be able to point out to you my conceptions of this in words?

e   SOC. JUN. What should hinder?

GUEST. You seem to think a thing of this kind easy. Let us consider it, therefore, in subcontrary genera. For often, and in many actions, when we admire the swiftness, vehemence, and acuteness of thought, body, or voice, we praise them, and at the same time employ one of the appellations of fortitude.

SOC. JUN. How so?

GUEST. In the first place, we say it is acute and strenuous, swift and virile, and in a similar manner vehement: and, universally, we praise all these natures, by applying this name to them in common.

307a SOC. JUN. We do.

GUEST. But what? Do we not often praise in many actions the species of quiet generation?

SOC. JUN. And very much so.

GUEST. Do we not, therefore, in praising these, assert things contrary to what we did in praising those?

SOC. JUN. How so?

GUEST. We say that each of these is quiet and temperate, and we admire these when they take place about cogitation; but about actions,

b   we admire the slow and the soft, about voice, the smooth and the grave, all rhythmical motion, and the whole of the muse which employs slowness opportunely; and to all these we give the appellation of the moderate, and not of fortitude.

SOC. JUN. Most true.

GUEST. But when both these take place unseasonably, we then blame each of them, and call them by contrary names.

SOC. JUN. How so?

GUEST. When they appear to be unseasonably acute, swift, and hard, we then call them insolent and insane; but when they are unseasonably

c   grave, slow, and soft, we call them timid and slothful. And we nearly find that these, and the nature of fortitude and temperance, are for the most part contrary to each other, as being hostile and seditious forms, and which are never mingled together in actions about things of this kind. We shall likewise find by investigation, that those who possess these in their souls, are discordant with each other.

SOC. JUN. Where do you say?

GUEST. In all those particulars which we have just now mentioned, and, it is probable, in many others. For, I think, praising some things as their own property, on account of their alliance to both, but blaming others as things foreign, they become very adverse to each other in many things.

SOC. JUN. They appear to do so.

GUEST. This difference, therefore, is the sport of these species. But a disease the most baneful of all others happens to cities about things of the greatest consequence.

SOC. JUN. About what things?

GUEST. About the whole apparatus of living, as it is likely it should. For those who are remarkably modest are always prepared to live a quiet life, attending privately to their own concerns, and being after a certain manner disposed to associate peaceably both with their fellow citizens and foreigners. Through this love, however, which is more unseasonable than is fit, when they do that which they wish to accomplish, they become secretly enervated, and render young men similarly affected. Hence, they are always subject to injuries; and in a short time themselves, their children, and the whole city, often by slow degrees, from being free, become slaves.

SOC. JUN. You speak of a severe and dire passion.

GUEST. But those that verge more to fortitude, do they not incite the cities to which they belong to war, through a more vehement desire of a life of this kind than is becoming, and thus rendering many nations and potentates hostile to their country, either entirely subvert it, or bring it in subjection to the enemy?

SOC. JUN. They do.

GUEST. How is it possible, therefore, we should not say, that in these things both genera are in the greatest degree adverse to each other?

SOC. JUN. It is impossible we should say otherwise.

GUEST. Have we not, therefore, found that which we were considering in the beginning, that certain parts of virtue, which are not small naturally, differ from each other, and that they likewise cause those that possess them to do the same?

SOC. JUN. It appears we have.

GUEST. Let us again too consider this.

SOC. JUN. What?

GUEST. Whether there is any thing belonging to synthetic sciences which has any one of its works, though it should be the vilest, composed from things evil and at the same time useful? Or shall we say, that every science always rejects things evil to the utmost of its power, and receives such as are apt and useful? and that from these, which are both similar and dissimilar, collected into one, it fabricates one certain power and idea?

SOC. JUN. Undoubtedly.

d GUEST. The truly political science, therefore, according to nature, will never be willing that a city should be composed from good and bad men; but it is very evident that it will first of all examine every thing by discipline, and, after the examination, will commit this employment to such as are able to instruct others, and at the same time be subservient to others, itself commanding and presiding: just in the same manner as the weaving art presides over the wool-combers, and others that prepare

e the materials for weaving, and gives such orders to the preparatory workmen as it thinks will best contribute to the work it has in view.

SOC. JUN. Entirely so.

GUEST. The royal science appears to me to do the very same, permitting those that instruct and educate others according to law, alone to exercise and teach that which being effected according to its temperature will produce worthy manners. But it punishes with death, exile, and the greatest disgrace, those that are unable to participate of fortitude, temperance, and such other things as tend to virtue, but through a depraved nature are violently impelled to impiety, insolence and injustice.

SOC. JUN. This is said to be the case.

309a GUEST. But those that are rolled like cylinders in ignorance and an abject spirit, it subjugates to servile employments.

SOC. JUN. Most right.

GUEST. It preserves and defends, therefore, such as are naturally qualified for acquiring the generous and the noble, when properly disciplined, and who through art can be mingled with each other. And

b such among these as verge more to fortitude, it considers as resembling strong thread in the loom on account of their solid manners; but such as verge more to modesty, as similar to fat and soft matter; and, that we may use an image from the weaving art, as resembling saffron-coloured thread. And such as tend contrary to these, it endeavours to bind together and connect after the following manner.

SOC. JUN. What manner?

c GUEST. In the first place, according to the allied, it harmonizes together the eternal part of their soul with a divine bond. But after that which is divine it harmonizes together their vivific part with human bonds.

SOC. JUN. How again is this?

GUEST. When true opinion becomes stably inherent in the soul respecting things beautiful, just and good, and the contraries to these, we say that the divine in the dæmoniacal genus is produced.

SOC. JUN. It is proper it should.

d GUEST. Do we, therefore, know that a politician and a good legislator ought alone to be able, with the Muse of the royal science, to effect this in those that are properly disciplined, and whom we have just now mentioned?

SOC. JUN. It is fit this should be the case.

GUEST. But he, Socrates, who cannot accomplish a thing of this kind, must by no means be called by the names which we are now investigating.

SOC. JUN. Most right.

GUEST. What then? Must not a brave soul, when it receives truth of
e this kind, become mild, and thus be willing in the highest degree to partake of things just? But when it does not receive it, must it not be considered as verging more to a certain savage nature?

SOC. JUN. Undoubtedly.

GUEST. But what? Will not a soul of a modest nature, when receiving these opinions, become truly temperate and moderate in a polity? But when it does not partake of the things we are speaking of, will it not be most disgracefully branded with stupidity?

SOC. JUN. Entirely so.

GUEST. Must we not say, that this connection and binding together of the evil with each other, and of the good with the evil, can never become stable, and that no science will ever seriously attempt to accomplish this with such as these?

SOC. JUN. For how can it?

310a GUEST. But in those alone who are endued with worthy manners from the first, and who are educated according to nature, this bond is naturally implanted through the laws. In these, too, this art is a remedy; and, as we said before, the natural virtue of the parts is the more divine bond of things dissimilar, and tending to contraries.

SOC. JUN. Most true.

GUEST. Since this divine bond exists, there is scarcely any difficulty in either understanding the other bonds which are human, or in bringing them to perfection when understood.

b SOC. JUN. How so? And what are these bonds?

GUEST. The communions of alliances and children, and those respecting private locations and marriages. For many respecting these things are not properly bound together for the purpose of begetting children.

SOC. JUN. Why?

GUEST. Is it worth while to relate how anxiously they pursue riches and power in these things?

SOC. JUN. It is not.

c GUEST. But it will be more just to speak of those who make the human race the object of their care, and to consider if they do any thing improperly.

SOC. JUN. It will.

GUEST. They do not indeed at all act from right reason, but pursue present pleasure; and in consequence of being delighted with those similar to themselves, and of not loving those that are dissimilar, they attribute the greatest part to molestation.

SOC. JUN. How so?

GUEST. Those that are modest seek after their own manners, and as much as possible marry those that are endued with them, and likewise marry their own offspring to such as resemble themselves. The genus

d about fortitude acts in the same manner, pursuing its own nature; when at the same time it is requisite that both genera should act in a manner entirely contrary.

SOC. JUN. How, and on what account?

GUEST. Because this is the natural condition of fortitude, that when it has been unmingled for many generations with a temperate nature, it is florid with strength in the beginning, but in the end becomes entirely efflorescent with insanity.

SOC. JUN. It is likely.

e GUEST. Again, a soul very full of shame, and void of audacious fortitude, when it has subsisted in this manner for many generations, naturally becomes unseasonably sluggish, and at last perfectly mutilated.

SOC. JUN. And this also is likely to happen.

GUEST. We have said that there is no difficulty in binding men with these bonds, if both genera have one opinion respecting things beautiful and good. For this is the one and entire work of royal weaving, *viz.* never to suffer temperate manners to subsist apart from such as are valiant, but, weaving together both these, from according opinions, honour, dishonour, and glory, to collect from these a web smooth, and, as it is said, well woven, and always to commit in common the authority of governors in cities to these.

SOC. JUN. How?

GUEST. Where it happens that one governor is sufficient, a president should be chosen who possesses both these; but where more than one is necessary, parts of these must be mingled together. For the manners of temperate governors are very cautious, just, and salutary; but they require acrimony, and a certain acute and practical temerity.

SOC. JUN. These things also appear so to me.

GUEST. Again, fortitude with respect to justice and caution is more indigent than those other virtues; but it excels them in actions. But it is impossible that all things pertaining to cities, both of a private and public nature, should subsist beautifully, unless both these are present.

SOC. JUN. Undoubtedly.

GUEST. We must say then that this end of the web of politic action is then rightly woven, when the royal art, connecting the manners of brave and temperate men by concord and friendship, collects together their life in common, producing the most magnificent and excellent of all webs; - and besides this, when, embracing in common all others in the city, both slaves and free-born, it holds them together by this texture, and governs and presides over the city in such a manner that nothing may in any respect be wanting which is requisite to its felicity.

SOC. JUN. You have finished, O guest, your description of the royal and political character most beautifully.

Additional Note

on the

POLITICUS

1 (See page 111, line 268d) The substance of this fable is beautifully explained by Proclus, in his fifth book on the Theology of Plato [V, 7, TTS vol. VIII, p. 315], as follows:

"This universe is very properly said to have twofold lives, periods and convolutions; one of these being Saturnian, and the other Jovian. According to the former of these periods, too, every thing good springs spontaneously, and every animated nature possesses a blameless and unwearied life; but the latter is the source of material error, and of an abundantly mutable nature. For, as there is a twofold life in the world, the one unapparent and more intellectual, but the other more natural and apparent, and the one being bounded by providence, but the other proceeding in a disorderly manner according to fate, - hence this latter, which is multiform, and perfected through nature, is suspended from the Jovian order; but the former, which is more simple, is intellectual and unapparent, and is suspended from that of Saturn. This the Elean guest clearly indicates, by calling one of the circulations Jovian, and the other Saturnian. Though Jupiter also is the cause of the unapparent life of the universe, is the supplier of intellect, and the leader of intellectual perfection, yet he leads upwards all things to the kingdom of Saturn, and, being a leader, together with his father gives subsistence to the whole mundane intellect. Each of these periods, indeed, viz. the apparent and unapparent, participates of both these Gods; but the one is more Saturnian, and the other is in subjection to the kingdom of Jupiter. That the mighty Saturn, therefore, is allotted the other kingdom of the Gods prior to him, the Elean guest clearly evinces in what he says prior to the fable, viz. that we have heard from many of the kingdom which Saturn obtained; so that, according to this wise man also, Saturn is one of the royal Gods. Hence, as his father Heaven contains the middle centres of the intelligible and intellectual Gods, he is the leader of the intellectual orders, and supplies the whole of intellectual energy, first to the gods; in the second place, to the genera superior to man; and in the last place, to partial souls such as ours, when they are able to extend themselves to the Saturnian place of survey. For this universe, and all the mundane Gods, perpetually possess this twofold life, and imitate the Saturnian intellection through unapparent and intellectual energy, but the demiurgic intellect of Jupiter through providential attention to secondary concerns; and, in short, through the apparent fabrication of things. But partial souls at one time energize intellectually, and consecrate themselves to Saturn, and at another time according to the characteristic of Jupiter, and with unrestrained energy provide for subordinate natures. When they revolve, however, analogously to these deities, they intellectually perceive intelligibles, and adorn sensibles, and live both these lives in the same manner as the Gods and the more excellent genera. For their periods are twofold, one intellectual and the other providential. Their paradigms also are twofold: of the one the Saturnian intellect, and of the other the Jovian; - since even the mighty Jupiter himself has a twofold energy; by intellect, indeed, adhering to intelligibles, but by demiurgic fabrication adorning sensibles.

"Since, therefore, the revolutions are twofold, not only in wholes but likewise impartial souls, in the Saturnian period, says the Elean guest, the generation of men is not from each other, as in apparent men, nor, as the first man with us is alone earth-born, so, in partial souls, the one first soul is earth-born; but this is the case with all of them. For they are led upwards from last and earthly bodies, and they receive an unapparent, deserting a sensible, life. But neither do they verge to old age, and change from younger to older, but on the contrary they become more vigorous, and proceed intellectually in a path contrary to generation, and resolve as it were that variety of life, which in descending they made a composite. Hence, likewise, all the symbols pertaining to youth are present with those souls when they pass into such a condition of being; for they lay aside every thing which adheres to them from generation. And when they are distributed about Saturn, and live the life which is there, he says fruits are produced in abundance from the trees, and many other things spring spontaneously from the earth. The inhabitants also are naked and without beds, and for the most part are fed, dwelling in the open air: for they possess an indissoluble temperament of the seasons. The grass likewise springing abundantly from the earth supplies them with soft couches. These and such like goods, souls derive from this mighty deity, according to the Saturnian period. For they are thence filled with vivific good, and gather intellectual fruits from wholes, but do not extend to themselves, from partial energies, perfection and beatitude. For doxastic nutriment possesses divisible and material apprehensions, but that which is intellectual, such as are pure, indivisible and spontaneous; which the spontaneous here obscurely signifies. The fruits also imparted from the earth signify the perfection of the prolific intellect of the Gods, and which illuminates souls with a sufficiency from themselves. For, through an unenvying abundance of goods, they are also able to impart to secondary natures felicity in a convenient measure. Neither, therefore, are they invested with garments, as when they proceed into generation, nor do they abound with additions of life, but are themselves pure, by themselves, from all composition and variety; and exciting their own intellect, they are extended by their intellectual father to these divine benefits. They likewise participate of total goods, being guarded by the intellectual Gods; and receiving from them the measures of a happy life, they pass the whole of their existence with facility. And lastly, establishing a sleepless and undefiled life in the generative powers of intelligibles, and being filled with intellectual fruits, and nourished with immaterial and divine forms, they are said to live the life which belongs to the government of Saturn."

THE

MINOS

A DIALOGUE

CONCERNING

LAW

INTRODUCTION

Law, considered according to its first subsistence in Deity, is justly defined by Plato to be *a distribution of intellect* (νου διανομη). As it originates, therefore, from deity, and is thence participated by the human soul, it does not depend for its being among men on arbitrary will and mutual compact, but is truly an evolution of one of those eternal ideas or forms which the soul essentially contains. He, therefore, who diligently attends to what is said by Plato in this dialogue, in his *Laws*, and *Republic*, concerning law, will find that it is a true mode of governing, which directs the governed to the best end through proper media, establishing punishments for such as transgress, and rewards for those that are obedient to this mode. Hence the institutions of princes, when they are not true, and do not proceed to the best end in a right path, are by no means laws, but decrees and edicts: for a work is frequently denominated legitimate from law, just from being legitimate, and good, right and true from being just; and therefore law is necessarily good and true. It also follows that law properly so called is eternal and perfectly immutable: for that which is changed by times, places and opinions, is not a law, but an institute.

According to Plato, too, it appears that there are four species of laws. The first of these are Saturnian, or, in other words, subsist in that deity, who according to ancient theologists is the summit of the intellectual order. These laws are mentioned by Plato in the *Gorgias*,[523a] where Socrates says, "This was the law in the times of Saturn, and now also subsists in the Gods." The second are Jovian, and are indicated in the *Laws*,[872e] where the Athenian guest says "that Justice follows Jupiter, being the avenger of those who desert the divine law." The third are fatal, as we learn from the *Timæus*,[41e] where it is said that the Demiurgus "disclosed to souls the laws of Fate." And the fourth are human. Since law, therefore, has a divine origin, all the illustrious framers of laws with the greatest propriety referred the invention of them to Deity. Hence Zoroaster, when he delivered laws to the Bactrians and Persians, ascribed the invention of them to Oromasis; Hermes Trismegistus the Egyptian legislator referred the invention of his laws to Mercury; Minos the Cretan lawgiver to Jupiter; Charondas the Carthaginian to Saturn; Lycurgus the Lacedæmonian to Apollo; Draco and Solon the Athenian legislators to Minerva; Pompilius the Roman lawgiver to Ægeria; Zamolxis the Scythian to Vesta; and Plato, when he gave laws to the Magnesians and Sicilians, to Jupiter and Apollo.

THE

MINOS

PERSONS OF THE DIALOGUE

SOCRATES AND MINOS

313a   SOC. What is law with us?

MIN. About what kind of law do you interrogate?

SOC. What is that by which law differs from law, according to this very thing, the being law? For consider what I ask you. For I ask as if I should inquire what gold is; and if you in a similar manner should ask me, about what kind of gold I inquire, I should think you would not rightly interrogate. For neither does gold differ in any thing from

b   gold, so far as it is gold, nor a stone from a stone, so far as it is a stone. And in like manner, neither does law differ in any thing from law; but all laws are the same. For each of them is similarly law; nor is one more, but the other less so. I ask you, therefore, the whole of this very thing, what law is; and if you have an answer at hand give it me.

MIN. What else, Socrates, will law be than things established by law?

SOC. Does speech also appear to you to be things which are spoken? or sight things which are seen? or hearing things which are heard? Or

c   is speech one thing, and are things spoken another? Is sight one thing, and are things seen another? Is hearing one thing, and are things heard another? And, is law one thing, and are things established by law another? Is this the case, or how does it appear to you?

MIN. This now appears to me to be the case.

SOC. Law, therefore, is not things established by law.

MIN. It does not appear to me that it is.

314a   SOC. What law, therefore, may be, let us thus consider. If some one should ask us respecting those things of which we have just now spoken, since you say that things visible are seen by the sight, what the sight is by which they are seen? we should answer him, that it is a sense which through the eyes manifests colours to us. And if he should again ask us what the hearing is by which things are heard? we should reply, that it

is a sense which through the ears manifests to us sounds. In like manner, if he should ask us, since legal institutions are legally established
b by law, what is law by which they are thus established? whether is it a certain sense, or manifestation? in the same manner as things which are learnt, are learnt by science rendering them manifest. Or is it a certain invention? just as things which are discovered are invented: as, for instance, things salubrious and noxious are discovered by medicine; but the conceptions of the Gods, as prophets say, by divination. For the divining art is with us an intention of such like things: Or is it not?

MIN. Entirely so.

SOC. Which of these, therefore, may we especially presume law to be? Shall we say it is these dogmas and decrees?

c MIN. It appears so to me. For what else can any one say law is? So that it appears the whole of this which you ask, *viz.* law, is the dogma of the city.

SOC. You call, as it seems, law, political opinion.

MIN. I do.

SOC. And perhaps you speak well; but perhaps we shall know better in the following manner. Do you say that some men are wise?

MIN. I do.

SOC. Are not the wise, therefore, wise by wisdom?

MIN. Yes.

SOC. But what? are the just, just by justice?

MIN. Entirely so.

SOC. Are the legitimate, therefore, also legitimate by law?

d MIN. Yes.

SOC. And the illegitimate, illegitimate by a privation of law?

MIN. Yes.

SOC. And are the legitimate just?

MIN. Yes.

SOC. But the illegitimate unjust?

MIN. Unjust.

SOC. Are not justice and law, therefore, things most beautiful?

MIN. They are.

SOC. And are not injustice and illegality most base?

MIN. Yes.

SOC. And does not one of these preserve cities and every thing else, but the other destroy and subvert them?

MIN. Yes.

SOC. It is necessary, therefore, dianoëtically to consider law as something beautiful, and to investigate it as good.

MIN. How should we not?

SOC. Have we not, therefore, said that law is the dogma of the city?

MIN. We have said so.

SOC. What then? Are not some dogmas good, and others bad?

MIN. They are.

SOC. Law however is not bad.

MIN. It is not.

SOC. It is not, therefore, right simply to determine that law is the dogma of the city.

MIN. It does not appear to me that it is.

SOC. The assertion, therefore, does not accord with the truth, that law is a base dogma.

MIN. It does not.

SOC. Law however appears also to me to be a certain opinion. And since it is not a base opinion, is not this, therefore, evident, that it is a good opinion, if law is opinion?

MIN. Yes.

SOC. But is not a certain good, a true, opinion?

MIN. Yes.

SOC. Is, therefore, true opinion the discovery of being?

MIN. It is.

SOC. Law, therefore, is the discovery of being.

MIN. But, Socrates, if law is the discovery of being, how is it that we do not always use the same laws about the same things, since beings are discovered by us?

SOC. Nevertheless law wishes to be the discovery of being; but men, as it seems, not always using the same laws, are not always able to discover that which law wishes, *viz.* being. But come, let us see if it will hence become evident to us, whether we always use the same laws, or different laws at different times; and if all of us use the same laws, or different persons different laws.

MIN. But this, Socrates, is not difficult to know, that neither do the same persons always use the same laws, nor different persons always different laws. Thus, for example, it is not a law with us to sacrifice men, but this is considered as unholy; but the Carthaginians sacrifice men, this being holy and legal with them; so that some of them sacrifice their sons to Saturn, as perhaps you have heard. And not only do Barbarian men use laws different from ours, but also those in Lycia. And as to the progeny of Athamas,[†] what sacrifices do they perform,

---

† Athamas was the son of Æolus, and king of Thebes in Bœotia.

d   though they are Greeks? You also know and have heard what laws we formerly used concerning the dead, cutting the throats of the victims before the dead body was carried out, and calling those that carry the sacrifices to the dead. And those still prior to these buried the dead at home; but we do none of these. Ten thousand instances likewise of this might be adduced. For the field of demonstration is very wide, that neither we always think invariably the same with ourselves, nor men with each other.

    Soc. It is by no means wonderful, O best of men, if you speak rightly, and this should be concealed from me. But till you by yourself

e   declare what appears to you, in a long discourse, and I again do the same, we shall never, as I think, agree. If however a common subject of speculation is proposed, we shall perhaps accord. If, therefore, you are willing, interrogating me, consider together with me in common. Or, if it is more agreeable to you, instead of interrogating, answer.

    Min. But I wish, Socrates, to reply to any question you may propose.

    Soc. Come then. Whether do you think that just things are unjust, and unjust things just? Or that just things are just, and unjust things unjust?

    Min. I indeed think that just things are just, and unjust things unjust.

316a   Soc. Is this opinion, therefore, entertained among all men, as well as here?

    Min. Yes.

    Soc. Among the Persians also?

    Min. And among the Persians too.

    Soc. But is this opinion always entertained?

    Min. Always.

    Soc. Whether are things which attract more, thought by us to be heavier, but things which attract less, lighter? or the contrary?

    Min. Not the contrary: but things which attract more are heavier, and things which attract less are lighter.

    Soc. Is this the case, therefore, in Carthage and in Lycia?

    Min. Yes.

b   Soc. Things beautiful, as it seems, are every where thought to be beautiful; and things base to be base: but things base are not thought to be beautiful, nor things beautiful base.

    Min. It is so.

    Soc. As we may say, therefore, in all things, beings are thought to be, and not non-beings, both with us and with all others.

    Min. It appears so to me.

SOC. He, therefore, who wanders from being wanders from that which is legitimate.

c   MIN. Thus, Socrates, as you say, these things always appear legitimate both to us and to others. But when I consider that we never cease transposing laws upwards and downwards, I cannot be persuaded by what you say.

SOC. Perhaps you do not perceive that these things thus transposed continue to be the same. But thus consider them together with me. Did you ever meet with any book concerning the health of the sick?

MIN. I have.

SOC. Do you know, therefore, to what art this book belongs?

MIN. I know that it belongs to the art of medicine.

SOC. Do you, therefore, call those who are scientifically skilled about these things, physicians?

MIN. I call them so.

d   SOC. Whether, therefore, do those that have a scientific knowledge think the same things about the same, or do some of these think differently from others about the same things?

MIN. They appear to me to think the same things.

SOC. Whether, therefore, do the Greeks alone accord with the Greeks about things of which they have a scientific knowledge, or do the Barbarians also both accord with each other about such things, and with the Greeks?

MIN. There is an abundant necessity that both Greeks and Barbarians who possess a scientific knowledge should accord in opinion with each other.

SOC. You answer well. Do they not, therefore, always accord?

MIN. Yes, always.

SOC. Do not physicians also write those things about health which they think to be true?

e   MIN. Undoubtedly.

SOC. Things medicinal, therefore, and medicinal laws, these are the writings of physicians.

MIN. Things medicinal, certainly.

SOC. Whether, therefore, are geometrical writings also geometrical laws?

MIN. Yes.

SOC. Of whom, therefore, are the writings and legitimate institutions concerning gardening?

MIN. Of gardeners.

SOC. Those laws, therefore, pertain to gardening.

MIN. They do.

SOC. Are they not, therefore, the laws of those who know how to manage gardens?

MIN. How should they not?

SOC. But gardeners possess this knowledge.

MIN. Yes.

SOC. But of whom are the writings and legitimate institutions concerning food?

MIN. Of cooks.

SOC. Those, therefore, are cooking laws.

MIN. Cooking.

SOC. And of those, as it seems, who know how to manage the preparation of food.

317a MIN. Yes.

SOC. But cooks, as they say, possess this knowledge.

MIN. They do possess it.

SOC. Be it so. But of whom are the writings and legal institutions concerning the government of a city? Are they not of those who scientifically know how to govern cities?

MIN. It appears so to me.

SOC. But do any others than politicians and kings possess this knowledge?

MIN. They alone possess it.

b   SOC. These writings, therefore, are political, which men call the writings of kings and good men.

MIN. You speak the truth.

SOC. Those, therefore, who possess a scientific knowledge do not at different times write differently about the same things.

MIN. Certainly not.

SOC. If, therefore, we see certain persons doing this, whether shall we say that those who act in this manner are scientific or unscientific?

MIN. Unscientific.

SOC. Shall we, therefore, say that what is right in every particular is legitimate, whether it be medicinal, or pertain to cooking, or to gardening?

MIN. Yes.

c   SOC. But with respect to what is not right, this we no longer assert to be legitimate.

MIN. No longer.

SOC. It, therefore, becomes illegitimate.

MIN. Necessarily so.

SOC. Hence, in writings concerning things just and unjust, and, in short, concerning the orderly distribution of a city, and the manner in which it ought to be governed, that which is right is a royal law; but that which is not right does not appear to be a royal law, because science is wanting: for it is illegal.

MIN. It is.

d SOC. We have rightly, therefore, acknowledged that law is the invention of being.

MIN. So it appears.

SOC. Further still, this also we should consider in it: who is it that scientifically knows how to sow seeds in the earth?

MIN. The husbandman.

SOC. Does he then sow fit seeds in each soil?

MIN. Yes.

SOC. The husbandman, therefore, is a good distributor of these things, and his laws and distributions in these particulars are right.

MIN. Yes.

SOC. But who is a good dispensator of pulsations for melodies, and distributes such things as are fit? And whose laws also, if he has any, are right?

e MIN. The laws of the piper, and those of the harper.

SOC. He, therefore, who is most legitimate in these things is in the most eminent degree a piper.

MIN. Yes.

SOC. But who in the best manner distributes nutriment to the bodies of men? Does not he do this who distributes that which is fit?

MIN. Yes.

SOC. The distributions, therefore, and the laws of this man are the best; and he who is most legitimate about these things is the most excellent distributor.

MIN. Entirely so.

SOC. Who is he?

MIN. The instructor of children.

318a SOC. Does he know how to feed the flock of the human body in the best manner?

MIN. Yes.

SOC. But who is he that feeds in the best manner a flock of sheep? What is his name?

MIN. A shepherd.

SOC. The laws, therefore, of the shepherd are the best for the sheep.

MIN. They are.

SOC. And those of the herdsman for oxen.

MIN. Yes.

SOC. But whose laws are the best for the souls of men? Are they not those of a king?

MIN. They are.

b   SOC. You speak well. Can you, therefore, tell me who among the ancients was a good legislator in the laws pertaining to pipes? Perhaps you do not recollect. Are you, therefore, willing that I should remind you?

MIN. Perfectly so.

SOC. Marsyas, then, and his beloved Olympus the Phrygian were of this description.

MIN. True.

SOC. The harmony produced by the pipes of these men is most divine, and alone excites and unfolds those that stand in need of the Gods.[†] It likewise alone remains to the present time as being divine.

c   MIN. These things are so.

SOC. But who among the ancient kings is said to have been a good legislator, and whose legal institutions even now remain as being divine?

MIN. I do not recollect.

SOC. Do you not know who they were that used the most ancient laws of the Greeks?

MIN. Do you speak of the Lacedæmonians, and Lycurgus the legislator?

SOC. These institutions, however, have not perhaps been established

d   three hundred years, or very little more than this. But do you know whence the best of their laws were derived?

MIN. They say, from Crete.

SOC. Do they, therefore, of all the Greeks use the most ancient laws?

MIN. Yes.

SOC. Do you know then who among these were good kings? I mean Minos and Rhadamanthus, the sons of Jupiter and Europa, by whom these laws were framed.

MIN. They say, Socrates, that Rhadamanthus was a just man, but that Minos was rustic, morose and unjust.

SOC. You relate, O best of men, an Attic and tragical fable.

e   MIN. Are not these things reported of Minos?

SOC. They are not by Homer and Hesiod, whose authority is greater than that of all the tragic poets from whom you assert these things.

---

† See the speech of Alcibiades in the *Banquet*.[215a]

MIN. But what do they say about Minos?

SOC. I will tell you, lest you as well as the many should be guilty of impiety. For there is not any thing which is more impious than this; *nor is there any thing of which we ought to be more afraid, than of offending against* THE GODS *either in word or in deed.*[†] And next to this

319a we should be fearful of offending against divine men. We should however be very cautious, when we praise or blame any man, that we do not speak erroneously; and for the sake of this it is necessary that we should learn to know good and bad men. For divinity is indignant when any one blames a man similar to himself, or praises one dissimilar to him: but the former of these is the good man. Nor ought you to think that stones, pieces of wood, birds and serpents are sacred, but that men are not so: for a good man is the most sacred, and a depraved man

b the most defiled, of all things. Now, therefore, since Homer and Hesiod pass an encomium on Minos, on this account I thus speak, *lest you, being a man sprung from a man, should sin in what you say against a hero the son of Jupiter.* For Homer,[‡] speaking of Crete, that there are many men and ninety cities in it, says that among these is Gnossus, a great city in which Minos reigned, who for nine years conversed with the mighty

c Jupiter. This then is Homer's encomium of Minos, which though short is such as he does not give to any one of his heroes. For that Jupiter is a sophist,[§] and that the art itself is all-beautiful, he evinces as well in many other places as here. For he says that Minos conversed nine years with Jupiter, and went to be instructed by him, as if Jupiter were a sophist. That Homer, therefore, does not bestow this honour of being instructed by Jupiter on any other hero than Minos alone, must be considered as a wonderful praise. Ulysses also, in speaking of the

d dead,[◊] represents Minos judging with a golden sceptre in his hand; but neither here nor in any other place does he speak of Rhadamanthus as judging, or as conversing with Jupiter. On this account I say that Minos is extolled by Homer beyond all other heroes. For that being the son of Jupiter, he was only instructed by Jupiter, contains no transcendency of praise. For the verse which says that Minos reigned nine years, and

---

[†] This among many other passages must convince the most careless reader, that Plato was a firm believer in the religion of his country.

[‡] Odyss. lib. xix, ver. 172 &c.

[§] That is, one endued with wisdom; for this is the original meaning of the word.

[◊] Odyss. lib. xi.

e　conversed with the mighty Jupiter, signifies that he was the associate of Jupiter; since οαροι are discourses, and οαριστης is an associate in discourse. Hence, for nine years Minos went to the cavern of Jupiter, learning some things, and teaching others, which during these nine years he had received from Jupiter. There are however some who conceive οαριστης to signify the associate of Jupiter in drinking and sport. But

320a　that those who thus conceive say nothing to the purpose, may be inferred from this, that, as both the Greeks and barbarians are numerous, there are none among these who abstain from banquets, and that sport to which wine belongs, except the Cretans and the Lacedæmonians, who were instructed by the Cretans. In Crete, too, this is one of the other laws which Minos established, that men should not drink with each other to intoxication. And this indeed is evident, that he made those things to be laws for his citizens which he thought to be

b　beautiful. For Minos did not, like a base man, think one thing, and do another different from what he thought; but his association with Jupiter was as I have said through discourse, in order to be instructed in virtue. Hence he established these laws for his citizens through which Crete is perpetually happy, and also Lacedæmon, from the time in which it began to use these laws, in consequence of their being divine. But Rhadamanthus was indeed a good man; for he was instructed by Minos.

c　He did not however learn the whole of the royal art, but that part of it which is of the ministrant kind, and which possesses authority in courts of judicature; and hence he is said to have been a good judge. For Minos employed him as a guardian of the laws in the city; but he used Talus[†] for this purpose through the rest of Crete. For Talus thrice every year went through the villages in order to preserve the laws in them, and carried with him the laws written in tables of brass; whence

d　also he was called brazen. Hesiod also asserts things similar to these of Minos. For, having mentioned his name, he says[‡] that he was the most royal of mortal kings, and that he reigned over many neighbouring men, having the sceptre of Jupiter, with which also he governed cities. And he calls the sceptre of Jupiter nothing else than the discipline of Jupiter, by which he governed Crete.

　　MIN. On what account then, Socrates, came the report to be spread
e　that Minos was an unlearned and morose man?

---

† A son of Cres, the founder of the Cretan nation.

‡ What Plato here cites from Hesiod is not to be found in any of the writings of that poet now extant.

SOC. On that account through which you, O best of men, if you are prudent, and every other man who intends to be celebrated, will be cautious never to offend a poet. For poets are able to effect much with respect to opinion, both in praising men and blaming them. In this particular, therefore, Minos erred when he warred on this city, in which there is much other wisdom, together with tragic and other poets of every description. But the tragedy here is ancient, not originating, as is generally thought, from Thespis, nor from Phrynicus; but, if you consider, you will find that it is a very ancient invention of this city.

321a Tragedy indeed is of all poetry the most pleasing to the vulgar, and the most alluring; to which applying ourselves we have taken vengeance on Minos, for which he has compelled us to pay those tributes. In offending us, therefore, Minos erred; whence, in reply to your question, he became infamous. For that he was a good man, a friend to law, and

b a good shepherd of the people, as I have before observed, this is the greatest token, that his laws are immutable, in consequence of having well discovered the truth concerning the government of a city.

MIN. You appear to me, Socrates, to have discovered a probable reason.

SOC. If, therefore, I speak the truth, do not the Cretans, the citizens of Minos and Rhadamanthus, appear to you to have used the most ancient laws?

MIN. They do.

c SOC. These, therefore, were the best legislators of the ancients, and were also shepherds of men; just as Homer likewise says, that a good general is the shepherd of the people.

MIN. Entirely so.

SOC. Come then, by Jupiter, who presides over friendship, if any one who is a good legislator and shepherd of the body should ask us what those things are which when distributed to the body will make it better, we should well and briefly answer, that they are nutriment and labour, the former of which by increasing, and the latter by exercising, give stability to the body.

MIN. Right.

d SOC. If, therefore, after this, that good legislator and shepherd should also ask us what those things are which being distributed to the soul make it better, what shall we answer, that we may not be ashamed of ourselves and of our age?

MIN. I am no longer able to answer this question.

SOC. It is however disgraceful to the soul of each of us, if we should appear to be ignorant of things pertaining to our souls, in which good and evil are contained, but to be knowing in particulars pertaining to the body, and to other things.

THE APOLOGY

OF

SOCRATES

INTRODUCTION

The elevation and greatness of mind for which Socrates was so justly celebrated by antiquity, are perhaps no where so conspicuously displayed as in this his *Apology*. In a situation in which death itself was presented to his view, he neither deviates from the most rigid veracity, nor has recourse to any of those abject arts, by which in similar circumstances pity is generally solicited and punishment sometimes averted. His whole discourse, indeed, is full of simplicity and noble grandeur, and is the energetic language of conscious innocence and offended worth.

The causes that occasioned this *Apology* were as follow: - Aristophanes, at the instigation of Melitus, undertook, in his comedy of *The Clouds*, to ridicule the venerable character of Socrates, on the stage; and the way being once open to calumny and defamation, the fickle and licentious populace paid no reverence to the philosopher, whom they had before regarded as a being of a superior order. When this had succeeded, Melitus stood forth to criminate him, together with Anytus and Lycon; and the philosopher was summoned before the tribunal of the Five Hundred. He was accused of making innovations in the religion of his country, and corrupting the youth. But as both these accusations must have been obviously false to an unprejudiced tribunal, the accusers relied for the success of their cause on perjured witnesses, and the envy of the judges, whose ignorance would readily yield to misrepresentation, and be influenced and guided by false eloquence and fraudulent arts. That the personal enemies indeed of Socrates, vile characters, to whom his wisdom and his virtue were equally offensive, should have accused him of making innovations in the religion of Greece, is by no means surprising; but that very many of modern times should have believed that this accusation was founded in truth, and that he endeavoured to subvert the doctrine of polytheism, is a circumstance which by the truly learned reader must be ranked among the greatest eccentricities of modern wit. For to such a one it will most clearly appear from this very *Apology*, that Socrates was accused of impiety for asserting that he was connected in a very transcendant degree with a presiding dæmon, to whose direction he confidently submitted the conduct of his life. For the accusation of Melitus, that he introduced other novel dæmoniacal natures, can admit of no other construction. Besides, in the course of this *Apology* he asserts, in the most unequivocal and solemn manner, his belief in polytheism; and this is indubitably confirmed in many places by Plato, the most genuine of his disciples, and the most faithful recorder of his doctrines. The testimony of Xenophon too on this point is no less weighty than decisive. "I have often wondered," says that historian and philosopher,[†] "by what arguments the Athenians who condemned Socrates persuaded the city that he was worthy of death. For, in the first place, how could they prove that he did not believe in the Gods in which the city believed? since it was evident that he often sacrificed at home, and often on the common altars of the city. It was also not unapparent that he employed divination. For a report was circulated, that signals were given to Socrates, according to his own assertion, by a dæmoniacal power; whence they especially appear to me to have accused him of introducing new dæmoniacal natures. He however introduced nothing new, nor any thing different from the opinion of those who, believing in divination, make use of auguries and oracles, symbols and sacrifices. For these do not apprehend that either birds, or things which occur, know what is advantageous to the diviners; but they are of opinion that the Gods thus signify to them what is beneficial; and he also thought the same. Again, in another place, he observes as follows: "Socrates[‡] thought that the Gods take care of men not in such a way as the multitude conceive. For they think that the Gods know some things, but do not know others. But Socrates thought that the Gods know all things, as well things said and done, as those deliberated in silence. That they are also everywhere present, and signify to men concerning all human affairs. I wonder, therefore, how the

---

[†] Πολλακις εθαυμασα, τισι ποτε λογοις Αθηναιους επεισαν οι γραψαμενοι Σωκρατην, ως αξιος ειη θανατου τη πολει. - Πρωτον μεν ουν ως ουκ ενομιζεν ους η πολις νομιζει θεους, ποιω ποτ᾽ εχρησαντο τεκμηριω; θυων τε γαρ φανερος ην πολλακις μεν οικοι, πολλακις δε επι των κοινων της πολεως βωμων· και μαντικη χρωμενος, ουκ αφανης ην· διετετρυλητο γαρ, ως φαιη Σεκρατης το δαιμονιον εαυτω σημαινειν, οθεν δη και μαλιστα μοι δοκουσιν αυτον αιτιασασθαι, καινα δαιμονια εισφερειν. ο δ᾽ ουδεν καινομενον εισεφερε των αλλων, οσοι μαντικην νομιζοντες, οιωνοις τε χρωνται, και φημαις, και συμβολοις, και θυσιαις. ουτοι τε γαρ υπολαμβανουσιν, ου τους ορνιθας, ουδε τους απαντωντας ειδεναι τα συμφεροντα τοις μαντευομενοις, αλλα τους θεους δια τουτων αυτα σημαινειν· κᾳκεινος ουτως ενομιζεν. p.441.

[‡] Και γαρ επιμελεισθαι θεους ενομιζεν ανθρωπων, ουχ ον τροπον οι πολλοι νομιζουσιν. ουτοι νεν γαρ οιονται πους θεους τα μεν ειδεναι, τα δ᾽ ουκ ειδεναι· Σωκρατης δε παντα μεν ηγειτο θεους ειδεναι, τα τε λεγομενα και πραττομενα, και τα σιγη βουλευομενα· πανταχου δε παρειναι και σημαινειν τοις ανθρωποις περι των ανθρωπειων παντων. θαυμαζω ουν, οπως ποτε επεισθησαν Αθηναιοι, Σωκρατην περι τους θεους μη σωφρονειν, τον ασβες μεν ουδεποτε περι τους θεους ουτ᾽ ειποντα ουτε πραξαντα· τοιαυτα δε και λεγοντα και πραττοντα περι θεων, οια τις αν και λεγων και πραττων ειη τε και νομιζοιτο ευσεβεστατος. p.443.

Athenians could ever be persuaded that Socrates was not of a sound mind respecting the Gods, as he never said or did any thing impious concerning them. But all his sayings and all his actions pertaining to the Gods were such as any one by saying and doing would be thought to be most pious." And lastly, in another place he observes, "That it was evident that Socrates worshipped the Gods the most of all men."[†]

After such unequivocal testimony, no other reason can be assigned for that strange position of the moderns, that Socrates ridiculed the religion of his country, than a profound ignorance of one of the most important tenets of the heathen religion, and which may also be considered as ranking among the first of the most magnificent, scientific, and divine conceptions of the human mind. The tenet I allude to is this, that the essential, which is the most perfect energy of deity, is deific; and that his first and immediate progeny must as necessarily be Gods, that is, beings transcendently similar to himself, and possessing those characteristics *secondarily* which he possesses *primarily,* as heat is the immediate offspring of fire, and coldness of snow. From being unacquainted with this mighty truth, which is coeval with the universe itself, modern theologists and sophists have dared to defame the religion of Greece, and, by offering violence to the sacred pages of antiquity, have made the great Socrates himself become the patron of their own shallow and distorted conceptions. But to return to the *Apology.*

Lysias, one of the most celebrated orators of the age, composed an oration, in a laboured and pathetic style, which he offered to Socrates to be pronounced as his defence in the presence of his judges. Socrates however refused it, observing, that a philosopher ought to be conspicuous for magnanimity and firmness of soul. Hence, in his *Apology*, he paid no attention to the splendour of diction, but trusted wholly to the intrinsic dignity of his sentiments. He contented himself with speaking to his judges as he used to do in common discourse, and with proposing questions to his accusers. Hence his defence was entirely the spontaneous effusions of his genius; simple and plain, yet nervous and dignified.

Several persons who assisted in the court upon this occasion, besides Plato, drew up the *Apology* of Socrates. Among the rest Xenophon compiled one from the relation of Hermogenes the son of Hipponicus, for he himself was not then at Athens. None of them are extant, however, but those of Plato and Xenophon. And of these, the first is in every respect worthy the greatest disciple of Socrates; but the other

---

† Φανερος ην θεραπευων τους θεους, μαλιστα των αλλων ανθρωπων. p.450.

presents us with an imperfect copy, because composed by a disciple that was absent. This imperfect copy, however, sufficiently proves that the substance of this *Apology* is accurate, how much soever it may have been amended by passing through such a hand as that of Plato.

THE APOLOGY

OF

SOCRATES

I know not, O Athenians, how you may be affected by my accusers: I indeed have through them almost forgotten myself, so persuasively have they spoken; though, as I may say, they have not asserted any thing which is true. But among the multitude of their false assertions I am most surprised at this, in which they say that you ought to beware

of being deceived by me, as if I were an eloquent speaker. For that they should not be ashamed of asserting that which will be immediately confuted by me in reality, since in the present instance I shall appear to you to be by no means eloquent, - this seems to me to be the consummation of impudence; unless they call him eloquent who speaks the truth. For, if they assert this, I shall indeed acknowledge myself to be a rhetorician, though not according to their conceptions. They have not then, as I said, asserted any thing which is true; but from me you will hear all the truth. Not, by Jupiter, O Athenians, that you will hear

from me a discourse splendidly decorated with nouns and verbs, and adorned in other respects, like the harangues of these men; but you will hear me speaking in such language as may casually present itself. For I am confident that what I say will be just, nor let any one of you expect it will be otherwise: for it does not become one of my age to come before you like a lad with a studied discourse. And, indeed, I very much request and beseech you, O Athenians, that if you should hear me apologizing in the same terms and modes of expression which I am accustomed to use in the Forum, on the Exchange and public Banks, and

in other places, where many of you have heard me, - that you will neither wonder nor be disturbed on this account; for the case is as follows: - I now for the first time come before this tribunal, though I am more than seventy years old; and consequently I am a stranger to the mode of speaking which is here adopted. As, therefore, if I were in reality a foreigner, you would pardon me for using the language and the

manner in which I had been educated, so now I request you, and this justly, as it appears to me, to suffer the mode of my diction, whether it be better or worse, and to attend to this, whether I speak what is just or not: for this is the virtue of a judge, as that of an orator is to speak the truth.

    In the first place, therefore, O Athenian, it is just that I should answer the first false accusations of me, and my first accusers, and afterwards
b the latter accusations, and the latter accusers. For many have been accusers of me to you for many years, and who have asserted nothing true, of whom I am more afraid than of Anytus and his accomplices, though these indeed are powerful in persuading; but those are still more so, who having been conversant with many of you from infancy, have persuaded you, and accused me falsely. For they have said, that there is one Socrates, a wise man, studious of things on high, and exploring every thing under the earth, and who also can make the worse to be the
c better argument. These men, O Athenians, who spread this report are my dire accusers. For those who hear it think that such as investigate these things do not believe that there are Gods. In the next place, these accusers are numerous, and have accused me for a long time. They also said these things to you in that age in which you would most readily believe them, some of you being boys and lads; and they accused me quietly, no one speaking in my defence. But that which is most irrational of all is this, that neither is it possible to know and tell their
d names, except some one of them should be a comic† poet. Such however as have persuaded you by employing envy and calumny, together with those who being persuaded themselves have persuaded others, - with respect to all these, the method to be adopted is most dubious. For it is not possible to call them to account here before you, nor to confute any one of them; but it is necessary, as if fighting with shadows, to make my defence and refutation without any to answer me. Consider, therefore, as I have said, that my accusers are twofold, some
e having accused me lately, and others formerly; and think that it is necessary I should answer the latter of these first; for you also have heard these my accusers, and much more than you have those by whom I have been recently accused. Be it so. I must defend myself then, O Athenians, and endeavour in this so short a space of time to remove
19a from you the calumny which you have so long entertained. I wish, therefore, that this my defence may effect something better both for you and me, and that it may contribute to some more important end. I think however that it will be attended with difficulty, and I am not entirely ignorant what the difficulty is. At the same time let this

† Meaning Aristophanes.

terminate as Divinity pleases. It is my business to obey the law, and to make my apology.

b   Let us repeat, therefore, from the beginning what the accusation was, the source of that calumny in which Melitus confiding brought this charge against me. Be it so. What then do my accusers say? For their accusation must be formally recited as if given upon oath. It is this: SOCRATES ACTS WICKEDLY, AND WITH CRIMINAL CURIOSITY INVESTIGATES THINGS UNDER THE EARTH, AND IN THE HEAVENS. HE ALSO MAKES THE WORSE TO BE THE BETTER ARGUMENT; AND HE TEACHES THESE THINGS TO OTHERS. Such is the accusation: for things

c of this kind you also have yourselves seen in the comedy of Aristophanes:† for there one Socrates is carried about, who affirms that he walks upon the air, and idly asserts many other trifles of this nature; of which things however I neither know much nor little. Nor do I say this as despising such a science, if there be any one wise about things of this kind, lest Melitus should charge me with this as a new crime, but because, O Athenians, I have no such knowledge. I adduce many of you

d as witnesses of this, and I call upon such of you as have at any time heard me discoursing, and there are many such among you, to teach and declare to each other, if you have ever heard me speak much or little about things of this kind. And from this you may know that other things also, which the multitude assert of me, are all of them of a similar nature: for no one of them is true. For neither if you have heard any one assert that I attempt to teach men, and that I make money by so

e doing, - neither is this true. This indeed appears to me to be a beautiful thing, if some one is able to instruct men, like Gorgias the Leontine, Prodicus the Cean, and Hippias the Elean. For each of these, in the several cities which he visits, has the power of persuading the young

20a men, who are permitted to apply themselves to such of their own countrymen as they please without any charge, to adhere to them only, and to give them money and thanks besides for their instruction. There is also another wise man, a Parian, who I hear has arrived hither. For it happened that I once met with a man who spends more money on the sophists than all others, - I mean Callias the son of Hipponicus. I therefore asked him, for he has two sons, O Callias, said I, if your two sons were two colts or calves, should we not have some one to take care

b of them, who would be paid for so doing, and who would make them beautiful, and the possessors of such good qualities as belong to their nature? But now, since your sons are men, what master do you intend

---

† See *The Clouds* of that poet, ver. 112 et seq. et ver. 188.

to have for them? Who is there that is scientifically knowing in human and political virtue of this kind? For I think that you have considered this, since you have sons. Is there such a one, said I, or not? There certainly is, he replied. Who is he? said I. And whence is he? And for how much money does he teach? It is Evenus the Parian, said he, Socrates, and he teaches for five minæ (15l.). And I indeed have considered Evenus as blessed, if he in reality possesses this art, and so elegantly teaches. I, therefore, should also glory and think highly of myself, if I had a scientific knowledge of these things; but this, O Athenians, is certainly not the case.

Perhaps, however, some one may reply: But Socrates, what have you done then? Whence have these calumnies against you arisen? For unless you had more curiously employed yourself than others, and had done something different from the multitude, so great a rumour would never have been raised against you. Tell us, therefore, what it is, that we may not pass an unadvised sentence against you. He who says these things appears to me to speak justly, and I will endeavour to show you what that is which has occasioned me this appellation and calumny. Hear, therefore; and though perhaps I shall appear to some of you to jest, yet be well assured that I shall tell you all the truth. For I, O Athenians, have acquired this name through nothing else than a certain wisdom. For of what kind is this wisdom? Perhaps it is human wisdom. For this in reality I appear to possess. Those indeed who I just now mentioned possessed perhaps more than human wisdom, which I know not how to denominate: for I have no knowledge of it. And whoever says that I have, speaks falsely, and asserts this to calumniate me. But, O Athenians, be not disturbed if I appear to speak somewhat magnificently of myself. For this which I say is not my own assertion, but I shall refer it to one who is considered by you as worthy of belief. For I shall adduce to you the Delphic Deity himself as a testimony of my wisdom, if I have any, and of the quality it possesses. You certainly then know Chærepho: he was my associate from a youth, was familiar with most of you, and accompanied you in and returned with you from your exile. You know, therefore, what kind of a man Chærepho was, and how eager in all his undertakings. He then, coming to Delphi, had the boldness to consult the oracle about this particular. Be not, as I said, O Athenians, disturbed: for he asked if there was any one more wise than I am. The Pythian priestess, therefore, answered that there was not any one more wise. His brother can testify to you the truth of these things; for Chærepho himself is dead.

b   Consider then on what account I assert these things: for I am going to inform you whence this calumny against me arose. When, therefore, I had heard this answer of the oracle, I thus considered with myself, What does the God say? and what does he obscurely signify? For I am not conscious to myself that I am wise, either in a great or in a small degree. What then does he mean in saying that I am most wise? For he does not lie, since this is not lawful to him. And for a long time, indeed, I was dubious what he could mean. Afterwards with considerable difficulty I betook myself to the following mode of investigating his meaning. I went to one of those who appear to be wise men, that here if any where I might confute the prediction, and evince to the oracle

c   that this man was more wise than I. Surveying, therefore, this man, (for there is no occasion to mention his name, but he was a politician;) while I beheld him and discoursed with him, it so happened, O Athenians, that this man appeared to me to be wise in the opinion of many other men, and especially in his own, but that he was not so. And afterwards I endeavoured to show him that he fancied himself to be wise, but was not. Hence I became odious to him, and also to many others that were

d   present. Departing, therefore, I reasoned with myself that I was wiser than this man. For it appears that neither of us knows any thing beautiful or good: but he indeed not knowing, thinks that he knows something; but I, as I do not know any thing, neither do I think that I know. Hence in this trifling particular I appear to be wiser than him, because I do not think that I know things which I do not know. After

e   this I went to another of those who appeared to be wiser than him; and of him also I formed the same opinion. Hence also I became odious to him and many others.

Afterwards however I went to others, suspecting and grieving and fearing that I should make enemies. At the same time however it appeared to me to be necessary to pay the greatest attention to the oracle of the God, and that, considering what could be its meaning, I should go to all that appeared to possess any knowledge. And by the

22a   dog,† O Athenians, (for it is necessary to tell you the truth,) that which happened to me was as follows. Those that were most celebrated for their wisdom appeared to me to be most remote from it; but others who were considered as far inferior to them possessed more of intellect. But

---

† Ραδαμανθυος ορκος ουτος, ο κατα κυνος, η χηνος, η πλατανου, η κριου, η τινος αλλου τοιουτου. Schol. Græc. in Plat. p. 5. *i.e.* "This is the oath of Rhadamanthus, who swore by the dog, or the goose, or the plane tree, or the ram, or something else of this kind."

it is necessary to relate to you my wandering, and the labours as it were which I endured, that the oracle might become to me unconfuted. For after the politicians I went to the poets both tragic and dithyrambic, and also others, expecting that I should here immediately find myself to be less wise than these. Taking up, therefore, some of their poems which appeared to me to be the most elaborately written, I asked them what was their meaning, that at the same time I might learn something from them. I am ashamed indeed, O Athenians, to tell you the truth; but at the same time it must be told. For, as I may say, all that were present would have spoken better about the things which they had composed. I discovered this, therefore, in a short time concerning the poets, that they did not effect by wisdom that which they did, but by a certain genius and from enthusiastic energy, like prophets and those that utter oracles. For these also say many and beautiful things, but they understand nothing of what they say. Poets, therefore, appeared to me to be affected in a similar manner. And at the same time I perceived that they considered themselves, on account of their poetry, to be the wisest of men in other things, in which they were not so. I departed, therefore, also from them, thinking that I surpassed them by the very same thing in which I surpassed the politicians.

In the last place, therefore, I went to the artificers. For I was conscious to myself that I knew nothing, as I may say, but that these men possessed knowledge, because I had found them acquainted with many and beautiful things. And in this indeed I was not deceived; for they knew things which I did not, and in this they were wiser than I. But, O Athenians, good artificers also appeared to me to have the same fault as the poets. For each, in consequence of performing well in his art, thought that he was also most wise in other things, and those the greatest. And this their error obscured that very wisdom which they did possess. I therefore asked myself in behalf of the oracle, whether I would choose to be as I am, possessing no part either of their wisdom or ignorance, or to have both which they possess. I answered, therefore, for myself and for the oracle, that it was advantageous for me to be as I am.

From this my investigation, O Athenians, many enmities were excited against me, and such as were most grievous and weighty, so that many calumnies were produced from them; and hence I obtained the appellation of *the wise man*. For those that hear me think that I am wise in these things, the ignorance of which I confute in others. It appears however, O Athenians, that Divinity is wise in reality, and that in this oracle he says this, that human wisdom† is but of little, or indeed of no worth; and it seems that he used my name, making me an example, as if he had said, He, O men, is the wisest among you, who, like Socrates, *knows* that he is in reality of no worth with respect to wisdom. These things, therefore, going about, I even now inquire and explore in obedience to the God, both among citizens and strangers, if any one of them appears to me to be wise; and when I find he is not, giving assistance to the God, I demonstrate that he is not wise. And in consequence of this employment I have no leisure worth mentioning either for public or private transactions; but I am in great poverty through my religious cultivation of the God.

Besides, the youth that spontaneously follow me, who especially abound in leisure, as being the sons of the most wealthy, rejoice on hearing men confuted by me; and often imitating me, they afterwards endeavour to make trial of others. In which attempt I think they find a numerous multitude of men who fancy that they know something, but who know little or nothing. Hence, therefore, those who are tried by them are angry with me, and not with them, and say that there is one Socrates a most wicked person, and who corrupts the youth. And when some one asks them what he does, and what he teaches, they have nothing to say, but are ignorant. That they may not however appear to be dubious, they assert things which may be readily adduced against all that philosophize, as, that he explores things on high and under the earth, that he does not think there are Gods, and that he makes the worse to be the better reason. For I think they are not willing to speak the truth, that they clearly pretend to be knowing, but know nothing. Hence, as it appears to me, being ambitious and vehement and numerous, and speaking in an elegant and persuasive manner about me, they fill your ears, both before and now calumniating in the extreme. Among these, Melitus, Anytus, and Lycon, have attacked me; Melitus indeed being my enemy on account of the poets; but Anytus on account of the artificers and politicians; and Lycon on account of the orators. So that, as I said in the beginning, I should wonder if I could remove such an abundant calumny from your minds in so short a time. These things, O Athenians, are true; and I thus speak, neither concealing nor subtracting any thing from you, either great or small; though I nearly know that I shall make enemies by what I have said. This however is

---

† This is the key to the profound meaning of Socrates when he said that he *knew* that he knew nothing. For, as I have elsewhere observed, he only intended by this to signify the nothingness of human when compared with divine knowledge.

an argument that I speak the truth, that this is the calumny which is raised against me, and that the causes of it are these. And whether now
b   or hereafter you investigate these things, you will find them to be as I have said. Concerning the particulars, therefore, which my first accusers urged against me, let this be a sufficient apology to you.

In the next place, I shall endeavour to reply to Melitus, that good man and lover of his country, as he says, and also to my latter accusers. For again, as being different from the former accusers, let us take the oath of these men for calumny. The accusation then is as follows: Socrates, it says, acts unjustly, corrupting the youth; and not believing in those Gods in which the city believes, he introduces other novel dæmoniacal natures. Such then is the accusation; of which let us examine every part.
c   It says, therefore, that I act unjustly by corrupting the youth. But I, O Athenians, say that Melitus acts unjustly, because he intentionally trifles, rashly bringing men into danger, and pretending to be studious and solicitous about things which were never the objects of his care. But that this is the case I will endeavour to show you.

d   Tell me then, O Melitus, whether you consider it as a thing of the greatest consequence, for the youth to become the best of men? - I do. - Come, then, do you therefore tell them what will make them better? For it is evident that you know, since it is the object of your care. For, having found me to be a corrupter of youth, as you say, you have brought me hither, and are my accuser; but come, inform me who it is that makes them better, and signify it to this assembly. Do you see, O Melitus, that you are silent, and have not any thing to say? Though, does it not appear to you to be shameful, and a sufficient argument of what I say, that this is not the object of your attention? But tell me, O
e   good man, who it is that makes them better. - The laws. - I do not, however, ask this, O best of men, but what man it is that first knows this very thing, the laws. - These men, Socrates, are the judges. - How do you say, Melitus? Do they know how to instruct the youth, and to make them better? - Especially so. - But whether do all of them know how? or do some of them know, and others not? - All of them. - You speak well, by Juno, and adduce a great abundance of those that benefit. But what? Can these auditors also make the youth better, or not? -
25a   These also. - And what of the senators? - The senators also can effect this. - But, O Melitus, do some of those that harangue the people in an assembly corrupt the more juvenile; or do all these make them better? - All these. - All the Athenians therefore, as it seems, make them to be worthy and good, except me, but I alone corrupt them. Do you say so? - These very things I strenuously assert. - You charge me with a very

great infelicity. But answer me: Does this also appear to you to be the case respecting horses, *viz.* that all men can make them better, but that there is only one person that corrupts them? or does the perfect contrary of this take place, so that it is one person who can make them better, or, at least, that those possessed of equestrian skill are very few;

b but the multitude, if they meddle with and make use of horses, corrupt them? Is not this the case, O Melitus, both with respect to horses and all other animals? It certainly is so, whether you and Anytus say so, or not. For a great felicity would take place concerning youth if only one

c person corrupted, and the rest benefited them. However, you have sufficiently shown, O Melitus, that you never bestowed any care upon youth; and you clearly evince your negligence, and that you pay no attention to the particulars for which you accuse me.

Further still, tell me, by Jupiter, O Melitus, whether it is better to dwell in good or in bad polities? Answer, my friend: for I ask you nothing difficult. Do not the depraved always procure some evil to those that continually reside near them; and do not the good procure

d some good? - Entirely so. - Is there then any one who wishes to be injured by his associates, rather than to be benefited? Answer, O good man: for the law orders you to answer. Is there any one who wishes to be injured? - There is not. - Come then, whether do you bring me hither, as one that corrupts the youth, and makes them depraved willingly, or as one who does this unwillingly? - I say that you do it willingly. - But what, O Melitus, is it possible that you, who are so much younger than I am, should well know that the depraved always procure some evil to those that are most near to them, and the good

e some good; but that I should have arrived at such ignorance as not to know that, if I make any one of my associates depraved, I shall be in danger of receiving some evil from him; and that I, therefore, do this so great an evil willingly, as you say? I cannot be persuaded by you, O Melitus, as to these things, nor do I think that any other man would:

26a but either I do not corrupt the youth, or I corrupt them unwillingly. So that you speak falsely in both assertions. But if I unwillingly corrupt them, the law does not order me to be brought hither for such-like involuntary offences, but that I should be taken and privately taught and admonished. For it is evident that, if I am taught better, I shall cease doing that which I unwillingly do. But you, indeed, have avoided me, and have not been willing to associate with and instruct me; but you have brought me hither, where the law orders those who require punishment, and not discipline, to be brought. Wherefore, O

Athenians, this now is manifest which I have said, that Melitus never paid the smallest attention to this affair.

b   At the same time, however, tell us, O Melitus, how you say I corrupt the youth. Or is it not evident, from your written accusation, that I teach them not to believe in the Gods in which the city believes, but in other new divine powers? Do you not say that, teaching these things, I corrupt the youth? - Perfectly so: I strenuously assert these things. - By

c   those very Gods, therefore, Melitus, of whom we are now speaking, speak in a still clearer manner both to me and to these men. For I cannot learn whether you say that I teach them to think that there are not certain Gods, (though I myself believe that there are Gods, for I am by no means an atheist, nor in this respect do I act unjustly,) not, indeed, such as the city believes in, but others, and that this it is for which you accuse me, that I introduce other Gods; or whether you altogether say that I do not believe there are Gods, and that I teach this doctrine also to others. - I say this, that you do not believe that there are Gods. - O wonderful Melitus, why do you thus speak? Do I then think,

d   unlike the rest of mankind, that the sun and moon are not Gods? - He does not, by Jupiter, O judges: for he says that the sun is a stone, and that the moon is earth. - O friend Melitus, you think that you accuse Anaxagoras; and you so despise these judges, and think them to be so illiterate, as not to know that the books of Anaxagoras the Clazomenian are full of these assertions. Besides, would the youth learn those things from me, which they might buy for a drachma at most in the orchestra,

e   and thus might deride Socrates if he pretended they were his own, ESPECIALLY SINCE THEY ARE LIKEWISE SO ABSURD.[†] But, by Jupiter, do I then appear to you to think that there is no God? - None whatever, by Jupiter. - What you say, O Melitus, is incredible, and, as it appears to me, is so even to yourself. Indeed, O Athenians, this man appears to me to be perfectly insolent and intemperate in his speech, and to have

27a   in reality written this accusation, impelled by a certain insolence, wantonness, and youthfulness. For he seems, as it were, to have composed an enigma in order to try me, and to have said to himself, Will the wise Socrates know that I am jesting, and speaking contrary to myself? Or shall I deceive him, together with the other hearers? For he appears to me to contradict himself in his accusation, as if he had said, Socrates is impious in not believing that there are Gods, but believing

---

† This assertion, among many others, affords an incontestable proof that Socrates believed in the religion of his country: for he here clearly says, that the doctrine of Anaxagoras, which made the sun and moon to be no Gods, is *absurd*.

that there are Gods. And this, indeed, must be the assertion of one in jest.

b   But let us jointly consider, O Athenians, how he appears to me to have asserted these things. And do you, O Melitus, answer us, and, as I requested you at first, be mindful not to disturb me if I discourse after my usual manner. Is there then any man, O Melitus, who thinks that there are human affairs, but does not think that there are men? Pray answer me, and do not make so much noise. And is there any one who does not think that there are horses, but yet thinks that there are equestrian affairs? or who does not think that there are pipers, but yet that there are things pertaining to pipers? There is not, O best of men. For I will speak for you, since you are not willing to answer yourself.

c   But answer also to this: Is there any one who thinks that there are dæmoniacal affairs, but yet does not think that there are dæmons? - There is not. - How averse you are to speak! so that you scarcely answer, compelled by these things. Do you not, therefore, say that I believe in and teach things dæmoniacal, whether they are new or old? But indeed you acknowledge that I believe in things dæmoniacal, and to this you have sworn in your accusation. If then I believe in dæmoniacal affairs, there is an abundant necessity that I should also believe in the existence of dæmons. Is it not so? - It is. - For I suppose you to assent, since you do not answer. But with respect to dæmons,[†] do we not

d   think either that they are Gods, or the sons of Gods? Will you acknowledge this or not? - Entirely so. - If, therefore, I believe that there dæmons as you say, if dæmons are certain Gods, will it not be as I say, that you speak enigmatically and in jest, since you assert that I do not think there are Gods, and yet again think that there are, since I believe in dæmons? But if dæmons are certain spurious sons of the Gods, either from Nymphs, or from certain others, of whom they are said to be the offspring, what man can believe that there are sons of the Gods, and yet that there are no Gods? For this would be just as absurd, as if some one

e   should think that there are colts and mules, but should not think that there are horses and asses. However, O Melitus, it cannot be otherwise but that you have written this accusation, either to try me, or because there was not any crime of which you could truly accuse me. For it is impossible that you should persuade any man who has the smallest degree of intellect, that one and the same person can believe that there

28a   are dæmoniacal and divine affairs, and yet that there are neither dæmons, nor Gods, nor heroes. That I am not, therefore, impious, O Athenians,

---

† For a copious account of dæmons, see note 37 [TTS vol. XI] on the *Banquet*.

according to the accusation of Melitus, does not appear to me to require a long apology; but what I have said is sufficient.

As to what I before observed, that there is a great enmity towards me among the vulgar, you may be well assured that it is true. And this it is which will condemn me, if I should happen to be condemned, *viz.* the hatred and envy of the multitude, and not Melitus, nor Anytus; which
b indeed has also happened to many others, and those good men, and will I think again happen in futurity. For there is no reason to expect that it will terminate in me. Perhaps, however, some one will say, Are you not ashamed, Socrates, to have applied yourself to a study, through which you are now in danger of being put to death? To this person I shall justly reply, That you do not speak well, O man, if you think that life or death ought to be regarded by the man who is capable of being useful though but in a small degree; and that he ought not to consider this alone when he acts, whether he acts justly, or unjustly, and like a
c good or a bad man. For those demigods that died at Troy would, according to your reasoning, be vile characters, as well others as the son of Thetis, who so much despised the danger of death when compared with disgraceful conduct, that when his mother, who was a goddess, on his desiring to kill Hector, thus I think addressed[†] him - My son, if you revenge the slaughter of your friend Patroclus, and kill Hector, you will yourself die, for said she, death awaits you as soon as Hector expires: - Notwithstanding this, he considered the danger of death as a trifle, and
d much more dreaded living basely, and not revenging his friends. For he says, May I immediately die, when I have inflicted just punishment on him who has acted unjustly, and not stay here an object of ridicule, by the crooked ships, and a burden to the ground? Do you think that he was solicitous about death and danger? For this, O Athenians, is in reality the case: wherever any one ranks himself, thinking it to be the best for him, or wherever he is ranked by the ruler, there as it appears to me he ought to abide, and encounter danger, neither paying attention to death nor to any thing else before that which is base.

e I therefore, O Athenians, should have acted in a dire manner, if, when those rulers which you had placed over me had assigned me a rank at Potidea, at Amphipolis, and at Delium, I should then have remained where they stationed me, like any other person, and should have encountered the danger of death; but that, when Divinity has ordered, as I think and apprehend, that I ought to live philosophizing, and exploring myself and others, I should here through fear of death or any

† *Iliad.* lib. xviii. ver. 94. &c.

29a   other thing desert my rank. For this would be dire: and then in reality any one might justly bring me to a court of judicature, and accuse me of not believing in the Gods, in consequence of not obeying the oracle, fearing death, and thinking myself to be wise when I am not. For to dread death, O Athenians, is nothing else than to appear to be wise, without being so: since it is for a man to appear to know that which he does not know. For no one knows but that death may be to man the greatest of goods; but they dread it, as if they well knew that it is the

b   greatest of evils. And how is it possible that this should not be a most disgraceful ignorance, I mean for a man to suspect that he has a knowledge of that of which he is ignorant? But I, O Athenians, differ perhaps in this from the multitude of men; and if I should say that I am wiser than some one in any thing, it would be in this, that not having a sufficient knowledge of the things in Hades, I also think that I have not this knowledge. But I know that to act unjustly, and to be disobedient to one more excellent, whether God or man, is evil and base. I shall never, therefore, fear and avoid things which for aught I

c   know may be good, before those evils which I know to be evils. So that neither if you should now dismiss me, (being unpersuaded by Anytus, who said that either I ought not to have been brought hither at first, or that, when brought hither, it was impossible not to put me to death, telling you that if I escaped, all your sons studying what Socrates had taught them would be corrupted,) if besides these things you should say to me, O Socrates, we now indeed shall not be persuaded by Anytus, but we shall dismiss you, though on this condition, that afterwards you no longer busy yourself with this investigation, nor philosophise, and if hereafter you are detected in so doing, you shall die, - if, as I said, you

d   should dismiss me on these terms, I should thus address you: O Athenians, I honour and love you: but I obey Divinity rather than you; and as long as I breathe and am able, I shall not cease to philosophise, and to exhort and indicate to any one of you I may happen to meet, such things as the following, after my usual manner. O best of men, since you are an Athenian, of a city the greatest and the most celebrated for wisdom and strength, are you not ashamed of being attentive to the

e   means of acquiring riches, glory and honour, in great abundance, but to bestow no care nor any consideration upon prudence† and truth, nor how your soul may subsist in the most excellent condition? And if any one of you should contend with me, and say that these things are the

---

† Meaning *intellectual prudence,* which is the contemplation of the forms contained in intellect.

objects of his care, I should not immediately dismiss him, nor depart, but I should interrogate, explore, and reason with him. And if he should not appear to me to possess virtue, and yet pretend to the possession of it, I should reprove him as one who but little esteems things of the greatest worth, but considers things of a vile and abject nature as of great importance. In this manner I should act by any one I might happen to meet, whether younger or older, a stranger or a citizen; but rather to citizens, because ye are more allied to me. For be well assured that Divinity commands me thus to act. And I think that a greater good never happened to you in the city, than this my obedience to the will of Divinity. For I go about doing nothing else than persuading both the younger and older among you, neither to pay attention to the body, nor to riches, nor any thing else prior to the soul; nor to be so much concerned for any thing, as how the soul may subsist in the most excellent condition. I also say that virtue is not produced from riches, but riches from virtue, as likewise all other human goods, both privately and publicly. If, therefore, asserting these things, I corrupt the youth, these things will be noxious; but if any one says that I assert other things than these, he says nothing. In addition to this I shall say, O Athenians, that whether you are persuaded by Anytus or not, and whether you dismiss me or not, I shall not act otherwise, even though I should die often.

Be not disturbed, O Athenians, but patiently hear what I shall request of you; for I think it will be advantageous for you to hear. For I am about to mention certain other things to you, at which perhaps you will be clamorous; though let this on no account take place. Be well assured then, if you put me to death, being such a man as I say I am, you will not injure me more than yourselves. For neither Melitus nor Anytus injures me; for neither can they. Indeed, I think it is not lawful for a better to be injured by a worse man. He may indeed perhaps condemn me to death, or exile, or disgrace; and he or some other may consider these as mighty evils. I however do not think so; but, in my opinion, it is much more an evil to act as he now acts, who endeavours to put a man to death unjustly. Now, therefore, O Athenians, it is far from my intention to defend myself, (as some one may think,) but I thus speak for your sake, lest in condemning me you should sin against the gift of Divinity. For, if you should put me to death, you will not easily find such another (though the comparison is ridiculous) whom Divinity has united to this city as to a great and generous horse, but sluggish through his magnitude, and requiring to be excited by a certain fly. In like manner Divinity appears to have united such a one as I am to the city,

that I might not cease exciting, persuading and reproving each of you,
and every where sitting among you through the whole day. Such
another man, therefore, will not easily arise among you. And if you
will be persuaded by me, you will spare me. Perhaps, however, you,
being indignant, like those who are awakened from sleep, will repulse
me, and, being persuaded by Anytus, will inconsiderately put me to
death. Should this be the case, you will pass the rest of your time in
sleep, unless Divinity should send some other person to take care of
you. But that I am such a one as I have said, one imparted to this city
by Divinity, you may understand from hence. For my conduct does not
appear to be human, in neglecting every thing pertaining to myself and
my private affairs for so many years, and always attending to your
concerns, addressing each of you separately, like a father, or an elder
brother, and persuading you to the study of virtue. And if indeed I had
obtained any emolument from this conduct, and receiving a recompense
had exhorted you to these things, there might be some reason for
asserting that I acted like other men; but now behold, even my accusers
themselves, who have so shamelessly calumniated me in every thing else,
have not been so impudent as to charge me with this, or to bring
witnesses to prove that I ever either demanded or solicited a reward.
And that I speak the truth, my poverty I think affords a sufficient
testimony.

Perhaps, therefore, it may appear absurd, that, going about and
involving myself in a multiplicity of affairs, I should privately advise
these things, but that I should never dare to come to your convention,
and consult for the city. The cause of this is that which you have often
heard me every where asserting, *viz.* because a certain divine and
dæmoniacal† voice is present with me, which also Melitus in his
accusation derided. This voice attended me from a child; and, when it
is present, always *dissuades* me from what I intended to do, but never
incites me. This it is which opposed my engaging in political affairs; and
to me its opposition appears to be all-beautiful. For be well assured, O
Athenians, if I had formerly attempted to transact political affairs, I
should have perished long before this, and should neither have benefited
you in any respect, nor myself. And be not indignant with me for
speaking the truth. For it is not possible that any man can be safe, who
sincerely opposes either you, or any other multitude, and who prevents
many unjust and illegal actions from taking place in the city; but it is

† See note 2 at the beginning of the *First Alcibiades* for a full account of the dæmon
of Socrates [TTS vol. IX, p 167, ff].

necessary that he who in reality contends for the just, if he wishes even
32a   but for a little time to be safe, should live privately and not engage in
public affairs.

I will present you with mighty proofs of these things, not words,
which you honour, but deeds. Hear then the circumstances which have
happened to me, that you may know that I shall not yield to any one
contrary to what is becoming, through dread of death; though at the
b   same time by not yielding I shall perish. For I, O Athenians, never bore
the office of magistrate† in the city, but I have been a senator: and it
happened that our Antiochean tribe governed, when you thought proper
to condemn the ten generals collectively, for not taking up the bodies of
those that perished in the naval battle;‡ and in so doing acted illegally,
as afterwards appeared to all of you. At that time I alone of the
Prytaneans opposed you, that you might not act contrary to the laws,
and my suffrage was contrary to yours. When the orators also
c   were ready to point me out and condemn me, and you likewise were
exhorting and vociferating to the same end, I thought that I ought rather
to encounter danger with law and justice, than adhere to you, not
establishing what is just, through fear of bonds or death. And these
things indeed happened while the city was yet a democracy; but when
it became an oligarchy, the Thirty sent for me and four others to the
Tholus,§ and ordered us to bring Leon the Salaminian from Salamis, in
order to be put to death;◊ for by these orders they meant to involve
d   many others in guilt. Then indeed I, not in words but in deeds, showed
them, if the assertion is not too rustic, that I made no account of death;
but that all my attention was directed to this, that I might do nothing
unjust or unholy. For that dominion of the Thirty, though so strong,
did not terrify me into the perpetration of any unjust action. But when
we departed from the Tholus, the four indeed went to Salamis, and
brought with them Leon; but I returned home. And perhaps for this I
should have been put to death, if that government had not been rapidly
dissolved. These things many of you can testify.

† The people of Athens were divided into tribes, and fifty men were chosen by
turns out of each, who governed thirty-five days, and were called Prytani or Senators.

‡ This battle was fought by Callicratidas, the Lacedæmonian general, against the ten
Athenian generals, who obtained the victory.

§ The Tholus was a kind of clerk's office, where the Prytani dined, and the clerks
sat.

◊ This happened in the second year of the 39th Olympiad.

e   Do you think, therefore, that I could have lived for so many years, if I had engaged in public affairs, and had acted in a manner becoming a good man, giving assistance to justice, and doing this in the most eminent degree? Far otherwise, O Athenians: for neither could any

33a other man. But I, through the whole of my life, if I do any thing publicly, shall appear to be such a man; and being the same privately, I shall never grant any thing to any one contrary to justice, neither to any other, nor to any one of these whom my calumniators say are my disciples. I however was never the preceptor of any one; but I never repulsed either the young or the old that were desirous of hearing me speak after my usual manner. Nor do I discourse when I receive money,

b but refrain from speaking when I do not receive any; but I similarly offer myself to be interrogated by the rich and the poor: and if any one is willing to answer, he hears what I have to say. Of these too, whether any one becomes good or not, I cannot justly be said to be the cause, because I never either promised or taught them any discipline. But if any one says that he has ever learnt or heard any thing from me privately which all others have not, be well assured that he does not speak the truth.

c Why therefore some have delighted to associate with me for a long time ye have heard, O Athenians. I have told you all the truth, that men are delighted on hearing those interrogated who think themselves to be wise, but who are not: for this is not unpleasant. But, as I say, I am ordered to do this by Divinity, by oracles, by dreams, and by every mode by which any other divine destiny ever commanded any thing to be done by man. These things, O Athenians, are true, and might easily

d be confuted if they were not. For if, with respect to the youth, I corrupt some, and have corrupted others, it is fit, if any of them have become old, that, knowing I gave them bad advice when they were young, they should now rise up, accuse and take vengeance on me; but if they themselves are unwilling to do this, that their fathers, or brothers, or others of their kindred, should now call to mind and avenge the evil which their relatives suffered from me. But in short many of

e them are here present, whom I see: - In the first place, Crito, who is of the same age and city that I am, and who is the father of this Critobulus; in the next place, Lysanias the Sphecian, the father of this Æschines; and further still, Antipho the Cephisian, the father of Epigenes. There are also others whose brothers are in this assembly, *viz.* Nicostratus the son of Zotidas, and the brother of Theodotus. And Theodotus indeed is dead, and so has no occasion for his brother's

assistance. Paralus also is here, the son of Demodochus, of whom
Theages was the brother; likewise Adimantus the son of Aristo, the
brother of whom is this Plato; and Æantidorus, of whom Apollodorus
is the brother. I could also mention many others, some one of whom
Melitus, especially in his oration, ought to have adduced as a witness.
If however he then forgot to do so, let him now produce him, for he has
my consent; and if he has any thing of this kind to disclose, let him
declare it. However, you will find the very contrary of this to be the
case, and that all these are ready to assist me who have corrupted and
injured their kindred, as Melitus and Anytus say. It might indeed
perhaps be reasonable to suppose that those whom I have corrupted
would assist me; but what other reason can the relatives of these have,
who are not corrupted, and who are now advanced in age, for giving me
assistance, except that which is right and just? For they know that
Melitus lies, and that I speak the truth. Be it so then, O Athenians: and
these indeed, and perhaps other such-like particulars, are what I have to
urge in my defence.

Perhaps, however, some one among you will be indignant on
recollecting that he, when engaged in a much less contest than this,
suppliantly implored the judges with many tears; that he also brought
his children hither, that by these he might especially excite compassion,
together with many others of his relatives and friends: but I do none of
these things, though, as it may appear, I am brought to extreme danger.
Perhaps, therefore, some one thus thinking may become more hostile
towards me, and, being enraged with these very particulars, may give his
vote with anger. If then any one of you is thus affected, I do not think
it by any means right; but if he should be, I shall appear to myself to
speak equitably to such a one by saying that I also, O best of men, have
certain relatives. For, as Homer says, I am not sprung from an oak, nor
from a rock, but from men. So that I also, O Athenians, have relations,
and three sons; one now a lad; but the other two, boys: I have not
however brought any one of them hither, that I might supplicate you on
that account to acquit me. Why is it then that I do none of these
things? It is not, O Athenians, because I am contumacious, nor is it in
contempt of you. And as to my fearing or not fearing death, that is
another question. But it does not appear to me to be consistent either
with my own glory or yours, or that of the whole city, that I should do
any thing of this kind at my age, and with the reputation I have
acquired, whether true or false. For it is admitted that Socrates surpasses
in something the multitude of mankind. If, therefore, those among you

who appear to excel either in wisdom, in fortitude, or any other virtue, should act in such a manner as I have seen some when they have been judged, it would be shameful: for these, appearing indeed to be something, have conducted themselves in a wonderful manner, thinking they should suffer something dreadful by dying, as if they would be immortal if you did not put them to death. These men, as it appears to me, would so disgrace the city, that any stranger might apprehend that such of the Athenians as excel in virtue, and who are promoted to the magistracy and other honours in preference to the rest, do not in any respect surpass women. For these things, O Athenians, ought not to be done by us who have gained some degree of reputation, nor should you suffer us to do them, if we were willing; but you should show that you will much sooner condemn him who introduces these lamentable dramas, and who thus makes the city ridiculous, than him who quietly expects your decision.

But exclusive of glory, O Athenians, neither does it appear to me to be just for a judge to be entreated, or to acquit any one in consequence of being supplicated; but in my opinion he ought to teach and persuade. For a judge does not sit for the purpose of showing favour, but that he may judge what is just: and he takes an oath that he will not show favour to any, but that he will judge according to the laws. Hence it is neither fit that we should accustom you, nor that you should be accustomed to swear: for in so doing neither of us will act piously. Do not, therefore, think, O Athenians, that I ought to act in such a manner towards you as I should neither conceive to be beautiful, nor just, nor holy; and especially, by Jupiter, since I am accused of impiety by this Melitus. For it clearly follows, that if I should persuade you, and, though you have taken an oath, force you to be favourable, I might then indeed teach that you do not think there are Gods; and in reality, while making my defence, I should accuse myself as not believing in the Gods. This however is far from being the case: *for I believe that there are* GODS *more than any one of my accusers;* and I refer it to you and to Divinity to judge concerning me such things as will be best both for me and you.†

That I should not, therefore, O Athenians, be indignant with you because you have condemned me, there are many reasons, and among others this, that it has not happened to me contrary to my expectation;

---

† After Socrates had thus spoken, votes were taken by the judges, and he was condemned by a majority of three voices. His speech after his condemnation commences in the paragraph immediately following.

but I much rather wonder that there should have been so great a number of votes on both sides. For I did not think that I should have wanted such a few additional votes for my acquittal. But now, as it seems, if there had been only three more votes, I should have escaped condemnation. Indeed, as it appears to me, I now have escaped Melitus; and I have not only escaped him, but it is perfectly evident that unless Anytus and Lyco had risen to accuse me, he had lost his thousand[†] drachmas, since he had not the fifth part of the votes on his side.

Melitus then thinks that I deserve death. Be it so. But what punishment,[‡] O Athenians, shall I assign to myself? Is it not evident that it will be such a one as I deserve? What then do I deserve to suffer or to pay, for not having during my life concealed what I have learned, but neglected all that the multitude esteem, riches, domestic concerns, military command, authority in public assemblies, and other magistracies? for having avoided the conspiracies and seditions which have happened in the city, thinking that I was in reality a more worthy character than to depend on these things for my safety? I have not, therefore, applied myself to those pursuits, by which I could neither benefit you nor myself; but my whole endeavour has been to benefit every individual in the greatest degree; striving to persuade each of you, that he should pay no attention to any of his concerns, prior to that care of himself by which he may become a most worthy and wise man; that he should not attend to the affairs of the city prior to the city itself; and that attention should be paid to other things in a similar manner. What then, being such a man, do I deserve to suffer? A certain good, O Athenians, if in reality you honour me according to my desert; and this such a good as it is proper for me to receive. What then is the good which is adapted to a poor man who is a benefactor, and who requires leisure that he may exhort you to virtue? There is not any thing more adapted, O Athenians, than that such a man should be supported at the public expense in the Prytaneum; and this much more than if some one

---

† An accuser was obliged to have one half of the votes, and a fifth part more, or else he was fined in a thousand drachmas, *i.e.* nearly 26l. 3s. 4d.

‡ When the criminal was found guilty, and the accuser demanded a sentence of death, the law allowed the prisoner to condemn himself to one of these three punishments, *viz.* perpetual imprisonment, a fine, or banishment. This privilege was first enacted on the behalf of the judges, that they might not hesitate to pass sentence on those who, by condemning themselves, owned their guilt. Socrates, therefore, in obedience to the laws, and in order to proclaim his innocence, instead of a punishment demanded a reward worthy of himself.

of you had been victorious in the Olympic games with horses, or in the two or four-yoked car. For such a one makes you *appear* to be happy, but I cause you *to be* so: and he is not in want of support, but I am. If, therefore, it is necessary that I should be honoured according to what is justly my desert, I should be honoured with this support in the Prytaneum.

Perhaps, therefore, in saying these things, I shall appear to you to speak in the same manner as when I reprobated lamentations and supplications. A thing of this kind, however, O Athenians, is not the case, but rather the following. I am determined not to injure any man willingly; though I shall not persuade you of this, because the time in which we can discourse with each other is but short. For if there was the same law with you as with others, that in cases of death the judicial process should not continue for one day only but for many, I think I should be able to persuade you. But now it is not easy in a short time to dissolve great calumnies. Being however determined to injure no one, I shall be very far from injuring myself, and of pronouncing against myself that I am worthy of evil and punishment. What then? Fearing lest I should suffer that which Melitus thinks I deserve, which I say I know not whether it is good or evil, that I may avoid this, shall I choose that which I well know to be evil, and think that I deserve this? Whether then shall I choose bonds? But why is it necessary that I should live in prison, in perpetual subjection to the eleven magistrates? Shall I pay a fine then, and remain in bonds till it is discharged? But this is what I just now said: for I have not money to pay it. Shall I then choose exile? For perhaps I shall be thought worthy of this. I should however, O Athenians, be a great lover of life, if I were so absurd as not to be able to infer that if you, being my fellow citizens, could not endure my habits and discourses, which have become to you so burthensome and odious, that you now seek to be liberated from them, it is not likely that others would easily bear them. It is far otherwise, O Athenians. My life would be beautiful indeed were I at this advanced age to live in exile, changing and being driven from one city to another. For I well know that, wherever I may go, the youth will hear me when I discourse, in the same manner as they do here. And if I should repel them, they also would expel me, persuading the more elderly to this effect. But if I should not repel them, the fathers and kindred of these would banish me on account of these very young men themselves.

Perhaps however some one will say, Can you not, Socrates, live in exile silently and quietly? But it is the most difficult of all things to persuade some among you, that this cannot take place. For if I say that in so doing I should disobey Divinity, and that on this account it is impossible for me to live a life of leisure and quiet, you would not believe me, in consequence of supposing that I spoke ironically. And if, again, I should say that this is the greatest good to man, to discourse every day concerning virtue, and other things which you have heard me discussing, exploring both myself and others; and if I should also assert that an uninvestigating life is to be rejected by man, much less, were I thus to speak, would you believe me. These things however, O Athenians, are as I say; but it is not easy to persuade you that they are so. And at the same time I am not accustomed to think myself deserving of any ill. Indeed, if I were rich, I would amerce myself in such a sum as I might be able to pay; but now I am not in a condition to do this, unless you would allow the fine to be proportioned to what I am able to pay. For thus perhaps I might be able to pay a mina of silver (3l.). But Plato here, O Athenians, Crito, Critobulus, and Apollodorus, exhort me to pay thirty minæ, (90l.) for which they will be answerable. I amerce myself, therefore, in thirty minæ; and these will be my securities for the payment.[†]

Now, O Athenians, your impatience and precipitancy will draw upon you a great reproach, and give occasion to those who are so disposed, to revile the city for having put that wise man Socrates to death. For those who are willing to reproach you will call me a wise man, though I am not. If, therefore, you had waited but for a short time, this very thing, my death, would have happened to you spontaneously. For behold my age, that it is far advanced in life, and is near to death. But I do not say this to all of you, but to those only who have condemned me to die. This also I say to them: Perhaps you think, O Athenians, that I was condemned through the want of such language, by which I might have persuaded you, if I had thought it requisite, to say and do any thing, so that I might escape punishment. Far otherwise: for I am condemned through want indeed, yet not of words, but of audacity and impudence, and because I was unwilling to say such things to you as you would have been much gratified in hearing, I at the same time weeping and lamenting, and doing and saying many other things unworthy of me, as I say, but such as you are accustomed to hear and see in others. But neither then did I think it was necessary, for the sake of avoiding danger, to do any thing illiberal, nor do I now repent that I have thus

---

† Socrates having amerced himself in obedience to the laws, the judges took the affair into consideration, and, without any regard to the fine, condemned him to die. After the sentence was pronounced, Socrates addressed them as in the next paragraph.

defended myself; but I should much rather choose to die, after having
made this apology, than to live after that manner. For neither in a
judicial process, nor in battle, is it proper that I or any other should
devise how he may by any means avoid death; since in battle it is
frequently evident that a man might easily avoid death by throwing
away his arms, and suppliantly converting himself to his pursuers.
There are also many other devices in other dangers, by which he who
dares to do and say any thing may escape death. To fly from death
however, O Athenians, is not difficult, but it is much more difficult to
fly from depravity; for it runs swifter than death. And now I indeed,
as being slow and old, am caught by the slower; but my accusers, as
being skilful and swift, are caught by the swifter of these two,
improbity. Now too, I indeed depart, condemned by you to death; but
they being condemned by truth, depart to depravity and injustice. And
I acquiesce in this decision, and they also. Perhaps, therefore, it is
necessary that these things should subsist in this manner, and I think
they subsist properly.

In the next place, I desire to predict to you who have condemned me,
what will be your fate. For I am now in that situation in which men
especially prophesy,[†] *viz.* when they are about to die. For I say, that
you, my murderers, will immediately after my death be punished,[‡] by
dying in a manner, by Jupiter, much more severe than I shall. For now
you have done this, thinking you should be liberated from the necessity
of giving an account of your life. The very contrary however, as I say,
will happen to you: for many will be your accusers, whom I have
restrained, though you did not perceive it. These too will be more
troublesome, because they are younger, and will be more indignant
against you. For, if you think that by putting men to death you will
restrain others from upbraiding you that you do not live well, you are
much mistaken; since this mode of liberation is neither sufficiently
efficacious nor becoming. But this is the most beautiful and the most
easy mode, not to disturb others, but to act in such a manner that you

---

† That men are often prophetic at the point of death is an opinion which may be
traced as far as to the time of Homer, and is doubtless of infinite antiquity.

‡ This prediction was fulfilled almost immediately after the death of Socrates. The
Athenians repented of their cruelty; and his accusers were universally despised and
shunned. One of them, Melitus, was torn in pieces; another, Anytus, was expelled from
the Heraclea, to which he fled for shelter; and others destroyed themselves. And, in
addition to this, a raging plague soon after desolated Athens.

39a

b

c

d

may be most excellent characters. And thus much I prophesy to those
of you who condemned me.

e   But to you who have acquitted me by your decision, I would willingly
speak concerning this affair during the time that the magistrates are at
leisure, and before I am brought to the place where it is necessary I
should die. Attend to me, therefore, O Athenians, during that time.
For nothing hinders our conversing with each other, as long as we are
permitted so to do; since I wish to demonstrate to you, as friends, the
40a   meaning of that which has just now happened to me. To me then, O
my judges (and in calling you judges I rightly denominate you,) a certain
wonderful circumstance has happened. For the prophetic voice of the
dæmon, which opposed me in the most trifling affairs, if I was about to
act in any thing improperly, prior to this, I was continually accustomed
to hear; but now, though these things have happened to me which you
b   see, and which some one would think to be the extremity of evils, yet
neither when I departed from home in the morning was the signal of the
God adverse to me, nor when I ascended hither to the place of
judgment, nor when I was about to speak, - though at other times it
frequently restrained me in the midst of speaking. But now, in this
affair, it has never been adverse to me, either in word or deed. I will
now, therefore, tell you what I apprehend to be the cause of this. For
this thing which has happened appears to me to be good; nor do those
c   of us apprehend rightly who think death to be an evil; of which this
appears to me to be a great argument, that the accustomed signal would
have opposed me, unless I had been about to do something good.

After this manner too we may conceive that there is abundant hope
that death is good. For to die is one of two things. For it is either to
be as it were nothing,† and to be deprived of all sensation; or, as it is
said, it is a certain mutation and migration of the soul from this to
d   another place. And whether no sensation remains, but death is like
sleep when unattended with any dreams, in this case death will be a
gain. For, if any one compares such a night as this, in which he so
profoundly sleeps as not even to see a dream, with the other nights and
days of his life, and should declare how many he had passed better and
e   more pleasantly than this night, I think that not only a private man, but
even the great king himself, would find so small a number that they
might be easily counted. If, therefore, death is a thing of this kind, I say
it is a gain: for thus the whole of future time appears to be nothing

---

†   The reader must not imagine by this that Socrates calls in question the
immortality of the soul; for this, as he will see, he demonstrates in the *Phædo*.

more than one night. But if again death is a migration from hence to another place, and the assertion is true that all the dead are there, what greater good, O my judges, can there be than this? For if some one arriving at Hades, being liberated from these who pretend to be judges, should find those who are true judges, and who are said to judge there, *viz.* Minos and Rhadamanthus, Æacus, and Triptolemus, and such others of the demigods as lived justly, would this be a vile journey? At what rate would you not purchase a conference with Orpheus and Musæus, with Hesiod and Homer? I indeed should be willing to die often, if these things are true. For to me the association will be admirable, when I shall meet with Palamedes, and Ajax the son of Telamon, and any other of the ancients who died through an unjust decision. The comparing my case with theirs will, I think, be no unpleasing employment to me. But the greatest pleasure will consist in passing my time there, as I have done here, in interrogating and exploring who among them is wise, and who fancies himself to be but is not so. What, O my judges, would not any one give for a conference with him who led that mighty army against Troy, or with Ulysses, or Sisyphus, or ten thousand others, both men and women, that might be mentioned? For to converse and associate with these would be an inestimable felicity. For I should not be capitally condemned on this account by those that dwell there; since they are in other respects more happy than those that live here, and are for the rest of time immortal, if the assertions respecting these things are true.

You, therefore, O my judges, ought to entertain good hopes with respect to death, and to be firmly persuaded of this one thing, that to a good man nothing is evil, neither while living nor when dead, and that his concerns are never neglected by the Gods. Nor is my present condition the effect of chance; but this is evident to me, that now to die, and be liberated from the affairs of life, is better for me. On this account the accustomed signal did not in this affair oppose me. Nor am I very indignant with those that accused and condemned me, though their intention in so doing was to injure me; and for this they deserve to be blamed. Thus much however I request of them: that you will punish my sons when they grow up, if they cause you the same molestation that I have; and if they shall appear to you to pay more attention to riches or any thing else than to virtue, and shall think themselves to be something when they are nothing, that you will reprobate them as I do you, as neglecting the care of things to which they ought to attend, and conceiving themselves to be of some consequence when they are of no worth. If ye do these things, your conduct both towards me and my sons will be just. But it is now time to depart hence, - for me indeed to die, but for you to live. Which of us however will arrive at a better[†] thing, is perfectly immanifest except to Divinity.

[†] It is always good for a good man to die with respect to himself; but it is often better for the community that he should live. It is likewise frequently better for a bad man to live than to die, in order that his latent vices may be called forth into energy; and besides this, he is frequently an instrument in the hand of Divinity of good to others. Socrates, therefore, with no less accuracy than profundity says, that Divinity only knows whether it is better for him to die, than for his accusers to live; for this could only be ascertained by a very extensive knowledge of futurity; and consequently could only be manifest to Divinity.

THE

CRITO

OR

CONCERNING TRUE AND JUST OPINION

The *Crito* is disposed after a manner so regular and plain, that it requires no Introduction. I shall therefore only observe, that it admirably teaches us to despise the opinions of the vulgar, to endure calamities patiently, and to consider the good of the whole as incomparably more important than that of a part.

THE

CRITO

PERSONS OF THE DIALOGUE

SOCRATES and CRITO

SCENE - The Prison of SOCRATES

43a SOC. Why came you at this early hour, Crito? Or is it not yet morning?

CRI. It is.

SOC. But what time of the morning is it?

CRI. It is now the break of day.

SOC. I wonder how the keeper of the prison came to admit you.

CRI. He is accustomed to me, Socrates, in consequence of my frequently coming hither; and he is also in a certain respect under obligations to me.

SOC. Did you come just now, or some time ago?

CRI. It is a considerable time since I came.

b SOC. But why did you not immediately call me, and not sit down in silence?

CRI. Not so, by Jupiter, Socrates; nor should I myself be willing to be for so long a time awake and in sorrow. But I have for some time admired you, on perceiving how sweetly you slept. And I designedly did not call you, that you might continue in that pleasant condition. Indeed I have often and formerly through the whole of your life considered you as happy on account of your manners, but far more so in the present calamity, because you bear it so easily and mildly.

c   SOC. But it would be absurd, Crito, if a man of my age were to be indignant when it is necessary for him to die.

CRI. And yet others, Socrates, equally old, when they have been involved in such-like calamities, have notwithstanding their age been indignant with their present fortune.

SOC. It is so. But why did you come to me so early?

CRI. I come, Socrates, bearing a message not unpleasant to you, as it appears to me, but bitter and weighty to me and to all your associates; and which I indeed shall bear most heavily.

d   SOC. What is it? Is it the ship[†] come from Delos, on the arrival of which it is necessary I should die?

CRI. Not yet; but it appears to me, from what certain persons coming from Sunium have announced, and who left it there, that it will arrive today. From these messengers, therefore, it is evident that it will be here today; and consequently it will be necessary for you, Socrates, to die tomorrow.

44a   SOC. But with good fortune, Crito: and if it please the Gods, be it so. Yet I do not think that it will arrive here today.

CRI. Whence do you infer this?

SOC. I will tell you. For on the day after, or on the very day in which the ship arrives, it is necessary that I should die.

CRI. Those that have power over these things say so.

SOC. I do not, therefore, think it will come this, but the next day. But I infer this from a certain dream which I saw this night a little before you came; and you appear very opportunely not to have disturbed me.

CRI. But what was that dream?

b   SOC. A certain woman, beautiful, of a pleasing aspect and in white raiment, seemed to approach, and calling me to say, The third day hence, O Socrates, you will arrive at the fertile Phthia.[‡]

CRI. What a strange dream, Socrates!

SOC. Manifest however, as it appears to me, O Crito.

---

† See the *Phædo* [58a - c].

‡ What this woman said to Socrates in a dream is taken from the ninth book of the *Iliad*, and belongs to the speech of Achilles on the embassy to him from Agamemnon. The original is ηματι κεν τριτατῳ Φθιην εριβωλον ικοιμην. As Socrates applied what is here said in the dream to a returning to his true country, the intelligible world, he confirms the explanation of the Trojan war which we have given from Proclus in the Notes on the *Phædrus*. [TTS vol. XI, note 7, p. 400.]

CRI. Very much so, as it seems. But, O blessed Socrates, be now persuaded by me, and save yourself. For, if you die, not one calamity only will befall me; but, exclusively of being deprived of you, an associate so necessary as I never have found any other to be, those who do not well know me and you, will think that I might have saved you if I had been willing to spend my money, but that I neglected to do so. Though what can be more base than such an opinion, by which I should appear to value riches more than my friends? For the multitude will not be persuaded that you were unwilling to depart hence, though we endeavoured to effect your escape.

SOC. But why, O blessed Crito, should we so much respect the opinion of the multitude? For the most worthy men, whose opinion ought rather to be regarded, will think these things to have been so transacted as they were.

CRI. Nevertheless you see, Socrates, that it is necessary to pay attention to the opinion of the multitude. For the present circumstances now evince that the multitude can effect not the smallest of evils, but nearly the greatest, if any one is calumniated by them.

SOC. I wish, O Crito, the multitude could effect the greatest evils, that they might also accomplish the greatest good: for then it would be well. But now they can do neither of these. For they can neither make a man wise, not destitute of wisdom; but they do whatever casually takes place.

CRI. Let these things be so. But answer me, Socrates, whether your concern for me and the rest of your associates prevents you from escaping hence, lest we should be molested by calumniators, as having fraudulently taken you from hence, and be forced either to lose all our property, or a great sum of money, or to suffer something else beside this? For, if you fear any such thing, bid farewell to it. For we shall be just in saving you from this danger, and, if it were requisite, from one even greater than this. But be persuaded by me, and do not act otherwise.

SOC. I pay attention to these things, Crito, and also to many others.

CRI. Do not, therefore, dread these things. For those who have agreed to save you, and to take you from hence, demand no great sum for this purpose. And, in the next place, do you not see how poor your calumniators are, and that on this account your liberty may be purchased at a small expense? My property too, which I think is sufficient, is at your service. And if, out of regard to me, you do not think fit to accept my offer, these guests here are readily disposed to pay what may be necessary. One also among them, Simmias the Theban, has bought with him a sum of money sufficient for this purpose. Cebes, too, and very many others are ready to do the same: so that, as I said, neither fearing these things, should you hesitate to save yourself, not should you be troubled on leaving the city (as in court you said you should) from not knowing how to conduct yourself. For in many other

c　places, wherever you may go, you will be beloved. And if you are disposed to go to Thessaly, you will there find my guests, who will pay you every attention, and will render your abode there so secure, that no one in Thessaly will molest you. Besides this, Socrates, neither do you appear to me to attempt a just thing, in betraying when you might same yourself; and in endeavouring to promote the earnest wishes of your enemies, who strive to destroy you. To this I may also add, that you appear to me to betray your own children, whom it is incumbent on you to maintain and educate; and, as far as pertains to you, leave them

d　to the guidance of chance; though it is likely that such things will happen to them as orphans are wont to experience. However, either it is not proper to beget children, or it is requisite to labour in rearing and instructing them when begotten. But you appear to me to have chosen the most indolent mode of conduct; though it is proper that you should choose such things as a good and brave man would adopt, especially as you profess to have made virtue the object of your attention through the

e　whole of life. I am, therefore, ashamed both for you, and those familiars who are our associates as well as yours, lest the whole affair concerning you should appear to have been accomplished through a certain cowardice on our part. And in the first place, your standing a trial which might have been prevented; in the next place, your defence; and, in the last place, the extremity to which you are now brought, will

46a　be placed to the account of our viciousness and cowardice, and will be considered as so many ridiculous circumstances which might have been avoided, if we had exerted ourselves even in a trifling degree. See, therefore, O Socrates, whether these things, besides being evil, will not also be disgraceful both to you and us. Advise then with yourself quickly, though indeed there is no time for consultation; for on the following night all this must be done. But, if we delay, it will be impossible to effect your escape. By all means, therefore, be persuaded by me, Socrates, and do not in any respect otherwise.

b　Soc. My dear Crito, your alacrity is very commendable, if it is attended with a certain rectitude; but if not, by how much the greater it is, by so much is it the more blameable. It is necessary, therefore, to consider whether these things ought to be done or not. For I am a man of that kind, not only now but always, who acts in obedience to that reason which appears to me on mature deliberation to be the best. And

the reasons which I have formerly adopted, I am not able now to reject in my present fortune, but they nearly appear to me to be similar: and
c I venerate and honour the same principles as formerly; so that, unless we have any thing better to adduce at present than these, be well assured that I shall not comply with your request, not though the power of the multitude should endeavour to terrify us like children, by threatening more bonds and deaths, and ablations of property.

CRI. How, therefore, may we consider these things in the best manner?

SOC. If, in the first place, we resume that which you said concerning opinions, considering whether it was well said by us or not, that to
d some opinions we ought to pay attention, and to others not; or rather indeed, before it was necessary that I should die, it was well said, but now it becomes evident that it was asserted for the sake of discussion, though in reality it was merely a jest and a trifle. I desire, however, O Crito, to consider, in common with you, whether that assertion appears to me in my present condition to be different, or the same, and whether that assertion appears to me in my present condition to be different, or the same, and whether we shall bid farewell to or be persuaded by it. But thus I think it is every where said by those who appear to say any thing pertinently, that, as I just now asserted of the opinions which men
e opine, some ought to be very much attended to, and others not. By the Gods, Crito, does not this appear to you to be well said? For you, so far as relates to human power, are out of danger of dying tomorrow, and such a calamity as the present will not seduce you into a false decision. Consider then: does it not appear to you to have been asserted with sufficient rectitude, that it is not fit to reverence all the opinions
47a of men, but that some should be honoured and others not? Nor yet the opinions of all men, but those of some and not those of others? What do you say? Are not these things well said?

CRI. Well.

SOC. Are not worthy opinions, therefore, to be honoured, but base opinions not?

CRI. They are.

SOC. And are not worthy opinions those of wise men; but base opinions those of the unwise?

CRI. Undoubtedly.

b SOC. Come then, let us again consider how things of this kind were asserted. Whether does he who is conversant in gymnastic exercises pay attention to the praise and blame and opinion of every man, or of that one man alone who is a physician, of the preceptor of boys in their bodily exercises?

CRI. Of that one alone.

SOC. Is it not, therefore, proper that he should fear the blame and embrace the praise of that one, but not the praise and blame of the multitude?

CRI. Evidently.

SOC. In this manner, therefore, he ought to act and exercise himself, and also to eat and drink, which appears fit to the one who presides and knows, rather than in that which may appear to be proper to all others.

CRI. Certainly.

c   SOC. Be it so. But if he is disobedient to that one, and disregards his opinion and his praise, but honours the opinion and praise of the multitude, who know nothing, will he not suffer some evil?

CRI. How is it possible he should not?

SOC. But what is this evil, whether does it tend, and to which of the things pertaining to him who is disobedient?

CRI. Evidently to his body, for this it corrupts.

SOC. You speak well. We must form the same conclusion, therefore, Crito, in other things, that we may not run though all of them. With respect, therefore, to things just and unjust, base and beautiful, good and evil, and which are now the subjects of our consultation, whether ought

d   we to follow the opinion of the multitude, and to dread it, or that of one man if there is any one knowing in these things, whom we ought to reverence and fear rather than all others; to whom if we are not obedient, we shall corrupt and injure that which becomes better by the just, but is destroyed by the unjust? Or is this nothing?

CRI. I think, Socrates, we ought to follow the opinion of that one.

e   SOC. Come then, if not being persuaded by the opinion of those that are judges, we destroy that which becomes better by the salubrious, but is corrupted by the insalubrious, can we live after this destruction? But is not this very thing of which we are speaking the body?

CRI. Yes.

SOC. Can we, therefore, live after the body is depraved and corrupted?

CRI. By no means.

48a   SOC. But can we live when that is corrupted which is injured by the unjust, but benefited by the just? Or shall we think that to be viler than the body, whatever it may be, pertaining to us, about which justice and injustice subsist?

CRI. By no means.

SOC. It is, therefore, more honourable.

CRI. By far.

SOC. We should not, therefore, O best of men, be so very much concerned about what the multitude say of us, but what that one man who knows what is just and unjust, and what truth itself is, asserts respecting us. So that you did not act rightly at first, in introducing the opinion of the multitude concerning things just, beautiful and good, and the contraries of these, as that to which we ought to pay attention. Though some one may say that the multitude are able to destroy us.

CRI. Some one, Socrates, may indeed say so.

SOC. True. But, O wonderful man, the assertion which we have discussed appears to me to be dissimilar and prior to this: and again consider whether this is still granted by us, that we are not to admit the merely living, but living well, to be a thing of the greatest consequence.

CRI. It is granted.

SOC. And is this also granted, or not, that it is the same thing to live well, beautifully, and justly?

CRI. It is.

SOC. From what has been assented to, therefore, this must be considered, whether it is just for me to endeavour to depart hence, the Athenians not dismissing me, or whether it is not just. And if it should appear to be just indeed, we should endeavour to accomplish it; but if not, we must bid farewell to the attempt. For as to the considerations which you adduce concerning money, opinion, and the education of children, see, Crito, whether these are not in reality the reflections of the vulgar, who rashly put men to death, and if it were in their power would recall them to life, and this without being at all guided by intellect. But by us, since reason requires it, nothing else is to be considered than as we just now said, whether we shall act justly in giving money and thanks to those who may lead me hence; or whether in reality, both we that are led from hence and those that lead us, shall not in all these things act unjustly. And if it should appear that we in so doing shall act unjustly, we must by no means pay attention to these things, rather than to the consideration whether we shall do any thing unjustly, not even if it should be necessary for us to die, staying here and being quiet, or to suffer any thing else whatever.

CRI. You appear to me, Socrates, to speak well; but see what is to be done.

SOC. Let us consider, O good man, in common; and if you can in any respect contradict what I say, contradict me, and I will assent to you; but if you cannot, cease, O blessed man, to repeat often to me the same thing, that I ought to depart hence, though the Athenians are unwilling.

For I shall think it a great thing if you can persuade me thus to act, but not if you attempt this contrary to my will. See then, whether the beginning of this consideration satisfies you, and endeavour to answer the interrogation in such a way as you especially think it proper.

49a   CRI. I will endeavour.

SOC. Shall we say then, that we should by no means willingly act unjustly? Or may we in a certain respect act unjustly, and in a certain respect not? Or is to act unjustly by no means neither good nor beautiful, as we have often confessed before, and as we just now said? Or are all those things which we formerly assented to dissipated in these few days; and has it for some time been concealed from us, that though we are so old, yet in seriously discoursing with each other, we have in

b   no respect differed from children? Or does it not thus subsist more than any thing, as we then said, whether the multitude admit it or not? And whether it be necessary that we should suffer things still more grievous, or such as are milder than these, at the same time shall we say or not that to act unjustly is evil and base to him who thus acts?

CRI. We shall say so.

SOC. By no means, therefore, ought we to act unjustly.

CRI. We ought not.

SOC. Neither, therefore, ought he who is injured to return the injury, as the multitude think, since it is by no means proper to act unjustly.

c   CRI. So it appears.

SOC. But what then? Is it proper to do evil to any one, O Crito, or not?

CRI. It is not proper, Socrates.

SOC. But what? Is it just to repay evil with evil, as the multitude say, or is it not just?

CRI. By no means.

SOC. For he who does evil to men, differs in no respect from him who acts unjustly.

CRI. Your assertion is true.

d   SOC. Neither, therefore, is it proper to return an injury, nor to do evil to any man, however you may be injured by him. But see, Crito, while you acknowledge these things, that you do not assent to them contrary to your opinion. For I know that these things appear to and are opined by very few. But those to whom these things appear, and those to whom they do not, disagree with each other in their decisions; and it is necessary that these should despise each other, while they look to each other's deliberations. Do you therefore consider, and very diligently, whether it thus appears to you in common with me, and whether

deliberating we should begin from hence, that it is never right either to do an injury, or to return an injury, or when suffering evil to revenge it be doing evil in return; or, whether you will depart and not
e   agree with us in this principle. For it thus appears to me both formerly and now; but if it in any respect appears otherwise to you, speak and inform me. And if you acquiesce in what has been said above, hear what follows.

CRI. But I do acquiesce and accord with you. Speak, therefore.

SOC. I will say then that which is consequent to this, or rather I will ask you, whether when a man has promised to do things that are just, he ought to do them, or break his promise.

CRI. He ought to do them.

50a   SOC. From these things then thus consider. If we should depart hence without the consent of the city, shall we do evil to certain persons, and those such as we ought not in the smallest degree to injure, or shall we not? And shall we acquiesce in those things which we assented to as being just, or shall we not?

CRI. I cannot reply to your question, Socrates: for I do not understand it.

SOC. But thus consider. If to us, intending to escape from hence, or in whatever manner it may be requisite to denominate it, the Laws and the Republic should present themselves in a body, and thus address us, -
Tell us, O Socrates, what is it you intend to do? Do you conceive that by this thing which you attempt, you will destroy any thing else than,
b   as far as you are able, us the Laws, and the whole city? Or does it appear to you to be possible for that city to subsist and not be subverted, in which Justice is not only without strength, but is likewise divested of its authority and corrupted by private persons? - What should we say, Crito, to these things, and to others of a similar kind? For much might be said, and particularly by rhetoricians, on the subversion of that law which provides that sentences once passed shall
c   not be infringed. Shall we say to them that the city has not passed an equitable sentence upon us? Shall we say this, or something else?

CRI. This, by Jupiter, Socrates.

SOC. Will not the Laws then thus address us? O Socrates, has it not been admitted by us and you, that you should acquiesce in the sentence which the city has passed? If, therefore, we should wonder at the Laws thus speaking, perhaps they would say, Be not surprised, O Socrates, at what we have asserted, but answer, since you are accustomed both to interrogate and reply. For what is the charge against us and the city, for
d   which you endeavour to destroy us? Did we not first beget you? And

was it not through us that your father married your mother, and planted you? Tell us, therefore, whether you blame these laws of ours concerning marriage as improper? I should say I do not blame them. But do you blame those laws concerning the nurture and education of children in which you were yourself instructed? Or did not the laws framed for this purpose order in a becoming manner when they commanded your father to instruct you in music and gymnastic? I should say they ordered well. Since then we begot and nourished and educated you, can you deny that both you and your progenitors are our offspring and servants? And if this be the case, do you think that there is an equality[†] of justice between us and you, and that it is just for you to attempt to do those things to us which we endeavour to do to you? Or will you admit that there is no equality of justice between you and your father, or master, if you happen to have either of them, so that you are not to return to these any evil you may suffer from them, nor, when they reproach you, contradict them, nor, when they strike you, strike them again, not do many other things of a similar nature; but that against your country and the Laws it is lawful for you to act in this manner, so that if we endeavour to destroy you, thinking it to be just, you also should endeavour, as far as you are able, to destroy in return, us the Laws and your country, and should say that in so doing you act justly, - you who in reality make virtue the object of your care? Or, are you so wise as to be ignorant that your country is more honourable, venerable and holy, than your mother and father, and all the rest of your progenitors, and ranks higher both among the Gods and among men endued with intellect? That it is also more necessary for a man to venerate, obey and assent to his country, when conducting itself with severity, than to his father? Likewise that he should be persuaded by it, and do what it orders? That he should quietly suffer, if it orders him to suffer? And that, if it commands him to be beaten, or confined in bonds, or sends him to battle to be wounded or slain, he should do these things, and that it is just to comply? And that he should neither decline nor recede from nor desert his rank; but in war, in a court of justice, and every where, the commands of the city and his country should be obeyed; or he should persuade his country to that which is naturally just; but that it is not holy to offer violence either to a mother or a father, and much less to one's country? - What shall we say to these

---

† Wholes in the order of nature are more excellent than parts; and in consequence of this, as being more honourable, there is no reciprocity of obligation between the two.

things, Crito? Shall we acknowledge that the Laws speak the truth or not?

CRI. To me it appears that they do.

SOC. Consider, therefore, O Socrates, perhaps the Law will say, whether our assertion is true, that your present attempt against us is unjust. For we are the authors of your birth, we nourished, we educated you, imparting both to you and all the other citizens all the good in our power, at the same time proclaiming, that every Athenian who is willing has the liberty of departing wherever he pleases, with all his property, if after having explored and seen the affairs of the city, and us the Laws, we should not be constituted according to his wishes. Nor does any one of us the Laws impede or forbid any one of you from migrating into some colony, or any other place, with all his property, if we and the city do not please him. But, on the other hand, if any one of you continues to live here after he has seen the manner in which we administer justice, and govern the city in other particulars, we now say, that he in reality acknowledges to us, that he will do such things as we may command. We also say, that he who is not obedient is triply unjust, because he is disobedient to his begetters, and to those by whom he was educated; and because, having promised to be persuaded by us, he is neither persuaded, nor does he persuade us, if we do any thing improperly; though at the same time we only propose, and do not fiercely command him to do what we order, but leave to his choice one of two things, either to persuade us, or to obey our mandates; and yet he does neither of these.

And we say that you also, O Socrates, will be obnoxious to these crimes if you execute what you intend to do; nor will you be the least, but the most obnoxious of all the Athenians. If, therefore, I should ask them the reason of this, they would perhaps justly reproach me by saying, that I promised to submit to all these conditions beyond the rest of the Athenians. For they would say, This, O Socrates, is a great argument with us, that both we and the city were pleasing to you; that you especially of all the Athenians would never have dwelt in it, if it had not been particularly agreeable to you. For you never left the city for any of the public spectacles except once, when you went to the Isthmian games, nor did you ever go elsewhere, except in your military expeditions. You never went any other journey like other men; nor had you ever any desire of seeing any other city, or becoming acquainted with any other laws; but we and our city were sufficient for you, so exceedingly were you attached to us, and so much did you consent to be governed by our mandates. Besides, you have procreated children in this city, in consequence of being pleased with it. Further still, in this very judicial process, you might have been condemned to exile, if you had been willing, and might then have executed with the consent of the city what you now attempt without it. Then however you carried yourself loftily, as one who would not be indignant, if it were requisite that you should die; but you preferred, as you said, death to exile. But now you are neither ashamed of those assertions, nor do you revere us

d the Laws, since you endeavour to destroy us. You also do that which the most vile slave would do, by endeavouring to make your escape contrary to the compacts and agreements according to which you consented to become a member of this community. In the first place, therefore, answer us this very thing, whether we speak the truth in asserting, that you consented to be governed by us in reality, and not merely in words? Do we in asserting this speak the truth? What shall we say to these things, Crito? Can we say any thing else than that we assent to them?

CRI. It is necessary so to do, Socrates.

e SOC. Do you not then, they will say, violate these compacts and agreements between us; which you consented to neither from necessity nor through deception, nor in consequence of being compelled to deliberate in a short time; but during the space of seventy years, in which you might have departed if you had been dissatisfied with us, and the compacts had appeared to you to be unjust? You however neither preferred Lacedæmon nor Crete, which you are perpetually saying are governed by good laws, nor any other city of the Greeks or Barbarians;

53a but you have been less out of Athens than the lame and the blind, and other mutilated persons. So much did the city and we the Laws please you beyond the rest of the Athenians. For who can be pleased with a city without the laws? But now you do not abide by the compacts. You will however abide by them if you are persuaded by us, Socrates, and do not become ridiculous by escaping from the city.

b For consider what advantage can be derived either to yourself or your friends by violating those compacts. For in consequence of your escaping from hence, it is nearly evident that your friends will be exposed to the danger either of banishment, or of the loss of their property. And as for yourself, if you retire to any neighbouring city, whether Thebes or Megara (for both are governed by good laws), you will be considered, Socrates, as an enemy to their polity. And such as have any regard for their country will look upon you as a corrupter of the laws. You will also confirm them in their good opinion of your

c judges, who will appear to have very properly condemned you. For he who is a corrupter of the laws will very much appear to be a corrupter of youth and of stupid men. Will you then avoid these well-governed cities, and men of the most elegant manners? Supposing you should, will it, therefore, be worth while for you to live? Or, should you go to these cities, will you not blush, Socrates, to discourse about the same things as you did here, *viz.* that virtue and justice, legal institutes, and the laws, should be objects of the greatest attention to men? And do you not think that this conduct of Socrates would be very indecorous? You must necessarily think so. But perhaps, avoiding these cities, you will go to Thessaly, to the guests of Crito. For there there is the greatest disorder and intemperance. And perhaps they will willingly hear you relating how ridiculously you escaped from prison, investing yourself with a certain apparatus, such as a skin, or something else which those that make their escape are accustomed to provide, and thus altering your usual appearance.

Do you think no one will say, that you, though an old man, and likely to live but a little longer, have dared to desire life with such sordid avidity, and to transgress the greatest laws? Perhaps this will be the case, though you should not have offended any one. But if you should, you will hear, Socrates, many things unworthy of you. You will however live obnoxious, and in subjection to all men. But what will you do in Thessaly besides feasting? having come to Thessaly as to a supper. And where shall we find those discourses concerning justice, and the other virtues? - But do you wish to live for the sake of your children, that you may nurture and instruct them? What then? Bringing them to Thessaly, will you there educate them, making them to be stranger guests, that they may also derive this advantage from you? Or, if you should not do this, but should leave them here, will they be better nurtured and educated in your absence? for your friends will take care of them. Do you suppose then that your children will be taken care of by your friends if you go to Thessaly, and that they will be neglected by them if you depart to Hades? If indeed any advantage is to be derived from those that call themselves your friends, it is proper to think that they will not.

But, O Socrates, being persuaded by us your nurses, neither pay more attention to your children, nor to life, not to any thing else than to justice, that, when you arrive at Hades, you may be able to defend all these particulars to the rulers there. For if, transgressing the laws, you should thus act, it will neither be better, nor more just, nor more holy to yourself, nor to any one of your friends; nor will it be more advantageous to you when you arrive at Hades. But you will depart, if c   you do depart, not injured by us the Laws, but by men. If however you should so disgracefully escape, returning injury for injury, and evil for evil, transgressing your agreements and compacts with us, and injuring those whom you ought not to injure in the smallest degree, *viz.* yourself, your friends, your country, and us; - in this case, we shall be indignant with you as long as you live; and in another life, our brothers the Laws who reside in Hades will not benevolently receive you; knowing that you attempted, as far as you were able, to destroy us. Let not Crito,

d   therefore, rather than us, persuade you to do what he says.

   Be well assured, my dear friend Crito, that I seem to hear these things, just as those who are agitated with Corybantic fury appear to hear the melody of pipes. And the sound of these words, like the humming of bees, in my ears, renders me incapable of hearing any thing else. You see then what appears to me at present; and if you should say any thing contrary to these things, you will speak in vain. At the same time, if you think that any thing more should be done, tell me.

   CRI. But, Socrates, I have nothing further to say.

e   SOC. Desist, therefore, Crito, and let us adopt this conduct, since Divinity persuades us thus to act.

THE

PHÆDO

A DIALOGUE

ON

IMMORTALITY OF THE SOUL

INTRODUCTION

The following dialogue is no less remarkable for the masterly manner of its composition, than for the different effects which the perusal of it is related to have formerly produced. For the arguments which it contains for the immortality of the soul, are said to have incited Cleombrotus to suicide, and to have dissuaded Olympiodorus, an eminent Platonic philosopher, from its perpetration. Indeed, it is by no means wonderful that a person like Cleombrotus, ignorant (as his conduct evinces) that the death so much inculcated in this dialogue is a philosophic, and not a natural death, should be led to an action which is in most cases highly criminal. This ignorance however is not peculiar to Cleombrotus, since I am afraid there are scarcely any of the present day who know that it is one thing for the soul to be separated from the body, and another for the body to be separated from the soul, and that the former is by no means a necessary consequence of the latter.

This philosophic death, or separation of the soul from the body, which forms one of the most leading particulars of the dialogue, is no other than the exercise of the cathartic virtues, of which the reader will find a copious explanation in the following notes. That these virtues are not figments of the latter Platonists, as some ignorant verbalists have rashly asserted, is not only evident from the first part of this dialogue, but from the Golden Pythagorean verses, which are certainly of greater antiquity than even the writings of Plato: for the following is one of the precepts in these verses -

Αλλ᾽ ειργου βρωτων, ων ειπομεν, εν τε καθαρμοις,
Εν τε γυσει ψυχης κρινω·

i.e. "Abstain from the foods of which we have spoken in the PURIFICATIONS and SOLUTION of the soul." And the employment of cathartic virtue entirely consists in *purifying* the soul and liberating it from all attachment to the body, as far as the condition of its union with it will permit.

Of the arguments adduced by Socrates in this dialogue, some, as will be shown in the notes, only demonstrate that the soul subsisted prior to, and will survive the dissolution of, the body, but do not prove that it has a *perpetual* existence; but others demonstrate, and with an invincible force, that the soul is *truly immortal*. Should it seem strange, and to those who are not deeply skilled in the philosophy of Plato it doubtless will, that Socrates in no part of this dialogue introduces that argument for the immortality of the soul which he adopts in the *Phædrus*, an argument drawn from the rational soul being the origin of motion, and which may be said to possess adamantine strength, - it is necessary to observe, in answer to this doubt, that, in the *Phædrus*, Socrates demonstrates the immortality of every rational soul, *viz.* the human, dæmoniacal and divine; but in the *Phædo* he alone demonstrates the immortality of the human soul.

But though some of the arguments in this dialogue are perfectly demonstrative, yet certain modern writers, from not understanding, have not only attempted to invalidate them, but have been induced to imagine that Socrates himself, convinced of their insufficiency, insinuates in the course of the dialogue the necessity of a divine revelation in order to obtain a full conviction of this most important truth. As this is an opinion no less dangerous than erroneous, I shall present the reader with the passage that gave occasion to it, and then unfold to him from ancient sources its genuine explanation.

About the middle of this dialogue,[85c] then, Simmias observes as follows:- "As to myself, Socrates, I am perhaps of the same opinion about these particulars as yourself; that to know them clearly in the present life is either impossible, or a thing very difficult to obtain. But not to argue about what has been said in every possible way, and to desist before, by an arduous investigation on all sides, weariness is produced, can only take place among indolent and effeminate men. For it is necessary in things of this kind either to learn or to discover the manner of their subsistence; or, if both these are impossible, then by receiving the best of human reasons, and that which is the most difficult of confutation, to venture upon this as on a raft, and fail in it through the ocean of life, unless some one should be able to be carried more safely and with less danger by means of a firmer vehicle, or a certain *divine reason*." Here, in the first place, it must be observed, that it is Simmias who thus speaks, an imperfect disciple of his great master, as is evident from many parts of this dialogue, and not Socrates himself. And in the next place, though it should be urged that Socrates himself is here said by Simmias to have admitted that "to know these particulars[†] clearly in the present life is either impossible or a thing very difficult to obtain," it must be observed, that Socrates thus speaks from a deep

---

† *Viz.* the particulars pertaining to the past and future existence of the soul [85c].

conviction that this sublime truth, the immortality of the soul, could not be fully comprehended by his auditors, who were very far from being masters in philosophy, and that this must be the case with the multitude in general. Hence, he says, it is either impossible or very difficult to obtain this knowledge. - To the *multitude* it is impossible, and to the *few* very difficult, because it requires many preparatory disciplines, and a genius naturally adapted to sublime speculations.

In the third place, by *a firmer vehicle, or a certain divine reason*, Socrates does not allude to a divine tradition, since this affords no higher evidence than that of opinion. It is well observed, therefore, by Olympiodorus, in his MS. Scholia on this dialogue, that by this θειος λογος, or *divine reason*, we must understand *self-beholding intellect*, which, agreeably to Plato's description of it in the *Phædrus*,[250b] associates with Deity itself. Τις ο ασφαλεστερος, και ακινδυνοτερος, και βεβαιοτερος, και θειος λογος; ου δηπου ως φασιν ο θεοθεν εκδοθεις, δοξαστικος γαρ ο γε τοιουτος· αλλ᾽ εστιν ο ειρημενος αυτοπτικος νους, ο θεῳ τῳ οντι συνων, ως εν Φαιδρῳ. In order however to understand what Olympiodorus means by *self-beholding intellect*, it is necessary to observe, that there are four modes of knowledge which we are able to acquire in the present life. The first of these results from opinion, by which we learn *that* a thing is, without knowing *the why*: and this constitutes that part of knowledge which was called by Aristotle and Plato παιδεια, or erudition; and which consists in moral instructions, for the purpose of purifying ourselves from immoderate passions. But the second is produced by the sciences; in which, from establishing certain principles as hypotheses, we educe necessary conclusions, and arrive at the knowledge of *the why* (as in the mathematical sciences); but at the same time we are ignorant with respect to the principles of these conclusions, because they are merely hypothetical. The third species of knowledge is that which results from Plato's dialectic; in which, by a progression through all ideas, we arrive at the first principle of things, and at that which is no longer hypothetical; and this by dividing some things and analysing others, by producing many things from one thing, and one thing from many. But the fourth species is still more simple than this; because it no longer uses analysations or compositions, definitions or demonstrations, but by a simple and self-visive energy of intellect speculates things themselves, and by intuition and contact becomes one with the object of its perception; and this energy is the *divine reason* which Plato speaks of in the present passage, and which far transcends the evidence of the most divine revelation; since this last is at best but founded in opinion, while the former surpasses even the indubitable certainty of science.

In short, that Socrates, and consequently Plato, firmly believed in this most important truth, is evident from the *Phædrus* and the tenth book of the *Republic*; and in the seventh Epistle[335a] of Plato there is the following remarkable passage:- πειθεσθαι δε ουτως αει χρη τοις παλαιοις τε και ιεροις λογοις η δη μηνυουσιν η μιν αθανατον ψυχην ειναι, δικαστας τε ισχειν, και τινειν τας μεγιστας τιμωριας, οταν τις απαλλαχθη του σωματος. *i.e.*"It is proper indeed always to believe in *ancient and sacred discourses*, which announce to us that the soul is immortal, and that it has judges of its conduct, and suffers the greatest punishments when it is liberated from the body." From which passage we also learn, that the immortality of the soul is a doctrine of the highest antiquity, and that it was delivered in the sacred writings of the heathens.

I shall only observe further, that the character of Socrates, as exhibited in this dialogue, in the *Crito*, and in the *Apology*, is so transcendently great, and displays such a perfection of justice, fortitude and piety, that it may be considered as a most splendid instance of the moral and intellectual excellence which human nature is capable of attaining, and an example of consummate wisdom and virtue, which will be imitated by the few in all future ages.

THE

PHÆDO

PERSONS OF THE DIALOGUE

ECHECRATES and PHÆDO

57a ECHEC. Were you present, Phædo, with Socrates that day when he drank the poison in prison? or did you hear an account of it from any other?

PHÆD. I myself, Echecrates, was present.

ECHEC. What then was his discourse previous to his death? and how did he die? for I should be very glad to hear the account: for scarcely does any one of the Phliasian[†] citizens now visit Athens; and it is some time since any stranger has arrived from thence who might afford us

b some clear information about these particulars. All indeed that we heard was, that he died through drinking the poison; but he who acquainted us with this had nothing further to say about other particulars of his death.

PHÆD. What! did you not hear the manner in which he was tried?

58a ECHEC. Yes: a certain person related this to us; and we wondered, as his sentence was passed so long ago, that he should not die till a considerable time after. What then, Phædo, was the reason of this?

PHÆD. A certain fortune happened to him, Echecrates: for, the day before his trial, the stern of that ship was crowned which the Athenians send every year to Delos.

ECHEC. But what is the meaning of this?

PHÆD. This is the ship, as the Athenians say, in which Theseus formerly carried the twice seven young children to Crete, and preserved

b both them and himself. The Athenians, therefore, as it is reported, then vowed to Apollo, that if the children were preserved, they would lead every year a sacred spectacle to Delos; which, from that time, they

---

† Phlius was a city of Peloponnesus situated not far from the Isthmus. Vid. Strab. lib. viii. Pausan. in Corinth. et Steph. de Urb. et Pop.

regularly send every year to the God. As soon, therefore, as the preparations for the sacred spectacle commence, the law orders that the city shall be purified, and that no one shall be put to death by a public decree till the ship has arrived at Delos, and again returned to Athens. But this sometimes takes a long time in accomplishing, when the winds impede their passage; but the festival itself commences when the priest of Apollo has crowned the stern of the ship. Now this, as I told you, took place on the day preceding the trial; and on this account that length of time happened to Socrates in prison between his sentence and his death.

c

ECHEC. And what, Phædo, were the circumstances respecting his death? what were his sayings and actions? and who of his familiars were present with him? or would not the magistrates suffer that any should be admitted to him, so that he died deprived of the presence of his friends?

d   PHÆD. By no means; but some, and indeed many, were present with him.

ECHEC. Endeavour to relate all these particulars to us in the clearest manner, unless you have some business which may prevent you.

PHÆD. But I am at leisure, and will endeavour to gratify your request: for indeed to call to mind Socrates, whether I myself speak or hear others, is to me always the most pleasant of all things.

ECHEC. Truly, Phædo, others who hear you will be affected in the same manner: but endeavour, as much as you are able, to narrate every circumstance in the most accurate manner.

e   PHÆD. And indeed I myself, who was present, was wonderfully affected; for I was not influenced with pity, like one present at the death of a familiar: for this man, O Echecrates, appeared to me to be blessed, when I considered his manner and discourses, and his intrepid and generous death. Hence it appeared to me, that he did not descend to Hades without a divine destiny, but that there also he would be in a

59a happy condition, if this can ever be asserted of any one. On this account I was entirely uninfluenced with pity, though apparently I ought not to have been, on so mournful an occasion; nor yet again was I influenced by pleasure through philosophical converse, as I used to be; for our discourses were of this kind. But, to speak ingenuously, a certain wonderful passion, and an unusual mixture of pleasure and grief, were present with me, produced by considering that he must in a very short time die. And, indeed, all of us who were present were nearly affected in the same manner, at one time laughing, and at another b weeping: but this was eminently the case with one of us, Apollodorus; for you know the man, and his manner of behaviour.

ECHEC. How is it possible that I should not?

PHÆD. He, therefore, was remarkably affected in this manner; and I myself, and others, experienced great trouble and confusion.

ECHEC. Who then, Phædo, happened to be present?

PHÆD. Of the natives, Apollodorus, Critobulus, and his father Crito, were present; likewise Hermogenes, Epigenes, Æschines, and Antisthenes,[†] and besides these, Ctesippus[‡] the Pœanian, Menexenus, and some other Athenians were present: but Plato I think was sick.

ECHEC. Were there no strangers?

c PHÆD. Yes: Simmias the Theban, Cebes,[§] and Phædondes; and among the Megarensians, Euclid and Terpsion.

ECHEC. But what! were not Aristippus[◊] and Cleombrotus there?

PHÆD. By no means: for they were said to be at Ægina.

ECHEC. Was any other person present?

PHÆD. I think those I have mentioned were nearly all.

ECHEC. Will you now then relate what were his discourses?

d PHÆD. I will endeavour to relate the whole to you from the beginning. For we were always accustomed to visit Socrates, myself and others meeting in the morning at the place where he was tried, for it was very near to the prison. Here we waited every day till the prison was opened, discoursing among ourselves, for it was not opened very early in the morning; but, as soon as we could be admitted, we went to Socrates, and generally spent the whole day with him. And then, indeed, we met together sooner than usual; for the day before, when we

e left the prison, we heard that the ship from Delos was returned. We determined, therefore, among ourselves, to come very early in the

---

† This Antisthenes, as principally imitating Socrates in his endurance and contempt of pleasure, was the author of the Cynic sect, and the preceptor of Diogenes.

‡ See the *Euthydemus*, in which the disposition of Ctesippus is described.

§ This Cebes is the author of the allegorical table now extant.

◊ A philosopher of Cyrene, and founder of the Cyrenaic sect. What is here said concerning the absence of Aristippus and Cleombrotus is well explained by Demetrius in his book περι Ερμηνειας. "Plato, he observes, says this in order to reprove Aristippus and Cleombrotus, who were feasting in Ægina at the time that Socrates was in prison, and did not fail to see their friend and master, though they were then at the entrance of the Athenian harbour. Plato however does not clearly relate these particulars, because his narration would have been an open defamation."

morning to the usual place; and we met together accordingly: but when we arrived, the gaoler, who used to attend upon us, told us to wait, and not to enter till he called us. For, says he, the eleven magistrates are now freeing Socrates from his bonds, and announcing to him that he must die to-day. But not long after this he returned, and ordered us to enter. When we entered, we found Socrates just freed from his fetters, but Xantippe (you know her) holding one of his children, and sitting by him. As soon, therefore, as Xantippe saw us, she began to lament in a most violent manner, and said such things as are usual with women in affliction; and among the rest, Socrates (says she), this is the last time your friends will speak to you, or you to them. But Socrates looking upon Crito, Crito (says he) let some one take her home. Upon which some of Crito's domestics led her away, beating herself, and weeping bitterly. But Socrates, sitting upright on the bed, drew up his leg, and, stroking it with his hand, said at the same time, What a wonderful thing is this, my friends, which men call *the pleasant and agreeable*! and how admirably is it affected by nature towards that which appears to be its contrary, *the painful*! for they are unwilling to be present with us both together; and yet, if any person pursues and receives the one, he is almost always under a necessity of receiving the other, as if both of them depended from one summit. And it seems to me (says he), that if Æsop had perceived this he would have composed a fable from it, and would have informed us, that Divinity, being willing to reconcile contending natures, but not being able to accomplish this design, conjoined their summits in a nature one and the same; and that hence it comes to pass, that whoever partakes of the one is soon after connected with the other. And this, as it appears, is the case with myself at present; for the pain which was before in my leg, through the bond, is now succeeded by a pleasant sensation.

But here Cebes replying, said, By Jupiter, Socrates, you have very opportunely caused me to recollect: for certain persons have asked me concerning those poems which you composed, *viz.* the Fables of Æsop which you versified, and your exordium to Apollo, and other pieces of composition; and, among the rest, Evenus lately inquired with what design you did this after coming here, when before you have never attempted any thing of the kind. If, therefore, you have any desire that I may have an answer ready for Evenus, when he again interrogates me on this occasion (and I am certain that he will do so), tell me what I must say to him. You may truly inform him (says he), Cebes, that I did not compose these verses with any design of rivalling him, or his poems

60a

b

c

d

e (for I knew that this would be no easy matter); but that I might try to explore the meaning of certain dreams, and that I might make a proper expiation, if this should happen to be the music which they have often ordered me to exercise. For in the past part of my life the same dream has often occurred to me, exhibiting at different times a different appearance, yet always advising me the same thing; for it said, Socrates, make and exercise music. And indeed, in the former part of my life, I considered that this dream persuaded and exhorted me respecting what I should do, in the same manner as those in the races are exhorted; for,

61a by persuading me to exercise music, it signified that I should labour in philosophy, which is the greatest music. But now since my sentence has taken place, and the festival of the God has retarded my death, it appeared to me to be necessary, that, if the music which the dream has so often exhorted me to undertake should happen to be of the popular sort, I should by no means resist its persuasions, but comply with the exhortation: for I considered that it would be more safe for me not to

b depart from hence before I had made an expiation by composing verses, and obeying the dream. Thus, in the first place, I composed some verses in honour of the God to whom the present festival belongs; but after the God, considering it necessary that he who designs to be a poet should make fables and not discourses, and knowing that I myself was not a mythologist, on these accounts I versified the fables of Æsop, which were at hand, and were known to me; and began with those first, that first presented themselves to my view.

Give this answer, Cebes, to Evenus: at the same time bid him farewell for me; and tell him, if he is wise he will follow me. But I shall depart, as it seems, to-day; for such are the orders of the Athenians. - Upon this

c Simmias replied, What is this, Socrates, which you command me to tell Evenus? for I often meet with him; and from what I know of him, I am certain that he will never willingly comply with your request. - What then (says Socrates), is not Evenus a philosopher? - To me he appears to be so (says Simmias). - Both Evenus, therefore, will be willing to follow me, and every one who is worthy to partake of philosophy; not perhaps indeed by violently[1] depriving himself of life, for this they say is unlawful. And at the same time, as he thus spoke, he withdrew his leg from the bed, and placed it on the ground; and afterwards continued to discourse with us, in a sitting posture, the remaining part of the time.

d Cebes,† therefore, inquired of him, How is this to be understood,

---

† Socrates and Cebes are here speaking about two different kinds of death; the latter about a physical, and the former about a pre-elective or free-will death.

Socrates, that it is not lawful to commit suicide, and yet that a philosopher should be willing to follow one who is about to die? - What (says he), Cebes, have not you and Simmias heard your familiar Philolaus[2] discourse concerning things of this kind? - We have not, Socrates, heard any thing clearly on this subject. - But I (says Socrates) speak in consequence of having heard; and what I have heard I will not enviously conceal from you. And perhaps it is becoming in the most eminent degree, that he who is about to depart thither should consider and mythologize about this departure: I mean, what kind of a thing we should think it to be. For what else can such a one be more properly employed about, till the setting of the sun?[†]

e

On what account then, Socrates, says Cebes, do they say that it is unlawful for a man to kill himself? for I myself have some time since heard from Philolaus, when he resided with us, and from some others, that it was not proper to commit such an action; but I never heard any thing clear upon the subject from any one. - Prepare yourself, then (says Socrates), for perhaps you may be satisfied in this particular: and perhaps it may appear to you wonderful, if this alone of everything else is something simple, and by no means happens to a man like other events, but still remains the same, even with respect to those to whom it is better to die than to live; though, perhaps, it may seem wonderful to you, that it should be better for those men to die, in whom it would be unholy to benefit themselves by suicide, and who ought to expect some other, as a benefactor on this occasion. - Then Cebes, gently laughing, Jupiter knows that (says he, speaking in his own tongue). - For this indeed (says Socrates) appears to be irrational; and yet, perhaps, it is not so, but has a certain reason on its side. For the discourse which is delivered about these particulars, in the arcana of the mysteries, *that we are placed as in a certain prison secured by a guard, and that it is not proper for any one to free himself from this confinement, and make his escape*, appears to me to be an assertion of great moment, and not easy to be understood. But this appears to me, O Cebes, to be well said, that the Gods take care of us, and that we who are men are one of the possessions belonging to the Gods. Or does not this appear to you to be the case? - It does to me (says Cebes). - Would not you, therefore, if any one of your servants[3] should destroy himself, when at the same time you did not signify that you was willing he should die, would you not

62a

b

c

[†] It was a law, says Olympiodorus [1.17], with the Athenians, to put no one to death in the day, just as it was an injunction with the Pythagoreans, not to sleep in mid-day, when the sun exhibits his most strenuous energy.

be angry with him? and if you had any punishment, would you not chastise him? - Entirely so (says he). - *Perhaps*, therefore, it is not irrational to assert, that a man ought not to kill himself before Divinity lays him under a certain necessity[†] of doing so, such as I am subject to at present.

d

e

63a

b

This, indeed (says Cebes), appears to be reasonable. But that which you said just now, Socrates, that philosophers would very readily be willing to die, appears to be absurd, if what we have asserted is agreeable to reason, that Divinity[4] takes care of us, and that we are one of his possessions; for it is irrational to suppose that the most prudent men should not be grieved, when departing from that servitude in which they are taken care of by the Gods, who are the best of governors. For such a one will by no means think that he shall be better taken care of when he becomes free: but some one who is deprived of intellect may perhaps think that he should fly from his master, and will not consider that he ought not to fly from a good master, but that he should by all means abide in his service. Hence he will depart from him in a most irrational manner: but he who is endowed with intellect will desire to live perpetually with one who is better than himself. And thus, Socrates, it is reasonable that the contrary of what you just now said should take place: for it is proper that the prudent, when about to die, should be sorrowful, but that the foolish should rejoice. - Socrates, therefore, upon hearing this, seemed to me to be pleased with the reasoning of Cebes; and looking upon us, Cebes (says he) never suffers any thing to pass without investigation, and is by no means willing to admit immediately the truth of an assertion. - But indeed (says Simmias), Cebes, O Socrates, appears to me to say something now to the purpose. For with what design can men, truly wise, fly from masters who are better than themselves, and, without any reluctance, free themselves from their servitude? And Cebes appears to me to direct his discourse to you, because you so easily endure to leave us, and those beneficent rulers the Gods, as you yourself confess. - You speak justly (says Socrates); for I think you mean that I ought to make my defence as if I was upon my trial. - By all means, says Simmias.

---

† Necessity is four-fold: for one kind is internal, and the other external; and each of these is twofold, *viz.* good and evil. But the paradigms of that which is inwardly good are the will of Divinity, and that of the just man; and of that which is inwardly evil, the pre-election of the depraved man. But of that necessity which is externally good, the paradigm is the will of Fate imparting precedaneous goods; and of that which is externally evil, the bestowing of things violent, contrary to nature, and corruptive.
[.25]

Be it so then (says Socrates): and I shall endeavour that this my apology may appear more reasonable to you than it did to my judges. For, with respect to myself (says he), O Simmias and Cebes, unless I thought that I should depart, in the first place, to other Gods[†] who are wise and good, and, in the next place, to men who have migrated from the present life, and are better than any among us, it would be unjust

c　　not to be troubled at death: but now believe for certain, that I hope to dwell with good men; though this, indeed, I will not confidently assert: but that I shall go to Gods who are perfectly good rulers, you may consider as an assertion which, if any thing of the kind is so, will be strenuously affirmed by me. So that, on this account, I shall not be afflicted at dying, but shall entertain a good hope that something remains for the dead; and, as it was formerly said, that it will be much better hereafter for the good than the evil. - What then Socrates, (says Simmias), would you have departed with such a conception in your intellect, without communicating it to us? Or will you not render us also partakers of it? For it appears to me, that this will be a common

d　　good; and at the same time it will be an apology for you, if you can persuade us to believe what you say. - I will endeavour to do so (says he). But let us first consider what that is which it appears to me Crito some time since was desirous of saying. What else (says Crito) should it be, Socrates, except what he who is to give you the poison has long ago told me, that you ought to speak as little as possible? For he says that those who dispute become too much heated, and that nothing of this kind ought to be introduced with the poison, since those who do not observe this caution are sometimes obliged to drink the poison twice

e　　or thrice. - Let him (says Socrates) only take care of his proper employment, as one who must administer the poison twice; and even, if the occasion requires, thrice. - I was almost certain (says Crito) that this would be your answer; but he enjoined me to do this, as I said, some time since. Permit him to do so (says Socrates); but I am desirous of rendering to you, as my judges, the reason, as it appears to me, why a man who has truly passed his life in the exercise of philosophy should

64a　　with great propriety be confident when about to die, and should possess good hopes of obtaining the greatest advantages after death; and in what manner this takes place I will endeavour, Simmias and Cebes, to explain:

---

† By *other Gods*, Socrates means such as are supermundane, or of an order superior to the ruling divinities of the world. In short, those Gods are here signified that are unconnected with body.

Those who are conversant with philosophy in a proper manner, seem to have concealed from others that the whole of their study is nothing else than how to die and be dead.[†] If this then is true, it would certainly be absurd, that those who have made this alone their study through the whole of life, should when it arrives be afflicted at a circumstance upon which they have before bestowed all their attention and labour. But here Simmias laughing, By Jupiter (says he), Socrates, you cause me to laugh, though I am very far from desiring to do so at present: for I think that the multitude, if they heard this, would consider it as well said respecting philosophers; and that men of the present day would perfectly agree with you, that philosophers should in reality desire death, and that they are by no means ignorant that men of this description deserve to suffer death. And indeed, Simmias, they would speak the truth, except in asserting that they are not ignorant of it: for both the manner in which true philosophers desire to die, and how they are worthy of death, is concealed from them. But let us bid farewell to such as these (says he), and discourse among ourselves: and to begin, Do you think that death is any thing? Simmias replied, Entirely so. Is it any thing else than a liberation of soul from body? and is not this to die,[‡] for the body to be liberated from the soul, and to subsist apart by itself? and likewise for the soul to be liberated from the body, and to be essentially separate? Is death any thing else but this? It is no other (says Simmias). - Consider then, excellent man, whether the same things appear to you as to me; for from hence I think we shall understand better the subjects of our investigation. Does it appear to you that the philosopher is a man who is anxiously concerned about things which are called pleasures, such as meats and drinks? - In the smallest degree, Socrates (says Simmias). - But what, is he sedulously employed in venereal concerns? - By no means. - Or does such a man appear to you to esteem other particulars which regard the observance of the body, such as the acquisition of excellent garments and sandals, and other

b

c

d

[†] It is well observed by Olympiodorus, that *to die* (ἀποθνῄσκειν) differs from *to be dead* (τεθνάναι). For the cathartic philosopher *dies* in consequence of meditating death; but the theoretic philosopher is *dead*, in consequence of being separated from the passions. [3.1]

[‡] Plato beautifully defines death to be a separation of the body from the soul, and of the soul from the body. For, with respect to souls that are enamoured with body, the body is indeed separated from the soul, but not the soul from the body, because it is yet conjoined with it through habitude or alliance, from which those shadowy phantasms are produced that wander about sepulchres. [7.2]

ornaments of the body? whether does he appear to you to esteem or despise such particulars, employing them only so far as an abundant necessity requires? - A true philosopher (says Simmias) appears to me to be one who will despise every thing of this kind. - Does it, therefore, appear to you (says Socrates), that the whole employment of such a one will not consist in things which regard the body, but in separating himself from the body as much as possible, and in converting himself to his soul? - It does appear so to me. - Is it not, therefore, first of all evident, in things of this kind, that a philosopher, in a manner far surpassing other men, separates his soul in the highest degree from communion with the body? - It appears so. - And to *the many*, O Simmias, it appears that he who accounts nothing of this kind pleasant, and who does not partake of them, is not worthy to live; but that he nearly approaches to death who is not concerned about the pleasures which subsist through the body. - You entirely speak the truth.

But what with respect to the acquisition[5] of wisdom? Is the body an impediment or not, if any one associates it in the investigation of wisdom? What I mean is this: Have sight and hearing in men any truth?[6] or is the case such as the poets perpetually sing, that

We nothing accurate or see or hear?

Though if these corporeal senses are neither accurate nor clear, by no means can the rest be so: for all the others are in a certain respect more depraved than these. Or does it not appear so to you? -Entirely so, says he. - When then does the soul touch upon the truth? for, when it endeavours to consider any thing in conjunction with the body, it is evidently then deceived by the body. - You speak the truth. - Must not, therefore, something of reality become manifest to the soul, in the energy of reasoning, if this is ever the case? - It must. - But the soul then reasons in the most beautiful manner, when it is disturbed by nothing belonging to the body, neither by hearing, nor sight, nor pain, nor any pleasure, but subsists in the most eminent degree, itself by itself, bidding farewell to the body, and, as much as possible neither communicating nor being in contact with it, extends itself towards real being. - These things are so. - Does not the soul of a philosopher, therefore, in these employments, despise the body in the most eminent degree, and, flying from it, seek to become essentially subsisting by itself? - It appears so. - But what shall we say, Simmias, about such things as the following? Do we say that the *just itself*[7] is something or nothing? - By Jupiter, we say it is something. - And do we not also say, that the *beautiful* and the *good* are each of them something? - How is it possible we should not? -

But did you ever at any time behold any one of these with your eyes? - By no means. - But did you ever touch upon these with any other corporeal sense? (but I speak concerning all of them; as for instance, about magnitude, health, strength, and, in one word, about the essence of all the rest, and which each truly possesses.) Is then the most true nature of these perceived through the ministry of the body? or rather shall we not say, that whoever among us prepares himself to think dianoëtically in the most eminent and accurate manner about each particular object of his speculation, such a one will accede the nearest possible to the knowledge of each? - Entirely so. - Will not he, therefore, accomplish this in the most pure manner, who in the highest degree betakes himself to each through his dianoëtic power, neither employing sight in conjunction with the dianoëtic energy, nor attracting any other sense, together with his reasoning; but who, exercising a dianoëtic energy by itself sincere, at the same time endeavours to hunt† after every thing which has true being subsisting by itself separate and pure; and who in the most eminent degree is liberated from the eyes and ears, and in short from the whole body, as disturbing the soul, and not suffering it to acquire truth and wisdom by its conjunction? Will not such a man, Simmias, procure for himself real being, if this can ever be asserted of any one? - You speak the truth, Socrates (says Simmias), in a transcendent‡ manner.

Is it not necessary, therefore (says Socrates), from hence, that an opinion of this kind should be present with genuine philosophers in such a manner, that they will speak among themselves as follows: In the consideration of things, this opinion, like a certain path, leads us in conjunction with reason from the vulgar track, that, as long as we are connected with a body, and our soul is contaminated with such an evil, we can never sufficiently obtain the object of our desire; and this object we have asserted to be truth? For the body[8] subjects us to innumerable occupations through necessary aliment, and fills us with love, desire, fear, all-various images, and a multitude of trifling concerns; not to

---

† The term *hunting*, says Olympiodorus, is adapted to intelligibles, because these are known by an unapparent power of the soul, in the same manner as hunters study to be invisible to the objects of their pursuit. Οικειον το θηρευειν επι των νοητων, διοτι αφανει δυναμει της ψυχης γινωσκεται ταυτα, καθαπερ και οι θηραται αφανες σπουδουσιν ειναι τοις θηραμασιν. [5.10]

‡ The word in the original is υπερφυως, which is literally *supernaturally*. And, as Olympiodorus says, it is very properly used here, because the discourse is about intelligibles. [5.12]

c   mention that, if we are invaded by certain diseases, we are hindered by them in our hunting after real being; so that, as it is said, *we can never truly, and in reality, acquire wisdom through the body.* For nothing else but the body and its desires cause wars, seditions, and contests, of every kind: for all wars arise through the possession of wealth; and we are compelled to acquire riches through the body, becoming subservient to d   its cultivation; so that on all these accounts we have no leisure for the exercise of philosophy. But this is the extremity of all evils, that if at any time we are at leisure from its attendance, and betake ourselves to the speculation of any thing, then invading us on all sides in our investigations, it causes agitations and tumults, and so vehemently impels us, that we are not able through its presence to perceive the truth; but it is in reality demonstrated to us, that, if we are designed to know any thing purely, we must be liberated from the body, and behold things e   with the soul itself. And then, as it appears, we shall obtain the object of our desire, and of which we profess ourselves lovers, *viz.* wisdom, when we are dead, as our discourse evinces; but by no means[9] while we are alive: for, if we can know nothing purely in conjunction with the body, one of these two consequences must ensue, either that we can never possess knowledge, or that we must obtain it after death; for then 67a   the soul will subsist apart by itself, separate from the body, but never before this takes place; and while we live in the body, as it appears, we shall approach in the nearest manner possible to knowledge, if in the most eminent degree we have no association with the body, nor any communication with it (except what the greatest necessity requires),[10] nor are filled with its nature, but purify ourselves from its defiling connection, till Divinity itself dissolves our bonds. And thus being pure, and liberated from the madness of body, it is proper to believe b   that we shall then associate with others who are similarly pure, and shall through ourselves know every thing genuine and sincere: and this perhaps is the truth itself; for it is by no means lawful that the pure should be touched by that which is impure. And such, O Simmias, in my opinion, ought to be the discourse and sentiments of all such as are lovers of learning in a proper manner. Or does it not seem so to you? - It does, Socrates, more so than any thing.

    If all this then (says Socrates) is true, my friend, much hope remains for him who arrives at that place to which I am now departing, that he shall there, if ever any where, sufficiently obtain that for the sake of c   which we take so much pains in the present life: so that the journey which is now assigned me will be accompanied with good hope; as will likewise be the case with any other man who thinks that he ought to prepare his dianoëtic part in such a manner that it may become as it were pure. - Entirely so (says Simmias). - But does not purification consist in this, as we formerly asserted in our discourse: I mean, in separating the soul from the body in the most eminent degree, and in accustoming it to call together and collect itself essentially on all sides from the body, and to dwell as much as possible, both now and hereafter, alone by itself, becoming by this means liberated from the body as from detaining bonds? - Entirely so (says he). - Is not death called a solution and separation of the soul from body? - Perfectly so (says he). - But those alone who philosophize rightly,[11] as we have said, always and especially providentially attend to the solution of the soul: and this is the meditation of philosophers, a solution and separation of the soul from the body; or do you not think so? - I do. - Would it not, therefore, as I said at first, be ridiculous for a man who has so prepared himself in the present life as to approach very near to death, to live indeed in the manner we have described, and yet, when death arrives, be afflicted? would not this be ridiculous? - How indeed should it not? - In reality, therefore (says he), O Simmias, those who philosophize rightly will meditate how to *die*; and *to be dead* will be to them of all men a thing the least terrible. But from hence consider as follows: for, if they are on all sides enemies to the body, but desire to possess the soul subsisting by itself, would it not be very irrational for them to be terrified and troubled when death approaches, and to be unwilling to depart to that place, where when they have arrived they may hope to enjoy that which they were lovers of in the present life (but they were lovers of wisdom), and to be liberated from the association of that nature to which they were always inimical? Or do you think it possible, that many should be willing, of their own accord, to descend into Hades, allured by the hope of seeing and conversing with departed beautiful youths, wives and children whom they have loved; and that the true lover of wisdom, who has exceedingly nourished this hope, that he shall never possess wisdom as he ought any where but in Hades, should be afflicted when dying, and should not depart thither with readiness and delight? For it is necessary, my friend, to think in this manner of one who is a true philosopher; since such a one is very much of opinion, that he shall never any where, but in that place, acquire the possession of wisdom with purity; and if this be the case, would it not be very irrational, as we just now said, for a man of this kind to be terrified at death? - Very much so, by Jupiter, says he.

This then will be an argument sufficient to convince you, that he whom you behold afflicted, when about to die, is not a philosopher, c but a lover of body; and this same person is a lover of riches and honours, either desiring the possession of one of these, or of both. - The case is entirely so (says he) as you represent it. - Does not then, O Simmias, that which is called fortitude eminently belong to such as are thus disposed? - Entirely so, (says he). - Does not temperance also, which even the multitude thus denominate as a virtue, through which we are not agitated by desires, but regard them with moderation and contempt; does it not, I say, belong to those only who despise the body in the

d most eminent degree, and live in the exercise of philosophy? - It is necessary, says he. - For, if you are willing (says Socrates) to consider the fortitude and temperance of others, they will appear to you to be absurdities. - But how, Socrates? You know (says he) that all others look upon death as the greatest of evils. - In the highest degree so, says he. - Those who are bold, therefore, among these, sustain death when they do sustain it, through the dread of greater evils. - They do so. - All men, therefore, except philosophers, are bold through fearing and dread,

e though it is absurd that any one should be bold through fear or cowardice. - Entirely so. - But what, are not the moderate among these affected in the same manner? and are they not temperate by a certain intemperance? Though this is in a certain respect impossible, yet a passion similar to this happens to them with respect to this foolish temperance: for, fearing to be deprived of other pleasures which at the same time they desire, they abstain from others, by others being vanquished. And though they call intemperance a subjection to pleasures; yet at the same time it happens to them, that, being vanquished by certain pleasures, they rule over others; and this is similar

69a to what I just now said, that after a certain manner they become temperate through intemperance. - It seems so, indeed. - But, O blessed Simmias, this is by no means the right road to virtue, to change pleasures for pleasures, pains for pains, fear for fear, and the greater for the lesser, like pieces of money: but that alone is the proper coin, I mean wisdom, for which all these ought to be changed. And indeed, for the sake of this, and with this every thing must in reality be bought and

b sold, both fortitude and temperance, justice, and, in one word, true virtue, which subsists with wisdom, whether pleasures and pains, and every thing else of this kind, are present or absent: but if these are separated from wisdom, and changed from one another, such virtue does not merit to be called even a shadowy description, but is in reality servile, and possesses nothing salutary and true. But that which is in

c reality true virtue[12] is a purification from every thing of this kind; and temperance and justice, fortitude, and prudence itself, are each of them a certain purification. And those who instituted the mysteries for us appear to have been by no means contemptible persons, but to have really signified formerly, in an obscure manner, *that whoever descended*[13] *into Hades uninitiated, and without being a partaker of the mysteries, should be plunged into mire; but that whoever arrived there, purified and initiated, should dwell with the Gods.* For, as it is said by those who

d   write about the mysteries,

> The thyrsus-bearers[14] numerous are seen,
> But few the Bacchuses have always been.

These few are, in my opinion, no other than those who philosophize rightly; and that I may be ranked in the number of these, I shall leave nothing unattempted, but exert myself in all possible ways. But whether or not my exertions will be properly directed, and whether I shall accomplish any thing when I arrive thither, I shall clearly know, very shortly, if Divinity pleases, as it appears to me. And this (says he), Simmias and Cebes, is my apology,[15] why upon leaving you, and the

e   rulers of the present life, I ought not to be afflicted and indignant, since I am persuaded that I shall there meet with masters and companions not less good than such as are here. This indeed is incredible to many; but if my apology shall have more influence with you than with the judges of the Athenians, it will have a good effect.

    When Socrates had thus spoken, Cebes, renewing the discourse, said,

70a   Other things, Socrates, appear to me to be well spoken; but what you have asserted about the soul will produce in men much incredulity, who think, when it is liberated from the body, that it is no longer any where, but that, on that very day in which a man dies, it is corrupted[16] and perishes, and this immediately as it is freed from the body; and, besides this, that on its departure it becomes dissipated like wind or smoke, makes its escape, and flies away, and is no longer any where: for if it remained any where essentially collected in itself, and liberated from those evils which you have now enumerated, there would be an abundant and fair hope, Socrates, that what you have asserted is true.

b   But it will perhaps require no small allurement and faith, in order to be persuaded that the soul remains, though the man dies, and that it possesses a certain power and prudence. - You speak the truth, Cebes (says Socrates); but what shall we do? Are you willing that we should discourse about these particulars, whether it is proper that this should be the case with the soul, or not? - Indeed (says Cebes), I shall hear with great pleasure your opinion on this subject. - For I do not think (answered Socrates) that any one who should hear this discussion, even

c   though he should be a comic poet, could say that I trifled, and
discoursed about things not accommodated to my condition. If it is
agreeable to you, therefore, and it is requisite to investigate these
particulars, let us consider whether the souls of dead men survive in
Hades, or not.

The assertion indeed, which we now call to mind, is an ancient one,
I mean that souls departing from hence exist in Hades, and that they
d   again return hither, and are generated from the dead. And if the case is
such, that living[17] natures are again generated from the dead, can there
be any other consequence than that our souls are there? for they could
not be again generated if they had no subsistence; and this will be a
sufficient argument that these things are so, if it is really evident that the
living cannot be generated from any thing else than the dead. But, if
this is not the case, it will be necessary to adduce some other reason. -
Entirely so (says Cebes). - You should not, therefore (says he), consider
this assertion with respect to men alone, if you wish to learn with
facility; but we should survey it as connected with all animals and
e   plants, and, in one word, with every thing which is endued with
generation. Are not all things, therefore, so generated, that they are
produced no otherwise than contraries from contraries, I mean those to
which any thing of this kind happens? as the beautiful is contrary to the
base, and the just to the unjust; and a thousand other particulars subsist
in the same manner. We should consider, therefore, whether it is
necessary, respecting every thing which has a contrary, that this contrary
should be generated from nothing else than that which is its contrary.
As for instance, is it not necessary that, when any thing becomes greater,
71a   it should become so from being before smaller? - It is so (says he). - And
is not the weaker generated from the stronger, and the swifter from the
slower? - Entirely so. - But what if any thing becomes worse, must it not
become so from the better? and if more just, must it not be generated
from the more unjust? - How should it not? - We have then (says he)
sufficiently determined this, that every thing is thus generated, viz.
contraries from contraries. - Entirely so. - But what, is there any thing
b   among these which has a middle subsistence between both (since all
contraries are two), so as to cause two generations from this to that, and
from that again to this? for between a greater and a lesser thing there is
increase and diminution; and hence we say that the one is increased, but
the other diminished. - It is so (says he). - And must not to be separated
and mingled, to be cooled and heated, and every thing in the same
manner, though sometimes we do not distinguish the several particulars
by names, must they not in reality be every where thus circumstanced,

be generated from each other, and be subject to a mutual generation of each into one another? - Entirely so (says he).

c   What then (says Socrates), is there any thing contrary to the being alive, as sleeping is contrary to waking? - Entirely so (says he). - But what is this contrary? - To be dead. - Are not these, therefore, generated from each other, since they are contraries? and since they are two, are there not two generations between them? - How should there not? - I will, therefore (says Socrates), tell you what one of these conjunctions is which I have just now spoken of, and what its generations are; do you

d tell me what the other is. But I say, that the one of these is *to sleep*, but the other *to awake*; and from sleeping awaking is generated, and from awaking sleeping; and the generations of these are on the one hand to be laid asleep, and on the other to be roused. Have I sufficiently explained this to you or not? - Perfectly so. - Do you, therefore (says he), inform me, in a similar manner, concerning life and death. Do you not say that *living* is the contrary of *to be dead*? - I do. - And that they are generated from each other? - Certainly. - What then is generated from that which is alive? - That which is dead (says he). - But what (says Socrates) is generated from *the dead*? - It is necessary to confess (says he) that this must be *the living*. - From the dead, therefore (says he), O Cebes, living things, and men who are alive, are generated. - It appears

e so, (says he). - Our souls therefore (says Socrates) subsist in Hades. - So it seems. - Is not, therefore, one of the generations subsisting about these manifest? for *to die* is, I think, sufficiently clear; is it not? - Entirely so (says he). - What then shall we do? shall we not render back a contrary generation in its turn, but say that nature is defective and lame in this particular? Or is it necessary to assign a certain contrary generation *to the being dead*? - Entirely so, (says he). - But what is this? - *To be restored back again to life*. - But (says Socrates), if there is such a thing as to

72a revive again, will not this reviving be a generation from the dead to the living? - Perfectly so. - This then is agreed upon by us, that the living are generated from the dead no less than the dead from the living: but, this being the case, it is sufficient argument to prove that the souls of the dead must necessarily exist somewhere, from whence they may again be generated. - It appears to me (says he), Socrates, that this must necessarily follow from what has been admitted.

    Take notice then (says he), O Cebes! that we have not unjustly made these concessions, as it appears to me: for if other things, when generated, were not always restored in the place of others, revolving as

b it were in a circle, but generation subsisted according to a right line, proceeding from one thing alone into its opposite, without recurring again to the other, and making an inflection, you know that all things would at length possess the same form, would be affected with the same passion, and would cease to be generated. - How do you say? (says he.) - It is by no means difficult (replies Socrates) to understand what I assert; but just as if there should be such a thing as falling asleep without recurring again to a vigilant state, generated from a sleepy condition, you know that all things would at length exhibit the delusions of Endymion, and would nowhere present themselves to the view, because

c   every thing else would suffer the same as happened to him, *viz.* would be laid asleep. And if all things were mingled together, without ever being separated, the doctrine of Anaxagoras would soon be verified; for all things would be at once collected in a heap. In the same manner, my dear Simmias, if all such things as participate of life should die, and after they are dead should abide in that lifeless form, and not revive again, would there not be a great necessity that all things should at length die, and that nothing should live? for if living beings are generated from

d   other things, and living beings die, how can it be otherwise but that all things must be extinguished through being dead? - It appears to me, Socrates (says Cebes), that it can not be otherwise; and in my opinion you perfectly speak the truth: - for to me, Cebes (says Socrates), it seems to be so more than any thing, and that we have not assented to this through deception; but that there is such a thing in reality as reviving again; that the living are generated from the dead; that the souls of the

e   dead have a subsistence; and that the condition of the good after this life will be better than at present; but of the evil, worse.

But (says Cebes, interrupting him), according to that doctrine, Socrates, which you are frequently accustomed to employ (if it is true), that learning, with respect to us, is nothing else than reminiscence;[18] according to this, it is necessary that we must have learned the things which we now call to mind in some former period of time. But this is impossible, unless our soul subsisted somewhere before it took up its residence in this human form; so that from hence the soul will appear

73a   to be a certain immortal nature. - But, Cebes (says Simmias, interrupting him), recall into my memory what demonstrations there are of these particulars; for I do not very much remember them at present. - The truth of this (says Cebes) is evinced by one argument, and that a most beautiful one; that men, when interrogated, if they are but interrogated properly, will speak about every thing just as it is. At the same time, they could never do this unless science and right reason resided in their natures. And, in the second place, if any one leads them to diagrams,

b   or any thing of this kind, he will in these most clearly discover that this is really the case. - But if you are not persuaded from this, Simmias (says Socrates), see if, from considering the subject in this manner, you will perceive as we do. For you do not believe how that which is called learning is reminiscence. - I do not disbelieve it (says Simmias); but I desire to be informed concerning this, which is the subject of our discourse, I mean reminiscence; and indeed, from what Cebes has endeavoured to say, I almost now remember, and am persuaded: but nevertheless I would at present hear how you attempt to support this

c   opinion. - We defend it then (says Socrates) as follows: we confess without doubt, that if any one calls any thing to mind, it is necessary that at some time or other he should have previously known this. - Entirely so (says he). - Shall we not confess this also (says Socrates), that when science is produced in us, after some particular manner, it is reminiscence? But I mean by a particular manner, thus: If any one, upon seeing or hearing any thing, or apprehending it through the medium of any other sense, should not only know it, but should also think upon something else, of which there is not the same, but a different science, should we not justly say, that he recollects or remembers the particular, of which he receives a mental conception? -

d   How do you mean? - Thus (says Socrates): In a certain respect the science of a man is different from that of a lyre. - How should it not? - Do you not, therefore, know that lovers when they see a lyre, or a vestment, or any thing else which the objects of their affection were accustomed to use, no sooner know the lyre, than they immediately receive in their dianoëtic part the form of the beloved person to whom the lyre belonged? But this is no other than reminiscence: just as any one, upon seeing Simmias, often recollects Cebes; and in a certain respect an infinite number of such particulars continually occur. - An

e   infinite number indeed, by Jupiter (says Simmias). - Is not then (says Socrates) something of this kind a certain reminiscence; and then especially so, when any one experiences this affection about things which, through time, and ceasing to consider them, he has now forgotten? - Entirely so (says Simmias). - But what (says Socrates), does it happen, that when any one sees a painted horse and a painted lyre, he calls to mind a man? and that when he beholds a picture of Simmias, he recollects Cebes? - Entirely so. - And will it not also happen, that on seeing a picture of Simmias he will recollect Simmias himself? - It certainly will happen so (says he).

74a   Does it not therefore follow, that in all these instances reminiscence partly takes place from things similar, and partly from such as are dissimilar? - It does. - But when any one recollects any thing from similars, must it not also happen to him, that he must know whether this similitude is deficient in any respect, as to likeness, from that particular of which he has the remembrance? - It is necessary (says he). - Consider then (says Socrates) if the following particulars are thus circumstanced: Do we say that any thing is in a certain respect equal? I do not say one piece of wood to another, nor one stone to another, nor any thing else of this kind; but do we say that equal itself, which is something different from all these, is something or nothing? - We say it

b   is something different, by Jupiter, Socrates (says Simmias), and that in a wonderful manner. - Have we also a scientific knowledge of that which is equal itself? - Entirely so (says he). - But from whence do we receive the science of it? Is it not from the particulars we have just now spoken of, *viz.* on seeing wood, stones, or other things of this kind, which are equals, do we not form a conception of that which is different from these? But consider the affair in this manner: Do not equal stones and pieces of wood, which sometimes remain the same, at one time

c   appear equal, and at another not? - Entirely so. - But what, can *equals themselves* ever appear to you unequal? or can equality seem to be inequality? - By no means, Socrates. - These equals, therefore, are not the same with equal itself. - By no means, Socrates, as it appears to me. - But from these equals (says he), which are different from equal itself, you at the same time understand and receive the science of *equal itself.* - You speak most true (says he). - Is it not, therefore, either similar to these or

d   dissimilar? - Entirely so. - But indeed (says Socrates) this is of no consequence: for while, in consequence of seeing one thing, you understand another, from the view of this, whether it is dissimilar or similar, it is necessary that this conception of another thing should be reminiscence. - Entirely so. - But what will you determine concerning this (says Socrates)? - Do we suffer any thing of this kind respecting the equality in pieces of wood, and other such equals as we have just now spoken of? and do they appear to us to be equal in the same manner as equal itself? and is something or nothing wanting, through which they are less equal than equal itself? - There is much wanting (says he). - Must we not, therefore, confess, that when any one, on beholding some particular thing, understands that he wishes this which I now perceive

e   to be such as something else is, but that it is deficient, and falls short of its perfection; must we not confess that he who understands this, necessarily had a previous knowledge of that to which he asserts this to be similar, but in a defective degree? - It is necessary. - What then, do we suffer something of this kind or not about equals and equal itself? - Perfectly so. - It is necessary, therefore, that we must have previously

75a known *equal itself* before that time, in which, from first seeing equal things, we understood that we desired all these to be such as *equal itself*, but that they had a defective subsistence. - It is so. - But this also we must confess, that we neither understood this, nor are able to understand it, by any other means than either by the sight, or the touch, or some other of the senses. - I speak in the same manner about all these. For they are the same, Socrates, with respect to that which your discourse wishes to evince. But indeed, from the senses, it is necessary to understand that all equals in sensible objects aspire after *equal itself*,

b and are deficient from its perfection. Or how shall we say? - In this manner: Before, therefore, we begin to see, or hear, and to perceive other things, it necessarily follows, that we must in a certain respect have received the science of *equal itself*, so as to know what it is, or else we could never refer the equals among sensibles to *equal itself*, and be convinced that all these desire to become such as *equal itself*, but fall short of its perfection. - This, Socrates, is necessary, from what has been previously said. - But do we not, as soon as we are born, see and hear,

c and possess the other senses? - Entirely so. - But we have said it is necessary that prior to these we should have received the science of *equal itself*. - Certainly. - We must necessarily, therefore, as it appears, have received it before we were born. - It appears so.

If, therefore, receiving this before we were born, we were born possessing it; we both knew prior to our birth, and as soon as we were born, not only *the equal*, *the greater*, and *the lesser*, but every thing of this kind: for our discourse at present is not more concerning *the equal*

d than *the beautiful*, *the good*, *the just*, and *the holy*, and in one word, about every thing which we mark with the signature of *that which is*, both in our interrogations when we interrogate, and in our answers when we reply: so that it is necessary we should have received the science of all these before we were born. - All this is true. -And if, since we receive these sciences, we did not forget each of them, we should always be born knowing, and should always know them, through the whole course of our life: for to know is nothing else than this, to retain the science which we have received, and not to lose it. Or do we not call oblivion

e the loss of science? - Entirely so (says he), Socrates. - But if, receiving science before we were born, we lose it at the time of our birth, and afterwards, through exercising the senses about these particulars, receive back again those sciences which we once before possessed, will not that which we call learning be a recovery of our own proper science? and

76a shall we not speak rightly when we call this a certain reminiscence? - Entirely so. - For this appears to be possible, that when any one perceives any thing, either by seeing or hearing, or employing any other sense, he may at the same time know something different from this, which he had forgotten, and to which this approaches, whether it is dissimilar or similar. So that, as I said, one of these two things must be the consequence: either that we were born knowing these, and possess a knowledge of all of them, through the whole of our life; or that we only remember what we are said to learn afterwards; and thus learning will be reminiscence. - The case is perfectly so, Socrates.

b   Which, therefore, will you choose, Simmias: that we are born knowing, or that we afterwards remember the particulars of which we formerly received the science? - At present, Socrates, I have no choice. - But what will be your choice in the following instance, and what will be your opinion about it? Can a man, who possesses science, render a reason concerning the objects of his knowledge, or not? - There is a great necessity (says he), Socrates, that he should. - And does it also appear to you, that all men can render a reason of the particulars concerning which we have just now spoken? - I wish they could (says Simmias); but I am much more afraid, that to-morrow there will no longer be any one here who can accomplish this in a becoming manner.

c   - You do not therefore think, Simmias, that all men know these particulars? - By no means. - They remember, therefore, the things which they have once learned. - It is necessary. - But when did our souls receive this science? for they did not receive them from those from whom we are born men. - Certainly not. - Before this period, therefore. - Certainly. - Our souls therefore, Simmias, had a subsistence before they were in a human form, separate from bodies, and possessed intellectual prudence. - Unless, Socrates, we received these sciences while we were making our entrance into the present life; for that space of time is yet

d   left for us. - Let it be so, my friend. But in what other time did we lose these? for we were not born possessing them, as we have just now acknowledged. Did we lose them at the very time in which we received them? Or can you mention any other time? - By no means, Socrates: but I was ignorant that I spoke nothing to the purpose.

Will then the case remain thus for us, Simmias? For if those things have a subsistence which we perpetually proclaim, viz. a certain something beautiful and good, and every such essence; and if we refer to

e   this all sensible objects, as finding it to have a prior subsistence, and to be ours, and assimilate these to it, as images to their exemplar; it is necessary that, as these have a subsistence, so likewise that our soul should have subsisted before we were born: but if these are not, this discourse will have been undertaken in vain. Is it not so? and is there not an equal necessity, both that these should have a subsistence, and that our souls should have had a being before we were born, and that the one cannot be without the other? - The same necessity, Socrates (says Simmias), appears to me to take place in a most transcendent manner; and the discourse flies to a beautiful circumstance, I mean that our soul subsisted before we were born, in a manner similar to that essence which you now speak of. For I possess nothing which is so clear to me as this, that all such things as the beautiful and the good subsist, in the most eminent degree, together with every thing else which you now mention; and, with respect to myself, it is sufficiently demonstrated. - But how does it appear to Cebes? says Socrates: for it is necessary that Cebes also should be persuaded. - In my opinion he is sufficiently so (says Simmias), although he is the most resolute of all men in not assenting to what is said. Yet I think he is sufficiently persuaded that our soul had a subsistence before we were born. But whether or not the soul remains after death, does not appear to me, Socrates (says he), to be yet demonstrated; but that doubt of the multitude, which Cebes mentioned, still presses hard upon me, whether, when a man dies, the soul is not dissipated, and this is the end of its existence. For what hinders but that it may be born, and may have had a subsistence elsewhere, and this before it came into a human body; and yet, after it departs, and is liberated from this body, may then die and be corrupted? - You speak well, Simmias (says Cebes); for it appears that the half only of what was necessary has been demonstrated, I mean that our soul subsisted before we were born: but it is necessary that you should demonstrate, besides this, that it no less subsists after we are dead, than it did before we were born, in order that the demonstration may be complete. - This, Simmias and Cebes (says Socrates), is even now demonstrated, if you are only willing to connect into one and the same the present discourse and that which we before assented to; I mean that every vital nature is generated from that which is dead. For if the soul had a prior subsistence, and it is necessary when it proceeds into the present life, and is generated man, that it should be generated from nothing else than death, and to be dead; how is it not necessary that it should also subsist after death, since it is requisite that it should be generated again? Its existence therefore, after death, is even now, as I said, demonstrated. But you and Simmias appear to me still more earnestly to discuss this assertion in a very pleasant manner, and to be afraid like boys, lest on the soul's departure from the body the winds should tear it in pieces, and widely disperse it, especially if any one should die during a stormy blast, and not when the heavens are serene. -

Upon this Cebes laughing, Endeavour (says he), O Socrates, to persuade
us of the contrary, as if we were afraid, or rather as if we were not
afraid; though, perhaps, there is some boy among us, by whom
circumstances of this kind may be dreaded: him, therefore, we should
endeavour to persuade not to be terrified at death, as if it was some
dreadful spectre. - But it is necessary (says Socrates) to charm him every
78a   day till he becomes well. - But from whence (says he), O Socrates, can
a man acquire skill in such enchantment, since you are about to leave us?
- Greece (says he), Cebes, is very spacious, in some part of which good
men may be found: and there are many barbarous nations, all which
must be wandered over, inquiring after an enchanter of this kind,
without sparing either riches or labour, as there is nothing for which
wealth can be more seasonably bestowed. But it is necessary that you
should inquire among yourselves; for perhaps you will not easily find
any one who is more able to accomplish this than yourselves. - Let these
things be so (says Cebes): but, if you please, let us return from whence
b   we made this digression. - It will be agreeable to me (says Socrates): for
how should it not be so? - You speak well, says Cebes.

Some such thing, therefore (says Socrates), we ought to inquire of
ourselves, viz. to what being the passion of becoming dissipated belongs;
and respecting what we ought to fear, lest this should take place; and to
whom a fear of this kind is proper: and after this, we should consider
whether it is soul or not; and, as the result of these speculations, should
either be confident or fearful concerning our soul. - You speak true (says
c   he). - Is it not, therefore, a passion natural to that which is collected
together, and a composite, that it should be dissolved so far as it is a
composite; and that, if there is any thing without composition, to this
alone, if to any other, it belongs not to suffer affections of this kind? -
This (says Cebes) appears to me to be the case. - But does it not follow,
that things which always subsist according to the same, and in a similar
manner, are in the most eminent degree incomposites; but that such
things as subsist differently at different times, and never according to the
same, are composites? - To me it appears so. - Let us return, therefore
d   (says he), to the particulars of our former discourse: Whether is *essence
itself* (which both in our inquiries and answers we established as having
a being) that which always subsists similarly, and according to the same,
or that which subsists differently at different times? And does *the equal
itself, the beautiful itself*, and every thing which truly is, ever receive any
kind of mutation? Or does not every thing which always truly is, and
has a uniform subsistence, essentially abide in a similar manner according
to the same, and never in any respect receive any mutation? - It is

necessary, Socrates (says Cebes), that it should subsist similarly, and according to the same. - But what shall we say concerning many beautiful things, such as men, horses, garments, or other things of this kind, which are either equal or beautiful; and of all such as are synonymous to these? Do these also subsist according to the same, or rather are they not entirely contrary to those, so that they neither subsist similarly according to the same, either with respect to themselves or to one another, or, in one word, in any manner whatever? - These (says Cebes) never subsist in a similar condition. These, therefore, may be touched, may be seen and perceived by the other senses; but those natures which always subsist according to the same, cannot be apprehended by any other means than the discursive energy of the dianoëtic power. But things of this kind are invisible, and cannot be seen. Are you willing, therefore (says he), that we should establish two species of beings, the one visible, and the other invisible? - Let us establish them (says he). - And that the invisible subsists always according to the same, but the visible never according to the same. - And this also (says he) we will establish. - Come then (says Socrates), is there any thing else belonging to us, than on the one hand body, and on the other soul? - Nothing else (says he). - To which species, therefore, shall we say the body is more similar and allied? - It is manifest to every one (says he), that it is allied to the visible species. - But what shall we say of the soul? Is it visible, or invisible? - It is certainly not visible to men, Socrates (says he). - But we speak of things which are visible or not so, with respect to the nature of men. Or do you think we speak of things visible to any other nature? - Of those which regard the nature of men. - What then shall we say respecting the soul, that it is visible, or cannot be seen? - That it cannot be seen. - The soul, therefore, is more similar to the invisible species than the body, but the body is more similar to the visible. - It is perfectly necessary it should be so, Socrates.

And have we not also formerly asserted this, that the soul, when it employs the body in the speculation of any thing, either through sight, or hearing, or some other sense (for to speculate through sense is to speculate through body), then, indeed, it is drawn by the body to things which never subsist according to the same, wanders† and is agitated, and

---

† The term *wandering*, says Olympiodorus, is common both to life and knowledge; but the term *agitated* belongs to life alone; and the term *giddiness* to knowledge alone. But giddiness is an evil. For as those who are thus affected, through the inward whirl which they experience, think that things external to them are in a similar condition, so the soul, through alone beholding sensibles, thinks that all things flow and are in motion. [13.18]

becomes giddy like one intoxicated, through passing into contact with
things of this kind? - Entirely so. - But when it speculates any thing,

d   itself subsisting by itself, then it departs to that which is pure, eternal,
and immortal, and which possesses a sameness of subsistence: and, as
being allied to such a nature, it perpetually becomes united with it,
when it subsists alone by itself, and as often as it is lawful for it to
obtain such a conjunction: and then, too, it rests from its wanderings,
and perpetually subsists similarly according to the same, about such
natures, as passing into contact with them; and this passion[19] of the soul
is denominated prudence. - You speak (says he), Socrates, in every
respect beautifully and true. - To which species, therefore, of things,
formerly and now spoken of, does the soul appear to you to be more

e   similar and allied? - It appears to me, Socrates (says he), that every one,
and even the most indocile, must admit, in consequence of this method
of reasoning, that the soul is both totally and universally more similar
to that which subsists perpetually the same, than to that which does not
so. - But to which is the body most similar? - To the other species.

But consider also as follows:[†] that, since soul and body subsist
together, nature commands that the one should be subservient and obey,

80a   but that the other should rule and possess dominion.   And in
consequence of this, which again of these appears to you to be similar
to a divine nature, and which to the mortal nature? Or does it not
appear to you that the divine nature is essentially adapted to govern and
rule, but the mortal to be governed and be subservient? - To me it does
so. - To which, therefore, is the soul similar? - It is manifest, Socrates,
that the soul is similar to the divine, but the body to the mortal nature.

b   - But consider (says he), Cebes, whether, from all that has been said,
these conclusions will result to us, that the soul is most similar to the
divine, immortal, intelligible, uniform and indissoluble nature, and
which always subsists similarly according to the same; but that the body
is most similar to the nature which is human, mortal, void of intellect,
multiform, dissoluble, and which never subsists according to the same.
Can we, my dear Cebes, produce any arguments to show that this is not
the case? - We cannot.

What then? in consequence of all this, must it not be the property of

c   the body, to be swiftly dissolved; but of the soul, on the contrary, to be
entirely indissoluble, or something bordering on such an affection? -
How should it not? - Do you conceive, therefore (says he), that when a

---

† This is the third argument derived from life, that the soul rules over the body.
For that which uses an instrument possesses dominion over it. [13.20]

man dies, the visible part of him, or the body, which is situated in a visible region (and which we call a dead body subject to dissolution, ruin, and dissipation), does not immediately suffer any of these affections, but remains for a considerable space of time; and if any one dies possessing a graceful body, that it very much retains its elegant form? for, when the body is bound and buried according to the manner in which the Egyptians bury their dead, it remains almost entire for an incredible space of time; and though some parts of the body may

d become rotten, yet the bones and nerves, and every thing of this kind, are preserved as one may say immortal. Is it not so? - Certainly. - Can the soul, therefore, which is invisible, and which departs into another place of this kind, a place noble, pure, and invisible, *viz.* into Hades,[†] to a beneficent and prudent God (at which place, if Divinity is willing, my soul will shortly arrive); can the soul, I say, since it is naturally of

e this kind, be immediately dissipated and perish on its being liberated from the body, as is asserted by the many? This is certainly, my dear Cebes and Simmias, far from being the case. But this will much more abundantly take place, if it is liberated in a pure condition, attracting to itself nothing of the body, as not having willingly communicated with it in the present life, but fled from it and collected itself into itself; an employment of this kind having been the subject of its perpetual meditation. But this is nothing else than to philosophize rightly, and to

81a meditate with facility, how *to be dead in reality*. Or will not this be a meditation of death? - Entirely so. - Will not the soul, therefore, when in this condition, depart to that which is similar to itself, a divine nature, and which is likewise immortal and prudent? and when it arrives thither, will it not become happy, being liberated from wandering and ignorance, terror and insane love, and from all other evils belonging to the human nature; and so, as it is said of the initiated,[‡] will in reality pass the rest of its time in the society of the Gods? Shall we speak in this manner, Cebes, or otherwise? - In this manner, by Jupiter (says Cebes).

b But I think that if the soul departs polluted and impure from the body, as having always been its associate, attending upon and loving the body,

---

† Pluto, says Olympiodorus, is celebrated as prudent and good, because he imparts to souls the virtue and science which they lost in the realms of generation. He is also Hades, because he wipes away the visible, which is, as it were, burnt in in the nature of the soul. [.348]

‡ The soul when living with Divinity may be said to be truly initiated, as flying both to its own *one* or summit, and that of divine natures. [.351]

and becoming enchanted by it, through its desires and pleasures, in such a manner as to think that nothing really is, except what is corporeal, which can be touched and seen, eaten and drunk, and employed for the purposes of venereal occupations, and at the same time is accustomed to hate, dread and avoid, that which is dark and invisible to the eye of sense, which is intelligible and apprehended by philosophy; do you think that a soul thus affected can be liberated from the body, so as to subsist sincerely by itself? - By no means (says he). - But I think that it will be contaminated by a corporeal nature, to which its converse and familiarity with the body, through perpetual association and abundant meditation, have rendered it similar and allied. - Entirely so. - But it is proper, my dear Cebes, to think that such a nature is ponderous and heavy, terrestrial and visible;[20] and that a soul of this kind, through being connected with such a nature, is rendered heavy, and drawn down again into the visible region from its dread of that which is invisible and Hades, and, as it is said, wanders about monuments and tombs; about which indeed certain shadowy phantoms of souls appear, being the images produced by such souls as have not been purely liberated from the body, but which participate of the visible nature; and on this account they become visible. - It is very reasonable to suppose so, Socrates. - It is reasonable indeed, Cebes: and likewise that these are not the souls of the worthy, but of the depraved, who are compelled to wander about such places; by these means suffering the punishment of their former conduct, which was evil; and they are compelled thus to wander till,[†] through the desire of a corporeal nature, which attends them, they are again bound to a body.

They are bound, however, as it is proper they should be, to such manners as they have exercised in the present life. - But what do you say these manners are, Socrates? - As for example, that such as are addicted to gluttony, arrogant injuries, and drinking, and this without any fear of consequences, shall enter into the tribes of asses and brutes of this kind. Or do you not think it proper that they should? - You speak in a manner perfectly becoming. - But shall we not say, that such as held in the highest estimation injustice, tyranny, and rapine shall enter into

---

† "Guilty souls", says the philosopher Sallust (De Diis et Mundo, cap. 19, TTS vol. VI, p. 23), "are punished on their departure from the present body; some by wandering about this part of the earth; others about certain of its hot or cold regions; and others are tormented by avenging dæmons. But, universally, the rational soul suffers punishment in conjunction with the irrational soul, the partner of its guilt; and through this that shadowy body derives its subsistence which is beheld about sepulchres, and especially about the tombs of such as have lived an abandoned life."

the tribes of wolves, hawks, and kites? Or where else can we say such souls depart? - Into tribes of this kind, certainly (says Cebes). - It will, therefore, be manifest concerning the rest into what nature each departs, according to the similitudes of manners which they have exercised. - It is manifest (says he); for how should it not be so? - Are not, therefore (says he), those among these the most happy, and such as depart into the best place, who have made popular and political[†] virtue their study, which they call indeed temperance and justice, and which is produced

b from custom and exercise, without philosophy and intellect? - But how are these the most happy? - Because it is fit that these should again migrate into a political and mild tribe of this kind; such as bees, wasps, or ants, or into the same human tribe again, and from these become moderate men. - It is fit.

c But it is not lawful for any to pass into the genus of Gods, except such as, through a love of learning, have philosophized and departed from hence perfectly pure. And for the sake of this, my dear Simmias and Cebes, those who have philosophized rightly abstain from all desires belonging to the body, and strenuously persevere in this abstinence, without giving themselves up to their dominion; nor is it because they dread the ruin of their families, and poverty, like the multitude of the lovers of wealth; nor yet because they are afraid of ignominy and the infamy of improbity, like those who are lovers of dominion and honours, that they abstain from these desires. - For it would not, Socrates, become them so to do (says Cebes). - It would not, by Jupiter

d (says he). - Hence those (says he), O Cebes! who take care of their soul, and do not live in a state of subserviency to their bodies, bidding farewell to all such characters as we have mentioned above, do not proceed in the same path with these during the journey of life, because such characters are ignorant how they should direct their course; but considering that they ought not to act contrary to philosophy, and to its solution and purification, they give themselves up to its direction, and follow wherever it leads. - In what manner, Socrates? - I will tell you (says he).

e The lovers of learning well know, that when philosophy receives their soul into her protection (and when she does so, she finds it vehemently bound and agglutinated to the body, and compelled to speculate things through this, as through a place of confinement, instead of beholding herself through herself; and besides this, rolled in every kind of

---

† It must here be obvious to the most careless reader, that, according to Plato, the *political* are not the *true* virtues.

ignorance: philosophy likewise beholds the dire nature of the confinement, that it arises through desire; so that he who is bound in an eminent degree assists in binding himself); the lovers of learning therefore, I say, know that philosophy, receiving their soul in this condition, endeavours gently to exhort it, and dissolve its bonds; and this she attempts to accomplish, by showing that the inspection of things through the eyes is full of deception, and that this is likewise the case with perception through the ears and the other senses. Philosophy too persuades the soul to depart from all these fallacious informations, and to employ them no further than necessity requires; and exhorts her to call together and collect herself into one. And besides this, to believe in no other than herself, with respect to what she understands, herself subsisting by herself, of that which has likewise a real subsistence by itself; and not to consider that as having a true being which she speculates through others, and which has its subsistence in others. And lastly, that a thing of this kind is sensible and visible; but that what she herself perceives is intelligible and invisible. The soul of a true philosopher, therefore, thinking that he ought not to oppose this solution, abstains as much as possible from pleasures and desires, griefs and fears, considering that when any one is vehemently delighted or terrified, afflicted or desirous, he does not suffer any such mighty evil from these as some one may perhaps conceive, I mean such as disease and a consumption of wealth, through indulging his desires; but that he suffers that which is the greatest, and the extremity of all evils, and this without apprehending that he does so. - But what is this evil, Socrates (says Cebes)? - That the soul of every man is compelled at the same time to be either vehemently delighted or afflicted about some particular thing, and to consider that about which it is thus eminently passive, as having a most evident and true subsistence, though this is by no means the case; and that these are most especially visible objects. Is it not so? - Entirely. -In this passion, therefore, is not the soul in the highest degree bound to the body? - In what manner? - Because every pleasure and pain, as if armed with a nail, fasten and rivet the soul to the body, cause it to become corporeal, and fill it with an opinion, that whatever the body asserts is true. For, in consequence of the soul forming the same opinions with the body, and being delighted with the same objects, it appears to me that it is compelled to possess similar manners, and to be similarly nourished, and to become so affected, that it can never pass into Hades in a pure condition; but always departs full of a corporeal nature; and thus swiftly falls again into another body, and, becoming as it were sown, is engendered; and lastly, that from these it becomes destitute of a divine, pure, and uniform association. - You speak most true, Socrates (says Cebes).

For the sake of these things therefore, O Cebes! those who are justly lovers of learning are moderate and brave, and not for the sake of such 84a as the multitude assert. Or do you think it is? - By no means; for it cannot be. - But the soul of a philosopher reasons in this manner; and does not think that philosophy ought to free him from the body, but that when he is freed he may give himself up to pleasures and pains, by which he will again be bound to the body, and will undertake a work which it is impossible to finish, reweaving a certain web of Penelope.[†] But procuring tranquillity with respect to these, and following the guidance of the reasoning power, and being always conversant with this, contemplating at the same time that which is true, divine, and not the subject of opinion, and being likewise nourished by such an object of contemplation, he will think that he ought to live in this manner while b he lives, and that when he dies he shall depart to a kindred essence, and an essence of this kind, being liberated from the maladies of the human nature. But from a nutriment of this kind the soul has no occasion to fear (while it makes these, O Simmias and Cebes! its study) lest, in its liberation from the body, it should be lacerated, and, being blown about and dissipated by the winds, should vanish, and no longer have anywhere a subsistence.

c When Socrates had thus spoken, a long silence ensued; and Socrates seemed to revolve with himself what had been said; as likewise did the greatest part of us: but Cebes and Simmias discoursed a little with each other. And Socrates at length looking upon them, What (says he), do our assertions appear to you to have been not sufficiently demonstrated? for many doubts and suspicions yet remain, if any one undertakes to investigate them sufficiently. If, therefore, you are considering something else among yourselves, I have nothing to say; but if you are doubting about those particulars which we have just now made the subject of our discourse, do not be remiss in speaking about and running over what has been said, if it appears to you in any respect that we d might have spoken better; and receive me again as your associate, if you think that you can be any ways benefited by my assistance. Upon this Simmias said, Indeed, Socrates, I will tell you the truth: for some time since each of us being agitated with doubts, we impelled and exhorted

---

† As Penelope, who is the image of Philosophy, unwove by night what she had woven by day, so Ignorance reweaves what Philosophy unweaves. Hence Philosophy dissolves the soul from, but Ignorance weaves it to, the body. [.358]

one another to interrogate you, through our desire of hearing them solved; but we were afraid of causing a debate, lest it should be disagreeable to you in your present circumstances. But Socrates, upon hearing this, gently laughed, and said, This is strange, indeed, Simmias; for I shall with difficulty be able to persuade other men that I do not consider the present fortune as a calamity, since I am not able to persuade even you; but you are afraid lest I should be more morose now than I was prior to the present event. And, as it seems, I appear to you to be more despicable than swans with respect to divination, who, when they perceive that it is necessary for them to die, sing not only as usual, but then more than ever; rejoicing that they are about to depart to that Deity in whose service they are engaged. But men, because they themselves are afraid of death, falsely accuse the swans, and assert that, in consequence of their being afflicted at death, their song is the result of grief. Nor do they consider that no bird sings when it is hungry or cold, or is afflicted with any other malady; neither the nightingale, nor the swallow, nor the lapwing, all which they say sing lamenting through distress. But neither do these birds, as it appears to me, sing through sorrow, nor yet the swans; but in my opinion these last are prophetic, as belonging to Apollo; and in consequence of foreseeing the good which Hades contains, they sing and rejoice at that period more remarkably than at any preceding time. But I consider myself as a fellow-servant of the swans, and sacred to the same Divinity. I possess a divining power from our common master no less than they; nor shall I be more afflicted than the swan in being liberated from the present life. Hence it is proper that you should both speak and inquire about whatever you please, as long as the eleven magistrates will permit. - You speak excellently well (says Simmias); and as you give me permission, I will both tell you what are my doubts, and how far Cebes does not admit what has been said. For, as to myself, Socrates, I am perhaps of the same opinion about these particulars as yourself; that to know them clearly in the present life is either impossible, or a thing very difficult to obtain. But not to argue about what has been said in every possible way, and to desist before by an arduous investigation on all sides weariness is produced, can only take place among indolent and effeminate men. For it is necessary, in things of this kind, either to learn or to discover the manner of their subsistence; or, if both these are impossible, then, by receiving the best of human reasons, and that which is the most difficult of confutation, to venture upon this as on a raft, and sail in it through the ocean of life, unless some one should be able to be carried more safely, and with less danger, by means of a firmer vehicle, or a certain *divine reason.*† I shall not, therefore, now be ashamed to interrogate, in consequence of the confession which you have made; nor shall I blame myself hereafter, that I have not spoken what appears to me at present: for, upon considering what has been said, both with myself and together with Cebes, your doctrine did not seem to be sufficiently confirmed.

e   And perhaps, my friend (says Socrates), you have the truth on your side; but inform me in what respect it did not seem to be sufficiently confirmed. - In this (says he); because any one may assert the same about harmony,[21] and a lyre, and its chords; that, for instance, harmony is something invisible and incorporeal, all-beautiful and divine, in a

86a   well-modulated lyre: but the lyre and its chords are bodies, and of a corporeal nature; are composites and terrestrial, and allied to that which is mortal. When any one, therefore, shall either have broken the lyre, or cut and burst the chords, some person may contend from the same reasoning as yours, that it is necessary the harmony should yet remain, and not be destroyed (for it cannot in any respect be possible that the lyre should subsist when the chords are burst, and the chords themselves are of a mortal nature; but the harmony, which is connate and allied to that which is divine and immortal, will become extinct, and perish prior to the mortal nature itself); because it is necessary that harmony should

b   be somewhere, and that the wood and chords must suffer putrefaction, before this can be subject to any passion. For I think, Socrates, that you yourself have also perceived this, that we consider the soul in the most eminent degree, as something of such a kind as to become the temperament of hot and cold, moist and dry, and such-like affections, for the reception of which our body is extended, and by which it is contained: and that the soul is the harmony of all these, when they are beautifully and moderately tempered with each other. If, therefore, the

c   soul is a certain harmony, it is evident that when our body suffers either intension or remission, through diseases and other maladies, the soul must from necessity immediately perish, though of the most divine nature (in the same manner as other harmonies perish, which either subsist in sounds or in the works of artificers); but the remaining parts of the body of each person must subsist for a long time, till they are

d   either burnt or become rotten. Consider then what we shall say to this discourse, if any one should think, since the soul is the temperament of things subsisting in the body, that it perishes the first, in that which is called death.

† See the Introduction to this Dialogue.

Socrates, therefore, beholding us, and laughing as he was accustomed to do very often, Simmias (says he) speaks justly. If any one of you, therefore, is more prompt than I am, why does he not reply to these objections? for he seems not to have handled this affair badly. But it appears to me, that before we make our reply we should first hear

e Cebes, and know what it is which he objects to our discourse; that, in consequence of some time intervening, we may deliberate what we shall say; and that afterwards, upon hearing the objections, we may either assent to them, if they appear to assert any thing becoming; or, if they do not, that we may defend the discourse we have already delivered. But (says he) tell me, Cebes, what it is which so disturbs you, as to cause your unbelief. - I will tell you (says Cebes): your discourse seems to me

87a to be yet in the same state, and to be liable to the same accusation as we mentioned before. For, that our soul had a subsistence before it came into the present form, is an assertion, I will not deny, of a very elegant kind, and (if it is not too much to say) sufficiently demonstrated: but that it still remains when we are dead, does not appear to me to have been clearly proved; nor do I assent to the objection of Simmias, that the soul is not stronger and more lasting than the body, for it appears to me to be much more excellent than all these. Why then, says reason, do you yet disbelieve? for, since you see that when a man dies that which is more imbecil still remains, does it not appear to you to be necessary that the more lasting nature should be preserved during this

b period of time? Consider, therefore, whether I shall say any thing to the purpose in reply. For I, as well as Simmias, as it seems, stand in need of a certain similitude: for to me these things appear to be asserted in the same manner, as if any one should say concerning an aged dead weaver, that the man has not yet perished, but perhaps still survives somewhere; and should exhibit as an argument in proof of this assertion a vestment woven by himself, which he wore, and which is yet safe and

c entire. And if he should ask some one not crediting his assertion, which is the more lasting, the genus of man or of a garment, whose subsistence consists in its use and in being worn; then should it be replied, that the genus of man is much more lasting, he might think it demonstrated, that the man is by a much stronger reason preserved, since that which is of a shorter duration has not yet perished. But I do not think, Simmias, that this is the case. For consider with yourself what I say: since every person must apprehend, that he who asserts this speaks foolishly. For this weaver, having worn and woven many such vestments, died *after*

d them being many, but I think *before* the last; and yet it cannot be any thing the more inferred on this account, that the man is viler or more imbecil than a vestment. And I think that the soul, with respect to the body, will receive the same similitude; and he who shall assert the same concerning these, will appear to me to speak in a very equitable manner; I mean that the soul is of a lasting nature, but the body more debile and less durable. But I should say that each soul wears many bodies, especially if it lives many years; for, if the body glides away like a stream, and is dissolved while the man yet lives, but the soul perpetually reweaves that which is worn and consumed, it will be necessary indeed,

e that when the soul is destroyed it should then be clothed with the last vestment, and should perish prior to this alone. But the soul having perished, then the body will evince the nature of its imbecility, and, becoming rapidly rotten, will be perfectly dissolved: so that, in consequence of this reasoning, it is not yet proper that we should be persuaded to believe with confidence, that our soul subsists somewhere

88a after we are dead. For, if any one should assent to him who asserts even more than you have done, and should grant that not only our soul had an existence before we were born into the present life, but that nothing hinders us from admitting that certain souls after death may still have a subsistence, exist in some future period, and often be born, and again perish (for so naturally strong is the soul, that it will preserve itself through frequent births); but this being granted, it may still follow, that it will not only labour in those many generations, but that, finishing its course, in some one of these deaths, it will entirely perish. But no one

b should say that this death and dissolution of the body, which also introduces destruction to the soul, can be known: for it is impossible that it can be perceived by any one of us. If this, however, be the case, it will not follow that he who possesses the confidence of good hope concerning death is not foolishly confident, unless he can demonstrate that the soul is perfectly immortal and undecaying: for otherwise it will be necessary, that he who is about to die should always fear for his soul, lest in the death, which is at hand, he should entirely perish through the separation of his body.

c When we heard them, therefore, speak in this manner, we were all of us very disagreeably affected, as we afterwards declared to each other; because, as we were in the highest degree persuaded by the former discourse, they again seemed to disturb us and to cast us into unbelief; and this in such a manner, as not only to cause us to deny our assent to the arguments which had been already adduced, but to such as might afterwards be asserted, fearing lest either we should not be proper judges of any thing, or that the things themselves should be unworthy of belief.

d   ECHEC. By the Gods, Phædo, I can easily pardon you: for, while I am now hearing you, I cannot refrain from saying to myself, In what arguments can we any longer believe? For the discourse of Socrates, which a little before was exceedingly credible, is now fallen into unbelief. For the assertion, that our soul is a certain harmony, gained my assent both now and always in a wonderful manner; and now it is mentioned, it recalls as it were into my memory a knowledge that I formerly was of the same opinion. And thus I am perfectly indigent again of some other reason, as if from the very beginning, which may persuade me that the soul of a dead man does not die together with the
e   body. Tell me therefore, by Jupiter, how Socrates pursued the discourse; and whether he, as you confess was the case with yourself, seemed troubled at these objections; or, on the contrary, answered them with facility; and whether he defended his doctrine sufficiently, or in a defective manner. Relate all these particulars to us as accurately as you can.

89a   PHÆD. Indeed, Echecrates, I have often admired Socrates; but never more so than at that time. That he should be able indeed to say something in reply, is perhaps not wonderful; but I especially admired, in the first place, this in him, that he received the discourse of the young men in such a pleasant, benevolent and wonderful manner; and, in the next place, that he so acutely perceived how we were affected by their objections; and lastly, that he so well cured our disturbance, recalled us, as if flying and vanquished, and caused us, in conjunction with himself, to pursue and consider the discourse.

         ECHEC. But how did he do this?

b   PHÆD. I will tell you: I happened at that time to sit at his right hand, upon a low seat near his bed; but he himself sat much higher than I did. Stroking me on the head, therefore, and compressing the hair which hung on my neck (for he used sometimes to play with my hairs), Tomorrow (says he), Phædo, you will perhaps cut off these beautiful locks. - It seems so, indeed (says I), Socrates. - But you will not (says he), if you will be persuaded by me. - But why not (says I)? - For both you and I (says he) ought to cut off our hair today, if our discourse must die, and we are not able to recall it to life again. And I indeed, if I was you,
c   and I found that discourse fled from me, would take an oath after the manner of the Argives, that I would never suffer my hair to grow, till, by contesting in disputation, I had vanquished the objections of Simmias and Cebes. - But (says I) Hercules is reported not to have been sufficient

against two. - Call upon me, therefore (says he), as your Iolaus[†] while the light yet lasts. - I call then (says I), not as Hercules upon Iolaus, but as Iolaus upon Hercules. - It is of no consequence (says he).

    But, in the first place, we must be careful that we are not influenced by a certain passion. - What passion (says I)? - That we do not become (says he) haters of reason,[‡] in the same manner as some become haters of men. For no greater evil can happen to any one than to be a hater of reasons. But a hatred of reason and a hatred of mankind are both produced in the same manner. For misanthropy is produced in us through very much believing without art in some particular person, and considering him as a man true, sincere, and faithful, whom in the course of a short acquaintance we find to be depraved and unfaithful; and that this is the case again with another. And when any one often suffers this disappointment, and especially from those whom he considered as his most intimate familiars and friends, at length, through finding himself thus frequently hurt, he hates all men, and thinks that there is nothing in any respect sincere in any one. Or have you never perceived that this is the case? - Entirely so (says I). - But is not this base (says he)? and is it not evident that such a one attempts to make use of men, without possessing the art which respects human affairs? For if, in a certain respect, he employed them with art, he would think, as the case really is, that men very good, or very bad, are but few in number; and that the greater part of mankind are those which subsist between these. - How do you mean (says I)? - In the same manner (says he) as about things very small and very great. Do you think that any thing is more rare than to find a very large or a very small man, or dog, or any thing else; and again any thing excessively swift or slow, beautiful or base, white or black? Or do you not perceive that the summits of the extremes of all these are rare and few, but that things subsisting between these are copious and many? - Entirely so (says I). - Do you not, therefore, think (says he) that if a contest of improbity should be proposed, those who hold the first rank among the base would be found to be but few? - It

(Marginalia left column: d, e, 90a, b)

---

    † Iolaus was the son of Iphiclus king of Thessaly. He assisted Hercules in conquering the Hydra, and burnt with a hot iron the place where the heads had been cut off, to prevent the growth of others.

    ‡ Four inevitable consequences attend the man who hates reason. In the first place, he must hate himself; for he is essentially rational. In the second place, he must hate truth; for this can only be discovered by the exercise of reason. In the third place, he must be a lover of that which is irrational. And, in the fourth place, he must be brutalized, as far as this is possible to man. [.399]

is agreeable to reason to think so (says I). - It is so, indeed (says he); but in this respect reasons are not similar to men (for I shall now follow you as the leader); but in this they are similar, when any one, for instance, without possessing the art belonging to discourse, believes that a certain discourse is true, and shortly after it appears to him to be false, as it is sometimes the one and sometimes the other, and the same thing happens

c to him about different discourses. And this is particularly the case with those who are familiar with contradictory arguments; for these you know think that they at length become most wise, and alone perceive that there is nothing sound and stable either in things or reasons; but that every thing is whirled upwards and downwards, as if existing in the river Euripus, and does not abide in any one condition for any portion of time whatever. - You speak perfectly true (says I). - Would it not then (says he), Phædo, be a passion worthy of commiseration, if, when a certain reason is true and firm, and is capable of being understood, yet

d some one falling from this should be involved in doubt, because he has heard reasons, which, though remaining the same, yet have at one time appeared to be true, and at another false; and should not accuse himself and his own want of skill, but at length through grief should transfer all the blame from himself to the reasons; and thus should pass the remainder of his life, hating and slandering reasons, and deprived of the truth and science of things? - By Jupiter (says I), such a one would be miserable indeed.

e In the first place, therefore (says he), we should be very careful against admitting an opinion, that no reasoning appears to be valid; but we should much rather think that we are not yet in a healthy condition, and that we ought vigorously and cheerfully to study how to be well. And this indeed ought to be the case with you and others, for the sake of the whole remainder of your life, but with me, for the sake of death

91a itself; as there is danger at the present time, lest I should not behave philosophically, but, like those who are perfectly unskilled, contentiously. For such as these, when they controvert any particular, are not at all concerned how that subsists about which they dispute; but are alone anxious, that what they have established may appear to the persons present to be true. And I seem to myself at present to differ alone in this respect from such as these: for I am not solicitous that my discourse may appear true to those who are present (except just as it may happen in passing), but that it may appear to be so in the most eminent degree to me myself. For I thus reason, my dear friend (and see

b in how fraudulent a manner), that if my assertions are true, it will be a beautiful circumstance to be persuaded of their truth; but that if nothing remains for the dead, I shall at least have the advantage of being less afflicted with my present condition than others. But this ignorance of mine will not continue long (for it would be bad if it should), but shortly after this will be dissolved; and being thus prepared (says he), Simmias and Cebes, I shall now return to the discourse. But, that you

c   may be persuaded by me, pay no attention to the person of Socrates, but be much more solicitous in assenting to the truth, if I should appear to you to assert any thing true; but if this should not be the case, oppose me with all your might, and beware, lest through too much ardour I should deceive both myself and you, and, acting in this respect like bees, should depart from you, leaving my sting behind.

But to begin (says he): In the first place, remind me of what you have said, if it should appear that I have forgotten it. For Simmias, I think, distrusted and was afraid lest the soul, though it is at the same time

d   more divine and beautiful than the body, should perish before it, as subsisting in the form of harmony. But Cebes appears to me to have admitted this, that the soul is more lasting than the body; but yet that it is perfectly uncertain, whether after the soul has worn out many bodies, and this often, it may not at length, leaving body behind, itself also perish; so that this will be death itself, I mean the destruction of the soul, since the body perpetually perishes without ceasing. Are not these the things, Simmias and Cebes, which we ought to consider? - They

e   both confessed that the particulars were these. - Whether, therefore (says he), do you reject the whole of our former discourse, or do you reject some things and not others? - They replied, We admit some things, and not others. - What then (says he) do you say about that discourse, in which we asserted that learning is reminiscence; and that, this being the

92a   case, our soul must necessarily have subsisted somewhere before it was bound in the body? - I indeed (says Cebes) was both then wonderfully persuaded by that discourse, and now firmly abide in the same opinion. - And I also (says Simmias) am affected in the same manner; and I should very much wonder should I ever conceive otherwise about this particular. - But (says Socrates) it is necessary, my Theban guest, that it should appear otherwise to you, if you still continue of the opinion, that

b   harmony is something composite, and that the soul is a certain harmony, composed from things extended through the body. For you will never assent to yourself asserting, that harmony was composed prior to the things from which it ought to be composed; or do you think you can? - By no means (says he), Socrates. - Do you perceive, therefore (says he), that you will not be consistent in your assertions, when you say that the soul had a subsistence before it came into a human form and into body, but that at the same time it was composed from things which then had not a being? For neither is harmony such as that to which you assimilate it; but the lyre, and the chords, and the sounds yet unharmonized, have a prior existence; but harmony is composed the last of all, and is the first dissolved. How, therefore, can this discourse be consonant with that? - In no respect (says Simmias). - But it certainly is proper (says he) that a discourse about harmony should be consonant, if this can ever be asserted of any other. - It is proper, indeed (says Simmias). - But this discourse of yours is not consonant. Consider, therefore, which of these assertions you will choose, that learning is reminiscence, or that the soul is harmony. - I prefer the former, Socrates, by much; for the latter gained my assent without a demonstration, through nothing more than a certain probability and specious appearance; from whence also it appears evident to the multitude of mankind. But I well know, that the discourses which frame their demonstrations from assimilative reasons only are nothing more than empty boastings; and unless a man defends himself against them, they will very much deceive him, both in geometry and all other speculations. But the discourse about reminiscence and learning was delivered through an hypothesis highly worthy of reception. For in this it was said that our soul had a subsistence somewhere before it came into the present body, as it is an essence possessing the appellation of that which truly is. But, as I persuade myself, I assent to this doctrine in a manner sufficient and proper; and hence it is necessary, as it appears to me, that I should neither assent to myself nor to any other asserting that the soul is harmony.

But what (says he), Simmias? Does it appear to you that it can either belong to this harmony, or to any composition, to subsist differently from the things from which it is composed? - By no means. - And indeed, as it appears to me, it can neither perform nor suffer any thing else, besides what these perform and suffer. - He agreed it could not. - It does not, therefore, belong to harmony to be the leader of the materials from which it is composed, but to follow them. - This also he granted. - It is far, therefore, from being the case, that harmony will either be moved or sound contrary, or in any other respect be adverse to its parts. - Very far, indeed, (says he). - But what, does not every harmony naturally subsist in such a manner as to be harmony, so far as it receives a congruous temperament? - I do not understand you. - But (says he) if it were possible that it could be congruously tempered with still greater vehemence, and more in quantity, would it not be more vehemently harmony and more in quantity; but if less vehemently and less in quantity, just the contrary? - Entirely so. - But can it be said of the soul, that, even in the smallest circumstance, one soul is more vehemently and more in quantity, or less vehemently and less in quantity, soul, than another? - By no means (says he). - Consider then (says he), by Jupiter, is it truly said, that one soul possesses intellect and virtue, and is good; but that another is foolish and vicious, and is bad? -

c   It is truly said. - Among those, therefore, who establish the soul as harmony, what can any one call virtue and vice in the soul? Will he call the one harmony, and the other discord? And that the one, that is to say the good soul, is harmonized; and, as it is harmony, possesses another harmony in itself; but that the other is discord, and does not contain in itself another harmony? - I know not what to reply (says Simmias); but it is manifest, that he who establishes this would make

d   some such reply. - But it has been granted (says he), that one soul is not more or less soul than another; and this is no other than to confess, that one harmony is not more vehemently and more in quantity, nor less vehemently and less in quantity, harmony, than another: is it not so? - Entirely so. - But that which is neither more nor less harmony, is neither more nor less harmonized: is it not so? - It is. - But can that which is neither more nor less harmonized participate more or less of

e   harmony?[22] or does it equally participate? - Equally. - The soul, therefore, since it is not more or less soul than another, is not more or less harmonized. - It is not. - But since it is thus affected, it will neither participate more of discord nor of harmony. - By no means. - And again, in consequence of this passion, can one soul participate more of vice or

94a   virtue than another, since vice is discord, but virtue harmony? - It cannot. - But rather, Simmias, according to right reason, no soul will participate of vice, since it is harmony: for doubtless the harmony, which is perfectly such, can never participate of discord. - It certainly cannot. - Neither, therefore, can the soul, which is perfectly soul, participate of vice: for how can it, in consequence of what has been said? In consequence of this reasoning, therefore, the souls of all animals will be similarly good; since they are naturally similarly souls, with respect

b   to the essence of soul. - To me it appears so, Socrates (says he). - If the hypothesis therefore was right, would it appear to you to be beautifully said, and that this consequence ensued, that the soul is harmony? - By no means (says he).

But what (says Socrates), among all the things which are inherent in man, would you say that any thing else governed except soul, if he be a prudent man? - I should not. - But whether does the soul govern, by assenting to the passions belonging to the body, or by opposing them?

My meaning is this, that when heat and thirst are present, the soul, if it governs, will frequently draw the body to the contrary, *i.e.* not to drink;

c and hunger being present, that it shall not eat; and in a thousand other instances we may behold the soul opposing the desires of the body: may we not? - Entirely so. - Have we not above confessed, that if the soul was harmony, it would never sound contrary to the intensions, remissions, or vibrations, or any other passion belonging to its component parts, but that it would follow, and never rule over them? - We have granted this (says he); for how could we do otherwise? - But what, does not the soul now appear to act just the contrary to this, ruling over all those particulars, from which it may be said it subsists, nearly opposing all of them through the whole of life, and exercising absolute dominion over them all manner of ways, punishing some of

d these indeed with greater difficulty, and accompanied with pain; some through gymnastic and medicine, and some by milder methods, and some again by threats, and others by admonishing desire, anger, and fear; addressing that which it opposes, as being itself of a different nature? just as Homer does in the *Odyssey*, where he says of Ulysses:

e His breast he struck, and cried, My heart sustain
This ill! for thou hast borne far greater pain.

Odyssey xx, 17.

Do you think that Homer devised this in consequence of thinking that the soul is harmony, and of such a kind as to be led by the passions of the body, and not such as is naturally adapted to lead and govern, and which is something much more divine than harmony? - By Jupiter, Socrates, I do not think that he did. - By no means, therefore, most excellent man, shall we do well, in asserting that the soul is a *certain*†harmony: for by thus asserting, as it appears, we shall neither agree with

95a Homer, that divine poet, nor be consistent with ourselves. - It is so, indeed (says he).

Let it then be so (says Socrates); and thus, as it appears, we have sufficiently appeased the patrons of the Theban harmony. But how, Cebes, and by what discourse shall we appease the patrons of Cadmus?[23] - You appear to me (says Cebes) to be likely to find out a way: for you have delivered this discourse against harmony in a wonderful manner,

b and beyond what I expected. For, while Simmias related his doubts, I thought it would be a most admirable thing, should any one be able to reply to his discourse. He therefore appears to me, in a manner

---

† That is, a harmony subsisting in, and therefore inseparable from, a subject. [.406]

perfectly extraordinary, not to have sustained the very first assault of
your discourse. I should not, therefore, be surprised if the arguments of
Cadmus met with the same fate. - My good friend (says Socrates), do not
speak so magnificently, lest a certain envy should subvert our future
discourse. These things, indeed, will be taken care of by Divinity. But
we, approaching near in an Homeric manner, will try whether you say
any thing to the purpose. This then is the sum of what you inquire:
you think it proper to demonstrate that our soul is without decay, and
c   immortal; that a philosopher who is about to die with all the confidence
of hope, and who thinks that after death he shall be far more happy
than in the present life, may not indulge a stupid and foolish confidence.
But you say, though it should be shown that the soul is something
robust and deiform, and that it subsisted before we were born, yet
nothing hinders but that all these arguments may not evince its
immortality, but only that the soul is more lasting than the body, that
it formerly existed somewhere for an immense period of time, and that
d   it knew and performed a multitude of things. But that, for all this, it
will be nothing the more immortal; but that, entering into the body of
a man, it will be the principle of destruction to itself, as if connected
with a disease: so that it will both lead a miserable life in the body, and
at last will perish in that which is called death. But you say it is of no
consequence whether it comes into body once or often, with respect to
our occasion of fear: for it is very proper that he who neither knows,
nor is able to render a reason, why the soul is immortal, should be
afraid of death, unless he is deprived of intellect. This, I think, Cebes,
e   is the sum of what you say; and I have repeated it often, that nothing
may escape our observation; and that, if you are willing, you may either
add or take away from our statement of the objections. But Cebes
replied, I have nothing at present either to add or take away; but these
are the objections which I make.

Socrates, therefore, after he had been silent for a long time, and
considering something by himself, said, You require, Cebes, a thing of
no small importance: for it is perfectly necessary to treat concerning the
cause of generation and corruption. If you are willing, therefore, I will
96a   relate to you what happened to me in this investigation; and afterwards,
if any thing which I shall say shall appear to you useful, with respect to
persuading you in the present inquiry, employ it for this purpose. - But
I am most assuredly willing (says Cebes). - Hear then my narration:
When I was a young man, Cebes, I was in a wonderful manner desirous

of that wisdom which they call a history of nature:[†] for it appeared to me to be a very superb affair to know the causes of each particular, on what account each is generated, why it perishes, and why it exists. And

b   I often tossed myself as it were upwards and downwards; considering, in the first place, whether after that which is hot and cold has received a certain rottenness, as some say, then animals are nourished; and whether the blood is that through which we become prudent, or air, or fire; or whether none of these, but the brain, is that which affords the senses of hearing, seeing, and smelling; so that memory and opinion are generated from these, and that from memory and opinion obtaining tranquillity, science is accordingly produced? And again considering the

c   corruptions of these, and the properties which take place about the heavens and the earth, I at length appeared to myself so unskilful in the speculation of these, as to receive no advantage from my inquiries. But I will give you a sufficient proof of the truth of this: for I then became so very blind, with respect to things which I knew before with great clearness (as it appeared both to myself and others) through this speculation, as to want instruction both in many particulars, which I thought I had known before, and in this, why a man is increased. For I thought it was evident to every one that this took place through eating

d   and drinking: for when, from the aliment, flesh accedes to flesh, bone to bone, and every where kindred to kindred parts, then the bulk which was small becomes afterwards great; and thus a little man becomes a large one. Such was then my opinion; does it appear to you a becoming one? - To me, indeed, it does (says Cebes). - But still further, consider as follows: for I thought that I seemed to myself sufficiently right in my opinion, when, on seeing a tall man standing by a short one, I judged that he was taller by the head; and in like manner one horse than

e   another: and still more evident than these, ten things appeared to me to be more than eight, because two is added to them, and that a bicubital is greater than a cubital magnitude, through its surpassing it by the half. - But now (says Cebes) what appears to you respecting these? - By Jupiter (says he), I am so far from thinking that I know the cause of these, that I cannot even persuade myself, when any person adds one to one, that then the one to which the addition was made becomes two; or

---

† What Socrates here calls *a history of nature*, is what the moderns call *experimental philosophy*. The danger of directing the attention solely to this study is, as Socrates justly observes, truly great. For by speculating no other causes than such as are instrumental, and which are involved in the darkness of matter, the mental eye becomes at length incapable of beholding true and primary causes, the splendid principles of all things.

97a that the added one, and that to which it is added, become two, through the addition of the one to the other. For I should wonder, since each of these, when separate from one another, was one, and not then two; if, after they have approached nearer to each other, this should be the cause of their becoming two, *viz.* the association through which they are placed nearer to each other. Nor yet, if any person should divide one, am I able to persuade myself that this division is the cause of its

b becoming two. For that former[†] cause of two being produced is contrary to this. For then this took place, because they were collected near to each other, and the one was applied to the other; but now, because the one is removed and separated from the other. Nor do I any longer persuade myself, that I know why one is produced; nor, in one word, why any thing else is either generated or corrupted, or is, according to this method of proceeding: but, in order to obtain this knowledge, I venture to mingle another method of my own, by no means admitting this which I have mentioned.

c But having once heard a person reading from a certain book, composed, as he said, by Anaxagoras[‡] - when he came to that part, in which he says that intellect orders and is the cause of all things, I was delighted with this cause, and thought that, in *a certain respect,*[§] it was an excellent thing for intellect to be the cause of all; and I considered that, if this was the case, disposing intellect would adorn all things, and place every thing in that situation in which it would subsist in the best manner. If any one, therefore, should be willing to discover the cause through which every thing is generated, or corrupted, or is, he ought to

d discover how it may subsist in the best manner, or suffer, or perform any thing else. In consequence of this, therefore, it is proper that a man should consider nothing else, either about himself or about others,

---

† Addition is no more the proper cause of two than division; but each of these is nothing but a concause. For one and one by junction become the subject or matter of the participation of the incorporeal duad; and this is likewise the case when one thing is divided.

‡ See an extract of some length from that work of Anaxagoras to which Plato here alludes, in the Notes on the first book of my translation of Aristotle's *Metaphysics* [TTS vol. XXIII, note 3, p. 291].

§ Socrates here uses the words *in a certain respect* with the greatest accuracy: for *intellect,* considered according to its highest subsistence in the intelligible order, may be said to be the cause of all things posterior to *The One;* but *The One,* being above intellect, is truly in every respect the cause of all.

except that which is the most excellent and the best: but it is necessary that he who knows this should also know that which is subordinate, since there is one and the same science of both. But thus reasoning with myself, I rejoiced, thinking that I had found a preceptor in Anaxagoras, who would instruct me in the causes of things agreeably to my own conceptions; and that he would inform me, in the first place, whether the earth is flat or round; and afterwards explain the cause and necessity of its being so, adducing for this purpose that which is better, and showing that it is better for the earth to exist in this manner. And if he should say it is situated in the middle, that he would, besides this, show that it is better for it to be in the middle; and if he should render all this apparent to me, I was so disposed as not to require any other species of cause. I had likewise prepared myself in a similar manner for an inquiry respecting the sun, and moon, and the other stars, their velocities and revolutions about each other, and all their other properties; so as to be able to know why it is better for each to operate in a certain manner, and to suffer that which it suffers. For I by no means thought, after he had said that all these were orderly disposed by intellect, he would introduce any other cause of their subsistence, except that which shows[†] that it is best for them to exist as they do. Hence I thought that in assigning the cause common to each particular, and to all things, he would explain that which is best for each, and is the common good of all. And indeed I would not have exchanged these hopes for a mighty gain! but having obtained his books with prodigious eagerness, I read them with great celerity, that I might with great celerity know that which is the best, and that which is base.

From this admirable hope however, my friend, I was forced away, when, in the course of my reading, I saw him make no use of intellect, nor employ certain causes, for the purpose of orderly disposing particulars, but assign air, æther, and water, and many other things equally absurd, as the causes of things. And he appeared to me to be affected in a manner similar to him who should assert, that all the actions of Socrates are produced by intellect; and afterwards, endeavouring to relate the causes of each particular action, should say, that, in the first place, I now sit here because my body is composed from bones and nerves, and that the bones are solid, and are separated by intervals from each other; but that the nerves, which are of a nature

---

† Concauses can never show that it is best for things to exist as they do; but this can only be effected by primary, *viz. effective, paradigmatic,* and *final* causes. [Cf. Aristotle, *Metaphysics*, 1,3, TTS vol. XXIII]

d capable of intension and remission, cover the bones, together with the
flesh and skin by which they are contained. The bones, therefore, being
suspended from their joints, the nerves, by straining and relaxing them,
enable me to bend my limbs as at present; and through this cause I here
sit in an inflected position - and again, should assign other such-like
causes of my conversation with you, *viz.* voice, and air, and hearing, and
a thousand other such particulars, neglecting to adduce the true cause,
e that since it appeared to the Athenians better to condemn me, on this
account, it also appeared to me to be better and more just to sit here,
and, thus abiding, sustain the punishment which they have ordained me.
99a For otherwise, by the dog, as it appears to me, these nerves and bones
would have been carried long ago either into Megara or Bœotia, through
an opinion of that which is best, if I had not thought it more just and
becoming to sustain the punishment ordered by my country, whatever
it may be, than to withdraw myself and run away. But to call things of
this kind causes is extremely absurd. Indeed, if any one should say that
without possessing such things as bones and nerves, and other particulars
which belong to me, I could not act in the manner I appear to do, he
would speak the truth: but to assert that I act as I do at present through
b these, and that I operate with this intellect, and not from the choice of
that which is best, would be an assertion full of extreme negligence and
sloth. For this would be the consequence of not being able to collect by
division, that the true cause of a thing is very different from that
without which a cause would not be a cause. And this indeed appears
to me to be the case with the multitude of mankind, who, handling
things as it were in darkness, call them by names foreign from the truth,
and thus denominate things causes which are not so. Hence, one placing
round the earth a certain vortex, produced by the celestial motion,
renders by this mean the earth fixed in the centre; but another places air
c under it, as if it was a basis to a broad trough. But they neither
investigate that power through which things are now disposed in the
best manner possible, nor do they think that it is endued with any
dæmoniacal strength: but they fancy they have found a certain Atlas,
more strong and immortal than such a strength, and far more sustaining
all things; and they think that the good and the becoming do not in
reality connect and sustain any thing. With respect to myself, indeed,
I would most willingly become the disciple of any one; so that I might
perceive in what manner a cause of this kind subsists. But since I am
deprived of this advantage, and have neither been able to discover it
myself, nor to learn it from another, are you willing, Cebes, that I
d should show you the manner in which I made a prosperous voyage to

discover the cause of things? - I am willing (says he) in a most transcendent degree.

It appeared to me therefore (says Socrates) afterwards, when I was wearied with such speculations, that I ought to take care lest I should be affected in the same manner as those are who attentively behold the sun in an eclipse: for some would be deprived of their sight, unless they beheld its image in water, or in a similar medium. And something of this kind I perceived with respect to myself, and was afraid lest my soul should be perfectly blinded through beholding things with the eyes of my body, and through endeavouring to apprehend them by means of the several senses. Hence I considered that I ought to fly to reasons, and in them survey the truth of things. Perhaps, indeed, this similitude of mine may not in a certain respect be proper: for I do not entirely admit that he who contemplates things in reasons, surveys them in images, more than he who contemplates them in external effects. This method, therefore, I have adopted; and always establishing that reason as an hypothesis, which I judge to be the most valid, whatever appears to me to be consonant to this, I fix upon as true, both concerning the cause of things and every thing else; but such as are not consonant I consider as not true. But I wish to explain to you what I say in a clearer manner: for I think that you do not at present understand me. - Not very much, by Jupiter, says Cebes.

However (says he), I now assert nothing new, but what I have always asserted at other times, and in the preceding disputation. For I shall now attempt to demonstrate to you that species of cause which I have been discoursing about, and shall return again to those particulars which are so much celebrated; beginning from these, and laying down as an hypothesis, that there is a certain something beautiful, itself subsisting by itself; and a certain something good and great, and so of all the rest; which if you permit me to do, and allow that such things have a subsistence, I hope that I shall be able from these to demonstrate this cause to you, and discover that the soul is immortal. - But (says Cebes), in consequence of having granted you this already, you cannot be hindered from drawing such a conclusion. - But consider (says he) the things consequent to these, and see whether you will then likewise agree with me. For it appears to me, that if there be any thing else beautiful, besides the beautiful itself, it cannot be beautiful on any other account than because it participates of the beautiful itself; and I should speak in the same manner of all things. Do you admit such a cause? - I admit it (says he). - I do not therefore (says Socrates) any longer perceive, nor am I able to understand, those other *wise* causes; but if any one tells me d   why a certain thing is beautiful, and assigns as a reason, either its possessing a florid colour, or figure, or something else of this kind, I bid farewell to other hypotheses (for in all others I find myself disturbed); but this I retain with myself, simply, unartificially, and perhaps foolishly, that nothing else causes it to be beautiful, than either the presence, or communion, or in whatever manner the operations may take place, of the beautiful itself. For I cannot yet affirm how this takes place; but only this, that all beautiful things become such through the beautiful itself. For it appears to me most safe thus to answer both

e   myself and others; and adhering to this, I think that I can never fall, but that I shall be secure in answering, that all beautiful things are beautiful through the beautiful itself. Does it not also appear so to you? - It does. - And that great things, therefore, are great, and things greater, greater through magnitude itself; and things lesser, lesser through smallness itself? - Certainly. - Neither, therefore, would you assent, if it should be said that some one is larger than another by the head, and that he who is lesser is lesser by the very same thing, *i.e.* the head: but you would

101a   testify that you said nothing else than that, with respect to every thing great, one thing is greater than another by nothing else than magnitude, and that through this it is greater, *i.e.* through magnitude; and that the lesser is lesser through nothing else than smallness, and that through this it is lesser, *i.e.* through smallness. For you would be afraid, I think, lest, if you should say that any one is greater and lesser by the head, you should contradict yourself: first, in asserting that the greater is greater, and the lesser lesser, by the very same thing; and afterwards that the greater is greater by the head, which is a small thing; and that it is

b   monstrous to suppose, that any thing which is great can become so through something which is small. Would you not be afraid of all this? - Indeed I should (says Cebes, laughing). - Would you not also (says he) be afraid to say that ten things are more than eight by two, and that through this cause ten transcends eight, and not by multitude and through multitude? And in like manner, that a thing which is two cubits in length is greater than that which is but one cubit, by the half, and not by magnitude? for the dread is indeed the same. - Entirely so (says he). - But what? one being added to one, will the addition be the

c   cause of their becoming two? or if one is divided, and two produced, would you not be afraid to assign division as the cause? Indeed you would cry with a loud voice, that you know no other way by which any thing subsists, than by participating the proper essence of every thing which it participates; and that in these you can assign no other cause of their becoming two, than the participation of the duad; and that it is proper all such things as are about to become two, should participate of this, and of unity, whatever is about to become one. But

d   you would bid farewell to these divisions and additions, and other subtilties of this kind, and would leave them to be employed in answering, by those who are wiser than yourself. And fearing, as it is said, your own shadow, and your own unskilfulness you would adhere to this safe hypothesis, and answer in the manner I have described. But if any one should adhere to this hypothesis, you would refrain from answering him till you had considered the consequences resulting from thence, and whether they were consonant or dissonant to one another. But when it is necessary for you to assign a reason for your belief in this hypothesis, you will assign it in a similar manner, laying down again another hypothesis, which shall appear to be the best among supernal natures, till you arrive at something sufficient. At the same time you

e   will by no means confound things by mingling them together, after the manner of the contentious, when you discourse concerning the principle and the consequences arising from thence, if you are willing to discover any thing of true beings. For by such as these, perhaps, no attention is paid to this. For these, through their wisdom, are sufficiently able to mingle all things together, and at the same time please themselves. But you, if you rank among the philosophers, will act, I think, in the manner I have described. - Both Simmias and Cebes said, You speak most truly.

102a   ECHEC. By Jupiter, Phædo, they assented with great propriety: for he appears to me to have asserted this in a manner wonderfully clear; and this even to one endued with the smallest degree of intellect.

PHÆD. And so indeed, Echecrates, it appeared in every respect to all who were present.

ECHEC. And well it might: for it appears so to us, now we hear it, who were not present. But what was the discourse after this?

b   PHÆD. If I remember right, after they had granted all this, and had confessed that each of the several species was something, and that others participating of these received the same denomination, he afterwards interrogated them as follows: If then you allow that these things are so, when you say that Simmias is greater than Socrates, but less than Phædo, do you not then assert that both magnitude and parvitude are inherent in Simmias? - I do. - And yet (says he) you must confess, that this circumstance of Simmias surpassing Socrates does not truly subsist

c   in the manner which the words seem to imply. For Simmias is not naturally adapted to surpass Socrates, so far as he is Simmias, but by the magnitude which he possesses: nor, again, does he surpass Socrates so far

as Socrates is Socrates, but because Socrates possesses parvitude with respect to his magnitude. - True. - Nor, again, is Simmias surpassed by Phædo, because Phædo is Phædo, but because Phædo possesses magnitude with respect to the parvitude of Simmias. - It is so. - Simmias, therefore, is allotted the appellation of both small and great, being situated in the middle of both; exhibiting his smallness to be surpassed
d   by the greatness of the one, and his greatness to the other's smallness, which it surpasses. And at the same time, gently laughing, I seem (says he) to have spoken with all the precision of an historian; but, notwithstanding this, it is as I say. - He allowed it. - But I have mentioned these things, in order that you may be of the same opinion as myself. For to me it appears, not only that magnitude is never willing to be at the same time both great and small, but that the magnitude which we contain never desires to receive that which is small, nor be surpassed; but that it is willing to do one of these two things,
e   either to fly away, and gradually withdraw itself, when its contrary the small approaches to it, or to perish when it arrives; but that it is unwilling, by sustaining and receiving parvitude, to be different from what it was. In the same manner as I myself receiving and sustaining parvitude, and still remaining that which I am, am nevertheless small. But that being great dares not to be small. And in like manner *the small*, which resides in us, is not willing at any time *to subsist in becoming to be* great, or *to be great*: nor does any thing else among contraries, while
103a   it remains that which it was, wish at the same time *to subsist in becoming to be*, and *to be*, its contrary; but it either departs or perishes in consequence of this passion. - It appears so to me (says Cebes) in every respect.

But a certain person, who was present, upon hearing this (I do not clearly remember who it was), By the Gods (says he), was not the very contrary of what you now assert admitted by you in the former part of your discourse, *viz.* that the greater was generated from the less, and the less from the greater; and that generation among contraries plainly took place from contraries? But now you appear to me to say, that this can never be the case. Upon this Socrates, after he had extended his head a little further, and had listened to his discourse, said, You very manfully
b   put me in mind; yet you do not understand the difference between what is now and what was then asserted. For then it was said, that a contrary thing was generated from a contrary; but now, that a contrary can never become contrary to itself, neither that contrary which subsists in us, nor that which subsists in nature. For then, my friend, we spoke concerning things which possess contraries, calling the contraries by the appellation

of the things in which they reside; but now we speak of things which
receive their denomination from the contraries residing in them. And
we should never be willing to assert that these contraries receive a
generation from one another. And at the same time, beholding Cebes,
he said, Did any thing which has been said by this person disturb you
also? - Indeed (says Cebes) it did not; and at such a time as this there are
not many things which can disturb me. - We ingenuously, therefore
(says he), assent to this, that a contrary can never become contrary to
itself. - Entirely so (says Cebes).

But still further (says he), consider whether you agree with me in this
also. Do you call *the hot* and *the cold* any thing? - I do. - Are they the
same with snow and fire? - They are not, by Jupiter. - *The hot*, therefore,
is something different from *fire*, and *the cold* from *snow*. - Certainly. -
But this also is, I think, apparent to you, that snow, as long as it is such,
can never, by receiving heat, remain what it was before, *viz.* snow, and
at the same time become hot; but, on the accession of heat, must either
withdraw itself from it, or perish. - Entirely so. - And again, that fire,
when cold approaches to it, must either depart or perish; but that it will
never dare, by receiving coldness, still to remain what it was, *i.e.* fire,
and yet be at the same time cold. - You speak truly (says he). - But (says
Socrates) it happens to some of these, that not only the species itself is
always thought worthy of the same appellation, but likewise something
else, which is not indeed that species, but which perpetually possesses
the form of it as long as it exists. But in the following instances my
meaning will perhaps be more apparent: for the odd number ought
always to possess that name by which we now call it: should it not? -
Entirely so. - But is this the case with the odd number alone (for this is
what I inquire)? or is there any thing else which is not indeed the same
with the odd, but yet which ought always to be called odd, together
with its own proper name, because it naturally subsists in such a
manner, that it can never desert the form of the odd? But this is no
other than what happens to the number three, and many other things.
For consider, does not the number three appear to you to be always
called by its proper name, and at the same time by the name of the odd,
though *the odd* is not the same as *the triad*? Yet the triad, and the
pentad, and the entire half of number, naturally subsist in such a
manner, that though they are not the same as *the odd*, yet each of them
is always odd. And again, two and four, and the whole other order of
number, though they are not the same as *the even*, yet each of them is
always even: do you admit this or not? - How should I not (says he)? -
See then (says Socrates) what I wish to evince. But it is as follows: It has

appeared, not only that contraries do not receive one another, but that even such things as are not contrary to each other, and yet always possess contraries, do not appear to receive that idea which is contrary to the idea which they contain; but that on its approach they either

c perish or depart. Shall we not, therefore, say that three things would first perish, and endure any thing whatever, sooner than sustain to be three things, and at the same time to be even? - Entirely so (says Cebes). - And yet (says Socrates) the duad is not contrary to the triad. - Certainly not. - Not only, therefore, do contrary species never sustain the approach of each other, but certain other things likewise cannot sustain the accession of contraries. - You speak most true (says he).

d Are you willing, therefore (says he), that, if we are able, we should define what kind of things these are? - Entirely so. - Will they not then, Cebes (says he), be such things as compel whatever they occupy, not only to retain their idea, but likewise not to receive a contrary to it? - How do you mean? - Exactly as we just now said. For you know it is necessary, that whatever things the idea of three occupies should not only be three, but likewise odd. - Entirely so. - To a thing of this kind, therefore, we assert, that an idea contrary to that form, through which it becomes what it is, will never approach. - It cannot. - But it becomes what it is through the odd: does it not? - Certainly. - But is not the

e contrary to this the idea of the even? - It is. - The idea of the even, therefore, will never accede to three things. - Never. - Are not three things, therefore, destitute of the even? - Destitute. - The triad, therefore, is an odd number. - It is. - The things which I mentioned then are defined, *viz.* such things, which, though they are not contrary to some particular nature, yet do not at the same time receive that which is contrary; just as the triad in the present instance, though it is not contrary to the even, yet does not any thing more receive it on this account: for it always brings with it that which is contrary to the even; and in like manner the duad to the odd, and fire to cold, and an abundant multitude of other particulars. But see whether you would

105a thus define, not only that a contrary does not receive a contrary, but likewise that the nature which brings with it a contrary to that which it approaches, will never receive the contrariety of that which it introduces. But recollect again, for it will not be useless to hear it repeated often. Five things will not receive the form of the even; neither will ten things, which are the double of five, receive the form of the odd. This,[†] therefore, though it is itself contrary to something

---

† That is, the double.

b else,† yet will not receive the form of the odd; nor will the sesquialter, nor other things of this kind, such as the half and the third part, ever receive the form of the whole, if you pursue and assent to these consequences. - I most vehemently (says he) pursue and assent to them.

Again, therefore (says Socrates), speak to me from the beginning; and this not by answering to what I inquire, but, in a different manner, imitating me. For I say this, in consequence of perceiving another mode of answering, arising from what has now been said, no less secure than that which was established at first. For, if you should ask me what that
c is, which, when inherent in any body, causes the body to be hot, I should not give you that cautious and unskilful answer, that it is heat, but one more elegant deduced from what we have just now said; I mean, that it is fire. Nor, if you should ask me what that is, which when inherent in a certain body, the body is diseased, I should not say that it is disease, but a fever. Nor, if you should ask what that is, which when inherent in a number, the number will be odd, I should not say that it is imparity, but unity, and in a similar manner in other particulars. But see whether you sufficiently understand my meaning. - Perfectly so (says he). - Answer me then (says Socrates), what that is, which when inherent in the body, the body will be alive? - Soul‡ (says he). - Is this then
d always the case? - How should it not (says he)? - Will soul, therefore, always introduce life to that which it occupies? - It will truly (says he). - But is there any thing contrary to life, or not? - There is. - But what? - Death. - The soul, therefore, will never receive the contrary to that which it introduces, in consequence of what has been already admitted. - And this most vehemently so (says Cebes).

But what? how do we denominate that which does not receive the idea of the even? - Odd (says he). - And how do we call that which does not receive justice, and that which does not receive music? - We call (says he)
e the one unjust, and the other unmusical. - Be it so. - But what do we call that which does not receive death? - Immortal (says he). - The soul does not receive death? - It does not. - The soul, therefore, is immortal. - Immortal. - Let it be so (says he). - And shall we say that this is now demonstrated? Or how does it appear to you? - It appears to me, Socrates, to be most sufficiently demonstrated. - What then (says he), Cebes, if it were necessary to *the odd* that it should be free from

---

† That is, the half.

‡ This, which is the fifth argument, properly and fully demonstrates the immortality of the soul from its essence.

destruction, would not three things be indestructible? - How should they
106a   not? - If, therefore, it was also necessary that a thing void of heat should
be indestructible, when any one should introduce heat to snow, would
not the snow withdraw itself, safe and unliquefied? For it would not
perish; nor yet, abiding, would it receive the heat. - You speak the truth
(says he). - In like manner, I think if that which is void of cold was
indestructible, that when any thing cold approached to fire, the fire
would neither be extinguished nor destroyed, but would depart free
b   from damage. - It is necessary (says he). - Hence (says Socrates) it is
necessary to speak in this manner concerning that which is immortal:
for, if that which is immortal is indestructible, it is impossible that the
soul, when death approaches to it, should perish. For it follows, from
what has been said, that it does not receive death, and of course it will
never be dead. Just as we said, that three things will never be even, nor
will this ever be the case with that which is odd: nor will fire ever be
cold, nor yet the heat which is inherent in fire. But some one may say,
What hinders but that the odd may never become the even, through the
accession of the even, as we have confessed; and yet, when the odd is
destroyed, the even may succeed instead of it? We cannot contend with
c   him who makes this objection, that it is not destroyed: for the odd is
not free from destruction; since, if this was granted to us, we might
easily oppose the objection, and obtain this concession, that the odd and
three things would depart, on the approach of the even; and we might
contend in the same manner about fire and heat, and other particulars:
might we not? - Entirely so. - And now, therefore, since we have
confessed respecting that which is immortal, that it is indestructible, it
must follow that the soul is, together with being immortal, likewise
indestructible: but if this be not admitted, other arguments will be
d   necessary for our conviction. But there is no occasion for this (says he).
For it is scarcely possible that any thing else should be void of
corruption, if that which is immortal and eternal is subject to
dissolution.

But I think (says Socrates) that Divinity, and the form itself of life, and
if any thing else besides this is immortal, must be confessed by all beings
to be entirely free from dissolution. All men, indeed (says he), by
Jupiter, must acknowledge this; and much more, as it appears to me,
e   must it be admitted by the Gods. Since, therefore, that which is
immortal is also incorruptible, will not the soul, since it is immortal, be
indestructible? - It is perfectly necessary. - When, therefore, death
invades a man, the mortal part of him, as it appears, dies; but the
immortal part departs safe and uncorrupted, and withdraws itself from

death. - It appears so. - The soul, therefore (says he), O Cebes, will,
107a more[†] than any thing, be immortal and indestructible; and our souls will
in reality subsist in Hades.   And therefore (says he), Socrates, I have
nothing further to object to these arguments, nor any reason why I
should disbelieve their reality: but if either Simmias, or any person
present, has any thing to say, he will do well not to be silent: for I
know not what other opportunity he can have, besides the present, if he
wishes either to speak or hear about things of this kind. - But indeed
(says Simmias) I have nothing which can hinder my belief in what has
b been said. But yet on account of the magnitude[24] of the things about
which we have discoursed, and through my despising human imbecility,
I am compelled to retain with myself an unbelief about what has been
asserted. - Indeed, Simmias (says Socrates), you not only speak well in
the present instance, but it is necessary that even those first hypotheses
which we established, and which are believed by us, should at the same
time be more clearly considered: and if you sufficiently investigate them,
you will follow reason, as it appears to me, in as great a degree as is
possible to man. And if this becomes manifest, you will no longer make
any further inquiry. - You speak true (says he).
c   But it is just, my friends (says he), to think that if the soul is immortal,
it requires our care and attention, not only for the present time, in
which we say it lives, but likewise with a view to the whole of time: and
it will now appear, that he who neglects it must subject himself to a
most dreadful danger. For, if death were the liberation of the whole
man, it would be an unexpected gain to the wicked to be liberated at the
same time from the body, and from their vices together with their soul:
but now, since the soul appears to be immortal, no other flight from
evils, and no other safety remains for it, than in becoming the best and
d most prudent possible. For when the soul arrives at Hades, it will
possess nothing but discipline and education, which are said to be of the
greatest advantage or detriment to the dead, in the very beginning of
their progression thither. For thus it is said: that the dæmon[25] of each
person, which was allotted to him while living, endeavours[26] to lead each
to a certain place, where it is necessary that all of them, being collected
together, after they have been judged, should proceed to Hades, together
e with their leader, who is ordered to conduct them from hence thither.
But there receiving the allotments proper to their condition, and abiding
for a necessary time, another leader brings them back hither again, in

---

† Socrates says, with great propriety, that the soul will be immortal *more than any*
thing. For soul is *essentially vital*; and *immortality is stability of life*.

108a   many and long periods of time. The journey, therefore, is not such as Telephus asserts it to be in Eschylus. For he says that a simple path leads to Hades: but it appears to me that the path is neither simple nor one. For there would be no occasion of leaders, nor could any one ever wander from the right road, if there was but one way. But now it appears to have many divisions and dubious turnings: and this I conjecture from our holy and legal rites. The soul, therefore, which is properly adorned with virtue, and which possesses prudence, willingly follows its leader, and is not ignorant of its present condition: but the soul which still adheres to body through desire (as I said before), being

b   for a long space of time terrified about it, and struggling and suffering abundantly about the visible place, is with violence and great difficulty led away by its presiding dæmon. And when it arrives at that place where other souls are assembled, all the rest fly from and avoid this unpurified soul, which has been guilty either of unjust slaughter, or has perpetrated such deeds as are allied to this, and are the works of kindred

c   souls; nor is any one willing to become either its companion or leader. But such a soul wanders about, oppressed with every kind of anxiety and trouble, till certain periods of time are accomplished: and these being completed, it is driven by necessity to an abode accommodated to its nature. But the soul which has passed through life with purity and moderation, obtaining the Gods for its companions and leaders, will reside in a place adapted to its purified condition.

    There are indeed many and admirable places belonging to the earth;[27] and the earth itself is neither of such a kind, nor of such a magnitude, as those who are accustomed to speak about it imagine, as I am persuaded from a certain person's account. - How is this, Socrates (says

d   Simmias)? For I myself also have heard many things about the earth; and yet perhaps not these particulars which have obtained your belief. I should therefore be glad to hear you relate them. - Indeed, Simmias (says he), the art of Glaucus does not appear to me to be necessary, in order to relate these particulars; but to evince their truth, seems to me to be an undertaking beyond what the art of Glaucus can accomplish. Besides, I myself perhaps am not able to accomplish this; and even though I should know how, the time which is allotted me to live, Simmias, seems by no means sufficient for the length of such a discourse. However, nothing hinders me from informing you what I am

e   persuaded is the truth, respecting the form of the earth, and the places which it contains. - And this information (says Simmias) will be sufficient. - I am persuaded, therefore (says he), in the first place, that if the earth is in the middle of the heavens, and is of a spherical figure, it

109a has no occasion of air, nor of any other such-like necessity, to prevent
it from falling: but that the perfect similitude of the heavens to
themselves, and the equilibrity of the earth, are sufficient causes of its
support. For that which is equally inclined, when placed in the middle
of a similar nature, cannot tend more or less to one part than another;
but, subsisting on all sides similarly affected, it will remain free from all
inclination. This is the first thing of which I am persuaded. - And very
properly so (says Cebes). - But yet further (says he), that the earth is
prodigiously great;[28] that we who dwell in places extending from Phasis
b   to the pillars of Hercules, inhabit only a certain small portion of it,
about the Mediterranean sea, like ants or frogs about a marsh; and that
there are many others elsewhere, who dwell in many suchlike places.
For I am persuaded, that there are every where about the earth many
hollow places of all-various forms and magnitudes; into which there is
a confluence of water, mists, and air: but that the earth itself, which is
of a pure nature, is situated in the pure heavens, in which the stars are
contained, and which most of those who are accustomed to speak about
c   such particulars denominate æther. But the places which we inhabit are
nothing more than the dregs of this pure earth, or cavities into which
its dregs continually flow. We are ignorant, therefore, that we dwell in
the cavities of this earth, and imagine that we inhabit its upper parts.
Just as if some one dwelling in the middle bottom of the sea, should
think that he resided on its surface, and, beholding the sun and the other
stars through the water, should imagine that the sea is the heavens; but
d   through sloth and imbecility having never ascended to the top of the sea,
nor emerged from its deeps into this region, has never perceived how
much purer and more beautiful it is than the place which he inhabits,
nor has received this information from any other who has beheld this
place of our abode. In the very same manner are we affected: for,
dwelling in a certain hollow of the earth, we think that we reside on its
surface; and we call the air heaven, as if the stars passed through this, as
through the heavens themselves. And this likewise, in the same manner
e   as in the above instance, happens to us through our imbecility and sloth,
which render us incapable of ascending to the summit of the air. For,
otherwise, if any one could arrive at its summit, or, becoming winged,
could fly thither, he would be seen emerging from hence; and just as
fishes, emerging hither from the sea, perceive what our region contains,
in the same manner would he behold the several particulars belonging
to the summit of the earth. And besides this, if his nature was sufficient
for such an elevated survey, he would know that the heavens which he
there beheld were the true heavens, and that he perceived the true light

110a and the true earth. For this earth which we inhabit, the stones which it contains, and the whole region of our abode, are all corrupted and gnawed, just as things in the sea are corroded by the salt: for nothing worthy of estimation grows in the sea, nor does it contain any thing perfect; but caverns and sand, and immense quantities of mud and filth, are found in it wherever there is earth. Nor are its contents to be by any means compared with the beauty of the various particulars in our place of abode. But those upper regions of the earth will appear to be

b yet far more excellent than these which we inhabit. For, if it is proper to tell you a beautiful fable, it is well worth hearing, Simmias, what kind of places those are on the upper earth, situated under the heavens.

It is reported then, my friend (says he), in the first place, that this earth, if any one surveys it from on high, appears like globes covered with twelve skins, various,[29] and distinguished with colours; a pattern of

c which are the colours found among us, and which our painters use. But there the whole earth is composed from materials of this kind, and such as are much more splendid and pure than our region contains: for they are partly indeed purple, and endued with a wonderful beauty; partly of a golden colour; and partly more white than plaster or snow; and are composed from other colours in a similar manner, and those more in number and more beautiful than any we have ever beheld. For the hollow parts of this pure earth, being filled with water and air, exhibit

d a certain species of colour, shining among the variety of other colours in such a manner, that one particular various form of the earth continually presents itself to the view. Hence, whatever grows in this earth grows analogous to its nature, such as trees, and flowers, and fruits: and again, its mountains and stones possess a similar perfection and transparency, and are rendered beautiful through various colours; of which the stones so much honoured by us in this place of our abode are

e but small parts, such as sardin-stones, jaspers, and emeralds, and all of this kind. But there nothing subsists which is not of such a nature as I have described; and there are other things far more beautiful than even these. But the reason of this is because the stones there are pure, and not consumed and corrupted, like ours, through rottenness and salt, from a conflux of various particulars, which in our places of abode cause filthiness and disease to the stones and earth, animals and plants, which

111a are found among us. But this pure earth is adorned with all these, and with gold and silver, and other things of a similar nature: for all these are naturally apparent, since they are both numerous and large, and are diffused every where throughout the earth; so that to behold it is the spectacle of blessed spectators. This earth too contains many other animals[30] and men, some of whom inhabit its middle parts; others dwell about the air, as we do about the sea; and others reside in islands which the air flows round, and which are situated not far from the continent. And in one word, what water and the sea are to us, with respect to utility, that air is to them: but what air is to us, that æther is to the inhabitants of this pure earth. But the seasons there are endued with such an excellent temperament, that the inhabitants are never molested with disease, and live for a much longer time than those who dwell in our regions; and they surpass us in sight, hearing, and prudence, and every thing of this kind, as much as air excels water in purity - and æther, air. And besides this, they have groves and temples of the Gods, in which the Gods dwell in reality; and likewise oracles and divinations, and sensible perceptions of the Gods, and such-like associations with them. The sun too, and moon, and stars, are seen by them such as they really are; and in every other respect their felicity is of a correspondent nature.

And in this manner indeed the whole earth naturally subsists, and the parts which are situated about it. But it contains about the whole of its ambit many places in its concavities; some of which are more profound and extended than the region which we inhabit: but others are more profound, indeed, but yet have a less chasm than the places of our abode; and there are certain parts which are less profound,† but broader than ours. But all these are in many places perforated into one another under the earth, according to narrower and broader avenues, and have passages of communication through which a great quantity of water flows into the different hollows of the earth, as into bowls; and besides this, there are immense bulks of ever-flowing rivers under the earth, and of hot and cold waters; likewise a great quantity of fire, mighty rivers of fire, and many of moist mire, some of which are purer, and others more muddy; as in Sicily there are rivers of mud, which flow before a stream of fire, which is itself a flaming torrent. And from these the several places are filled, into which each flows at particular times. But all these are moved upwards and downwards, like a hanging vessel, situated in the earth. This hanging vessel too, through a certain nature of this kind, is one of the chasms of the earth; and this the greatest, and

---

† Plato, says Olympiodorus, directs his attention to the four quarters of the globe: for since there are two which we inhabit, *viz.* Europe and Asia, there must also be two others according to the antipodes. [2.139] Καταστοχαζεται δε των τεσσαρων τμηματων, επειδη δυο καθ᾽ ημας εισιν, η Ευρωπη και η Ασια· ωστε δυο αλλοι κατα τους αντιποδας. [139.7 - 8]

112a totally perforated through the whole earth. And of this Homer† thus speaks:

> Far, very far, where under earth is found
> A gulf, of every depth, the most profound:

which he elsewhere and many other poets denominate Tartarus.‡ For into this chasm there is a conflux of all rivers, from which they again
b flow upwards. But each derives its quality from the earth through which it flows. And the reason why they all flow into, and again out of this chasm, is because this moisture cannot find either a bottom or a basis. Hence it becomes elevated, and fluctuates upwards and downwards: and this too is the case with the air and spirit[31] which are situated about it. For they follow this moisture, both when they are impelled to more remote places of the earth, and when to the places of our abode. And as in respiration the flowing breath is perpetually expired and inspired, so there the spirit, which is elevated together with the moisture, causes certain vehement and immense winds during its ingress and departure. When the water, therefore, being impelled, flows
c into that place which we call downwards, then the rivers flow through the earth into different channels, and fill them; just as those who pour into another vessel the water which they have drawn. But when this water, departing from thence, is impelled hither, it again fills the rivers on the earth; and these, when filled, flow through channels and through the earth; and when they have severally passed through the avenues, which are open to each, they produce seas, lakes, rivers, and fountains.
d Flowing back again from hence under the earth, and some of them streaming round longer and more numerous places, but others round such as are shorter and less numerous, they again hurl themselves into Tartarus; and some indeed much more profoundly, but others less so, than they were drawn: but the influxions of all of them are deeper than the places from which they flow upwards. And the effluxions of some are in a direction contrary to their influxions, but in others both take place according to the same part. There are some again which entirely flow round in a circle, folding themselves like snakes, once or often

---

† *Iliad* lib. viii.

‡ Tartarus, says Olympiodorus, is the extremity of the universe, and subsists oppositely to Olympus. But Tartarus is a deity, the inspective guardian of that which is last in every order. Hence, says he, we have a celestial Tartarus, in which Heaven concealed his offspring; a Saturnian Tartarus, in which also Saturn concealed his offspring; and also a Jovian of this kind, which is demiurgic. [2.140]

about the earth; and being bent downwards as much as possible, they are
again hurled forth on each side till they arrive at the middle, but never
beyond this. For each part of the earth becomes steep to both these
streams.

The other rivers, indeed, are many, great, and various: but among this
abundance there are certain streams, four in number,[32] of which the
greatest, and which circularly flows round the earth the outermost of all,
is called the Ocean. But that which flows opposite, and in a contrary
direction to this, is Acheron; which, flowing through other solitary
places, and under the earth, devolves its waters into the Acherusian
marsh, into which many souls of the dead pass; and abiding there for
certain destined spaces of time, some of which are more and others less
extended, they are again sent into the generations of animals. The third
river of these hurls itself forth in the middle, and near its source falls
into a mighty place, burning with abundance of fire, and produces a lake
greater than our sea, and hot with water and mud. But it proceeds from
hence in a circle, turbulent and miry, and, surrounding the earth, arrives
both elsewhere and at the extremities of the Acherusian marsh, with the
water of which it does not become mingled; but, often revolving itself
under the earth, flows into the more downward parts of Tartarus. And
this is the river which they still denominate Pyriphlegethon; the streams
of which send forth disseveverd rivers to various parts of the earth. But
the fourth river, which is opposite to this, first falls as it is said into a
place dreadful and wild, and wholly tinged with an azure colour, which
they denominate Styx: and the influxive streams of this river form the
Stygian marsh. But falling into this, and receiving vehement powers in
its water, it hides itself under the earth, and, rolling round, proceeds
contrary to Pyriphlegethon, and meets with it in the Acherusian marsh,
in a contrary direction. Nor is the water of this river mingled with any
thing, but, revolving in a circle, it hurls itself into Tartarus, in a course
opposite to Pyriphlegethon. But its name, according to the poets, is
Cocytus.

These being thus naturally constituted, when the dead arrive at that
place into which the dæmon leads each, in the first place they are
judged, as well those who have lived in a becoming manner, and piously,
and justly, as those who have not. And those who appear to have
passed a middle kind of life, proceeding to Acheron, and ascending the

vehicles† prepared for them, arrive in these at the Acherusian lake, and dwell there; till being purified, and having suffered punishment for any injuries they may have committed, they are enlarged; and each receives the reward of his beneficence, according to his deserts. But those who appear to be incurable, through the magnitude of their offences, because they have perpetrated either many and great sacrileges, or many unjust slaughters, and such as are contrary to law, or other things of this kind - these, a destiny adapted to their guilt hurls into Tartarus, from which they will *never* be discharged.³³ But those who are found to have committed curable, but yet mighty crimes, such as those who have been guilty through anger of any violence against their father or mother, and have lived the remainder of their lives penitent for the offence, or who have become homicides in any other similar manner; with respect to these, it is necessary that they should fall into Tartarus: but after they have fallen, and have dwelt there for a year, the waves hurl them out of Tartarus; and the homicides indeed into Cocytus, but the violators of fathers and mothers into Pyriphlegethon. But when, being borne along by these rivers, they arrive at the Acherusian marsh, they here bellow and invoke one part those whom they have slaughtered, and another part those whom they have injured. But, invoking these, they suppliantly entreat that they would suffer them to enter into the lake, and forgive them. And if they persuade them to do this, they depart, and find an end to their maladies: but if they are unable to accomplish this, they are carried back again into Tartarus, and from thence again into the rivers. And they do not cease from suffering this, till they have persuaded those they have injured to forgiveness. For this punishment was ordained them by the judges. But those who shall appear to have lived most excellently, with respect to piety - these are they, who, being liberated and dismissed from these places in the earth, as from the abodes of a prison, shall arrive at the pure habitation on high, and dwell on the ætherial earth.‡ And among these, those who are sufficiently

---

† These vehicles are aërial: for souls are moved locally according to the vehicles which are suspended from them. And these aërial vehicles, as being corruptible, are naturally adapted to receive punishment. [2.146]

‡ Observe here, that those who have lived a holy and guiltless life, without philosophy, will after death dwell on the summit of the earth; and their bodies will consequently consist of the most attenuated air. Those who have philosophized politically, says Olympiodorus, will live in the heavens with luciform bodies. And those that are perfectly purified will be restored to the supermundane place, without bodies. [.551]

purified by philosophy shall live without bodies, through the whole of the succeeding time, and shall arrive at habitations yet more beautiful than these, which it is neither easy to describe, nor is the present time sufficient for such an undertaking.

But for the sake of these particulars which we have related, we should undertake every thing, Simmias, that we may participate of virtue and prudence in the present life. For the reward is beautiful, and the hope

d   mighty. To affirm, indeed, that these things subsist exactly as I have described them, is not the province of a man endued with intellect. But to assert that either these or certain particulars of this kind take place, with respect to our souls and their habitations - since our soul appears to be immortal - this is, I think, both becoming, and deserves to be hazarded by him who believes in its reality. For the danger is beautiful; and it is necessary to allure ourselves with things of this kind, as with inchantments: and, on this account, I produced the fable which you have just now heard me relate. But, for the sake of these, it is proper that the man should be confident about his soul, who in the present life bidding

e   farewell to those pleasures which regard the body and its ornaments, as things foreign from his nature, has earnestly applied himself to disciplines, as things of far greater consequence; and who having adorned his soul not with a foreign but its own proper ornament, *viz.* with temperance and justice, fortitude, liberty and truth, expects a migration

115a   to Hades, as one who is ready to depart whenever he shall be called upon by Fate. You, therefore (says he), Simmias and Cebes, and the rest who are here assembled, will each depart in some period of time posterior to the present; but

Me now calling, Fate demands:

(as some tragic poet would say) and it is almost time that I should betake myself to the bath. For it appears to me better to wash myself before I drink the poison, and not to trouble the women with washing my dead body.

b   When, therefore, he had thus spoken, - Be it so, Socrates (says Crito): but what orders do you leave to these who are present, or to myself, or respecting your children, or any thing else in the execution of which we can particularly oblige you? - None such as are new (says he), Crito, but that which I have always said to you; that if you take care of yourselves, you will always perform in whatever you do that which is acceptable to myself, to my family, and to your own selves, though you should not promise me any thing at present. But if you neglect yourselves, and are unwilling to live according to what has been now and formerly said, as vestiges of direction in your course, you will accomplish nothing, though you should now promise many things, and in a very vehement manner. - We shall take care, therefore (says Crito), to act as you desire. But how would you be buried? - Just as you please (says he), if you can but catch me, and I do not elude your pursuit. And at the same time gently laughing, and addressing himself to us, I cannot persuade Crito (says he), my friends, that I am that Socrates who now disputes with you, and methodizes every part of the discourse; but he thinks that I am he whom he will shortly behold dead, and asks how I ought to be buried. But all that long discourse which some time since I addressed to you, in which I asserted that after I had drunk the poison I should no longer remain with you, but should depart to certain felicities of the blessed, this I seem to have declared to him in vain, though it was undertaken to console both you and myself. Promise, therefore (says he), for me to Crito, just the contrary of what he promised to my judges. For he promised that I should not run away; but do you engage that when I die I shall not stay with you, but shall depart and entirely leave you; that Crito may more easily bear this separation, and may not be afflicted when he sees my body either burnt or buried, as if I suffered some dreadful misfortune; and that he may not say at my interment, that Socrates is laid out, or is carried out, or is buried. For be well assured of this (says he), excellent Crito, that when we do not speak in a becoming manner, we are not only culpable with respect to our speech, but likewise affect our souls with a certain evil. But it is proper to be confident, and to say that my body will be buried, and in such a manner as is pleasing to you, and which you think is most agreeable to our laws.

When he had thus spoken he rose, and went into a certain room, that he might wash himself, and Crito followed him: but he ordered us to wait for him. We waited, therefore, accordingly, discoursing over and reviewing among ourselves what had been said; and sometimes speaking about his death, how great a calamity it would be to us; and sincerely thinking that we, like those who are deprived of their father, should pass the rest of our life in the condition of orphans. But when he had washed himself, his sons were brought to him (for he had two little ones, and one considerably advanced in age), and the women belonging to his family likewise came in to him: but when he had spoken to them before Crito, and had left them such injunctions as he thought proper, he ordered the boys and women to depart; and he himself returned to us. And it was now near the setting of the sun: for he had been absent for a long time in the bathing-room. But when he came in from washing, he sat down; and did not speak much afterwards. For then the servant of the eleven magistrates came in, and standing near to him, I do

c   not perceive that in you, Socrates, which I have taken notice of in others; I mean, that they are angry with me, and curse me, when, being compelled by the magistrates, I announce to them that they must drink the poison. But, on the contrary, I have found you at the present time to be the most generous, mild, and the best of all the men that ever came into this place: and, therefore, I am well convinced that you are not angry with me, but with the authors of your present condition. You know those whom I allude to. Now, therefore (for you know

d   what I came to tell you), farewell, and endeavour to bear this necessity as easily as possible. And at the same time bursting into tears, and turning himself away, he departed. But Socrates looking after him, And thou too (says he), farewell; and we shall take care to act as you advise. And at the same time turning to us, How courteous (says he) is the behaviour of that man! During the whole time of my abode here, he has visited and often conversed with me, and proved himself to be the best of men; and now how generously he weeps on my account! But let us obey him, Crito, and let some one bring the poison, if it is bruised;

e   but if not, let the man whose business it is bruise it himself. But, Socrates (says Crito), I think that the sun still hangs over the mountains, and is not yet set. And at the same time I have known others who have drunk the poison very late, after it was announced to them; who have supped and drunk abundantly; and who have enjoyed the objects of their love. Therefore, do not be in such haste; for there is yet time enough. Upon this Socrates replied, Such men, Crito, act with great propriety in the manner you have described (for they think to derive some advantage by so doing), and I also with great propriety shall not

117a   act in this manner. For I do not think I shall gain any thing by drinking it later, except becoming ridiculous to myself through desiring to live, and being sparing of life when nothing of it any longer remains. Go, then (says he), be persuaded, and comply with my request.

Then Crito, hearing this, gave the sign to the boy that stood near him. And the boy departing, and having stayed for some time, came, bringing with him the person that was to administer the poison, and who brought it properly prepared in a cup. But Socrates, beholding the man - It is well, my friend (says he); but what is proper to do with it? for you are knowing in these affairs. - You have nothing else to do (says he),

b   but when you have drunk it to walk about, till a heaviness takes place in your legs; and afterwards lie down: this is the manner in which you should act. And at the same time he extended the cup to Socrates. But Socrates received it from him - and indeed, Echecrates, with great cheerfulness; neither trembling, nor suffering any alteration for the worse in his colour or countenance: but, as he was accustomed to do, beholding the man with a bull-like aspect, What say you (says he) respecting this potion? Is it lawful to make a libation of it, or not? - We only bruise (says he), Socrates, as much as we think sufficient for the

c   purpose. - I understand you (says he): but it is certainly both lawful and proper to pray to the Gods, that my departure from hence thither may be attended with prosperous fortune; which I entreat them to grant may be the case. And at the same time ending his discourse, he drank the poison with exceeding facility and alacrity. And thus far, indeed, the greater part of us were tolerably well able to refrain from weeping: but when we saw him drinking, and that he had drunk it, we could no longer restrain our tears. But from me, indeed, notwithstanding the violence which I employed in checking them, they flowed abundantly; so that, covering myself with my mantle, I deplored my misfortune. I

d   did not indeed weep for him, but for my own fortune; considering what an associate I should be deprived of. But Crito, who was not able to restrain his tears, was compelled to rise before me. And Apollodorus, who during the whole time prior to this had not ceased from weeping, then wept aloud with great bitterness; so that he infected all who were present, except Socrates. But Socrates, upon seeing this, exclaimed - What are you doing, excellent men? For, indeed, I principally sent away the women, lest they should produce a disturbance of this kind. For I

e   have heard that it is proper[†] to die joyfully and with propitious omens. Be quiet, therefore, and summon fortitude to your assistance. - When we heard this we blushed, and restrained our tears. But he, when he found during his walking that his legs felt heavy, and had told us so, laid himself down in a supine position. For the man had ordered him to do so. And at the same time he who gave him the poison, touching him at intervals, considered his feet and legs. And after he had vehemently pressed his foot, he asked him if he felt it. But Socrates answered he did

---

† The Pythagoreans, says Olympiodorus, thought it proper to die joyfully, because death is a good and sacred thing; and because sometimes a contrary conduct destroys that impulse by which the soul is led back to her true felicity. Besides this, when the soul departs in sorrow, a crowd of dæmons who are lovers of body are by this mean evocated; and who, in consequence of rejoicing in a life conversant with generation, render the pneumatic vehicle of the soul heavy. [.559]

118a not. And after this he again pressed his thighs: and thus ascending with his hand, he showed us that he was cold and stiff. And Socrates also touched himself, and said, that when the poison reached his heart he should then leave us. But now his lower belly was almost cold; when uncovering himself (for he was covered), he said (which were his last words): Crito, we owe a cock[†] to Æsculapius. Discharge this debt, therefore, for me, and do not neglect it. - It shall be done (says Crito): but consider whether you have any other commands. To this inquiry of Crito he made no reply; but shortly after moved himself, and the man covered him. And Socrates fixed his eyes. Which when Crito perceived, he closed[34] his mouth and eyes. This, Echecrates, was the end of our associate; a man, as it appears to me, the best of those whom we were acquainted with at that time, and, besides this, the most prudent and just.

† Should it be asked, says Olympiodorus, why Socrates desired that a cock might be offered for him to Æsculapius, we reply, that by this mean he might heal the diseases which his soul had contracted in generation. Perhaps too, says he, according to the oracle, he was willing to return to his proper principles, celebrating Pæon. [.561] Olympiodorus adds, that Socrates is said by Plato to have been the best of men, because he was in every respect good; the most prudent, according to knowledge; and the most just, according to desire. [.562]

Additional Notes

on the

PHÆDO

1 (See page 237, line 61c) Socrates says, that perhaps the philosopher will not destroy himself, for this is not lawful. This the text shows through two arguments, the one mythical and Orphic, but the other dialectic and philosophic. But before we consider the text, says Olympiodorus, let us show by appropriate arguments that suicide is not lawful. Divinity possesses twofold powers, anagogic and providential; and the powers which are providential of things secondary are not impeded by the anagogic, and which are converted to them, but he energizes at once according to both. In like manner, nothing hinders but that a philosopher, since he is an imitator of Divinity, (for philosophy is an assimilation to Deity,) may at once energize cathartically, and with a providential care of secondary natures: for there is nothing great in living cathartically when separated from the body after death; but, while detained in the body, it is generous to be intent on purification. The second argument is this: As a divine nature is always present to all things, and some things participate of it more or less, through their proper aptitude or inaptitude; so also it is necessary that the soul should be present to the body, and should not separate itself from it. But the body participates or does not participate of it, through its proper aptitude or inaptitude. Thus, in the *Theætetus*,[173c] the Coryphæan philosopher is represented as not knowing where the Forum is situated, but as being even ignorant that he is ignorant of sensible particulars; and this while he is in the body. The third argument is as follows: It is necessary that a voluntary bond should be voluntarily dissolved; but that an involuntary bond should be dissolved with an involuntary solution, and not in a promiscuous manner. Hence a physical life, being involuntary, must be dissolved with an involuntary solution, *i.e.* by a physical death; but the impassioned life in us, which subsists according to pre-election or free will, must be dissolved with a voluntary solution, *i.e.* with purification, or the exercise of the cathartic virtues.

With respect to the text, it shows through two arguments, as we have observed, that suicide is not lawful; and of these the mythical argument, according to Olympiodorus, is as follows:- According to Orpheus, there are four governments: the first that of Heaven, which Saturn received, cutting off the genitals of his father. After Saturn, Jupiter reigned, who hurled his father into Tartarus. And after Jupiter Bacchus reigned, who they say was lacerated by the Titans, through the stratagems of Juno. It is also said that the Titans tasted his flesh, and that Jupiter being enraged hurled his thunder at them; and

[margin: 1.2]

[margin: 1.3]

that from the ashes of their burnt bodies men were generated.† Suicide, therefore, is not proper, not, as the text seems to say, because we are in a certain bond the body, (for this is evident, and he would not have called this arcane,) but suicide is not lawful, because our body is Dionysiacal: for we are a part of Bacchus, if we are composed from the ashes of the Titans who tasted his flesh. Socrates, therefore, fearful of disclosing this arcane narration, because it pertained to the mysteries, adds nothing more than that we are in the body, as in a prison secured by a guard; but the interpreters, when the mysteries were declining, and almost extinct, owing to the establishment of a new religion, openly disclosed the fable.

But the allegory of this fable, says Olympiodorus, is of that kind as when Empedocles asserts that the intelligible and sensible worlds were generated according to parts; not that they were produced at different times, for they always are, but because our soul at one time lives according to the intelligible, and then the intelligible world is said to be generated, and at another time according to the sensible world, and then the sensible world is said to be generated. So likewise with Orpheus, those four governments do not subsist at one time, and at another not, for they always are; but they obscurely signify the gradations of the virtues according to which our soul contains the symbols of all the virtues, the theoretic and cathartic, the politic and ethic. For it either energizes according to the theoretic virtues, the paradigm of which is the government of Heaven, and on this account Heaven receives its denomination παρα του τα ανω οραν, *from beholding the things above*; or it lives cathartically, the paradigm of which is the kingdom of Saturn, and on this account Saturn is denominated as *a pure intellect, through beholding himself*, οιον ο κορονους τις ων δια το εαυτον οραν; and hence he is said to devour his own offspring, as converting himself to himself: or it energizes according to the political virtues, the symbol of which is the government of Jupiter; and hence Jupiter is the demiurgus, as energizing about secondary natures: or it lives according to the ethical and physical virtues, the symbol of which is the kingdom of Bacchus; and hence it is lacerated, because the virtues do not alternately follow each other.

But Bacchus being lacerated by the Titans signifies his procession to the last of things; for of these the Titans are the artificers, and Bacchus is the monad of the Titans. This was effected by the stratagems of Juno, because this goddess is the inspective guardian of motion and progression; and hence, in the *Iliad*, she continually excites Jupiter to a providential attention to secondary natures.

---

† Παρα τω Ορφει τεσσαρες βασιλειαι παραδιδονται. πρωτη μεν η του Ουρανου, ην ο Κρονος διεδεξατο εκτεμων τα αιδοια του πατρος. μετα δη τον Κρονον ο Ζευς εβασιλευσε καταταρταρωσας τον πατερα. επειτα τον Δια διεδεξατο ο Διονυσος, ον φασι κατ' επιβουλην της Ηρας τους περι αυτον Τιτανας σπαραττειν, και των σαρκων αυτου απογευεσθαι· και τουτους οργισθεις ο Ζευς εκεραυνωσε, και εκ της αιθαλης των ατμων των αναδοθεντων εξ αυτων υλης γενομενης γενεσθαι τους ανθρωπους. [3.2 - 9]

1.6 Bacchus also, says Olympiodorus, presides over generation, because he presides over life and death. Over life, because over generation; but over death, because wine produces an enthusiastic energy, and at the time of death we become more enthusiastic, as Proclus testifies together with Homer; for he became prophetic when he was dying. Tragedy and comedy also are referred to Bacchus; comedy from its being the sport of life, and tragedy through the calamities and the death in it. Comic, therefore, do not properly accuse tragic writers as not being Dionysiacal, when they assert that these things do not pertain to Bacchus. But Jupiter hurled his thunder at the Titans, the thunder manifesting conversion: for fire moves upwards. Jupiter, therefore, converts them to himself. And this is the mythical argument.

1.7 But the dialectic and philosophic argument is as follows:- The Gods take care of us, and we are their possessions: it is not proper, therefore, to free ourselves from life, but we ought to convert ourselves to them. For if one of these two things took place, either that we are the possessions of the Gods, but they take no care of us; or, on the contrary, that we are not the possessions of the Gods, it might be rational to liberate ourselves from the body: but now, as neither of these takes place, it is not proper to dissolve our bonds.

1.8 On the contrary, however, it may be said that suicide according to Plato is necessary. And, in the first place, he here says that a philosopher will not *perhaps* commit suicide, unless Divinity sends some great necessity, such as the present: for the word *perhaps* affords a suspicion that suicide may *sometimes* be necessary. In the second place, Plato admits that suicide may be proper to the worthy man, to him of a middle character, and to the multitude and depraved: to the worthy man, as in this place; to the middle character, as in the *Republic*,[407d] where he says that suicide is necessary to him who is afflicted with a long and incurable disease, as such a one is useless to the city, because Plato's intention was that his citizens should be useful to the city, and not to themselves; and to the vulgar character, as in the *Laws*,[854a] when he says that suicide is necessary to him who is possessed with certain incurable passions, such as being in love with his mother, sacrilege, or any thing else of this kind.

Again it may be said, from the authority of Plotinus [En. I, 9, TTS vol. III, p.417], that suicide is sometimes necessary, and also from the authority of the Stoics, who said that there were five ways in which suicide was rational. For they assimilated, says Olympiodorus, life to a banquet, and asserted that it is necessary to dissolve life through such-like causes as occasion the dissolution of a banquet. A banquet, therefore, is dissolved either through a great necessity unexpectedly intervening, as through the presence of a friend suddenly coming; or it is dissolved through intoxication taking place; and through what is placed on the table being morbid. Further still, it is dissolved after another manner through a want of things necessary to the entertainment; and also through obscene and base language. In like manner life may be dissolved in five ways. And, in the first place, as at a banquet, it may be dissolved through some great necessity, as when a man sacrifices himself for the good of his country. In the second place, as a banquet is dissolved through intoxication, so likewise it is necessary to dissolve life through a delirium following the body: for a delirium is a physical intoxication. In the third place, as a banquet is dissolved through what is placed on the table being morbid, thus too it is necessary that life should be dissolved when the body labours under incurable diseases, and is no longer capable of being ministrant to the soul. In the fourth place, as a banquet it dissolved through a want of things necessary to the entertainment, so suicide is proper when the necessaries of life are wanting. For they are not to be received from depraved characters; since gifts from the defiled are small, and it is not proper for a man to pollute himself with these. And, in the fifth place, as a banquet is dissolved through obscene language, so likewise it is necessary to dissolve life when compelled by a tyrant to speak things arcane, or belonging to the mysteries, which a certain female Pythagorean is said to have done. For, being compelled to tell why she did not eat beans, she said, I may eat them if I tell. And afterwards being compelled to eat them, she said, I may tell if I eat them; and at length bit off her tongue, as the organ of speech and taste.

1.9   What then shall we say? for the discourse is brought to a contradiction. And how can it be admitted that suicide is unlawful? Or, may we not say that a liberation from life is not necessary so far as pertains to the body; but that it is rational when it contributes a greater good to the soul? Thus, for instance, suicide is lawful when the soul is injured by the body. As, therefore, it is unholy not to give assistence to a friend when he is scourged, but, if he is scourged by his father, it is not becoming to assist him; so here suicide is unlawful when committed for the sake of the body, but rational when committed for the sake of the soul; since this is sometimes advantageous to it.

I only add, that according to Macrobius it is said, in the arcane discourses concerning the return of the soul, "that the wicked in this life resemble those who fall upon smooth ground, and who cannot rise again without difficulty; but that souls departing from the present life with the defilements of guilt are to be compared to those who fall from a lofty and precipitous place, from whence they are never able to rise again." "Nam in arcanis de animæ reditu disputationibus fertur, in hac vita delinquentes similes esse super æquale solum cadentibus, quibus denuo sine difficultate præsto sit surgere: animas vero ex hac vita cum delictorum sordibus recedentes, æquandas his, qui in abruptum ex alto præcipitique delapsi sunt, unde facultas nunquam sit resurgendi." Somn. Scip. cap. xiii. Suicide, therefore, is in general unlawful, because it is not proper to depart from life in an unpurified state.

1.13   2 (See page 238, line 61d) Philolaus, says Olympiodorus, was a Pythagorean, and it was usual with the Pythagoreans to speak through ænigmas. Hence silence was one of the peculiarities of this sect; through silence indicating the arcane nature of Divinity, which it is necessary a philosopher should imitate. But Philolaus said in ænigmas that suicide is not proper: for he says, we ought not to turn back when going to a temple, nor cut wood in the way. By the latter of these he manifests that we should not divide and cut life; for life is a way: and by the former he indicates the meditation of death. For the life of a future state is sacred; since our father and country are there. He says, therefore, that he who lives cathartically should not turn back, *i.e.* should not cut off the cathartic life. But Cebes met with Philolaus in Bœotia; for he associated with him in Thebes. Olympiodorus also, after observing that it was the custom of the Pythagoreans to live as in a common life, making all their possessions common, adds as follows:- "If, therefore, any one among them was found to be unadapted to philosophy, they led him out together with his property, made a cenotaph or empty tomb, and lamented as if it were for one who was going a journey. But a certain person named Cylo coming among them, and experiencing this treatment, set fire to the school, and all the disciples were burnt except two, Philolaus and Hipparchus. Philolaus, therefore, came to Thebes in order to perform funeral sacrifices to his deceased preceptor. He also performed them to Lysias, who was there buried, and in whose name Plato has written a dialogue, which is inscribed, *Lysias*, or *Concerning Friendship*". Ει τις ουν ανεπιτηδειος ευρεθη προς φιλοσοφιαν, εξηγον αυτον μετα της ουσιας, και κενοταφιον εποιουν, και ωσπερ περι αποιχομενον αποδυροντο. Κυλων δε τις εισελθων και πεπονθως τουτο υφηψε πυρ τω διδασκαλειω, και παντες εκαυθησαν πλην δυο Φιλολαον και Ιππαρχον. ηλθεν ουν ο Φιλολαος εις Θηβας αφειλον χοας τω οικειω διδασκαλω τεθνεοτι, και εκει τεθαμμενω ποιησασθαι τω Λυσιδι, ου και κατα ομωνυμιαν γεγραπται τω Πλατωνι διαλογος, Λυσις η Περι Φιλιας. [13.16 - 22]

.19   3 (See page 238, line 62c) How from human affairs, says Olympiodorus, do we conjecture that things pertaining to the Gods subsist in a similar manner? For they are not like us, passive. May we not say that he assimilates them analogously, but politically and economically? For it is evident that the paradigms of every mundane providential care are previously comprehended in the Gods. But reconciliation and vengeance must be conceived to take place in a very different manner in the Gods. For the former is the rising of their proper light when the darkness of guilt is dispersed; and the latter is a secondary punishing providence, about the apostatizing soul.

.29   4 (See page 239, line 62d) Every thing naturally provides for things subordinate; but the Gods exert a providential energy prior to all things, and according to hyparxis. For each is *a goodness*, because the highest God is *The Good*, and providence is the energy of goodness, and imparts essential good. Divinity too may be said to take care of man, because from being worse he makes him better; but man cultivates Divinity because he is made better by him. Observe too, that as, in the universe, intellect subsisting after the Gods is first converted to them, so likewise in us *intellect* is extended to Divinity, but *ignorance* turns from a divine nature. By intellect, however, here, we must understand, not that alone which is gnostic, but also that which is orectic or appetitive, both in the universe and in us: for intellect possesses both desire and knowledge, because it is the first animal. This being admitted, we shall no longer be disturbed by the doubt, whether orectic is better than gnostic perfection; or, in other words, whether virtue is better than science: for the one is not perfect without the other.

.32   Should it be inquired how the Gods are our masters, since a *master*, so far as a master, does not consider the good of his servant, but his own good; for in this he differs from a *governor*; and should it also be said, What good can the Gods derive from man? we reply with Olympiodorus, that the Gods make all things precedaneously on account of themselves; and that they are excellent in proportion as they are exempt from other things. But they *govern* according to a certain coordination with us; and by how much the more we subject ourselves to, by so much the more do we participate of them, as wholly giving ourselves up to them, and neglecting that which is properly our own.

4.1   5 (See page 242, line 65a) Socrates having shown from *life* that the philosopher is willing to die, now proves this from *knowledge* as follows:- The philosopher despises the senses: he who does this despises also the body, in which the senses reside: he who despises the body is averse to it: he who is averse to it separates himself from the body: and he who separates himself from the body is willing to die; for death is nothing else than a separation of the soul from the body.

4.2   But it is here necessary to observe, that there are three energies of the soul: for it either converts itself to things subordinate, and acquires a knowledge of sensibles; or it converts itself to itself, and sees all things in itself, because it is an omniform image containing the reasons of all things; or it extends itself to the intelligible, and beholds ideas. As there are, therefore, three energies of the soul, we must not suppose that the politic, cathartic and theoretic characters differ from each other in this, that the political character knows sensibles; the cathartic, the reasons in the soul; and the theoretic, ideas - since no one is in reality a philosopher who has not a knowledge of all things: but they differ in this, that the political philosopher is conversant with pleasures and pains; for he attends to the body as an instrument, and his end is not a privation, but a moderation of the passions. But the cathartic and theoretic philosophers attend to the body as a neighbouring trifle, that it may not become an impediment to their energies; and the end with them is a liberation from the passions.

4.7   6 (See page 242, line 65b) Plato says that there is no truth in the senses, because they do not properly know: for passion is mingled with their knowledge, in consequence of being obtained through media. For intellect is said to know accurately, because that which understands is the same with the intelligible, or the object of intellection. Besides, sense cannot sustain the accuracy of sensibles. Thus, for instance, the eye cannot bear to look at that

which is white in the extreme.   For sensible objects, when they are
transcendent, destroy the senses.   Sense, however, may be said to be always true
and accurate when it is compared with assimilative knowledge, such as that of
images in mirrors.   When, therefore, sense is said, as it is by Aristotle [*Posterior
Analytics*, 100a3], to be the principle of science, it must not be considered as the
producing principle, but as agitating the soul to a recollection of universals, and
as performing the office of a messenger and herald, by exciting our soul to the
evolution of the sciences.   The poets who assert that the senses know nothing
accurately are Parmenides, Empedocles, and Epicharmus.

5.1   7 (See page 242, line 65d)   The energy of our soul, as we have before
observed, is triple: for it either converts itself to things subordinate, obtaining
a knowledge of and adorning them, or it converts itself to itself, and acquires
a knowledge of itself, or it converts itself to natures more excellent than its
own.   Socrates, therefore, having shown that the philosopher is willing to die,
from a conversion to things subordinate, because he flies from the body,
despising it; and having also shown this from a conversion to himself, because
he attends to the body no further than extreme necessity obliges him; he now
also shows that he is willing to die, from a conversion to things more excellent.
For he wishes to know ideas; but it is impossible for the soul to know these
while energizing with the body, or having this communicating with it in the
investigation of them.   For, if sense possesses something impartible, as is evident
from the collected nature of its perception: for it knows, for instance, at once,
that this particular thing is white, and not black; since, if it knew this divisibly,
it would be just as if I should perceive one part of a thing, and you another;†
much more therefore does the rational soul perceive impartibly.   It differs
however from sense in this, that sense knows, but does not know that it
knows; for it is not converted to itself, since neither body, nor things which
possess their being in body, are converted to themselves; but the rational soul
knows both sensibles and itself: for it knows that it knows.   If this then be the
case, the soul will not receive, as its associate in investigation, either the body
or the senses, or the instruments of sense, if it wishes to know things
accurately.

6.1   8 (See page 243, line 66b)   The *vital irrational* part of our nature is an
impediment to the rational soul.   But this is twofold: for it is either beheld
about the body alone, as fears, desires and loves, or about things external, as
wars, and the accumulation of wealth.   The *gnostic irrational* part also becomes
an impediment, as, for instance, the phantasy, which is always a hindrance to
6.2   our intellectual conceptions.   For there are two passions which it is difficult to

† For these partible perceptions would never produce a perception of that which
is white, as one thing.

wipe away; in knowledge the phantasy, and in life ambition; since these are the things with which the soul becomes first invested, and which she, in the last place, lays aside. For the first vital vehicle of the soul is ambition, and the first gnostic is the phantasy. Hence, says Olympiodorus, Ulysses required the assistance of the mercurial moly, and right reason, in order to fly from Calypso, or the phantasy which like a cloud becomes an impediment to reason, the sun of the soul. For the phantasy is a veil; and hence some one calls it *long veiled*. On this account, Ulysses first came to Circe, that is, Sense, as being the daughter of the Sun. The phantasy, therefore, is an impediment to our intellectual conceptions; and hence (Olympiodorus adds), when we are agitated by the inspiring influence of Divinity, if the phantasy intervenes, the enthusiastic energy ceases: for enthusiasm and the phantasy are contrary to each other. Should it be asked, whether the soul is able to energize without the phantasy? we reply, that its perceptions of universals prove that it is able. It has perceptions, therefore, independent of the phantasy; at the same time, however, the phantasy attends it in its energies, just as a storm pursues him who sails on the sea.

5.3   9 (See page 244, line 66e) Socrates says this in consequence of looking to the knowledge which the soul can participate in the present life, and to that which it possesses when it obtains hereafter the supreme perfection of its nature. For that it is possible according to Plato to live while connected with this body not only *cathartically* but *theoretically*, and this through the whole of life, is evident from his Coryphæan philosopher in the *Theætetus*,[173c] who is represented as continually astronomizing above the heavens (του ουρανου υπεραστρονομουντες), and investigating the nature of every *whole* in the universe; and also from those guardians in his *Republic* who ascend through dialectic as far as to *The Good* itself. To live here however *theoretically* in *perfection* is impossible, on account of the occupations and molestations of the body, which do not permit us to enjoy the theoretic energy without impediment and distracted attention.

3.5   10 (See page 244, line 67a) There are three energies pertaining to the irrational nature; *viz.* physical and necessary, as to be nourished and to sleep; physical but not necessary, as venereal enjoyments; and those which are neither physical nor necessary, as the decoration of the body, and such things as pertain to variety of clothing: for that these last are neither physical nor necessary is evident from their not being used by other animals. As there are, therefore, these three energies, the philosopher, says Olympiodorus, neither uses those which are physical and not necessary, nor those which are neither physical nor necessary. For emissions in sleep are sufficient to him for the discharge of the seed; and he pays no attention to external decoration. He likewise uses those which are physical and necessary, no further than necessity requires. This being the case, the philosopher is willing to die, and consequently meditates death.

.132   11   (See page 245, line 67d)   Those only, says Olympiodorus, who philosophize rightly, *i.e.* with an undeviating energy, *especially* and *always providentially* attend to a solution from the body; possessing the *providential* energy from Prometheus, but the *especially* and the *always* from Hercules. For the never-failing and the strenuous make the solution strong. In consequence, too, of being deprived of good we are afflicted, and fall into evil. We rejoice, therefore, when we are liberated from evil, and meet with good; so that, according to each of these, it is necessary to be delighted with death, both as liberating us from the hated body, and as affording us the enjoyment of what we truly desire. As fire too tends downwards by violence and through a certain artifice, but spontaneously ascends, because its *wholeness*† is on high; in like manner the soul's attention to the body is the effect of compulsion, and its ascent to true being spontaneous, because its separate wholeness is there.

.138   12 (See page 246, line 69c) The first of the virtues are the physical, which are common to brutes, being mingled with the temperaments, and for the most part contrary to each other; or rather pertaining to the animal. Or it may be said that they are illuminations from reason, when not impeded by a certain bad temperament: or that they are the result of energies in a former life. Of
.139 these Plato speaks in the *Politicus*[306a] and the *Laws*.[963c] The ethical virtues, which are above these, are ingenerated by custom and a certain right opinion, and are the virtues of children when well educated. These virtues also are to be found in some brute animals. They likewise transcend the temperaments, and on this account are not contrary to each other. These virtues Plato delivers in the *Laws*.[653a] They pertain however at the same time both to reason
.140 and the irrational nature. In the third rank above these are the political virtues, which pertain to reason alone; for they are scientific. But they are the virtues of reason adorning the irrational part as its instrument; through prudence adorning the gnostic, through fortitude the irascible, and through temperance the desiderative power; but adorning all the parts of the irrational nature through justice. And of these virtues Plato speaks much in the *Republic*.[434d]
.141 These virtues, too, follow each other. Above these are the cathartic virtues, which pertain to reason alone, withdrawing from other things to itself, throwing aside the instruments of sense as vain, repressing also the energies through these instruments, and liberating the soul from the bonds of generation. Plato particularly delivers to us these virtues in this dialogue. Prior
.142 to these, however, are the theoretic virtues, which pertain to the soul, introducing itself to natures superior to itself, not only gnostically, as some one may be induced to think from the name, but also orectically: for it hastens to become, as it were, intellect instead of soul; and intellect, as we have before observed, possesses both desire and knowledge. These virtues are the converse

† See the introduction to the *Timæus*.

of the political: for, as the latter energize about things subordinate according to reason, so the former about things more excellent according to intellect. These virtues Plato delivers in the *Theætetus*.[173c]

8.2   According to Plotinus [En I, 2, 7, TTS vol. III, p. 177], there is also another gradation of the virtues besides these, *viz.* the paradigmatic. For, as our eye, when it is first illuminated by the solar light, is different from that which illuminates, as being illuminated, but afterwards is in a certain respect united and conjoined with it, and becomes as it were solar form; so also our soul at first indeed is illuminated by intellect, and energizes according to the theoretic virtues, but afterwards becomes, as it were, that which is illuminated, and energizes uniformly according to the paradigmatic virtues. And it is the business indeed of philosophy to make us intellect; but of theurgy to unite us

8.3   to intelligibles, so as that we may energize paradigmatically. And as, when possessing the physical virtues, we know mundane bodies (for the subjects to virtues of this kind are bodies); so, from possessing the ethical virtues, we know the fate of the universe, because fate is conversant with irrational lives. For the rational soul is not under fate; and the ethical virtues are irrational. According to the political virtues we know mundane affairs, and according to the cathartic supermundane; but as possessing the theoretic we know intellectual, and from the paradigmatic intelligible natures. Temperance also pertains to the ethical virtues; justice to the political, on account of compacts; fortitude to the cathartic, though not verging to matter; and prudence to the theoretic.

8.4   Observe too, that Plato calls the physical virtues servile, because they may subsist in servile souls; but he calls the ethical σκιογραφιαι, because their possessors only know *that* the energies of such virtues are right, but do not

8.6   know *why* they are so. It is well observed too here, by Olympiodorus, that Plato calls the cathartic and theoretic virtues, those which are in reality true virtues. He also separates them in another way, *viz.* that the politic are not telestic, *i.e.* do not pertain to mystic ceremonies, but that the cathartic and theoretic are telestic. Hence, says Olympiodorus, the cathartic are denominated from the purification which is used in the mysteries; but the theoretic from perceiving things divine, απο του τα θεια οραν. On this account he accords with the Orphic verses, that

> The soul that uninitiated dies,
> Plung'd in the blackest mire in Hades lies.

8.7   For initiation is the Bacchic mysteries of the virtues (τελετη γαρ εστιν η των αρετων βακχεια). Olympiodorus also further observes, that by the thyrsus-bearers, Plato means those that energize according to the political virtues, but by the Bacchuses those that exercise the cathartic virtues. For we are bound in matter as Titans, through the great partibility of our nature; but we rise from the dark mire as Bacchuses. Hence we become more prophetic at the time of death: and Bacchus is the inspective guardian of death, because he is likewise of every thing pertaining to the Bacchic sacred rites.

It is here too necessary to observe, that all the virtues exhibit their proper characters, these being every where common, but subsisting appropriately in each. For the characteristic property of fortitude is the not declining to things subordinate; of temperance, a conversion from an inferior nature; of justice, a proper energy, and adapted to being; and of prudence, the election and selection .150 of things good and evil. Observe too, with Olympiodorus, that all the virtues are in the Gods: for many Gods, says he, are adorned with their appellations; and all goodness originates from the Gods. Likewise prior to things which sometimes participate the virtues, as is our case, it is necessary there should be .151 natures which always participate them. In what order, therefore, do the virtues first appear? Shall we say in the psychical? For virtue is the perfection of the soul; and election and pre-election are the energies and projections of the soul. Hence the Chaldæan oracles conjoin fontal virtue with fontal soul, or, in other words, with soul subsisting according to cause. But may it not also be said, that the virtues naturally wish to give an orderly arrangement to disorder? If this be admitted, they will originate from the demiurgic order. How then will they be cathartic there? May we not say, that through the cathartic virtues considered according to their causal subsistence in Jupiter the demiurgus, he is enabled to abide in his accustomed mode, as Plato says in the *Timæus*? [42e] And further still, according to ancient theologists, he ascends to the tower of Saturn.

.165 13 (See page 247, line 69c) It is requisite, says Olympiodorus, that dialectic conceptions should either begin from divine ænigmas, unfolding the arcane truth which they contain; or that they should become established in them as in a port, and rest in the demonstrations of them; or that they should accomplish both these. Olympiodorus further observes that what is here said .166 imitates the mystic and mundane circle of souls; for these, says he, flying from an impartible and Bacchic life, and energizing according to that which is Titannic, become fettered and imprisoned. Abiding however in punishment, and attending to themselves, they are purified from Titannic defilements, and, passing into a collected from a dispersed subsistence, they become Bacchuses, *i.e.* entire and perfect, according to the Bacchus that abides on high. In the .167 mysteries too, says Olympiodorus, popular purifications first take the lead; in the next place, such as are more arcane than these; in the third place, things permanently abiding are introduced; in the fourth place, perceptions with the eyes closed (μυησεις); and, in the last place, an inspection of the things themselves (εποπτειαι). οτι εν τοις ιεροις ηγουντο μεν αι πανδημοι καθαρσεις· ειτα επι ταυταις απορρητοτεραι· μετα δε ταυτας συστασεις παρελαμβανοντο· και επι ταυταις μυησεις· εν τελει δε εποπτειαι. Hence, says he, the ethical and political virtues are analogous to the apparent purifications; but such of the cathartic virtues as reject every thing external, to the more arcane purifications. The energies also which are theoretic about intelligibles, are analogous to the things which permanently abide; but the contractions of these energies into the impartible are analogous to the perceptions with the eyes closed; and the simple intuitive perceptions of simple forms, to epoptic vision, or an inspection of the things themselves.

.168　　　Olympiodorus further observes, that the scope of the mysteries is to lead back souls to that end from which as a principle they made their first descent; and in which also Bacchus established them, seating them in the throne of his proper father; or, in other words, in the whole of that life of which Jupiter is the source. He, therefore, who is initiated, necessarily dwells with the Gods, according to the scope of the initiating deities. But the greatest and most mystical sacrifices (τελεται), says he, are twofold; the one here, being certain preparations; and the other hereafter. The latter also, he adds, are in his opinion twofold; some taking place about the pneumatic vehicle, as here about the shelly body (περι τον οστρεινον), and others about the luciform vehicle. For there are three gradations of mystic as well as of philosophic ascent. For philosophers are led back to their pristine condition in the three thousandth year, as it is said in the *Phædrus*;[249a] and a chiliad, or a thousand, signifies a perfect and periodic life. He, therefore, who is uninitiated, as remaining most remote from his proper end, lies in mire here, and much more there; for he is merged in the impurity of matter.

.170　　　14 (See page 247, line 69d) The thyrsus, says Olympiodorus, is a symbol of material and partible fabrication, on account of its divulsed continuity, whence also it is a Titannic plant. For it is extended before Bacchus instead of his paternal sceptre, and through this they call him into a partial nature. Besides, says he, the Titans are thyrsus-bearers; and Prometheus concealed fire in a reed, whether by this we are to understand that he draws down celestial light into generation, or impels soul into body, or calls forth divine illumination, the whole of which is ungenerated, into generation. Hence Socrates Orphically calls the multitude thyrsus-bearers, as living Titannically. Olympiodorus

.171　　further adds, that he who lives Bacchically, now rests from his labours, is liberated from his bonds, and dismisses his guard, or rather his confined life; and such a one is a cathartic philosopher. Some too, says he, prefer *philosophy*,

.172　　as Porphyry and Plotinus, and many other philosophers; but others prefer the *hieratic discipline*, or the discipline pertaining to sacred ceremonies, as Iamblichus, Syrianus, and Proclus, and all the *hieratic* philosophers. Plato, however, knowing that much may be said on both sides, collects the arguments into one, by calling the philosopher a Bacchus.

.174　　　15 (See page 247, line 69d) The apology of Socrates is twofold, one to the Athenian judges, and the other to the most genuine of his associates. The one contending for the safety of the animal, *i.e.* of the composite of soul and body, but the other for the separate and proper life of the soul. The one also being a mixture of science and opinion, but the other of intellect and science. The one proceeding from the political life, but the other from the cathartic life. And the one evincing that the death which is apparent and known to all men is good; but the other, that this must be asserted of the true death, and which is only known to philosophers.

.177   16 (See page 247, line 70a) Some, says Olympiodorus, immortalize the soul from the rational part as far as to the animated habit, as the Pythagorean Numenius. Others as far as to nature, as Plotinus [En. IV, 3]. Others as far as to the irrational part, as among the ancients Xenocrates and Speusippus, but among the moderns Iamblichus and Plutarch. Others again as far only as to the rational soul, as Proclus and Porphyry. Others as far only as to intellect; for they suppose that the doxastic part is corrupted, as many of the Peripatetics. And others as far as to the whole soul; for they admit that partial souls are corrupted into the whole soul of the universe.

.207   17 (See page 248, line 70d) The design of what is here said is not to show that the soul is immortal, but that it continues for a certain time after the dissolution of the body. Iamblichus, however, as we are informed by Olympiodorus, thought that each of the arguments in the *Phædo* demonstrated the immortality of the soul. But, as Olympiodorus justly observes, Iamblichus said this in consequence of energizing according to intellect enthusiastically, which, says he, was usual with him.

10.3   Proclus, or rather Syrianus, as we learn from Olympiodorus, collects that life and death are generated from each other, because life is a conjunction and death
10.4   a disjunction. But these are contraries; and contraries change into each other; for that contraries change into each other, the text shows in a threefold respect. First, from induction. Secondly, from generations themselves, and the ways which lead to them: for if the ways change into each other, as for instance whitening into blackening, much more must the ends change into each other, *viz.* the white into the black. Thirdly, because nature would be mutilated, if one of two contraries changed into the other, and the other not; and also because in time the other would fail, and nothing would be contrary, the remainder not having any thing into which it can change. Just as if a vigilant should be changed into a sleepy state, but not on the other hand a sleepy into a vigilant state, the delusion of Endymion, as Socrates says, would take place; for not only he, but all things, would sleep. Endymion, however, is said to have slept perpetually, because he applied himself in solitude to the study of astronomy. Hence, too, he is said to have been beloved by the moon.

It is likewise necessary to observe that Plato here speaks of things which are properly contraries; and that, if he also makes mention of relatives, these, from the participation of contraries, change into each other.

11.1   18 (See page 250, line 72e) Socrates, having shown from life and death that
the soul remains after its separation from the body, now shows, from discipline
being reminiscence, that it subsisted prior to the body; so that from both these
positions it may be collected that the soul endures for a much longer time than
11.2   the body. Olympiodorus however again informs us that Iamblichus thought
that each of these positions evinced the immortality of the soul. For, says he,
if life and death are always from each other, the soul is perpetual; and if also
disciplines are reminiscences, according to this also the soul lives for ever. So
that, by uniting both the arguments, he concludes that the soul is without
generation and incorruptible.   However, as Olympiodorus justly observes,
neither nor both of these positions demonstrate that the soul is immortal, but
that it subsists for a certain time prior and posterior to the body. Hence Plato,
perceiving that he had not yet sufficiently demonstrated the thing proposed,
introduces other arguments in proof of it; and the fifth alone properly
demonstrates the immortality of the soul from its essence.

11.3   Since however, says Olympiodorus, the discourse is now about reminiscence,
and memory is proximate to reminiscence, and oblivion is opposed to memory,
let us define what each of these three is, from their appellations. Reminiscence,
therefore, is renewed memory,[†] as its name evinces.   But memory is
permanency of intellect.[‡] And oblivion is as it were a certain dimness of the
sight.[§] For as dimness is an impediment to the sight, so oblivion is a dimness
of our knowledge, as it were of our sight. For memory, which is permanency
of intellect, is first beheld in intellect; since it is a stable collection of
knowledge: just as *the ever* is stability of being, and *immortality* is stability of
life; for it is inextinguishable life.   In like manner memory is stability of
knowledge. As, therefore, our soul does not possess infinite power according
11.4   to knowledge, though it does according to life, hence oblivion intervening,
reminiscence is a certain regeneration as it were of knowledge.   Memory
likewise first subsists in intellect, because intellect always understands and abides
in itself; but secondarily in divine souls, as possessing transitive intellections,
and not knowing all things without time, and collectively; and it subsists, in the
third place, in our souls, in which oblivion also intervenes. Memory likewise
is similar to eternity, perpetually subsisting about the same; but reminiscence,
to time, through its transition.

           But as Socrates shows from reminiscence that the soul subsisted prior to the
body, the following Platonic arguments in defence of the soul's pre-existence
.279   are offered to the earnest consideration of the reader. Unless the soul then had
a being prior to her connexion with the present body, she never would be led
to search after knowledge. For if the objects of her investigation were things

      † Αναμνησις εστι ανανεωσις μνημης.

      ‡ Μνημη δε μονη του νου.

      § Ληθη δε οιον λημη τις.

which she had never before been acquainted with, how could she ever be certain that she detected them? Indeed it would be as impossible on this hypothesis for the soul to know any thing about them, even when she perceived them, as it would be to tell the meaning of the words of an unknown language on hearing them pronounced. The Peripatetics, in order to subvert .280 this consequence, have recourse to an intellect in capacity, which is the passive recipient of all forms. The doubt however still remains. For how does this intellect understand? For it must either understand the things which it already knows, or things which it does not know. But the Stoics assert, that natural conceptions are the causes of our investigating and discovering truth. If, therefore, these conceptions are in capacity, we ask the same question as before; but if they are in energy, why do we investigate things which we know? Lastly, the Epicureans affirm that anticipations are the causes of our investigations. If then they say that these anticipations subsist distinctly, investigation must be vain; but if indistinctly, why do we seek after any thing besides these anticipations? Or, in other words, why do we seek after distinct knowledge, of which we have no anticipation?

.285 Again, there are numberless instances of persons that are terrified at certain animals, such as cats, lizards, and tortoises, without knowing the cause of their terror. Thus the nephews of Berius, says Olympiodorus, that were accustomed to hunt bears and lions, could not endure the sight of a cock. The same author adds, that a certain apothecary could look undisturbed at asps and snakes, but was so exceedingly frightened at a wasp, that he would run from it crying aloud, and stupefied with terror. Thus too, says he, Themison the physician could apply himself to the cure of every disease except the hydrophobia; but if any person only mentioned this disease, he would be immediately agitated, and suffer in a manner similar to those afflicted with this malady. Now it is impossible to assign any other satisfactory cause of all this, than a reminiscence of having suffered through these animals in a prior state of existence.

.288 Further still, infants are not seen to laugh for nearly three weeks after their birth, but pass the greatest part of this time in sleep; however, in their sleep they are often seen both to laugh and cry. But how is it possible that this can any otherwise happen than through the soul being agitated by the whirling motions of the animal nature, and moved in conformity to the passions which .291 it had experienced in another life? Besides, our looking into ourselves, when we are endeavouring to discover any truth, evinces that we inwardly contain .292 truth, though concealed in the darkness of oblivion. The delight too which attends our discovery of truth, sufficiently proves that this discovery is nothing more than a recognition of something most eminently allied to our nature, and which had been, as it were, lost in the middle space of time, between our former knowledge of the truth and the recovery of that knowledge. For the perception of a thing perfectly unknown and unconnected with our nature, would produce terror instead of delight; and things are pleasing only in proportion as they possess something known and domestic to the natures by which they are known.

13.19   19 (See page 258, line 79d) Olympiodorus here inquires how Plato calls *prudence* a *passion* of the soul. To which he replies, that all the virtues are *passions*. For it is evident, says he, that things which participate *suffer*. Hence also *being*, considered as participating *The One*, is said by Plato to *suffer* or be *passive* to *The One*. Since, therefore, the soul participates of the prudence which subsists in intellect, or, in other words, of intellectual prudence, on this account he calls prudence the passion of the soul. Or we may say, that since the whole soul is through the whole of itself self-motive, so far as it *moves itself* it *acts*, but so far as it is *moved* it *suffers*.

.352   20 (See page 260, line 81c) The irrational nature is the image of the rational soul. This nature also is corporeal, consisting of a corporeal life, and a certain body more attenuated than this visible body. This image, Plato says, becomes heavy, and is seen about sepulchres. Hence souls that are still bound to the visible nature through a strong propensity to body, are said to follow this phantom; and thus they become visible through participation of the visible, or sympathy towards it. But such souls, says Olympiodorus, are not only willing,
.353   but are compelled to wander about sepulchres, as a punishment of their sympathy about the body. He adds, that the image having a connate desire
.354   towards the outward body, sometimes also draws to it the soul, with the consent of Justice.

.361   21 (See page 265, line 85e) Harmony has a triple subsistence. For it is either harmony itself, or it is that which is first harmonized, and which is such according to the whole of itself; or it is that which is secondarily harmonized, and which partially participates of harmony. The first of these must be assigned to intellect, the second to soul, and the third to body. This last too is corruptible, because it subsists in a subject; but the other two are incorruptible, because they are neither composites, nor dependent on a subject. Simmias, therefore, reasons falsely in what he here says, in consequence of looking to the third species of harmony only. Hence, the rational soul is analogous to a musician, but the animated body to harmonized chords: for the former has a subsistence separate, but the latter inseparable from the musical instrument.

.405   22 (See page 273, line 93d) As every rational soul is an incorporeal harmony separate from a subject, it does not admit of intensions and remissions; and, therefore, one rational soul is neither more nor less harmony than another, so far as each is *essentially* harmony. One soul, however, may be more similar to intellect, or harmony itself, than another, and, so far as it is more similar, will be more harmony in *energy*. Hence, virtue may be considered as the concord, and vice as the discord, of the rational and irrational nature; the former being produced from the rational harmonizing the irrational part, in consequence of being a harmony more energetic; and the latter arising from the irrational being unharmonized by the rational part, because in this case the essential harmony of the soul is more dormant than energetic. The reasoning, therefore, of Socrates does not apply to that harmony which is separate, but to that which is inseparable from body.

.378   23 (See page 274, line 95a) "Cadmus," says Olympiodorus, "is the sublunary world, as being Dionysiacal, on which account Harmony is united to the God, and as being the father of the four Bacchuses. But they make the four elements to be Dionysiacal, *viz. fire*, to be *Semele*; *earth*, *Agave*, tearing in pieces her own offspring; *water*, *Ino*; and lastly, *air*, *Autonoe*". There is great beauty in conjoining *Harmonia*, or *Harmony*, the daughter of Venus and Mars, with Cadmus. For Venus is the cause of all the harmony and analogy in the universe, and beautifully illuminates the order and communion of all mundane concerns. But Mars excites the contrarieties of the universe, that the world may exist perfect and entire from all its parts. The progeny, therefore, of these two Divinities must be the *concordant discord* or *harmony* of the sublunary world. But Socrates (as Forster well observes in his notes on this dialogue) represents Cebes as another Cadmus, because, according to his doctrine, men after they are buried, like the teeth of the serpent slain by Cadmus, will revive in another form, and in a short time like the Cadmæan men will entirely perish.

24 (See page 288, line 107b) Simmias says this, in consequence of not having arrived at the summit of philosophical attainments, and, therefore, not seeing the full force of this fifth argument of Socrates. For it possesses a most wonderful and invincible strength; and by those that understand it will be acknowledged to have all the force of geometrical demonstration. Socrates himself insinuates as much as this, when he says in reply to Simmias, that by sufficiently investigating the hypotheses on which this argument is founded, we shall follow reason in as great a degree as is possible to man, and at length make no further inquiry. That is, we shall at length perceive this truth by the projecting energies of intellect, which is a degree of evidence, as I have already observed in the Introduction to this dialogue, superior to that of any tradition however divine.

.94   25 (See page 288, line 107d) Since there are in the universe, says Olympiodorus, things which subsist differently at different times, and since there are also natures which are conjoined with the superessential unities, it is necessary that there should be a certain middle genus, which is neither immediately suspended from Deity, nor subsists differently at different times according to better and worse, but which is always perfect, and does not depart

from its proper virtue; and is immutable indeed, but is not conjoined with the superessential. The whole of this genus is dæmoniacal. There are also different
.95 genera of dæmons: for they are placed under the mundane Gods. The highest of these subsists according to *the one* of the Gods, which is called an unific and divine genus of dæmons. The next according to the intellect which is suspended from Deity, and is called intellectual. The third subsists according to soul, and is called rational. The fourth according to nature, which is denominated physical. The fifth according to body, which is called corporeal-
.96 formed. And the sixth according to matter, and this is denominated material. Or after another manner it may be said, Olympiodorus adds, that some of these are celestial, others ethereal, others aërial, others aquatic, others terrestrial, and others subterranean. With respect to this division, it is evident that it is derived from the parts of the universe. But irrational dæmons originate from the aërial governors, whence also the Oracle[†] says, "being the charioteer of the aërial, terrestrial and aquatic dogs."

$$\eta \epsilon \rho \iota \omega \nu \ \epsilon \lambda \alpha \tau \eta \rho \alpha \ \kappa \upsilon \nu \omega \nu \ \chi \theta \text{ο} \nu \iota \omega \nu \ \tau \epsilon \ \kappa \alpha \iota \ \upsilon \gamma \rho \omega \nu.$$

.97 Our guardian dæmons, however, belong to that order of dæmons which is arranged under the Gods that preside over the ascent and descent of souls.

26 (See page 288, line 107d) Olympiodorus observes here, that the dæmon endeavours to lead the soul, as exciting its conceptions and phantasies; at the same time, however, yielding to the self-motive power of the soul. But in consequence of the dæmon exciting, one soul follows voluntarily, another violently, and another according to a mode subsisting between these. Olympiodorus further observes that there is one dæmon who leads the soul to
.491 its judges from the present life; another, who is ministrant to the judges, giving completion, as it were, to the sentence which is passed; and a third who is again allotted the guardianship of life.

.114 27 (See page 289, line 108c) With respect to the earth which is here mentioned, Olympiodorus informs us, that some of the ancients considered it as incorporeal, others as corporeal, and each of these in a twofold respect. For those who considered it as incorporeal said that it was either an idea, or nature; but of those who considered it as corporeal, some asserted that it was the whole world, and others the sublunary region. Plato, however, as is evident from the text, appears to speak of this our earth.

† See TTS vol. VII, p. 43.

.115 Olympiodorus adds, that as the earth is a *pleroma*[†] of the universe, it is a God. For, if the universe is a God, it is evident that the parts from which it derives its completion must also be Gods. Besides, if the earth contains Divinities, much more must it be itself a God, as Timæus also says. Hence, intellect and a rational soul must be suspended from it, and consequently it must have a luciform prior to this apparent body.

.117 Again, that the universe is spherical, may be shown from its final cause. For a sphere imitates *The One*, because it is the best and most indissoluble of figures, as being free from angles, and the most capacious of all things. This is also evident from its paradigmatic cause, because *animal itself*, or the extremity of the intelligible order, to which looking, the demiurgus fabricated the world, is all-perfect. And further still, this is evident from its producing cause. For the demiurgus made it to be perpetual and indissoluble, and both the circle and sphere are figures of this kind.

.118 Further still, as every part of the whole, which ranks as a whole, imitates the universe in the *whole* and the *all*, so likewise in figure. Every whole, therefore, in the universe, is spherical, and consequently this must also be true of the

.119 earth. It is likewise evident that the earth is in the middle. For, if the universe is spherical, it subsists about the centre: the parts of the universe, therefore, which rank as wholes will also subsist about centres, and consequently this will be the case with the earth. Let it, however, be admitted, that it subsists about a centre, but whence is it evident that it subsists about the centre of the universe? We reply, that if it is the most gross of all the bodies, it will be the last of them; for the most attenuated of bodies, as being able to pervade through each other, possess the higher place, conformably to the order of attenuation; and the earth the lower.

.125 28 (See page 290, line 109a) That the earth is very great, says Olympiodorus, is evident from the Atlantic island surpassing in magnitude both Asia and Libya. It is also evident from the putrefaction of the places which we inhabit, since such places cannot rank as first. It is likewise evident from the summits of things secondary wishing to be assimilated to the extremities of things prior to them; so that the summit of earth must be attenuated and pellucid, similar to the most precious stones and metals. And lastly, this is evident from the profundity of the hollows in which we dwell, and the height of the mountains; for these evince that the spheric superficies of the earth is larger than that

.126 which is generally considered as its surface. On this summit of the earth, therefore, the true heavens are visible. They are also seen near, and not through æther only, and with more beautiful eyes. According to Ammonius

.128 Hermeas, too, whom Olympiodorus calls the Interpreter, the stars themselves, as I have before observed, are not seen by us here, but inflammations of them

---

† A whole, which gives completion to the universe.

in the air. And perhaps, says he, this is the meaning of that assertion of Heraclitus, "enkindling measures and extinguishing measures." For he certainly did not say this of the sun itself, but of the sun with reference to us.

.131   Olympiodorus further observes, that there is a triple division of the earth, according to the three Saturnian deities Jupiter, Neptune, and Pluto: for to these, says Homer, heaven and earth are common. But if common, it is evident that these two are divided among them. Hence, in the heavens, the inerratic sphere belongs to Jupiter; from thence, as far as to the sphere of the sun, to Neptune; and the remaining part of the heavens to Pluto. If there is also a division of the earth according to the universe, it must be divided into celestial, terrestrial, and middle. For Olympian earth is honoured, as well as that which is properly terrestrial. There must, therefore, be a certain middle earth. If, likewise, there is a division of the earth conformably to that of an animal, for the earth is an animal, it must be divided into the head, middle parts, and feet.

.132   It is also beautifully observed by Olympiodorus, that each of the elements has the dodecahedron in common, as preparatory to becoming a sphere. Hence, says he, the earth has from itself the cubic, water the icosahedric, air the octahedric, and fire the pyramid; but from the supermundane Gods the dodecahedron is imparted to all of them, as preparatory to intellectual participation, which is sphericity, or the reception of a spherical figure.

.133   29 (See page 291, line 110b) The earth is distinguished with colours, says Olympiodorus, according to the *physical* variety of colours; according to the defluxions of celestial illuminations from Mars and the Sun; and according to incorporeal lives, which proceed as far as to sensible beauty. With respect to

.134   the elements likewise on the summit of the earth, water there is as vapour, and as moist air; but air is æther, and æther is the summit of æther. If, also, there are mountains there, it is evident, says he, that from their nearness they reach the heavens. In short, he adds, the æthers of the elements are there, as the Chaldæan oracles say.

.137   30 (See page 292, line 111a) These forms of life, says Olympiodorus, on the summit of the earth, subsist between the forms of perpetual animals and those that live but for a short time. For a medium is every where necessary. But the excellent temperature of the seasons and the elements causes the inhabitants there to die easily, and to live long. And what is there wonderful in this, says Olympiodorus, since this in a certain respect is the case with the Æthiopians,

.138   through the symmetry of the air? He adds, if also Aristotle relates, that a man lived here without sleep, and nourished by the solar-form air alone, what ought we to think of the inhabitants which are there? Καὶ τι θαυμαστον, οτι και οι Αιθιοπες ωδε πως εχουσι δια την των αερων συμμετριαν. και ει ενταυθα ιστορει Αριστοτελης ανθρωπον αυπνον και μονω τω ηλιοειδει τρεφομενον αερι, τι χρη περι των εκει οιεσθαι. [137.4 - 5]

.141   31 (See page 293, line 112b) As fire, water, and air, are in the middle of the earth, much vapour must be there, as Olympiodorus justly observes, water being analysed into vapour through fire. Earth also being an animal, and living, must be willing to respire, as it were, and must make certain refluxes by its inspirations and expirations. Further still, its luciform must be its first vehicle, and its apparent must be this corporeal bulk. It must, therefore, require a middle, or aërial vehicle, the province of which is to cherish and move more attenuated bodies, through its all-various motion.

.142   Olympiodorus further observes, that of Tartarus, and Earth which is conjoined with Heaven, Typhon, Echidna, and Python, form as it were a certain Chaldaic triad, the inspective guardian of all inordinate fabrication. [See also TTS vol. VII, p. 43.]

.145   32 (See page 294, line 112e) The four rivers which are here mentioned are, says Olympiodorus, according to the Interpreter (*i.e.* Ammonius Hermeas), the four elements in Tartarus. Of these Ocean is water; Cocytus, or rather Styx, is earth; Pyriphlegethon is fire; and Acheron is air. But Styx is opposed to Pyriphlegethon, as heat to cold; and Acheron to Ocean, as air to water. Hence also Orpheus[†] calls the Acherusian lake aërial. However, says Olympiodorus, the position of the rivers does not correspond to this interpretation. For Ocean is first, and in the higher place. Under this is Acheron. Under this again, Pyriphlegethon; and in the last place, Cocytus. Besides, all of them are called rivers, though the elements are different. It is better therefore, says he, to consider the allotments, and the places themselves of souls, as receiving a fourfold division, according to depth. And prior to the places, we should consider the divine idioms, *viz.* the definitive, according to Ocean; the cathartic, according to Acheron; that which punishes through heat, according to Pyriphlegethon; and that which punishes through cold, according to Cocytus.

33 (See page 295, line 113e) Let not the reader imagine, that by the word *never*, here, an eternal duration is implied; for Divinity does not punish the soul as if influenced by anger, but, like a good physician, for the sake of healing the maladies which she has contracted through guilt. We must say, therefore, as Olympiodorus well observes, that the incurable soul is punished *eternally*, calling eternity her life and the partial period of her existence. "For, in reality

.147   (says he), souls which have offended in the highest degree cannot be sufficiently purified in one period, but are *continually* in life, as it were, in Tartarus; and this period is called by Plato eternity."

---

† Διο και Οτην Αχεροισιαν λιμνην αεριαν καλει. [Fr. 125]

.150 34 (See page 300, line 118a) The meaning of the Attic symbols respecting those that die is, according to Olympiodorus, as follows: The closing of the mouth and eyes signifies the cessation of external energy, and the conversion of the soul to that which is inward. The being laid on the earth recalls to our memory, that the soul is conjoined with wholes. The washing of the dead body indicates purification from generation. The anointing the parts of the body signifies a divulsion from the dark mire of matter, and that divine inspiration is evocated. But the burning signifies the being led to that which is on high, and to an impartible nature. And the being laid in the earth indicates a conjunction with intelligibles. Τινων συμβολα τα περι τους αποιχομενους πατρια αττικα. το μεν ουν καμμυειν, του παυειν μεν της εξω ενεργειας, προς δε την εισω επιστρεφειν. το δε επι γης τιθεναι του αναμιμνησκειν οπως αν τοις ολοις η ψυχη συναφθειη. το δε λουειν, το αποκαθαιρειν της γενεσεως. το δε μυριζειν, το αποσπαν μεν του βορβορου της υλης, την δε θειαν επιπνοιαν προκαλεισθαι. το δε καιειν, το περιαγειν εις το ανω, και το αμεριστον. το δε εντιθεναι τη γη το συναπτειν τοις νοητοις. [150. 1 - 7]

THE

GORGIAS

A DIALOGUE

CONCERNING

THE PRINCIPLES

WHICH LEAD TO POLITICAL FELICITY

INTRODUCTION

0.2 It is necessary in the first place, says Olympiodorus,† to investigate the dramatic apparatus of the dialogue; in the second place, its scope; in the third place, the division of it; in the fourth place, the persons in it, and the analogy of the persons; and in the fifth place, (that which is investigated by many, though it does not deserve to be discussed, and was not doubted by men of greater antiquity,) on what account Plato introduces Gorgias here, who was very far from being contemporary with Socrates.

0.3 The dramatic apparatus then is as follows: Gorgias, the Leontine, came from the Leontines in Sicily, as an ambassador to the Athenians, respecting a confederation, and the war against the Syracusians. He had also with him Polus, who delighted in rhetoric; and he dwelt in the house of Callicles, the public orator of the Athenians. This Callicles, too, was delighted with skilful rhetoricians, but made pleasure the end of life, and deceived the Athenians, always addressing them in the language of Demosthenes, "What do you wish? What shall I write? In what can I gratify you?" Gorgias, therefore, displayed his art, and so captivated the Athenian people, that they called the days in which he exhibited *festivals*, and his periods *lamps*. Whence Socrates, perceiving the people thus deceived, and being able to extend good to all the youth, formed the design of saving the souls both of the Athenians and of Gorgias himself. Taking, therefore, with him Chærepho the philosopher, who is mentioned by Aristophanes, they went to the house of Callicles, and there their conferences and investigations of theorems took place. But he went with Chærepho, and did not go alone, that he might show how scientific men conducted themselves and discoursed. And thus much for the apparatus of the dialogue.

0.4 With respect to its scope, it has appeared to be different to different persons. For some say that the design of Plato was to discourse concerning rhetoric; and they inscribe it "Gorgias, or concerning Rhetoric;" but improperly: for they characterize the whole from a part. Others again say, that the dialogue is concerning justice and injustice; showing that the just are happy, and the unjust unfortunate and miserable. Likewise, that by how much the more unjust a man is, by so much the more is he miserable; that in proportion as his injustice is extended by time, in such proportion is he more miserable; and that if

---

† In his MS. Scholia on this Dialogue. [The references throughout this introduction and the notes are this Scholia, which is arranged into 50 lectures and a proemial, with each lecture being divided into sections. The reference number refers to lecture and then section number as given in the full translation of it by Jackson, Lycos and Tarrant (*Olympiodorus, Commentary on Plato's Gorgias*, Brill, Leiden, 1998)].

it were immortal, he would be most miserable. These too receive the scope of the dialogue from a part, *viz.* from the arguments against Polus. Others say that its scope is to speak concerning the demiurgus. But these also collect the scope from a part; because in the fable in the latter part of this dialogue the demiurgus is mentioned. These, however, speak absurdly, and foreign from the purpose. We say, therefore, that its scope is *to discourse concerning the principles which conduct us to political felicity.*

0.5   Since, then, we have mentioned principles and a polity, let us speak concerning principles universally, and concerning political felicity, and also what the principles are of the political science. The principles, therefore, of every thing are six. *Matter*, as with a carpenter wood. *Form*, the writing table, or something of this kind. *That which makes*, as the carpenter himself. *The paradigm*, that to which directing his phantasy, he made the table. *The instrument*, the saw perhaps, or the axe. And *the end*, that on account of which it was made. The multitude, therefore, and rhetoricians, not looking to truth, say that *the matter* of the political science is the body which is preserved; *the form*, luxury; *the producing cause*, rhetoric; *the paradigm*, a tyranny; *the instrument*, persuasion; and *the end*, pleasure. And such are their assertions. We however say that the *matter* is soul, and this not the rational, but that which consists of three[†] parts: for it imitates a polity. And as in cities there are governors, soldiers, and mercenaries; so, in us, reason is analogous to the governor; anger to the soldier, subsisting as a medium, and being obedient to reason, but commanding and ranking the mercenaries, that is desire. The *matter*, therefore, is the soul considered as divided into three parts. For the political character wishes to be angry and to desire, with respect to such things as are proper, and when it is proper. Just as the lowest string of a musical instrument accords with the highest, and emits the same sound with it, though more acute. For thus desire is conjoined with reason. But *the form* is justice and temperance. *The producing cause* is a philosophic life. But *the paradigm* is the world. For the political philosopher arranges all things in imitation of the universe, which is replete with excellent order. For this universe is *order* (κοσμος) according to Plato, and not disorder (ακοσμια). Manners and discipline are *the instrument*. And *the end* is good. It must, however, be observed, that good is twofold, one of which pertains to us

---

† *i.e.* Of reason, anger, and desire.

in the present life, but the other we possess hereafter.[†] *Political good*, therefore, belongs to us in the present, but *theoretic good* will be our portion in another life. To Gorgias, therefore, the discourse is about the *producing cause*; to Polus, about the *formal*; and to Callicles, about the *final*. Nor is it wonderful if all appear to be in all. For in the producing cause the rest are found, and in the others all: for there is a certain communion among them, and they pervade through each other. But they derive their order from that which abounds.

Hence, therefore, the division of the dialogue becomes apparent. For it is divided into three parts: into the discourse with Gorgias; into that with Polus; and into that with Callicles. It is necessary also to observe, that justice and temperance are peculiarly said to be the form of the political science. For it is necessary to know that all the virtues contribute to political felicity, but especially these two. Hence Plato always makes mention of these, as being neglected by men. For they wish to know the other two, though not perfectly, yet fictitiously, and under a false appellation. Hence they say, Such a one is a prudent man; he knows how to enrich himself. And in a similar manner with respect to fortitude; but they neglect the other two. There is, however, occasion for these, since they proceed through all the parts of the soul. For as he who in the city performs his proper work, and gives to every man that which is his due, is said to be just; in like manner justice rules in the soul, when reason, anger, and desire, respectively perform the office accommodated to each. If this be the case, temperance then subsists in the soul, when each part does not desire that which is foreign to its nature.

In the next place, it is worth while to inquire into the number and analogy of the persons. Five persons, therefore, are introduced, *viz.* Socrates, Chærepho, Gorgias, Polus, and Callicles. Of these, Socrates is analogous to that which is intellectual and scientific; Chærepho to right opinion; Gorgias to distorted opinion; for he was not entirely vanquished by injustice, but was dubious whether he should be persuaded or not. But Polus is analogous to injustice, and to one who is alone ambitious; and Callicles is analogous to a swinish nature, and which is a lover of pleasure. Some, however, doubt on what account the orators are three, but the philosophers two; and why the number of the orators in indivisible,[‡] but that of the philosophers divisible. We

---

† Though a few are able to exercise the *theoretic* as well as the *political* virtues in the present life, yet we can only possess the good of the former in perfection hereafter. - For an accurate account of these virtues, see the Notes on the *Phædo* [p. 309].

‡ For three, being an odd number, in indivisible.

say, however, that this in not true. For Socrates imitates the *monad*[†] looking to *The One*. And divinity (or *The One*) is simple, produced from nothing. Hence the hymn to him says, "From whom all things emerge into light; but thy subsistence alone is not on account of any thing."[‡] Chærepho also imitates the monad, but that which is material and inseparable from matter; but Socrates the separate monad. And as subordinate do not proceed to better, or better to subordinate natures, without a medium, on this account Chærepho has a middle order; and consequently it is incumbent on him to transmit that which the extremes possess.

0.9   It now remains to inquire how Plato makes mention of Gorgias. I say, therefore, in the first place, that there is nothing absurd in a writer recording unknown men, and introducing them as discoursing with each other. And, in the second place, we say that Socrates and Gorgias were contemporaries. For Socrates lived in the third year of the 77th Olympiad: and Empedocles the Pythagorean, the preceptor of Gorgias, associated with him. To which we may add, that Gorgias wrote a treatise concerning Nature, not inelegant, in the 84th Olympiad; so that this was twenty-eight or a few more years before Socrates. Besides, Plato, in the *Theætetus*, says that Socrates, when a very young man, met with Parmenides, when he was very much advanced in years, and found him to be a most profound man. But Parmenides was the preceptor of Empedocles, who was the preceptor of Gorgias. And Gorgias was very old: for, according to history, he died in the one-hundred-and-ninth year of his age. So that these two lived about the same time.

I shall only observe, in addition to what Olympiodorus has said, that Plato does not condemn all orators, but those only who study to persuade their hearers to embrace whatever they please, whether it be good or bad, false or true; such as were Lysias the Theban, Tisias, and Gorgias. But, in the *Phædrus*, he prefers Pericles and Isocrates to all the other orators, because they combined eloquence with philosophy. He also adds, that a legitimate orator ought to understand the reasons of things, the laws of manners, the powers of words, and the different dispositions of men; that he should know how to compose words adapted, as much as possible, to the genius of his hearers; and that he should not be so anxious that what he says may be pleasing to men, as that it may be acceptable to Divinity.

---

† The *monad* is the united subsistence of separated multitude; but *The One* is the summit of multitude.

‡ Εξ ου παντα πεφηνη· συ δ᾽ ουδενος ουνεκα μουνος.

THE

GORGIAS

PERSONS OF THE DIALOGUE

CALLICLES,   CHÆREPHO,
SOCRATES,   GORGIAS,
AND POLUS

447a   CAL. In this manner, Socrates, they say it is requisite to engage in war and contention.

SOC. But have we not, according to the proverb, come after the festival? and are we not late?

CAL. And, indeed, after a very elegant festival. For Gorgias, a little before, exhibited to us many and beautiful things.

SOC. But Chærepho, O Callicles, was the cause of our being so late: for he compelled us to waste our time in the forum.

b   CHÆR. It is, however, of no consequence, Socrates: for I can apply a remedy, as Gorgias is my friend, who either now, or at some future time, will, if you please, exhibit the same things to us.

CAL. But what, Chærepho, does Socrates desire to hear Gorgias?

CHÆR. We are certainly come hither for this very purpose.

CAL. Whenever, therefore, you please, come to me at my house: for Gorgias resides with me, and will exhibit to you whatever you desire.

c   SOC. You speak well, Callicles. But will he be willing to discourse with us now? For I wish to inquire of the man what the power of his art is, and what it is he professes and teaches. But the other things which you speak of, he may show us some other time.

CAL. There is nothing like asking[1] him, Socrates: for this is one of the things which he exhibited. He, therefore, just now promised all that are in the house, that he would answer any question that might be asked him.

SOC. You certainly speak well. Ask him, therefore, Chærepho.

CHÆR. What must I ask him?

d   SOC. What he is.

CHÆR. How do you say?

Soc. Just as, if he should happen to be an artificer of shoes, he would answer you that he was a shoemaker. Or do you not understand what I say?

Chær. I do; and I will ask him. Tell me, O Gorgias, did Callicles here say true, that you promised to answer whatever should be asked you?

448a Gorg. He spoke truth, Chærepho: for I just now made this promise: and I say that no one has asked me any thing new for many years.

Chær. You will, therefore, answer easily, Gorgias.

Gorg. We shall make trial of this, Chærepho.

Pol. Do so, by Jupiter: but if you please, Chærepho, discourse with me: for Gorgias appears to me to be weary; as he has just now discussed many particulars.

Chær. But what, Polus, do you think that you can answer better than Gorgias?

b Pol. Of what consequence is it, if you are answered sufficiently?

Chær. It is of no consequence: but, since you are willing, answer me.

Pol. Ask.

Chær. I ask you then, if Gorgias were knowing in that art[2] in which his brother Herodicus is skilled, by what name we might justly call him? Might we not call him the same as his brother?

Pol. Entirely so.

Chær. Calling him, therefore, a physician, we should rightly denominate him?

Pol. We should.

Chær. But if he were skilled in that art in which Aristopho, the son of Aglaophon, is skilled, or his brother, what should we then rightly call him?

c Pol. Evidently, a painter.

Chær. But now, since he is knowing in a certain art, what can we properly call him?

Pol. O Chærepho! there are many arts in men which are from skill[3] skilfully discovered. For skill causes our life to proceed according to art; but unskilfulness according to fortune. Of each of these, different persons differently participate: but the best participate of the best; in the number of which is Gorgias here, who participates of the most beautiful of arts.

d Soc. Polus, Gorgias, appears to be very well furnished for discourse; but he does not fulfil his promise to Chærepho.

Gorg. In what principally, Socrates?

Soc. He does not appear to me altogether to answer what he was asked.

Gorg. But do you, if you please, ask him.

Soc. Not if you yourself would be willing to answer me; for this would be much more agreeable to me. For it is evident to me that Polus, from what he said, has applied himself more to what is called the rhetoric art than to the art of discourse.

e Pol. Why do you say so, Socrates?

Soc. Because, Polus, when Chærepho asked you in what art Gorgias was skilled, you praised indeed his art, as if any one had blamed it, but you did not say what the art itself is.

Pol. Did I not answer, that it was the most beautiful of arts?

Soc. Very much so. But no one asked you concerning the quality of the art of Gorgias, but what it was, and what Gorgias ought to be called;

449a in the same manner as Chærepho proposed to you before, and you answered him beautifully, and with brevity. Now, therefore, inform me in the same manner, what the art of Gorgias is, and what we ought to call Gorgias. Or rather, do you, O Gorgias, tell us yourself what we ought to call you, as knowing in a certain art.

Gorg. A person skilled in rhetoric.

Soc. Ought we, therefore, to call you a rhetorician?

Gorg. And a good one, Socrates, if you wish to give me a name; which, as Homer says, I pray may be the case.

Soc. But I do wish.

Gorg. Denominate me, therefore.

b Soc. Shall we say too, that you are able to make other rhetoricians?

Gorg. I profess this not only here, but elsewhere.

Soc. Are you willing therefore, Gorgias, we should proceed in the mode of discourse we just now adopted, *viz.* by question and answer, employing on some other occasion that prolixity of speech which Polus just now began to use? But do not deceive me in what you promised, but be willing to answer with brevity what is asked you.

c Gorg. There are, Socrates, certain answers which must necessarily be prolix: however, I will endeavour to answer you in the shortest manner possible. For this is one of the things which I profess, *viz.* that no one can say the same things in fewer words than myself.

Soc. I have occasion, Gorgias, for this brevity: and I request that you will now give me a specimen of it, reserving prolixity of speech for another time.

Gorg. I will give you a specimen; and such a one that you will say you never heard a shorter discourse.

SOC. Come, then (for you say that you are knowing in the rhetorical
d   art, and that you can make others rhetoricians), is not rhetoric
conversant with a certain thing, in the same manner as the weaving art
is employed about the making of garments?

GORG. It is.

SOC. And is not music, therefore, conversant with the production of
melodies?

GORG. Yes.

SOC. By Juno, Gorgias, I am delighted with your answers, because
they are the shortest possible.

GORG. I entirely think, Socrates, that I shall give you satisfaction in
this respect.

SOC. You speak well. But answer me in this manner respecting the
rhetorical art, and inform me of what thing it is the science.

GORG. Of discourses.

SOC. Of what discourses, Gorgias? Is it of such discourses as those
employ who show the sick by what mode of living they may become
well?

e   GORG. It is not.

SOC.   The rhetorical art, therefore, is not conversant with all
discourses.

GORG. It certainly is not.

SOC. But yet it enables men to speak.

GORG. It does.

SOC. Does it impart the power of intellection in those things in which
it imparts the ability of speaking?

GORG. Undoubtedly.

450a   SOC. Does not, therefore, the medicinal art, of which we just now
spoke, render us able to understand and speak about the maladies of the
sick?

GORG. Necessarily so.

SOC. The medicinal art, therefore, as it appears, is conversant with
discourses.

GORG. It is.

SOC. And is it not conversant with discourses about diseases?

GORG. Especially so.

SOC. The gymnastic art, therefore, is also conversant with discourses
about the good and bad habit of bodies.

GORG. Entirely so.

b   Soc. And, indeed, other arts, O Gorgias, will subsist in this manner. For each of them will be conversant with those discourses which are employed about that particular thing of which each is the art.

GORG. It appears so.

Soc. Why, therefore, do you not call other arts rhetorical, since they are conversant with discourses, and you call this very thing which is employed about discourses, rhetoric?

GORG. Because, Socrates, all the science of other arts is conversant, as I may say, with manual and such-like operations; but nothing belonging to the rhetorical art is manual, since all its action and authority subsist
c   through discourses. On this account, I think that the rhetorical art is conversant with discourses, and I affirm that in this I speak rightly.

Soc. I understand what kind of an art you wish to call it; but perhaps I may comprehend it yet still more clearly. However, answer me. Have we not arts?

GORG. Yes.

Soc. I think that, with respect to all the arts, some are very much employed in operation, and stand very little in need of discourse; but others do not require it at all, but accomplish their design in silence; such as the arts of painting and statuary, and many others. You appear, therefore, to me to say that the rhetorical art is not conversant with such arts as these. Or do you not?

d   GORG. You apprehend my meaning very well, Socrates.

Soc. But there are other arts which accomplish the whole of their intention through discourse, and either require, as I may say, nothing of operation, or very little, such as the arithmetic, logistic, pettutic,† and many other arts; some of which have discourses nearly equal to their
e   operations; but with many the discourses surpass the operations: and, universally, all their action and authority subsist through discourses. You appear to me to say that rhetoric ranks among things of this last kind.

GORG. You speak the truth.

Soc. Yet I do not think you are willing to call rhetoric any one of these, though you said that the rhetorical art was that which possessed its authority through discourse. For some one disposed to be troublesome might ask, Do you therefore, Gorgias, say that the arithmetical is the rhetorical art? But I do not think that you call either the arithmetical, or the geometrical, the rhetorical art.

451a   GORG. You think rightly, Socrates, and apprehend me perfectly well.

---

† The art of chess.

SOC. Now, therefore, complete the answer to my question. For, since rhetoric is one of those arts which very much use discourse, and there are other arts of this kind, endeavour to tell us about what particular thing in discourse the authority of rhetoric is exercised. Just as if any one should ask me respecting the arts which I lately mentioned, O Socrates, what is the arithmetical art, I should say as you did just now, b that it is one of the arts which possesses all its power through discourse. And if he should again ask me about what it is conversant, I should answer, About the knowledge of the even and the odd, *viz.* what the nature is of each. But if he should further ask me, What do you call the logistic art? I should answer, that this also is one of those arts which possess all their authority through discourse. And if he should ask me about what it is conversant, I should answer, like those who write decrees in the Senate-house, that the logistic in other respects subsists in c the same manner as the arithmetical art (for each is employed about the even and the odd); but that it differs in this, that it considers the amount of the even and the odd, both with respect to themselves and to each other. And if any one should ask me about what the discourses of astronomy are employed, in consequence of my saying that it ranked among those arts the whole of whose authority consists in discourse, I should say that they are employed about the lation of the stars, of the sun and the moon, *viz.* how they are related to each other with respect to swiftness.

GORG. And you would answer very properly, Socrates.

d SOC. Now then do you answer, Gorgias. For rhetoric is one of those arts which accomplish every thing, and derive all their authority through discourse. Is it not?

GORG. It is.

SOC. Tell me then, what that particular thing is, about which the discourses are conversant which rhetoric employs.

GORG. The greatest and the best, Socrates, of human concerns.

SOC. But Gorgias, what you now say is ambiguous, and in no respect e clear. For I think you have heard that convivial song, which is sung at banquets, in which the singers thus enumerate: that to be well is the best thing; but to be beautiful ranks in the second place; and, as the author of the song says, to be rich without fraud, in the third place.[4]

GORG. I have heard it; but why do you say this?

452a SOC. Because there those artificers will immediately present themselves to you, who are celebrated by the author of this song; *viz.* the physician, the master of gymnastic, and the collector of wealth. And, in the first place, the physician will say: Gorgias, O Socrates, deceives you. For his art is not employed about that which procures the greatest good to men, but this is the province of my art. If, therefore, I should ask him, What are you who assert these things? he would perhaps say that he is a physician. What then do you say? Or is the employment of your art the greatest good? How is it possible, perhaps he will say, Socrates, it should not, since the work of my art is health?

b For what can be a greater good to men than health? But if after this the master of gymnastic should say, I should wonder, Socrates, if Gorgias could show you that there is greater good in his art than I can evince there is in mine, I should again say to him, And what are you, O man? and what is your work? he would say, I am a master of gymnastic, and my employment consists in rendering the bodies of men beautiful and strong. But after the master of gymnastic, the collector of wealth would say, despising all others, as it appears to me, Consider, Socrates, whether

c there is any greater good than riches, either with Gorgias, or any other person? I should therefore say to him, What then, are you the artificer of this good? He would say that he is. And what are you? A collector of money. What then? Do you think that riches are the greatest good to men? Undoubtedly, he will say. To this we shall reply, Gorgias here contends that his art is the cause of greater good than yours. It is

d evident, therefore, that after this he will say, And what is this good? Let Gorgias answer. Think then, Gorgias, that you are thus interrogated by them and me, and answer, What is this, which you say is the greatest good to men, and of which you are the artificer?

GORG. That which is in reality, Socrates, the greatest good, and is at the same time the cause of liberty to men, and of their being able to rule over others in their own city.

SOC. What then do you say this is?

e GORG. The ability of persuading by words in a court of justice judges, in the senate-house senators, and in a public assembly the hearers, and in every other convention of a political nature. Likewise through this art you will make the physician and the master of gymnastic your slaves. And as to the collector of money, it will appear that he exercises his employment, not for himself, but for you who are able to speak, and persuade the multitude.

453a SOC. Now you appear to me, Gorgias, very nearly to evince what kind of an art rhetoric is in your opinion: and if I understand you, you say that the rhetorical art is an artificer of persuasion, and that the whole of its employment and its very summit terminate in this. Or are you able to say any thing further respecting rhetoric, than that it is able to cause persuasion in the souls of the hearers?

GORG. I have nothing further to say, Socrates; but you appear to me to have sufficiently defined it. For this is its summit.

b   SOC. But hear, Gorgias. For I well know, as I persuade myself, that if ever any one, discoursing with another, wished to know that about which he discoursed, this is my case. And I think that you are likewise affected in the same manner.

GORG. But to what purpose is all this, Socrates?

SOC. I will now tell you. I very clearly perceive that I do not know what the rhetorical persuasion is which you speak of, or with what particulars it is conversant: and though I conjecture what I think you say, and about what you speak, yet I do not the less cease to ask you, what you assert rhetorical persuasion to be, and about what it is

c   employed. Though I, therefore, suspect that for the sake of which it subsists, yet I do not ask on your account, but for the sake of discourse, that it may proceed in such a manner as to render apparent in the highest degree the subject of the present discussion. For consider whether I appear to interrogate you justly: just as I should ask you what kind of a painter is Zeuxis, and you should answer me that he paints animals, - might I not justly inquire of you, what are the animals which he paints, and how he paints them?

GORG. Entirely so.

d   SOC. And would not my inquiry be made on this account, because there are many other painters who paint many other animals?

GORG. It would.

SOC. But if there were no one besides Zeuxis that painted animals, you would have answered properly.

GORG. Undoubtedly.

SOC. This being the case, then, inform me respecting rhetoric, whether it appears to you that the rhetorical art alone produces persuasion, or whether this is effected by other arts? But my meaning is this: Does he who teaches any thing persuade that which he teaches, or not?

GORG. He does persuade, Socrates, and the most of all things.

e   SOC. Again, if we should speak respecting the same arts as we did just now, does not the arithmetical art teach us such things as pertain to number; and does not an arithmetician do the same?

GORG. Entirely so.

SOC. Does he not, therefore, also persuade?

GORG. He does.

SOC. The arithmetical art, therefore, is the artificer of persuasion.

GORG. It appears so.

454a SOC. If, therefore, anyone should ask us what persuasions it produces, and about what, we should reply, that it produces preceptive persuasions about the quantity of the even and the odd. And in like manner we might show, that the other arts which we just now mentioned are effective of persuasions, and what these persuasions are, and about what they are employed. Or might we not?

GORG. We might.

SOC. The rhetorical art, therefore, is not alone effective of persuasion.

GORG. True.

SOC. Since, therefore, it does not alone effect this, but likewise other arts accomplish the same thing, we may justly after this make the inquiry concerning the rhetorical art as we did about the painter; *viz.* what kind of persuasion rhetoric produces, and about what its persuasion is employed. Or does it not appear to you to be just to make such inquiry?

b GORG. It does.

SOC. Answer then, Gorgias, since this appears to you to be the case.

GORG. I say, therefore, Socrates, that rhetoric is the cause of the persuasion which is produced in courts of justice, and in other public associations, as I just now said; and likewise that this persuasion is employed about things just and unjust.

SOC. And I likewise did suspect, Gorgias, that you would give this answer respecting rhetorical persuasion. But do not wonder if a little after this I shall ask you a thing of such a kind as indeed appears to be evident, but which I shall notwithstanding repeat. For, as I before observed, I ask not for your sake, but that the discourse may be brought to a conclusion in an orderly manner, that we may not accustom ourselves by conjecture to snatch from each other what is said. But do you finish your hypothesis in such a manner as is most agreeable to you.

GORG. You appear to me to act rightly, Socrates.

SOC. Come then, let us also consider this. Do you say that to learn is any thing?

GORG. I do.

SOC. Again, do you say that to believe is any thing?

GORG. I do.

d SOC. Whether, therefore, does it appear to you, that to learn and to believe are the same, and likewise that discipline and faith are the same, or that they differ from each other?

GORG. I think, Socrates, that they differ from each other.

Soc. And you think well: but you may know that you do so from hence. For if any one should ask you, Are there such things Gorgias, as false and true belief? you would, I think, say there are.

Gorg. I should.

Soc. But what, is there such a thing as true and false science?

Gorg. There is not.

Soc. It is evident, therefore, that true and false science are not the same.

Gorg. True.

e   Soc. But those that learn, and those that believe, are persuaded.

Gorg. They are.

Soc. Are you willing, therefore, that we should establish two species of persuasion, one of which produces faith without knowledge, but the other science?

Gorg. Entirely so.

Soc. Whether, therefore, does the rhetorical art produce persuasion in courts of justice, and other numerous assemblies, respecting things just and unjust? And is it that persuasion from which faith without knowledge is produced, or that from which knowledge arises?

Gorg. It is evident, Socrates, that it is that from which faith is produced.

455a   Soc. The rhetorical art, therefore, as it seems, is the artificer of the persuasion which produces belief, and not of that which teaches respecting the just and unjust.

Gorg. It is so.

Soc. A rhetorician, therefore, does not teach courts of justice, and other numerous assemblies, respecting things just and unjust, but only procures belief concerning these. For he, doubtless, is not able to teach so great a multitude in a short time things of such great importance.

Gorg. He, doubtless, is not.

Soc. But come, let us see what we should say concerning the rhetorical art. For I, indeed, as yet am not able to understand what I

b   say. When an assembly, then, is held in a city, respecting the choice of physicians, or shipwrights, or any other kind of artists, does the rhetorician then do any thing else than refrain from giving his advice? For it is evident that, in each election, he who is the most consummate artist ought to be chosen. Nor in consultations respecting the building of walls, or the construction of ports or docks, will any other advice be attended to but that of architects. Nor, again, in the election of commanders, or any military order, in times of war, or in deliberations respecting the capture of certain places, will rhetoricians be consulted, but those that are skilled in military affairs. Or how do you say, Gorgias, respecting things of this kind? For since you say that you are a rhetorician, and are able to make other rhetoricians, it is very proper to inquire of you about the things pertaining to your art. And believe that I shall benefit you by acting in this manner. For, perhaps, some one who is now within the house may wish to become your disciple: and I nearly perceive a collected multitude who, perhaps, are ashamed to interrogate you. These, therefore, being interrogated by me, think that you also are asked by them, What would be the consequence, Gorgias, if we should associate with you? About what particulars shall we be able to give advice to the city? Whether about the just alone and the unjust; or respecting those things which Socrates just now mentioned? Endeavour, therefore, to answer them.

GORG. But I will endeavour, Socrates, clearly to unfold to you all the power of the rhetorical art. For you have beautifully led the way. For you doubtless know that these docks and walls of the Athenians, and the structure of the ports, were partly the consequence of the advice of Themistocles, and partly of Pericles, but were not built from the advice of artificers.

SOC. These things are said, Gorgias, respecting Themistocles: but I myself heard Pericles when he gave us his advice respecting the middle wall.

GORG. And when an election is made respecting the particulars of which you speak, you see, Socrates, that rhetoricians are the persons that give advice, and whose opinion respecting these things vanquishes.

SOC. Wondering, therefore, that this is the case, Gorgias, I some time ago asked you, what the power of the rhetorical art is. For, while I consider it in this manner, it appears to me to be something divine with respect to its magnitude.

GORG. If you knew all, Socrates, you would find, as I may say, that it comprehends under itself all powers. But of this I will give you a great example. For I have often, with my brother, and other physicians, visited certain sick persons, who were unwilling either to drink the medicine, or suffer themselves to be cut or burnt by the physician, in consequence of the inability of the physician to persuade them; but these I have persuaded by no other art than the rhetorical. I say further, that if a rhetorician and a physician should in any city verbally contend with each other in a place of disputation, or any other assembly, which ought to be chosen in preference, a rhetorician or a physician, the decision would by no means be given in favour of the physician, but of the rhetorician, if he was willing to be chosen. And if the rhetorician should contend with any other artist, he would persuade his hearers that he ought to be chosen in preference to any other. For there is not any thing about which the rhetorician will not speak more persuasively to the multitude than any other artist. Such, therefore, and so great is the power of this art. Indeed, Socrates, the rhetorical art ought to be used

d   like every other contest. For in other contests it is not proper for any one to strike, pierce, and slay his friends, because he has learned to contend in boxing, in the pancratium, and with arms, so as to be superior both to friends and enemies. Nor, by Jupiter, if some one going to the palæstra, whose body is in a flourishing condition, and becoming a pugilist, should afterwards strike his father and mother, or any other of his kindred or friends, it would not on this account be

e   proper to hate, and expel from cities, the masters of gymnastics, and those who instruct men to fight with arms. For they impart these arts to their pupils, in order that they may use them justly against enemies, and those that injure others, defending themselves, but not offering violence to others. But such a one, as I have just mentioned, acting perversely, does not rightly employ his strength and art. The teachers,

457a therefore, are not base characters, nor is art to be blamed, nor is it to be considered as on this account base: but I think those are to be considered so who do not use these arts properly. The same may be said of the rhetorical art. For a rhetorician is able to speak against all

b   men, and about every thing; so that, in short, he can persuade the multitude respecting whatever he pleases more than any other: but yet physicians ought not to suffer in our opinion, nor other artificers, because this can be done by rhetoricians. But the rhetorical art, as well as that pertaining to contest, is to be used justly. In my opinion, however, if any one becoming a rhetorician acts unjustly through this

c   power and art, it is not proper to hate and expel from cities the teacher of rhetoric; for he imparts the knowledge of it for just purposes, but the other applies it to contrary purposes. It is just, therefore, to hate, banish, and slay him who does not use rhetoric properly, but not him by whom it is taught.

    Soc. I think, Gorgias, that you are skilled in a multitude of arguments, and that you have perceived this in them, that it is not easy

d   for men to dissolve their conference respecting things of which they endeavour to discourse, by mutually defining, learning from others, and teaching themselves: but that, if they contend about any thing, and the one says that the other does not speak with rectitude or clearness, they are indignant, and think it is said through envy of themselves, and through a desire of victory, and not in consequence of exploring the thing proposed in the disputation: and that some, indeed, depart in a shameful manner, after they have reviled others, and spoken and heard such things about themselves as cause those that are present to be indignant, that they have deigned to become auditors of such men as these. But on what account do I assert these things? Because you now appear to me to speak not altogether conformably to what you first said respecting the rhetorical art. I am afraid, therefore, to confute you, lest you should think that I do not speak with an ardent desire that the thing itself may become manifest, but that my discourse is directed to you. If, therefore, you are such a man as I am, I shall willingly interrogate you; but if not, I shall cease my interrogations. But among what kind of men do I rank? Among those who are willingly confuted, if they do not speak the truth, and who willingly confute others when they assert what is false; and who are not less pleased when they are confuted than when they confute. For I consider the former to be as much a greater good than the latter, as for a man to liberate himself from the greatest evil rather than another. For I do not think that any evil happens to men of such a magnitude as false opinion respecting the things which are the subject of our present discourse. If, therefore, you say that you are a man of this kind, let us converse; but if it appears to you that we ought to desist, let us bid farewell to our discussion, and dissolve the discourse.

GORG. But indeed, Socrates, I profess myself to be such a man as you have mentioned. Perhaps, however, it is proper to attend to those that are present. For, some time since, before I came to you, I evinced many things to the persons now present: and now, perhaps, if we discourse, we shall extend our discussion to a great length. Some attention, therefore, ought to be paid to the persons present, lest we should detain any of them, when at the same time they wish to do something else.

CHÆR. Do but attend, Gorgias and Socrates, to the clamour of these men, who wish to hear if you say any thing. As to myself, therefore, I am not so engaged, that, leaving these and the former discourses, I can do any thing better.

CAL. By the Gods, Chærepho, I also have been present at many conferences; but I do not know that I was ever so delighted as with the present disputation: so that you will gratify me, should you be even willing to discourse the whole day.

SOC. But indeed, Callicles, nothing prevents, with respect to myself, if Gorgias is willing.

GORG. After this, Socrates, it would be shameful that I should not be willing, especially as I have announced that any one might ask what he pleased. But if it is agreeable to these men, discourse, and ask any question you please.

e   SOC. Hear then, Gorgias, the particulars which I wondered at in the discourse which you just now made. For, perhaps, what you said is right, and I did not rightly apprehend you. Did you not say that you could make any one a rhetorician, who was willing to be instructed by you?

GORG. I did.

SOC. And, therefore, that you could enable him to speak in a persuasive manner about every thing to the multitude, not by teaching but persuading?

459a   GORG. Entirely so.

SOC. You say, therefore, that a rhetorician is more capable of persuading with respect to what pertains to the health of the body, than a physician.

GORG. I did say that this was the case in a crowd.

SOC. Is not, therefore, that which takes place in a crowd the same as that which takes place among the ignorant? For, doubtless, among those endued with knowledge, the rhetorician will not be more capable of persuading than the physician.

GORG. You speak the truth.

SOC. Will it not, therefore, follow, that if the rhetorician is more capable of persuading than the physician, he will be more capable of persuading than one endued with knowledge?

GORG. Entirely so.

b   SOC. And this, not being a physician?

GORG. Yes.

SOC. But he who is not a physician must, doubtless, be ignorant of those things in which a physician is skilled.

GORG. It is evident.

SOC. He, therefore, who is ignorant will be more capable of persuading among the ignorant than he who is endued with knowledge, since a rhetorician is more capable of persuading than a physician. Does this happen to be the case, or any thing else?

GORG. In this instance this happens to be the case.

SOC. Can the same thing, therefore, be said respecting a rhetorician and the rhetorical art, in all the other arts? I mean, that the rhetorical

c   art has no occasion to know how things themselves are circumstanced, but that it discovers a certain device of persuasion, so as that a rhetorician may appear to the ignorant to know more than those endued with knowledge.

GORG. Is there not great facility in this, Socrates, that a man who has not learned the other arts, but has learned this one, may become in no respect inferior to artificers?

SOC. Whether, from this being the case, a rhetorician is inferior, or not, to others, we will shortly consider, if it contributes any thing to our disputation. But let us now first of all consider this: Whether a rhetorician is affected in the same manner respecting the just and the unjust, the base and the becoming, good and evil, as respecting that which pertains to health, and other things of which there are other arts: I mean, that he does not know what is good, or what is evil, what is becoming, or what is base, what is just, or what is unjust; but is able to devise persuasion respecting them, so as among the ignorant to appear more knowing than one endued with knowledge, at the same time that he is himself ignorant? Or is it necessary that he should know these? and is it requisite that he who is about to learn the rhetorical art should, when he comes to you, previously possess a knowledge of these? But if he does not, shall we say that you, who are a teacher of rhetoric, will not instruct such a one in any of these things (for it is not your province), but that you will cause him to appear knowing in such particulars among the multitude, at the same time that he is ignorant of them, and to seem to be a good man when he is not good? Or, in short, are you not able to teach him the rhetorical art, unless he previously knows the truth respecting these things? Or how do such-like particulars take place, Gorgias? And, by Jupiter, as you just now said, unfold to me what the power is of the rhetorical art.

GORG. But I think, Socrates, that if such a one should happen to be ignorant, he would learn these things from me.

SOC. Granted: for you speak well. And if you make any one a rhetorician, it is necessary that he should know things just and unjust, either before he is under your tuition, or afterwards, in consequence of being instructed by you.

GORG. Entirely so.

SOC. What then? Is he who learns things pertaining to building, tectonic, or not?

GORG. He is.

SOC. And is he, therefore, who learns things pertaining to music, a musician?

GORG. Yes.

SOC. And he who learns things pertaining to medicine, a physician? And so, according to the same reasoning, in other things, he who learns any thing is such as science renders its votaries.

GORG. Entirely so.

SOC. Does it not, therefore, follow from this reasoning, that he who learns just things is just?

GORG. Entirely so.

SOC. But does not he who is just act justly?

GORG. Yes.

c   SOC. Is it not, therefore, necessary that a rhetorician should be just, and that he who is just should be willing to act justly?

GORG. It appears so.

SOC. A just man, therefore, will never be willing to act unjustly.

GORG. It is necessary.

SOC. But, from what has been said, it is necessary that a rhetorician should be just.

GORG. It is.

SOC. A rhetorician, therefore, will never be willing to act unjustly.

GORG. It does not appear that he will.

d   SOC. Do you remember, therefore, that you said a little before, that the preceptors of youth ought not to be called to account, nor expelled from cities, if a pugilist does not use in a becoming manner the pugilistic art, and acts unjustly? And that, in a similar manner, if a rhetorician unjustly uses the rhetoric art, the preceptor is not to be called to account, nor expelled from the city, but he who acts unjustly, and does not properly use the rhetorical art? Were these things said, or not?

GORG. They were said.

e   SOC. But now it appears that this very same rhetorician will never act unjustly. Or does it not?

GORG. It appears so.

SOC. And in the former part of our discourse, Gorgias, it was said that the rhetorical art is conversant with discourses, not those respecting the even and the odd, but those respecting the just and the unjust. Was not this asserted?

GORG. It was.

SOC. I, therefore, in consequence of your asserting these things, thought that the rhetorical art could never be an unjust thing, as it 461a always discourses concerning justice. But, since a little after you said that a rhetorician might use the rhetorical art unjustly, I wondered at the assertion; and thinking that what was said did not accord with itself, I said, that if you should think it a gain to be confuted, as it is my opinion, then it would be worth while to discourse, but if not, we should bid farewell to discussion. Afterwards, however, while we were considering, you seem to have again confessed that it was impossible a rhetorician could use the rhetorical art unjustly, and be willing to do an injury. To determine, therefore, sufficiently, how these things take place, requires, by the dog, Gorgias, no brief discussion.

POL. But what, Socrates? Do you really form such an opinion of the rhetorical art as you now say? Or do you think Gorgias is ashamed that he has not acknowledged to you, that a rhetorician knows things just, beautiful, and good, and that if any one goes to him who is ignorant of these things, he will instruct him in them? From this confession, something contrary will, perhaps take place in the discourse. This, however, is what you love, since you lead interrogations to things of this kind. But what man do you think will deny that he knows things just, and teaches them to others? To bring the discourse, therefore, to things of this kind, is very rustic.

SOC. O most excellent Polus! we designedly procure associates and children, that when, through being advanced in years, we fall into error, you that are younger being present may correct our life both in words and deeds. And now, if I and Gorgias err in any respect in what we have asserted, do you who are present correct us: for it is just so to do. And I wish you would retract any thing that has been granted, if it appears to you that it has not been properly admitted, if you only take care of one thing for me.

POL. What is that?

SOC. That you would avoid in future prolixity of discourse, which at first you attempted to use.

POL. But what, may I not be permitted to speak as much as I please?

SOC. O best of men, you would be used very unworthily, if, having come to Athens, where liberty of speech is permitted more than in any part of Greece, you alone should here be deprived of this liberty. But, on the contrary, consider if you should speak in a prolix manner, and be unwilling to answer what is asked you, should not I be used unworthily, if it is not permitted me to depart, and not hear you? But if you are at all concerned for what has been said, and wish to correct it (as you just now said), then, retracting whatever you think fit, and alternately asking and being asked, confute in the same manner as I and Gorgias. For, indeed, you say that you know the same things as Gorgias. Or do you not?

POL. I do.

SOC. Will not you, therefore, also exhort any one to ask you whatever he pleases, as knowing how to answer him?

POL. Entirely so.

b   Soc. And now you may do whichever of these you please, *viz.* either
ask or answer.

POL. I shall do so. And do you answer me, Socrates. Since Gorgias
appears to you to doubt respecting the rhetorical art, what do you say
he is?

Soc. Do you ask me what his art is?

POL. I do.

Soc. It does not appear to me to be any art, that I may speak the
truth to you.

POL. But what does the rhetorical art appear to you to be?

c   Soc. A thing which you say produces art, in the book which I just
now read.

POL. What do you call this thing?

Soc. A certain skill.

POL. Does the rhetorical art, therefore, appear to you to be skill?

Soc. To me it does, unless you say otherwise.

POL. But of what is it the skill?

Soc. Of procuring a certain grace and pleasure.

POL. Does not the rhetorical art, therefore, appear to you to be a
beautiful thing, since it is capable of imparting delight to mankind?

d   Soc. But what, O Polus? Have you already heard me saying what the
rhetorical art is, that you after this ask me, if it does not appear to me
to be a beautiful thing?

POL. Have I not heard you say that it is a certain skill?

Soc. Are you willing, therefore, since you honour gratification, to
gratify me in a trifling thing?

POL. I am.

Soc. Ask me then now, whether cooking appears to me to be an art?

POL. I ask you then, what kind of an art is cooking?

Soc. It is no art, Polus.

POL. But tell me what it is.

Soc. I say, then, it is a certain skill.

POL. Inform me what skill.

e   Soc. I say it is the skill of procuring grace and pleasure, Polus.

POL. But is cooking the same as rhetoric?

Soc. By no means, but a part of the same study.

POL. Of what study are you speaking?

Soc. Lest it should be too rustic to speak the truth, I am averse to
speak, on account of Gorgias, lest he should think that I deride his
463a   pursuit. But I do not know whether this is that rhetoric which Gorgias
studies. For just now, it was by no means apparent to us, from the

disputation, what is his opinion. But that which I call rhetoric, is a part of a certain thing which does not rank among things becoming.

GORG. Tell me, Socrates, what this thing is; and do not be in the least ashamed because I am present.

SOC. This thing therefore, Gorgias, appears to me to be a certain study, not of a technical nature, but belonging to a soul which sagaciously conjectures, which is virile, and endued with a natural skill of conversing with men. But I call the summit of it adulation. It likewise appears to me that there are many other parts of this study, and that one of these is cookery; which, indeed, appears to be an art, but, according to my doctrine, is not an art, but skill and exercise. I likewise call rhetoric a part of this study, together with the sophistic artifice, and that which pertains to the allurements of outward form. And these four parts belong to four things. If, therefore, Polus wishes to inquire, let him; for he has not yet heard what part of adulation I assert rhetoric to be: but he does not perceive that I have not yet answered, and asks me if I do not think that rhetoric is beautiful. But I shall not answer him, whether I think rhetoric is beautiful or base, till I have first of all answered what rhetoric is. For it will not be just, Polus, to do otherwise. But if you wish to hear, ask me what part of adulation I assert rhetoric to be.

POL. I ask, then, and do you answer me what part it is.

SOC. Will you, therefore, understand when I have answered? For rhetoric, according to my doctrine, is an image of the politic art.

POL. What then? Do you say that it is something beautiful, or that it is something base?

SOC. I say that it is something base: for I call things evil base; since it is requisite I should answer you, as now knowing what I assert.

GORG. By Jupiter, Socrates, but neither do I myself understand what you say.

SOC. It is likely, Gorgias: for I do not yet speak any thing clearly. But Polus here is a young man and acute.

GORG. However, dismiss him; and inform me how it is you say that rhetoric is an image of the politic part.

SOC. But I will endeavour to tell you what rhetoric appears to me to be. And if it is not what I assert it to be, let Polus here confute me. Do you not call body something, and likewise soul?

GORG. Undoubtedly.

SOC. Do you not, therefore, think that there is a certain good habit of each of these?

GORG. I do.

SOC. But what? Is this only a habit which appears to be good, but which is not in reality? As, for instance, many appear to have their bodies in a good condition, when at the same time no one, except a physician, and some one skilled in gymnastics, can easily perceive that these are not in a good condition.

GORG. You speak the truth.

SOC. I say that a thing of this kind takes place both in body and soul, which causes both body and soul to appear to be in a good condition, when at the same time they are not so.

b   GORG. These things take place.

SOC. But come, I will explain to you in a still clearer manner, if I am able, what I say. As there are two things, I say there are two arts: and one of them, which pertains to the soul, I call politic; but the other, belonging to the body, I cannot in like manner distinguish by one appellation. But since the culture of the body is one, I call the two parts c   gymnastic and medicine. But in the politic art I establish legislation, as corresponding to gymnastic, and justice as reciprocating with medicine. These communicate with each other, as subsisting about the same thing, *viz.* medicine communicates with gymnastic, and justice with legislation; but at the same time they differ in a certain respect from each other. But since these are four, and always procure remedies, looking to that which is best, one part of them curing the body, and the other the soul, the adulatory power perceiving this, I do not say knowing, but conjecturing it, in consequence of giving to itself a fourfold distribution, d   and entering under each of the parts, it feigns itself to be that under which it enters. And it is not, indeed, in the least concerned for that which is best; but always, through that which is pleasant, hunts after folly, and deceives; so as to appear to be of great worth. Cookery, therefore, enters under medicine, and feigns that it knows the best aliment for the body. So that if a cook and a physician should contend with each other among boys, or among men as stupid as boys, which of them possessed the knowledge of good and bad aliment, the physician e   would die through hunger. This, therefore, I call adulation; and I say, 465a O Polus, that a thing of this kind is base. For this I say to you, that it looks to the pleasant without regarding that which is best. But I do not call it an art, but skill, because it has no reason by which it can show what the nature is of the things which it introduces; so that it is unable to tell the cause of each. But I do not call that an art which is an irrational thing. If you are doubtful respecting these things, I am willing to give you a reason for them. The adulation, therefore, pertaining to b   cookery is, as I have said, placed under medicine; but after the same manner, the artifice respecting the allurements of outward form is placed under gymnastic: and this artifice is productive of evil, is deceitful, ignoble, and illiberal, deceiving by figures and colours, by smoothness and the senses; so as to cause those who attract to themselves foreign beauty, to neglect that which is properly their own, and which is procured through gymnastic. That I may not, therefore, be prolix, I

c wish to tell you, after the manner of geometricians (for perhaps you can now follow me), that the artifice respecting the allurements of outward form is to gymnastic as cookery to medicine. Or rather thus, that the artifice respecting the allurements of outward form is to gymnastic as the sophistic to the legislative power: and that cookery is to medicine as rhetoric to justice. As I have said, they are thus distinguished by nature: but as sophists and rhetoricians are proximate to each other, they are mingled in the same, and about the same things, and do not possess anything by which they can benefit themselves, or be benefited by other

d men. For, if the soul did not preside over the body, but the body over itself, and cookery and medicine were not considered and judged of by the soul, but the body itself judged, estimating things by its own gratifications; then, friend Polus, that doctrine of Anaxagoras would abundantly take place, (for you are skilled in these things,) *viz.* that all things would be mingled together in the same, things salubrious, medicinal, and pertaining to cookery, subsisting undistinguished from each other. You have heard, therefore, what I assert rhetoric to be, *viz.* that it is a thing reciprocating with cookery in the soul, as that in the

e body. Perhaps, therefore, I have acted absurdly, since, not permitting you to use prolixity of discourse, I myself have made a long oration. I deserve however to be pardoned: for, if I had spoken with brevity, you would not have understood me, nor have been able to make any use of

466a my answer to you, but would have required an exposition. If, therefore, when you answer, I in my turn am not able to reply, do you also extend your discourse: but, if I can, suffer me to reply; for it is just. And now, if you can make any use of this answer, do so.

POL. What then do you say? Does rhetoric appear to you to be adulation?

SOC. I said, indeed, that it was a part of adulation. But cannot you remember, Polus, though so young? What then will you do when you become advanced in years?

POL. Do, therefore, good rhetoricians appear to you to be considered in the same place as vile flatterers in cities?

b SOC. Do you propose this as a question, or as the beginning of a certain discourse?

POL. As a question.

SOC. They do not then appear to me to be considered in the same place as vile flatterers in cities.

POL. How not *to be considered?* Are they not able to accomplish the greatest things in cities?

SOC. They are not, if you allow that to be endued with power is good to him who is endued with it.

POL. But this indeed I do say.

SOC. Rhetoricians, therefore, appear to me to possess the least power of all men in cities.

c   POL. But what, do they not like tyrants slay, take away possessions, and banish from cities whomever they please?

SOC. By the dog, Polus, I am doubtful with respect to each of the things said by you, whether you assert these things yourself, and exhibit your own opinion, or interrogate me.

POL. But I interrogate you.

SOC. Be it so, my friend. But do you not ask me two things at once?

POL. How two things?

d   SOC. Did you not just now say, that rhetoricians like tyrants slew whomever they pleased, deprived them of their possessions, and expelled them from cities?

POL. I did.

SOC. I therefore say to you that these are two questions, and I shall give you an answer to both. For I say, Polus, that rhetoricians and tyrants possess the least power of all men, in cities, as I just now said.

e   For, in short, they accomplish nothing which they wish to accomplish; and yet they do that which appears to them to be best.

POL. Is not this, therefore, to possess the power of accomplishing great things?

SOC. It is not, as says Polus.

POL. Do I say not? On the contrary, I say it is.

SOC. By Jupiter, not you. For you said that to be able to do great things is good to him who possesses this power.

POL. And I now say so.

SOC. Do you think, therefore, it is a good thing, if any one void of intellect does that which appears to him to be best? And do you call this the ability of accomplishing something great?

POL. Not I.

SOC. Will you not, therefore, evince that rhetoricians are endued with intellect, and, confuting me, show that rhetoric is an art, and not adulation? For, if you do not confute me, rhetoricians and tyrants, who

467a do in cities whatever they please, will not by so doing obtain any thing good. But power is, as you say, good; though, for a man to do without intellect whatever he pleases, you also have acknowledged to be evil. Or have you not?

POL. I have.

SOC. How then can rhetoricians or tyrants be able to accomplish any thing great in cities, unless Polus evinces, against Socrates, that they do whatever they please?

b POL. Is it possible any one can speak so absurdly?

SOC. I do not say that they accomplish what they wish: but confute me if you can.

POL. Did you not just now acknowledge, that they accomplished things which appeared to them to be best?

SOC. And I now acknowledge this.

POL. Do they not, therefore, do that which they wish to do?

SOC. I say they do not.

POL. But do they do that which they think fit?

SOC. I say they do.

POL. You speak importunately and unnaturally.

c SOC. Do not accuse me, most excellent Polus, that I may speak to you in your own way; but, if you are capable of interrogating me any further, evince in what it is I am deceived; but if not, do you yourself answer.

POL. But I am willing to answer, that I may also know what you say.

SOC. Whether, therefore, do men appear to you to wish this, which every individual accomplishes, or that for the sake of which they accomplish this which they accomplish? As for instance, whether do those who take medicines from a physician appear to you to wish this which they do, *viz.* to drink the medicine, and suffer pain; or do they wish to be well, for the sake of which they take the medicine?

POL. They doubtless wish to be well, for the sake of which they drink the medicine.

d SOC. Does not the like happen to navigators, and to those who are engaged in other employments, *viz.* that the object of their wishes is not that which each of them does (for who would wish to sail, to encounter dangers, and to be entangled with a multiplicity of affairs?); but, in my opinion, the object of their wishes is that for the sake of which they venture on the sea, *viz.* to acquire riches. For they sail for the sake of wealth.

POL. Entirely so.

SOC. In like manner, with respect to all other things, he who does any thing for the sake of some particular thing does not wish this which he does, but that for the sake of which he does it.

e   POL. It is so.

SOC. Is there any thing, therefore, in the whole of existence, which is neither good nor evil? Or is there a medium between these, which is neither good nor evil?

POL. It is abundantly necessary, Socrates, that there should.

SOC. Do you not, therefore, say that wisdom and health, riches, and other things of this kind, are good, but the contraries of these evil?

POL. I do.

468a   SOC. But do you say that things which are neither good nor evil are of such a kind, that they sometimes partake of good, sometimes evil, and sometimes of neither; such as to sit, to run, to walk, and to sail; and again, such things as stones, wood, and other things of this kind? Are not these the things which you speak of? Or do you denominate other certain things neither good nor evil?

POL. I do not: but these are the things.

SOC. Whether, therefore, do men, when they act, accomplish these things which subsist as media, for the sake of things good, or things good for the sake of these media?

POL. Doubtless, the media for the sake of things good.

b   SOC. Pursuing good, therefore, we both walk when we walk, thinking it is better so to do; and, on the contrary, we stand when we stand, for the sake of the same good. Or is it not so?

POL. It is.

SOC. Do we not, therefore, when we slay, or banish, or deprive any one of his possessions, think that it is better for us to do these things than not to do them?

POL. Entirely so.

SOC. Those, therefore, that do all these things do them for the sake of good.

POL. I say so.

SOC. Do we not, therefore, grant that we do not wish those things which we do for the sake of something, but that for the sake of which c   we do these things?

POL. We especially admit this.

SOC. We do not, therefore, simply wish to slay, exterminate, or deprive any one of his possessions; but if these things are useful we wish to do them, but by no means if they are noxious. For we desire good things, as you say, but not such as are neither good nor evil, nor yet such as are evil. Do I, therefore, Polus, appear to you to speak the truth, or not? Why do you not answer?

POL. You speak the truth.

d   SOC. Does it not follow, therefore, if we assent to these things, that if any one slays, exterminates from a city, or takes away the possessions of another, whether he is a tyrant or a rhetorician, thinking that it is better for him so to do, though it is worse, - does it not follow, that in so doing he acts in a manner which to him seems fit?

POL. Yes.

SOC. Does he, therefore, do the things which he wishes to do, if these things are evil? Why do you not answer?

POL. But he does not appear to me to do the things which he wishes.

e   SOC. Will, therefore, a man of this kind be able to accomplish great things in a city, if to be able to accomplish great things is something good, according to your concession?

POL. He will not.

SOC. I therefore said true, when I said that a man might do that in a city which seemed fit to him, and yet not be able to accomplish great things, nor do that which he wished to do.

POL. As if, Socrates, you would not admit, that it is possible for you to do what you please in a city, rather than that it is not possible, and that you would not be envious when you saw any one slaying or taking away the possessions of another, or confining in bonds whomever he pleased.

SOC. Do you speak justly or unjustly?

469a   POL. Whichever of these he may do, is he not in each of these actions to be envied?

SOC. Good words, I beseech you, Polus.

POL. But why?

SOC. Because it is not proper, either to envy those that are not to be envied, or the unhappy; but they ought to be pitied.

POL. But what? Does this appear to you to be the case respecting the men of whom I speak?

SOC. Undoubtedly.

POL. Does he, therefore, who justly slays any one whom he thinks fit, appear to you to be miserable, and an object of pity?

SOC. He does not to me, indeed; nor to me does he appear to be an object of envy.

POL. Did you not just now say that he was miserable?

b   SOC. I said, my friend, that he was miserable who slew another unjustly, and that, besides this, he was to be pitied; but that he who slew another justly was not to be envied.

POL. He indeed who dies unjustly is an object of pity, and is miserable.

SOC. But less so, Polus, than he who slays another; and less than he who dies justly.

POL. How so, Socrates?

SOC. Thus: because to do an injury is the greatest of evils.

POL. But is this really the greatest of evils? Is it not a greater evil to suffer an injury?

SOC. By no means.

POL. Would you, therefore, rather be injured than do an injury?

c   SOC. I should rather indeed have no concern with either of these. But if it were necessary that I should either do an injury, or be injured, I should choose the latter in preference to the former.

POL. Would you not, therefore, receive the power of a tyrant?

SOC. I would not, if you say that to tyrannize is what I say it is.

POL. But I say it is that which I just now mentioned, *viz.* for a man to do in a city whatever he pleases; to slay or banish any one, and do every thing according to his own opinion.

d   SOC. O blessed man, attend to what I say. If in a crowded forum, taking a dagger under my arm, I should say to you, O Polus, a certain wonderful power and tyranny has just now fallen to my lot: for, if it appears to me that any one of these men whom you see ought immediately to die, he dies; and if it appears to me that any one of them ought to lose his head, he is immediately beheaded; or if his garment should be torn asunder, it is immediately torn. Such mighty power do

e   I possess in this city. If, therefore, in consequence of your not believing me, I should show you the dagger, perhaps on seeing it you would say: After this manner, Socrates, all men are capable of effecting great things, since thus armed you may burn any house that you please, all the docks and three-banked galleys of the Athenians, together with all their ships as well public as private. But this is not to possess the ability of effecting great things, - I mean, for a man to do whatever he pleases. Or does it appear to you that it is?

POL. It does not after this manner.

470a   SOC. Can you, therefore, tell me why you blame a power of this kind?

POL. I can.

SOC. Tell me then.

POL. Because it is necessary that he who acts in this manner should be punished.

SOC. But is not being punished an evil?

POL. Entirely so.

SOC. Will it not, therefore, O wonderful man, again appear to you, on the contrary, that to be able to accomplish great things is good, if acting in a useful manner follows him who does what he pleases? And this, as it appears, is to be able to effect great things: but the contrary to this is evil, and the ability of accomplishing small things. But let us also consider this. Have we not acknowledged that it is sometimes better to do the things which we just now spoke of, *viz.* to slay, exterminate, and deprive men of their possessions, and sometimes not?

POL. Entirely so.

SOC. This then, as it appears, is acknowledged both by you and me.

POL. It is.

SOC. When, then, do you say it is better to do these things? Inform me what boundary you establish.

POL. Answer yourself, Socrates, to this question.

SOC. I say therefore, Polus, if it is more agreeable to you to hear it from me, that it is better when any one does these things justly, but worse when he does them unjustly.

POL. It is difficult to confute you, Socrates; but may not even a boy convince you that you do not speak the truth?

SOC. I shall give the boy, therefore, great thanks, and I shall be equally thankful to you if you can confute me, and liberate me from my nugacity. But be not weary in benefiting a man who is your friend, but confute me.

POL. But, Socrates, there is no occasion to confute you by ancient examples. For those things which happened lately, and even but yesterday, are sufficient to convince you, and to show you that many unjust men are happy.

SOC. Who are these?

POL. Do you not see Archelaus here, the son of Perdiccas, governing Macedonia?

SOC. If I do not, at least I hear so.

POL. Does he, therefore, appear to you to be happy or miserable?

SOC. I do not know, Polus; for I have not yet associated with the man.

POL. What then? if you associated with him, would you know this? And would you not otherwise immediately know that he is happy?

SOC. I should not, by Jupiter.

POL. It is evident then, Socrates, you would say, that neither do you know that the great king[†] is happy.

SOC. And I should say the truth. For I do not know how he is affected with respect to discipline and justice.

POL. But what? Is all felicity placed in this?

SOC. As I say, it is, Polus. For I say that a worthy and good man and woman are happy; but such as are unjust and base, miserable.

471a POL. This Archelaus, therefore, according to your doctrine, is miserable.

SOC. If, my friend, he is unjust.

POL. But how is it possible he should not be unjust, to whom nothing of the government which he now possesses belongs? as he was born of a woman who was the slave of Alcetas, the brother of Perdiccas; who according to justice was himself the slave of Alcetas; and, if he had been willing to act justly, would have served Alcetas in the capacity of a slave; and thus, according to your doctrine, would have been happy. But now he is become miserable in a wonderful degree, since he has committed

b the greatest injuries. For, in the first place, sending for his master and uncle, as if he would restore the government which Perdiccas had taken from him, and entertaining and intoxicating both him, and his son Alexander, who was his uncle, and nearly his equal in age, he afterwards hurled them into a cart, and, causing them to be taken away by night, destroyed both of them by cutting their throats. And though he has committed these injuries, he is ignorant that he is become most miserable, and does not repent of his conduct. But, a little after, he was

c unwilling to nurture and restore the government to his brother, the legitimate son of Perdiccas, a boy of about seven years of age, and who had a just right to the government, though by so doing he would have been happy: but hurling the youth into a well, and there suffocating him, he told his mother Cleopatra that he fell into the well and died, through pursuing a goose. This man, therefore, as having acted the most unjustly of all in Macedonia, is the most miserable, and not the most

d blessed, of all the Macedonians. And, perhaps every one of the Athenians, beginning from you, would rather be any other of the Macedonians than Archelaus.

SOC. In the beginning of our conference, Polus, I praised you, because you appeared to me to be well instructed in rhetoric, but to have neglected the art of discourse. And now, without relating any thing further, this is a discourse by which even a boy might convince me.

---

† *i.e.* the king of Persia.

And, as you think, I am now convicted, by this narration, of having said that he who acts unjustly is not happy. But whence, good man? For, indeed, I did not grant you any of the particulars which you mention.

POL. You are not willing to grant them. For the thing appears to you as I say.

SOC. O blessed man! For you endeavour to confute me in a rhetorical manner, like those who in courts of justice are thought to confute. For there some appear to confute others, when they procure many respectable witnesses of what they say; but he who opposes them procures one certain witness, or none at all. But this mode of confutation is of no worth with respect to truth. For sometimes false witness may be given against a man, by many men of great reputation. And now, respecting what you say, nearly all Athenians and strangers accord with you in these things. And if you were willing to procure witnesses against me to prove that I do not speak the truth, Nicias, the son of Niceratus, and his brothers with him, would testify for you, by whom there are tripods placed in an orderly succession in the temple of Bacchus. Or, if you wish it, Aristocrates the son of Scellius, of whom there is that beautiful offering in the Pythian temple. Or again, if you wish it, the whole family of Pericles, or any other family, that you may think proper to choose out of this city, will testify for you. But I, who am but one, do not assent to you. For you do not force me, but, procuring many false witnesses against me, you endeavour to eject me from my possessions and the truth. But I, unless I can procure you being one, to testify the truth of what I say, shall think that I have not accomplished any thing worthy to be mentioned respecting the things which are the subject of our discourse. Nor shall I think that you have accomplished any thing, unless I being one, alone testify for you, and all those others are dismissed by you. This, therefore, is a certain mode of confutation, as you and many others think: but there is also another mode, which I on the contrary adopt. Comparing, therefore, these with each other, we will consider whether they differ in any respect from each other. For the subjects of our controversy are not altogether trifling; but they are nearly something the knowledge of which is most beautiful, but not to know it most base. For the summit of these things is to know, or to be ignorant, who is happy, and who is not. As, for instance, in the first place, respecting that which is the subject of our present discourse, you think that a man can be blessed who acts unjustly and is unjust; since you are of opinion that Archelaus is, indeed, unjust, but happy. For, unless you say to the contrary, we must consider you as thinking in this manner.

POL. Entirely so.

SOC. But I say that this is impossible. And this one thing is the subject of our controversy. Be it so then. But will he who acts unjustly be happy if he is justly punished?

POL. In the smallest degree; since he would thus be most miserable.

e   SOC. If, therefore, he who acts unjustly happens not to be punished, according to your opinion he is happy.

POL. So I say.

SOC. But, according to my opinion, Polus, he who acts unjustly, and is unjust, is miserable. And indeed, he is more miserable if, when acting unjustly, he is not justly punished; but he is less miserable if he is punished, and justice is inflicted on him both by Gods and men.

473a   POL. You endeavour, Socrates, to assert wonderful things.

SOC. And I shall endeavour, my associate, to make you say the same things as I do: for I consider you as a friend. Now, therefore, the things about which we differ are these. But do you also consider. I have already said in some former part of our discourse, that to do an injury is worse than to be injured.

POL. Entirely so.

SOC. But you say it is worse to be injured.

POL. I do.

SOC. And I say that those who do an injury are miserable; and I am confuted by you.

POL. You are so, by Jupiter.

b   SOC. As you think, Polus.

POL. And perhaps I think the truth.

SOC. But, on the contrary, you think that those who act unjustly are happy, if they escape punishment.

POL. Entirely so.

SOC. But I say that they are most miserable: and that those who suffer punishment for acting unjustly are less miserable. Are you willing to confute this also?

POL. But it is more difficult to confute this than that, Socrates.

SOC. By no means, Polus: but it is impossible that this should be the case. For that which is true can never be confuted.

POL. How do you say? If a man acting unjustly is detected in attempting to acquire absolute power by stratagem, and in consequence c   of being detected is put on the rack, is castrated, and has his eyes burnt; and after he has suffered many other mighty and all-various torments, sees his wife and children suffering the same, and at last is either crucified, or incrusted with pitch; will he be more happy, than if, having escaped punishment, he obtains despotic power, and passes through life ruling in the city, doing whatever he pleases, and envied, and accounted happy, both by his citizens and strangers? Do you say that these things cannot be confuted?

SOC. You terrify, and do not confute us, generous Polus: but just now you testified for us. At the same time remind me of a small particular, whether you say that such a one endeavours to gain absolute power unjustly?

POL. I do.

SOC. By no means, therefore, will either of these be more happy, neither he who has unjustly obtained the tyranny, nor he who is punished. For, of two that are miserable, one cannot be more happy than the other; but he is the more miserable of the two who escapes punishment, and obtains the tyranny. Why do you laugh at this, Polus? Is this another species of confutation, to laugh when any one asserts something, and not confute him?

POL. Do you not think you are confuted, Socrates, when you say such things as no man would say? For only ask any man if he would.

SOC. O Polus, I am not among the number of politicians. And last year, when I happened to be elected to the office of a senator, in consequence of my tribe possessing the chief authority, and it was requisite I should give sentence, I excited laughter, through not knowing how to give sentence. Do not, therefore, now order me to pass sentence on those who are present. But if you have no better modes of confutation than these(as I just now said), assign to me a part of the discourse, and make trial of that mode of confutation which I think ought to be adopted. For I know how to procure one witness of what I say, *viz.* him with whom I discourse; but I bid farewell to the multitude. And I know how to decide with one person, but I do not discourse with the multitude. See, therefore, whether you are willing to give me my part in the argument, by answering to the interrogations. For I think that you and I, and other men, are of opinion, that to do an injury is worse than to be injured; and not to suffer, than to suffer punishment.

POL. But I, on the contrary, think that neither myself nor any other man is of this opinion. For would you rather be injured than do an injury?

SOC. Yes; and so would you, and all other men.

POL. Very far from it: for neither I, nor you, nor any other, would say so.

SOC. Will you not, therefore, answer?

POL. By all means. For I am anxious to know what you will say.

SOC. Tell me then, that you may know, as if I asked you from the beginning: whether does it appear to you, Polus, worse to do an injury, or to be injured?

POL. It appears to me it is worse to be injured.

SOC. But which is the more base? To do, or to suffer, an injury? Answer me.

POL. To do an injury.

SOC. Is it not, therefore, worse, since it is more base?

POL. By no means.

d   SOC. I understand. You do not think, as it seems, that the beautiful and the good are the same, and likewise the evil and the base.

POL. I do not.

SOC. But what will you say to this? Do you not call all beautiful things, such as bodies, colours, figures, sounds, and pursuits, beautiful, without looking at anything else? As, for instance, in the first place, with respect to beautiful bodies, do you not say that they are beautiful, either according to their usefulness to that particular thing to which each is useful, or according to a certain pleasure, if the view of them gratifies the beholders? Have you any thing else besides this to say, respecting the beauty of body?

POL. I have not.

e   SOC. Do you not, therefore, denominate other things beautiful after this manner, such as figures and colours, either through a certain pleasure, or utility, or through both?

POL. I do.

SOC. And do you not in a similar manner denominate sounds, and every thing pertaining to music?

POL. Yes.

SOC. And further still, things which pertain to laws and pursuits are certainly not beautiful, unless they are either advantageous or pleasant, or both.

POL. It does not appear to me that they are.

475a   SOC. And does not the beauty of disciplines subsist in a similar manner?

POL. Entirely so. And now, Socrates, you define beautifully, since you define the beautiful by pleasure and good.

SOC. Must not, therefore, the base be defined by the contrary, viz. by pain and evil?

POL. Necessarily so.

SOC. When, therefore, of two beautiful things, one is more beautiful than the other, or when some other thing transcends in beauty either one or both of these, it must be more beautiful either through pleasure, or advantage, or both.

POL. Entirely so.

b SOC. And when, of two things, one is more base, it must be more base through transcending either in pain or evil. Or is not this necessary?

POL. Entirely so.

c SOC. But, in the first place, let us consider whether to do an injury surpasses in pain the being injured; and whether those suffer greater pain that injure, than those that are injured.

POL. This is by no means the case, Socrates.

SOC. The former, therefore, does not transcend the latter in pain.

POL. Certainly not.

SOC. Will it not therefore follow, that, if it does not transcend in pain, it will no longer transcend in both?

POL. It does not appear that this will be the case.

SOC. Must it not, therefore, transcend in the other?

POL. Yes.

SOC. In evil?

POL. So it appears.

SOC. Will it not therefore follow, that to do an injury, since it transcends in evil, is worse than to be injured?

POL. Evidently so.

d SOC. If, therefore, something else were not admitted by the multitude of mankind, and by you formerly, it would follow that to do an injury is worse than to be injured.

POL. It would.

SOC. Now, however, it appears to be worse.

POL. So it seems.

SOC. Would you, therefore, admit that which is worse and more base, rather than that which is less so? Do not hesitate to answer, Polus (for you will not be injured by so doing), but answer generously, committing yourself to discourse as to a physician; and either admit or reject what I ask.

e POL. But I should not, Socrates, prefer that which is worse and more base to that which is less so.

SOC. But would any other man?

POL. It does not appear to me that he would, according to this reasoning.

SOC. I therefore spoke the truth when I asserted, that neither I, nor you, nor any other man, would rather do an injury than be injured; for it would be worse to do so.

POL. So it appears.

SOC. Do you not therefore see, Polus, that, when argument is compared with argument, they do not in any respect accord? But all others assent to you, except myself. However, you, who are only one, are sufficient for my purpose, both in assenting and testifying; and I, while I ask your opinion alone, bid farewell to others. And thus is this affair circumstanced with respect to us. But, after this, let us consider that which was the occasion of doubt to us in the second place, *viz.* whether it is the greatest of evils for him to be punished who acts unjustly, as you think, or whether it is not a greater evil not to be punished in this case, as I, on the contrary, think. But let us consider this affair in the following manner: Do you call it the same thing for him to suffer punishment who has acted unjustly, and to be justly punished?

POL. I do.

SOC. Can you therefore deny that all just things are beautiful, so far as they are just? Consider the affair, and answer me.

POL. It appears to me that they are, Socrates.

SOC. Consider also this: When a man performs any thing, must there not necessarily be something which is passive to him as an agent?

POL. It appears so to me.

SOC. Does it, therefore, suffer that which the agent performs, and of the same kind as that which he performs? But my meaning is this: If any one strikes, is it not necessary that something should be struck?

POL. It is necessary.

SOC. And if he who strikes, strikes vehemently and swiftly, must not that which is struck be in the same manner struck?

POL. Yes.

SOC. A passion, therefore, of such a kind is in that which is struck, as the striker produces.

POL. Entirely so.

SOC. If, therefore, any one burns, is it not necessary that something should be burned?

POL. Undoubtedly.

SOC. And if he burns vehemently, or so as to cause pain, must not that which is burned be burned in such a manner as he who burns burns?

POL. Entirely so.

SOC. And will not the same reasoning take place if any one cuts? For something will be cut.

POL. Yes.

d SOC. And if the cut is great or deep, or attended with pain, that which is cut will be cut with such a cleft as the cutter cuts.

POL. It appears so.

SOC. In short, see if you grant what I just now said respecting all things, *viz.* that such as the agent produces, such does the patient suffer.

POL. I do grant it.

SOC. These things, therefore, being admitted, whether is the being punished, to suffer, or to do something?

POL. Necessarily, Socrates, it is to suffer something.

SOC. Must it not, therefore, be by some agent?

POL. Undoubtedly. And by him who punishes.

SOC. But does not he who rightly punishes, punish justly?

e POL. Yes.

SOC. Does he act justly, or not, by so doing?

POL. Justly.

SOC. Must not, therefore, he who is punished, in consequence of being punished, suffer justly?

POL. It appears so.

SOC. But is it not acknowledged that just things are beautiful?

POL. Entirely so.

SOC. Of these, therefore, the one does, and the other (who is punished) suffers, that which is beautiful.

POL. Yes.

477a SOC. But if things are beautiful, are they not also good? For they are either pleasant or useful.

POL. It is necessary they should.

SOC. He therefore who is punished suffers that which is good.

POL. It appears so.

SOC. He is benefited, therefore.

POL. Yes.

SOC. Does it not, therefore, follow (as I understand advantage), that the soul becomes better if it is punished justly?

POL. It is probable.

SOC. The soul, therefore, of him who is punished is liberated from vice.

POL. It is.

b   SOC. And hence it is liberated from the greatest evil. But consider thus: In the acquisition of wealth, do you perceive any other human evil than poverty?

POL. No other.

SOC. But what, in the constitution of the body? do you call imbecility, disease, deformity, and things of this kind, evils, or not?

POL. I do.

SOC. Do you think, therefore, that in the soul also there is a certain depravity?

POL. Undoubtedly.

SOC. Do you not then call this injustice, ignorance, timidity, and the like?

POL. Entirely so.

c   SOC. Since, therefore, riches, body, and soul, are three things, will you not say that there are three depravities, want, disease, injustice?

POL. Yes.

SOC. Which, therefore, of these depravities is the most base? Is it not injustice, and, in short, the depravity of the soul?

POL. Very much so.

SOC. But, if it is the most base, is it not also the worst?

POL. How do you say, Socrates?

SOC. Thus. That which is most base is always so either by procuring the greatest pain, or injury, or both, from what has been previously acknowledged by us.

POL. Especially so.

SOC. But is it not at present acknowledged by us, that injustice, and the whole depravity of the soul, are most base?

d   POL. It is.

SOC. Are not these, therefore, either most troublesome, and most base, through transcending in molestation, or from the injury which attends them, or from both?

POL. It is necessary.

SOC. Is therefore to be unjust, intemperate, timid, and unlearned, the cause of greater pain than to be poor and diseased?

POL. It does not appear to me, Socrates, to be so, from what has been said.

SOC. Another depravity of the soul, therefore, transcending in a certain mighty detriment, and wonderful evil, is the most base of all things; since, according to your assertion, it is not so, from transcending in pain.

e   POL. So it appears.

SOC. But, indeed, that which transcends in the greatest of all detriments must be the greatest evil of all things.

POL. It must.

SOC. Injustice, therefore, intemperance, and the other depravity of the soul, are each of them the greatest evil of all things.

POL. So it appears.

SOC. What is the art, therefore, which liberates from poverty? Is it not that which procures money?

POL. Yes.

SOC. But what is that art which liberates from disease? Is it not the medicinal?

478a POL. Necessarily so.

SOC. And what is that which liberates from depravity and injustice? If you cannot answer this question with the like facility, consider thus: Whither, and to whom, do we conduct those that are diseased in body?

POL. To physicians, Socrates.

SOC. But whither do we conduct those who act unjustly, and live intemperately?

POL. You say, to the judges.

SOC. And is it not, therefore, that they may be punished?

POL. I say so.

SOC. Do not then those that punish rightly punish by employing a certain justice?

POL. It is evident they do.

b SOC. The art, therefore, which procures money liberates from poverty; the medicinal art, from disease; and punishment, from intemperance and injustice.

POL. So it appears.

SOC. Which, therefore, of these do you consider as the most beautiful?

POL. Of what things are you speaking?

SOC. Of the art of procuring money, the medicinal art, and punishment.

POL. Punishment, Socrates, excels by far.

SOC. Does it not, therefore, again produce either abundant pleasure, or advantage, or both, since it is the most beautiful?

POL. Yes.

SOC. Is it, therefore, pleasant to be cured by a physician? and do those who are cured rejoice?

POL. It does not appear to me that they do.

SOC. But it is beneficial to be cured. Is it not?

c POL. Yes.

SOC. For it liberates from a great evil: so that it is advantageous to endure pain, and be well.

POL. Undoubtedly.

SOC. Will the man, therefore, who is cured by a physician be thus most happy with respect to his body, or ought this to be said of him who has never been diseased?

POL. Evidently of him who has never been diseased.

SOC. For, as it seems, a liberation from disease would not be felicity; but, on the contrary, this is to be asserted of the non-possession of it from the first.

POL. It is so.

d　SOC. But what? Which of two men is the more miserable, he who is diseased in body, or he who is diseased in soul? He who is cured by a physician, and liberated from disease, or he who is not cured, and is diseased?

POL. He who is not cured, as it appears to me.

SOC. Will it not, therefore, follow, that to suffer punishment will be a liberation from the greatest of evils, depravity?

POL. It will.

SOC. For punishment produces a sound mind, makes men more just, and becomes the medicine of depravity.

POL. It does.

SOC. He, therefore, is most happy who possesses no vice in his soul, since this appears to be the greatest of evils.

e　POL. It is evident.

SOC. But he doubtless ranks in the second degree of felicity, who is liberated from vice.

POL. It is likely.

SOC. But this is the man who is admonished, reproved and suffers punishment.

POL. He is.

SOC. He, therefore, lives in the worst manner who possesses injustice, and is not liberated from it.

POL. It appears so.

SOC. Is not, therefore, such a one, a man who, having committed the greatest injuries, and employing the greatest injustice, causes it to come
479a　to pass, that he is neither admonished, nor restrained in his conduct, nor punished; just as you said was the case with Archelaus, and other tyrants, rhetoricians, and powerful noblemen?

POL. It seems so.

SOC. For the conduct of these, O best of men, is nearly just as if some one afflicted with the greatest diseases should prevent the physicians from inflicting on him the punishment of his bodily maladies, fearing as if he were a child to be burned and cut, because these operations are attended with pain. Or does it not appear so to you?

POL. It does.

SOC. And this through being ignorant, as it seems, of the nature of health and the virtue of body. For, from what has been now acknowledged by us, those who escape punishment, Polus, appear to do something of this kind; *viz.* they look to the pain attending punishment, but are blind to its utility; and are ignorant how much more miserable it is to dwell with a soul not healthy, but corrupt, unjust and impious, than to have the body diseased. Hence they do every thing that they may escape punishment, but are not liberated from the greatest evil; and procure for themselves riches and friends, and the ability of speaking in the most persuasive manner. But if we have assented to the truth, Polus, do you perceive what consequences follow from our discourse? Or are you willing that we should collect them?

POL. I am, if agreeable to you.

SOC. Does it, therefore, happen that injustice and to act unjustly are the greatest evil?

POL. It appears so.

SOC. And it likewise appears that to suffer punishment is a liberation from this evil.

POL. It does appear.

SOC. But not to suffer punishment is a continuance of the evil.

POL. Yes.

SOC. To act unjustly, therefore, ranks in the second degree of evils, as to magnitude; but, when acting unjustly, not to suffer punishment is naturally the greatest and the first of all evils.

POL. It is likely.

SOC. Are we not, therefore, my friend, dubious about this thing? you considering Archelaus as happy, who commits the greatest injustice, and suffers no punishment; but I on the contrary thinking, that whether it is Archelaus, or any other man whatever, who when acting unjustly is not punished, it is proper that such a one should surpass in misery other men; and that always he who does an injury should be more wretched than he who is injured, and he who escapes than he who suffers punishment. Are not these the things which were said by me?

POL. Yes.

SOC. Is it not, therefore, shown that these assertions are true?

POL. It appears so.

480a   SOC. Be it so. If these things then are true, Polus, what is the great utility of rhetoric? For from what has been now assented to by us, every one ought especially to guard himself from acting unjustly, as that through which he will possess a sufficiency of evil. Is it not so?

POL. Entirely so.

SOC. But if any man acts unjustly himself, or some one committed to his care, he ought willingly to betake himself thither, where with the
b   utmost celerity he may be punished by a judge, just as if he was hastening to a physician; lest, the disease of injustice become inveterate, it should render the soul insincere and incurable. Or how must we say, Polus, if the things before acknowledged by us remain? Is it not necessary that these things should after this manner accord with those, but not in any other way?

POL. For what else can we say, Socrates?

SOC. For the purpose, therefore, of apologizing, either for our own injustice, or that of our parents, or associates, or children, or country,
c   rhetoric affords us, Polus, no utility. Unless, on the contrary, any one apprehends that he ought especially to accuse himself, and afterwards his domestic associates, and any other of his friends, whom he may find acting unjustly; and that conduct of this kind ought not to be concealed, but should be led forth into light, that he by whom it is committed may be punished, and restored to health. Likewise, that he should compel both himself and others to lay aside fear, and with his eyes shut, and in a virile manner, deliver himself up, as to a physician, to be cut and burnt, purusing the good and the beautiful, without paying any regard
d   to pain: delivering himself to be beaten, if he has acted in such a manner as to deserve this chastisement; and in like manner to bonds, to fines, to exile, and even to death; being the first accuser of himself, and all his familiars, without sparing either himself or them, but employing rhetoric for this very purpose; that, the crimes becoming manifest, they may be liberated from the greatest of evils, injustice. Shall we speak in this manner, Polus, or not?

e   POL. These things appear to me, Socrates, to be absurd; but from what has been before said, they will, perhaps, be assented to by you.

SOC. Must not, therefore, either those objections be solved, or these things necessarily follow?

POL. This, indeed, must be the case.

SOC. But again. let us transfer the affair to the contrary side, if it is requisite that any one should act basely, whether he is an enemy, or some other person, only admitting that he is not injured by an enemy;

for this is to be guarded against. If, then, an enemy injures another, we
should endeavour by all possible means, both by actions and words, that
he may not be punished, nor brought before a judge: but, if he is
brought before him, we should devise some method by which he may
escape, and not suffer punishment. And if this enemy has by force
taken away a great quantity of gold, he should not restore it, but,
possessing, spend it on himself and his associates in an unjust and
impious manner. Likewise, if he acts in such a manner as to deserve
death, we should be careful that he does not die at any time, but, that
being a depraved character, he may be immortal; but, as this is not
possible, that he may live being such for an extended period of time.
Rhetoric, Polus, appears to me to be useful for purposes of this kind;
since to him who has no intention to act unjustly, its utility, if it has
any, is not, in my opinion, great: for it certainly has not at all appeared
in the former part of our discourse.

CAL. Inform me, Chærepho, does Socrates assert these things
seriously, or in jest?

CHÆR. He appears to me, Callicles, to jest in a transcendent degree:
but there is nothing like asking him.

CAL. There is not, by the Gods! and I desire to do it. Tell me,
Socrates, whether we must say that you are in earnest or in jest? For,
if you are in earnest, and these things which you say are true, is not our
human life subverted, and are not all our actions, as it seems, contrary
to what they ought to be?

SOC. If there were not a certain passion which, remaining the same,
is different in different men, but some one of us should suffer a certain
passion different from others, it would not be easy for such a one to
exhibit his own passion to another. I speak in this manner from
considering, that I and you now happen to suffer the same thing; for,
being two, we each of us love two things: I, indeed, Alcibiades the son
of Clinias, and Philosophy; and you likewise two, the Athenian people,
and Demus the son of Pyrilampes. I continually, therefore, perceive
you, though you are skilful, unable to contradict the objects of your
love, however they may oppose you, and in whatever manner they may
assert a thing to take place; but you are changed by them upwards and
downwards. For, in the convention, if, when you say any thing, the
Athenian people says it is not so, - changing your opinion, you speak
conformably to theirs: and you are affected in the same manner towards
the beautiful son of Pyrilampes; for you cannot oppose the wishes and
discourses of the objects of your love. So that, if any one, in
consequence of what you say being the effect of compulsion through

these, should wonder at its absurdity, perhaps you would say to him, if
482a you wished to speak the truth, that unless some one causes the objects
of your love to desist from such assertions, neither can you desist from
them. Think, therefore, that it is proper to hear other things of this
kind from me; and do not wonder that I speak in this manner; but cause
Philosophy, the object of my love, to desist from such assertions. For
she says, my friend, what you now hear from me; and she is much less
insane than the other object of my love. For Clinius, here, says
different things at different times; but the assertions of Philosophy are
b always the same. But she says things which will now cause you to
wonder: you have, however, been present at her discourses. Either,
therefore, confute her for what I just now said, and evince, that to act
unjustly, and when acting unjustly not to suffer punishment, is not the
extremity of all evils: or, if you suffer this to remain unconfuted, then,
by the dog, one of the deities of the Egyptians, Callicles will not accord
with you, O Callicles, but will dissent from you through the whole of
c life: though I think, O best of men, that it is better for my lyre to be
unharmonized and dissonant, and the choir of which I might be the
leader (for many men do not assent to but oppose what I say), than that
I, being one, should be dissonant and contradict myself.

CAL. You appear, Socrates, to employ a juvenile audacity in your
discourses, as being in reality a popular orator: and now you assert these
things in a popular manner, suffering that same passion of Polus, which
he accused Gorgias of suffering from you. For he said that Gorgias,
when asked by you, whether if any one ignorant of things just, and
d willing to learn rhetoric, should come to him, he would teach him, was
ashamed, and said that he would teach him; and this because men are
accustomed to be indignant if any one denies a thing of this kind.
Through this concession, Gorgias was compelled to contradict himself.
But you were delighted with this very circumstance; for which he then
very properly, as it appeared to me, derided you. And now he again
e suffers the very same thing. But I, indeed, do not praise Polus for
granting you, that to do an injury is more base than to be injured. For,
from this concession, he being impeded by you in his discourse, had not
any thing further to say, being ashamed to mention what he thought.
For you in reality, Socrates, lead to these troublesome and popular
assertions, while you profess to be in search of truth; assertions which
are not naturally, but only legally beautiful. For these for the most part
are contrary to each other, *viz.* nature and law. If any one, therefore,
483a is ashamed, and dares not say what he thinks, he is compelled to
contradict himself. But you, perceiving this subtle artifice, act

fraudulently in discourses. For, if any one asserts that things which are according to nature are according to law, you privately ask him, if things which belong to nature belong to law; as in the present disputation respecting doing an injury and being injured, when Polus spoke of that which is more base according to nature, you pursued that which is more base according to law. For, by nature, every thing is more base which is worse, as to be injured; but, by law, it is worse to

b do an injury. For to be injured is not the passion of a man, but of some slave, to whom to die is better than to live; and who, being injured and disgraced, is incapable of defending either himself or any other person committed to his care. But I think that those who establish laws are imbecil men, and the multitude. Hence they establish laws with a view

c to themselves and their own advantage, and make some things laudable, and others blamable, with the same intention. They likewise terrify such men as are more robust, and who are able to possess more than others, by asserting that to surpass others in possessions is base and unjust; and that to endeavour to possess more than others is to act unjustly. For, in my opinion, these men are satisfied with possessing an equal portion, in consequence of being of a more abject nature. Hence, to endeavour to possess more than the multitude is, according to law, unjust and base; and they call this committing an injury. But I think

d nature herself evinces, that the better should possess more than the worse, and the more powerful than the more imbecil. But she manifests in many places, both in other animals, and in whole cities and families of men, that the just should be established in such a manner, as that the more excellent may rule over, and possess more than, the less excellent. For, with what kind of justice did Xerxes war upon Greece? or his

e father on the Scythians? or ten thousand other things of this kind which might be adduced? But I think that they do these things according to the nature of the just, and indeed, by Jupiter, according to the law of nature; not, perhaps, according to that law which we establish, while we fashion the best and most robust of our fellow-citizens, receiving them from their childhood like lions, and enslaving them by incantations and fascination; at the same time asserting that the equal ought to be preserved, and that this is beautiful and just. But, in my opinion, if

484a there should be any man found with sufficient strength of mind, - such a one, shaking off these things, and breaking them in pieces, abandoning and trampling upon your writings, magical allurements, incantations, and laws contrary to nature, will, by rebelling, from being a slave, appear to be our master; and in this case, that which is just according to nature will shine forth. It appears to me that Pindar also evinces the b truth of what I assert, in the verses in which he says, that "Law is the king of all mortals and immortals; and that he does that which is most just violently, and with a most lofty hand. And this, he adds, I infer from the deeds of Hercules, who drove away the oxen of Geryon unbought."† He nearly speaks in this manner; for I do not perfectly remember the verses. He says then, that Hercules drove away the oxen

c of Geryon, without having either purchased them, or received them as a gift; as if this was naturally just, that oxen, and all other possessions, when the property of the worse and inferior, should yield to the better and more excellent. Such then is the truth of the case: but you will know that it is so, if, dismissing philosophy, you betake yourself to greater things. For philosophy, Socrates, is an elegant thing, if any one moderately meddles with it in his youth; but, if he is conversant with it more than is becoming, it corrupts the man. For, if he is naturally of

d a good disposition, and philosophizes at an advanced period of life, he must necessarily become unskilled in all things in which he ought to be skilled, who designs to be a worthy, good, and illustrious man. For these men are unskilled in the laws of the city, and in those arguments which he ought to use, who is conversant with the compacts of men, both in public and private. They are likewise entirely unskilled in human pleasures and desires, and, in short, in the manners of men. When, therefore, they engage in any private or political undertaking, they become ridiculous. Just as, in my opinion, politicians are

e ridiculous when they meddle with your disputations and arguments. For that saying of Euripides here takes place: "Every one shines in this, and to this hastens; consuming the greater part of the day, in order that

485a he may become better than himself."‡ But that in which a man is inferior he avoids and slanders; and praises that in which he excels through his benevolence towards himself, thinking that after this manner he praises himself. But I think it is most right to partake of both these. Of philosophy, indeed, it is beautiful to participate, so far as pertains to discipline, nor is it base for any one to philosophize while he is a youth: but it is a ridiculous thing, Socrates, for a man still to philosophize when he is advanced in years. And I own myself similarly

b affected towards those who philosophize, as to those who stammer and sport. For when I see a boy who it yet becomes to discourse, thus

---

† These words are cited from some one of the lost writings of Pindar.

‡ These verses are taken from the *Antiope* of Euripides, and are edited by Barnes among the fragments of that tragedy.

stammering and engaged in play, I rejoice, and his conduct appears to me
c   to be elegant and liberal, and such as is proper to the age of a boy. But
when I hear a little boy discoursing with perspicuity, it appears to me
to be an unpleasant circumstance, offends my ears, and is, in my
opinion, an illiberal thing. And when any one hears a man stammering,
or sees him engaged in play, he appears to be ridiculous, unmanly, and
deserving chastisement. I therefore am affected in the same manner
towards those who philosophize. For, when I see philosophy in a
young man, I am delighted, and it appears to me becoming, and I
consider the young man as liberal; but when I find a youth not
philosophizing, such a one appears to me illiberal, and who will never
think himself worthy of any beautiful or generous thing. But when I
d   behold a man advanced in years, yet philosophizing, and not liberated
from philosophy, such a one, Socrates, appears to me to require
chastisement. For to this man, as I just now said, it happens that he
becomes effeminate, though born with the best disposition in
consequence of his avoiding the middle of the city, and the forum, in
which, as the poet says, men become greatly illustrious; and that,
concealing himself from the public view, he passes the remainder of his
life with three or four lads, muttering in a corner; but he never
e   utters any thing liberal, great and sufficient. But I, Socrates, am affected
in an equitable and friendly manner towards you. For it seems that the
same thing now happens to me which happened to Zethus towards
Amphion in Euripides, whom I have already mentioned; since it occurs
to me to say to you what he said to his brother: that you neglect,
486a   Socrates, what you ought to attend to, and destroy the generous nature
of your soul, by adorning it with a certain juvenile form; and that in
consultations pertaining to justice you do not speak with rectitude, nor
apprehend what is probable and persuasive, nor consult for others in a
strenuous manner. Though, friend Socrates, (do not be angry with me,
for I speak to you with benevolence,) does it not appear to you
shameful, that any one should be affected in such a manner as I think
you are, and others who always make great advances in philosophy? For
now, if some one arresting you, or any other, should lead you to prison,
asserting that you had acted unjustly, when you had not, you know you
b   would not be able in any respect to benefit yourself; but, being seized
with a giddiness, you would yawn, and not have any thing to say: and
that ascending to a court of justice, and meeting with an accuser
perfectly vile and base, you would die, if he wished to punish you with
death. And indeed, Socrates, how can that art possess any wisdom,
which, when possessed by a man of a naturally good disposition, renders

him worse, and neither able to assist himself, nor preserve either himself
or any other from the greatest dangers, but causes him to be plundered
c   by enemies of all his possessions, and live in the city devoid of honour?
Indeed (if I may speak in a more rustic manner), it may be allowable to
slap the face of such a man with impunity. But, good man, be persuaded
by me, and desist from confuting. Cultivate an elegant knowledge of
things, and employ yourself in studies which will cause you to appear
wise, leaving to *others* these graceful subtilties, whether it is proper to
call them deliriums, or mere trifles,

Which leave *you* nothing but an empty house:

and emulating, not those men who are able to confute such trifling
d   things as these, but those with whom there are possessions, renown, and
many other goods.

SOC. If, Callicles, I should happen to have a golden soul, do you not
think I should gladly find one of those stones by which they try gold,
particularly if it was one of the best sort; to which if I should introduce
my soul, and it should acknowledge to me my soul was well cultivated,
should I not then well know that I was sufficiently good, and that it was
not necessary any further trial should be made of me?

e   CAL. Why do you ask this, Socrates?

SOC. I will now tell you. I think that I, in meeting with you, met
with a gain of this kind.

CAL. Why so?

SOC. I know that you agree with me in those opinions which my soul
entertains of certain particulars, and that you acknowledge them to be
487a   true. For I perceive that he who intends sufficiently to explore, whether
the soul lives uprightly or not, ought to possess three things, all which
you possess, *viz.* science, benevolence, and freedom of speech. For I
meet with many who are not able to make trial of me, through not
being wise as you are; but others are wise, indeed, but are unwilling to
speak the truth to me, because they are not concerned about me as you
are. But these two guests, Gorgias and Polus, are wise, indeed, and my
friends, but are deficient in freedom of speech, and are more bashful
b   than is becoming. For how should it be otherwise? since they are so
very bashful that each dares to contradict himself, before many men, and
this too about things of the greatest consequence. But you possess all
these requisites, which others have not. And you are both well
instructed, as many of the Athenians affirm, and are benevolent to me.
c   I will tell you what argument I use. I know that your four, Callicles,

mutually partake of wisdom, *viz.* you, and Tisander the Aphidnan,[†] Andron the son of Androtion, and Nausicydes the Cholargean. I likewise once heard you deliberating how far wisdom is to be exercised: and I know that this opinion prevailed among you, that we should not strenuously endeavour to philosophize with accuracy; but you admonished each other to be cautious, lest, through being more wise than is proper, you should be corrupted without perceiving it. Since, therefore, I hear you giving me the very same advice as you gave your most intimate associates, it is to me a sufficient argument, that you are truly benevolent to me. And besides this, that you can use freedom of speech, and not be ashamed, both you yourself say, and the oration, which you a little before made, testifies. But the case is this: If, in the things which are now discussed by us, you in any particular consent with me, this may be considered as sufficiently explored by you and me, and as no longer requiring any further examination. For you would never have assented to such a thing, either through a defect of wisdom, or too much bashfulness. Nor yet, again, would you have assented in order to deceive me: for you are, as you acknowledge, my friend. In reality, therefore, your and my assent has now its true end. But the consideration, Callicles, of those things respecting which you reproved me, is of all things the most beautiful, *viz.* what kind of person a man ought to be, what he ought to study, and how far he should study, both when an elderly and a young man. For, with respect to myself, if there is any thing pertaining to my life in which I do not act rightly, I well know that I do not voluntarily err, but that this happens through my ignorance. Do you, therefore, as you began to admonish me, not desist, but sufficiently show me what this is which I ought to study, and after what manner I may accomplish it. And if you find me now assenting to you, but afterwards not acting conformably to the concessions which I have made, then consider me as perfectly indolent: and in this case, as being a man of no worth, you should afterwards no longer admonish me. But, resuming the subject from the beginning, inform me how you and Pindar say, that it is naturally just for the more excellent to take away by force the possessions of the less excellent, and for the better to rule over the worse, and possess more than the depraved. Do you say that the just is any thing else than this? Or do I rightly remember?

CAL. These things I then said, and I now say.

SOC. But whether do you call the same thing better and more excellent? For I could not then understand what you said: whether you

---

† Aphidnæ and Cholarges were two Attic villages.

call the stronger the more excellent, and say it is requisite that the more imbecil should listen to the more strong; just as you then appeared to show me, that great invaded small cities, according to natural justice, because they are more excellent and strong; (as if the more excellent, the stronger, and the better, were the same;) or is it possible that a thing can be better, and at the same time inferior and more imbecil? and that it can be more excellent, and at the same time more depraved? or is there the same definition of the better and the more excellent? Define this for me clearly, whether the more excellent, the better, and the more strong, are the same, or different?

CAL. But I clearly say to you, that they are the same.

SOC. Are not, therefore, the multitude naturally more excellent than one person; since they establish laws for one, as you just now said?

CAL. Undoubtedly.

SOC. The laws, therefore, of the multitude are the laws of such as are more excellent.

CAL. Entirely so.

SOC. Are they not then the laws of such as are better? For the more excellent are, according to your assertion, far better.

CAL. Yes.

SOC. Are not, therefore, the legal institutions of these naturally beautiful, since those who establish them are more excellent?

CAL. I say so.

SOC. Do not, therefore, the multitude think (as you just now said) that it is just to possess the equal, and that it is more base to do an injury than to be injured? Are these things so, or not? And here take care that you are not caught through bashfulness. Do the multitude, or not, think that to possess the equal, but not more than others, is just? and that it is most base to do an injury than to be injured? Do not deny me an answer to this, Callicles; that, if you assent to me, I may be confirmed in my opinion by you, as being a man whose assent is sufficient to the clear knowledge of a thing.

CAL. The multitude, then, do think in this manner.

SOC. Not by law therefore only is it more base to do an injury than to be injured, or just to have equality of possessions, but likewise according to nature. So that you appear not to have spoken the truth above, nor to have rightly accused me, in saying that law and nature are contrary to each other; which I also perceiving, I have acted fraudulently in my discourse with you, by leading him to law, who says a thing is according to nature; and to nature, who says a thing is according to law.

CAL. This man will not cease to trifle. Tell me, Socrates, are you not ashamed, at your time of life, to hunt after names, and, if any one errs in a word, to make it an unexpected gain? For, did you think I said any thing else, than that the more excellent were better? Did I not some time since tell you, that I considered the better and the more excellent as the same? Or did you suppose I said, that if a crowd of slaves, and all sorts of men of no worth, except perhaps they might possess bodily strength, should be collected together, and establish certain things, that these would be legal institutions?

SOC. Be it so, most wise Callicles: do you mean as you say?

CAL. Entirely so.

SOC. But I, O divine man, some time since conjectured that you said something better than this; and therefore I asked you, desiring clearly to know what you said. For you doubtless do not think that two are better than one, nor that your slaves are better than you because they are stronger. But again from the beginning tell me who those are which you say are better, when at the same time they are not stronger. And, O wonderful man, previously instruct me in a milder manner, that I may not leave you.

CAL. You speak ironically, Socrates.

SOC. By Zethus, Callicles, your familiar, you have now said many things ironically to me. But come, tell me who you say are better.

CAL. Those that are more worthy.

SOC. You see, therefore, that you yourself mention names, but evince nothing. Will you not tell me whether you say that the better and more excellent are more prudent, or that this is the case with certain others?

CAL. But, by Jupiter, I say that these are more prudent, and very much so.

SOC. Often, therefore, according to your assertion, one wise man is better that ten thousand men that are unwise; and it is proper that he should govern, but the others be governed, and that the governor should possess more than the governed. For you appear to me to wish to say this (for I do not hunt after words), if one man is more excellent than ten thousand.

CAL. But these are the things which I say. For I am of opinion that this is the just according to nature, *viz.* that he who is better and more prudent should rule over and possess more than such as are depraved.

SOC. I attend to what you say. But what will you again now say? If we, who are many, were crowded together in the same place as at present, and abundance of food and drink was placed for us in common, but we were men of all-various descriptions, some of us being strong,

and others weak, and one of us should happen to be more skilful
respecting these things, as being a physician, but at the same time should
be (as is likely) stronger than some, and weaker than others, - would not
this man, since he excels us in prudence, be better and more excellent
with respect to these things?

CAL. Entirely so.

c   SOC. Ought he, therefore, to have more of this food than us, because
he is better? or is it proper that in governing he should distribute all
things; but that, in consuming and using them for his own body, he
should not possess more than others, unless with detriment to himself?
But that he should possess more than some, and less than others. But
if he is the most imbecil of all, then he who is best should possess the
least of all. Is it not so, O good man?

d   CAL. You speak of meat and drink, and physicians, and trifles; but I
do not speak of these.

SOC. Whether, therefore, do you say that a more prudent is a better
man? Do you say so, or not?

CAL. I do.

SOC. And do you not say that he who is better than others ought not
to possess more than others?

CAL. He ought not to possess more of meat and drink.

SOC. I understand you. But perhaps he ought of clothes: and it will
be proper that he who is most skilled in weaving should have the largest
garment, and should walk about invested with garments more numerous
and more beautiful than those of others.

CAL. What kind of garments do you mean?

e   SOC. But with respect to shoes, indeed, it is requisite that he who is
more prudent than others, and is the best of men, should have more of
them than others. And a shoemaker perhaps ought to walk with the
largest shoes on his feet, and to have them in the greatest abundance.

CAL. About what kind of shoes do you talk in this trifling manner?

SOC. But if you will not assert such things as these, perhaps you will
the following: for instance, perhaps it will be requisite that a
husbandman who in cultivating the land is a prudent, worthy and good
man, should possess more seeds than others, and sow them more
abundantly in his own ground.

CAL. How you always say the same things, Socrates?

SOC. Not only the same things, Callicles, but likewise respecting the
same things.

491a CAL. Sincerely, by the Gods, you are always speaking about shoemakers, fullers, cooks, and physicians, as if these were the subject of our discourse.

SOC. Will not you, therefore, tell me, what the things are of which he who is better and more prudent than others, by possessing more than others, possesses justly? Or will you neither endure me suggesting, nor speak yourself?

CAL. But I said some time since what these particulars are. And in the first place, I do not call those that are better than others shoemakers, b or cooks, but those who are skilled in the affairs of a city, so as to know after what manner, it will be well inhabited, and who are not only prudent but likewise brave, able to accomplish what they conceive to be best, and are not wearied through effeminacy of soul.

SOC. You see, most excellent Callicles, that you and I do not reason about the same things. For you say that I always assert the same things; and I, on the contrary, that you never say the same things about the same. But at one time you define the better and more excellent to be c the stronger, but at another time those that are more prudent: and now again you come with something else; for certain persons that are braver are said by you to be better and more excellent characters. But, O good man, tell me at length, who you say those better and more excellent characters are, and about what they are conversant.

CAL. But I have said that they are such as are prudent and brave, with respect to the affairs of a city. For it is fit that these should govern d cities: and this is the just, that these should have more than others, the governors than the governed.

SOC. But what of these governors considered with respect to themselves? Ought they to have more, as governors, or as governed?

CAL. How do you say?

SOC. I speak of every one as governing himself. Or is there no occasion for a man to govern himself, but only others?

CAL. What do you mean by a man governing himself?

SOC. Nothing various, but just as the vulgar call a man who is temperate and master of himself, one that governs his pleasures and desires.

e CAL. How pleasant you are! You speak of the foolishly temperate.

SOC. How so? There is not any one who is ignorant that this is not what I say.

CAL. But this is very much what you say, Socrates; since how can the man be happy who is a slave to any one? But this which I now freely tell you, is becoming and just according to nature; *viz.* that he who

intends to live properly, should suffer his desires to be as great as possible, and should not restrain them: but to these, as the greatest
492a possible, it will be sufficient to be subservient, through fortitude and prudence, and always to fill them with such things as they require. This, however, I think, is not possible to the multitude. And hence they blame such persons as I have mentioned, concealing their own impotency through shame; and say that intemperance is base, enslaving, as I said before, men of a better nature than themselves; and in consequence of their inability to satisfy their own pleasures, they praise
b through their slothfulness temperance and justice. For what in reality can be more base and evil than temperance, to men who from the first happen to be either the sons of kings, or who are naturally sufficient to procure for themselves a tyranny, or a dynasty? who, when it is lawful for them to enjoy good things without any impediment, impose a master on themselves, viz. the law, discourse, and the censure of the
c multitude? Or how is it possible that they should not become miserable through the beauty of justice and temperance, while they impart no more to their friends than to their enemies; and this while they possess the supreme authority in their own city? But in reality, Socrates, that which you say you pursue subsists in the following manner: Luxury, intemperance, and liberty, if attended with proper assistance, are virtue and felicity; but these other things are nothing more than ornaments, compacts contrary to nature, the nugacities of men, and of no worth.
d   SOC. In no ignoble manner, Callicles, do you freely attack the discourse: for you now clearly say what others think, indeed, but are unwilling to say. I beg, therefore, that you would not by any means relax, that it may in reality become evident how we ought to live. Tell me then: do you say that desires ought not to be repressed, if any one intends to be that which he ought to be? and that, suffering them to be
e as great as possible, he ought to procure their full satisfaction from some other person? and that this constitutes virtue?
     CAL. I do say these things.
     SOC. Those, therefore, that are not in want of any thing are not rightly said to be happy.
     CAL. For thus stones and dead bodies would be most happy.
     SOC. But, indeed, as you also say, life is a grievous thing. For I
493a should not wonder if Euripides[5] spoke the truth when he says: "Who knows whether to live is not to die, and to die, is not to live?" And we, perhaps, are in reality dead. For I have heard from one of the wise, that we are now dead; and that the body is our sepulchre; but that the part of the soul in which the desires are contained is of such a nature that it

can be persuaded, and hurled upwards and downwards. Hence, a certain elegant man, perhaps a Sicilian, or an Italian, denominated, mythologizing, this part of the soul a tub, by a derivation from the probable and the persuasive; and likewise he called those that are stupid, or deprived of intellect, uninitiated. He further said, that the intemperate and uncovered nature of that part of the soul in which the desires are contained was like a pierced tub, through its insatiable greediness. But this man, Callicles, evinced, directly contrary to you, that of such as were in Hades (which he called *aeides*, or the invisible) those were most miserable who were not initiated, and that their employment consisted in carrying water to a pierced tub in a similarly pierced sieve. The sieve, therefore, as he who spoke with me said, is the soul. But he assimilated the soul of the unwise to a sieve, because, as this is full of holes, so their soul is unable to contain any thing, through incredulity and oblivion. These assertions may, indeed, in a certain respect, be very justly considered as unusual: but they evince what I wish to show you, if I could but persuade you to change your opinion, that, instead of having an insatiable and intemperate life, you would choose one that is moderate, and which is sufficiently and abundantly replete with things perpetually present. But can I in any respect persuade you? And will you, changing your opinion, say that the moderate are more happy than the intemperate? Or shall I not at all persuade you? And will you nothing the more alter your opinion, though I should deliver in fables many things of this kind?

CAL. You have spoken this more truly, Socrates.

SOC. But come, I will exhibit to you another image from the same gymnasium, as that which I just now exhibited to you. For consider, whether you would speak in this manner concerning the life of a temperate and intemperate man, - I mean, as if two men had each of them many tubs; and that the tubs belonging to one of these were entire and full, one of wine, another of honey, a third of milk, and many others of them with a multitude of many other things. Likewise, that each of these various liquors was rare and difficult to be obtained, and was procured with many labours and difficulties. Let us suppose, therefore, that this man whose tubs are thus full neither draws any liquor from them, nor is at all concerned about them, but, with respect to them, is at rest. Let it be possible also to procure liquors for the other, though with difficulty; but let his vessels be pierced, and defective, and let him always be compelled, both night and day, to fill them, or if he does not, to suffer the most extreme pain. Will you therefore say, since such is the life of each, that the life of the

intemperate is more happy than that of the moderate man? Can I in
any respect persuade you by these things, that a moderate is better than
an intemperate life? Or shall I not persuade you?

CAL. You will not persuade me, Socrates. For he whose vessel is full
has not any pleasure whatever: but this is, as I just now said, to live like
a stone, when once filled, neither rejoicing nor grieving: but living
pleasantly consists in an abundant influx.

b   SOC. Is it not therefore necessary, if there is an influx of many things,
that there should also be an abundant efflux? and that there should be
certain large holes as passages for the effluxions?

CAL. Entirely so.

SOC. On the contrary, therefore, you speak of a certain life of the
bird called Charadrius, and not of that of a dead body, or a stone But
tell me, do you speak of any such thing as the being hungry, and, when
hungry, of eating?

CAL. I do.

c   SOC. And of the being thirsty, and, when thirsty, of drinking?

CAL. I say so; and likewise that he who possesses all other desires, and
is able to satisfy them, will live rejoicing in a happy manner.

SOC. Well done, O best of men! Proceed as you have begun, and do
not be hindered by shame. But it is likewise requisite, as it seems, that
neither should I be restrained by shame. And, in the first place, inform
me whether he who is scabby, and itches, who has abundantly the
power of, and passes his life in, scratching, lives happily?

d   CAL. How absurd you are, Socrates, and perfectly vulgar!

SOC. Hence it is, Callicles, that I have astonished Polus and Gorgias,
and made them ashamed. But do not you be astonished, nor ashamed:
for you are brave: but only answer.

CAL. I say, then, that he who scratches himself lives pleasantly.

SOC. Does he not, therefore, live happily, if he lives pleasantly?

CAL. Entirely so.

e   SOC. I again ask you, whether this will be the case if he only itches
in his head, or any other part of the body. See, Callicles, what you
should answer, if any one asks you respecting all the parts of the body
in succession. And all the parts being thus affected, would not, in short,
this life of catamites be dire, base, and miserable? Or will you also dare
to call these happy, if they possess in abundance what they require?

CAL. Are you not ashamed, Socrates, to bring the discourse to things
of this kind?

SOC. Do I bring it hither, o generous man? Or does not he rather,
who says in so shameless a manner, that such as rejoice, however they

may rejoice, are happy; and does not define what pleasures are good, and
what are evil? But further still, now tell me, whether you say that the
pleasant and the good are the same: or that there is something pleasant
which is not good?

CAL. But my assertion would not dissent from itself, if that which I
say is different I should also say is the same.

SOC. You subvert, Callicles, what was said in the first part of our
discourse; nor can you any longer sufficiently investigate things with me,
if you speak contrary to your opinion.

CAL. But you, Socrates, do the same.

SOC. Neither, therefore, do I, nor you, act rightly in so doing. But,
O blessed man, see whether it is not a good thing to rejoice in
perfection. For many base consequences, and a multitude of other
things, appear to attend the particulars which I just now obscurely
signified, if they should take place.

CAL. It is as you think, Socrates.

SOC. But do you in reality, Callicles, strenuously assert these things?

CAL. I do.

SOC. Let us, therefore, enter on the discussion, as if you were serious.

CAL. And extremely so.

SOC. Come, then, since it is agreeable to you, divide as follows: Do
you call science any thing?

CAL. I do.

SOC. And did you not just now say, that there is a certain fortitude,
together with science?

CAL. I did say so.

SOC. You spoke, therefore, of these two, as if fortitude was something
different from science.

CAL. Very much so.

SOC. But what? Are pleasure and science the same, or different?

CAL. They are certainly different, O most wise man.

SOC. Is fortitude also different from pleasure?

CAL. Undoubtedly.

SOC. Come, then, that we may remember these things, *viz.* that
Callicles of Acharne said that the pleasant and the good are the same;
but that science and fortitude are both different from each other and the
good; and that Socrates of Alopecia did not assent to these things. Or
did he assent to them?

CAL. He did not assent.

e SOC. But I think that neither will Callicles when he rightly beholds himself. For tell me, do you not think that those who do well are affected in a manner entirely contrary to those who do ill?

CAL. I do.

SOC. If these, therefore, are contrary to each other, must they not necessarily subsist in the same manner as health and disease? For, certainly, a man is not at the same time well and diseased, nor at the same time liberated from health and disease.

CAL. How do you say?

496a SOC. Taking any part of the body you please, as, for instance, the eyes, consider whether some man is diseased with an ophthalmy.

CAL. Undoubtedly.

SOC. He certainly is not, if at the same time his eyes are well.

CAL. By no means.

SOC. But what? When he is liberated from the ophthalmy, is he then also liberated from the health of his eyes, and lastly, at the same time liberated from both?

CAL. In the least degree.

b SOC. For I think this would be wonderful and absurd. Or would it not?

CAL. Very much so.

SOC. But I think he will alternately receive one, and lose the other.

CAL. So I say.

SOC. And will he not, therefore, in a similar manner receive and lose strength and weakness?

CAL. Yes.

SOC. And swiftness and slowness?

CAL. Entirely so.

SOC. And with respect to things good, and felicity, and the contraries of these things, evil and infelicity, will he alternately receive and be liberated from each of these?

CAL. Entirely so.

c SOC. If, therefore, we should find certain things from which a man is at the same time liberated, and which he at the same time possesses, certainly these would not be good and evil. Do we mutually assent to these things? Well consider, and answer me.

CAL. But I assent in a transcendent degree.

SOC. Let us then recur to what we assented to before. Do you say that to be hungry is pleasant, or troublesome? I say, to be hungry.

CAL. That it is troublesome.

SOC. But it is pleasant for him who is hungry to eat?

CAL. It is.

d SOC. I understand you: but to be hungry you say is troublesome. Do you not?

CAL. I do.

SOC. And is it not likewise troublesome to be thirsty?

CAL. Very much so.

SOC. Whether, therefore, shall I ask you any more questions? Or do you acknowledge that all indigence and desire is troublesome?

CAL. I do acknowledge it: but do not ask me.

SOC. Be it so. But do you say it is any thing else than pleasant, for a man who is thirsty to drink?

CAL. I say it is nothing else.

SOC. In this thing, therefore, which you speak of, to be thirsty is, doubtless, painful. Is it not?

e CAL. It is.

SOC. But is not to drink a repletion of indigence, and a pleasure?

CAL. Yes.

SOC. Do you no therefore say that drinking is attended with joy?

CAL. Very much so.

SOC. And do you not say that to be thirsty is painful?

CAL. Yes.

SOC. Do you, therefore, perceive what follows? I mean, that you say he who is in pain at the same time rejoices, when you say that he who is thirsty drinks. Or does not this happen together, according to the same place and time, whether you consider the soul or the body? For I think it is of no consequence which of these you consider. Are these things so, or not?

CAL. They are.

SOC. But you say it is impossible that he who is happy should at the same time be unhappy.

497a CAL. I do say so.

SOC. But you have granted that he who is disquieted may rejoice.

CAL. It appears so.

SOC. To rejoice, therefore, is not felicity, nor to be disquieted, infelicity? So that the pleasant is something different from the good?

CAL. I know no what these particulars are, Socrates, which you sophistically devise.

SOC. You know, though you pretend not, Callicles. In consequence

b of trifling, too, you proceed to what was before said; that you may know how wise you are to admonish me. Does not each of us at the same time cease from being thirsty, and at the same time receive pleasure from drinking?

CAL. I do not know what you say.

GORG. By no means, Callicles, act in this manner; but answer at least for our sakes, that the discourse may be brought to a conclusion.

CAL. But this is always the way with Socrates, Gorgias, *viz.* he asks and confutes trifling things, and such as are of no worth.

GORG. But of what consequence is this to you? This is altogether no concern of yours: but suffer Socrates to argue in whatever manner he pleases.

c CAL. Ask, then, since Gorgias thinks proper, these trifling and vile questions.

SOC. You are happy, Callicles, because you are initiated in great mysteries prior to the small: but I do not think this is lawful. Answer me, therefore, the question which you left unanswered, *viz.* whether each of us does not at the same time cease to be thirsty, and to receive delight?

CAL. I say so.

SOC. And with respect to hunger, and other desires, do we not at the same time cease to feel them, and to receive delight?

CAL. We do.

d SOC. Do we not, therefore, at one and the same time experience a cessation of pains and pleasures?

CAL. Yes.

SOC. But do we not at the same time experience a cessation of things good and evil, as you did acknowledge: but now do you not acknowledge this?

CAL. I do. But what then?

SOC. That things good are not the same with such as are pleasant, nor things evil with such as procure molestation. For, from these we are liberated at once, but not from those, because they are different. How, therefore, can things pleasant be the same with such as are good, or things troublesome with such as are evil? But, if you please, consider

e the affair thus: for I think that neither in this will you accord with yourself. Consider now. Do you not call the good good, from the presence of good things, in he same manner as you call those beautiful to whom beauty is present?

CAL. I do.

SOC. But what? Do you call those good men who are foolish and timid? For you did not just now; but you said that good men were brave and prudent. Or do you not call the brave and prudent, good?

CAL. Entirely so.

SOC. But what? Have you ever seen a stupid boy rejoicing?

CAL. I have.

SOC. And have you not also seen a stupid man rejoicing?

CAL. I think I have. But to what purpose is this?

498a SOC. To none: but answer.

CAL. I have seen such a one.

SOC. But have you seen a man endued with intellect grieving and rejoicing?

CAL. I say I have.

SOC. But which rejoice and grieve the more; the wise, or the foolish?

CAL. I do not think there is much difference.

SOC. This is sufficient. But have you ever in war seen a coward?

CAL. Undoubtedly I have.

SOC. What then? On the departure of the enemies, which have appeared to you to rejoice the more, cowards or the brave?

b   CAL. Both have appeared to me to rejoice more: or, if not, certainly in nearly the same degree.

SOC. It is of no consequence. Cowards, therefore, also rejoice?

CAL. And very much so.

SOC. And those that are stupid, likewise, as it seems?

CAL. Yes.

SOC. But, when enemies approach, do cowards only grieve? or is this also the case with the brave?

CAL. With both.

SOC. Do they, therefore, similarly grieve?

CAL. Perhaps cowards grieve more.

SOC. But, when the enemies depart, do they rejoice more?

CAL. Perhaps so.

c   SOC. Do not, therefore, as you say, the stupid and the wise, cowards and the brave, similarly grieve and rejoice, but cowards more than the brave?

CAL. I say so.

SOC. But the wise and the brave are good, but cowards and the stupid, bad?

CAL. They are.

SOC. The good and the bad, therefore, rejoice and grieve similarly?

CAL. I say so.

SOC. Are, therefore, the good and the bad similarly good and bad? or are the good yet more good, and the bad more bad?

d   CAL. But, by Jupiter, I do not know what you say.

SOC. Do you not know that you said the good were good, through the presence of things good, and the bad through the presence of things evil? And that pleasures were good things, and pains bad?

CAL. I do know it.

SOC. Are not, therefore, good things, *viz.* pleasures, present with those that rejoice, if they rejoice?

CAL. Undoubtedly.

SOC. Are not, therefore, those that rejoice good, in consequence of things good being present?

CAL. Yes.

SOC. But what? Are not things evil, *viz.* pains, present with those that are disquieted?

CAL. They are present.

e   SOC. But do you not say that the evil are evil, through the presence of things evil? Or do you no longer say so?

CAL. I do.

SOC. Those, therefore, that rejoice, are good; but those that are disquieted are evil?

CAL. Entirely so.

SOC. And those that are more so, more, but those that are less so, less? and those that are similarly so, similarly?

CAL. Yes.

SOC. Do you say, therefore, that the wise and the stupid rejoice and grieve similarly; and that this is likewise the case with cowards and the brave? Or that cowards rejoice and grieve more than the brave?

CAL. I do.

SOC. Collect, therefore, in common with me, what will be the consequence of what we assented to. For, as it is said, it is beautiful to
499a speak and consider twice, and even thrice, beautiful things. Do we say, then, that he who is prudent and brave is good, or not?

CAL. We do.

SOC. But that he is a bad man who is stupid and a coward?

CAL. Entirely so.

SOC. And again, that he who rejoices is good?

CAL. Yes.

SOC. But that he is a bad man who is disquieted?

CAL. Necessarily so.

SOC. Likewise, that to be disquieted, and rejoice, are similarly good and evil; but perhaps more evil than good?

CAL. Yes.

SOC. Does not, therefore, a bad man become similarly bad and good,
b   with the good man, or even more good? Do not these things follow,
and likewise those prior things, if any one says that the same things are
pleasant and good? Are not these consequences necessary, Callicles?

CAL. A while ago, Socrates, I said that I listened and assented to you,
considering that if any one grants you any thing, though in jest, this you
gladly lay hold of after the manner of lads. Just as if you could think
that either I or any other person did not believe that some pleasures are
better, and others worse.

SOC. Hey-day, Callicles, how crafty you are! And you use me as if I
c   were a boy: at one time asserting that these things subsist in this
manner, and at another in a different manner; and thus deceiving me.
Though, from the first, I did not think that I should be voluntarily
deceived by you, because you are my friend. But now I am deceived.
And now, as it seems, it is necessary, according to the ancient proverb,
that I should make good use of the present opportunity, and receive
what you give. But it appears that what you now say is this, that with
respect to pleasures some are good, and others bad. Is it not so?
d   CAL. Yes.

SOC. Are, therefore, the profitable good, but the noxious evil?

CAL. Entirely so.

SOC. And are those profitable which accomplish a certain good, but
those evil, which effect a certain evil?

CAL. I say so.

SOC. Do you, therefore, speak of such things as the following; as, for
instance, in the body, those pleasures of eating and drinking which we
just now spoke of; and do you think that if some of these produce in
the body health or strength, or some other corporeal virtue, they are
good, but that the contraries of these are evil?
e   CAL. Entirely so.

SOC. And in the like manner, with respect to pains, are you of
opinion that some are worthy, and others base?

CAL. Undoubtedly.

SOC. Are not, therefore, such pleasures and pains as are worthy, to be
chosen and embraced?

CAL. Entirely so.

SOC. But such as are base, not.

CAL. It is evident.

SOC. For it appeared, if you remember, that all things are done by us,
viz. by me and Polus, for the sake of things good. Does it, therefore,
appear also to you, that the good is the end of all actions? Likewise,

that all other things ought to be done for its sake; but that it is not to
be obtained for the sake of other things? Will you then make a third
with us in the same opinion?

500a

CAL. I will.

SOC. Both other things, therefore, and such as are pleasant, ought to
be done for the sake of things good, but not things good for the sake of
such as are pleasant?

CAL. Entirely so.

SOC. Is every man, therefore, able to choose such pleasant things as
are good, and likewise such as are evil? Or must this be the province of
a man endued with art?

CAL. Of a man endued with art.

SOC. But let us again recall to our memory what I said to Polus and
Gorgias. For I said (if you remember) that there were certain
preparations, some as far as pleasure, preparing this alone, but ignorant
of the better and the worse; but others that knew the nature both of
good and evil. I likewise placed among the preparations respecting
pleasures, cooking as a skill pertaining to the body, but not an art; but
among the preparations respecting the good I placed the medicinal art.
And, by Jupiter, the guardian of friendship, Callicles, do not think that
you ought to jest with me, nor answer me casually contrary to your
opinion, nor again receive my assertions as if I was in jest. For you see
that our discourse is about this, after what manner it is proper to live,
than which, what can any man endued with the smallest degree of
intellect more seriously discuss? I mean, whether we should adopt that
mode of life to which you exhort me, engaging in such employments of
a man, as speaking among the people, cultivating rhetoric, and managing
political affairs, after the manner which you adopt; or whether we
should betake ourselves to a philosophic life, and consider what it is in
which it differs from the former life. Perhaps, therefore, as I just now
said, it is best to make a division; and after we have divided, and
assented to each other, to consider, if these two species of life have an
existence, in what they differ from each other, and which of them ought
to be pursued. But perhaps you do not yet understand what I say.

CAL. I do not.

SOC. But I will speak to you still more clearly. Since you and I have
agreed that there is something good, and likewise something pleasant,
and that the pleasant is different from the good, but that in each of them
there is a certain exercise and preparation of acquisition, one being the
hunting after the pleasant, and the other of the good; do you, in the first
place, grant me this, or do you not grant it?

b

c

d

e CAL. I do grant it.

SOC. But come, consent with me in what I said to these men, if I then appeared to you to speak the truth. But I said that cooking did not appear to me to be an art, but skill; and that medicine is an art. For I

501a said that medicine considers the nature of that which it cures, and the cause of the things which it does, and that it is able to give an account of each of these: but that cooking very inartificially proceeds to pleasure, to which all its attention is directed, neither considering in any respect the nature nor the cause of pleasure, but being entirely irrational, numbering nothing (as I may say), depending wholly on use and skill, and only preserving the memory of that which usually takes place, by

b which also it may impart pleasures. In the first place, therefore, consider whether these things appear to you to have been sufficiently said, and that there are also certain other studies of this kind respecting the soul, some of which depend on art, and bestow a certain attention to that which is best in the soul; but others neglect this, considering, in the same manner as cooking with respect to the body, only the pleasure of the soul, and in what manner it may be procured; neither considering which is the better or the worse of pleasures, nor attending to any thing

c else than gratification only, whether it is better or worse. For to me, Callicles, these things appear to take place; and I say that a thing of this kind is flattery, both respecting body and soul, and any thing else the pleasure of which is sedulously attended to by any one, without paying any regard to the better and the worse. But whether do you entertain the same opinion respecting these things with us, or do you oppose them?

CAL. I do not, but grant them, that your discourse may come to an end, and that I may gratify Gorgias here.

d SOC. But whether does this take place respecting one soul, but not respecting two and many souls?

CAL. It does not. But it takes place respecting both two and many souls.

SOC. May it not, therefore, be lawful to gratify souls collected together, without paying any attention to what is best?

CAL. I think so.

SOC. Can you, therefore, tell me what those studies are which effect this? Or rather, if you are willing, on my asking, assent to whichever appears to you to be one of these, but to that which does not do not

e assent. And, in the first place, let us consider the piper's art. Does it not appear to you to be a thing of this kind, Callicles; viz, which only pursues our pleasure, but cares for nothing else?

CAL. It does appear to me.

SOC. Are not, therefore, all such studies as these like the harper's art in contests?

CAL. Yes.

SOC. But what? Does not the erudition of choirs, and the dithyrambic poesy, appear to you to be a thing of this kind? Or do you think that Cinesias[†] the son of Meles is in the smallest degree solicitous that he may say any thing by which his hearers may become better? Or is he not rather solicitous about that which may gratify the crowd of spectators?

502a   CAL. It is evident, Socrates, that this latter is the case respecting Cinesias.

SOC. But what with respect to his father Meles? Does he appear to you to play on the harp, looking to that which is best? Or does he not also regard that which is most pleasant? For in singing he pleasingly pains the spectators. But consider, does not the whole of the harper's art, and dithyrambic poesy, appear to you to have been invented for the sake of pleasure?

CAL. To me it does.

b   SOC. But what of the venerable and wonderful poesy of tragedy? What does it strive to accomplish? Do its endeavour and study, as appears to you, alone consist in gratifying spectators? or also in striving not to say any thing which may be pleasing and grateful to them, but at the same time base; and that, if any thing happens to be unpleasant and useful, this it may say and sing, whether it gratifies the spectators or not? According to which of these modes does the poesy of tragedy appear to you to consist?

c   CAL. It is evident, Socrates, that it is more impelled to pleasure, and the gratification of the spectators.

SOC. Did we not, therefore, Callicles, just now say that a thing of this kind is flattery?

CAL. Entirely so.

SOC. Come then, if any one should take from all poesy, melody, rhythm, and measure, would any thing else than discourses remain?

CAL. Necessarily nothing else.

SOC. Are not, therefore, these discourses delivered to a great multitude of people?

d   CAL. I say so.

---

† A bad dithyrambic poet, according to the Scholiast ad *Ranas* Aristoph.

SOC. Poesy, therefore, is a certain popular speech. Or do not poets appear to you to employ rhetoric in the theatres?

CAL. To me they do.

SOC. Now, therefore, we have found a certain rhetoric among a people consisting of boys, and at the same time women and men, slaves and the free-born; and which we do not altogether approve. For we said that it was adulation.

CAL. Entirely so.

SOC. Be it so. But what shall we say that rhetoric is, which subsists among the Athenian people, and the people consisting of free-born men in other cities? Do the rhetoricians appear to you always to speak with a view to that which is best, directing their attention to this, that the citizens through their discourses may become the best of men? Or are they also impelled to the gratification of the citizens? and, neglecting public for the sake of private advantage, do they converse with the people as with boys, alone endeavouring to gratify them, without being in the least concerned whether through this they become better or worse?

CAL. This which you ask is not a simple thing. For some rhetoricians are solicitous in what they say for the good of the citizens: but other are such as you represent them.

SOC. It is sufficient. For, if this also is twofold, one part of it will be adulation, and base harangue; but the other, which causes the souls of citizens to become most excellent, will be beautiful; and will always strive to speak such things as are best, whether they are more pleasant or more unpleasant to the hearers. But you never have seen this kind of rhetoric. Or, if you can say some one of the rhetoricians is a character of this kind, why have you not informed me who he is?

CAL. But, by Jupiter, I cannot instance to you any rhetorician of present day.

SOC. But what? Can you instance any one of the ancient rhetoricians who was the means of rendering the Athenians better, after he began to harangue them, when previous to this they had been worse? For I do not know who such a one is.

CAL. But what? Have you not heard that Themistocles was a good man, and likewise Cimon and Miltiades, Pericles here, who died lately and whose harangues you also have heard?

SOC. Yes; if that virtue, Callicles, which you before spoke of is true, viz. for a man to replenish both his own desires and those of others. But if this is not the case, but, as we were afterwards compelled to confess, those desires are to be embraced, the replenishing of which renders a man better, but not those which render him worse, and if there is a certain art of this, as we also acknowledged, can you say that any one of these was a man of this kind?

CAL. I have not any thing to say.

SOC. But if you seek in a becoming manner you will find. Let us however, sedately considering, see if any one of these was a character of this kind. Is it not true that a good man, who says what he says with a view to the best, does not speak casually, but looking to something? in the same manner as all other artists, each of whom regards his own work, and does not rashly choose what he introduces to his work, but so that the subject of his operation may have a certain form - as, for instance, if you are willing to look to painters, architects, shipwrights, and all other artificers, and to consider how, whichever of them you please, places whatever he places in a certain order, and compels one thing to be adapted to and harmonize with another until the whole thing is constituted with regularity and ornament. And indeed, both other artificers, and those which I just now mentioned, who are employed about the body, *viz.* the masters of gymnastic, and physicians adorn in a certain respect, and orderly dispose the body. Do we grant that this is the case, or not?

CAL. It is the case.

SOC. A house, therefore, when it acquires order and ornament, will be a good house, but a bad one, when it is without order?

CAL. I say so.

SOC. And will not this in like manner be the case with a ship?

CAL. Yes.

SOC. And may we not assert the same things also respecting our bodies?

CAL. Entirely so.

SOC. But what with respect to the soul? Will it be in a good condition, when it acquires disorder, or when it acquires a certain order and ornament?

CAL. It is necessary, from what has been said, to grant that the latter must be the case.

SOC. What then, in the body, is the name of that which subsists from order and ornament? Perhaps you will say it is health and strength.

CAL. I do.

SOC. But what again is the name of that which subsists in the soul from order and ornament? Endeavour to find and mention it, in the same manner as the former name.

CAL. But why do not you say what it is, Socrates?

SOC. If you had rather, I will. But, if I speak well, do you assent to me; if not, confute, and do not indulge me. To me then it appears that the name belonging to the orderly disposition of the body is the healthful, from which health and every other virtue of the body are produced in the body. Is it so, or not?

CAL. It is.

d SOC. But the name belonging to the orderly disposition and ornament of the soul is the legitimate and law; whence also souls become legitimate and adorned with modest manners: but these are justice and temperance. Do you assent, or not?

CAL. Be it so.

SOC. Will not, therefore, that good rhetorician who is endued with art, looking to these things, introduce all his orations and actions to souls? and, if he should bestow a gift, bestow it, and, if he should take any thing away, take it; always directing his attention to this, that justice may be produced in the souls of his fellow-citizens, and that they may be liberated from injustice: likewise that temperance may be produced e in them, and that they may be liberated from intemperance: and, in short, that every virtue may be planted in them, but vice expelled? Do you grant this, or not?

CAL. I do grant it.

SOC. For where is the utility, Callicles, in giving a body diseased, and in a miserable condition, abundance of the most agreeable food and drink, or any thing else, which will not be more profitable to it than the contrary, but even less, according to a just mode of reasoning? Is this the case?

505a CAL. Be it so.

SOC. For I think it is not advantageous for a man to live with a miserable body; for thus it would be necessary to live miserably. Or would it not?

CAL. Yes.

SOC. Do not, therefore, physicians for the most part permit a man in health to satisfy his desires, (as, for instance, when hungry to eat as much as he pleases, or when thirsty to drink,) but never permit, as I may say, a diseased man to be satiated with things which he desires? Do you also grant this?

CAL. I do.

b SOC. But is not the same mode, O most excellent man, to be adopted respecting the soul; *viz.* that as long as it is depraved, in consequence of being stupid, intemperate, unjust and unholy, it ought to be restrained from desires, and not permitted to do any thing else than what will render it better? Do you say so, or not?

CAL. I say so.

SOC. For such a mode of conduct will indeed be better for the soul.

CAL. Entirely so.

SOC. Is not, therefore, to restrain any one from what he desires to punish him?

CAL. Yes.

SOC. To be punished, therefore, is better for the soul than intemperance, contrary to what you just now thought.

c   CAL. I do not know what you say, Socrates: but ask something else.

SOC. This man will not suffer himself to be benefited by suffering this of which we are speaking, *viz.* punishment.

CAL. I am not at all concerned about any thing which you say; and I have answered you these things for the sake of Gorgias.

SOC. Be it so. But what then shall we do? Shall we dissolve the conference in the midst?

CAL. You know best.

d   SOC. But they say it is not lawful to leave even fables in the midst, but that a head should be placed on them, that they may not wander without a head.

CAL. How importunate you are, Socrates! But, if you will persuaded by me, you will bid farewell to this discourse, or carry it on with some other person.

SOC. What other, then, is willing? for we must not leave the discourse unfinished.

CAL. Cannot you yourself finish the discourse, by either speaking to yourself, or answering yourself?

e   SOC. In order, I suppose, that the saying of Epicharmus may be verified, *viz.* I being one am sufficient to accomplish what was before said by two. And it appears most necessary that it should be so. But, if we do this, I think it will be proper that all of us should in a friendly manner strive to understand what is true, and what false, respecting the subjects of our discourse. For it will be a common good to all for this

506a   to become manifest. I will, therefore, run over the affair in the manner in which it appears to me to take place. But, if I shall seem to any of you not to grant myself things which truly are, it will be proper that you should apprehend and confute me. For I do not say what I do say as one endued with knowledge, but I investigate in common with you. So that, if he who contends with me appears to say any thing to the purpose, I will be first to concede to him. But I say these things on condition that you think it fit the discourse should be completed: but if you do not assent to this, let us bid farewell to it, and depart.

GORG. But it does not appear to me, Socrates, proper to depart yet, but that you should pursue the discourse. It likewise seems to me that this is the opinion of the rest of the company. For I also am willing to hear you discussing what remains.

SOC. But indeed, Gorgias, I should willingly have discoursed still longer with Callicles here, till I had recompensed him with the oration of Amphion, instead of that of Zethus. But as you are not willing, Callicles, to finish the discussion in conjunction with me, at least attend to me, and expose me if I shall appear to you to assert any thing in an unbecoming manner. And if you confute me, I shall not be indignant with you, as you are with me, but you will be considered by me as my greatest benefactor.

CAL. Speak then yourself, good man, and finish the discourse.

SOC. Hear me then repeating the discourse from the beginning. Are the pleasant and the good the same? - They are not the same, as I and Callicles have mutually agreed. - But whether is the pleasant to be done for the sake of the good, or the good for the sake of the pleasant? - The pleasant for the sake of the good. - But is the pleasant that, with which when present we are delighted; and the good that, through which when present we are good? - Entirely so. - But we are good, both ourselves, and all other things that are good, when a certain virtue is present. - To me this appears to be necessary, Callicles. - But, indeed, the virtue of each thing, of an instrument, and of the body, and again of the soul, and every animal, does not fortuitously become thus beautiful, but from order, rectitude, and art, which are attributed to each of them. - Are these things, therefore, so? For I say they are. -The virtue of every thing, therefore, is disposed and adorned by order. - So, indeed, say I. - Hence, in each thing, a certain order becoming inherent, which is domestic to each, renders each thing good. - It appears so to me. - The soul, therefore, which has a certain order of its own, is better than the soul which is without order. -It is necessary.- But the soul which has order is orderly. - For how is it possible it should not? - But an orderly soul is temperate. - This is very necessary. - A temperate soul, therefore, is good. I, indeed, am no able to say any thing besides these things, O friend Callicles. But do you, if you have any thing else, teach me.

CAL. Proceed, good man.

SOC. I say, then, if a temperate soul is good, the soul which is affected in a manner contrary to that of the temperate is vicious. But such a soul will be destitute of intellect, and intemperate. - Entirely so. - And, indeed, a temperate man acts in a proper manner, both towards Gods and men. For he would not be temperate if he acted in an improper

b manner. - It is necessary that these things should be so. - And besides this, by acting in a proper manner towards men he will act justly, and by a proper conducts towards the Gods he will act piously. But it is necessary that he should be just and holy, who acts in a just and holy manner. - It must be so. - It is likewise necessary that such a one should be brave. For it is not the province of a temperate man either to pursue or avoid things which ought neither to be pursued nor avoided: but it is proper that he should both avoid and pursue things and men, pleasures and pains, and bravely endure when it is requisite. So that

c there is an abundant necessity, Callicles, that the temperate man, being just, brave, and pious, as we have described him, should be a perfectly good man: likewise, that a good man should do in a becoming and beautiful manner whatever he does; and that he who acts well should be blessed and happy. And lastly, it is necessary that the unworthy man, and who acts ill, should be miserable. But such a man will be one who is directly contrary to the intemperate man, *viz.* he will be the intemperate character which you praised. I, therefore, lay down these things, and assert they are true. But if they are true, temperance must

d be pursued and cultivated, as it appears, by him who wishes to be happy, and he must fly from intemperance with the utmost celerity. He must likewise endeavour to live in such a manner as not to require any degree of punishment: but if he does require it, or any other of his family, - or if this is the case with a private person, or a city, - justice must be administered, and punishment inflicted, if such wish to be happy. This appears to me to be the mark with our eye directed to which it is proper to live: and all concerns, both private and public, should tend to this, *viz.* if any one wishes to be happy, to act in such a

e manner that justice and temperance may be ever present with him; not suffering his desires to be unrestrained, and endeavouring to fill them; which is an infinite evil, and causes a man to live the life of a robber. For a character of this kind can neither be dear to any other man, nor to Divinity. For it is impossible there can be any communion between them: but where there is no communion there can be no friendship.

508a The wise too, Callicles, say that communion, friendship, decorum, temperance, and justice, connectedly comprehend heaven and earth, Gods and men. And on this account, my friend, they call this universe *kosmos,* or *order,* and not *akosmia,* or *disorder,* and *akolasia,* or *intemperance.* However, you appear to me not to attend to these things, and this though you are wise. But you are ignorant that geometric equality is able to accomplish great things, both among Gods and men. On the contrary, you think that every one should strive to possess more than others: for you neglect geometry. - Be it so, then. - However, this our discourse must either be confuted, *viz.* it must be shown that those who are happy are not happy from the possession of justice and temperance, and that those who are miserable are not miserable from the possession of vice; or, if our discourse is true, we must consider what consequences result from it. Indeed, Callicles, all those former things are the consequences concerning which you asked me if I was speaking in earnest. For I said that a man should accuse himself, his son, and his friend, if he acted in any respect unjustly, and that rhetoric was to be used for this purpose. Hence, those things which you thought Polus granted through shame are true, *viz.* that by how much it is more base to do an injury than to be injured, by so much is it the worse; and that he who would be rightly skilled in rhetoric ought to be just, and endued with a scientific knowledge of things just; which, again, Polus said that Gorgias acknowledged through shame.

This then being the case, let us consider what are the things for which you reprove me, and whether they are well said, or not. You assert, then, that I can neither assist myself, nor any of my friends or domestics, nor save myself from the greatest dangers: but that I am obnoxious to the arbitrary will of any one, like men of infamous characters (though this is nothing more than the juvenile ardour of your discourse), so as either to be struck in the face, or deprived of my property, or expelled from the city, or which is the extremity of injustice, to be slain. And to be thus circumstanced, according to your doctrine, is the most shameful of all things. But, according to my doctrine, (which has indeed been often mentioned, yet nothing hinders but that it may again be repeated,) I do not say, Callicles, that to be struck in the face unjustly is a most shameful thing; nor yet for my body, or my purse, to be cut; but that to strike and cut unjustly me and mine, is a thing more shameful and base. And that to defraud, enslave, break open the house, and, in short, to injure in any respect me and mine, is to him who does the injury more base and shameful than to me who am injured. These things, which appeared to us to subsist in this manner in the former part of our discourse, are contained and bound in adamantine reasons, though it is somewhat rustic to make such an assertion. However, unless you can dissolve these reasons, or some one more robust than yourself, it is impossible that he who speaks otherwise than I now speak can speak in a becoming manner. For I always assert the same thing, *viz.* that I know not how these things subsist: and that no one of those whom I have ever met with, as at present, if unable to say otherwise, would be ridiculous. I therefore again determine that these things thus subsist. But, if this is the case, and injustice is the greatest of evils to him that acts unjustly; and it is still a greater evil, if the greatest of evils to him that acts unjustly; and it is still a greater evil, if possible, though this is the greatest, for him who acts unjustly not to be punished; what assistance will that be, which, when a man is unable to afford himself, he is in reality ridiculous? Will it not be that which averts from us the greatest detriment? But there is an abundant necessity that this should be the most shameful assistance, *viz.* for a man to be incapable of assisting either himself, or his friends and domestics; that the next to this should be that which pertains to the second evil; and the third, that which pertains to the third evil; and thus in succession, according to the magnitude of each evil. Thus also does the beauty of being able to give assistance, and the deformity of not being able, subsist. Does the thing take place in this manner, or otherwise, Callicles?

CAL. No otherwise.

SOC. Since, therefore, these things are two, to do an injury, and to be injured, we say that to do an injury is a greater, but to be injured, a less evil. By what means, then, may a man so assist himself as to possess both these advantages - I mean, that which arises from not doing an injury, and that which is the consequence of not being injured? Is it by power, or will? But I say thus: Will a man, if he is unwilling to be injured, not be injured? Or, if he has procured the power of not being injured, will he not be injured?

CAL. It is evident that he will not, if he has procured the power.

SOC. But what with respect to acting unjustly? Whether, if any one is unwilling to do an injury, is this sufficient (for in this case he will not commit an injury), or is it requisite that for this purpose he should procure a certain power and art, as one who will do an injury, unless he has learned and cultivated these? Why do you not answer me this question, Callicles: whether I and Polus appear to you to be rightly compelled to acknowledge this, or not? since we confess that no one is willing to act unjustly, but that those who injure others do it unwillingly.

CAL. Let it be so, Socrates, that your discourse may be brought to conclusion.

SOC. For this purpose, therefore, a certain power and art, as it appears, are to be procured, in order that we may not act unjustly.

CAL. Entirely so.

SOC. What then is the art which will enable a man not to be injured in any respect, or at least in the smallest degree? Consider, if it appears to you in the same manner as to me. For to me it appears thus: that he ought either to govern in a city, or obtain the tyranny, or be the associate of the most powerful person in a polity.

CAL. Do you see, Socrates, how ready I am to praise you, if you say any thing beautifully? This you appear to me to have said in a manner entirely beautiful.

b

SOC. Consider also, whether I appear to you to speak well in what follows: Those seem to me to be friends in the highest degree, concerning whom ancient and wise men say, "similar to similar." Does it not also appear to you?

CAL. To me it does.

SOC. Does it not therefore follow, that when a tyrant who is rustic and unlearned governs, if there is any one in the city much better than him the tyrant will fear such a one, and will never be able to be cordially his friend?

c

CAL. It does follow.

SOC. Nor yet, if any one in the city should be much worse than the tyrant, would he be able to be his friend. For the tyrant would despise him, nor ever pay attention to him as a friend.

CAL. This also is true.

SOC. It remains, therefore, that he alone would be a friend to such a one deserving to be mentioned, who, in consequence of being endued with similar manners, would praise and blame him, be willing to be governed, and to be subject to him that governs. Such a one in this city will be able to accomplish great things, and no one will injure him with impunity. Is it not so?

d

CAL. Yes.

SOC. If, therefore, any young man in this city should thus think with himself, "After what manner may I be able to accomplish great things, and be injured by no one?" this, as it appears, must be the way, *viz.* he must immediately from his youth be accustomed to rejoice and be afflicted with the same things as his master, and render himself in the highest degree similar to him. Is it not so?

CAL. Yes.

e

SOC. Will it not therefore follow, that such a man will not be injured, and, as you say, that he will be able to accomplish great things in a city?

CAL. Entirely so.

SOC. Will he not, therefore, be able to refrain from acting unjustly? Or will this be far from being the case, if, when the governor is unjust, he is similar to him, and is able to accomplish great things with him? But I think that the very contrary will take place, and that such a one will render himself able to act unjustly in the highest degree, without being punished for his unjust conduct. Will he not?

CAL. It appears so.

511a   SOC. Will not, therefore, the greatest evil be present with him, in consequence of being corrupted and depraved in his soul, through the imitation and power of his master?

CAL. I do not know whither you are always turning the discourse, Socrates, upwards and downwards. Or do you not know, that he who is imitated can, if he pleases, slay and take away the possessions of him who is not imitated?

b   SOC. I know it, good Callicles, unless I am deaf; for, a little before, I often heard this from you and Polus, and nearly, indeed, from all in the city. But do you also hear me: for he may indeed slay whom he pleases; but, being a depraved character, he may slay one who is worthy and good.

CAL. And is not this a circumstance grievous to be borne?

SOC. Not to a man endued with intellect, as the discourse evinces. Or do you think that a man should endeavour to live to a most extended period, and should apply himself to those arts which always preserve us from dangers - in the same manner as that rhetoric which preserves in courts of justice, and which you exhorted me to cultivate?

c   CAL. I do indeed, by Jupiter, and I rightly advised you.

SOC. But what, O best of men, does the science of swimming also appear to you to be a venerable thing?

CAL. By Jupiter, it does not.

SOC. And, indeed, this also saves men from death, when they fall into such a danger as requires the aid of this science. But if this science

d   appears to you to be a small thing, I will mention to you a greater than this, viz. that of piloting a ship, which not only saves lives, but also bodies and possessions, from extreme danger, in the same manner as rhetoric. And this, indeed, is moderate and modest, and is not haughty with a grandeur of ornament, as if it accomplished something transcendent. But since it accomplishes the same things as the judicial art, if it saves any from Ægina hither, it demands, I think, two oboli; but if from Egypt, or Pontus, if it demands a great sum, on account of

e   the great benefit it has conferred, through saving those I just now mentioned, viz. ourselves and children, our riches and wives, and conducting them to port, this sum is usually two drachms. And the man who possesses this art, and accomplishes these things, going out of the ship, walks near the sea and the ship, in a moderate garb. For he knows, I think, how to reason with himself, that it is uncertain whom he may assist of those that sail with him, not suffering them to be merged in the sea, and whom he may injure, as knowing that neither the bodies nor souls of those who depart from his ship are in any respect better than they were when they entered into it. He will, therefore, reason with himself, that the case is not as if some one who is afflicted in his body with great and incurable diseases should happen not to be suffocated, because this man is indeed miserable for having escaped death, and has not derived any advantage from him; but that if any one labours under many and incurable diseases in that which is more honourable than body, *viz.* in his soul, such a one ought to live; and that he will benefit him, whether he saves him from the sea, or from a court of justice, or from any thing else. But he knows that it is not better for a depraved man to live; because he must necessarily live badly. On this account, it is not usual for a pilot to be arrogant, though he saves us; nor yet, O wonderful man, for an artificer of machines, who is sometimes able to save a multitude in no respect inferior to that which is saved by the general of an army, or a pilot, or any other person. For sometimes he saves whole cities. Does it appear to you that he is to be compared with a lawyer? Though, if he should wish to speak, Callicles, such things as you are accustomed to speak, extolling his own art, he would overwhelm you with words, asserting and calling on you to consider that you ought to be the artificers of machines, as if other things were of no consequence. For he would have enough to say. But you nevertheless would despise him and his art, and would call him by way of reproach a maker of machines. Nor would you be willing to give your daughter to his son in marriage, nor his daughter to your son. Though, if you consider what the particulars are from which you praise your own profession, with what justice can you despise the artificer of machines, and the rest whom I have just now mentioned? I know that you will say that your profession is better, and consists of better things. But if that which is better is not what I say it is, but this very thing is virtue, *i.e.* for a man to save himself and his possessions, whatever kind of man he may happen to be, then your reprehension of the artificer of machines, of the physician, and of other arts, which are instituted for the sake of preservation, is ridiculous.

But, O blessed man, see whether or not the generous and the good are not something else than to save and be saved. For perhaps to live for a period of time however extended, is not to be wished, nor too much sought after, by him who is truly a man; but leaving these things to the care of Divinity, and believing in prophetic women, that no one can avoid fate, he will afterwards consider by what means he may pass the remainder of his life in the most excellent manner. But will this be effected by rendering himself similar to the polity in which he dwells? If this then were the case, it is necessary that you should become most similar to the Athenian people, if you wish to be dear to them, and to be able to accomplish great things in the city. But consider whether this is advantageous to you and me; and whether we should not, O divine man, be exposed to the same misfortune which they say happened to the Thessalian[†] women in drawing down the moon. But, indeed, our choice of this power in the city should be with the most friendly. If however you think that any man whatever is able to deliver a certain art of this kind, which will cause you to possess mighty power in this city, even when you are dissimilar to the polity, and whether this power is for the better, or the worse, - in this case you appear to me, Callicles, not to consider the affair in a proper light. For it is not requisite that you should be a mimic, but that you should be naturally similar to them, if you design to effect a genuine friendship with the Athenian people, and, by Jupiter, besides this with Demus the son of Pyrilampes. Whoever, therefore, shall render you most similar to these will also render you, since you desire to be skilled in civil affairs, both a politician and a rhetorician. For every one is delighted with orations adapted to his own manners, but is indignant with such as are foreign from them; unless you, O beloved head, say otherwise. Can we say any thing against these things, Callicles?

CAL. I do not know how it is, but you appear to me, Socrates, to speak well. But yet that which happens to many happens also to me: for I am not entirely persuaded by you.

SOC. For the love of Demus, Calilicles, which is resident in your soul, opposes me: but if we should often and in a better manner consider these things, you would perhaps be persuaded. Remember, therefore, that we said there were two preparations, which in every thing were subservient to the cultivation both of body and soul: one associating with these with a view to pleasure; but the other with a view to that

---

† According to Suidas (in Proverbio επι σαυτω την σεληνην καθελκεις) the Thessalian women who drew down the moon are said to have been deprived of their eyes and feet. And hence, says he, the proverb is applied to those who draw down evils on themselves. It is necessary to observe that witches formerly were able to cause the *appearance* of drawing down the moon to take place. See my Notes on Pausanius, vol. I [TTS vol. XXXI, note 97, p. 413].

which is best, not by gratifying, but opposing. Are not these the things which we then defined?

CAL. Entirely so.

SOC. Is not, therefore, the one of these which looks to pleasure ignoble and nothing else than adulation?

e CAL. Let it be so, if you please.

SOC. But the other endeavours that this which we cultivate may be the best possible, whether it is body or soul.

CAL. Entirely so.

SOC. Whether, therefore, we are after this manner to take upon ourselves the care of a city and its citizens, I mean when the citizens are rendered the best possible? For without this, as we have found in what has been previously said, it is of no use to bestow any other benefit; *viz.* unless the dianoëtic part of those who are to receive either abundance

514a of riches, or dominion over certain persons, or any other power, is beautiful and good. Shall we lay this down, as being the case?

CAL. Entirely so, if it is more agreeable to you.

SOC. If, therefore, Callicles, when publicly transacting political affairs, we should publicly exhort each other to the art of building either walls, or docks, or temples, or, in short, buildings of the largest kind, whether would it be necessary that we should consider and examine for ourselves, in the first place, if we knew or were ignorant of the art of building, and

b by whom we were instructed in it? Would this be requisite, or not?

CAL. Entirely so.

SOC. In the second place, therefore, this ought to be considered, whether we have ever built any private edifice, either for any one of our friends, or for ourselves; and whether this edifice is beautiful or deformed. And if on considering we find that our masters were good

c and illustrious, and that we have built, in conjunction with our masters, many beautiful edifices, and many without their assistance, after we left our masters, - if we find this to be the case, ought we not, if endued with intellect, to betake ourselves to public works? But if we can neither evince that we had a master, and have either raised no buildings, or many of no worth, would it not in this case be stupid in us to attempt public works, and to exhort each other to such an undertaking?

d Shall we say that these things are rightly asserted, or not?

CAL. Entirely so.

SOC. And is not this the case with all other things? And if we should engage publicly in medical affairs, exhorting each other as if we were skilful physicians, ought not you and I to consider as follows: By the Gods, how is Socrates affected in his body with respect to health? Or is there any other person, whether a slave or free-born, who by the help of Socrates is liberated from disease? And indeed I think I may consider other things of this kind respecting you. And if we do not find any

e   one, stranger or citizen, man or woman, whose body has been benefited by our assistance, will it not, by Jupiter, Callicles, be truly ridiculous, that we should proceed to that degree of folly as to attempt, according to the proverb,[†] to teach a potter in making a tub, before we have transacted many things privately, as they might happen to occur, and have happily accomplished many things, and been sufficiently exercised in the medical art, and should endeavour to exhort others like ourselves to exercise medicine publicly? Does it not appear to you that a conduct of this kind would be stupid?

CAL. It does.

515a   SOC. But now, O best of men, since you have just begun to transact public affairs, and you exhort me to the same, reproaching me at the same time that I do not engage in them, ought we not mutually to consider as follows: What citizen has Callicles made a better man? Is there any one who, being before depraved, unjust, intemperate, and unwise, has through Callicles become a worthy and good man, whether he is a stranger or a citizen, a slave or free-born? Tell me, Callicles, if

b   any one should ask you these things, what would you say? Whom would you assert to be a better man from associating with you? Are you averse to answer, if there is as yet any private work of this kind accomplished by you, before you engage in public affairs?

CAL. You are contentious, Socrates.

SOC. But I do not ask through a love of contention, but in consequence of really wishing to know, after what manner you think government ought to be conducted by us. Or would you, when applying yourself to public affairs, attend to any thing else than that we

c   citizens may be rendered the best of men? Or have we not often acknowledged that this ought to be done by a politician? Have we, or not, acknowledged this? Answer. We have acknowledged it. I will answer for you. If, therefore, a good man ought to procure this for his city, now having recollected, inform me respecting those men whom you a little before mentioned, if they any longer appear to you to have

---

† This proverb, according to Zenobius, is applied to those who pass over the first disciplines, and immediately apply themselves to the greater. Just as if some one learning the potter's art should attempt to make a tub before he had learned how to make tables, or any other small utensil.

d   been good citizens, - I mean Pericles and Cimon, Miltiades and Themistocles.

CAL. To me they do.

SOC. If, therefore, they were good men, did not each of them render their fellow-citizens better instead of worse? Did they render them so, or not?

CAL. They did.

SOC. When Pericles, therefore, began to speak to the people, were they not worse than when he addressed them for the last time?

CAL. Perhaps so.

SOC. It is not proper to say 'perhaps', O best of men; but this must be a necessary consequence from what has been granted, if he was a good citizen.

e   CAL. But what then?

SOC. Nothing. But besides this inform me, whether the Athenians are said to have become better men through Pericles, or on the contrary were corrupted by him. For I hear that Pericles rendered the Athenians indolent, timid, loquacious, and avaricious, having first of all rendered them mercenary.

CAL. You hear these things, Socrates, from those whose ears are broken.

SOC. However, I no longer hear these things; but both you and I clearly know that Pericles at first was much celebrated, and was not condemned by the Athenians by any ignominious sentence, at the very time when they were worse; but when he had made them worthy and good, then towards the close of his life they fraudulently condemned

516a   him, and were on the point of putting him to death as if he had been an unworthy man.

CAL. What then? Was Pericles on this account a bad man?

SOC. Indeed, a person of this kind who has the care of asses, horses, and oxen, appears to be a bad character, if, receiving these animals neither kicking backwards, nor pushing with their horns, nor biting, he causes them to do all these things through ferocity of disposition. Or

b   does not every curator of an animal appear to you to be a bad man, who, having received it of a milder nature, renders it more savage than when he received it? Does he appear to you to be so, or not?

CAL. Entirely so, that I may gratify you.

SOC. Gratify me also in this, by answering whether man is an animal, or not.

CAL. Undoubtedly he is.

SOC. Did not Pericles, therefore, take care of men?

CAL. Yes.

SOC. What then? Is it not requisite, as we just now acknowledged, that they should become through him more just, instead of more unjust, and being a good politician, took care of them?

c   CAL. Entirely so.

SOC. Are not, therefore, the just mild, as Homer[†] says? But what do you say? Is it not so?

CAL. Yes.

SOC. But, indeed, he rendered them more savage than when he received them: and this against himself; which was far from being his intention.

CAL. Are you willing I should assent to you?

SOC. If I appear to you to speak the truth.

CAL. Be it so, then.

SOC. If, therefore, he rendered them more savage, must he not also have rendered them more unjust, and worse characters?

d   CAL. Be it so.

SOC. From this reasoning, therefore, it follows, that Pericles was not a good politician.

CAL. You, indeed, say not.

SOC. And, by Jupiter, you say so too, from what you have acknowledged. But again, tell me respecting Cimon. Did not those who were the objects of his care punish him by an ostracism, and so as that for ten years they might not hear his voice? And they acted in a similar manner towards Themistocles, and, besides this, punished him with exile. But they decreed that Miltiades, who fought at the battle of Marathon, should be hurled into the Barathrum; and unless the Prytanis

e   had defended him, he would have fallen into it. Though these, if they had been good men, as you say they were, would never have suffered these things. Indeed it can never happen that good charioteers should at first not be thrown from their cars; but, when they have disciplined their horses, and have themselves become better charioteers, that they should then be thrown from them. This is never the case, either in driving a chariot, or in any other employment. Or does it appear to you that it is?

CAL. It does not.

SOC. Our former assertions, therefore, as it appears, are true, *viz.* that

517a   we do not know any good politician in this city: but you acknowledge that you know of none at present, but that formerly there were some;

† *Odyssey* vii, ver. 120.

and the names of these you have mentioned: but these have appeared to be equal to the politicians of the present day. So that, if they were rhetoricians, they did not use rhetoric truly (for otherwise they would not have fallen into disgrace), nor yet did they employ adulation.

b CAL. But indeed, Socrates, it is far from being case, that any one of the present day will ever accomplish such undertakings as were accomplished by any one of those I mentioned.

SOC. Neither, O divine man, do I blame these men, so far as they were servants of the city; but they appear to me to have been more skilful ministers than those of the present day, and more adapted to procure for the city such things as it desired. But in persuading, and at the same time compelling, the citizens to repress their desires, and not indulge them, by means of which they would become better men, in this those former politicians in no respect differed from such as exist at c present; for this, indeed, is alone the work of a good citizen. But, with respect to procuring ships, walls, and docks, and many other things of this kind, I also agree with you, that those were more skilful than these. I, therefore, and you, act ridiculously in this disputation. For during the whole time of our conversation we have not ceased to revolve about the same thing, and to be mutually ignorant of what we said. I think, therefore, that you have often acknowledged and known, that there is d this twofold employment, both respecting the body and soul: and that the one is ministrant, by which we are enabled, if hungry, to procure food for our bodies, and, if thirsty, drink; if cold, garments, coverlids, shoes, and other things which the body requires. And I will designedly speak to you through the same images, that you may more easily understand. If any one then supplies these things, being either a victualler, or a merchant, or an artificer of some one of them, *viz.* a e baker, or a cook, a weaver, shoemaker, or tanner, it is by no means wonderful that, being a person of this kind, he should appear, both to himself and others, to be a curator of the body; I mean, to all those who are ignorant that, besides all these, there is a certain gymnastic and medicinal art, to which the care of the body in reality pertains; to which it belongs to rule over all these arts, and to use their respective works; in consequence of knowing what is good and bad in solid or liquid 518a aliment, with respect to the virtue of the body, while all the other arts are ignorant of this. On this account, it is necessary that these arts should be servile, ministrant, and illiberal, respecting the concerns of the body; but that gymnastic and medicine should be justly the mistresses of these. That the very same things, likewise, take place in the soul, you appeared at the same time to grant me, as if knowing what I said; but a

little after you asserted that there had been worthy and good citizens in
this city. And when I asked you who they were, you appeared to me

b   to exhibit just such men, with respect to political concerns, as if, in
consequence of my asking about gymnastic affairs, who have been, or
are at present, good curators of bodies, you should seriously answer me,
that Thearion the baker, and Mithæcus, who wrote on the Sicilian art
of cooking, and Sarambus the victualler, were wonderful curators of
bodies; the first of whom made admirable bread; the second procured
admirable food; and the third admirable wine. Perhaps, therefore, you

c   will be indignant if I should say to you, O man, you understand nothing
respecting gymnastic. You have told me of men who are the ministers
and purveyors of desires, but you do not understand any thing beautiful
and good concerning them; who, if it should so happen, while they fill
the bodies of men, and render them gross, and are praised by them for
so doing, at the same time destroy their ancient flesh. These, therefore,
through their unskilfulness, do not accuse men given to feasting, as the

d   causes of the diseases with which they are infested, and of the loss of
their ancient flesh, but those who happen to be then present, and give
them some advice. But, after a long time, when repletion introduces
disease, in consequence of having taken place without the healthful, then
they accuse and blame their advisers, and would injure them if they

e   were able; but praise those ministers of their desires, and the causes of
their maladies. And now you, O Callicles, act in a manner most similar
to this; for you praise those who delight such-like men with feasting, and
who satiate them with the objects of their desire, and say that they make
the city great; but who do not perceive that the city is swollen, and
inwardly in a bad condition, through those ancient men. For, without
temperance and justice, they have filled the city with ports and

519a docks, with walls and tributes, and such-like trifles. When, therefore,
this accession of imbecility arrived, they accused the advisers that were
then present, but praised Themistocles, Cimon, and Pericles, who were
the causes of the maladies: but you perhaps, unless you are careful, they

b   will apprehend, together with my associate Alcibiades, since they have
destroyed those ancient particulars, besides those which they have
acquired; though you are not the causes, but perhaps the con-causes, of
the evils. Indeed, I perceive that a very stupid affair takes place at
present, and I hear that it has taken place with respect to ancient men.
For I see that when a city conducts itself towards any political character,
as one that acts unjustly, such a one is indignant, and complains as
suffering grievously, though he has conferred many benefits on the city.

c   Are, therefore, such unjustly destroyed by the city, according to their assertion? But, indeed, their assertion is entirely false. For he who presides over a city can never be unjustly cut off by the city over which he presides. For those who profess themselves to be politicians, appear to be the same with those that call themselves sophists. For the sophists, though wise in other things, act absurdly in this respect. Proclaiming themselves to be teachers of virtue, they often accuse their disciples of acting unjustly towards them, by defrauding them of their wages, and other testimonies of gratitude for the benefits they receive

d   from them. But what can be more irrational than such an accusation? - I mean, that men who have become good and just, being freed from injustice by their preceptor, and having obtained justice, should yet act unjustly from that very thing which they have not? Does not this, my friend, appear to you to be absurd? You compel me in reality, Callicles, to make a public harangue, because you are unwilling to answer me.

CAL. But cannot you speak unless some one answers you?

e   SOC. I seem, indeed, as if I could. For now I extend my discourses, since you are not willing to answer me. But, O good man, tell me, by Jupiter, the guardian of friendship, does it not appear to you irrational, that he who says he can make another person a good man, should blame this man, that, having become good through his instructions, and being so now, he is, notwithstanding, an unworthy character?

CAL. To me it appears so.

SOC. Do you not, therefore, hear those who profess to instruct men in virtue speaking in this manner?

520a   CAL. I do. But why do you speak about men of no worth?

SOC. But what will you say respecting those men, who, while they assert that they preside over the city, and are careful that it may be the best possible, again accuse it, when it so happens, as the worst of cities? Do you think that these differ in any respect from those? O blessed man! a sophist and a rhetorician are the same, or they are something near and similar, as I and Polus have said. But you, through ignorance,

b   think that rhetoric is something all-beautiful, and despise the sophistic art. In reality, however, the sophistic art is as much more beautiful than rhetoric, as the legislative than the judicial profession, and gymnastic than medicine. But I think public speakers and sophists alone ought not to complain that the thing which they teach is evil to themselves; or, if they do, that they must accuse themselves at the same time of not having in any respect benefited those whom they profess to have benefited. Is it not so?

c   CAL. Entirely so.

Soc. And, indeed, it will be proper to impart benefit to these alone, if they asserted what is true. For, if some one should receive any other benefit, as, for instance, the power of running swiftly, through the instructions of a master of gymnastic, perhaps he would be averse to recompense him, if the master of gymnastic benefited him without having made an agreement that he should be paid for his trouble as soon as he had enabled him to run swiftly. For men, I think, do not act unjustly through slowness, but through injustice. Or do they not?

d   CAL. Yes.

Soc. If, therefore, any one should take away this, - I mean injustice, - would it not follow, that there would be no occasion to fear lest he should suffer injustice; but that to him alone it would be safe to impart this benefit, if any one is in reality able to form good men? Is it not so?

CAL. I say so.

Soc. Hence, as it appears, there is nothing base in taking money for giving advice about other things, as, for instance, respecting building, or other arts.

e   CAL. So it appears.

Soc. But with respect to this action, - I mean, how any one may be rendered the best of men, and may govern his own family, or the city, in the most excellent manner, - it is reckoned base to withhold advice, unless money is given to the adviser. Is it not so?

CAL. Yes.

Soc. For it is evident that the reason is this: that.of all benefits, this alone renders him who is benefited desirous of making a recompense. So that it appears to be a beautiful sign, if he who imparts the benefit is in his turn benefited; but by no means if he is not. Are these things so, or not?

521a   CAL. They are.

Soc. Define, therefore, to which mode of healing the maladies of a city you exhort me: whether to that of contending with the Athenians, that they may become the best of men, as if I were a physician; or to that by which I may minister to their wants, in order to obtain their favour. Tell me the truth, Callicles. For it is but just, that, as you began to speak to me freely, you should continue to impart your conceptions. And now speak well and generously.

CAL. I say, therefore, that I exhort you to act as ministrant to the city.

b   Soc. You exhort me, therefore, most generous man, to employ flattery.

CAL. Unless you had rather be the prey of the Mysians; which will be the case, if you do not act in this manner.

SOC. Do not say, what you often have said, that any one who is willing might slay me, lest I again should say, that an unworthy would slay a good man; nor yet that he might take away whatever I possessed, lest I also should again say, that after he has taken away my possessions he would not derive any advantage from them; but that, as he has unjustly deprived me of them, he will also, having received them, use

c them unjustly; and if unjustly, basely; and if basely, wickedly.

CAL. You appear to me, Socrates, to believe that you shall never suffer any of these things, as being one who lives at a distance, and that you shall never be brought before a court of justice by a man, perhaps, entirely depraved and vile.

SOC. I am therefore, O Callicles, in reality stupid, unless I think that any one in this city may suffer whatever may happen to take place. But this I well know, that if I was brought before a court of justice, and I

d should be in danger respecting any one of these particulars which you mention, he who brings me thither will be a depraved man. For no worthy man will bring one who is innocent before a court of justice. Nor would it be any thing wonderful, if in this case I should be condemned to death. Are you willing I should tell you why I should expect these things?

CAL. By all means.

SOC. I think that I, in conjunction with a few Athenians, (that I may not say alone,) apply myself to the true political art, and alone of those of the present day perform things political. As, therefore, the discourses which I make are not composed for the sake of the popular favour, but with a view to that which is best, and not to that which is most pleasant, - and as I am not willing to do those elegant things which you

e now advise me to do, - I should not have any thing to say in a court of justice. But the same discourse occurs to me which I addressed to Polus. For I should be judged in the same manner as a physician would be judged among boys, when accused by a cook. For consider what would be the apology of such a man, when apprehended by these, if any one should accuse him as follows: O boys, this man fabricates for you many

522a evils, and corrupts both you and the youngest of you. For, by cutting, burning, emaciating, and almost suffocating you, he makes you desperate; and likewise by giving you the most bitter potions, and compelling you to be hungry and thirsty; not delighting you, as I do, with many pleasant and all-various dainties. What do you think the physician would have to say in such a bad situation? If he spoke the truth, would he not say, I have done all these things, boys, for the sake of health? But, upon this, in what manner do you think these judges would exclaim? Would they not loudly exclaim?

CAL. Perhaps it may be proper to think so.

b   SOC. Do you not think, therefore, that he would be perfectly at a loss what to say?

CAL. Entirely so.

SOC. And I also know that I should be affected in the very same manner, on coming into a court of justice. For I should not be able to mention any pleasures which I had imparted to them, and which they consider as benefits and advantages. But I neither emulate those that impart them, nor those to whom they are imparted. And if any one should say that I corrupt young men, by causing them to doubt, or accuse elderly men, by employing bitter discourses, either privately or publicly, I should not be able to say that which is the truth, that I assert

c   and do all these things justly; and that it is your province, O judges, to act in this manner, and to do nothing else. So that, perhaps, I should suffer whatever might happen to be the consequence.

CAL. Does, therefore, Socrates, that man appear to you to be in a good condition in a city who is thus circumstanced, and is unable to help himself?

SOC. He does, if he is in that condition, Callicles, which you have often allowed, viz. if he can assist himself, and has not either said or done any thing unjustly respecting men or Gods. For it has often been acknowledged by us, that this is the best aid which any one can impart

d   to himself. If, therefore, any one can prove that I am incapable of affording this assistance either to myself or another, I shall be ashamed, whether I am convicted of this impotence before many, or a few, or alone, by myself alone. And if I should be punished with death on account of this impotency, I should be indignant. But if I should die through the want of adulatory rhetoric, I well know that you would behold me bearing death easily. For no one fears to die, who is not entirely irrational and effeminate: but he fears to act unjustly; since, for

e   the soul to come to Hades full of unjust actions, is the extremity of all evils. But, if you please, I wish to show you by a certain narration that this is the case.

CAL. Since you have finished the other things which remained to be completed, finish this also.

523a   SOC. Hear then, as they say, a very beautiful narration; which you indeed will, I think, consider as a fable; but I consider it as a relation of facts. For the particulars of the ensuing narration are true. As Homer says, then, Jupiter, Neptune, and Pluto,[6] divided the government among themselves, after they had received it from their father. This law,[†] therefore, respecting men subsisted under Saturn, and always was, and now is, established among the Gods, *viz.* that the man who has passed through life in a just and holy manner, when he dies, departing to the islands of the blessed, shall dwell in all felicity, removed from evil; but that he who has lived unjustly and impiously shall go to the prison of punishment and justice, which they call Tartarus. But the judges of these, during the reign of Saturn, and even recently, Jupiter possessing the government, were living judges of the living, judging on that very day on which any one happened to die. In consequence of this they judged badly. On this account, therefore, Pluto, and those to whom the care of the islands of the blessed was committed, went to Jupiter, and informed him that men came to them who were unworthy, whether they were accusers or the accused. But Jupiter said, I will prevent this in future. For now judgements are badly exercised; because those that are judged are judged clothed; for they are judged while living. Many, therefore, says he, whose souls are depraved are invested with beautiful bodies, are noble by birth, and rich; and when judgement of their conduct takes place, many witnesses appear in their behalf, testifying that they have lived justly. Hence the judges are astonished at these things, and are at the same time themselves clothed, while judging, as prior to their soul being concealed they have a veil before their eyes and ears, and the whole of their body.[7] All these things, indeed, are placed before them, as well their own vestments as the vestments of those that are judged. In the first place, therefore, says he, they must be deprived of the power of foreseeing death: for now they do foresee it. Hence, Prometheus[8] must be ordered to make this faculty in them cease: and afterwards they must be judged divested of all these things; for it is requisite that they should be judged when dead. It is likewise requisite that the judge should be naked and dead, speculating the soul itself, with the soul itself, every one dying suddenly, destitute of all his kindred, and leaving all that ornament on the earth, that the judgment may be just. I therefore having known these things before you, have made my sons judges; two indeed from Asia,[9] Minos and Rhadamantus; and one from

---

† Neither *was* nor *will be* can be asserted of a divine nature: for *was* is past, and no longer is, and *will be* is imperfect, and is not yet. But nothing of this kind can be conceived of Divinity. As, therefore, Plato introduces this as a fable, on this account he uses the term *was;* since the fable is not poetic, but philosophic, he also introduces the word *always.* [47.8]

524a   Europe, Æacus. These then, after their death, shall judge in the
meadow, in the highway, where two roads extend, the one to the islands
of the blessed, and the other to Tartarus. And Rhadamanthus shall
judge those from Asia, but Æacus those from Europe. But I will confer
this additional dignity upon Minos, that he shall decide whatever may
be inscrutable to the other judges, that the judgement respecting the path
of men may be most just.

   These are the things, O Callicles, which I have heard, and believe to
b   be true: and from this narration I infer that a thing of the following
kind must take place. Death, as it appears to me, is nothing else than
the dissolution of two things, *viz.* of the soul and the body from each
other. But when they are mutually separated, each of them possesses its
own habit, not much less than when the man was living; and the body
conspicuously retaining its own nature, attire, and passions. So that, for
c   instance, if the body of any one while living was large by nature, or
aliment, or from both, the body of such a one when dead will also be
large; and if corpulent, it will be corpulent when dead; and so with
respect to other things. And if any one while living was studious to
obtain long hair, the hair also of the dead body of such a one will be
long. Again, if any one while living had been whipped, and retained
vestiges of the blows in his body scars from scourges, or other wounds,
d   his dead body also is seen to preserve the same marks. And if the limbs
of any one were broken or distorted while he lived, these also will be
conspicuous when he is dead. And, in short, whatever was the
condition of the body of any one while living, such will be its condition
entirely, or for the most part, for a certain time, when dead. The same
thing also, Callicles, appears to me to take place respecting the soul; *viz.*
that all things are conspicuous in the soul, after it is divested of body,
as well whatever it possesses from nature,[10] as those passions which the
man acquired in his soul, from his various pursuits. When, therefore,
e   they come to judge,† those from Asia to Rhadamanthus, Rhadamanthus
stopping them contemplates the soul of each, not knowing to whom it
belongs; but often seizing the soul of the great king, or of any other
king or potentate, he beholds nothing sound in such a soul, but sees that
it has been vehemently whipped, and that it is full of scars, through the
perjuries and injustice impressed in it by its several actions; that all

----

   † Plato here presents us with a fable, but he does not suffer it to be poetical, but
likewise adds demonstrations: for this is the peculiarity of philosophical fables. See the
general Introduction to this work.

525a things in it are distorted† through falsehood and arrogance, and that nothing is right, in consequence of its having been educated without truth. He likewise sees that such a soul through power, luxury, and intemperate conduct, is full of inelegance and baseness. On seeing however a soul in this condition, he directly[11] sends it into custody with disgrace; whither when arrived, it will suffer the punishment which it

b deserves. But it is proper that every one who is punished if he is rightly punished by another, should either become better, and derive advantage from his punishment, or become an example‡ to others, that others perceiving his sufferings may be terrified and made better. But those are benefited and suffer punishment both from Gods and men, who have been guilty of curable offences: but at the same time the advantage which they derive both here and in Hades, takes place through torments

c and grief: for they cannot by any other means be liberated from injustice. But those who have acted unjustly in the extreme, and have through such crimes become incurable, serve as examples to others. And these no longer derive any advantage, as being incurable: but others are benefited on perceiving these suffering through the whole of time the greatest, most bitter, and most horrid of punishments for their guilt, being indeed suspended in the prison of Hades as examples, spectacles,

d and warnings to the unjust men that come thither. One of whom I say Archelaus will be (if Polus says true), and every other tyrant who resembles him. I think too, that the greatest part of these examples will consist of tyrants, kings, and potentates, and such as have governed the affairs of cities. For these through their power commit the greatest and the most impious crimes. Homer also testifies the truth of these assertions. For he makes those to be kings and potentates, that are

e punished in Hades through the whole of time, *viz*. Tantalus, Sisyphus and Tityus;[12] but he does not make Thersites, or any other private unworthy individual, oppressed by the greatest punishments as if incurable: for I do not think he could be guilty of incurable offences; on which account, he was more happy than those who could. But, Callicles, men extremely unworthy are among the number of the powerful: at the same time, nothing hinders but that good men also may

526a subsist among these; and when this is the case they deserve the greatest admiration. For it is a difficult thing, Callicles, and deserves much

---

† For when the soul is defiled and wounded by the passions nothing in it is *straight*. [50.6]

‡ For the soul by suffering becomes herself amended, and is an example to those that behold her. [50.7]

praise, for a man who has great power of acting unjustly, to pass through life justly. Yet there are a few men of this kind; for they have existed both here and elsewhere, and I think there will be hereafter

b   worthy and good men, who will be endued with the virtue of administering justly things committed to their trust. A character of this kind, and of great celebrity among the other Greeks, was Aristides the son of Lysimachus. But the greater part, O most excellent man, of potentates are bad men. As I said, therefore, after Rhadamanthus has taken any soul into his custody, he does not know any thing else respecting it, neither who it is, nor from whom it originated. But he only knows that it is a depraved soul; and seeing this, he sends it to Tartarus; signifying at the same time whether it appears to be curable or incurable. But the soul arriving thither suffers the punishments due to

c   its offences. Sometimes, too, Rhadamanthus beholding the soul of one who has passed through life with truth, whether it is the soul of a private man, or of any other - but I say, Callicles, especially of a philosopher, who has transacted his own affairs, and has not been engaged in a multiplicity of concerns in life - when this is the case, Rhadamanthus is filled with admiration, and dismisses the soul to the islands of the blessed. The same things also are done by Æacus. And

d   each of them judges, holding a rod† in his hand. But Minos, who is the inspector, is the only one that sits having a golden‡ sceptre, as the Ulysses of Homer§ says he saw him:

> A golden sceptre in his hand he holds,
> And laws promulgates to the dead.

I therefore, Callicles, am persuaded by these narrations, and consider how I may appear before my judge, with my soul in the most healthy condition. Wherefore, bidding farewell to the honours of the multitude, and looking to truth, I will endeavour to live in reality in the best

e   manner I am able, and when I die to die so. I likewise call upon all other men, and you also I exhort to this life, and this contest, instead of that which you have adopted, and which I say is to be preferred to all the contests here. And I upbraid you because you will not be able to

---

† By the *rod*, says Olympiodorus, the straight, and the equality of justice, are signified. [50.11]

‡ Again, says Olympiodorus, the *sceptre* signifies *equality*, but *golden the immaterial*. For gold alone does not rust, to which all other material natures are subject. [50.12]

§ *Odyssey* xi, ver. 756.

assist yourself, when that judicial process shall take place of which I have just been speaking. But when you shall come before that judge who is the son of Ægina, and he laying hold of shall examine you, you will there yawn, and be seized with a giddiness, no less than I am here. Some one too, perhaps, will strike you ignominiously on the face, and treat you in a manner disgraceful. These things, however, perhaps appear to you to be nothing more than the tales of an old woman, and you accordingly despise them. Nor would it be at all wonderful that these things should indeed be despised by us, if by investigation we could find any thing better and more true. But now you three, who are the wisest of all the Greeks existing at present, *viz.* you, Polus, and Gorgias, see it cannot be shown that it is requisite to live any other life than this, which appears also to be advantageous hereafter. But among so many arguments, while others are confuted this alone remains unmoved, *viz.* that we ought to be more afraid of doing injury than of being injured; and that a man ought more than any thing to endeavour not to appear to be good, but to be so in reality, both in private and public. Likewise, that if any one is in any respect vicious, he should be punished; and that this is the next good to the being just, *viz.* to become just, and to suffer through chastisement the punishment of guilt. And further, that all adulation, both respecting a man's self and others, and respecting a few and a many, is to be avoided; and that rhetoric, and every other action, is always to be employed with a view to the just. Being, therefore, persuaded by me, follow me to that place, whither when you arrive you will be happy, both when living and dead, as my discourse evinces. Suffer, too, any one to despise you as stupid, and to load you with disgrace if he pleases. And, by Jupiter, do you, being confident, permit him to strike this ignominious blow. For you will not suffer any thing dire, if you are in reality worthy and good, and cultivate virtue: and afterwards, when we have thus exercised ourselves in common, then, if it shall appear to be requisite, we will betake ourselves to political concerns, or deliberate on whatever we please, as we shall then be better qualified to deliberate than now. For it is shameful, in the condition we appear to be in at present, to boast of ourselves with juvenile audacity, as if we were something; we who are never unanimous about the same things, and things of the greatest consequence; at such a degree of unskilfulness have we arrived. Let us employ, therefore, as a leader, the reasoning which now presents itself to the view,- I mean, that which signifies to us that the best mode of life consists in cultivating justice and the other virtues. This, then, let us follow, and exhort others to the same, but not that, in which you confiding exhorted me: for it is, Callicles, of no worth.

Additional Notes

on the

GORGIAS

2.1   1 (See page 329, line 447c) Rhetoric, says Olympiodorus, is twofold; the one being art, and the other skill. It is worth while, therefore, to inquire, on what account skill is not art? It is justly then observed in the *Phædrus* [270a ff], that he who intends to discourse about any thing should first define, and afterwards teach: for he who does not do this must necessarily totally err. Thus, for instance, in investigating if the soul is immortal, we ought not immediately to show that it is immortal; but, previous to this, we should make a division, and say that soul is not one thing, but many things. For there is both rational and irrational soul: and there is also a plantal soul, - whence likewise we say that plants live. We say, then, that the rational soul is both immortal and not immortal. It is not immortal, indeed, if we consider the immortal according to a subsistence perpetual and uniform; but it is immortal both in its essence and energy.

2.2   Again, the definition of art is twofold. For art is a method proceeding in an orderly path in conjunction with phantasy. Olympiodorus adds in conjunction with phantasy, in order to distinguish it from nature. For nature also proceeds in an orderly way, but not with phantasy. Again, art is a system of conclusions, coexercised to a certain end, beneficial to some of the purposes of life. According to the first definition, therefore, rhetoric, falsely so denominated, may be called an art. For it proceeds in an orderly path; in the first place, arranging the proem; and afterwards the state or condition (κατασταϲιϲ), and what is consequent to this. But it is not an art according to the second definition, since this can only apply to true rhetoric, which assigns the causes of what it asserts. Indeed, not only rhetoric, falsely so called, is an
2.3   art, according to the first definition, but also cookery, and the dressing of hair. For to cook is not the province of any casual person, but of one who possesses skill, and proceeds in a certain way. In like manner, the decoration of the hair has a knowledge of ointments, and knows how to adorn the hairs. The rhetoric, therefore, which knows not how to assign the cause of what it asserts, but proceeds to both sides, *i.e.* to the true and the false, is not an art. For art is that which has one good end. But true rhetoric, which subsists under the political character, is an art. For, as the rational physician knows how to cure an ophthalmy, so likewise the empiric. But the former, who also acts according to art, can assign the causes of what he does, which the empiric cannot. Again,
2.4   if some one should ask in what art differs from science, since art also assigns causes, we reply, that science produces the knowledge of things whose subsistence is perpetual and uniform, but art the knowledge of things flowing.

Shall we say, therefore, that the physiologist is not scientific who investigates things flowing and material? By no means: for his investigation is not of things material, but he refers them to universals, and explores the hypostasis of universal physical natures. So that Plato reprobates false and not true rhetoric.

3.9   2 (See page 330, line 448b) There are two kinds of rhetoric, says Olympiodorus; but of these the genera, and the ends, and the ways, are different. For the genus of true rhetoric is art; but, of the false, skill. Again, the end of the true is good; but, of the false, persuasion, whether the thing persuaded to be done, or not, be good or bad. And again, the way of the true is to know the powers of the soul; but, of the false, not to know them. *Doctrinal* faith also is the way of the true; but *credible* that of the false. For the geometrician wishes to persuade, but in a demonstrative way, and not from credibility, as the rhetorician. As, therefore, the medicinal art announces health through different auxiliaries, so rhetorics proceed through different forms. As a knife, therefore, is not of itself either good or bad, but is beneficial, or the contrary, to him who uses it; so rhetoric is not of itself beautiful, but is beneficial who uses it.

3.2   3 (See page 330, line 448c) Experiment ($\pi\epsilon\iota\rho\alpha$), says Olympiodorus [3.2], differs from skill ($\epsilon\mu\pi\epsilon\iota\rho\iota\alpha$). For skill is asserted of actions, but experiment of things artificial according to a part. And again, experiment is conversant with things partial, but skill with things more universal. Skill, therefore, does not produce art, if skill is of things subordinate; for, if it did, superior would be produced from inferior natures. But it may be said, Do we not arrive at skill from experiment, and at art from skill? We reply, that experiment, indeed, contributes to skill, and skill to art; but they are not producing causes. This, however, takes place from our possessing the gnostic reasons of things, and being excited by sensibles. As, therefore, he who makes the sparks which have a long time been concealed in ashes apparent, is not said to have made light, but to have rendered it manifest; and in like manner, he who purifies the eye from an ophthalmy does not produce light, but contributes to the presence of it to the eye: so the reasons in us require that which may cause us to recollect. For we are analogous to a geometrician sleeping. So that skill is not effective.

4 (See page 334, line 451e) These verses, according to the Greek Scholia of Ruhnkenius, are by some ascribed to Simonides, and by others to Epicharmus. But they form a part of one of those songs which were sung at entertainments, and were called σκολια, *scolia*. They mostly consisted of short verses, and were sung by the few of the company that were best skilled in music. These *scolia* were chiefly used by the Athenians; yet they were not unknown in other parts of Greece, where several celebrated writers of scolia lived, such as Anacreon of

Teos, Alcæus of Lesbos, Praxilla of Sicyon, and others. Their arguments were of various kinds; some of them being ludicrous and satirical, others amorous, and many of them serious. Those of a serious nature sometimes contained a practical exhortation or sentence, such as that which is now cited by Plato. And sometimes they consisted of the praises and illustrious actions of great men.

But the following additional information on this subject, from the MS. Scholia of Olympiodorus on this dialogue, will I doubt not be gratefully received by all lovers of antiquity, as the whole of it is not to be found in any other writer.

5.5 Olympiodorus then, after observing that Plato admitted music in his republic, though not the popular, but that which adorns the soul, adds as follows: "The ancients especially used music in their banquets; since banquets excite the passions. A choir, therefore, was formed. And if they danced from the left hand to the right hand part, a thing of this kind was called *progression* (προοδος); but if to the left hand, *epode* (εποδος); and if to the middle, it was called *mesodos* (μεσοδος). Again, if, turning in a backward direction, they went to the right hand part, it was called *strophe* (στροφη); but if to the middle, *mesodos* (μεσοδος); and if to the more left hand parts, *antistrophe* (αντιστροφη). Of these also Stesichorus makes mention. But these things were symbolical: for they imitated the celestial motions. For the motion from the left to the right hand parts is western; but that from the right to the left, eastern. In like manner those that began to sing, and who moved to the middle, and ended the dance, obscurely signified by all this the earth, which is a certain *beginning*, as being the centre; a *middle*, through its position; and an *end*, as being the dregs of the universe. When, therefore, the music partially ceased, they used wine mixed with myrtle; and some one taking it, and singing, did not give it to the person next to him, but to the one opposite to him. Afterwards, he gave it to the first, and he again to the second, and the communication became *scolia*. And the part here is called *scolion.*" Μαλιστα τοινυν εν τοις συμποσιοις μουσικη εκεχρηντο· επειδη τα συμποσια οιατε ην εις παθος κινησα· χορος ουν εγενετο· και ει μεν απο αριστερων επι το δεξιον μερος εφεροντο, εκαλειτο προοδος το τοιουτον· ει δε επι το αριστερον εποδος· ειδε επι το μεσον, μεσοδος. και παλιν, ει επι το οπισθεν στραφεντες επι το δεξιον μερος ιεσαν, στροφη εκαλειτο· ει δε επι το μεσον, μεσοδος· ει δε επι το αριστερον αντιστροφη· τουτων μεν ουν και Στεσιχορος μεμνηται· συμβολικα δε ταυτα ησαν· επιμιμουνται γαρ τας ουρονιας κινησεις· η μεν γαρ απο των αριστερων εις τα δεξια δυτικη εστιν· η δε απο των δεξιων επι τα αριστερα ανατολικη· ωσαυτως και οι αρχομενοι αδειν και μεσουντες και ληγοντες, την γην ηνιττοντο, η τις αρχη μεν εστιν ως κεντρον· μεση δε δια την θεσιν· τελευτη δε ως υποσταθμη του παντος· επει τοινυν εξελιμπανη κατα μερος η μουσικη, μυρριναις εκεχρηντο. και εκαμβανε τις αυτην, και αδων ου παρειχετο μετ' αυτον, αλλα τω κατα αντικρυ αυτου· ειτα εκεινος τω πρωτω · και παλιν εκεινος τω δευτερω· και σκολια η μεταδοσις εγενετο· και ενταυθα το σκολιον μερος ειρηται.

Information similar to the above may be found in the Greek Scholia of Hephestion, but by no means so complete.

29.3   5 (See page 380, line 493a) Euripides (in Phryxo) says, that to live is to die, and to die to live. For the soul coming hither, as she imparts life to the body, so she partakes of a certain privation of life; but this is an evil. When separated, therefore, from the body, she lives in reality: for she dies here, through participating a privation of life, because the body becomes the cause of evils. And hence it is necessary to subdue the body.

30.1   The meaning of the Pythagoric fable which is here introduced by Plato is as follows: We are said then to be dead, because, as we have before observed, we partake of a privation of life. The sepulchre which we carry about with us is, as Plato himself explains it, the body. But Hades is the unapparent, because we are situated in obscurity, the soul being in a state of servitude to the body. The tubs are the desires, whether they are so called from hastening to fill them as if they were tubs, or from desire persuading us that it is beautiful. The initiated, therefore, *i.e.* those that have a perfect knowledge, pour into the entire tub: for these have their tub full, or in other words, have perfect virtue. But the uninitiated, *viz.* those that possess nothing perfect, have perforated tubs. For those that are in a state of servitude to desire always wish to fill it, and are more inflamed; and on this account they have perforated tubs, as being never

30.2   full. But the sieve is the rational soul mingled with the irrational. For the soul is called a circle, because it seeks itself, and is itself sought; finds itself, and is itself found. But the irrational soul imitates a right line, since it does not revert to itself like a circle. So far, therefore, as the sieve is circular, it is an image of the rational soul, but, as it is placed under the right lines formed from the holes, it is assumed for the irrational soul. Right lines, therefore, are in the middle of the cavities. Hence, by the sieve, Plato signifies the rational in subjection to the irrational soul. The water is the flux of nature: for, as Heraclitus says, moisture is the death of the soul.

47.2   6 (See page 415, line 523a) The ineffable principle of things did not produce sensibles by his own *immediate* energy: for there would have been a privation of order, if we had been directly produced by the first cause. And, in the progression of things, the similar is always unfolded into subsistence prior to the dissimilar. By how much greater, therefore, one cause is than another, by so much does one effect surpass another. Hence, he who possesses science in a higher degree produces more illustrious disciples. It is necessary, therefore, that other powers greater than we are should be produced by the first cause, and thus that we afterwards should be generated from these: for we are the dregs of the universe. These mighty powers, from their surpassing similitude to the first God, were very properly called by the ancients Gods; and were considered by them as perpetually subsisting in the most admirable and profound union with each other, and the first cause; yet, so as amidst this union to preserve their own essence distinct from that of their ineffable cause.

But these mighty powers are called by the poets a *golden chain*, on account of their connection with each other, and incorruptible nature. One of these powers you may call *intellectual;* a second *vivific;* a third, *Pæonian,* and so on; which the ancients desiring to signify to us by name have symbolically denominated. Hence (says Olympiodorus, in MS. Comment. in Gorgiam) we ought not to be disturbed on hearing such names as a Saturnian power, the power of Jupiter and such-like, but explore the things to which they allude. Thus, for instance, by a Saturnian power rooted in the first cause, understand a pure intellect: for Κρονος, or Saturn, is κορος νους, *i.e. ο καθαρος,* or, a pure intellect. Hence, those that are pure, and virgins, are called κοραι. On this account, too, poets[†] say that Saturn devoured his children, and afterwards again sent them into the light, because intellect not only seeks and procreates, but produces into light and profits. On this account, too, he is called αγκυλομητις, or *inflected counsel,* because an inflected figure verges to itself. Again, as there is nothing disordered and novel in intellect, they represent, Saturn as an old man, and as slow in his motion: and hence it is astrologers say, that such as have Saturn well situated in their nativity are prudent, and endued with intellect.

47.4 Further still: the ancient theologists called life by the name of Jupiter, to whom they gave a twofold appellation, δια and ζηνα, signifying by these names that he gives *life through* himself. They also assert that the sun is drawn by four horses, and that he is perpetually young, signifying by this his power, which is motive of the whole of nature subject to his dominion, his fourfold conversions, and the vigour of his energies. But they say that the moon is drawn by two bulls: by *two,* on account of her increase and diminution; but by *bulls,* because, as these till the ground so the moon governs all those parts which surround the earth.

Plato says, therefore, that Jupiter and Neptune distributed the government from Saturn; and since Plato does not fashion a political but a philosophical fable, he does not say, like the poets, that they received the kingdom of Saturn by violence, but that they divided it. What then are we to understand by receiving law from Saturn? We reply that law is the distribution of intellect; and we have before observed that Saturn signifies intellect. Hence law is thence derived.

Again, mundane natures, says Olympiodorus, are triple; for some are celestial, others terrestrial, and others between these, *viz.* the fiery, aërial, aquatic. And of these, Jupiter possesses the celestial, Pluto the terrestrial, and Neptune those between. Again, through these things the powers presiding over these natures are signified. For Jupiter on this account has a sceptre, as signifying the judicial; but Neptune a trident, as presiding over the triple nature in the middle; and

† This is asserted by Hesiod in his *Theogony* [453 ff].

Pluto a helmet, on account of the obscure. For, as a helmet conceals the head, so this power (*i.e.* Pluto) belongs to the unapparent. Nor must it be thought 47.5 that philosophers worship stones and images as things divine: but since, living according to sense, we are not able to arrive at an incorporeal and immaterial power, images are devised for the purpose of recalling to the memory divine natures; that, seeing and reverencing these, we may form a conception of incorporeal powers. This, therefore, is also said by the poets, that Jupiter mingling with Themis begot three daughters, Equity, Justice, and Peace. Equity, therefore, reigns in the inerratic sphere: for there the same motion subsists perpetually, and after the same manner, and nothing is there distributed. But Justice rules in the planetary spheres: for here there is a separation[†] of the stars; and where there is separation, there justice is necessary, that an harmonious distribution may be made according to desert. And Peace reigns over terrestrial natures, because contention is among these; and where there is contention, there peace is necessary. But there is a contention here of the hot and the cold, the moist and the dry. Hence they say that Ulysses wandered on the sea by the will of Neptune. For they signify by this, that the Odyssean life was neither terrestrial nor celestial, but between these. Since, therefore, Neptune is the lord of the middle natures, on this account they say that Ulysses wandered through the will of Neptune, because he had the allotment of Neptune. Thus also they speak of the sons of Jupiter, Neptune, and Pluto, regarding the allotments of each. For we say that he who has a divine and celestial polity is the son of Jupiter; that he who has a terrestrial polity is the son of Pluto; and that he is the son of Neptune whose polity or allotment is between these. Again, Vulcan is a certain power residing over bodies; and hence he says of himself in Homer:

> *All day* I fell . . . .

because his attention to bodies is perpetual. On this account also, he operates with bellows (εν φυσαις εργαζεται) *viz.* in natures (αντι του εν ταις φυσεσι). 47.6 For this power leads forth nature to the care of bodies. Since, therefore, Plato makes mention here of the islands of the blessed, of punishment, and a prison, let us unfold what each of them is. Geographers then say that the islands of the blessed are about the ocean, and that souls depart thither that have lived well. This, however, is absurd, for souls thus would live a stormy life. What then shall we say? The solution is this: Philosophers assimilate the life of men to the sea, because it is turbulent, prolific, bitter, and laborious. But it is necessary to know that islands are raised above the sea, being more elevated. Hence, they call that polity which transcends the present life and generation, the islands of the blessed; and these are the same with the Elysian fields. On this account, also, Hercules accomplished his last labour in the Hesperian

---

† *Viz.* the planets are distributed into different spheres, and are not all of them contained in one sphere, like the fixed stars.

regions, signifying by this, that, having vanquished a dark and terrestrial life, he afterwards lived in day, that is, in truth and light.

47.7   Philosophers, then, are of opinion that the earth is cavernous, like a pumice stone, and that it is perforated as far as to its ultimate centre. They likewise think that about the centre there are different places, and certain fiery, cold, and Charonian powers, as the exhalations of the earth evince. The last place, therefore, is called Tartarus. Hence it is necessary to know that souls have lived viciously remain in this place for a certain time, and are punished in their pneumatic vehicle: for those that have sinned through the sweetness of pleasure can only be purified by the bitterness of pain.

Again, souls that are hurled into Tartarus are no longer moved: for it is the centre of the earth, and there is not any place beneath it. For, if they were moved, they would again begin to ascend; since all beyond the centre is upwards. Hence, the prison is there of dæmons and terrestrial presiding powers: for by Cerberus, and things of this kind, they signify dæmoniacal powers.

48.1   7 (See page 415, line 523d) Such, says Olympiodorus, is the fable, which, agreeably to the nature of a fable, does not preserve *together* things which always subsist together, but divides them into prior and posterior. It also first speaks of the more imperfect, and afterwards of the perfect: for it is necessary to advance from the imperfect to the perfect. When the fable, therefore, says that the judges were living judges of the living, judging on that very day in which any one happened to die, and that in consequence of this they judged badly; this signifies that we judge badly, but divine judges well. For they know

48.2   who ought to be sent to Tartarus, and who to the islands of the blessed. The fable, therefore, looking to our judgement, and beginning from the imperfect, says that formerly they judged badly; but, proceeding to the perfect, it says that they now judge justly. Jupiter does not effect this from himself, but at the request of Pluto, because subordinate convert themselves to superior natures.

Again, let us show what is meant by the judges being formerly in bodies, but now naked. Here, therefore, again the fable divides, and calls us from the more imperfect to the perfect. It is necessary to know, therefore, that our life is obscurely signified by this, both in the present state of existence, and hereafter. For, in this life, both we and those that we judge are in bodies; and hence deception takes place. In consequence of this, from judging passively, we do not send to Tartarus a depraved character, as one who is miserable, but, on the contrary, to the islands of the blessed. But, in another life, both the judges and those that are judged are naked.

48.6   8 (See page 415, line 523e) *Prometheus*, says Olympiodorus, is the inspective guardian of the descent of rational souls: for to exert a *providential energy* is the employment of the rational soul, and, prior to any thing else, to know itself.

Irrational natures, indeed, perceive through percussion, and prior to impulsion know nothing; but the rational nature is able, prior to information from another, to know what is useful. Hence, *Epimetheus* is the inspective guardian of the irrational soul, because it knows through percussion, and not prior to it. Prometheus, therefore, is that power which presides over the descent of rational souls. But *fire* signifies the rational soul itself; because, as fire tends upwards, so the rational soul pursues things on high. But you will say, Why is this fire said to have been stolen? Because that which is stolen is transferred from its proper place to one that is foreign. Since, therefore, the rational soul is sent from its proper place of abode on high, to earth, as to a foreign region, on this account the fire is said to be stolen. But why was it concealed in a reed? Because a reed is cavernous (συριγγωδης), and therefore signifies the flowing body (το ρευστον σωμα), in which the soul is carried. But why was the fire stolen, contrary to the will of Jupiter? Again, the fable speaks as a fable: for both Prometheus and Jupiter are willing that the soul should abide on high; but as it is requisite that she should descend, the fable fabricates particulars accommodated to the persons. And it represents, indeed, the superior character, which is Jupiter, as unwilling; for he wishes the soul always to abide on high: but the inferior character, Prometheus, obliges her to descend. Jupiter, 48.7 therefore, ordered *Pandora* to be made. And what else is this than *the irrational soul,*[†] which is of a feminine characteristic? For, as it was necessary that the soul should descend to these lower regions, but, being incorporeal and divine it was impossible for her to be conjoined with body without a medium, hence she becomes united with it through the irrational soul. But this irrational soul was called Pandora, because each of the Gods bestowed on it some particular gift. And this signifies that the illuminations which terrestrial natures receive take place through the celestial bodies.[‡]

49.2   9 (See page 415, line 523e) Asia is eastern, but Europe has a more western situation. But eastern parts are analogous to celestial natures, through light; but Europe through its curvature to terrestrial natures. Through these two, therefore, *viz.* Asia and Europe, a celestial and terrestrial polity are signified. There is also a middle polity, which Plato signifies through the doctrine of the extremes. For, having spoken of a celestial and terrestrial polity, he also

---

† The reader must remember, that the true man, or the rational soul, consists of *intellect, the dianoëtic power,* and *opinion;* but the summit of the irrational life is the *phantasy,* under which *desire,* like a many-headed savage beast, and *anger,* like a raging lion, subsist.

‡ For the irrational soul is an *immaterial body,* or in other words, *vitalized extension,* such as mathematical bodies which we frame in phantasy; and the celestial bodies are of this kind.

manifests that which has a middle subsistence; just as above, having spoken of those that are sent to the islands of the blessed, and those that are hurled into Tartarus, he likewise manifests souls which are characterized by a middle life.

49.3   In the next place, in order to know what is meant by the meadow, and the roads in which they judge, it is necessary to observe that the ancients call generation moist, on account of its flowing nature, and because the mortal life flourishes here. The place of judgement, therefore, is said to be in æther, after the places under the moon, and this is called a meadow through its moisture and variety.

49.6   10   (See page 416, line 524d)   We must not think from this, says Olympiodorus, that vice is natural to the soul. For, since the soul is incorporeal and immortal, if it naturally possessed vice, vice also would be immortal; which is absurd. By the term *from nature*, therefore, Plato means the soul living in conjunction with things base; so that vice is as it were coessentialized with it, the soul becoming subservient to the temperaments of the body. The soul, therefore, suffers punishment for this, because, being in short self-motive, and connected with anger and desire, and certain corporeal temperaments, she does not harmonize these, and lead them to a better condition, by her self-motive power. For, as a physician very properly scourges him who has an ophthalmy, not because he labours under this disease, but because he has touched and agitated his eyes, and has not preserved the form enjoined by the physician; in like manner the demiurgus punishes souls, as not subduing by their self-motive power the passions which were imparted to them for their good: for it is necessary that they should be vanquished, and employed to a good and not to a bad purpose.

50.2   11   (See page 417, line 525a)   Again, Olympiodorus observes as follows: It is necessary to know that souls which have moderately sinned, are punished but for a short time, and afterwards being purified ascend. But when I say they ascend, I do not mean locally, but vitally: for Plotinus says that the soul is elevated, not with feet, but by life. But souls that have committed the greatest crimes are *directly* sent to Tartarus; Plato using the word ευθυς *directly* instead of *swiftly*; a right line being the shortest of lines which have the same extremities. It is here however worth while to doubt why Plato says that they are always judged, and are never purified. What then, is there never any cessation of their punishment? If however the soul is always punished, and never enjoys good, she is always in vice. But punishment regards some good. It is not proper, therefore, that the soul should always continue in a state contrary to nature, but that she should proceed to a condition according to nature. If, therefore, punishment does not in any respect benefit us, nor bring us to a better condition, it is inflicted in vain. Neither God, however, not nature does any thing in vain.

50.3 　　What then are we to understand by the *ever*? We reply as follows: There are seven spheres, that of the moon, that of the sun, and those of the other planets; but the inerratic is the eighth sphere. The lunar sphere, therefore, makes a complete revolution more swiftly: for it is accomplished in thirty days. That of the sun is more slow: for it is accomplished in a year. That of Jupiter is still slower: for it is effected in twelve years. And much more that of Saturn; for it is completed in thirty years. The stars, therefore, are not conjoined with each other in their revolutions, except rarely. Thus, for instance, the sphere of Saturn and the sphere of Jupiter are conjoined with each other in their revolutions, in sixty years. For, if the sphere of Jupiter comes from the same to the same in twelve years, but that of Saturn in thirty years, it is evident that when Jupiter has made five, Saturn will have made two revolutions: for twice thirty is sixty, and so likewise is twelve times five; so that their revolutions will be conjoined in sixty years. Souls, therefore, are punished for such like periods. But the seven planetary spheres conjoin their revolutions with the inerratic sphere, through many myriads of years; and this is the period which Plato calls αει χρονον, for ever. Souls, therefore, that have been patricides or matricides, and universally souls of this description, are punished *for ever i.e.* during this period. Should however some one say, If a soul that has been guilty of parricide should die to-day, and sixty months, or years, or days after, a conjunction of the revolutions of the seven planets with the inerratic sphere should take place, will such a soul be punished only for that time? we reply, that such a soul is punished for as many years as are sufficient to effect this conjunction of revolutions. Thus, for instance, if this conjunction should take place in a thousand years, such a person when he dies will be punished for a thousand years. This time, therefore, and this period are denominated by Plato *always*; since it is impossible for the soul to be punished to infinity. Hence the soul converts herself to herself gradually, and again receives an organ on the earth adapted to her desert. It is necessary, therefore, to know that a pneumatic vehicle is suspended from the soul, and that this is punished by becoming either very much heated or refrigerated. It may also be said, that certain dreadful things present themselves to the view, such as the tragedian speaks of, *viz.* virgins with a bloody aspect, and the like.

50.4 　　It is likewise necessary to know that punishment makes the soul more sane, and renders her more adapted to be purified. We must not, therefore, think that punishments are purification itself. For, if the soul should be punished without being converted to herself, she would not be purified. When, therefore, she becomes sober and converted to herself, as being self-motive, then she is purified; since a physician also purifies a depraved body, but he does not render it strong by his purification. The diseased person however recovers his health afterwards, by taking care of himself, and not acting in a disorderly and irregular manner by the assumption of improper food. And again, as he who comes from health to disease forgets what he did when he was well, but as he recovers his health again remembers; so the soul coming into the present life forgets the punishments which she formerly endured, and thus acts erroneously. For, if she was always conscious of this, she would not sin. This forgetfulness, however, happens to her for a good purpose: for, if she remembered, and did not err through fear, she would preserve through fear her proper good, and thus would no longer be well conditioned, or act like a self-motive nature. She becomes oblivious, therefore, that she may explore good as being self-motive; since we also love servants, and consider them as of more worth when they serve us voluntarily, and not through fear.

Souls, therefore, are punished here, but they appear to be especially purified hereafter; since a life without body is more adapted to them. If however some one should ask, why the poor also are not punished who have the will to act unjustly, but only the powerful; since the poor, if they had instruments subservient to their will, such as wealth and the like, would likewise sin, we reply, that the poor also if they had an unjust will in the present life are punished; but the measures are different. For he whose injustice extended no further than to his will, is not punished similarly with him whose will has proceeded into energy, and who has acted unjustly.

50.1   12 (See page 417, line 525e) Ulysses, says Olympiodorus, descending into Hades, saw among others Sisyphus and Tityus and Tantalus. And Tityus he saw lying on the earth, and a vulture devouring his liver; the liver signifying that he lived solely according to the desiderative part of his nature, and through this was indeed internally prudent; but earth signifying the terrestrial condition of his prudence. But Sisyphus, living under the dominion of ambition and anger, was employed in continually rolling a stone up an eminence, because it perpetually descended again; its descent implying the vicious government of himself; and his rolling the stone, the hard, refractory, and as it were rebounding condition of his life. And lastly, he saw Tantalus extended by the side of a lake, and that there was a tree before him, with abundance of fruit on its branches, which he desired to gather, but it vanished from his view: and this indeed indicates that he lived under the dominion of the phantasy; but his hanging over the lake, and in vain attempting to drink, implies the elusive, humid, and rapidly-gliding condition of such a life.

THE

PHILEBUS

A DIALOGUE

CONCERNING

THE CHIEF GOOD OF MAN

INTRODUCTION

The design of this dialogue is to discover what is the chief good of man; and in order to effect this in the most perfect manner, it is divided into twelve parts. In the first part, therefore, Plato proposes the subject of discussion, *viz.* what the good of man is, and whether wisdom or pleasure is more conducive to the attainment of this good. In the second part, he explains the condition of a voluptuous life, and also of a life according to wisdom, that it may be seen which of the two most contributes to felicity, and also whether some third state of life will appear, which is better than either of these; and that, if this should be the case, it may be seen whether pleasure or wisdom is more allied to the perfection of this life. In the third part, he shows how this discussion should be conducted, and that division and definition should precede demonstration. In the fourth, he describes the conditions of the good, and shows that neither wisdom nor pleasure is the chief good of man. In the fifth part, he investigates the genus of pleasure, and also of wisdom, and unfolds those two great genera of things *bound* and *the infinite*, principles the next in dignity to the ineffable cause of all; from which two he exhibits that which is mixt, and presages the cause of the mixture. In the sixth part, because through those genera certain sparks of knowledge are enkindled, he enters on the comparison between pleasure and wisdom. In the seventh, he more largely explains the cause of the mixture, and continues the comparison more clearly. In the eighth part, the principles and genera being now unfolded, he investigates the differences; inquires, in what pleasure and pain consist, which among these are properly produced from passion, and how many parts they contain. In the ninth part, he investigates, in what science properly consists, and, having divided it, shows that a certain third life presides over wisdom, and wisdom over pleasure. In the tenth part, it appears how pleasure and wisdom are mingled together, and that our good consists in a composition of this kind. In the eleventh part, he inquires what it is in that composition from the dominion of which felicity is produced; in which part both our good and good itself become conspicuous. And, in the twelfth and last part, all the kinds of good which are pursuable as ends are enumerated in order, according to the relative value of each of them to man.

"The subject of this dialogue," says Mr. Sydenham, "is introduced by stating the different opinions of Socrates and Philebus concerning the nature of that good wherein the happiness of man is to be found;

opinions which, it seems, they had just before severally avowed. Philebus, a man strongly prepossessed with the doctrine of Aristippus, had asserted that this good was pleasure, meaning pleasurable sensation, or pleasure felt through the outward senses. On the other hand Socrates had supposed the sovereign good of man to be placed in mind, and in the energies of mind on mental subjects. Philebus, in support of his own assertion, had been haranguing for a long time together, after the manner of the sophists, until he found his spirits and imagination, or perhaps his stock of plausible arguments, quite exhausted. He had, therefore, desired his friend Protarchus, a young gentlemen who appears to have been a follower of Gorgias, to take up the controversy, and carry it on in his stead and behalf. Protarchus had consented, and had engaged himself so to do. Immediately on this engagement, at this very point of time the present dialogue commences: accordingly it is carried on chiefly between Socrates and Protarchus. But as Philebus is the principal person whose opinion combats against that of Socrates, and as no higher character is given to Protarchus than that of accessary, or second to Philebus, in this argumentative combat, the dialogue now before us, very properly and consistently with the rule which Plato seems to have laid down to himself in naming his dialogues, has the name given to it of Philebus."

This admirable dialogue is replete with some of the most important dogmas of the Platonic theology, as will appear from our notes upon it; and by those who are capable of knowing wholes from parts it may be collected from what is here said, that intellect has not the same order with the first cause of all. For, if our intellect is the image of the first intellect, and the good of the whole of our life is not to be defined according to this alone, it necessarily follows that the cause of good is established above intellectual perfection. *The Good*, therefore, or the ineffable principle of things, has a super-intellectual subsistence, agreeably to what is asserted in the Sixth Book of the *Republic*.[509b]

I shall only add, as is well observed by Mr. Sydenham, that the apparent form of this dialogue is *dramatic*; the genius of it, *didactic*; and the reasoning, for the most part *analytical*.

Note: Thomas Taylor added as notes much of Damascius' *Commentary on the Philebus*, at that time considered to be written by Olympiodorus, a full translation of which was translated by L G Westerink, North Holland Publishing House, 1959. We have followed Westerink's pagination. PT.

THE

PHILEBUS

PERSONS OF THE DIALOGUE

SOCRATES, PROTARCHUS, PHILEBUS

SCENE - The LYCEUM.

11a   SOC. Consider† now, Protarchus, what the doctrine of Philebus is, which you are taking upon yourself to second and support; and what things said by me you are going to controvert, if they should be found

b   such as are not agreeable to your mind. Will you permit me to state, in a summary way, the difference between my positions and those of Philebus?

PROT. By all means.

SOC. Philebus then says, that the good of all animals is joy, and pleasure, and delight,‡ and whatever else is congenial to them, and harmonizes with all other things of the same kind. And what I contend for is, that those things are not the best; but that to be wise, and to understand,[1] and to remember, and whatever is of kin to them, right opinions, and true reasonings, are better things than pleasure, and more

c   eligible to all beings universally, that is, to such as are capable of receiving the participation of them; and that to all beings which have that capacity, the actual partaking of them is of all things the most advantageous, not only to those beings which are, but to those also

---

† The beginning of this dialogue supposes that much conversation had passed, immediately before, between Socrates and Philebus. -S.

‡ This part of the sentence, to give it a literal translation, runs thus: *that it is good for all animals to rejoice, and (to feel) pleasure and delight*, etc. - But in translating it we chose to give it that meaning which is rightly presumed by Socrates to be agreeable to the sentiments of Philebus; for otherwise there would be no opposition between the opinion of Philebus and his own. -S.

which are to come. Do we not, O Philebus, you and I, severally lay down some such hypotheses as these?

PHIL. Exactly such, O Socrates!

SOC. And will you, Protarchus, take up the controversy, as I have just now stated it?

PROT. Of necessity I must.[†] For Philebus, the champion of our side, is tired and gives out.

SOC. Now it is right and proper for us to discover, by all means possible, the full force and meaning of both those hypotheses; and not to give over till we have determined the controversy between them.

PROT. I agree with you, it is.

SOC. Let us agree in this too, besides.

PROT. In what?

SOC. That we should, each of us,[‡] endeavour to set forth what state and what affection[2] of the soul is able, according to our different hypotheses, to procure for every man a happy life. Is it not our business so to do?

PROT. Certainly it is.

SOC. Well then: You say that it is that of rejoicing; we, that it is that of understanding and thinking rightly.

PROT. True.

SOC. But what if there should appear some other, preferable to both of these, but more nearly of kin to pleasure? should we not in this case be both of us confuted, and obliged to yield the preference to a life which gives the stable possession of those very things wherein you place human happiness? However, at the same time it must be agreed, that a life of pleasure would be found more eligible than a life of knowledge or intellection.

PROT. Without doubt.

---

† Necessity is threefold: for it is either self-perfect, associating with *The Good*; or material, with which indigence and imbecility associate; or it is as that which is referred to an end, as navigation with a view to gain. Thus Proclus. - T.

‡ The Greek of this sentence, in all the editions of Plato, is αυτων εκατερος. But all the translators interpret, as if they read in the MSS ημων εκατερος: a reading which is clearly agreeable to the sense of the passage, and makes it easier to be understood. In the printed reading the word αυτων must refer to λογων, which is more remote, and has been rather implied than expressed; αυτων εκατερος will then mean *the argument of each*; but to say, *the argument should endeavour*, is in a style too figurative and bold to be used by any prosaic writer. - S.

SOC. But if that better state of the soul should appear to be more nearly allied to knowledge, in that case, knowledge would be found to have the advantage over pleasure, and pleasure must give place. Do you not agree with me, that these things are so? or how otherwise say ye that they are?

PROT. To me, I must confess, they seem to be as you represent them.

SOC. But to Philebus how seem they? What say you, Philebus?

PHIL. To me pleasure seems, and will always seem, to be the superior, whatever it be compared with. And you, Protarchus, will be at length convinced of it yourself.

PROT. After having resigned to me the management of the debate, you can no longer be the master of what should be yielded to Socrates, and what should not.

b PHIL. You are in the right. But, however, I have discharged my duty; and I here call the Goddess herself to witness it.

PROT. We too are witnesses of the same; and can testify your making of the assertion which you have just made. But now, as to that examination, O Socrates! which is to follow after what you and I have agreed in, whether Philebus be willing to consent, or however he may be disposed, let us try to go through with it, and bring it to a conclusion.

SOC. By all means, let us; beginning with that very Goddess who, according to him, is called Venus, but whose true name is Pleasure.[3]

PROT. Perfectly right.

c SOC. The fear[4] which I have always in me concerning the proper names of the Gods, is no ordinary kind of fear; but surpasses the greatest dread. Hence, in the present case, with regard to Venus, whatever name be agreeable to the Goddess, by that would I choose to call her. But as to pleasure,[†] how various a thing it is, I well know. And with this, as I just now said, ought we to begin, by considering and inquiring into the nature of pleasure first. For we hear it called, indeed, by one single name, as if it were one simple thing: it assumes, however, all sorts of

d forms, even such as are the most unlike one to another. For observe: we say that the intemperate man has pleasure; and that the temperate man has pleasure also, - pleasure in being what he is, that is, temperate. Again: we say that pleasure attends on folly, and on the man who is full of foolish opinions and foolish hopes; that pleasure attends also on the

---

† Pleasure subsists together with motion; for it is the attendant of it. But the motion of intellect is an immutable energy; that of soul, a mutable energy; and that of an animal, a passive energy. But that of a plant is passion only. - T. [.35]

man who thinks wisely, - pleasure in that very mental energy, his thinking wisely. Now any person who would affirm these pleasures to be of similar kind, would be justly deemed to want understanding.

PROT. The pleasures which you mention, O Socrates, are indeed produced by contrary causes; but in the pleasures themselves there is no contrariety. For how should pleasure not be similar to pleasure, itself to itself, the most similar of all things?[†]

SOC. Just so, colour too, my friend, differs not from colour in this respect, that it is colour, all. And yet, we all of us know that black, besides being different from white, happens to be also its direct contrary. So figure, too, is all one with figure, after the same manner, in the general. But as to the parts of that one general thing, some are directly contrary to others; and between the rest there happens to be a kind of infinite diversity. And many other things we shall find to be of this nature. Believe not then this position, that things the most contrary are all of them one. And I suspect that we shall also find some pleasures quite contrary to other pleasures.

PROT. It may be so. But how will that hurt my side of the question?

SOC. In that *you* call them, dissimilar as they are, by another name; (shall we say?) for all *pleasant* things you call *good*. Now that all pleasant things are pleasant, admits of no dispute. But though many of them are evil, and many indeed good, as I readily acknowledge, yet all of them you call good; and at the same time you confess them to be dissimilar in their natures, when a man forces you to this confession. What then is that, the same in every pleasure, in the evil pleasures equally with the good, from which you give to all pleasures the denomination of good?

PROT. What is that, O Socrates, which you say? Do you imagine that any person, after having asserted that pleasure is the good, will admit your supposition? or will suffer it to pass uncontradicted, that only some pleasures are good, but that other pleasures are evil?

---

† This was the very language, or manner of expression, used by a sect of philosophers called Cyrenaics, from Cyrene, the native city of Aristippus, their master. For the Cyrenaics held, says Laërtius, μη διαφερειν ηδονην ηδονης, *that pleasure differs not from pleasure.* Whence it appears probable, that Philebus derived his notions and expressions on this point from some of the disciples of Aristippus, if not from Aristippus himself. For this philosopher, after he had for some time conversed with Socrates, for the sake of whose conversation he came to Athens, departed thence, and went to Ægina; where he professed the teaching of philosophy, and where he resided till after the death of Socrates. - S.

c SOC. However, you will acknowledge that pleasures are unlike one to another, and some even contrary to others?

PROT. By no means; so far as they are pleasures, every one of them.

SOC. We are now brought back again to the same position, O Protarchus! There is no difference between pleasure and pleasure; all pleasures are alike, we must say: and the similar instances, just now produced, in colours and in figures, have had, it seems, no effect upon

d us. But we shall try, and talk after the manner of the meanest arguers, and mere novices in dialectic.

PROT. How do you mean?

SOC. I mean, that if I, to imitate you, and dispute with you in your own way, should dare to assert that two things, the most unlike, are of all things the most like to each other, I should say nothing more than what you say: so that both of us would appear to be rawer disputants than we ought to be; and the subject of our dispute would thus slip out of our hands, and get away. Let us resume it, therefore, once more: and, perhaps, by returning to similitudes,[5] we may be induced to make some concessions each of us to the other.

e PROT. Say how.

SOC. Suppose me to be the party questioned; and suppose yourself, Protarchus, to interrogate me.

PROT. Concerning what?

SOC. Concerning prudence, and science, and intelligence, and all the rest of those things which in the beginning of our conversation I said were good, when I was asked what sort of a thing good was; must I not acknowledge these to be attended with the same circumstance which attends those other things celebrated by you?

PROT. What circumstance?

SOC. The sciences, viewed all of them together, will seem to both of us not only many, and of diverse kinds, but dissimilar too, some to

14a others. Now if besides there should appear a contrariety[†] in any way, between some of them and others, should I deserve to be disputed with any longer, if, fearful of admitting contrariety between the sciences, I were to assert that no one science was dissimilar to any other science? For then the matter in debate between us, as if it were a mere fable, being destroyed, would vanish: while we saved ourselves by an illogical retreat. But such an event ought not to happen, except this part of it,

---

† *Contrariety* in the sciences is nothing more than *diversity*. For one science is not in opposition to, or hostile to, another; since secondary are subservient to prior sciences, and from them derive their proper principles. - T.

- the saving of ourselves. And now the equality, which appears thus far between your hypothesis and mine, I am well enough pleased with. The pleasures happen to be found many and dissimilar; many also and diverse are the sciences. The difference, however, between your good and mine, O Protarchus, let us not conceal: but let us dare to lay it fairly and openly before us both; that we may discover, (if those who are closely examined will make any discovery,) whether pleasure or wisdom ought to be pronounced the chief good of man, or whether any third thing, different from either: since it is not, as I presume, with this view that we contend, that my hypothesis, or that yours, may prevail over its antagonist; but that which hath the truth on its side, we are both of us to contend for and support.

PROT. This is certainly our duty.

SOC. But this point further we should, both of us together, settle on the surest ground.

PROT. What point do you mean?

SOC. That which puzzles and perplexes all persons who choose to make it the subject of their conversation: nay, sometimes some others, who have no such intention, are led to it unawares in conversation upon other subjects.

PROT. Express what you mean in plainer terms.

SOC. I mean that which fell in our way but just now, the nature of which is so full of wonders. For that many are one,[†] and that one is many, is wonderful to have it said; and either of those positions is easy to be controverted.

PROT. Do you mean such positions as this, - that I Protarchus, who am by nature one person, am also many? and such as these others, - that myself, and other persons the reverse of me, - the great also and the little, the heavy and the light, are one and the same? with a thousand positions more which might be made of like kind?

SOC. The wonders, O Protarchus, which you have now spoken of, relating to the one and many, have been hackneyed in the mouths of the vulgar; but by the common agreement, as it were, of all men, they are now laid aside, and are never to be mentioned: for they are considered as childish and easy objections, and great impediments also to discourse. It is now also agreed, never to introduce into conversation, as an instance of one and many, the members or parts into which any single thing may be considered as divisible. Because, when a respondent has once admitted and avowed, that all these [*members* or *parts*] are that *one*

---

† See the *Parmenides*. - T.

thing, which is thus at the same time *many*, he is refuted and laughed at by his questioner, for having being driven to assert such monstrous absurdities as these, - that a single one is an infinite multitude, and an infinite multitude only one.

15a   PROT. What other things, then, not hackneyed among the vulgar, nor as yet universally agreed on, do you mean, O Socrates, relating to this point?

SOC. I mean, young man, when a thing is proposed to be considered, which is one, but is not of the number or nature of things generated and perishable. For as to the ones of this latter sort, it is agreed, as I just now said, to reject them, as unworthy of a serious confutation. The ones which I mean are such as man, ox, beauty, good. When these *henads*,† or such as these, are proposed for subjects of debate, much serious attention is given them; and when they come to be divided, any one of them into many, much doubt and controversy arises.

PROT. Upon what points?

b   SOC. In the first place, whether such monads should be deemed to have true being. In the next place, how it is that these monads, every one of them being always the same, and never generated, nor ever to be destroyed, have, notwithstanding, one and the same stability common to them all.⁶ And lastly, Whether we should suppose every such monad to be dispersed and spread abroad amongst an infinity of things generated or produced, and thus, from being one, to become many; or whether we should suppose it to remain entire, itself by itself,‡ separate and apart from that multitude. But, of all suppositions, this might appear the most impossible, that one and the same thing should be in a

c   single one, and in many, at the same time. These points, O Protarchus, which regard such instances as I have mentioned, and not such as were mentioned by you, these are they, which, for want of being rightly

---

† Plato, says Olympiodorus, calls the summits of forms *monads* and *henads*. He calls them *henads*, with reference to the appropriate multitude of which they are the leaders; but *monads*, with reference to the superessential. Or we may say, that there are twofold summits of forms, the one *essential*, and the other *characterized by unity*, as it is said in the *Parmenides*.[131a] - See the Notes on the first hypothesis of the *Parmenides*. From hence the ignorance of Cudworth is apparent, who, in his *Intellectual System*, p. 555, considers the doctrine of *henads* derived from the first one, or *The One Itself*, as a fiction of the latter Platonists. - T. [.44]

‡ In the Greek we here read - αυτην αυτης χωρις. But it is presumed that we ought to read - αυτην εφ' αυτης χωρις. - S.

settled, create all the difficulties and doubts we meet with in discourse;
but when once they are settled rightly, they clear the way with ease.

PROT. Then, it seems, we are to labour these points first.

SOC. I should think we ought.

PROT. And that we consent to it, you may take for granted, all of us
here. Philebus, indeed, it is best perhaps, at present, not to discompose
by asking him questions, now that he is quiet.

d   SOC. Very well; but in what way shall we begin the discussion of
these points in so wide a field of controversy? Shall we begin thus?

PROT. How?

SOC. We say, in speaking of these monads, (each of which is one, but,
on a logical examination of it, appears to be divisible into many,) that
they run throughout every sentence in our discourse, every where and
always; and that, as their being shall never have an end, so neither does
it first begin in the present age. Now this perpetual attendant upon all
speech proceeds, as it seems to me, from something immortal and
undecaying within ourselves. And hence it is, that the youth every

e   where, when they have thus had a taste of it, are overjoyed at their
having thus found a treasure of wisdom. Transported, therefore, with
the delight it gives them, they apply it to every subject of discourse:
sometimes they collect particulars from all quarters, and roll them into
one; then they unroll them again, and part them asunder. After having
in this way puzzled themselves in the first place, they question and
puzzle the next person at hand, whether he be their equal in age, or

16a   younger than themselves, or older, sparing neither father nor mother,
nor any one else who will attend to them, scarcely other animals more
than man: it is certain they would not exempt any who speak a foreign
language only, could they but find somewhere an interpreter.

PROT. Do you not see, O Socrates, how numerous we are, and that
all of us are young? and are you not afraid that, if you rail at us, we
shall all join Philebus, and attack you jointly? However (for we
apprehend your meaning), if you can by any means or contrivance easily

b   rid us of these perplexities, which hinder the progress of our inquiry,
and can devise some better way of managing the argument, do you but
give your mind to the prosecution of it, and we shall do our utmost to
follow and attend you. For the present debate is of no trifling concern,
Socrates.

SOC. Indeed it is not, O boys! as Philebus called you. No better way
then is there, nor can there be, than that, which I am always a great
lover of; but often before now it has slipped away from my sight, and
has left me, as it were, in a desert, at a loss whither to turn me.

PROT. Let us but know what way you mean.

c   SOC. To point out the way is not very difficult; but to travel in it, is the most difficult of all things. For all such human inventions as depend on art are, in this way, discovered and laid open. Consider then the way which I am speaking of.

PROT. Do but tell it us then.

SOC. A gift[7] of the Gods to men, as it appears to me, by a certain Prometheus[8] hurled from the Gods along with a fire the most luminous. From the men of ancient times, men better than we are, and dwelling nigher to the Gods, this tradition of it hath descended to us, - that those

d   beings said to be for ever derive their essence from one and many; and therefore have in themselves bound and infinity connatural to them: that, being in the midst of things so constituted as they are, we ought to suppose and to search for some one idea in every thing around us; for that, since it is there, we shall, on searching, be sure to find it: that, after we have found it, we are next to look for two, if two only are next; otherwise three, or some other number: again, that every one of this number we are to examine in like manner: until at length a man not only perceives, that the one, with which he began, is one, and many, and infinite, but discovers also how many it contains: for, that a man never should proceed to the idea of infinite, and apply it immediately to any number, before he has fully discovered all the definite number

e   which lies between the infinite and the one: but that, having completed this discovery, we should then finish our search; and dismissing into infinity every one of all those numbers, we should bid farewell to them. The Gods, as I before said, have given us to consider things in this way, and in this way to learn them, and teach them one to another. But the

17a   wise men of these days take any monad whatever, and divide it into many with more conciseness than they ought, and with more prolixity too, since they never come to an end: for immediately after the monad they introduce infinity, overlooking all the intermediate numbers; the express mention of which, or the omission of them, distinguishes such dialectical and fair debates as ours, from such as are contentious and sophistical.

PROT. Part of what you say, Socrates, I seem to apprehend tolerably well: but the meaning of some things which you have now said, I should be glad to hear you express in plainer terms.

b   SOC. The whole of what I have said, Protarchus, is evident in letters. In these, therefore, which have been taught you from your childhood, you may easily apprehend my meaning.

PROT. How in letters?

SOC. Voice, that issues out of the human mouth, may be considered as one general thing, admitting of an infinite number of articulations, not only in all men taken together, but also in every individual man.

PROT. Without doubt.

SOC. Now we are not made knowing in speech, or sound articulate, through the knowledge either of the infinity or of the oneness of its nature: but to know how many, and what, are the parts into which it is naturally divided, - this it is which makes any of us a grammarian, or skilled in grammar.

PROT. Most certainly.

SOC. And further, that by which a man comes to be skilled in music is this very thing.

PROT. How so?

c　SOC. Musical sound,[9] which is the subject matter of this art, may be considered in itself as one general thing.

PROT. Without dispute.

SOC. And let us suppose two kinds of it, the grave and the acute, and a third kind between those two, the homotonous, or how otherwise?[10]

PROT. Musical sound in general is so to be distinguished.

SOC. But with the knowledge of this distinction only, you would not yet be skilled in music; though without knowing it you would be, as to music, quite worthless.

PROT. Undoubtedly.

d　SOC. But, my friend, when you have learnt the intervals between all musical sounds, from the more acute to the more grave, how many they are in number, and into what sorts they are distinguished; when you have also learnt the bounds of these intervals, and how many systems are composed out of them;[11] (which our predecessors having discovered, delivered down to us, who come after them, by the name of harmonies;[12] and having discovered other such affections[13] in the motions of the body, and in words,† measuring these by numbers, they have taught us to call them rhythms‡ and metres; bidding us to infer from hence, that every *one-and-many* ought to be searched into and examined

e　in the same way;) when you have learnt all those things, and comprehend them in this ample manner, with all their several diversities and distinctions, then are you become skilled in music. And by

---

† In the printed Greek of this passage we read only, - ευτε ταις κινηδεδιν αυ του δωματος - immediately after which, - εντε ρημαδιν, - ought to follow, but is omitted. -S.

‡ Rhythm, in general, is an order of homogeneous motions measured by time.

considering in the same way the nature of any other kind of being, when you thus fully comprehend it, you are become in that respect intelligent and wise. But the infinite multitude of individuals, their infinite variety, and the infinite changes incident to each, keep you *infinitely far off* from intelligence and wisdom: and as they make you to be behind other men in every path of knowledge, they make you inconsiderable, and of no account, not to be numbered amongst the knowing in any subject; because you never consider any thing thoroughly, and are unable to give a true account of it, never looking at the definite number which it contains.

18a   PROT. Excellently well, O Philebus, as it appears to me, has Socrates spoken in what he has now said.

PHIL. It appears so too to me myself. But how does all this speech of his concern our controversy? What was the design or drift of it?

SOC. A very pertinent question, O Protarchus, this, proposed to us by Philebus.

PROT. Indeed it is: and by all means give it an answer.

SOC. That will I do, as soon as I have gone through the little yet remaining of the subject on which I have been speaking. For, as the man who applies himself to the consideration of any kind of things whatever ought not, as I have said, to throw his eye at once upon the infinite, but upon some definite number in the first place; so, on the

b   other hand, when a man is obliged to set out from the infinite, he ought not to mount up immediately to the one, but to some certain number, in each of whose ones a certain multitude is contained; and thus gradually rising from a greater to a less number, to end in one. As an instance of what I have now said, let us resume the consideration of letters.

PROT. In what way?

SOC. Whoever it was, whether some God, or some divine man, (the Egyptian reports say that his name was Thoth,[†]) who first contemplated the infinite nature of the human voice, he observed, that amongst the infinity of the sounds it uttered the vowel sounds[‡] were more than one,

c   they were many. Again, other utterances he observed, which were not

---

† See the Notes on the *Phædrus*, [TTS vol. XI, note 33, p. 421] - T.

‡ That is, sounds purely vocal; whence the letters by which they are distinguished are called vowels; in the utterance of which sounds the voice solely is employed, whilst the other organs of speech remain inactive. - S.

indeed vowels,[14] but partook, however, of some kind of vocal sound;[†] and that of these also there was a certain number.[‡] A third sort of letters also he set apart, those which are now called mutes by us.[15] After this he distinguished every one of these letters which are without any vocal sound, whether perfect or imperfect:[16] the vowels also, and those of middle sort, every one of them, he distinguished in the same manner: and when he had discovered how many letters there were of each sort, to every one, and to all of them together, he gave the name of element. But perceiving that none of us could understand any one of them by itself alone, without learning them all, he considered that this connection, or common bond between them, was one; and that all these letters made in a manner but one thing: and as he perceived that there was one art in all these, he called it, from its subject matter, the art of letters.

d

PHIL. This which Socrates now says, O Protarchus, I understand still more plainly than what he said just before; and am at no loss to apprehend what relation each of the subjects about which he has spoken has to the other. But as to that article in which his argument on the first of those subjects appeared to me to be defective, I am at a loss still.

SOC. To know what those instances are to the purpose; is not this your meaning?

PHIL. Just so. This very thing it is that Protarchus and myself are all this while in search of.

e

SOC. In search still, do you say, when you are just now arrived at it?

PHIL. How so?

SOC. Was not the point originally in dispute between us this: Whether wisdom or pleasure was the more eligible?

PHIL. Certainly it was.

SOC. And do we not admit that each of them is one thing?

PHIL. Without doubt.

SOC. Now then must come this question, arising naturally from what was said a little before the mention of music and grammar, - In what way (or by what division) are wisdom and pleasure, each of them, one and many? or how is it, that neither of them breaks into infinite multitude directly; but that each contains some certain number before it pass into infinity?

---

† These were by the old grammarians called ημιφωνα, *semi-vowels*; because, in their very formation by the organs of speech, they are, of necessity, so far accompanied by the voice, as to give a half-vocal sound, without the open aid of any vowel. - S.

‡ The Greek grammarians enumerate eight of these semi-vowels. -S.

19a PROT. Upon no trivial question, O Philebus, on a sudden has Socrates, after having led us a large round-about way, I know not how, thrown us. And now consider, which of us two shall answer to the question he has proposed. It would be ridiculous in me, who have undertaken the support of your argument, to make an absolute revolt on account of my disability in regard to the present question; and so to remit over again to you the task of giving an answer to it: but I think

b it would be much more ridiculous for both of us to fail. Consider, then, what we shall do in this case, where Socrates seems to interrogate us concerning the species of pleasure; - whether it is divisible into different species, or not; and, if it be, what is the number of these species, and how they differ in their nature: and the like questions he seems to put to us concerning knowledge and intelligence.

SOC. Your conjecture is perfectly right, O son of Callias! and, if we are not able to answer to these questions upon every monad, as to its likeness, sameness, and contrariety, - unless, I say, we can do this, - the instances just now produced have shown, that none of us, in any matter we had to handle, would ever be of any worth at all.

c PROT. The case, O Socrates, seems indeed to be not very different from your representation of it. Well, it is certainly a fine thing to know all things, for a wise and prudent person: but I think the best thing next to that is for a man not to be ignorant of himself. With what design I have now said this, I shall proceed to tell you. This conversation, O Socrates, you have granted to us all, and have given yourself up to us, for the purpose of investigating what is the best of human goods. For, when Philebus had said that it consisted in pleasure, and delight, and joy, and all things of the like nature, you opposed him on this point, and said, it consisted not in these things, but in those which we often

d repeat the mention of; and we are right in so doing, that the opinions on each side, being always fresh in our memories, may the more easily be examined. You then, it seems, say, what I shall be right in again repeating, that intellect, science, art, and whatever is allied to them, are better things than Pleasure with her allies; and therefore, that the possession, not of these, but of those greater goods, ought to be the object of our aim. Now these positions being laid down severally on each side, as subject-matters of our debate, we in a jocose way threatened, that we would not suffer you to go home quietly before it

e was brought to a fair determination. You complied, and promised us to contribute all you could towards the accomplishment of that end. We insist therefore that, as children say, you must not take away again what is fairly given. But, in the present inquiry, forbear proceeding in your usual way.

SOC. What way do you mean?

20a   PROT. Bringing us into straits and embarrassments; propounding questions to which we should not be able on the sudden to give a proper answer. For we are not to imagine that our present inquiry is brought to a conclusion, merely because all of us are at a loss what to answer. If, therefore, we are unable to extricate ourselves from these difficulties, you must help us out; for so you promised. Consider, then, what to do on this occasion; whether to distinguish pleasure and knowledge, each of them, into their proper species; or whether to pass it by, if you choose to take a different way, and can find some other means of deciding the matter now controverted between us.

b   SOC. No harm then need I be afraid of any longer to myself, since you have said this.[†] For your leaving to my own choice what ways and means to make use of, frees me from all apprehensions on my own private account. But, to make it still easier to me, some God, I think, has brought things to my remembrance.

PROT. How do you mean? What things?

SOC. Having formerly heard, either in a dream,[‡] or broad awake, certain sayings, I have them now again present to my mind; - sayings concerning pleasure and knowledge, that neither of them is of itself good, but some third thing, different from both of those, and better

c   than either. Now if this should discover itself to us clearly, pleasure is then to be dismissed from any pretensions to the victory. For we should then no longer expect to find that pleasure and good are the same thing: or how say you?

PROT. Just so.

SOC. We shall have no occasion then, in my opinion, for distinguishing the several species of pleasure. And in the progress of our inquiry it will appear more evidently still that I am in the right.

---

    † Alluding to those jocular threats employed by the young gentlemen, then in the Lycæum, and gathered around Socrates, to engage him in this dialectic inquiry. - S.

    ‡ Olympiodorus here justly observes, that we possess the reasons of things as in a dream, with respect to a separate life supernally perfected; but as in a vigilant state with respect to the exertion of them through sense. Perhaps however, says he, it is better to consider the vigilant state with respect to the distinct evolution, but the dreaming state, with respect to the indistinct subsistence of knowledge. -T. [.72]

PROT. Having begun so happily, proceed, and finish with the same success.

SOC. Let us, first, agree upon a few little points beside.

PROT. What are those?

SOC. In what condition or state of being is *The Good*? Must it of necessity be perfect?[17] or may it want perfection?

PROT. Of all things, O Socrates, it is the most perfect.

SOC. Well; and is it also sufficient?

PROT. Without doubt: and in this respect it excels all other things.

SOC. But further: This also, I presume, is of all things the most necessary to say of it, that every being to whom it is known, hunts after, and desires it, as choosing the possession of it above all things; and, indeed, caring for no other things, except such as are constantly attended with the enjoyment of good.

PROT. There is no possibility of contradicting this.

SOC. Now, then, let us consider and judge of the life of pleasure and the life of knowledge: and to do this the better, let us view them each apart from the other.

PROT. How do you mean?

SOC. Thus: Let us suppose a life of pleasure, unaccompanied by intelligence; and, on the other hand, a life of intelligence, unaccompanied by pleasure. For, if either of them be good, it must be complete and sufficient, in want of no aid from any other quarter. But, if either of them should appear to be indigent of aught, or insufficient, we are no longer to imagine this to be that real and true good we are in search of.

PROT. In such a case, how could we?

SOC. Shall we then examine their pretensions thus separately, making your own mind the judge?

PROT. With all my heart.

SOC. Answer then to my questions.

PROT. Propose them.

SOC. Would you, Protarchus, accept the offer, were it made you, to live all your life with a sense and feeling of pleasures the most exquisite?

PROT. Undoubtedly. Why not?

SOC. Suppose you were in full possession of this, would you not think that something beside was still wanting to you?

PROT. I certainly should not.

SOC. Consider now, whether you would not be in want of wisdom, and intelligence, and reasoning, and such other things as are the sisters of these; at least whether you would not want to *see* something.

PROT. Why should I, when I had in a manner all things, in having continual joy?

SOC. Living thus then continually all your life, would the most exquisite pleasures give you any joy?

PROT. Why not?

SOC. Having neither intellect, nor memory, nor science, nor opinion, - in the first place of this very thing, your possession of joy, you must of necessity be ignorant, and unable to say whether you then had any joy, or not, being void of all just discernment or knowledge of things present.

PROT. I must.

c SOC. Being also void of memory, it would be impossible for you to remember that you ever had any joy; or to preserve even the least memorial of a joy then present: wanting also right opinion, you could not so much as think you had any joy, though in the midst of it: unable also to reason or draw consequences, you could not possibly conclude that ever you should have any joy to come. Thus you would live the life, not of a man, but of a sea-sponge, or of an oyster. Are these things so? or ought we to think otherwise concerning them?

d PROT. A life of mere pleasure must be such as you have described it.

SOC. Do we think, then, that such a life is eligible?

PROT. The description of it, O Socrates, has silenced me entirely for the present.

SOC. Nay; let us not shrink so soon from pursuing our inquiries; but proceed to the consideration of that other life, the life of intellect.

PROT. What kind of life is that?

e SOC. Let us consider, whether any of us would choose to live with wisdom, and intellect, and science, and a perfect memory of all things; but without partaking of pleasure, whether great or small; and, on the other hand, without partaking of pain; wholly exempt from all feelings of either kind.

PROT. To me, O Socrates, neither of these lives appears eligible; and I think never would appear so to any other man.

22a SOC. What think you of a middle life, where both of them are mixed together - a life composed of the other two?

PROT. Composed of pleasure do you mean, on the one hand, and of intellect and wisdom on the other hand?

SOC. Just so: such a life do I mean.

PROT. Every man would certainly prefer such a kind of life to either of the other two.

SOC. Perceive we now what the result is of our discoursing thus far on the subject now before us?

b PROT. Perfectly well; it is this: that three lives have been proposed for our consideration, and that neither of the two first-mentioned appears sufficient or eligible for any one, neither for man, nor any other animal.

SOC. Is it not evident, then, with regard to the point in controversy, that neither of those two lives can give the possession of the good? for, whichever of them had such a power, that life would be sufficient, perfect, and eligible also to all those animals[†] who are capable of living in the continual enjoyment of the good all their lives. And whoever of us should give any other life the preference to that, would make his election contrary to the nature of the truly eligible, though not willingly, because through ignorance, or some unhappy necessity.

PROT. What you say is highly probable indeed.

c SOC. That we ought not to think that Goddess of Philebus to be the same thing with the good, has been shown, I think, sufficiently.

PHIL. Neither is that intellect of yours, O Socrates, the good; for it will be found deficient in the same respects.

SOC. Mine perhaps, O Philebus, may; but not that intellect which is divine and true; for it is otherwise, I presume, with this. However, I do

d not contend for the chief prize of victory, in behalf of the life of intellect against the middle or mixed life. But what to do with the second prize, and which life to bestow it on, is next to be considered. For the cause of that happiness which the mixed life affords, one of us, perhaps, may ascribe to intellect, the other of us to pleasure. And thus, neither of these two would be man's sovereign good, and yet one or other of them may perhaps be supposed the cause of it. Now on this point I would still more earnestly contend against Philebus, - that not pleasure, but intellect, is the nearest allied, and the most similar to that, whatever it be, by the possession of which the mixed life becomes eligible and good. And if this account be true, pleasure can never be said to have any just pretensions either to the first or to the second prize

---

† In the Greek, - πασι φυτοις και ζωοις, *to all plants and animals*. But are plants capable of living a life of sensual pleasure? or brute animals, a life of science and understanding? We are, therefore, inclined to think, that Plato's own words were πασι τοις ζωοις· for immediately he subjoins an explanation of his meaning, and limits the word πασι, *all*, to such only as are endued with reason; and that the word φευ was written in the margin of some manuscript, opposite to the words πασι τοις by a reader, astonished at the boldness of the expression πασι τοις ζωοις, and not sufficiently attentive to the qualifying words subjoined. - S.

e　　of excellence. Still further is she from coming in for the third prize, if any credit may be given for the present to that intellect of mine.

PROT. Indeed, O Socrates, it seems to me that Pleasure is now fallen:
23a　your reasons have been like so many blows given her; under the force of which, fighting for the master-prize, she lies vanquished. But I think, however, that we must say it was prudent in Intellect not to contend for that prize; for she would otherwise have met with the same fate. Now if Pleasure should also lose the prize of second value, as already she has lost the highest, she must entirely fall into disgrace with her own lovers: for even to them she would no longer appear to merit such honour as they paid to her before.

SOC. Well then; is it not the better way to dismiss her now directly, and not give her pain, by inspecting into her too nicely, and discovering all her imperfections?

PROT. What you now say goes for nothing, Socrates.

b　　SOC. Do you mean, because I supposed an impossible thing when I supposed that pain might be given to pleasure?

PROT. Not on that account only, but because you are sensible that none of us will give you a discharge before you have brought these arguments to a conclusion.

SOC. Ah! the copious matter of argument, O Protarchus, still behind! and scarcely is any part of it very manageable on the present occasion.[†] For, whoever stands forth as the champion of Intellect to win the second prize for her, must, as it appears to me, take another way of combating, and has need of other weapons different from those reasons I before made use of: some, however, of the same may, perhaps, be of use again. Must we then proceed in that manner?

PROT. By all means.

c　　SOC. But let us begin cautiously, and endeavour to lay down right principles.

PROT. What principles do you mean?

SOC. All things which are now in the universe let us divide into two sorts, or rather, if you please, into three.

---

† Aldus's edition of Plato, by omitting the word οὐδε in this sentence, gives a quite contrary turn to it. Stephens, in his edition, has inserted the οὐδε: and this reading we have preferred to the former; because it makes much better sense, and is agreeable also to Ficinus's translation from the Medicean manuscript. It is strange that Grynæus, who undertook to revise that translation, should depart from it here, where it is evidently right, to follow the erroneous reading in the Aldine edition. Cornarius, Serranus, Bembo, and Grou, were not so misled. - S.

PROT. You should tell us what difference between things it is, with respect to which you make that division.

SOC. Some things which have been already mentioned let us reassume.

PROT. What things?

SOC. God, we said, has exhibited[18] *the infinite*, and also *the bound* of beings.

PROT. Very true.

d SOC. Let us take these for two of the species of things; and for a third let us take that, which is composed of those two mixed together. But I deserve, methinks, to be laughed at for pretending thus to distinguish things, and to enumerate their several species.

PROT. Why so, my good friend?

SOC. A fourth kind appears to have been omitted by me.

PROT. Say, What?

SOC. Of that commixture, the combination of the former two, consider the cause: and beside those three species, set me down this cause[†] for a fourth.

PROT. Will you not want a fifth species too, for a cause of disunion and separation?

e SOC. Perhaps I may; but not, I believe, at present. However, should there be occasion for it, you will pardon me, if I go in pursuit of a fifth life.

PROT. Certainly.

SOC. Of these four species, then, in the first place dividing the three, and perceiving that two of these, when both are divided, and their divisions separated, are, each of them, many;- then, gathering together the many of each, and uniting them again, let us endeavour to understand in what manner each of them is, at the same time, one and many.

24a PROT. Would you but express your meaning more plainly, I might, perhaps, apprehend it.

SOC. I mean, then, by the two, which I propose to be now considered, the same which I mentioned at the first; one of them *the infinite*, and the other *bound*. That *the infinite* is, in some manner, many, I will attempt to show: and let *bound* wait a while.

PROT. It shall.

SOC. Give me now your attention. It is, I confess, a difficult and doubtful thing, that, which I would have you to consider. Consider it,

† That is, the ineffable principle of things. -T.

however. First, with regard to hotter and colder, in things, see if you can think of any bound. Or would not the more and the less, residing
b in the kinds themselves of things, hinder, so long as they reside there, an end from being fixed to them? For, if ever they receive an end, to an end also are their very beings then brought.

PROT. Most certainly true.

SOC. And in speaking of either the colder or the hotter of any two things, we constantly attribute to them the more and the less.

PROT. And very much so.

SOC. Reason then constantly suggests to us that the *colder* and the *hotter* have no end: and being thus without any end, they are altogether boundless.

PROT. I am strongly inclined to agree with you, Socrates in this point.

SOC. Well have you answered, my friend Protarchus; and well have
c you reminded me, that the *strongly*, which you mentioned, and the *faintly*, have the same power as the *more* and the *less*. For, wherever they reside, they suffer not any thing to be just *so much*; but infusing either the more *intense* or the more *remiss* into every action, they always produce in it either the *more* or the *less*; while the just *so much* flies away and vanishes from before them. For, as it was just now observed, were they not to drive away the just *so much*, did they permit *this*, and
d the *moderate*, to enter into the regions of the *more* and the *less*, or of the *intense* and the *remiss*, these very beings must quit their own places: because, if they admitted the just *so much*, the *hotter* and the *colder* would be gone. For the *hotter*, and in like manner the *colder*, is always advancing forward, and never abides in the same spot: but the just *so much* stops, and stays, having finished its progress. Now, according to this reasoning, the *hotter* must be *boundless*; and so must also be the *colder*.

PROT. So it appears indeed, Socrates. But, as you rightly said, it is not easy to apprehend these things. Questions, however, relating to
e them, again and again repeated, might perhaps show that the questioner and the respondent were tolerably well agreed in their minds concerning them.

SOC. You say well: and we should try so to do. But at present, to avoid lengthening out this argument, by enumerating every infinite, consider, whether we may take this for the characteristic mark of the nature of all infinites.

PROT. What mark do you mean?

SOC. Whatever things appear to us to be increasing or diminishing, or to admit of intenseness and remission, or the too much, and all other

25a such attributes, we ought to refer all these to the genus of the infinite; collecting, as it were, all of them in one, agreeably to what was before said; that whatever things were divided and separated we ought to assemble together and combine, as well as we are able, affixing to all of them the mark of some one nature;- if you remember.

PROT. I remember it well.

SOC. Every thing, then, which rejects all such attributes, and admits only such as are quite the contrary, - in the first place, the equal and equality, and, after the equal, the double, and every other relation which

b one number bears to another, and one measure to another, - all these things, I say, in summing up, and referring them to bound, think you not that we should do right? or how say you?

PROT. Perfectly right, O Socrates.

SOC. Well: but the third thing made up, and consisting of the other two, what characteristic shall we assign to this?

PROT. You, as I presume, will show it to me.

SOC. Divinity indeed may; if any of the Gods will hearken to my prayers.

PROT. Pray, then, and *survey*.

SOC. I survey: and some God, O Protarchus, is now, methinks, become favourable to us.

c PROT. How do you mean? and by what sign do you know it?

SOC. I will tell you in plain words: but do you follow them closely.

PROT. Only speak.

SOC. We mentioned just now the hotter and the colder; did we not?

PROT. We did.

SOC. To these then add the drier and the moister; the more numerous and the fewer; the swifter and the slower; the larger and the smaller; and whatever things beside, in our late account of them, we ranked under one head, - that which admits of the nature of the more and the less.

d PROT. You mean the infinite.

SOC. I do: and mingle together with this that which we spoke of next afterward, - the race of bound.

PROT. What race do you mean?

SOC. Those things which we did not (as we ought to have done) assemble together under one head, in the same manner as we assembled together the race of the infinite. But you will now, perhaps, do what was then omitted. And when both the sorts are assembled, and viewed

e together, the race of bound will then become manifest.

PROT. What things do you speak of? and how are they to be assembled?

SOC. I speak of that nature in which are comprised the equal and the double; and whatever else puts an end to contest between contrary things; and, introducing number, makes them to be commensurate one with another, and to harmonize together.

PROT. I apprehend your meaning to be, that, from the commixture of those two, a certain progeny will arise between them in every one of their tribes.

SOC. You apprehend me rightly.

PROT. Relate then the progeny of these commixtures.

SOC. In *diseases*, does not the right commixture of those two produce the *recovery of health*?

26a   PROT. Entirely so.

SOC. And in the acute and the grave, in the swift also and the slow, which are all of them infinite, does not the other sort, received among them, and begetting bounds, constitute the perfection of all the Muse's art?

PROT. Certainly so.

SOC. And in weather excessively either cold or hot, does not the entrance of that other kind take off the excess, the vehement, and the infinite, - generating in their stead, not only the moderate and the measured, but symmetry also, and correspondence between their measures?

PROT. Without dispute.

b   SOC. And do not propitious seasons, and all their fair productions, arise to us from hence, from the mixture of things which are infinite with things which have a bound?

PROT. Doubtless.

SOC. A thousand other things I forbear to mention; as, for instance, strength and beauty, the attendants upon health of body; and in the soul other excellencies, very many and very noble. For Venus herself, O good Philebus! observing lawless lust, and all manner of vice every where reigning, the love of pleasure being in all men boundless, and their desires of it insatiable, she herself established a law and an order, setting bounds to pleasure and desire. This you said was to lessen and to impair pleasure; but I maintain, that, on the contrary, it preserved pleasure from decay. And you, Protarchus! what think you of it?

c   PROT. For my part, I am entirely of your mind, Socrates.

SOC. I have shown you then those three kinds, if you apprehend my meaning.

PROT. Partly, I suppose, I do. By one of those three, I suppose, you mean the infinite; by another, the second sort, you mean that which in all beings is the bound; but what you mean by the third sort, I have no strong apprehension of.

SOC. Because the care of that third sort, my friend, has amazed you with its multitude. And yet, the infinite also appeared to contain many tribes: but as they were all of them stamped with the character of more and less, they were seen clearly to be one.

PROT. True.

SOC. Then, as to bound; that neither contained many, nor found we any difficulty in admitting the nature of it to be one.

PROT. How could we?

SOC. It was not at all possible, indeed. Of those two sorts, then, all the progeny, - all the things produced into being through those measures, which are effected in the immoderate, when bounds are set to the infinite, - in summing up all these things together, and comprehending them in one, understand me to mean, by the third sort, this one.

PROT. I understand you.

SOC. Now, besides these three, we are further to consider, what that kind is which we said was the fourth. And as we are to consider it jointly, see whether you think it necessary, that all things which are produced into being should have some cause of their production.

PROT. I think it is: for, without a cause, how should they be produced?

SOC. The nature then of the efficient differs from the cause in nothing but in name: so that the efficient and the cause may be rightly deemed one.

PROT. Rightly.

SOC. So, likewise, the thing effected, and the thing produced into being, we shall find to differ in the same manner, in nothing but in name, or how?

PROT. Just so.

SOC. In the nature of things, does not the efficient lead the way? and does not the effect follow after it into being?

PROT. Certainly.

SOC. Cause, therefore, is not the same thing with that which is subservient to cause in the producing of its effect, but a thing different.

PROT. Without doubt.

SOC. Did not the things which are produced into being, and the things out of which they are all of them produced, exhibit to us the three genera?

PROT. Clearly.

b   SOC. That, then, which is the artificer of all these, the cause of them, let us call the fourth cause; as it is fully shown to be different from those other three.

PROT. Be it so.

SOC. But the four sorts having been now described, every one of them distinctly, we should do well, for memory's sake, to enumerate them in order.

PROT. No doubt of it.

c   SOC. The first then I call infinite; the second bound; the third essence[†] mixt and generated from these: and in saying[‡] that the cause of this mixture and this production is the fourth, should I say aught amiss?

PROT. Certainly not.

SOC. Well now: what is next? How proceeds our argument? and with what design came we along this way? Was it not this? We were inquiring who had a right to the second prize of victory; whether Pleasure had, or Wisdom: was it not so?

PROT. It was.

SOC. Now then, since we have thus divided these genera, may we not happily form a more finished judgment concerning both the very best and the second-best of those things which originally were the subjects of dispute between us?

PROT. Perhaps we may.

SOC. We made no difficulty, I think, of setting down for conqueror, the mixt life, the life of pleasure and wisdom together. Was it not so?

d   PROT. It was.

SOC. We perceive then of what sort the mixt life is, and to which kind it is to be referred.

PROT. Evidently.

SOC. And I think we shall agree, that it is part of the third sort. For the mixt life is not to be referred solely to any one of the infinites, mixed with some one only of the bounds: it is a life of all such things together as are infinite in their own nature, but are under the restraint

---

† As essence, therefore, is plainly asserted by Socrates to be mixt and generated from bound and infinity, it is evident that *bound* and *infinity* are superessential. For cause is every where superior to its effect. -T. [.117]

‡ The edition of Plato by Aldus, and that by Stephens, in this place erroneously give us to read λεγω, instead of the evidently right reading, which is λεγων, exhibited in the Basil editions. -S.

of bound. So that the mixt life, this winner of the prize, may be rightly said to be a part of the third sort.

PROT. Most rightly.

SOC. It is well. But that life of yours, O Philebus, a life of pleasure simple and unmixed, to which of the three sorts may we rightly say that it belongs? But before you pronounce, answer me first to this question.

PHIL. Propose it then.†

SOC. Concerning pleasure and pain; have they in their own nature any bounds? or are they among those things which admit the more and the less?‡

PHIL. Pleasure, O Socrates! to be sure, admits the more. For it would not comprehend every good in it, if it were not by nature infinite, with respect to the multitude which it contains, and the increase which it is capable of.

SOC. Nor can pain be imagined, O Philebus, to comprehend every evil. So that we must consider of some other thing, different from the nature of the infinite, for the imparting of any good to pleasures. It is admitted, that your life of pleasure is the issue of things unbounded, and belongs, therefore, to the infinite. But to which of the sorts before mentioned, O Protarchus and Philebus, may we refer wisdom, and science, and intellect, without being guilty of impiety? For it appears to me that we incur no trifling danger in answering the present question, whatever be our answer, whether right or wrong.

PHIL. You magnify that God of yours, O Socrates, very highly, methinks.

SOC. So do you, my friend, that Goddess of yours. The question, however, ought to be answered by us.

PROT. Socrates says what is right, O Philebus, and we must do as he says we ought.

PHIL. Have not you, Protarchus, taken upon yourself my part in the debate?

PROT. It is true that I have. But in the present case I find myself much at a loss how to answer. I must therefore request, O Socrates, that

---

† Aldus, in his edition of Plato, gave these words to Protarchus; though nothing is more plain than that Plato meant them for Philebus. The Basil editors restored them to the right owner: and it is strange that Stephens either knew it not, or did not acknowledge it. -S.

‡ In all the editions of the Greek we here read εστι instead of εστον. We are ignorant of any authority for using so strange an enallage; and therefore we suppose it an erroneous reading. -S.

you yourself will take the office of prophet to us; lest, by some mistake, I should offend the combatant† whom you favour, and by singing out of tune should spoil the harmony.‡

c   SOC. You must be obeyed, Protarchus. Indeed there is nothing difficult in your injunctions. But, in asking you to which of the two above mentioned kinds intellect and science were to be referred, - when I was magnifying, as Philebus says, the subject of my question, - the joke, which I intended to soften the solemnity of it, confused your thoughts, I find, in good earnest.

PROT. Very thoroughly so, I confess, O Socrates.

SOC. And yet it was an easy question. For, on this point, there is a consent and harmony among all the wise, dignifying thus themselves, - that *Intellect is king of heaven and earth.* And this which they say is perhaps§ well said. But let us, if you are willing, consider the nature of this genus more amply, and not in so concise a manner.

d   PROT. Consider it in what manner you think best, without regarding the length of the inquiry: for the length will not be disagreeable to us.

SOC. Fairly spoken. Let us begin, then, by proposing this question.

PROT. What?

SOC. Whether shall we say that the power of the irrational principle governs all things in the whole universe, fortuitously and at random? or shall we, on the contrary, agree with our ancestors and predecessors, in affirming that a certain admirable intellect and wisdom orders all things together, and governs throughout the whole?

---

† This evidently is a metaphor taken from the contentions usual at that time between dramatic poets during the feasts of Bacchus, for the fame of superiority in their art. For the Grecians of those days had an emulation to excel in the musical entertainments of the mind, as well as in the gymnic exercises of the body. To inspire them with that emulation, combats in poetry and music, as well as in gymnastic, were instituted by their legislators; and the contenders in either kind were alike termed αγωνισται, combatants. The metaphorical combatants meant by Protarchus are Mind and Pleasure. -S.

‡ In continuing the metaphor taken from theatrical contests, Protarchus likens himself to one of the chorus in a tragedy or comedy, and Socrates to the κορυφαιος, or χορηγος, the chief or leader of the whole band. For, in the chorus songs, it was the office of the chief, or president, to lead the vocal music, keeping it in time and tune with the instrumental: and in the dialogue scenes, wherever the chorus bore a part, their president spoke alone for them all. -S.

§ Socrates does not say this as being himself doubtful whether Intellect is king of heaven and earth, but because those with whom he was conversing had not arrived at a scientific knowledge of this dogma. -T.

e   PROT. Alike in nothing, O Socrates, are these two tenets. That which you mentioned just now is, in my opinion, impious. But, to hold that Intellect disposes all things in a beautiful order, is agreeable to that view which we have of the world, of the celestial bodies, and of the whole circumvolution of the heavens. For my own part, I should never speak nor think any otherwise on this subject.

29a   SOC. Is it then your pleasure that we add our voices to those of the ancients, and openly avow that tenet to be ours; not contenting ourselves with a bare repetition of the sayings of others, in hopes of escaping danger to ourselves; but resolved to run all risk together, and to share in undergoing the censures of some great and formidable man, when he asserts that in the whole of things there is no order?[†]

PROT. How can I do otherwise than join with you in this?

SOC. Attend now to the argument which comes on next to be considered.

PROT. Propose it then.

SOC. In the bodies of all animals, somehow, we discover that fire, water, and air, must be in their composition by nature; and earth, which gives support to the other ingredients in their frame, we see plainly: as mariners say, when they are tossed about in a thunder-storm at sea, and descry land.

b   PROT. True: and tossed about indeed are we too in these discourses; but for a port to anchor in we are entirely at a loss.

SOC. Let us proceed then: Concerning each of those elementary ingredients in our frame, understand this.

PROT. What?

SOC. That which there is in us of each element is small and inconsiderable; no where in any part of our frame have we it at all unmixed and pure; neither has it in us a power worthy of its nature. Take one of them for a sample, by which you may estimate all the rest. Fire in some manner there is in us; fire[‡] there is also in the universe.

PROT. Most certainly.

---

    † That the person here alluded to is Critias, one of the thirty oligarchic tyrants, cannot be doubted of by those who are acquainted with his character, and the injurious treatment he gave to Socrates. A considerable fragment of his atheistic poetry is extant in Sextus Empiricus, p. 562. -S.

    ‡ Socrates is here speaking of the difference between the *wholes* of the universe, and the *parts* to which these wholes are prior, as being their cause. See the Introduction to the *Timæus* [TTS vol. X]. -T.

c   Soc. Now the fire which is in our composition is weak and inconsiderable: but that which is in the universe is admirable for the multitude of it, for the beauty which it exhibits, and for every power and virtue which belong to fire.

PROT. Perfectly true.

Soc. Well then: is the fire of the universe generated, fed, and ruled by the fire which we have in us? or, on the contrary, does my fire, and yours, and that of every other living thing, receive its being, support, and laws, from the fire of the universe?

PROT. This question of yours does not deserve an answer.

d   Soc. Rightly said. And you would answer in the same manner, I suppose, if your opinion was asked concerning the earthy part of every animal here, compared with the earth in the universe; and just so concerning the other elementary parts of animal bodies mentioned before.

PROT. What man, who made a different answer, would ever appear to be of sound mind?

Soc. Scarcely would any man. But attend to what follows next. Wherever we find these four elements mixed together and united, do we not give to this composition the name of body?

PROT. We do.

e   Soc. Apprehend the same thing then with regard to this, which we call the world. This should be considered as a body in the same manner, being composed of the same elements.

PROT. You are perfectly in the right.

Soc. To the whole of this great body, then, does the whole of that little body of ours owe its nourishment and whatever it has received, and whatever it possesses? or is the body of the universe indebted to ours for all which it is and has?

PROT. There is no reason, O Socrates, for making a question of this point, neither.

30a   Soc. Well: what will you say to this point then?

PROT. What point?

Soc. Must we not affirm these bodies of ours to be animated with souls?

PROT. It is evident that we must.

Soc. But from whence, O my friend Protarchus, should our bodies derive those souls of theirs, if that great body of the universe, which has all the same elements with our bodies, but in much greater purity and perfection, was not, as well as ours, animated with a soul?

PROT. It is evident, O Socrates, that from no other origin could they derive them.

b   SOC. Since, therefore, O Protarchus, we acknowledge these four genera, bound, infinite, the compound of both those, and the genus of cause, to be in all bodies; and since we find, that in this part of the universe to which we belong there are beings of that fourth sort, - causes, which produce souls, build up bodies for those souls to dwell in,[19] and heal those bodies when diseased; - causes, also, which create and frame other compositions, and amend them when impaired; - causes these, to every one of which we gave a particular name, betokening a particular kind of wisdom or skill: - since, I say, we are persuaded of these things, surely we can by no means think that the whole heaven, in the larger parts of which are the same four genera, and these undepraved and pure, can have any other cause than a nature who is full of contrivance and design, and in whom the most beautiful and noble things all unite.

c   PROT. It would not be at all reasonable to think it can.

  SOC. If this then be absurd, we may the better assert, as a consequence of our reasoning, that in the universe there are, what we have several times repeated, *infinite* in great quantity, and *bound* sufficient; and besides these, a *cause,* not inconsiderable or mean, which, by *mixing* them properly together, marshals and regulates the years, the seasons, and the months, - a cause, which with the greatest justice we may term *wisdom* and *intellect.*

  PROT. With the greatest justice, indeed.

  SOC. But further, wisdom and intellect could never be without soul.[†]

  PROT. By no means.

d   SOC. You will affirm, then, that in the nature of Jupiter there is a kingly soul and a kingly intellect, through the power of cause;[‡] and that in the other Gods there are other beautiful things, whatever they are, by

---

† That is, soul is consubsistent with wisdom and intellect. If this be the case, it is evident that when Plato in the *Timæus* [41a] speaks of the *generation* of soul by the *demiurgus,* whom he there expressly calls *intellect,* he does not mean by *generation* a *temporal* production, but an *eternal procession* from cause. And in the same manner, what he there says of the *generation* of the universe is to be understood. Hence, those are to be derided who assert that the world, according to Plato, was produced in time. - T.

‡ That is to say, a kingly soul, and a kingly intellect, subsist in Jupiter, the artificer of the universe according to cause. For Jupiter, as a Deity, is a superessential unity, in which all things have a causal subsistence. -T.

which their Deities love to be distinguished, and from which they delight in taking their respective denominations.

PROT. Certainly I shall.

SOC. The discourse we have now had together on this subject, O Protarchus, think it not idle, and to no purpose. For it supports that doctrine of our ancestors, that the universe is for ever governed by intellect.

PROT. Indeed it does.

e   SOC. And besides, it has furnished us with an answer to my question, - to what genus intellect is to be referred; in making it appear that intellect is allied to that which we said was the cause of all things, one of our four genera. For now at length you plainly have our answer.

PROT. I have; and a very full and sufficient answer it is: but I was not aware what you were about.

SOC. A man's attention to serious studies, O Protarchus, is sometimes, you know, relaxed by amusements.

31a   PROT. Politely said.

SOC. And thus, my friend, to what genus intellect belongs, and what power it is possessed of, has been now shown tolerably well for the present.

PROT. It has, indeed.

SOC. And to what genus also belongs pleasure, appeared before.

PROT. Very true.

SOC. Concerning these two, then, let us remember these conclusions, - that intellect is allied to cause, and is nearly of this genus; and that pleasure is infinite in her own nature, and belongs to that genus which, of itself, neither has nor ever will have in it either a beginning, or a middle, or an end.

b   PROT. We shall not fail to remember them both.

SOC. Now we ought to consider next, in which genus either of those two things, intelligence and pleasure, is found to have a seat; and in what state or condition those beings must be in whom either of them is produced, at the time of its production. And first in the case of pleasure: for, as we inquired to which genus she belonged, before we considered of which sort was intellect; so, with regard to the points also now proposed, she is the first to be examined.[†] But, separately from the

---

† Cornarius and Stephens, both of them, perceived the Greek of this sentence to be erroneous. But the emendations proposed by them appear insufficient. Ficinus's translation from the Florentine MS. helps to restore the right reading thus: - Δει δη, - ιδειν ημας· και πρωτον περι την ηδωην, ωσπερ - ουτω και ταυτα προτερον [sc. δει ιδειν].-S.

consideration of pain, we should never be able fully to explore the nature of pleasure.

PROT. Well: if we are to proceed in this way, let us then in this way proceed.[†]

SOC. Are you of the same opinion with me concerning their rise and production?

c PROT. What opinion is that?

SOC. Pain and pleasure appear to me, both of them, to arise, according to nature, in that which is a common genus.

PROT. Remind us, friend Socrates, which of the genera mentioned before is meant by the term common.

SOC. What you desire, O wonderful man! shall be done, to the best of my ability.

PROT. Fairly said.

SOC. By this common genus, then, we are to understand that which, in recounting the four sorts, we reckoned as third.

PROT. That which you mentioned next after both the infinite and bound: that in which you ranked health, and also, as I think, harmony.

d SOC. Perfectly right. Now give me all possible attention.

PROT. Only speak.

SOC. I say, then, that whenever the harmony in the frame of any animal is broken, a breach is then made in its constitution, and at the same time rise is given to pains.

PROT. You say what is highly probable.

SOC. But when the harmony is restored, and the breach is healed, we should say that then pleasure is produced: if points of so great importance may be dispatched at once in so few words.

e PROT. In my opinion, O Socrates, you say what is very true: but let us try if we can show these truths in a light still clearer.

SOC. Are not such things as ordinarily happen, and are manifest to us all, the most easy to be understood?

PROT. What things do you mean?

SOC. Want of food makes a breach in the animal system, and at the same time gives the pain of hunger.

PROT. True.

SOC. And food, in filling up the breach again, gives a pleasure.

32a PROT. Right.

---

† In the edition of Plato by Aldus, and in that also by Stephens, this sentence, by a strange mistake, is printed as if it were spoken by Socrates. -S.

SOC. Want of drink also, interrupting the circulation of the blood and humours, brings on us corruption, together with the pain of thirst; but the virtue of a liquid, in moistening and replenishing the parts dried up, yields a pleasure. In like manner, preternatural suffocating heat, in dissolving the texture of the parts, gives a painful sensation: but a cooling again, a refreshment agreeable to nature, affects us with a sense of pleasure.

PROT. Most certainly.

SOC. And the concretion of the animal humours through cold, contrary to their nature, occasions pain: but a return to their pristine state of fluidity, and a restoring of the natural circulation, produce pleasure. See, then, whether you think this general account of the matter not amiss, concerning that sort of being which I said was
b   composed of infinite and bound, - that, when by nature any beings of that sort become animated with soul, their passage into corruption, or a total dissolution, is accompanied with pain; and their entrance into existence, the assembling of all those particles which compose the nature of such a being, is attended with a sense of pleasure.

PROT. I admit your account of this whole matter; for, as it appears to me, it bears on it the stamp of truth.

SOC. These sensations, then, which affect the soul by means only of the body, let us consider as one species of pain and pleasure.

PROT. Be it so.

SOC. Consider now the feelings of the soul herself, in the expectation
c   of such a pain or such a pleasure, - antecedent to the pleasure expected, an agreeable feeling of hope and alacrity, - antecedent to the pain expected, the uneasiness of fear.

PROT. This is, indeed, a different species of pleasure and pain, independent of the body, and produced in the soul herself through expectation.

SOC. You apprehend the matter rightly. Now the consideration of these feelings of pain and pleasure, which immediately affect the soul
d   herself, (and seem to be produced in her, each of them, unmixed and genuine,) will, as I imagine, clear up that doubt concerning pleasure, - whether the whole kind be eligible, or whether a particular species of it be the proper object of our choice. And in the latter case, pleasure and pain (in general), like heat and cold, and all other things of this sort, will deserve sometimes to be embraced, and at other times to be rejected; as not being good in themselves, but admitting the nature of good to be superadded to them only at some times, and some of them only.

PROT. You are perfectly in the right. It must be in some such way as this that we ought to investigate the things we are in pursuit of.

e   SOC. If, then, what we agreed in be true, - that animal bodies feel pain, when any thing befalls them tending to their destruction, - pleasure, when they are using the means of their preservation, - let us now consider what state or condition every animal is in, when it is neither suffering aught that tends to its destruction, nor is engaged in any action, or in the midst of any circumstances, tending to its preservation. Give your earnest attention to this point, and say, whether it is entirely necessary, or not, that every animal at that time should feel neither pain nor pleasure, in any degree, great or small.

PROT. It is quite necessary.

33a   SOC. Besides the condition then of an animal delighted, and besides the opposite condition of it under uneasiness, is not this a different, a third, state or condition of an animal?

PROT. Without dispute.

SOC. Be careful then to remember this judgement of ours. For on the remembering of it, or not, greatly will depend our judgment concerning the nature of pleasure. But, to go through with this point, let us, if you please, add a short sentence more.

PROT. Say what.

SOC. You know, nothing hinders a man who prefers the life of wisdom from living all his life in that state.

b   PROT. In the state, do you mean, of neither pleasure nor uneasiness?

SOC. I do: for, when we compared together the different lives, it was supposed, that whoever should choose the life of intellect and wisdom was not to have pleasure either in a great or in a small degree.

PROT. That was the supposition.

SOC. He must live, therefore, such a life.[†] And perhaps it is by no means absurd, to deem that life to be of all lives the most Godlike.

PROT. It is not indeed probable, that the Gods feel either the pleasurable sensation, or its opposite.

SOC. Highly indeed, is it improbable. For neither of them is consistent with the divine nature. But we shall consider further of this

---

† In the Greek, the first words of this sentence of Socrates, and the first word also of the next sentence, spoken by Protarchus, ought for the future to be printed thus, - Ὀυκουν and not Ουκὸυν. - The wrong accentuation of these passages in all the editions seems owing to the error of Ficinus, who mistook both the sentences for interrogations: and the mistakes are continued by Grynæus. Serranus's translation is guilty of the same mistakes: but in those of Cornarius, Bembo, and Grou, they are corrected. -S.

c point afterwards, if it should appear to be of any service to our argument; and shall apply it to the purpose of winning the second prize for intellect, though we should not be able to make use of it so as to win for her the first.

PROT. Very justly said.

SOC. Now that species of pleasure which we said is proper to the soul herself, is all produced in her by means of memory.

PROT. How so?

SOC. But, before we consider of this point, I think we should premise some account of memory, - what it is: and still prior to an account of memory, some mention too, methinks, ought to be made of sense, if we are to have this subject appear tolerably plain to us.[†]

d PROT. Explain your meaning.

SOC. Of those things which are incident to our bodies in every part, coming from all quarters around us, and affecting us in various ways, - some spend all their force upon the body, without penetrating to the soul, leaving this entirely untouched and free; others extend their power through the soul as well as through the body; and some of this latter sort excite a vehement agitation in them both, jointly and severally. Do you admit this?

PROT. Be it admitted.

SOC. If we should say of those things, the power of which is confined to the body, and reaches not the soul, that the soul is deprived of knowing them; but of other things which befall us, and have a power to pervade both the body and the soul, that of these the soul hath the knowledge; should we not thus say what is most true?

e PROT. Without dispute.

SOC. But when I say that the soul is deprived of knowing the former sort, do not suppose my meaning to be, that oblivion happens to her in this case. For oblivion is the departure of memory. But of the accidents now spoken of the soul never had a memory. And of that which neither is nor ever was, it is absurd to say that any loss can happen to us. Is it not?

PROT. Undoubtedly.

SOC. Only then alter the terms.

PROT. In what manner?

34a SOC. Instead of saying that the soul is deprived of knowing what the body suffers, when she is not affected by any motions produced in the

---

† The Greek of this passage, it is presumed, ought to be read thus - ειπερ μελλει ταυθ᾽ ημιν κ.τ.λ. -S.

body by those ordinary occurrences, - what we termed a privation of knowledge, let us now term insensibility.

PROT. I apprehend your meaning.

SOC. But when the soul and the body are affected, both of them in common, by any of those occurrences, and in common also are moved or agitated,[†] - in giving to this motion the name of sensation, you would not speak improperly.

PROT. Very true.

SOC. Now then do we not apprehend what it is which is commonly called sense or sensation?

PROT. What should hinder us?

SOC. And of memory,[‡] if one should say that it was the retaining of sensations, it would not be ill defined, in my opinion.

b PROT. I think so too.

SOC. Do we not hold, that memory differs from remembrance?

PROT. Perhaps it does.

SOC. Do they not differ in this respect?

PROT. In what respect?

SOC. When the soul alone, unaided by the body, recovers and resumes within herself as much as possible the state which heretofore she was in, when she was affected jointly with the body, we say that the soul then remembers. Do we not?

c PROT. Certainly we do.

SOC. So we do also, when the soul, after having lost the memory of something which she had sensibly perceived, or of something which she had learnt, recalls and recollects the memory of it again, herself within

---

† In the Greek of this passage, instead of γιγνομενα, the participle singular, agreeing with σωμα, we ought to read γιγνομενα, the plural, agreeing with the two preceding substantives, ψυχην and σωμα, coupled together; according to a rule, the same in the grammars of the Greek and Latin languages. For the words of this sentence, placed in the order of their grammatical construction, are these, - Τῳ κοινῃ κινεισθαι την ψυχην και το σωμα, κοινῃ γιγνομενα εν ενι παθει, - ταυτην την κινησιν κ.τ.λ. If Stephens had perceived this, he would not have adopted Cornarius's alteration of the text. -S.

‡ Memory, says Olympiodorus, is triple, viz. irrational, rational, and intellectual. Each of these likewise is twofold, viz. phantastic, sensitive; dianoëtic, doxastic, essential, divine. -T. [.159]

herself: and all this we term remembrance, and a recovery of things slipt out of our memory.[†]

PROT. Very true.

SOC. Now the end for the sake of which we have been considering these faculties of the soul is this.

PROT. For the sake of what?

SOC. That we may apprehend,[‡] as well and as clearly as we are able, what is the pleasure of the soul abstracted from the body, and at the same time may apprehend also what is desire. For the nature of both these things seems to be discovered in some measure by showing the nature of memory and of remembrance.

PROT. Let us then, O Socrates, now explain how such a discovery follows from perceiving the nature of these faculties of ours.

d   SOC. In treating of the rise of pleasure, and of the various forms which she assumes, it will be necessary for us, I believe, to consider a great variety of things. But, before we enter on so copious a subject, we should now, I think, in the first place, consider the nature and origin of desire.

PROT. Let us then: for we must not lose any thing.

SOC. Nay, Protarchus! we shall lose one thing, when we shall have found the objects of our inquiry; we shall lose our uncertainty about them.

PROT. You are right in your repartee. Proceed we then to what is next.

e   SOC. Was it not just now said, that hunger, and thirst, and many other things of like kind, were certain desires?

PROT. Without doubt.

SOC. What is it, then, which is the same in all these things, - that, with respect to which we give to all of them, notwithstanding the great difference between them, one and the same appellation?

---

† In the printed Greek we here read - αναμνησεις και μνημας - So that *memory* and *remembrance* are now confounded together; and the difference but just before made between them is annulled. It is therefore apprehended, that we ought to read - αναμνησεις και μνημης ανακτησεις. -S.

‡ All the editions of Plato give us here to read - Ινα μη - λαβοιμεν κ.τ.λ. From this sentence, thus absurdly printed, Cornarius, in his marginal lemmas, extracted the following curious precept, - "Voluptas & cupiditas animæ, absque corpore, vitanda." *Pleasure and desire in the soul herself, abstracted from the body, are both to be avoided.* The French translator has judiciously rejected the negative particle in this sentence. -S.

PROT. By Jupiter, Socrates! it is, perhaps, not easy to say: it ought, however, to be declared.

SOC. Let us resume the mention of that with which we began the consideration of this subject.

PROT. Of what in particular?

SOC. Do we not often speak of being thirsty?

PROT. We do.

SOC. And do we not mean by it some kind of emptiness?

PROT. Certainly.

SOC. Is not thirst a desire?

PROT. It is.

SOC. A desire of drink is it?

PROT. Of drink.

35a SOC. Of being replenished by drink: is it not?[†]

PROT. I suppose it is.

SOC. Whoever of us then is emptied, desires, it seems, a condition the reverse of what has befallen him. For whereas he is emptied, he longs to be filled again.

PROT. Most evidently so.

SOC. Well now: is it possible that a man, who at the first[‡] is empty, should apprehend, either by sense or by memory, what it is to be full, - a condition, in which he neither is at the time, nor ever was heretofore.

PROT. How can he?

b SOC. We are agreed, that the man who desires has a desire of something.

PROT. Without dispute.

SOC. Now it is not the condition in which he is that he desires. For he suffers thirst, that is, an emptiness: but he desires to be full.

PROT. True.

SOC. Something, therefore, belonging to the man who is thirsty must apprehend in some manner what it is to be full.

PROT. It must, of necessity.

SOC. But it is impossible that this should be his body: for his body is supposed to suffer emptiness.

PROT. Right.

---

† A future editor of Plato may consider, in the Greek of this sentence, whether διά should not be inserted before the word πόματος. -S.

‡ That is, at the beginning of his sensitive life. -S.

SOC. It remains, therefore, that his soul apprehends what it is to be full, by means of her memory.

PROT. Plainly so.

c   SOC. For, indeed, by what other means could his soul have such an apprehension?

PROT. Hardly by any other.

SOC. Perceive we now, what consequence follows from this reasoning of ours?

PROT. What consequence?

SOC. It proves that desire doth not arise in the body.

PROT. How so?

SOC. Because it shows that the aim and endeavour of every animal is to be in a condition opposite to the feelings with which the body is at that time affected.

PROT. It certainly shows this.

SOC. And the inclination by which it moves toward this opposite condition, shows the remembrance of a condition opposite to those present feelings and affections.

PROT. Clearly.

d   SOC. Our reasoning, then, in proving that memory leads us toward the objects of our desire, shows at the same time what is the general inclination and desire of the soul; and what is the moving principle in every animal.

PROT. Perfectly right.

SOC. Our conclusion, therefore, will by no means admit of an opinion that the body suffers hunger, or thirst, or is affected with any other such desire.

PROT. Most true.

SOC. Let us observe this also further, regarding these very subjects now under consideration. Our reasoning seems to me as if it meant to exhibit in those very things a certain kind of life.

e   PROT. What things do you mean? and what kind of life do you speak of?

SOC. I mean the being filled, and the being emptied, and all other things tending either to the preservation of animal life, or to the destruction of it; and whatever things ordinarily give pain, - yet, coming in a change from things contrary, are sometimes grateful.

PROT. True.

SOC. But what when a man is in the midst of these contrary conditions, and is partaking of them both?

PROT. How do you mean in the midst?

SOC. When he is afflicted with an anxious sense of his present bad condition, but at the same time has a remembrance of past delights; he may enjoy an intermission of his pain, without having as yet the cause of it removed;[†] now do we affirm, or do we deny, that he is at that time in the midst of two contrary conditions?

PROT. It must be affirmed.

SOC. Is he afflicted or delighted wholly?

PROT. By Jupiter, he is in a manner afflicted doubly: in his body, from his present condition; in his soul, from a tedious expectation, longing for relief.

SOC. How is it, O Protarchus, that you suppose his affliction to be doubled? Is not a man whose stomach is empty sometimes in a state of hopefulness, with assurance of having it filled? and on the contrary, is he not at other times in a condition quite hopeless?

PROT. Certainly.

SOC. Do you not think that, when he is in hopes of being filled, he is delighted with the remembrance of fulness? and yet that, being empty at the same time, he is in pain?

PROT. He must be so.

SOC. In such a state, therefore, man and other animals are at the same time afflicted and delighted.

PROT. It seems so to be.

SOC. But what think you when a man is empty, and hopeless of obtaining fulness? must he not, in such a condition, suffer double pain? with a view to which particular condition it was, that just now you supposed the memory of past delight, in all cases, to double the present pain.

PROT. Most true, Socrates.

SOC. Now of this inquiry into these feelings of ours we shall make this use.

PROT. What use?

SOC. Shall we say that all these pains and pleasures are true? or that they are all false? or that some of them are true, and others false?

PROT. How should pleasures or pains, O Socrates, be false?

---

† Thus have we rendered into English the Greek of this sentence as it is printed. But we are much inclined to adopt the emendation καὶ παύεται μεν, proposed by Stephens in the margin of his edition: only changing καὶ into η. If our learned readers are of the same opinion, and think with us, that two different cases are here stated by Socrates; in both of which there is a mixture of anxiety and delight, but not a mixture of the same kind; then, instead of - *he may enjoy*, the translation should be - *or when he enjoys*, &c. -S.

SOC. How is it then, O Protarchus, that fears may be either true or false? that expectations may be true, or not? Or, of opinions, how is it that some are true, and others false?

d   PROT. Opinions, I admit, may be of either kind: but I cannot grant you this of those other feelings.

SOC. How say you? We are in danger of starting a disquisition of no small importance.

PROT. That is true.

SOC. But whether it has any relation to the subjects which have preceded, this, O son of an illustrious father![20] ought to be considered.

PROT. Perhaps, indeed, it ought.

e   SOC. Tell me then: for, as to myself, I am continually in a state of wonderment about these very difficulties now proposed.

PROT. What difficulties do you mean?

SOC. False pleasures are not true; nor true pleasures false.[21]

PROT. How is it possible they should?

SOC. Neither in a dream, then, nor awake, is it possible, as you hold, not even if a man is out of his senses through madness, or has lost the soundness of his judgment any other way, is it possible for him ever to imagine that he feels delight, when he is by no means sensibly delighted; or to imagine that he feels pain, when actually the man feels none.

PROT. All of us, O Socrates, constantly suppose these facts to be as you have now stated them.

37a   SOC. But is it a right supposition? or should we examine whether it is right, or not?

PROT. We ought to examine it, I must own.

SOC. Let us then explain a little more clearly what was just now said concerning pleasure and opinion. Do we not hold the reality of our having an opinion?

PROT. Certainly.

SOC. And the reality of our having pleasure?

PROT. To be sure.

SOC. Further: it is something, that which is the object of our opinion.

PROT. Without doubt.

SOC. And something also that is with which whatever feels a pleasure is delighted.

PROT. Most certainly.

SOC. In the having, then, of an opinion, whether we are right or wrong in entertaining that opinion, the reality of our having it abides still.

b   PROT. How can a man lose an opinion whilst he has it?

SOC. In the enjoying also of any pleasure, whether we do right or wrong to enjoy it, it is certain that the reality of the enjoyment still remains.

PROT. To be sure, these things are so.

SOC. On what account is it, then, that we are used to call some opinions true, and others false; yet to pleasures only we allow the attribute of true; notwithstanding that pleasure and opinion, both of them, equally admit reality in the having of them?

PROT. This ought to be considered.

c SOC. Is it that falsehood and truth are incident to opinion, so that, by the supervening of one or other of these, opinion becomes something beside what in itself it is; and every opinion is thus made to have the quality of being either false or true. Do you say that this ought to be considered?

PROT. I do.

SOC. And beside this: supposing that opinions universally do admit of attributes and qualities; whether only pleasure and pain are what they are in themselves simply, and never admit any quality to arise in them; ought we not to settle this point also by agreement between us?

PROT. It is evident that we ought.

SOC. But it is easy enough to perceive, that these also admit the accession of some qualities. For of pleasures and pains we agreed awhile since, that some are great, others little; and that each sort admits of vehemence and of intention.

d PROT. Very true.

SOC. And if either to any pleasure, or to any opinion, there be added the quality of evil, shall we not affirm the opinion thus to become evil, and the pleasure evil in the same manner?

PROT. Without doubt, O Socrates.

SOC. And what, if rectitude, or the opposite to rectitude, accede to any of them, shall we not say, that the *opinion* is *right*, if rectitude be in it? and shall we not ascribe the same quality to *pleasure*, on the same supposition?

PROT. Of necessity we must.

e SOC. And if the object of our *opinion* be mistaken by us, must we not in such a case acknowledge that our *opinion* is *erroneous*, and not right; and that we are not right ourselves in entertaining such an opinion?

PROT. Certainly we must.

SOC. But what, if we discover ourselves to be mistaken in the object of our *grief* or of our *pleasure*, shall we give to this *grief*, or to this *pleasure,* the epithet of *right,* or *good,* or any other which is fair and honourable?

PROT. We certainly cannot, where a mistake is in the pleasure.

SOC. And surely pleasure is apt to arise in us oftentimes, accompanied, not with a *right* opinion, but with an opinion which is *false.*

38a   PROT. Indisputably so. And the opinion, O Socrates, then and in that case, we should say was a false opinion. But to the *pleasure* itself no man would ever give the appellation of *false.*

SOC. You are very ready, O Protarchus, at supporting the plea made use of by Pleasure on this occasion.

PROT. Not at all so. I only repeat what I have heard.

SOC. Do we make no difference, my friend, between such a pleasure as comes accompanied with right opinion or with science, and that kind of pleasure which often arises in every one of us at the same time with false opinion or ignorance?[†]

b   PROT. It is probable, I own, that no little difference is between them.

SOC. Let us now come to the consideration of what the difference is.

PROT. Proceed in whatever way you think proper.

SOC. I shall take this way then.

PROT. What way?

SOC. Some of our opinions are false, and others of them are true: this is agreed.

PROT. It is.

SOC. Pleasure and pain, as it was just now said, oftentimes attend on either of them indifferently; on opinions, I mean, either true or false.

PROT. Certainly so.

SOC. Is it not from memory and from sense that opinion is produced in us, and that room is given for a diversity of opinions on every subject?

c   PROT. Most undoubtedly.

---

† Stephens's edition of Plato agrees with all the prior editions in giving us to read ανοιας in this place: but that learned printer, in his latter annotations, p. 75, justly observes, that instead of ανοιας we ought to read αγνοιας. That emendation was made before Stephens by Cornarius, in his Eclogæ, p. 333. Ignorance is here opposed to knowledge, as false opinion is opposed to true. The Medicean manuscript exhibits the right reading, as appears from the Latin of Ficinus. -S.

Soc. I ask you, then, whether or not, as to these things, we deem ourselves to be of necessity affected thus?

Prot. How?

Soc. Oftentimes, when a man looks at something which he discovers at a great distance, but does not discern very clearly, will you admit that he may have an inclination to judge of what he sees?

Prot. I do admit the case.

Soc. Upon this, would not the man question himself in this manner?

Prot. In what manner?

d   Soc. What is that which appears as if it was standing under some tree by the cliff there? Do you not suppose that he would speak those words to himself, looking at some such appearances before him, as I have mentioned?

Prot. No doubt of it.

Soc. Hereupon, might not this man then, making a conjecture, say to himself, by way of answer, - It is a man?

Prot. Certainly.

Soc. But walking on, perhaps he might discern it to be but the work of some shepherds, and would say again to himself, - It is only a statue.

Prot. Most certainly he would.

e   Soc. And if he had any companion with him, he would speak out aloud what he had first spoken within himself, and repeat the very same words to his companion: so that what we lately termed an opinion would thus become a speech.

Prot. Very true.

Soc. But if he were alone, this very thing would be a thought still within him; and he might walk on, keeping the same thought in his mind, a considerable way.

Prot. Undoubtedly.

Soc. Well now: does this matter appear to you in the same light as it does to me?

Prot. How is that?

Soc. The soul in that case seems to me to resemble some book.

Prot. How so?

39a   Soc. The memory, coinciding with the senses, together with those passions of the soul which attend this memory and the present sensation, seem to me as if they concurred in writing sentences at that time within our souls. And when the scribe writes what is true, true opinions and true sentences are by him produced within us: but when our scribe writes what is false, then what we think, and what we say to ourselves, is contrary to the truth.

PROT. I heartily agree to your account of this matter, and acknowledge those joint scribes within the soul.

b   SOC. Acknowledge also another workman within us, operating at that time.

PROT. What is he?

SOC. An engraver, who follows after the scribe; engraving within the soul images of those thoughts, sentences, and sayings.

PROT. How and when is this done?

SOC. It is, when that which a man thinks and says to himself, concerning the object of his sight, or of any other outward sense, he separates from the sensation which he has of it; and views somehow within himself the image of that thought, and of that saying. Or is there no such thing as this ever produced within us?

c   PROT. Nothing is more certain.

SOC. The images of true thoughts and true sentences, are they not true? and the images of those which are false, are they not themselves also false?

PROT. Undoubtedly.

SOC. Now if we have pronounced thus far rightly, let us proceed to the consideration of one point further.

PROT. What is that?

SOC. Whether all the operations of this kind, such as are naturally performed within our souls, regard only things present and things past, but not things to come; or whether any of them have a reference to these also?

PROT. Difference of time makes no difference in these matters.

d   SOC. Did we not say before, that pleasures and pains of the soul, by herself, arise in us prior to those pleasures and pains which affect the body? so as that we feel antecedent joy and grief in the prospect of things to come hereafter.

PROT. Very true.

SOC. Those writings, then, and those engravings, which, as we held just now, are performed within us, do they respect the past and the present time only? and have they no concernment with the future?

e   PROT. About the future very much are they concerned, and chiefly.

SOC. In saying this, do you mean that all these things are expectations of the future; and that we are, all of us, throughout life, full of expectations?

PROT. The very thing I mean.

SOC. Now then, since we are thus far agreed, answer to this further question.

PROT. What is it?

SOC. A man who is just, and pious, and entirely good, is he not beloved by Divinity?

PROT. Undoubtedly.

SOC. And what of the unjust and entirely bad man? is not the reverse of it true of him?

PROT. How can it be otherwise?

SOC. Now every man, as we said just now, is full of a multitude of expectations.

PROT. True.

SOC. Sayings there are, written within every one of us, to which we give the name of expectations.

PROT. There are.

SOC. And phantasies also, engraven in us. Thus, for instance, a man often sees in imagination plenty of money flowing into him, and by those means many pleasures surrounding him; and views himself, engraven within himself, as highly delighted.

PROT. That often is the case.

SOC. Of these engravings, shall we say that good men, because of the divine favour, have generally those which are true; and bad men, generally those of the contrary sort? or shall we deny it?

PROT. It cannot be denied.

SOC. Bad men, then, have pleasures engraven within them also; but these are of the false sort.

PROT. No doubt of it.

SOC. Wicked men, therefore, delight mostly in false pleasures; the good, in pleasures which are true.

PROT. It must of necessity be so.

SOC. According to this account, there are, in the souls of men, such pleasures as are false; though in a most ridiculous manner they imitate, and would fain pass for, true pleasures: pains also there are with the like qualities.

PROT. Such pleasures and such pains there are.

SOC. May not a man who indulges fancy at random, and embraces opinions of any kind whatever, always really† think and believe some

40a

b

c

---

† In the Greek of this sentence, before the word αει, we ought to read οντως instead of ουτως. This appears from a sentence soon after, concerning a man *really delighted* with the thoughts of *things unreal.* Both the sentences refer to what was said before, where the same word is used in the same sense as it is here. -S.

things to be, which neither are nor ever were, and sometimes such as never will be?

PROT. Certainly.

d SOC. And they are the false semblances and seemings of these unreal things, which produce in him those false opinions, and occasion him to think thus falsely. Are they not?

PROT. They are.

SOC. Well then: should we not say of the pains and pleasures felt by those bad men, that their condition corresponds with the case of false opinions?

PROT. How do you mean?

SOC. May not a man who courts and embraces pleasure at random, pleasure in general, of any kind whatever, may not such a man always really feel delight from things which are not, and sometimes from things which never were, - often too, and perhaps the most frequently, from things which will never be?

e PROT. This must of necessity be granted.

SOC. Should not the same be said of fears and desires, and all things of the like sort, that these also are sometimes false?

PROT. Certainly.

SOC. Well now: can we say of opinions, that they are bad, or that they are good, any otherwise than as they prove to be false, or prove to be true?[†]

PROT. No otherwise.

41a SOC. And I should think, that pleasures too we apprehend not to be bad on any other account, than as they are false.

PROT. Quite the contrary, O Socrates. For hardly would any man put to the account of falsehood any of the evils brought on by pain and pleasure; since many and great evils accede to them from other quarters.

SOC. Pleasures which are evil, through the evil they occasion, we shall
b speak of by and by, if we shall continue to think it requisite: but we are now to speak of a multitude of pleasures felt by us, and frequently arising in us, - pleasures which are false in yet another way. And this other way of considering pleasure we shall have occasion, perhaps, to make use of in forming a right judgment of the several sorts of it.

---

† It is observed by Cornarius, that after the word ψευδεῖς in the Greek of this sentence, all the printed editions omit the words καὶ ἀληθεῖς; the sense evidently demands them; and they are not wanting in the Medicean MS., as appears from Ficinus' Latin translation. -S.

PROT. By all means let us speak of these, if any such pleasures there are.

SOC. And there are such, O Protarchus, in my opinion. But as long as this opinion lies by us unexamined, it is impossible for it to become certain or incontestable.

PROT. Fairly said.

SOC. Now, therefore, let us advance to this other argument, like champions to the combat.

PROT. Come we on then.

c   SOC. We said, if we remember, a little while since, that as long as the wants of the body, which are called desires in us, remain unsatisfied, the body all that time will be affected distinctly, and in a different manner from the soul.

PROT. We remember that it was so held.

SOC. In such a case, that within us, which desired, would be the soul, desiring to have her body in a state contrary to its present condition; and that which felt uneasiness or pain from the condition it was in, would be the body.

PROT. Things would be thus with us.

SOC. Now compute these things together, and consider the amount.

PROT. Say what.

d   SOC. In such a case, it comes out that pains and pleasures are placed together, each by the other's side; and that together, each by the other's side, arise in us a feeling of emptiness, and a desire of its contrary, fulness: for so it has just now appeared.

PROT. It is indeed apparent.

SOC. Has not this also been said? and does it not remain with us a point settled between us by agreement?

PROT. What?

SOC. That pain and pleasure, both of them, admit of the more and of the less; and that they both are of the infinites.

PROT. It was so said and agreed.

SOC. Is there not, then, some way in which we may judge of pain and pleasure rightly?

e   PROT. What way, and how do you mean?

SOC. In judging of them, are we not wont, in every case, readily to try them by these marks, - which of them is the greater, and which is the less, - which of them hath the nature of its kind the most, - and which is more intense than the other, - in comparing either a pain with a pleasure, or one pain with another pain, or one pleasure with another pleasure?

PROT. Such comparisons are often made: and from these comparisons we are wont to form our judgment and our choice.

SOC. Well now: in the case of magnitudes, does not the distance of visible objects, some of which are seen remote, and others near, render their real magnitudes uncertain, obscuring the truth of things, and producing false opinions? and does not the same thing hold true with regard to pains and pleasures? is not the same effect produced by the same means in this case also?

PROT. Much more feelingly, O Socrates.

SOC. But in this case it happens contrary to what was in the case mentioned a little before.

PROT. What happens, say you?

SOC. In that case, the true and the false opinions entertained by us impart to the pains and pleasures which attend them, their own qualities of truth and falsehood.

PROT. Very right.

SOC. But, in the case which I am now speaking of, the pains and pleasures being viewed afar off and near, continually changing [their aspects with their distances], and being set in comparison together, [it happens that] the pleasures [at hand] compared with the [remote] pains, appear greater and more intense [than they really are], and [that] the pains, compared with the pleasures, [have an appearance] quite the contrary.

PROT. Such appearances must of necessity arise by these means.

SOC. As far, therefore, as the pains and pleasures appear less or greater than they really are, if from the reality you separate this appearance of what neither of them is, and take it by itself thus separated, you will not say that it is a right appearance; nor will you venture to assert, that this additional part of pain and pleasure is right and true.

PROT. By no means.

SOC. After these discoveries, let us look if we can meet with pleasures and pains still falser, and more remote from truth, than those already mentioned, which are not only in appearance what they are called, but are felt also by the soul.

PROT. What pleasures and pains do you speak of?

SOC. We have more than once said, that when the frame of any animal is on its way to dissolution, through mixtures and separations, repletions and evacuations, the increase of some, and the diminution of other parts of it, that in such a condition of its body, pains, aches, and oppressions, with many other uneasy feelings, to which are given various names, are wont to arise in us.

PROT. True: this observation has been again and again repeated.

SOC. And that, when all things in our bodily frame return to their natural and sound state, together with this recovery, we receive some pleasure from within ourselves.

PROT. Right.

SOC. But how is it when none of these changes are operating in our bodies?

PROT. At what times, O Socrates, may this be?

e SOC. The question, O Protarchus, which you have now put to me is nothing to the purpose.

PROT. Why not?

SOC. Because it will not hinder me from putting again my question to you.

PROT. Repeat it then.

SOC. I shall put it thus: If at any time none of those things were passing within us, what condition should we of necessity be in, as to pleasure and pain, at such a time?

PROT. When no motion was in the body either way, do you mean?

SOC. Exactly so.

PROT. It is plain, O Socrates, that we should feel neither any pleasure nor any pain at such a time.

43a SOC. Perfectly well answered. But now in your question I suppose you meant this, - that some or other of those things were of necessity passing within us continually at all times; agreeably to this saying of the wise, - "that all things are in perpetual flow, going upward and downward."

PROT. So they tell us: and this saying of theirs is, methinks, worthy of regard.

SOC. Undoubtedly it is: for it is said by men who are worthy, themselves, to be regarded. But this subject, which we have thus lighted on, I would willingly decline. Now I have it in my thoughts to avoid it this way; but you must accompany me.

PROT. What way?

b SOC. Be it so, then, let us say to these wise men: but you, Protarchus, answer me to this question: Do animals feel all the alterations which they continually undergo? or, whilst we are growing, or suffering in any part of our bodies any other change, are we sensible of these internal motions? Is not quite the contrary true? for almost every thing of this kind passing within us passes without our knowledge.

PROT. Certainly so.

Soc. It was, therefore, not right in us to say, as we did just now, that all the alterations which happen to our bodies, and all the motions within them, produce either pains or pleasures.

Prot. Certainly not right.

c   Soc. And it would be better, and less liable to censure, to lay down this position.

Prot. What position?

Soc. That great changes within give us pains and pleasures; but that such as are inconsiderable, or only moderate, produce neither pleasures nor pains.

Prot. This is more justly said than the other sentence, indeed, Socrates.

Soc. If, then, these things are so, we meet with the life mentioned before recurring to us here again.

Prot. What life?

Soc. That which is exempt from all sensations, both of pain and pleasure.

Prot. Very true.

Soc. Hence, we find there are three kinds of life proposed to our consideration: one of them full of pleasure, another full of pain; the d   third neutral, and free from both. Or how otherwise would you determine upon these points?

Prot. No otherwise I, for my part: for three different kinds of life appear to me in what has been said.

Soc. To have no pain, therefore, cannot be the same thing as to have pleasure.

Prot. Certainly it cannot.

Soc. But whenever you hear a man say, that it is the most pleasurable of all things to live all one's life free from pain, what do you take to be his thought and meaning?

Prot. He means and thinks, as I take it, that it is a pleasure not to have any pain.

e   Soc. Well now: let there be any three things whatever: to instance in things of honourable name, let us suppose one of them to be gold, another to be silver, and the third to be neither gold nor silver.

Prot. We shall suppose so.

Soc. That which is neither, is it possible for it any way to become either gold or silver?

Prot. By no means.

Soc. The middle life, therefore, if it were said to be pleasurable, or if it were said to be painful, would not be spoken of in either way, rightly and agreeably to the true nature of things; nor would any person who entertains either of those opinions concerning it think rightly.

PROT. Certainly not.

SOC. And yet, my friend, we find that there are persons who actually speak and think thus amiss.

PROT. it is very evident.

SOC. Do these persons really feel pleasure[†] whenever they are free from pain?

PROT. So they say.

SOC. They must imagine, then, that they are pleased; for otherwise they would not say so.

PROT. They do, it seems, imagine it.

SOC. They have a wrong opinion then of pleasure; if it be true that pleasure, and freedom from pain, have each a distinct nature, different from that of the other.

PROT. Different, indeed, we have concluded them to be.

SOC. And are we willing to abide by our late conclusion, that the subjects still under examination are three distinct things? or do we choose to say that they are only two? Do we now say that pain is man's evil, and that deliverance from pain is man's good, and is that to which is given the appellation of pleasure?

PROT. How come we, O Socrates, to propose this point to be reconsidered by us now? for I do not apprehend your drift.

SOC. In fact, O Protarchus, you do not apprehend who are the direct enemies to Philebus.

PROT. To whom do you give that character?

SOC. To persons who are said to have a profound knowledge of nature: these persons say that pleasures have no reality at all.

PROT. What do they mean?

SOC. They say that all those things which Philebus and his party call pleasures are but deliverances from pain.

PROT. Is it your advice, then, O Socrates, that we should hearken to these persons? or how otherwise?

---

† We have ventured to suppose an error in the Greek of this passage; and that we ought to read χαιρουσιν ουτοι, instead of the printed words - χαιρειν οιονται. For, without such an alteration, Socrates in his next sentence (where these very words - χαιρειν οιονται - appear again, and where they are very proper) is guilty of mere tautology; and his argumentation proceeds not the least step, but halts during that whole sentence. -S.

SOC. Not so: but to consider them as a kind of diviners, who divine
not according to any rules of art; but, from the austerity of a certain
genius in them not ignoble, have conceived an aversion to the power of
Pleasure, and deem nothing in her to be solid; but all her attractive
d charms to be mere illusions, and not [true] pleasure. It is thus that we
should regard these persons, especially if we consider their other harsh
maxims. You shall in the next place hear what pleasures seem to me to
be true pleasures: so that, from both the accounts compared together, we
may find out the nature of Pleasure, and form our judgment of her
comparative value.

PROT. Rightly said.

SOC. Let us then follow after them, as our allies, wherever their
austerity shall lead us. For I suppose they would begin their argument
with some general principle, and propound to us some such question as
this, - whether, if we had a mind to know the nature of any particular
e quality of things, for instance, the nature of the hard, whether or no we
should not comprehend it better by examining the hardest things, than
we should by scrutinizing a various multitude of the less hard. Now,
Protarchus, you must make an answer to these austere persons, as if you
were making it to me.

PROT. By all means: and I make this answer to them, - that to
examine such bodies as exceed all others in hardness is the better way.

SOC. In like manner, then, if we had a mind to know the nature of
pleasure in general, we are not to consider the multitude of little or
mean pleasures, but those only which are called extreme and exquisite.

45a PROT. Every man would grant you the truth of this your present
argument.

SOC. The pleasures which are always within our reach, those which
we often call the greatest, do they not belong to the body?

PROT. There is no doubt of it.

SOC. Are the [bodily] pleasures which are produced in those persons
who labour under diseases, greater than the pleasures [of the same kind]
felt by those who are in health? Now let us take care not to err, by
making too precipitate an answer.

PROT. What danger is there of erring?

b SOC. Perhaps we might pronounce in favour of those who are in
health.

PROT. Probably we should.

SOC. But what? are not those pleasures the most excessive which are
preceded by the strongest desires?

PROT. This cannot be denied.

SOC. The afflicted with fevers, or with diseases of kin to fevers, are they not more thirsty than other persons? do they not more shake with cold? and suffer they not in a greater degree other evils which the body is subject to? Do they not feel their wants more pressing? and feel they not greater pleasures when they have those wants supplied?[†] Or shall we deny all this to be true?

PROT. Your representation of those cases clearly is right.

c   SOC. Well then: should we not be clearly right in saying, that whoever would know what pleasures are the greatest must not go to the healthy, but to the sick, to look for them? Be careful now not to imagine the meaning of my question to be this, - whether the sick enjoy pleasures more, in number, than the healthy: but consider me as inquiring into high degrees of pleasure; and by what means, and in what subjects, the vehemence or extreme of it always is produced. For we are to find out, we say, what the nature is of pleasure, and what those persons mean by pleasure who pretend that no such thing as pleasure has any being at all.

d   PROT. Tolerably well do I apprehend your argument.

SOC. And possibly, O Protarchus, you will equally well show the truth of it. For, tell me; in a life of boundless luxury see you not greater pleasures (I do not mean more in number, but more intense and vehement,) than those in the life of temperance? Give your mind to the question first, and then answer.

PROT. I apprehend what you say: and the great superiority of the pleasures enjoyed in a luxurious life I easily discern. For sober and temperate persons are on all occasions under the restraint of that maxim,
e   now become a proverb, which advises them to avoid the too much of any thing; to which advice they are obedient. But an excess of pleasure, even to madness, possessing the souls of the unwise and intemperate, as it makes them frantic, it makes them conspicuous, and famed for being men of pleasure.

SOC. Well said. If this, then, be the case, it is evident that the greatest pleasures, as well as the greatest pains, are produced in a morbid and vicious disposition of the soul or of the body; and not when they are in their sound and right state.

46a   PROT. Certainly so.

---

† In all the editions of the Greek we here read ἀποπληρουμενων· but certainly we ought to read ἀποπληρουμενοι. -S.

Soc. Ought we not then to instance in some of these pleasures, and to consider what circumstances attend them on account of which it is that they are styled the greatest?

Prot. That must be done.

Soc. Consider now what circumstance attends the pleasures which are produced in certain maladies.

Prot. In what maladies?

Soc. In those of the base or indecent kind; - pleasures, to which the persons whom we termed austere have an utter aversion.

Prot. What pleasures do you mean?

Soc. Those which are felt in curing the itch, for instance, by friction; and in other maladies of like kind, such as need no other medicine. Now the sensation thence arising in us, in the name of the gods, what shall we say of it? Pleasure is it? or shall we term it pain?

Prot. A mixt sort of sensation, O Socrates, seems to arise from this malady, partaking of both pain and pleasure.

b Soc. It was not, however, for the sake of Philebus that I brought this last subject into our discourse: it was because we should never be able to determine the point now before us, unless we had taken a view of these mixt pleasures, and of others also which depend on these. Let us proceed, therefore, to consider such as have an affinity with them.

Prot. Such, do you mean, as partake of pleasure and pain by means of their commixture?

Soc. That is my very meaning. Of these mixt feelings, then, some
c belong to the body; and in the body are these generated. Others are of the soul; and these have in the soul their residence. We shall find also pleasures mingled with pains, where the soul and the body have, each of them, a share. Now these mixtures [though composed of contraries] are, in some cases, termed only pleasures; in other cases, only pains.

Prot. Express yourself more fully.

Soc. When a man, whether in a sound or in a decaying state of his body, feels two contrary sensations at the same time; as when, chilled with cold, he is warming himself; or sometimes, when overheated, he is cooling himself; with a view, I suppose, to his enjoying one of those sensations, and to his deliverance from the other: in such cases, what is called the bitter-sweet, through the difficulty met with in driving away
d the bitter part, causeth a struggle within, and a fierce meeting together of opposite qualities and sensations.

Prot. It is perfectly true, what you have now said.

SOC. Are not some of these mixt sensations composed of pain and pleasure in equal proportion? and in others is not one of them predominant?

PROT. Without doubt.

SOC. Among those, then, in which there is an overplus of pain, I reckon that of the malady termed the itch, and all other pruriencies and itchings, when nothing more than a slight friction or motion is applied to them, such as only dissipates what humours are at the surface, but reaches not the fermentation and turgescence of those humours which lie deep within. In this condition, the diseased often apply heat to the parts which pain them, and then the opposite extreme, through impatience, and uncertainty which way to take. Thus they excite inexpressible pleasures first, and then the contrary, in the interior parts, compared with the pains felt in the exterior, which yet are mixed with pleasures, according as the humours are driven outwardly or inwardly. For by violently dispersing the morbific matter where it is collected, and by compelling it together from places where it lies dispersed, pleasures and pains are at once excited, and arise by each other's side.

PROT. Most true.

SOC. Now wherever, in any case of this kind, a greater quantity of pleasure is mingled, the smaller quantity of pain creates but a slight uneasiness, no more than what serves to tickle: whilst, on the other hand,[†] the great excess of pleasure spread throughout convulseth the whole frame, and sometimes causeth involuntary motions; operating also every change of colour in the countenance, every variety of posture in the limbs, and every different degree of respiration; - and within the soul it energizes in transports, uttered madly in exclamations.

PROT. Entirely so.

SOC. Further: a man in such a condition, O my friend! is apt to say of himself, and others are apt to say of him, that he is dying, as it were, through excess of pleasure. From this time for ever after he is wholly intent on pursuing the like pleasures; and the more so, the more he happens to be intemperate, and less under the government of prudence. Thus he calls these pleasures the greatest, and accounts him the happiest of men who spends his whole time, as far as possible, in the enjoyment of them.

PROT. You have described all this, O Socrates, just as it happens to the bulk of mankind, according to their own sense and opinion.

---

† In the Greek, as it is printed, we read το δ' αυτης ηδονης: but we should choose to read το δ' αυ της η. -S.

c   SOC. But all this, O Protarchus, relates only to such pleasures mixed
with pains as arise solely in the body, in its superficial parts and interior
parts alternately. And as to those feelings of the soul which meet with
a contrary condition of the body, when pleasure in the one is mixed
with pain in the other, so as that both are ingredients in one
composition, we spake of those before; such as a desire of fullness, under
a sense of emptiness in the body; when hope administers delight, while
the emptiness gives a pain. We did not, indeed, consider them at that
time as evidences of the present point; but we now say, that in all those
d   cases (and the number of them is infinite) where the condition of the
soul is different from that of the body, a mixture of pain and pleasure
happens to be produced.
       PROT. You are, I believe, perfectly in the right.
       SOC. Among the mixtures of pain and pleasure, there is a third kind
remaining, yet unmentioned.
       PROT. What kind is that?
       SOC. That where such pleasures and pains as we said arise frequently
in the soul, herself by herself, are mixed together.
       PROT. In what cases, say we, are these mixtures found?
e   SOC. Anger, fear, and desire, and lamentation, love, emulation, and
envy, and all other such passions of the soul herself, do you not suppose
them to give pain and uneasiness to the soul?
       PROT. I do.
       SOC. And shall we not find these very passions fraught with
wondrous pleasures? In the passions of resentment and anger, do we
need to be reminded of what the poet says,[†] - that

> . . . . though resentment raise
> Choler, like smoke, in even the prudent breast;
> The luscious honey from its waxen seat
> Distils not half such sweetness.

And do we not remember, in lamentations and desires, the pleasures we
have felt mingled with the pains which those passions produce?
       PROT. It is true: our passions do affect us in the manner you have
mentioned, and no otherwise.
48a   SOC. And have you not observed, at tragic spectacles presented on the
stage, with how much pleasure the spectators shed tears?
       PROT. I certainly have.

[†] Homer, in the eighteenth book of his *Iliad*, ver. 108 &c.

SOC. But have you attended to the disposition of your soul at the acting of a comedy? Do you know that there also we feel pain mixed with pleasure?

PROT. I do not perfectly well comprehend that.

b　　SOC. It is not perfectly easy, O Protarchus, at such a time, to comprehend what mixed passions possess the soul in every case of that kind.

PROT. Not at all easy, I believe.

SOC. However, let us consider what our feelings are at that time; and the more attentively, on account of their obscurity; that we may be able to discover with the greater ease what mixture there is of pain and pleasure in other cases.

PROT. Say on, then.

SOC. The passion known by the name of envy, will you set it down for a sort of pain in the soul, or how?

PROT. Even so.

SOC. And yet the man who envies another will plainly appear to be delighted with the evils which befall him.

c　　PROT. Clearly so.

SOC. Now ignorance is an evil; and so is what we term want of sense.

PROT. Undoubtedly.

SOC. From these premises you may perceive what is the nature of ridicule and the ridiculous.

PROT. You must tell me what it is.

SOC. Every particular vice takes its name from some particular bad habit in the soul. But total viciousness, the habit of wickedness in all respects, is the direct contrary of that habit which the Delphic inscription adviseth us to acquire.

PROT. That of knowing one's self do you mean, O Socrates?

d　　SOC. I do. And the contrary to this advice of the oracle would be, - not to know one's self in any respect at all.

PROT. Certainly it would.

SOC. Try now to divide this ignorance of ourselves into three kinds.

PROT. How, say you, should this be done? for I am not able to do it.

SOC. Do you say that I should make this division in your stead?

PROT. I not only say it, but desire you so to do.

SOC. Well then: whoever is ignorant of himself, must he not be thus ignorant, in one or other of these three respects?

PROT. What three?

e　　SOC. First, with respect to external possessions, in imagining himself wealthier than he really is.

PROT. Many persons there are who labour under this sort of ignorance.

SOC. Yet more numerous are they, in the next place, who imagine themselves handsomer in their persons, nobler in their air, or graced with some other corporeal advantage in a higher degree than actually they are.

PROT. Very true.

SOC. But the number is by far the greatest, I presume, of such as are mistaken in themselves, with respect to the third kind of excellence, that which belongs to the soul, by fancying themselves possessed of more virtue than in truth they have.

PROT. Nothing is more certain.

SOC. Among the virtues and excellencies of the soul, is not wisdom that to which the generality of mankind lay claim with the greatest earnestness, and in regard to which they are full of contention, opinionativeness, and false notions?

PROT. Evidently so.

SOC. Now the man who should say that ignorance and error, in any of these respects, were evils, would say what is true.

PROT. Very right.

SOC. But we are to make still another division of this ignorance of a man's self, O Protarchus, if we would discover the odd mixture of pain and pleasure in that mirthful envy which is excited by comedy, - a division into two sorts.

PROT. Into what two sorts do you mean?

SOC. To those persons who foolishly entertain any such false opinion of themselves it necessarily happens, as it does to all men in general, that strength and power attend on some; while the fate of others is quite the contrary.

PROT. It must be so.

SOC. According to this difference then between them, distinguish those ignorant persons into two sorts. And all those whose self-ignorance is attended with weakness, and with a want of power to be revenged on such as laugh at them, you may justly say that they are open to ridicule, and may call their characters properly ridiculous. But as to the others, who have power to take their revenge, if you should say that these are to be dreaded, as being powerful and hostile, you would give a very right account of them. For such ignorance, armed with power, is powerful to do mischief; and not only itself is hostile and hurtful to all persons within its reach, but so likewise are all its images and representatives. But self-ignorance, without strength and power, is to be ranked among the things which are ridiculous, and is a proper object of ridicule.

PROT. There is much of truth in what you say. But I do not as yet perceive clearly what mixture there is of pain and pleasure in our feelings on such occasions.

SOC. You are, in the first place, to apprehend the force of envy in these cases.

PROT. Show it me then.

d SOC. Is not sorrow, on some occasions, felt unjustly? and is it not the same case with joy and pleasure?

PROT. No doubt can be made of it.

SOC. There is neither injustice, nor envy, in rejoicing at the evils which befall our enemies.

PROT. Certainly there is not.

SOC. But if at any time, when we see an evil happening to our friends, we feel no sorrow, - if, on the contrary, we rejoice at it, - are we not guilty of injustice?

PROT. Without dispute.

SOC. Did we not say that it was an evil to any person to be ignorant of himself?

PROT. We did, and justly too.

e SOC. If there be in any of our friends a false conceit of their own wisdom, or of their own beauty, or of whatever else we mentioned, when we divided ignorance of one's self into three kinds, is not this conceit an object of ridicule, where it is attended with impotence and weakness; but an object of hatred, if power and strength[†] are joined with it? or do we deny, what I just now said, that the having of such a false opinion, if it be not hurtful to others, is an object of ridicule?

PROT. You said what is entirely true.

SOC. And do we not acknowledge this false conceit to be an evil, as being built on ignorance?

PROT. Most heartily.

SOC. Whether do we feel delight or sorrow when we laugh at it?

50a PROT. It is plain that we feel delight.

SOC. Did we not say, that whenever we feel delight from the evils which happen to our friends, it is envy which operates in us that unjust delight?

---

† It is hoped that no future editor of Plato will be either so absurd, or so careless, as to follow all the former editors in printing μη (instead of αν η) ερρωμενα, in the Greek of this passage. -S.

PROT. It must be envy.

SOC. Our reasoning then shows, that when we laugh at what is ridiculous in a friend, mixing thus delight with envy, we mix together pleasure and pain. For we acknowledged long ago that envy gives uneasiness and pain to the soul; and we have admitted, that laughing yields delight. Now in these cases they arise, both of them, at the same time.

PROT. True.

b SOC. We see, then, from the conclusion of our argument, that in mournful spectacles, and no less in comedies, not only as they are acted on the stage, but as they are presented to us also in the tragedy and comedy of real life, and in a thousand intermediate occurrences, pains and pleasures are blended together.

PROT. It would be impossible, O Socrates, for a man not to acknowledge this, were he ever so zealous an advocate for the opposite side.

c SOC. When we entered on the present subject, we proposed to consider anger, desire and grief, fear and love, jealousy and envy, and such other passions of the soul, promising ourselves to find in them those mixed feelings which again and again we had been speaking of: did we not?

PROT. We did.

SOC. Do we perceive that we have dispatched already all which relates to grief, and envy, and anger?

PROT. We perceive it clearly.

SOC. But there is much yet remaining.

PROT. Very true.

SOC. For what reason, principally, do you suppose it was that I explained to you the mixed feeling which a comedy occasions in us? Do

d you not conceive, that it was to show myself able to explain to you with much more ease, the like mixture of pain and pleasure in fear, in love, and in the other passions? and that after you had seen the truth of it in one instance, you might discharge me from the necessity of proceeding to the rest, or of lengthening out the argument any further; but might receive it for a truth, without limitation or exception, that the body without the soul, and the soul without the body, and both together likewise, are, in many things, which affect them severally or jointly, full of a sense of pleasures mingled with pains. Say, then, whether you will dismiss me, or make it midnight before we finish. But I imagine that, after I shall have added a few things more, I shall obtain from you my dismission: for I shall be ready to give you an account of all these things

e   at large tomorrow; but at present am desirous of proceeding to what
remains on this subject; that we may come to a decision to the point in
controversy, as Philebus hath enjoined us.

PROT. You have well spoken, O Socrates; and as to what remains, go
through with it in whatever way it is agreeable to yourself.

SOC. Well then: after the mixed pleasures we are to proceed, by a kind
of natural necessity, to the several pleasures which are unmixed and
pure.

51a PROT. Perfectly well said.

SOC. The nature of these I shall endeavour to explain to you, by
converting to my own use, with a little alteration, what is said of them
by others. For I do not entirely give credit to those persons who tell us,
that all pleasure consists in a cessation from uneasiness and pain. But,
as I said before, I make use of these persons as witnesses, in confirmation
of this truth, - that some things there are which seem to be pleasures,
but by no means are so in reality; and of this also, - that some other
pleasures there are, many and great in imagination, accompanied with
pains, but at the same time with relief from greater pains, amid the
distresses of the body and of the soul.

b   PROT. But what pleasures are those, O Socrates, which a man would
deem rightly of, in supposing them to be true?

SOC. The pleasures[22] which are produced in us from seeing beauteous
colours and beauteous figures; many pleasures also of the smell, and
many others arising in us from the hearing of sounds; in a word,
whatever pleasures we feel from perceiving the presence of any thing,
whose absence we are insensible of, or at least occasions no pain in us,
all these are unmixed and pure.

PROT. How do you explain this general account, O Socrates?

c   SOC. The meaning of it, indeed, is not directly obvious: but we must
endeavour to make it evident. I mean, then, by beauteous figures, not,
as most men would suppose I meant, the beauty of living forms, or their
statues; but the straight and the round, whether in surfaces,[†] or in
solids;[‡] according to which are fashioned the turner's works, and those
of the carpenter, by means of his rules and angles. For the figures
which I mean, if you apprehend me, have no relative beauty, like those

† That is, rectilinear plane figures, such as triangles, rectangles, and circles. -S.

‡ Such as pyramids and cubes, spheres, cylinders and cones. -S.

other beauteous forms;† but in their own nature, separately considered,
are always absolutely beautiful; and the beholding of them gives us
certain peculiar pleasures, not at all similar to the pleasures excited in us
d   by any kind of motion. And as to colours, I mean such as bear the like
stamp of absolute beauty,‡ and yield also pleasures of a peculiar nature.
But do we apprehend these things? or what say we to them?

PROT. I endeavour, O Socrates, to comprehend your full meaning: but
endeavour you yourself to explain thoroughly the whole of it.

SOC. As to sounds, I mean such as are smooth, clear, and canorous,
conveying some pure and simple melody,§ without relation to any other
sounds, but singly of themselves musical: of such I speak, and of the
connatural pleasures which attend them.

PROT. That such pleasures also there are, I readily acknowledge.

e   SOC. The pleasures felt by us from certain odours are, indeed, of a
kind less divine than the pleasures just now mentioned; but in respect of
their being equally pure, and not, of necessity, mixed with pains, I rank
them all under the same head. For in whatever pleasures there happens
to be found this quality of entire freedom from pain, all these I oppose
to those other pleasures with which pain is complicated. Now, if you
observe, we have already spoken of two different kinds of pleasure.

PROT. I do observe.

52a   SOC. To these let us now add the pleasures taken in the mathematical
sciences; unless we are of opinion that such pleasures are of necessity
preceded by a thirst of learning them; and that, when tasted and
enjoyed, they raise a thirst of more and more; so that, from our
beginning to learn them, they are all along attended with uneasiness.

PROT. I think that such uneasiness is not at all necessary.

---

† The parts of every mathematical simple figure, whether it be right-lined or
circular, are, all of them, similar and commensurable. - The beauty of figure in all
animals, on the contrary, arises from the proportions of dissimilar parts, measured, not
by any common measure, but by the respective ends and uses for which they are
severally designed by nature. -S.

‡ Such as the beautiful colours of many flowers; or as those of a clear morning or
evening sky: not such as the colour of a complexion, the tincture of a skin, - in the
human species, - a colour belonging only to that species, and relatively agreeable, as it
indicates health of body, and a purity of the blood and humours. -S.

§ Such is that of many species of birds, whose whistling is all monotonous. Such
also is that of the Æolian harp, on which the vibrations are made solely by the air in
motion. -S.

SOC. Well: but suppose that, having attained to full possession of them, we happen afterwards to lose some part through forgetfulness, do you see no uneasiness arising hence?

PROT. None at all from the nature of the thing itself: but when the knowledge is wanted to be applied to some use in human life, then a man is uneasy at having lost it, on account of its usefulness.

b   SOC. And we are at present, my friend, actually concerned about those feelings only which arise in us from the nature of the knowledge itself, without any regard to the usefulness of it in computing or measuring.

PROT. You are right then in saying, that, in mathematical knowledge, a forgetfulness frequently befalls us, without giving us any uneasiness.

SOC. These pleasures, therefore, the pleasures of science, we must acknowledge to be unmixed with pains. But these pleasures belong not to the vulgar multitude, being enjoyed only by a very few.

PROT. All this must certainly be acknowledged.

c   SOC. Now, then, that we have tolerably well distinguished between the pure pleasures and those which are rightly called impure, let us further add these distinctions between them, - that the vehement pleasures know not moderation nor measure; while those of the gentler kind admit of measure, and are moderate: and that greatness and intenseness, and the contrary qualities, the frequency also and the rareness of repetition, are attributes of such pleasures only as belong to the boundless genus, - to that which is perpetually varying in its quantities and motions through the body and through the soul, - while the pleasures to which the like variations never happen, belong to the contrary genus, and are allied to all things wherein symmetry is found.

d   PROT. Perfectly right, O Socrates.

SOC. The pleasures, beside these assortments of them, are to be further distinguished thus.

PROT. How?

SOC. We should consider whether the purity and the simplicity of pleasures serve to discover what true pleasure is: or whether the truth of pleasures may best be known from their intenseness, their multitude, their greatness and their abundance.

PROT. What is your view, Socrates, in proposing this to be considered?

SOC. To omit nothing by which the nature of pleasure, and that of knowledge, may be set in the clearest light; and not to leave it undiscovered, whether or no some kinds of each of them are pure, while e   other kinds are impure; that thus, what is pure and simple in each being brought before us to be judged of, you and I, and all this company, may the more easily form a right judgment.

PROT. Very rightly said.

SOC. Well then: all those kinds of things which we commonly say are pure, let us consider of in the following way: but first let us choose out some one among them for an instance to consider of.

PROT. Which would you have us choose?

53a   SOC. Among the principal of those kinds, let us, if you please, consider the white kind of things.

PROT. By all means.

SOC. In what way, then, might we have any thing which is called white, with the most perfect and pure whiteness? whether by having the greatest number of things which are white, and the largest of the kind in size, or by having what is white in the highest degree, and not tinged with the least degree of any other colour?

PROT. Evidently, by having what is of the most simple and unmixed whiteness.

b   SOC. Rightly said. Shall we not then determine that this pure white is the truest, and at the same time the most beautiful of all whites; and not that which is of the largest size, and whose number is the greatest?

PROT. Most certainly we shall.

SOC. In pronouncing, then, that a little of purely white is whiter, and of a more beautiful and true whiteness, than a great quantity of the mixed white, we shall say what is entirely right.

PROT. Without the least doubt.

SOC. Well then: I suppose we shall have no occasion to produce many such instances to prove the truth of our conclusion concerning pleasure; the instance already brought seems sufficient for us to perceive at once,

c   that a little of pleasure, pure, and free from pain, is more pleasant, more true, and perfect, as well as more comely, than pleasure where pain is mingled, be there ever so much of it, or be it ever so vast and vehement.

PROT. By all means: the instance you gave in whiteness, is an argument from analogy, sufficient for the proof of it.

SOC. But what think you now of this? Have we not heard it said concerning pleasure, that it is a thing always in generation, always produced anew, and having no stability of being, cannot properly be said to be at all? For some ingenious† persons there are who endeavour to show us, that such is the nature of pleasure; and we are much obliged to them for this their account of it.

PROT. Why so?

d   SOC. I shall recount to you the whole of their reasoning on this point, my friend Protarchus, by putting a few questions to you.

PROT. Do so: and begin your questions.

SOC. Are there not in nature two very different kinds of things: this, in itself alone complete; that, desirous always of the other?

PROT. How do you mean? and what things do you speak of?

SOC. One of them is by nature always of high dignity and value; the other, falling far short of it, and always indigent.

PROT. Express yourself a little more clearly.

SOC. Have we not seen some of the fair sex who excelled in beauty and in virtue? and have we not seen their lovers and admirers?

PROT. Often.

e   SOC. Analogous then to these two different sorts of persons, see if you cannot discover two different kinds of things, to one or other of which different kinds belongs every thing, commonly said to have a being: the third be to the saviour.[23]

PROT. Speak your meaning, O Socrates, in plainer terms.

SOC. I mean nothing, O Protarchus, but what is very simple and easy to be seen. But our present argument is pleased to sport itself. However, it means no more than this, - that there is a kind of things which are always for the sake of some other; and there is also a kind of things for whose sake always is produced whatever hath any final cause of its production.

PROT. I find it difficult to understand your meaning, after your many explanations of it.

SOC. Perhaps, young man, it will be understood better as we proceed in the reasoning on this subject.

54a   PROT. I make no doubt of it.

SOC. Let us now make another division of things into two different kinds.

PROT. What kinds are they?

---

† In the Greek - κομψοι, neat and trim, that is, in their reasonings and discourses; - subtle arguers, or fine logicians; - a character which distinguished the school of Zeno the Eleatic. It will presently be seen, that the persons here spoken of philosophized on the principles of the Eleatic sect, and probably were some of the same Zeno's Athenian disciples. -S.

Soc. The generation[†] of all things is one kind of things; and the being of all is a different kind.

PROT. I admit your difference between being and generation.

Soc. You are perfectly in the right. Now, whether of these two is for the sake of the other? Shall we say that generation is for the sake of being? or shall we say that being is for the sake of generation?

PROT. Whether or no that which is termed being, is what it is for the sake of generation, is this your present question?

Soc. Apparently it is.

b   PROT. In the name of the Gods, how can you ask so strange a question?

Soc. My meaning in that question, O Protarchus, is of such a kind as this other; - whether you would choose to say that ship-building is for the sake of shipping, rather than you would say that shipping is for the sake of ship-building: and all other things of like kind, O Protarchus, I include in the question which I ask you.

PROT. But for what reason, O Socrates, do you not give an answer to it yourself?

Soc. I have no reason to refuse that office; do you but go along with me in my answer.

PROT. Certainly I shall.

c   Soc. I say, then, that for the sake of generation, it is true, that medicines are composed; the instrumental parts, prepared by nature, and all the materials of it, provided: but that every act of generation is for the sake of some being; generation in every species, for the sake of some being belonging to that species; and universally, all generation, for the sake of universal being.

PROT. Most evidently so.

Soc. If pleasure, then, be of such a nature as to be generated always anew, must not the generating of it be always for the sake only of some being?

PROT. Without doubt.

Soc. Now that, for the sake of which is always generated whatever is generated for some end, must be in the rank of things which are good:

---

† *Essence* and *generation,* says Olympiodorus, are fourfold. For that which is sensible is generation, and the intelligible is essence. In a similar manner, that which is subcelestial is generation, and that which is celestial is essence. Further still, in the third place, generation is a procession to form, and form itself is essence. In the fourth place, mutation about a subject is generation, and the subject itself is essence; as, for instance, quality about body. But every where generation is for the sake of essence: for essence is the cause of generation. -T. [.216]

and that which is generated for the sake of any other thing, must of necessity, my friend, be placed in a different rank of things.

PROT. Certainly it must.

d   SOC. Shall we not be right, then, in placing pleasure in a rank of things different from that of good; if it be true, that pleasure has no stable being, but is always generated anew?

PROT. Perfectly right.

SOC. Therefore, as I said in beginning this argumentation, we are much obliged to the persons who have given us this account of pleasure, - that the essence of it consists in being always generated anew, but that never has it any kind of being. For it is plain, that these persons would laugh at a man who asserted, that pleasure and good were the same thing.

PROT. Certainly they would.

e   SOC. And these very persons would certainly laugh at those men, wherever they met with them, who place their chief good and end in generation.

PROT. How, and what sort of men do you mean?

SOC. Such, as in freeing themselves from hunger, or thirst, or any of the uneasinesses from which they are freed by generation, are so highly delighted with the action of removing those uneasinesses, as to declare they would not choose to live without suffering thirst and hunger, nor without feeling all those other sensations which may be said to follow from such kinds of uneasiness.

55a   PROT. Such, indeed, there are, who seem to be of that opinion.

SOC. Would not all of us say that corruption was the contrary of generation?

PROT. It is impossible to think otherwise.

SOC. Whoever, then, makes such a life his choice, must choose both corruption and generation, rather than that third kind of life, in which he might live with the clearest discernment of what is right and good, but without the feeling of either pain or pleasure.

PROT. Much absurdity, as it seems, O Socrates, is to be admitted by the man who holds that human good consists wholly in pleasure.

SOC. Much, indeed. For let us argue further thus.

PROT. How?

b   SOC. Since no good nor beauty is in bodies, nor in any other things beside the soul; is it not absurd to imagine, that in the soul pleasure should be the only good; and that neither fortitude, nor temperance, nor understanding, nor any of the other valuable attainments of the soul, should be numbered among the good things which the soul enjoys?

Further too, is it not highly irrational to suppose, that a man afflicted with pain, without feeling any pleasure, should be obliged to say that evil only, and no good, was with him at the time when he was in pain, though he were the best of all men? And is it not equally absurd, on the other hand, to suppose that a man in the midst of pleasures must be, during that time, in the midst of good; and that the more pleasure he

c feels, the more good he is filled with, and is so much the better man?

PROT. All these suppositions, O Socrates, are absurdities in the highest degree possible.

SOC. It is well. But now let us not employ ourselves wholly in searching into the nature of pleasure; as if we industriously declined the examination of intellect and science; but in these also, if there be any thing putrid or unsound, let us have the courage to cut it all off, and throw it aside; till, coming to a discovery of what is entirely pure and sound therein, the discovery may be of use to us in comparing the truest parts of intellect and science with the truest parts of pleasure, and in forming our judgment concerning the superiority of either from that comparison.

PROT. Rightly said.

d SOC. Do we not hold, that mathematical science is partly employed in the service of the mechanic arts, and partly in the liberal education and discipline of youth? or how think we on this subject?

PROT. Exactly so.

SOC. Now, as to the manual arts,[†] let us consider, in the first place, whether some of these depend not on science more than others; and whether we ought not to look on those of the former sort as the more pure, and on these others as the more impure.

PROT. Certainly we ought.

SOC. And in each of these we should distinguish and separate the leading arts from the arts which are led and governed by them.

PROT. What arts do you call the leading arts? and why do you give that epithet to them?

SOC. I mean thus; from all the arts were a man to separate and lay

e aside those of numbering, of measuring, and of weighing, what remained in every one of them, would become comparatively mean and contemptible.

PROT. Contemptible, indeed.

---

† In the Greek of this passage it is presumed that we ought to read χειροτεχνιαις, and not, as it is printed, χειροτεχνικαις, - and also to read εστι instead of ενι. -S.

SOC. For room would be then left only for conjecture, and for exercise of the senses, by experience and habitual practice; and we should then make use of no other faculties beside those of guessing and aiming well, (to which, indeed, the multitude give the name of arts) increasing the strength of those faculties by dint of assiduity and labour.

56a PROT. All which you have now said must, of necessity, be true.

SOC. The truth of it is evident in all musical performances throughout. For, in the first place, harmony is produced, and one sound is adapted to another, not by measuring, but by that aiming well which arises from constant exercise. It is evident too in musical performances on all wind-instruments: for in these the breath, by being well aimed as it is blown along, searches and attains the measure of every chord beaten. So that music has in it much of the uncertain, and but a little of the fixed and firm.

PROT. Very true.

b SOC. And we shall find the case to be the same in the arts of medicine and agriculture, in the art of navigation also, and the military art.

PROT. Most clearly so.

SOC. But in the art of building we shall find, as I presume, many measures made use of, and many instruments employed; by which it is made to surpass in accuracy many things which are called sciences.

PROT. How so?

SOC. It is so in ship-building, and house-building, and in many other works of carpentry. For in these, I think, the art useth the straight-rule, c and the square, the turning-lath and the compasses, the plummet and the marking-line.

PROT. You are entirely right, O Socrates, it is so as you say.

SOC. The arts, therefore, as they are called, let us now distinguish into two sorts; - those which music is at the head of, as they are less accurate than some others; and these others which partake of accuracy the most, at the head of which is architecture.

PROT. This distinction is allowed of.

SOC. And let us set down those arts for the most accurate which we lately said were the prime or leading arts.

PROT. You mean, if I mistake not, arithmetic, and those other arts which you mentioned together with it but just now.†

d SOC. The very same. But, O Protarchus, must we not say that each of these arts is twofold? or how otherwise?

PROT. What arts do you speak of?

---

† Namely, *mensuration* and *statics*. -S.

SOC. Arithmetic, in the first place. Must we not say of this, that the arithmetic of the multitude is of one sort, and that the arithmetic of those who apply themselves to philosophy[†] is of another sort?

PROT. What is the difference by which the one may be distinguished from the other?

SOC. The difference between them, O Protarchus, is far from being inconsiderable. For the multitude in numbering, number by unequal ones put together; as two armies of unequal force; two oxen of unequal size; two things, the smallest of all, - or two, the greatest, - being compared with others of the same kind. But the students in philosophy would not understand what a man meant, who, in numbering, made any difference between some and other of the ones which composed the number.

PROT. You are perfectly right in saying that no inconsiderable difference lies in the different manner of studying and using numbers; so as to make it probable that two different sorts there are of arithmetic.

SOC. Well: and what of calculation in trade, and of mensuration in building? Does the latter of these arts not differ from mathematical geometry? nor the other from calculations made by the students in pure mathematics. Shall we say that they are, each of them, but one art? or shall we set down each of them for two?

PROT. For my part, I should give my opinion agreeably to your division of arithmetic; and should say that each of these arts also was twofold.

SOC. You would give a right opinion. But with what design I brought these distinctions on the carpet do you conceive?

PROT. Perhaps I do. But I could wish that you yourself would declare what was your design.

SOC. These distinctions seem to me to have shown to us, that in science there is that very circumstance attending it which we had before discovered to be in pleasure; the one thus answering to the other. For, having found that some sort of pleasure was purer than some other sort, we were inquiring whether the same difference was to be found with regard to science; and whether one sort of this also was purer than some other.

PROT. It is very manifest that your distinctions between the several arts were introduced for this very purpose.

---

† Meaning the students in mathematics. For the study of the mathematical sciences was deemed by Plato the best introduction to the knowledge of intelligible things. -S.

SOC. Well then: have we not discovered, in what has been said, that some arts are clearer than others, having more light within them; and that others are more involved in obscurity and darkness?

PROT. Evidently so.

SOC. And has not the course of our argument led us to take notice of some art, bearing the same name with some other art; and first, to suppose them both to be, as they are commonly imagined, but one art; then, to consider them as two different arts; to examine each with regard to its clearness and purity; and to inquire which of the two has in it the most accuracy, whether that which is cultivated by students in philosophy, or that which is exercised by the multitude?

PROT. Our argument seems to bring on this inquiry.

SOC. And what answer, O Protarchus, should we make to such a question?

PROT. O Socrates, we are now advanced so far as to discover an amazingly wide difference between the parts of our knowledge in point of clearness.

SOC. It will, therefore, be the easier for us to answer to that question.

PROT. Without doubt. And let us affirm, that those leading arts greatly excel the others with regard to clearness; and that such of those brighter arts themselves as are studied by real students in philosophy, display, in measures and in numbers, their vast superiority to all other arts, with regard to accuracy and truth.†

SOC. Granting these things to be what you say they are, let us, on the credit of what you have said, boldly answer to those persons who are so formidable in argumentation, thus:

PROT. How?

SOC. That there are two sorts of arithmetic; and that, dependant on these, there is a long train of arts, each of them, in like manner, twofold under one denomination.

PROT. Let us give to the persons whom you call formidable that very answer, O Socrates, with a confidence of its being right.

SOC. Do we then affirm, that in these sciences there is an accuracy the highest of all.

PROT. Certainly.

---

† This whole sentence, beginning with the words "and let us affirm," is, in Stephens's edition, very improperly given to Socrates; and consequently the sentence following, with equal impropriety, to Protarchus. The Basil editions are both right; the Aldine not clear. -S.

SOC. But the power of dialectic, O Protarchus, if we gave to any other science the preference above her, would deny that superiority.

58a   PROT. What power is it to which we are to give that name?

SOC. Plainly that power, O Protarchus, by which the mind perceives all that accuracy and clearness of which we have been speaking. For I am entirely of opinion, that all persons, endued with even the smallest portion of understanding, must deem the knowledge of the real essence of things - the knowledge of that kind of being whose nature is invariable - to be by far the most certain and true knowledge. But you, Protarchus, to what art or science would you give the distinction of pre-eminence?

b   PROT. As to me, O Socrates, I have often heard Gorgias maintaining in all places, that the art of persuasion has greatly the advantage over all other arts in overruling all things, and making all persons submit to it, not by constraint, but by a voluntary yielding; and therefore, that of all arts it is by far the most excellent. Now I should not chose to contradict or oppose either you or him.

SOC. As much as to say, if I apprehend your meaning rightly, that you cannot for shame desert your colours.

PROT. Let your opinion of these matters now prevail; and the ranks of the several arts be settled as you would have them.

SOC. Am I now to blame for your making a mistake?

PROT. What mistake have I made?

SOC. The question, my friend Protarchus, was not which art, or
c   which science, is superior to all the rest, with regard to greatness, and excellence, and usefulness to us; but of which art the objects are the brightest, the most accurate, and true, though the art itself brought us little or no gain: this it is, which is the present subject of our inquiry. Observe, then, Gorgias will have no quarrel with you: for you may still allow to his art the preference above all others, in point of utility and profit to mankind. But, as I said before concerning white, that be there
d   ever so little of it, so it be pure, it excels a large quantity of an impure white, with regard to the truth of whiteness; just so is it with the study which I have been commending; it excels all others with regard to truth itself. And now that we have considered this subject attentively, and discussed it sufficiently, laying aside all regards to the usefulness of the sciences and arts, as well as to the reputation which they bear in the world, and thoroughly sifting them to find out the purity of intellect and wisdom, - if there be in the soul any faculty of loving truth above all things, and of doing whatever she does for the sake of truth, - let us consider whether it is right to say that we have this faculty improve

chiefly by dialectic, or whether we must search for some other art fitter for that purpose, and making it more her proper business.

PROT. Well: I do consider the point proposed; and I imagine it no easy matter to admit that any other science or art seeks and embraces truth so much as this.

SOC. Say you this from having observed that many of the arts, even such as profess a laborious inquiry after truth, are, in the first place, conversant only with opinions, and exercise only the imagination; and that methodically, and according to a set of rules, they then search into things which are the subjects only of such opinions?† and do you know, that the persons who suppose themselves to be inquiring into the nature of things are, all their lives, inquisitive about nothing more than this outward world, how it was produced, what causeth the changes which happen therein, and how those changes operate their effects? Should we acknowledge all this so to be, or how otherwise?

PROT. Just so.

SOC. Whoever of us then addicts himself to the study of nature in this way, employs his time and care, not about the things which always are in being, but about things which are either newly come into being, or which are to come, or which have been already, and are past.

PROT. Very true.

SOC. What clearness, therefore, what certainty, or exact truth, can we expect to find in these things, none of which had ever any stability or sameness in them, nor ever will have any, nor have such of them as now exist any, even during their existence?

PROT. How can it be expected?

SOC. Concerning things in which there is not the least stability, how can we form any stable notions?

PROT. I suppose it not possible.

SOC. Of those things, then, there is neither intelligence, nor any sort of science to be acquired; at least not such as contains the highest degree of certainty.

---

† Meaning, as we presume, such as the philosophers of the Ionic sect, by Aristotle styled φυσικοι, *naturalists*. For we learn from D. Laertius that Archelaus, a disciple of Anaxagoras, and the last professor and teacher of the doctrine of those philosophers, did, in the time of Socrates, introduce into Athens their way of philosophizing; which was none other than that spoken of in this passage. It seems therefore probable, that the Athenian scholars of Archelaus are the very persons whose studies are here shown to fall short of attaining to the knowledge of truth, or the true nature of things. The same judgment of Socrates concerning these Ionic physiologers we find recorded by Xenophon in Memorabil. lib. i, cap 1, sec. 11. -S.

PROT. It is not probable that there is.

SOC. We ought, therefore, both you and I, to lay aside the consideration of what Gorgias or Philebus said, and to establish on a firmer basis this truth.

c　　PROT. What truth?

SOC. This: - Whatever is in us of stable, pure, and true, it has for the objects of it - either the beings which always are, and remain invariable, entirely pure and unadulterate; or [if these are beyond the reach of our sight] then such as are the nearest allied to them, and are second in the ranks of being: for all other things come after those first beings; second, and so on in order.

PROT. Perfectly right.

SOC. The noblest, therefore, of the names given to things of this kind, is it not perfectly right to assign to those of this kind, which are the noblest?

PROT. It is reasonable so to do.

d　　SOC. Are not intellect and wisdom the noblest of those names?

PROT. They are.

SOC. Rightly then are these names in accurate speech appropriated to the intelligence and contemplation of real being.

PROT. Certainly so.

SOC. And the things for the excellency of which I at the first contended, are the very things to which we give these names.

PROT. Clearly are they, O Socrates.

e　　SOC. Well now: were a man to say that the nature of intellect and the nature of pleasure lay severally before us, like two different sorts of materials before some workman, for him to mix or join together, and from them, and in them, to compose his designed work, - would he not make a fair comparison suitable to the task which our inquiry has engaged us in?

PROT. A very fair comparison.

SOC. Should we not, then, in the next place, set about mixing them together?

PROT. Why should we not?

SOC. Would it not be our best way to begin this work by recollecting and repeating those things over again?

PROT. What things?

SOC. Those we have often mentioned before. For, I think, the
60a　proverb says well: - "Again and again that which is right, by repeating it, to recall into our minds."

PROT. Undoubtedly.

SOC. In the name of Jupiter, then, come on. The whole of our controversy began, I think, with stating the point in question, to this effect.

PROT. How?

SOC. Philebus affirms that pleasure is the right mark set up by nature for all animals to aim at; that they all ought to pursue pleasure; that the good of them all is this very thing, pleasure; and that *good* and *pleasant*, these two attributes, belong but to one subject, as they both have but

b   one and the same nature: on the other hand, Socrates denies this to be true; and maintains, in the first place, that as the two names, *good* and *pleasant*, are two different names, different also are the things so denominated; in the next place, that the nature of good differs from that of pleasure; and that intelligence, or mind, partakes of the properties of good more than pleasure does, and is allied nearer to its nature. Were not some such positions as these, O Protarchus, severally laid down by us?

PROT. They were.

SOC. But was not this point agreed on between us at that time, and do we not still agree in it?

PROT. What point?

SOC. That the nature of good itself is more excellent than the nature of any other thing in this respect?

c   PROT. In what respect?

SOC. This: that whatever animal being hath the constant, entire, and full possession of good itself, such a being has no want of any thing beside, having always a most perfect and complete sufficiency. Is it not so?

PROT. It certainly is.

SOC. Have we not endeavoured to consider separately a life of pleasure and a life of intellect, each unmixed with the other, - a life of pleasure without intellect, and in like manner, a life of intellect without the smallest degree of pleasure?

PROT. We have.

d   SOC. Did either of those lives appear to us at that time to be sufficient for the happiness of any man?

PROT. How was it possible?

SOC. But if at that time any mistake was committed, let it be now revised and rectified. In order to which, let us take memory, science, wisdom, and right opinion, comprehending them all in one idea, and consider whether any man, without having something of that kind, would accept of pleasure, were it offered to him, either in the greatest abundance, or in the most exquisite degree; whether, indeed, he would regard the having or the receiving of any thing whatever; as he would not, in that case, have a right thought or opinion of his having any pleasure; neither would he know what he felt or had at present; nor would he remember in what condition or circumstances he had been at any time before. In like manner concerning wisdom, consider, whether a man would choose to have it without a mixture of any pleasure in the least, rather than to have the same wisdom attended with pleasures of certain kinds; and whether a man would prefer the having of all possible pleasures, without wisdom, to the having of them accompanied with some portion of wisdom.

PROT. It is impossible, O Socrates, for a man to make any such choice as you have supposed. And there is no occasion to repeat these questions again and again.

SOC. Not pleasure, then, nor wisdom, either of them alone, can be the perfect and consummate good, eligible to all men, that which we are inquiring after.

PROT. Certainly not.

SOC. Of this good, then, we are to give a clear and full description, or at least some sketch, that we may know where the second prize of excellence, as we called it, ought to be bestowed.

PROT. Perfectly right.

SOC. Have we not, then, taken a way by which we may find out our chief good?

PROT. What way do you mean?

SOC. As if we were in search of any particular man, and were already well informed of the place of his abode, we should have made a great progress toward finding the man himself.

PROT. Without doubt.

SOC. And our reasoning has now declared to us clearly, what it pointed to before, that, not in the unmixed life, but in the mixed, we are to seek for happiness.

PROT. Certainly so.

SOC. But in a proper and well-tempered mixture we may reasonably hope to discover what we are in search of with more certainty than we could by an ill-made composition.

PROT. With much more.

SOC. Let us, then, set about mixing and making the composition, first praying to the Gods for their assistance; whether it be Bacchus,[24] or Vulcan, or some other of the Gods, who presides over the mixture of these ingredients.

PROT. Let us, by all means, do so.

SOC. And now, as it were, two cisterns, or vases, are set before us; the vase of pleasure,† as of honey; and the vase of intellect, cool and sober, as of some hard and healthful water. These, then, we are to mix together in the best manner we are able.

PROT. With all my heart.

d SOC. Come, then: but first say, whether by mingling all pleasure with all wisdom we may best obtain our end, the having of a proper and due mixture.

PROT. Perhaps we might.

SOC. But it is dangerous to make the experiment. And I believe that I can point out a way to mix them with more safety.

PROT. Say what say.

SOC. Concerning pleasures, I think, we held, that some more truly deserved that name than others of them; and of arts, that some were more accurate and exact than others.

PROT. Undoubtedly so.

e SOC. And that the sciences also differed one from another in like manner: for that some kinds of science have for their objects only such things as arise into being and afterwards perish; whereas another kind directs its view to things which are neither generated nor destroyed, but always are in being, always have the same properties, and preserve always the same relations. And this kind of science, with regard to the truth of it, we deemed more excellent than the other kinds.

PROT. Entirely right.

SOC. In the first place, therefore, mixing together the purest parts of pleasure and of wisdom, when they have been thus distinguished from the less pure, if we view those purest parts of each in combination, are they not, thus combined, sufficient to furnish out, and present us with, an ample view of that life which is desirable? or is any thing further, any ingredient of a different kind, wanting to perfect the composition?

62a PROT. So as you propose, and only so, it seems to me necessary for us to do.

SOC. Let us, then, suppose a man to have in his mind the idea of justice itself, so as to know what it is in its own essence, and to be able

---

† Pleasure is compared to honey, says Olympiodorus, because it possesses sweetness and the ecstatic. And hence the Pythagoric saying, that souls fall into generation through honey (διο και πυθαγορειος λογος, δια μελιτος πιπτειν εις γενεσιν τας ψυχας). But intellect is compared to water, because it is sober. [.229]

to give an account of it in consequence of that knowledge. Let us also suppose him to have the like knowledge of all other beings.

PROT. Be such a man supposed.

SOC. Will this man now sufficiently possess science by knowing the nature of the circle, and of the divine sphere itself; whilst he is ignorant
b   of that sphere, and of those circles with which the eyes of men are conversant? Will that knowledge of his be sufficient for his use in building, and in other arts where lines and circles are to be drawn?

PROT. Ridiculous we should call our condition here, O Socrates, if our knowledge were thus confined to things ideal and divine.

SOC. How do you say? Arts which are neither certain nor pure, using untrue rules, and conversant with untrue circles, are we to throw such arts into the composition, and mix them with the other ingredients?

PROT. It is necessary for us; if, whenever we are any where abroad, we are desirous of finding our way home.

c   SOC. Are we to add music too? - an art which, not long since we said, is wanting in purity, as being full of conjecture and imitation?

PROT. Of necessity we must, as it appears to me, if the life which we are to lead shall ever deserve to be called life, or be at all worth the having.

SOC. Would you, then, like a door-keeper, when he is pushed and pressed by a throng of people, yield to them, set the doors wide open, and suffer all the sciences to rush in, the less pure mingling themselves among the perfectly pure?

d   PROT. I see not, O Socrates, for my part, how any man would be hurt by receiving all the other sciences, if he was already in possession of the first and highest.

SOC. I may safely then admit them all to come pouring in, like the torrents of water in that fine poetical simile of Homer's,[†] rushing down into a valley from the mountains which surround it.

PROT. By all means, let them be all admitted.

SOC. Let us now return to the vase of pleasure. For when we thought of mixing pleasure and knowledge together, the purer parts of pleasure did not present themselves immediately to our minds: but, from our affectionate regard to science, we suffered all kinds of it to crowd in before any of the pleasures.

e   PROT. Very true.

† *Iliad*, lib. iv, ver. 453.

SOC. It is now time for us to consult about the pleasures; whether we should let them all come thronging in, or whether we should admit those of the true sort first.

PROT. It makes a great difference in point of safety, to let in, the first, such only as are true.

SOC. Let these, then, be admitted. But how shall we proceed? Must we not do, as we did with the several kinds of science, admit as many pleasures also as are of the necessary sort?

PROT. Without doubt, the necessary pleasures also, by all means.

63a   SOC. But now, as we held it both safe and advantageous in going through life to be acquainted with every art, - if we are of the same opinion with regard to pleasures, - if we hold it conducive to our good, and at the same time harmless, to enjoy every sort of pleasure in the course of our lives, - in this case, we are to intermix all sorts of pleasure with all the kinds of science.

PROT. What say we then as to this point? and how ought we to act?

SOC. This question, O Protarchus, should not be put to us. But the pleasures themselves, and the other assembly also, that of the sciences and arts, are to be examined, each party concerning the other, in this manner.

b   PROT. In what manner?

SOC. Friends, we shall say, [*addressing our question to the pleasures first*] whether we ought to call you pleasures, or whatever is your right name, would ye choose to live in the same place with all kinds of wisdom, or to live without wisdom? To this interrogatory they must, I think, answer thus:

PROT. How?

SOC. That seeing, as was said before, were wisdom and pleasure to be left, each of them, alone, single, and destitute of aid, neither of them would have any virtue of power at all, nor would any advantage arise

c   from either, - we deem it best that all the kinds of wisdom should dwell with us, one kind of wisdom with each of us, one who is suitable to the peculiar nature of its companion, and is perfectly acquainted with her power and influence.

PROT. And well have ye now answered, we shall say to them.

SOC. After this, we are to demand of wisdom and intellect, in the same manner, thus:- Have ye any occasion for pleasures to be mixed among you? On the other side, we may suppose wisdom and intellect to interrogate us; and what sort of pleasures, they would perhaps say, is it that ye mean?

PROT. Probably they would.

d   SOC. And to this question of theirs our answer would be this:- Beside those true pleasures, we should say, do ye further want the pleasures of the intense and exquisite kind to dwell with you? How is it possible, O Socrates, they would then perhaps say, that we should want these? These, who give a thousand hindrances to all our proceedings; and who, by their fury and madness, are always creating disturbance in the souls where we dwell; - these, who had they been there first, would never

e   have suffered us to have admittance; and who entirely spoil our children, there born, by letting forgetfulness in upon them, for want of care to guard the dwelling-place. But the other pleasures mentioned by you, the true and the pure, you are to know that they are nearly related to us, and belong to our family: and beside these, the pleasures who are accompanied by health and sobriety; such, also, as are the followers of

64a all virtue, like the train of some Goddess, every where attending her; let all of these come and mix amongst us. But those pleasures who are always found in company with folly, and with all kinds of vice, it is very absurd for a man to mingle with intellect, - if he desires to see a mixture as clear, untroubled, and well-attempered as possible to be made; - and if he would from thence try to discover what the nature is of good, not only in man, but also in the universe; from which discovery some notion is to be gained, by a sort of divination, of what the idea is of good itself. Shall we not say that intellect and science, in thus answering, have spoken prudently and consistently with themselves, pleading in their own cause, and at the same time in behalf of memory and right opinion?

PROT. By all means ought we.

SOC. But in our mixture it is necessary to add this also; for without it no one thing could ever be.

b   PROT. What is that?

SOC. Whatever has not truth mixed with it in the composing of it, can never be produced into true existence; or, could it be produced, it never can be lasting.

PROT. How is it possible that it should?

SOC. Certainly no way. Now if any thing further be yet wanting to perfect our composition, declare it, you and Philebus. For the mixture which we have now made in speculation, appears to me to have been as perfectly well composed as if it were some incorporeal world meant for the good government of an animated body.

PROT. And be assured, O Socrates, that to me it has had the same appearance.

c   Soc. Might we not, then, rightly say, that we were now arrived at the dwelling-place of the good, and were standing in its vestibules?

Prot. I think we might.

Soc. And now what should we deem to be the greatest excellence in the composition, and to be also the chief cause that such a mixture must be grateful to all? For when we shall have discerned what this is which is so grateful and so excellent, we shall then consider to which of the two, to pleasure or to intellect, it is related the most nearly, and familiar the most intimately, in the constitution of the universe.

d   Prot. Right: it will be of the greatest service to us in determining this point.

Soc. And there is, indeed, no difficulty in discovering the cause, why some mixtures are most valuable, and others good for nothing.

Prot. Explain your meaning.

Soc. No person is ignorant of this.

Prot. Of what?

Soc. That in every mixture, whatever it be, and whatever be the quantity of it,[†] if measure pervades it not, and if thence it obtains not symmetry and proportion, all the ingredients must of necessity be spoiled, besides the spoiling of the whole composition. For, in such a case, no one thing is really tempered by any other thing; but a confused

e   and disorderly assemblage is made of various things jumbled together; which, like a concurrence of bad accidents in life, is a real misfortune to the persons who are to use it.

Prot. It is very true.

Soc. The power of the good then is transferred, we find, into that province where dwells the nature of the beautiful. For every where, from measure and mediocrity, and from symmetry and proportion, arise beauty and virtue.

Prot. Certainly so.

Soc. And we said before that truth also was an ingredient in the composition.

Prot. We did.

65a   Soc. If, then, we are not able to discover the nature of good itself in one single idea, - yet, taking it in three ideas together, in beauty,

---

† In all the editions of the Greek we here read - οπωσουν, *however it be made.* But this is contradictory to the meaning of the sentence; for the meaning is this, - that "every right and good mixture must be made *in one certain manner only, viz. by measure.*" - We may fairly therefore presume, that Plato wrote, not οπωσουν, but οποσαουν, (or, by elision, οποσουν,) with a view to the magnitude of the universe. -S.

symmetry, and truth,[25] we may conceive it as one thing; and most justly attributing to it the cause of whatever is graceful of agreeable in the composition, we may most truly say, that by means of this, as being good itself, the whole proves to be such as it is, thus agreeable, and thus graceful.

PROT. Most truly, indeed.

b   SOC. Now then, O Protarchus, any person may be a competent judge between pleasure and wisdom to decide, whether of the two is nearest allied to the supreme good, and of higher value than the other is, both to men and Gods.

PROT. What the decision must be is clear. However, it is the better way to go through the recital of it in explicit words.

SOC. Each of those three, then, let us compare, severally, with pleasure, and again with intellect. For we are to see and determine whether of these two it is that each of those three is most congenial to, and to give sentence accordingly.

PROT. Do you speak of beauty, and truth, and mediocrity?

c   SOC. I do. Now take, in the first place, O Protarchus, truth; and look at all the three together, intellect, truth, and pleasure: and after you have considered them a sufficient time, say whether, in your opinion, intellect, or whether pleasure, is nearer of kin to truth.

PROT. What need is there of time to consider of this point? for, I presume, that very great is the difference between intellect and pleasure in this respect. Of all things in the world, pleasure is the most addicted to lying: and it is said, that in the pleasures of Venus, which seem to be the greatest, even perjury is pardoned by the Gods; it being supposed that pleasures, like children, have not the least intellect in them to know what they say. But intellect is either the same thing with truth, or it is of all things the most like to it, and the truest.

SOC. Next, then, consider mediocrity in the same manner;† and say whether you think that pleasure possesses more of it than wisdom, or that wisdom possesses more of it than pleasure.

PROT. This which you have now proposed for a subject of consideration is not less easy than the other. For there cannot, in my opinion, be found any thing more immoderate in its nature than pleasure and extravagant joy; nor any thing which has more of measure in it than intellect and science.

d

---

† Cornarius, and Stephens after him, rightly observe, that in the Greek of this sentence we ought to read ωσαυτως, and not, as it is printed, ως ουτως. -S.

e   SOC. You have well said. But proceed further now to the third. Do you say that intellect partakes of beauty more than any species of pleasure partakes of it? and that intellect is more excellent than pleasure in this respect? or that the contrary is true?

PROT. Did ever any man then, O Socrates, whether awake or dreaming, see or imagine wisdom and intellect to be in any matter, or in any manner, unhandsome or unbecoming, whether in reflecting on the past, or in perceiving the present, or in looking forward to the future?

SOC. Right.

PROT. But whenever we see any person immersed in pleasures, in 66a those pleasures too which are of all perhaps the greatest, - when we behold what a ridiculous figure the man makes in the very act of enjoying them, - or view what is of all spectacles the most unseemly, the consequence of his enjoyment, - we ourselves are ashamed; and all such things, as far as possible, we conceal, veiling them with night and darkness, as not being fit objects for the light to look on.

SOC. Every where then, O Protarchus, you will declare, speaking yourself to all persons about you, and publishing abroad by messengers, that the possession of pleasure is neither of supreme nor of secondary worth: but that whatever is of all things the most excellent and valuable, is to be found in measure, in the moderate, and the seasonable, and in all things† of that kind, whose nature and essence we ought to deem eternal.

PROT. Their supreme excellence appears from what has been said and proved.

b   SOC. And that the next in value are symmetry and beauty, the perfect and the sufficient, and whatever else is congenial to these.

PROT. So it seems.

SOC. In the third degree of excellence, if I divine aright, you would not greatly mistake the truth if you were to place intellect and wisdom.

PROT. Perhaps I should not.

SOC. And is not the fourth rank due to those things which we assigned to the soul herself, as her own proper goods, sciences, and arts,

---

† Mons. Grou has observed, very justly, that the word ειρησθαι, in the latter part of this sentence, is an error in the text: and instead of it, he proposes the word ηρησθαι. Grynæus, the corrector of Ficinus's translation of Plato, seems, in his rendering the Greek word in this place into Latin by the words *sortita esse* (*to have obtained an allotment of*,) either to have read ειληχθαι in some manuscript, or else to have thus amended the text by a happy conjecture of his own. -S.

c   and right opinions, a fourth order of goods, following next after the first three? ought we not here to place them, if they are more nearly related to the good than they are to pleasure?

PROT. Perhaps we ought.

SOC. Then follow, fifth in order, the pleasures of that sort which we described to be unmixed with pain, and denominated pure, such as those consequent to sensation, but belonging to the soul herself when she is engaged in the sciences.†

PROT. It may be so.

SOC.

> With the sixth race . . . . (says Orpheus)
> Close we the finish'd series of our song.‡

d   Our disquisition, too, seems to be now finished, and to close with passing our sixth sentence. After all this, nothing remains for us to do but to affix a head, as it were, to the whole body of our inquiry.

PROT. It is fit that we should.

SOC. Come, then: the third to the saviour. Let us commemorate him whose aid brought the argument to a conclusion; calling him to witness the truth of it.

PROT. Whom do you mean?

SOC. Philebus laid down this position: that the good was all and every kind of pleasure in full abundance.

PROT. By commemorating the saviour, it seems then, Socrates, you meant that we should resume the original argument of our inquiry.

e   SOC. Well: but let us observe what followed. I, viewing with dislike that position just now mentioned, - the tenet, not of Philebus only, but of thousands beside in all ages, - on the other hand asserted, that intellect was a thing far better and more beneficial to human life than pleasure.

PROT. That was your position.

---

† In the Greek of this sentence, the word ἐπιστήμας ought to be either quite expunged, or changed for the word ἡδονας, or immediately preceded by the preposition περι. The purest pleasures, those of science, are certainly not sciences themselves.

‡ This verse of Orpheus we meet with again in Plutarch's Treatise concerning the Delphic Inscription Εἰ, and in no other ancient author whom we are acquainted with. It is introduced by Plutarch no otherwise than as a part of the present passage in Plato, which is there quoted; and not so as to give us any light into the poet's own meaning in that verse. But if we may form a probable conjecture from Plato's application of it, it was the end of a description of five different ages of the world, with regard to men's manners and ways of life. -S.

SOC. But then, suspecting that many other things had pretensions to the same character of being the good, I engaged, if something† should appear better than both of those, to combat for the second prize, in behalf of intellect against pleasure; that pleasure, in her claim to so much as this, might be defeated.

PROT. You did engage so to do.

67a SOC. Afterwards, on trial, it was very sufficiently proved that neither of our favourites answered the character of complete good.

PROT. Perfectly true.

SOC. Intellect, therefore, and pleasure, were, both of them, quite dismissed from having any thing to do in the controversy concerning good itself; as each of them wanted self-sufficience, and that power which attends the sufficient and perfect.

PROT. Very right.

SOC. But after we had discovered a third thing preferable to either of those two, we found the nature of intellect to approach nearer to the nature of this conqueror, and to be much more familiar with this form than pleasure.

PROT. We certainly did.

SOC. The sixth‡ *and lowest* place, then, according to the judgment now given as the result of this inquiry, belongs to the power of pleasure *unbounded.*

PROT. So it appears.

b SOC. But the first place belongs to her, as bulls§ would say, and horses,[26] and all beasts whatever of the savage kind: for it appears so from the manner in which they pursue pleasure. And on the credit of

---

† All the editions of Plato give us to read το instead of τι in this sentence. Ficinus, however, translates as if in the Medicean manuscript he read τι, which undoubtedly is the true reading; and herein he is followed by all the translators who came after him. -S.

‡ A very gross error has infected all the editions and all the translations of Plato in this place. For in all the editions we read πεμπτον the *fifth,* instead of εκτον the *sixth.* Now the *fifth* rank was before assigned solely to the *pure* pleasures. The *sixth* and last rank, therefore, remains to *Pleasure,* one of the three great subjects of this dialogue; to *pleasure,* pretending to be the only or the chief good of man, and by Philebus avowed and contended for as such; *pleasure in general* and undistinguished; *pleasure at random,* from whatever quarter it comes; - in Plato's own words, vol. ii, p. 40, edit. Steph. παραπαν, οπωσουν, και εικη χαιρειν. But the very next sentence of Socrates puts it beyond all doubt, that pleasure of sense, *sensual pleasure,* is here meant. -S.

§ In the Greek of this sentence, we presume that the word ουκ ought to be changed into ως. -S.

these animals, just as the judgment of diviners depends on the flight of
birds, sentence is pronounced by the multitude, that pleasures have the
greatest power in making our lives happy. For the loves and joys of
brute animals they deem a stronger evidence, and fitter to be credited,
than the sayings of men prophetically uttered in all places through
inspiration of the philosophic muse.

PROT. That you have said what is most agreeable to truth, O Socrates,
we are, all of us, now agreed.

SOC. Now then ye will dismiss me.

PROT. There is a little, O Socrates, still remaining to be considered.
For you must not quit the company before it breaks up: and I will put
you in mind of what you have left unsaid.†

---

† This dialogue both begins and ends abruptly. Hence Olympiodorus asks, why
it is without a beginning and an end? And he solves this question very properly as
follows: "Shall we say that this is because *The Good* is uncircumscribed, and has neither
beginning nor end? But it may be said, that on the contrary it is necessary *The Good*
should have a beginning and end; a beginning of such a kind, that there is not another
beginning prior to it, and an end beyond which there is not any other end. Perhaps
therefore, it is better to say with our preceptor, that the mixt life has an end, and such
a one as is adapted to all animals. So that the dialogue is very properly without a
beginning, for the purpose of indicating that there is a certain good beyond that which
it investigates. And again, for the same reason, it is without an end: for there is also
another end more ancient than its end." [.11]

.13   1 (See page 437, line 11b) How is intellect, says Olympiodorus, spoken of
with relation to pleasure? For, in the first place, appetite (*orexis*) rather is
divided in opposition to knowledge; but appetite and pleasure are not the same.
And, in the next place, there is a certain pleasure in knowledge. To this we
may reply, that there is a pleasure in knowledge, in consequence of its
participation of appetite. For to be pleasantly affected when we apprehend the
object of knowledge, arises from the assumption of appetite. But to the other
question we may reply, that the investigative is analogous to the orectic power:
for investigation, being as it were a gnostic orexis (appetite), is a way to a
certain end; just as orexis hastens to a certain thing. But the possession of the
object of appetite is analogous to knowledge, which is the possession of truth.

.14   Again, the vital and the orectic are not the same. For life is also predicated
of knowledge; since knowledge moves, and that which knows is moved, which
is especially the peculiarity of life. But that which knows is moved when it
investigates, not when it has arrived at the end, which knowledge signifies.

.15   Again, good is predicated both of knowledge and orexis: for knowledge is
beneficial, and is the cause of union with the object of knowledge. But the
good of orexis is, as it were, practic, and we wish not to know, but to be
passive to it, and we embrace it more nearly, but do not endure to have it at
a distance. But we can endure the object of knowledge, though at a distance;

.16   for we wish to know and not to be it. What, however, shall we say the orectic
is? For it is not common good; since this also pertains to knowledge. Nor is
it something unknown: for orexis subsists together with knowledge. It is,
therefore, a certain good which is known. Hence, it moves from itself the
perceiver. But this is the beautiful; since orexis, considered according to its
common acceptation, is nothing else than love; though love is a strenuous
orexis. For the more and the less produce no alteration according to species;
but the strenuous is intenseness alone. Further still, the pleasant is the
attendant of orexis; but the pleasant is apparent beauty. For apparent good is
benignant and lovely to all animals. But may not the beautiful be thus related
to the good, according to indication? For, in the first place, the good is above
idea; but the beautiful is the formal object of love; just as being is the formal
object of knowledge. Orexis, however, differs in species from love. For, if
orexis is assumed in common, it is extended to one common good. But, if the
ends are separated, the powers also which hasten towards them must be
separated. For the contact which, according to its idiom, is called friendship,
φιλια, and which makes a union with good, is one thing, and the power which

harmonizes with this must be called desire, εφεσις; but the power which, according to indigence, urges the multitude is another; and a thing of this kind is denominated love, ερως, and hastens to the beautiful. - T.

2 (See page 438, line 11d) In the Greek, - εξιν και διαθεσιν - All the differences between εξις and διαθεσις are accurately shown by Aristotle in his *Categories*, cap. viii [TTS vol. XX, 8b25], and in his *Metaphysics*, V, 19 [TTS vol. XXIII, 1022b1]. In the sentence now before us, the difference between them is this: διαθεσις ψυχης, *an affection of the soul*, is the soul's present but transient state; εξις ψυξης, *a state of the soul*, is the soul's permanent affection. Thus we say of a man, that he is in a joyous state of mind, when the joy with which he is affected is of some standing, and is likely to continue: but of a man in whose soul joy is just now arisen, we say, that he is seized (that is, affected suddenly) with joy. And thus again we say that the mind is in a thoughtful state, when it has been for some time actually thinking, and is not easy to be diverted from thinking on: but when a thought arises suddenly within us, in an unthinking state of mind, and amidst the wanderings of fancy, usually mean *habit* and *disposition*. But the affinity between this their usual meaning, and that which they have in the passage now before us, will appear, from considering, that, as the soul acquires certain habits of acting, through frequently-repeated acts of the same kind, - so she is fixed in some certain state, through frequent impressions made on her where she is passive, or through frequent energies of her own where she is active; a state, to which those impressions from without, and those energies within, gradually lead her;- and also that, in like manner as some certain previous disposition of the soul is necessary to every single act which is voluntary, so is it also necessary to the receiving of every impression from without, and to the performing of every energy within. - S.

.18 3 (See page 439, line 12b) Why is Pleasure, says Olympiodorus, a Goddess, according to Philebus? May we not say, As that which is the object of desire, and as an end? But why is Venus a Goddess? Shall we say, As lovely? Perhaps they are Goddesses, because they are both concerned in the procreations of
.19 animals, the one as a presiding power, the other as a passion. Why, too, is Pleasure not considered as a Goddess by any of the ancients?[†] Because, says Proclus, it neither is a precedaneous good, nor immediately beautiful, nor has a middle subsistence, and different from both these. We must say, however, that Pleasure, according to Iamblichus, is a Goddess, and is recognized in temples by Proclus the Laodicean.

† *Viz.* by none of the Greek theologists.

.21   Again, no one of the ancients says that Venus is Pleasure. What then is the reason of this? May we not say, that it is because Venus has a copulative power, and that a certain pleasure follows copulation? And also, that this pleasure is accompanied with much of the deformed? Venus, however, is beautiful, not only that Venus which is divine, but that also which belongs to nature. And in theology, the idiom of *Venus* is different from that of Ευφροσυνη, Delight. -T.

.24   4 (See page 439, line 12c) Why does Socrates, says Olympiodorus, so much venerate the names of the Gods? Shall we say, Because formerly things adapted were consecrated to appropriate natures, and because it is unbecoming to move things immovable? or, that names are adapted to the nature of the Gods, according to what is said in the *Cratylus?*[390d] or, that these names are vocal

.25   images of the Gods, according to Democritus? But how does a worthy man fear? Either very properly the divine wrath; or this fear is a veneration, but not a certain passion attended with dread. I shall only observe, in addition to what is said by Olympiodorus, that this passage, among a multitude of others, proves, beyond all possibility of contradiction, that Socrates believed in the existence of divine beings, the immediate progeny of the ineffable cause of all, or, in other words, was a polytheist. -T.

5 (See page 441, line 13d) The sense and the reasoning require a small alteration to be here made in the Greek copies of Plato, by reading, instead of τας ομοιας, - τας ομοιοτητας, *similitude*, or rather τα ομοια, *similes*. - Similes of the kind here meant are by Aristotle, in his *Art of Rhetoric*, II, edit. Du Vall [TTS vol. XXII, 1393b], justly styled τα Σωκρατικα, *Socratic*, because frequently employed by Socrates. They are not such as those for which the imagination of a poet skims over all nature, to illustrate some things by superficial resemblances to them in other things: neither are they such as the memory of an orator ransacks all history for, to prove the certainty of some doubtful fact by examples on record, which agree with it in a few circumstances: but they are such as the reason of an accomplished master of dialectic chooses out from subjects near at hand, to prove the truth of some uncertain or controverted position, by the analogy it bears to some other truth which is obvious, and clear, and will be readily admitted. Such a simile, bearing the plainest and most striking analogy with what is to be proved, is actually produced, immediately after this preface to it, by Socrates. But not a word is there in what follows concerning similar pleasures; and τας ομοιας, *alike* or *similar*, cannot be joined with, or belong to, any preceding noun, beside ηδονας. As to the word *returning*, in the present sentence, it refers to those similes produced before of colour and of figure. -S.

6 (See page 443, line 15b) This second question supposes the first question decided in favour of the true being of the monads. For, if universals are held to be only names, invented to denote unreal fancies or factitious notions, it is trifling and idle to inquire whence they derive stability; this being an affection, or property, of real beings only, - unless it be as merely nominal, notional, or fantastic, as those things are to which it is attributed. - The sentence now before us in the Greek is printed thus: πως αυ ταυτας, μιαν εκαστην ουσαν αει την αυτην, και μητε γενεσιν μητε ολεθρον προσδεχομενην, ομως ειναι βεβαιοτητα μιαν ταυτην. The Greek text must here be faulty; and, to make good sense of it, it is necessary to make a small alteration or two, - by reading εχειν instead of ειναι, and και αυτην instead of ταυτην. In translating this passage, we have presumed it ought to be so read; and the meaning, intended to be conveyed by it, we suppose to be this: - "it must needs seem strange, that distinct beings, not generated, some of them by others, but all equally eternal, without intercommunity or interchange between them, should, nevertheless, have one and the same nature, that of *monad* or *unity*, and one and the same property of their being, that of *stability*." -S.

7 (See page 445, line 16c) This gift is the *dialectic* of Plato, of which we have given an ample account in the Introduction to, and Notes on, the *Parmenides* [TTS vol. XI]. I shall only observe at present, that this vertex of the sciences consists of four parts, *viz. division, definition, demonstration,* and *analysis.* Of

.54

these, the *divisive* art, says Olympiodorus, is connate with the progression of things; but the *analytic* with their conversion. And the *definitive* and *demonstrative* arts, which have a middle situation, are similar to the hypostasis, or subsisting nature of things. The *definitive*, however, is analogous to that hypostasis which subsists from itself; but the *demonstrative* to that which is suspended from its cause. - T.

.60

8 (See page 445, line 16c) Prometheus, says Olympiodorus, does not produce good, as unfolding into light, but as a Titan. For he employs a providential care upon rational essences which proceed to the extremity, just as Epimetheus provides for irrational natures. For irrational natures proceed to a care of things subordinate, and having proceeded, distribute the whole of divine

.61

Providence. Again, the fire which Prometheus stole, and gave to men, is every anagogic essence and perfection, distributed through him to the last of things. Hence it is said to have been *stolen*, because an *anagogic* essence is *deduced*; but through him, because it is alone deduced Titanically, - but other Gods give subsistence to a form of this kind.

.62

Again, that every generated nature is one and many, is nothing wonderful; for these natures are partible, and participate of many habitudes; but how is this the case with every intelligible essence? In the first place, we may say that each is a monad, and also a number, according to the series of the monad; as, for instance, the beautiful, and things beautiful. In the second place, that the monad is both that which it is, and all other things according to commixtion. In the third place, it both consists from the genera of being and one idiom. In the fourth place, the idiom is multiplied together with the many; but there is a certain impartible summit in all the many. In the fifth place, this summit is an united form, but there is also something in it above form. And, in the sixth place, this summit is at the same time the united, but not *The One.* Further still, as all things are from one and many, it is necessary that these two principles should be arranged prior to all things; the former being the cause to all things of unity, and the latter of multitude. They must likewise evidently be posterior to the first cause; for that is *at once* the cause of all things.

.63 Again, in the extremities of things infinite multitude is beheld, but in the summit a monad presubsists, according to every form. But infinite multitude would not be generated, unless in the monad which generates it an infinite
.64 power was preassumed. Nor would every individual in infinites be bounded, unless bound proceeded to the last of things. Progression subsists through all appropriate media, from the monad to infinite multitude. And, in the first place, this is seen in multitude capable of being participated. For progression is not immediately from *The One* to the infinite, but to two and three, and the following numbers. And, in the next place, the progression of bodies is of this kind, for it has no vacuum together with its variety. In the third place, the generative power of the monad being both one and many, at once generates all things according to the whole of itself; things secondary being always consequent to such as are prior.

.65 Further still, says Olympiodorus, the divisive method proceeds together with the progression of forms, not cutting off the continuity of subjection, nor introducing a vacuum, but proceeding through all the media, from the one to
.66 the infinite. The business of the divisive method is first to place *The One* every where before the many. Secondly, to place the finite before infinite multitude. Thirdly, always to define according to quantity, the lesser before the greater number. Fourthly, to omit no number of things which give completion to progression. Fifthly, to select numbers adapted to respective forms; the triadic, for instance, or the hebdomadic, to Minerva, and in a similar manner in all the rest. For different numbers proceed according to different forms; as also of the Gods, there are different numbers according to different Divinities. For of monads themselves, one progression is monadic, as that of the monad; another dyadic, as that of the dyad; and in a similar manner with the rest: so that there is not a division of all things into two. Sixthly, to divide through forms, but not through form and negation, according to the opinion of Aristotle: for no number is produced from form and negation. Seventhly, to produce every monad into division in its proper order, whether it be in that of bound, or in that of infinity: for each is every where. Ninthly, to produce things oppositely divided, according to antithesis, whether certain media are discovered, or not. Tenthly, not to leave the media in the extent ($\epsilon\nu$ $\tau\omega$ $\pi\lambda\alpha\tau\epsilon\iota$). Eleventhly, to

ascribe different numbers appropriately to different orders, as the number twelve to supermundane natures, and the number seven to intellectuals. Twelfthly, to see where the lesser numbers are more excellent, and where they are subordinate, and in a similar manner with respect to the greater. For the mundane decad is subordinate to the supermundane duodecad; but the intellectual hebdomad is superior to it.

.68 Again, the analytic art is subordinate to the divisive: for the latter is from a cause, but the former from a sign; and the latter from on high surveys things more subordinate, but the former beholds downwards things on high; and the latter stops at nothing sensible, but the former at first stands in need of sense.

.69 Thus, the latter giving subsistence and producing, nearly makes the whole of the proceeding essence; but the former converting, confers on that which has proceeded a departure from the subordinate, and an adherence to the more excellent nature. On which account progression is more essential than conversion, and is therefore more excellent. So that procession is superior to conversion, and the essential to the anagogic. In the descent of the soul, however, since progression is here an apostasy from better natures, ascent which corresponds to conversion is better than progression or descent. - T.

 9 (See page 446, line 17b) In the Greek, the term used here, as well as just before, (where this translation hath the word *voice*, is φωνη. It there signified *articulated* vocal sound, or *speech*: it here signifies *musical* sound of the voice, or *vocal music*. We see then that φωνη, *human voice*, is by Plato supposed to be a common genus, divisible into those two sorts or species. It is expressly so laid down by Nicomachus, (Harmonic. Enchirid. p. 3, edit. Amst.) in these words:- Της ανθρωπινης φωνης οι απο του Πυθαγορικου διδασκαλειου δυο εφασκον, ως ενος γενους, ειδη υπαρχειν· και το μεν συνεχες ιδιως ωνομαζον· το δε διαστηματικον. Such [writers concerning music] *as came out of the Pythagorean School say, that of human voice* [in general], *as of one genus, there are two species. One of these two they properly named continuous, the other discrete.* These two technical terms he afterward explains, by showing us that the *continuous* is that voice which we utter in discoursing and in reading; (and therefore, by Aristoxenus and by Euclid termed φωνη λογικη·) and that the *discrete* is the voice issued out of our mouths in singing; (and thence termed φωνη μελωδικη·) for, in this latter case, every single sound is distinguished by a certain or measured tone of the voice. The same division of φωνη is laid down, and a similar account of it is given, by Aristoxenus in Harmonic. Element. p. 8 & 9, edit. Amst. -S.

 10 (See page 446, line 17d) Homotony of sound is made when a string of some stringed instrument of music, having the same degree of tension with a similar string of some other, yields, in conjunction with it, the same musical tone; or when two different voices utter at the same time musical sounds,

neither of which is more acute, or more grave, than the other. In both cases, the sameness of the sound is also termed ομοφωνια: for φωνη, voice, is (metaphorically) attributed to all musical instruments; (see Nicomachus, p. 5 and 6) as, on the other hand, tone is (by an easy metaphor) attributed to the human voice, modulated by the will in the trachea, or aspera arteria: for this natural wind-instrument, in English aptly named the wind-pipe, while it transmits the air breathed out from the lungs, receives any degree of tension it is capable of, at the pleasure of the mind. In like manner, a repetition of the same tone from a single human voice, as well as from a single monochord, is termed a monotony. - S.

11 (See page 446, line 17d) *An interval* is the distance [or difference κατα τοπον, with regard to place] between any two musical sounds, (between that which is acute relatively to the other, and that other which is relatively a grave,) however near together they may be, or however remote from each other, on any scale of music. In proportion to the nearness or remoteness of these two sounds, the interval between them is, in mathematical language, said to be small or great; that is, it is short or long. So that different musical intervals, like all other different distances from place to place, essentially differ one from another in magnitude or length. And on this essential difference are founded all the other diversities of the intervals.

The bounds of each interval are those two musical sounds, from either of which there is made an immediate step or transition to the other. Of all musical sounds the three principal were: υπατη *the most grave,* νητη *the most acute,* and μεση *the middle* between those other two, on the most ancient scale of music; which consisted of only seven sounds, produced by striking on the same number of strings, all of different lengths. We account those three just now mentioned the principal, because the first and easiest division of any quantity, whether it be continuous or discrete, is into two equal parts, or halves: the most distinguishable points or bounds of it, therefore, however it be afterwards subdivided, are the two extremes and the middle. Accordingly Plato, in his 4th book *De Republica,* edit. Cantab. p. 314, speaking of the νεατη, the υπατη, and the μεση, the highest, the lowest, and the middle sound in music, calls them ορους τρεις αρμονιας, the *three bounds of harmony;* and likens to them the three most evidently distinguished parts of the soul, - the rational part, the highest; the concupiscible, the lowest; and the irascible, between them both.

A system is a composition of three or more musical sounds; or (what amounts to the same thing) it is an extent, comprehending two or more intervals. Of these systems the general diversities are laid down by Aristides, p. 15 & seq. But in his definition of a system (as it is printed) an important error deserves notice. For we there read - πλειονων η δυοιν, *more than two:* instead of which we ought to read - δυοιν η πλειονων, *two or more;* or else - πλειονων η ενος, *more than one:* which last are the very words used by Aristoxenus, Euclid, and Gaudentius, in their definitions of a system. The error probably arose from some manuscript copy of Aristides happening to be not easily legible in this place. The transcriber of it, therefore, we suppose, consulted Baccheius; who in his definition of a system useth the words - πλειονων η δυοιν. These words are right indeed in Baccheius, because they are by him applied to φθογγων, musical sounds, agreeably to our first definition; but they would be wrong in Aristides, where he is speaking, not of φθογγων, but of διαστηματων, the intervals of those sounds, agreeably to our second definition. On the many diversities and variations to be made in so large a field of systems, are founded those many different forms, figures, or modes of harmony, or sorts of tunes, (the Greek writers call them ειδη, μορφαι, σχηματα, τροποι and τονοι αρμονιας) the general kinds of which, according to Aristides, p. 25, are these - the Doric, the Phrygian, and the Lydian. If this be true, all the other modes are to be considered as subordinate to these three; and indeed they seem, some of them, to be intensions, others to be remissions, and others to be mixtures, of those the more moderate and simple. - S.

12 (See page 446, line 17d) The word αρμονια, *harmony*, was used in different senses by the old Grecian writers. We learn from Nicomachus, that the most ancient writers on music gave the name of harmony to that most perfect consonance, the diapason. Aristoxenus and Euclid mean, by the term harmony, that kind of melody which is called enharmonic. Plato and Aristotle, when they speak of harmony in the singular number, without the addition of an epithet denoting the sort, mean by that term the idea which is commonly now-a-days expressed by the term music; probably, because it was the first discovered of those sciences, as well as the first invented of those arts, which were anciently comprehended together in one general idea, expressed in one word, and termed music. But when the same great philosophers speak of harmonies in the plural number, they mean those different forms or modes of harmony whose specific differences depend on the different systems, or on the different order of those systems of which they are severally composed. To the term harmony in this latter sense only, (as it signifies a mode of harmony,) agrees the following definition of it, given us by Theo, and, long after him, by Psellus:- Αρμονια εστι συστηματων συνταξις. *A harmony* (not harmony in general) *is a composition* (or an ordering together) *of systems*. On this definition Bouillaud, in his Notes to Theo, p. 250, judiciously observes, - *Vocat hic harmoniam quos alii appellant* τροπους *seu* τονους. On this subject we shall only observe further, that the synthesis of harmony, presented to us by Plato, in the whole passage now before us, beginning from simple φθογγοι, or musical sounds, (which are the elements or primary constituent parts of harmony,) is exactly the same, and proceeds in the same order, with that synthesis which is taught by all the ancient Greek writers on music: one proof among many, this, of Plato's knowledge in the theory of music. Agreeably to which observation, Plutarch, in his Treatise περι Μουσικης, informs us, that Plato applied his mind closely to the science of music; having attended the Lectures of Draco the

Athenian, and those of Metellus of Agrigentum. Or if we suppose that Plato, in this part of the present dialogue, did no more than faithfully record the doctrine of Socrates, our supposition is very justifiable; for Socrates in his old age studied music under Connus. - S.

13 (See page 446, line 17d) That is, such relations and proportions, (or, to make use of musical terms,) such steps and transitions, intervals and bounds, systems and compositions, in the motions of the body, and in words, as are analogous to the affections of musical sounds, called by those very names. The Greek word, which we have rendered into English by the word *affections*, in the passage of Plato now before us is $\pi\alpha\theta\eta$, and, translated literally, signifies *passions*. For, whatever situation, condition, or circumstance, any being or thing is placed in by some other, - or by its relation to some other, - in whatever way it is acted on, or affected by, that other, - such situation, &c of the being or thing so placed, so acted on, or so affected, was by the Greek philosophers termed a $\pi\alpha\theta\sigma\varsigma$, *passion* of such being; because in that respect the being is passive. - S. I shall only observe, in addition to what Mr Sydenham has said, that the word *passion* always signifies, both with Plato and Aristotle, *a participated property* of any being. -T.

14 (See page 448, line 18b) In the Greek of this passage, as it is printed by Aldus and by Stephens, we here read - $\phi\omega\nu\eta\varsigma \ \mu\epsilon\nu \ o\nu, \ \phi\theta\sigma\gamma\gamma\sigma\upsilon \ \delta\epsilon \ \mu\epsilon\tau\epsilon\chi\sigma\nu\tau\alpha$ $\tau\iota\nu\sigma\varsigma\cdot$ - a reading which may be tolerably well supported by what soon follows. But the margin of the first Basil edition of Plato has suggested to us a reading, in which appears a distinction more obvious and plain than there is between $\phi\omega\nu\eta$ and $\phi\theta\sigma\gamma\gamma\sigma\varsigma$, *voice* and *sound of the voice*. For, in that margin, we are directed to read the word $\sigma\nu\tau\alpha$ (found, perhaps, in some manuscript copy of Plato) immediately after the word $\phi\omega\nu\eta\varsigma$, and before the words $\mu\epsilon\nu \ o\nu$, in this sentence. Now these two words $\phi\omega\nu\eta\varsigma \ \sigma\nu\tau\alpha$, put together, very little differ from $\phi\omega\nu\eta\epsilon\nu\tau\alpha$, a word which gives to this part of the sentence a meaning quite agreeable to the tenor of the whole of it, and to the language of all grammarians. -S.

15 (See page 448, line 18c) Socrates, by expressing himself in this manner, concerning the general name of this third sort of letters, as if it were then newly given them at Athens, seems to disapprove it. Perhaps the ancient term $\sigma\upsilon\mu\phi\omega\nu\alpha$, *consonants*, - a term applied by the new grammarians to the $\eta\mu\iota\phi\omega\nu\alpha$, *semi-vowels*, as well as to the $\alpha\phi\omega\nu\alpha$, *mutes*, - was, in his judgment, properly applicable to those letters only which yield of themselves no sound at all. For mutes, as they are called, cannot be pronounced even imperfectly and obscurely, as semi-vowels can, without the concurrence of some vowel, some sound perfectly vocal. - S.

16 (See page 448, line 17c) In the Greek, - αφθογγα και αφωνα· - evidently meaning such as are neither vowels nor semi-vowels. It should seem, therefore, that by φωνη Plato meant a perfect and clear vocal sound, such as we utter in pronouncing a vowel singly; and that by φθογγος he meant that imperfect and obscure sound of the voice made in the forming and pronouncing of a semi-vowel, unaided by a vowel. Now if this be true, then may the printed reading of that passage, to which belongs note 14 above, be justified. Aristotle, however, who treats of this subject in his *Poetics*, cap. 20 [TTS vol. XXII], recognizes not any such distinction between φωνη and φθογγος: for he attributes φωνη ακουστη, *a vocal sound*, such as may be heard, to the semi-vowels no less than to the vowels; and states the difference between these two sorts of letters thus:- The voice in uttering the vowels proceeds ανευ προσβολης, that is, it *makes no allision* against any parts of the mouth, those upper organs of speech, so as to be impeded in its free and full exit: but the expressing of the semi-vowels is μετα προσβολης, the voice in uttering them *makes such allision*, and meets with some degree of *resistance* by the allision it is, indeed, articulated; but by the resistance, the passages through the mouth being straitened, it becomes weaker, and is diminished, - except it be in some syllable; for here a vowel will never fail to assist in the delivery, by giving the voice a free passage into the air. Now Aristotle is indisputably right in attributing to a semi-vowel, by itself, φωνην, *vocem*, a vocal sound: but his learned commentator Victorius is equally right in giving to this vocal sound the epithets *obscura, tenuis and exilis*; since it is but half of the full and whole vowel-sound: and Plato may fairly be allowed to distinguish the half-sound by a particular name, and to call it φθογγος. But we know not how to agree with him, if he says that a semi-vowel does not partake of the vowel-sound; because the half of any thing whatever seems to partake, to be a part, or to have a share of its whole. For this reason it is that we incline to that emendation of the printed Greek text proposed in note 14. - S.

17 (See page 451, line 20d) *The desirable*, says Olympiodorus, proceeds from the intelligible father;[†] *the sufficient* from power; and *the perfect* from the paternal intellect. In reality, however, perfection is the third from essence: for the middle is life. But if this be true, it is evident that *the end* is different from *perfection*; for the latter is the last; but the former the first, to which essence, life, and intellect, and therefore all things converge. So that in every form, in a similar manner, *the end* will be the summit, and that which connectedly contains the whole; but *perfection* will be the third, subsisting after essence and life: for it is necessary that a thing should be, and should live, that it may become perfect.

---

† That is, from the summit of the intelligible order. - See the *Parmenides*.

.79 Again, *the perfect* is spread under *the sufficient*, in the same manner as *the full* under *the superfull*, and *the sufficient* under *the desirable*. For things when full excite to desire. The *first end*, likewise, is above *the desirable, the sufficient*, and *the perfect*. For that is simple and ineffable; and hence Socrates does not say that it is composed from the elements; but that these elements possess indefinitely a portion of *The Good*. It is better, however, to call the coordinated common contraction (συναιρεμα) of the three a portion of the good, though this is anonymous. For *The Good* is all things, and not only these three; nor is it alone the end, but is truly all things prior to all. Besides, the end which is now the object of consideration is knowable, so that there will be another end more common than this. -T.

18 (See page 455, line 23c) Proclus, in Platon. Theol. [TTS vol. VIII, p. 189], observes, that Plato here, according to the theology of his country, establishes two principles after *The One*. And, according to Philolaus, the nature of beings is connected from things *bounded* and things *infinite*. If beings, therefore, subsist from *bound* and *the infinite*, it is evident that these two must be prior to beings, or, in other words, must be superessential. Hence, as *bound* and *the infinite* are superessential, Socrates with great propriety says that "God has *exhibited* them." For their procession from the highest God is ineffable, and they may be rather said to be *arcane manifestations* from him than his *productions*. Mr. Sydenham, from being unacquainted with the sublime theology of the Greeks, has totally mistaken the profound meaning of this passage in his translation, which is as follows:- "The Gods, we said, have shown us the infinite of things, and also their bound." For the original is τον θεον ελεγομεν που, το μεν απειρον δειξαι των οντων, το δε περας.

Should it be asked, says Olympiodorus, how the two elements *bound* and *infinity* are better than that which is mixed, since these two elements are the principles of being; we reply, that these principles must be considered as total orders more simple than that which is mixt; and that secondary principles proceed from these two, in the first mixt, which are subordinate to the mixt, in the same manner as elements are every where subordinate to that which is composed from them.

.105 Again, neither is perfect separation in the second† order: for the fabrication of form first pertains to intellect; and the first intellect is pure intellect. Hence, Iamblichus says that the monads of forms subsist in this, meaning by monads that which is unseparated in every form. On this account it is intellectual as in intellectuals, and is the cause of formal essence, just as the second is the cause of life, and the third of the fabrication of form in intellectuals.

† The reader must remember that the intelligible order consists of *being, life,* and *intellect,* and that each of these receives a triadic division. - See the Notes on the *Parmenides*.

.106   Again, the egg, the paternal intellect, occult number; and, in short, that which is the third from *bound*, respectively signify the third God, according to theologists, and consequently each is the same as that which is mixt from bound and infinity.

.107   Further still, the one principle which gives subsistence to, and is the end of, all things, contains the final as superior to the producing; for hypostasis is through the ends. But the first principle is both these according to *The One*: and the two principles *bound* and *infinity* according to the producing cause.

.108   Again, Socrates establishing that which is mixt as a certain cause of union, the cause of separation is also investigated. This cause, however, will be the *difference* which subsists after the intelligible, as we learn from the *Parmenides*.[143a] For the intelligible is united alone. But it would be better to make *The One* the cause of all things; *bound* the cause of union; *infinite* of separation; and *the mixt* that which participates of both. Observe, too, that the
.109   more and the less are every where, but in intelligibles according to a superior and inferior degree of power. - T.

    19 (See page 465, line 30b) In the Greek of this passage we read - ψυχην τε παρεχον και σωμα σκιαν εμποιουν. - Ficinus translates the two last words of it thus:- *"dum imprimit umbram."* But this being obscure, an error in the Greek manuscripts was justly suspected by the subsequent translators, Cornarius and Serranus; the former of whom proposes instead of σκιαν to read υγειαν; and the latter imagines that we should read σωμασκιαν as one word. Grynæus and Bembo never attempt an emendation of the printed Greek, even where it is most apparently erroneous. And Mons. Grou has taken the easy way of not translating the two last words. But all the difficulty vanishes, if, instead of σκιαν we read σκηνος, a *tabernacle* or *tent*; a word metaphorically used by the Pythagoreans to signify the human body, as being but a slight temporary dwelling for the soul. See Timæus the Locrian, in several passages; and a fragment of Ocellus the Lucanian, de Lege, in Stobæus's Eclogæ Phys. cap. 16. See also Æschines the Socratic, p. 128, edit. Horrei; the Greek index to which will furnish the learned reader with examples of the same metaphor, used by several Greek writers in the succeeding ages. -S.

    20 (See page 476, line 36d) We cannot conceive to what purpose this compliment to Protarchus is here introduced, unless it be by way of a simile; to represent the dignity and excellence of the matters before discussed; and, by reminding Protarchus of his illustrious birth, to signify to him, - that, as he ought not to degenerate from his ancestors, so neither ought any new matters to be brought upon the carpet, if, in their weight and value, they fall short of those which have preceded. Perhaps also an intimation is thus given by Plato to his readers, that one of the subjects of inquiry just now mentioned by Socrates, - that concerning *opinions*, - immediately related to that other

concerning *pleasures*, as to their truth or falsehood. In the Greek of this passage, it is probable that the printed reading κεινου του ανδρος is erroneous; and that Plato wrote κλειτου ανδρος; but that, in after ages, a reader of some manuscript copy of this dialogue, where instead of κλειτου was written κλεινου, (and Heschius interprets κλεινος by the more usual terms ενδοξος, ονομαστος,) on collating it with another MS. copy, where he found κλειτου written, wrote του in the margin of the former copy, opposite to the syllable νου, with which, perhaps, a new line began; that afterwards a transcriber of this copy received του into the text of his own transcript, just before ανδρος, supposing it to be a word casually omitted in the former copy; and that, last of all, when κλεινου του ανδρος was discovered to be a solecism in the Greek syntaxis, κλεινου, a word very uncommon, was easily changed into κεινου, and the construction was thus purified. -S.

21 (See page 476, line 36e) In the Greek we read only, - ψευδεις, αι δ' αληθεις ουκ εισιν ηδοναι. All the translators of Plato into other languages justly suppose this sentence to be imperfect in the beginning of it; but in their way of supplying the words omitted, it is nothing more than a repetition of the question proposed before, without any new additional matter. Socrates, in fact, is now entering on a proof of the distinction between the true pleasures and the false: and we presume, that he here builds his proof on that prime axiom on which is founded all demonstration, *viz.* "Things cannot be what they are, and yet different from what they are, at the same time." In the passage, therefore, now before us, it seems probable that the sentence, to be made agreeable to the sense of it, is to be completed thus, - Αληθεις αι μεν ψευδεις, ψευδεις αι δ' αληθεις, ουκ εισιν ηδοναι. The error of omitting the first words is easy to be accounted for. -S.

.207 22 (See page 497, line 51b) Of pleasures, says Olympiodorus, those that excite a vehement agitation are such as are attended with pain, but the energetic alone are such as are beheld in a perfect animal when energizing. Again, of

.208 pure pleasures, the corporeal are such as the vision of commensurate light; those pertaining to the soul are such as result from the speculation and apprehension of a certain intelligible; but those which belong to both, *viz.* to body and soul, are such as those of health, in which the soul also rejoices; the pleasure in this case beginning from the motion of the soul, but descending as far as to the body. -T.

23 (See page 501, line 53e) This whole sentence in all the editions of the Greek is thus printed, - Τουτοις τοινυν εοικοτα δυοιν ουσι, δυ' αλλα ζητει, κατα παντα οσα λεγομεν ειναι το τριτον ετερω. - A sentence quite unintelligible to us. Mons. Grou very justly apprehends some error in the text. We presume, that

this sensible and elegant translator never saw the emendation proposed by Cornarius; for that, otherwise, he would have embraced it, and have made his version, as we have ours, agreeable to that emendation: which is no more than a change of the last word - ετερῳ into σωτηρι. The sentence, thus amended, concludes with this proverbial saying, - *the third to the saviour.* It was a form of words anciently used at the feast of every victor in the Olympic games, when he made an accustomed libation out of the third cup or glass, Δu σωτηρι, *to Jupiter,* in his character of *saviour* in all difficulties and dangers. A speech so well known to all the Grecians, easily passed into a proverb: and it is alluded to as such by Plato in his *Charmides,*[167a] in his *Republic,*[498b] and in his *Seventh Epistle.*[334d] -S.

.228   24 (See page 512, line 61c) There are Gods, says Olympiodorus, that preside over temperament; over the physical and mundane, Vulcan; but over the psychical and supermundane, Bacchus. The mingling idiom, indeed, proceeds as far as to the last hyparxis. Thus, for instance, Vulcan being the leader of physical temperament, first produces this idiom in himself; afterwards, in the mundane intellect which presides over nature; in the third place, in a soul of this kind, in a similar manner; and lastly, in the physical world according to hyparxis. In like manner, Bacchus unfolding in himself the principle of psychical temperament after a divine manner, in the next place establishes this in intellect intellectually, according to hyparxis in soul, and in a binding mode in the animated body. And still higher than these, Jupiter is the principle of intellectual temperament. There are also other principles of temperament more partial than Bacchus and Vulcan. Plato mentions these two, as being about to mingle all the supermundane and mundane mixtures; but he omits the Jovian temperament, as being superior to the things proposed in this dialogue. -T.

.338   25 (See page 518, line 65a) The one principle of all things, says Olympiodorus, presides over every thing, according to that which he is. Hence, the light proceeding from him is truth, and subsists as the object of desire to all things. On this account, too, this light is the first beauty, the cause of things beautiful, bounding every thing in its proper measure; and hence it is celebrated as measure. Again, the one principle is not a contracted comprehension of the three monads, beauty, symmetry, and truth: for it is the cause of all things. But that which is mixed is the contraction of all things, as .239   the end, and not as the contraction of essences; so that the one principle may be more justly denominated the end of ends. Again, the three monads subsist .240   arcanely in the first principle; unically, and according to one, in bound; multiformly, and as it were according to the parturition of separation, in infinity; but according to the first separation, though not perfectly divided, nor .241   yet intellectually, in the third God, who is the cause of the mixed, so far as it is mixed. Again, *The Good* is analogous to truth: for the good to every thing is to be that which it in reality is; but the just is analogous to symmetry. For this is the measure of that which pertains to every thing, in the same manner .243 as the commensurate. Further still, Iamblichus says, that the three monads proceeding from *The Good* adorn intellect; but it is immanifest what intellect, whether that which subsists after life, or the paternal intellect which is celebrated in essence. Besides, in the Orphic writings, these three monads .244 become apparent in the mythological egg. The followers of Syrianus, however, make a division, and survey truth in the *first being*, as being perfectly replete with that which it is, and in no respect admitting in itself non-being. But they survey beauty in *life*, as being prolific, and rejoicing in progressions. For, after that which is perfectly without separation, life introduces a parturition, as it were, of separation. And they contemplate symmetry in *intellect*, because in this forms are first separated and harmoniously coordinated. You may also divide them into the principles after the one principle of all things. For you may justly ascribe *truth* to *bound*; *beauty* to *infinity*, through its progression; and *symmetry* to *that which is mixed*.

Proclus, in Theol. Plat. [TTS vol. VIII, p. 198], observes, "that Iamblichus appears to him to have bounded the intelligible in these three monads, symmetry, truth, and beauty; and through these to have unfolded the intelligible Gods in the Platonic theology." He adds, "it is also apparent why Socrates speaks of this triad as subsisting in the vestibules of *The Good*. (See p. 467.) For that which is primarily being, in consequence of its union with *The Good*, participates of this triad. Hence, because *The Good* is the measure of all things, the first being is commensurate. Because *The Good* is prior to being, the first being truly subsists. And because the former is desirable, the latter shines forth as the beautiful itself." -T.

26 (See page 521, line 67b) Porphyry, in his Treatise περι αποχης εμψυχων, lib. iii, sec. 1. writes thus: Σωκρατης προς τους ηδονην διαμφισβητουντας ειναι το τελος, ουδ᾽ αν παντες, εφη, συες και τραγοι τουτῳ συναινοιεν, πεισθησεσθαι αν εν τῳη δεσθαι το ευδαιμον ημων καισθαι, εστ᾽ αν νους εν τοις πασι κρατη. "To certain persons who were disputing on this point, - whether pleasure was the ultimate end *of man*, Socrates said that, were all the swine and goats in the world to join in applauding this man, *(the advocate for pleasure)* yet he should never be persuaded that human happiness consisted in being pleased, so long as mind excelled and prevailed in all things." If Porphyry in this alluded to the very emphatical passage in Plato now before us, he seems to have improved the force of it not a little; unless, in his copy of this dialogue, he read συες και τραγοι instead of βοες και ιπωοι. -S.

THE
SECOND ALCIBIADES

A DIALOGUE

CONCERNING

PRAYER

INTRODUCTION

The *Second Alcibiades*, which in the supposed time of it is subsequent to the first of the same name, is on a subject which ranks among the most important to a rational being; for with it is connected piety, which is the summit of virtue. Hence, as all nations in the infinity of time past have believed in the existence of certain divine powers superior to man, who beneficently provide for all inferior natures, and defend them from evil; so likewise they worshipped these powers by numerous religious rites, of which prayer formed no inconsiderable part. The exceptions, indeed, to this general belief of mankind are so few that they do not deserve to be noticed. For we may say, with the elegant Maximus Tyrius,[†] that, "if through the whole of time there have been two or three atheists, they were grovelling and insensate men, whose eyes wandered, whose ears were deceived, whose souls were mutilated, a race irrational, barren, and useless, resembling a timid lion, an ox without horns, a bird without wings." All others, as well those engaged in public affairs, as philosophers who explored the hidden causes of things, most constantly believed that there were Gods, *viz.* one first ineffable source of all things, and a multitude of divine powers proceeding from, and united with, him; and always endeavoured to render these divine natures propitious, by sacrifice and prayer. Hence, the Chaldeans among the Assyrians, the Brahmins among the Indians, the Druids among the Gauls, the Magi among the Persians, and the tribe of priests among the Egyptians, constantly applied themselves to the worship of Divinity, and venerated and adored the Gods by various sacred ceremonies, and ardent and assiduous prayers.

As the leading design, therefore, of the following dialogue is to show the great importance of prayer, I persuade myself, that I cannot do any thing more illustrative of this design, or more beneficial to the reader, than to present him with the divinely luminous conceptions of Porphyry, Iamblichus, Proclus, and Hierocles on prayer, together with what the pseudo Dionysius has stolen from the Platonic philosophers on this subject. As these observations never yet appeared in any modern language, and as they are not to be equalled in any other writer for their profundity and sublimity, I trust no apology will be requisite for their

---

† In his Dissertation *What God is according to Plato*. See TTS vol. VI, p. 7.

length.   Previous to their insertion, therefore, I shall only give the following definition of prayer, *viz.* that it is a certain force supernally imparted to the soul, elevating and conjoining her to Divinity, and which always unites in a becoming manner secondary with primary natures.

Porphyry then observes,[†] that prayer especially pertains to worthy men, because it is a conjunction with a divine nature. But the similar loves to be united to the similar. And a worthy man is most similar to the Gods. Since those also that cultivate virtue are enclosed in body as in a prison, they ought to pray to the Gods that they may depart from hence. Besides, as we are like children torn from our parents, it is proper to pray that we may return to the Gods, as to our true parents: and because those that do not think it requisite to pray, and convert themselves to more excellent natures, are like those that are deprived of their fathers and mothers. To which we may add, that as we are a part of the universe, it is fit that we should be in want of it: for a conversion to the whole imparts safety to every thing. Whether, therefore, you possess virtue, it is proper that you should invoke that which causally comprehends[‡] the whole of virtue. For that which is all-good will also be the cause to you of that good which it is proper for you to possess. Or whether you explore some corporeal good, there is a power in the world which connectedly contains every body. It is necessary, therefore, that the perfect should thence be derived to the parts of the universe. Thus far Porphyry, who was not without reason celebrated by posterior philosophers for his ἱεροπρεπη νοηματα, or conceptions adapted to sacred concerns.

Let us now attend to Iamblichus,[§] whom every genuine Platonist will acknowledge to have been justly surnamed *the divine.*

As prayers, through which sacred rites receive their perfect consummation and vigour, constitute a great part of sacrifice, and as they are of general utility to religion, and produce an indissoluble communion between the Divinities and their priests, it is necessary that we should mention a few things concerning their various species and wonderful

---

[†] Vide Procl. in Tim. 64B [TTS vol. XV]. -T.

[‡] The word used by Porphyry here is προειληφος, which always signifies in Platonic writings *causal comprehension;* or the occult and indistinct prior to the actual and separate subsistence of things. After this manner numbers subsist causal in the monad. -T.

[§] De Myst. sec. 5, cap. 26. [TTS vol. XVII] -T.

effects. For prayer is of itself a thing worthy to be known, and gives greater perfection to the science concerning the Gods. I say, therefore, that the *first* species of prayer is *collective,* producing a contact with Divinity, and subsisting as the leader and light of knowledge. But the *second* is the *bond of consent and communion with the Gods,* exciting them to a copious communication of their benefits prior to the energy of speech, and perfecting the whole of our operations previous to our intellectual conceptions. But the *third* and most perfect species of prayer is *the seal of ineffable union with the Divinities,* in whom it establishes all the power and authority of prayer: and thus causes the soul to repose in the Gods, as in a divine and never-failing port. But from these three terms, in which all the divine measures are contained, suppliant adoration not only conciliates to us the friendship of the Gods, but supernally extends to us three fruits, being, as it were, three Hesperian apples of gold.† The *first* pertains to *illumination;* the second, to *a communion of operation;* but through the energy of the *third* we receive *a perfect plenitude of divine fire.* And sometimes, indeed, supplication *precedes;* like a forerunner, preparing the way before the sacrifice appears. But sometimes it *intercedes as a mediator:* and sometimes *accomplishes the end of sacrificing.* No operation, however, in sacred concerns can succeed without the intervention of prayer. Lastly, the continual exercise of prayer nourishes the vigour of our intellect, and renders the receptacles of the soul far more capacious for the communications of the Gods. It likewise is the *divine key* which unfolds to men the penetralia of the Gods; accustoms us to the splendid rivers of supernal light; in a short time perfects our inmost recesses, and disposes them for the ineffable embrace and contact of the Gods; and does not desist till it raises us to the summit of all. It likewise gradually and silently draws upwards the manners of our soul, by divesting them of every thing foreign from a divine nature, and clothes us with the perfections of the Gods. Besides this, it produces an indissoluble communion and friendship with Divinity, nourishes a divine love, and enflames the divine part of the soul. Whatever is of an opposing and contrary nature in the soul it expiates and purifies; expels whatever is prone to generation, and retains any thing of the dregs of mortality in its ethereal and splendid spirit; perfects a good hope and faith concerning the reception of divine light; and in one word, renders those by whom it is

---

† This particular respecting the *apples of gold* is added from the version of Scutellius, who appears to have made his translation of Iamblichus from a more perfect manuscript than that which was used by Gale. -T.

employed the familiars and domestics of the Gods. If such, then, are the advantages of prayer, and such its connection with sacrifice, does it not appear from hence, that the end of sacrifice is a conjunction with the demiurgus of the world? And the benefit of prayer is of the same extent with the good which is conferred by the demiurgic causes on the race of mortals. Again, from hence the *anagogic, perfective,* and *replenishing* power of prayer appears; likewise how it becomes efficacious and unific, and how it possesses a common bond imparted by the Gods. And in the third and last place, it may easily be conceived from hence how prayer and sacrifice mutually corroborate, and confer on each other a sacred and perfect power in divine concerns.

The following translation (64D ff) of Proclus on the *Timæus,* containing the doctrine of Iamblichus on prayer, with the elucidations of Proclus, may be considered as an excellent commentary on the preceding observations.

All beings are the progeny of the Gods, by whom they are produced without a medium, and in whom they are firmly established. For the progression of things which perpetually subsist and cohere from permanent causes, is not alone perfected by a certain continuation, but immediately subsists from the Gods, from whence all things are generated, however distant they may be from the Divinities: and this is no less true, even though asserted of matter itself. For a divine nature is not absent from any thing, but is equally present to all things. Hence, though you consider the last of beings, in these also you will find Divinity: for *The One* is every where; and in consequence of its absolute dominion, every thing receives its nature and coherence from the Gods. But as all things proceed, so likewise they are not separated from the Gods, but radically abide in them, as the causes and sustainers of their existence: for where can they recede, since the Gods primarily comprehend all things in their embrace? For whatever is placed as separate from the Gods has not any kind of subsistence. But all beings are contained by the Gods, and reside in their natures after the manner of a circular comprehension. Hence, by a wonderful mode of subsistence, all things proceed, and yet are not, nor indeed can be, separated from the Gods; (for all generated natures, when torn from their parents, immediately recur to the wide-spreading immensity of non-being,) but they are after a manner established in the divine natures: and, in fine, they proceed in themselves, but abide in the Gods. But since in consequence of their progression it is requisite that they should be converted, and return, and imitate the egress and conversion of the Gods to their ineffable cause, that the natures, thus disposed, may again be contained by the Gods, and the first unities, according to a *telesiurgic,* or perfective triad, they receive from hence a certain secondary perfection, by which they may be able to convert themselves to the goodness of the Gods; that after they have rooted their principle in the Divinities, they may again, by conversion, abide in them, and form as it were a circle, which originates from, and terminates in, the Gods. All things, therefore, both abide in, and convert themselves to, the Gods; receiving this power from the Divinities, together with twofold symbols according to essence: the one, that they may abide there; but the other, that having proceeded, they may convert themselves: and this we may easily contemplate, not only in souls, but also in inanimate natures. For what else ingenerates in these a sympathy with other powers but the symbols which they are allotted by nature, some of which contract a familiarity with *this* and some with *that* series of Gods? For nature supernally depending from the Gods, and being distributed from their orders, impresses also in bodies the symbols of her familiarity with the Divinities. In some, indeed, inserting solar symbols, but in others lunar, and in others again the occult characters of some other God. And these, indeed, convert themselves to the Divinities: some as it were to the Gods simply, but others as to particular Gods; nature thus perfecting her progeny according to different peculiarities of the Gods. The Demiurgus of the universe, therefore, by a much greater priority, impressed these symbols in souls, by which they might be able to abide in themselves, and again convert themselves to the sources of their being: through the symbol of unity, conferring on them stability; but through intellect affording them the power of conversion.

And to this conversion prayer is of the greatest utility: for it conciliates the beneficence of the Gods through those ineffable symbols which the father of the universe has disseminated in souls. It likewise unites those who pray with those to whom prayer is addressed; copulates the intellect of the Gods with the discourses of those who pray; excites the will of those who perfectly comprehend good, and produces in us a firm persuasion, that they will abundantly impart to us the beneficence which they contain: and lastly, it establishes in the Gods whatever we possess.

But to a perfect and true prayer there is required, first, a knowledge of all the divine orders to which he who prays approaches: for neither will any one accede in a proper manner, unless he intimately beholds their distinguishing properties: and hence it is that the Oracle[†] admonishes, "*that a fiery intellection obtains the first order in sacred veneration.*" But

---

† *Viz.* one of the Chaldean Oracles [TTS vol. VII, p. 44]. -T.

afterwards there is required a conformation of our life with that which is divine; and this accompanied with all *purity, chastity, discipline,* and *order.* For thus while we present ourselves to the Gods, they will be provoked to beneficence; and our souls will be subjected to theirs, and will participate the excellences of a divine nature. In the third place, a certain contact is necessary, from whence, with the more exalted part of the soul, we touch the divine essence, and verge to a union with its ineffable nature. But there is yet further required an accession and inhesion, (for thus the Oracle calls it, while it says, *"the mortal adhering to fire will possess a divine light,"*) from whence we receive a greater and more illustrious part of the light proceeding from the Gods. In the last place, a union succeeds with the unity of the Gods, restoring and establishing unity to the soul, and causing our energy to become one with divine energy: so that in this case, we are no longer ourselves, but are absorbed, as it were, in the nature of the Gods; and residing in divine light, are entirely surrounded with its splendour. And this is, indeed, the best end of prayer, the conjunction of the soul's conversion with its permanency; establishing in unity whatever proceeds from the divine unities; and surrounding our light with the light of the Gods.

Prayer, therefore, is of no small assistance to our souls in ascending to their native region: nor is he who possesses virtue superior to the want of that good which proceeds from prayer, but the very contrary takes place; since prayer is not only the cause of our ascent and reversion, but with it is connected piety to the Gods, that is, the very summit of virtue. Nor, indeed, ought any other to pray than he who excels in goodness: (as the Athenian guest in Plato admonishes us,) for to such a one, while enjoying by the exercise of prayer familiarity with the Gods, an efficacious and easy way is prepared for the enjoyment of a blessed life. But the contrary succeeds to the vicious: since it is not lawful for purity to be touched by impurity. It is necessary, therefore, that he who generously enters on the exercise of prayer should render the Gods propitious to him; and should excite in himself divine conceptions, full of intellectual light: for the favour and benignity of more exalted beings is the most effectual incentive to their communication with our natures. And it is requisite, without intermission, to dwell in the veneration of Divinity: for, according to the poet, *"the Gods are accustomed to be present with the mortal constantly employed in prayer."* It is likewise necessary to preserve a stable order of divine works, and to produce those virtues which purify the soul from the stains of generation, and elevate her to the regions of intellect, together with *faith, truth,* and *love:* to preserve this triad and hope of good, this immutable perception of divine light, and segregation from every other pursuit; that thus solitary, and free from material concerns, we may become united with the solitary unities of the Gods; since he who attempts by multitude to unite himself with unity, acts preposterously, and dissociates himself from Divinity. For as it is not lawful for any one to conjoin himself by that which is not, with that which is; so neither is it possible with multitude to be conjoined with unity. Such, then, are the consequences primarily apparent in prayer, *viz.* that its essence is the cause of associating our souls with the Gods; and that on this account it unites and copulates all inferior with all superior beings. For, as the great *Theodorus*[†] says, *all things pray, except the FIRST.*

But the perfection of prayer, beginning from more common goods, ends in divine conjunction, and gradually accustoms the soul to divine light. And its efficacious and vigorous energy both replenishes us with good, and causes our concerns to be common with those of the Gods. We may also rationally suppose that the causes of prayer, so far as they are *effective,* are the vigorous and efficacious powers of the Gods, converting and calling upwards the soul to the Gods themselves. But that, so far as they are *perfective,* they are the immaculate goods of the soul, from the reception of which, souls are established in the Gods. And again, that so far as they are *paradigmatical,* they are the primary fabricating causes of beings; proceeding from *The Good,* and conjoined with it by an ineffable union. But that so far as they are *formal,* or possess the proportion of forms, they render souls similar to the Gods, and give perfection to the whole life of the soul. Lastly, so far as they are *material,* or retain the proportion of matter, they are the marks or symbols conferred by the Demiurgus on the essences of souls, that they may be wakened to a reminiscence of the Gods who produced both them and whatever else exists.

But we may also describe the modes of prayer, which are various, according to the genera and species of the Gods. For of prayers, some are *fabricative;* others of *a purifying nature;* and others, lastly, are *vivific.* I call those *fabricative* which are offered for the sake of showers and winds. For the fabricative Gods (δημιουργοι) are also the causes of these: on which account, it is customary with the Athenians to pray to such Divinities for the sake of obtaining winds procuring serenity of weather. But I call those prayers of *a purifying nature,* which are instituted for the purpose of averting diseases originating from pestilence, and other contagious distempers: such as are written in our temples. And lastly,

---

† *Viz.* Theodorus Asinæus, a disciple of Porphyry. -T.

those prayers are *vivific* with which we venerate the Gods who are the causes of vivification, on account of the origin and maturity of fruits. Hence it is that prayers are of a perfective nature, because they elevate us to these divine orders: and those who consider such prayers in a different manner, do not properly apprehend in what their nature and efficacy consist. But again, with respect to the things for which we pray, those which regard the *safety of the soul* obtain the first place; those which pertain to *the proper disposition and strength of the body,* the second; and those claim the last place which pertain to *external concerns.* And lastly, with respect to the distribution of the times in which we offer up prayers, it is either according to the seasons of the year, or the centres of the solar revolution; or we establish multiform prayers according to other suchlike conceptions.

With the above admirable passages the following extract from Iamblichus de Myst. I, 12 [TTS vol. XVII] may be very properly conjoined. Its design is to show, that the Gods are not agitated by passions, though they appear to be moved through the influence of prayer.

Prayers are not to be directed to the Gods, as if they were passive, and could be moved by supplications: for the divine irradiation which takes place through the exercise of prayer, operates spontaneously, and is far remote from all material attraction; since it becomes apparent through divine energy and perfection; and as much excels the voluntary motion of our nature, as the divine will of *The Good* surpasses our election. Through this volition, the Gods, who are perfectly benevolent and merciful, pour their light without any parsimony on the supplicating priests, whose souls they call upwards to their own divine natures; impart to them a union with themselves, and accustom their souls, even while bound in body, to separate themselves from its dark embrace, and to be led back by an ineffable energy to their eternal and intelligible original. Indeed it is evident that the safety of the soul depends on such divine operations. For while the soul contemplates divine visions, it acquires another life, employs a different energy, and may be considered, with the greatest propriety, as no longer ranking in the order of man. For it often lays aside its own proper life, and changes it for the most blessed energy of the Gods. But if an ascent to the Gods, through the ministry of prayer, confers on the priests purity from passion, freedom from the bonds of generation, and a union with a divine principle, how can there be any thing passive in the efficacy of prayer? For invocation does not draw down the pure and impassive Gods to us who are passive and impure; but, on the contrary, renders us who are become through generation impure and passive, immutable and pure.

But neither do invocations conjoin, through passion, the priests with the Divinities, but afford an indissoluble communion of connection, through that friendship which binds all things in union and consent. Nor do invocations incline the intellect of the Gods towards men, as the term seems to imply; but, according to the decisions of truth, they render the will of men properly disposed to receive the participations of the Gods; leading it upwards, and connecting it with the Divinities by the sweetest and most alluring persuasion. And on this account the sacred names of thé Gods, and other divine symbols, from their anagogic nature, are able to connect invocations with the Gods themselves.

And in chapter 15 of the same section, he again admirably discourses on the same subject as follows:

That which in our nature is divine, intellectual, and one, or (as you may be willing to call it) intelligible, is perfectly excited by prayer from its dormant state; and when excited, vehemently seeks that which is similar to itself, and becomes copulated to its own perfection. But if it should seem incredible that incorporeal natures can be capable of hearing sounds, and it is urged, that for this purpose the sense of hearing is requisite, that they may understand our supplications; such objectors are unacquainted with the excellency of primary causes, which consists in both knowing and comprehending in themselves at once the universality of things. The Gods, therefore, do not receive prayers in themselves through any corporeal powers or organs, but rather contain in themselves the effects of pious invocations; and especially of such as though sacred cultivation are consecrated and united to the Gods: for, in this case, a divine nature is evidently present with itself, and does not apprehend the conceptions of prayers as different from its own. Nor are supplications to be considered as foreign from the purity of intellect: but since the Gods excel us both in power, purity, and all other advantages, we shall act in the most opportune manner, by invoking them with the most vehement supplications. For a consciousness of our own nothingness, when we compare ourselves with the Gods, naturally leads us to the exercise of prayer. But through the benefits resulting from supplication we are in a short time brought back to the object of supplication; acquire its similitude from intimate converse; and gradually obtain divine perfection, instead of our own imbecility and imperfection.

Indeed he who considers, that sacred prayers are sent to men from the Gods themselves; that they are certain symbols of the divine natures; and that they are only known to the Gods, with whom in a certain respect they possess an equal power; I say, he who considers all this, cannot any longer believe that supplications are of a sensible nature, and that they are not very justly esteemed intellectual and divine: and must acknowledge it to be impossible that any passion should belong to things the purity of which the most worthy manners of men cannot easily equal.

Nor ought we to be disturbed by the objection which urges, that material things are frequently offered in supplications; and this as if the Gods possessed a sensitive and animal nature. For, indeed, if the offering consisted solely of corporeal and composite powers, and such as are only accommodated to organical purposes, the objection would have some weight: but since they participate of incorporeal forms, certain proportions, and more simple measures; in this alone the correspondence and connection of offerings with the Gods ought to be regarded. For, whenever any affinity of similitude is present, whether greater or less, it is sufficient to the connection of which we are now discoursing: since there is nothing which approaches to a kindred alliance with the Gods, though in the smallest degree, to which the Gods are not immediately present and united. A connection, therefore, as much as is possible, subsists between prayers and the Gods: at the same time prayers do not regard the Divinities as if they were of a sensitive or animal nature; but they consider them as they are in reality, and according to the divine forms which their essences contain.

In the third place, let us attend to the admirable observations on prayer of Hierocles, who, though inferior in accuracy and sublimity of conception to Iamblichus and Proclus, yet, as Damascius well observes, (in this Life of Isidorus apud Phot.) he uncommonly excelled in his dianoëtic part, and in a venerable and magnificent fluency of diction. The following is a translation of his Comment on the Pythagoric verse:

.... Αλλ᾽ ερχευ επ᾽ εργον
Θεοισιν επευξαμενος τελεσαι.

i.e. "Betake yourself to the work, having implored the Gods to bring it to perfection."

The verse briefly describes all that contributes to the acquisition of good, *viz.* the self-moved nature of the soul, and the co-operation of Divinity. For, though the election of things beautiful[†] is in our power, yet, as we possess our freedom of the will from Divinity, we are perfectly indigent of his co-operating with and perfecting the things which we have chosen. For our endeavour appears to be similar to a hand extended to the reception of things beautiful; but that which is

---

† By things beautiful, with Platonic writers, every thing excellent and good is included. -T.

imparted by Divinity is the supplier and the fountain of the gift of good. And the former, indeed, is naturally adapted to discover things beautiful; but the latter to unfold them to him by whom they are rightly explored. But prayer is the medium between two boundaries, *viz.* between investigation by us, and that which is imparted by Divinity, properly adhering to the cause which leads us into existence, and perfects us in well-being. For how can any one receive well-being unless Divinity imparts it? And how can Divinity, who is naturally adapted to give, give to him who does not ask, though his impulses arise from the freedom of his will? That we may not, therefore, pray only in words, but may also corroborate this by deeds; and that we may not confide only in our own energy, but may also beseech Divinity to co-operate with our deeds, and may conjoin prayer to action, as form to matter; and, in short, that we may pray for what we do, and do that for which we pray, the verse conjoining these two, says, "Betake yourself to the work, having implored the Gods to bring it to perfection." For neither is it proper alone to engage with alacrity in beautiful actions, as if it were in our power to perform them with rectitude, without the co-operation of Divinity; nor yet should we be satisfied with the words of mere prayer while we contribute nothing to the acquisition of the things which we request. For thus we shall either pursue atheistical virtue (if I may be allowed so to speak) or unenergetic prayer; of which the former, being deprived of Divinity, takes away the essence of virtue; and the latter, being sluggish, dissolves the efficacy of prayer. For how can any thing be beautiful which is not performed according to the divine rule? And how is it possible that what is done according to this should not entirely require the co-operation of Divinity to its subsistence? For virtue is the image of Divinity in the rational soul; but every image requires its paradigm, in order to its generation, nor is that which it possesses sufficient, unless it looks to that from the similitude to which it possesses the beautiful. It is proper, therefore, that those should pray who hasten to energetic virtue, and having prayed, that they should endeavour to possess it. It is likewise requisite that they should do this, looking to that which is divine and splendid, and should extend themselves to philosophy, adhering at the same time in a becoming manner to the first cause of good. For that tetractys,[†] the fountain of

---

† This *tetractys* which is the same as the *Phanes* of Orpheus, and the αυτοζωον, or *animal itself*, of Plato, first subsists at the extremity of the intelligible order, and is thence participated by Jupiter, the fabricator of the universe. See the Introduction to the *Timæus* [TTS vol. X]. -T.

perennial nature, is not only the eternal cause of being to all things, but likewise of well-being, expanding proper good through the whole world, like undecaying and intellectual light. But the soul, when she properly adheres to this light, and purifies herself like an eye to acuteness of vision, by an attention to things beautiful, is excited to prayer; and again, from the plenitude of prayer she extends her endeavours, conjoining actions to words, and by divine conferences giving stability to worthy deeds. And discovering some things, and being illuminated in others, she endeavours to effect what she prays for, and prays for that which she endeavours to effect. And such indeed is the union of endeavour and prayer.

In the last place, the pseudo Dionysius has decorated his book *On the Divine Names* with the following admirable observations on prayer, stolen[†] from writers incomparably more sublime than any of the age in which he pretended to have lived.

Divinity is present to all things, but all things are not present to him; but when we invoke him with all-sacred payers, an unclouded intellect, and an aptitude to divine union, then we also are present to him. For he is neither in place, that he may be absent from any thing, nor does he pass from one thing to another. But, indeed, to assert that he is in all things, falls far short of that infinity which is above, and which comprehends, all things. Let us therefore extend ourselves by prayer to the more sublime intuition of his divine and beneficent rays. Just as if a chain, consisting of numerous lamps, were suspended from the summit of heaven, and extended to the earth. For if we ascended this chain, by always alternately stretching forth our hands, we should appear indeed to ourselves to draw down the chain, though we should not in reality, it being present upwards and downwards, but we should elevate ourselves to the more sublime splendours of the abundantly-luminous

---

† Fabricius, in the 4th vol. of his Bibliotheca Græca, has incontestably proved that this Dionysius lived several hundred years after the time of St Paul; and observes, that his works are, doubtless, composed from Platonic writings. In confirmation of this remark, it is necessary to inform the learned reader, that the long discourse on Evil in the treatise of Dionysius, περι θειων ονοματων, appears to have been taken almost verbatim from one of the lost writings of Proclus *On the Subsistence of Evil*, as will be at once evident by comparing it with the Excerpta from that work, preserved by Fabricius in Biblioth. Græc. tom. viii. p. 502. -T.

rays. Or, as if we ascended into a ship, and held by the ropes[†] extended to us from a certain rock, and which were given to us for our assistance; we should not in this case draw the rock to us, but we in reality should move both ourselves and the ship to the rock. Just as, on the contrary, if any one standing in a ship pushes against a rock fixed in the sea, he indeed effects nothing in the firm and immovable rock, but causes himself to recede from it: and by how much the more he pushes against, by so much the more is he repelled from the rock. Hence, prior to every undertaking, and especially that which is theological, it is necessary to begin from prayer, not as if drawing down that power which is every where present, and is at the same time no where, but as committing and uniting ourselves to it by divine recollections and invocations.

I shall only add, that the ancients appear very properly to have placed this dialogue in the class which they called *maieutic:* and, as Mr Sydenham justly observes, "the outward form of it, from the beginning to the end, is *dramatic;* the *catastrophe* being a change of mind in Alcibiades, who resolves to follow the advice of Socrates, by forbearing to specify, in his addresses to Divinity, his wants and his wishes, till he shall have attained to a sense of his real indigence through the knowledge of his real good, the only right and proper object of prayer."

[†] This part is stolen from the Commentaries of Simplicius on Epictetus, as is evident from the following extract: Ταυτην την ημων επιστροφην προς αυτον (θεον) ως αυτου προς ημας λεγομεν· τοιουτον τι πασχοντες, ειον οι πετρας τινος παραλιας καλων εξαψαντες, και τω εκεινον επισπασθαι εαυτους τε και το ακατιον τη πετρα προσαγοντες· και δι' απειριαν του γινομενου δοκουντες ουκ αυτοι προσιεναι τη πετρα, αλλα την πετραν κατ' ολιγον επ' αυτους ιενα· μεταμελειαι δε, και ικετειαι, και ευχαι, και τα τοιαυτα, αναλογουσι τω καλω. p. 223, 8vo. *i.e.* "We speak of this our conversion to Divinity, as if it was a conversion of him to us; being affected in somewhat the same manner as those who, fastening a rope to a certain rock in the sea, and drawing both themselves and the boat to the rock by pulling it, appear, through their ignorance of this circumstance, not to approach themselves to the rock, but think that the rock gradually approaches to them. For repentance, supplication, prayer, and things of this kind, are analogous to the rope."

THE

SECOND ALCIBIADES

PERSONS OF THE DIALOGUE

SOCRATES, ALCIBIADES

SCENE - The Way to the TEMPLE of JUPITER[1]

138a   SOC. Alcibiades! are you going to the temple to make your petitions to the God?

ALC. Your conjecture is perfectly right, Socrates.

SOC. Indeed your countenance appears close and cloudy; and your eyes are turned toward the ground, as if you were wrapped in some profound thought.[2]

ALC. What profound thoughts could a man have at such a time, Socrates?

b   SOC. Thoughts, Alcibiades, such as seem to me of the highest importance. For tell me, in the name of Jupiter, do you not think, when we happen, whether in private or in public, to be making our petitions to the Gods, that sometimes they grant a part of those petitions, and reject the rest; and that to some of their petitioners they hearken, but are deaf to others?

ALC. No doubt of it.

SOC. Do you not think, then, that much previous consideration is requisite to prevent a man from praying unwittingly for things which are very evil, but which he imagines very good; if the Gods at that time

c   when he is praying to them should happen to be disposed to grant whatever prayers he happens to make? As Œdipus, they say, inconsiderately[3] prayed the Gods that his sons might divide their patrimony between them by the sword.[†] Instead, therefore, of praying for his family, as he might have done, that the evils which it then suffered might be averted, he cursed it by praying[4] that more might be superadded. The event of which curse was this, that not only what he prayed for was accomplished, but from that accomplishment followed other evils, many and terrible, which there is no need to enumerate.[‡]

ALC. But, Socrates, you have now spoken of a man who was insane, for who, think you, in his sound mind would venture to make such sort of prayers?

SOC. Whether is it your opinion, that to be insane is to be in a state of mind contrary to that which is sound?

ALC. I am quite of opinion that it is.

d　　SOC. And are you not of opinion, too, that there are men who want understanding and men who have not that want?

ALC. I am.

SOC. Come, then, let us consider what sort of men these are. You have admitted, that men there are who want understanding, men who do not want it, and other men, you say, who are insane.

ALC. True.

SOC. Further now; are there not some men in a good state of health?

ALC. There are.

SOC. And are there not others in a bad state of health?

139a　　ALC. Certainly.

SOC. These, then, are not the same men with those.

ALC. By no means.

SOC. Whether now are there any men who are in neither of those states?

ALC. Certainly, none.

SOC. For every man must of necessity either *have* good health, or *want* good health.

ALC. I think so too.

SOC. Well: do you think after the same manner with regard to the having of understanding, and the want of understanding?

ALC. How do you mean?

---

† The same relation of this curse is given by Euripides, in Phænissæ, ver. 68; by Sophocles, in Œdipus Colon. ver. 1437, 1447, et seq. (where Œdipus himself reiterates the curse:) and by the Scholiast on Æschylus, in Septem apud Thebas, ver. 613, 713, 729, and 853. -S.

‡ The particulars are briefly related by Appollodorus, in Bibliothen. lib. iii. cap. 6 and 7. -S.

SOC. Do you think it to be necessary,[5] that a man should either *have*
b   or *want* a good understanding? Or is there, besides, some third and
middle state, in which a man neither *has* nor *wants* a good
understanding?

ALC. There certainly is not.

SOC. Every man, then, of necessity must be either in the one or in the
other of those two conditions.

ALC. So it seems to me.

SOC. Do you not remember that you admitted this, that insanity was
contrary to soundness of understanding?

ALC. I do.

SOC. And do you not remember that you admitted this also, that
there was no middle or third state, in which a man neither *has* nor *wants*
a good understanding?

ALC. I admitted this too.

SOC. But how can two different things be contrary to one and the
same thing?

ALC. It is by no means possible.

c   SOC. Want of understanding, therefore, and insanity, are likely to be
found the same thing.

ALC. It appears so.

SOC. If then we should pronounce that all fools were madmen,[†] we
should pronounce rightly, Alcibiades.

ALC. We should.

SOC. In the first place, your equals in age, if any of them happen to
be fools, as indeed they are, and some of your elders too, all these we
must pronounce madmen. For consider, are you not of opinion, that in
this city there are few wise men, but a multitude of fools, whom you
call madmen?

ALC. I am of that opinion.

SOC. Can you imagine then, that, living in the same city with so
d   many madmen, we should live with any ease or comfort? or that we
should not have suffered from them long ago, have been buffeted, and
pelted, and have met with all other mischiefs which madmen are wont
to perpetrate? But consider, my good sir, whether we live not here in
a different state of things.

---

† That the philosophers of the Stoic sect derived from Socrates that celebrated
paradox of theirs, παντας τους αφροιας μαινεσθαι, *that all fools are mad,* is a just
observation of Cicero's in Tuscul. Disputat. l. iii, § 5: and Dr Davis, in his notes
thereon, shows the justness of it, by referring to the passage in Plato now before us. -S.

ALC. What is then the truth of the case, Socrates, with respect to the multitude? For it is not likely to be what I just now imagined.

SOC. Neither do I think it is so myself. But we should consider it in some such way as this.

ALC. In what way do you mean?

SOC. I will tell you. We presume that some men there are who are ill in health: do we not?

ALC. Certainly we do.

e   SOC. Do you think it necessary then that every man, who is ill in health, should have the gout, or a fever, or an ophthalmy?[†] do you not think that a man, without suffering from any of these diseases, may be ill of some other? For diseases, we suppose, are of many various kinds, and not of those only.

ALC. I suppose they are.

SOC. Do you not think that every ophthalmy is a disease?

ALC. I do.

SOC. And do you think that every disease, therefore, is an ophthalmy?

ALC. By no means, not I. Yet still I am at a loss about your meaning.

140a   SOC. But if you will give me your attention, in considering the matter, both of us together, we shall go near to find the truth of it.

ALC. I give you, Socrates, all the attention I am master of.

SOC. Was it not agreed by us, that every ophthalmy was a disease; though not every disease an ophthalmy?

ALC. It was agreed so.

SOC. And I think it was rightly so agreed. For all persons who have a fever have a disease; not all, however, who have a disease have a fever;

b   neither have they all of them the gout, nor all of them an ophthalmy. Every thing indeed of this kind[6] is a disease; but they whom we call physicians say that diseases differ in their effects on the human body. For all diseases are not alike, neither are they all attended with like symptoms; but each of them operates with a power peculiar to itself, and

---

† We have no single word in our language to denote that disease of the eyes, called by the Grecian physicians οφθαλμια, the word here used by Plato. They meant by it such a ferous inflammation of the eyes, or defluxion of humours on them, as in Latin is called *lippitudo*. -S.

yet diseases are they all. Just as it is with respect to workmen; for workmen we suppose some men are, do we not?[†]

ALC. Certainly we do.

SOC. Such as shoemakers, smiths, statuaries, and a great multitude of others, whom it is needless to enumerate distinctly. All these have
c different parts of workmanship divided amongst them; and they all are workmen. They are not, however, smiths, nor shoemakers, nor statuaries, indiscriminately all of them together. Just so folly is divided amongst men. And those who have the largest share of it, we call madmen; such as have a portion somewhat less, we call senseless and stupefied:[‡] but if we choose to speak of these in gentler terms, some of us say they are magnanimous;[§] others call them simpletons; and others
d again, harmless and inexperienced in the world and speechless.[◊] You will also find, if you reflect, many other names given them beside these. But they are all comprised under the general term, folly or want of understanding. There is, however, a difference between them, as one art differs from another, one disease from another. Or how otherwise doth the case seem to you?

ALC. To me exactly as you represent it.

SOC. This point, therefore, being settled, let us from hence return back again. For it was proposed, I think, in the beginning of our inquiry, to be considered by us, what sort of men wanted understanding,

---

† In the Socratic manner of arguing from answers given to interrogations, the interrogating party asserts nothing positively; nor even lays down the most certain principles for a foundation of the future reasoning, until they are admitted for truths by the responding party. -S.

‡ In the Greek, εμβροντητους, literally to be translated thunder-stricken. For the effect of lightning, (when attended by thunder,) and indeed of all ætherial or electrical fire, is to stupefy, at least for a time, whatever animal it strikes. -S.

§ This euphemismus is applied in the way of raillery or good-humour, to such men as want sense or understanding in the common affairs of human life; as men really magnanimous, being usually regardless of things really little and appearing so to them, are looked upon as fools or as senseless by the multitude, to whom those little things appear great and important. -S.

◊ In the Greek, Eννεους, a word which, in the proper sense of it, is applied only to infants before they have attained to the use of speech. This epithet, and the two preceding it, are used in the way of extenuation or apology; the first for the wholly useless or unserviceable in any affair; the next for the silly or easy to be imposed on; the last for the silent from want of ideas, having nothing to say. -S.

and what sort were men of good understanding. For it was agreed that some there were of each sort. Was it not?

ALC. It was so agreed.

e SOC. Whether then do you suppose, that such persons have a good understanding who know how they ought to act, and what they ought to say?

ALC. I do.

SOC. And what persons do you apprehend to be wanting in understanding? are they not such as are ignorant in both those cases?

ALC. These very persons.

SOC. Will not these persons then, who are ignorant of what they ought to do and to say, both say and do what they ought not without being sensible of it?

ALC. It appears so.

141a SOC. Well then, Alcibiades, of this sort of persons, I said, was Œdipus. And you may find many in our own times, who, though they are not seized with sudden anger, as he was, yet pray for things hurtful to themselves; not suspecting evil in them, and imagining nought but good. Œdipus indeed, as he did not wish for any thing good, so neither did he imagine the thing he prayed for to be good. But some others there are, whose minds are in a disposition quite contrary to that of Œdipus. For you yourself, in my opinion, if the God to whom you are going to offer your petitions should appear to you, and, before you had made any petition to him, should ask you, "whether your desires would be satisfied with your becoming tyrant of Athens;" and (if you held this favour cheap, and no mighty grant) should add further, "and tyrant of all Greece;" and, if he should perceive that you deemed it still too little for you, unless you were tyrant† of all Europe, should promise you that also; and not merely promise, but make you so immediately on the spot, if you were in haste to have all the Europeans acknowledge Alcibiades, the son of Clinias, for their lord and master; in this case, it is my opinion, that you yourself would march away full of joy, as if the greatest good had befallen you.

b

ALC. I believe, Socrates, that I should; and that so would any other man whatever, had he met with such an adventure.

c SOC. You would not, however, accept of absolute dominion over the estates and persons of all the Grecians and Barbarians together, on condition of giving your life in exchange for it.

---

† The word *tyrant*, every where in Plato, signifies a despotic or arbitrary monarch. - S.

ALC. I suppose not. For why should I, when it could be of no use to me?

SOC. And, if you knew that you should make an ill use of it to your own detriment, would you not also in such a case refuse it?

ALC. Certainly I should.

SOC. You see, then, how dangerous it is, either inconsiderately to accept of it, when offered, or to wish and pray for it of yourself; since a man, by having it, may suffer great detriment, if not the total loss of
d   his life. In confirmation of this, we could mention many persons who longed after tyranny, and laboured to obtain it, as if some mighty good were to be enjoyed from it; but having obtained it, were, from plots and conspiracies to deprive them of it, forced to part with their very lives. Nay, it cannot, I suppose, have escaped your own hearing, what happened as it were but yesterday, that Archelaus, tyrant of the Macedonians, was murdered by his favourite; for this favourite was no less fond of the tyranny, than the tyrant was of him; and imagined that,
e   by obtaining the tyranny himself, he should be made a happy man; but that, after he had held the tyranny three or four days, he himself was, in his turn, secretly murdered by some others, who had conspired against him. Amongst our own fellow citizens, also, you see, (for this we have not from the report of others, but have been eye witnesses of it ourselves,) that of those who succeeded in their ambition to command
142a our armies, some were banished,[†] and still at this day live in exile from the city; others lost their lives;[‡] and such as seem to have fared the best, such as had gone through many terrifying dangers[§] in their campaigns, and were returned to their own country, have ever afterwards suffered at home, from sycophants and detractors, a siege as fierce and as dangerous as any from open enemies in the field, so that some of them

---

[†] Thucydides, the son of Melesias, had been banished by ostracism, four or five years before what we suppose the time of this dialogue; and we no where read, that ever he was recalled from exile; nor indeed is it probable that he was, at least during the life of Pericles. - S.

[‡] This was the case of Callias, the son of Calliades; he was slain in battle, about the time when the above-mentioned Thucydides was banished from Athens. See Thucydides the Historian, lib. i. § 61, 2, and 3. -S.

[§] In the Greek, διὰ πολλῶν κινδυνων ἐλθοντες και φοβων. - But we should be glad to have the authority of some ancient manuscript, for reading the last word in this sentence πονων, instead of φοβων· not only because the word πονων conveys a better meaning, but because also the words οι κινδυνοι τε και πονιο in the next sentence evidently appear to have respect to the mention of them both, made just before. -S.

b at length wished they had never known how to command an army, much rather than ever to have born the burden of that command. Indeed if the dangers and toils, which they underwent, had tended to their advantage, they would have had something plausible to plead in behalf of their ambition: but their case is quite the reverse of that. In the same manner, with respect to the having of children, you will find many men who wish and pray for them; but after they have[†] them, are brought, on that very account, into the greatest calamities and griefs: for some, whose children were incurably wicked, have spent all their after

c days in sorrow; and some, who had good children, but lost them by some bad accident, have been reduced to a state of mind no less miserable than the others, and, like them, have wished that their children never had been born. And yet, notwithstanding the evidence of these and many other cases of like kind, it is rare to find a man who would refuse those gifts of fortune, were they offered to him; or who, could he obtain them by his prayers, would forbear to pray for them.

d Few men would reject even a tyranny, if offered them; or the chief command of an army; or many other things, which often bring more mischief than benefit to the possessor. Nay, there are few men, of those who happen not to have them at present, who would not be glad if ever they came into their possession. And yet such, as obtain them, every now and then recant their wishes, and pray to be disencumbered of what they before prayed to have. I suspect, therefore, that in reality men accuse the Gods unjustly,[‡] in saying, that the evils which they suffer come from them:

> For on themselves they draw, through their own crimes,

e (or follies should we say?)

> More griefs than fate allots to human life.

And to me, Alcibiades, it seems probable, that some wise man or other, happening to be connected with certain persons void of understanding, and observing them to pursue and to pray for things, which it were better for them still to be without, but which appeared to them good,

---

† Perhaps the word ηδη in the Greek, which, as it is printed, precedes the word γενεσθαι, should be transferred from thence hither, that we might here read ηδη γενομενων. -S.

‡ This passage evidently alludes to a speech of Jupiter in Homer's *Odyssey*, lib. i. v. 32, *et seq.* -S.

composed for their use a common prayer;[7] the words of which are nearly these -

143a   Sov'reign of Nature! grant us what is good,
        Be it, or not, the subject of our pray'rs;
        And from thy suppliants, whate'er is ill,
        Tho' supplicating for it, still avert.

Now in this prayer, it seems to me, that the poet says what is right; and that whoever makes use of it, incurs no danger. But if you have any thing to say against it, speak your mind.

ALC. It is a difficult matter, Socrates, to speak against any thing which
b   is rightly said. But what I am thinking of is, how many evils are brought on men by ignorance: since to this it seems owing, that we labour to procure for ourselves the greatest mischiefs, without knowing what we are about; and how extreme our ignorance is, appears in our praying for them. And yet no man would imagine that to be his own case; and every one supposes himself sufficiently knowing, to pray for things the most advantageous to himself, and to avoid praying for things the most mischievous: for to pray for these things would in reality be like a curse, and not a prayer.

SOC. But perhaps, my good friend, some man or other, who happens to be wiser than you or I, might say, that we are wrong, in laying the
c   blame so rashly on ignorance, unless we proceed to specify what things we mean the ignorance of. To some persons also, in certain conditions and circumstances, ignorance is a good; though it be an evil to those others we have been speaking of.

ALC. How say you? Is it possible there should be any thing, which it is better for any person in any condition whatever to be ignorant of than to know?

SOC. I think it is: are not you of the same opinion?

ALC. Not I, by Jupiter.

SOC. Well now; - but observe, I am not going to charge you with having a will, disposed to have ever perpetrated[8] a deed, like that of
d   Orestes, upon his own mother, as it is reported; or like that of Alcmæon, or whoever else happened to act in the same manner.

ALC. Mention not such a horrid deed, I beseech you, Socrates.

SOC. The man, who acquits you of a disposition to have acted in that manner, you ought not, Alcibiades, to bid him avoid the mention of such a deed; but much rather ought you to lay that injunction on a man who should express a contrary opinion of you; since the deed appears to you so horrid, as not to admit a casual mention of it in conversation.

But do you think that Orestes, had he been a wise and prudent man, and had he known how it was best for him to act, would have dared to be guilty of any such action?

ALC. By no means.

e   SOC. Nor, I suppose, would any other man.

ALC. Certainly, not.

SOC. The ignorance therefore of what is best is an evil thing; and whoever is ignorant of that best will always suffer evil.

ALC. So I think.

SOC. And did not he think so too? and do not all other men think the same?

ALC. I cannot deny it.

SOC. Further then, let us consider this also. Supposing, that it should come into your head all at once, from a sudden fancy of its being the best thing you can do, to take a dagger with you, and go to the house of Pericles, your guardian and your friend; and supposing that, when you came there, upon your asking if Pericles was within, with intention

144a   to kill him only and no other person, you should receive this answer, He is within; - I do not say, that you have a will or inclination to verify any of these suppositions; I say no more than this - supposing you should be seized with such a fancy,[†] (and nothing, I think, hinders a man, who is ignorant of what is best, from being at some time or other so seized,) in that case an opinion might be conceived, that the worst thing a man can do is, in some circumstances, the best: do not you think it might?

ALC. Certainly so.

SOC. If then, upon being admitted to his presence, you should see and yet not know him, but should mistake him for some other person, I ask you, whether you would, notwithstanding that, be so furious as to kill him?

b   ALC. No, by Jupiter; I do not imagine that I should.

SOC. For you would not be so furious as to kill any person, whom chance threw in your way; but him only at whom you aimed. Is it not for this reason that you would not kill him?

ALC. Without doubt.

---

† In the Greek, ει, οιμαι, δοξει σοι οπερ ουθεν κωλυει, κ.τ.λ. The word οιμαι here seems to be out of its proper place, and to belong to the *parenthetical* part of this sentence, thus, ει δοξει σοι· οπερ, (or rather, as Stephens conjectures, οτιπερ,) οιμαι, ουθεν κωλυει δεπου τω γε αγνοουντι το βελτιστον παραστηναι ποτε δοξαν· ωστε, κ.τ.λ. -S.

SOC. And if you attempted the same thing ever so often, and still mistook Pericles, whenever you were about to execute your design, you never would lay violent hands on him.

ALC. Certainly I should not.

SOC. Well; and can you think that Orestes would ever have laid violent hands on his mother, if in like manner he had mistaken her for some other person?

c ALC. I think he would not.

SOC. For he too had it not in his mind to kill any woman he should chance to meet with, nor the mother of any man whatever, but his own mother only.

ALC. It is true.

SOC. To mistake therefore, and not to know things of that kind, is better for men who are in such dispositions, and who are seized with such imaginations.

ALC. It appears so to be.

SOC. Do you now perceive, that for some persons, in some circumstances, to be ignorant of some things, is a good, and not, as you just now imagined it, an evil?

ALC. It seems to me probable.

d SOC. Further; if you are willing to consider what follows after this, though it be strange and paradoxical, you may perhaps be of opinion that there is some truth in it.[†]

ALC. Above all things, Socrates, tell me what.

SOC. That the acquisition of other sciences, without the science[‡] of what is best, is, I may venture to say, likely to be found rarely beneficial, and generally hurtful to the person who has acquired them.[§] And consider it in this way: do you not think it necessary that, when we are about to engage in any affair, or to speak on any subject, we

---

† Immediately before ειναι, which is the last word of this sentence in the Greek, the word τι seems to be omitted.

‡ The words των αλλων επιστημων, in the Greek of this sentence, are sufficient to show, that, presently afterwards, we ought to read ανευ της του βελτιστου [sc. επιστημης]. And this reading, if it wanted confirmation, is indisputably confirmed by a subsequent passage, in which the very same paradoxical position, having been proved, is repeated as a conclusion from the proofs. -S.

§ The last word of this sentence in the Greek, we presume, should be read, not αυτα, as it is printed; but, either αυτας [sc. επιστημας], or αυτο [sc. κτημα]. The latter of these two emendatory readings is confirmed by that passage, to which we have referred in the preceding note.

should really know, or at least should fancy that we know, the subject
e   we are about to speak on, or the affair we are going so readily to engage
in?

ALC. I do think it is.

SOC. And do not our public orators, either knowing, or fancying that
they know, what the city ought to do, give us accordingly their counsel
off hand on every occasion? Some of them, on the subject of war and
peace; others, when the affair of building walls, or that of furnishing the
145a port-towns with proper stores, is in debate. In a word, all the
negotiations between our city and any other, and all our domestic
concerns, are they not conducted just as these orators advise?

ALC. True.

SOC. Observe then, how we proceed in this argument, if possible.
Some men you call wise, and others you call foolish.

ALC. I do.

SOC. Foolish do you not call the many, and wise the few?

ALC. Just so.

SOC. And do you not give those different epithets to those two sorts
of persons, in consideration of something in which they differ?

SOC. I do.

b   SOC. Whether do you call him a wise man, who knows how to
harangue the people on those subjects of debate we mentioned, without
knowing what advice is the best in general, and what on the present
occasion?

ALC. Certainly not.

SOC. Nor him neither, I suppose, who hath the knowledge of military
affairs, but knows not when it is best to go to war, nor how long a time
to continue it. Is not my supposition just?

ALC. It is.

SOC. Neither then do you call him a wise man, who knows how to
procure another man's death, or the confiscation of his estate, or the
banishment of him from his country, without knowing on what
occasion, or what person, it is best so to persecute.

ALC. Indeed I do not.

c   SOC. The man, therefore, who possesses any knowledge of such a
kind, if that knowledge of his be attended with the knowledge also of
what is best, (and this I presume to be the same with the knowledge of
what is beneficial; Is it so?

ALC. Certainly it is.)

SOC. We shall say, that he is a wise man, and sufficiently well able to judge for himself, and to be also a counsellor to the city. But of the man who has not the knowledge of what is beneficial,[†] we shall say the contrary. Or what is your opinion that we ought to say?

ALC. Mine agrees with yours.

SOC. Well now; let us suppose a man skilled in horsemanship, or in shooting with a bow, or in wrestling, or boxing, or other combat; or in any thing else which art teaches: what do you say concerning him who knows what is executed best, in that art which he has learnt? The man, for instance, who knows what is performed best in horsemanship, do you not say of him, that he is skilled in the horseman's art?

ALC. I do.

SOC. And the man who knows what is performed best in wrestling, I presume you say of him, that he is skilled in the wrestler's art. Of a man who has the like knowledge in music, you say, that he is skilled in the musician's art. And of men who have the like knowledge in the performances of other arts, you speak after a like manner: or how otherwise?

ALC. No otherwise than just as you say.

SOC. Do you think now, that a man, skilled in any of these arts, must of necessity be a wise man? or shall we say, that he wants much of being so?

ALC. Much indeed does he, by Jupiter.

SOC. Suppose then a commonwealth, composed of good bowmen and musicians, of wrestlers too and other artists; and mixed with these, such persons as we just now mentioned,[‡] such as understand military affairs, and such as know how to persecute a man to death; and superadded to them, your politicians, swollen with the pride of managing state-affairs; all these people void of the science of what is best; and not a man of them knowing when, or in what case, it is best to exercise the particular skill or knowledge that each man is master of; what sort of a commonwealth do you think this would prove?

ALC. But a bad one, Socrates, I think for my part.

---

† In the Greek, as it is printed, we here read ποιουντα, a word which is foreign to the sense. From what goes before, we conjecture the right reading to be either ωφελουντα, that is, ωφελειν επισταμενον, or else τοιουτον, that is, *such a one* as before described, ῳ παρεπεται η του βελτιστου επιστημη, whose particular knowledge or skill is attended with the science of what is best. -S.

‡ Instead of οις αρτι ειρηκαμεν, printed here in the Greek, we suspect that we ought to read ων α. ει. -S.

SOC. Neither would you, I suppose, hesitate to pronounce it so, when you saw every one of these men ambitious of being honoured, and making it his chief business in the commonwealth,

To attain to more, and still more, excellence,[9]

(by excellence I mean that which is the best in his own art,) but in what is best for the public, and best also for himself,[†] generally mistaken; as being, I suppose, without rational principles, and governed only by opinion. In this case, should we not be right in pronouncing that such a commonwealth was full of great disorder and of lawless doings?

b

ALC. Right indeed, by Jupiter.

SOC. Did we not think it necessary for us, either to fancy that we know, or really to know previously, the business we are going to engage in, or offhand to speak upon?

ALC. We did.

SOC. And did we not also think, that if a man engages in any business which he knows, and his knowledge of it be attended with the knowledge of what is beneficial, he will be in a way of profiting both the public and himself?[10]

c

ALC. How could we think otherwise?

SOC. But that if it be attended with ignorance of what is beneficial, the contrary will happen; he will neither profit the public nor himself?[‡]

ALC. Certainly we thought he would not.

SOC. And what? are you still of the same opinion? or have you in any respect altered your way of thinking about these matters?

ALC. Not at all: I think as I did still.

---

† In the Greek, αυτον αυτω βελτιστου, Stephens perceiving this to be quite ungrammatical, proposes, by a very scholar-like as well as sensible emendation, that instead of αυτον we should read αυτου. But perhaps the word αυτον was altogether intruded here by some transcriber, inattentive to the grammatical construction of this sentence, but who observed the words αυτον αυτω used in many following, sentences which have the same meaning with that now before us. -S.

‡ This sentence, interrogative also, is thus printed in the Greek; Εαν δε γ', οιμαι, ταναντια τουτων, ουτε τη πολει, ουτ αυτον αυτω: it plainly respects that passage cited in the last preceding note. The sense of it therefore must be the same with the sense of that: to express which sense exactly, we presume that we ought here to read, as follows: Εαν δ' αγνοια [sc. του ωφελιμου παρεπεται], ταναντια τουτων, κ.τ.λ. There is thus, we see, but little alteration made, even in the letters; and the corruption of this passage was not perhaps made with more ease, than that with which the genuine reading has been restored. -S.

SOC. Let me ask you then, whether you did not say that you called the many fools, and the few wise men?

ALC. I acknowledge it.

SOC. And do we not still say, that the many are mistaken in their opinion of what is best, for that they are generally, I suppose, without rational principles, and only governed by opinion?

d ALC. We still say the same.

SOC. It is the interest, therefore, of the many not to be knowing in any affairs, nor to conceit themselves knowing; if what affairs they know, or conceit they know, they will be the more forward to engage in; and, engaging in them, will receive more harm than benefit.

ALC. What you say is very true.

SOC. Do you see then; do I not appear to have been actually in the
e right, when I said, that the acquisition of other sciences, without the science of what is best, is rarely beneficial, and generally hurtful, to the person who has acquired them?

ALC. If I did not think so at that time, yet now, Socrates, I do.

SOC. It is incumbent therefore on every civil state, and every private person, if they would manage their affairs rightly, to depend absolutely on this science; just as the sick patient depends on his physician; or as the mariner, who would escape the dangers of the voyage, depends on
147a the commander of the vessel. For[11] without this science, the more vehemently an inward gale† impels a man, whether it arise from the consideration of his wealth, or bodily strength, or some other advantage of the same kind with either of those, so much the greater miscarriages will of necessity it seems befall him, from those very advantages. And, in like manner, the man who has acquired what is called much learning, and many arts, but is destitute of this science, and is driven along by each of the others, will not he meet with, and justly too indeed, a very tempestuous voyage? and supposing him to continue still at sea, without
b a commander of the vessel in which he sails, it will not be long‡ before he perishes. So that to such a man very applicable, I think, is that verse where the poet says of some person, in dispraise of him,

---

† In the Greek, το της ψυχης, by which we understand το της ψυχης πνευμα in the nominative case *before* επουριση, and not as Cornarius imagined, το πλοιον, or ακατιον, in the accusative case *after* that verb. -S.

‡ In the Greek, χρονον ου μακρον βιου θεων. Stephens proposes βιου θεων to be read for the two last words. And we embrace his proposal of reading βιου, but conjecture the right reading of the very last word to be rather βιων. -S.

Much knew he, and in many things had skill;
But whate'er things he knew, he knew them ill.

ALC. How, Socrates, doth this verse of the poet fall in with what we are speaking of? for to me it seems nothing to the purpose.

SOC. Very much to the purpose is it. But poets, you must know, write enigmatically almost all of them, but this poet more especially. For it is the genius of poetry in general to use an enigmatical language; and it is not for any ordinary person to understand it. But when, besides this difficulty, the poetical genius, so enigmatical in itself, seizes a man who is backward in communicating his knowledge, unwilling to tell us plainly what he means, and desirous to conceal his wisdom as much as possible from the world,[†] it appears in the highest degree difficult to find out the real meaning of any such poet. For you can by no means think that Homer,[‡] so very divine a poet as he was, could be ignorant, how impossible it was for a man, who possessed any science whatever, not to know it well. But he expresses himself enigmatically, I suppose, by using, instead of the words *evil*,[§] and *to know*, the derivative words, *ill*, and *he knew*.[◇] If then we use the two proper words, there is formed this sentence, in plain prose indeed, but

---

† From this passage it appears, what opinion either Plato himself, or other learned men in his time, entertained of Homer, as a philosopher. For he here represents the great poet as possessed of some profound knowledge, which he thought proper and prudent to conceal from the bulk of mankind; and therefore making the discovery of it so difficult, on purpose that only those, whose genius led them to philosophy, and whose outward circumstances of fortune permitted them to follow their genius, might be able to make such a discovery from his writings. -S.

‡ We see, that the ancient poem, entitled, from the name of the hero of it, Margites, in which was the verse above cited, is expressly attributed to Homer by Plato in this place; as it also is by Aristotle, in his *Poetics* iv, and in his *Nichomachean Ethics* vi, 7 [TTS vol. XXII]. What ancient writers have acceded to their opinion, and what others have differed from it, may be seen in Fabricii Bibliotheca Græca, ii, c. 2, § 24, n° 17. -S.

§ In the Greek, αντι του κακου, we suspect the right reading to be αντι του κακον, that is, αντι του ονοματος KAKON, instead of the noun *evil*: as αντι του επιστασθαι, just after, means αντι του ρηματος απαρεμφατου και πρωτοτυπου ΕΠΙΣΤΑΣΘΑΙ, instead of the infinitive and primitive verb *to know*. -S.

◇ We have here a specimen of Plato's uncommon skill in philosophical or universal grammar. It appears, not only by his deducing the adverb ΚΑΚΩΣ, *ill*, from the substantive noun KAKON, *evil*, but also by (what shows a much deeper theory of words, considered as the parts of speech,) his deriving ΗΠΙΣΤΑΤΟ, *he knew*, a verb of the indicative mode, from the infinitive, or most general verb, ΗΠΙΣΤΑΣΘΑΙ, *to know*. See Mr Harris's *Hermes*, b. i, ch. xi, and viii. -S.

expressive of the poet's meaning, - *He was knowing and skilled in many things, but to know all those things was to him an evil.* - It is evident then, that if much knowledge was to him an evil, what knowledge he had was worthless, and he himself was some worthless fellow; supposing any credit to be due to the conclusions from our past reasonings.

e   ALC. And I think, Socrates, it is their due: for I should hardly give credit to any other rational conclusions, if I denied it to those.

SOC. And you think rightly too. But in the name of Jupiter, let us proceed. For you see, how great are the perplexities attending the subject in which we are engaged; you see also, what the nature is of those perplexities. And you seem to me to have a share in them yourself; as you never rest from changing your thoughts over and over again upon this subject; discarding the opinions, which you had before

148a   so ardently embraced, and continuing no longer in the same mind. Should the God then, to whom you are going to make your prayers, appear to you, now after all our conclusions; and should he ask you, before you had presented any petition whatever to him - whether or no your desires would be satisfied, if you obtained any of those dominions mentioned in the beginning of our argument; - or should he leave to yourself the naming of what you wished for; - in which way, think you, could you best avail yourself of this opportunity? whether in accepting any of the grants offered you, or in naming some other thing you wished for?

ALC. Now, by the Gods, Socrates, I should not know what to say to

b   such a proposal. Indeed, I think, that it would be rash in me to make any decisive answer at all; and that great caution is absolutely requisite in such a case; to prevent a man from praying unwarily for things evil, while he imagines them to be good; and from doing as you said, soon afterwards recanting his choice, and praying to be delivered from what he had before prayed to have.

SOC. Did not then the poet, whom I cited in the beginning of this argument, know somewhat more than we do, in supplicating Jupiter to avert from us what is evil, even though we prayed for it?

ALC. Indeed I think so.

c   SOC. The Lacedæmonians, therefore, O Alcibiades! admiring and imitating this of the poet, or whether they had of themselves considered the subject in the same manner as he did, every one of them in private, and all of them in public, make a prayer similar to his: for they beseech the Gods to grant them such good things as at the same time are beautiful; and nothing more were they ever heard to pray for.

Accordingly, no people have hitherto been more prosperous than they.
And if it has happened to them not to prosper in all things, it was not
d   because they prayed amiss; but because the Gods, I presume, have it in
their choice, either to grant a man that for which he prays, or to send
him the reverse. I have a mind to relate to you somewhat else on this
subject, what I once heard from certain elderly men; - that, in the
differences between the Athenians and the Lacedæmonians, it so fell out,
that whenever they came to a battle, whether by land or by sea, our city
was always unsuccessful, and was never able to get one victory: - that the
Athenians therefore, uneasy at these miscarriages, and at a loss for
e   some contrivance to put an end to their pressing evils, held a council,
and came to this conclusion, - that their best way would be to send to
Ammon,† and consult him what they should do; and at the same time
to ask him this question farther, - on what account the Gods always give
victory to the Spartans their enemies, rather than to them; though of all
the Grecians, we, said they, bring them the greatest number of sacrifices,
and those the fairest in their kinds; and though we, beyond all other
people, have decorated their temples with the presents that are hung up
in them; and in honour of the Gods have made yearly processions, the
149a   most solemn and the most costly; and have paid them a greater tribute
in money than all the rest of the Grecians put together: whilst the
Lacedæmonians, they said, never regard any of these things; but, on the
contrary, worship the Gods in so slighting a manner, as to make their
sacrifices commonly of beasts full of blemishes; and, in all other
instances, fall far short of us, said they, in honouring the Gods; at the
same time that the riches they are masters of are not less than ours.
When the ambassadors had thus spoken, and had inquired of the Oracle,
what they should do to find an end of their present misfortunes, the
b   prophet made no other answer than this; (for without doubt the God
did not permit him:) sending for the Athenian ambassadors, he spake to
them these words, - Thus saith Ammon; he saith, that he prefers the
pious addresses of the Lacedæmonians to all the sacrifices of all the
Grecians. - These words, and no more, spake the prophet. Now it seems
to me, that, by pious addresses, the God means only that prayer of

---

† The oracle of Ammon was highly celebrated for the truth of its predictions. It
had been anciently consulted by Hercules and by Perseus. Long afterwards it was
consulted by Crœsus, when he was meditating to stop the progress of Cyrus's arms in
Asia. In what veneration it was held by the Romans we learn from the ninth book of
Lucan. And from the present passage in Plato, as also from the lives of Lysander,
Cimon, and Alexander, in Plutarch, it appears to have been, among the Grecians of
those days, in as great vogue and credit as any oracles of their own. -S.

theirs. And it is indeed much more excellent than the prayers of any
c   other people. For the rest of the Grecians, when they have either led
up to the altar oxen with their horns gilded, or brought rich offerings
and presents to hang up in the temples, pray for whatever they happen
to desire, whether it be really good or evil. The Gods therefore, when
they hear their impious addresses, accept not of their costly processions,
sacrifices, and presents. So that much caution and consideration seem to
me requisite on this subject, what is fit to be spoken to the Gods, and
what is not. You will also find in Homer sentiments similar to those
d   I have been expressing: for he tells us, that the Trojans, on a certain
night, taking up their quarters without the city walls,

> In honour of the blest Immortals, slew
> Unblemish'd hecatombs:[†] . . . .

and that the smoke from these sacrifices was by the winds wafted up
into heaven:[‡]

> Sweet odorif'rous smoke; yet by the Gods
> Rejected, and the sav'ry taste refus'd.
> For strong aversion in their holy minds
> Was rooted, against Troy's devoted tow'rs,
> Against th' injurious might of Troy's proud king,
> And 'gainst the Trojan people, who withheld
e   Helen, unjustly, from her wedded lord.[§]

It was of no advantage therefore, it seems, to them to sacrifice, or to
offer presents, to the Gods whom they had made their enemies. For the

---

† In the Greek, Ερδειν αθανατοισι τελειεσσας εκατομβας; a line this not found in
the copies of Homer now extant; but in Barnes's edition, supplied from this passage of
Plato; and by Ernestus shown to be genuine, from the next line, which supposes the
mention made of a sacrifice just before. -S.

‡ Κνιστη δ' εκ πεδιου ανεμοι φερον ουρανον εισω. This line of Homer appears in
all the editions of that poet. Plato is here obliged to take this sentence quite out of the
metre; because he is relating, only at second hand and as told by Homer, a fact, the
narration of which Homer himself puts immediately into the mouth of the muse: and,
for the same reason, we have given a prosaic translation of it. In the preceding line, as
also in those which follow, Plato was able to preserve the metre, while he only changed
the indicative verbs into infinitive. -S.

§ The verses, here translated, are not found in any of the editions of Homer, except
in that of Barnes; but, as Ernestus judiciously observes, they are altogether worthy of
that greatest of all poets. -S.

divine nature, I presume, is not of such a kind as to be seduced by presents, like those whose trade it is to make the most of their money, and who care not by what means they are enriched. Besides, we plead very foolishly, in our expostulations with the Gods, if we think to get the better of the Lacedæmonians by such arguments. For it would be a sad thing indeed, if the Gods regarded our presents and our sacrifices, 150a and not the disposition of the soul, when a religious and just man addressed them. Nay, in my opinion, they have much more regard to this, than they have to those pompous processions and costly sacrifices. For nothing hinders, but that any, whether private persons or civil states, let them have sinned against the Gods and against men ever so greatly, may be well able to pay the Gods such a tribute yearly. But they not being to be bribed, disdain all that outward worship; as faith the divine Oracle, and as also saith the Prophet of the Gods. It seems, therefore, that justice and prudence are honoured, above all things, by the Gods, and by men too, such as have good sense and understanding. b Now the prudent and the just are no other persons than such as know what behaviour and what speech is proper to be used in our intercourse, whether with Gods or with men. But I should be glad to hear from you what your thoughts are on this subject.

ALC. For my part, I am of the same opinion with you, Socrates, and with the Oracle. And indeed it would ill become me to give my vote opposite to the judgment of the God.

SOC. Do you not remember, that you acknowledged your being much at a loss concerning prayer; for fear you should unwarily pray for evil c things, imagining them to be good?

ALC. I do remember it.

SOC. You perceive then, that it is not safe for you to go and make your prayer at the temple, as you intended; lest your addresses should happen to be impious, and the God hearing them should wholly reject your sacrifice, and you perhaps should draw upon your own head some farther evil. It seems to me, therefore, that your best way is to be at d quiet. For because of your magnanimity, (that fairest of names given to folly,) I suppose you would not be willing to make use of the Lacedæmonian prayer. It is necessary, therefore, that a man should wait till he has learnt what disposition he ought to be in towards the Gods and towards men.

ALC. But, Socrates, how long will it be before that time comes? and who is he that will instruct me? for I should be very glad, methinks, to see that man, and to know who he is.

SOC. It is he, whose care you are the object of. But as Homer[†] says of Minerva, that she removed the mist from before the eyes of Diomede,

> That he might clearly see, and Gods from men
> Plainly distinguish, ...

e so must he in the first place, as it seems to me, remove from your soul the mist that now happens to surround it; and after that he will apply those medicines, by means of which you will clearly distinguish good from evil. For, at present, I think you would not be able so to do.

ALC. Let him then remove that mist, or any other obstruction that he pleases: for he will find me readily disposed to follow any of his prescriptions, whoever the man is, if by those means I may become a better man than I am at present.

151a SOC. It is wonderful to consider how greatly he is disposed towards the making you so.

ALC. Till that time therefore, I think, it is the better way to defer my sacrifice.

SOC. You think rightly too. For it is a safer way than to run so great a risk.

ALC. It is undeniable, O Socrates. In the mean time, however, since you seem to me to have counselled well, I shall put this crown[‡] about b your brows. And to the Gods we shall present crowns,[12] and all other accustomed offerings, then, when I see that day arrived. Nor will the time be long before its arrival, if it so please the Gods.

SOC. Well, I accept of this: and should have pleasure in seeing the time come, when you yourself[§] shall have received some other thing in return for your present to me. And as Creon, when Tiresias, showing him his crown [of Gold], said, it had been given him [by the Athenians],

---

† *Iliad.* lib. v, ver. 127. -S.

‡ All those, who went to the temples with intent to petition the Gods for any particular favour, carried along with them crowns or garlands; and these they wore whilst they were praying. It was by such a crown, held by Alcibiades in his hand, that Socrates, in meeting him, conjectured rightly whither he was going.

§ In the Greek, αλλο δε [f. αλλο τι] αντι των παρα σου δοθεντων ηδεως ιδοιμι δεξαμενον εμαυτον. In which sentence the last word is, we doubt not, a corrupt reading, and was by Plato written σεαυτον. For we cannot apprehend how a man who has received a present can be said to make a return for it, by his own receiving of any other present from the same or any other person. -S.

in honour of his science, as the first-fruits of [their]† victory obtained over the enemy, is by Euripides‡ made to say,

> This crown, a happy omen and presage,
> I deem, of conquest on our Theban side.
> For you know well, how tempest-tost a sea
> We sail on . . . .

c   I, in the same manner, deem this honour, you have now done me, to be a good presage. For, as I think myself sailing on a sea, no less tempest-tost than that of Creon, I should be glad to bear away the crown of victory from the rest of your admirers.§

---

† In this sentence all the words, enclosed within hooks, we have translated from Euripides, to render this passage of Plato clearer to those who have not read the Phænissæ of that poet, from which tragedy it is taken. -S.

‡ See the Phænissæ, v. 865.

§ The fine turn, which Socrates here gives to his acceptance of the crown, presented to him by Alcibiades, is perfectly in character, being, at the same time, most ingenious, elegant, wise, modest, and polite. He accepts it not as an ensign of divine honour, as it was meant by the donor; but as a token of (future) victory; victory over his competitors for the friendship of Alcibiades, whom they endeavoured to corrupt, and success in his own endeavours to engage him wholly in the study of wisdom and the pursuit of virtue. -S.

Additional Notes

on the

Second Alcibiades

1 (See page 555, title lines) At Athens were two edifices, built in honour of Jupiter. One of these was a most magnificent temple, called the Olympium, and situate in the lower city. The other was only a chapel in the upper city, sacred to Ζευς ο σωτηρ, *Jupiter the* [universal] *saviour*, and adjoining to another chapel, sacred to Αθηνα η σωτειρα, *Minerva the saviour* [of Athens]. Both these chapels stood at the entrance of the treasury; one probably on each side, as guardians of the public money: and this treasury stood at the back of that beautiful temple of Minerva, called the Parthenon. Now had Socrates met Alcibiades in the ascent, which led first to the Parthenon, and thence to the chapels behind it, no reason appears for his supposing that Alcibiades was going to pay his devotions to Jupiter, rather than to Minerva, the guardian Deity of Athens. But the masculine article τον, used in this place by Plato before the noun θεον, forbids us to imagine that Minerva could be here meant. For at Athens, as Minerva was styled η θεος, *the Goddess*, by way of eminence, so Jupiter was styled either simply θεος, *God*, or ο θεος, *the God*, as being Supreme. Beside this, we are to observe, that in the chapel of Jupiter in the upper city, he was worshipped in a particular character, as the preserver of his votaries in dangers from which they had escaped; as not only is to be presumed from the title of Saviour, by which he was there invoked, but also is clearly proved from the Plutus of Aristophanes, act. 5, sc. 2, and from the oration of Lycurgus against Leocrates, p. 168 and 253, edit. Taylor. Now there is not the least appearance that Alcibiades had had any signal deliverance from danger, or that he was now going to offer a thanksgiving sacrifice, as it was customary to do on such occasions. From all this we justly may conclude, that the scene of this dialogue lies in a street leading to the temple of Olympian Jupiter in the lower city. -S.

2 (See page 555, line 138a) The first symbolical precept which the Pythagorean philosophers gave to their disciples was this: "When you go from your house with intention to perform your devotions at the temple, neither speak nor do any thing in the way thither concerning any business of human life" - A precept recorded, among others of like kind, by Iamblichus, in the last of his λογοι προτρεπτικοι, and rightly there interpreted, p. 134, to this purport: - that a man ought to purify his mind, by abstracting it from earthly cares, and from all objects of sense, whenever he contemplates divine things; because these are abstracted or pure from matter themselves; and pure naturally joins and

unites with homogeneous pure. Further, divine things being stable, and always the same, but human things unstable, and for ever changing; they are in this respect also heterogeneous, and, as the same great Platonist elsewhere elegantly speaks, incommensurable, the one sort of things with the other; so that they mix not amicably together in the mind. -S.

3 (See page 555, line 138b) This sentence is evidently meant to prove the necessity of much consideration before a man prays; by showing, from the example of Œdipus, the mischiefs often consequent to rash and unpremeditated prayer. An opposition, therefore, seems intended between the αυτικα in this passage, and the προμηθεια, *premeditation,* or *previous consideration,* above recommended. Accordingly, we have ventured, against the opinion of Ernestus, in his Notes to Xenophon's Memorab. lib. iv, cap. 7, to give this *opposed meaning* here to the word αυτικα, by rendering it in English *inconsiderately:* a meaning very little different from the primary and usual sense of the word, in which it signifies the same with παραυτικα, that is, *immediately, directly, without delay.* -S.

4 (See page 556, line 138c) Curses in those ancient days were prayers addressed to the Infernal Deities, - to Tartarus, - to primæval Night, but chiefly to the daughters of Night, the Eumenides. For no Deities who dwelt in light were imagined to be the authors of evil ever to any. In conformity with these practices and opinions, Sophocles, in the last of the two passages cited from him in note 7, and Statius, in his Thebaid, lib. i. ver. 56 et seq., give to this curse, pronounced by Œdipus against his sons, the form of a prayer, addressed to those powers of darkness. Hence appears the ignorance of the author of the κυκλικη Θηβαις, or old Greek ballad of the Siege of Thebes, cited by the scholiast on Sophocles, p. 577, edit. P. Steph. For, after he has told a very silly tale, how the two sons of Œdipus, having had an ox killed for a sacrifice, sent a joint of it to their father who was then blind, - and how Œdipus had expected the prime piece of all, - he concludes this part of the story in manner and form following; that is to say, being interpreted (as it ought to be) in ballad style and ballad metre,

> As soon as e'er he understood
>   'Twas only the ache-bone,
> For him to mean, unworthy food;
> Against the ground, in wrathful mood,
>   He straightway dash'd it down.
>
> Then pray'd he to th'immortals all,
>   But chief to Jove on high,
> That each by th'other's hand might fall;
> And so to Pluto's darksome hall
>   They both at once might fly. -S.

5 (See page 557, line 139a) In all the printed editions of the Greek we here read, Δοκει σοι οιον τε ειναι, *Do you think it possible, &c.*. And Cornarius, as if he found this reading in the Hessenstein manuscript, translates it into Latin thus: *Videtur tibi fieri posse,* &c. Ficinus and Stephens translate it, as if they had read in their manuscripts, Δοκει σοι δειν ειναι, *Do you think that a man ought to be* &c. Neither of these readings can be right, because they, both of them, make this dialectical question to be *foolish* as well as *impertinent*: and because also either of them spoils the argumentation. To make the inference, in the next sentence of Socrates, just and conclusive, we must here read Δοκει σοι αναγκαιον ειναι, as we have supposed in translating it. The necessity of making this emendation in the Greek text was seen also by Dacier, as appears from his French translation. -S.

6 (See page 558, line 140b) That is, every continued indisposition of the body; whether the whole body suffer from it throughout, as in a fever; or whether it be seated in any organical part serving to motion, as in the gout; or serving to sensation, as in an ophthalmy. Plato, in his choice of similitudes and instances, where they are requisite to illustrate his subject, (and he never uses any but on such occasions,) is always so exquisitely curious, and often, as here, so scientifically judicious, that, with respect to this ingredient in good writing on ideal or intellectual subjects, we know of no writer who is his equal. -S.

7 (See page 563, line 142e) It is necessary to observe, that this prayer is adapted solely to that part of mankind (and a very numerous part it is) who have not arrived at a *scientific* knowledge of divine concerns, and therefore know not what to pray for as they ought. See an excellent remark on this passage from Proclus in a note on the *Republic* [TTS vol. IX, p. 571]. Mr Sydenham, from mistaking the intention of this prayer, has made Socrates assert, without any authority from the text, that the author of it composed it for his own use as well as that of the ignorant. Hence he translates, "composed for *his own* use and theirs a common prayer." -T.

8 (See page 563, line 143c) That part of the story of Orestes, which is here alluded to, is well known to those who are versed in Greek learning, from the Χοηφοροι of Æschylus, the *Electra* of Sophocles, and the *Electra* of Euripides. - For the story of Alcmæon, we refer them to the old Scholia on Homer's *Odyssey*, lib. xi, v. 326; or to Servius's Commentary on Virgil's *Æneid*, lib. vi, v. 445. It is told more at large by Apollodorus, in lib. iii, cap. 6 and 7. But lest such of our readers, as happen to be unlearned in the history of ancient Greece, should mistake the meaning of this passage, they are to be informed that Orestes and Alcmæon were guilty of so atrocious a crime, as the murder of

their own mothers, out of a mistaken notion of filial piety, and an ignorance of the bounds of duty towards a father. Orestes was the son of Agamemnon and Clytemnestra. His mother, in the absence of his father during the siege of Troy, carried on an amour with Ægisthus, consingerman to Agamemnon. At her husband's return home, after the destruction of Troy, she and her paramour procured his death; which was afterwards avenged by his children: for Orestes, at the instigation of his sister Electra, slew the adulterous pair together. Alcmæon was the son of Amphiaraus and Eriphyle. This lady betrayed her husband into a situation in which he must inevitably lose his life. He knowing how she had acted, and foreseeing the event, enjoined his son Alcmæon to avenge his death on Eriphyle, by taking away her life. In neither of these cases, cited here by Plato, does there appear any malice in the young princes against their mothers; no spirit of revenge for personal injuries done to them; no lust of riches or of dominion; in short, no selfish passion or appetite whatever; no other intention than to perform an imagined act of duty to their fathers, by doing such an act of justice on their mothers as belonged not to them to execute. It appears, that both of these unhappy princes perpetrated a deed so unnatural, from erroneous notions of duty, justice, and honour; that is, through want of moral wisdom, or true prudence. We apprehend, therefore, that the drift of Plato in this passage is to prove, from these sad instances of the fatal effects of ignorance in the laws of nature and reason, the necessity of applying our minds to the study of moral science, in order to act rightly and to be happy. -S.

9 (See page 568, line 146a) Plutarch, towards the end of his treatise περι αδολεσχιας, *Concerning Talkativeness,* cites the two following verses, which appear to be taken out of some ancient Greek poet,

> Νεμει το πλειστον ημερας τουτῳ μερος,
> Ιν᾿ αυτος αυτου τυγχανη κρατιστος ων.

> He makes it the chief business of the day,
> T'attain to more, and still more, excellence.

In the passage now before us, we find the *latter* of these two verses cited by Plato, word for word. The *former* of them indeed he has a little altered; but only just so much as to adapt it to his own purpose; which could not be done without weaving it into his own prosaic style. -S.

10 (See page 568, line 146c) This interrogative sentence of Socrates no less evidently refers to a former sentence beginning with these words, *The man therefore* - a sentence that will greatly help us in amending this; the Greek of which, as it is printed, runs thus: Ουκουν καν μεν πραττη α τις οιδεν, η δοκει

ειδεναι, παρεπεται δη το ωφελιμως και λυσιτελουντως ημας εχειν, και τη πολει και αυτον αυτω Now in this sentence the words η δοκει ειδεναι not only are not found in the sentence to which this refers, and the sense of which it repeats with but little variation in the words, but they also convey a meaning contrary to the mind of Socrates. For he takes every occasion to inculcate, that only a man's real knowledge, shown by his speeches, or his actions, and not his own false conceit of it, nor other men's too high opinion of it, can be of any lasting advantage either to himself or to others. Of equal moment with this interpolation, (a fault to which the words οιηθηναι ειδεναι in the preceding sentence, where they are used rightly, seem to have given occasion,) is another fault in the sentence now before us, an omission of the words η του βελτιστου επιστημη, or others to the same purport. For, without some such words, this sentence, in which Socrates delivers his opinion in the way of a question, is quite contradictory to his opinion, delivered but a little before in that sentence above referred to. Our supposition, that such words are here omitted in the printed editions of Plato, but ought to be inserted, is confirmed by the Latin of Ficinus, who translated faithfully from a manuscript copy of Plato, (probably the Medicean,) with which Grynæus afterwards compared and corrected that translation. For both Ficinus and Grynæus, in their Latin, insert these words; "*addit autem scientiam optimi.* In this sentence also are wanting the words εδοκει ημιν; unless Plato purposely omitted them, as thinking it needless to repeat them, after they had been expressed in the question immediately preceding. There remains yet another fault in this sentence, the word ημας, a word which the grammatical construction by no means admits of. If our conjectural emendation of this sentence, which we now beg leave to offer to the learned, should appear to be a just one, it will appear at the same time, on examination, that all the faults in it, as printed, are owing originally to a mere *transposition* of some of the words in transcribing it, an error frequently found in ancient manuscripts, and the cause of those many additional errors, as well in printed as in written copies, which were afterwards committed with intention to correct the former. The proposed reading is this; Ουκουν, καν μεν πραττη α τις οιδε, παρεπεται δε ειδεναι το ωφελιμον, [or παρεπεται δε η του βελτιστου επιστημη, as Ficinus and Grynæus seem to have read,] εδοκει ημιν, λυσιτελουντως εχειν τη πολει, και αυτον αυτω. -S.

11 (See page 569, line 147a) Of this passage in the Greek, Monsieur Dacier says, "C'est un des plus difficiles endroits de Platon." Indeed, as it is printed, it is quite unintelligible. For, after a comma put at the word πλειν, it proceeds thus; οσωπερ αν μη προτερον επουρισῃ το της ψυχης. Ανευ γαρ ταυτης, η περι, κ.τ.λ. But what if it were printed thus? Putting a full stop at πλειν, let the next sentence immediately begin, Ανευ γαρ ταυτης, οσωπερ αν λαβροτερον επουρισῃ το της ψυχης, η περι, κ.τ.λ. All the difficulty is now vanished by this slight transposition, and an easy alteration of μη προτερον to λαβροτερον, a

word perhaps mistaken by the writer to whom it was read, from his not being so thoroughly well versed in the language of Homer, as a man must be before he can every where understand the language of Plato. Προτερον therefore being, as we suppose by this mistake, written in some manuscript copy of this dialogue, it is probable that some reader of it afterwards, who saw the absurdity of that word, condemned it by writing in the margin μη προτερον, and that the next half-learned transcriber, instead of omitting προτερον, took μη also into the text.   Both these spurious words are rightly omitted in the Hessenstein manuscript, as we are informed by Cornarius; but the genuine word, in the mean time, was lost. -S.

12   (See page 575, line 151b)   The learned archbishop Potter, in his Archæolog. Græc. b. ii, ch. 4, very justly observes, that crowns and garlands were some of the presents offered to the Gods by their petitioners, to obtain some future benefit.   And from the passage now before us we infer, that the very same crowns or garlands, worn by those petitioners during their prayers in the temples, they used, at their departure, to take off from their own heads, and to put them on the heads of the divine images; from whence afterward the priest took, and hung them up on the side walls of the temple.   Plato here exhibits Alcibiades giving to Socrates the very honour which he had designed for the image of Jupiter.   By this, we presume, he meant to signify, that whoever could teach wisdom and virtue, as Alcibiades supposed of Socrates, was to be esteemed and honoured as a divine man. -S.

Glass-Ceramics
and Photo-Sitalls

Glass-Ceramics
and Photo-Sitalls

Anatolii I. Berezhnoi
Laboratory of Glass and Glass-Ceramics
Moscow, USSR

Translated from Russian by
Stanley A. Mersol

Translation Editor
Alexis G. Pincus
I I T Research Institute
Chicago, Illinois

⊕ PLENUM PRESS • NEW YORK — LONDON • 1970

Anatolii Ivanovich Berezhnoi was born in 1928. A 1952 graduate
of the Silicate Faculty of the Moscow Chemical-Technological
Institute, he received his doctorate from the same Institute in 1955
with a dissertation entitled "Investigation of Some Physical and
Mechanical Properties of Thermally Treated Glasses." From 1955
to 1957 he worked as an instructor at the Chemical Engineering
Institute at Ivanovo. Since 1957 he has served as the director of
a glass and glass-ceramics laboratory in a scientific research institute in Moscow. Among his current research projects is the investigation of photosensitive glass. The author of a number of technical
works concerning glass technology, Dr. Berezhnoi also holds patents
in this field. In addition, he contributes regularly to chemical
review journals as well as to the series "Silicate Materials," published by The All-Union Institute of Scientific and Technical
Information, Academy of Sciences of the USSR, Moscow.

The Russian text, originally published by Mashinostroenie Press
in Moscow in 1966, has been corrected by the author for this edition. The present translation is published under an agreement
with Mezhdunarodnaya Kniga, the Soviet book export agency.

GLASS-CERAMICS AND PHOTO-SITALLS
SITALLY I FOTOSITALLY
СИТАЛЛЫ И ФОТОСИТАЛЛЫ
Анатолий Иванович Бережной

Library of Congress Catalog Card Number 69-12509

SBN 306-30400-7

Preface

In the decade since glass-ceramics first became mass-produced articles of commerce, they have become a popular subject for research and invention, as attested to by the 773 references cited in this book. Discovered almost accidentally during research on photosensitive glasses, thermally crystallized glass-ceramics have been distinguished by the rapid pace of their utilization for distinctive new products.

This promise has been recognized throughout the world, and original contributions have appeared from nearly every country having an ongoing glassmaking capability. Particularly numerous have been the publications and the ideas, scientific and technological, issuing from the USSR. For several years, the annual All-Union Conference on the Glassy State has been dominated by papers on catalyzed crystallization of glasses. With regard to new product lines, we learn about slag-based sitalls (glass-ceramics) and also about specialty items derived by radiation-assisted crystallization in glasses, photo-sitalls.

A. I. Berezhnoi has written a comprehensive review of the publications on this topic, which includes a balanced weighting to the contributions from the USSR and the USA, and also introduces advances from Britain, Czechoslovakia, Romania, Japan, and other centers of activity.

The pattern of publications in itself serves as a demonstration of nucleation and growth. This book appears at a time when the initial growth process for glass-ceramic technology is preparing to enter a second stage with regard to concepts, compositions, microstructures, processing techniques, properties, and applications. The book is impressive not only for the large amount of work reviewed, but for the service it performs in revealing the vaster areas where data and knowledge remain inadequate.

A. G. Pincus

Foreword to the
American Edition

Research and development in science and technology demonstrate conclusively that technological progress, which one associates with continuous improvement in the state of the art, with cost reduction, and with more efficient application of technological processes, is not possible without the discovery of new materials possessing certain necessary specific properties or a combination of a number of valuable, sometimes unique, properties.

Glass-crystalline materials, such as glass-ceramics and photosensitive glass-ceramics,* which have been developed during the last decade in the USA, USSR, and Japan, as well as elsewhere, are a class of new materials especially needed by modern technology. The interest in these new materials is unusually great. This can be explained by the fact that glass-ceramics possess an extremely favorable combination of mechanical, thermal, chemical, electrical, and physical properties. By heat treatment of special glasses, scientists succeeded in preparing materials with a fine-crystalline structure and with significantly higher mechanical strengths, as well as with better thermal stability and electrical insulating properties, than hold for the original glasses. The discovery of original technological possibilities for some photosensi-

---

* The following terms are synonymous: glass-ceramic (US and Great Britain), vitroceramic (continental Europe), sitall or sital (USSR), glass-porcelain (Romania), and quasiceramic (Poland). Other terms used in the US include devitrified ceramic, crystallized glass, nucleated glass, and melt-formed ceramic. The following are trade names: Pyroceram and Fotoceram (Corning Glass Works), Cer-Vit (Owens-Illinois), Hercu-Vit (PPG Industries), Re-X (General Electric Co.), Nucerite (Ritter-Pfaudler Corp.), Slagceram (British Iron and Steel Research Association), Vitrokeram (Germany), Devitroceram and Miraklon (Japan), Minelbite (Hungary), Kriston (Czechoslovakia), Disilital (Poland), and Slagsital (USSR).

tive glasses made it possible to produce microminiaturized articles characterized by complex shapes and accurate dimensions,
which found applications in electronics and in other branches of
industry. These properties of these new materials naturally attracted the attention of experts in the various branches of science,
as substantiated by the sharp increase in published work associated with the theory and the practice of preparing and using glass-
crystalline materials.

The author of the present book is pleased to point out the significant contributions to this field by American scientists — mainly,
Stookey, Armistead, Schuler, Shaver, Maurer, and their co-workers
at Corning Glass Works — whose widely known works on photosensitive glasses and glass-ceramics gave an impetus, from the year
1957 on, to intensive and thorough investigation in this area of research throughout the world, notwithstanding the fact that the actual phenomenon of the crystallization of glass had been known very
much earlier, and that there are numerous works in the literature
devoted to this problem, in which attempts are described to con-
sciously utilize this phenomenon for the preparation of crystallized
materials, from Reaumur bottles to stone casting.

In attempting to briefly characterize the present situation
concerning glass-ceramics and photosensitive glass-ceramics, we
must realize that, in spite of the scientific and technological progress achieved during the past decade, and in spite of the fact that
a great deal of scientifically sound data have been obtained with respect to the interdependencies among the composition of the original glass, the mechanism of its crystallization, and the properties
of the glass-crystalline materials prepared, there still exist all
too many unresolved problems, such as those associated with the
necessity of discovering new additives capable of catalyzing the
crystallization of a still larger number of glasses of various compositions, and with the development of new and more efficient heat-
treatment procedures for these glasses so as to further enhance
the thermal, mechanical, dielectric, and chemical properties of
glass-ceramics and photosensitive glass-ceramics. These problems constitute the fundamental link in the chain of continuing investigation of the controlled crystallization of glass, and are at the
center of interest for scientists preoccupied with the synthesis, the
perfection of the production technology, the study of properties, and
the determination of the areas of application of glass-crystalline
materials.

In this book, I have attempted to cover as thoroughly as possible all pertinent work on the theory of crystallization and on the composition, properties, production technology, and areas of application of photosensitive glasses, of glass-ceramics, and of photosensitive glass-ceramics, in order to compare, systematize, and generalize at least where such was possible. Compared to the Russian-language edition, the present book has been supplemented by the presentation of fundamental results of some very recent work by the author and co-workers on the preparation of homogeneous photosensitive glass and on the mechanical, thermal, and chemical properties of photosensitive glasses and photosensitive glass-ceramics.

It should be especially emphasized that the present book is only a first attempt to generalize the results of the most important investigations in the area of photosensitive glasses, of glass-ceramics, and of photosensitive glass-ceramics. In the systematization of such extensive literature material, the author encountered certain difficulties, which cannot be considered to have been fully overcome. The author will therefore be very grateful for any critical comments that the readers of this book may have.

A. I. Berezhnoi

January 14, 1968

Foreword to the
Russian Edition

Glass-ceramics, or glass-crystalline materials, are new inorganic materials of immense technological significance. They are prepared by the crystallization of glasses or melts of various compositions taking place throughout the bulk of the preshaped article. Crystallization produces a very fine-grained and uniform structure, resulting in very good mechanical, thermal, and mechanical properties of these articles.

Several areas for the practical application of glass-ceramics are known at the present time; for example, these materials are used in radio technology, in electronics, in the chemical industry, and in food processing as electrical insulators, wear- and acid-resistant sheets, refractory tubing, and so on. As a result of the experimental work, new varieties of glass-ceramics and articles made from them are being developed all the time.

Prior to the present book, there was no monograph available in the literature on glass-ceramics, even though workers in the budding glass-ceramics industry, contributors to numerous scientific research organizations, who have been preoccupied with the physical, chemical, and technological aspects of the problem of glass-ceramics, and students in many specialties have deeply felt the necessity of such a publication.

The present book by A. I. Berezhnoi discusses in detail and at the appropriate level most of the questions pertaining to the problem of glass-ceramics, and, to a significant degree, fills the above-indicated gap.

N. A. Toropov

Contents

Glass-Ceramics
and Photo-Sitalls

Introduction

Workers in the glass industry are quite familiar with the problem of "devitrification," i.e., the formation of undesirable crystals on the surface or within the bulk of the fused glass and of the articles made from it. The presence of individual crystals debases the optical and mechanical properties of glass which is the reason most of the investigations in the glass industry are directed toward the preparation of glasses which are stable with respect to crystallization. It is true that controlled precipitation of fluorides and phosphates was used to produce opaline glasses, just as controlled precipitation of gold, copper, or cadmium sulfoselenides was used to produce ruby glasses, and controlled precipitation of titanium oxide was used to produce opaque enamel.

The first known attempt to modify the glass itself and to change it into almost entirely crystalline material was undertaken by the French chemist Reaumur more than 200 years ago [1, 119, 413, 486]. He placed glass bottles filled with a mixture of sand and gypsum into a mixture of these same materials, heated them up to read heat in an annealing furnace, and held them there at temperature for a long time.

The result of this experiment was the preparation of "porcelain" products which were fully crystallized and capable of withstanding high temperatures without deforming.

Reaumur determined that crystallization always started from the surface of the glass, and that crystals grew inward in the form of filaments until they met in the center. The intermediate polycrystalline product proved to have low strength, in view of the fact that the crystals had a higher thermal expansion coefficient than the glass itself, and were experiencing tensile stresses during cooling. The final, completely crystallized product was also found to have a low strength, due to the growth of large oriented crystals.

1

During the last 40 years, technologists in a number of countries have conducted experiments to obtain silicate materials having a crystalline structure. Thus, in Germany, in the 1920's, Becker [2] proposed the crystallization of three-component glasses of the following composition: $100\,SiO_2 \cdot 40\,Na_2O \cdot 30\,CaO$; here, it was recommended that the fusion of these glasses should not be done over a long period of time, so as to preserve the minute inclusions of the reheated batch which were to serve as the nuclei for subsequent crystallization.

In order to speed up the purification and the crystallization processes, it was specified that CaF_2 and Na_3AlF_6 be added to the initial batch [3, 4]. Articles made of crystallized glass may be used as heat-resistant and mechanically strong smelting containers. Later, Becker recommended the addition of Al_2O_3, kaolin, and clay, as well as fluorine compounds, so as to create nuclei in the melt before it is melted [5-7].

Wagner [8-11] also proposed compositions of fluorine-containing glasses for the preparation of recrystallized and chemically stable glass products.

Trenzen [12] was able to prepare glass products from crystallized glass by smelting mixtures of common sodium potassium glass and wollastonite slag. Here, wollastonite dissolved in the melt, and the crystallization took place during the shaping process.

Gehlhoff [13] described a method of preparation of electrical insulators from crystallized masses based on glasses which do not produce coarsely crystalline spherulites during crystallization.

At the beginning of the 1930's, technologists in the Soviet Union investigated on a wide scale the possibility of using rocks for glass manufacturing. It was determined that crystallized glasses have higher strength and lower brittleness. Already, in 1932, Kitaigorodskii [14] wrote the following in a report prepared for a conference on new structural materials:

"The overwhelming majority of glasses and glass bodies change their glassy structure to a crystalline structure upon a given treatment with time. The greater the crystallizing capability of the alloy and the lower the rate of growth of the crystals, the finer will be the crystalline structure of the material. When the crystallization capability is small and the rate of crystallization is high, the structure will be composed of a relatively small number of large crystals. The crystallizing capability and the rate of crystallization depend on the chemical composition of the alloy and on the temperature conditions of its cooling.

"Therefore, by changing the chemical composition, temperature, and duration of heat treatment, one is able to control the crystallization process and influence the formation of a particular crystalline structure desired. The latter, in turn, produces the necessary physical and chemical properties of the glass material prepared and of the articles made from it.

"Notable advantages of the crystalline mass as opposed to its glassy source are the absence of brittleness, and higher mechanical and chemical strength. Such properties are the predetermining factor for the wide application of this material for construction and industrial purposes. This material is also of great importance in highway construction. Recrystallized slabs and plates may be used, for example, for steps, ladders, roofing, pavement, and balconies.

"In order to make the glass articles and glass bodies more lightweight, one may recrystallize blocks and slabs made of foamed glass, which remind one of pumice, and which in fact are synthetic pumice or synthetic tuff. As was shown by experiments, this material is an excellent construction and tiling material."

A method for producing cordierite porcelain by means of the crystallization of glass during heat treatment was patented by Sugiura [15] in 1951, who, however, did not pay any attention to the question of controlling the formation of crystallization nuclei, as a result of which the crystalline grains were several hundreds of microns in size.

Sersale [16] succeeded in obtaining glass-crystalline materials which were similar to ceramics and had a higher hardness, and in which wollastonite was the principal crystalline phase.

The Romanian scientists Lungu and Popescu-Has [17] investigated the process of homogeneous crystallization of glass, with the purpose of producing from it a nontransparent porcelainlike body. The technology for the preparation of such bodies is similar to the processing of common glasses, the only difference being that, in the former, the annealing operation is either replaced or supplemented by the crystallization process. It was shown that glasses of a specific composition in the $SiO_2-MgO-Na_2O(K_2O)$, $SiO_2-MgO-Al_2O_3-Na_2O(K_2O)$, and $SiO_2-MgO-Al_2O_3-CaO$ systems with the addition of fluorides can be made to crystallize at a high viscosity, of the order of $10^{10}-10^{13}$ poise. This makes it possible to change glass into "porcelain" without deformation and to obtain a degree of crystallization close to that of porcelain by the precipitation of only one of the silicates. The length of the crystals in the crystallized glass was 1-5 μ; for bodies with a higher quantity of fluorine, it was less than 1 μ; and in bodies impoverished of fluorine, the crystals were up to 20 μ long. The crystallized glass had certain advantages over porcelain-type ceramic bodies; these were primarily greater homogeneity, high mechanical strength, and high thermal stability.

Albrecht and co-workers [18, 19] proposed a method which is suitable for the preparation of solid glass-crystalline materials. He obtained these materials from glasses containing a high quantity of alumina, lithium oxide, and less than 50% SiO_2. The temperature for the melting of this glass was 1450-1500°C. Complete crystallization was achieved after cooling to 800°C and subsequent holding at this temperature. The holding time at this temperature can be shortened considerably if mineralizers — such as tin oxide or titanium oxide — are added to the glass. The crystalline material contained minerals of the augite group.

Still, all the above-mentioned materials found only limited applications, due to the difficulties arising during the shaping process, and due to the absence of controlled crystallization.

On May 23, 1957, Corning Glass Works issued a number of publications dealing with the development of a number of new fine-grained glass-crystalline materials [20-31]. These materials are prepared by controlled crystallization from glasses of specific compositions with minute additions of TiO_2 or salts of photosensitive Ag, Au, and Cu metals, which are necessary for the formation of seed crystallization nuclei, around which myriads of microscopically fine crystals emerge.

These new materials differ from glass in that they are basically crystalline, and they differ from ceramics by having a much smaller crystal size.

The results of tests on the new materials indicate that they have properties better than many common engineering materials. They excel in having a high hardness and high mechanical strength, they possess excellent electrical insulating properties, and have a high softening temperature and good thermal stability. It suffices to state that they are several times stronger than laminated glass, lighter than aluminum, and may be harder than high-carbon steel. It is not surprising, therefore, that glass-crystalline materials show promise in having a wide area of application for the future inasmuch as they are capable, thanks to this favorable combination of electrical, mechanical, and thermal properties, of satisfying many of the demands confronting contemporary technology.

Glass-crystalline materials show promise for use in aviation and atomic technology, as well as in rocket construction. Unlimited potential possibilities exist for their use in lieu of many present engineering, structural, electrical insulation, and optical materials.

The production of Pyroceram is assessed as being one of the most important technological achievements in the materials science area since the discovery of thermally stable borosilicate glass at the beginning of the twentieth century.

The development of new materials is associated with investigations of photosensitive glasses, many of which were carried out on a large scale by Stookey at Corning Glass Works; one significant portion of his work is concerned with this particular area of research.

The investigations leading to the development of photosensitive glass started with Dalton's discovery [32, 33] that in the coloration of copper-ruby glass produced by striking (i.e., where precipitation is accomplished by heating the initially colorless glass), development became easier if the glass was exposed to ultraviolet light prior to heat treatment.

In 1947, Stookey started investigating a number of compositions in which the above phenomenon could be intensified sufficiently so as to make photography in glass possible. This was achieved on glasses colored with copper [34]. Later, it was determined that different results were obtained by using gold together with suitable sensitizing agents and color modifiers [35]. It was found that the metallic particles obtained by the photographic method act as centers of formation and growth of nonmetallic crystals in certain glass compositions. This led to the preparation of photosensitive opaline glass, called "Fotolite" [36]. In investigations of glasses colored with silver, photosensitive glasses were obtained [37]. In contrast to the usual photographic imprint, the image in a photosensitive glass is not produced only on the surface of the glass, but also inside of it. Next, it was observed that the crystallized nonmetallic, nontransparent portions of the new glasses dissolve significantly faster in acids than the adjoining transparent portions. Thanks to this "photographic process," chemical machining of photosensitive glass became possible [38]; such glass was called "Fotoform" glass. In this manner, it became possible to prepare, on a large scale, objects of complex configuration and accurate dimensions to be used for the most varied purposes.

At a temperature higher than the softening point of glass, the "Fotoform" glass plate acquires a dark-brown color, while the structure of the heat-treated sample undergoes radical physical changes, transforming from noncrystalline glass into crystalline ceramic-like material, "Fotoceram" [40].

This material has better dielectric properties, is several times stronger than transparent glass, has a higher softening temperature, and is stable in water, oils, and organic solvents.

The "Fotoform" glass and the scope of its treatment possibilities are of special interest in electronics technology, since this glass can be used to fabricate miniature parts, such as, for example, micromodular plates and thin panels for printing systems equipped with through-holes of small dimensions and high tolerances [41]. These holes may be coated by a given metal using known methods so as to produce current-conducting paths between the upper and the lower sides of the plate, which is capable of operating at temperatures of up to 250°C without warping or otherwise damaging the metallic coating [42].

The compositions of glass-crystalline materials are as varied as those of glasses, which makes the properties of these materials most varied as well. Depending on the size and the composition of the crystals formed, materials with an exceptionally broad range of electrical, mechanical, and chemical properties can be prepared. Five thousand compositions of new materials had already been prepared by 1961 [43], and one has every reason to assume that this number is still very far from the maximum possible.

Systematic investigations with the purpose of preparing glass-crystalline materials or synthetic stones based on blast-furnace slags by employing sulfides of heavy metals as catalysts for their crystallization have been carried out in Hungary [44, 45], where a cast ceramic material, Minelbite, has recently been prepared in the $Na_2O-CaO-MgO-Al_2O_3-SiO_2$ system; Minelbite has excellent wear resistance and improved chemical stability.

In the USSR, Kitaigorodskii and Bondarev [46] developed a technically efficient and economically profitable method for producing glass-ceramics from metallic slags. Slag glass-ceramics excel in having a uniform, fine-crystalline microstructure, high mechanical strength, high wear resistance, and good chemical and thermal stability.

Intense investigations of new glass-based materials are presently going on in many countries. The most renowned of these materials are Pyroceram and Fotoceram in the USA, "sitalls" (glass-ceramics) and "photositalls" (photosensitive glass-ceramics) in the USSR [47, 48], Vitrokeram in Germany [49], Devitroceram [50] and Miraklon [709] in Japan, "glass-porcelain" in Romania [51, 52], Minelbite in Hungary [53], Kriston in Czechoslovakia [54], and quasi-ceramic or Disilital in Poland [706, 707].

In the Soviet Union, one of the fundamental areas in the study of inorganic glasses is the investigation of new glass-crystalline materials and new physical-chemical bases for catalyzed crystallization [55, 56].

Because it has a very favorable combination of the desired physical properties, this prospective new class of materials attracted the attention of builders, engineers, and scientific workers throughout the world. An active program of studies exists to develop glass-crystalline materials which, among other things, retain their strengths up to 1370°C and higher [57], have a higher hardness and wear resistance, and have thermal expansions in line with the thermal expansion of various materials. Proposals have been made to develop a manufacturing process which will make it possible to obtain an almost ideal polycrystalline structure, having a small grain size, a uniform grain-size distribution, a disordered crystal distribution, and the absence of pores and defects. One may hope to obtain new combinations of crystal composition and microstructure, which will result in new properties.

The growing scope of new areas of application for glass-crystalline materials indicates that these materials have a high practical value.

Note: When describing experiments which were carried out in the USSR prior to the introduction of the International System of Units, we use the units in which the measurements were performed. In particular, the stresses are always expressed in kg/cm^2. When going over to the units of the International System, one may take $1 \ kg/cm^2 \approx 98,000 \ kN/m^2 \approx 0.1 \ MN/m^2$, with the errors being 0.06% and 2%, respectively.

Chapter I

Photosensitive Glasses

In this chapter, the general characteristics of photosensitive glasses are given, and the theory of the photosensitive process is explained. Actual compositions and the process technology for photosensitive glasses are described in Chapter III.

1. GENERAL CONSIDERATIONS

Corning Glass Works announced in June 1947 that it had succeeded in producing a photosensitive glass. Under this designation are to be understood normal silicate glasses which contain ingredients which are capable of forming a photographic image in the glass after being irradiated with ultraviolet light and after subsequent heat treatment. This light sensitivity must not be confused with the change in color observed in some glasses following irradiation with ultraviolet light — a phenomenon which has been called "solarization" — since the causes of this latter color change are not very deep, and may be considered as pertaining to color tinting rather than to the coloration of glass. All effects of solarization are reversible, and can be eliminated upon slight heating, although in order to completely restore its initial properties, the glass must be heated to 400-500°C.

Stookey [58] compares photosensitive glass with photographic emulsion on the basis that it contains metal compounds and sensitizers distributed throughout the medium. However, a significant difference between photosensitive glass and emulsion is that the emulsion is a nonuniform suspension of silver halide grains in a turbid medium, whereas photosensitive glass is an actual solution of the compounds in the optically homogeneous transparent glass.

Irradiation with ultraviolet light does not produce any visible changes in glass; however, after it is heated to the annealing temperature, the metal particles precipitate in it, forming the developed image. These particles may be grown up to certain controlling sizes and cause the glass to be colored red, yellow, blue, purple, red-orange, or amber.

The high resolution capability of photosensitive glasses and the absence of cloudiness and graininess are due to the fact that the sizes of the coloring particles in them may be less than 10 nm, i.e., considerably less than the sizes of the particles in the photographic silver halide emulsion (approximately 30 nm). Stookey [58, 59] thinks that in some cases these particles are dispersed metal atoms, and that they are not capable of dissipating light.

The photosensitive properties of glasses may be summarized by the general principle that ions of some of the metals which are present in the glass with varying degrees of oxidation are capable of forming active centers which are the nuclei of future crystals. Metal ions become deposited on these nuclei during the subsequent heat treatment and form metallic particles of colloidal dimensions, because of which colloidal colors of considerably higher intensity than those in solarized glass appear. The formation of particles of colloidal size (which takes place by the transfer of electrons) makes this process — in contrast to the solarization process — irreversible during heating. However, the image obtained in such a photosensitive glass may nevertheless be ruined due to the solution of colloidal particles at a sufficiently high temperature and upon prolonged heating, although,after this, the glass itself is nevertheless suitable for the production of another image.

Two fundamental types of photosensitive glass are known: (1) transparent colored glass, the coloring of which is produced by the formation of colloidal gold, silver, or copper particles after exposure and development; and (2) nontransparent glass, in which the image is formed by the precipitation of the nonmetallic crystalline phase on these metallic particles, which results in considerable dissipation of light. The three-dimensional character of the image may produce a stereoscopic effect.

2.   COMPOSITIONAL CHARACTERISTICS OF PHOTOSENSITIVE GLASSES

From the point of view of their composition, photosensitive glasses are similar to normal silicate glasses, and differ from them only in that they contain small additions of photosensitive metals and sensitizers, i.e., intensifiers of photosensitivity, which become heat-reducible and optical sensitizers. When these additions are correctly selected, the majority of silicate glasses can be made photosensitive. These glasses must not, however, contain components such as PbO, which absorb the effective short-wave radiation without giving up electrons. Elements such as arsenic and vanadium which accept electrons and thereby decrease the yield of metallic atoms must also not be present in these glasses. According to Weyl [60], these elements enter with cerium oxide into the following reactions:

$$2Ce^{3+} + As^{5+} + h\nu = 2Ce^{4+} + As^{3+}$$
$$Ce^{3+} + V^{3+} + h\nu = Ce^{4+} + V^{2+}.$$

The presence of small amounts of metallophilic ions (Bi^{3+}, Sn^{2+}, and Sb^{3+}) is essential, especially for copper-containing glasses, although excessive concentrations, such as of Sn^{2+}, may increase the activation energy of the diffusion process of the metal at low temperatures.

The addition of such glass-forming oxides as B_2O_3, P_2O_5, and Al_2O_3 changes the equilibrium between Ce^{3+} and Ce^{4+}, Ag^+ and Ag, and Cu^+ and Cu, and thereby has an effect on the photosensitivity of a glass, the increase in the "acidity" of which propitiously shows up by the stabilization in it of the silver ion.

In order to retain photosensitivity, the presence of not less than 5% of R_2O oxides is essential. The following are the oxides which, according to Stookey and Schuler [61], may be added to a glass in quantities of 15% without changing its photosensitive properties; the oxides are to be added to $SiO_2 + R_2O$ (with R_2O being not less than 5% of the total content):

R_2O_3: B_2O_3, Al_2O_3

RO: MgO, CaO, SrO, ZnO, BaO

R_2O: Li_2O, Na_2O, K_2O.

For the production of photosensitive glasses, materials with a relatively high degree of purity (Fe < 0.05%, TiO_2 < 0.02%), such as is necessary for ultraviolet transparency of glass, should be used.

In pure borate and phosphate glasses, the color develops spontaneously during the cooling of the melt or during the secondary heating (stress annealing), which makes it impossible to produce images in these glasses.

Nonetheless, nonsilicate alumoborophosphate photosensitive glasses are known. For instance, glasses of the composition* $(25-46)P_2O_5$, $(8-9)B_2O_3$, $(17-30)Al_2O_3$, $(5-12)Na_2O$, $(6-25)K_2O$, $(0-3)Li_2O$, $(6-7)ZnO$, $(2-3)NaF$, and $(1-2)AlF_3$ are capable of forming images of dark-red color [62] after $AgNO_3$ has been introduced into them after irradiation by x-rays or γ-rays for 5 min and after heat treatment at 390-395°C for 1 min. Moreover, by using irradiation at high temperatures, one may considerably expand the range of composition of photosensitive glasses [63].

Photosensitive Metals. The fundamental photosensitive metals are gold, silver, and copper, with silver being used more than the other two metals. Palladium, although not photosensitive, can be activated and can change the color of glass by giving a gray tint to glasses which normally would be colored red.

According to Weyl [60], regardless of whether gold is introduced in the glass in the form of Cassius' purple, metallic gold, or gold chloride, the majority of it is present in the glass in the form of a solution proper, i.e., in a noncombined state, characterized by atomic dispersion.

Sodium silicate, borate, and other glasses in which the photosensitive metal has a solubility close to zero are characterized by a steep solubility curve for this metal, i.e., by a low solubility capability at striking temperatures, and by the impossibility for recrystallization to take place. According to Weyl [60], such glasses, having a relatively low viscosity, will precipitate practically all the gold in the form of drops or crystals.

The behavior of silver-containing glasses was studied by Zsigmondy [64], who expressed the opinion that these glasses contain both metallic silver in a true solution and ionic silver in the form of Ag^+ and silver silicates, phosphates, and borates.

---

* Here, and throughout this book, all compositions are given in wt.% unless specifically noted otherwise.

According to Weyl [60], the oxidizing conditions of melting make it possible to retain in glass relatively high concentrations of Ag_2O, which plays a role analogous to Na_2O. Based on this, the conclusion was made that Ag^+ ions participate in the formation of the glass structure as network modifiers. In equilibrium with these Ag^+ ions is a small amount of atomic silver. Considering that Ag^+ and Ag^0 are colorless, Weyl suggests that one distinguish the atomic silver from the ionic silver by intense fluorescence of the former after irradiation with ultraviolet light.

According to Weyl [60], the equilibrium between Ag^+ and Ag^0 atoms is influenced by the oxidation—reduction conditions (batch composition, furnace atmosphere), by the high melting temperature, capable of preserving metallic Ag, and by the glass composition, on which depends not only the Ag^0/Ag^+ equilibrium, but also the solubility of metallic silver. Silver dissolves in glass more readily than does gold, especially in the presence of polyvalent Bi and Sn ions.

Stookey [65] determined that Au- or Ag-containing glasses should be melted in oxidizing conditions, whereas Cu-containing glasses should be melted in reducing conditions.

In sodium—calcium—silicate glasses, the solubility of elemental copper is very small, although it may be somewhat increased due to the Pb^{2+} or Sn^{2+} additions. In these glasses, which melt under reducing conditions, an equilibrium is established between the Cu^+ copper ions and elemental copper [60], so that the colorless copper-ruby glass contains atomic copper and Cu^+ copper ions which participate in the glass structure in the same manner as the alkali ions. At high temperatures, cuprous oxide ions are formed which, during cooling, become atomic copper and result in glass which is supersaturated with elemental copper.

Sensitizers. Thermal Reducing Agents. Among these are counted the compounds of several polyvalent ions, such as tin and antimony, traces of which (approximately 0.02%) intensify the capability of the metal to develop a color during the heat-treatment process, and decrease the time of irradiation with ultraviolet light necessary to produce a latent image, thereby also improving its contrast [61]. One should try to avoid introducing excess amounts of thermal reducers, so as not to cause spontaneous coloration during the melting or the treatment of glass.

    Weyl [60] thinks that in silicate glasses containing small
amounts of tin compounds the presence of both Sn^{2+} and Sn^{4+}, between which an equilibrium is established, is possible. This
equilibrium may also include neutral atoms of the metal. Weyl
considers the stannous oxide to be a cation-modifier of the network,
whereas tin dioxide takes part in the formation of the network structure of glass, in which the SnO_4^{4-} groups may interact with the SiO_4^{4-}
groups. In view of this, the solubility of tin dioxide, as well as
that of other oxides which are capable of entering the silicon oxide
lattice, such as aluminum, titanium, and zirconium oxides, is
rather insignificant, and increases in proportion to the alkali content. Stannous oxide ions in the silicate glass are relatively stable
and are able, in glass, to easily form both the tin dioxide as well
as metallic tin. The ions of stannous and stannic oxides may take
part in the chemical reactions during the melting of glass and may
act as oxidizing or as reducing agents. In copper- and silver-containing glasses, stannous oxide is, according to Weyl, capable of
influencing the oxidation—reduction equilibrium according to the
equation: $Sn^{2+} + 2Cu^+ = Sn^{4+} + 2Cu$. Similar reactions, including the transfer of electrons between tin atoms and the photosensitive metal, are important for gold–ruby and also for photosensitive
gold-containing glasses.

    The increase in the solubility of the metal in a glass of the
"gold-ruby" type due to the presence of Sn is explained by Weyl
[60] in terms of the tendency of the stannous and stannic oxides to
link the atoms of the metal into compounds. Upon the cooling of
such a glass which has been sufficiently supersaturated, metallic
crystallization nuclei arise, although a significant portion of the
metals remains in the dissolved state. The glass is considered to
be supersaturated with respect to the metal present. A secondary
heating of the glass to the striking temperature results in the
growth of nuclei and the appearance of coloring.

    The effect of polyvalent ions, including thermal reducers,
on the coloring of silver-containing glass was studied by Sakaino
[66], who determined that the Sn, Cr, and Co ions showed an
effective influence on the development of coloring during heat
treatment. The Sn, Sb, Fe, Cr, and Ce ions are capable of
intensifying coloring when the glasses are irradiated with ultraviolet light.

Optical Sensitizers. Optical sensitizers differ from thermal reducers in that the photosensitive effects are caused by the action of the active ultraviolet rays, which are absorbed by the sensitizer [67]. Optical sensitizers increase the sensitivity of the metal to some wavelengths of the rays, which they absorb. They speed up the photographic process without any loss of contrast. The most important optical sensitizer is cerium, the content of which, in the form of CeO_2, should, for all practical purposes, not exceed 0.02% [67].

The introduction of optical sensitizers in the composition of photosensitive glasses makes it possible to increase their photo-sensitivity and to decrease by ten times the time for irradiation with ultraviolet light necessary for the formation of the normal latent image [68].

It was also found that by replacing the optical sensitizer, i.e., cerium ions, by thermally reducing ions such as Sn^{2+} or Sb^{3+}, one can, with the aid of the photographic process, regulate the con-centration of the metallic atoms, and thus the number of the nuclei, which may vary from 0 to 10^9 per 1 mm^3 [69, 70].

While investigating the photosensitive glasses of the lithium—aluminum—silicate system, we determined that the oxides of other rare-earth elements, such as Sm_2O_3 and Pr_3O_4, taken individually or in combination are more effective optical sensitizers than CeO_2, since, in addition to the increased photosensitivity, they extend the range of the spectral photosensitivity of the glasses, and lower their development temperature. The Pr-containing glasses show a greater difference between the temperatures of the start of crys-tallization for irradiated and for nonirradiated samples than do glasses containing Sm.

3. THE PHOTOGRAPHIC PROCESS

Photosensitive glasses may be irradiated by ultraviolet or other types of short-wave radiation, such as x-rays or γ-rays. The most active ultraviolet band, and one having a sufficiently narrow wavelength range, is the band ranging from 260 to 360 nm. Rays with wavelengths less than 260 nm become absorbed in the thin surface layer of the glass. Nor are rays with wavelengths greater than 360 nm effective, since they just go through the glass without activating it.

If the radiation with the shorter wavelength is filtered off — such as by common photographic film — and if ultraviolet light with wavelengths ranging from 330 to 350 nm is used, then the photosensitive glass may be irradiated by the contact-printing method through an ordinary film or glass negative. It is possible to achieve a more uniform degree of exposure, more uniform crystallization, and a depth of coloring of the sample (down to 50 mm), regardless of the fact that a portion of the activating radiation is being absorbed by the photographic negative material and by the glass. The shorter wavelengths (less than 315 nm) are absorbed to a large degree by the thin surface layer of the glass, and, after development, produce an image which is close to the glass surface, and the color of which, in the barium silicate gold-containing glass, changes from blue to amber with increasing exposure time [58].

Ultraviolet rays of wavelength less than 300 nm ruin the film of the negative, and this makes it necessary to protect the films by means of filters which absorb the harmful radiation and let the useful radiation pass through.

The coloring, the depth of penetration, the intensity, and the contrast of the image developed through heat treatment can be regulated by changing the light source, the filter, the time of exposure, and the heat treatment.

The development time is influenced by, in addition to other factors, the type of coloring and by the desired depth of its penetration.

In order to obtain an average density image by direct irradiation with rays of effective wavelengths, the radiation dosage required should be 2 mW-min/cm^2, and when the ordinary film negative is used as a filter, this dosage should be 2-10 times larger because of the absorption of light by the negative [58].

The image can be developed within several hours at the annealing temperature of glass, it can be developed within 1 h at a temperature lying somewhere between the annealing and the softening temperatures, and it can be developed in 8 min at the softening temperature [67]. The coloring and the depth of penetration of the image are basically determined by the conditions of exposure, and to a degree by the development. The more intense is the exposure during radiation, the faster the coloring develops during heat treatment. The color penetration may depend on the thickness of the article since the deeper layers will be given less exposure than surface layers, and the image in them will develop more slowly. In barium glass containing Au and CeO_2, the orange and the red colors, which develop at higher exposures, develop faster than purple and blue colors. The intensity and the depth of penetration of the color gradually increase with temperature, exposure time, and the concentration of the pigment. The most effective sources for ultraviolet radiation are mercury and carbon arcs. In order to avoid diffuseness of the image, the light source should be small and set up in such a manner as to produce a parallel beam of rays. In some cases, in order to obtain special designs, several light beams are used, and the glass sample is rotated in a plane inclined to the light beam; other special techniques are also used [39].

At temperatures below 500°C, the coloring of photosensitive glasses is stable and does not require "fixation." Stookey [58] shows that nonirradiated portions of the glass do not undergo changes during the development of the image, and are capable of developing a new image during secondary irradiation and heat treatment, in contrast to the Fotoform glass (see page 157). The previously formed image, however, may, under the influence of the secondary irradiation cycle and heat treatment, somewhat change its color and depth of penetration. The basic requirement of the heating procedure is to ensure the necessary uniform heating of all portions of the glass product from room temperature to 650°C, and to carefully control the temperature.

Normal indoor light has no effect on photosensitive glass, provided neither ultraviolet light nor sunlight is present.

4.   THE LATENT IMAGE AND ITS PROPERTIES

If a sample of photosensitive glass is subjected to irradiation, one cannot observe any changes in it visually. The latent image can be observed only after its development. As can be seen from Fig. 1, the formation of a latent image leads to an insignificant change in the transmission of glass toward the side of increased absorption in the ultraviolet or the visible spectral region. This, however, according to Stookey [67], is not a true measure of the latent image, inasmuch as in some cases, analogous changes can also be observed in glass in the absence of photosensitive metals.

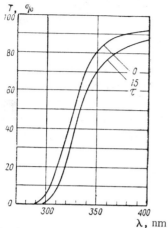

Fig. 1. Solarization of photosensitive glass. T) Light transmission; λ) wavelength; τ) time of irradiation in hours (0 indicates no irradiation).

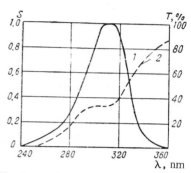

Fig. 2. Spectral sensitivity of photosensitive components. λ) Wavelength; S) relative sensitivity; T) light transmission per 1 mm of glass thickness. Curve 1 is the sensitivity of photoactive materials; curve 2 is the light transmission of the photosensitive glass.

Under the influence of sunlight or ionizing radiation, Cu-containing photosensitive glasses acquire a light blue-gray color, while the Ag-containing glasses acquire a yellow color. This insignificant change in the color, or "solarization," is accompanied by the appearance in these glasses of a wide absorption band in the 300–370 nm region, which is typical for Cu or Ag compounds. However, in Au-containing glasses, no absorption bands characteristic for any Au compound were observed. Based on these measurements, Stookey [67] thinks that in Cu- and Ag-containing glasses, the latent image is formed during irradiation by ultraviolet light in the absorption regions corresponding to the Cu or Ag compounds, while in Au-containing glasses, it arises in the absorption regions corresponding to other glass components and during the irradiation by ultraviolet light with a wavelength of 254 nm and shorter. The introduction of CeO_2 into Au-containing glasses makes it possible to obtain a latent image during irradiation with light with a longer wavelength (350 nm) and in the absorption regions corresponding to the Ce ions (Fig. 2).

During the determination of the transmission coefficient for photosensitive glass up to and after irradiation, it was observed that the end of the light transmission curve, lying in the long-wave

ultraviolet spectral region, is shifted to the side of the long wavelengths (see Fig. 1). Consequently, a portion of the incident light,
larger than previously, will be absorbed after irradiation in the
wavelength region examined, i.e., the solarization effect, such as
can also be observed in various other glasses, will arise.

Barth [71] thinks that during irradiation of photosensitive
glasses, the solarization and the formation of the latent image occur simultaneously but independently of each other. This is proven
by the facts that the rapidly attained limit of the final solarization
value does not depend on the intensity of the latent image, and that
the decrease in light transmission due to solarization may be reduced as a result of heat treatment without this having any effect
on the latent image. The intensity of the latent image depends not
only on irradiation, but also on the concentration of those glass
components which are influenced by the ultraviolet light.

It must be mentioned, however, that the absorption bands of
the latent image which arise in photosensitive glasses when they
are irradiated by x-rays may change under the influence of heat
treatment [72].

Stookey [67] studied some properties of the latent image. He
investigated the effect of time at various temperatures as well as
of the heating rate.

Deep cooling to liquid-air temperatures and heating to 580°C
showed no effect on the latent image, which was always developed
after the glass was held in this temperature region and after it
was heated to the development temperature. Heating to higher
temperatures (higher than 600°C) resulted in the irreversible destruction of the latent image, which no longer showed up even in
cases of exposures 50 times longer than normal.

Irradiated photosensitive glass containing 0.01% Au and
0.049% CeO_2 was heated rapidly, by immersing 1-mm-thick plates
into a tank containing salt melted at a temperature of 600°C or
higher, and this also destroyed the latent image. Once the image
has been developed, it is retained in the glass up to its melting
point at 1150°C or higher. If the latent image is destroyed by the
heating of the glass at higher temperatures, then thermal luminescence is observed. If irradiated photosensitive glass is held in
darkness for a long time (1 yr), no change in the latent image is

observed, nor does a high-frequency electrical field (10-100 MHz) applied during the irradiation of the development have any effect on it.

5. THE DEVELOPED IMAGE

The development time for a latent image decreases with increasing temperature, and also depends on the viscosity of the glass, on the type of photosensitive metal present, on its state in the glass, on the presence of thermal reducers, and on the intensity of exposure during irradiation [67]. The minimum development temperature for Ag-containing glasses lies 100°C lower than their annealing temperatures, and that for Au-containing glasses lies 20°C lower than their annealing temperatures, whereas the maximum development temperatures for both types of glass are limited because of the deformation of the glass at the annealing temperature. The time—temperature and viscosity—temperature dependencies for the development are shown in Fig. 3, from which it is seen that for glass with a softening temperature of 709°C and an annealing temperature of 523°C, the average development temperature lies between 580 and 680°C; the average development time here is 10-60 min. For glasses which contain a thermal reducer or which are subjected to a more intense exposure, lower development times are necessary. In conformity with previous investigations [65], Stookey confirmed the presence of crystalline gold in the irradiated portions of the glass which were colored as a result of heat treatment, and he also confirmed the absence of crystalline gold in the adjacent portions of glass, which were subjected to heat treatment, but were not irradiated.

In order to obtain a high-quality developed photographic image in a photosensitive glass, the correct determination of its optical density is of great importance, for it may serve as a measure of its photosensitivity. Riess and co-workers [73] determined the blackening density of photosensitive glass subjected to irradiation of various intensities and developed at 550-565°C at various times, using the formula

$$D = \log_{10} I_0/I, \tag{1}$$

where I_0 is the intensity of the light going through the unexposed glass sample, and I is the intensity of the light going through the exposed and the developed glass.

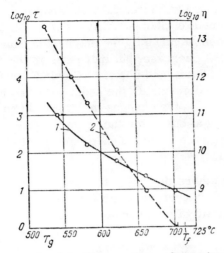

Fig. 3. Normal development time and viscosity as a function of temperature. τ) Development time in minutes; η) viscosity of glass in poise; T_g = 523°C and is the annealing temperature for glass; T_f = 709°C and is the softening temperature for the given glass. Curve 1 is the development time; curve 2 is the viscosity.

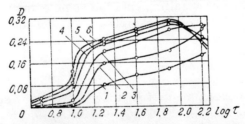

Fig. 4. Density as a function of exposure for several development times. τ) Time, in minutes; D) density. The development times for the curves are as follows: 1) 200; 2) 400; 3) 600; 4) 1000; 5) 1600; 6) 2600 sec.

Table 1. The γ Values for a Photosensitive Glass

Development time, sec	200	400	600	1000	1600	2600
Gradient γ	0.44	0.80	0.85	0.98	1.41	2.40

Figure 4 shows the curves they obtained for the various stages of development of photosensitive glass. Curves 1, 2, and 3 differ from the normal curve by the anomalous change in the density, which does not decrease, but increases in the region of overexposure (τ = 15-80 min and higher). Curve 6 corresponds to the completely developed glass. In the underexposure region (τ = 5-10 min), the curves for the changes in density do not show deviations from the normal curve for the bromine—silver photographic emulsion. The region for the correct exposure lies between τ = 10 and τ = 15 min.

The above authors think that the gradient γ, i.e., the slope of the curve in the correct exposure region, is an important determining characteristic of photosensitive glass. It is given by

$$\gamma = dD/d(\log \tau), \tag{2}$$

where dD is the gradually increasing change in the density as dependent on the correspondingly increasing change in log τ. The γ values for the investigated samples of photosensitive glass are shown in Table 1, which has been taken from [74].

Barth [71] determines the intensity of the coloration during the darkening of the developed image as a logarithm of the ratio between the light flux Φ falling onto the sample and the light flux ΦT which passes through the sample (at wavelengths λ = 250-700 nm):

$$S = \log \Phi/\Phi_T. \tag{3}$$

After the development of photosensitive glass samples of the composition (in mole %): 74.0 SiO_2, 0.6 B_2O_3, 19.0 Na_2O, 6.5 Al_2O_3, 1.7 Na_2SiF_6, 0.2 KBr, 0.02 Sb_2O_3, 0.04 Ag, and 0.05 CeO_2, which had been irradiated for various lengths of time, their respective curves for the transmission coefficient τ were obtained as presented in Fig. 5. The graphs for the dependence of the darkening S on the logarithm of the irradiation time (Fig. 6) are analogous to the curves for normal photosensitive materials.

The intensity of coloring of the developed image in the direction of irradiation decreases as one goes deeper into the sample because of the absorption and weakening of the light flux causing the formation of the latent image [71]. The decrease in the color-

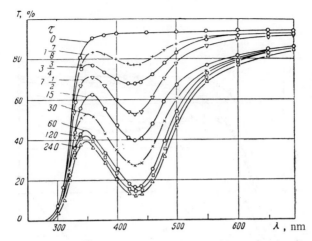

Fig. 5. The transmission of silver-containing glasses after irradiation for various times. λ) Wavelength; T) light transmission; τ) irradiation time in minutes.

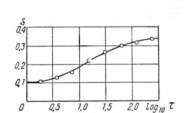

Fig. 6. Dependence of darkening on the irradiation time. τ) Irradiation time in minutes; S) darkening.

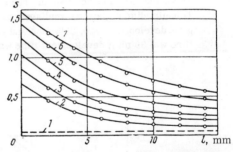

Fig. 7. Change in the darkening relative to the depth of the sample. l) Depth; S) darkening. Irradiation times for the curves are as follows: 1) 0; 2) 15; 3) 30; 4) 60; 5) 120; 6) 240; 7) 480 min.

ing intensity is shown in Fig. 7, from which it is seen that at a certain depth all curves come together in a horizontal line, which corresponds to the darkening of the nonirradiated glass. This means that at a given depth the action of the ultraviolet rays is weakened to such an extent that no formation of a latent image or coloring of glass occurs. Thus, in order to make ultraviolet light penetrate

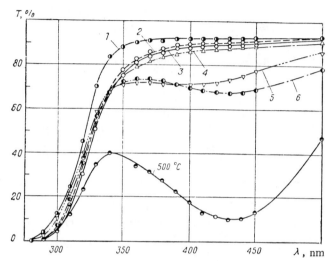

Fig. 8. Transmission of glasses developed at various temperatures.
λ) Wavelength; T) transmission. The curves for glasses are as follows:
1) nonirradiated glass; 2) irradiated, but not developed, glass; 3-6)
glass developed at 300, 350, 400, and 450°C, respectively. Exposure
time was 30 min; development time was 1 h.

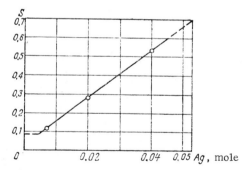

Fig. 9. Dependence of the darkening of glasses on the
change in the silver content. Here, S is the darkening.
Exposure was at 510°C for 30 min, and the development
time was 30 min.

to a sufficient depth, Barth [71] recommends that such an irradiation exposure be selected that there is an overexposure by several orders of magnitude at the surface. The coloring intensity increases with increasing development time and tends to acquire a definite limiting value depending on the time of irradiation and the silver concentration (see Fig. 6).

The dependence of the transmission coefficient of the photosensitive glass samples on the development temperature is represented in Fig. 8, where it can be seen that curve 2 for the irradiated, but undeveloped, glass is shifted to the right as compared to curve 1 for the nonirradiated glass [71]. Thus, development at 300°C somewhat decreases the shifting of the curve toward the side of longer wavelengths, and the coloring of the glass does not vary. At 400°C, absorption bands corresponding to the yellowish-brown color are formed; however, in the region $\lambda < 350$ nm, the curve is nevertheless shifted toward the side of shorter wavelengths. Only at 450°C and within the entire measured region did there occur a decrease in the transmission coefficient and a clear formation of the absorption bands corresponding to an increase in the coloring intensity [71].

The darkening of the developed image also depended on the chemical composition of the photosensitive glass. It increased linearly with silver concentration (Fig. 9) which, however, one cannot increase arbitrarily, due to the fact that if the concentration is excessive, the glass body may spontaneously assume a yellowish-brown color during melting or fabrication [71]. The allowable concentrations of silver and the glass compositions are given in Chapter III.

The dependence of darkening on the content of cerium oxide in the glass turned out to be more complex. From Fig. 10, it is seen that the sample with the higher cerium oxide content (0.5 mole) is darkened considerably more than the sample with the lower cerium oxide content, which made Barth [71] conclude that darkening cannot serve as a criterion for the photosensitive properties of a glass without taking into consideration the transmission coefficient. Glass with an excessively high CeO_2 content did not change transmission coefficient after development, i.e., it was no longer photosensitive (curve 2 in Fig. 10). At the optimum Ce content (0.01 mole of CeO_2), a maximum in darkening took place (Fig. 11) [71].

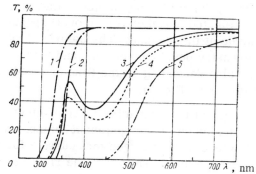

Fig. 10. Transmission of glasses containing various amounts of cerium. λ) Wavelength; T) transmission. The curves are for glasses with the following respective contents of cerium: 1) 0.01 mole, nonirradiated glass; 2) 0.5 mole, both nonirradiated and irradiated; 3-5) 0.10, 0.05, and 0.01 mole, respectively, irradiated at 510°C for 30 min and developed in a time of 45 min.

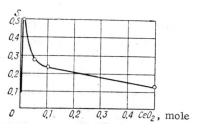

Fig. 11. Dependence of the darkening of glasses on the cerium content present. S is the darkening.

With increasing Na_2O content, as well as during the substitution of the aluminum ion, with its relatively small radius, by the barium ion, the coloring intensity of the developed image increased (Figs. 12 and 13).

6. PHOTOSENSITIVE OPALINE GLASSES

Stookey [67] was the first to demonstrate the possibility of obtaining a nontransparent or opaline image by means of nonmetallic crystals precipitating during the heat-treatment process on the particles of the photosensitive Au, Ag, or Cu metals in the previously irradiated portions of the photosensitive glass. The obtaining of the opaline photographic image in this case is based on the fact that a sufficiently high viscosity of glass hinders the penetration of the crystallization beyond the limits of irradiated portions of the glass. The nonmetallic crystals themselves are transparent and colorless; however, due to the fact that their index of refrac-

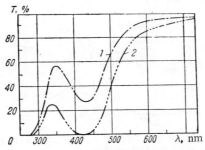

Fig. 12. Dependence of the transmission of glasses on the
Na$_2$O content present. λ) Wavelength; T) transmission.
Curve 1 is for glasses containing 19 moles Na$_2$O; curve 2
is for glasses containing 24 moles Na$_2$O. Irradiation at
505°C for 20 min with development time being 15 min.

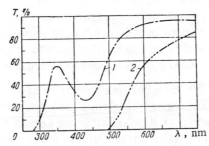

Fig. 13. Change in the transmission of glass upon re-
placement of Al$_2$O$_3$ with BaO. λ) Wavelength; T) transmission. 1) Initial glass; 2) the same glass with 2% Al$_2$O$_3$
replaced by 1.2% BaO. Irradiation at 505°C for 30 min,
with the development time being 15 min.

tion is different from that of glass, and due to the coloring effect
of the metallic particles, the image obtained becomes opaline and
colored. A white and an easily developed image may be obtained
inside the transparent glass by decreasing the concentration of the
photosensitive metal, which nevertheless still causes the formation of crystallization nuclei.

Stookey [75] determined that a complex, stepwise heat treatment is needed for the development of the image in photosensitive
opaline glasses, including heating up to a temperature higher than
600°C in order to develop metallic particles and have them grow

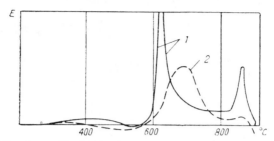

Fig. 14. Differential thermal analysis curves for opaline
glass. T) Temperature; E) exothermal effect. 1) Glass
irradiated for 180 min; 2) nonirradiated glass.

to the critical size, a decrease of the temperature to 520°C or
lower in order to start the heterogeneous crystallization of light-
scattering crystals on the metallic crystallization nuclei, and a
secondary heating to a temperature higher than 550°C, necessary
for the growth of nonmetallic crystals. The number of nuclei may
be regulated by a change in the irradiation exposure and in the
primary stage of heat treatment. The growth of crystals basically
depends on the secondary stage of the heat treatment.

Upon excessive irradiation exposures of Au-containing
photosensitive glass, a red color appeared after the development;
however, no formation of light-scattering crystals was observed,
which Stookey [75] explains either by the excessively small Au particle size and their incapability of acting as crystallization nuclei,
or by the fact that they are located too close to each other, so that
the matrix substance cannot precipitate on these particles and thus
form the crystals. These propositions were later developed and
confirmed by Maurer [76].

Tashiro and Sakka [77] investigated the change in the transparency of the opaline photosensitive glass of the composition
$81SiO_2$, $12.5Li_2O$, $2.5K_2O$, $4Al_2O_3$, $0.03CeO_2$, and $0.027Au$ as a
function of the exposure time. Glass samples in the form of 2-mm-
thick plates were exposed to ultraviolet light from a high-pressure,
500-W mercury lamp at a distance of 10 cm, with the exposure
time ranging from 1 to 1000 min, and were held first at 510°C for
30 min and then at 620°C for 60 min so as to excite the formation
of crystallization nuclei, i.e., the metallic gold particles and lithium metasilicate crystals, respectively. The precipitation of the

lithium metasilicate crystals at 620°C and of lithium disilicate at 880°C was confirmed by the maxima on the differential thermal analysis curves for this glass (Fig. 14). The size of lithium meta-silicate crystals precipitating out in the transparent glass was 70 nm. Nontransparent glasses contained coarser particles. Tashiro and Sakka [77] determined that: (1) with increasing exposure time of up to 30 min, the transparency decreases due to the formation of lithium metasilicate crystals; (2) with increasing exposure time within the range 30-180 min, transparency also increases, and the sample subjected to a 180-min exposure was almost transparent, although it had a dark-red color; this increase in the transparency is associated with the decrease of the crystals to sizes at which they are no longer capable of dissipating the visible light; and (3) with exposure times greater than 180 min, the transparency again decreased.

7. THEORY OF THE PHOTOSENSITIVE PROCESS

Of considerable importance for the formation of the latent image in a photosensitive glass is the state in it of the dissolved Au, Ag, or Cu. Some investigators [65] think that gold is dissolved in fused glass in the form of Au^+ or Au^{3+} ions which at the strik-ing temperatures are reduced to the metal. Others propose that gold first dissolves in the glass in the form of atoms; that during the cooling stage of the glass, a supersaturated solution of the metallic, but still colorless, gold is formed in the form of par-ticles, the sizes of which are greater than the atomic size; and, finally, that these particles grow and a coloring appears upon sec-ondary heating [65]. The coloring of glass fundamentally depends on the concentration of the photosensitive metal introduced into the batch, and on the degree of oxidation of the melt. It was shown in practice that the coloring becomes intensified with increasing con-centration of the metal present and with a decreasing degree of oxidation of the melt. The decrease in the degree of oxidation of the melt, which is ordinarily achieved by the introduction of highly active reducers, enhances the precipitation of the photosensitive metal compounds in the form of elemental metal. A combination of suitable reducers with oxidizing agents may lead to the best re-sults. Thus, polyvalent ions in combination with nitrates allow glass to remain colorless during melting and permit it to become colored during slow cooling or during reheating.

According to Weyl [78], gold may be present in the glass melt in the form of ions or in the form of atoms. The gold atoms may condense in the form of colloidal particles. If these particles grow to sizes of 3-5 μ, then they may color glass, but they can also serve as crystallization nuclei. At the same time, according to Badger et al. [79], the gold ions may be reduced at a low temperature to their atomic state by the tin ions.

Stookey [65] conclusively showed that in fused glass, gold is present in the oxidized colorless state. The formation of elemental metal and the coloring of glass is possible at temperatures lower than the melting point only in glasses melted under reducing conditions, which can be done by adding tin or other polyvalent ions to the glass. In glasses which do not contain reducers, gold remains in the ionic state all the way down to room temperature. Such glasses are sensitive to ultraviolet rays, i.e., the reduction of gold ions and the formation of the metal by the photochemical method is possible. The same is true of glasses containing silver or copper.

According to Stookey [67], the mechanism of photosensitivity consists in the following. The initial, nonirradiated glass contains uniformly dispersed Au, Ag, or Cu ions. Besides one of the ions of these metals, optical sensitizers may also be present in the glass, such as cerium ions or some Ag and Cu compounds. The role of the optical sensitizers is to reduce the Au, Ag, or Cu ions under the influence of the ultraviolet rays. The glass is generally irradiated at room temperature. The result of the irradiation is that some of the ions present in the glass give up electrons. These electrons are designated as photoelectrons. Photoelectrons are capable of forming a metastable activated state localized on other ions, such as on the ions of the metal, or on the structural defects of glass.

The reduction of the Au, Ag, or Cu ions and the coloring of glass does not occur as yet. Only with increasing temperatures, when the viscosity of glass decreases, is the reduction of such ions possible, with the formation of neutral metal particles, as a result of which the glass becomes colored, i.e., the latent image develops. Thus, the coloring of the glass occurs as a result of the reaction between the photochemically active components of the glass, the amount of which present in the glass is very small. The remaining glass components may change the photosensitivity only when they show an effect on the state of the photochemically active components of the glass.

Rapid heating or exposure at a high temperature destroys the latent image, since the excited electrons instantaneously return to their initial equilibrium state in the ion from which they had been released. This process is accompanied by the thermal luminescence of the glass.

According to Stookey [67], the development of the latent image during heating includes two stages: the formation of neutral metallic atoms due to the trapping of the metals by the ions which had been freed of photoelectrons, and the subsequent growth of particles, which can take place both by their accretion or coalescence, and by the deposition of the metal ions on the metallic atoms.

A somewhat different mechanism for the formation of the latent image in Cu-containing photosensitive glasses is proposed by Weyl [60], who thinks that the photochemical reduction of Cu^+ ions to the Cu atoms is already possible during the irradiation of the glass. According to this hypothesis, the first stage of the formation of the latent image consists in the absorption by the Cu^+ of a quantum of light and in the formation of the excited ion. Glasses containing Cu^+ ions fluoresce, which is explained by the returning of the excited ion to its fundamental state. It is possible, however, that this Cu^+ ion gives up one electron and changes into Cu^{2+}; thus

$$Cu^+ + h\nu \rightarrow Cu^{2+} + e^-. \tag{4}$$

Regardless of the low quantum efficiency of this process, the fluorescence decreases with increasing irradiation by ultraviolet light due to the decrease in the Cu^+ ion concentration.

At the secondary stage of the latent-image formation, the Cu^+ reduces to atomic copper [60]; thus

$$Cu^+ + e^- = Cu^0. \tag{5}$$

This reaction goes faster than reaction (4), the rate of which also determines the rate of the latent-image formation. The formation of the latent image is expressed by Weyl [60] using the equation

$$2Cu^+ + h\nu = Cu^{2+} + Cu, \tag{6}$$

indicating that the irradiated portion of the glass differs from the nonirradiated portion in having a lower concentration of the Cu^+ ions and by a higher concentration of the Cu atoms. In portions with the higher concentration of the copper atoms, recrystallization takes place at a higher rate upon heating or at lower temperatures according to

$$xCu \rightarrow Cu_x. \tag{7}$$

The effect of Ce, which makes for better contrast and finer detail in the image, is based on the following reactions:

$$Ce^{3+} + h\nu \rightarrow Ce^{4+} + e^-, \tag{8}$$

$$Ce^{3+} + Cu^+ + h\nu \rightarrow Ce^{4+} + Cu. \tag{9}$$

According to Weyl [60], CeO_2 in the sodium—calcium—silicate glass dissociates during melting into Ce^{3+} and O^{2-}. The Ce^{3+} absorbs ultraviolet radiation and fluoresces just like the Cu^+ ion.

In silver-containing glasses, in analogy with the copper-containing glasses, the silver ion, by taking on an electron, changes into atomic silver [60]; thus

$$Ag^+ + e^- \rightarrow Ag^0. \tag{10}$$

The atomic silver is able to color glass only during heating, when the formation of silver aggregates takes place according to the following reaction [60]:

$$x \cdot Ag \rightarrow Ag_x. \tag{11}$$

These particles can later serve as crystallization nuclei for the prime glass body.

According to other investigators [80, 81], the quantum of light, during its interaction with the photosensitive silver-containing glass, depending on its energy, either excites the silver ion or oxidizes it, with the formation of a free electron:

$$Ag^+ + h\nu \begin{cases} \nearrow (Ag^+)^* & \text{(a)} \\ \searrow Ag^{++} + e^- & \text{(b)} \end{cases} \tag{12}$$

It is proposed that the free electrons forming according to reaction (12b) nevertheless remain linked with the silver ion until the heat treatment of glass, during which process they neutralize it according to the reaction

$$Ag^+ + e^- \longrightarrow Ag^0 + h\nu_1, \; \nu_1 < \nu. \tag{13}$$

By analogy with copper-containing glasses, entrapment of an electron by the Ag^+ ion is also possible up to the heat treatment, i.e., during irradiation.

According to Tucker [82], when electron paramagnetic resonance spectra of photosensitive silver-containing calcium metaphosphate glass irradiated by x-rays were investigated, neutral silver atoms, emerging during the entrapment of the electrons by the Ag^+ ion, and Ag^{2+} ions, forming during the entrapment of the "holes" by the Ag^+ ions, were observed.

The most effective electron source is apparently the Ce^{3+} ion. In the absence of cerium, the photosensitivity of silver-containing glasses is weak, or the reaction (12b), giving free electrons, may proceed only under the influence of irradiation with a wavelength $\lambda < 280$ nm, radiation which is already almost entirely absorbed in the surface layer of the glass. Cerium increases the number of free electrons present according to reaction (8), which is also capable of proceeding under the influence of radiation with $\lambda > 280$ nm.

According to Bondarev and Borodai [81], the energy corresponding to the active radiation (280–360 nm) for photosensitive glasses is 4.4–3.8 eV, while the ionization potentials are equal to 7.58, 21.5, 35.8, and 51.8 eV for silver, and 6.54 and 33.3 eV for cerium.

This noncorrespondence is explained by the fact that due to the influence of the electric and the magnetic fields of the adjacent atoms, ions, and molecules, the energy levels of the silver or the cerium ions may vary greatly, as a result of which ionization of other ions and atoms is possible.

According to Stookey [67], the photochemical process may be represented by (1) the following reaction:

$$A^x + h\nu \rightleftarrows A^{x+1} + e^\omega, \tag{14}$$

where A^x is the ion A absorbing light and having a valency x, h_ν is the quantum of absorbed energy, and e^ω is the excited photoelectron; and (2) the reaction

$$M^y + ye^\omega \rightleftarrows (M^0)^\omega \rightarrow M^0 + \omega, \tag{15}$$

where M^y is the metal ion of valency y (y = 1 for Cu, Ag, and, possibly, Au), $(M^0)^\omega$ is the metal atom with the excess energy imparted by the photoelectron, and ω is the excess energy given off in the form of heat or light.

Typical reactions are, in accord with the above [67]:

The sensitization of gold with cerium,

$$Ce^{3+} + Au^+ + h\nu \rightarrow Ce^{4+} + Au^0 + \omega. \tag{16}$$

The action of copper as self-sensitizer,

$$2Cu^+ + h\nu \rightarrow Cu^{2+} + Cu^0 + \omega. \tag{17}$$

The action of silver as self-sensitizer,

$$2Ag^+ + h\nu \rightarrow Ag^{2+} + Ag^0 + \omega. \tag{18}$$

Thermal luminescence during rapid heating,

$$Ce^{4+} + e^\omega \rightarrow Ce^{3+} + h\nu. \tag{19}$$

As can be seen from the last reaction, thermal luminescence consists in the addition of an entrapped electron to the Ce^{4+} ion and in the release of a quantum of light energy.

When investigating the dependence of the photosensitive properties of lithium aluminosilicate glasses on the silver and cerium concentrations, the present author, together with A. I. Gel'berger, S. E. Piterskikh, and others, observed that the known absorption band at 270 nm appeared (Fig. 15) when glasses without additions, glasses with Ag but without Ce, and glasses with Ce but without Ag were irradiated. The irradiation was done at 80° by ultraviolet light from a PRK-7 lamp at a distance of 420 mm. With increasing exposure, the intensity of this band increased to saturation. During heating of irradiated samples, the 275-nm band disintegrated, which indicates the disintegration of the electronic centers formed

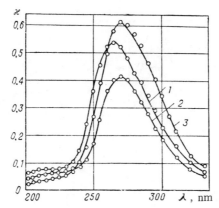

Fig. 15. Absorption spectra for irradiated glasses. λ)
Wavelength; $\varkappa$) absorption. 1) Glass without additions;
2) glass with 0.02% Ag; 3) glass with 0.03% CeO_2. Irradiation at 250°C for 1 h.

during irradiation. At the same time, the 405-nm band emerged
in the visible region. The disintegration of centers during increased temperature was accompanied by luminescence of the
samples, i.e., so-called thermal luminescence (Figs. 16a, b). Two
thermal luminescence peaks were observed, one at 160 and another
at 350°C, with both of them heavily dependent on the silver content,
with the CeO_2 content being constant. With decreasing silver content, the magnitude of both peaks increased. At constant silver
content, the intensity of the thermal luminescence peaks increased
with increasing cerium concentration. Therefore the occupancy of
the electronic levels depends on the cerium content.

The intensity of the peak of the 405-nm band depended on the
CeO_2 content and attained the highest magnitude at 0.02-0.04 wt.%
CeO_2. The disintegration of the latent image (the 275-nm band) is
accompanied by the formation of the atomic centers* of silver,
which are characterized not only by the appearance of the 405-nm
absorption band, but also by the change in the luminescence spectra. The intensity of the luminescence peak at 525 nm relative to

---

* Later [83], we determined that these centers are apparently formations which are
more complex than merely atomic, and should, in our opinion, more correctly be
called molecular-like aggregates.

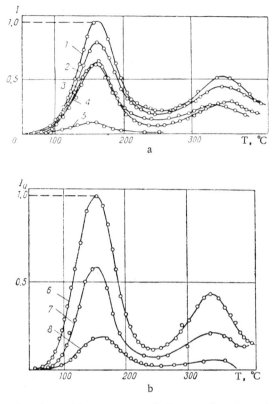

Fig. 16. Thermal luminescence of glasses with various silver and cerium contents. T) Heating temperature; I) intensity of thermal luminescence in units of the experimental conditions. a) Curves 1-5 represent glasses containing 0.03% CeO_2 and 0.01, 0.02, 0.04, 0.08, and 0.12% Ag, respectively; b) curves 6-8 represent glasses containing 0.02% Ag and 0.16, 0.08, and 0.04% CeO_2, respectively.

that of the peak at 418 nm increased with increasing concentration of silver, CeO_2 content being constant, which is caused by the intensification of the luminescence of atomic centers as compared to the luminescence produced by the constant cerium content.

As a result of this investigation on the effect of Ag and CeO_2 content on the photosensitive properties of glass, the role of these additions in the mechanism of the latent and the visible image formation has been clarified.

When glasses are irradiated, the formation of electronic centers occurs. The levels for the localization of the electrons are determined by the framework, i.e., by the structural network of the glass. The filling up of the electron levels is associated with the formation of the latent image, which is characterized by the absorption of the irradiated glass in the ultraviolet region and by the intensity of the peaks of the thermal luminescence spectra (see Fig. 16). Both characteristics are determined by the cerium content in the glass being studied.

With increasing cerium concentration — with cerium the electron donor in photosensitive glasses — the number of electronic centers increases, i.e., the latent-image density increases.

Increasing the temperature results in disintegration of the electronic centers and in reduction of the silver ions, which is accompanied by an increase in the 405-nm absorption peak. Also, the reduction of the silver ions is accompanied by a recombination process, i.e., the entrapment of the electrons by the Ce^{4+} ions. With increasing CeO_2 concentration, the probability of recombination increases, and the intensity of the absorption peak in the visible region decreases. The study of the absorption spectra and the luminescence of irradiated and heat-treated glasses showed that from 0.02-0.04% CeO_2 should be introduced into the glass in order to obtain a visible image having the best density.

With increasing Ag content, the probability of the entrapment of electrons by Ag ions increases, which is accompanied by increasing absorption in the visible region. At the same time, the probability of recombination decreases, and so does the intensity of the thermal luminescence peaks.

The intensity of the absorption peak in the visible region of the glasses irradiated and heat treated at a temperature of 400°C increases linearly within the concentration range of 0.01-0.08% silver.

At silver concentrations of 0.01% and less, absorption in the visible region occurs only after very long irradiation times.

The density of the latent image increases with increasing cerium concentration up to 0.16%, whereas the density of the visible image attains a maximum value at a concentration of 0.04% CeO_2.

The density of the latent image does not depend on the silver content. With increasing silver concentration, the density of the visible image increases linearly.

The properties of the latent image in photosensitive lithium aluminosilicate glasses, based on the absorption spectra, were investigated by Berezhnoi and Polukhin [84]. Since glass without cerium has a very low photosensitivity at room temperature, i.e., it becomes colored only weakly during subsequent heat treatment, the hypothesis was put forward that the appearance of the 270-nm band attests to the nucleation of centers in the structural network of the glass, the role of which in photosensitive processes is small compared to that of the centers which are formed in a glass when cerium is present.

The observed dependence of the intensity of the 270-nm band on cerium concentration makes it possible to assume that this band is a complex one and that it consists of several overlapping bands. Differential absorption spectra were taken; in this method, which had not been used previously for the investigation of photosensitive glasses, bands appear in the spectrum which characterize only the centers dependent on cerium, and bands which pertain to the centers in the structural network of the glass do not appear. The gist of this method consists in the fact that the spectrum of the glass with the higher cerium concentration was taken relative to that of the glass with the lower cerium concentration, which served as the standard prior to the irradiation plus heat treatment of both glasses; the same was then done after the treatment of both glasses, and the difference in the pre- and post-treatment spectral curves for the optical density was calculated.

The irradiation of these glasses was by a PRK-7 mercury lamp at a distance of 5 cm, the spectra were taken on an SF-4 spectrophotometer, and the samples investigated had a thickness of 0.5 mm. Good reproducibility of the results was observed on many of the samples studied.

Lithium aluminosilicate glasses with CeO_2 concentrations of 0.02%, 0.04%, 0.08%, and 0.16%, and an Ag concentration of 0.02% were selected for the investigation. Figure 17a shows the spectra of the glasses with CeO_2 concentrations of 0.04%, 0.08%, and 0.16%, which were taken relative to the glass with CeO_2 concentration equal to 0.02%. From these spectra, it can be seen that the ratio

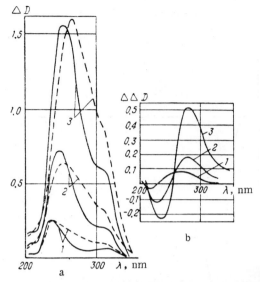

Fig. 17. Absorption spectra for cerium-containing glasses. λ)
Wavelength; ΔD) difference between the optical density of the
given glass and that of the standard glass; $\Delta\Delta D$) increment in
the optical-density difference. a) Absorption spectra taken
with respect to the glass having a concentration of 0.02% CeO_2.
Curves are for glasses with CeO_2 concentrations as follows: 1)
0.04; 2) 0.08; 3) 0.16%. Solid curves: prior to irradiation;
dashed curves: after irradiation. b) Increment in the optical-
density difference after irradiation for glasses 1-3.

between the trivalent and the quadrivalent cerium [85, 86] within
the concentration range given remains constant. One must focus
attention on the dependence of the position of the maximum of the
quadrivalent Ce on the CeO_2 concentration. The position of this
maximum shifts with increasing CeO_2 concentration toward the
long-wave side, from 230 nm at a concentration of 0.02% to 250
nm at a concentration of 0.14%. Figure 17 also shows spectra of
the same samples taken in an analogous manner after irradiation.
The differences in the optical densities obtained after and prior to
irradiation are shown in Fig. 17b, from which it can be seen that
during the irradiation, a maximum appears at 285 nm and a minimum appears in the region of 220-240 nm. The intensities of both
the maximum and the minimum are proportional to the CeO_2 con-

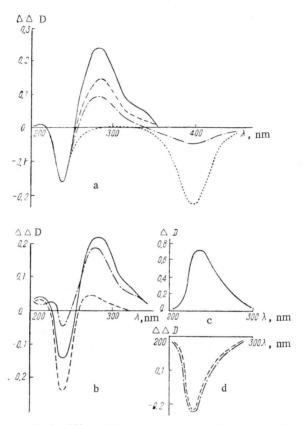

Fig. 18. Changes in the differential absorption spectra of cerium- and samarium-containing glasses following various cycles of irradiation and heat treatment. λ) Wavelength; △D) difference in optical density between the given glass and the given reference glass; △△D) gain in the optical-density difference. a) Gain in the difference between the spectral absorption curves for glasses containing 0.08 and 0.02% CeO₂. Solid curve: irradiated vs. nonirradiated glass; dashed curve: denotes glass irradiated at 50°C and heat treated at 200°C vs. nonirradiated glass; dot-dashed curve: glass irradiated at 50°C and heat treated at 200 and 250°C vs. nonirradiated glass; dotted curve: glass irradiated at 50°C and heat treated at 200, 250, and 300°C vs. nonirradiated glass. b) Gain in the difference between the spectral absorption curves for glasses containing 0.08 and 0.02% CeO₂. Solid curve: irradiated vs. nonirradiated glass; dashed curve: glass subjected to five cycles of irradiation at 50°C and heat treated at 350°C vs. nonirradiated glass; dot-dashed curve: glasses which were additionally irradiated after five cycles of irradiation at 50°C and heat treated at 350°C vs. nonirradiated glass. c) Absorption spectrum of glass containing 0.08% Sm₂O₃, taken with respect to a glass containing 0.01% Sm₂O₃ (nonirradiated). d) Gain in the difference between the spectral absorption curves for glasses containing 0.08 and 0.01% Sm₂O₃. Dashed curve: irradiated vs. nonirradiated glass; dot-dashed curve: glass irradiated at 50°C and heat treated at 350°C vs. nonirradiated glass.

centration. With increased irradiation dosage, the maximum and the minimum show up even more clearly. Figure 18a shows the difference in the optical densities after and prior to irradiation with increased dosage for glasses with a CeO_2 concentration of 0.08%, taken with respect to the glass with a CeO_2 concentration of 0.02%. It can be seen from Fig. 18a that a noticeable reflection point in the spectral curve is observed at 315 nm, which is caused by the change in the state of the Ce^{3+} ions after irradiation.

After a 2-h heat treatment of these glasses at 200°C, a decrease in the intensity of the maximum at 285 nm is observed without, however, the formation of a visible image. Subsequent heat treatment at 250°C results in a further decrease in the intensity of the maximum at 285 nm and in the formation of a weak visible image at 400 nm, with the intensity of the 400-nm band less in the case of a higher Ce concentration. Finally, glass heat treated at 300°C shows a complete disappearance of the 285-nm maximum and a marked increase in the visible image at 400 nm. As to the 240-nm minimum, its intensity remains unchanged during the above heat-treatment stages.

Analogous results were obtained for glasses in which Sm was used as the sensitizer instead of Ce (see Fig. 18c). After irradiation of such glasses, no maximum is observed at 285 nm, whereas the minimum at 240 nm is again present and its intensity does not vary with heat treatment.

We also investigated CeO_2-containing glass subjected to multiple irradiation cycles at room temperature and subsequently heat treated at 350°C. As can be seen from Fig. 18b, this glass shows an increased minimum at 240 nm. Subsequent irradiation again results in the appearance of a maximum at 285 nm and a much weaker minimum at 240 nm. The ratio between the intensity of the maximum and that of the minimum is approximately 4:1 (see Fig. 18a), whereas during the initial irradiation, their ratio was approximately 2:1. This indicates that the intensity of the 285-nm maximum does not depend on the intensity of the minimum at 240 nm.

This glass with the addition of only Ag has a low photosensitivity, which, however, increases considerably in the presence of Ce ions. The appearance of centers in the glass after irradiation, the number of which depends linearly on the Ce concentration, makes it possible to assume that these centers are directly related to the increase in photosensitivity.

Fig. 19. Energy schematic for photosensitive processes in glass.

The 285-nm band, in our opinion, characterizes the centers which, during the irradiation of the glass, result from the Ce^{3+} centers either as a result of their ionization or as a result of their localization near their electrons which had been freed from the structural network of the glass during irradiation. The fact that these centers indeed come from the Ce^{3+} centers is confirmed by the decrease in the absorption at 315 nm, i.e., in the region of the maximum of the Ce^{3+} absorption. With regard to the minimum at 240 nm, it apparently is due to the reduction of the Ce^{4+} ions to trivalent cerium. Centers are thereby formed which are either analogous to the centers characterized by the 285-nm band, or to the centers of trivalent cerium which pass over into the centers characterized by the 285-nm band. During heat treatment, the centers characterized by the 285-nm band break down and apparently change into centers of trivalent cerium or into Ce^{4+}. Visible-image centers are also formed thereby, characterized by the 405-nm band. It is perfectly obvious that the 285-nm band cannot characterize those centers in the structural network of glass forming as a result of the liberation of electrons during the ionization of ions of trivalent cerium, since, in this case, we would have an analogous band in the glass containing Sm (see Fig. 18b). Experiments with repeated irradiation show that the intensity of the band at 285 nm depends to a considerably larger degree on the decrease in the absorption at 315 nm than on the minimum at 240 nm. This is in good agreement with the results of Stroud [87, 88], who showed that the effective absorption cross section of Ce^{4+} ions is very much larger than that of Ce^{3+} ions. If we follow the Stroud interpretation, according to which ionization of the ions of trivalent cerium, as well as the formation of Ce^{3++} centers (which, in our glass, are characterized by the 285-nm band), occurs during irradiation, we may suggest the energy schematic for active photosensitive processes in glass given in Fig. 19. The possibility of applying the band theory to photosensitive glasses was shown previously [61]. During the irradiation of a glass, ionization of the Ce^{3+} ion and the localization of the electrons at the C level takes place. During heat treatment of a glass, the electrons become liberated from the C level and fall onto the A' and B' levels, corresponding to the excited states of the atomic Ag centers and those of Ce^{3+} ions, respectively, from which they can either drop to the fundamental states of these centers on levels A and B, respectively, or they can return to the conduction band by virtue of the thermal energy. It is obvious that a glass will have better photosensitivity, the larger the number of electrons dropping onto level A, which in turn depends to a significant degree on the position of levels A' and B' relative to the conduction band. The deeper is the A' level and the shallower is the B' level, the more photosensitive will the glass be. Experiments on the temperature quenching of luminescence make it possible to determine the depth of the A' and B' levels. As is known, the atomic center of silver has yellow luminescence, whereas the Ce^{3+} ion has blue luminescence. Experiments which we carried out on glasses of various compositions showed that the depths of the A' and B' levels in photosensitive glasses are of the same order of magnitude, and are of the order of hundredths of an electron volt. We also investigated a photosensitive glass which differed from the given glass by having a significantly larger Al content. It turned out that in this glass the depth of the B' level is an order of magnitude greater than the depth of the A' level. The physically greater depth of the B' level corresponds to the higher temperature stability of luminescence of the Ce^{3+} ions. Thus, our experimental data essentially confirm the energy schematic shown in Fig. 19 for the photosensitive processes. One must mention still another noteworthy experimental fact. Although the density of the latent image is proportional to the Ce concentration up to concentrations of 0.16% CeO_2, the visible image is less dense at this concentration than, for instance, at a concentration of 0.04% CeO_2. The resolution of this contradiction requires even deeper probing into the nature of photosensitive processes in glasses.

As a result of the present investigation, we determined that:

1. The centers appearing in the glass after irradiation and having an absorption band at approximately 285 nm are responsible for the increased photosensitivity of Ag-containing glasses with ions of trivalent cerium present.

2. At relatively high concentrations of cerium, the intensity of the visible image decreases, while the intensity of the 285-nm band is strictly proportional to the Ce concentration.

3. The photosensitivity of glasses essentially depends on the equilibrium conditions between the Ce^{3+} ions and the atomic Ag centers. These equilibrium conditions are determined by the depth of the excited levels of the Ce^{3+} ions and of the atomic centers with respect to the conduction band.

The formation of the latent and the developed image in photosensitive glasses containing both Au and Ag was studied by Gurkovskii [89], who observed a shift in the maximum on the spectral absorption curves of these glasses with increasing Au or Ag content. Based on these data, that author concluded that a series of continuous Au and Ag solid solutions existed in the glasses investigated, and he proposed that neutral metal atoms may be serving as the sensitivity centers in photosensitive glasses.

8. IRRADIATION OF PHOTOSENSITIVE GLASSES AT HIGH TEMPERATURES

The effectiveness of using high temperatures during the irradiation of photosensitive glasses is well-known [60, 67]. It was also reported that silver-containing glasses became colored when irradiated with ultraviolet light at 400°C [90]. Borgman et al. [63] found that glass with the composition 76 SiO_2, 8 Al_2O_3, 12 Li_2O, 4 K_2O, 0.03 CeO_2, and 0.02 Ag becomes colored during irradiation at temperatures higher than 220°C. The intensity of coloring thereby increased significantly, which reflects increased intensity of the photographic process. The authors point out that for glasses of various compositions, the temperature range within which glass possesses photosensitivity changes. They deduce a linear dependence between the development temperature and the temperature of irradiation up to 220°C (Fig. 20), assuming that at temperatures less than 220°C, trapping centers exist in the glass to capture the photoelectrons, and prevent the reduction of the metal until the electrons are freed by heating. The depth of the traps, according to these authors, depends on the temperature, as a result of which the binding energy of the trapped electron also depends on the temperature at which it was trapped. It has been mentioned that the thickness of the colored layer decreased with increasing temperature of irradiation, from 7 mm at 20°C to 1 mm at 515-535°C; at temperatures higher than 540°C, only the surface layer, with a thickness of 0.1 mm, became colored, and at temperatures higher than 550°C, the glass lost its photosensitivity, which is explained

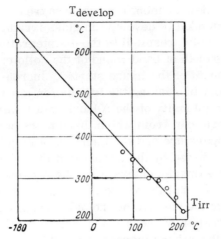

Fig. 20.   Dependence of the development temperature of glass
on the temperature at which it is irradiated.

by the authors by a decrease in the electronic bonds during the
softening of glass, corresponding to a displacement of its fundamental absorption band toward the long-wavelength side, and, as a
result of this, by a decrease in the transparency of glass to ultraviolet rays. The maximum photosensitivity value for glass of the
above composition was attained at an irradiation temperature of
300-400°C, with the lower limit of photosensitivity lying below 180°C.

In order to explain the linear dependence of the development
temperature of Ag-containing glasses on the irradiation temperature, Borgman and Chistoserdov [91] studied the changes in their
absorption spectra as a result of irradiation by a PRK-7 lamp followed by heat treatment. It was determined that irradiation at
20°C created the absorption band A with a maximum at 270 nm. An
increase in the irradiation temperature resulted in a tremendous
increase in the intensity of the A band at the same irradiation dosage. Irradiation at temperatures higher than 220°C resulted in the
appearance of a new band B which heavily overlaps band A, and a
weak absorption band of colloidal Ag with a maximum at 410 nm.
Thus, the visible image started to form directly during the irradiation process. At temperatures higher than 270°C, the A band did
not appear, and only the B band with a maximum at 250 nm and the
colloidal band (both with a much higher intensity) were formed, so

that no additional development through heat treatment was necessary. Heating intended to develop the glass irradiated at temperatures lower than 220°C resulted in the disintegration of the A band,
after which the growth of band B and of the colloidal band began,
i.e., the development of the image started. Increasing the irradiation dosage without increasing the irradiation temperature resulted,
by increasing the intensity of the A band, in a lowering of the development temperature, from which the authors concluded that the
development temperature and the intensity of colloidal coloring
are entirely determined by the intensity of the A band, which belongs to the latent-image centers, i.e., the A centers. In the
opinion of these authors, there are traps of a certain type in the
glass which, after the capture of photoelectrons, change into A centers, the concentration of these traps increasing with temperature.
The intensity of the A band increased rapidly during the first 30
min of irradiation, whereupon a slower increase in the intensity
was noted, which the authors explain by the filling up of all the
traps available at any given temperature, as a result of which, the
further slow growth in the latent-image density occurs through the
filling up of new traps which accidentally appear during the thermal vibration of the structure. The system of the A centers appearing during the irradiation is stable only to a certain temperature, at which, as has been mentioned by these authors, its breakdown begins, as does the capture of the liberating electrons by the
Ag^+ ions. The higher the center concentration, the easier their
system becomes a nonequilibrium one, and the lower is the development temperature of the glass; at temperatures higher than 270°C,
the capture of photoelectrons for a given glass is not possible, as
a result of which, a direct reduction of the Ag^+ ions occurs during
the irradiation process.

The same authors [72] studied the absorption bands arising
at various temperatures in photosensitive glasses upon x-ray irradiation. It was found that only one broad band I with maxima at
355 nm and 300 nm appeared in glasses with photosensitive additions but without Ce. In glasses containing Ce, a rather short-
wave band II which heavily overlapped with band I also appeared.
Band I could easily be produced by heating to 170°C or by the influence of the visible light (optical decolorization). Band II disintegrated upon heating to 300°C; here, a band III with a maximum
at 260 nm for Ag-containing, and at 245 nm for Au-containing,

glasses appeared. Upon heating to higher than 410-470°C, this band also broke down, and an absorption band IV with a maximum at 240-250 nm appeared in all glasses. The sensitivity of glasses to x-ray irradiation did not depend on the Ce content. The intensity of the colloidal coloring of Ag-containing glasses depended heavily on the optical and thermal decolorization of the irradiated glass, and rapidly decreased if the development was preceded by optical decolorization of band I, and only slightly increased after thermal decolorization during slow heating. This behavior was not observed for Au-containing glasses. Based on the experimental data obtained, the authors believe that the centers responsible for absorption band I appear directly during irradiation. Their properties are similar to those of the F-centers although, by nature, they are of the impurity type, since they appear only in the presence of the impurity Ag^+ or Au^+ ions. The bands indigenous to the basic composition of the glass are thereby not produced, i.e., the impurity centers compete with the structural defects. The authors consider the I centers to be the latent-image centers, which is confirmed by the connection between the optical decolorization of the I band and the weakening of the subsequent colloidal coloring in Ag-containing glasses.

By comparing the data obtained in [63, 72, 91], the authors came to the conclusion that ultraviolet and x-rays produce entirely different processes in photosensitive glasses, and that the nature of the latent-image centers in these cases also is different. An opposite deduction for γ-rays was arrived at by Tashiro et al. [92]. Cerium, which tremendously increases the sensitivity to ultraviolet rays, showed no effect on the sensitivity of glasses to x-rays.

Borgman and Chistoserdov [93] described the formation of the latent image due to the filling up of the free traps by photoelectrons during irradiation at high temperatures by the following equation:

$$\frac{dn}{dt} = -anN; \tag{20}$$

the increase in the density of this image with time they described by the equation

$$n_1 = n_0(1 - e^{-aNt}), \tag{21}$$

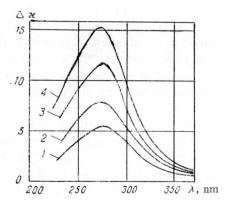

Fig. 21. Relationship between ultraviolet radiation absorption and the exposure temperature of glass. λ) Wavelength; $\Delta\varkappa$) increment to the absorption coefficient per 1 cm of the path in the glass. The curves pertain to the following exposure temperatures, °C: 1) 47; 2) 110; 3) 170; 4) 215.

where N is the free-electron concentration in the glass during irradiation; n_0 is the concentration of free traps prior to irradiation; n is the number of free traps at the irradiation time t; n_1 is the number of filled-up traps in the same time t; and α is the probability of entrapment of the electron.

The authors explain the increase in the photosensitivity of glasses upon heating by the fact that, in the temperature range studied for the latent-image formation the magnitude αN varies only slightly for constant irradiation intensity with increasing temperature, whereas n_0, under the same conditions, is increased by 9-10 orders of magnitude. Linked with the fact that after the cooling of the previously heated and irradiated glass, n_0 and the photosensitivity acquire their initial values, these authors associate the growth in n_0 with increasing temperature with reversible changes in the glass structure. However, the sharp peaks and inflection points on the curves showing the dependence of the formation of the metallic colloidal centers and absorption bands of the latent image on irradiation temperature at the points of polymorphic transformations of silica (120, 165, and 210°C), such as have been observed by Borgman et al. [94], did not increase, but rather decreased the effectiveness of irradiation at this rearrangement of the glass structure.

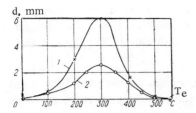

Fig. 22. Depth of penetration of ultraviolet irradiation into glass as a function of the irradiation temperature. d)
Depth of the penetration of crystallization; T_e) irradiation temperature.
Curves 1 and 2 were taken for glasses
of the same type but of different smelt-
ings.

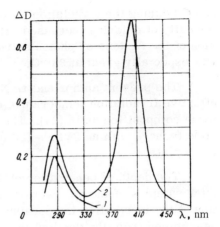

Fig. 23. Change in the optical density of
glasses irradiated at 70 and 400°C for 1 h.
λ) Wavelength; ΔD) change in the optical
density. Curve 1 denotes irradiation at
70°C; curve 2 denotes irradiation at 400°C.

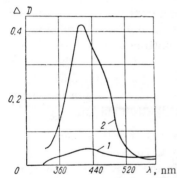

Fig. 24. Determination of the depth of
penetration of ultraviolet light. λ)
Wavelength; ΔD) change in optical
density. Curve 1 denotes irradiation at
70°C; curve 2 denotes irradiation at
400°C.

Yokota [95] observed a ten-
fold increase in the photosensitivity of glass of composition 80
SiO_2, 0.02 CeO_2, 12.5 Li_2O, 0.5
K_2O, 2.5 Al_2O_3, and 0.006 AgCl,
when irradiated at 200°C as compared to the same glass irradiated
at 100°C. Figure 21 shows the increase in the intensity of the 270-
nm absorption band with increasing temperature of a glass sample
irradiated for 60 min. Since this
behavior was observed for glasses
with Ce but without Ag, the author
thinks that, in this case, the photo-
electrons liberated in connection with the ionization of the Ce^{3+}
ions are responsible for the 270-nm absorption band. After heat
treatment of irradiated glasses at 580°C for 40 min, the 410- to 420-
nm colloidal absorption band appeared and the 270-nm band vanished. At a temperature higher than 280°, colloidal coloring ap-

peared during the irradiation process in a spontaneous manner, the intensity of coloring increased with irradiation time, and the diffusion of the Ag ions or photoelectrons associated with the coloring was especially great at 330°C.

The present author and L. N. Il'chenko determined the most effective irradiation temperature of the photosensitive glass of the same composition as in [63]. The irradiation was done in a crucible furnace with an SVDSh-120 lamp through a transparent quartz glass plate.

The depth of penetration of the ultraviolet light into 10-mm-thick samples of the photosensitive glass was measured as a function of the irradiation temperature. The depth of penetration was determined from the depth of the propagation of the crystalline phase which, in this glass, forms following heating at a rate of 3 deg/min to a temperature of 610°C and holding at this temperature for 1 h. The results of the experiments are presented in Fig. 22, where it can be seen that the largest penetration thickness was observed at the irradiation temperature of 300°C. For photosensitive glasses of other compositions, the optimum irradiation temperature may be determined in an analogous fashion. The degree of influence of the high temperatures may also be judged by the height of the colloidal absorption band at 405 nm, which is primarily determined by the number of crystallization nuclei.

Figure 23 shows the change in the ΔD of optical density for the glass irradiated by the PRK-7 lamp at 70 and 400°C for 1 h. The intensity of the latent image lying in the ultraviolet spectral region is 1.5 times greater for glass irradiated at 400°C than for glass irradiated at 70°C. Furthermore, a colloidal absorption band was observed having a height, based on our experimental data, corresponding to a 20-h irradiation at a temperature of 70°C and development at 500°C. Thus, we determined that as a result of the irradiation of photosensitive glasses at 400°C, the exposure time necessary for the formation of the latent image is decreased by 20-30 times as compared to irradiation at room temperature.

The depth of penetration of the ultraviolet light, determined from the depth of crystallization after irradiation for 1 h, was 0.3-0.5 mm when irradiated at 60°C, and more than 2.5 mm when irradiated at 400°C. For illustration purposes, the following example may be cited. Two 2.5-mm-thick plates of photosensitive glass

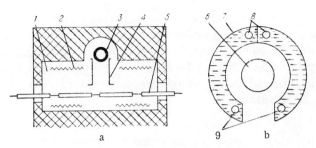

Fig. 25. Schematic of the continuous-operation conveyer setup for the irradiation of glass at elevated temperatures. a) Continuous furnace; b) ultraviolet light source.

were irradiated by the PRK-7 lamp for 1 h at temperatures of 70 and 400°C, respectively. The plates were subsequently polished to a thickness of 0.4 mm and were subjected to heat treatment at 500°C for 7 h. The dependencies of the optical density of these plates on the wavelength were found to be as shown in Fig. 24, which indicates the effectiveness of irradiating photosensitive glasses at elevated temperatures.

Based on the experimental investigations performed, Berezhnoi et al. [96] proposed an experimental arrangement for the irradiation of photosensitive glasses by ultraviolet rays at elevated temperatures, by which it would be possible to mechanize and automatize what are among the most labor-consuming processes in the fabrication of articles of photosensitive glasses and glass-ceramics — namely, the primary and secondary irradiation processes — and thus to sharply increase productivity.

Figure 25a shows the principal schematic for the proposed furnace, and Fig. 25b shows the setup with the ultraviolet source. The furnace consists of a tunnel 1, in which the required temperature is provided by the heating elements 2, and which contains the source of the ultraviolet light 3, a screen 4, and a conveyer 5. A temperature of approximately 300°C is maintained in the furnace, which means that the lamp 6, which emits the ultraviolet light, must be cooled. This is done by cooling the jacket 7, which is equipped with incoming tubes 8 and outgoing tubes 9, by continuously flowing water. The jacket 7 has such a configuration as to direct only those rays which are perpendicular to its surface onto the glass, making it possible to avoid scattering of the ultraviolet light, which could lead to the formation of oblique faces in the manufactured articles.

The zone of irradiation by the ultraviolet rays is located directly under the lamp. In order for reflected or oblique rays not to strike objects located outside the irradiation zone, the latter is bounded by screens 4, which form a well, ensuring that the irradiation is uniform and that the rays are perpendicular to the plane of the irradiated glass.

The rate of motion of the conveyer belt is determined by the time that the glass spends in the irradiation zone, which ranges from 1 to 5 min, depending on its composition, sensitivity, etc.

This experimental setup is applicable both for the primary and the secondary irradiation of photosensitive glasses. However, for primary irradiation, negatives on fused silica are used, which is transparent to ultraviolet rays and capable of withstanding temperatures up to 350°C; frames are provided to facilitate close contact between the negative and the photosensitive glass at 300–350°C.

Chapter II

The Formation of Nuclei and the Crystallization of Glass

The development of a new area of glass technology, the production of glass-crystalline materials, became possible because of the discovery of the catalytic crystallization method, the essence of which is that the growth of crystals starts simultaneously from a large number of nuclei which are uniformly distributed in the preshaped glass article.

If the formation of nuclei of the new phase of the material proceeds within a different phase of the same material — such as during the condensation of liquid drops in water vapor or during the emergence of crystals in the melt — in the absence of or without the help of foreign particles, then Stookey [119] calls this "homogeneous" crystallization, to distinguish it from "heterogeneous" crystallization — also called catalyzed crystallization — which occurs when the nuclei of the new phase are formed on surfaces having a different chemical composition than this new phase.

In contrast to the term "catalyst" commonly used in chemistry, by which is understood a substance which speeds up a reaction but does not enter into the reaction products, the term "crystallization catalyst" is an arbitrary term, by which we understand a substance capable of influencing not only the rate of the phase transformation, but also, for instance, the succession of the precipitation of the crystalline phases, i.e., a substance capable of changing the course of this transformation. By employing the term "catalyst," one emphasizes that heterogeneous formation of nuclei takes place. The terms "agent for the formation of nuclei," "agent of crystallization," and "crystallization catalyst" are synonymous.

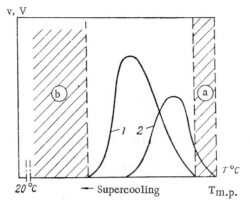

Fig. 26. Schematic for the crystallization of a viscous
liquid. T) Heating temperature; v) rate of formation of
the nuclei; V) rate of crystal growth. Curve 1 represents
the rate of formation of nuclei; curve 2 represents the
rate of growth of crystals. a) Metastable supercooling
zone; b) metastable zone of high viscosity.

Stookey [97] classifies catalyzed crystallization in glass into
(1) crystallization of the "dissolved substance," where crystallization of small amounts of the catalyst dissolved in the glass does
not produce a significant change in the glass structure, and (2)
"crystallization of the solution," during which the very structure
of glass changes, since the process includes ions entering into the
structural network of glass. According to Stookey, ruby, opaline, and
some photosensitive glasses belong to the former type of crystallization, whereas glass-crystalline materials belong to the latter
type.

1. HOMOGENEOUS, OR SPONTANEOUS, CRYSTALLIZATION

Stookey [98] presents a survey of works dealing with the formation of nuclei in various systems. Ostwald [99] (see also [98])
showed that spontaneous crystallization may occur only in highly
supersaturated solutions and cannot take place in the metastable
supersaturation zone. Experimental investigations by Tamman
[100] (also see [98]) on the crystallization of supercooled liquids
and inorganic glasses determined the existence of two metastable
regions. In one of these regions, located below the melting point

(zone a in Fig. 26), the nuclei are not formed at any measurable rate; however, the crystals, if they have been formed at all, are capable of growing. The second metastable region (zone b) is in the low-temperature region and is characterized by a low rate of formation of nuclei, since the high viscosity of glass here inhibits spontaneous crystallization and the growth of crystals. The existence of the first metastable region in later investigations [98, 101] is explained by the significantly lower melting points of the finest nuclei than of macroscopic crystals.

Theoretical investigations of the process of nucleus formation based on thermodynamic equilibrium were started by Gibbs [102] (also see [98]), who states that the growth of the new phase B at the expense of the initial phase A is possible if these phases are in nonequilibrium with respect to each other, i.e., if phase A is in a metastable equilibrium with phase B, and that the nuclei of phase B are in the form of very small particles of phase B, distinguished by a large surface and by large surface energy and surface tension. For a droplet not extremely small, the total free surface energy is equal to $S\sigma$, or $4\pi r^2\sigma$, where σ is the surface tension, r is the radius of the droplet, and S is the surface area.

By making use of the thermodynamic equilibrium principle, Gibbs [102] (also see [98]) deduced the amount of work W required for the formation of critical-size nuclei of phase B:

$$W = \frac{1}{3}\sigma S_c = \frac{4}{3}\pi r_c^2. \tag{22}$$

For the smallest stable nuclei capable of spontaneous growth,

$$p'' - p' = \frac{2\sigma}{r_c}$$

and

$$W = \frac{16}{3}\frac{\pi\sigma^3}{(p''-p')^2}, \tag{23}$$

where σ is the surface tension; p'' and p' are the vapor pressures inside the droplet and in the matrix solution, respectively; and r_c and S_c are the radius and the surface area, respectively, of the droplet of critical size, i.e., of the stable nucleus.

Mathematical relationships for the spontaneous formation of nuclei by the condensation of the supersaturated vapor are given by Thompson [103]. Other investigators [104-106] obtained the following expression for the rate of homogeneous crystallization by making use of the kinetic theory of gases and the concept of thermal fluctuations:

$$J = Ae^{-\Delta F^*/kT}, \tag{24}$$

where J is the rate of formation of the nuclei (the number of nuclei formed in 1 sec in 1 cm^3); A is a constant; and ΔF^* is the maximum free activation energy of the formation of these nuclei.

The rate of nucleus formation is dependent on the rate of diffusion of the atoms or molecules across the interphase boundary if one or both phases are in the form of a viscous liquid or a solid. Becker [107] gave the following general equation for the rate of formation of nuclei of homogeneous crystallization in condensed systems of the type liquid—liquid, solid—liquid, or liquid—solid:

$$J = A \exp\left[-(\Delta F^* + q)kT\right], \tag{25}$$

where q is the free activation energy for the diffusion of molecules across the interphase boundary.

According to Kuznetsov [108], the spontaneous formation of nuclei in the supercooled liquid may be explained on the basis of the molecular-kinetic theory of matter. The molecules, which are in continuous thermal motion have, at the given temperature, completely determined kinetic and potential energies, which diminish with decreasing temperature. The molecules of the liquid, which, in comparison with the molecules of the crystal, have larger reserves of kinetic energy, are not capable of forming stable crystallization nuclei, since, due to thermal motion, any accidental clustering of them will rapidly break up. However, with decreasing temperature and, consequently, with decreasing kinetic energy of the molecules, the clusters formed by them become more stable. Therefore, the appearance of nuclei is possible at a certain given temperature. If the nucleus has very small dimensions, i.e., when a considerable number of its molecules lie at the surface, then it is unstable and may again disappear, since the stored potential energy is greater for the surface-layer molecules than for the inner molecules. When the nucleus attains a certain given size at which the number of surface molecules is small in comparison with the number of internal molecules, it is not annihilated, but grows at the expense of the molecules of the supercooled liquid.

For spontaneous crystallization to take place in the solution, not only is the formation of local clusters of molecules of the dissolved substance or the fluctuation in density necessary, but so is the presence of an arrangement of the molecules corresponding to their arrangement in the crystalline lattice. The investigations discussed above proved that there are individual clusters of molecules in the melt or the solution with spatial arrangements identical to their arrangements in the crystals.

An atomistic treatment of the process of nucleus formation in a homogeneous melt, and of the energy barrier which makes possible the glass formation, was given by Weyl [109, 111, 112], and Weyl and Marboe [110]. The formation of the nuclei necessitates the overcoming of a high energy barrier. This is why high-melting materials tend more toward crystallization than toward glass formation. The formation of nuclei from a liquid may be represented as a process which is the reverse of melting. It is known that melting is the result of the accummulation of defects in solids at increased temperature. This is why Weyl and Marboe [113, 114] associate the rate of nucleus formation of supercooled liquids with defects or with asymmetrical groupings. The presence of asymmetry produces disproportionation of the bonding forces and decreases the energy barrier for the formation of the nuclei. This is visually confirmed by the fact that crystallization more often than not starts from the surface of the glass body. Materials which exhibit insignificant disproportionation of their bonding forces, such as quartz or albite, are difficult to crystallize from their melts.

The growth rate of nuclei depends on the concentration of the precipitating molecules, on the temperature, and on the catalysts present. The catalysts, even when present in low quantities, decrease the energy barrier for the formation of the nuclei.

A number of anomalies which arise when trying to interpret some kinetic phenomena of solids (diffusion, viscosity, melting, nucleation) only on the basis of the concept of the cation—anion bonding force are explained by Weyl on the basis of the concept of screening, which takes into consideration not only the ionic field force introduced by Dietzel [115], but also the polarizability of the ion and the fact that it is needed for screening. The ions with higher polarizability have a greater capability for screening.

The energy barrier for the formation of nuclei includes the temporarily partly unshielded state of the cations. The energy necessary for the creation of this state and the thermal energy kT present up to the melting point of the material under consideration determine its capability to form nuclei or for glass formation. Materials with a higher cation coordination, such as that of Na^+ ion in NaF, and Ti^{4+}, Sn^{4+}, and Zr^{4+} ions in TiO_2, SnO_2, and ZrO_2 more easily allow the time change of the coordination number, i.e., the temporarily unshielded state of the cations, and therefore can easily be crystallized. For atoms with a high charge and a low coordination number, i.e., in the case of low anion/cation ratio, the partly unshielded state of the cations needs a high energy. An increase in the anion/cation ratio shows up favorably in the crystallization. The substitution of one O^{2-} ion by two F^- ions or by two OH^- ions is a well-known method for decreasing viscosity and for speeding up the formation of the nuclei. To this group of phenomena also belongs the catalyzed crystallization of glassy quartz when small amounts (up to 5%) of Na_2O are added to it.

The demand for coordination and the high charge of the Si^{4+} ions in quartz make the formation of vacancies in it very difficult or impossible. The absence of long-range order in glass does not permit the additions to play the role of "foreign atoms." Therefore, the effect on the formation of nuclei of some disproportionation of the bonds in a glass caused by the presence of foreign atoms is minimal.

According to Kleber [744], the formation of nuclei is a kinetic process, and depends on two basic factors: (1) on the work proper of nucleus formation, which he determines as the energy consumed for nucleus formation under the condition that all the structural elements of which the nucleus consists are already in position at the point of its emergence, and (2) the activation energy which must be expended in order to move the structural elements to the point of emergence of the nucleus. The work proper for nucleus formation depends on the difference between the energy expended to overcome the surface tension forces at the interphase boundary during the emergence of the new surface of the nucleus and the energy which is expended during the glass—crystal transformation. If the structural elements of the nucleus are already at the point of its emergence — which, for instance, is the case when insignificant amounts of Au, Ag, or Cu are distributed uniformly throughout the bulk of the glass and are enriched by droplike microphases which, according to the data of Vogel [745] form in photosensitive glass as a result of microsegregation — then the work of formation of the nucleus becomes very small. Furthermore, homogeneous formation of these nuclei becomes considerably easier if the microportions of the segregations which precipitate throughout the bulk of the material have the same stoichiometric composition with respect to the nucleus and the same magnitude. The formation of the nucleus and the crystallization inside the droplike microphases which have precipitated as a result of the microsegregation proceed considerably easier than in the amorphous region, which differs considerably in composition from the nucleus.

An interpretation of homogeneous crystallization from the point of view of statistical-thermodynamic theory was given by Hillig [116], who thinks that a glass-forming system is more or less capable of homogeneous precipitation of the nuclei, and that heterogeneous catalysis with the aid of nuclei is not very important in obtaining the uniform crystallization of glass.

An analogous statistical-thermodynamic approach to explain the formation of crystalline nuclei during the spontaneous crystallization of glasses was developed by Filipovich [117, 735], who describes the rate of formation of these nuclei by the following formula, which results from the general theory for statistical fluctuations and holds true for the various phase transformations:

$$I = N^* N_1^* = \left(\tilde{N} e^{-\frac{\Delta\Phi^*}{kT}} \right) \left(A e^{-\frac{\Delta\Phi_A^*}{kT}} \right), \qquad (26)$$

where I is the number of growing nuclei of critical size arising in a unit volume per unit time at temperature T; $N^* = N \exp(-\Delta\Phi_A^*/kT)$ is the average number of nuclei of critical size which are formed and which are resorbed in the unit volume; $N_1^* = A \exp(-\Delta\Phi_A^*/kT)$ is the rate of growth of a clump of critical size; N is a factor proportional to the number of spots where the nuclei appear; A is a factor determined by the activation mechanism for nucleus growth; $\Delta\Phi^*$ is the barrier, or the gain in the thermodynamic potential of the system during the emergence of a critical-size nucleus of a new phase; and $\Delta\Phi_A^*$ is the barrier of the thermodynamic potential, which is overcome during the transfer of this nucleus to a state of further growth.

The author associates the emergence of nuclei of spontaneous crystallization in complex glasses with the diffusion and chemical differentiation of atoms and structural groups which form clusters in regions whose composition is similar to that of the precipitating crystals. Two mechanisms are possible for the crystallization of multicomponent glasses: a mechanism including precrystallization metastable immiscibility, and a mechanism without it. In the first case, metastable glass-forming microregions with the composition of the future crystals are formed during the segregation process thanks to the formation of amorphous nuclei of critical size. These regions then rapidly become ordered and crystallize. In the second case, the microregions with the composition of the future crystals, which emerge in a fluctuating manner thanks to the increase in the thermodynamic potential, are not stable and may become resorbed unless their ordering takes place. The formation of these regions proceeds simultaneously with their crystallization. Equation (26) describes the probable results of these two complex cooperative processes. The initial, or nucleation, stages of crystallization have an important significance for the sitallization* of glass. The number of nuclei which form uniformly throughout the glass during its low-temperature treatment, which determines the number of future microcrystals, must be rather large, of the order of 10^{12} cm^{-3} or more. At relatively low temperatures, those phases — including the metastable phases — nucleate first for which the $\Delta\Phi^* + \Delta\Phi_A^*$ barrier is the smallest, and kinetically precipitate from the glass with the least difficulty [118].

As a rule, practical glasses do not crystallize during cooling. The absence of crystallization in a supercooled glass may be explained either by a small rate of formation of the nuclei or by the small rate of growth of crystals at all temperatures.

According to Stookey [119], the crystallization of glasses is inhibited primarily by an excessively low rate of nucleus formation,

---

* Also known as "ceramming" in the USA.

in the absence of which, the growth of crystals may neither begin
nor proceed. Stookey [119] explains the absence of centers of
homogeneous crystallization in glasses not containing catalysts in
the following manner. In Eq. (25), the rate J of nucleus formation
will be significantly greater than zero only in the case when
$(\Delta F^* + q) < 1$. In conformity with the laws of thermodynamics,
nuclei cannot be in equilibrium at a temperature higher than the
melting point, while the free energy ΔF^* of activation for the formation of these nuclei is infinitely large. At a temperature lower
than the melting point, this energy decreases with decreasing temperature. The free energy q of activation for diffusion and the viscosity in glass are relatively high even at high temperatures and
increase with decreasing temperature. From this it follows, according to Stookey [119], that J will be equal to zero, and the
spontaneous crystallization will not begin, if the sum of the free
energies of activation of the processes for nucleus formation and
for the diffusion of the crystallizing particles into the glass tends
toward infinity, which, for all practical purposes, is the case for a
majority of practical glasses. In opaline, ruby, and photosensitive
glasses, which contain small quantities of the dissolved supersaturated phase and which are marked by a low $(\Delta F^* + q)$ value at
some temperature, the curve for the temperature dependence of
the rate of formation of the nuclei of homogeneous crystallization
will be similar to the curve in Fig. 26. At the liquidus temperature, J = 0, since $\Delta F = \infty$, whereas, at low temperatures, J approaches zero due to the high viscosity of glass and to the large
value for the free activation energy q of diffusion. Consequently,
J will attain a maximum at a certain intermediate temperature [119].

2. HETEROGENEOUS, OR CATALYZED, CRYSTALLIZATION

In investigations of the heterogeneous formation of nuclei in
water and in supercooled metals [120-122], the important role of
the metastable zone was confirmed, and the necessity was under-
lined for the catalyst to be wetted by the crystallizing phase, and
also for the structures and interatomic distances of the two to be
similar. The greater the difference in the structures, the higher
is the degree of supercooling necessary for the formation of nuclei. Mechanical agitation, vibration, and the presence of positively or negatively charged ions have a significant effect on this
process.

Turnbull [122] obtained the following equation for the rate of formation of nuclei in condensed systems, based on (24) and (25):

$$J_c = A' \exp \{ - [\Delta F^* f(\theta) + q] \, kT \}, \tag{27}$$

where J_C is the rate of formation of the nuclei on the surface of the catalyst; ΔF^* is the maximum free energy of formation of these nuclei; θ is the contact angle between the liquid and the solid surface of the catalyst; q is the free activation energy of diffusion; and $f(\theta)$ is the decrease in the surface energy as a result of the wetting.

Stookey [119] shows that ΔF^* is exceptionally small at the melting temperature of the crystalline phase, that it decreases with increasing degree of supercooling or supersaturation, and that it also depends on the degree of matching of the crystalline structures of the catalyst and the crystallizing phase. In the presence of an effective catalyst, ΔF^* is much lower in comparison with the free energy of formation for the nuclei of homogeneous crystallization, and this is why the rate of nucleation is many times larger in the presence of a catalyst than in its absence [119].

It turned out that glass may be stimulated toward crystallization by introducing catalyzing particles and by subsequent heat treatment, which is necessary for the formation of nuclei to start as well as for the growth of crystals.

Catalyzed crystallization of glass, which ensures that a uniform fine-crystalline product is obtained, consists in the introduction of submicroscopic particles of the catalyst, which are capable of high dispersion at a lower temperature than the temperature region of the rapid growth of crystals of the basic crystallizing phase. The fused glass with the dissolved catalyst is cooled until the catalyst no longer forms nuclei uniformly distributed in the glass, or no longer precipitates spontaneously throughout the bulk of the glass in the form of submicroscopic particles. The glass is then again heated to the appropriate temperature for a time sufficient for the formation of the nuclei of heterogeneous crystallization (curves 1 and 2 in Fig. 27) and for the growth of crystals from the basic glass components with the aid of the catalyst particles (curve 3 in Fig. 27).

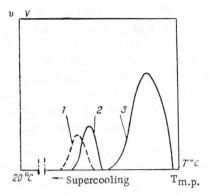

Fig. 27. Schematic of the crystallization of glass for the preparation of glass-ceramics. T) Temperature of heating; v) rate of formation of nuclei; V) rate of crystal growth. Curve 1) Rate of formation of nuclei; curve 2) rate of growth of the nucleating crystals; curve 3) rate of growth of crystals from nuclei.

Stookey [119, 123] established the following criteria for the selection of effective catalysts:

1. Ready solubility of the catalyst in the glass at the melting and heat-treatment temperatures, and limited solubility in the glass at low temperatures.

2. Low free energy of activation for homogeneous nucleation from the melt at low temperatures, which is made possible by the low interfacial energy between the dissolved and the crystalline phases, and by the high degree of supersaturation during cooling.

3. A higher diffusion rate at low temperatures as compared with the major glass components, i.e., a relatively low free activation energy for the diffusion process [see Eq. (27)].

4. A low interfacial energy at the boundary between the glass and the catalyst crystal for effective wetting [see Eq. (27)].

5. Closeness in the crystal structure and lattice parameters for the catalyst crystal and the precipitating crystalline phase. The allowable deviation should not exceed 15%.

In contrast with this, Weyl [109] thinks that the rate of nucle-us formation depends, to a large degree, on the distribution of the chemical bonds inside the system, and that the structural factors — in particular, similar crystal structures between the catalyst and the crystallizing phase — are inadequate to produce this process by themselves. For instance, despite the similar structures of cristo-balite and silica glass, the transition of glass into cristobalite pro-ceeds very slowly and necessitates a catalyst.

On the other hand, in spite of the fact that solid NaCl is dis-tinguished by a significantly high melting point compared to fused NaCl (which has better viscosity), the formation of nuclei and crys-tallization during cooling of the melt proceed very fast, which is not the case in glassy NaCl [109].

According to Weyl [109], the nucleation of the crystalline phase and the oriented growth of crystals with similar lattice pa-rameters (epitaxial growth) are entirely different phenomena. By recognizing the large effect of external and internal interphase sur-faces on the formation of nuclei in glass, the author at the same time thinks that this process, in contrast to epitaxial growth, does not need any preferred lattice parameter, and that the function of the colloidal particles of gold and platinum as catalysts of this pro-cess certainly are not based on epitaxy. Synthetic formation in glasses of a large number of ultramicroscopic Au, Ag, Cu, Pt, or TiO_2 particles produces interphase surfaces, intensifying the crys-tallization of the compounds, the components of which predominate in glass. Weyl explains the formation of nuclei from noble metals in glass by the fact that, in the metallic state, the electrons are most effectively used for the screening of positively charged nu-clei. Metallicity is the property of the indefinitely extending three-dimensional network of the atoms, in which some electrons may play the role of the "degenerate electron gas." For very small col-loidal particles of the metal, these conditions are not fulfilled, which leads to some loss in metallicity. However, the metallicity may also be increased by the proper screening of small colloidal particles. For instance, when colloidal Pt, Au, Ag, and Cu interact with a fused glass body, containing tetrahedra with different de-grees of screening, they will interact preferentially with those tet-rahedra which contain the largest number of polarizable ions and which are the most screened, i.e., with tetrahedra containing the largest number of nonbridging O^{2-} ions. The preferential adsorp-

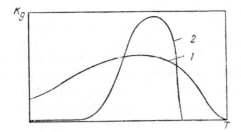

Fig. 28. Typical temperature dependencies of the growth rate of crystals. T) Heating temperature; K_g) growth rate of the crystals. Curve 1) Gently sloping maximum; curve 2) sharp maximum.

tion of these structural units by the particles of the colloidal Pt or Au, Ag, and Cu forms a phase which has a higher basicity, a higher degree of screening, and a higher polarizability than the basic substance. Such a division of the system into larger elements of greater and lesser basicity intensifies the formation of nuclei and the crystallization during phase segregation. Bulk metal, such as a platinum crucible, cannot produce such a division of glass into more-basic and more-acidic elements, because the surface atoms of the bulk metal may attract electrons from the inner layers, thereby increasing their electronic density and decreasing the degree of descreening.

Thus, the need for the screening of colloidal particles of the noble metal leads to the preferential adsorption of more polarizable and more basic structural units of the glass, and this division stimulates the formation of nuclei.

In examining the tendency of glasses to heterogeneous crystallization, Meyer [124] (in contrast to Stookey) ascribes a greater significance to the temperature dependence of the growth rate of crystals K_g than to that of the rate of nucleus formation K_V on the basis of the fact that glass with a high K_V rate is still capable of being worked well if its K_g rate is sufficiently small. While attempts are being made to find such compositions in the processing of glass for which both K_V and K_g have as low a value as possible, the goal in the processing of glass-ceramics is, according to Meyer [124], for crystallization to be characterized by some optimum value.

On the one hand, K_g must be sufficiently small within the temperature region for the manufacture of glass articles so that this process is not inhibited by the blowing, pressing, drawing, and casting methods. On the other hand, K_g must be sufficiently large within the temperature region of crystallization so as to effect a relatively rapid completion of crystallization. During the manufacture of glass, K_v must, for all practical purposes, be equal to zero, while within the region of the transformation temperature, it should attain a maximum value.

Both the absolute height of the maximum of the K_g—T curve and the shape of the curve have a significance. Meyer [124] considers glasses with sloping K_g curves, the maximum of which ranges from 10 to 25 μ/min (Fig. 28, curve 1), to be the most favorable for the preparation of glass-ceramics. Glasses with such curves will already crystallize at a marked rate of devitrification below the softening temperature. In glasses with a sharp maximum of K_g (see Fig. 28, curve 2), the crystallization proceeds in a heavily softened state, which makes these glasses unsuitable for the sitallization of preshaped glass products. Of special significance for sitallization is the value for the crystallization rate directly above the softening point, i.e., approximately in the region of viscosity values of 10^{12}-10^{13} poise. A direct measurement of this rate is difficult here, and to calculate its value for any given melt one must know the shape of the viscosity—temperature curve [124].

3. TWO-PHASE SEPARATION AND CATALYZED CRYSTALLIZATION OF GLASS DURING THE PREPARATION OF GLASS-CERAMICS

Until recently, the prevalent point of view concerning the mechanism of heterogeneous crystallization during the preparation of a glass-ceramic of uniform, fine-crystalline structure was that the formation of such a structure occurs in two stages: the catalysts previously dissolved in the melt segregate out depending on the cooling of the glass, thereby forming nuclei which, after reaching the critical size, cause the crystallization from the glass of the second crystalline phase during the subsequent heat-treatment process [125].

A second mechanism was then proposed, according to which the necessary prerequisite for the formation of nuclei in the processing of glass-ceramics is separation into two phases, or immiscibility, in the liquid—liquid system [119, 126]. During the cooling of the glass melt or during the heating of the previously cooled glass containing TiO_2, the segregation of the fine-crystalline TiO_2 or titanate proceeds first, and during further heat treatment, catalyzes the crystallization of the fundamental glass body. Stookey [127] explains the mechanism for the influence of such crystallization agents as TiO_2 in terms of the tendency of glass or glass melt toward segregation into two glassy or liquid phases. He thinks that the segregation of the immiscible phase proceeds homogeneously, in view of the fact that the free energy at the interphase boundaries of the two phases is small and proportional to the cube of the surface energy at these boundaries. The segregated globules then crystallize either homogeneously or heterogeneously. These globules can indeed either act or not act as nuclei or catalysts for the subsequent crystallization of the transparent glassy phase.

Vogel [745] also thinks that the transformation of glass into glass-ceramic proceeds as a result of not purely homogeneous, but homogeneous—heterogeneous formation of nuclei. During heat treatment of the sitallizing glass of the $SiO_2-TiO_2-Li_2O-MgO-ZnO$ system, relatively large phase-separation regions first appear. Depending on the time of heat treatment and the tendency of the system to a higher degree of ordering, secondary phase separation occurs with the formation of very small TiO_2-enriched drop-like regions and with the segregation of the TiO_2 nuclei, which results in spontaneous crystallization in larger-size drops due to the oriented or epitaxial segregation of the material on these nuclei. In time, the crystallization process goes beyond the boundaries of the drops and, as shown by electron microscopy, continues until the growth fronts of the crystalline spherulites no longer collide with each other; this in turn prevents their further growth and, moreover, results in a microcrystalline structure. In the meantime, in photosensitive glass of lithium disilicate (32.5 mol.% Li_2O, 67.5 mol.% SiO_2) composition with additions of 0.001 mol.% Au_2O and 0.01 mol.% CeO_2, coarse $Li_2O \cdot 2SiO_2$ spherulites were observed to grow without interruption after irradiation and heat treatment, since their growth in this glass — which has a low crystallization capability and is not good for obtaining a fine-grained image —

was not prevented by the sharp change in composition which usually takes place on the phase boundaries of immiscible regions, nor by the approaching growth fronts of other spherulites, which limits the size of the crystals.

According to Weyl [128], the formation of nuclei in a glass which does not contain highly polarizable cations is made possible by separation in the liquid phase, which is characterized by a lower energy barrier and by a decreased surface energy at the boundary between two liquids when compared to the interphase surfaces between the liquid and the crystal or between two crystalline phases.

By examining the phase diagram of the system in question, one may foresee the separation into two phases, one can foretell the precipitation in glass of other primary phases different from TiO_2 and capable of catalyzing the crystallization of the fundamental glass body, and one may also select the composition of a suitable catalyst [129-132]. For the preparation of glass-ceramics, those systems are also of significance in which the segregated region is in the liquid phase; among these is the latent segregated region situated below the liquidus temperature.

Roy [126] shows that the fundamental requirement of the glass composition for glass-ceramics is that it be located close to the region of immiscibility of the two liquid phases on the phase diagram, or that there be present abnormal sloping (e.g., an S-shape) in the liquidus curves. The latter criterion also indicates the tendency toward phase separation, although to a somewhat lesser degree. In regions immediately adjacent to the region of separation into two liquid phases the liquid has a rather specific structure which consists of submicro-heterogeneous groupings 10 to 100 Å in size of one type of glass rich in SiO_2 and included in or mixed with the glass matrix rich in network-modifying cations. Depending on how far it is from stable coexistence of the two immiscible liquids, the structure of the liquid becomes normalized and the glass becomes uniform. Figure 29 shows the possible transformations occurring in glasses with such a fine heterogeneous structure during their subsolidus crystallization during the cooling process. Outwardly transparent glass may be obtained by cooling the liquid. Depending on the composition, this glass may alter its structure at room temperature, or during the quench-

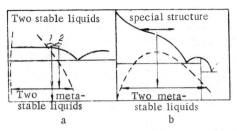

Fig. 29. Regions of possible subsolidus metastable immiscibility.

ing process by expanding the region of decreased viscosity. Figures 29a and 29b show the position of the region of metastable immiscibility below the liquidus temperature. Figure 29a also shows the region of the stable coexistence of two liquids above the liquidus temperature. The melt of composition 1 undergoes spontaneous phase separation during the cooling process and forms a porcelain-like structure during crystallization. In order to obtain an analogous effect in a glass of composition 2, which is farther removed from the region of stable immiscibility, additional heat treatment of the previously cooled glass is needed.

The ease with which nuclei form in the presence of immiscibility regions or of abnormally sloping liquidus curves may be caused by the facilitation of the diffusion process when the composition of the liquid phase is close to the composition of the crystallizing phase, or by the decrease in the free energy surface between the segregating phase and the melt. Surface-active substances at the solid—liquid interphase boundary lower the surface energy and thereby decrease the work of nucleus formation [126]. Since TiO_2 displays immiscibility in silicate systems, it may possess surface-active properties.

An explanation based on crystal-chemistry concepts of the immiscibility of systems with an open region of phase separation (shown on the phase diagram by the well-known bell-shaped curve) was given by Warren and Pincus [133]. Total miscibility is determined by the fact that the network-forming cations in the melt — namely, the glass-forming Si^{4+}, B^{3+}, and P^{5+} — strive to become bonded by strong ionic chemical bonds to all the closest oxygen ions. By the introduction of network-modifying cations, a redistribution of the oxygen ions may occur. The stronger the modifier—oxygen bond, the greater is the probability of forming self-sustained cation—oxygen regions of a given chemical composition with decreased glass-forming cation content, i.e., the greater is the tendency toward immiscibility. When the modifier—oxygen bond has a low energy, there is no differentiation of the melt into one region enriched with modifying cations and another with glass-forming cations, and the melt remains homogeneous.

Dietzel [115] showed that the tendency of the melt to form two immiscible liquids is determined by the magnitude of the electrostatic force field of the cation, z/r^2 (where z is the valency of the cation and r is its ionic radius in Å), or z/a^2 (where $a = r_a + r_k$). By increasing this ratio, the modifier cation becomes more completely surrounded by nonsaturated oxygen ions, which results in the segregation of the melt into two liquid phases. By making use of these quantitative characteristics, one can calculate the limiting composition regions of immiscibility; for the $CaO-SiO_2$ system, this results in a relatively good agreement with experimental data.

Inasmuch as the surface energy on the interphase boundaries between two liquids is significantly less than on the interphase boundaries between the glassy and the crystalline phases, segregation into two liquid or glassy phases occurs significantly easier than the formation of nuclei from the glassy phase. After phase separation, the formation of nuclei is possible at the given temperature, without considerable expenditure of diffusion work, such as is needed for the glass melt of the same composition but of a single homogeneous phase [134]. The extent of separation into two liquids depends on the differences in their densities and temperatures, among other factors.

Hinz and Kunth [134] show that it is necessary that glass-forming properties not be present in one of the segregating phases, and that the amount of the latter, moreover, must be insignificant in comparison with the amount of the glass-forming phase, so that the segregation process may be controlled and a large amount of uniformly distributed nuclei are produced. Massive formation of these nuclei only starts during rapid cooling, and it develops fully after heat treatment of this glass — which outwardly differs only slightly from the nonsegregating glass — at a temperature below the liquidus temperature. The precipitation of the first crystallites of colloidal size during the segregation process proceeds as the result of homogeneous formation of nuclei. The existence of segregated regions below the liquidus temperature may be assumed not only on the basis of the S-shaped liquidus curve for the binary systems, but also from the characteristic shape of these regions on the ternary phase diagrams. For instance, the latent segregation region, marked on the $BaO—SiO_2$ phase diagram by the sharply defined S-shaped curve at the SiO_2 side, and the open segregation region in the $BaO—B_2O_3$ system are significantly broadened in the ternary $BaO—B_2O_3—SiO_2$ phase diagram [135].

Latent segregation, even though developed only in the supercooled metastable state, may result in the same effect as open segregation, i.e., in the formation of two supercooled liquids having different tendencies toward crystallization. Glass-ceramics having a fine-crystalline structure may be prepared if one of these phases has an improved crystallization capability.

In the opinion of Hinz and Kunth [134], the segregation phenomenon is not common nor imperative for all glasses, but takes place only in special glasses, the tendency of which toward immiscibility may be foreseen by studying the corresponding phase diagrams with the aid of the above-mentioned criteria. The necessary conditions for the production of glass-ceramics containing TiO_2 or other catalysts are: (1) the presence of overt or latent segregation regions on the phase diagrams of the respective systems; the composition of the mixture selected must lie in these regions or near them; (2) increased tendency toward crystallization of one of the segregating phases, and the capability toward glass-formation of the other phase.

As examples of overt and latent segregation, Hinz and Kunth [134] list first systems containing TiO_2. The $TiO_2—SiO_2$ system has a very wide segregation region, from 10 to 93% SiO_2 [136]. The oxides MgO, CaO, SrO, FeO, MnO, and ZnO form with SiO_2 systems which segregate into two liquid phases [137]. In systems with the alkali oxides K_2O, Na_2O, and Li_2O, at the side enriched with SiO_2, an S-shaped tendency in the liquidus curves, i.e., a latent segregation region, is observed [134]. Furthermore, the $Li_2O—SiO_2$ system must possess an apparent segregation region in the range 92-99% SiO_2 [138]. By introducing into the $TiO_2—SiO_2$ system a third oxide, such as CaO or MgO, which shows an apparent or a latent segregation region on the phase diagram with SiO_2, phase separation extends over the entire ternary system [134, 139, 140].

Vitroceram with a fine-crystalline structure was prepared by Hinz and Kunth [134, 141] from lithium-containing glasses with an addition of 3-4% TiO_2 as the crystallization catalyst. It is known that compositions containing Li_2O, together with CaO, ZnO, BaO, or Na_2O with TiO_2, form finely dispersed segregation regions, a fact which is made use of in the production of white enamels [134, 142].

An effect analogous to that of TiO_2 is produced by ZrO_2; a segregation region forms in the ZrO_2-SiO_2 system [143]. According to the Geller and Lang [144] data this system does not have immiscible regions; however, from the extended liquidus field, one may assume the presence of a latent segregation region.

The Cr_2O_3 in the $Cr_2O_3-SiO_2$, $CaO-Cr_2O_3-SiO_2$, and $MgO-Cr_2O_3-SiO_2$ systems causes large segregation regions [145, 146], which fact is utilized in the production of glass-ceramics from copper-containing slags containing less than 1% Cr_2O_3 for the catalyst [134, 736].

The presence of large segregation regions in the $FeO-FeS-SiO_2$ system [147] is explained by Hinz and Kunth [134] as being the reason for the successful application of the sulfides of heavy metals in the preparation of glass-ceramics from metallurgical slags and from mineral mixtures of the albite—anorthite—diopside system [44, 53, 148-153]. The ions of sulfides and selenides possess good polarizability, which produces the separation of Fe^{2+}, Mn^{2+}, Ni^{2+}, and other ions by the joining of an electron. Olivine crystals and colloidal metallic particles having a high melting point serve as the catalyst which is insoluble in the melt. In the presence of sulfide additions, selenides of heavy metals, elemental metal, or olivine, crystallization proceeds throughout the bulk of the glass at rather low temperatures when the formation of nuclei prevails over the rate of their growth. Additions are also used to prepare glass-ceramics by a two-stage process, including the precipitation of the "pseudophase," rich in fluorine and crystallizing rapidly, and subsequent crystallization of glass [51, 52, 134]. Large segregation regions are observed in systems of the $MeF_2-MeO-SiO_2$ type [154, 155]. Opaque glasses may be prepared near the segregation region of the $MgO-SiO_2$ system due to the precipitation of the secondary, finely dispersed liquid phase during the rapid cooling of the melt [134]. Latent segregation regions were found in the glass-forming portions of the fluorine—beryllium systems $LiF—BeF_2$, $NaF—BeF_2$, and $KF—BeF_2$ — which are analogous to the $MgO—SiO_2$, $CaO—SiO_2$, and $SrO—SiO_2$ oxide systems — as well as in the corresponding ternary fluorine-containing systems [128, 134, 156]. There is also a technological application for phosphate-containing segregating systems, in which both of the liquid phases are in the form of hardened emulsion [156], in contrast to the fluorine-containing opaque glasses, where one phase, which is present in smaller amounts, precipitates in the crystalline form, and the other phase, which is present in larger amounts, remains glassy.

Although admitting that many glasses which yield good glass-ceramics are capable of segregating, Filipovich [117] nevertheless does not believe that it has been proven that the heavily developed interphase surface resulting from the metastable immiscibility between the glass-forming phases is the catalyst, and that the crystallization of the immiscible phases may be considered as being catalyzed. In his opinion, metastable immiscibility, as a bona fide physicochemical property of glasses, may lead, not to the development of the interphase surface, but to the formation of very fine glass-forming regions which, in turn, independently of the role of the surface, cause the development of fine crystals, as determined by the size of the immiscibility regions. In our opinion, such a mechanism for the crystallization of immiscible glasses differs only slightly from the one described above, since the formation of very fine glass-forming regions cannot help but be accompanied by the development of new interphase regions catalyzing the crystallization of these glasses.

Maurer [157, 158] determined that the segregation of titanium-containing glasses into two liquid phases, or the development of isotropic regions ("emulsions"), facilitates the process of nucleus formation due to the lower surface energy at the interphase surfaces between two liquids as compared to the surface energy at the interphase boundary between the crystal and the liquid. The activation energy for the process of nucleus formation at the interphase boundaries of these emulsions and inside one of these phases is smaller than in the initial homogeneous glass, in view of the difference in the chemical composition of one of the precipitating phases from that of the initial glass. The presence of a gradient in the chemical composition of the segregation region enhances formation of the nuclei.

Kitaigorodskii and Khodakovskaya [159] observed the emergence of heterogeneities and their influence on the subsequent crystallization of glass to be used for the preparation of glass-ceramics, by observing microimmiscibility during the precrystallization period of heat treatment in a glass of the $SiO_2-Al_2O_3-MgO$ system. The absence of a crystalline phase in the microimmiscibility regions was confirmed by x-ray analysis.

Investigations of various systems performed by Galakhov [160] showed that glasses whose compositions lie near the immiscibility region or at the portions of the phase diagram characterized by the tendency toward immiscibility give, upon crystallization, a regular, finely dispersed structure. In order to successfully develop new types of glass-ceramics, the present author believes that it is necessary to determine the submicroimmiscibility boundaries on the phase diagrams. The metastable immiscibility regions in glasses and the microheterogeneities associated with them may be determined experimentally by electron microscopy [161-163] and by small-angle x-ray scattering methods [164, 165]. When investigating immiscibility in fluorine-containing and rare-earth silicate systems, I. Ya. Bondar' and N. A. Toropov determined that immiscibility depends on the size and the charge of the cation, the nature of the anion—cation bond, their mutual polarization, and the coordination state. With decreasing ionic radius of the cation, the phase-separation boundaries increase.

Opalescence caused by metastable immiscibility [167] takes place in glasses of the Li_2O-SiO_2 system containing 20-29 mol.% Li_2O following heat treatment at 480-620°C. Kalinina et al. [167] believe that separation into two phases starts with the formation of amorphous seeds of the metastable glassy phases, in which the nuclei are then formed. They look upon metastable immiscibility as an independent phenomenon characteristic of glass as a supercooled liquid, and not as a precrystallization phenomenon.

When investigating the changes in the physical properties of glasses of the $Li_2O-Al_2O_3-SiO_2$ system with TiO_2 additions, Buzhinskii et al. [168] also came to the conclusion that upon heating of these glasses from low annealing temperatures upward, segregation into two droplike glassy phases occurs, resulting in an increased viscosity of the glass. With decreasing heat-treatment temperature, the size of the drops decreases, but their number increases. Only after the two phases are separated does a rearrangement of the structure occur within the new phase, with the formation of a crystalline lattice. The segregation process is caused only by the saturation of the glass with the newly formed phase, and occurs at different temperatures depending on the time of heat treatment.

The theory of the immiscibility phenomena in fused and glassy silicate systems and the corresponding phase diagrams were examined by Toropov and Barzakovskii [169], who emphasize the importance and significance of knowing the metastable regions of submicroimmiscibility — independently of whether they are located above or below the liquidus temperatures — in the development of the theoretical bases for the production of glass-ceramics. In total agreement with the literature data, it is confirmed that in order to obtain a fine-crystalline structure in a glass-ceramic, it is necessary to select the composition of the glass either in those concentration portions of the phase diagram where immiscibility phenomena take place, or in the portions which are directly adjacent to the regions of immiscibility.

The kinetics of the formation of atomic clusters of one type in the microregion in segregating glasses and alloys is not explained by all authors in terms of the formation of nuclei and of their diffusion-controlled growth. In some borosilicate glasses which have a tendency toward phase separation, there was no indication of nucleation in any of the segregating phases. In these glasses, precipitation of the particles occurred, a phenomenon known as spinodal decomposition [747]. Due to the presence of breaks in the miscibility in the corresponding phase diagrams, and as a result of the spinoidal decomposition, the perfectly uniform glasses of the $Na_2O—SiO_2$ system separate into regions rich in SiO_2 and into noncrystalline microphases rich in alkalis [748].

4. MECHANISM OF THE ACTION BY TiO_2 DURING CATALYZED CRYSTALLIZATION OF TITANIUM-CONTAINING GLASSES

It is known that glasses containing from 2 to 20% TiO_2 crystallize with the formation of a uniform structure, which is caused, in contrast to surface crystallization, by internal, or homogeneous, formation of nuclei throughout the glass article. Therefore, it was first assumed that TiO_2 has an effect similar to that of metals in photosensitive glasses, where epitaxial growth of nonmetallic crystals takes place on the metallic particles uniformly precipitated throughout the bulk.

However, when Ohlberg et al. [170] investigated glass of the composition 56 SiO_2, 7 TiO_2, 20 Al_2O_3, 17 MgO, they noticed that rutile was the last phase to crystallize, from which they deduced that it is unlikely that the silicate phases were catalyzed by the TiO_2 crystals. The same opinion was expressed by Hillig [116], who thinks that even in glass containing 40 mol.% TiO_2, rutile by itself is not capable of homogeneous nucleus formation, and that a two-stage mechanism for the nucleus formation — including as a necessary prerequisite the TiO_2 phase — is not probable. However, in glasses devoid of TiO_2 or with a low concentration of TiO_2, only surface crystallization was observed, even after long-term heat treatment [170]. From this, it followed that there is a certain minimum TiO_2 concentration which is necessary for the internal process of nucleus formation in glasses of the magnesium aluminosilicate system. It is the opinion of Ohlberg et al. [170] that the mechanism of the action by TiO_2 does not lie in the TiO_2 crystals acting as nuclei, but rather in the fact that TiO_2 speeds up the segregation process of glass and its subsequent crystallization. This was confirmed by other investigators.

Vogel [132, 745] showed by electron-microscope methods that segregation of microphases, such as he observed in many glasses, is a "precrystalline state" of glass, and that controlled precipitation of microphases is a fundamental process in the production of any glass-ceramics. Thus, he ascribed the round segments of the crystal growth observed in glass-ceramics to this precrystalline state (see Fig. 30, showing the slowly cooled and partially crystallized glass, and Fig. 31, showing further development of segregation and crystallization due to the slow cooling of the glass; many segregation regions overlap).

Vogel and Gerth [171, 172, 745] believe that the catalyzed crystallization of glass is determined primarily by two processes: phase separation in the glass, which is enhanced by TiO_2, and the subsequent epitaxial growth of the basic precipitating crystalline

Fig. 30. Glass containing droplike segregation regions. The glassy portion at the top right can easily be etched with hydrofluoric acid.

Fig. 31. Glass at the stage of the completion of crystal growth. The sample can easily be etched with hydrofluoric acid.

phase on the nuclei formed. It is assumed that aggregation of certain atoms or their groups takes place during the cooling of the glass melt. The degree of order of these groupings depends on the cooling rate. During rapid cooling, the orientation process cannot be completed, and the melt hardens in the form of uniform glass. However, secondary heating results in droplike phase separation and in the appearance of an interphase boundary between two glassy phases, one of which is structurally more developed than the other. Analogous views were developed by Moriya [173] and con-

firmed on borosilicate glass samples, in which droplike heterogeneous regions of easily leached-out phases high in alkali ions
were observed [174-180].

The various glasses investigated by Vogel and Gerth [172]
were separated into two phases, one of which was enriched with
network-modifying cations and the other with glass-forming cations. The shape of the drop was especially discernible for the
phase having a maximum surface tension.

According to Vogel and Gerth [172], TiO_2 has a double function during the crystallization of titanium-containing glasses. On
the one hand, TiO_2, similarly to other cations with a high charge,
enhances the separation of glass into two phases. On the other
hand, in agreement with the dependence between the field force and
the formation of crystalline compounds (as shown by Dietzel [115,
181, 182]), the TiO_2 itself may become separated into its different
crystalline modifications, thereby forming nuclei which increase
in size during the primary and secondary stages of heat treatment,
and then cause epitaxial growth of fundamental components of the
separating microphases. The sizes of the crystals of the fundamental precipitating phase depend on the sizes of the droplike portions and on the degree of development of their interphase boundaries.

It has been proposed that analogous processes may take place
in the preparation of photosensitive glass-ceramics, with the only
difference being that instead of TiO_2, there are the droplike phases
Cu^+, Ag^+, or Au^{3+} and Ce^{3+} ions, which, just like TiO_2, have a
double function: they speed up the separation of the phases, and
after irradiation of the photosensitive glass-ceramic with ultraviolet light, they form nuclei for the epitaxial growth of the primary segregating phase [172].

We first observed droplike microsegregation experimentally
in photosensitive lithium aluminosilicate glass which was subjected
to precrystallization heat treatment so as to create better conditions for the formation of nuclei and to increase the amount of the
crystalline phase. It was determined that intermediary cooling of
the photosensitive glass from 500 to 250°C, after first holding it in
the low-temperature region, such as at 500°C, for 3 h, determines
the "precrystalline state" of the glass and enhances the droplike
segregation of the microphases. The early stages of the formation

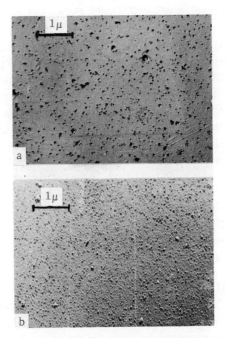

Fig. 32. Early stages of the formation of nuclei in light-sensitive lithium aluminosilicate glass subjected to the following treatment: a) irradiation for 90 min with a PRK-7 lamp, heated to 500°C and held there for 3 h; b) nonirradiated glass, heated to 570°C and held there for 5 h.

of droplike segregation regions in the photosensitive glass investigated, which had been subjected to precrystallization low-temperature heat treatment, are clearly seen on electron micrographs (Fig. 32). In agreement with the data cited above [172], one may assume that inside these droplike microphases there are Ag$^+$ ions which first speed up the phase separation and, after the photosensitive glass is irradiated with ultraviolet light, form nuclei on which the epitaxial growth of crystals of the primary nonmetallic segregating phase begins. The products of the high-temperature crystallization of a photosensitive glass which had undergone precrystallization heat treatment with intermediary cooling and which had been held for a given time in the low-temperature region and showed the presence of droplike phase segregation had increased mechanical strength and minimal deformation.

Small amounts of F^-, Cl^-, Br^-, I^-, and SO_4^{2-} ions also act as catalysts for the crystallization and facilitate its control. According to Vogel [745, 746], the significance of small additions of sensitizers — halogens or sulfates — in photosensitive glasses is that they make possible a finer control of the ratio between the amounts of the droplike microphases present, such as emerge during the phase separation. Here, the action of the fluorides is explained by noting that fluorine, although also capable of partially replacing oxygen, nevertheless cannot, because of its univalency, serve as the bridge between two SiO_4 tetrahedra, as a result of which, the mobility of other network modifiers and the degree of phase separation increase. The analogous action of Cl, Br, I, and sulfate ions, which have a large size and are incapable of replacing oxygen, is explained by the author in terms of their penetrating into the structural network of glass and expanding it, thereby causing a higher mobility of the network modifiers.

The capability of noble metals to produce phase separation in photosensitive glasses has also been demonstrated by Weyl [109], as has been mentioned previously. Such a mechanism for the action of these metals seems to us to be quite probable.

By investigating light-scattering heterogeneities in glass of the composition 56 SiO_2, 20 Al_2O_3, 15 MgO, 9 TiO_2, Maurer [157, 158] came to the conclusion that the catalytic action of TiO_2 consists in the formation of isotropic regions or emulsions, one of which is extremely unstable and can easily be crystallized. The formation of nuclei from emulsions requires a lesser activation energy compared to the formation of nuclei in the absence of phase separation. Thus, the formation of emulsions with the aid of TiO_2 is the path which the system follows during its crystallization. A similar kinetics of crystallization is characteristic only for multi-component glasses.

Bobovich [183] studied the mechanism of the action of TiO_2 in glass having the spodumene composition using the combination scattering method, and expressed the opinion that Ti in this glass is in tetrahedral coordination, whereas Al is in the octahedral coordination. After preliminary heat treatment, the TiO_4 tetrahedra become TiO_6 octahedra which are interlinked at the corners, due to the change in the Al coordination, which is confirmed by the diffuse character of the spectral bands caused by the presence of

titanium—oxygen octahedra. At this point, the precrystallization
period in glass is being concluded. During further heat treatment,
the titanium—oxygen octahedra become partially linked by ribs,
which leads to the formation of crystallites similar to rutile or of
a more complex composition. These crystallites serve as the nuclei of the fundamental crystalline phase. This author, however,
admits that, in addition to rutile, other crystals of the composition
$mAl_2O_3 \cdot nTiO_2$ may also form nuclei.

Kondrat'ev and co-workers [184, 185] investigated the crystallization of glasses of the $Li_2O—Al_2O_3—SiO_2—TiO_2$ system and also observed a double role played by Ti, although somewhat different from that pointed out by Vogel and Gerth. On the one hand, Ti
is capable of forming liquids of the $Al_2O_3 \cdot TiO_2$ type already in the
melt, which then serve as nuclei. The structure of the compound
$Al_2O_3 \cdot TiO_2$ can be represented as octahedral complexes of Ti and
Al, which are joined by the AlO_4 nodes. The amount of the compound present is determined not only by the amount of Ti, but also
by the amount of octahedral Al, which gives the condition $[Al_2O_3] >$
$[R_2O]$.

On the other hand, if the amount of Ti present is greater than
the amount necessary for the formation of the compound $Al_2O_3 \cdot$
TiO_2, then titanium is present in the network of the glass in the
form of TiO_4 tetrahedra. At the points where TiO_4 is present inter-
stitially, the local dielectric permeability ε greatly increases,
which results in a weakening of the interaction between the polar
and the structural groupings, i.e., in a decrease in the autosolva-
tion effect [186]. During the precrystallization and crystallization
periods, the polar groupings split up, which facilitates their ordering and crystallization.

Podushko and Kozlova [187] confirm that the action of the
catalyst in glasses of the $Li_2O—Al_2O_3—SiO_2$ system with additions
of 2-11% TiO_2 consists in the creation of structural defects during
the cooling of the melt, among which they list phase separation,
cracks, and other areas with weakened energy bonds. It is on
these defects that nuclei then appear, the composition of which corresponds to the composition of the fundamental crystalline phase.
The quantity of the defects present, which depends on the glass
composition and the catalyst concentration, determines the quantity
of the nuclei formed and the crystal size of the precipitating crystalline phase.

Buzhinskii et al. [168] expressed an opposite opinion with respect to the question of the composition of the nuclei in titanium-containing glasses of this system, asserting that very fine particles of rutile already precipitate in glass with a certain titanium concentration when it is being cooled, and that they do not thereby produce any changes in the properties of the glass. During heat treatment at annealing temperatures and higher, titanium oxides — which thereby alter their structural form — iron oxides, and fundamental glass components precipitate on the nuclei formed. Drops are formed which differ in composition from the initial glass, and in this manner separation into two phases is produced, which then is followed by crystallization.

Zhunina et al. [188] propose that the mechanism of TiO_2 as a crystallization catalyst of limited solubility in glasses of the $CaO-MgO-Al_2O_3-SiO_2$ system consists in the formation of finely dispersed TiO_2 particles — the nuclei of the fundamental crystallizing phase of pyroxene. However, the immiscibility caused by TiO_2 complicates its positive effect as a catalyst. The possibility of the transition of TiO_2 into Ti_2O_3 and the change in the coordination number of titanium is admitted.

In work by other investigators [189-191], it is confirmed that in the preparation of glass-ceramics in the $Li_2O-Al_2O_3-SiO_2$ system, the switching of covalent bonds and the transition into octahedral coordination of titanium which is present in microimmiscibility regions are of considerable importance because of the lowering of the coordination of other cations, such as aluminum or gallium, the donor—acceptor interaction of which with oxygen is weaker. The coordination transition of titanium occurs by the mechanism of covalent transformation diffusion, which is extremely energy consuming and which thus determines the slow rate of the process.

In order to verify the concept that phase separation in glass is the source for the formation of nuclei in the $MgO-Al_2O_3-SiO_2-TiO_2$ system, Ohlberg et al. [170] heat treated glass of the composition 56 SiO_2, 20 Al_2O_3, 17 MgO, 7 TiO_2 at 900°C for short periods of time. Electron micrographs of freshly cleaved surfaces of such heat-treated samples after etching in a 1% solution of HF for 30 sec are presented in Fig. 33.

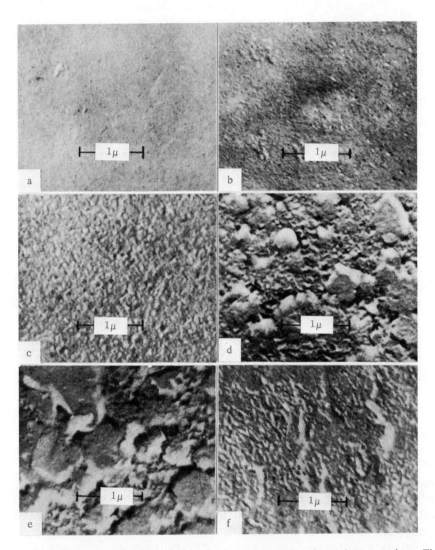

Fig. 33. Formation of nuclei and growth of crystals in glass during heat treatment. The glass has the following composition: $56\,SiO_2$, $17\,MgO$, $7\,TiO_2$. a) Surface after melting, with no crystallization present; b) heating to 900°C for 5 min, with no crystallization present; c) the same for 7 min, with no crystallization present; d) the same for 10 min, 20% crystallization; e) the same for 20 min, 60% crystallization; f) the same for 25 min, 80% crystallization.

Although in the first three samples the average size of the heterogeneity regions increased from 200 to 400 Å, it was not possible, using x-ray structural analysis, to observe the presence of crystals. However, in the sample treated at 900°C for 10 min, x-ray analysis showed the presence of crystals or their aggregates with sizes ranging from 2500 to 4000 Å. After heat treatment for 20 min, these sizes increased to 3000-5000 Å, and after 25 min, the degree of crystallization reached 80%. Heat treatment for 1.5 h at a lower temperature of 815°C produced less than 5% of a crystalline phase, identified as MgO · 2TiO$_2$ (?) in the sample. After heat treatment for 3 h at 850°C, the degree of crystallization increased by more than 50%, while β-quartz solid solution appeared as the crystalline phase. The mechanism for the formation of nuclei in the glass investigated is represented by the authors in the following manner. During the cooling period, glass separates into two finely dispersed droplike phases, which increase in size during secondary heating until no more crystallization takes place. The MgO · 2TiO$_2$ (?) present in amount of less than 5% is the catalyst for the crystallization of the primary phase β-quartz solid solution.

The presence of magnesium dititanate or rutile crystals as the primary phase during the crystallization of titanium-containing glasses was observed by other investigators [192, 193], according to whom the critical size of these crystallization catalysts was 2000 Å.

Droplike immiscibility regions 0.2-0.4 μ in size were also observed in glass having the composition 65 SiO$_2$, 20 TiO$_2$, 10 Li$_2$O, 5 CaO [170]. On electron micrographs of freshly cleaved surfaces of the samples (Fig. 34), these drops differ from the crystals in having a perfectly round form and a smooth cleavage surface [194]. After a 1-h heat treatment at 705°C, crystallization started at the interphase surfaces of droplike regions, with the amount of crystalline phase being only 3%. After a 2-h heat treatment, the degree of crystallization increased to 8%. Crystallization was never observed in those portions of the glass which did not contain the drops. Prolonged heat treatment for 24 h at a lower temperature (680°C) resulted in a 90% crystallization of the sample. The crystalline phases were α-quartz, lithium silicates, and an unidentified phase. In these glasses, as well as in glasses of the MgO—Al$_2$O$_3$—SiO$_2$—TiO$_2$ system, Ohlberg et al. [170] assume a two-stage process

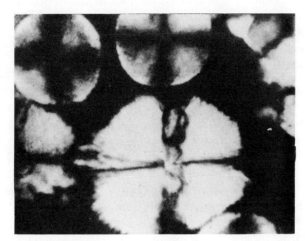

Fig. 34. Freshly cleaved surface of glass directly after melting.

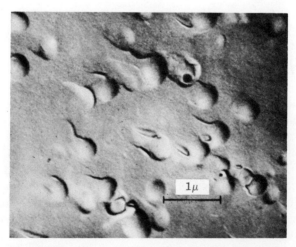

Fig. 35. Droplike phase separation of glass and its crystallization.

of the nucleus formation. First, segregation of the glass occurs due to the presence of minute quantities of the catalyst and the tendency of glass to separate into two phases, and then the particles of the catalyst, because of their growth to the critical size of 2000-4000 Å, become nuclei of heterogeneous crystallization of the primary crystallizing phase.

Glass of the composition 53 SiO_2, 19 Al_2O_3, 15 MgO, 13 Li_2O was heat treated for 96 h at 595° and then for 30 min at 650°, and separation into droplike regions with sizes ranging from 1 to 30 μ was observed with the normal optical microscope [170]. The degree of crystallization of β-quartz solid solution was 8%. After heat treatment for 19 h at 650°C, the degree of crystallization increased to 85%, with the primary crystalline phases being β-spodumene and β-quartz solid solution. The metastable glass drops, their sizes ranging to 60 μ, which formed as a result of the phase separation, differed from the crystalline spherulites by having a spherical form, a lower birefringence, and by not having a radial structure (Fig. 35). In contrast to the preceding two glasses, the crystallization of the glass of the $Li_2O-MgO-Al_2O_3-SiO_2$ system started not on the interphase surfaces between the drops and the primary glassy material, but within the drops themselves.

Hillig [116] investigated two series of glasses in the ternary $BaO-SiO_2-TiO_2$ system, the compositions of which were determined by the formulas $25BaO \cdot (75 - x)SiO_2 \cdot xTiO_2$ and $(25 + y)BaO \cdot (70 - y)SiO_2 \cdot 5TiO_2$. In the shortened notation used below, $(x - 15)$, for example, will indicate glass in which x = 15.

In glasses of the ternary systems at the lowest TiO_2 concentrations and with slight supercooling, a uniform precipitation of the phase α-BaO $\cdot$ $2SiO_2$ was observed, which made it possible at first to assume immiscibility. However, according to Hillig [116], the possibility of a liquid—liquid emulsion being formed is precluded by x-ray investigations of the crystalline phase and the transmission of glass immediately after heating above the secondary liquidus temperature, even in the case when it was slowly cooled to a temperature lower than 700°C.

Within the composition $(x - 15)$, the first precipitating crystalline phase was the compound α-BaO $\cdot$ $2SiO_2$, which then rapidly transformed into β-BaO $\cdot$ $2SiO_2$. With increasing TiO_2 content, the process of the homogeneous formation of nuclei weakened, aided by a decrease in the α-BaO $\cdot$ 2SiO$_2$ liquidus, increased viscosity of the glass, and increased temperature range of critical super-cooling. In the $(x-15)$ composition, homogeneous formation of nuclei was not observed.

However, with the TiO$_2$ content increased to 50 mol.%, the process of the homogeneous formation of nuclei again took place. The ability of titanium-containing glasses to become supercooled without the heterogeneous formation of nuclei led Hillig [116] to the conclusion that TiO$_2$ is not effective as a catalyst, and that it is not true that a two-stage mechanism for the formation of nuclei in glass exists with separation into two phases and with TiO$_2$ taking part. Instead, as has previously been mentioned, Hillig proposes that a homogeneous formation of α-BaO $\cdot$ 2SiO$_2$ nuclei and a uniform precipitation of the secondary crystalline phase β-BaO $\cdot$ 2SiO$_2$ take place throughout the bulk of the glasses investigated. The fact that TiO$_2$ also shows a somewhat significant influence on this process is explained by the partial effect of TiO$_2$ on the free energy of the system at the interphase surfaces. The primary influence on the magnitude of this free energy, the change in which determines the behavior of glass with respect to nucleus formation, is exerted by the chemical, stereochemical, and polarization effects among the ions penetrating the glass structure.

5. IMMISCIBILITY AND CRYSTALLIZATION IN GLASSES CONTAINING SMALL AMOUNTS OF PLATINUM OR PLATINUM-GROUP METALS

It has been established [195-198] that very small amounts of Pt introduced into a glass by means of platinum chloride form sub-microscopic colloidal particles in the melt which act as nuclei, producing segregation in the liquid phase, change in coloring, light scattering, and crystallization even during rapid cooling. In addition to the platinum chloride, palladium and rhodium chlorides can also be introduced, which, during the melting, reduce to finely dispersed metal. Phosphate glasses of the composition Na$_2$O $\cdot$ P$_2$O$_5$ and 0.5Na$_2$O $\cdot$ 0.5SiO$_2$ $\cdot$ P$_2$O$_5$ changed in color from yellow to gray with increasing Pt concentration. At a Pt concentration higher than 0.1%, crystallization of the metal took place in the form of hexagonal plates of microscopic size. At 0.002-0.008 wt.% Pt, partial crystallization of the sodium metaphosphate glasses took place. The coloring of the glasses depended on the oxidation—

reduction conditions during melting and on the Pt concentration. For instance, gray glasses became yellow in the presence of an oxidizer, and yellow glasses acquired a gray color under reducing conditions. Sodium metaphosphate glasses containing 0.0005-0.001% Pt had a gray color; at a 0.002-0.006% Pt concentration, crystallization of glasses occurred, preceded by separation into two phases, which was confirmed by electron-microscope and x-ray analyses. Here, the crystalline phase which precipitated in the glass in the presence of Pt differed from the phase which precipitated during the crystallization of the same glass in the absence of Pt, although it was not possible to identify this phase.

Karkhanavala and Weyl [195] showed that Pt and other noble metals cause the separation of glass of the $Li_2O—SiO_2$ system into two phases at a temperature lying somewhat higher than the liquidus temperature of the melt. This phenomenon, which was also observed in sodium phosphate glasses, is explained by the authors in terms of the emergence of various structural groups in the melt under the influence of platinum nuclei. The transition from one group to another is continuous; however, the various groups differ in having a different ratio of R_2O to glass-forming oxides. A necessary condition for the growth of groups and the emergence of interphase boundaries is a decrease in the free energy of the system during the phase separation. In the absence of Pt, the gain in energy during the formation of larger-size groups is not sufficient to overcome the immiscibility entropy, while in the presence of Pt, one of the structural groups becomes selectively adsorbed on it, the sizes of the groups increase, and phase separation takes place.

In order to study the dependence between immiscibility and the crystallization of sodium phosphate glasses with Pt additions, composition was varied by a slight change in the Na_2O/P_2O_5 ratio near 1. Platinum was introduced into glasses of the composition 0.55 Na_2O, 0.45 P_2O_5, and 0.47 Na_2O, 0.53 P_2O_5. It was determined that with the Na_2O/P_2O_5 ratio increasing from 0.89 to 1.2, i.e., with increasing Na_2O content, the effectiveness of Pt as a catalyst increased, inasmuch as the crystallization of the respective glasses started at small concentrations (0.05, 0.002, and 0.0005% Pt). By assuming that the liquid phase, which, during phase separation, became adsorbed on the Pt particles, contains more P_2O_5 than the remaining melt, the authors think that the Na_2O/P_2O_5 ratio in the bulk increases, and the more so, the more Pt is introduced. The smallest amount of Pt is needed for the crystallization of glass with an Na_2O/P_2O_5 of 1.2, since the slightest loss of P_2O_5 from the melt increases the content of Na_2O and facilitates crystallization. For glass with an Na_2O/P_2O_5 ratio equal to 0.89, more Pt is needed, in order to produce better phase separation and to remove such a quantity of P_2O_5 from the fundamental melt which would enhance the subsequent crystallization.

The phase separation of lithium silicate glasses and the existence in them of discontinuous and continuous structural groups was confirmed by electron-microscope and chromatographic methods [200], by the measurement of their electrical properties [201], and also by etching with hydrofluoric acid the glasses experiencing phase separation [202].

The rate of crystallization of glass of the composition $Li_2O \cdot 4SiO_2$ rapidly increased in the presence of Pt [203]. For instance, in order to obtain the same degree of crystallization at 650°C, glass without Pt had to be held at that temperature for 4 h, whereas glass with 0.001% Pt had to be held there for 45 min, and glass with 0.010% Pt for 20 min. Total nontransparency of glass with 0.010% Pt was achieved after 45 min, while that of glass without Pt was achieved after 16 h. Glass containing 0.010% Pt had a gray color and was distinguished by a uniform distribution of crystals with a size of approximately 500 Å in the absence of separate crystalline or glassy segments. The crystal sizes in glass without Pt was 0.5-1 μ. The primary crystals had the lithium disilicate composition and were present in glass with 0.010% Pt after a 16-h heat treatment at 650°C in an amount almost twice that in glass without Pt.

Rindone [204] also determined that the amount of lithium disilicate crystallizing from glass of the composition $Li_2O \cdot 4SiO_2$ at 600 and 650°C was not constant, but varied depending on the Pt concentration for any given crystallization time, and went through a maximum. At 600°C, the optimum Pt concentration was in the range 0.004-0.007%, and at 650°C, it was in the range 0.008-0.011%, whereas a significant decrease in the amount of the crystallizing $Li_2O \cdot 2SiO_2$ was observed when the Pt concentration was 0.025%. This Rindone explains by the appearance at this Pt concentration of an additional crystalline phase, the β-quartz solid solution

Table 2. Rate of Crystallization of $Li_2O \cdot SiO_2$

Pt content, %	Rate of crystallization, in min, at temperature, °C			
	600		650	
	initial	final	initial	final
0	0.008	0.022	0.210	0.003
0.001	0.051	0.013	1.070	0.004
0.005	0.975	0.002	4.750	0.000
0.010	0.750	0.002	5.000	0.000
0.025	0.157	0.003	1.000	0.001

phase, the maximum amount of which at 650°C was 20%, which remained constant after a 4-h treatment. At 600°C, the maximum amount (12%) of β-quartz solid solution was achieved after a 32-h heat treatment.

The rates of crystallization of lithium disilicate as a function of Pt concentration at 600 and 650°C are presented in Table 2 [204].

By means of calculations, Rindone showed the strong effect that Pt has in lowering the activation energy of the crystallization process of $Li_2O \cdot 2SiO_2$. In the absence of Pt, this activation energy was 120 kcal/mole; in the presence of 0.005% Pt, it rapidly decreased to 50 kcal/mole; with further increase in the Pt concentration, it again increased to 60 kcal/mole. Electron microscope investigation of the freshly cleaved surface of the $Li_2O \cdot 4SiO_2$ glass showed that in the absence of Pt, the size of the regions of granularity was approximately 250 Å, whereas in glass containing 0.005% Pt, these increased, attaining sizes of 500 Å. The presence of these microheterogeneities is interpreted as proof for the existence in lithium aluminosilicate glasses of structural groups enriched with lithium.

Rindone only partially associates the capability of Pt to form $Li_2O \cdot 2SiO_2$ nuclei with the crystallochemical similarity between some of the parameters of their crystal lattices. The (111) face of the Pt crystal differs by not more than 5% from the (002) face of $Li_2O \cdot 2SiO_2$. He ascribes a more important role in the formation of microheterogeneous structural groups enriched with lithium to the size of the platinum centers, which must be significantly smaller than the sizes of the regions enriched with lithium, and which, in his opinion, are of the order of 50 Å. In the series of glasses with a high Pt concentration, Pt crystals 1 μ in size and better were observed. Nuclei of rather small size are the most effective, as is observed at small Pt concentrations (approximately 0.005%).

Closely associated with the size of the nuclei is their number, since with increasing Pt concentration, the average size of the nuclei increases, the proportion of microheterogeneous regions having the size of less than 250 Å decreases, and therefore the rate of crystallization also decreases. Very small Pt concentrations, of the order of 0.001%, are also ineffective, inasmuch as they do not markedly increase the crystallization rate. At the optimum Pt concentration of 0.005%, as shown by calculations, each gram of glass contains 10^{13} platinum centers, 50 Å in size, which form 10^{15} microheterogeneity regions of up to 500Å in size [204].

Thus, the presence in lithium silicate glasses of discrete regions enriched with lithium or silicon has been confirmed. According to Rindone [204], this phenomenon is not the result of microscopic phase segregation or of incomplete homogenization, but rather is peculiar to the glass itself. Nevertheless, in the presence of platinum centers and due to the adsorption process, an intensive growth of microheterogeneity regions enriched with lithium took place, which can easily be crystallized at 600 and 650°C.

Catalyzed crystallization of glasses of the composition 12.5 Li_2O, 12.5 K_2O, 4 Al_2O_3, 81 SiO_2, and 0.00001, 0.001, or 0.1 Pt was investigated by Tashiro et al. [205], who observed an increase in mechanical strength during multistage heat treatment of samples with increased Pt content. The optimum Pt concentration for the total crystallization of these glasses and to ensure a high mechanical strength of the crystallized samples was 0.01% Pt. Samples of the composition 15 MgO, 23 Al_2O_3, 62 SiO_2, and x Li_2O (where x is equal to 4, 6, 8, 12), without Pt and with an addition of 0.01% Pt, were heated to 1050-1100°C at a rate of 5°C/min and held at temperature for 1 h. It was determined that the effect of Pt on the increase in mechanical strength of the crystallized samples depended on the Li_2O content. Samples with a high (12%) Li_2O content had the maximum flexure strength. Samples with 6% Li_2O present showed only a slight increase in mechanical strength.

Rindone [206-208] observed that crystals which formed during the crystallization of lithium silicate glasses showed a high degree of orientation with respect to the surface of the glass, and that the introduction in this glass of platinum crystallization nuclei had a tremendous effect on the degree of this orientation.

This investigation was done on glass of the composition $Li_2O \cdot 4SiO_2$, from which lithium disilicate was crystallized. However, orientation was also found in other lithium silicate glasses, the compositions of which varied to $Li_2O \cdot 2.75SiO_2$. The glass samples investigated were subjected to heat treatment at 600°C for times ranging from 10 min to 32 h. The degree of orientation was determined by x-ray analysis at the surface and at depths ranging from 1 to 30 μ below the starting surface, for which the sample was etched in a 24% HF for 15 sec. The lithium disilicate crystals were always oriented along the [002] plane parallel to the glass surface. The measure for the relative degree of orientation was taken as the ratio between the intensity of the x-rays diffracted from the [002] plane and the intensity of the x-rays diffracted from the [111] plane.

When the duration of heat treatment was increased from 20 min to 32 h for a glass without Pt, the intensity of x rays diffracted from the [002] plane increased from 16 to 600 units, whereas the intensity of the x rays diffracted from the [111] plane decreased from 17 to 2 units. The addition of Pt significantly inhibited this behavior. For instance, after heat treatment for 32 h, the degree of orientation in glass containing 0.025% Pt was two orders of magnitude less than that in glass without Pt.

The depth of propagation of the oriented layer of crystals changed depending on the Pt concentration and the duration of heat treatment. In Pt-containing glasses heat treated at 600°C for 20 min, 30 min, 40 min, 60 min, and 4 h, the maximum orientation was observed at a depth of from 0.5 to 3 μ, but not on the surface proper. After attaining this maximum, the orientation no longer increased, whereas in glasses without Pt, the orientation increased with depth. With increasing Pt concentration, the orientation rapidly increased in all samples, including those which were heat treated at 600°C for 32 h. The exact reasons for the observed preferred orientation of the $Li_2O \cdot 2SiO_2$ crystals parallel to the [002] plane have not been determined. The decrease in orientation in glasses with Pt is explained by Rindone [206-208] in terms of the presence of a large number of platinum crystallization nuclei associated with the regions enriched with lithium and having a size of 500 Å, as well as the possibility of epitaxial growth of $Li_2O \cdot 2SiO_2$ crystals on the platinum nuclei. The greatest importance here is ascribed to the size of the platinum crystallization nuclei, and not to the oriented growth of crystals, since sizes sufficiently small enable the possibility of the formation of regions enriched with lithium and determine the magnitude of the surface free energy at the interphase boundaries and the need for nuclei in screening. The formation of new interphase surfaces in glasses with Pt decreases the activation energy of nucleus formation and intensifies the crystallization, which destroys the orientation of the $Li_2O \cdot 2SiO_2$ crystals as compared to glasses without Pt.

On examining the process of heterogeneous crystallization on impurities from the point of view of crystallization theory [211-213], Rabinovich and co-workers [209, 210] affirmed, though without sufficient evidence, that the crystallization of lithium silicate — including photosensitive and sodium phosphate glasses — is caused exclusively by the crystallographic relationship between Pt, Au, Ag, or Cu and the crystals of the corresponding phases, and not by microsegregation of the glass or by the formation in it of microheterogeneous structural groups, such as was experimentally established in the investigations discussed above of Weyl and Karkhanavala, Rindone, and Vogel and Gerth, and which was theoretically substantiated by Weyl. Rabinovich acknowledged the shortcomings of his deductions [209], reporting that he does not have the data confirming the hypothesis as to the crystallographic mechanism of the crystallization of phosphates on the Pt particles in sodium phosphate glasses. The formation of microimmiscibility regions or of submicroheterogeneous structural groups as the result of preferred adsorption on the Pt particles of network-modifying cations as the stage preceding the oriented growth of crystals in glasses containing additions of noble metals has conclusively been confirmed by electron microscopy, by the measurement of electrical properties, by the etching of these glasses in hydrofluoric acid, and by other methods. After the completion of this stage, there follows the oriented or epitaxial growth of crystals of the primary phase on the nuclei of critical size formed.

6. FORMATION OF NUCLEI AND GROWTH OF COLLOIDAL PARTICLES IN PHOTOSENSITIVE GLASSES

The formation of nuclei and their growth in the gold-containing photosensitive glass of the composition 71.5 SiO_2, 23 Na_2O, 4 Al_2O_3, 1 ZnO, 0.3 Sb_2O_3, 0.13 CeO_2, and 0.01 Au was studied by Maurer [76] using the light-scattering method [214]. In order to study the spontaneous precipitation of Au particles, an increased amount of Sb_2O_3, equal to 1.5%, was introduced into the glass. The samples were subjected to the influence of x-ray irradiation with intensities of 12,500, 17,500, 25,000, 50,000, and 75,000 R. In addition to light scattering, light absorption was also studied. For the initial glass, the absorption coefficient was approximately 0.01 cm^{-1}, and the Rayleigh ratio was approximately $3 \cdot 10^{-6}$ cm^{-1}. The precipitation and the growth of Au particles was achieved after the sample was held at 530° for 5 min, and after the viscosity of the glass was $4 \cdot 10^{11}$ poise. The results of the measurements of the absorption and scattering of light for five different exposures showed that at each given exposure, a constant number of nuclei is formed, which increases in proportion to the duration of irradiation. The Au precipitates on the nuclei formed. With decreasing irradiation dosage, the number of nuclei decreases, while the size of the particles formed and the scattering produced by them increase, which is explained by the reduction of gold by antimony. Thus, at low exposures, larger-size particles grew in the glass. If the samples which had been subjected to exposures of 37,000, 50,000, and 75,000 R, and which had been heat treated until all the Au precipitated out were again irradiated by twice the original irradiation dosage, no more Au could be precipitated upon additional heating. Based on these experiments, Maurer concluded that irradiation determines only the number of Sb and Au nuclei formed in the supersaturated solution, and that the constant of the growth of the particles does not depend on the exposure. With increasing Sb concentration, the rate of nucleus formation increased, which resulted in spontaneous precipitation of Au. The particle growth constant for glass with 0.01% Au and 0.3% Sb_2O_3 was calculated to be equal to 1.51, while for glass with a somewhat smaller Au content and 1.5% Sb_2O_3, it was equal to 0.82. A fivefold increase in the concentration scarcely increased the growth constant. Therefore, Maurer [76] thinks that the growth of particles and the formation of nuclei of critical size is determined by diffusion and the interaction between the antimony and the gold ions, and not by the migration of neutral Au atoms. The probability of nucleus formation increases with increasing Sb content. For calculations of the number and the size of the Au particles at their initial stage of precipitation, a spherical particle shape was assumed, although electron-microscope investigation showed that in the gold-ruby glass, the particles were in the form of cubes. Nonetheless, photosensitive glasses sometimes showed the presence of particles of a spherical shape. The growth constant G for five samples of the photosensitive glass at 530° was taken to be equal to $4.98 \cdot 10^{-26}$ $cm^3 \cdot sec^{-3/2}$, and the rate of formation of nuclei in glass with a high Sb content was determined to be equal to $5.25 \cdot 10^5 \; cm^{-3} \cdot sec^{-1}$. Calculations showed that for the formation of one nucleus, three photoelectrons are necessary, from which it follows that either three univalent or one trivalent Au ion participate in this process. If in 1 cm^3 there are $2 \cdot 10^{18}$ Au ions, then, therefore, only one out of 10^6 Au ions could be neutralized at maximum irradiation exposures. Knowing the growth constant, Maurer [76] determined the coefficient of diffusion of the Au ions which, according to the calculations, was found to be equal to $6.8 \cdot 10^{-13} \; cm^2 \cdot sec^{-1}$. For silver-containing glasses, this coefficient was lower at the same temperatures, which the author explains by the difference in the ionic radii.

Thus, as a result of Maurer's investigation [76], it was determined that in photosensitive glasses with a high Sb content, as a result of the reduction of Au ions by the antimony at elevated temperatures, a continuous process of the formation and growth of nuclei occurs due to the precipitation of the Au particles from the supersaturated solution. In photosensitive glasses with a lowered Sb content, such a process does not take place, and the precipitation of Au occurs here only on a certain, very limited number of nuclei arising as the result of reduction by photoelectrons of an insignificant number of Au ions. From this example, one can see the importance for the technology of photosensitive glass-ceramics of the presence of the thermal reducers Sb_2O_3 or SnO_2 in the initial photosensitive glass. Reduction of photoelectrons occurs only in the early stages of the process of the formation of a definite number of nuclei. It was determined that the number of nuclei growing in photosensitive glass depends only on the intensity and the duration, i.e., the dosage, of irradiation, and does not depend on heat treatment. The growth rate of the particles did not depend on the irradiation dosage and was the same for all exposures. In the formation of a single nucleus of homogeneous crystallization, three photoelectrons participate, reducing only 10^{-7}-10^{-6} of the total number of all Au atoms present, and producing a marked precipitation of Au. The reduction of Au ions occurs as the result of diffusion and interaction between the Sb and Au ions. The particles grow to a practically total precipitation of all Au present in the glass. The completeness of the Au precipitation is determined by the antimony—gold equilibrium. The final sizes of the particles depend on the number of the growing nuclei, which is determined by the irradiation exposure, and generally attain several hundreds of angstroms [76].

Berezhnoi and Il'chenko [83] studied several stages in the precipitation process of silver in photosensitive glasses of the lithium aluminosilicate system, which had first been subjected to irradiation by ultraviolet light and to heat treatment. The study of the nucleation mechanism of colloidal particles in crystals, glasses, photographic emulsions, or solutions makes it possible to fully expose the pattern of formation of the new phase by establishing the steps in its formation and by complementing or confirming the existing theoretical hypotheses.

According to Shatalov [215], "the creation of colloids in alkali halide crystals goes through three compulsory stages: the stage of atomic F-centers, the stage of aggregates of F-centers similar to molecules which are constructed in the fundamental crystal lattice, and the stage of colloidal inclusions possessing the metallic conductivity proper."

Colloid formation in silver halide crystals and photoemulsions based on them proceeds through the formation of nuclei of a fine structure, both in the form of atomic centers of silver and their aggregates [216]. The presence of analogous structural centers was also determined during the sputtering of Ag films on quartz glass substrate. Particles of freshly prepared silver sols in solutions have an amorphous structure. Depending on the degree of aging, the particles go over into the crystalline state. The rate of this transition increases with increasing temperature [217].

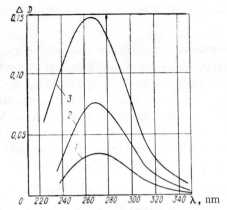

Fig. 36. Change in the absorption bands of glass with irradiation time. λ) Wavelength; ΔD) change in optical
density. The irradiation times for curves 1, 2, and 3 were
1, 6, and 20 min, respectively.

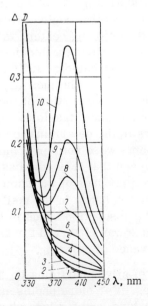

Fig. 37. Kinetics of the appearance of
coloration in silver-containing glass.
λ) Wavelength; ΔD) change in the optical density. Data are for glass with a
thickness of 2.1 mm irradiated for 240
min and heat treated at 300°C. For
curves 1-10, the irradiation times are
0, 15, 30, 35, 60, 75, 90, 110, 130, and
170 min, respectively.

It is of interest to look at the stages in the colloidal forms of glasses, which occupy a position intermediate between crystals and solutions.

For these measurements, photosensitive glass containing 0.02% Ag was used. Glasses from different factories but of the same composition differed in photosensitivity. Samples 30 × 15 × 0.38 mm in size were irradiated at 80°C at a distance of 420 mm from a PRK-7 lamp. Heat treatment was done in an electric muffle furnace preheated to the given temperature. Absorption spectra were taken on an SF-4 spectrophotometer with respect to a nonirradiated sample subjected to the same heat treatment.

When photosensitive glasses are irradiated with ultraviolet rays or x-rays, photochemical reactions take place in them, as described on page 34. The captured electrons localize on the defects of the structural network of the photosensitive glass, thereby forming absorption bands, the intensity of which increases with increasing irradiation time (see Fig. 36).

During the heating of these glasses, an amber-green color develops, which is associated with the precipitation of the silver particles. The characteristic curves illustrating the kinetics of the appearance of the band in the visible spectral region are shown in Fig. 37. Since the concentration of the coloring centers is very small, the most photosensitive glass, No. 3, having a thickness of 2.1 mm and irradiated for 240 min and heat treated at 300°C, was used. The samples were periodically cooled for the measurements. Besides an increase in absorption in the visible portion of the spectrum, a decrease in the absorption bands in the ultraviolet region was observed. In order to avoid errors in the determination of the differential optical density, measurements were not performed beyond 340 nm. From Fig. 37, it can be seen that it is not possible to measure the half-width of the absorption bands of the samples heat treated to 130 min, because absorption bands in the visible portion of the spectrum overlap with the absorption bands in the ultraviolet region. A similar occurrence was observed for all samples at the first stage of the appearance of coloring.

The process of the precipitation of silver particles is different for samples from different factories. For more photosensitive glasses, it proceeds at a lower temperature, and for less photosensitive glasses more heating is necessary. For glasses from

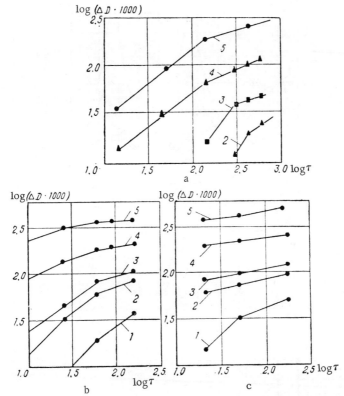

Fig. 38. Change in the optical density of glass at λ = 405 nm as a function of exposure and heat treatment. τ) Heat-treatment time (min); ΔD) difference in the optical density. Heat treatment at: a) 350°C; b) 400°C; c) 450°C. The exposure times for curves 1-5 are 10, 60, 100, 419, and 1000 min, respectively.

the same factory, the process of the precipitation of Ag depends on the dosage of the ultraviolet light which is acting on the glass (Fig. 38). In order to develop glasses which have been exposed for a lesser time, a higher temperature is needed. The temperature range for the start of the development varies from 50 to 200°C. For instance, samples of glass No. 2 irradiated for 10 and 1000 min were developed at 550 and 350°C, respectively.

Figure 39 shows absorption curves for samples of glass No. 1 which were heat treated at 300, 400, and 500°C, respectively. For treatment at 300°C, the most intensive bands correspond to the ir-

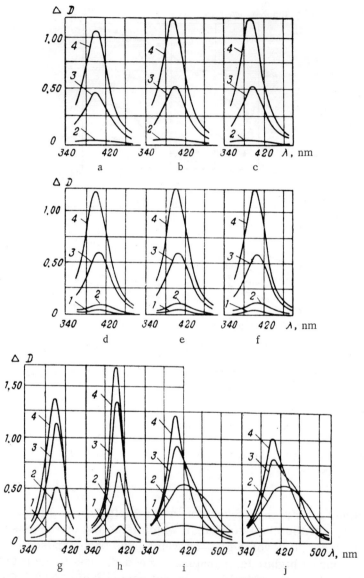

Fig. 39. Absorption of glass after irradiation and heat treatment. λ) Wave-length; ΔD) difference in the optical density. The heat-treatment conditions were as follows: a-c) Heated to 300°C for 60, 180, and 420 min, respective-ly; d-f) heated to 400°C for 60, 180, and 420 min, respectively; g-j) heated to 500°C for 5, 65, 480, and 780 min, respectively. The irradiation times for curves 1, 2, 3, and 4 are 3, 20, 190, and 3000 min, respectively.

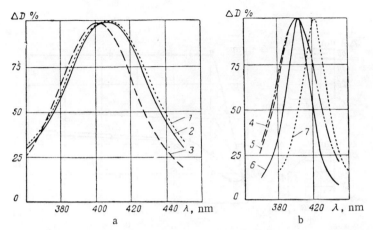

Fig. 40. Normalized absorption curves for glass. λ) Wavelength; ΔD) differ-ence in the optical density. a) Irradiation for curves 1-3, respectively, for 20, 180, and 3000 min, heat treatment at 400°C for 180 min; b) irradiation for 3000 min, heat treatment for curves 4-6, respectively, at 300, 400, and 500°C. Curve 7 represents the calculated values for very small colloidal particles.

radiation times of 3000 and 190 min. The band for 20 min develops extremely poorly. With the temperature increasing to 400°C, all absorption bands become more intense. An absorption band ap-pears for a sample irradiated for 3 min. The change in the dura-tion of heat treatment at these temperatures does not result in a noticeable change in the absorption bands. The maxima of absorp-tion for samples irradiated for 3000 min lie at 400 nm, and, for samples irradiated for lesser times, at 405 nm. The half-width of the absorption bands for glasses which had received a lesser radi-ation dosage is maximal (62 and 64 nm), and for the samples which had been irradiated for 3000 min, it is minimal (56 nm); therefore, normalized curves which correspond to different irradiation times do not coincide (see Fig. 40a). Heat treatment at 500°C results in a displacement of the maxima toward the long-wavelength side and in a broadening of the curves (Fig. 39). By means of accurate spectrophotometric measurements, it was determined that with the heat-treatment time fixed, the maxima of the absorption curves for samples which had received a larger dosage of ultraviolet light are displaced to the left — however, not farther than 397 nm.

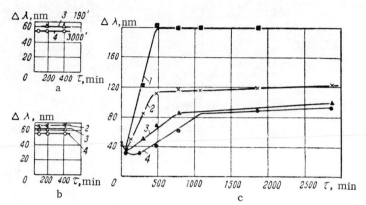

Fig. 41. Half-width of the absorption bands of glass. τ) Heat-treatment time; $\Delta\lambda$) half-width of the absorption band. The temperatures of heat treatment were: a) 300°C; b) 400°C; c) 500°C. The irradiation times for the respective curves were: 1) 3; 2) 20; 3) 190; 4) 3000 min.

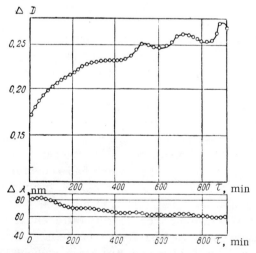

Fig. 42. Optical density of glass for λ = 405 nm, and half-width of the absorption bands. τ) Time of heat treatment at 500°C; ΔD) difference in the optical density; $\Delta\lambda$) half-width of the absorption band.

It is known that the half-width of the absorption band depends only on the size of the colloidal particles, and not on their number. With increasing size of the colloidal particles, the half-width of the absorption bands increases. Figure 41 shows measurements indicating the dependence of the half-width of the absorption bands on the duration of heat treatment at various temperatures. During heat treatment in the temperature region 300-400°C, the half-width of these bands did not change. For curves obtained at 500°C, an increase in the half-width with increasing duration of heat treatment was observed, which corresponded to the growth of colloidal particles. The slope of the curves is maximal for glasses which received a lesser irradiation dosage, and the saturation state for them is attained fastest. For glasses which received a large irradiation dosage, a lesser slope is observed, and the saturation state is attained slowest. Practically no changes in half-width are observed starting with the heat-treatment time of 1000 min. Attention is attracted by the characteristic minimum which is observed on all curves at the start of heat treatment (see Fig. 41). The appearance of an analogous minimum on the curves showing the dependence of the half-width of the absorption bands on the duration of heat treatment was also observed for glass samples of other factories. For glass No. 2, this phenomenon was investigated at various temperatures; for samples heat treated at 500°C the half-width of the bands continuously decreased with increasing duration of heat treatment (Fig. 42).

This is shown more markedly after the heating of glass at 550°C (see Fig. 43). It should be noted that for all irradiation exposures, the decreasing branches of the curves of the change in half-width practically combine into a single line starting with 20 min of heat treatment. Further on, one can expect a different slope of the $\Delta\lambda - \tau$ curves and a different attainment of saturation, analogous to that represented in Fig. 41. Figures 42 and 43 show not only the half-width curves, but also the curves of the dependence of the optical density on the duration of heat treatment. From a comparison of these dependencies, it can be seen that the maximum steepness of the optical density curves corresponds to the minimum on the half-width curves. When the curves for the half-width of the absorption bands diverge, the curves of the change in the optical density approach saturation. The minimum half-width of the absorption bands shown in Figs. 42 and 43 is equal to 35 nm.

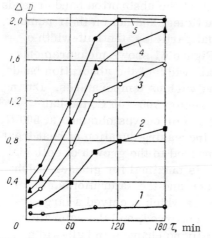
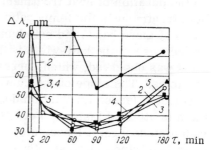

Fig. 43. Optical density of glass for λ = 405 nm and half-width of the absorption bands. τ) Heat-treatment time at 550°C; ΔD) difference in the optical density; $\Delta\lambda$) the half-width of the absorption band. The irradiation times for curves 1-5 were 5, 60, 200, 360, and 720 min, respectively.

The effect of irradiation on colloidal particles growing in alkali halide crystals was first described by Savost'yanova [218]. Following this, the effect of secondary light irradiation on fine-structure nuclei was studied by Kirillov [216]. For photosensitive glasses, we observed an analogous effect of secondary light action, and used this as a means of investigating the structure of the nucleating or growing silver particles. It turned out that these particles have a different sensitivity to the secondary light irradiation depending on the preceding heat and light treatment of the samples.

Table 3 gives results obtained during the secondary irradiation of samples of photosensitive glass No. 2 of thickness 0.1 mm which had first been irradiated for 5, 60, and 300 min, respectively, and which had then been heat treated for 60 min at various temperatures and then irradiated again. The secondary light irradiation for 5, 60, and 300 min was done through a plate of windowpane glass with a thickness of 2 mm, which transmitted radiation from a mercury lamp starting from 365 nm.

Table 3 shows the relative positions of the absorption bands in the ultraviolet and the visible spectral regions. Here, "0" designates the absorption bands of a sample after primary irradiation;

Table 3. Absorption Bands after Secondary Light Irradiation

Temp. of heat treatment, °C	Spectral region	Absorption bands for primary irradiation of given duration		
		5 h	60 h	300 h
100	UV V	$0 > \tau > 5 > 60$ No bands	$0 > \tau > 5 > 60$ No bands	$0 > \tau > 5 > 60$ No bands
200	UV V	$0 > \tau > 5 > 60 > 300$ No bands	$0 > \tau > 5 > 60 > 300$ No bands	$0 > \tau > 5 > 60 > 300$ No bands
300	UV V	$0 > \tau > 5 > 60 > 300$ $0 > 300 > 60 = 5 = \tau$ $D \leqslant 0.01$	$0 > \tau > 5 > 60 > 300$ Bands indistin-guish., $D \leqslant 0.01$	$0 > \tau > 5 > 60 > 300$ $\tau = 5 = 60 > 0 > 300$ Shape irregular, $D \leqslant 0.02$
400	UV V	$0 > 300 > \tau > 60 > 5$ $300 > 0 > 60 = 5 = \tau$ Shape irregular $D \leqslant 0.02$	$0 > 300 > 60 = \tau > 5$ $300 = 60 = 5 = \tau > 0$ Shape irregular, $D \leqslant 0.04$	$0 > 300 > 60 = \tau > 5$ $300 > 60 = 5 > \tau > 0$ Shape close to the Gauss curve
500	UV V	$0 > 300 > \tau = 60 = 5$ $300 > \tau = 60 = 5 > 0$ $D \leqslant 0.02$	$0 > \tau = 300 = 60 = 5$ $300 > 60 > 5 = \tau > 0$	$0 > \tau = 300 = 60 = 5$ $300 > 60 > 5 = \tau > 0$

Sub-data, 400 °C, 300 h:

	D_{max}	λ_{max}, nm	$\Delta\lambda$, nm
τ	0.085	410	78
5	0.092	406	80
60	0.093	403	78
300	0.095	401	78

Sub-data, 500 °C:

	D_{max}	λ_{max}, nm	$\Delta\lambda$, nm	D_{max}	λ_{max}, nm	$\Delta\lambda$, nm
$\tau = 5$	0.090	410	44	0.200	410	48
60	0.100	405	38	0.230	405	42
300	0.105	403	36	0.240	403	40

T designates the absorption bands of the same sample subjected to heat treatment at the various given temperatures; and 5, 60, and 300 designate the absorption bands of the same sample subjected to secondary irradiation for 5, 60, or 300 min, respectively. Measurements of the half-widths and the positions of the maxima of the absorption bands in the visible spectral region were made where possible, and the results of these measurements are also presented in Table 4. The relative positions of the absorption bands in the visible and in the ultraviolet spectral regions as a result of the primary irradiation, heat treatment, and secondary irradiation are indicated by the mathematical symbols "greater than" and "equal to." For instance, in Table 3, we find the following for the case of primary irradiation for 60 min and heat treatment at 300°C in the ultraviolet region: $0 > T > 5 > 60 > 300$. This means that the absorption band in the sample after primary irradiation is positioned higher than in the same sample after heat treatment, which, in turn, is positioned higher than in the sample which received secondary irradiation for 5 min, etc. The spectral regions are denoted in Table 3 by UV for ultraviolet and V for the visible.

Analogous experiments were carried out on glass samples with thicknesses of 0.2 and 1.0 mm under the action of unfiltered radiation from a PRK-7 lamp.

Based on the experimental results obtained, one can formulate the following generalizations:

1. The maxima for the absorption of glasses irradiated for 5, 60, and 300 min lie in the ultraviolet portion of the spectrum, in the 270- to 280-nm region. Heat treatment results in their displacement toward the short-wave region, with the displacement being larger, the higher is the temperature of heat treatment. Secondary irradiation without a light filter increases the absorption bands in the ultraviolet spectral region of heat-treated glasses, while irradiation with a light filter decreases these bands; the longer the irradiation time, the greater is the decrease. This is observed up to heat-treatment temperatures of 400°C. At 500°C, the absorption bands in the ultraviolet spectral region are entirely superimposed on the absorption bands of heat-treated samples.

2. When silver particles are present after heat treatment of glass at 100, 200, and 300°C (exposures of 5 and 60 min), the ab-

sorption bands in the visible spectral region either do not appear at all or cannot be identified.

3. At low intensities of the absorption bands, not exceeding 0.020 with respect to the optical density, secondary light irradiation does not result in a change in the absorption band in the visible spectral region, whereas irradiation after heat treatment at 300°C develops an absorption band of an irregular form, which is arranged approximately parallel to the axis of the wavelengths and is higher than the corresponding curve for the heat-treated sample. Such an effect was observed for samples irradiated for 5 and 60 min and heat treated at 400°C, and also for samples irradiated for 5 min and heat treated at 500°C.

4. For samples subjected to longer irradiation or to heat treatment at higher temperatures (300 min at 400°C, 60 min at 500°C, 300 min at 500°C), the absorption bands have the shape of a Gauss curve. With increasing dosage of secondary light irradiation, a displacement of the absorption maxima to the left and a decrease in the half-width of the curves is observed.

5. The observed effects are extremely small, and the maximum change in the optical density is 12%, which attests to the considerable instability of the nuclei formed with respect to the secondary light irradiation.

In analogy to the processes taking place in crystals and preceding the process of colloid formation, one may also expect the precipitation of atomic centers of silver in glass. Gorbachev et al. [219] think that atomic centers are absorbed in the visible spectral region with a maximum at 405 nm. These centers, they believe, precipitate during the heat treatment of photosensitive glass at temperatures not higher than 400°C, after which their amalgamation into small particles with sizes less than 20 nm is assumed. Granting a definite structure for the silver aggregates, we should obtain perfectly identical absorption bands for glasses which have received a different dosage of ultraviolet rays. The results of our experiments show just the opposite. Absorption bands of glasses irradiated for different times have different half-widths and different positions of maxima, and, if normalized, are not superimposed (see Fig. 40a). Therefore, the silver aggregates which precipitate at 300-400°C have a different structure and may not be thought of as atomic. Weyl [60], by studying the luminescence at various temperatures of silver-containing glasses reduced in a hydrogen atmosphere, obtained the most intense luminescence at 100-120°C. No coloring of the glasses was observed in this case.

Thus, absorption bands corresponding to atomic centers are not observed experimentally. One may assume that they are either positioned in the ultraviolet spectral region, or that the effective absorption cross section of these centers in the visible spectral region is extremely small. The absorption bands we observed (see Fig. 40) must then be ascribed either to colloidal particles or to silver aggregated in a dispersed state, which is the state intermediate between the atomic and the colloidal states.

Using Savost'yanova's method, we calculated from the Mie formulas [220], using Minor's data [221], the absorption curve for the smallest colloidal particles relative to the wavelength of the visible light. In comparing this curve with experimental curves (see Fig. 40b), it follows that, while the curves at 300-400°C fail to coincide with the calculated curve both with respect to the half-width and with respect to the position of the maxima, the curves at 500°C only fail to coincide with respect to the position of the maxima, but do attain half-widths which are equal to the half-width of the calculated curve. The noncoincidence of the maxima may be explained by the inaccuracy of the interpolation curves, since, with increasing temperature, the absorption coefficient of bulk Ag also increases [222]. Therefore, the absorption maximum for silver particles precipitating at temperatures of 300-500°C and "frozen" due to the high viscosity of glass will be shifted toward the short-wavelength side. The assumption that colloidal particles of different degrees of dispersion precipitate at 300-400°C, because of which the experimental curves are broadened, does not agree with the observations at 500°C, when the half-width of the experimental absorption bands attains a minimum. The reason for this could be the resorption of large colloidal particles, which, however, does not seem very probable. Finally, one may assume that in centers which precipitate at temperatures of 300-400°C, a rigid metallic structure with collectivized conduction electrons inside the Ag aggregates is absent, and thus the deviation of the optical constants of Ag from the optical constants of the bulk metal results in a large half-width of the experimental absorption bands. As was shown above, these centers are not colloidal particles, nor are they atomic centers; one can consider them to be molecular-like aggregates of a different degree of dispersion.

By analyzing the results of the secondary light action on silver particles, we obtain additional information on the nature of the centers forming in photosensitive glasses:

1. Absorption bands in the visible spectral region cannot be caused by the atomic centers of silver, because the secondary light action would lead to their rapid decolorization, as has been observed for the atomic centers of the alkali metal in alkali halide crystals during the action of the light in the absorption region proper of the F-centers.

2. The different behavior of absorption bands after secondary light action is more than likely caused by the different structure of the molecular-like aggregates, which form absorption bands in the visible spectral region.

It is known that the process of producing stable nuclei of a latent image in silver halide emulsions proceeds from the emergence of the atomic Ag^0, through the subcenters Ag_2^+, to the positively charged group made of four silver atoms Ag_4^+, for the formation of which three electrons are necessary [223]. For photosensitive glasses, one may assume the emergence of analogous silver aggregates, which subsequently will serve as the crystallization nuclei for metallic silver. After heat treatment at 300 and 400°C, the required amorphous aggregates are formed. The aggregation of the particles results in increased intensity of coloring only when the contact of the "conglomerating" particles is so close that collectivization of conduction electrons takes place [224].

The absence of a shift of the maxima into the region of longer wavelengths and the constancy of coloring may be explained by the absence of such a close contact between the colloidal particles.

At 500°C, a decrease in the half-width of the experimental absorption bands is observed which corresponds to the crystallization process of silver, with the optical constants of the bulk metal having been attained. One may think that it is exactly at that moment that silver single crystals are formed having a regular crystalline structure, because the half-widths of the calculated and the experimental curves coincide. Since the process of the decrease in the half-width takes place independently of exposure, one may assume that temperature is the determining factor for the crystallization. Apparently, at 500°C (for some glasses, at 550°C), the silver particles having the regular crystalline structure are energetically more stable than the molecular-like aggregates. An analogous effect is produced by secondary irradiation if the glass samples have an optical density of better than 0.1 in the absorption-band maximum. With increasing duration of heat treatment at 500°C, the growth of Ag single crystals takes place, and a displacement of the absorption-band maxima toward the long-wavelength spectral region and a broadening of the curves are observed. For samples irradiated for a shorter period of time, a maximum growth rate and a maximum size of the silver particles are observed.

By analogy to the assumption in the theory of Mott and Gurney [225], describing the growth of colloidal particles in silver halide crystals, and confirmed by the results of numerous experiments, one may assume that in glasses, too, the growth of colloidal particles is realized by the repeated alternation of the motion of the electrons and the Ag ions to the centers of colloid formation. Photoelectrons charge these particles negatively, and the ions are reduced on their surface to neutral atoms. The process continues as long as ions or electrons are being used up, as a result of which, limiting sizes of colloidal particles will be observed.

Based on the experiments performed, the process of the formation and growth of colloidal Ag particles in photosensitive glass may be represented in the following manner. During irradiation of photosensitive glass by ultraviolet light, the photoelectrons excited from the Ce^{3+} and Ag^+ ions and from the structural network of the glass localize at the defects of the network. Heating the glass to 300-400°C liberates these electrons from their traps, and they then interact with the Ag ions to form molecular-like aggregates of varying degrees of dispersion. The molecular-like silver aggregates do not have a rigid crystalline structure, no conduction electrons are collectivized, and the viscosity of glass and the fact that the temperature is too low inhibit this process. When glass is heated to 500°C (for some glasses, to 550°C), the crystallization of molecular-like aggregates takes place with the formation of Ag single crystals, which is attested to by a decrease in the half-width of the absorption bands. The longer the duration of heat treatment, the more is the growth of silver particles enhanced. Nonetheless, after the $\Delta\lambda - \tau$ curves reach a state of saturation, further heat treatment does not result in a change in the size of the precipitating particles.

The emergence and the growth of particles or nuclei in photosensitive glasses containing Ag and Ce has also been studied by Yokota and Simidzu [226] and Yokota [227]. The heating of the glass produced the diffusion of ions to the places where the electrons become entrapped by lattice defects, and caused the formation of Ag particles, which was deduced based on the appearance of additional absorption bands. These authors determined the size and the amount of Ag particles present by comparing the experimental results with the results calculated using the Mie theory on absorption coefficients and diffusion. Heating glass during irradiation markedly increased its photosensitivity. At temperatures in excess of 350°C, development of the image occurred during irradiation. The activation energy for the transition of an electron of a Ce^{3+} ion from the excited state to the conduction band was determined to be equal to 0.11 eV.

By examining the formation of nuclei in gold-containing ruby glass as a function of heat treatment, Weyl [60] indicates that the growth of these — at first, invisible — nuclei into crystals of colloidal sizes may be the result of two different processes: recrystallization and coagulation.

Recrystallization depends on the diffusion coefficient and on the different diffusion rates of large and small crystals. Small crystals possess a better solubility due to their higher surface energy and lower melting point. Even for an extremely limited solubility of dispersed crystals, the smaller crystals dissolve, while the coarser crystals grow and increase in size. Tin and other metallophilous ions increase the solubility of the noble metal in glass at low temperatures.

In glasses not having an adequate dissolving capability relative to the particles of noble metals during the submersion time, recrystallization becomes attenuated, whereas the growth of particles from submicroscopic to colloidal sizes proceeds due to coagulation as the result of collisions. The secondary particles which appear here differ from the regularly grown crystals with regard to structure and light absorption. In view of the fact that nuclei which are composed of several hundreds of metal atoms have a lower mobility than simple atoms, the collisions between particles leads, according to Weyl [60], not to a regular growth of one of the lattices, but to the appearance of two separate lattices and, furthermore, to the appearance of dendritic aggregates or clusters of a large number of smaller crystals.

In order to verify the theory developed by Smoluchowski [229, 230] concerning the coagulation of gold particles, Ehringhaus and Wintgen [228] (also see Weyl [60]), investigated the effect of heat treatment on the size of the Au particles and on the light absorption of fused borates containing varying amounts of Au. It was found that at 925°C and at a concentration of $2 \cdot 10^{-3}\%$ Au, the ratio between the radius of attraction R between the particles and the radius a of the particle is approximately equal to two, i.e., prior to coagulation, the Au particles must come into contact with each other. However, at lower Au concentrations, this ratio significantly increased, approaching 14, which the authors [228] explain either by the presence of impurities playing the role of nuclei or by the additional precipitation of Au on the larger-size particles and the growth of these particles due to recrystallization.

The mechanism of coloring titanium-containing glasses of various systems with the addition of a small amount of Ag was studied by Sakaino and Moriya [231], who determined a rapid precipitation of Ag in phosphate glasses, which is explained by the change in the equilibrium

$$Ti^{3+} \rightleftarrows Ti^{4+} \tag{28}$$

and the action of Ti^{3+} as a thermal reducer, namely:

$$Ag^+ + Ti^{3+} \rightarrow Ag^0 + Ti^{4+} \tag{29}$$

The change in the absorption spectrum in the 460-nm region in silicate glasses containing Ti and Ag is ascribed to the precipitation of TiO_2 around Ag microcrystals.

Fanderlik [232] studied the photochemical process of the formation of nuclei in photosensitive Au- and Ag-containing glasses of the following compositions: 72.5 SiO_2, 12.5 Li_2O, 5 K_2O, 10 Al_2O_3, 0.02 CeO_2, 0.01 Au ("Fopl 40"); and 72.5 SiO_2, 12.5 Li_2O, 5 K_2O, 10 Al_2O_3, 0.02 CeO_2, 0.08 Ag ("Fopl 17"). He determined that with increasing irradiation dosage, the depth of propagation of coloration in heat-treated glasses first increased, attained a maximum, and then decreased. This phenomenon is explained by the emergence or nucleation at large irradiation dosages of a significant number of neutral Au or Ag atoms which, during the heat treatment, form lithium silicate nuclei which are considerably larger in size.

Berezhnoi and Polukhin [757] investigated the mechanism of the formation and growth of colloidal particles of silver in photosensitive glasses of the following compositions (in wt.%): Glass No. 1, 4 K_2O, 12 Li_2O, 8 Al_2O_3, and 76 SiO_2; Glass No. 2, 4 K_2O, 8 Li_2O, 12 Al_2O_3, 76 SiO_2, activated by 0.02 Ag and 0.03 CeO_2. For the measurement of the electronic absorption spectra of these glasses, polished samples 0.5 mm thick were used.

When photosensitive glass is exposed to ultraviolet light, the known band of the supplementary optical absorption occurs at 275 nm which apparently belongs to the electron or hole centers forming after irradiation [219] (Figs. 44a and 45a, curves 1). During heat treatment of irradiated photosensitive glass, the liberation of photoelectrons from the entrapment centers occurs, and some of the Ag^+ ions are reduced to their atomic state. During the early stages of heat treatment (300-450°C), this process is characterized by the disappearance of the optical absorption band induced during irradiation at 275 nm, and by the appearance of a relatively weak absorption band at 410 nm (Figs. 44 and 45, curves 2). The band at 410 nm is due to the absorption by very fine colloidal particles of silver which apparently form as a result of the coagulation of silver atoms. The latter process proceeds very rapidly and directly follows the reduction process of silver atoms, since it was not possible to observe absorption by isolated atomic centers of silver.

The absorption produced by the atomic centers of silver can be observed in alkali halide crystals prepared by condensation, at low temperatures, of the vapors of a mixture of the alkali halide crystals containing 1-2% AgCl and the same amount of the excess alkali metal. The corresponding absorption band was observed by Kaiser [758], and is positioned at 285 nm for the KCl crystal.

The intensity of the absorption band at 410 nm displays a rapid (within approximately 1-2 h) intermediary saturation at a heat-treatment temperature of 450°C, with the level of saturation

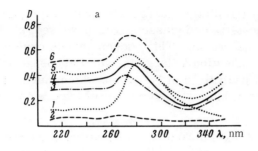

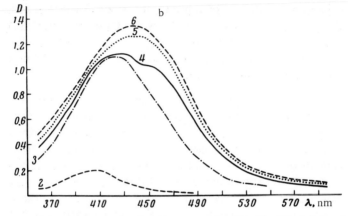

Fig. 44. Supplementary absorption spectrum for glass No. 1 in (a) the ultraviolet and (b) the visible spectral regions. 1) After irradiation. After passing through the following successive stages of heat treatment: 2) 2 h at 450°C; 3) 2 h at 520°C; 4) 2 h at 520°C; 5) 4 h at 520°C; 6) 4 h at 520°C.

increasing with increasing time of exposure. After further heat treatment at 500°C, a spasmodic increase in the intensity of the absorption band is observed. This indicates that precipitation is occurring of the still unreduced silver ions on the colloidal particles which had previously been formed through the coagulation of the silver atoms. Thus, a further increase in the size of the colloidal particles of silver takes place.

The latter process may be comprehended as being based on Weyl's concept of screening [109–114], according to which the colloidal particles of the metal form more easily, the higher the polarizability of the medium. Consequently, the formation of very fine colloidal particles of the metal from silver atoms in a medium

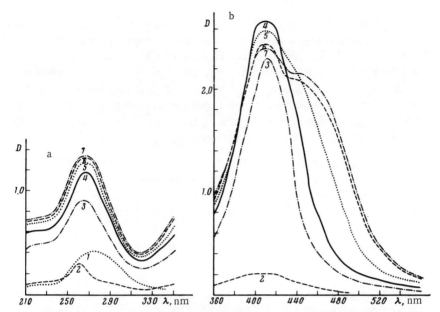

Fig. 45. Supplementary absorption spectrum for glass No. 2 in the (a) ultraviolet and
(b) the visible spectral regions. 1) After irradiation. After passing through the following successive stages of heat treatment: 2) 2 h at 450°C; 3) 2 h at 520°C; 4) 4 h at
520°C; 5) 6 h at 520°C; 6) 12 h at 520°C; 7) 14 h at 520°C.

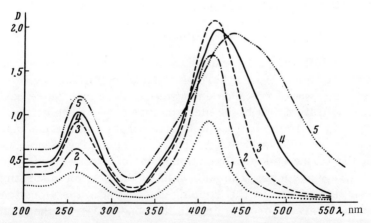

Fig. 46. Supplementary absorption spectrum for glass No. 2 (irradiation time, 125 min)
after passing through the following successive stages of heat treatment: 1) 2 h at 500°C;
2) 2 h at 500°C; 3) 4 h at 500°C; 4) 9 h at 500°C; 5) 5 h at 530°C.

with polarizability insufficiently high causes, with increasing temperature, phase separation of the surrounding medium. This results in enrichment of the regions directly adjacent to the colloidal particles, which are highly polarized by the ion concentrations
(including Ag^+ or Li^+ or K^+ ions), and in impoverishment of the
regions which are at a distance from the colloidal particles. The
phase separation process continues until the disturbance exerted
by the colloidal particle on the surrounding medium is screened.

It must be mentioned that the growth in the absorption band
at 410 nm is accompanied by the normal increase in absorption at
260-280 nm in the ultraviolet spectral region, the intensity of
which is considerably less (Figs. 44-47). In alkali halide crystals
in which colloidal particles of silver have formed, there also exist,
as a rule, two absorption bands, one in the visible spectral region,
the other in the ultraviolet. The intensity of the ultraviolet band
is less here, too. For instance, it has been noted [758, 759] that
absorption bands of the colloidal particles of silver in a KCl crystal are observed at 400-420 and 280-285 nm. As has been mentioned above, the ultraviolet absorption band is also characteristic
for isolated atomic centers of silver in an alkali halide crystal.
One may conclude that this band also characterizes the intra-
atomic absorption in the case of colloidal particles of silver. Insofar as the absorption band at 410 nm is concerned, it is caused by
the plasma resonance of the collective vibrations of valence electrons in individual colloidal particles [760]; that is why this absorption band is characteristic only for colloidal particles, and not
for isolated atomic centers of silver.

The following expression has been obtained [761] for the
plasma frequency ω_0 of spherical colloidal particles: $\omega_0^2 =$
$\frac{1}{3}(ne^2/m\varepsilon)$, where n is the density of the electrons taking part in
plasma vibrations, m is the electron mass, e is the electron
charge, and ε is the optical dielectric constant of the medium in
which the particle is located. Thus, the plasma frequency depends
basically on the bulk concentration of the electrons taking part in
collective vibrations. The half-width of the plasma absorption
band is determined by the damping coefficient of the vibration,
which is inversely proportional to the conductivity of the particle
material, which, in turn, is directly proportional to the average
length of the electron free path, with that length normally limited

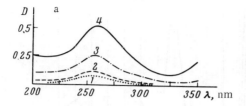

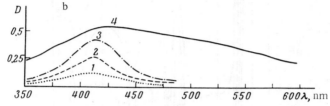

Fig. 47. Supplementary absorption spectrum for glass No. 2 in (a) the ultraviolet and (b) the visible spectral regions (irradiation time, 25 min) after going through the following successive stages of heat treatment: 1) 2 h at 500°C; 2) 2 h at 500°C; 3) 4 h at 500°C; 4) 9 h at 500°C; 5) 5 h at 530°C.

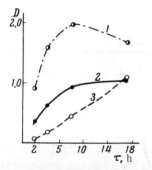

Fig. 48. Increase in the absorption as a function of the duration of heat treatment at 500°C (from data of Fig. 46) at: 1) 415; 2) 260; 3) 470 nm.

by the size of the particles. In this connection, when the particle size increases, the absorption band ought to narrow down.

By employing the above formula, one may calculate the position of the absorption maximum for colloidal particles of a given metal in various different media if one knows the dielectric constants ε or the indices of refraction of the respective media.

We calculated the frequencies of the plasma absorption bands for colloidal particles of potassium and lithium for the glasses studied by using the absorption data for these colloidal particles in crystals [760]. The index of refraction of the glasses studied was equal to 1.52. According to the calculations, there is an absorption band for lithium colloidal particles at 470 nm, and one for potassium colloidal particles at 800 nm. It is

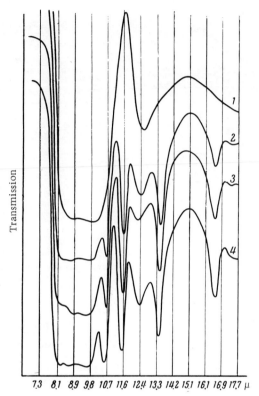

Fig. 49. Infrared transmission spectra for glass No. 1, which was first irradiated and then crystallized at various temperatures. 1) Initial glass. Successive heat treatment: 2) 2 h at 600°C; 3) 2 h at 700°C; 3) 2 h at 800°C.

reasonable to expect the appearance of these absorption bands in the glasses investigated, since highly polarized phases are mainly being formed when lithium and potassium ions take part.

Upon further heat treatment at 500°C, a saturation in the intensity of the ultraviolet band was observed (Fig. 45, curves 4-7; Fig. 48), which attests to the fact that the deposition of silver has terminated. However, even after the saturation in the intensity of the ultraviolet absorption band was achieved, the absorption band in the visible spectral region continued to be deformed. As can be seen from Figs. 44-48, a distinct increase in absorption at 470 nm is observed. The more the absorption increases at 470 nm, the

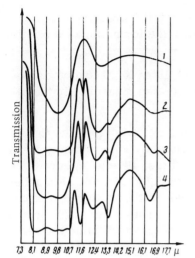

7,3 8,1 8,9 9,8 10,7 11,6 12,4 13,3 14,2 15,1 16,1 16,9 17,7 μ

Fig. 50. Infrared transmission spectra for glass No. 1, heat treated at 600°C for 2 h, as a function of exposure time. 1) Original glass. Glass irradiated for: 2) 5 min; 3) 25 min; 4) 125 min.

more markedly the absorption decrease at 410–415 nm (Figs. 45b, 48). Further heat treatment often results in the shifting of the total absorption maximum in the visible spectral region to 430–440 nm.

The increase in absorption at 470 nm clearly indicates the appearance of colloidal particles of lithium, with their interaction with the colloidal particles of silver also present. This is possible only when lithium becomes deposited directly on the colloidal particles of silver. The more lithium deposited, the larger, apparently, is the contact area between lithium and silver, and lithium, which diffuses into the silver, becomes dissolved in it. The electron concentration in colloidal particles is somewhat decreased, which is the reason the total absorption maximum shifts into the intermediary position at 430–440 nm (Figs. 44, 46, 47). The slight increase in the absorption in the 360-nm region (Fig. 45, curves 5–7; Fig. 46, curve 5; Fig. 47, curve 4) is apparently due to the broadening of the absorption band in the visible region due to an increase in the damping coefficient. This fact can easily be explained if one assumes that when lithium becomes dissolved in silver, an alloy with a poorer conductivity is formed. At small exposures, one may obtain an especially wide absorption band in the visible spectral region (Fig. 47, curve 4). Moreover, in this case, the intensity of the visible band is comparable to the intensity of the ultraviolet band. This obviously indicates that the formation of colloidal alloys takes place here.

No absorption was observed in the 800-nm region. This points to the absence of potassium colloids. Although the laws obtained regarding the change in the absorption band in the visible region do not completely eliminate the possibility of insignificant alloying between potassium and silver, we nevertheless consider such a possibility as very unlikely, especially since we do not know of any data at all demonstrating whether the formation of a similar alloy is even possible.

The transmission by thin films of glass No. 1 and of glass-crystalline thin films made from it were also measured in the infrared spectral region.

The chemical composition of glass No. 1 is closer to that of the disilicate than to that of the metasilicate. This is demonstrated by the infrared spectrum of this glass (Figs. 49 and 50, curves 1). After the crystallization of samples irradiated at 600°C, a number of sharp, narrow absorption lines appear on the background of the almost-invariable spectrum of this glass. These lines are located at 10.7, 11.6, 13.5, and 16.6 μ, and correspond to lithium metasilicate crystals. From this, one may conclude that lithium metasilicate already precipitates in significant amounts at low crystallization temperatures.

Infrared spectra indicate that crystallization does not start everywhere, but only on the nuclei by means of the above-described phase separation. As is known, the metasilicate is more polarizable than the disilicate. It is also known that lithium metasilicate does not form glass. The rate of precipitation of the crystalline phase increases with increasing exposure time, which is explained by the formation of a large number of nuclei during long exposures (Fig. 50). This is clearly supported by the long-wave lines for the metasilicate, which are less intensive, and which are, consequently, off the saturation absorption.

It must be mentioned that infrared spectra of nonirradiated glass after its crystallization are very similar to the spectra of the irradiated glass. Here, nonirradiated glasses frequently do not show colloidal absorption bands after precrystallization heat treatment. One may assume that in this case crystallization takes place on spontaneously forming submicroscopic colloidal particles of the metal. By "submicroscopic," we have in mind particles of such small sizes that plasma resonance does not take place.

As a result of this investigation, the mechanism of the formation and the growth of colloidal particles of silver in photosensitive glasses was more accurately defined. First, the formation of colloidal particles takes place through the coagulation of silver atoms,

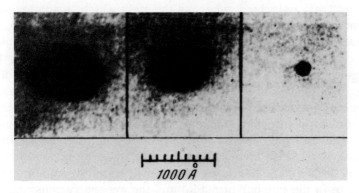

Fig. 51. Gold particles in photosensitive glass. Electron micrographs obtained by electron transmission through a glass foil 900 Å thick.

and then their growth occurs due to the phase separation process taking place in the glass.

Phase separation results in the formation around the colloidal particle of a screening or shielding layer composed of a phase which has better polarizability than the matrix glass phase. The primary crystalline phase precipitating is lithium metasilicate, which has a better polarizability than the matrix glass phase.

7. CRITICAL SIZE OF STABLE NUCLEI FOR HETEROGENEOUS CRYSTALLIZATION

Stookey [39] observed experimentally that very small particles of a catalyst are not capable of producing nuclei for another crystalline phase. This is especially true for photosensitive glasses, in which the Au crystals which precipitate during the photochemical reaction become the catalysts for the crystallization of lithium metasilicate.

In order to verify the above-mentioned effect and to determine the critical size of colloidal particles at which their catalytic action begins, Maurer [233] investigated the scattering and absorption of light by a photosensitive glass of the composition 81 SiO_2, 10 Li_2O, 5 K_2O, 4 Al_2O_3, 0.15 Sb_2O_3, 0.02 CeO_2, and 0.005 Au. The measurements of the scattering of light in the glass at the various stages of precipitation of the colloidal particles were based on the fact that the light which is scattered by the metallic colloid is almost entirely polarized, whereas the light which is scattered by the anisotropic lithium metasilicate crystals is depolarized. At the early stages of the precipitation of the particles, the depolarized component of the scattered light in the absence of crystals changes only little; however, it increases noticeably, depending on the growth of the colloidal particles to the sizes at which the rate of nucleus formation becomes significant. It was assumed that at the moment of the sharp increase in the depolarized component of the scattered light, the particles precipitating in glass attained critical size. With increasing exposure to x-ray irradiation, the size of the metallic particles decreased, which is explained by the increase in the number of nuclei and the generally constant amount of the precipitating metal present. At some intermediate exposure, the average size of the given number of particles becomes equal to the critical size necessary for the effective formation of nuclei.

By measuring the scattering of the plane-polarized light as a function of the time of the precipitation of the particles, it was determined that approximately $4 \cdot 10^4$ sec are needed for a noticeable formation of nuclei of lithium metasilicate to begin; after the expiration of this time, the anisotropic crystals of lithium metasilicate start to depolarize the scattered light, because of which, the intensity of polarization increases. By making use of the experimental data obtained, Maurer [233] calculated the average particle diameter for three irradiated samples after heat treatment for $4 \cdot 10^4$ sec to be equal to 38 Å. For an exposure of 4000 R, the value was 80 Å; for 7000 R, it was 75 Å; and for 10,000 R, it was 74 Å. With irradiation dosage increased to 40,000 R and higher, crystallization of samples held at 495°C for 70 h and at 600°C for 10 h disappeared, as was evident from the blurring. The particle size in the sample obtained by a dosage of 15,000 R was 76 Å, and the size obtained by a dosage of 40,000 R was 44 Å. The Au particles investigated by electron microscopy had a hexagonal shape and rounded corners (Fig. 51). It is assumed that these particles are heavily rounded rhombohedral dodecahedra with a size of approximately 100 Å.

Thus, the catalyst of the crystallization process must have a sufficiently large critical size (approximately 80 Å); after this size is reached, the rate of nucleus formation sharply increases. According to Maurer [233], one of the possible reasons for this phenomenon is the decrease in the activation energy with increasing size of the catalyst and the approach of the dimensions of its surface to the critical size of the lithium metasilicate nuclei. If one assumed a dodecahedral shape of the particles of the catalyst, then the area of the surface of one of the Au particles with a size of approximately 80 Å is approximately $(40 \text{ Å})^2$ which, according to Maurer [233], is too much for lithium metasilicate nuclei of critical size. Another possible reason is the appearance of mechanical stresses in the nuclei as a result of distortion of their shape when contacted with the catalyst, and the subsequent damping of the process of their formation because of this. At exceedingly small radii of curvature of the nucleus — for instance, when the size of the particles of the catalyst is less than 20 Å — the stress energy necessary for the formation of a crystalline lattice and, consequently, the free activation energy of the rate of formation of nuclei become very large, while the rate of this process becomes insignificant.

Stookey [119] expresses doubt that the minimum size of the Au crystal capable of catalyzing lithium silicate crystallization is 80 Å, i.e., not less than 10,000 atoms, as determined by Maurer [233], since this number is very much larger than the three to four atoms necessary for homogeneous nucleation of the Au crystal itself.

However, Fletcher's data [234], showing that the critical minimum size of the particles for condensation, sublimation, and freezing of water on extraneous nuclei is approximately 100 Å, indicate, according to Stookey [119], the existence of a generally effective critical size for the nuclei of heterogeneous crystallization in the various media themselves.

According to Lillie [235], the critical size of nuclei in various glassy systems may vary from 10 to 250 Å in diameter, while the ratio between the diameter of the nucleus and the diameter of the crystal is approximately equal to 1 : 50.

8. EFFECT OF THE CATALYST ON THE COMPOSITION OF PRECIPITATING CRYSTALS. NUMBER AND SIZE OF THE CRYSTALS

As has been mentioned previously, Stookey [119] ascribes great significance to the specific action by the catalyst, which tends to accelerate the crystallization of compounds which are crystallographically compatible with it. Because of this, one can control not only the number, the distribution, and the size of the crystals, but also their composition. In practice, this means that, depending on the structure of the catalyst, both equilibrium and non-equilibrium products of catalyzed crystallization can be precipitated. Generally, in the case of a similarity between the structures of the catalyst and of the crystalline phase A in whose crystallization field is a selected glass composition, the precipitation of the phase A occurs. However, in some cases, when a catalyst with a different structure is introduced, instead of the phase A, the metastable phase B is precipitated, which, upon heat treatment, may be transformed into phase A. If, after the crystallization of the metastable phase B from the variable composition of the remaining glass, other crystalline phases continue to precipitate, then phase A may not form at all, i.e., only crystallization of metastable phases will take place [119].

According to Stookey [119], from 10^9 to 10^{15} crystals of the catalyst may precipitate in a 1 mm^3 of glass, each of which initiates the growth of one crystal. During the simultaneous growth of such a large number of crystals, total crystallization is achieved, with the average size of the crystals varying from 1 μ in the first case to 100 Å in the second case. In the photosensitive glass of the composition 81.5 SiO_2, 12.0 Li_2O, 3.5 K_2O, 3.0 Al_2O_3, 0.02 Ag, and 0.03 CeO_2 which had been irradiated to saturation and which developed images, the average size of the crystal was measured to be 4 μ, which corresponds to a content of 10^{10} crystals per 1 cm^3 of a photographic image [39].

Chapter III

Production Technology and Chemical Compositions for Photosensitive Glasses and Photosensitive Glass-Ceramics

The photosensitive-glass compositions described in this chapter were classified basically according to the type of photosensitive additions introduced into them, as well as according to certain other distinguishing peculiarities characteristic for each group of glasses. It is necessary to state, however, that such a classification is rather conditional, since, in a number of tables, glass compositions containing Cu, Au, or Ag are given at the same time.

1. COPPER-CONTAINING PHOTOSENSITIVE GLASSES

The compositions and methods of production of Cu-containing photosensitive glasses were proposed by Dalton [236, 238] and Stookey [239]. Acidic glasses, in which copper is in the state of a true copper silicate solution, are colored green or blue. During rapid cooling of glasses with the low Cu content, which were melted under reducing conditions, they are obtained colorless and acquire a red "ruby" color only during a subsequent heat-treatment process, due to the formation of colloidal Cu or Cu_2O particles. The development of coloration in Cu-containing glasses depends on the rate of cooling of the melt, on the duration and temperature of subsequent heat treatment, and also on the presence in the glass composition of a small amount of SnO_2, which intensifies the sensitivity of glass to heat treatment.

In glasses irradiated by ultraviolet or other short-wave rays, the coloration appears at lower temperatures and at lesser times of heat treatment, whereas, in some cases, the blue color already develops during the irradiation process. Spectral analysis did not show the presence in such glasses of copper in an oxidized state. By heating the irradiated glass to the annealing temperature, copper-ruby is obtained. The initial blue color does not depend on the amount of SnO_2 present in glass.

Into the initial batch from which the copper-containing glass is to be melted a small quantity of SnO_2 is added, as well as a reducer, such as sodium cyanide, NaCN, or abietic acid, $C_{19}H_{29}CO_2H$, plus copper in an amount corresponding to a content of not less than 0.05% Cu_2O in the finished glass. The higher the Cu content, the shorter is the irradiation time by ultraviolet light of the shaped glass articles. However, if the copper content is too high, it is hard to obtain a colorless glass after cooling, particularly for thick articles, where the preservation of heat during cooling is equivalent to the heat treatment necessary for the development of coloring. For rapidly cooled, thin products, relatively high copper concentrations are allowable, which makes it possible to shorten the irradiation time. For instance, glass fibers containing approximately 1% Cu_2O, which are at first colorless, acquire a light-blue color after irradiation for 10 sec, whereas during the subsequent heat treatment, they become red. Without irradiation after heat treatment in an oxidizing air atmosphere, no color is produced.

Table 4 presents four recommended [236-239] batch compositions for the melting of Cu-containing photosensitive glasses. Both NaCN and abietic acid are weak reducers. Strongly oxidizing conditions lead to the formation of stable cupric ions, which give glass a blue color and which cannot be reduced to the metal by heat treatment. On the other hand, strongly reducing conditions produce the deposition of metallic copper with the formation of a cloudy brownish color. An intermediate state of reduction makes an almost colorless glass which, after secondary heating, develops a satisfactory ruby color.

Since tin oxide is absent in batch No. 1, the glass melted from it is capable of being colored blue during irradiation. However, during heat treatment, it is not possible to obtain a satisfactory red color in this glass. Batch Nos. 2, 3, and 4 give glasses which can be colored both red and blue, with glass based on batch No. 4 capable of serving for the production of glass fibers and thin-walled glass products [236-239].

Table 4. Batch Compositions for the Melting of Cu-Containing
Glasses

Component	Content (in parts by wt.) of various batches			
	1	2	3	4
SiO_2	330	330	330	330
Na_2CO_3	139	139	139	139
$Al(OH)_3$	10.5	10.5	10.5	10.5
$Ca(OH)_2$	52	52	52	52
Cu_2O	0.5	0.5	0.5	0.5
NaCN	3.8	3.8	—	—
SnO_2	—	1.2	1.2	1.2
$C_{19}H_{29}CO_2H$	—	—	2.5	10

Table 5. Batch Compositions for the Melting of Cu-Containing
Glasses with CeO_2 Additions

Component	Contents (in parts by wt.) of various batches			Component	Contents (in parts by wt.) of various batches		
	1	2	3		1	2	3
SiO_2	330	330	330	SnO_2	—	1.2	1.2
Na_2CO_3	139	139	139	CeO_2	0.2	0.2	0.2
$Al(OH)_3$	10.5	10.5	10.5	Sugar	1—3	1—3	—
$CaCO_3$	70	70	70	NH_4Cl	—	—	8—9
Cu_2O	0.5	0.5	0.5				

In the glasses described, it is possible to obtain photographic images by using a negative which is capable of transmitting active radiation. The copper-containing glass can be directly covered by the photographic emulsion, and the negative can be procured
on it by conventional methods; the glass can then be irradiated
through the negative, after which the emulsion is removed and the
glass is subjected to heat treatment, yielding a ruby-red image. It
is also possible to obtain colored images in glass by the projection
photoprinting method and subsequent heat treatment [236-239].

In order to increase the photosensitivity of copper-containing glasses and to intensify the contrast of the details in the image, Stookey [240] proposed introduction of small quantities of CeO_2 (not more than 0.05%) into the initial batch of these glasses. Table 5 gives the batch compositions which were suggested by Stookey for the melting of these glasses.

Sugar and ammonium chloride are reducers − the latter a very weak one − capable of achieving an extremely accurate reduction of copper in these photosensitive glasses so as to obtain coloring of the required density. The amount of reducer needed depends on, among other factors, the size and the type of the melt container, and for given melting conditions, it can easily be determined experimentally. For instance, the batch compositions listed above with the indicated quantities of the reducer present are suitable for melting in closed pots with a capacity of 400 kg [240].

2. GOLD-CONTAINING PHOTOSENSITIVE GLASSES

By irradiating and striking Au-containing glasses, colors can be obtained which, with increasing exposure time, change from blue to lilac to purple to light-brown to dark-red. Table 6 presents the batch compositions of photosensitive glasses containing Au [68, 241].

Cryolite was introduced into batch No. 2 for fining purposes. Other fluorides, such as CaF_2, Na_2SiF_6, and NaF, can also be used as fining agents provided that no impurities are present in them which would lower photosensitivity. The products made from these glasses are transparent; however, upon heating to 500-600°C, they either partially or wholly limit their transparency, depending on the fluorine content, thereby becoming capable of scattering light. If some areas are irradiated while still in the transparent state, then, upon heat treatment, the irradiated opacified portions become colored, in contrast to nonirradiated, thermally opacified portions. Thus, it is possible to produce colored ornaments and images which are in sharp contrast on a nontransparent background [241].

Stookey [242] determined that glasses which do not contain PbO and which do contain primarily BaO, SrO, or ZnO may be made nontransparent and photosensitive if fluorides and small

Table 6. Batch Compositions for the Melting of Au-Containing Glasses

Component	Content (in parts by wt.) of various batches			Component	Content (in parts by wt.) of various batches		
	1	2	3		1	2	3
SiO_2	100	100	100	CeO_2	0.052	0.052	0.052
Na_2CO_3	42	37	42	$NaNO_3$	—	6	—
$Al(OH)_3$	3.3	3.3	3.3	cryolite	—	10	—
$BaCO_3$	15	15	15	SnO_2	—	—	0.029
Au	0.013	0.013	0.013				

Table 7. Batch Compositions for the Melting of Nontransparent Au-Containing Glasses with Fluoride Additions

Component	Content (in parts by wt.) of various batches										
	1	2	3	4	5	6	7	8	9	10	11
SiO_2	100	100	100	100	100	100	100	100	100	100	100
Na_2CO_3	22	22	22	22	22	38	22	22	33	46	46
K_2CO_3 (85%)	10	10	10	10	10	—	10	10	—	—	—
$Al(OH)_3$	15	15	15	15	15	4	15	15	4	—	—
$BaCO_3$	16	16	16	16	16	—	16	—	—	—	—
ZnO	—	—	—	—	—	12	—	12	—	—	—
$SrCO_3$	—	—	—	—	—	—	—	—	19	—	—
Na_2SiF_6	5	5	5	5	5	5	5	5	10	—	—
Na_3AlF_6	—	—	—	—	—	—	—	—	—	14	14
$NaNO_3$	—	—	—	4	—	2	—	—	2	4	4
Sugar	1	—	—	—	—	—	—	—	—	—	—
NH_4Cl	—	1.8	—	—	—	—	—	—	—	—	—
NaCl	1.8	—	1.8	1.8	1.8	1.8	1.8	1.8	—	1	1
CeO_2	—	0.05	—	—	0.05	0.05	—	—	0.07	—	0.04
SnO_2	0.35	0.35	—	—	—	—	0.03	—	—	—	—
Au	—	—	0.02	0.014	0.014	0.02	0.03	—	0.02	0.014	0.014
CuO	0.15	0.15	—	—	—	—	—	—	—	—	—
AgCl	—	—	—	—	—	—	—	0.13	—	—	—

amounts of Au, Ag, or Cu are added to them. He was unable to obtain an opaline image in glasses with a small content of BeO, MgO, CaO, or CdO, since these glasses either have a tendency toward spontaneous cloudiness, or it is difficult to opacify them. The batch compositions recommended by Stookey [242] for the preparation of nontransparent glasses are listed in Table 7.

The chlorides NaCl and NH_4Cl are capable of opacifying glasses. Gold- and silver-containing glasses must be melted under oxidizing conditions; this is why no reducer is introduced into their initial batch. The amount of opacifiers for all glasses and the amount of reducers for Cu-containing glasses depend on the size of the melt container and on the glass type. The prescribed amounts in Table 7 are calculated on melting in crucibles with a capacity of 0.5 kg. The Au-containing glasses are more photosensitive than Ag- or Cu-containing glasses, and they are capable of producing a wider range of colors. Compounds of As, Sb, U, Tl, Fe, V, Mn, Se, Pb, etc. absorb ultraviolet rays and decrease photosensitivity [242]. Therefore, the amount of lead present should not exceed 2-3%, and, preferably, lead should not be present at all. The amount of B_2O_3 present should not exceed 4-5%, and that of Al_2O_3 should not exceed 5-6%. The presence of Cu is harmful to the photosensitivity of Au- and Ag-containing glasses. Stookey [242] recommends that Au be introduced in amounts of 0.01-0.03% in the form of a solution in aqua regia, which is added to the batch. With respect to Ag-containing glasses, one should preferably introduce 0.05-0.3% Ag (based on AgCl). Copper should be introduced in amounts of 0.1-1.0% (based on Cu_2O). Large amounts of SnO_2 decrease the photosensitivity of Au-containing glasses and produce coloring during the heat-treatment process independently of irradiation; however, it is worthwhile to introduce amounts of up to 0.02% in order to obtain various shades, since SnO_2 enhances the development of the red color in Cu-containing glasses [242].

The presence of very small amounts (0.05%) of CeO_2 noticeably increases the photosensitivity of glasses containing Au, Ag, or Cu, and it decreases their irradiation time by a factor of ten [242]. The introduction of oxidizers ($NaNO_3$, KNO_3) does not have a significant effect on the rate of the photosensitive reaction; however, it intensifies the colors obtained during irradiation and striking [242].

The irradiation time is determined by the glass composition, by the coloring desired, the intensity of the light source, and the distance from the light source to the object. For instance, in order to produce a blue color in glass containing Au and CeO_2, it is enough to irradiate it for 5 min by ultraviolet light from a source at a distance of 200 mm from the glass surface, and then to heat it to 550°C and hold it there for 30 min. For Cu-containing glasses, larger irradiation dosages are needed. The striking temperature depends on the degree of activity of the ultraviolet irradiation on the Au, Ag, or Cu contained in the glass, and is generally in the range of 500-600°C. According to Stookey [242], long-term heat treatment at lower temperatures is equivalent in effectiveness to short-term heat treatment at elevated temperatures.

Fining of photosensitive glasses during melting is difficult because it is impossible to introduce into their composition such an effective fining agent as As_2O_3, the presence of which, even in amounts of less than 0.1%, destroys photosensitivity. Therefore, it is recommended that instead of As_2O_3, approximately 0.1% Sb_2O_3 be introduced, which serves not only as a fining agent, but also as an intensifier of photosensitivity. However, an increase in Sb_2O_3 content decreases photosensitivity, and its presence in the amount of 1% destroys it entirely [242].

Table 8 lists the batch compositions of Au-containing, transparent, photosensitive glasses with Sb_2O_3 or $CaSO_4$ additions which are well-fined during melting [243, 244].

For fining agents which at the same time intensify photosensitivity Sb_2O_3 in amounts of 0.02-0.03% and $CaSO_4$ in the amount of approximately 1% are used. Batches 3, 4, and 5 are suitable for the production of sheet glass. Table 9, taken from Stookey [243, 244], gives the suggested batch compositions for Au-containing glasses with Sb_2O_3 additions, which become well-fined during melting, and which can be made nontransparent by the introduction of fluorides.

The amount of opacifiers introduced varies depending on the weight of the batch and the melting conditions. The batches listed above give transparent, colorless, and bubblefree photosensitive glasses after melting for 4 h at 1350°C in crucibles with a capacity of not more than 0.45 kg of the material, which then become opaline after secondary heating at 500-600°C.

Table 8. Batch Compositions for the Melting of Au-Containing
Glasses with Sb_2O_3 or $CaSO_4$ Additions

Component	Content (in parts by wt.) of various batches								
	1	2	3	4	5	6	7	8	9
SiO_2	100	100	100	100	100	100	100	330	330
Na_2CO_3	42	31	26	26	26	30	30	139	139
$NaNO_3$	—	8	8	8	8	7	7	—	—
$Al(OH)_3$	3.3	8	4	4	4	—	—	10.5	10.5
$BaCO_3$	15	15	16	16	16	—	17	—	—
ZnO	—	—	—	—	—	13	—	—	—
$CaCO_3$	—	—	15	15	15	—	—	70	70
CeO_2	0.052	0.05	0.05	0.05	0.05	0.05	0.05	0.2	0.2
SnO_2	—	—	—	—	—	—	—	—	1.2
$CaSO_4$	—	—	0.85	—	—	—	—	—	—
Sb_2O_3	0.025	0.026	0.026	0.026	0.026	0.02	0.02	0.03	0.03
Na_2SO_4	—	—	—	—	0.85	—	—	—	—
Au	0.013	0.03	0.025	0.025	0.025	—	0.014	—	—.
AgCl	—	—	—	—	—	0.14	0.14	—	—
CuO	—	—	—	—	—	—	—	0.5	0.5
Sugar	—	—	—	—	—	—	—	2	—
NH_4Cl	—	—	—	—	—	—	—	—	9

The irradiation time is determined experimentally. For instance, direct irradiation for 5 min by a carbon arc at 60 A at a
distance of 200 mm from the glass and subsequent heating for 30
min at 550°C produces a blue color in glass containing Au, CeO_2,
and an oxidizer [243, 244].

The color of the developed image depends on the type of
photosensitive addition, the intensity of irradiation, and the duration of heat treatment. Gold-containing glasses can, with increasing dosage of irradiation or time and temperature of heat treatment, first be colored blue, and then lavender, purple, chestnut
brown, and red. Copper-containing glasses are colored red, and
Ag-containing glasses are colored yellow or amber.

Gold- and silver-containing glasses are similar in their reactions. Consequently, Ag and Au can both be present simultaneously, while the presence of significant amounts of Cu in such

Table 9. Batch Compositions for the Melting of Nontransparent
Au-Containing Glasses with Sb_2O_3 Additions

Component	Content (in parts by wt.) of various batches					
	1	2	3	4	5	6
SiO_2	100	100	100	100	100	100
Na_2CO_3	22	22	38	33	46	22
K_2CO_3	10	10	—	—	—	10
$NaNO_3$	—	—	2	2	4	—
$Al(OH)_3$	13	15	4	4	—	15
$BaCO_3$	16	16	—	—	—	—
ZnO	—	—	12	—	—	12
SrO	—	—	—	19	—	—
Na_2SiF_6	5	5	5	10	—	5
Na_3AlF_6	—	—	—	—	14	—
$NaCl$	—	1.8	1.8	—	1	1.8
NH_4Cl	1.8	—	—	—	—	—
CeO_2	0.05	0.05	0.05	0.07	0.04	0.05
SnO_2	0.35	—	—	—	—	—
Sb_2O_3	0.05	0.025	0.02	0.02	0.03	0.03
CuO	0.15	—	—	—	—	—
Au	—	0.014	0.02	0.02	0.014	—
$AgCl$	—	—	—	—	—	0.13

glasses is not allowable, since it results in the annihilation of
photosensitivity.

Because of the improved photosensitivity of the above-described glasses due to the presence of CeO_2 and Sb_2O_3, Stookey
[243, 244] thinks that it is possible to irradiate them with ultraviolet radiation or sunlight through conventional photographic negatives. The images obtained thereby are, from the point of view of
fine detail and contrast, equal to the chemically developed images
printed by conventional techniques on photographic paper.

Stookey [245, 246] suggested photosensitive glasses in which
the image is obtained by differential precipitation of lithium disilicate crystals. These glasses contain 10-25% Li_2O. Introduced as
photosensitive metals were 0.004-0.05% Au, 0.019-0.22% Ag, and
0.032-1.0% Cu, and as sensitizers, 0.05% CeO_2 and up to 0.04%

SnO_2. These glasses may contain up to 35% BaO and up to 10% RO, Al_2O_3, or R_2O. The compositions containing both Li_2O and BaO contain 55-75% SiO_2, 10-25% Li_2O, and 3-35% BaO. In barium-containing glasses, a small amount of barium disilicate can also be precipitated, although the lithium disilicate is always the primary component causing opacification [245].

In Au-containing glasses of this type, an addition of 0.03% SnO_2 or Sb_2O_3 prevents the appearance of a blue color and produces only red tinting in irradiated surface layers. Opacification occurs after tinting and is observed only under the surface of the glass, which is tinted red, thanks to which one can obtain a transparent red image superimposed on the nontransparent white background.

The larger the Au content and the higher the irradiation dosage, the greater are the intensity and the depth of color propagation. An interesting characteristic of these and other photosensitive glasses containing SnO_2 or Sb_2O_3 is their capability to produce tinting without opacification or opacification without tinting, which can be achieved in the very same glass by introducing into it a small amount of a photosensitive metal which is not sufficient for tinting, but is sufficient for opacification. An analogous effect can also be obtained at a higher content of the photosensitive metal by selecting such an irradiation time or intensity as would produce opacification, but would not produce tinting during the subsequent heat treatment. In Table 10, from Stookey [245, 246], certain batch compositions of photosensitive glasses of this type are presented, in which the images contain lithium disilicate crystals.

By irradiating these glasses for 1-10 min with an electric arc (60 A, 35 cm from the sample) and by subsequently heating them from 1 min to 1 h at 540-600°C, one can obtain a blurring of the irradiated portions. After irradiation for 5-10 min and after heating at 600°C for several minutes, the glass made from batch No. 1 gives a pinkish, opaline color in the irradiated portions, while glass made from batch No. 7 gives a white color. An increase in the exposure time or in the amount of the reducer NH_4Cl present in batch No. 7 leads to the appearance of a reddish tint in the nontransparent portions. The depth of penetration of the image into the glass is 1-5 mm and better, and it increases with increasing time and intensity of irradiation, as well as with increasing content of the photosensitive metal present. It was shown by x-ray

Table 10. Batch Compositions for the Melting of Au-, Ag-, and Cu-Containing Glasses with Lithium Disilicate Crystals in the Image

Component	Content (in parts by wt.) of various batches						
	1	2	3	4	5	6	7
SiO_2	100	100	100	100	100	100	100
Li_2CO_3	34.4	32	41	39	32	37.1	39.4
Na_2CO_3	1.9	—	—	1.9	—	—	3.2
$NaNO_3$	3.2	—	3.8	1.7	—	—	—
CeO_2	0.04	—	0.047	0.024	—	0.04	0.046
Au	0.0093	0.0047	0.016	—	—	—	—
$Al(OH)_3$	—	7.1	4.3	4.2	7.1	—	4.2
Sb_2O_3	—	0.014	—	—	—	—	—
$CaCO_3$	—	—	24.3	—	—	—	—
SnO_2	—	—	0.016	—	—	—	0.032
$BaCO_3$	—	—	—	16	—	—	16
Na_2SiF_6	—	—	—	0.56	—	—	—
AgCl	—	—	—	0.11	0.09	0.09	—
Li_2SO_4	—	—	—	—	—	4.2	—
CuO	—	—	—	—	—	—	0.11
NH_4Cl	—	—	—	—	—	—	2.1

analysis that the portions of the glass which were irradiated and blurred after heat treatment contain lithium disilicate crystals of microscopic size [245, 246].

Glasses were also developed in which the precipitation of metallic gold on the colloidally dispersed nuclei, the precipitation of barium disilicate, and the formation of a nontransparent image associated with it occur by means of the irradiation of certain portions by short-wave radiation and by the subsequent heat treatment [247, 248]. The glass compositions contain 50-65% SiO_2, 5-15% R_2O, and 15-45% BaO, together with insignificant amounts of Au, CeO_2, and SnO_2. Characteristic for glasses with a high BaO content is the possibility of introducing as the photosensitive metal only Au in amounts of 0.004-0.05%, and not Ag or Cu, which are ineffective. If necessary, the degree of opacification can be decreased by either introducing up to 4% Al_2O_3, up to 3% B_2O_3, CaO, MgO, or ZnO, or up to 12% SrO [247, 248]. The photosensitivity of glasses

Table 11. Batch Compositions for the Melting of Au-Containing
Glasses with Barium Disilicate Crystals in the Image

Component	Contents (in parts by wt.) of various batches					
	1	2	3	4	5	6
SiO_2	100	100	100	100	100	100
Na_2CO_3	14.3	14.3	14.3	40.7	25.7	22
$NaNO_3$	4.7	4.7	4.7	5.6	4.7	4
K_2CO_3	17.7	17.7	17.7	—	—	—
$BaCO_3$	55.5	55.5	55.5	86.4	42.7	36.6
$Al(OH)_3$	5.0	5.0	5.0	—	—	—
CeO_2	0.06	—	—	0.07	0.06	0.05
Sb_2O_3	0.02	—	—	—	—	—
Au	0.013	0.013	0.013	0.024	0.013	0.06
SnO_2	—	0.02	—	—	—	—
SrO	—	—	—	—	23.7	—

sharply decreases or entirely disappears in the presence of reducers or various compounds of As, Pb, Tl, V, U, Fe, Mn, or Se.

The introduction of 0.04-0.05% CeO_2 noticeably intensifies the photosensitivity of glasses, which makes it possible to shorten the irradiation time or, at constant exposure, to achieve a greater degree of crystallization than in glasses without CeO_2. Red, and not blue, color develops in glasses with additions of up to 0.03% SnO_2 or Sb_2O_3 in the surface layers during heat treatment, and opacification occurs only in untinted portions, which leads to the superposition of a transparent red image on a nontransparent white background.

As in the glasses examined above [245, 246], the color intensity in the presence of SnO_2 and Sb_2O_3 increases with increasing Au content, whereas the depth of color penetration increases with increasing irradiation time. Table 11 [247, 248] gives the batch compositions which may be employed.

Glass made from batch No. 1 gives the best opacification, and has the composition 60 SiO_2, 6 K_2O, 26 BaO, 2 Al_2O_3, 0.04 CeO_2, 0.02 Sb_2O_3, and 0.0075 Au.

The temperature of heat treatment necessary for opacification is 600-700°C. Glass from batch No. 1 gives a white opacified background after being irradiated by an electric arc (60 A, 35 cm from the glass) for 2 min and after being held for several minutes at 700°C; for a 5-min exposure, the color turns blue; for a 20-min exposure, it turns lilac; and for a 40-min exposure, it becomes pink.

X-ray analysis of crystallized portions of these glasses showed the presence of barium disilicate crystals, which were not there in transparent portions.

Miyake et al. [249] obtained barium-containing glasses with Au which, after irradiation and development, gave both blue and red images. Glasses with the composition 51-60 SiO_2, 12-14 R_2O, 1-6 Al_2O_3, 20-27 BaO, 3-6 B_2O_3, 0.04-0.07 Au, and 0.06-0.12 CeO_2 did not show color shades after they were irradiated by 300- to 370-nm ultraviolet rays for 5 min, but after development at 620°C for 10 min, produced a clear blue image with a moderate contrast. Addition of Na_2O prevented the spontaneous coloring of glass during melting. Glasses of the composition 65-70 SiO_2, 14-19 R_2O, 3-7 Al_2O_3, 6-9 BaO, 0.035-0.040 Au, and 0.06-0.07 CeO_2 gave, under the same irradiation and heat-treatment conditions, a clear red image of the same contrast [250]. Introduction of not more than 1% F, 3% Cl, and 3% Na_2O improved the technological properties of this glass.

Stookey [251] (also see [252, 253]) proposed fluoride-containing photosensitive glasses with Au in which only irradiated portions become nontransparent after irradiation and after heat treatment, and which contain 55-75 SiO_2, 12-18 Na_2O, K_2O, or Li_2O; 0-5 B_2O_3, 2-12 Al_2O_3, 0-3 BeO, MgO, or CaO, or their mixture; 0-10 ZnO and 0-10 BaO (where ZnO + BaO must not exceed 10%); 0.001-0.01 Au; 0.005-0.05 CeO_2; 0-0.2 Sb_2O_3; and 1.8-2.4 fluorine in the form of Na_2SiF_6 or Na_3AlF_6. Increasing the SiO_2 or the Al_2O_3 content or decreasing the Na_2O content increases the melting temperature and degrades or completely eliminates the photosensitivity. Decreasing the SiO_2 or Al_2O_3 content decreases the chemical stability and produces spontaneous coloration during the subsequent heat treatment, while too large an amount of Na_2O or a deficiency of Al_2O_3 decreases or prevents the crystallization of irradiated portions. One may add B_2O_3 to the glass, but only in quantities of not more than 5%, since, in quantities greater than this, it causes excessive softening of the glass and decreases its photosensitivity. Additions of greater than 3% BeO, MgO, or CaO, or of 10% ZnO or BaO mixed or separately cause spontaneous changes of both the irradiated and the nonirradiated portions of the glass. One must avoid adding elements or oxides which color glass and absorb ultraviolet radiation, such as oxides and other compounds of Se, Te, Fe, Cu, U, V, and Mn, and also noncoloring oxides of As and Pb. Excessive amounts of CeO_2 are also unwanted.

Gold should preferably be introduced into the batch in the form of a solution of aurous hydrochloric acid containing, for instance, 10 g of gold per 100 cm^3. Less than 0.001% gold is not effective, and more than 0.01% gold causes massive coloring of the glass after irradiation and heat treatment. With 0.001-0.01% Au, the crystallized portions of the glass do not become colored [251-253].

Cerium may be introduced in the form of CeO_2 or a preparation containing 75% CeO_2. Less than 0.005% CeO_2 in the glass is not effective. More than 0.05% CeO_2 is detrimental, since it absorbs the short-wave rays.

The presence of Sb_2O_3 facilitates the development of the image in irradiated glass during the heat-treatment process, since the striking then takes place at a lower temperature and within a shorter time period, because of which the irradiation intensity, and even the Au content in the glass, may be reduced. More than 0.2% Sb_2O_3 causes spontaneous coloring of the glass by gold throughout the bulk of the article. The Sb_2O_3 also acts as a fining agent. Fluorine in the form of sodium or potassium silicon fluoride, cryolite, or an alkali metal fluoride should be introduced into the batch in such a quantity that its amount in the glass following losses from volatilization during melting should be 1.8-2.4%. Typical batch compositions are listed in Table 12 [251-253].

Sodium chloride in batch No. 1 somewhat facilitates the crystallization of NaF, but not to such a degree that its presence is a necessity.

Batch No. 1 was fused in a small tank furnace designed to produce 830 kg of glass. The maximum melting temperature was 1380°C, and the material was held at this temperature for 10 h.

Table 12. Batch Compositions for the Melting of Au-Containing
Glasses with Nontransparent Irradiated Portions
after Heat Treatment

Component	Content (in parts by wt.) of various batches							
	1	2	3	4	5	6	7	8
Gravel	1000	1000	1000	1000	1000	1000	1000	1000
Na_2CO_3	346	265	294	378	383	229	249	311
$NaNO_3$	39	41	82	93	41	41	40	90
$Al(OH)_3$	225	100	240	271	209	144	86	262
Borax	22	38	23	30	—	79	77	26
$CaCO_3$	—	—	53	—	—	26	—	—
$BaCO_3$	—	211	137	155	—	158	—	150
ZnO	—	—	—	—	—	—	144	—
10%-solution of gold, cm^3*	0.3	0.6	0.6	0.8	0.7	0.9	0.9	0.9
Cerium hydrate (75% CeO_2)	0.22	0.24	0.24	0.25	0.25	0.3	0.3	0.48
Sb_2O_3	1.37	1.2	1.2	—	—	0.6	0.6	0.28
NaCl	3	—	—	—	—	—	—	—
Na_2SiF_6	72	62	73	96	—	59	57	83
Na_3AlF_6	—	—	—	—	88	—	—	—

* Here and below, the indicated amounts of Au solution in cm^3 correspond to concentrations ranging from 0.001 to 0.01 wt.% Au in the glass.

After this, the glass was cooled to 1200°C during a 10-h interval.
The actual glass compositions deviate slightly from the given calculations because of the volatilization of fluorine. For instance,
the composition calculated for batch No. 1 is as follows: 69.8
SiO_2; 16.6 Na_2O, 10.1 Al_2O_3, 0.5 B_2O_3, 0.002 Au, 0.01 CeO_2, 0.09
Sb_2O_3, and 2.9 F. The actual fluorine content found in this glass
was 2.27% F. Taking this into consideration, the calculated glass
composition for batch No. 1 will be as follows: 70.2% SiO_2, 16.7
Na_2O, 10.2 Al_2O_3, 0.5 B_2O_3, 0.002 Au, 0.01 CeO_2, 0.09 Sb_2O_3, and
2.27 F. This glass had a softening temperature of 651°C, the upper and the lower annealing temperatures being 460°C and 429°C,
respectively, with $\alpha = 83.7 \cdot 10^{-7}$ deg^{-1} in the temperature range
0-300°C [251-253].

Glasses of the above compositions are colorless and transparent after melting. Heat treatment of glasses irradiated by short-wave radiation produces crystallization in irradiated portions of the glass, while the nonirradiated portions remain colorless and transparent.

Irradiation time varies from 1-2 min to 1 h and more, depending on the power of the light source and its distance from the object. For instance, the average time of irradiation by a carbon arc at 60 A, located at a distance of 30.5 cm from the glass, reaches 15 min. The heat-treatment time of irradiated samples for the given irradiation dosage varies from 5 min at a temperature 50°C higher than the softening point of glass, to 6 h at a temperature 100°C lower than the softening point. The duration of heat treatment is a logarithmic function of temperature, decreasing with increasing temperature. A very rapid heating of glass to temperatures higher than 500°C is not allowed because it results in the disintegration of the latent image, which could not be developed anyway. For batch No. 1 glasses, heating at a moderate rate from room temperature to 650°C and then holding there for 20 min is equivalent to heating at the same rate to 580°C and holding at that temperature for 2 h.

Stookey [252] surmises that the appearance of a pink color during this preliminary, but important and necessary, stage in latent-image development is caused by the nucleation of submicroscopic centers of colloidal gold in irradiated portions of the glass still transparent after heat treatment, when sufficient amounts of Au and Sb are present. However, batch No. 1 glass, which contains the minimum amount of Au, remains colorless after preliminary heat treatment. After the preliminary heat treatment, the glass is cooled to a temperature below 520°C, as a result of which submicroscopic centers of an opacifier, such as sodium fluoride, are formed on the Au nuclei. The formation at 520°C of such, still invisible, nuclei of sodium fluoride and the opacification of the developed image are possible only in the presence of Au nuclei. Opacification proceeds during the subsequent heating of the glass at a temperature and a time which are sufficient for the growth of the nuclei of sodium fluoride and for the formation of crystals. In order to obtain such an opacified image, glass from batch No. 1 must be heated for 1 h at 540°C or for several seconds at 700°C [251-253].

Gurkovskii [254, 255] investigated the fluorine-containing photosensitive glass with Au with the following composition: 74 SiO_2, 9.0 CaO, 16.0 Na_2O, 1.0 K_2O, 0.04 Au, and 0.1 CeO_2. Melting under oxidizing conditions in chamotte 3-liter crucibles was done according to the following procedure. Three charges were introduced at 1410°C every 45 min; then they were held at 1410°C for 1 h; temperature was increased from 1410 to 1450°C over a time of 1.5 h; temperature was then increased from 1450 to 1480°C over a time of 1 h; and the charges were held at 1480°C for 4 h. The shaped articles were irradiated with a PRK-7 lamp for 3 min and then subjected to striking at 580°C for 7.5, 15, 60, and 120 min. The color of the image thereby changed from purple-blue to purple-red.

Increasing the Au content while holding the CeO_2 content constant increased the sensitivity of these glasses to radiation. As a result of testing samples with different Au and CeO_2 contents, it was determined that the best sensitivity of glasses to radiation is attained at 0.04% Au and 0.1% CeO_2. For practical purposes, amounts of 0.02% Au and 0.1% CeO_2 are sufficient.

Photosensitive glasses colored with both Au and Ag were studied. Results show that the addition of Ag to Au-containing glasses may increase their sensitivity to radiation, with a concomitant change in the color from purple to mustard yellow. It was determined that in glasses containing both Au and Ag, the growth of mixed crystals takes place, without which no image formation is possible. Glasses of the composition 68.5-71 SiO_2, 15.5-17.5 Na_2O, 0-2 K_2O, 0-2 Al_2O_3, 3-4 Na_2SiF_6, 7-9 ZnO, 0.04 SnO_2, 0.014 Sb_2O_3, and 0.01-0.02 Au, melted in a kiln with a capacity of 450-500 kg, were colored ruby after striking [256].

3. PALLADIUM-CONTAINING PHOTOSENSITIVE GLASSES

Introduction of Pd [257] expands the palette of colors for photosensitive glasses; work is going on to increase the solubility of Pd in glass and to improve the fining of opacified Pd-containing glass. Palladium by itself is not photosensitive; however, it becomes activated in the presence of definite quantities of Au or Ag and is effective in glass in amounts of up to 0.02%.

Table 13. Batch Compositions for the Melting of Brownish
Pd-Containing Glasses with Au

Component	Content (in parts by wt.) of various batches								
	1	2	3	4	5	6	7	8	9
SiO_2	100	100	100	100	100	100	100	100	100
Na_2CO_3	24	24	27	27	27	41	41	27	28
$NaNO_3$	8.5	8.5	3.5	4	4	4	4	4	8
K_2CO_3	6	6	6	6	6	—	—	6	—
$BaCO_3$	15	15	15	15	15	15	—	15	14
Al_2O_3	5	5	4	3	3	3	3	3	16
Na_3AlF_6	3.5	3.5	2.5	2	2	—	—	2	—
Au	0.035	0.035	0.014	0.038	0.0385	0.036	0.036	—	0.023
Pd	0.0035	0.014	0.0035	0.011	0.011	0.0068	0.091	0.0069	0.0029
CeO_2	0.07	0.07	0.07	0.055	0.06	0.06	0.06	0.055	0.059
Sb_2O_3	0.035	0.035	0.035	—	0.055	—	—	—	0.059
$CaCO_3$	—	—	—	—	—	21	21	—	—
Borax	—	—	—	—	—	—	—	—	2.33
Na_2SiF_6	—	—	—	—	—	—	—	—	7
AgCl	—	—	—	—	—	—	—	0.028	—

If Pd is present in very small amounts (0.001%), then the glass colored by Au or Ag acquires an additional brownish tint, which then becomes a distinct brown color of various intensities when larger amounts of Pd are present. According to Stookey [257], a concentration of 0.02% Pd is the solubility limit of Pd in silicate glasses, and thus quantities larger than 0.02% Pd are not recommended. The optimum Au content in Pd-containing glass is 0.01-0.03%. It is recommended that Ag be introduced in amounts of up to 0.03% (with respect to AgCl); larger amounts of Ag make glass nonphotosensitive. The presence of CeO_2 in amounts of 0.05% not only increases photosensitivity, but also increases by approximately 20 times the solubility of Pd in glass. To intensify photosensitivity, one can also use up to 0.1% Sb_2O_3.

One must avoid the presence of reducers, as well as of oxides of As, Fe, Mn, V, Se, Tl, and U. This glass must be melted under heavily oxidizing conditions, for which reason oxidizers, such as saltpeter, are included in the batch. Therefore, it is not possible to use Cu in Pd-containing glasses. The presence of PbO in amounts exceeding 2% is also detrimental. The RO oxides, such as CaO and BaO, increase photosensitivity. Recommended batch compositions, taken from [257], are presented in Table 13.

After 5 h of melting at 1350°C, batch No. 9 gives a transparent glass which, after irradiation and heat treatment at 600°C, becomes brown opal in irradiated portions and white opal in non-irradiated portions.

Stookey [257] recommends the following batch compositions for the preparation of Au-containing glasses with lowered Pd content (in parts by weight): 100 SiO_2, 24 Na_2CO_3, 8.5 $NaNO_3$, 6 K_2CO_3, 15 $BaCO_3$, 5 Al_2O_3, 3.5 Na_3AlF_6, 0.035 Au, 0.0009-0.0035 Pd, 0.07 CeO_2, 0.035-0.14 Sb_2O_3. At 0.035 Sb_2O_3 and when the Pd content changes from 0.0009 to 0.0035, the color of the glasses obtained ranges from brownish-pink to brown. At a content of 0.0026 Pd and 0.07-0.14 Sb_2O_3, the glasses become well-fined, and with increasing Sb_2O_3 content, they acquire a chocolate-brown color. With 0.0026 Pd and 0.035 Sb_2O_3 present, the glass obtained has a neutral gray color with an azure tint.

4. SILVER-CONTAINING PHOTOSENSITIVE GLASSES

Photosensitive glasses containing silver are of special interest, because it is precisely these glasses that have primarily been used for the production of photosensitive glass-ceramics. Silver-containing photosensitive glasses were first proposed by Armistead [37]. One can obtain photosensitive glass colored yellow or amber by introducing 0.05-0.3% Ag (based on AgCl) in a glass of the following composition: 75 SiO_2, 15 R_2O, and 10 RO [258]. One may introduce oxidizers into the batch, but not reducers. One may introduce B_2O_3 in amounts of up to 10% if the R_2O content is not less than 15%, since at a lesser R_2O content, B_2O_3 destroys the photosensitivity of these glasses. The Al_2O_3 content may reach 2%. One must avoid introducing materials which absorb ultraviolet rays. The glasses whose batch compositions are presented in Table 14 (taken from [258]) are especially photosensitive.

Additions of up to 0.05% CeO_2 increase the photosensitivity and the contrast of the image. The presence of up to 0.2% SnO_2 intensifies the coloring. Introduction of Au in amounts of 0.01-0.03% gives a combination of red coloration from Au and yellow from Ag.

Table 14. Batch Compositions for the Melting of Yellow
Ag-Containing Glasses

Component	Content (in parts by wt.) of various batches								
	1	2	3	4	5	6	7	8	9
SiO_2	100	100	100	100	100	100	100	100	100
Na_2CO_3	43	—	30	38	34	34	34	34	30
85% K_2CO_3	—	44	—	—	—	—	—	—	—
ZnO	14	14	13	17	—	—	—	—	—
$CaCO_3$	—	—	—	—	24	—	—	—	—
$Cd(OH)_2$	—	—	—	—	—	15	—	—	—
$BaCO_3$	—	—	—	—	—	—	17	—	17
PbO	—	—	—	—	—	—	—	13	—
Ag_2S	0.14	0.14	—	0.28	0.14	0.14	0.14	0.14	—
AgCl	—	—	0.14	—	—	—	—	—	0.14
$NaNO_3$	—	—	7	—	—	—	—	—	7
CeO_2	—	—	0.05	—	—	—	—	—	0.05
SnO_2	—	—	—	0.28	—	—	—	—	—
Na_2SiF_6	—	—	1.3	—	—	—	—	—	1.3
Au	—	—	—	—	—	—	—	—	0.014

After irradiation for 10-60 min by an electric arc (25 A at a distance of 20 cm from the glass), heat treatment at 470-500°C for 1-3 h is necessary for the development of the image.

Silver-containing photosensitive glasses were prepared in which, as with the Au-containing glasses, only the irradiated parts become nontransparent after irradiation and heat treatment [259-261]. Silver-containing glasses are distinguished by improved photosensitivity, and the coloring in them develops significantly faster and at a lower heat-treatment temperature, because of which one can avoid softening and deformation of the glass.

These glasses contain primarily 55-75% SiO_2 and one or more of the R_2O oxides (up to 2 Li_2O, 5-18 Na_2O, or up to 13 K_2O), of which Na_2O must be present, with a total R_2O content of 12-18%. These glasses also contain 2-12 Al_2O_3, 0.0001-0.3 Ag (based on AgCl), 0.005-0.05 CeO_2, 1.8-3 F, and one of the following halogens: 0.01-0.2 Cl, 0.02-0.4 Br, or 0.03-0.6 I in the form of their respective compounds. Of R_2O oxides, the use of only Na_2O is preferred, although Li_2O and K_2O can also be used together or separately within the ranges indicated. The introduction of Li_2O in amounts higher than listed decreases the softening temperature of the glass and enhances its devitrification. Higher amounts of K_2O than those listed increase the refractoriness of the glass and produce spontaneous opacification. As a melting catalyst, and also to improve the working properties of the glass, not more than 5% B_2O_3 may be used.

In order to increase the chemical stability of this glass, not more than 2% RO may be added, with BeO, MgO, and CaO possibly being introduced in amounts of up to 3% total, together or individually; ZnO, SrO, and BaO may be introduced in amounts up to 12%, and CdO in amounts up to 5%. The most beneficial of these oxides is ZnO. The analytically determined amount of F remaining in the glass should be within the range 1.8-3.0%. The presence of less than 1.8% F results in very mild cloudiness, while more than 3% causes spontaneous opacification. Crystals of alkali metal fluorides, in particular NaF, were found in opacified portions of the glass [259].

Chlorine, bromine, and iodine in the above-stated quantities intensify the photosensitivity of the glass thanks to their activating effect on silver. The amount of halogen remaining in the glass must be (in %): 0.01-0.2 Cl, 0.02-0.4 Br, and 0.03-0.6 I. Smaller amounts of halogens are ineffective, and larger amounts cause spontaneous opacification. These three halogens may be used either individually or together; however, their total content should not exceed the above-stated limits.

The batch compositions recommended by Stookey [259-261] are presented in Table 15.

The calculated composition of the glass melted from batch No. 1 is: 69.4 SiO_2, 16.7 Na_2O, 10.1 Al_2O_3, 0.6 B_2O_3, 0.0017 Ag (on the basis of AgCl), 0.01 CeO_2, 0.09 Sb_2O_3, 2.9 F, and 0.25 Br. However, in view of the volatilization of the halogens, the glass melted from batch No. 1 at 1400°C in a large commercial furnace contained 2.6% F and 0.2% Br, based on chemical analyses. Therefore, the actual composition of this glass is: 69.6 SiO_2, 16.8 Na_2O, 10.1 Al_2O_3, 0.6 B_2O_3, 0.0017 Ag (on the basis of AgCl), 0.01 CeO_2, 0.09 Sb_2O_3, 2.6 F, and 0.2 Br.

Table 15. Batch Compositions for the Melting of Au–Containing Glasses with Nontransparent Irradiated Portions after Heat Treatment

Component	Content (in parts by wt.) of various batches												
	1	2	3	4	5	6	7	8	9	10	11	12	13
SiO_2	267	348	350	348	348	364	350	336	336	364	353	267	350
Na_2CO_3	99	130	133	122	130	138	133	116	56	136	138	99	125
$NaNO_3$	—	—	—	14	—	—	—	—	—	—	—	—	14
K_2CO_3	—	—	—	—	—	—	—	—	62	—	—	—	—
$Al(OH)_3$	60	52	52	52	52	82	52	38	38	82	49	60	52
Borax (anhydrous)	3.3	—	—	—	—	4	—	—	—	4.2	9	—	—
$CaCO_3$	—	—	—	—	13	—	—	—	—	—	7.5	—	—
ZnO	—	25	25	25	18	—	25	—	—	—	16	—	25
$BaCO_3$	—	—	—	—	—	—	—	64	64	—	—	—	—
$AgNO_3$	0.0078	0.01	0.01	0.02	0.02	0.01	0.01	0.01	0.01	0.02	0.03	0.01	1
AgCl	—	—	—	—	—	—	—	—	—	—	—	—	—
Ce hydrate (75%)	0.05	0.125	0.1	0.125	0.125	0.1	0.1	0.1	0.1	0.15	0.1	0.05	0.1
CeO_2	—	—	—	—	—	—	—	—	—	—	—	—	—
Sb_2O_3	0.36	0.5	—	0.5	0.5	0.5	0.3	0.5	0.5	0.5	0.5	—	0.3
SnO_2	—	—	0.3	—	—	—	—	—	—	—	—	—	—
25%-solution of Au, cm^3	—	—	—	36	—	—	—	—	—	—	—	—	—
Na_2SiF_6	19	25	19.5	25	25	22	19	22	18	18	22	19	19
NH_4Cl	—	—	—	—	—	—	—	—	—	4	—	—	—
NaCl	—	—	—	—	1	—	—	—	—	—	—	—	—
NaBr	1.3	1.75	1.75	1.75	—	—	1.75	—	1.75	—	1.75	1.3	1.75
KBr	—	—	—	—	—	2	—	1.75	—	—	—	—	—
NaI	—	—	—	—	—	—	—	—	—	—	—	—	—
Corn starch	—	0.4	0.4	—	0.4	—	0.3	—	—	—	—	—	—

The presence of ZnO in batch No. 2 imparts a good chemical stability to this glass. The actual composition of this glass is: 69.1 SiO_2, 16.5 Na_2O. 6.6 Al_2O_3, 4.8 ZnO, 0.002 Ag (on the basis of AgCl), 0.02 CeO_2, 0.1 Sb_2O_3, 2.6 F, and 0.2 Br.

Either NaBr or NaI may be used as a weak reducer. If NaCl is used, then instead of NH_4Cl, a different reducer, such as corn starch (batch No. 5), is added. Addition of organic reducers, such as starch, sugar, or urea, augments by five times the reaction rate of the photosensitive process. At the same time, excessive amounts of reducers produce spontaneous opacification during heat treatment.

If the Ag content in glass is more than 0.5%, then it is desirable to introduce the oxidizer $NaNO_3$ so as to increase its solubility. For Au-containing glasses (batch No. 4), the use of oxidizers is obligatory [259-261].

Glasses without prior irradiation are transparent even after secondary heating.

A two-stage heat treatment is used to develop the image in glasses irradiated for 10 sec to 1 h by ultraviolet light using a carbon arc at a current of 60 A and 30 cm distant from the object. The first stage consists in heating the glass for 1 min at a temperature 50° higher than the temperature of the beginning of the softening or for 1 h at a temperature 150° lower than the temperature. During the first stage, no cloudiness occurs, although at a content of 0.002% Ag, a yellow transparent image may appear. Stookey [259-261] proposes that submicroscopic, colloidally dispersed Ag particles may form in irradiated portions, which also are the cause of the yellow coloring. The glass is then cooled to below 500°C. No visible changes are observed, although alkali metal fluorides are precipitated on the Ag particles, forming almost-invisible nuclei of the primary precipitating phase. Cooling to even lower temperatures, such as to room temperatures, has no further effect on the formation of nuclei. The second stage includes secondary heating for 3-15 min to temperatures 100°C lower than the softening temperature. At this stage, the nuclei of the fluorides grow, forming crystals which produce opacification of the irradiated portions of the glass. The degree of opacification increases with increasing irradiation exposure and increasing heat-treatment time. For glasses with a higher fluorine content, the second stage of heat treatment may be omitted, since opacification already occurs during the first stage. However, as a rule, two-stage heat treatment is necessary. By changing the irradiation dosage, the temperature, and the time of heating, one can vary the color produced in glasses of the same composition. By decreasing the exposure, by increasing the time or the temperature of the first stage of heat treatment, and by not exceeding 550°C during the second stage of heat treatment, one obtains, consecutively, a yellow, brown, orange, pink, purple, blue, and green color. Introduction of Sb_2O_3 and SnO_2 in various ratios imparts a grayish or a pinkish tint to the opaline image. The total Sb_2O_3 and SnO_2 content present must not exceed 0.2%, with SnO_2 not exceeding 0.1%. Pink coloring can also be attained by introducing up to 0.01% Au. A colored background may be obtained by the addition of a colorant into the batch, such as CoO or MnO_2.

Stookey [259-261] observed reversibility of the opaque image. Thus, if the previously irradiated sample which had been subjected to the first stage of heat treatment is again irradiated and subjected to heat treatment, then the portions of the image which had been irradiated twice become transparent on the generally nontransparent background.

The addition to the batch of corn starch or some other reducer in amounts larger than those normally used, but not exceeding 0.6%, also produces the effect of reversibility of the opaline image; nonirradiated portions become opacified after heat treatment, and the irradiated portions remain transparent.

Stookey [262-264] prepared nontransparent lithium silicate glasses characterized by enhanced photosensitivity and a large difference in the rate of dissolution in HF. It was found that the transparent glassy phase of such a glass has a lower solubility in HF than the crystalline opacified phase, which can be dissolved entirely in the time during which the transparent phase becomes only slightly corroded. Stookey [262] called the ratio between the rate of solution of the crystallized portions and the rate of solution of the glass proper the solubility differential.

Glass which melts under reducing conditions contains 70-85% SiO_2, at least one R_2O oxide, including certainly 9-15% Li_2O, 0-8 Na_2O, K_2O, or their mixture, with the total R_2O content being 9-23, and 0.001-0.02 Ag (on the basis of AgCl). These fundamental components should total not less than 84%. One may introduce up to 10% Al_2O_3 and up to 0.05% CeO_2. Preferred glasses contain 78-83 SiO_2, 10-13 Li_2O, 2-5 K_2O, up to 10 Al_2O_3, 0.001-0.020 Ag (on the basis of AgCl), and 0.05 CeO_2.

The peculiarity of these glasses, in comparison with those previously known [243, 245], consists in their low Ag content and the fact that they melt under reducing conditions. Previously, the necessity of melting Ag-containing glasses under oxidizing conditions was always emphasized, since glasses melted under reducing conditions with the normal amount of Ag present generally lost their photosensitivity. It turned out that glasses of the above compositions not only did not lose their photosensitivity during melting under reducing conditions, but, on the contrary, intensified it. The decrease in the Ag content here also decreases the cost of this glass.

The introduction of K_2O increases the solubility of the glass in HF, with the largest solubility differential belonging to glasses which contain K_2O and do not contain Na_2O. This is explained by the predominance of the lithium metasilicate phase in the crystallized portions of glasses containing K_2O, which is considerably more soluble in HF than lithium disilicate, quartz, and cristobalite, which are found in the crystallized portions of glasses containing Na_2O, but not containing K_2O. The proportion of lithium metasilicate present increases significantly with increasing K_2O content [262-264].

For a photosensitive addition, it is recommended that only Ag be introduced into these glasses, since under reducing conditions Au will become deposited as metal and the glass will lose its photosensitivity. Copper requires very strong reducing conditions, which is also unacceptable for these glasses.

At a content of SiO_2 < 70%, the glass is easily soluble in HF, which results in the lowering of the solubility differential. The presence of Al_2O_3 increases the solubility differential, and, at a content of up to 10%, it decreases the crystallization capability. An excess of SiO_2 or Al_2O_3 makes the glass refractory and crystallizable during the melting and the heat-treatment process. Glasses deficient in Li_2O and with an excess of Na_2O or K_2O do not show cloudiness after exposure and heat treatment. An excess of Li_2O

Table 16. Silver-Containing Glasses with Increased Photosensitivity and a High Solubility Differential

Component	Content (in wt.% *) of various glasses								
	1	2	3	4	5	6	7	8	9
SiO_2	77.5	85	82.5	82.5	80	79	72.5	80	81.5
Li_2O	12.5	10	12.5	12.5	12.5	9	12.5	12.5	12
Na_2O	—	—	2.5	—	7.5	2	—	—	—
K_2O	—	—	—	25	—	2.5	5	5	3.5
Al_2O_3	10	5	2.5	2.5	—	7.5	10	2.5	3.0
$AgCl$	0.002	0.002	0.006	0.002	0.002	0.002	0.002	0.002	0.002
CeO_2	0.02	0.02	0.003	0.02	0.02	0.02	0.02	0.02	0.02

* Here and below, the content of the various additions present brings the total to above the 100% made up by the basic components.

or K_2O increases the solubility of glass and decreases the solubility differential.

Table 16 shows some glasses of the above-discussed compositions, taken from [262-264], which are characterized by increased photosensitivity and a high solubility differential.

As a reducer in these glasses, one may introduce a small amount of starch which, for instance for glass No. 4, amounts to approximately 0.35%. A higher amount of reducing agent is not allowable, since it causes the precipitation of Ag. Melting in a closed container necessitates a smaller amount of the reducer than melting in an open container.

The value of the solubility differential depends not only on the glass composition and the degree of its reduction, but also on irradiation dosage and on the temperature and duration of heat treatment. For instance, for glass No. 3, the maximum degree of opacification and a solubility differential in 10% HF equal to 23 : 1 was attained by irradiation for 6 min through a filter made of windowpane glass 3 mm thick using a carbon arc light at 60 A at a distance of 30 cm from the object, and by heat treatment at 650°C for 1 h. In order to obtain a solubility differential of 46 : 1 in glass No. 4 with somewhat different reducer content, irradiation for 80 min and heat treatment for 4 h at 640°C were necessary under the

same experimental conditions. In order to avoid the formation during etching of fluorides insoluble in HF, the total amount of RO
oxides present, including PbO, should not exceed 3%. The amount
of B_2O_3 present may be 2-3%. One should avoid the presence of
SnO_2, which intensifies the effect of the reducer.

Stookey [265] determined that one may impart a neutral tint
to Ag-containing opacified glasses by adding to them the nonphotosensitive colorants NiO and CoO in amounts which are not sufficient for detrimental coloring of transparent portions of the glass
object. The best results are obtained by introducing 0.01-0.3% NiO
and 0.001-0.3% CoO. Here, the crystallized portions of the glass
were more intensely colored than the transparent glass, which is
explained by the increase in the length of the light path due to multiple internal reflections by the crystals. In contrast to other
colorants, NiO and CoO in the amounts indicated do not decrease
the photosensitivity of the glass. Transparent portions of the
colored glass plate 3 mm thick had a transmission of not less than
70% in the visible range.

In order to produce glass plates having semitransparent lines
or bands of a neutral color, NiO and CoO may be introduced into
any of the opacifiable photosensitive glasses described previously.
Approximate batch compositions, taken from [265], for the melting
of similar glasses are presented in Table 17.

To the batches presented in Table 17 are added 0.01-0.3 NiO
and 0.001-0.3% CoO. Smaller amounts are not effective, and larger
amounts decrease the light transmission (less than 70% at the glass
plate thickness of 3 mm). A neutral gray tint is obtained when the
ratio of NiO to CoO is approximately 10:1 by weight. An increase
in the CoO content gives a bluish tint, and an increase in the NiO
content gives a brownish tint.

In order to obtain a two-dimensional photographic image of
optical scales and grids characterized by a better color intensity
than is the case for conventional photosensitive glasses, Stookey
[266] proposed the application of a silver photographic emulsion on
the surface of the alkali silicate glasses, with subsequent burning
in of silver under reducing conditions. The Ag ions diffuse into
the glass to a depth of several microns, and, after being reduced to
metallic Ag, they produce a sufficiently dense and accurately reproducible two-dimensional image of an amber or a brown color.

Table 17. Batch Compositions for the Melting of Opacified Glasses Colored by Nickel and Cobalt Oxides

Component	Content (in parts by wt. 10% solution of Au, in cm^3)			
	1	2	3	4
SiO_2	1000	1000	1000	1000
Na_2CO_3	370	346	19	143
$NaNO_3$	—	39	17	47
K_2CO_3	—	—	—	177
Li_2CO_3	—	—	390	—
$BaCO_3$	—	—	160	555
$Al(OH)_3$	225	225	42	50
Borax (anhydrous)	12.5	22	—	—
AgCl	—	—	1.1	—
$AgNO_3$	0.03	—	—	—
10% solution of Au (in cm^3)	—	0.3	—	1.2
Ce hydrate (75% CeO_2)	0.2	0.22	0.32	0.8
Sb_2O_3	1.4	1.37	—	0.2
Na_2SiF_6	71	72	5.6	—
NaBr	5.0	—	—	—
NaCl	—	3	—	—

5. PRODUCTION TECHNOLOGY OF THE PHOTOSENSITIVE GLASS "FOTOFORM"

Stookey [267] discovered a method of leaching, or selectively etching, photosensitive glasses containing crystals of lithium silicate, barium disilicate, or alkali metal fluorides in the nontransparent image. The compositions of such glasses (see Tables 11, 12, and 17) and the methods of obtaining a nontransparent image in them have been presented above.

The method is based on the difference in the rates of solution of the crystalline and the glassy phases, where the crystallized portions may be dissolved entirely in a period of time during which the transparent glassy part is only slightly etched away. After the solution of the crystallized part, either a depression or a through-hole remains in the glass article, because of which it proved possible to "cut" designs in the glass which are complex in shape and have precise dimensions; this could be done without heavy erosion, such as is characteristic for the acid etching process of conventional glasses, all portions of which dissolve in the acid at the same rate. The difference in the dissolving rates may be determined in the following manner. The small polished glass plate, which consists of crystallized and glassy portions, is immersed into an agitated 10% HF solution at room temperature. Within a given time, say after 15 min, the plate is taken out of the solution and rinsed with water, and, by measuring the thicknesses remaining of both the crystallized and the glassy parts, their rates of solution are determined and the solubility differential is calculated (see page 148).

Especially effective are glasses which contain lithium metasilicate crystals in the opaline image (see Table 17), lithium metasilicate being considerably more soluble in dilute HF than lithium disilicate.

In contrast to these glasses, the nontransparent image in photosensitive barium silicate glasses (see Table 11), which contains barium disilicate crystals, is less soluble in dilute HF than is the transparent glassy part. This is explained by the formation of insoluble fluorides, which produce a screening effect and which inhibit the reaction from proceeding further. Consequently, in such glasses, the transparent part of the glass dissolves, while the nontransparent part remains. It must be mentioned that photosensitive glasses of this type have practically no practical applications at present.

In glasses in which the opacified image contains alkali metal fluorides (see Table 12), the nontransparent part is completely soluble in HF, while the glassy part does not undergo substantial changes.

Increasing the concentration or the temperature of the acid solution decreases the solubility differential. It is recommended that the etching be done at room temperature in a 20% solution of HF. Stookey [267] showed that under approximately equal conditions, the solubility differential for the acid concentration in 1 wt.% HF is 50:1; for 10% HF, it is 30:1; and for 20% HF it is 13.5:1. Elsewhere [268], it is stated that increasing the acid concentration results in a larger difference in the etching rates, i.e., the solubility differential increases; in our opinion, this is not very probable. We determined that etching of lithium aluminosilicate photo-

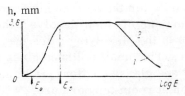

Fig. 52. Depth of etching after development (1) without cooling and (2) with cooling. h) Depth of etching; E) exposure; E_0) initial exposure; E_s) saturation exposure.

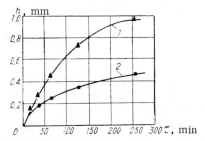

Fig. 53. Depth of propagation of the crystalline phase. h) Height of the step between the irradiated and the non-irradiated portions of the glass after complete dissolution of the crystalline phase; τ) time of irradiation. Curve 1) irradiation by an erythemic lamp; curve 2) irradiation by a bactericidal lamp.

sensitive glasses can best be done in HF solution at a concentration of 12-15% at 45°C. Application of mechanical or ultrasonic vibrations can reduce the etching time to 5-10 min.

By the method described above, one can produce glass articles with three-dimensional designs in the form of intaglio or with relief, the hillocks and the depressions of which correspond to portions of the halftone photographic negative of varying density. The image may extend to a certain depth, or it may go through the entire thickness of the glass sample, being at various angles to its surface, which makes it possible to obtain through-holes of any shape, with the minimum diameter being approximately 0.6 mm when the bridge thickness between two neighboring holes is equal to 0.25 mm [267].

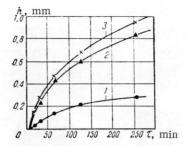

Fig. 54. Dependence of the step height on etching time.
h) Step height; τ) etching time. Light source is an erythemic lamp. Etching time, min: curve 1) 90; 2) 230;
3) 350.

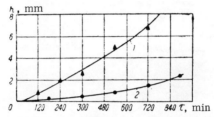

Fig. 55. Dependence of the depth of propagation of crystallization on the duration of heat treatment. h) Depth of
propagation of crystallization; τ) time of heat treatment.
Curve 1) irradiation by an erythemic lamp; curve 2) irradiation by a bactericidal lamp.

Etching to various depths can be achieved by controlling the
irradiation time and the duration of heat treatment during image
development. Schuler [269] showed that the nuclei (metal particles)
emerging during very long exposures are exceedingly small, and
the quantity of the precipitating crystalline phase is not sufficient
to produce etching to a significant depth (Fig. 52). Heat treatment
with intermediary cooling favors the formation of nuclei and increases the amount of the crystalline phase and the depth of etching.

The present author, together with L. N. Il'chenko, investigated the depth of etching of a developed image as dependent on the
irradiation time by a monochromatic light source and on heat treatment. Used as sources were a bactericidal lamp emitting light at
a wavelength of 254 nm and an erythemic lamp emitting light in the

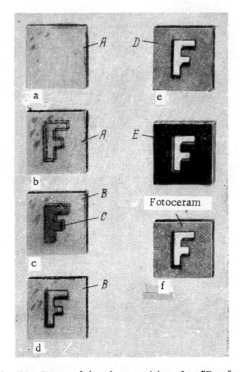

Fig. 56. Forms of the photosensitive glass "Fotoform" a)
Original plate (photosensitive form A); b) latent image
obtained by irradiation of the glass through a photographic negative; c) image developed by heat treatment; the
irradiated portions are milky-white (form C); the remaining portions are transparent and nonphotosensitive (form
B); d) form C etched out by hydrofluoric acid; e) form B
transformed by further heat treatment either into the
dark-brown form D or into the black form E, f) Fotoceram
obtained from form B by special heat treatment.

wavelength range 220-350 mm. Figure 53 shows the height of the
step between irradiated and nonirradiated portions of the glass
after complete solution of the crystalline phase in the areas irradiated by the lamps. The difference in the curves can apparently be
explained by the change in the spectral composition of the ultraviolet light, producing a photochemical effect. With decreasing
wavelength, its absorption by glass increases, which also limits

the depth of propagation of the crystalline phase. It must be mentioned that the height of this step increases with the time of etching in the HF solution (Fig. 54). The largest discrepancies were found in glasses which received the higher irradiation dosages. We also investigated the dependence of the depth of penetration of the crystalline phase on the duration of heat treatment at a constant temperature for samples of photosensitive glasses subjected to ultraviolet irradiation at different wavelengths. The dependence established was found to be close to exponential (Fig. 55).

In 1953, a transparent glass called "Fotoform" was synthesized [39, 40, 43, 270-272] which, in its original form-A (Fig. 56), is a modified lithium silicate containing traces of silver and cerium compounds, and therefore possessing photosensitivity.

Upon heating the initial nonirradiated form-A glass at a temperature close to the softening temperature, photosensitivity disappears and form-B glass appears which, in its external appearance and mechanical and electrical properties, does not differ from the initial glass. After irradiating Fotoform A through a negative by the contact or projection printing technique, and by heating it first to 500°C and then to 600-650°C, a fine-crystalline, milky-white, nontransparent structure (form C) appears in the irradiated portions, consisting primarily of lithium metasilicate crystals mixed with the Li-impoverished glass, and characterized by such a developed surface that it dissolves in dilute HF approximately 15 times faster than Fotoform B (in a 5% solution of HF, the rate of solution of form C is approximately 1 mm/h). The increased solubility of the crystallized portions is explained by Stookey [39] and Weyl [109] by the existence of stresses arising during crystallization and by the open texture of these portions. Indeed, it seems to us that the most decisive effect on the solubility in HF comes, in addition to the surface area, from the chemical-mineralogical composition of the precipitating crystalline phases. Stookey [39] determined, by x-ray analysis, that the irradiated and crystallized portions of the photosensitive glass whose composition is listed on page 124, contain approximately 35% of crystalline lithium metasilicate mixed with glass impoverished with lithium. Between these crystals are densely entangled layers of one or several other phases, including glasses with a lower index of refraction, the values of which changed from 1.515 prior to the development to 1.590 after crystallization.

With further heat treatment, form B, i.e., the remaining non-irradiated material, may be transformed into the brown nontransparent form D and the black form E (see Fig. 56).

Using a special heat-treatment technique, a crystalline ceramic body with high strength and high melting point, called "Fotoceram," can be prepared.

Using the photochemical method, various products of complex configuration and exact dimensions can be prepared from Fotoform glass. Both for the contact as well as the projection (shadow) photographic technique, a parallel beam of ultraviolet rays may be used. The heat-treatment procedure must be adhered to very strictly during the development of the image so as to avoid crystallization in the nonirradiated portions which, after heat treatment, are to be transformed into form B. Due to crystallization, the irradiated portions (form C) form an opacified image which propagates either to a given depth or through the entire thickness of the plate. The image enclosed in the Fotoform glass is abrasion-proof, cannot be contaminated, and retains the original dimensions due to the absence of shrinkage during the transitions of the original material into forms B and C.

Due to the difference in the rates of solution of forms B and C in HF, the crystallized portions surrounding the image contour in perfect detail may be totally dissolved. In this way, the detail is "cut" from the plate, which is why this process is called "photochemical machining." During the acid etching of conventional glass, the surface of which is covered by an appropriate wax mask, tapers are formed at an angle of 45° at the edges of the etched portions, which is caused by the fact that the rate of solution of the glass is the same at the surface and in depth (Fig. 57). The ratio of the depth of etching to its width is thereby limited. In Fotoform glass, with a solubility differential of 15:1, in contrast to conventional glasses, one can produce through-holes having a depth 10 times greater than their width, with the slope of the sidewalls being approximately 4° [270]. This slope may be increased to 30°. When etching glass from one side, holes of conical shape are formed; when etching from two sides, hourglass-shaped holes are formed (see Fig. 57). Etching from two sides is preferred, since finer holes can be produced this way which are located closer to each other, and the hourglass shape of the holes facilitates the in-

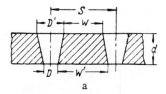 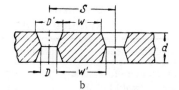

a   b

Fig. 57. Allowable dimensions of holes obtained by etching in Fotoform glass. a) Etching from one side. D_{min} = d : 8, but not less than 0.25 mm; d_{max} = 8D, but not more than 6 mm; D' = D + d : 10; W'_{min} = 0.10 + d : 10. b) Etching from two sides. D_{min} = d : 10, but not less than 0.25 mm; d_{max} = 10D, but not less than 6 mm; W'_{min} = 0.10 mm; D' = D + d : 20; W' = 0.10 + d : 20.

stalling of metallic outlets from both sides and the metallization of these holes in the fabrication of printed circuits.

Since the original may be drawn to a large scale and then reduced optically, a high accuracy and fineness in the detail are possible with Fotoform glass, depending first of all on the accuracy of the original and the quality of the negative taken from it, and also on the size of the crystals in irradiated portions and on the care with which the etching process has been controlled. If the detail has a length-to-width ratio of greater than 2, a correction must be made in the negative for the slight change in the image dimensions occurring during its development at the low-temperature treatment [273].

Relief designs with depressions of various shapes can be obtained with the aid of special protective methods and of selective etching. A combination of depressions and through-holes is achieved by masking with wax during the etching of nonthrough-holes first from one and then from both sides [268]. The depth of the through-holes is determined by the time spent in the etching tank after wax has been removed from the side in question. Holes with slight conicity may be obtained by masking with wax only from the side at which the lesser conus base should appear.

The photochemical method is characterized by: (1) its simplicity and accuracy, (2) the reproducibility of the dimensions of the details, (3) its capability to be used as an assembly-line technological production method, (4) the possibility of its being automatized, (5) the ease with which the transition can be made from one production assortment to another, and (6) its economical opera-

Table 18. Dimensional Tolerances for the Components of
Articles Made from Fotoform Glass

Component	Nominal dimensions, mm	Range of deviation, mm
Inner diameter of the hole or length (width) of the slit	Up to 6 > 6.3-25.4 > 25.4-76.2	± 0.025 ± (0.038-0.051) ± (0.065-0.125)
Intercenter hole distances	Up to 25 > 25.4-101.6 >101.6-177.8	± 0.025 ± (0.060-0.076) ± 0.125
Concentricity of holes or designs exposed simultaneously	Up to 25 > 25.4-101.6 > 101.6-177.8	± 0.025 ± (0.060-0.076) ± 0.125
Concentricity of holes or designs exposed separately	−	± 0.150
Outer dimensions at the edge: after cutting after grinding by conventional techniques after grinding of higher quality after etching	 − − − Up to 25.4 > 25.4-101.6 >101.6	 ± 0.8 ± 0.125 ± 0.050 ± 0.050 ± 0.125 ± 0.25
Deviation from plane-parallelity	−	0.002 per 1 mm of length

tion, since such difficult operations as grinding, boring, and cutting are eliminated, and no expensive equipment, such as presses or dies, are needed.

Nets or grids containing up to 50,000 holes/cm^2 can be prepared from Fotoform glass, with the grid spacing less than 0.01 mm; sturdy honeycombed panels can also be prepared in which the spacing between the holes is one tenth of their depth. Crude Fotoform can be drawn out in the form of plates with dimensions of up to 305 × 460 mm and thicknesses of 1.3, 1.6, 1.9, 2.9, 3.6, 4.3, and 6.0 mm [274]. Plates of intermediate thicknesses can be obtained by grinding, whereas thicker plates may be prepared by combining several mechanically treated plates with a thickness of 6 mm or

Table 19. Distance between the Holes in Perforated Screens Made from Fotoform Glass and the Respective Tolerances

Etching from one side (Fig. 57a)						Etching from two sides (Fig. 57b)					
d, mm	1.39	2.03	3.17	3.81	4.47	6.35	1.39	2.03	3.17	3.81	4.47	6.35
$S-D$, mm	0.18	0.25	0.38	0.48	0.55	0.78	0.07	0.12	0.20	0.22	0.27	0.40

D, mm	S, mm											
0.15	0.33						0.22					
0.25	0.43	0.50					0.32	0.37				
0.38	0.56	0.63	0.76	0.86			0.45	0.50	0.58	0.60		
0.50	0.68	0.75	0.88	0.98	1.05		0.57	0.62	0.70	0.62	0.77	
0.63	0.81	0.88	1.01	1.11	1.18	1.41	0.70	0.75	0.83	0.85	0.90	1.03
1.27	1.45	1.52	1.65	1.75	1.82	2.05	1.34	1.39	1.47	1.49	1.54	1.67
2.54	2.72	2.79	2.92	3.02	3.09	3.32	2.61	2.66	2.74	2.76	2.81	2.94
6.35	6.53	6.60	6.73	6.83	6.90	7.13	6.42	6.47	6.55	6.57	6.62	6.75
12.70	12.88	12.95	13.08	13.18	13.25	13.48	12.77	12.82	12.90	12.92	12.97	13.10

Notes. Here, d is the thickness of the screen plate prior to etching, D is the hole diameter, and S is the intercenter distance of the holes. Tolerances for the hole diameters are as follows. Up to 6.3 mm, ± 0.025 mm, >6.3-25.4 mm, ± 0.052 mm; >25.4 mm, ± 0.13 mm. Tolerances for the distances between the hole axes are as follows: up to 25.4 mm, ±0.025 mm; >25.4-101.6 mm, ± 0.076 mm; > 101.6-177.8 mm, ± 0.13 mm. Tolerances for the distances between the edges of the holes are as follows: for the edge length of up to 25.4 mm, ± 0.052 mm; for the edge length >25.4-101.6 mm, ± 0.13 mm; for the edge length >101.6 mm, ±0.25 mm.

less. Tables 18 and 19 list the tolerances allowed for the dimensions of articles made from forms B and C of Corning catalog number 8603 Fotoform photosensitive glass [273-275, 480]. In some cases, one can maintain even closer tolerances than those listed in Table 18.

6. PRODUCTION TECHNOLOGY AND SOME CHEMICAL COMPOSITIONS FOR PHOTOSENSITIVE GLASS-CERAMICS

Besides selective solubility in dilute HF, photosensitive glasses have the capability of being transformed, without distortions in shape and size (except for a 3% volume shrinkage), into almost entirely crystalline, nonporous, fine-grained material exceeding the original glass in strength, viscosity, hardness, thermal stability, temperature of deformation, and electrical resistivity [39, 40].

The problem of obtaining homogeneous and well-fined photosensitive lithium aluminosilicate glass is one of the most difficult in this area. I investigated the possibility of obtaining homogeneous photosensitive glass by melting it in high-temperature furnaces provided with mechanical stirring of the melt, i.e., by employing the method used for the melting of optical glasses. A comparative analysis of the quality of the glass obtained by production melting procedures with respect to its homogeneity, photosensitivity, bubble content, light absorption, and optical constants showed that the high reactivity of the lithium aluminosilicate photosensitive glass and its chemical interaction with the clay-based refractories of the glass-founding kiln — and especially with the stirrer — at sufficiently high melting temperatures (1480-1490°C) and after long-term stirring resulted in a (1) marked dissolution of the refractory in the glass mass, enriching it with Al_2O_3 and SiO_2, (2) a decrease in the coefficient of refraction n_D and coefficient of dispersion $n_F - n_C$, and (3) an increase in the light absorption of the glass. This made it very difficult to obtain homogeneous glass with a stable photosensitivity. In addition, difficulties arise in connection with the fact that appropriate fining agents are not present, and that it is not possible to add to the photosensitive glass the effective fining agents normally used in the glass-making industry, such as As_2O_3, and also in view of the intense evolution of the gaseous inclusions from the dissolving refractory into the glass mass during melting.

Determinations of the degree of homogeneity of the photosensitive glass by measuring the transmission of the system "immersed liquid—tested glass" as a function of the wavelength of the light source [762] showed that glasses melted by different procedures possessed a high degree of homogeneity, as characterized by the half-width of the transmission curve, which lay within the range 102-131 Å, as compared to 145 Å for insufficiently homogeneous photosensitive glass melted in a batch-operated tank furnace without stirring.

Decreasing the intensity and duration of stirring of the glass melt, and slightly decreasing the melting temperature resulted in a regular decrease in the SiO_2 + Al_2O_3 content in the glass; this also decreased the volatilization and increased the concentration of Li_2O + K_2O in the glass. It was shown thereby that the most homogeneous glass also possessed the best photosensitivity. Thus, decreasing both the time and the intensity of the stirring procedure of the glass mass, both at high temperatures at the fining stage and at lower temperatures at the cooling stage, resulted in a decrease in the dissolution of the refractory and in an improvement of the homogeneity and photosensitivity of this glass, which, due to the reduced time at the high fining temperature, apparently retains a large amount of nonoxidized active cerium in a trivalent state.

The crystalline product consists primarily of lithium silicate, the crystals of which, as shown by Stookey, are bonded by several percent of potassium aluminosilicate glass. The microstructure of the crystallized material is represented by crystals with a flat habit. In order to produce such material, the glass articles which have been etched in HF are subjected to high-temperature heat treatment, the essential stage of which is the formation at 600°C of a rigid crystalline skeleton, which makes it possible to heat glass to an even higher temperature without concomitant deformation.

Stookey [276, 277] determined that further high-temperature treatment of irradiated photosensitive glass, or of the glass article etched from it, results in it being transformed — without substantial changes in its shape and size — into an almost entirely crystallized ceramiclike material "Fotoceram," which differs from corresponding ceramics by having higher mechanical strength and by the presence in its microstructure of crystalline silicates as well as of quartz, which is stable at high temperatures. Because of shrinkage during the drying and the firing processes, ceramic articles with highly accurate dimensions cannot be prepared, and if they also contain small amounts of quartz, they can easily be broken when subjected to sudden changes in temperatures. This is explained by the fact that it is not possible to retain high-temperature quartz in such ceramic articles, since, during the cooling process, it transforms into other modifications which are unstable at elevated temperatures.

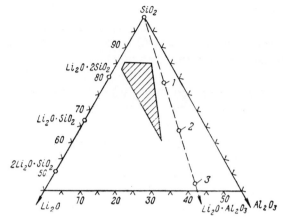

Fig. 58. Region of photosensitive glasses in the $Li_2O-Al_2O_3-SiO_2$ system. The contents of the components are shown in wt.%. 1) Petalite; 2) spodumene; 3) eucryptite.

The photosensitive glasses proposed by Stookey [276, 277] have the following composition: 60-85 SiO_2, 5.5-15 Li_2O, 2-25 Al_2O_3, 0.001-0.03 Au, and 0.001-0.3 Ag (in the form of AgCl) or 0.001-1.0 Cu (on the basis of Cu_2O). The compositions of these glasses are shown on the ternary diagram of the $Li_2O-Al_2O_3-SiO_2$ system given in Fig. 58 [278]. These primary components should be present in amounts not less than 90% of the total content, and the ratio between Al_2O_3 and Li_2O should be not more than 1.7:1; otherwise, these glasses lose their photosensitivity. In order to increase photosensitivity, up to 0.05% CeO_2 is introduced, and in order to facilitate the formation of the metallic nuclei, not more than 0.2% SnO_2 can be introduced. In order to lower the melting temperature of this glass, one can add to it Na_2O and K_2O, in addition to Li_2O, although these oxides remain in the glassy phase during the subsequent crystallization process, together with a slight proportion of the Li_2O, and thus lower the total content of the crystalline phase in the crystallized article. Therefore, the amount of Na_2O and K_2O present in the original photosensitive glass should not exceed a total of 4%, with the total R_2O content being up to 19%. On the other hand, it is shown that the introduction of up to 4% K_2O increases the amount of the precipitating lithium metasilicate, which increases the solubility differential of glass in HF, reaching, according to some data [279], values of 50:1 or 100,000:1 [39].

Table 20. Compositions of Glasses for the Production of Fotoceram

Component	Composition (in wt.%) of various glasses											
	1	2	3	4	5	6	7	8	9	10	11	12
SiO_2	80	81	81	77.5	81.5	80	80.8	80.8	80	73.5	65	79.8
Li_2O	12.5	12.5	12.5	12.5	6.5	8.5	12.5	12.4	12.4	12.5	15	10.2
Na_2O	—	—	—	—	4	4	—	—	—	—	—	—
K_2O	2.5	2.5	2.5	—	—	—	2.5	2.5	2.5	4	—	5
CeO_2	0.03	0.03	0.03	0.02	0.03	0.03	0.025	0.025	0.03	—	0.03	0.012
SnO_2	—	—	—	—	—	—	0.15	0.015	0.01	0.01	0.01	—
Au	0.003	0.018	0.027	0.002	0.006	0.006	—	—	—	—	—	0.001
$AgCl$	—	—	—	—	—	—	0,18	0,27	—	—	—	0.16
Cu_2O	—	—	—	—	—	—	—	—	0.003	0.1	0.8	—
Al_2O_3	4	4	4	10	8	7.5	4	4	4	10	20	4
ZnO	1	—	—	—	—	—	—	—	1	—	—	1
Softening temp., °C	634	620	620	661	668	667	620	620	634	629	675	620
Annealing temp., °C	457	461	461	482	489	470	461	461	457	457	510	463

The crystallized portions of glasses of the following composition etch well in a HF solution: 75–85 SiO_2, 9–15 Li_2O, 2–10 Al_2O_3, and 0.001–0.03 Au or 0.001–0.3 Ag (in the form of AgCl) or 0.001–1 Cu (in the form of Cu_2O), with the sum total of the primary oxides to be not less than 94% [38]. A better photosensitive addition for these glasses is Ag in the amount of 0.001–0.20% (in the form of AgCl). Especially suitable for etching are glasses containing 78–83 SiO_2, 10–13 Li_2O, 0–4 Na_2O, 0–4 K_2O, 4–10 Al_2O_3, and/or 0.001–0.03 Au or 0.001–0.3 Ag (in the form of AgCl) or 0.001–1 Cu (in the form of Cu_2O), and up to 0.05 CeO_2. The total content of R_2O must be 10–17%, and that of the fundamental components not less than 94%.

One may introduce up to 6% ZnO, SrO, CdO, BeO, PbO, or their mixtures, up to 10% MgO and CaO or their mixtures, which crystallize well with the fundamental glass components, and up to 5% B_2O_3. With the maximum Li_2O content, the presence of up to 10% B_2O_3 is allowable. One may also add fining agents Sb_2O_3 and As_2O_3, their exact amounts not being stated. The As_2O_3, as pointed out earlier, destroys photosensitivity. These additional components make it possible to increase the amount of the residual glassy phase present, and thus their total content should not exceed 10%. Table 20 lists the recommended [276, 277] compositions of photosensitive glasses for the production of Fotoceram.

Glasses of the compositions listed in Table 20 are melted at 1350–1400°C for 3–4 h in open crucibles with a 0.45–liter capacity. Glasses with Au (Nos. 1–3) and with a large Ag content (Nos. 7, 8, 12) are melted under neutralized or oxidizing conditions; glasses with a low Ag concentration (Nos. 4–6) and glasses containing Cu (Nos. 9–11) are melted under reducing conditions. In order to create oxidizing conditions, oxidizers are introduced into the batch, and if reducing conditions are required, starch or NH_4Cl is added in amounts determined experimentally, since they depend on the dimensions and the type of melt container and on the duration and the temperature of melting.

The concentrations of photosensitive additions cited are for all practical purposes limiting, since an increase in them only causes an unnecessary consumption of precious metals, and can, under the given conditions, result in spontaneous coloring of glass during the melting process or during fabrication.

The shaping of glass articles is done by pressing, blowing, rolling, and drawing. Additional shaping can be imparted to these products by irradiation and heat treatment; pressing of the billets and joining them together are also used. Glass products may be shaped by powder technology methods, such as by slip casting, after which they are subjected to irradiation and heat treatment. The mechanical strength of such articles is less than that of the articles prepared using photochemical technology, yet it is four times higher than the strength of analogous articles fabricated by shaping and simple sintering of powders of conventional glasses.

In order to form a maximum number of submicroscopic particles of Au, Ag, or Cu — the future nuclei — in the irradiated portions, it is recommended that during the low-temperature heat-treatment process, the articles be held within the temperature range between the annealing temperature (viscosity being $10^{-13.4}$ poise) and the softening temperature (viscosity being $10^{7.6}$ poise), say at 520°C, for 2 min, or that they be heated from 500 to 600°C at a rate not exceeding 5 deg/min. If the glass article is heated too rapidly in the temperature range 520-600°C, then nuclei do not form in sufficient quantities, as a result of which, it is difficult to reach the necessary degree of opacification and the subsequent crystallization at higher temperatures.

In connection with this, doubt is cast on the results obtained by Vaisfel'd et al. [280], who report that repeated thermal shock, i.e., sudden heating at 500-700°C, of irradiated photosensitive glass makes it possible to obtain a more uniform fine-crystalline structure than slow heating. In our opinion, this is a result not of thermal shock, but of the additional precipitation of nuclei during multiple cycles of irradiation and heat treatment. Furthermore, sudden and multiple cyclic heating to high temperatures of the originally nonthermally stable glass inevitably causes it to break down.

If the glass article is heated to 500-600°C for a period sufficient for the formation of a maximum number of nuclei, then heating it further to a temperature below the softening point may, according to Stookey [276, 277], be done at any rate whatever, as long as it does not result in the cracking of the glass articles. The transformation of glass at the low-temperature crystallization stage is associated with the necessity of heating it to a temperature which is higher than the softening point of glass. A heat-treatment

procedure is selected such that a crystalline structure can successfully be formed in the glass, such as would then play the role of a
rigid skeleton inhibiting the deformation of the article. The higher
the temperature and the lower the viscosity of a glass, the faster
such a structure is formed. For instance, at 520°C this time is
20 h; at a temperature 50° lower than the softening point, it is only
1 h; and at a temperature near the softening point, it is 10-20 min.
The heating rate near these temperatures must be equal to 5
deg/min or somewhat higher. According to Stookey [276, 277],
the type of crystalline phase precipitating during the preliminary
low-temperature heat treatment is determined by the glass composition. The K_2O present fosters the formation of the metasilicate, and the Na_2O present favors the precipitation of lithium disilicate.

The favorable effect of K_2O on the formation of lithium metasilicate is explained by Hinz et al. [749] by saying that a known
portion of K_2O possibly enters the crystal lattice of the metasilicate phase, as proven by the deviations they observed in the intensities of the primary x-ray diffraction lines. It is the opinion of
these authors that the major portion of K_2O nevertheless is retained in the glassy phase.

When the glass contains more than 3% K_2O, less than 80%
SiO_2, and less than 5% Al_2O_3, practically all Li precipitates at first
in the form of lithium metasilicate. If the glass contains less than
3% K_2O, more than 80% SiO_2, and less than 5% Al_2O_3, then lithium
disilicate crystals are formed as a result of lithium metasilicate
reacting with SiO_2. When more than 5% Al_2O_3 is present, the formation of β-spodumene is possible as the result of the previously
precipitated lithium metasilicate reacting with Al_2O_3.

While investigating the photosensitive glasses of the lithium
aluminosilicate system, we determined the optimum temperature
for heat treatment, which corresponds to the largest difference
between the rates of solution of the crystallized and the glassy portions. For this purpose, moldings from the glass investigated,
which had been irradiated with ultraviolet light, were crystallized
in a gradient furnace and were subjected to solution in 10% HF. By
determining the decrease in the diameter of the molding after etching, the rate of solution of the material was found, the dependence
of which on the crystallization temperature is shown schematically

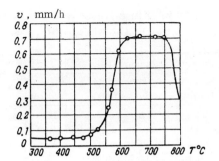

Fig. 59. Rate of solution of the crystalline phase in hydrofluoric acid.

in Fig. 59. By examining this graph, it can be seen that there
exists an optimum temperature range which fosters the precipitation of the largest amount of lithium metasilicate which, in turn,
is responsible for the high solution rate of the crystallized portions.

Analogous dependencies were obtained by Chistoserdov et al.
[281] for photosensitive glasses of the same system. However, in
contrast to the results of Stookey, these dependencies are apparently based on an erroneous interpretation of measurements of the
solubility of standards of primary crystalline phases in the lithium
aluminosilicate system in a 10% solution of HF; according to these
authors, the maximum rate of solution of the portions of the glasses
from this system irradiated and crystallized at 550-600°C is explained by the precipitation in them as the primary phase, not lithium metasilicate, but solid solutions of spodumene—eucryptite mixtures with SiO_2. This assertion is actually in contradiction with
the results of their own experiments, as well as with the experimental data obtained by us and presented in Table 21.

Table 21 shows that, according to the data of Chistoserdov
et al. [281], eucryptite has the maximum solubility in dilute HF,
and not spodumene—eucryptite mixtures, whereas our data show
this to be true for lithium metasilicate; the latter is in good agreement with literature data cited above. Doubtful and difficult to explain is the assertion [281] that the irradiated and crystallized
samples undergo changes in phase composition at room temperature with the passing of time.

Table 21. Solubility in Dilute HF of Standards of Crystalline
Phases in the $Li_2O—Al_2O_3—SiO_2$ System

Compound	Data of Chistoserdov et al. [281]		Data of Berezhnoi and Kim	
	Percent dissolv.	Experimental conditions	Percent dissolv.	Experimental conditions
Eucryptite	93.4	Powder suspension	16.4	Powder suspension was
Li metasilicate	60.8	was treated by a	48.6	treated by a 10% solu-
Li disilicate	58.1	1% solution of	37.8	tion of HF for 15 min
Spodumene	56.1	HF for 1 h at 20°C	38.5	at 20°C.
Quartz	0.3		0.5	

The high-temperature crystallization of the photothermally opacified glass article must be performed at temperatures ranging from 800 to 950°C if it is to be transformed into a photosensitive glass-ceramic. At temperatures higher than these, the crystals begin to melt. During the high-temperature heat-treatment process, lithium metasilicate transforms into lithium disilicate if the glass contains not less than 8-10% Al_2O_3 and if the amount of SiO_2 present is sufficient for the formation of β-spodumene. In addition to these phases, quartz also forms if the SiO_2 concentration is greater than 80%. The glassy phase consists of K_2O, Na_2O, and residual amounts of SiO_2 and Al_2O_3. The duration of heat treatment depends on the temperature and on the glass composition. For instance, the same degree of crystallization of the glass of composition No. 1 (Table 20) is attained when heating it at 900°C for 20 min and when heating at 800°C for 1 h [276, 277]. At a high Li_2O content and at a low SiO_2 content, the formation of not only lithium disilicate, but also of lithium metasilicate, is possible. The latter may also be present when SiO_2 is present in amounts sufficient for the total transformation of lithium metasilicate into lithium disilicate, but only if heat treatment is performed either at a very low temperature or for a period which is not sufficient for this transformation to be completed. The amount of the glassy phase present also increases in this case. For instance, glasses with a high SiO_2 content and a relatively low K_2O and Al_2O_3 content (compositions Nos. 1-3, 7-9), after being heated at 600°C for 1 h or at 615°C for 40 min, contained only lithium metasilicate crystals which were wholly transformed into lithium disilicate and a certain amount of quartz after being heated at 890°C for 1 h. The

Table 22. Electrical Properties of Initial Glass
and of Fotoceram

Material	Electrical resistivity, Ω-cm	Power factor, % at		Loss factor at		Dielectric constant	
		60 Hz	1 MHz	60 Hz	1 MHz	60 Hz	1 MHz
Initial glass	$5 \cdot 10^{11}$	23	1.5	2.24	0.10	9.75	6.9
Fotoceram	$3 \cdot 10^{16}$	0.53	0.27	0.029	0.014	5.5	5.2

crystalline phases precipitating during the high-temperature heat-treatment process are responsible for the physical, mechanical, and dielectric properties of photosensitive glass-ceramics. Thus, if, for example, the glass of composition No. 7 (Table 20) has a linear thermal expansion coefficient equal to $\alpha = 85 \cdot 10^{-7}$, a flexure strength equal to 840 kg/cm^2, and Mohs hardness 5, then the crystalline product, consisting primarily of lithium disilicate and a small amount of quartz, has $\alpha = 100 \cdot 10^{-7}$, a flexure strength equal to 2415 kg/cm^2, and Mohs hardness 7. The increase in the linear thermal expansion coefficient here is explained by the fact that lithium disilicate has an α value exceeding $100 \cdot 10^{-7}$. Because of the close packing of lithium disilicate crystals and their mutual adherence, the photosensitive glass-ceramic has a strength which is four to six times higher than the original glass and, in spite of the high α values, a relatively good thermal stability. The material does not deform at temperatures below 950°C. A comparison between the electrical properties of No. 7 glass and of Fotoceram at a temperature of 24°C is presented in Table 22 (from [277]).

The present author, together with E. I. Kim, studied the dependence of the formation of crystalline phases on the temperature of heating of photosensitive glasses of the lithium aluminosilicate system. The results obtained are presented in Table 23. Over the temperature range 575-650°C, lithium metasilicate and β-spodumene are formed as the primary crystalline phases. The mass ratio of these phases depends on the crystallization procedure; however, in the majority of cases, lithium metasilicate predominates over β-spodumene.

Table 23. Formation of Crystalline Phases at Various
Crystallization Temperatures

Crystallization temperature, °C	Crystalline phase	
	Primary	Secondary
575-595	Lithium metasilicate, β-spodumene	β-Eucryptite, lithium disilicate
620	Lithium metasilicate, β-spodumene; more rarely, lithium disilicate	β-Eucryptite
660	β-Spodumene, β-eucryptite; more rarely, lithium disilicate	β-Eucryptite, β-quartz
700; 750	β-Spodumene, β-eucryptite; more rarely, lithium disilicate	Lithium metasilicate
800	β-Eucryptite	β-Spodumene, lithium metasilicate, lithium disilicate
850	β-Eucryptite	Lithium disilicate, β-spodumene, β-quartz
900	Fusion of crystals and their transition into the glassy state	

β-Spodumene is formed as the primary crystalline phase up to a temperature of 750°C.

Over the temperature range 600-750°C for some compositions, lithium disilicate is formed as the primary crystalline phase, together with β-spodumene. The β-eucryptite which forms in small amounts in the temperature range 575-650°C appears at a higher temperature (up to 750°C) as the primary crystalline phase, together with β-spodumene. At a temperature of 800°C and higher, the β-eucryptite is the sole primary crystalline phase present; lithium disilicate and β-spodumene are formed here in insignificant amounts. At 660 and 850°C, the presence of quartz is noticed; here, cristobalite also forms in very insignificant amounts. At 900°C, the melting and vitrification of crystals is observed.

Irradiation of photosensitive glasses with ultraviolet rays caused their earlier crystallization. The glasses we irradiated were crystallized at a temperature of 575-595°C, while nonirradiated glasses crystallized at 650-660°C. Thus, the difference in the temperatures for the start of crystallization between the irradiated and the nonirradiated glasses was 60-75°C.

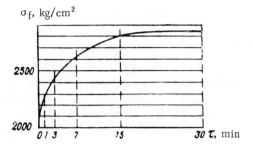

σ_f, kg/cm^2

Fig. 60. Mechanical strength of crystallized glass. τ)
Irradiation time; σ_f) flexure strength.

Irradiation of glass, regardless of the irradiation time, had
no effect on the phase composition of the samples. The mineralogical composition of irradiated and nonirradiated samples crystallized at the same temperature was the same, although slight vari-
ances in the secondary phases were sometimes observed.

Irradiation, nevertheless, had a considerable effect on the
structure of the crystallized samples. In the majority of the
samples which were not irradiated, surface crystallization was observed, as well as a coarsely crystalline structure with crystal
size ranging from 20-40 to 400 μ. Moreover, in some samples,
anisotropic regions were observed, giving extinctions in polarized
light. These regions consisted of crystals oriented in the same
direction and bonded with glass. When comparing samples subjected to irradiation for varying times (up to 30 min), it can be
seen that the size of the anisotropic regions is inversely proportional to irradiation time. With increasing irradiation time, the
length of the crystals decreased, with their width remaining constant at less than 1 μ. In the sample irradiated for 30 min, a uniform microcrystalline structure was observed with crystal size
less than 1 μ.

By determining the mechanical strength of the samples subjected to irradiation for various times, we found that there is a
regular increase in strength with increasing exposure time up to
a certain point, beyond which no further change in the structure
and the strength of the given material was observed (Fig. 60).

Shmeleva and Ivanova [282] studied the products of the high-
temperature crystallization of photosensitive glasses, in which

bands in the form of gas bubbles of various shapes and SiO_2-enriched tensile microzones were observed at the interphase boundaries between the glass and the crystals. It is asserted that microvacancies are nucleated due to the rupture of the material in tensile microzones and during the crystallization process. These authors think that crystallization throughout the bulk of these glasses can be achieved only because of the presence of gas micronodules whose walls are silica-enriched. This fosters the formation of solid solutions with SiO_2. One cannot possibly agree with these conceptions, since the micronodules described are not typical for the crystallization of lithium silicate glasses and are, above all, a result of inadequate fining of glass during the melting process. The authors do not present any proof that tensile and rupture microzones do exist in their material. Furthermore, a displacement of the Becke band due to bubble contours does not, as the authors assert, constitute a direct proof that the "boundary" layer of the bubble is SiO_2-enriched, since Becke bands always exist at the boundary between two media with different indices of refraction. Finally, it is not very likely that the brown color of the crystallized material would be produced by the formation of micronodules. The "black" material, which is interpreted by the authors as a result of the extremely fine distribution of gas vacancies in the crystalline material, is, according to our data, cristobalite, which is observed as "black" material due to the optical effect. Under the microscope, the fine-grained cristobalite aggregates are sometimes shown to be nontransparent, i.e., black, under transmitted light, even if composed of transparent and colorless particles.

In order to come up with photosensitive glass-ceramics with improved dielectric properties, we investigated high-silica glasses in the SiO_2—CaO—Li_2O system with additions of 0.5-3% K_2O. Glasses have been prepared, some of which have been melted at 1540-1560°C, with the photosensitive additions Ag_2O and CeO_2, which were then irradiated with a PRK-7 lamp and crystallized. It was determined that irradiation had a significant effect on the photosensitive glasses of this system, by producing crystallization at lower temperatures. The difference in the temperatures for the start of the crystallization between nonirradiated glasses and glasses irradiated for 6 h was 75°C. Preliminary irradiation of glass had a tremendous effect on the structure of the crystalliza-

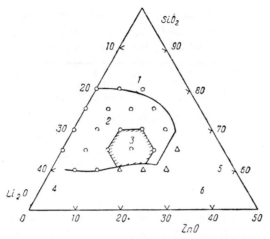

Fig. 61. Region of compositions of gold-containing glasses in the $Li_2O-K_2O-ZnO-SiO_2$ system. Additional components (mol.%) are: $3K_{2O}$, 0.005Au, and $0.01CeO_2$. 1) Excessive viscosity; 2) photographic formation of nuclei; 3) glass-formation region, in which $2Li_2O \cdot SiO_2$ is precipitated; 4) devitrification; 5) spontaneous crystallization; 6) absence of photosensitivity. The content of primary components present is given in mol.%.

tion product, but, as in the previous example, did not have an effect on its phase composition.

The primary crystalline phases in the majority of the glasses investigated were represented by lithium disilicate in the temperature range 540-640°C, by the low-temperature quartz modification at 650-700°C, by the high-temperature quartz modification in the temperature region 700-950°C, and by tridymite in the temperature region 950-1280°C. At other temperatures, some of these compounds formed as secondary phases.

In addition to the above, the following were present as secondary phases in small amounts. Kaliophilite in the temperature range 540-700°C, β-wollastonite at 600-900°C, and β-eucryptite in the temperature range 800-900°C. At 1280°C, β-wollastonite was observed to be present in small amounts.

In some glasses, a difference was observed in the phase composition of irradiated and nonirradiated samples. Cristobalite at 700°C and petalite at 600-650°C were observed as the primary

Table 24. Crystalline Phases (in mol.%) Precipitating in Glasses
of the Composition 17 Li_2O, 0.3 K_2O, $(80 - m)SiO_2$, $mZnO$,
0.005 Au, and 0.01 CeO_2

m	0	5	10	15
Phases precipitating	$Li_2O \cdot SiO_2$	$Li_2O \cdot SiO_2$	$Li_2O \cdot SiO_2$ $2Li_2O \cdot SiO_2$ $Li_2O \cdot 2SiO_2$ SiO_2	$2Li_2O \cdot SiO_2$ SiO_2

crystalline phases in these glasses. Irradiated samples had a
more finely crystalline and a more uniformly granular structure
than nonirradiated glasses.

Soga et al. [283] undertook to investigate gold-containing
photosensitive glasses of the following basic composition: 15-20
Li_2O, 1-5 K_2O, 10-20 ZnO, and 60-70 SiO_2 (Fig. 61). Glass of the
composition (in mol.%) 17 Li_2O, 3 K_2O, 15 ZnO, 65 SiO_2, 0.01 CeO_2,
and 0.005 Au was irradiated by ultraviolet rays for 60 min at a
distance of 6 cm from a mercury—quartz high-pressure lamp with
a power of 500 W, heated to 520°C at a rate of 5 deg/min, held
there for 30 min to give the colloidal gold (nuclei) a change to precipitate, and then heated at the same rate to 620°C, held there for
60 min to give the $2Li_2O \cdot SiO_2$ crystals a change to precipitate,
and subsequently etched in an agitated 5% solution of HF at 18°C.

In glasses containing less than 10 mol.% ZnO, either lithium
met- or lithium disilicate precipitates (Table 24). The addition of
K_2O together with Au and CeO_2 made it possible for the orthosili-
cate to precipitate [283].

An interesting result of the work of Soga et al. [283] is the
high rate of solution in HF of glasses containing more than 10
mol.% ZnO (Fig. 62), and an increase in the solubility differential
due to the addition to the glass of a small amount of Al_2O_3 (Fig. 63).
The rate of solution of the crystallized portions of the glass containing 15 mol.% ZnO was equal to 0.02 mm/min, while the solubility differential was equal to 10:1. The material crystallized at
700°C had a satisfactory mechanical strength and satisfactory dielectric properties.

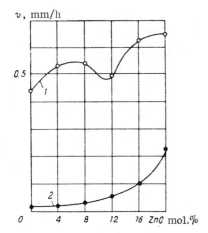

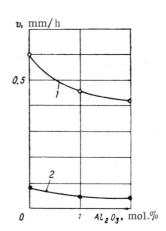

Fig. 62. Linear rate of dissolution v of a glass of the $Li_2O-K_2O-ZnO-SiO_2$ system. The composition of the glass (mol.%) is: $17Li_2O$, $3K_2O$, $xZnO$, $(80-x)SiO_2$. Irradiation by ultraviolet light, heat treatment at 520°C for 30 min, and then at 620°C for 60 min. 1) Crystallized glass; 2) initial glass.

Fig. 63. Effect of Al_2O_3 on the linear solution rate v of glass of the composition (mol.%): $17Li_2O$, $3K_2O$, $15ZnO$, $65SiO_2$, $0.005Au$, and 0.01 CeO_2. 1) Crystallized glass; 2) initial glass.

Stookey [284-286] proposed a method for the preparation of highly uniform and finely grained glass-crystalline materials using heat treatment only (without irradiation) of glasses containing photosensitive additions of Au, Ag, or Cu, and one of the platinum-group metals.

For this purpose, glasses of the type $R_2O \cdot BaO \cdot SiO_2$ and $Li_2O \cdot Al_2O_3 \cdot SiO_2$, designated from here on as type 1 and type 2, respectively, were employed. The R_2O in these glasses is Li_2O, Na_2O, and K_2O; they contain (0.001-1)% Cu or (0.001-0.10)% Au. Type 1 glasses contain: $(50-85)SiO_2$; $(3-45)BaO$; $(0-25)Li_2O$, $(0-10)Na_2O$, and $(0-10)K_2O$; $(0-10)RO$ in addition to BaO; and $(0-10)Al_2O_3$. The total R_2O content is (5-25)%, and the sum total of Na_2O and K_2O should not be more than 15% if the BaO concentration is more than 20%, and not more than 8% if the BaO concentration is less than 20%. The overall total RO content present should not be more than 45%.

Type 2 glasses contain: $(60-85)SiO_2$; $(2-25)Al_2O_3$, and $(6-15)Li_2O$; here, the Al_2O_3-to-Li_2O ratio must be not more than

Table 25. Glass Compositions for the Preparation of
Glass-Ceramics without Irradiation

Component	Contents (in wt.%) of various glasses								
	1	2	3	4	5	6	7	8	9
SiO_2	74.7	75.8	75.4	55.1	55.9	55.5	80.5	80.5	80.5
Li_2O	18	18	18	1	1	1	12	12	12
Na_2O	1	1	1	6	6	6	—	—	—
K_2O	—	—	—	—	—	—	3	3	3
Al_2O_3	2	2	2	2	2	2	4	4	4
BaO	3	3	3	35	35	35	—	—	—
Cu	0.8	—	—	0.4	—	—	0.8	—	—
Ag	—	0.2	—	—	0.1	—	—	0.05	—
Au	—	—	0.1	—	—	0.05	—	—	0.005
Pt	—	—	0.01	—	—	—	0.05	—	—
Pd	—	0.95	—	—	—	—	—	—	—
Sb_2O_3	0.5	—	0.5	—	—	—	0.5	0.5	—
SnO_2	—	—	—	0.5	—	0.5	—	—	0.5

1.7 : 1; 0-4 Na_2O and K_2O are also present either individually or jointly. The total content of SiO_2, the R_2O oxides, and Al_2O_3 should not be less than 97%.

The approximate compositions of these glasses are presented in Table 25, taken from [284-286].

The melting at 1400°C for 4 h, the shaping, and the heat treatment of the articles are done under reducing conditions, due to which metallic Au, Ag, or Cu ions are reduced to metal in the form of colloidal particles, and the glass becomes nonphotosensitive. Excessively strong reducing conditions enhance excessive growth and deposition of the colloidal particles, whereas, under insufficient reduction, the glass remains photosensitive and does not crystallize under the effect of heat treatment alone. The reducing conditions needed are created by the introduction into the batch of small amounts of starch or sugar. For Cu-containing glasses, 0.5-1% starch is needed; for Ag-containing glasses, 0.2-0.5% starch; and for Au-containing glasses, 0.05-0.1% starch. For the fining agent, the use of Sb_2O_3 is recommended instead of As_2O_3, which is less effective under reducing conditions.

Table 26. Compositions of Glasses Containing Platinum-Group Metals

Component	Contents (in wt. %) of various glasses															
	1	2	3	4	5	6	7	8	9	10	11	12	13	14	15	16
SiO_2	81	81	81	81	81	81	76	76	76	76	56	56	56	56	56	56
Li_2O	14.5	14.5	14.5	14.5	14.5	14.5	18	18	18	18	1	1	1	1	1	1
Al_2O_3	4.5	4.5	4.5	4.5	4.5	4.5	2	2	2	2	2	2	2	2	2	2
Na_2O	—	—	—	—	—	—	1	1	1	1	6	6	6	6	6	6
BaO	—	—	—	—	—	—	3	3	3	3	35	35	35	35	35	35
Ru	0.02	—	—	—	—	—	0.02	—	—	—	0.05	—	—	—	—	—
Rh	—	0.02	—	—	—	—	—	—	—	—	—	0.10	—	—	—	—
Pd	—	—	0.10	—	—	—	—	0.05	0.002	—	—	—	0.001	—	—	—
Os	—	—	—	0.02	—	—	—	—	—	—	—	—	—	0.02	—	—
Ir	—	—	—	—	0.02	—	—	—	—	—	—	—	—	—	0.02	—
Pt	—	—	—	—	—	0.001	—	—	—	0.05	—	—	—	—	—	0.10

It was observed that reducing conditions during the heat treatment of a glass are created by the presence in the glass of up to 1% polyvalent Sb, Sn, Se, and Te ions, which, during melting, are reduced to lower-valency oxides, which are stable at high temperatures, but partially remain present in the cooled glass. During secondary heating, these polyvalent elements are capable of being oxidized, thereby reducing the Au, Ag, or Cu ions to the metal. A small addition of alkali-metal nitrate to the batch results in a uniform distribution of the colloidal particles of the metal in the glass, because the nitrate keeps the metal-catalyst, which is uniformly dissolved in the glass, in the ionic state. This uniform distribution of the metal particles is also retained after the reduction of the ions.

Introduction into the glass of, in addition to Au, Ag, or Cu, one or more of Ru, Rh, Pd, Os, Ir, or Pt in amounts of 0.001-0.1 wt.% results in a uniform, fine-crystalline structure after heat treatment by the following procedure. The glass article is heated to 580-650°C at a rate of 5 deg/min, held at 580°C for 8 h or at 650°C for 0.5 h, and then heated to 700-850°C at the same rate and held for 8 h at 700°C or for 1 h at 850°C. Depending on the amount of Li_2O, BaO, and SiO_2 in the glass, the microstructure of the crystallized products consisted of lithium metasilicate or disilicate, barium disilicate, and quartz or cristobalite.

Table 26, from [287, 288], presents glass compositions in the $R_2O-BaO-SiO_2$ and $Li_2O-Al_2O_3-SiO_2$ systems with platinum-group metals added for the preparation of glass-ceramics, the glasses being characterized by a uniform, fine-crystalline structure. These glasses differ from those previously considered by their insensitivity to the melting atmosphere (because of the presence of platinum-group metals only) and by the circumstance that introduction of $NaNO_3$ and As_2O_3 into their batch is recommended for the purpose of better fining. The melting and the heat-treatment procedures for these glasses are the same as for the glasses listed in Table 25.

7. METAL-COATING OF ARTICLES MADE FROM PHOTOSENSITIVE GLASS-CERAMICS

Photosensitive glass-ceramics are characterized by the ease with which they are metal-coated and by the very high coupling strengths between them and metallic coatings applied by such techniques as chemical and electrical copper-plating, nickel-plating, and the burning in of pastes prepared from silver-, gold-, and copper-based materials. The break-off and tear-off strengths of such coatings on photosensitive glass-ceramics are considerably better than the strength of the coupling for the laminated board generally used for the fabrication of printed circuits [41]. Heat applied during sealing has no effect on the strength of the coupling, since photosensitive glass-ceramics do not change during such an increase in temperature. Metal-coated printed circuits on photosensitive glass-ceramics are capable of operating without impairment at temperatures of approximately 400-500°C and under high humidity if the metallic conductors, the sealed-on parts, and their bracing supports are sufficiently stable under such conditions [289]. Printed circuits on photosensitive glass-ceramics (Figs. 64 and 65), which are connected through through-holes by means of metallization, have a good thermal conductivity when sealed by the submersion technique; the latter enhances the formation of a smooth and uniform sealing layer during the metallization of through-holes [273].

The thickness of the copper conducting layer of the printed circuit on a photosensitive glass-ceramic board metallized from two sides may range from 0.05 to 0.15 mm [290]. The photosensitive glass-ceramic may be metal-coated by burning in a silver-containing paste applied by the silkscreen method, by ultrasonic sealing, and also by the deposition of electrolytic copper coating through a silken filter with the subsequent application of metal to the copper. The high coupling strength obtained thereby makes it possible to seal and unseal the components repeatedly (more than 20 times) without damaging the printed circuit [42].

In one of the techniques used [291], those portions on the functional photosensitive glass-ceramic board which do not have a circuit imprinted on them are masked, whereupon the board is coated with a thick copper layer using the electrochemical technique. The metal-coated portions are thereupon coated with gold, which plays the role of a protective coating during the subsequent etching procedure. The leads or ends of the microelements coated with gold are joined to the board simply by heating them with an iron.

Fig. 64. Printed-circuit board made of photosensitive glass-
ceramic.

Fig. 65. Burnished printed-circuit board made of Fotoceram. a) All
board surfaces are coated with copper; b) finished design; unnecessary
copper was removed by etching.

Fig. 66. Reticulated boards of a printing rig made of Fotoceram coated with copper.

Corning Glass Works [292, 293] puts out reticulated boards made of Fotoceram with a circuit design imprinted on them (Fig. 66). The design of the circuit is then transferred by the photographic technique to a board which is coated with copper and with a photoresist which can be etched away wherever it was irradiated. The etching of the photoresist and the copper takes 15 min, after which the board is ready to be put together.

We conducted experiments on the metal-coating of photosensitive glass-ceramics by the chemical and electrical copper- and nickel-plating techniques.

The essence of the chemical copper- and nickel-plating processes consists in the reduction of the metal from their salts using various reducers. Techniques have been developed for the reduction of copper salts by, among other agents, sugar, Rochelle salt, formaldehyde, glycol, and phenylhydrazine [294]; among these techniques is one for the preparation of a thin film from a complex Cu^+ compound. During the acidification of a solution of this complex, Cu^{2+} is formed, and metallic copper precipitates. For the reduction of nickel, a hydrophosphite is generally employed, with the coatings forming here constituting a complex system including phosphorus, in addition to nickel, thereby changing both the physical and the chemical properties of the coating [295].

During chemical deposition of the metals, the preliminary preparation of the surface has a large effect on the quality of the coatings and on the strength of their adhesion with the basic material. This preliminary preparation includes: degreasing, sensitization, and activation. The selection of the degreasing method depends on the type of the material to be metal-coated, and also on the degree of contamination of the surface. Sensitization speeds up the reduction process, improves the adhesion, and makes it possible to obtain a more uniform coating. As the sensitizer, a solution of $SnCl_2$ with concentration ranging from 0.1 to 10 g/liter is generally employed. Salts of noble metals Ag, Pd, and Au are reduction activators of copper and nickel from their salts.

Prior to chemical deposition of the metal, the article was degreased by boiling in alkali solutions. After being carefully rinsed by distilled water and after being dried, its surface was treated with a stannic dichloride solution. The article was then desiccated, and the activator solution was applied to those portions of the surface which had been metal-coated. Chemical nickel-plating was done in a solution recommended in [295] at a temperature of 80–85°C for 5-30 min. If the nickel coating was applied as the basis for the subsequent electrodeposition of copper or some other metal, the individual parts were nickel-plated for 5 min, after which copper was electrolytically grown on the nickel layer.

The photolithography method was employed to produce nickel coatings of a definite pattern on flat articles made of photosensitive glass-ceramics. First, all articles were covered with nickel, then the photosensitive emulsion was applied, and the articles were irradiated through a negative with ultraviolet light. After development in warm water and after polymerization at 250°C, the nickel was etched away from those portions which had not been covered with the protective layer. The strength of the adhesion between the photosensitive glass-ceramic and the nickel coating obtained in this manner amounted to 165-200 kg/cm^2, on the average.

The well-known [294] solutions for the chemical deposition of copper were used. It was determined that a decrease in the nickel chloride content present in the solution resulted in increased strength of the sealed joint, which may be explained by the greater thickness of the copper deposit, since the rate of the process increased due to the heightened activity of the Cu^{2+} ions in the solution. Degreasing was done most effectively in hot potash solutions and in a 10% solution of NaOH. Of significant importance was the concentration of the activator $PdCl_2$. The best results were obtained at a content of 0.4-0.6% $PdCl_2$ in the solution. The optimum duration for copper-plating was 30 min. In order to increase the thickness of the coating, the copper or nickel layers produced on the photosensitive glass-ceramic by the chemical deposition method were built up by the electrolytic method. We observed that electrolytic coatings 5-15 μ thick, which were deposited at a current density of 0.5-1 A/dm^2, increased the strength of the sealed joint of the article made of photosensitive glass-ceramic, characterized by the breaking load of 800-1500 g.

The present author and Ya. L. Ryzhik investigated silver coatings on photosensitive glass-ceramics which have a high electrical conductivity and provide for soft seal timing.

By considering glass-ceramics as ceramic materials with a very fine crystalline structure, one may also consider that the mechanism of adhesion of the metallic coating with a ceramic is the same as that with a glass-ceramic. It was determined that the most important role in the adhesion of silver is played by the flux which is present in most of the compositions of silver pastes. During annealing, the flux either interacts in the liquid state with the ceramic — most probably with the glassy phase — or it diffuses into this glassy phase without fusion, which produces a strong bond between the ceramic and silver. Of significance here are the quantity and the composition of the flux and of the glassy phase of the material.

The present author and Ya. L. Ryzhik attempted to find the technique of applying silver coatings on photosensitive glass-ceramics of the lithium aluminosilicate system which would result in the strongest adhesion. As a result of the experiments performed, a composition for the silver paste was selected which is based on silver oxide and which also contains rosin dissolved in turpentine as the binder and bismuth—lead—borate glass as the flux.

Table 27. Schematic for the Fabrication of Crystallized
Photosensitive Glass Samples

Technological operation	Flow sheet showing order of operations during fabrication of samples				
	I	II	III	IV	V
Irradiation with ultraviolet light	1	1	1	1	2
Heat treatment following the low-temperature crystallization procedure	—	—	2	2	1
Etching in a 10% solution of HF for 5 min	—	2	—	—	3
30 min	—	—	3	—	—
Heat treatment following the high-temperature crystallization procedure	2	3	4	3	4

The sintering temperature of the powdered glass is about 410°C, and its spreading temperature, as determined from the wetting of the ceramic, is approximately 520°C.

It is known that the adhesion strength of the coating depends not only on the flux content in the silver paste, but also on the sealing temperature [296]. An understanding of these dependencies for coatings on photosensitive glass-ceramics makes it possible to determine the optimum technological conditions for their silver-plating.

Also of considerable interest are the surface peculiarities of articles made of photosensitive glass-ceramics; these are the result of the photochemical treatment of the photosensitive glass and are capable of influencing the strength of the adhesion of the coating.

The adhesion strength of the silver coating, determined by the breakaway force of a brass rod sealed perpendicularly to the surface, was expressed by the formula

$$\sigma = \frac{P}{S},\tag{30}$$

where P is the breakaway load in kg, and S is the area of the fracture zone in cm^2.

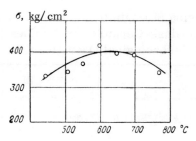

Fig. 67. Adhesion strength between the silver coating and the photosensitive glass-ceramic at various burning-in temperatures. T) Burning-in temperature; σ) adhesion strength at breakaway.

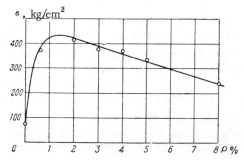

Fig. 68. Adhesion strength between silver coating and photosensitive glass-ceramic at various contents of bismuth—lead—borate glass in the paste. P) Content in percent of bismuth—lead—borate glass in the past; σ) adhesion strength at breakaway.

Polished blocks of photosensitive glass 30 × 10 × 10 mm in size were used as samples, which, depending on their projected purpose, were subjected to the appropriate technological operations and were crystallized according to the high-temperature crystallization procedure under the same conditions under which articles made of photosensitive glass-ceramics are prepared (see Table 27).

After a rosin—alcohol flux was applied to the surface of the sample which had been silver-plated by triple burning in of the

Table 28. Adhesion Strength between Silver Coating and
Photosensitive Glass-Ceramic for Samples Fabricated
by the Different Technological Operations Given in Table 27

Sample type	I	II	III	IV	V
Breakaway stress (kg/cm^2)	410	390	90	370	370

silver-containing paste, the surface of the sample was tin-plated
through a paper stencil by a POS 61 solder. Triple silver-plating
was used so as to produce coatings 15-25 μ thick, which would be
able to withstand the sealing process without dissolving.

The adhesion strength was characterized by the average
value of 15 measurements. Figure 67 shows the dependence of the
adhesion strength between a silver coating and a photosensitive
glass-ceramic (type-I sample) on the temperature of burning-in
paste containing 2% of bismuth—lead—borate glass. With increasing temperature, the adhesion strength increases, and attains a
maximum value at 600-700°C, which is apparently associated with
the thinning of the flux and the softening of the glassy phase. At
temperatures in excess of 700°C, a slight decrease in the breakaway stresses was noted, which may be explained by the increase
in the oxide film on the silver coating.

The dependence of the adhesion strength on the content of
bismuth—lead—borate glass in the paste is presented in Fig. 68.
The burning-in temperature here was 600°C. The maximum values
for the breakaway stresses are obtained at a content of 0.5-4% of
glass in the paste. However, the coatings tinned better if the glass
content was not more than 2%.

It must be mentioned that at breaking stresses of approximately 350 kg/cm^2, breakaway of the silver layer together with
small portions of the photosensitive glass-ceramic took place in a
number of cases; with increasing load, this phenomenon was observed more frequently and over a larger area. Consequently, the
adhesion strength of the coatings with the photosensitive glass-
ceramic samples exceeded the strength of the samples themselves.

Some special photosensitive glass-ceramic articles need to
have those surfaces metal-coated which became exposed after etch-

ing away the crystalline portions with a hydrofluoric acid solution and which underwent subsequent changes during high-temperature crystallization. Unfortunately, one cannot reproduce this surface on the samples, because of the difficulties associated with the etching of the glass and the appearance of conicity.

In this case, the adhesion strength of the silver coating may be studied indirectly by examining the effect of the crystals remaining on the etched surface upon "under-etching," and also by examining the effect of "over-etching" photosensitive glass.

Experiments with type-II samples (over-etching) metal-coated by burning in at 600°C the silver paste with a 2% content of bismuth—lead—borate glass showed that in this case the adhesion strength of the coating corresponds to the strength of the type-I samples (Table 28).

From Table 28 it follows that incomplete etching away of the crystallized part of the sample during treatment in a HF solution (type-III sample) sharply decreases the adhesion strength. While the reasons for this are uncertain, we believe that the observed phenomenon can be explained by the greater rate of diffusion of the glassy phase as opposed to the crystalline phase in the photosensitive glass which had been crystallized following a low-temperature procedure, which results in an impoverishment of the surface layers relative to the glass phase. As another explanation, one may cite the deposition of reaction products in individual microsections of the etched surface, which, upon further heat treatment, produce a protective layer which, in turn, inhibits the interaction of the glassy phase with the flux of the paste. The effect of recrystallization is precluded here, inasmuch as the adhesion strengths on type-IV and type-I samples are practically the same.

As confirmation of the above statements, one ought to consider the increase to 200 kg/cm² in the adhesion strength of the silver coating of type-III samples as the etching time is increased to 1 h. This is associated with surface propagation of crystallization during low-temperature heat treatment due to the limited penetration of ultraviolet rays inside the sample; here, etching the surface of the samples causes those subsurface layers to be exposed in which the degree of crystallization is smaller, i.e., in which the amount of noncrystallized glass present is larger, which makes the experimental conditions of these tests similar to those for tests with type-II samples.

Of no less interest is the adhesion strength between the silver coating and the surface of the photosensitive glass-ceramic which does not serve as the etching boundary of the crystallized portion. Such a surface was reproduced on type-V samples in studies of the peculiarities produced on photosensitive glass-ceramic surfaces by the partial surface crystallization of glass in nonirradiated portions during treatment following the low-temperature crystallization procedure. As shown by the profile patterns of these samples, due to the difference in the etching rates of glass and of the crystals forming at the surface, the relief of the latter undergoes substantial changes, which are basically retained during the high-temperature crystallization process.

In spite of the better developed surface, type-V samples showed the same adhesion strength of the silver coating as type-II samples, both of which had been subjected to etching during the fabrication process.

As a result of our investigation, the effect of the burning-in temperature and the content of the flux present in the paste containing silver oxide on the adhesion strength between the silver coating and the photosensitive glass-ceramic was determined. The optimum conditions for the silver-coating of photosensitive glass-ceramics were determined: a content of 0.5-2% of the flux present and a burning-in temperature of 600°C.

Incomplete etching away of the crystallized portions results in a weakening of the adhesion of the silver coating at that part of the surface of the photosensitive glass-ceramic which has been exposed by etching.

Upon complete solution of the crystalline portions and upon etching of the glass, the adhesion strength is the same as for coatings on crystallized photosensitive glass which had not been etched. The silver coating also had this same adhesion strength upon metal-coating of the matrix of the surface of the photosensitive glass-ceramic which had not been etched.

The following original method for producing a metallic coating on glass-ceramics has been proposed by English Electric Company [297]. During the crystallization of glass in a controlled reducing atmosphere, the metal ions which are present in the glass diffuse to the surface of the product, where they become reduced and where they form a metallic film possessing good adhesive

Table 29. Compositions of Self-Metallizing
Thermosensitive Glasses

Component	Contents (in wt.%) of various glasses							
	1	2	3	4	5	6	7	8
SiO_2	59	58.4	59	59.3	56.6	62.8	63.7	80.1
Li_2O	9.8	9.7	9.8	9.9	9.4	17.7	18	10.7
ZnO	26.6	26.3	26.6	26.7	25.5	—	—	—
MgO	—	—	—	—	—	—	—	3.6
Al_2O_3	—	—	—	—		10.7	10.9	—
P_2O_5	2.6	2.6	2.6	2.6	2.5	4.3	4.4	2.6
CuO	2	2	1	0.5	5	3.5	2	2
SnO	—	1	1	1	1	1	1	1

properties. The compositions of glasses listed in [297] are presented in Table 29.

As crystallization agents, orthophosphates of lithium or zinc
and P_2O_5 are introduced into these glasses; as sources of copper,
Cu oxide, carbonate, or nitrate are used. The glass is melted at
1250-1450°C in refractory crucibles containing increased amounts
of zircon or sillimanite. In order to produce a metallic coating,
the preshaped glass article is placed in an electric furnace with a
reducing atmosphere, the latter being maintained by feeding H_2 or
a mixture of 90% N_2 and 10% H_2 into the furnace. The article is
heated at a rate of 2 deg/min almost to the softening point, and is
held at that temperature for 1 h. The article is then heated at a
rate of 5 deg/min to the final crystallization temperature (850-
1000°C), and is held at that temperature for 1 h. The rate of cooling is approximately 10 deg/min [297].

The film quality is improved if heat treatment is started in
an oxidizing atmosphere. The glass articles are first heated in an
air atmosphere or in an air—oxygen mixture to a temperature
which is 50-200°C below the softening point and are then held at
this temperature for 1 h. Nitrogen, and then hydrogen, are fed into the furnace, and the process follows the procedure which has
been described above.

During heat treatment, the Cu ions diffuse to the glass surface and become reduced to the metal. Small (up to 2%) amounts

of SnO_2 facilitate the reduction. The glass transforms into a glass-ceramic which is coated with a copper film, but which has, nevertheless, poor conductivity, due to the presence of a surface film composed of silicate glass. This film can easily be dissolved within 5-6 min in a 2% solution of HF. The resistivity of the copper film prepared in this manner is equal to 0.04-1 Ω when the distance between the electrodes is 1 cm. This resistivity may be reduced by electrochemical buildup of the copper coating. In order to produce a printed-circuit design on such a metal-coated glass-ceramic, the necessary design is imprinted on its surface by the photographic technique, while the unprotected portions of the metal are removed by treatment in an iron chloride solution.

Chapter IV

Chemical Compositions and Production Technology of Glass-Ceramics

As a result of further research, it became possible to prepare glass-ceramics from nonphotosensitive glass. Inexpensive crystallization catalysts were found, exposure to ultraviolet light was eliminated, and the production of glass-ceramics was simplified to such an extent that, for all practical purposes, it differed only slightly from conventional glass production [298, 299]. Raw materials for the production of glass-ceramics can be available nonstrategic materials, such as are used in the production of ordinary glass.

At the present time, glass-ceramics are prepared from glasses of more than 5000 compositions, and methods have been worked out for controlling the growth of crystals and the chemical-mineralogical composition of the crystalline phases precipitating, making it possible to prepare glass-ceramics with previously specified physical and mechanical properties [43].

In the production of many types of glass-ceramics, TiO_2 is used as the crystallization catalyst, being introduced into the glass batch in amounts of 2-20 wt.%. This compound, which supplies nuclei with diameters of approximately 50 Å, may cause many components of glass to crystallize, such as magnesium silicates and aluminates, lithium aluminosilicates, and quartz.

Sakaino [50] used zirconia for the preparation of glass-ceramics from glass of the $MgO-Al_2O_3-SiO_2-P_2O_5$ system. It was found [300] that a glass in the $Li_2O-Al_2O_3-SiO_2$ system which is close to spodumene may be transformed into a thermally stable glass-ceramic with the aid of small additions of ZrO_2 and P_2O_5 and upon heat treatment. In the opinion of Tashiro and Wada [300], a

193

Table 30. Structural Characteristics of Some Catalysts and of Some Crystalline Phases Which Precipitate with the Aid of These Catalysts

Catalyst			Crystallizing phase		
Element	Crystalline structure	Lattice, Å	Chemical formula	Crystalline structure	Lattice, Å
Au	FCC	4.070	NaF	Cubic	4.62
Ag		4.079	Li_2SiO_3	Rhombo-hedral	5.43 4.66 9.41
Cu		3.608	$BaSi_2O_5$		4.63 7.69 13.53
Pt		3.914			

serious disadvantage of ZrO_2 is its insufficient solubility in glasses, especially those with a low Li_2O content. It was shown that ZrO_2, introduced through the zircon $ZrSiO_4$, can easily be converted into a solution at the melting temperature if the glass contains a small amount of P_2O_5.

The method of controlling the nucleation process with the aid of fluorine additions was proposed by Lungu and Popescu-Has [51, 52, 301]. Glass-ceramics in the mica—spodumene system were prepared by the rapid precipitation of fine crystals during the crystallization of a glass whose batch consisted primarily of lithium oxide, fluorine, and mica [302].

McMillan and Partridge [716] found that the most effective crystallization catalysts for the preparation of glass-ceramics are fluorides of those metals whose oxides enter into the composition of glasses of the lithium—potassium—magnesium—aluminosilicate system, such as LiF, MgF_2, and AlF_3, as well as cadmium sulfoselenide CdS · CdSe [717] present in the amounts of 0.5-2.0% in the finished glass.

Fine crystals with sizes of the order of 1 μ were precipitated from glass by adding to it transition-group elements, including vanadium [303]. This makes it possible to employ such varied elements as iron, nickel, and chromium. It is believed that the transition elements added not only form nuclei, but also enable their emergence in the glass [124].

In order to prepare glass-ceramics based on blast-furnace slags, sulfides of the heavy metals Fe and Mn in amounts of 4-5% are employed as catalysts [53]. The catalytic action of these sulfides is caused by the appearance of phase separation and by an increase in the glass—crystal interphase surface. The Fe^{2+}, Mn^{2+}, Cd^{2+}, and Cu^{2+} ions in the silicate glass are heavily polarized, and can easily accept two electrons, thus forming the corresponding crystalline compounds. This is further made possible by the paramagnetism of the sulfides of heavy metals.

As catalysts for the crystallization of various glasses for the preparation of glass-ceramics, one can employ platinum [203, 304-308] and other noble metals. Table 30, from [119], lists the structural characteristics of the catalysts of this type, and of crystalline phases which may be precipitated under the action of any of these catalysts.

In the production of glass-ceramics by sintering and by the crystallization of the glassy powder, finely dispersed powders of Li_2CO_3, $LiAlO_2$, $MgCO_3$, $MgSiO_3$, and $Al(NO_3)_3$ were found to be effective catalysts [309].

Table 31, based on [310], classifies methods of preparing glass-ceramics based on the various glassy systems according to the type of catalysts introduced into them. The numbers given below the formulas of the materials designate the oxide content in the glass in wt.%. Temperatures given are the crystallization temperatures.

This classification does not include by far all of the glassy systems and catalysts which are employed for the preparation of glass-ceramics. Thus, for instance, the use of such compounds as Nb_2O_5, Ta_2O_5 [311], WO_3, MoO_3 [312], lithium carbonate, and petalite [313], as catalysts for the crystallization of silicate glasses is well-known.

Here, the action of TiO_2, Nb_2O_5, Ta_2O_5, and other crystallization catalysts in glasses of the $K_2O—SiO_2—TiO_2$, $K_2O—SiO_2—Nb_2O_5$, and $K_2O—GeO_2—Ta_2O_5$ systems where these oxides may be present in amounts of order 30-75% is explained by Janakiramarao [713, 714] in terms of the incompatibility of the TiO_6, NbO_6, and TaO_6 groups with the SiO_4 and GeO_4 groups which, under favorable conditions of concentration, temperature, and time, results in phase

Table 31. Classification of Glass-Ceramics and the Methods of Their Preparation, According to the Type of Catalysts Used

(a) Method of irradiation by ultraviolet and γ-rays

Au^+, Ag^+, Cu^+ Metallic   Primary   Secondary

$Li_2O-Al_2O_3-SiO_2$ Nuclei $\rightarrow$ Crystals   Crystals
Glass   600° C   900° C

(b) Method utilizing TiO_2
Ti^{4+}
$Li_2O-Al_2O_3-SiO_2$ Glass

                     $\rightarrow$ Oxide nuclei $\rightarrow$ Glass-ceramic
$MgO-Al_2O_3-SiO_2$ Glass

(c) Method utilizing Pt
Pt^+, Li_2O-SiO_2 Glass $\left.\begin{array}{l}\end{array}\right\}$ $Li_2O\cdot2SiO_2$
                                       $Li_2O\cdot SiO_2$, $Li_2O\cdot Al_2O_3\cdot2SiO_2$
                                       SiO_2
Pt^+, $Li_2O-MgO-Al_2O_3-SiO_2$ Glass $MgO\cdot SiO_2$ $Li_2O\cdot Al_2O_3\cdot4SiO_2$
(0.01) (12) (10—20) (0—10) (80—90)

(d) Method without using catalysts
$Li_2O-MgO-Al_2O_3-SiO_2$ Glass $\rightarrow$ $Li_2O\cdot Al_2O_3\cdot2SiO_2 \rightarrow 750 \sim 850°$
(4) (15—23) (15—27) (54—62)
    $\rightarrow Li_2O\cdot Al_2O_3\cdot4SiO_2$ 900 $\sim$ 1100°

(e) Method utilizing fluorides
F^-
$\underbrace{Li_{\frac{1}{3}}\cdot Na_{\frac{1}{3}}\cdot Mg_3(Si_3AlO_{10})F_2}_{(75)} + \underbrace{Li_2O\cdot Al_2O_3\cdot4SiO_2}_{(25)}$ Glass $\left.\begin{array}{l}\end{array}\right|$ Mica
                                             $\rightarrow Li_2O\cdot Al_2O_3\cdot4SiO_2$,
$Li_2O-Al_2O_3-SiO_2-CaF_2$ Glass $CaO\cdot SiO_2$
(5) (20 — 26) (54) (20)

(f) Method utilizing ZrO_2
Zr^{4+}
$Li_2O - MgO - Al_2O_3 - SiO_2 - ZrO_2 - P_2O_5$ Glass $\rightarrow$
(14)   (14)   (6)   (69)   (10)   (17)

                     $\rightarrow \left\{\begin{array}{l} Li_2O\cdot Al_2O_3\cdot2SiO_2 \\ 2MgO\cdot SiO_2 \\ 2MgO\cdot P_2O_5,\ SiO_2 \\ 650 - 850° \end{array}\right\} \rightarrow \left\{\begin{array}{l} Li_2O\cdot Al_2O_3\cdot4SiO_2 \\ 2MgO\cdot SiO_2 \\ ZrO_2\cdot SiO_2,\ SiO_2 \\ 950 - 1100° \end{array}\right.$

(g) Method utilizing P_2O_5
$Li_2O-SiO_2-P_2O_5$ Glass
(20)   (80)   (2—5)

   $Li_2O-K_2O-Al_2O_3-SiO_2-P_2O_5$ Glass $\rightarrow \left\{\begin{array}{l} Li_2O\cdot2SiO_2 \\ Li_2O\cdot SiO_2 \end{array}\right.$
   (12.5) (2.5)   (4)   (81)   (2—7) SiO_2

   $Li_2O - PbO - SiO_2 - P_2O_5$ Glass
   (20) (15—25) (80)   (2—5)

(h) Method utilizing ZnO

$Li_2O - ZnO - Al_2O_3 - SiO_2$ Glass $\left\{\begin{array}{l} 2ZnO\cdot SiO_2 \\ SiO_2 \end{array}\right\} \rightarrow \left\{\begin{array}{l} 2ZnO\cdot SiO_2,\ SiO_2 \\ Li_2O\cdot Al_2O_3\cdot2SiO_2 \\ Li_2O\cdot Al_2O_3\cdot4SiO_2 \\ Li_2O\cdot SiO_2 \end{array}\right.$

(4—8) (30—50) (0—20) (45—60) $\rightarrow$

Table 31 (continued)

(i) Method using transition elements
   Cr^{3+}
   Li$_2$O—K$_2$O—CaO—Al$_2$O$_3$—SiO$_2$—Cr$_2$O$_3$ Glass   →
     (7)   (4)   (10)   (24)   (558.5) (1—3)

$$→ Li_2O \cdot Al_2O_3 \cdot 2SiO_2 → \begin{cases} Li_2O \cdot Al_2O_3 \cdot 2SiO_2 \\ CaO \cdot SiO_2 \end{cases}$$

   V^{5+}, Ni^{2+}
   Li$_2$O—Al$_2$O$_3$—SiO$_2$—V$_2$O$_5$ Glass
   (13.3) (15.2) (71.5) (16.2)

   Li$_2$O—Al$_2$O$_3$—SiO$_2$—NiO Glass
   (13.3) (15.2) (71.5)   (13)

$$→ Li_2O \cdot SiO_2 → \begin{cases} Li_2O \cdot Al_2O_3 \cdot 4SiO_2 \\ Li_2O \cdot 2SiO_2, SiO_2 \end{cases}$$

---

separation and the emergence of ordered microheterogeneous regions, which migrate to the nuclei which are uniformly distributed throughout the bulk of the glass, or the appearance of "micelles" of a definite chemical composition.

A very effective catalyst was found to be As$_2$O$_3$, especially in combination with MoO$_3$, WO$_3$, and Sb$_2$O$_3$. A semitransparent, high-strength glass-ceramic with crystal size less than 1 μ was obtained by heat treatment of glass of the composition 81.0 SiO$_2$, 4.0 Al$_2$O$_3$, 12.5 Li$_2$O, 2.5 K$_2$O, and 4.0 As$_2$O$_3$ [314].

Below we classify practically all the glass-ceramics given in the literature according to the basic glass-forming systems in which they have been prepared.

1. GLASS-CERAMICS IN THE Li$_2$O—Al$_2$O$_3$—SiO$_2$ AND MgO—Al$_2$O$_3$—SiO$_2$ SYSTEMS WITH TiO$_2$ ADDITIONS, CHARACTERIZED BY A LOW LINEAR THERMAL EXPANSION COEFFICIENT

Glass-ceramics with a small linear thermal expansion coefficient α may be prepared from glasses in which compounds with a small α precipitate during crystallization. Some of these compounds of interest in the production of glass-ceramics are listed in Table 32, which is from [141].

Stookey [320-323] observed that a relatively large number of glasses which during crystallization produce β-spodumene (Li$_2$O · Al$_2$O$_3$ · 4SiO$_2$), β-eucryptite (Li$_2$O · Al$_2$O$_3$ · 2SiO$_2$), or solid solutions

Table 32. Compounds with a Low Linear Thermal Expansion Coefficient

Compound	Formula	Linear thermal expansion coefficient, $\alpha \cdot 10^7 \, (°C)^{-1}$	Temp., °C	Source
α-Cordierite	$2MgO \cdot 2Al_2O_3 \cdot 5SiO_2$	$+10$	?	[315]
β-Eucryptite	$Li_2O \cdot Al_2O_3 \cdot 2SiO_2$	-90	1200	[316]
		$\begin{cases} \alpha_a = \alpha_\theta = +182.1 \\ \alpha_c = -176 \end{cases}$	800	[317]
β-Spodumene	$Li_2O \cdot Al_2O_3 \cdot 4SiO_2$	$+9$	1200	[316]
Petalite	$Li_2O \cdot Al_2O_3 \cdot 8SiO_2$	$+3$	1200	[316]
Aluminotitanate	$Al_2O_3 \cdot TiO_2$	$\begin{cases} \alpha_a = +118 \\ \alpha_\theta = +194 \\ \alpha_c = -26 \end{cases}$	1000*	[318]
Beryl	$3BeO \cdot Al_2O_3 \cdot 6SiO_2$	From $+5$ to $+23$	225—300	[319]
Zinc orthosilicate†	$2ZnO \cdot SiO_2$	Approx. $+16$	350	[319]

* At temperatures below 300°C, the α of aluminotitanate is very low.
† The synthetic product contains approximately 95% Zn_2SiO_4.

containing one or both of these phases were found to be suitable for the preparation of glass-ceramics with an exceptionally low α. Compositions lying in the cordierite ($2MgO \cdot 2Al_2O_3 \cdot 5SiO_2$) crystallization field give, after heat treatment, dense and strong glass-ceramics with low or average values for α and with good dielectric properties at high frequencies. The size of the crystals varies from 0.1 to 20 μ, and the amount of crystalline phase present is more than 50%. These glasses contain primarily four components: SiO_2, Al_2O_3, and TiO_2 in amounts of 90-95 wt.%, and one or more of the following oxides: Li_2O, MgO, CaO, ZnO, SrO, CdO, BaO, PbO, MnO, FeO, CoO, and NiO. The total content of the R_2O oxides present should not exceed 10%; otherwise, the amount of the glassy phase in the glass-ceramic will increase. Introduction of up to 5% Na_2O and up to 5% K_2O is permissible.

The optimum amount of TiO_2 is determined by the composition of the glass, and increases with decreasing SiO_2 content, as well as in the presence of Na_2O or K_2O. It is most advantageous to introduce 8-15 wt.% TiO_2. The presence of more than 20% TiO_2 results in the precipitation of crystalline TiO_2 and in a decrease in the content of desirable crystalline compounds, or it produces spontaneous crystallization during the cooling of glass from the melt. Increasing the TiO_2 content within the range 2-20% increases the number of nuclei present, which facilitates crystallization and decreases the heat-treatment temperature.

Stookey [320-323] recommends that the crystallization process take place during the cooling of glass within the temperature region between the temperature of the peak of nucleus formation, and the temperature lying somewhat above the annealing temperature. The temperature of the peak of nucleus formation is generally 50° higher than the annealing temperature of the glass. Practically no formation of nuclei occurs at the annealing temperature or below it, due to the high viscosity of glass. Nucleation is completed, however, almost entirely within 1 h at a temperature which is somewhat below the temperature of the peak of the nuclei formation, while at the annealing temperature, this would take 100 h. Insufficient cooling of the glass product results in the formation of a small amount of coarse crystals of various sizes. Therefore, it is recommended that before secondary heating the product be cooled to a temperature which is 100-300°C below the temperature of the peak nucleus formation, and that it then be reheated to the above temperatures to enable the crystallization of crystalline compounds on the emerging nuclei of the matrix. The time at the temperature of the peak of nucleus formation is 0.5-2 h. The deformation temperature of glass containing a large number of dissolved crystallizing compounds is determined by the compound with the lowest liquidus temperature. In order to avoid deformation, the heating rate of glass to a temperature lying 20-25°C lower than the solution temperature of the fundamental crystalline phase must not exceed 5 deg/min. Whether the correct rate of heat treatment has been selected can approximately be determined by the magnitude of the flexure of a glass block with a cross section of

Table 33. Glasses in the Li₂O–Al₂O₃–SiO₂ and MgO–Al₂O₃–SiO₂ Systems with TiO₂ Additions, and the Glass-Ceramics Prepared from Them, Having Low and Medium α Values

Composition No.	SiO₂	Al₂O₃	TiO₂	Li₂O	MgO	CaO	CaF₂	Na₂O	K₂O	B₂O₃	ZrO₂	BeO	F	BaO	Crystalline temp., °C	Time, h	$\alpha \cdot 10^7$ (°C)⁻¹	Density, g/cm³	σf, kg/cm²	Crystalline phases*
1	69.8	14.9	7	4.3	—	—	—	1	—	3	—	—	—	—	900	2	11.4	—	1141	—
2	57.6	15.2	12.1	5.2	—	—	—	1.6	—	4.7	3.6	—	—	—	—	—	22.0	2.57	—	(6), (7)
3	61.7	15.3	10.7	4.3	—	—	—	0.9	0.1	3.1	3.9	—	—	—	900	2	17.2	2.55	—	(6), (7)
4	73.1	13.5	4.5	4.9	—	—	2.1	1.7	0.2	—	—	—	—	—	—	—	—	—	—	—
5	58.7	13.7	13.7	3.9	8.8	—	—	1.0	0.2	—	—	—	—	—	950	0.5	—	—	—	—
6	56.1	12.1	13.8	3.0	3.9	11,1	—	—	—	—	—	—	—	—	950	0.5	—	—	—	—
7	67.4	14.4	7.0	4.2	1.2	1.8	—	—	—	3.0	—	—	—	—	950	2	—	—	—	—
8	63.7	12.1	13.8	3.1	3.9	3.4	—	1.0	—	—	—	—	—	—	900	1	64.4	—	1246	—
9	64.8	18.5	7.4	—	—	—	—	—	—	—	—	9.3	—	—	1250	1.5	—	—	—	—

No.	1	2	3	4	5	6	7	8	9	10	11	12	13	14	15	16	17	18
10	42.8	30.2	13.0	—	14.0	—	—	—	—	—	—	—	1200	16	16.5	2.65	1680	(4), (8)
11	45.8	25.3	11.1	—	17.8	—	—	—	—	—	—	—	1300	16	22.6	2.68	1211	(4), (8)
12	45.5	30.5	11.5	—	12.5	—	—	—	—	—	—	—	1345	1	14.1	2.62	2625	(4), (7)
13	50.2	26.5	11.4	—	11.9	—	—	—	—	—	—	—	1250	2	21.5	2.60	2100	(4), (7)
14	52.5	26.5	11.4	—	11.9	—	—	—	—	—	—	—	1300	16	28.3	—	1610	(4), (7)
15	56.0	20.0	9.0	—	15.0	—	—	—	—	—	—	—	1250	1	56.0	2.59	2184	(4), (8), (7), (5)
16	57.8	8.9	11.1	—	22.2	—	—	—	—	—	—	—	1300	16	39.9	—	—	(4), (7), (5)
17	46.7	28.9	10.2	0.9	13.3	—	—	—	—	—	—	—	1300	16	17.7	—	1400	(4), (8)
18	58.1	19.1	9.1	—	13.7	—	—	—	—	—	—	—	1300	16	63.3	2.56	2345	(4), (8), (5)
19	60.4	21.4	9.1	—	9.1	—	—	—	—	—	—	—	1200	1	52.9	—	1890	(4), (3), (7), (8)
20	64.2	13.8	8.2	—	13.8	—	—	—	—	—	—	—	1200	16	—	2.55	—	(4), (7), (5), (8)
21	67.5	12.5	11.1	—	8.9	—	—	—	—	—	—	—	—	—	—	2.49	—	—
22	53.3	26.7	11.1	—	3.6	5.3	—	—	—	—	—	—	1250	3	33.8	2.65	1750	(4), (1)
23	48.9	26.7	11.1	—	5.3	8.0	—	—	—	—	—	—	1250	3	29.6	2.67	1351	(4), (7), (2)
24	45.2	29.5	10.8	—	10.4	—	2.3	—	—	—	1.8	—	1100	6	—	—	—	(4), (7)
25	44.5	31.1	11.1	—	5.3	8.0	—	—	—	—	—	—	1250	3	—	2.72	784	(4), (7)
26	50.4	26.9	13.0	—	3.6	6.1	—	—	—	—	—	—	1200	2.5	41.7	—	1204	—
27	54.6	19.1	9.1	—	10.9	—	—	—	1.8	—	—	4.5	1200	6	29.1	—	1141	(5), (7)

* 1) Aluminotitanate; 2) wollastonite; 3) quartz; 4) cordierite; 5) cristobalite; 6) spodumene; 7) rutile; 8) Mg titanate.

6 × 6 mm, which, between supports 100 mm apart,   should not be more than 13 mm [320-323]. Depending on the extent of crystallization, the deformation temperature gradually increases, and for the final article, it may reach 1300°C.

The selection of glass composition for glass-ceramics is based on the study of equilibrium phase diagrams corresponding to the crystallization of the systems, on which the melting points and the eutectics of the various crystalline phases, as well as some of their physical properties, are shown [324, 325].

Table 33, from [320-323], shows the chemical composition of glasses to be used for the preparation of glass-ceramics, in which the primary crystalline phases (shown first in the table) are spodumene or cordierite.

Glasses of compositions Nos. 12 and 15 were melted in a small tank furnace and were shaped by the pressing or the drawing method. The crystallization procedure included heating at a rate of 5 deg/min to 800-820°C, holding at these temperatures for 0.5-2 h, and then further heating at a rate of 3-5 deg/min to 1250-1350°C, with holding at these temperatures for 1-2 h. The absence of Na_2O or K_2O favors a more fully completed crystallization of the glasses.

During crystallization, glasses Nos. 1-7 precipitate lithium-containing minerals, such as β-spodumene. This is why glass-ceramics based on these glasses have relatively low α values. It is possible to prepare glass-ceramics whose α value is close to zero.

Glasses containing BeO (composition No. 9) precipitate beryl ($3BeO \cdot Al_2O_3 \cdot 6SiO_2$) during crystallization, and have a low α. Glass-ceramics of this type have, besides low expansion, a high deformation temperature, as well as a relatively high mechanical strength and hardness. However, the batch for the founding of these glasses is toxic due to the presence of BeO.

In glasses Nos. 10-27, which contain a significant amount of MgO, cordierite crystallizes out. The glass-ceramics here are characterized by a low α and a high mechanical strength, as well as by a high hardness and high thermal stability, with low values for the dielectric constant (approximately 5 for composition No. 15).

Pyroceram 9606, as it is known in the US, is prepared in the $MgO-Al_2O_3-SiO_2$ system with the addition of a small amount of TiO_2 [43, 119]. The fundamental crystalline phases present are cordierite, cristobalite, and rutile. Another material — namely, the material known by laboratory number BDQ-115 — has the same chemical composition but different crystalline phases, including spinel $MgAl_2O_4$ and an enstatite, $MgSiO_3$, which is achieved using the same crystallization procedure.

The composition of Pyroceram 9608 includes the oxides SiO_2, Al_2O_3, Li_2O, MgO, and TiO_2, and the crystalline phases represented by β-spodumene, cordierite, and rutile [119].

Corning Glass Works [326, 327, 712] developed glass-ceramics in the lithium aluminosilicate system, the α values of which vary from negative values to $15 \cdot 10^{-7}$. The calculated compositions of these glasses contain: 53-75 SiO_2, 3-7 TiO_2, 2-15 Li_2O, and 12-36 Al_2O_3, the ratio Li_2O/Al_2O_3 ranging from 0.1 to 0.6, and the total content of SiO_2, Li_2O, TiO_2, and Al_2O_3 being not less than 95%. In order to speed up the melting process and to increase the thermal stability of this glass, it is permitted to introduce up to 5% of oxides R_2O or RO, of which amount not more than 3% is Na_2O or K_2O, up to 5% is MgO, ZnO, BaO, or PbO, and up to 3% is CaO.

When there is an excess of SiO_2 or Al_2O_3 and a deficiency of Li_2O relative to the above ranges for the various glass components, these glasses cannot be melted very well and are difficult to shape. With decreasing SiO_2 content or with increasing Li_2O content, the chemical stability of these glasses and glass-ceramics becomes worse, and α increases. An excess of TiO_2 leads to a spontaneous crystallization, and a deficiency in TiO_2 leads to incomplete crystallization of this glass.

The melting time for these glasses at a maximum temperature of 1550°C is 16 h. Instead of the expensive Li_2CO_3, one may introduce either petalite or spodumene into the batch, and, as the oxidizer or fining agent, one may introduce As_2O_5, nitrates of the alkali metals and barium, or Pb_3O_4 in amounts up to 1%. The simultaneous presence of TiO_2 and FeO results in undesirable coloring of the glass and the glass-ceramic, which is the reason raw materials with a low iron content are employed.

Table 34. Glasses Used for the Preparation of Glass-Ceramics
with Low α Values

Component	Contents (in wt.%) of various compositions													
	1	2	3	4	5	6	7	8	9	10	11	12	13	14
SiO_2	73.5	69.5	65.5	65.5	61.3	53.0	54.5	68	68.2	67.8	66.8	68	70.7	70.7
TiO_2	6.0	5.5	4.5	4.5	5	7	5.5	5	5.7	5.5	5.5	6	4.8	4.8
Li_2O	4.3	7.5	9	4	7.7	14	5.5	4.5	3.8	3.9	5.5	4	2.6	2.6
Al_2O_3	16.2	17.5	21	26	26	26	34.5	20.5	21.4	20.8	20.2	21	18.1	18.1
PbO	—	—	—	—	—	—	—	2	—	—	—	—	—	—
BaO	—	—	—	—	—	—	—	—	—	1	—	—	—	—
ZnO	—	—	—	—	—	—	—	—	—	1	—	—	—	1
CaO	—	—	—	—	—	—	—	—	—	—	2	—	—	—
K_2O	—	—	—	—	—	—	—	—	—	—	—	1	—	—
Na_2O	—	—	—	—	—	—	—	—	0.9	—	—	—	—	—
MgO	—	—	—	—	—	—	—	—	—	—	—	—	3.8	2.8

For the sitallization of an article which is several centi-
meters thick, it is first heated at a rate of 5 deg/min from 650 to
800°C, and then kept at these temperatures from 2 h to 10 min, respectively. Articles which have small dimensions can be heated
at a rate of 100 deg/min and higher. The same result can be
achieved by cooling the shaped glass product to 750°C and then
heating it at a rate of 0.5-100 deg/min to 800°C. The maximum
effective temperature of preliminary heat treatment is 125-150°C
higher than the annealing temperature of the glass. The final heat
treatment consists in heating the article within the temperature
range 800-1175°C for 1-4 h for such a time that α does not decrease by more than 75% as a result of the segregation of β-spod-
umene or eucryptite as the primary crystalline phases. The deformation temperature of the glass-ceramic is 1200-1300°C.

Table 34, based on data given in [326, 327], gives the compositions of glasses in the $Li_2O-Al_2O_3-SiO_2$ system with TiO_2 additions, and Table 35 gives their properties and the heat-treatment
procedure used, as well as the properties of the glass-ceramics
obtained. For all the glass-ceramics in Table 35, β-spodumene
is the primary crystalline phase, with the exception of the glass-
ceramic from composition No. 6, which has β-eucryptite as the

Table 35. Properties of Glasses Given in Table 34, Their Heat-Treatment Procedure, and the Properties of the Glass-Ceramics Obtained

| Comp. No. | Glass properties | | Anneal. temp., °C | Heat treatment | | | | Glass-ceramics properties | | | |
| | α·10⁷ 1/°C | Specific gravity, g/cm³ | | Preliminary | | Finite | | α·10⁷ 1/°C | Specific gravity, g/cm³ | σ$_f$, kg/cm² | Crystalline phase |
				heating, °C	time, h	heating, °C	time, h				
1	42.0	2.3429	678	800	2	1150	4	−0.7	2.4591		Rutile
2	59.9	2.4022		740	2	1000	2	12.7	2.4514		Rutile
3	66.6	2.4190		740	2	1000	2	14.5	2.4206		Rutile
4	38.0	2.4078	703	900	2	1090	2	5.3	2.5061	1405	Corundum
5	60.9	2.4247		700	2	1100	2	8.6	2.4322	1420	Rutile
6	85.6	2.4867		570	2	1100	2	−7.7	2.4438		Aluminum titanate
7	46.7	2.4500	688	900	2	1090	2	12.8	2.5553	1270	Rutile
8	43.1	2.4138	676	800	4	1150	4	2.8	2.5021		Aluminum titanate
9	42.3	2.3828	671	800	1	1150	4	6.9	2.4703	1500	Rutile
10	40.1	2.4430	672	800	1	1150	4	2.7	2.5089	1250	Rutile
11	44.5	2.3964	680	800	1	1150	4	7.6	2.4795	1390	Anatase
12	42.5	2.3751	683	800	2	1150	2	8.5	2.4609		Aluminum titanate
13	33.9	2.3973	689	800	1	1200	4	5.1	2.4786		Cordierite, rutile
14	33.6	2.4035	682	800	1	1100 / 1175	2 / 2	6.9	2.5073	2060	

primary phase. Secondary crystalline phases present are also listed in this table.

Table 35 indicates doubt as to whether the density of the glass of composition No. 6 is greater than that of the glass-ceramic corresponding to it.

The flexure strength σ_f was determined on a 6.35-mm-diameter rod whose surface was subjected to abrasion by silicon carbide powder in a ball mill for 15 min. The distance between the supports was 100 mm, and the sample was loaded at two points each at a distance of 31 mm from the nearest support. Glass rods whose surface has been worked this way had a flexure strength of 350-420 kg/cm^2. The glass-ceramics obtained can, because of their low α values, be heated or cooled at any rate within the temperature range below their deformation temperature. Slow cooling at a rate of 2 deg/min after the completion of crystallization of compositions Nos. 13 and 14, which contain MgO, increased the cordierite content in these glass-ceramics, and also increased their strength and the α value.

In the Glass Research Scientific Institutes of the Soviet Union [328], glass-ceramics have been prepared based on, among others, glasses in the following systems: $SiO_2-Al_2O_3-CaO-MgO-F$, $SiO_2-Al_2O_3-B_2O_3-PbO-F$, and $SiO_2-Al_2O_3-CaO-MgO-TiO_2$.

After special heat treatment, some of these materials can sustain temperatures higher than 1400°C without softening, in addition to having increased thermal stability and a number of other valuable properties.

In the $Li_2O \cdot 2SiO_2-Li_2O \cdot Al_2O_3 \cdot 4SiO_2$ system with addition of up to 16% V_2O_5, a glass-ceramic was obtained with a crystal size of approximately 1 μ [77], while in the $CaO \cdot TiO_2 \cdot SiO_2-Li_2O \cdot Al_2O_3 \cdot 4SiO_2-Li_2O \cdot 2SiO_2$ system, a glass-ceramic was prepared in which the primary crystalline phases were β-spodumene, $2CaO \cdot SiO_2$, and lithium silicate [329]. The more closely the composition approached $Li_2O \cdot Al_2O_3 \cdot 4SiO_2$, the more the coefficient α decreased, even attaining negative values. Irradiation of samples with ultraviolet, x-rays, and γ-rays made it possible to decrease the size of the crystals in the crystallized material.

Tashiro and Wada [300, 739] investigated series of glasses of the following composition (in parts by weight), with the purpose

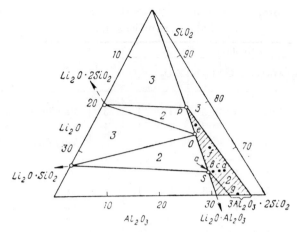

Fig. 69. Compositions of the glasses of the $Li_2O-Al_2O_3-SiO_2$ system catalized by ZrO_2. See text for compositions of glasses in the shaded triangle. Series A: points a, b, c, d. Series B: point d. Series C: points e, f, d, g. The numbers inside the diagram show the amount of the crystalline phases for the respective regions. P) Petalite; O) lithium orthoclase; S) spodumene.

of preparing thermally stable glass-ceramics in the $Li_2O-Al_2O_3-SiO_2$ system with SrO_2 and P_2O_5 additions:

Series A: $65SiO_2$, $(35-x)Al_2O_3$, xLi_2O, yK_2O, 3 P_2O_5, $zZrO_2$ (x = 5, 6, 7, 8; y = 0.1; z = 1, 2, 3, 4).

Series B: $65SiO_2$, $30Al_2O_3$, $5Li_2O$, $1K_2O$, pP_2O_5, $zZrO_2$ (p = 1, 3, 5; z = 1, 2, . . . , 7).

Series C: $(95-q)SiO_2$, qAl_2O_3, 1 K_2O, pP_2O_5, 4 ZrO_2 (q = 20, 25, 30, 35; p = 1, 3, 5).

The investigated basic compositions without ZrO_2, P_2O_5, and K_2O are shown in Fig. 69, where point a corresponds to the composition of spodumene. The melting temperature of the glasses was 1500-1600°C. Samples 3 × 5 × 50 mm in size were subjected to gradual heating from room temperature to 650, 750, 800, and 1200°C, and were held at each of these temperatures for 30 min. The glass-ceramic of the following composition (in mol.%) had the best thermal stability: 65 SiO_2, 30 Al_2O_3, 5 Li_2O, 1 K_2O, 3 P_2O_5, and 4 ZrO_2 (point d in Fig. 69). Its $\alpha_{20-500°} = 13.6 \cdot 10^{-7}$, and $\sigma_f = 640$ kg/cm².

Table 36. Compositions and Properties of Crystallized Glasses
Taken from Fig. 69

Point on Fig. 69	Content (wt.%)						Foam	Viscosity	$\alpha \cdot 10^7$ 1/°C	σ_f, kg/cm²
	SiO_2	Al_2O_3	Li_2O	P_2O_5	ZrO_2	K_2O				
e	75	20	5	5	4	1	3	Very high	−3.8	520
	75	20	5	3	4	1	4	Very high	3.8	560
	75	20	5	1	4	1	5	Very high	3.8	550
f	70	25	5	5	4	1	2	High	10.8	610
	70	25	5	3	4	1	2	High	10.8	640
	70	25	5	1	4	1	4	High	10.8	580
d	65	30	5	5	4	1	0	Medium	13.6	610
	65	30	5	3	4	1	1	Medium	13.6	640
	65	30	5	1	4	1	3	Medium	13.6	700
g	60	35	5	5	4	1	0	Low	17.4	770
	60	35	5	3	4	1	0	Low	17.4	830
	60	35	5	1	4	1	1	Low	17.4	820

It was determined that with increasing P_2O_5 content, the solubility of ZrO_2 in glass at elevated temperatures increased, which
resulted in increased strength of the glass-ceramic. However, the
introduction of P_2O_5 in the amounts of more than 5 mol.% (p in
series B) increased the viscosity of the glass and made melting
more difficult. A greater amount of Li_2O instead of Al_2O_3 (x > 6 in
series A) had a bad effect on the uniform crystallization of glass,
producing deformation, cracking, or buckling of samples. Replacing SiO_2 by Al_2O_3 decreased the viscosity of the glass and increased
the solubility of ZrO_2; however, the Al_2O_3 concentration should not
be greater than 30 (q in series C), or the α of the glass-ceramics
prepared attains values greater than $15 \cdot 10^{-7}$ and increases further with increasing Al_2O_3 content.

The interdependence between the chemical composition and
the properties of the crystallized glasses of the $Li_2O-Al_2O_3-SiO_2$
system catalyzed by ZrO_2 is shown in Table 36, as taken from

[300]. The numbers in the column labeled "Foam" characterize the degree to which the fused glass is covered by foam; 0 denotes the absence of foam. The coefficient α as listed holds within the temperature region 20-500°C, and σ_f was measured on unground samples heated to 1200°C for 2 h.

Glass-ceramics with low α values were obtained in the lithium aluminosilicate system with 2-6% additions of ZrO_2 to the glass of the following composition: 48-73 SiO_2, 14-35 Al_2O_3, and 4-10 Li_2O [330]. The total content of SiO_2 + Al_2O_3 + Li_2O present should not be less than 85%. One may add up to 3% R_2O, up to 6% PbO, ZnO, CdO, BaO, SrO, CaO, MgO, La_2O_3, ThO_2, and B_2O_3, and 1-1.8% TiO_2 at a low content of ZrO_2. Heat treatment of this glass so as to transform it into glass-ceramic consisted in successive heating to 650-750°C and then to 1100-1150°C, with the material being held at each stage for 2 h.

Hinz and Kunth [141] were able to obtain glass-ceramics (Vitrokerams in their terminology) in the cordierite—spodumene and eucryptite—spodumene systems with TiO_2 additions, with α being approximately 20-30 and 0-10 · 10^{-7} (°C)$^{-1}$, respectively. In crystallization products at temperatures above 1250°C, mixed lithium and magnesium spinel crystals were observed, as well as cordierite and spodumene, which is in agreement with [331].

In the eucryptite—spodumene system, each compound is capable of entering the crystalline lattices of the other in significant amounts. Eucryptite, for instance, forms mixed crystals containing up to 68% of spodumene, and spodumene can absorb up to 16% eucryptite [332]. With decreasing temperature, these crystals transform into eucryptite at 972°C and into spodumene at 500°C, with a concomitant phase separation of the system, which is occurring, however, very slowly [333]. The mixed crystals thus formed also have low α values [314, 315, 332, 334-336].

In the compositions investigated [141], which are listed in Table 37, the Li_2O was partially or totally replaced by ZnO in the cordierite—spodumene system, whereas, in the eucryptite—spodumene system, it was partially or totally replaced by MgO. Here, TiO_2 was added to the batch, as were small amounts of $MgSO_4$, the latter so as to speed up the melting and fining process.

Table 37. Fundamental Glass Compositions for the Preparation of Glass-Ceramics with Low α Values in the Cordierite—Spodumene and Eucryptite—Spodumene Systems

Comp. No.	Content in glass (wt.%)					Crystalline phase, moles			Remarks
	SiO_2	Al_2O_3	MgO	Li_2O	ZnO	Spod-u-mene	Eu-cryp-tite	Cor-di-erite	
1	54.6	33.0	10.5	1.9	—	2	—	1	
2	56.6	31.9	8.4	3.1	—	1	—	1	
3	58.7	30.7	6.1	4.5	—	1	—	2	
4	52.8	32.0	10.1	—	5.1	2	—	1	Li_2O replaced by ZnO
5	53.1	30.95	7.95	—	8.0	1	—	1	LiO replaced by ZnO
6	55.0	31.2	8.2	1.5	4.1	1	—	1	One-half of Li_2O replaced by ZnO
7	53.7	33.5	11.4	1.4	—	3	—	1	
8	52.5	32.7	11.1	—	3.7	3	—	1	Li_2O replaced by ZnO
9	56.6	29.5	5.8	2.2	5.9	1	—	2	One-half Li_2O replaced by ZnO
10	58.3	29.1	4.6	3.4	4.6	1	—	3	One-third Li_2O replaced by ZnO
11	53.25	36.15	—	10.6	—	—	3	1	
12	51.0	34.6	—	7.6	6.9	—	3	1	One-fourth Li_2O replaced by ZnO
13	52.8	35.8	3.5	7.9	—	—	3	1	One-fourth Li_2O replaced by MgO
14	48.7	33.1	—	4.8	13.4	—	3	1	One-half Li_2O replaced by ZnO
15	50.5	34.3	3.4	5.0	6.8				One-fourth of Li_2O replaced by ZnO and one-fourth by MgO

The melting of the glasses was done at 1500–1600°C in an induction electric furnace in a neutral or a slightly reducing atmosphere. The reducing atmosphere resulted in a partial reduction of TiO_2 and in the appearance of a dark-brown or black coloring of these glasses. Crystallization of the samples was done in an annealing furnace by heating them at a rate of 5 deg/min to 1100°C and holding them at that temperature for 1 h. The amount of TiO_2 added decreases with increasing Li_2O content.

Increasing the TiO_2 content resulted in a significant increase in the α values of the samples not containing Li_2O. In the eucryptite—spodumene system, a fine-crystalline structure was attained by introducing 4 parts by weight of TiO$_2$ per 100 parts of the batch. Addition of CaO was found effective in reducing the tendency toward spontaneous crystallization of glass of composition No. 11, which has good melting properties; however, α was thereby noticeably increased, whereas the addition of B$_2$O$_3$ to this glass decreased the refractoriness of the resulting glass-ceramic.

Urnes [337] investigated glasses of the composition 20 Li$_2$O—3Al$_2$O$_3$—77SiO$_2$ and 20Li$_2$O—10Al$_2$O$_3$—70SiO$_2$, and he came to the conclusion that in order to produce uniform crystallization, it is not necessary to add a crystallization catalyst, inasmuch as Li$_2$O, when uniformly distributed throughout the bulk of the glass, is an excellent mineralizer.

On the other hand, Vertsner and co-workers [163, 338] determined that bulk crystallization of glass of the spodumene composition takes place only when not less than 4% TiO$_2$ is added to it, which enhances microsegregation of the glass. Lesser amounts of TiO$_2$ do not produce the necessary phase separation, because of which the crystallization of such glasses, for all practical purposes, does not differ from the crystallization of glasses not containing TiO$_2$. These data were confirmed by Kind [339], who observed a sharp change in the character of the crystallization of spodumene glass when more than 3% TiO$_2$ was added to it. The high-temperature spodumene was the primary crystalline phase precipitating. Also possible is the simultaneous precipitation of several crystalline phases, including aluminum titanates.

Crystallization of spodumene and eucryptite glass compositions at pressures in excess of 100 kbar and temperatures in excess of 800°C was studied by Blinov and Roy [340], who were first able to synthesize the α-spodumene in a reproducible manner. In glasses of the eucryptite composition, metastable crystallization of β-quartz solid solution and β-eucryptite was observed. Kitaigorodskii et al. [341] postulate that it may be possible that a large number of solid solutions, including β-eucryptite, β-spodumene, and petalite, may coexist in the crystallization products of glasses of the Li$_2$O—Al$_2$O$_3$—SiO$_2$ system of variable composition. In fact, Eppler [342] observed metastable solid solutions of the β-eucryptite and β-quartz when investigating the glass formation and crystallization of glasses of the composition 10-40 Li$_2$O, 0-25 Al$_2$O$_3$, and 50-80 SiO_2. The junction point of the three solid solutions – namely, of lithium metasilicate, β-spodumene, and β-eucryptite – was located near the composition 62.5 SiO_2, 17 Al_2O_3, and 20 Li_2O.

The crystallization of spodumene, eucryptite, and other glasses of stoichiometric composition was investigated by Kolesova [343], who thought that the structural network of spodumene glass is formed by networks of AlO_4 and SiO_4 tetrahedra, while the aluminum atoms enter the anion framework. Upon heating at temperatures in excess of 700°C, the network-like α-spodumene changes into the high-temperature β-spodumene, which also crystallizes out from the glass of this composition. As the result of the crystallization of eucryptite glass, the high-temperature β-eucryptite is obtained in all cases, with its structure consisting of impoverished AlO_4 and SiO_4 tetrahedra. In all glasses investigated, only those atoms which did not enter the anion framework and having a coordination number of 4 with respect to oxygen crystallized out.

Glass-ceramics composed of more than 50% β-eucryptite have zero or negative α values [344].

In order to produce a glass-ceramic with a fine-grain structure and average α values, Hinz and Baiburt [345] investigated the compositions of the glasses in the cordierite system given in Table 38. These glasses became well-fined during melting and had a dark-yellow color.

By means of differential thermal and x-ray structural analyses, it was determined that magnesium aluminotitanate is the primary crystalline phase formed (when samples are heated to 900°C), and that clinoenstatite, spinel, or sapphirine can also be formed at the same time. As a result of the subsequent transformation of the crystallization products at 1000-1100°C, cordierite and additional amounts of magnesium aluminotitanate were precipitated. Upon heating at 1200°C and above, coarse crystals of cordierite and, to an extent, of the titanate were obtained. The size of the crystals in the glass-ceramic developed thereby was 1 μ or less.

These data are not confirmed by Chistoserdov and coworkers [346], who determined that during the crystallization of glasses in the $MgO-Al_2O_3-SiO_2-TiO_2$ system, the formation of α-cordierite takes place through the intermediary μ-phase. In

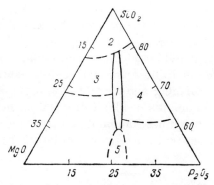

Fig. 70. Range of compositions for the preparation of glass-
ceramics containing ZrO_2 and P_2O_5 from glasses of the MgO—
$SiO_2-P_2O_5$ system. 1) Good glass-crystalline materials; 2) nonuniform glass; 3) deformation; 4) spontaneous crystallization;
5) cracking.

Table 38. Glass Compositions in the $MgO-Al_2O_3-SiO_2$ System with TiO_2 Additions

Component	Contents (in wt.%) of various glasses					
	1	2	3	4	5	6
SiO_2	45.2	41.7	42.1	42.7	44.7	39.1
MgO	17.4	21.7	15.2	14.0	11.9	21.7
Al_2O_3	24.3	23.5	29.6	30.2	30.3	26.1
TiO_2	13.1	13.1	13.1	13.1	13.1	13.1

glasses containing 10–18% TiO_2, the formation of geikielite, and
sometimes clinoenstatite, was also observed in addition to that of
α-cordierite. The precipitation of μ-cordierite as the primary
crystalline phase in glasses of the cordierite composition containing 8–20% TiO_2 was also observed by Kalinin and Podushko [347].
However, Kitaigorodskii et al. [348] did not observe the presence
of μ-cordierite during their investigation of the catalyzed crystallization of glasses of the cordierite system with the addition of 10
mol.% TiO_2. They believe that the first crystalline phase to precipitate out at 850°C is a solid solution based on the high-temperature β-quartz solid solution. Almost at the same time, solid solutions of aluminum titanate and magnesium dititanate (850-900°C)
and of rutile (950-1200°C) are being formed.

Glass-ceramics with low α values were prepared by the sintering and crystallization of the powder of glass of the following composition: 54 SiO_2, 27 Al_2O_3, 16 MgO, CaO, or BaO, and 3 B_2O_3. Any of the following could be added as catalysts: carbonates, silicates, or aluminates of lithium and magnesium; aluminum nitrate [309, 349]; ZrO_2 or $ZrSiO_4$; and Cr_2O_3 in the form of ammonium bichromate and bichromates of alkali or alkaloid metals [350]. At 1000°C, cordierite, anorthite, diopside, eucryptite, spodumene, or spinel crystallized out from the glass powder of the above composition.

Effective catalysts for the preparation of glass-ceramics in the cordierite system are the reaction products between glass and carbon which had been added to the batch [351]. For the preparation of electrical insulator, glass-ceramics of the following compositions are suggested: (1) 3-35 MgO, 25-80 SiO_2, 3-35 BaO, and 10-35 flux; (2) 22-30 MgO, 40-50 SiO_2, 10-18 Al_2O_3, 8-13 flux; (3) 10-30 MgO, 30-50 SiO_2, 7-40 fluorides, and 2-25 Al_2O_3 or B_2O_3; and (4) 4-30 Li_2O, 50-80 SiO_2, and 3-25 Al_2O_3 [352].

Figure 70 shows the narrow compositional range of glasses in the $MgO-SiO_2-P_2O_5$ system in which glass-ceramics with α ranging from 10 to 80 · 10^{-7} (°C)$^{-1}$ and $\sigma_f > 5000$ kg/cm^2 can be obtained [310].

Tashiro [353] suggested magnesium-containing porcelain with an α value of approximately 20-40 · 10^{-7} (°C)$^{-1}$ and the deformation temperature in excess of 1000°C. The original glass has the following composition: 7-23 MgO, 20-35 Al_2O_3, 45-68 SiO_2, 0.5-6 Li_2O, and 0.001-0.1 Pt. One may add not more than 10% Na_2O, K_2O, CaO, SrO, and B_2O_3. Besides cordierite, β-spodumene and β-eucryptite are the primary crystalline phases present.

A glass-ceramic with $\alpha = 100 · 10^{-7}$ (°C)$^{-1}$ and $\sigma_f = 2800$ kg/cm^2 was prepared from glasses of the following composition: 40-68 SiO_2, 8-32 Al_2O_3, 7-14 TiO_2, and 8.5-23 MgO. The glasses are heated at 990°C for 8-24 h, and at 1160°C for 0.25-0.5 h [354].

Crystallization of glasses in the $SiO_2-Al_2O_3-MgO-K_2O$ system with F, P_2O_5, TiO_2, ZrO_2, SnO_2, and talc additions was investigated by Sil'vestrovich and Rabinovich [355, 356]. A stepwise crystallization procedure was used in the temperature region 600-1300°C. Most of these glasses started to crystalline intensely only at 900-950°C. The crystalline phases precipitating were cordierite, spinel, and muscovite. The size of the crystals in the fluorine-containing crystallized glass was 3-5 μ. Glass to which ZrO$_2$ has been added also showed coarsely crystalline, though uniform, structure.

2. GLASS-CERAMICS IN THE RO—Al$_2$O$_3$—SiO$_2$ SYSTEM WHERE RO IS CaO, ZnO, CdO, BaO, PbO, MnO, FeO, OR CoO WITH TiO$_2$ OR ZrO$_2$ ADDITIONS. GLASS-CERAMICS TRANSPARENT TO INFRARED RADIATION

Table 39, which is based on data from [320, 381], shows the compositions of titanium-containing glasses in CaO—Al$_2$O$_3$—SiO$_2$ and ZnO—Al$_2$O$_3$—SiO$_2$ systems to be used for the preparation of glass-ceramics in which anorthite, CaO · Al$_2$O$_3$ · 2SiO$_2$, and gahnite (zinc spinel), ZnO · Al$_2$O$_3$, or willemite, 2ZnO · SiO$_2$, are found to be the primary crystalline phases present. These glass-ceramics have high mechanical strength, high hardness, good wear resistance, and a high deformation temperature.

Glass-ceramics with low α values, which were prepared by sintering powder of the glass of composition 48 Al$_2$O$_3$, 30 CaO, and 13 (K$_2$O + Li$_2$O) at 1200°C for from 15 min to 6 h, contained crystalline calcium aluminate and compounds of the melilite group [350].

During the investigation of calcium aluminate glasses, Kreidl and Weidel [357] were the first to prepare glass-ceramics which are transparent to infrared radiation. The glass investigated had the following composition: 31.04 CaO, 49.92 Al$_2$O$_3$, 3.96 Na$_2$O, 2.0 K$_2$O, 1.38 MgO, 5.23 BaO, 1.36 TiO$_2$, 2.09 ZrO$_2$, 2.7 Fe$_2$O$_3$, and 0.304 Cu$_2$O. When this glass is subjected to heat treatment, it transforms almost entirely into crystalline nontransparent material, with the size of the crystals ranging up to 1 μ. This material transmits infrared rays, has high mechanical and dielectric properties, is insoluble in water, and may expeditiously be used in lieu of conventional electrical-insulation materials. Its softening temperature is 400°C higher than the softening temperature of the original glass, and exceeds 900°C. The melting temperature of this glass is 1510°C. It is stirred at 1480°C for 15 h by the conventional stirrer equipped with slanting blades at a rate of 150 rpm, after which the temperature is decreased to 1450°C and the

Table 39. Glasses in the $CaO-Al_2O_3-SiO_2$ and $ZnO-Al_2O_3-SiO_2$ Systems with TiO_2 Additions, and Glass-Ceramics Prepared from Them

Comp. No.	Content in glass (wt.%)								Heat treatment		Properties of glass-ceramics			Crystalline phases*
	SiO_2	Al_2O_3	TiO_2	MgO	CaO	BaO	ZnO	PbO	crystal. temp., °C	time, h	$\alpha \cdot 10^7$ 1/°C	density, g/cm³	σ_f, kg/cm²	
1	48.9	24.9	11.1	—	15.1	—	—	—	1200	1	—	2.75	—	(1), (6)
2	54.3	22.2	11.1	—	13.3	—	—	—	1275	16	—	—	—	(1), (6), (5)
3	54.3	17.7	11.1	—	17.8	—	—	—	1200	1	—	2.71	—	(1), (7), (5)
4	57.8	16.0	11.1	—	15.1	—	—	—	1100	16	—	2.80	—	(7), (5), (1)
5	62.3	13.3	11.1	—	13.3	—	—	—	1100	16	—	2.71	—	(5), (1), (7), (8)
6	66.7	15.5	11.1	—	6.7	—	—	—	1300	16	—	2.48	—	(5), (1), (2)
7	71.1	12.5	11.1	—	5.3	—	—	—	1300	16	—	—	—	(5), (1), (6)
8	53.4	26.7	11.1	—	8.9	—	—	—	1200	16	—	2.68	1218	(1), (5)
9	43.5	17.4	8.7	—	4.3	—	26.1	—	—	1	38.3	—	—	(4), (3), (5), (6)
10	43.5	17.4	8.7	4.3	—	—	26.1	—	1200	1	36.7	—	1505	(4), (5), (6)
11	44.6	17.9	10.7	8.9	—	—	17.9	—	1145	2	—	—	5600	—
12	43.5	17.4	8.7	—	—	4.3	26.1	—	1250	1	31.7	—	—	(4), (3), (6)
13	43.5	17.4	8.7	—	—	—	26.1	4.3	1200	1	193	—	833	—
14	48.5	14.6	2.9	—	—	—	34.0	—	1200	2.5	193	3.13	945	(3), (5), (4), (6)
15	50.9	23.2	7.4	—	—	—	18.5	—	1250	16	189	2.99	—	(4), (5), (6), (6)
16	58.2	14.6	2.9	—	—	—	24.3	—	1100	2	183	—	1330	(4), (5), (3), (6)
17	49.0	19.6	2.0	—	—	—	39.4	—	1250	2	165	—	385	(4), (5), (3), (6)
18	46.3	18.5	7.4	—	—	—	27.8	—	1100	45	—	—	1095	(4), (5), (3), (6)
19	41.7	9.3	7.4	—	—	—	41.6	—	1250	2	—	3.23	—	(3), (4), (5), (6)
20	60.2	18.5	7.4	—	—	—	13.9	—	1250	2	—	—	—	(4), (6), (5), (6)
21	38.5	14.4	3.8	—	—	—	43.3	—	—	—	—	—	—	(4), (5), (3)

*1) Anorthite; 2) anatase; 3) willemite; 4) gahnite; 5) cristobalite; 6) rutile; 7) sphene; 8) tridymite.

melt is poured into a metallic mold. Annealing at 750°C takes 24 h.
For crystallization purposes, glass blocks with dimensions of
76 × 76 × 6.3 cm are heated to 900°C, and are held at that temperature for 6 h. Transmission in the infrared region for this material starts with 1.75-2.00 μ, attains a maximum (85%) between
3.75 and 4.75 μ, and terminates near 6.0 μ.

The compositions of these glasses may contain up to 65-100
mol.% CaO · $AlO_{1.5}$, out of which up to 25 mol.% may be replaced
by the oxides of Zr, Fe, Sr, Mg, and Ba. It is also possible to add
up to 35 mol.% Na_2O, K_2O, Ag_2O, Cu_2O, La_2O_3, ZrO_2, SiO_2, CeO_2,
B_2O_3, P_2O_5, among others. Another example for the composition
of such a glass is as follows: 40.74 CaO, 33.95 Al_2O_3, 5.09 Na_2O,
1.70 K_2O, 2.72 MgO, 2.72 BaO, 1.36 La_2O_3, 3.40 SiO_2, 6.79 Fe_2O_3,
and 1.53 Cu_2O. The melting temperature of this glass is 1427°C,
and the pouring temperatures is 1400°C. The melting temperature
of the glasses of this system is determined by the CaO · Al_2O_3 content and lies within the range 1370-1540°C. The processing temperature is 50-100°C lower than the liquidus temperature. The
temperature of heat treatment is higher than the annealing temperature, but lower than the liquidus temperature. The duration
of heat treatment ranges from several minutes to 5-10 h, depending on the temperature of the treatment and the composition of the
initial glass.

Some new refractory glass-ceramics developed by Owens-
Illinois Glass Co. [715] and known as "Cer-Vit" have the interesting characteristic that they transmit infrared radiation, but do not
heat up very much during this process; the α values of these
glass-ceramics may vary from $-20 \cdot 10^{-7}$ to $+80 \cdot 10^{-7}$ (°C)$^{-1}$, and
it is possible to produce glass-ceramics having zero α values.

For electron tubes operating at frequencies of 10,000 MHz,
polycrystalline materials with good dielectric and mechanical
properties were developed by heating to 1400-1635°C mixtures of
60-95% Al_2O_3 and 40-5% of glass of the following composition: 15-
75 SiO_2; up to 45 Al_2O_3; and 10-60 CaO or BaO. The softening temperature of such material may reach 1400-1475°C, the α values
may be in the range 54-64 $\cdot 10^{-7}$ (°C)$^{-1}$, and the σ_f may range from
1620 to 2950 kg/cm^2 [358].

For the preparation of glass-ceramics with lower α values,
glass of the composition 48-72 SiO_2, 20-29 Al_2O_3, 8-29 CaF_2, 2-7

Li_2O, and 0.2-0.5 PbO was melted at 1300-1500°C. The glass article was heated at a rate of 300 deg/h to above the annealing temperature, held at that temperature for 2 h for the formation of nuclei, whereupon it was again heated to a temperature somewhat below the softening point and held there for 1 h [359].

Glass-ceramics with high dielectric properties were prepared from glasses having a high ZnO content [360]. The basic composition of these glasses is as follows: 2.0-27.0 Li_2O, 10-59 ZnO, and 34-81 SiO_2. The total content of the basic components must be not less than 90%. The remaining 10% may include Na_2O, K_2O, Al_2O_3, MgO, CaO, B_2O_3, PbO, among others. As crystallization agents, it is recommended that 0.02-0.03% Au, 0.02-0.03% AgCl, or 0.5-1.0% Cu_2O be used. In the glass-ceramics prepared from such mixtures, the range of α values was $42.6-174.0 \cdot 10^{-7}$, the breakdown voltage ranged from 34 to 50 kV/mm and the range of $\tan \delta$ was $13-60 \cdot 10^{-4}$ at 1 MHz.

Glasses with a somewhat lower ZnO concentration containing 45-65 SiO_2, 10-27 Al_2O_3, 15-35 ZnO, 2-10 Li_2O, 2-8 SnO_2, and 2-5 B_2O_3 could be used to produce glass-ceramics with increased refractoriness and increased mechanical strength when heated from 500 to 900°C at a rate of 20 deg/h and after being held at 900°C for 3 h [361]. The primary crystalline phases present were spodumene, eucryptite, and the compounds $2ZnO \cdot SiO_2$ and $ZnO \cdot Al_2O_3$.

Thermally stable glass-ceramics can also be produced from glasses in the $Li_2O-ZnO-Al_2O_3-SiO_2$ system when prepared from a mixture of sphalerite with petalite or spodumene [362]. The primary crystalline phases were willemite, hernite, and β-spodumene; σ_f attained values of 1515 kg/cm^2, and the α values were in the range $30.5-34.3 \cdot 10^{-7}$ (°C)$^{-1}$.

Compositions for the glasses in the $CdO-Al_2O_3-SiO_2$ and $BaO-Al_2O_3-SiO_2$ systems to which TiO_2 has been added so as to produce glass-ceramics with medium α values, a high mechanical strength, and a high temperature of deformation are represented in Table 40 [320, 321]. In compositions containing BaO, dibarium trisilicate was observed to be present as the primary crystalline phase.

Table 40. Glasses in the CdO—Al$_2$O$_3$—SiO$_2$ and BaO—Al$_2$O$_3$—SiO$_2$ Systems with TiO$_2$ Additions, and the Glass-Ceramics Prepared from Them

Comp. No.	Content in glass (wt.%)									Heat treatment		Properties of glass-ceramics			Crystalline phases
	SiO$_2$	Al$_2$O$_3$	TiO$_2$	ZrO$_2$	CdO	MgO	BaO	CaO	ZnO	Crystallization temp., °C	time at temp., h	$\alpha\cdot10^7$, 1/°C	density, g/cm³	σ_f, kg/cm²	
1	44.3	17.7	11.5	26.5	—	—	—	—	—	1150	3	75	—	1120	—
2	44.7	22.3	10.7	—	22.3	—	—	—	—	1250	2	102	3.11	1330	—
3	45.9	22.9	8.3	—	22.9	—	—	—	—	1100	40	91	—	343	—
4	36.4	22.7	9.1	—	31.8	—	—	—	—	1100	2	42	—	875	—
5	54.6	13.6	9.1	—	22.7	—	—	—	—	1100	20	—	—	910	—
6	27.3	27.3	9.1	—	36.3	4.8	—	—	—	—	—	—	—	—	—
7	48.5	21.6	10.1	—	15.0	4.7	—	—	—	—	—	—	—	—	—
8	47.9	18.3	11.3	—	—	—	17.8	—	—	1150	2	39.7	2.86	—	Trisilicate and meta-silicate of Ba
9	39.5	13.2	12.3	—	—	—	35.0	—	—	1150	2	38.5	2.97	—	
10	43.8	13.2	12.3	—	—	—	30.7	—	—	780	20.5	51.2	5.85	—	
11	48.2	13.2	12.3	—	—	—	26.3	—	—	1100		91.7	3.17	—	
12	43.8	17.6	12.3	—	—	—	26.3	—	—	1250	15	32.8	3.08	560	Trisilicate and meta-silicate of Ba
13	48.2	17.6	12.3	—	—	—	21.9	—	—	1300	0.5	—	2.99	—	=
14	52.5	17.6	12.3	—	—	—	17.6	—	—	1300	0.5	35.7	3.10	651	=
15	39.5	21.9	12.3	—	—	—	26.3	—	—	1250	15	—	3.03	—	=
16	43.9	21.9	12.3	—	—	—	21.9	—	—	1300	0.5	—	2.96	—	=
17	46.0	24.1	12.3	—	—	—	17.6	—	—	1300	0.5	—	2.93	—	=
18	41.7	26.3	12.3	—	—	—	19.7	—	—	1300	0.5	—	—	—	
19	46.2	20.1	12.5	—	—	—	17.4	3.8	—	1150	2	—	—	—	Trisilicate and meta-silicate of Ba
20	44.7	17.9	10.6	—	—	—	17.5	—	9.3	1150	2	—	—	—	—

Glass-ceramics prepared from glasses containing mixtures of two or more RO oxides — such as from glasses of compositions Nos. 6-8, 22, 23, 25, and 26 of Table 34, Nos. 9-13 of Table 39, and Nos. 7, 8, 19, and 20 from Table 40 — have properties which are intermediary between the properties of the glass-ceramics prepared from glasses containing each one of these oxides individually.

Glass-ceramics with a high dielectric constant ε and a low dielectric loss are prepared from glasses of the $BaO-Al_2O_3-SiO_2-TiO_2$ system which, as a result of the heat treatment to which they are subjected, precipitate, as the primary crystalline phase, compounds which have ferroelectric properties, such as barium titanate [363, 364]. Additions of SiO_2 and Al_2O_3 speed up the glass-formation process. Adding a small (up to 1.5%) amount of fluorine in the form of fluorides of metals of the first or the second group of the periodic chart speeds up the melting process, enhances a more rapid formation of $BaTiO_3$, and prevents the precipitation of other undesirable crystalline compounds, as it also improves the dielectric properties of the glass-ceramic. These glasses contain (in cation-mol.%) the following: 30-45 BaO, 15-40 TiO_2, 7-26 SiO_2, 3-30 $AlO_{1.5}$, and 0.5-1.5 F_2. The amount of $AlO_{1.5}$ relative to the SiO_2 should not exceed the ratio $^4\!/_3$. The total content of BaO, TiO_2, SiO_2, $AlO_{1.5}$, and F_2 present must be in excess of 90%. In order to prevent the formation of other titanium compounds, such as barium titanosilicate, the BaO should be present in excess (up to 100%) relative to its stoichiometric equivalent 1:1 in $BaTiO_3$, as calculated from the TiO_2 content. This excess must always be greater than the minimum TiO_2 content. A more narrow range of compositions for which the presence of the given amount of F_2 is optimal includes (in cation-mol.%): 30-40 BaO, 15-40 TiO_2, 9.5-26 SiO_2, and 7-25 $AlO_{1.5}$ [363, 364].

Deviations from the above amounts of BaO and TiO_2 lead to a decrease in the amount of the precipitating ferroelectric crystalline compound $BaTiO_3$ and to a lowering of ε. This occurs both in case of an excess of SiO_2 or a deficiency of $AlO_{1.5}$. However, too little SiO_2 or too much $AlO_{1.5}$ makes spontaneous crystallization of the glass melt possible, no matter what its cooling rates are. Some examples of calculated compositions of these glasses, taken from [363, 364], are listed in Table 41, which also presents the temperature and the duration of heat treatment of these glasses, as well as the ε and the tan δ at 25°C of the glass-ceramics obtained.

Table 41. Compositions of Glasses in the BaO—TiO$_2$—SiO$_2$—Al$_2$O$_3$ System, Their Heat-Treatment Procedure, and the Dielectric Properties of the Glass-Ceramics Obtained

Component	Content (in cation-mol.%) of various compositions							
	1	2	3	4	5	6	7	8
BaO	44.3	31.2	35.7	37.8	33.4	36.6	36.4	36.1
TiO$_2$	22.5	23.0	28.2	32.3	19.7	35.0	35.2	36.1
SiO$_2$	15.6	21.4	16.5	14.9	21.7	13.2	9.9	16.7
AlO$_{1.5}$	16.2	23.3	17.2	13.7	23.7	13.9	17.2	9.8
F$_2$	0.6	0.5	1.3	0.5	0.6	0.5	0.6	0.6
CaO	1.4	1.1	2.4	1.3	1.5	1.3	1.3	1.3
Excess of BaO	97.0	35.6	26.6	17.0	69.6	4.6	3.4	—
Heat treatment procedure								
Temperature, °C	1000	1000	925	925	925	1000	1075	915
Time at temperature, h	2	2	3	3	2	2	2	2,5
Dielectric properties of glass-ceramics								
ε	240	260	820	1370	300	860	840	600
tan δ	1.5	2.8	3.1	2.8	3.2	3.1	2.9	2.4

Component	Content (in cation-mol.%) of various compositions							
	9	10	11	12	13	14	15	16
BaO	36.1	36.7	36.7	36.8	36.9	37.9	35.2	33.7
TiO$_2$	31.8	32.4	32.4	32.5	32.5	32.0	37.4	36.9
SiO$_2$	14.8	14.2	14.2	14.2	14.1	14.3	16.4	8.0
AlO$_{1.5}$	17.3	15.4	15.4	15.6	15.6	15.8	9.8	18.4
F$_2$	—	0.6	0.6	0.6	0.5	0.7	1.2	1.2
CaO	—	1.3	—	—	—	—	1.2	3.0
MgO	—	—	1.3	—	—	—	—	—
ZnO	—	—	—	0.9	—	—	—	—
SrO	—	—	—	—	0.9	—	—	—
Excess of BaO	13.5	13.3	13.3	13.3	13.5	18.4	—	—
Excess of TiO$_2$	—	—	—	—	—	—	6.3	9.5
Heat treatment procedure								
Temperature, °C	1075	1075	1000	1075	1075	925	950	950
Time at temperature, h	2	2	3	2	2	3	2	2
Dielectric properties of glass-ceramics								
ε	800	1340	1370	1220	1320	1350	500	1300
tan δ	3.6	3.0	2.9	3.2	2.5	2.8	2.2	1.2

These glasses are melted under neutralizing or oxidizing conditions at 1400°C or higher for 1-8 h in pots or tank furnaces. Because of the low viscosity of the melt (approximately 1 poise at 1400°C), refining agents cannot be employed. As oxidizers, it is recommended to use barium nitrate or other nitrates. In order to avoid spontaneous crystallization during the processing, such as during the pressing of bars up to 12.7 mm thick, the rolling of thin sheets, or centrifugal casting of the products, the melt is quenched from 700°C within 2-10 sec. Thin glass sheets are suitable for the production of layerlike condensers, which are prepared by soldering these glass sheets to metallic foil at 700°C under pressure. In order to produce articles having a greater thickness, the melt is poured into cold water and the granulate is ground into powder, from which slip is prepared. The article which has been shaped by the slip-casting method is then sintered without crystallization at the softening temperature, whereupon it is subjected to sitallization by being heated at 850°C for 1 h, or at 1150°C for 0.5 min. The primary crystalline phase is $BaTiO_3$.

By adding up to 10 cation-mol.% of the oxides of Ca, B, Ga, P, As, Tl, V, Ge, In, Ce, Zr, Sb, Nb, Fe, Cd, La, Sn, Zn, Bi, and Pb, one can change the Curie point slightly (approximately by 20°) and also improve the glass formation, although the temperature coefficient of ε is thereby decreased. Adding oxides of In, Ce, Zr, Nb, Sb, or Fe lowers the Curie point to 80°C, adding oxides of Mg, Sn, or Co lowers it to 50°C, and adding ZnO lowers it to room temperature. Adding Bi_2O_3 increases the Curie point. Adding oxides of Zn, Mn, or Ni decreases $\tan \delta$. If, in addition to SiO_2, such glass-formers as B_2O_3 and P_2O_5 are added to the glasses of the above compositions, the ε of these glass-ceramics sharply decreases from the values listed in Table 41 — namely, to 30-80 or 130-230, respectively.

Glass-ceramics with α approximately 50-90 · 10^{-7} (°C)$^{-1}$ and σ_f ranging up to 2000 kg/cm² were obtained by heating glasses of the composition 45-65 SiO_2, 10-27 Al_2O_3, 3-15 MgO, 5-25 BaO, 1-10 Na_2O, 1-10 Li_2O, and 0.2-5 F at a rate of 30 deg/h from 400 to 1000°C, followed by the subsequent annealing of the articles produced [365].

Compositions of the glasses in the $PbO-Al_2O_3-SiO_2$, $MnO-Al_2O_3-SiO_2$, $FeO-Al_2O_3-SiO_2$, and $CoO-Al_2O_3-SiO_2$ systems with

TiO$_2$ additions, their heat-treatment procedures, the properties of the glass-ceramics obtained, and the crystalline phases present in these glass-ceramics are listed in Table 42, taken from [320, 321].

Tykachinskii et al. [366] synthesized a glass in the SiO$_2$—Al$_2$O$_3$—B$_2$O$_3$—PbO system from which glass-ceramics with enhanced mechanical and thermal properties could be obtained by a two-stage crystallization process. The composition of this glass was 48-43 SiO$_2$, 22-27 Al$_2$O$_3$, 18-23 B$_2$O$_3$, 8-13 PbO, and 2-6 F. The glass articles are shaped by pressing, drawing, casting, or other methods, are held at 800°C for the purpose of forming nuclei, and are then heated to 1200°C and above so as to complete the crystallization process. These glass-ceramics attain a σ_f of 2500 kg/cm^2, are thermally stable to 1230°C, and have a softening temperature higher than 1400°C.

A number of glass-ceramics was prepared [367] based on glasses in boron and boron-free aluminosilicate systems. One of the most promising of these is glass-ceramic 4-23, which is based on a glass in the SiO$_2$—Al$_2$O$_3$—B$_2$O$_3$ system. It has a softening temperature higher than 1450°C, a good thermal stability, and a mechanical strength which is three to four times higher than that of the respective glass.

A glass-ceramic with a softening temperature lower than 700°C, a dielectric constant higher than 15, and a power factor of not more than 0.003 was prepared from glasses of the following composition: 50-70 TiO$_2$, 10-11 PbO, 13-14 BaO, 19-20 SiO$_2$, 4-5 SnO$_2$, 5-6 CaO, 3-4 SrO, 2-3 ZrO$_2$, 2-3 Sb$_2$O$_3$, 9-10 K$_2$O, 4-5 Na$_2$O, 2-3 Li$_2$O, 2-3 B$_2$O$_3$, and 0.5-1.5 MgO [368]. The melt of this glass homogenizes well at 1100-1250°C.

Employing as the crystallization catalyst a mixture of ZrO$_2$ with one of the oxides TiO$_2$, V$_2$O$_3$, CoO, NiO, MoO$_3$, Fe$_2$O$_3$, or ThO$_2$ and adding it to glass of the composition 40.2 SiO$_2$, 31.0 Al$_2$O$_3$, 6.0 MgO, 1.0 F, 8.0 ZrO$_2$, 1.5 TiO$_2$, 0.2 SnO$_2$, and 5 CaO made it possible to obtain a glass-ceramic whose σ_f ranged from 7000 to 10,000 kg/cm^2 [369]. The basic crystalline phases were tridymite, sapphirine, and mullite. Heat treatment included holding for 0.5-1 h at the following, successively increasing, temperatures: at the temperature of the nucleus formation (viscosity $\eta = 10^{13.5}$ poise); within the temperature range where the crystallization develops ($\eta = 10^{10}$ poise); and within the temperature range

Table 42. Glasses in the $PbO-Al_2O_3-SiO_2$, $MnO-Al_2O_3-SiO_2$, Additions, and Glass-Ceramics

Comp. No.	Content in glass (wt.%)							
	SiO_2	Al_2O_3	TiO_2	NiO	CoO	B_2O_3	PbO	MnO
1	26.6	17.8	11.1	—	—	—	44.5	—
2	31.1	17.8	11.1	—	—	—	40.0	—
3	35.5	17.8	11.1	—	—	—	35.6	—
4	38.4	17.8	11.1	—	—	—	32.7	—
5	26.6	15.5	11.1	—	—	—	46.8	—
6	31.1	15.5	11.1	—	—	—	42.3	—
7	31.1	13.3	11.1	—	—	—	44.5	—
8	35.6	13.3	11.1	—	—	—	40.0	—
9	17.8	13.3	11.1	—	—	—	57.8	—
10	17.8	8.9	11.1	—	—	—	62.2	—
11	17.8	4.4	11.1	—	—	—	66.7	—
12	15.6	4.4	11.1	—	—	—	68.9	—
13	48.2	23.6	9.1	—	—	—	—	19.1
14	50.9	23.6	9.1	—	—	-.-	—	16.4
15	43.8	25.9	10.7	—	-.-	—	—	19.6
16	48.2	23.6	9.1	—	—	—	—	19.1
17	46.1	22.6	13.0	—	—	—	—	18.3
18	44.2	21.6	16.7	—	—	—	—	17.5
19	40.8	22.8	9.1	—	—	—	—	27.3
20	44.1	29.4	2.0	-.-	—	—	—	—
21	42.4	28.3	5.7	—	—	—	—	—
22	45.5	22.7	9.1	—	22.7	—	—	—
23	45.5	18.2	9.1	—	27.2	—	—	—
24	49.1	18.2	9.1	—	23.6	—	-.-	-.-
25	49.1	21.8	9.1	—	20.0	—	—	—
26	40.9	25.4	9.1	—	24.6	—	—	—
27	46.1	19.1	8.7	21.7	—	4.4	—	—

FeO—Al_2O_3—SiO_2, and CoO—Al_2O_3—SiO_2 Systems with TiO_2 Obtained from Them

	Heat treatment		Properties of glass-ceramics			Crystalline phases*
FeO	crystal. temp., °C	time at temp., h	$\alpha \cdot 10^7$ 1/°C	density, g/cm^3	σ_f, kg/cm^2	
—	1100	18	36.0	4.04	—	
—	1100	18	36.1	3.83	—	
—	1100	18	42.7	3.62	—	
—	1000	3	59.2	3.50	—	
—	1100	18	40.0	4.07	—	
—	1100	4	38.3	3.90	—	
—	—	—	38.3	3.99	—	
—	—	—	—	3.75	—	
—	750	17	25.9	4.80	—	
—	750	—	36.8	5.24	—	(6)
—	750	2	—	5.51	—	
—	780	2	41.6	5.76	—	(6)
—	1100	15	101	2.88	1162	(2), (5), (1), (4)
—	1100	15	108	2.82	1085	(2), (3), (5), (1)
—	1100	16	93.6	2.94	1743	(5), (7), (4), (1)
—	1100	2.5	111	2.93	728	(2), (5), (1), (4)
—	1100	2	128	2.88	1162	(5), (2), (1), (3)
—	1100	2	129	3.04	1491	(5), (2), (1), (4)
—	1100	2,5	20.6	2.86	728	(3), (5), (1)
24,5	1200	4	—	—	—	
23,6	1200	4	—	—	—	
—	1100	16	170	3.06	—	
—	1100	16	—	2.94	—	
—	1200	1	—	—	—	
—	1200	1	—	—	—	
—	1250	2	174	3.18	—	
—	1200	4	—	—	—	

* 1) Quartz, 2) cristobalite, 3) cordierite, 4) mullite, 5) pyrophanite, 6) lead titanate, 7) tridymite.

where the crystallization is completed ($\eta = 10^{7.65}$ poise), which is 75-150°C higher than the softening temperature of the glass. The glass products were subjected to heat treatment in a continuous furnace.

The presence of PbO in glass of the composition 45-65 SiO_2, 10-27 Al_2O_3, 15-35 ZnO, 0.5-10 Li_2O, 3-10 MgO, and 1.5-15 PbO makes it possible to prepare a structurally dense and mechanically and thermally strong glass-ceramic [370]. Small amounts of TiO_2, Al_2O_3, and Na_2O, and fining agents are added to the glass. The product is heated from 500 to 900°C at a rate of 20 deg/h, and is held at the maximum temperature for 3 h. The crystalline phases are cordierite and spodumene.

The addition of oxides CaO, BaO, MgO, PbO, ZnO, CoO, B_2O_3, Fe_2O_3, Bi_2O_3, Sb_2O_3, As_2O_3, and P_2O_5 in amounts of less than 20% facilitated the crystallization of glass of the composition 56-67 SiO_2, 12-20 Li_2O, and 11 Al_2O_3, and resulted in the preparation of a white glass-ceramic similar in its looks to plastic with the crystal size ranging from 0.5-1 μ, with increased mechanical strength, and with α approximately 55-100 · 10^{-7} (°C)$^{-1}$ [371]. The heat treatment of this glass includes heating at a rate of 2 deg/min within the temperature range 500-620°C, holding at temperature for 30 min, and then heating to 720°C and holding at that temperature for 1 h.

Glasses with a substantial amount of Fe and Mn present produce glass-ceramics which are stable with respect to thermal and impact loads [372]. Articles made from glass of the composition 45-65 SiO_2, 10-27 Al_2O_3, 1-10 B_2O_3, 1-10 Li_2O, 10-27 FeO, 5-25 MnO, and a small amount of MgO are heated to the given temperature in the temperature region 400-1000°C at a rate of 0.5 deg/min, held at temperature for 3 h, and then annealed.

3. GLASS-CERAMICS IN THE $CaO-Al_2O_3-P_2O_5-SiO_2$ SYSTEM AND IN OTHER SYSTEMS WITH P_2O_5 ADDITIONS, HAVING THE PROPERTIES OF ENGLISH HARD PORCELAIN

Stookey [373, 374] proposed glasses in the $CaO-P_2O_5-Al_2O_3-SiO_2$ system which, through heat treatment, can be transformed into glass-ceramics which are similar to English hard porcelain with regard to their composition and properties. These

Table 43. Calculated Compositions for the Glasses of the
CaO—Al_2O_3—P_2O_5—SiO_2 System for Glass-Ceramics with
the Properties of English Hard Porcelain

Component	Contents (in wt.%) of various compositions							
	1	2	3	4	5	6	7	8
SiO_2	30.0	30.1	36.1	40.0	40.0	40.0	42.0	45.5
$Ca_2P_2O_7$	48.2	50.1	43.3	38.6	39.6	41.6	39.6	35.0
Al_2O_3	20.0	28.0	19.0	20.0	19.0	17.0	17.0	18.3
CaO	0.9	0.9	0.8	0.7	0.7	0.7	0.7	0.6
MgO	0.9	0.9	0.8	0.7	0.7	0.7	0.7	0.6

glasses have the following compositions: 30-48 SiO_2, 34-54 $Ca_2P_2O_7$,
and 15-21 Al_2O_3. The weight ratio of $Ca_2P_2O_7$: Al_2O_3 is not less
than 1.85, and the total content of the basic components is not less
than 95%. One may add 5% CaF_2; 2% K_2O, Na_2O, or Li_2O; 5% MgO,
ZnO, BaO, or PbO; and also not more than a 4% excess of CaO or
a 2% excess of P_2O_5 relative to their amounts in $Ca_2P_2O_7$.

The characteristic peculiarity of these glasses is the absence
in them of crystallization catalysts, the role of which is played, according to Stookey [373, 374], by the hardened droplets of the phosphate-containing glass which are dispersed throughout the bulk of
the glass and which already segregate during the cooling of the
melt, thereupon serving as the nuclei on which crystals characteristic of the English hard porcelain then grow during the heat-
treatment process.

The following serve as raw materials for the melting of
these glasses: feldspar, clay, and bone ash containing 96.3%
$Ca_2P_2O_7$, an excess of approximately 1.5% CaO relative to the theoretical amount, and small amounts of MgO, SiO_2, Al_2O_3, and RO
oxides as impurities. In order to avoid any coloring, such as from
iron impurities, pure materials — namely, sand, limestone, phosphorus salts, and Al_2O_3 — are used.

Typical compositions for these glasses, as taken from [373,
374], are shown in Table 43.

These glasses are melted at 1550°C for approximately 16 h.
One may add 0.1-1% As_2O_3 as the fining agent. In order to prevent

the reduction of the phosphate, oxidizing conditions are created by employing As_2O_3, $Ca(NO_3)_2$, or $Al(NO_3)_3$.

Heat treatment consists in heating the products in the temperature range 850-1050°C at a rate of 3-5 deg/min and holding them at 1050°C until α is not greater than $50-70 \cdot 10^{-7}$ (°C)$^{-1}$ for the original glass and not greater than $90-100 \cdot 10^{-7}$ (°C)$^{-1}$ or higher for the glass-ceramic. Heat treatment may also include holding at from 950 to 1000°C for from 2 to 0.5 h, respectively, which prevents the article from being deformed when held at the final temperature of 1050°C. However, if the heating rate does not exceed 5 deg/min, one may omit this intermediary procedure. Some properties of the initial glasses of the $CaO-Al_2O_3-P_2O_5-SiO_2$ system, and of the glass-ceramics prepared from them, which are similar to English hard porcelain are listed in Table 44, as taken from [373, 734].

The primary crystalline phases are calcium orthophosphate $Ca_3(PO_4)_2$ and β-cristobalite.

The above-mentioned amounts of the primary components SiO_2, $Ca_2P_2O_7$, and Al_2O_3 are critical, in view of the fact that either a deficiency of Al_2O_3 or an excess of $Ca_2P_2O_7$ makes the melting and the shaping of the glass more difficult, while an increase in the Al_2O_3 content to 16% increases the melting temperature to 1650°C. An excess of SiO_2 or Al_2O_3 or a deficiency in $Ca_2P_2O_7$ impair the capability of the glass with regard to crystallization, whereas a deficiency in SiO_2 results in spontaneous crystallization of the glass during cooling.

The utilization of phosphates as catalysts for the crystallization of glasses of various systems makes it possible to obtain glass-ceramics of a white color with a fine-grained structure (the size of the crystals ranging from 0.1 to 6 μ), having a higher mechanical strength than when Au, Ag, or Cu are used, and also with lower dielectric losses [375]. Phosphates speed up the melting and the fining processes of the glass, they improve its forming properties, their activity as catalysts does not depend on oxidation—reduction conditions in the furnace, and they are inexpensive. For the preparation of glass-ceramics based on lithium aluminosilicate glasses, preference should be given to $LiPO_3$, $Mg_3(PO_4)_2$, $AlPO_4$, $Ca_3(PO_4)_2$, $Zn_3(PO_4)_2$, Na_3PO_4, and K_3PO_4. The compositions of some glasses containing phosphates as the catalysts are shown

Table 44. Properties of Original Glasses and Glass-Ceramics Similar to English Hard Porcelain

Comp. No.	Original glass		Glass-ceramic		
	$\alpha \cdot 10^7$ 1/°C	density, g/cm^3	$\alpha \cdot 10^7$ 1/°C	density, g/cm^3	σ_f, kg/cm^2
1	69	2.631	108	2.647	—
2	68	639	128	657	1180
3	61	599	117	609	1190
4	54	561	108	578	1040
5	55	560	117	572	—
6	57	556	129	583	750
7	53	550	130	571	565
8	52	2.527	122	2.537	—

in Table 45 (taken from [375]), where the values for the linear thermal coefficient α are also listed for the corresponding glass-ceramics within the temperature region 20-500°C.

These glasses are melted at 1200°C (composition No. 1) or at 1450°C (composition No. 10) in electric or gas furnaces, lined with sillimanite or zirconium-containing refractories. The pre-shaped products are annealed at 500°C (composition No. 1) or 750°C (composition No. 10) and then heated at a rate of 4-5 deg/min to the temperature where softening begins, and are held at that temperature for 1 h, so that nuclei can form. More-refractory glasses with a high Al$_2$O$_3$ content are held for an additional hour at a temperature lying 40-50° higher than the softening point. The nucleating crystallization prevents deformation at these temperatures. Further heating is done, at the same rate, to the temperature of the final crystallization, which is 850°C for all compositions listed except for glasses Nos. 5, 8, and 16, for which it is 1200°C.

The crystallized articles are cooled at a normal rate, although rates of approximately 600 deg/h are allowable. The primary crystalline phases in the lithium and magnesium aluminosilicate glasses were β-spodumene and its solid solutions with quartz, β-eucryptite, α-quartz, α-cristobalite, clinoenstatite, forsterite, cordierite, and lithium metasilicate and disilicate, with a small amount of the glassy phase present.

Table 45. Phosphate-Containing Glasses for the Preparation of Glass-Ceramics with High Mechanical and Dielectric Properties

Comp. No.	Contents of glass (wt. %)									$\alpha \cdot 10^{-7}$ $(^\circ C)^{-1}$, of glass-ceram.
	Li_2O	MgO	Al_2O_3	SiO_2	P_2O_5	K_2O	B_2O_3	ZnO	CaO	
1	24.1	—	—	72.9	3.0	—	—	—	—	95.0
2	19.3	—	—	77.7	3.0	—	—	—	—	117.5
3	22.2	—	18.9	55.9	3.0	—	—	—	—	78.0
4	12.1	—	3.9	78.5	3.0	2.5	—	—	—	102.0
5	13.6	15.5	—	67.9	3.0	—	—	—	—	115.2
6	11.0	3.7	—	82.3	3.0	—	—	—	—	142.0
7	—	24.4	20.3	52.3	3.0	—	—	—	—	31.0
8	—	19.7	17.9	59.4	3.0	—	—	—	—	28.9
9	16.3	7.4	18.6	54.7	3.0	—	—	—	—	—1.9
10	8.4	2.7	28.7	57.2	3.0	—	—	—	—	—38.7
11	5.0	13.7	17.3	61.0	3.0	—	—	—	—	12.1
12	12.9	11.7	7.7	64.7	3.0	—	—	—	—	63.8
13	10.5	7.0	—	72.1	3.0	—	6.4	—	—	124.0
14	7.8	2.8	19.4	62.4	3.0	4.6	—	—	—	11.5
15	4.7	2.6	27.2	58.2	3.0	4.3	—	—	—	1.9
16	4.7	2.6	27.4	58.6	3.0	—	—	3.7	—	—0.9
17	8.1	2.8	19.8	63.6	3.0	—	—	—	2.7	1.2

The α values of these glass-ceramics ranged from $-38 \cdot 10^{-7}$ to $142 \cdot 10^{-7}$ $(^\circ C)^{-1}$ in the temperature range 20–500°C, which makes it possible to solder them to various metals for the construction of vacuum-tight seals. Glass-ceramics Nos. 9 and 15–17 have α close to zero, which makes it possible for them to sustain sharp drops in temperature, such as quenching in cold water of an article heated to 800°C.

Glass-ceramic No. 12 has $\tan \delta = 29 \cdot 10^{-4}$ at 1 MHz and $15 \cdot 10^{-4}$ at 10 MHz. Glass-ceramic of composition No. 4 has $\sigma_f = 2800$ kg/cm^2, and its dielectric strength is more than 40 kV. In the lithium aluminosilicate system with 2–4% P_2O_5 additions, glass-ceramics were obtained whose σ_f attains 2500–4000 kg/cm^2 [376]. Adding RO (CaO, BaO, MgO, PbO, ZnO, CdO) and R_2O_3 (B_2O_3, Fe_2O_3, Bi_2O_3, Sb_2O_3, As_2O_3) oxides to the glass containing 55–67 SiO_2, 12–20 Li_2O, 11 Al_2O_3, and 7–15 P_2O_5 facilitates its crystallization and makes it possible to obtain glass-ceramics with crystal sizes of 0.5-1 μ [377]. It was determined that the size of the crystals decreases with increasing Al$_2$O$_3$ content [378]; however, the σ_f was highest for glass-ceramics containing 1% Al$_2$O$_3$.

Glass-ceramics with porcelain properties were synthesized from glasses of the composition 78-80 SiO$_2$, 8-20 Li$_2$O, 4-10 Al$_2$O$_3$, not more than 7 P$_2$O$_5$, and 5 R$_2$O (exclusive of Li$_2$O) by heating them at a rate of 2 deg/min to temperatures lying 30-50° below the temperature of the beginning of softening, and with the aid of subsequent heating necessary for the formation of fine, uniformly distributed crystals [379].

Glass-ceramics with a high softening temperature and low α values were prepared from lithium aluminosilicate glasses with additions of 1-7% P$_2$O$_5$ and 1-5 ZrO$_2$ [380]. For this, not less than 90% of the batch was composed of the glass of the following composition: 50-70 SiO$_2$, 12-35 Al$_2$O$_3$, 2-10 Li$_2$O, 1-5 ZrO$_2$, and 1-7 P$_2$O$_5$; in order to improve the forming properties, not more than 3% R$_2$O (in addition to Li$_2$O), 6% MgO, ZnO, BaO, PbO, 2% TiO$_2$, and 3% P$_2$O$_5$ were added. The glass was heated at a rate of 5 deg/min from 650-750 to 800°C, held there for 30 min, and then again heated to 900-1200°C and held at the maximum temperature for 4 h.

Partridge and McMillan [381] determined that with the aid of metal phosphates one may catalyze the crystallization of a wide range of compositions of silicate glasses, including 34-88 SiO$_2$, up to 27 Li$_2$O, and small amounts of Al$_2$O$_3$, MgO, and ZnO. In order to improve the forming properties of this glass and to control the crystallization process, one may add small amounts of Na$_2$O, K$_2$O, CaO, SrO, BaO, PbO, and B$_2$O$_3$. The P$_2$O$_5$ concentration in the melted glass varies from 0.5 to 6%. It is desirable to add phosphates of those metals whose oxides are the primary components of the glass, such as phosphates of lithium or aluminum in lithium aluminosilicate glass. One may also add ammonium phosphates or phosphoric acids, although they are more volatile during the melting process. The melting temperature may vary from 1000 to 1500°C. The products are shaped by casting, pressing, drawing, or blowing methods. For sitallization, the glass articles are heated at a rate of 4-5 deg/min to a temperature exceeding by 0-50°C the dilatometric softening temperature of the glass, and are

held there for 1 h. The heating is thereupon continued at a rate of
3-5 deg/min until a temperature of 800-1200°C is reached, and
the product is held at the final temperature for 1 h.

4. GLASS-CERAMICS IN THE PbO−ZnO−B$_2$O$_3$− SiO$_2$ SYSTEM. CRYSTALLIZING SOLDER (SEALING) GLASSES

In the PbO−ZnO−B$_2$O$_3$−SiO$_2$ system, solder (or sealing)
glasses which crystallize at low temperatures were obtained for
the sealing of small parts of cathode-ray tubes for color television; the α range of these glasses is 80-105 · 10^{-7} (°C)$^{-1}$ in the
temperature region 0-300°C [382]. The characteristic property of
these glasses is that they do not crystallize right after being
heated to the softening temperature, at which sealing takes place,
and that because they retain their viscosity, they are capable of
successfully wetting the fine parts to be soldered or sealed together, thereby forming a tight soldered junction which does not
contain cracks or other sources of lowered mechanical strength.
At 450°C, the crystallization is completed within 1 h. Since heat-
sensitive materials are introduced inside the cathode-ray tube,
the maximum sealing temperature does not exceed 450°C, whereas the softening temperature of the glass is 385°C. The compositions of these glasses are as follows: 75-82 PbO, 6.5-12 B$_2$O$_3$,
7-14 ZnO, 1.5-3 SiO$_2$, and 0-3 Al$_2$O$_3$. The total concentration of
these basic components should not be less than 95%. Instead of
PbO and ZnO, one may introduce up to 5% CdO or Fe$_2$O$_3$, which do
not raise the given softening temperature of the glass. In order
to increase the strength of the soldered junction and the adhesiveness, one may add up to 4% BaO and up to 1% Li$_2$O or Na$_2$O. It is
permissible to add up to 1% Sb$_2$O$_3$, As$_2$O$_3$, and CoO. Typical compositions of solder glasses in the PbO−ZnO−B$_2$O$_3$−SiO$_2$ system
with α = 80-105 · 10^{-7} are given with their softening temperatures
T$_s$ in Table 46, based on data from [382]. At a content above 12%
B$_2$O$_3$ and 3% SiO$_2$, the glasses crystallize slowly and incompletely.
Glasses containing less than 6.5% B$_2$O$_3$ or more than 14% ZnO crystallize very rapidly and do not produce good soldered junctions.
Glasses containing less than 6.5% B$_2$O$_3$, more than 3% SiO$_2$, and
less than 75% PbO have very high softening temperatures.

Table 46. Compositions of Solder Glasses and Their Softening Temperatures

Component	Contents (in wt.%) of various compositions							
	1	2	3	4	5	6	7	8
PbO	77.5	75.5	76	76	77.5	75	75	76.5
ZnO	10	11	11	11	10	10	10	11
B$_2$O$_3$	7.5	9	9	9	10	9	9	9
SiO$_2$	2.5	2	2	2.5	2.5	2.5	2.5	2.5
Al$_2$O$_3$	2.5	0.5	—	1	—	1	1	1
BaO	—	2	2	—	—	—	—	—
Na$_2$O	—	—	—	0.3	—	—	—	—
Li$_2$O	—	—	—	0.2	—	—	—	—
CdO	—	—	—	—	—	—	2.5	—
Fe$_2$O$_3$	—	—	—	—	—	2.5	—	—
T$_s$, °C	372	370	366	370	366	382	379	374

Table 47. Composition of Vitrokeram Elements

Component	Contents (in wt.%) of various compositions						
	1	2	3	4	5	6	7
PbO	77.5	77.5	80	77.5	71.5	75	74.5
ZnO	10	10	10	10	10	10	10
B$_2$O$_3$	7.5	9	6.5	8.5	7.5	10	8
Al$_2$O$_3$	2.5	1	1	2.5	3.5	2	1
SiO$_2$	2.5	2.5	2.5	1.5	2.5	3	1
CuO	—	—	—	—	—	—	5
Sb$_2$O$_3$	—	—	—	—	—	—	0.5

The presence of PbO in amounts greater than 82% increases the expansion coefficient of the crystallized glass, roughly corresponding to materials with $\alpha \approx 105 \cdot 10^{-7}$ (°C)$^{-1}$.

One may add up to 3% Al$_2$O$_3$, which serves as an inhibitor of crystallization during the formation of the soldered junction and increases the chemical stability of glass; the amount of Al$_2$O$_3$ present is decreased with increasing ZnO content. Crystals containing PbO and B_2O_3 enter into the composition of the crystalline phase, as do lead borates; ZnO goes over into the remaining glassy phase, which, at a ZnO content below 7%, is not very refractory at all, thereby decreasing the strength and the thermal stability of the soldered junction.

Analogous glasses having in their composition not more than 4% BaO and 0-0.5% Na_2O and Li_2O also have a softening temperature not higher than 385°C and, at 450°C, form a glass-crystalline soldered junction within 1 h [383].

Table 47, which is based on data from [384], presents the compositions of glasses crystallizing in the $PbO-ZnO-B_2O_3-SiO_2$ system (called vitrokeram elements by the author) for soldering with materials whose α range is $80-120 \cdot 10^{-7}$ (°C)$^{-1}$. As crystallization catalysts, one may add small amounts of Au or Ag to these glasses.

It is recommended that the melting of these chemically active glasses be performed under strictly controlled conditions with respect to time and temperature, in a platinum crucible placed in a furnace heated to 1050°C and held at that temperature for 10 min, whereupon the melt is rapidly cooled by being poured onto a steel plate so as to prevent crystallization. The glass frit obtained is ground and sieved.

Martin [385, 386] developed solder glasses which slowly crystallize at 700°C and above for soldering materials whose α is approximately $30-50 \cdot 10^{-7}$ (°C)$^{-1}$, such as borosilicate and aluminosilicate glasses, glass-ceramics with average α values, zircon, electrical porcelain, molybdenum, and tungsten. These glasses contain 60-70 ZnO, 19-25 B_2O_3, and 10-16 SiO_2. The total concentration of these three components is not less than 90%. One may add PbO, As_2O_3, Sb_2O_3, and fining agents. Glasses containing more than 70% ZnO possess very good flow and crystallizability properties. At a content of less than 65% ZnO, these glasses are very sensitive to moisture, which enhances their crystallization, resulting in a coarse-grained and friable structure. An excess or a deficiency of B_2O_3 and SiO_2 relative to the ranges indicated also results in too rapid a crystallization of the glass. Typical compositions of the glasses in the $ZnO-B_2O_3-SiO_2$ system arc shown in Table 48, based on data from [385, 386].

Table 48. Compositions of Slowly Crystallizing Solder Glasses
with $\alpha \approx 30\text{-}50 \cdot 10^{-7}$ (°C)$^{-1}$

Component	Contents (in wt.%) of various compositions						
	1	2	3	4	5	6	7
ZnO	65	65	65	65	62.5	60	60
B$_2$O$_3$	22.5	20	25	23	22.5	22.5	22.5
SiO$_2$	12.5	15	10	10	12.5	12.5	12.5
Al$_2$O$_3$	—	—	—	2	—	—	—
MgO	—	—	—	—	2.5	—	—
BaO	—	—	—	—	—	5	—
PbO	—	—	—	—	—	—	5

These glasses are melted at 1300°C until a uniform melt is obtained, which is then poured on a metallic plate or into water so as to prevent crystallization, with the latter capable of disintegrating the glass. In order to improve its chemical durability, it is desirable to add up to 2% Al$_2$O$_3$ to the glass. The primary crystalline phases precipitating are ZnO · B$_2$O$_3$, 5ZnO · 2B$_2$O$_3$, and willemite, 2ZnO · SiO$_2$, the α range of which is $25\text{-}35 \cdot 10^{-7}$ (°C)$^{-1}$. The α values of the crystalline cement are less than that of the original glass. For instance, glass of composition No. 1 has $\alpha = 42 \cdot 10^{-7}$ (°C)$^{-1}$ within the temperature region 0-300°C, whereas glasses obtained by sintering the glass powder for 1 h at 700 and 750°C have $\alpha = 36 \cdot 10^{-7}$ and $24 \cdot 10^{-7}$ (°C)$^{-1}$, respectively [385, 386]. Thus, increasing the crystallization temperature decreases the α of the glass-ceramic. At temperatures higher than 300°C, the α of all these glass-ceramics approaches the α of borosilicate glass, which is equal to $33 \cdot 10^{-7}$ (°C)$^{-1}$.

Low-melting crystallizing glasses of the composition 71-180 PbO, 6-11 B$_2$O$_3$, and 9-15 ZnO produced well-crystallized seals or soldered junctions with metal, ceramic, or glass when approximately 1% Pd, Pt, Rh, Au, V$_2$O$_5$, Al$_2$O$_3$, TiO$_2$, SnO$_2$, ZrSiO$_4$, AgCl + SnO$_2$, or CaF$_2$ + NaF was added to them [387]. The thickness of the half-crystallized glass at the soldered junction was approximately 0.2 mm, and the residual stresses in the soldered junction reached 0.15 kg/mm^2.

Pirooz proposed several series of crystallizing solder glasses making it possible to join various materials by soldering at relatively high temperatures. Glass of the composition 11-29 PbO, 18-32 B_2O_3, 34-46 ZnO, 7-14 SiO_2, and 8-16 CuO had a softening temperature less than 600°C and an α range within the temperature range 0-425° of approximately 45-65 · 10^{-7} [388]. Glass with the composition 16-18 PbO, 12-15 B_2O_3, 48-52 ZnO, and 18-20 SiO_2 was designated to be used for joining by soldering with materials whose $\alpha \approx 50 \cdot 10^{-7}$ [389]. The liquidus temperature of this glass is 1093°C, and the softening temperature is between 600 and 700°C. Crystallization of this glass was performed at 675-750°C during 1 h. For joining materials whose α is approximately 35-50 · 10^{-7} (°C)$^{-1}$, glass is used whose composition is 5 PbO, 17-19 B_2O_3, 59-61 ZnO, 14-16 SiO_2, and 2-3 CuO [390]. Its liquidus temperature is equal to 1038°C, and its softening point ranges between 600 and 700°C. A time of 1 h is needed for crystallization at 675-750°C.

Solder glasses for joining small parts made of glass, ceramics, or metals have the composition 73 PbO, 24 B_2O_3, and 3 V_2O_5 are characterized by the absence of porosity and a high dielectric strength of the soldered junction [391]. The glasses are applied to the junction by multiple immersion into the melt of preheated small parts until a glass layer 3 mm thick is reached, after which the joined parts are placed into a furnace, where they are first heated to 450 and then to 525°C, being held at each of these temperatures for 1 h. This is followed by cooling at a rate of 10 deg/min to a temperature below 300°C. Solder glass of the composition 75-95 PbO, 6.5-12 B_2O_3, 7-14 ZnO, 1.5-3 SiO_2, and 0-3 Al_2O_3 has the same softening temperature as given previously [382] — namely, not higher than 385°, has a crystallization temperature of 450°, and is capable of being soldered well with materials whose α values are within the range 80-105 · 10^{-7} [393]. A crystallizing solder glass with fluorine additions was proposed by Sack [394] and has the following composition: 64.0-69.0 SiO_2, 18.0-20.0 B_2O_3, 0.8-1.8 Al_2O_3, 0.4-0.8 Na_2O, 7.0-9.5 K_2O, 1.0-4.0 BaO, 0.2-1.5 F, and 0.5-2.0 KCl.

Electrically conducting crystallizing glass for joining by soldering the cone and the screen of a cathode-ray tube envelope was obtained by adding powdered Ag (4.5-6%) or 5-7% Ag_2O to glass of the following composition: 75-82 PbO, 7-14 ZnO, 6.5-12.0

B$_2$O$_3$, 1.5-3 Na$_2$O, and 0.3 Al$_2$O$_3$ [392]. During the process of soldering together small parts at 450-475°C in a gas furnace, the silver
oxide becomes reduced to the metal which, in turn, provides the
conductivity and the safe electrical contact between the aluminum
film on the screen and the Aquadag on the cone.

Cement No. 95, which was developed by Corning Glass Works
[395, 396] for joining soft glasses and metals with $\alpha \approx 80\text{-}90 \cdot 10^{-7}$
(°C)$^{-1}$ has the following composition: 77.5 PbO, 9.0 B$_2$O$_3$, 10.0 ZnO,
2.5 SiO$_2$, and 1.0 Al$_2$O$_3$. It is prepared in the form of a powder suspension of the glass in a solution of nitrocellulose in amyl acetate,
and is applied to the portions to be joined by a small brush, by
spraying, or by immersion. The weight ratio between the glass
and the solvent in the suspension applied by a hand-operated tube
is equal to 12:1, whereas a more liquid suspension is needed for
application by twofold immersion. The glass powder, the solvent,
and the prepared suspension must be preserved under hermetic
conditions. Prior to the application of the emulsion, the surface
to be joined is degreased and purified of any contaminants. The
first immersion results in a thin coating layer which, because of
the partial drying, collects a considerable amount of the suspension during the second immersion, which, in turn, results in the
formation of beading. The drying prior to heat treatment may be
done in air over a period of several hours or in a special desic-
cator at 115°C for 15-30 min.

In order to prevent deformation and to produce a partially
crystallized, hard, and strong junction, the crude frit is generally
heated to the soldering temperature at a rate of 10-15 deg/min. At
rates of less than 2 deg/min, crystallization of the solder is possible before the soldered junction is formed. Glass "47572" is
held at 440° for 60 min, at 425°C from 90-120 min, and at 455°C
for 30 min. Glass "95" is heated at 440°C for 1 h and then at
470°C for 0.5 h. In order to produce a seal or soldered junction
from cement "45," the glass must be held at 750°C for 60 min and
then at 760°C for 30 min. The rate of cooling depends on the size,
shape, and differences in the α values of the soldered parts. Usually, this rate is 3-15 deg/min.

A typical temperature procedure for soldering or sealing
with Vitrokeram-cement the small parts of cathode-ray tubes [384]
consists in heating to 285°C and holding there for 15 min for the

purpose of burning out the binder, then increasing the temperature to 385°C and holding there for 30 min for the purpose of softening the glass and subsequently increasing the temperature to 450°C and holding there for 30 min for the purpose of crystallization, which starts at temperatures above 390°C.

When installing Pyroceram "9606" envelopes in a vacuum apparatus which is operating at the high temperatures of the surrounding medium, glass "7574" is applied in the form of a 0.5-mm-thick paste over the couplings of the small sealed parts [397]. Portions of the tungsten conductors which are to be sealed are first glazed by heating at 620°C in air, whereupon they are soldered together in a nitrogen atmosphere at 720°C for 1 h. The heating and the cooling rate is 3 deg/min. To protect the tungsten portions of the conductor from oxidation, they are coated electrolytically with a layer of gold 0.0025-0.009 mm thick.

The parts which had been sealed with crystallized glass may be separated by immersing them in a 10% solution of HNO_3 at 50-60°C. One may etch a hollow into the seal or soldered junction made of the crystallized glass and then, by means of thermal shock, create stresses in it to break the seal [398, 399]. Another method of creating rupture stresses in the seal is to heat it to a temperature 50° higher than the soldering temperature. Then a pressure of 1.4-4.2 kg/cm^2 is created in the hollow glass article, depending on the size of the seal [400, 401].

One must observe certain safety precautions when working with a hot or an extremely volatile solvent, such as the suspension of nitrocellulose in amyl acetate or that of collodion in butyl acetate, or when working with glasses with a high lead content.

5. HIGH-SILICA GLASS-CERAMICS IN THE $SiO_2 - Na_2O - K_2O$ SYSTEM WITH FLUORINE ADDITIONS, CHARACTERIZED BY A HIGH LINEAR THERMAL EXPANSION COEFFICIENT

Stookey [402-404] synthesized glass-ceramics with an α range of $175-300 \cdot 10^{-7}$ (°C)$^{-1}$ by using high-silica glasses, and found that these glass-ceramics are very compatible with such metals and alloys as copper, brass, and aluminum. Articles made of these glass-ceramics have a glassy surface layer with a significantly lower α than is the case for inner layers, which causes the

Table 49. Compositions of High-Silica Glasses for
Glass-Ceramics with $\alpha \approx 175\text{-}300 \cdot 10^{-7}$ $(°C)^{-1}$

Component	Contents (in wt.%) of various compositions					
	1	2	3	4	5	6
SiO_2	86.5	85.5	87	89.5	92.5	87
Na_2O	9.5	7.5	11	8.5	7.5	8
Al_2O_3	4.0	7.0	2	2.0	—	2
$CaO \cdot MgO$	—	—	—	—	—	3
F	2.8	4.3	3.6	3.6	—	—

Component	Contents (in wt %) of various compositions						
	7	8	9	10	11	12	13
SiO_2	85.5	87.5	89.5	85.5	87.5	89.5	86.5
Na_2O	14.5	12.5	10.5	14.5	12.5	10.5	—
K_2O	—	—	—	—	—	—	13.5
F	—	—	—	3.5	3.5	3.5	3.5

emergence of compressive stresses and a high mechanical strength.
They may be used for the fabrication of dinnerware, since they are
not scratched by silverware.

These glasses contain 85-92 SiO_2, 6.5-15 Na_2O or K_2O, 0-8
Al_2O_3, and 0-5 F. The total SiO_2, Na_2O, and K_2O content should not
be less than 92%. The crystallization of these glasses does not depend on the presence of fluorine, since the NaF and KF crystals
which appear in these glasses at temperatures below 900°C form
an additional phase which does not speed up crystallization. Fluorine speeds up only the melting, and makes it possible to form on
the surface of the product a glazing with decreased α due to the diffusion of the previously forming sodium or potassium fluorides in
the glassy phase at a temperature above 900°C. Typical compositions of these glasses are shown in Table 49, based on data from
[402-404].

The melting of the glasses made from the batch to which
small amounts of the fining agent As_2O_3 and the oxidizer $NaNO_3$ or
KNO_3 were added is performed at 1400°C for 4 h in pots or in a
tank furnace.

Table 50. Properties and Heat-Treatment Procedure for High-Silica Glasses and for Glass-Ceramics Prepared from Them

Comp. No.	Properties of glasses		Heat treatment				Properties of glass-ceramics			Crystalline phase
			stage 1		stage 2					
	$\alpha \cdot 10^7$ 1/°C	Density g/cm³	Temp. heated to, °C	Time at temp., h	Temp. heated to, °C	Time at temp., h	$\alpha \cdot 10^7$ 1/°C	Density, g/cm³	σ_f kg/cm²	
1	50	—	720	1	820	1	—	—	1530	Tridymite
			950	2	1150	5	—			
			820	1	950	—				
2	—	—	1150	5	—	—	—	—	2210	
3	56	—	720	2	975	4	236	—	1270	
3	56	—	720	2	840	5	306	—	730	
4	37	2.269	680	8	—	—	>316	2.349	820	Cristobalite
4	37	2.269	720	0,5	—	—	>316	2.347	790	
4	37	2.269	720	2	—	—	>316	2.347	750	
4	37	2.269	720	2	890	1	>316	2.340	1240	
4	37	2.269	720	2	975	4	267	—	1400	
5	41	—	720	3	900	10	261	2.312	—	Tridymite
6	48	2.297	960	2	1150	4	218	2.322	880	
7	76	2.344	720	2	900	8	177	2.367	700	
8	66	2.323	720	2	900	8	191	2.352	710	
9	56	2.308	720	2	900	8	209	2.347	795	
10	66	2.319	720	2	900	8	218	2.334	1600	
11	58	2.312	720	2	900	8	223	2.326	1420	
12	—	—	720	2	900	8	224	2.299	995	
13	43	2.282	720	2	900	8	224	2.294	1035	

An excess of SiO_2 or a deficiency of R_2O makes melting more difficult, due to the higher viscosity of the glass. A deficiency in SiO_2, an excess of R_2O, or a content of more than 8% Al_2O_3 prevents crystallization of glass during heat treatment. The presence of Al_2O_3 in amounts of 1.5-8% increases the chemical stability of the glass and the glass-ceramic.

For the sitallization of the glass article, the latter is heated within the temperature range 650-1250°C for such a time that α does not exceed $175 \cdot 10^{-7}$ (°C)$^{-1}$. If the temperature of the long-term heat treatment does not exceed 900°C, tridymite is the primary crystalline phase, and the α range for the glass-ceramic will be 175-280 · 10^{-7}. If this temperature is above 900°C, then the primary crystalline phase will be cristobalite, and the α of the glass-ceramic will be above 300 · 10^{-7}. Table 50, which is based on data from [402-404], gives the heat-treatment procedure, the α values in the temperature region 0-300°, and the strength characteristics of the glasses of the compositions listed in Table 49, and the properties of the glass-ceramics prepared from these glasses.

The high α values of the glass-ceramic obtained by the crystallization of the glass at a temperature below 900°C can partially be explained by the transformations of cristobalite near 200-275°C or of tridymite near 117-163°C, which are accompanied by a sharp decrease in density. Silicate articles containing large amounts of coarsely crystalline cristobalite or tridymite may break as a result of such transformations, whereas the glass-ceramics discussed here are characterized by a very fine, uniform crystalline structure and are stable with respect to these transformations.

6. GLASS-CERAMICS WITH A HIGH Nb_2O_5 CONTENT, CHARACTERIZED BY A HIGH DIELECTRIC PERMEABILITY. GLASS-CERAMICS BASED ON NONSILICATE GLASSES

Based on glasses with a high Nb_2O_5 content, glass-ceramics were obtained containing as crystalline phases such ferroelectric compounds as niobates of Na, K, Cd, Ba, and Pb. Precipitation of other ferroelectric compounds is also possible, such as: titanates of Ba or Cd, cadmium zirconates, ferrites of Pb or La, iron germanates, and others. These glass-ceramics show hysteresis effects, such as are characteristic of ferroelectrics [364].

Table 51, which is based on data from [405], shows the compositions and the melting points of these glasses, their dielectric constants, the tan δ values, and the primary crystalline phases present in the glass-ceramics prepared. Composition No. 2 has an annealing temperature of 600°C and an optimum heat-treatment temperature of 905°C. Precipitation of the ferroelectric crystalline phase begins at 690°C, and the remelting at 1170°C. The duration of heat treatment at 905°C is 2 h.

Table 51. Compositions of Niobium-Containing Glasses, Their Melting Points, and Dielectric Properties, and the Phase Compositions of the Glass-Ceramics Obtained

Component	Contents (in cation-mol.%) of various compositions				
	1	2	3	4	5
$NbO_{2.5}$	42.7	45.0	40.3	41.3	45.8
$NaO_{0.5}$	28.3	29.7	27.0	27.7	14.9
CdO	7.1	7.4	6.8	6.9	7.2
BaO	—	—	7.3	—	—
TiO_2	—	—	—	6.6	—
$KO_{0.5}$	—	—	—	—	13.7
SiO_2	21.9	17.9	18.6	17.5	18.4

Temperature of the first melting of the crystalline phase, °C

	1000	1000	1000	925	925

Dielectric properties of the glass-ceramics

ε	375	590	520	990	308
$\tan\delta$, %	2.4	2.1	1.6	1.5	2.6

Crystalline phases with a high ε

	(1); (2); (6)	(1): (2); (6)	(1); (2); (4); (6); (7)	(1); (2); (5); (6)	(1); (3); (2); (6)

Component	Contents (in cation-mol.%) of various compositions			
	6	7	8	9
$NbO_{2.5}$	42.6	43.8	40.5	29.8
$NaO_{0.5}$	28.2	26.6	29.6	33.8
CdO	7.0	7.1	9.8	7.2
$TaO_{2.5}$	3.5	—	—	—
ZrO_2	—	4.5	—	—
WO_3	—	—	2.0	12.7
SiO_2	18.7	18.3	18.1	16.5
$BO_{1.5}$	—	—	—	—
$PO_{2.5}$	—	—	—	—

Temperature of the first melting of the crystalline phases, °C

	1000	1000	850	775

Table 51 (continued)

Component	Contents (in cation-mol.%) of various compositions			
	6	7	8	9
	Dielectric properties of the glass-ceramics			
ε	1138	520	645	90
$\tan\delta$, %	2.2	1.5	2.3	1.1
	Crystalline phases with a high ε			
	(1); (2); (9); (11)	(1); (2); (10)	(1); (2); (8)	(1); (2); (8)

Component	Contents (in cation-mol.%) of various compositions				
	10	11	12	13	14
$NbO_{2.5}$	—	34.0	45.1	39.1	18.3
CdO	10.5	—	—	—	—
ZrO_2	30.0	—	—	—	—
$NaO_{0.5}$	—	—	22.6	—	—
BaO	10.3	11.1	—	19.4	—
PbO	23.8	12.5	11.3	10.2	36.2
SrO	—	10.5	—	8.8	—
$FeO_{1.5}$	—	—	—	—	18.3
$AlO_{1.5}$	5.2	16.2	—	2.3	—
$BO_{1.5}$	—	—	—	11.6	—
SiO_2	20.2	15.7	21.0	17.1	27.2
F_2	1.1	2.0	—	—	—
	Temperature of the first melting of the crystalline phases, °C				
	925	1000	1075	1000	800
	Dielectric properties of the glass-ceramics				
ε	161	148	214	1200	182
$\tan\delta$, %	1.0	0.1	1.4	3.7	3.0
	Crystalline phases with a high ε				
	(12); (14); (10)	(4); (15); (13); (18); (19)	(1); (13); (19)	(4); (15); (13); (7); (18); (19)	(13); (16); (17); (19); (20)

Remarks:

(1)—$NaNbO_3$ (6)—$CdNbO_{3.5}$ (11)—$Cd_{0.5}TaO_3$ (16)—$Pb_2NbF_2O_6$
(2)—$Cd_{0.5}NbO_3$ (7)—$BaNbO_{3.5}$ (12)—$BaZrO_3$ (17)—$Pb_2Nb_2O_7$
(3)—$KNbO_3$ (8)—WO_3 (13)—$Pb_{0.5}NbO_3$ (18)—$SrNbO_{3.5}$
(4)—$Ba_{0.5}NbO_3$ (9)—$NaTaO_3$ (14)—$PbZrO_3$ (19)—$PbNbO_{3.5}$
(5)—$CdTiO_3$ (10)—$CdZrO_3$ (15)—$SrNbO_{3.5}$ (20)—Fe_2O_3

The content of oxides of the elements capable of forming ferroelectric compounds must not be more than 90%. Glass-ceramics containing less than 39.4 cation-mol.% of these oxides have relatively low ε values. A small residual glassy phase is necessary for maintaining sufficient mechanical strength of these glass-ceramics. All of these glass-ceramics are characterized by an unusually high electrical resistivity, attaining 10^{11} Ω-cm at 400°C, and a high electrical strength, approximately $4 \cdot 10^5$ V/cm for direct current and $2 \cdot 10^5$ V/cm for alternating current.

Anderson and Friedberg [406] studied the crystallization of glass of the composition (in mol.%) 20 PbO, 20 Nb_2O_5, and 60 SiO_2, with the addition of 15% Al_2O_3 over the 100%, for the sake of precipitating the ferroelectric lead metaniobate compound $PbNb_2O_6$ and preparing glass-ceramics having high ε values intended for use in condensers. When the glass melt was cooled from 1250°C at a rate ranging from 60 to 5 deg/h, rhombohedral and orthorhombic $PbNb_2O_6$ crystals, as well as one or more of secondary phases, precipitated. Heat treatment of this glass at 1000°C for 1 h resulted in the crystallization of 46% of the rhombohedral $PbNb_2O_6$. The highest value of ε = 83.6 (at room temperature) corresponded to the maximum content (56%) of the orthorhombic $PbNb_2O_6$ in the sample, which was obtained by cooling the melt from 1250°C at a rate of 45 deg/h. On curves of the temperature dependence of ε and of the dissipation coefficient of the glass-ceramic, peaks were observed at 480 and 500°C, at which ε attained a value of 161.3.

Glass-ceramics are known in which the Nb_3O_5, GeO_2, and Ta_2O_5 content ranges from 0.1-5% [407] to 25-70% [408, 713, 714].

Glass-ceramics can also be prepared from nonsilicate glasses containing GeO_2, B_2O_3, and P_2O_5 as the primary glass-formers (compositions Nos. 1-4 of Table 52). Glasses containing SiO_2, Al_2O_3, and TiO_2 and not containing one of the metallic oxides (compositions Nos. 5-6) are characterized by a high hardness, but also have a high melting temperature — namely, 1680° and above [320, 321].

Table 52. Compositions of Crystallizing Nonsilicate Glasses
and of Glasses with a High Melting Temperature

Component	Contents (in wt.%) of various compositions					
	1	2	3	4	5	6
GeO_2	61.9	—	—	—	—	—
B_2O_3	—	33.9	—	—	—	—
P_2O_5	—	—	62.5	62.4	—	—
SiO_2	—	—	—	—	75	65
Al_2O_3	9.5	6.8	13.4	14.9	10	17
TiO_2	4.8	8.5	10.7	9.1	15	18
ZnO	23.8	50.8	13.4	—	—	—
CdO	—	—	—	13.6	—	—
Crystallization temp., °C	1100	1200	1150	1050	1450	1450
Time at temperature, h	2	1	1	1	1	1

7. GLASS-CERAMICS CLOSE IN COMPOSITION TO SYNTHETIC MICAS (MICA GLASS-CERAMICS). ROMANIAN PORCELAIN MADE FROM GLASS

The Romanian scientists Lungu and Popescu-Has [17, 51, 52, 301, 409-412] synthesized glass-ceramics with a fine-crystalline, porcelainlike structure, by crystallizing fluorine-containing glasses at a high viscosity, of the order of 10^{10}-10^{13} poise, and by precipitating only one silicate type. These authors explain the catalytic action of fluorine by the closeness in the crystal lattice constants between the fluorides and the silicates precipitating on them — in particular, by the equality between the ionic radii of O^{2-} and F^-. The transparent and homogeneous glass obtained by the usual rate of cooling from the melt was transformed upon heating into a homogeneous crystalline mass, the degree of crystallization of which depended on the composition and the temperature of heat treatment. "Porcelain" made from glass was obtained in the following most simple glass-forming systems: SiO_2—MgO—Na_2O; SiO_2—MgO—K_2O; SiO_2—MgO—Al_2O_3—Na_2O; SiO_2—MgO—Al_2O_3—K_2O; SiO_2—MgO—Al_2O_3—CaO. The size of the crystals measured 5 μ

on the average; in glass bodies with a higher fluorine content, it was less than 1 μ, and in glass bodies with a low fluorine content, it measured up to 20 μ. X-ray analysis showed that there is a similarity between the structures of the crystals formed and the structure of the mica of the phlogopite type: (Na, K, Ca, . . .) · (Mg, Al, Fe, . . .)$_{23}$[(Al, Si)$_4$(O$_{10}$, F$_2$)]. Allowing for the possible substitution of the F$^-$ ions by the O^{2-} ions in the composition of the crystal, these authors assume that crystallization takes place during the appearance of temporary formations of fluoride or oxyfluoride crystals with a hexagonal lattice, out of which the subsequent development of crystals with a lower fluorine content takes place. The composition of the final crystals formed depends on the number of preliminary crystals dissolving. Under the microscope, only one type of crystal has been observed.

The degree of crystallization as dependent on composition has been determined from the changes in the density and in α. In glasses of the SiO$_2$—Al$_2$O$_3$—MgO—Na$_2$O system, it depended on the total content of Al$_2$O$_3$ + MgO. The composition of the crystals formed lay within the limits NaAl$_2$ · [AlSi$_3$O$_{10}$/F$_2$] and KNaMg$_3$ · [AlSi$_3$O$_{10}$/F$_2$]. Gradual substitution of MgO by Al$_2$O$_3$ lead to an increase in α and in the volume of the crystallized bodies. When held at constant crystallization temperature, the viscosity of the bodies and the resistance to deformation under constant load increased, which made it possible, in turn, to increase the crystallization temperature without lowering the viscosity and without deformation. The σ_f of porcelain made from glass was 2000 kg/cm^2, and the impact strength was 8 kg-cm/cm^2.

The same authors [413] obtained porcelain from glasses of a complex composition in which part of the oxygen was replaced by fluorine, with the molar ratio (SiO$_2$ + Al$_2$O$_3$) : (MgO + CaO + BaO + ZnO + PbO + Na$_2$O + K$_2$O) lying between 1.5 and 4, and the atomic ratio O : F lying between 5 and 15. Fluorine is introduced in the form of fluorides, which, in amounts of 8-20 wt.%, replace the corresponding oxides. The oxide-based batch has the following composition: 70-85 (SiO$_2$ + Al$_2$O$_3$), 10-25 (MgO + CaO + BaO + ZnO + PbO), 0-10 (Na$_2$O + K$_2$O), and 3-8F$_2$. The melting temperature for these glasses in batch-operated furnaces ranges from 1300 to 1500°C, and increases with increasing Al$_2$O$_3$ content. The articles are formed by casting, pressing, blowing, or rolling. The temperature of heat treatment lies between 600 and 1000°C. The crystalline phase present is represented primarily by one silicate type surrounded by the glassy phase. These glass-ceramics are suitable for the production of electrical insulators [414], structural materials, and kitchenware.

Glass-ceramics are known in which fluorine-phlogopite and fluorine aluminosilicates of the alkali metals are present as the primary crystalline phases [415].

Moriya et al. [416] synthesized thermally stable glass-ceramics whose composition they consider to be a mixture of mica — $Li_{1/3}$, $Na_{2/3}$, Mg_3, $(SiAlO_{10})F_2$ — and spodumene. The glass was heated to a temperature slightly higher than the temperature of the exothermal peak on the differential-thermal-analysis curve and held there for 2 h; for the sake of stabilizing the microcrystals formed, the glass was heated again to 950°C for 1 h, and then to 1000°C for 2 h.

An unstable glass with poor forming properties was obtained from the mixture corresponding to pure mica. The glass-ceramic with a uniform fine-crystalline structure had a composition corresponding to 75 mol.% mica and 25 mol.% spodumene. The crystalline phases present were β-spodumene and mica. With increasing mica content, the crystallization of β-spodumene was facilitated.

By analogous heat treatment of a glass melted at 1500°C from a mixture of 5–90 mol.% mica [$(Na, K)Mg_3(Si_3AlO_{10})]F$ with 95–10 mol.% lithium aluminosilicate glass it was possible to obtain a dense and refractory glass-ceramic with good fabricating properties, with β-spodumene and mica crystals of several microns, and with a range of α values of 10–$60 \cdot 10^{-7}$ $(°C)^{-1}$ [417].

By investigating the crystallization of glasses close in composition to synthetic phlogopite mica, it was determined that it is possible to obtain a uniform crystalline structure without employing crystallization catalysts. The crystallization process was done in two stages and was accompanied by the formation of an intermediate unstable pseudocrystalline phase, from which phlogopite crystals were subsequently grown, appearing first at the interphase boundary between this phase and glass, and then throughout the bulk of the pseudocrystalline phase. Mica crystals were never formed from the original glassy phase [418].

Glass-ceramics of a micalike structure based on the synthetic potassium fluorine-phlogopite were prepared by Tresvyatskii, Parkhomenko, and co-workers [718-721], who demonstrated the possibility of isomorphous homovalent and heterovalent substitution of the interlayer potassium ion in phlogopite-type micas by other ions of alkali and alkali-earth metals, and who worked out the processing technology for easily formed cast and sintered mica glass-ceramics. They show the advantages of using ceramics technology for the preparation of mica glass-ceramics from powdery mica glass by pressing the billets and subsequently sintering the articles, the microstructure of which contain no glassy phase and no graphite impurities; in addition, the grain size of the mica crystals is 10-15 μ, as compared to 500-800 μ for cast mica crystalline materials. Of considerable interest is the possibility of controlling the properties of mica glass-ceramics by changing the composition due to the formation of solid solutions during the melting of micas both of the homovalent and the heterovalent type.

Glass-ceramics with a mica crystalline phase were synthesized from natural raw materials, such as from kaolin and hydromicas [722], as well as by the crystallization of a finely ground mixture of lead borate glass with mica of the fluorine-phlogopite or taeniolite type [750].

8. GLASS-CERAMICS IN THE $Na_2O - Al_2O_3 - SiO_2$
    SYSTEM WITH $\alpha \approx 60-120 \cdot 10^{-7}$ $(^\circ C)^{-1}$.
    GLASS-CERAMICS BASED ON ROCKS

Corning Glass Works [420, 421] developed glass-ceramics in the $Na_2O - Al_2O_3 - SiO_2$ system in which nepheline ($Na_2O \cdot Al_2O_3 \cdot 2SiO_2$) is the primary crystalline phase, whereas, if a small amount of CaO is added, plagioclase (a solid solution of albite $- Na_2O \cdot Al_2O_3 \cdot 6SiO_2 -$ and anorthite $- CaO \cdot Al_2O_3 \cdot 2SiO_2$) is the primary crystalline phase. These glass-ceramics have a relatively high mechanical strength and α values of approximately $60-120 \cdot 10^{-7}$. The glasses have the following composition (in mol.%): 50-68 SiO_2, 16-34 Al_2O_3, 7-34 Na_2O, 0-23 CaO, and 0-16 K_2O. The total amount of Na_2O, CaO, and K_2O is 23-24 mol.%, with the molar ratio $(Na_2O + CaO + K_2O) : Al_2O_3$ not exceeding 1.7. It is permissible to add up to 10% B_2O_3, P_2O_5, PbO, BaO, or other oxides not having a significant effect on the fundamental properties of the glass and the glass-ceramic.

Table 53. Compositions of Glasses in the Nepheline—Plagioclase System

Component	Contents (in mol.%) of various compositions								
	1	2	3	4	5	6	7	8	9
SiO_2	61.7	51.8	54.1	51.8	58.7	63.1	57.4	51.8	59.7
Na_2O	21.8	27.9	17.5	23.9	17.1	16.6	21.3	23.9	20.0
Al_2O_3	16.5	20.3	28.4	24.3	24.2	20.3	21.3	24.3	20.3
CdO	3.9	4.0	4.2	—	—	—	—	—	—
TiO_2	8.4	8.6	9.0	7.9	7.9	7.8	7.8	—	—
Cr_2O_3	—	—	—	—	—	—	—	0.11	0.11

Component	Contents (in mol.%) of various compositions								
	10	11	12	13	14	15	16	17	18
SiO_2	64.5	57.4	57.4	57.4	57.4	51.8	58.7	64.5	57.4
Na_2O	17.5	21.3	21.3	21.3	21.3	23.9	17.1	17.5	21.3
Al_2O_3	18.0	21.3	21.3	21.3	21.3	24.3	24.2	18.0	21.3
FeO	—	—	—	—	—	3.0	3.0	2.8	1.9
TiO_2	—	—	—	—	—	4.9	4.9	4.7	4.8
Cr_2O_3	0.11	0.009	0.18	0.23	0.46	—	—	—	—

Component	Contents (in mol.%) of various compositions								
	19	20	21	22	23	24	25	26	27
SiO_2	57.4	57.4	57.4	51.8	58.7	64.5	58.7	57.4	57.4
Na_2O	21.3	21.3	21.3	23.9	17.1	17.5	17.1	21.3	21.3
Al_2O_3	21.3	21.3	21.3	24.3	24.2	18.0	24.2	21.3	21.3
FeO	2.9	4.1	4.0	—	—	—	—	—	—
MnO	—	—	—	2.7	2.7	2.6	2.5	2.6	3.5
TiO_2	4.8	4.8	6.1	8.9	8.8	8.5	4.7	8.7	8.7

Table 53 (Continued)

Component	Contents (in mol.%) of various compositions								
	28	29	30	31	32	33	34	35	36
SiO_2	63.1	67.2	63.1	51.8	58.7	64.5	60.2	51.0	51.0
Na_2O	16.6	16.3	16.6	23.9	17.1	17.5	20.9	19.0	30.0
Al_2O_3	20.3	16.5	20.3	23.4	24.2	18.0	18.9	30.0	19.0
NiO	2.3	2.3	6.0	—	—	—	—	—	—
ZnO	—	—	—	4.1	4.1	4.0	4.0	—	—
TiO_2	7.8	7.2	7.8	6.2	6.2	6.0	8.6	4.8	4.7
MgO	—	—	—	—	—	—.	—	4.0	4.0

Component	Contents (in mol.%) of various compositions								
	37	38	39	40	41	42	43	44	45
SiO_2	53.0	55.0	55.0	65.0	68.0	57.4	57.4	63.1	61.0
Na_2O	24.0	15.0	25.0	19.0	16.0	21.3	21.3	16.6	20.2
Al_2O_3	23.0	30.0	20.0	16.0	16.0	21.3	21.3	20.1	18.8
MgO	4.1	4.0	4.0	4.0	4.0	4.0	4.0	5.5	3.3
TiO_2	4.8	4.8	4.7	4.8	4.7	3.9	8.7	7.8	3.0

Component	Contents (in mol.%) of various compositions								
	46	47	48	49	50	51	52	53	54
SiO_2	61.0	61.0	61.0	61.0	61.0	61.0	61.0	61.0	61.0
Na_2O	20.2	20.2	20.2	20.2	20.2	20.2	20.2	20.2	20.2
Al_2O_3	18.8	18.8	18.8	18.8	18.8	18.8	18.8	18.8	18.8
MgO	4.0	4.0	3.3	3.4	4.7	7.0	9.0	7.5	4.5
TiO_2	4.7	6.0	10.0	12.0	4.7	4.7	4.7	3.0	5.4

Component	Contents (in mol.%) of various compositions								
	55	56	57	58	59	60	61	62	63
SiO_2	61.1	61.1	61.1	57.2	62.1	61.9	56.7	61.5	61.5
Na_2O	20.2	20.2	20.2	18.1	17.5	15.3	8.6	8.7	7.6
Al_2O_3	18.8	18.8	18.8	21.2	18.0	18.0	21.0	17.8	17.8

Table 53 (Continued)

Component	Contents (in mol.%) of various compositions								
	55	56	57	58	59	60	61	62	63
CaO	—	—	—	3.5	2.4	4.8	13.7	12.0	13.2
MgO	5.5	7.0	8.0	4.0	3.9	3.9	4.0	3.9	3.9
TiO_2	6.5	8.3	9.5	8.7	8.5	8.5	8.6	8.4	8.4

Component	Contents (in mol.%) of various compositions						
	64	65	66	67	68	69	70
SiO_2	57.9	59.0	58.9	58.9	58.9	57.2	56.8
Na_2O	19.1	13.7	20.7	20.7	20.7	21.2	21.2
K_2O	1.5	5.4	—	—	—	—	—
Al_2O_3	21.5	21.9	20.0	18.3	16.1	21.3	21.3
B_2O_3	—	—	0.4	2.2	4.4	—	—
P_2O_5	—	—	—	—	—	0.3	0.7
MgO	4.0	4.1	4.0	4.0	4.0	4.7	4.7
TiO_2	8.9	8.9	4.7	4.7	4.7	4.0	4.0

Component	Contents (in mol.%) of various compositions					
	71	72	73	74	75	76
SiO_2	60.6	59.3	58.3	55.8	56.3	61.0
Na_2O	20.1	19.7	19.3	15.8	15.9	20.2
K_2O	—	—	2.2	1.4	1.4	—
CaO	—	—	—	5.4	5.5	—
Li_2O	—	—	2.2	—	—	—
NiO	0.6	2.7	—	—	—	—
BaO	—	—	—	0.9	—	—
Al_2O_3	18.7	18.3	18.0	20.7	20.9	18.8
MgO	4.0	4.0	3.9	4.0	7.4	1.0
TiO_2	4.7	4.8	4.7	5.0	4.9	5.0
ZnO	—	—	—	—	—	1.0

Table 54. Heat-Treatment Procedure for Glasses of the
Nepheline−Plagioclase System, and Properties of the
Glass-Ceramics Obtained

Comp. No.	Heat treatment						Properties of glass-ceramics			
	stage 1		stage 2		stage 3					
	Temp., °C	Time at temp., h	Temp., °C	Time at temp., h	Temp., °C	Time at temp., h	$\alpha \cdot 10^7$ 1/°C	Density, g/cm³	σ_f, kg/cm²	Color
1	800	2	900	8	1000	8	—	—	1220	White
2	800	1	950	4	1000	6	—	—	1235	White
3	800	2	900	4	1000	6	—	—	995	White
4	790	3	900	3	1060	3	—	—	—	Green
5	790	3	900	3	1060	3	—	—	—	Blue
6	800	2	1000	8	—	—	109	2.644	970	Blue
7	800	2	1000	8	—	—	—	—	—	Green
8	700	3	800	3	1020	3	—	—	—	Gray
9	700	3	800	3	1020	3	—	—	—	Gray
10	700	3	800	3	1020	3	—	—	—	Gray
11	800	3	900	3	1050	3	—	—	—	Grayish
12	800	3	900	3	1100	3	120	2.523	—	Green
13	800	3	1020	3	—	—	—	—	—	Green
14	700	3	900	3	1035	3	—	—	—	Green
15	815	3	1030	3	—	—	—	—	—	Brown
16	740	3	845	3	1020	3	—	2.681	—	Brown
17	815	3	1030	3	—	—	—	2.592	—	Copper
18	750	1	1060	8	—	—	—	—	760	Olive
19	720	2	900	4	1060	4	—	—	730	Gray
20	720	2	900	4	1060	4	118.5	2.663	—	Brown
21	750	2	850	2	1020	2	—	—	800	Gray
22	800	3	900	3	1015	3	—	—	—	Brown
23	800	3	900	3	1040	3	—	2.709	—	Brown
24	800	3	900	3	1015	3	—	2.627	—	Brown
25	740	3	850	3	1020	3	—	2.669	—	—
26	800	2	900	8	1000	8	—	—	1400	Yellow
27	830	3	1080	12	—	—	—	—	1010	Yellow

Table 54 (Continued)

Comp. No.	Heat treatment						Properties of glass-ceramics			Color
	stage 1		stage 2		stage 3					
	Temp., °C	Time at temp., h	Temp., °C	Time at temp., h	Temp., °C	Time at temp., h	$\alpha \cdot 10^7$ $1/°C$	Density, g/cm^3	σ_f, kg/cm^2	
28	800	2	920	6	1000	12	111	2,625	1220	Green
29	750	1	900	8	—	—	112	2,590	1165	Yellow
30	850	4	1000	8	—	—	—	—	1370	Green
31	740	3	850	3	1020	3	—	—	—	White
32	740	3	850	3	1020	3	—	—	—	.
33	740	3	850	3	1020	3	—	2.643	—	.
34	800	3	900	3	1040	3	—	2.683	—	.
35	800	3	900	3	1000	3	—	—	—	.
36	800	3	900	3	1000	3	—	—	—	.
37	800	3	900	3	1015	3	—	—	—	.
38	800	3	900	3	1000	3	—	—	—	.
39	800	3	900	3	1015	3	—	—	—	.
40	800	3	900	3	1000	3	—	—	—	.
41	800	3	900	3	1000	3	—	—	—	.
42	800	2	900	6	1080	12	—	—	1130	.
43	850	6	1000	8	—	—	120	2,608	1060	.
44	850	6	1000	9	—	—	—	—	935	.
45	800	3	900	3	1050	3	—	—	—	.
46	800	3	900	3	1020	3	118	—	805	.
47	800	3	900	3	1000	3	—	—	680	.
48	800	3	900	3	1000	3	—	—	940	.
49	800	3	900	3	1000	3	—	—	680	.
50	850	3	1030	3	—	—	—	—	—	.
51	850	3	1050	3	—	—	—	—	—	.
52	850	3	1030	3	1030	3	—	—	—	.
53	800	3	900	3	1030	3	—	—	—	.
54	800	3	900	3	1000	3	117	2.614	—	.
55	800	3	900	3	1055	3	—	—	905	.
56	800	3	900	3	1000	3	116	2.643	800	.
57	800	3	900	3	1055	3	—	—	800	.
58	800	1,5	900	3	1055	8	107	2.656	910	.
59	800	1	900	3	1000	6	—	—	650	.

Table 54 (Continued)

Comp. No.	Heat treatment						Properties of glass-ceramics			
	stage 1		stage 2		stage 3		$\alpha \cdot 10^7$ $1/°C$	Density, g/cm^3	σ_f kg/cm^2	Color
	Temp., °C	Time at temp., h	Temp., °C	Time at temp., h	Temp., °C	Time at temp., h				
60	800	1	900	3	1000	6	—	—	—	White
61	830	3	1080	12	—	—	67	2.758	1310	"
62	800	1.5	900	3	1050	8	66	2.718	1310	"
63	800	1.5	900	3	1050	8	—	—	1270	"
64	800	1.5	1100	12	—	—	—	—	1000	"
65	830	3	920	3	1080	12	—	—	695	"
66	800	3	900	3	1000	3	—	—	—	"
67	800	3	900	3	1000	3	—	—	—	"
68	800	3	900	3	1000	3	—	—	—	"
69	1020	2	—	—	—	—	—	—	960	"
70	1020	2	—	—	—	—	—	—	800	"
71	750	2	850	2	1060	2	—	—	800	"
72	750	2	850	2	1060	2	—	—	860	"
73	780	1	1020	2	—	—	—	—	—	"
74	750	4	900	1	1040	3	112	2.697	1160	"
75	780	1	1020	2	—	—	110	2.686	1030	"
76	900	3	900	3	1015	3	—	—	—	"

As crystallization catalysts for these glasses, compounds with the ilmenite-type hexagonal-close-packed structure, rather than TiO_2, have been found to be effective. Among such compounds are included the titanates of Fe, Zn, Mg, Cd, Mn, Co, Ni, and Cr. Generally, one adds 0.08-0.50% Cr_2O_3 and one of the above-mentioned titanates. The amount of TiO_2 present in these titanates is 2.9-12%, that of RO is 1.9-10%. The total content of the titanates should be not less than 6%. Deficiencies of Cr_2O_3, of RO · TiO_2, or of RO and TiO_2 individually result in incomplete crystallization, while excesses of these result in the spontaneous crystallization of the melt while it is being cooled. The compositions of glasses for the preparation of glass-ceramics with a relatively high strength and $\alpha = 60-120 \cdot 10^{-7}$ (°C)$^{-1}$ are presented in Table 53 (based on data from [419-421]), where the amounts of catalysts present are shown above 100%.

These glasses are melted at 1400°C or above for 4 h in crucibles, pots, or tank furnaces in a neutral atmosphere. From 0.6 to 0.8 wt.% As_2O_3 is added to the batch as the fining agent. Excess SiO_2 and Na_2O and a deficiency of Al_2O_3 hinder the crystallization process. A deficiency of SiO_2 and Na_2O or an excess of Al_2O_3 results in spontaneous crystallization of the glass during the cooling of the melt. It is recommended that not more than 5 mol.% CaO at a Na_2O content of not less than 15 mol.% be added. A higher CaO content causes an increase in the size of the crystals during the heat-treatment process. If the Na_2O content is 7-10 mol.%, then the presence of more than 10 mol.% CaO is allowable. An excess of K_2O causes deformation of the articles during crystallization.

The heat-treatment procedure which results in the most complete crystallization consists in heating at a rate of 5 deg/min to 800-850°C, holding for 1-4 h, and then further heating to 1000-1080°C and holding for 6-12 h. One may also make use of other intermediate temperatures, such as 900-950°C, for which the time at temperature is 3-8 h. Table 54 presents the heat-treatment procedure for the glasses of Table 53, as well as the α values between 0 and 300°C, the specific weight, flexure strength σ_f, and the color of the glass-ceramics obtained [419-421].

Depending on the degree of substitution of Na_2O by CaO, the α of the glass-ceramics varies from $120 \cdot 10^{-7}$ to $60 \cdot 10^{-7}$, i.e., with increasing CaO content, α decreases. Glasses consisting primarily of Na_2O, Al_2O_3, and SiO_2 only (compositions Nos. 46, 69, and 70) are especially suitable for the drawing of sheet glass from the melt. Adding greater amounts of CaO makes it possible to obtain glass-ceramics with a low α.

Crystallized materials of the cast-rock type are produced from fused natural rocks, such as from fused basalt. The synthetic batch for the preparation of such materials consists of quartz sand, dolomite, and other materials. The best results are obtained by employing raw material of the following composition: 43.5-47.0 SiO_2, 11.0-13.0 Al_2O_3, 4.0-7.0 Fe_2O_3, 5.0-6.0 FeO, 0.2-0.3 MnO, 2.0-3.9 TiO_2, 10.0-12.0 CaO, 8.0-11.0 MgO, 2.0-3.5 Na_2O, and 1.0-2.0 K_2O [422].

In order to increase the mechanical strength of the sitallized cast rock based on basalt, it is worthwhile to add 6% FeS to the original batch [740].

For the production of low-melting glass-ceramics, Toropov [423] recommends that various clay materials, tailings from nepheline—apatite ore concentrations, and other mineral raw materials be used. He believes that in the near future it shall be possible to use formable silicate magmatic deposits, which have become accessible due to the development of very deep drilling technology, for the production of sitallized cast rock.

Lukinskaya [424] showed that it is possible to prepare glass-ceramics based on aegirite — $NaFe[Si_2O_6]$, a mineral from the group of alkali igneous rocks — nepheline syenites, and others. Aegirite raw material of the following composition was used: 44.66 SiO_2, 7.40 Al_2O_3, 31.45 Fe_2O_3, 4.24 CaO, 1.84 MgO, 2.59 SO_3, and 8.59 Na_2O. The melting temperature ranged from 1250 to 1350°C. By a two-stage heat treatment at 600 and 800°C, with the material held at each of these two temperatures for 6 h, an incompletely crystallized material was obtained consisting of aegirite crystals of size less than 1 μ, and of hematite crystals of sizes ranging from fractions of a micron to 0.4 mm.

Nikandrov [425], while studying inexpensive low-melting glass-ceramics based on the natural mineral diopside, investigated the crystallization of diopside glasses of the following composition: 24.4 CaO, 17.5 MgO, 52.5 SiO_2, and 5.6 Al_2O_3. For crystallization catalysts, Ag, Cu, Cr_2O_3, and TiO_2 impurities, as well as apatite, were added in amounts ranging from 0.01 to 5%. The most effective addition was found to be that of fluor-apatite, which produced crystallization of glass throughout its bulk by heating to 820°C and holding for 10 h, or by heating to 960°C and holding for 1 h. This effect is explained by Nikandrov by the presence of immiscible regions in the systems when apatite is added, and by the crystallographic compatibility between the diopside and the apatite structures.

Zhunina et al. [188] used low-melting clays with Cr_2O_3 additions, and synthesized glasses located within the diopside and the pyroxene field and precipitating crystals of these compounds. When 8–10% Na_2SiF_6 or $Ca_3(PO_4)_2$ is added to the glass of the composition 57.85 SiO_2, 18.1 Al_2O_3, 3.25 Fe_2O_3, 10.48 CaO, 66.5 MgO, and 4.01 ($Na_2O + K_2O$), a material with uniformly distributed crystals of sizes 1–3 μ was obtained [426].

Budnikov et al. [427] studied the crystallization of glasses based on perlite—acidic volcanic ore with Li_2O, Na_2O, Ag, and Cu additions. These glasses were melted at 1300-1350°C for 2-3 h. Glass-ceramics having a hardness 3-4 times higher than that of steel were obtained by heating these glasses to 520-540°C at a rate of 3-4 deg/min, holding at temperature for 1 h, cooling to room temperature, and reheating to 77°C and holding for 2 h. The crystalline phases present were spodumene, lithium silicates, and lithium aluminosilicates. Samples containing 87.5% of perlite had the highest hardness.

9. GLASS-CERAMICS BASED ON BLAST-FURNACE SLAGS (SLAG GLASS-CERAMICS), CHARACTERIZED BY HIGH WEAR RESISTANCE AND GOOD CHEMICAL STABILITY

Löcsei [53] studied the $Na_2O—CaO—MgO—Al_2O_3—SiO_2$ system by employing blast-furnace slags with additions of a sulfide of the heavy metals as crystallization catalyst. He synthesized certain glasses which, by slip casting and subsequent crystallization, yielded a glass-ceramic, called "Minelbite," characterized by high wear resistance and high chemical stability. These glasses were melted at 1430°C in a reducing atmosphere from raw materials of the following composition (in parts by weight): 100 blast-furnace slag, 50 sand, 8.5 Na_2CO_3, 10 Na_2SO_4, 10 clay. The blast-furnace slag had the following composition (in wt.%): 34.0 SiO_2, 1.0 TiO_2, 3.9 MgO, 3.6 MnO, 0.3 Na_2O, 9.9 Al_2O_3, 40.6 CaO, 2.3 BaO, 2.2 Fe_2O_3, 0.3 K_2O, and 1.9 S. The clay was composed of 80% SiO_2 and 20% Al_2O_3. "Minelbite," characterized by high chemical stability and a high content of diopside crystals, had the following composition: 56.1 SiO_2, 7.9 Al_2O_3, 21.9 CaO, 2.6 MgO, 1.5 BaO, 2.0 MnO, 5.0 Na_2O, 1.0 K_2O, 1.5 Fe_2O_3, and 0.5 TiO_2. The total amount of the crystallization catalyst present constituted 4-5%, taking into consideration the iron content in the batch and the addition of 1.5-2.0% of the sulfide. "Minelbite 2," characterized by a higher content of feldspar, has the composition: 60.9 SiO_2, 14.2 Al_2O_3, 9.0 CaO, 5.7 MgO, 0.4 BaO, 2.0 MnO, 3.2 Na_2O, 1.9 K_2O, 2.5 Fe_2O_3, and 0.2 TiO_2. Minelbite 2 is characterized by a high wear resistance.

Table 55. The Final Heat-Treatment Procedure for the
Preparation of the Glass-Ceramic "Minelbite"

Procedure No.	1	2	3	4	5	6	D				E			
Temperature, °C	800	860	950	830	900	1000	800	820	840	860	800	830	860	900
Time at temp., h	2,3 & 5	1, 2, 3 & 5		1, 2, 3 & 4			1	2	2	2	1	2	2	2

Heat treatment for the glasses of the $Na_2O-CaO-MgO-Al_2O_3-SiO_2$ system so as to transform the cast glass articles into the glass-ceramic Minelbite is done in two stages. According to Löcsei [53], the preliminary heat treatment consists in heating the material to 800°C and holding it there for 1 h; the final heat-treatment procedure is presented in Table 55.

The degree of crystallization of the articles may be controlled using the density values d and the α values, which vary from d = 2.70 g/cm^3 and $\alpha = 96 \cdot 10^{-7}$ (°C)$^{-1}$ for the original glass to d = 3.10 g/cm^3 and $\alpha = 72 \cdot 10^{-7}$ (°C)$^{-1}$ for Minelbite. The size of the crystals in both cases is less than 1 μ. An increase in the ratio between the feldspar and the diopside content increases mechanical strength, thermal stability, wear resistance, and chemical stability. The glass-ceramics have the best mechanical properties if the compositions of the glasses corresponding to them in the albite—anorthite—diopside system lie along the eutectic lines.

Löcsei [45] also proposed a method of producing glass-ceramics from a mixture containing blast-furnace slag and other raw materials. A mixture of the following rather wide composition range can be used: 50-62.0 SiO_2, 5.5-12.0 Al_2O_3, 3-7.5 R_2O, 20.0-33.0 RO, 1.5-10.0 MnO, 0.1-5.0 FeO, and 0.3 sulfide ions; or, preferably, a mixture of the following more narrow composition range can be used: 54.0-58.5 SiO_2, 6.5-8.5 Al_2O_3, 4.5-6.0 R_2O, and 25.0-29.0 RO (of which there are 25-100 MgO, 1.8-3.5 MnO, 0.1-5.0 FeO, and 0.5-1.0 sulfide ions). These mixtures are then melted at 1400-1500°C in a reducing atmosphere. It is recommended that sulfides of Ca, Mg, Fe, and Mn be added, although the necessary sulfide ions may be obtained by the reduction of sulfides, such as $CaSO_4$, in the melt, for which purpose powdered coke or some other

Table 56. Compositions of the Raw Materials for Mixtures with Slags

Raw material	Content (in wt.%) for the oxides present							
	SiO_2	Al_2O_3	Fe_2O_3	CaO	BaO	MgO	MnO_2	R_2O
Aplite	77.5	12.6	1.2	—	—	—	—	7.0
Phonolite	57.6	20.6	3.6	1.9	—	0.3	—	13.1
Slags	36.7	7.0	0.9	41.6	1.2	5.5	6.1	0.4
Manganese ore	10.0	6.7	15.0	3.3	—	—	65.0	—
Dolomite	3.1	2.5	0.5	27.0	—	19.3	—	—
Sand	63.7	0.3	0.1	—	—	31.0	—	—

Table 57. Batch Compositions from Mineral Raw Materials

Raw material	Contents (in wt.%) for various batches											
	1	2	3	4	5	6	7	8	9	10	11	12
Aplite	50	50	50	—	—	50	30	30	25	16	30	30
Phonolite	—	—	—	31.5	31.5	—	15	25	25	16	25	25
Blast-furnace slags	—	—	—	—	—	—	—	—	—	31	—	—
Na_2SO_4	5	6	6	2.5	3.3	—	3	—	2	3.5	1	3
$MgSO_4$	5	5	—	19.4	—	5	6	—	3	—	6	6
$CaSO_4$	—	—	2	—	2	—	—	6	6	—	—	—
Dolomite	38	48.4	51.4	—	48.3	28	10	10	—	—	38	10
Manganese ore	3	4	3	3	3	10	4	4	4	4	4	4
Talc	27.5	—	—	60.6	—	27.5	34	34	30	36	—	34
Sand	—	15.7	17.7	—	38.6	—	—	—	—	—	22	—
Coke powder	5	5	5	4	4	4	4	3	5	4	1	1

reducer is added. The compositions of the raw materials on an oxide base and the compositions of original batches for the preparation of glass-ceramics are given in Tables 56 and 57, as taken from [45].

One may add 1-2% of flux to the mixture, such as boric acid, borax, or fluorspar. The articles may be shaped by casting from the melt or by pressing of the glass powder (with particles less than 0.1 mm in size), with subsequent rapid heating from 750 to 960°C for 1 h, cooling to 800°C for 2-3 h or longer, and further rapid cooling for sintering and crystallization purposes.

The crystallization of cast products is done at 750-1000°C. The heat-treatment procedure depends on the chemical composition of the material, on the size of the articles, and on the requirements with regard to the fine-crystalline structure. For instance, batch No. 1 was melted at 1400-1500°C in order to produce a homogeneous melt, from which moldings 40 mm long were then formed by molding or by pressing. The crystallization procedure included heating to 820°C, increasing the temperature to 900°C for 4 h, cooling the article at a rate of 30-60 deg/h to 500°C, and then further cooling at a rate of 50-80 deg/h to the end. The size of the crystals after such heat treatment was 1-2 μ or less for batch No. 2. The compression strength attained values of 5000 kg/cm^2, the flexure strength had a value of $\sigma_f = 460$ kg/cm^2, and the wear resistance of the material was better than that of steel. The heat-treatment temperature of the material made from batches Nos. 6 and 11 was 770-860°C. Samples of composition No. 12 were heated at 850-970°C for 4.5 h and then cooled following the above-mentioned procedure. All these glass-ceramics are characterized by a high corrosion resistance with respect to concentrated HCl, H_2SO_4, or HNO_3 acids at temperatures up to 100°C. Samples with a constant of not less than 25% MgO had the highest thermal stability, since with increasing MgO content, the α decreases. The highest wear resistance is shown by samples from batches Nos. 11 and 12. The dielectric strength of all glass-ceramics was between 16 and 22 kV/mm, while for a 5-mm-thick sample, the range was 50-59 kV. The dielectric constant was equal to 6-8.5; tan δ was 12-20 · 10^{-4} [45].

Methods of preparing sitallized cast rock based on blast-furnace slags, natural rocks, or other mineral raw material have also been described by Becker [2-7, 428], Wagner [8-11], Wolf [429], Voldan [430], and others.

Kitaigorodskii and Bondarev [46, 431-434] developed a technically effective and economically advantageous method for the preparation of glass-ceramics from inexpensive tailings, such as from fused metallurgical slags. For the production of slag glass-ceramics, conventional apparatus and furnaces as used in the glass industry are quite applicable. In addition to fused slags, one may also employ waste slags, although their working and the preparation of the batch require additional outlay and expenditure. Slag glass-ceramics differ from natural rocks in having a very fine-grained structure; the size of the crystals is not more than 2 μ, which makes it possible to achieve flexure strengths of up to 2500 kg/cm^2, high wear resistance, and high chemical and thermal stability [435, 436]. The primary crystalline phases present in slag glass-ceramics may be anorthite, CaO · Al$_2$O$_3$ · 2SiO$_2$; fluorite, CaF$_2$; or sphene, CaO · TiO$_2$ · SiO$_2$ [436, 437]. Various ways of crystallizing blast-furnace slags based on the CaO—Al$_2$O$_3$—SiO$_2$ system were examined by Toropov [422], who also came up with a classification scheme for slags according to the typical crystalline phases precipitating during their crystallization from the melt.

The Polish investigators Ziemba and Chlopicka [723] obtained slag glass-ceramics based on inexpensive metallurgical slags, and found that these glass-ceramics had good mechanical and electrical insulating properties, and a reasonably high chemical stability, as characterized by the second or third hydrolytic class. The slag glass-ceramic of the brand ZN-164 had the composition 58.9 SiO$_2$, 5.8 Al$_2$O$_3$, 0.2 Fe$_2$O$_3$, 0.2 TiO$_2$, 28.5 CaO, 3.9 MgO, 0.4 MnO, 1.24 R$_2$O, and had an $\alpha = 62 \cdot 10^{-7}$ (°C)$^{-1}$. The slag glass-ceramic of the brand 2S-143a had $\alpha = 84 \cdot 10^{-7}$, and was of the composition 56.9 SiO$_2$, 6.5 Al$_2$O$_3$, 0.3 Fe$_2$O$_3$, 32.2 CaO, 3.0 MgO, 0.6 R$_2$O, and 0.4 S.

Hinz and Wihsmann [736] developed glass-ceramics with a dense and stable monomineral pyroxene microstructure by employing copper-containing slags of the following composition (in %): 46-50 SiO$_2$, 16-22 CaO, 15-19 Al$_2$O$_3$, 6-9 MgO, 3-5 (K$_2$O + Na$_2$O), 3-5 FeO (primary components); 0.2-0.3 Cu, 0.2-0.3 MnO, 0.1-1.0 TiO$_2$, 0.35 BaO, 0.35 ZnO, 0.45 S (secondary components); 0.03-0.3 C, and Pb, Co, Ni, Ag, Sn, V, Be, and Cr (traces). It was determined that the primary components have a definite effect on the behavior of slags during melting, casting, and crystallization, as well as on their mineral composition, mechanical, thermal, and chemical properties, while 3% C and 0.1-0.3% Cr have a favorable effect on the formation of a uniform, fine-crystalline microstructure almost without glassy phase, and significantly increase the crystallizing capability of the slags. A significant role during the crystallization of these slags is played by the presence of a small amount of Mn,

while the remaining secondary components may be excluded or replaced by others without altering the properties of the slag glass-
ceramic. The mechanism of the action of Cr is based on the relatively low solubility of Cr_2O_3 in copper-containing slags, and on
the phase separation, which, at a high Cr content ($> 2\%$ Cr), was
observed already as being present in the melt, at $\geq 0.3\%$ Cr, was
observed during cooling, and , at $< 0.3\%$ Cr, was observed during
the secondary heating process. The primary slag mass then crystallized on the phase which was separated out during the phase
separation process, and which was enriched with Cr_2O_3 (spinel).

The addition of carbon to the composition of the industrial
flame, which reacted especially well with slag, resulted in a uniform and spontaneous crystallization of copper-containing slags,
although not as fine-crystalline a structure was obtained here as
in the case of Cr. This was explained [736] by the fact that it is
impossible for C to be uniformly distributed in the melt, as Cr can
be. In view of the violent combustion of carbon, it is necessary
to add approximately 3% C to the batch so as to maintain an effective amount of it in the slag (0.03-0.3%). Calcination of the slag in
air at 800-1000°C resulted in a partial combustion of C and in a
significant lowering of the crystallizing capability of the slag.

10. COLORED GLASS-CERAMICS

Tables 53 and 54 already showed the compositions of glasses
and the respective heat-treatment procedures for the preparation
of glass-ceramics which may be colored by adding various pigments. Glass-ceramics in the nepheline—plagioclase system containing as crystallization catalysts titanates of MgO, ZnO, or CdO
have a white color, while those containing titanates of MnO, CoO,
NiO, FeO, or Cr_2O_3 may be colored gray, green, blue, brown, or
yellow, depending on the type of coloring oxide and on its amount
[419-421].

Morrisey [438-440] proposed a method of decorating the surface layer of glass-ceramics to a depth of 1 mm or more by spraying, sputtering, or using the silk screen method to apply to the surface of the article, prior to its crystallization, one or more of such
pigments as Fe, Co, Ni, or one of their oxides, together with an inert diluent not reacting with the glass-ceramic, such as TiO_2,
Al_2O_3, MgO, ZnO, sillimanite, ZrO_2, or SiO_2. The diluent improves

Table 58. Glass Compositions for the Preparation of Colored
Glass-Ceramics

Component	Contents (in wt.%) of various compositions				
	A	B	C	D	E
SiO$_2$	71.0	69.2	67.9	71.0	56.0
Li$_2$O	2.5	3.9	4.3	2.5	—
Al$_2$O$_3$	18.0	20.5	20.4	18.0	19.7
TiO$_2$	4.5	5.4	5.4	4.5	9.0
MgO	3.0	—	—	4.0	14.7
ZnO	1.0	—	1.0	—	—
BaO	—	1.0	1.0	—	—

the uniformity of coloration, especially when Co or its compounds
are used as the pigments; however, when the dilution is very high
(up to 90% by weight), the intensity of coloration is decreased and
the pigment is rendered practically ineffective. Prior to the application, the pigment mixed with the diluent and the binder (water,
alcohol, or special oil) is ground in a ball mill. To improve the
adhesive properties, it is recommended that 10 wt.% polyethylene
glycol be added to the mixture prior to heat treatment. The article
with the applied coating is heated at 900-1175°C for 1-4 h or more.
The coloring process proceeds simultaneously with the crystallization of the glass due to the solid-phase reaction between the compound of the crystals of the glass-ceramic and the atoms of the pigment, which are penetrating the lattices of these crystals. Chromium compounds, especially fluorides, produce a green color only in
a mixture with compounds of Fe, Co, or Ni. Compositions of
glasses for the preparation of colored glass-ceramics are shown
in Table 58 [438-440]. These glasses are melted at 1400°C for 4 h.
As fining agent, As$_2$O$_3$ is added to the batch.

Pigments and diluents for the compositions listed in Table
58, their recommended amounts, and the color of the glass-ceramics obtained are shown in Table 59 [438-440].

One must avoid having larger amounts of alkali-metal compounds within the pigment, in view of their volatility and their capability of causing a rough surface on the glass-ceramic.

Table 59. Concentration of Pigments and the Color of
Pigmented Glass-Ceramics

No.	Comp. from Table 58	Pigment (parts by wt.)	Diluent (parts by wt.)	Color of the glass-ceramic
1		$30Co_3O_4$	$70SiO_2$	Dark blue
2		$40NiO$	60 sillimanite	Gray
3		$10CoF_2$	$80TiO_2$	Light blue
4		$3Co_3O_4$, $5Fe_2O_3$	$23TiO_2$	Grayish blue
5		$15NiO$	$70TiO_2$, $15Cr_2O_3$	Grayish green
6		$20NiO$	$80TiO_2$	Light gray
7		$30Fe_2O_3$	$70TiO_2$	Light yellow
8	A	$Ni(NO_3)_3 \cdot 6H_2O$	—	Light green
9		$10Co_3O_4$, $10Fe_2O_3$	$10Cr_2O_3$	Dark green
10		$3Co_3O_4$, $5Fe_2O_3$	—	Bluish gray
11		$5Co_3O_4$, $5CoF_2 \cdot 2H_2O$	$90TiO_2$	Dark blue
12		$20Fe_2O_3$	$80MgO$	Light yellow
13		Fe_2O_3	—	Reddish yellow
14		$20NiO$	Al_2O_3	Light gray
15		$5Co_3O_4$	$50TiO_2$, $10CrF_3$	Green
16		$2NiO$	$80TiO_2$, $1Cr_2O_3$	Greenish rusty brown
17	B	$20Co_3O_4$	$80TiO_2$	Purple
18	C	$20Co_3O_4$	$80TiO_2$	Purple
19	D	$20Co_3O_4$	$80TiO_2$	Gray
20	E	$20Co_3O_4$	$80TiO_2$	Blue

Kitaigorodskii, Litvinov, and co-workers [441-445] synthesized glass-ceramics colored by compounds of Ni, Co, Cr, V, Fe, and Mn, which were added to the original glasses above the 100% content in the amounts of 0.10-9.0 wt.%. X-ray and electron-microscopic analyses showed that the pigments containing Ni or Co are the aluminates $NiAl_2O_4$ and $CoAl_2O_4$, i.e., minerals from the spinel group, which impart to the glass-ceramics a greenish blue or a dark-blue color, respectively. With increasing pigment concentration in the phase composition of the glass-ceramics, the content of nickel and copper aluminates gradually increases, and the crystal size also increases. During this process, the aluminum-containing phases of the glass-ceramic become impoverished with Al_2O_3,

which goes on to form color centers, i.e., the spinels of the pigment. Adding 4% Fe_2O_3 colored the glass-ceramic dark brown due
to the formation of the $FeO \cdot Al_2O_3$ spinel. Vanadium compounds
in the form of 3-9% V_2O_5 enter the glassy phase of the glass-
ceramic and give it a yellow color. Compounds of Ni and Co somewhat increase α, and decrease the thermal stability, the temperature of the beginning of softening, and σ_f, although these changes
are insignificant if the amount of pigment added does not exceed
1-2%.

Glass-ceramics having a dark-green color were prepared in
the $Li_2O—Al_2O_3—SiO_2$ system by introducing small amounts of
Cr_2O_3 [446]. Adding 0.1-8 CuO, 0.1-8 NiO, 0.1-8 V_2O_5, and 0.1-15
FeO individually or jointly to glass of the composition 45-65 SiO_2,
10-27 Al_2O_3, 3-15 MgO, 5-25 BaO, 1-10 Na_2O, and 1-10 Li_2O made
it possible to obtain glass-ceramics of various colors by heating
the glasses from 400 to 1000°C at a rate of 30 deg/h, holding for
3 h, and annealing [447]. Glasses of the composition 45-65 SiO_2,
10-25 Al_2O_3, 5-15 Li_2O, 0.5-25 MgO, and 1.0-5.0 Na_2O with additions of 0.01-2.50 V_2O_5, Fe_2O_3, CoO, NiO, TiO_2, and F give colored
glass-ceramics after heat treatment at 500-900°C for 3 h and subsequent slow cooling [448]. Lithium aluminosilicate glasses with
a high ZnO content, the basic compositions of which, based on [361],
were presented on page 218, make it possible to produce glass-
ceramics having various colors by adding such pigments as 0.1-5
Fe_2O_3, 0.1-2 Cr_2O_3, 0.1-4 $AgNO_3$, 0.1-3 CuO, 0.5-1 CoO, 0.2-1.5 Se,
0.2-5 CdO, 0.2-3 V_2O_5, taken individually or in combinations [449-
451].

Vargin [452] successfully used additions of 0.03% CoO and
0.1% NiO to titanium-containing lithium aluminosilicate glasses as
color indicators to study the changes in the structure of these
glasses during crystallization, when the coordination number of Ni
and Co changes from 6 to 4, with a concomitant change in color
from yellow for the Ni-containing glass to purple for the corresponding glass-ceramic. With increasing crystallization temperature, these structural changes are expressed more strongly. In
glasses of the $Na_2O—Al_2O_3—SiO_2$ system, the coordination number
of Ni^{2+} depends on the coordination of Al, i.e., on the $Na_2O : Al_2O_3$
ratio. If this ratio is less than 1, then Ni^{2+} has a sixfold coordination, which imparts a purple color to the glass.

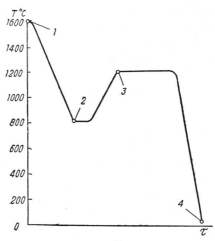

Fig. 71. Heat-treatment procedure for the preparation of glass-ceramics by cooling the fused glass body. τ) Time; T) temperature. 1) Solution of the crystallization catalyst in the glass; 2) precipitation of finely dispersed particles of the crystallization catalyst; 3) growth of crystals of the glass-ceramic on the particles of the crystallization catalyst; 4) cooling of the glass-ceramic to room temperature.

11. PRODUCTION TECHNOLOGY OF GLASS-CERAMICS

The production of glass-ceramics consists of the following fundamental technological stages [43]:

1. Melting of the batch containing the necessary amounts of catalysts at a temperature 100°C higher than the melting point of its most refractory components; 1600°C is a typical temperature (Fig. 71). The crystallization catalyst dissolves in the fused glass.

2. Shaping of the glass products and cooling them to a temperature at which the submicroscopic particles of the catalyst will precipitate, a temperature which is usually 50° higher than the annealing temperature of glass, and may reach 800°C. The products are held at this temperature for 1 h so as to precipitate the maximum number of particles of the catalyst.

3. Heating at a rate of several degrees per minute to the temperature of the formation and growth of crystals (1200°C), and

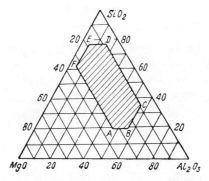

Fig. 72. Compositions of glasses of the MgO—Al_2O_3—SiO_2 system, requiring special crystallization procedures.

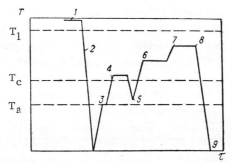

Fig. 73. Typical temperature crystallization procedure for glasses of the MgO—Al_2O_3—SiO_2 system.

holding at that temperature for 4 h so as to complete at least 80% of the crystallization process.

4. Cooling of the sitallized product to room temperature.

Stookey [43] indicates that it is necessary to carefully control all operating temperatures, times, and heating and cooling rates, since deviations from the appropriate values may result in nonreproducibility of the properties of the glass-ceramic. In addition, by changing the temperatures and heat-treatment procedures, one may obtain, from the same glass, glass-ceramics with different crystalline phases and properties. The rate of heating after the nuclei have been formed must be restrained so as to prevent deformation of the article.

For a large number of glasses of the $MgO-Al_2O_3-SiO_2$ system (Fig. 72, region ABCDEF), as well as for certain other glasses, the complete temperature cycle of heat treatment for the preparation of glass-ceramics may be more complex than is represented in Fig. 71, and may include several intermediate stages of cooling and of gradual heating [453]. From glass which has been melted at a temperature higher than the temperature of the liquidus T_1 (Fig. 73, section 1), one may shape articles using pressing, blowing, or rolling methods; they are then cooled to the annealing temperature T_a (point 3) at a rate of 190-200 deg/h, although annealing is not always obligatory. The temperature can also be lowered to the room temperature (Fig. 73, section 2). Increasing the temperature to T_c or somewhat higher (point 4) and holding it at that temperature for 1 h causes the precipitation of submicroscopic particles of the catalyst throughout the bulk of the glass. This precipitation is intensified during a subsequent cooling of 50-100°C at a rate of 2.5-8 deg/min to point 5, which leads to cloudiness of the glass. The temperature is then again increased at a rate of 2-10 deg/min to a temperature lying 50-100°C higher than T_c (point 6), and the particles of the catalyst increase in size, attaining diameters of $10\,\mu$. Their growth stops after holding in at this temperature for 2-4 h. The final temperature of crystallization, at which 85-95 wt.% of the glass transforms into glass-ceramic with the crystal size approximately $25\,\mu$, is 100-200°C lower than the liquidus temperature T_1 (points 7 and 8). The glass-ceramic obtained is cooled to room temperature (point 9).

Of all the technological stages for the production of glass-ceramics, Kitaigorodskii [159, 435] emphasizes, in particular, the precrystallization period within the softening temperature region or 150-200°C lower. By changing the temperatures of this preliminary heat treatment, one may lower the temperature at which the primary crystalline phase precipitates, and one may control the composition of the crystalline phases and the sizes of the crystals, thus affecting the properties of the glass-ceramic.

According to data of Vertsner et al. [338], the most important technological stage in the preparation of glass-ceramics based on glass of spodumene composition with TiO_2 additions is within

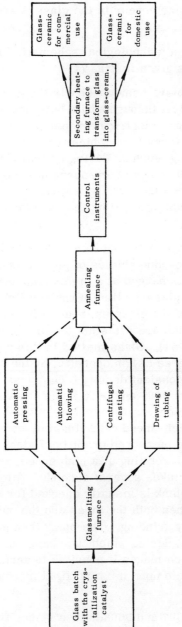

Fig. 74. Technological process for the production of articles made from glass-ceramics of the Pyroceram type.

the temperature region 650-850°C, at which temperature fine crystals 0.005-0.1 μ in size appear in the glass, their amount increasing with temperature.

An example of a technological schematic for the production of glass-ceramics is given in Fig. 74.

In order to achieve homogeneity in the glass and uniform distribution of the catalyst throughout its bulk, and to reproduce the physical, chemical, and electrical properties of the glass-ceramics, the melting of the glasses from which they are made must be accompanied by stirring, such as during optical glass-melting [57]. Out of more than 5000 types of Pyroceram prepared in the US, four types have experienced the most widespread use, since they are very suitable for mass production; they are known under the numbers 9605-9608 [43].

In order to produce Pyroceram 9606, which serves as the material for the nose-cone shields of guided missiles, the batch is stirred carefully and charged at a highly controlled rate into a batch-operated tank glass-melting furnace which has a capacity for holding 40 tons of the glass melt, and which is lined with special refractories which are resistant to corrosion and do not contaminate the glass [454]. Glass melted in this manner is characterized by a high degree of homogeneity, by the absence of bubbles and cords, and by a constant density. The glass used for the production of Pyroceram 9605 and 9606 has a low viscosity at high melting and forming temperatures. It is possible to mold articles from this glass by high-speed centrifugal or by conventional gravitational casting. The measured quantity of glass enters a steel conical mold which is rotating at a high speed, which is why the shaping of the cones takes several seconds. After annealing, the transparent glassy blank is visually checked for the absence of internal defects, and then both the inner and the outer side are subjected to preliminary grinding. The blank then undergoes the sitallization process, during which the change in dimensions remains below 1%, which makes it possible to achieve accurate dimensions of the article upon minimal final mechanical treatment [21].

Pyrocerams 9607 and 9608 have a viscosity in their fused states which is close to the viscosity of borosilicate glass, and they are most suitable, using the pressing method, for the forming of crucibles, heating grills, Petri dishes, flat plates, lenses, and other articles with thin and thick sides. By blowing by hand, one can also produce vials, cylinders, and Petri dishes; by mechanized blowing, one can produce bottles, beakers, flasks, and other industrial products. Pyroceram 9608, as a material of general designation, is being produced in large tank furnaces which operate around the clock. Articles made from it can be manufactured by all automatic processes for the molding of glass; they can be produced by pressing, blowing, drawing, rolling, or casting [455-460]. From the glass melt to be used for Pyrocerams 9607 and 9608, one may draw sheet glass, as well as tubing or molding of various dimensions. Finally, articles made of glass-ceramics may be produced through ceramics technology by pressing the powder of the glass with the addition of the proper catalyst [309, 461], or by casting from a thermoplastic mass based on glass powder to which paraffin binder has been added, and subsequently sintering the blanks.

Voss [462-464] proposed a method of producing glass-ceramic articles without significant deformation by the stepwise crystallization of glass of the composition 71 SiO_2, 2.5 Li_2O, 18 Al_2O_3, 4.5 TiO_2, 3 MgO, and 1 ZnO with small additions of oxidizers and clarifiers $NaNO_3$ and As_2O_3 · 1.5% Na_2O and As_2O_3 which, remaining in the glass, have no significant effect on the properties of the glass-ceramic. This glass is melted in a batch-operated tank furnace at 1600°C. The molded article is heated at a rate of 5 deg/min to 800°C, where it is held for 1 h; it is then again heated at the same rate to 1080-1120°C held at 1080°C for 2 h and at 1120°C for approximately 2 h. The deformation of the heating grills and small pots after such heat treatment amounted to 10 mm, which was found to be acceptable. During this procedure, the α varies from $34 \cdot 10^{-7}$ for the glass to 10-$15 \cdot 10^{-7}$ $(°C)^{-1}$ for the glass-ceramic. If the glass was held in the temperature range 1150-1175°C for 4 h, then σ_f for the glass-ceramic attained a value of 1470 kg/cm^2 and α a value of $10 \cdot 10^{-7}$ $(°C)^{-1}$ [465].

Brown and King [466-468] developed a method of producing glass-ceramic articles having accurate dimensions, high σ_f values, and low α values using glasses capable of forming, after crystallization, compression layers on the surface, and having the following composition: 55-75 SiO_2, 3-7 TiO_2, 58-82 (SiO_2 + TiO_2), 2-15 Li_2O, and 12-13 Al_2O_3. The weight ratio of Li_2O to Al_2O_3 was equal to

0.1-0.6; the total content of SiO_2, TiO_2, Li_2O, and Al_2O_3 must not be less than 95%. The most advantageous composition is 71 SiO_2, 2.5 Li_2O, 18 Al_2O_3, 4.5 TiO_2, 3 MgO, 1 ZnO, and minute amounts of $NaNO_3$ and As_2O_3. The melting temperature of this glass is 1600°C. Glass rods 127 mm long, with a diameter of 6.35 or 2.7 mm were heated at a rate of 7 deg/min to 800°C, held there for 1 h, then heated at a rate of 1 deg/min to 1000°C and held there for 10 h, and finally heated at the same rate to 1175°C and held at that temperature for 4 h. The σ_f of the sample 6.35 mm in diameter was 1418 kg/cm^2, with α equal to $5.1 \cdot 10^{-7}$ (°C)$^{-1}$, and the flexure point at 7.2 mm. After grinding the 12.7-mm diameter rod until it measured 6.35 mm in diameter, σ_f became 799 kg/cm^2, which is 619 kg/cm^2 less than the original strength. The ground rods were then heated to 1100°C and held there for 4 h, which resulted in $\sigma_f = 1404$ kg/cm^2 and $\alpha = 7 \cdot 10^{-7}$ (°C)$^{-1}$ at a deformation of 0.076 mm.

Corning Glass Works [469] proposed a method of heat treating glass of the composition 40-68 SiO_2, 8-32 Al_2O_3, 7-14 TiO_2, and 8.5-23 MgO to yield a glass-ceramic with $\sigma_f = 2800$ kg/cm^2 at α not less than $100 \cdot 10^{-7}$ (°C)$^{-1}$ within the temperature region 0-300°C. The preshaped article is heated at 990°C for 8-24 h or at 1160°C for 0.25-0.5 h, and subsequently cooled.

Corning Glass Works [470] developed a method for mechanically working Pyroceram articles by diamond tools, such as drills with a diamond tip and diamond grinding wheels, since conventional steel and carbide instruments proved to be unsuitable for drilling holes in these articles. Grinding with diamond wheels makes it possible to obtain a flat surface with deviations less than 0.025 mm. Holes for the attachment of handles on heating grills and on flat plates made of Pyroceram have a diameter of 6.35 mm, holes for the heating cables for the electrically heated base are 9.7 mm in diameter, and the holes for installing the thermostat are 11.1 mm in diameter. The thickness of the perforated walls is 6.35 and 9.5 mm. The upper part of the heating base with an area of 645 cm^2 and the heating grills bordering on it must be ground, so that the deviations from the plane do not exceed 0.1 mm. The heating grills and the heating bases are first placed on a special mandrel, whereupon they are braced onto a grinder and are ground simultaneously four pieces at a time. After being ground by diamond, the articles are ground by corundum powder and are polished with a mixture of TiO_2 and ZrO_2 powders.

It is possible to prepare foamed glass-ceramics from glasses of the following composition (in %): 60.5 SiO_2, 14.6 Al_2O_3, 8.72 BaO, 16.7 CaO, and 5.0-15 TiO_2. For this purpose, 0.5% Sb_2O_3, 4% MnO_2, 1% SiC, and 0.5% carbon black are added to the initial glass batch as foaming agents. The foamed glass-ceramic "F-6" had the following composition (in %): 58 SiO_2, 16 Al_2O_3, 6 Na_2O, 12 CaO, 8 MgO, and 6 F (over 100%). Carbon black was found to be the best foaming agent. The specific gravity of the foamed glass-ceramic was 0.3-1.8 g/cm^3, with the water absorption being less than 1%. Foamed glass-ceramic can also be obtained by foaming the glass body with gas introduced into the furnace from below, with the furnace held at a temperature sufficient for the formation of nuclei in the glass [742]. With a further increase in the temperature, the growth of crystals occurs, which forces out of the glass body the gases which had dissolved in it, thereby forming pores in the glass in the form of cells, which are retained during the subsequent cooling and crystallization processes, transforming the material into a foamed glass-ceramic.

In conclusion, let us briefly discuss two methods of strengthening glass by producing compression layers on its surface with the aid of controlled crystallization upon thermal or ionic exchange during the thermochemical treatment. According to the first method [471-477], glasses containing (in parts by weight) 65-72 SiO_2, up to 4 Li_2O, and 22.5-36 Al_2O_3 (the weight ratio $Li_2O : Al_2O_3$ not more than 0.311), 0.1-3.5 TiO_2, 0.1-5 B_2O_3, 0.4-2 Na_2O, and 0.5-10 PbO (the total amount of all the components being not more than 110 parts by weight) are heated at temperatures corresponding to a viscosity of 10^7-10^{10} poise for 1-40 h until submicroscopic crystals of β-eucryptite, the α of which is less than that of the original glass, are formed in their surface to a depth of 0.1 mm. This results in the emergence in the surface layer of compression stresses and in an increase in strength to 1050-1400 kg/cm^2 [474]. Analogous results were obtained on glasses having the composition (in parts by weight) 52-65 SiO_2, up to 4 Li_2O, and up to 40 Al_2O_3, with the total content of the primary components being not less than 100 parts by weight [475]. Glass of the composition 66.7 SiO_2, 26.2 Al_2O_3, 5.3 Li_2O, 0.1 K_2O, 0.3 Na_2O, 0.1 B_2O_3, 0.8 TiO_2, and 0.5 As_2O_3, and other glasses having a similar composition, after being heated in air at 860°C for 64 h or at 960°C for 0.25 h, increased their σ_f to 6000-7000 kg/cm^2 due to the formation in their surface layer to a depth of 0.06-0.08 mm of transparent hexagonal crystals of lithium aluminosilicates with low α values and due to the appearance of compressive stresses [476]. The strengthened glasses were quite transparent, in view of the closeness between the indices of refraction for the crystals and the glass.

The second method of strengthening glass containing 45-80 SiO_2 and 7-25 Na_2O or K_2O is by substituting Na ions by Li ions in its surface layer, which also results in the emergence of compressive stresses, since the radius of the Li ion is less than that of the Na or K ions [478, 479]. To achieve this, the glass is reheated in the melt of a salt or a mixture of Li salts whose melting point is lower than the softening point of glass; this condition is satisfied by the nitrate, sulfate, chloride, bromide, or iodide of lithium. The treatment is done in the temperature range corresponding to viscosities ranging from $10^{14.5}$ to $10^{7.6}$ poise for a period of time sufficient for the diffusion of Li ions into the surface layer of the glass to a depth of 0.05-0.1 mm. In glasses containing Al_2O_3, the Li ions, which react with SiO_2 or Al_2O_3, form β-spodumene crystals, which also lowers the α of the surface layer. The most significant strengthening and increase in chemical stability was obtained for glass of the following composition: 55-66 SiO_2, 10-20 Al_2O_3, 10-13 Na_2O or K_2O, 8-12 TiO_2, 2-5 ZrO_2, and 2 B_2O_3. The articles turn out to be semitransparent or transparent in proportion to the amount of β-spodumene formed, while their tensile strength reaches values ranging from 4200 to 4900 kg/cm^2. Glass of the composition 57.2 SiO_2, 23.7 Al_2O_3, 11.0 Na_2O. 1.1 Li_2O, 6.2 TiO_2, and 0.5 As_2O_3, when treated in a melt of the salts 95% Li_2SO_4 + 5% Na_2SO_4 at 860° for 5 min, remained transparent and had an unusually high σ_f, its values ranging between 70 and 80 kg/mm^2 [476]. X-ray analysis showed the presence of crystals of a solid solution of β-eucryptite and quartz in the surface layer of the glass.

Chapter V

Properties of Glass-Ceramics, Photosensitive Glasses, and Photosensitive Glass-Ceramics

Photosensitive glasses possess a number of valuable properties, such as high strength, good stability, grain-free image, accurate reproducibility, multiplicity of contrast shades possible, and constancy of size in two and three dimensions, i.e., three-dimensionality of the image, which may extend to a certain depth or through the entire thickness of the glass plate. Consequently, the image in a photosensitive glass cannot be scratched away, and it can easily be purified of contaminants which can normally be removed only with difficulty from engraved or etched images. When photosensitive glass is transformed into forms B and C, no shrinkage is produced, which makes it possible to retain unchanged the dimensions of the transferred image.

Properties of photosensitive glasses of various shapes and of photosensitive glass-ceramics (based on data from [70, 270, 273-275, 480-482]) are presented in Table 60, where the properties of sodium calcium silicate and borosilicate glasses are also given for comparison purposes.

Glass-ceramics possess a favorable combination of many important properties, including a relatively high hardness, a fine-crystalline structure, resistance to moisture and gas penetration, considerable mechanical strength, a high temperature of deformation, good thermal stability, and excellent electrical-insulating properties. By controlling the size, the density, and the chemical and mineralogical composition of the crystals, it is possible to obtain glass-ceramics with previously specified properties, satisfying special requirements. The properties of glass-ceramics depend not only on the chemical composition, but also on the conditions of heat treatment [726].

275

Table 60. Properties of Photosensitive Glasses of Various Shapes and of Photosensitive Glass–Ceramics

Properties	Photosensitive glass				Fotoceram	Sodium calcium silicate glass	Borosilicate glass
	Foto-form	Type B	Type C	Type E			
Physical properties:							
Density, g/cm^3	2.34	2.36	2.37	2.37	2.39—2.46	2.47	2.23
Water absorption				Zero			
Gas penetrability				Impenetrable by gases			
Thermal properties:							
Softening temperature, °C	637	452	634	—	700—900	520	570
Annealing temperature, °C	—	452	634	634	650	510	555
Lower annealing temperature, °C	—	422—452	596	586	600	478	515
Heat capacity, cal/°C							
at 25°	—	—	—	—	0.209	—	—
at 200°	—	—	—	—	0.256	—	—
Heat conductivity, cal/sec–cm^2–°C							
at 25°	—	—	—	—	0.0056	—	—
at 200°	—	—	—	—	0.0050	—	—
Linear thermal expansion coeff. (0–300°), $\alpha \cdot 10^7$ (°C)$^{-1}$	83.7	83.0	86.0	86.0	100—104	—	—
Mechanical properties:							
Elastic modulus, kg/mm^2	—	7000—7800	7000—8400	—	7000—9500	6500—6860	6500—6860

Poisson ratio	—	0.20—0.22	0.18—0.22	—	0.20—0.22	0.22	0.20—0.22
Shear modulus, kg/cm²	—	3200	3600	—	4000	—	—
Flexure strength, kg/cm²	280—420	615	1130	—	1400—2520	—	—
Tensile strength, kg/cm²	—	7.1	—	—	21	—	—
Permissible operating stress, kg/cm²	—	70	70	—	210	70	70
Knoop microhardness at 100-g loads, kg/mm²	—	507	566	—	581	—	481
Mohs hardness	5.5	—	—	—	7—8	—	—
Electrical properties:							
Dielectric constant at 60 Hz, 20°	9.75	—	—	—	5.5	—	—
at 1 MHz, 20°	6.9	6.5	5.7	5.7	5.2—5.6	—	—
at 1 MHz, 200°	6.9	8.3	6.3	—	5.2—6.3	—	—
Scattering coeff. at 1 MHz, 20°	—	—	—	—	0.0062	—	—
Loss coeff. at 1 MHz, 20°	—	0.033	0.017	0.017	0.034	0.001	0.02
Power factor at 1 MHz, 20°	—	0.005	0.003	0.003	0.006	—	—
at 1 MHz, 200°	—	0.130	0.021	0.021	0.014	—	—
Electrical resistivity at 25°, Ω-cm	—	$5 \cdot 10^{12}$	$6 \cdot 10^{15}$	$6 \cdot 10^{15}$	$6 \cdot 10^{15}$	$1 \cdot 10^{11}$	$3 \cdot 10^{13}$
Specific resistance of the surface, Ω/mm², for untreated surface	—	—	—	—	10^{8}	—	—
for treated surface	—	—	—	—	$4 \cdot 10^{12}$	—	—

Glass-ceramics may be perfectly opaque, being colored white or some other color, or they may be transparent, having a light-brownish, amethystlike tint. The first transparent glass-ceramic samples had a yellowish-brown color, while the first opaline samples had a grayish-white color [460]. Pyrocerams 9605 and 9608 are opaque and are colored white. The color of Pyroceram 9606 may change from white to cream. Pyroceram 9607 may be transparent and may have a light-brownish tint. Phosphate-containing glass-ceramics are colored white and have a smooth and shiny surface [381].

1. MICROSTRUCTURE

Glass-ceramics have a dense microcrystalline structure similar to that of ceramic materials based on pure oxides, characterized by randomly oriented crystals of a very small size and by the absence of porosity. The size of the crystals ranges from fractions of a micron to several microns. For instance, in phosphate-containing glass-ceramics, the crystals have sizes ranging from 0.5 to 6 μ, compared to 20-50 μ for conventional ceramics [381]. The crystals are cemented to each other by a small amount of the glassy phase [483, 484].

A comparison given by Stookey [485, 486] between the microstructures of glass-ceramics and of ceramics showed that the conventional sintering process, such as is characteristic for the preparation of traditional ceramic materials, does not make it possible to avail oneself of all the possible combinations of crystal composition, and that the properties of ceramics are frequently determined to a larger degree by the presence of voids and other defects than by the actual properties of the crystals. The hot-pressing method produces more dense, finer-grained polycrystalline ceramic materials, but is expensive and the articles produced thereby can have only limited sizes; glass-ceramics, on the other hand, have a microstructure which is very close to the ideal polycrystalline structure. Table 61, which is taken from [486], shows several characteristics of the microstructure which depend on the processing and which have an effect on the properties of ceramics, as well as of glass-ceramics.

By electron-optical, optical, and x-ray investigations, as well as by the low-angle x-ray scattering method, it was shown that particles several angstroms in size emerge during the effective

Table 61. Characteristics of the Microstructure and Those
Properties of the Articles Which Are Influenced By It

Characteristics of the microstructure	Properties of the articles
Porosity	Strength
Size	Optical properties
Concentration	Electrical properties
Composition of crystals	
Structure	Thermal properties
Orientation	Chemical properties
Homogeneity of the materials	All properties

process of the nucleus formation. The most complete crystallization, according to Stookey's data [485], is achieved when the average size of the crystal is 200-300 Å. During the early stages of
crystallization, the crystals grow as spherulites until they come in
contact with the neighboring particles. Upon further heating, crystals of an angular form are formed and recrystallization takes
place, with a concomitant decrease in the number of crystals and
an increase in their size. Crystals $0.5-1\,\mu$ in size had angular surfaces with rounded corners. Larger crystals were highly angular.

Alekseev and Fedorova [487] used x-rays to study the early
stages of crystallization of glass composed of spodumene, petalite,
and eucryptite, with additions of 5% TiO_2, and showed that the formation of the crystal from the nucleus happens abruptly. The rate
of this process is significantly greater than the growth rate of the
crystals. The sizes of the crystals forming are not less than 100 Å.

Figures 75a-d are electron micrographs showing individual
stages in the transformation of a titanium-containing magnesium
aluminosilicate glass into a glass-ceramic. Figure 76 shows the
microstructure of the glass-ceramic based on spodumene glass
with TiO_2 additions, and Fig. 77 shows the microstructure of Corning 8603 Fotoceram [708].

The process of the formation of the microstructure of glass-
ceramics as dependent on the heat-treatment procedure of original
glasses in the $Li_2O-Al_2O_3-TiO_2-SiO_2$ and $BaO-Al_2O_3-SiO_2$ systems was studied by Williams and Carrier [488] using electron-
microscope and x-ray methods. Heating of glass of the Li_2O-
$Al_2O_3-TiO_2-SiO_2$ system at 800°C for 1 h resulted in the appear-

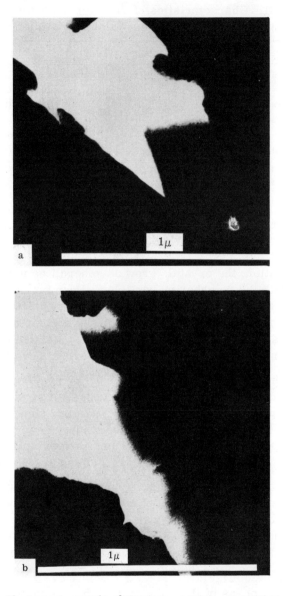

Fig. 75. Electron micrographs of titanium-containing magnesium aluminosilicate glass, showing individual stages of the nucleus formation process. a) A thin lamella of glass, cooled directly after fusion. The lamella in the center attests to the amorphous nature of the glass. b) Secondary heating at 740°C for 20 h, causing the emergence of a large number
of nuclei 40-50 Å in diameter.

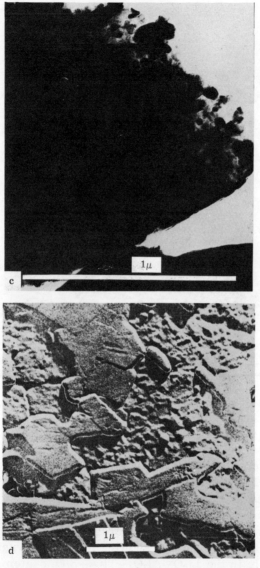

Fig. 75. c) Secondary heating at 820°C for 2 h and at 1050°C for 15 min.
The particles show angular shapes of the crystals. The number present
decreased, but their size increased to 0.1 μ. d) Secondary heating at
820°C for 2 h and at 1250°C for 8 h. The sample was ground and etched
in a 1.2% solution of HF for 2 min. Seen are randomly oriented crystals of cordierite. The carbon replica was first shadowed by 80% Pt—
20% Pd.

Fig. 76. Electron micrograph of titanium-containing spodumene
glass. This glass was cooled and subsequently heated to 800°C,
held there for 1 h, and then heated to 1150°C and held there for
4 h. The sample was etched for 0.5 min in a 1% solution of HF.
Seen are randomly oriented spodumene crystals in the form of
blocks, and acicular rutile crystals approximately 1 μ in size.
This is a replica.

ance of β-eucryptite crystals 60-90 Å in size which, after heating
at 930°C for 1 h, increased to 100-120 Å. When the temperature
was increased to 940°C, the sizes of the crystals increased to 200-
1000 Å, during which process one portion of the hexagonal β-
eucryptite was transformed into tetragonal β-spodumene. Figure
78 is an electron micrograph showing the microstructure of a
glass-ceramic in the $Li_2O—Al_2O_3—TiO_2—SiO_2$ system obtained by
stepwise crystallization of the glass first at 800°C for 1 h, and
then at 1150°C for 4 h. Careful analysis of the microstructure obtained showed the presence of 5% by volume acicular crystals of
aluminum titanate, 84% by volume polygonal crystals of β-spodu-
mene, and 11% by volume of the glassy phase. These crystals attained sizes of 2,000-10,000 Å [488].

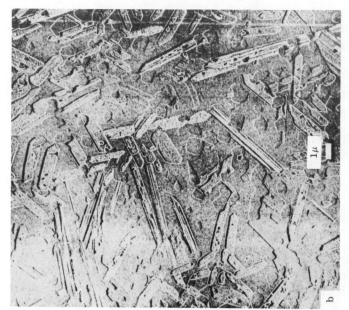

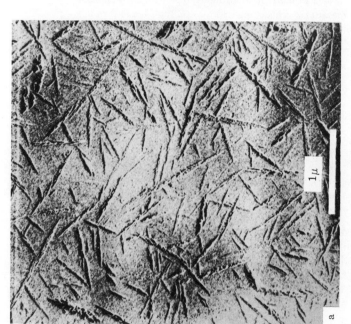

Fig. 77. Electron micrographs of Corning Code 8603 photosensitive glass. a) The glass exposed to x rays of intensity of 10,000 R and heat treated at 600°C for 1 h. The glass was polished and then etched in a 0.5% solution of HF for 5 sec. Seen are dendritic crystals of lithium metasilicate and the beginning of the process of "chemical machining." This is a replica. b) Glass exposed to x rays of intensity 160,000 R and heat treated at 600 and 650°C for 1 h. The glass was polished and etched in a 0.5% solution of HF for 1 min. Seen are acicular and columnar crystals of lithium disilicate. This is a replica.

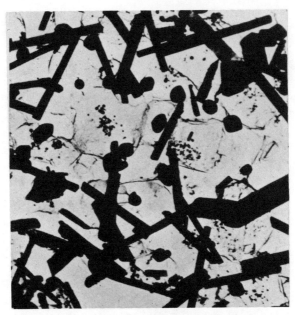

Fig. 78. Electron micrograph of a glass-ceramic of the lithium silicate and lithium aluminosilicate type with TiO$_2$ additions. The material was heat treated at 800°C for 1 h and then at 1150°C for 4 h. Insoluble acicular crystals are shown.

In glasses of the BaO—Al$_2$O$_3$—SiO$_2$ system, the first mullite crystals 300 Å in size appeared after heating at 950°C for 2 h, and at 1000°C after being heated for 10 h. The crystal size increased to 800 Å at 1100°C and to 1200 Å at 1250°C (Fig. 79). After heating to 1400°C and holding at that temperature for 10 h, the crystals attained sizes of the order of 1000–10,000 Å, and after being held for 10 h at 1650°C, they attained sizes in excess of 10,000–30,000 Å (Fig. 80). Chemical analysis showed that the content of the mullite crystals present was 38 wt.%. The different dissolving rates in HF and HCl of crystalline mullite in samples prepared under various heating conditions, as well as infrared spectra of leached-out mullite, attested to the changes in the mullite structure as dependent on the heat-treatment temperature [488].

Korelova et al. [489] studied the microstructure of crystallized two-component lithium silicate glasses with Li$_2$O contents of 23–42 mol.% as a function of the temperature and the time of heat

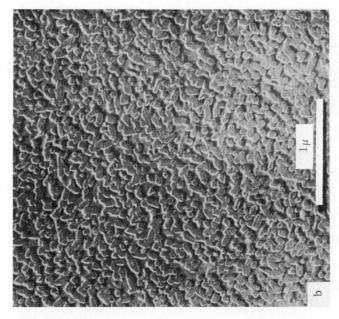

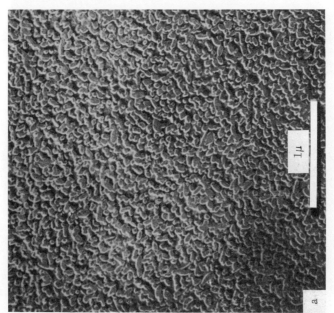

Fig. 79. Electron micrographs of glass-ceramics in the BaO—Al$_2$O$_3$—SiO$_2$ system. a) Material heat treated at 950°C for 2 h and then at 1100°C for 10 h. b) Material heat treated at 950°C for 2 h and then at 1250°C for 10 h.

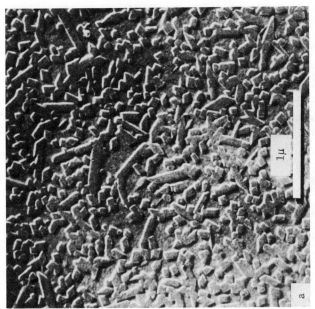

Fig. 80. Electron micrographs of glass-ceramics in the BaO—Al$_2$O$_3$—SiO$_2$ system. a) Material heat treated at 950°C for 2 h and then at 1400°C for 10 h. b) Material heat treated at 950°C for 2 h and then at 1650°C for 10 h.

treatment. When glass containing 23.4 mol.% Li_2O was slowly
cooled, droplike phase-separation regions 0.1-0.2 μ in size were
observed, and the glass obtained was opaque. Upon rapid cooling,
the glass retained its transparency, but also contained microheterogeneities 300 Å in size. Heating the glass at 480°C for 96 h
caused opalescence of the glass and, due to the precipitation of
$Li_2O \cdot 2SiO_2$ crystals, resulted in an increase in the size of the
microheterogeneities to 0.05-0.16 μ. Total crystallization of lithium disilicate with the formation of coarse (150-200 μ in size)
spherulites of a radial structure occurred when the glass was
heated to 620°C and held at that temperature for 5 h. Increasing
the time held at 480 and 620°C to 20 h at each of these two temperatures did not change the character of the microstructure, but
resulted in a decrease in the size of the spherulites to 15-25 μ.
Heat treatment at 480 and 620°C for 24 h each and at 1000°C for
18 h caused the crystallization of cristobalite, which significantly
changed the microstructure of these samples. Glasses with 37.1
and 41.6 mol.% Li_2O crystallized at 480°C during a period of 24 h,
with the precipitation of lithium metasilicate and disilicate in the
form of spherulites 30-40 μ in size, which decreased to 15-30 μ
with increasing time and temperature of heat treatment.

Klemm and Volkmann [490] conducted an electron-microscope investigation of the microstructure of glass-ceramics based
on several brands of Jena glass so as to determine whether these
materials might be usable as mirrors for astronomical telescopes.
Because of different hardnesses in the various axial directions,
and because of dissimilar orientation, the crystals polished differently, which resulted in unevenness of the relief of the order of
approximately 0.1 μ. Crystals in the form of dendrites measured
0.1-2 μ, and the magnitude of the unevenness of the relief in this
case was 0.08 μ. The formation of dendritic crystals in the glass-
ceramic was accompanied by the formation of microcracks, which
made this material unsuitable for the preparation of a high-quality
optically polished surface. Nevertheless, glass-ceramics of the
"Cer-Vit" type [715] are capable of being treated so that a high-
quality optically polished surface can be obtained.

Of importance in the selection of optimal conditions for the
crystallization of glasses and in controlling the properties of the
glass-ceramics obtained is the development of a quantitative x-
ray method for the determination of the amount of the crystalline

and the glassy phases present in the microstructure of glass-ceramics. However, as of the present time, no such method has been developed; the applicability of the method proposed by Ohlberg and Strickler [491] is limited due to a number of assumptions which must be verified relative to each glass tested. It was assumed, for instance, that during the crystallization process, only the intensity of the scattering of x-rays from the glassy phase changes, and not the nature of the diffusion rings for the original glass, while it is known that in the case of sodium-containing, partially crystallized glass, the distribution of the scattering intensity of the glassy phase does change. It was further assumed that the absorption coefficients for the original glass and the glassy phase remaining in the glass-ceramic are very close in value, which obviously is not true due to the difference in the chemical compositions of the original glass and of the residual glassy phase in the glass-ceramic. The proposed method is based on the assumption that the intensity of scattering for the amorphous phase must decrease in proportion to the increase in the amount of the crystalline phase which had formed from the amorphous phase. The percent crystallization of glass, according to [491], can be given by the expression

$$100\% \cdot (I'_g - I'_x)/I'_g, \qquad (31)$$

where I'_g and I'_x are the intensity of scattering for the amorphous phase for the original and the partially crystallized glass, respectively. By measuring the scattering for the mechanical mixture of crystalline compounds corresponding in composition to that of the original glass, a correction was introduced for background scattering caused by air, the apparatus, and the Compton effect. Measurement is done at a given scattering angle 2θ, and the degree of crystallization is determined from the following expression [491]:

$$100\% \cdot (I_g - I_x)/(I_g - I_\beta), \qquad (32)$$

where I_g, I_x, and I_β are, respectively, the intensity of scattering from the amorphous phases of the original glass, from the partially crystallized glass, and from the mechanical mixture of crystalline compounds, all measured at one given value of the angle 2θ.

This method cannot be employed if the degree of crystallization of the glass is less than 10%. For the measurements, Cu K_α radiation was used, with a monochromatized nickel filter. To re-

cord the radiation, a xenon proportional recorder was employed
in combination with a Norelco diffractometer and an amplitude
analyzer. All samples to be tested were ground and screened
through a 325-mesh sieve. Checking the value obtained from Eq.
(32) by measuring the scattering at an angle of $2\theta = 22.5°$ on
samples of fused silica, its mixture with quartz, and pure quartz,
showed the experimentally obtained values and the calculated
values to agree to within 5%. The same result was obtained for a
titanium-containing glass-ceramic of the cordierite type, in which
the degree of crystallization was determined as equal to 76.2% [491].

Carrier [724] proposed a quantitative method for determining the degree of crystallization of glass-ceramics the sizes of
whose crystals measured not less than 0.1μ; this method is based
on the determination of the ratio between the number of intersections by the crystals of the transparent grid superimposed on the
electron micrograph of the replica with the polished surface of the
glass-ceramics, and the total number of intersections over the entire area of the electron micrograph. If only one crystalline phase
is present in the microstructure of the glass-ceramic, then the degree of crystallization in wt.% is calculated by multiplying the
vol.% by the ratio between the density of this crystalline phase and
the density of the glass-ceramic. In case two or more crystalline
phases are present, this method is supplemented by x-ray analysis
and electron-diffraction determination of each of these phases,
after extracting them, if possible, from the glassy matrix.

The degree of crystallization, the size, and the distribution
of crystalline particles in the microstructure of multiphase glass-
ceramics can be determined by a combination of electron microscopy and direct electron transmission of thin samples of the glass-
ceramic (the thickness being of the order of 1000 Å) [725]. The
degree of crystallization in this case is found by determining (in %)
the area of the projections of the crystalline particles on the area
of the image.

2. PHYSICAL PROPERTIES

a. Density

The density of glass-ceramics varies in the range 2.40-2.72
g/cm^3 [492-497], i.e., their density is lower than that of aluminum.
The change in density of glass during its crystallization was studied

by a number of investigators [498-501]. Tykachinskii and Sorkin [500] showed that the density of glass of the $Li_2O-Al_2O_3-SiO_2$ system with TiO_2 additions decreases at the start of heat treatment, which is explained by the transition of this glass into an equilibrium state; after this, the density remains constant for a while and, starting from a certain point at the holding temperature, and depending on the temperature, it sharply increases. For instance, at 690°C, the beginning of a density increase was noted after glass was held at that temperature for 3.5 h; at 700°C, such an increase was noted after the glass was held there for 2 h; and at 710°C the increase occurred after it was held there for 75 min. An approximately asymptotic approach of density to a certain limiting value was observed.

A somewhat different behavior in the change in density of glass of this same system at various stages of sitallization was observed by Buzhinskii et al. [168], who, in addition to observing an increase in density, also observed a decrease in density in the final period III of crystallization during the precipitation in glass of spodumene and β-eucryptite crystals. The increase in density during period I of heat treatment within the range of annealing temperatures when crystals were not as yet observed amounted to 1.2%; in period II of heat treatment, after the primary crystalline phase (β-eucryptite) precipitated, the increase in density amounted to 0.9%. These changes in density are associated with the amount of the crystalline phase present, and are explained by these authors not in terms of densification, but by an increase in the glass during the period of its crystallization of Al^{3+} present in the sixfold coordination. A decrease in density from 2.462 g/cm³ for the original glass of eucryptite composition to 2.421-2.422 g/cm³ for the glass-ceramic produced by holding the glass at 800-1000°C for a time ranging from 2 min to 1 h was noted by Baum [502].

The presence in the structure of glass-ceramics catalyzed by phosphates of quartz (density 2.65 g/cm³) makes them denser than glass-ceramics which contain cristobalite (density 2.32 g/cm³). If there is a crystalline phase in the structure of a glass-ceramic with a higher density, such as $Li_2O \cdot ZnO \cdot SiO_2$, then, regardless of the presence of a large amount of the cristobalite, the density of the phosphate-containing glass-ceramic does not decrease significantly [381].

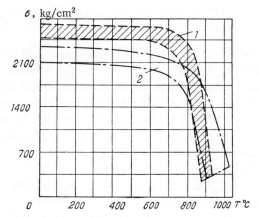

Fig. 81. Flexure strength of glass-ceramics as a function of temperature. 1) Pyroceram 9605; 2) Pyroceram 9606.

b. Porosity

Glass-ceramics are nonporous, and possess zero water absorption and gas penetrability [503-507], which is the reason they can be employed in very-high-vacuum apparatus [508, 509].

3. MECHANICAL PROPERTIES

a. Strength

It must be taken into account that the increased mechanical strength of glass-crystalline materials is primarily caused by their microcrystallinity, i.e., by the exclusively small size of the crystals they are composed of, the crystal size varying from 1 to 0.1 μ.

However, as a matter of fact, the mechanical strength of glass-ceramics and photosensitive glass-ceramics is a function of a still larger number of variables than is the case for glasses. Thus, besides the chemical composition of the original glass, factors such as the following also have an effect on the strength of glass-crystalline materials: (1) internal strength of the crystals and the glassy phase; (2) strength of the coupling at the boundaries of contact between the crystalline grains; (3) the quantitative ratio between the crystalline and the glassy phases; and (4) the difference in thermal expansion coefficients of the latter [763, 764].

For photosensitive glass-ceramics, the crystal size may be controlled by varying the ultraviolet radiation dosage.

In the opinion of Tashiro [764], the increased mechanical strength of glass-crystalline materials of the lithium aluminosilicate system with a high content of lithium oxide (up to 12%) and a low content of Al_2O_3 (from 4-10%) at SiO_2 concentrations ranging from 77 to 81% is rather puzzling. Nevertheless, he pointed out the possible interdependence between σ_f of the glass-ceramic and the thermal expansion coefficient of the primary crystalline phase. With decreasing thermal expansion coefficient of the crystalline phase, the σ_f of the glass-ceramic decreases, which the author explains by the possible emergence of tensile stresses in the glassy phase, which have a harmful effect on the mechanical strength.

Glass-ceramics are several times stronger than glasses, and they are also stronger than the majority of ceramic materials and some metals [510-520]. Their flexure strength may attain values of 2500-3000 kg/cm^2, and for some experimental samples, it can even attain values of 4200 and 5600 kg/cm^2, i.e., glass-ceramics may attain greater flexure strength values than those of quartz glass, stainless steel, and titanium [521]. The strength-to-specific weight ratio for Pyroceram 9605 is equal to 14.1, which is comparable to 13.3 for dense alumina, 14.3 for aluminum, and 10.1 for stainless steel. The high strength-to-specific-weight ratio, their light weight, and good thermal properties make glass-ceramics excellent prospective candidates to replace metals presently used in aviation [522-525]. The permissible operating stresses for Pyroceram 9606 are 210-280 kg/cm^2. Having a softening temperature of 1250°C, this material is capable of retaining its strength under load at 700°C for 1000 h.

Although glass-ceramics only insignificantly decrease in strength upon heating to 700-780°C, the flexure strength of Pyrocerams 9605 and 9606 at temperatures higher than approximately 790°C drops rather rapidly (Fig. 81). Glass-ceramics do not possess viscosity and ductility, and are classified as brittle materials, even though their impact strength is considerably higher than that of glass [526].

Hinz and Baiburt [345] showed that the σ_f of glass-ceramics depends primarily on the degree of homogeneity and the microstructure of the samples, with the phase composition playing only

a secondary role. The low strength of samples containing cordierite was explained in terms of their coarse-grained structure. They
explain the scatter in the results of the measurements by the difference in the homogeneity of the samples which, in turn, depends on
the melting and casting conditions. The high melting point, i.e.,
the relatively low viscosity of the fused materials prior to casting,
made it possible to obtain a uniform crystalline structure and a
high σ_f.

In order to produce glass-ceramics having a maximum
strength, Stookey [486] believes that it would be of considerable interest to study the effect on strength of a decrease to very small
crystal sizes, such as to molecular sizes. It is not yet clear what
degree of strength could be obtained by reducing the crystal size
to such small dimensions, and at the same time preventing the
structure from becoming amorphous. The strength of a ceramic
with grain size greater than 20 μ is inversely proportional to the
square root of its grain size and is independent of surface cracks
[527]. The internal strength of such glass must be more than
70,000 kg/cm^2; however, under the influence of surface cracks,
this is reduced to 400-700 kg/cm^2. It is assumed that the strength
of glass-ceramics must increase considerably with decreasing crystal size to the point where phase boundaries practically disappear.
However, this is accompanied by a simultaneous effect of surface
microcracks on the strength of such glass-ceramics [486].

The anisotropy of aluminum titanate or eucryptite crystals,
i.e., nonuniformity of the properties along the directions of the
various axes, decreases the strength of sintered ceramics due to
the emergence of microcracks or due to reduced areas [528]. In
the opinion of Stookey [486], glass-ceramics containing eucryptite
or other anisotropic crystals experience the influence of these
factors to a lesser degree, in view of the significantly smaller size
of the crystals and the higher strength. Nevertheless, to take
glass-ceramics catalyzed by phosphates as an example, it was observed that glass-ceramics containing cristobalite as the primary
crystalline phase had lower strength than glass-ceramics in which
quartz was the primary crystalline phase [381]. This is caused by
the larger (by 5%) decrease in volume during the transformation
of α-cristobalite into its β phase within the temperature range
220-270°C, as well as by the appearance of stresses and microcracks. The volumetric changes of quartz near 575°C are only 2%,

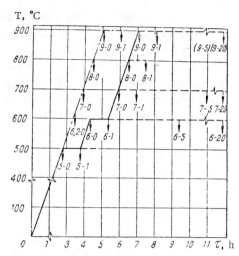

Fig. 82. Heat-treatment procedure for the production of glass-ceramics. Solid curves, series N; dashed curves, series H.

Table 62. Mechanical Strength of Sintered Ceramics and Glass-Ceramics Having the Same Crystal Composition

Primary crystalline phase	σ_f (kg/cm^2)	
	Sintered ceramic	Abraded glass-ceramic
Cordierite	350—1050	1750
β-Spodumene	350—700	1400
β-Eucryptite	140	1120

which is why they exert a lesser effect on the strength of the glass-ceramic. The σ_f of glass-ceramics of a simple composition is always higher than the σ_f of the ceramic with analogous composition (see Table 62, as based on [486]).

Watanabe et al. [529] tested the strength of photosensitive glass of the composition 80.8 SiO$_2$, 4.0 Al$_2$O$_3$, 12.4 Li$_2$O, 2.5 K$_2$O, 0.025 CeO$_2$, 0.015 SnO$_2$, and 0.18 AgCl, and of its crystallization products at various stages of heat treatment, in order to explain to what degree the strength of a photosensitive glass-ceramic is a function of microcrystalline structure, chemical composition, physical characteristics of the crystals formed, chemical composition of the residual glassy phase, or of other factors.

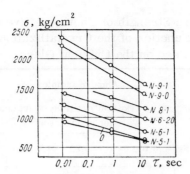

Fig. 83. Static fatigue of abraded glass-ceramic samples at the various stages of heat treatment. τ) Loading time; σ) strengh; 0) untreated sample. Tests were performed on samples immersed in distilled water.

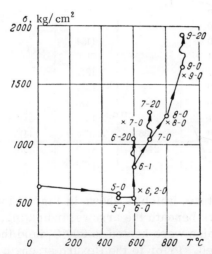

Fig. 84. Strength of abraded glass-ceramic samples as a function of heat-treatment procedure at constant loading time. T) Temperature of heat treatment; σ) strength. The loading time was 0.82 sec. X) Series H; o) series N.

Glass samples in the form of rods 1.27-1.9 mm in diameter were heated during sitallization at a rate of 3 deg/min to 900°C (series H in Fig. 82), or they were held for an additional hour at 500 and 600°C (series N in Fig. 82). In order to test their strength properties, they were rapidly cooled from the given temperature

Table 63. Flexture Strength of Photosensitive Glass-Ceramic
Samples as a Function of the Crystallization Procedure
Used on the Original Glass

Heat-treatment procedure		Abraded samples			Nonabraded samples
heating	time at temp.	σ_f (kg/cm^2) at time of application of load, sec			
°C	h	0.012	0.82	15	0.82
Freshly drawn glass		979	781	593	Above 5600
500	0	952	758	613	Above 4900
500	1	900	742	594	Above 4900
600	0	946	734	609	4865
600	1	1213	963	750	3570
600	5	—	959	—	—
600	20	1593	1161	997	—
700	0	—	1154	—	2464
700	1	—	1130	—	—
700	7	—	1212	—	—
700	20	—	1356	—	—
800	0	—	1326	—	1831
800	1	—	1342	1149	—
900	0	2236	1693	1415	2667
900	1	2442	1203	1574	—
900	5	—	1830	—	2254

to room temperature, which is shown in Fig. 82 by arrows pointing down, the numbers beneath the arrows, indicating, for instance, by 9-1 that the samples were heated to 900°C, held there for 1 h, and then rapidly cooled. Prior to the flexure strength tests, which were performed in distilled water, the samples were subjected to sand-blast treatment and were exposed to water vapors in an dessicator for 15-20 h. Each strength value obtained was the average of 20 measurements, and the results are presented in Table 63 and in Fig. 83 (in the form of static fatigue curves) [529].

From the results obtained, it follows that the strength of abraded samples increases with increasing heating time, and after such samples have undergone a full heat-treatment cycle, their strength is double that of the original untreated glass, with the material at all stages of heat treatment exhibiting static fatigue similar to the fatigue of the conventional sodium calcium silicate glass.

The change in strength as a function of the degree of heat treatment is shown in Fig. 84, from which it can be seen that at the early stages (points 5—0, 5—1) of heat treatment, the σ_f decreases insignificantly, which the authors [529] explain in terms of annealing of the samples which had previously undergone rapid cooling. The formation of nuclei (points 5—1, 6—0) did not have a marked effect on strength, in spite of the loss of transparency and the appearance of a yellow color. Depending on how long the material is subjected to heat treatment, the original glass transforms into photosensitive glass-ceramic of a white color and, because of the crystallization taking place, an increase in strength results. The strength of samples subjected to continuous heating at 500 and 600°C (points of series H in Fig. 84), for all practical purposes, does not differ from the strength of samples of the series N, which were subjected to heat treatment at these temperatures and held at each temperature for 1 h. Based on these results, the authors [529] concluded that, in order to produce photosensitive glass-ceramics of maximum strength, these holding temperatures may be eliminated as long as this does not result in the deformation of the articles. We find it impossible to agree with this conclusion, inasmuch as our investigations relative to the effect of various crystallization procedures on the strength of photosensitive glass-ceramics showed that holding the materials at the given temperatures for a given time — especially during the intermediate graduated cycles of cooling and heating — is exceptionally important for the formation and the growth of the maximum number of nuclei, as well as for the prevention of deformation of the articles and for obtaining very high strengths.

The prolongation of holding time at intermediate temperatures had only a slight effect on the strength of abraded samples. In order to reach a maximum strength, it sufficed to heat the sample at 900°C for 1 h, since further heat treatment only slightly changed the strength obtained. Higher temperatures were not very applicable, inasmuch as this material had a melting point of approximately 950°C [529].

A comparison between the behavior of abraded and nonabraded samples showed that the strength of nonabraded samples decreased with increasing degree of heat treatment up to a temperature of 800°C, while at the same stages of heat treatment, the strength of the abraded samples increased. Within the tempera-

Table 64. Dependence of the Ratio Between the
Strengths of Abraded and Nonabraded Samples on
Heat-Treatment Procedure

Heat-treatment procedure		σ_a/σ_0
heating, °C	time at temp., h	
Freshly drawn glass		0.14
500	0	0.15
500	1	0.15
600	0	0.15
600	1	0.27
700	0	0.47
800	0	0.72
900	0	0.63
900	5	0.81

ture range 800-900°C, the strength of nonabraded samples increased somewhat.

Watanabe et al. [529] think that the increased strength of abraded photosensitive glass-ceramics is caused primarily by an increase in the wear resistance, and not by a high internal strength, which is also confirmed by data of Table 64 [529], where σ_a/σ_0 denotes the ratio between the strength of abraded samples to that of nonabraded samples.

The gradual decrease in the strength of nonabraded samples with increasing heat-treatment time is explained by Watanabe et al. [529] by the fact that the photosensitive glass-ceramic is similar to glass containing Griffith cracks of increasing sizes. The increase in the strength of abraded samples may be caused, according to them, either by the limiting of the size of the cracks due to the growth of mutually joined crystals, or by the increase during the heat-treatment process of the hardness and wear resistance of

the residual glassy phase, which continuously changes its composition during crystallization. The existence in the photosensitive glass-ceramic of static fatigue similar to that indigenous to glass gave the authors [529] a basis for assuming that its strength and wear resistance depend to a significant degree on the changes in the chemical composition and the properties of the glassy phase, while microcrystallinity is not the most important factor. This conclusion is rather unusual, since the properties of glass-ceramics are generally associated with their microcrystalline structure, although, as early as 1950, Kitaigorodskii [14] pointed out the important role played by the glassy phase. In order to check the validity of this conclusion, special investigations of glass-ceramics and photosensitive glass-ceramics should be set up, although the primary difficulty here is that no quantitative method exists at present for the determination of the composition and the relative amounts in these materials of the crystalline and the glassy phases.

In order to improve the mechanical strength of photosensitive glass-ceramics, the present author investigated the effect of chemical composition, the degree of homogeneity of the original photosensitive glass, the radiation exposure, and the structural changes occurring in glass during the heat-treatment process, on the mechanical strength and thermal expansion of the crystallized material.

The σ_f was determined for samples in the form of square plates $9.6 \times 9.6 \times 3$ mm in size or in the form of disks 9.6 mm in diameter machined from photosensitive glasses 1, 2, and 3 of varying degree of homogeneity. In addition, glasses 1 and 3 differed from glass 2 by having a somewhat higher content of Al_2O_3 and a lower content of alkali oxides. Each σ_f value represented an average of 25-100 measurements. The irradiation time of photosensitive glass samples using ultraviolet light from a PRK-7 lamp at a distance 250-300 mm from the object varied from 0 to 1000 min. The results of these tests are given in Table 65.

By examining the data of Table 65, it can be seen that even for different crystallization temperatures, there exists an optimum irradiation exposure for the photosensitive glass (64 or 60 min) to which there corresponds a maximum σ_f equal to 2750 or 2880 kg/cm^2. Materials with this kind of strength were characterized by a dense, fine-crystalline microstructure, with a crystal size of less than 1 μ and with the smallest amount of the glassy phase present. With the exposure increased beyond the optimum for a given photosensitive glass, crystal growth occurs, with a concomitant decrease in mechanical strength. A decrease in the crystal size with increasing exposure time is explained by the increase in the num-

Table 65. Dependence on Irradiation Time of σ_f for
Photosensitive Glasses Crystallized According to
Different Heat-Treatment Procedures *

Glass 1		Glass 2		Glass 3	
Irradiation time, min	σ_f, kg/cm^2	Irradiation time, min	σ_f, kg/cm^2	Irradiation time, min	σ_f, kg/cm^2
16	2640	16	2080	10	2640
32	2650	32	2480	20	2760
64	2890	64	2750	30	2415
		128	2400	40	2700
		256	2480	60	2880
				90	2265
				120	2400

* Crystallization temperature and total heat treatment time for the three glasses, are, respectively: 1) 750°C and 16 h; 2) 825°C and 140 min; 3) 825°C and 16 h.

ber of nuclei in the form of colloidal Ag particles, while the total amount of the precipitating metal remains unchanged [233]. At intermediate exposure, the average size of a given number of particles becomes equal to the critical size necessary for the effective formation of nuclei. Corresponding to the optimum intermediate exposure, at which the majority of the nuclei attains the critical size, there is a maximum σ_f value (see Table 65). However, as the irradiation exposure is further increased, the nuclei become too small to serve as effective catalysts for the crystallization of photosensitive glass; some of the crystals in this case apparently lose their heterogeneous character and are no longer characterized by epitaxial growth which, in turn, results in an increase in the crystal size.

A preliminary investigation of the dependence on the crystallization procedure of σ_f for photosensitive glass-ceramics (Fig. 85) was performed on the insufficiently homogeneous photosensitive glasses 1 and 2 melted in a tank furnace without stirring the melt (see page 162).

One of the first experimental heat-treatment procedures, No. 3 (Fig. 85), was characterized by a moderate initial rate of temperature increase, by the absence of intermediate cooling, and by further graduated heating to 750°C with a considerably larger total cycle time above 15 h. The σ_f of samples of glass 1 crystal-

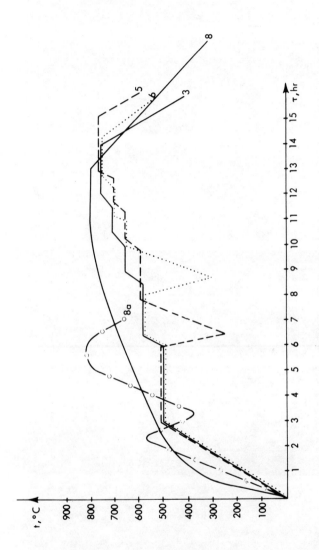

Fig. 85. Experimental heat-treatment procedures for photosensitive glass-ceramic samples subjected to mechanical strength tests.

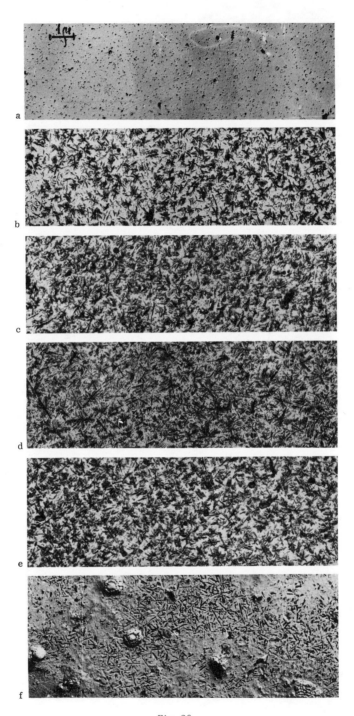

Fig. 86

lized according to this procedure attained very high values, lying within the range 2600-3600 kg/cm^2. Because of the relatively low final crystallization temperature, the material contained acicular crystals of lithium metasilicate 1-2.5 μ in size, and it contained short prismatic β-quartz crystals as the secondary phase, with the total amount of the crystalline phase not exceeding 60%. In order to provide better conditions for the formation of nuclei [269] and to increase the amount of the crystalline phase present, procedure No. 5 was tried (Fig. 85), differing from procedure No. 3 only by intermediate cooling from 500 to 250°C and a further increase in temperature to 580°C.

Intermediate cooling of photosensitive glass, as well as holding within the low-temperature range, such as at 500°C for 3 h (see Fig. 86a), also resulted in the droplike phase separation of the microphases which were discussed previously (see page 76).

As a result of introducing intermediary cooling (procedure No. 5 in Fig. 85), a further, even more marked increase in the σ_f of the photosensitive glass-ceramic was noted, to values of 3400-4100 kg/cm^2; a decrease in the deformation of the article to 0-5% and a noticeable decrease in the amount of the glassy phase in the microstructure of the material were also noted, with acicular lithium metasilicate crystals also being present in the microstructure, but having a crystal size ranging from 0.6 to 0.2 μ as compared to the 1-2.5 μ for the procedure not including intermediary cooling. Intermediary cooling of photosensitive glass 2 from 590 to 300°C (procedure No. 6 in Fig. 85), with the material being held at the final temperature of 750°C for 90 min, resulted in an even greater increase in σ_f, to 3930-5580 kg/cm^2. The strength of the articles obtained by crystallization of photosensitive glass according to the procedure including intermediary cooling did not, on the average, exceed 3200 kg/cm^2.

The increase in σ_f at individual stages of the temperature crystallization procedures Nos. 5 and 6 (Fig. 85) was studied for samples of photosensitive glass 2, the initial strength of which was

---

Fig. 86. Formation of nuclei and the growth of crystals in photosensitive glass subjected to the following heat treatment: (a) Holding at 500°C for 3 h; (b) holding at 500°C for 3 h, then cooling from 500°C to 250°C, and reheating to 580°C; (c) as above, plus holding at 580°C for 2 h; (d) as above, plus holding at 650°C for 1 h; (e) as above, plus holding at 700°C for 1 h; (f) as above, plus holding at 750°C for 2 h.

1320 kg/cm^2. After the material was heated to 500°C at a rate of 2.8 deg/min and held there for 3 h, the σ_f increased to 1620 kg/cm^2. As a result of intermediary cooling from 500 or 590°C to 250°C, and the subsequent increase in temperature to 580°C, the formation and the growth of numerous lithium metasilicate crystals took place, increasing their size from 0.1 to 0.3-0.6 μ (Fig. 86b), although the σ_f became 1560 kg/cm^2. With the temperature increasing first to 580°C and then to 650°C, and with holding of the material at these temperatures for 2 h and 1 h, respectively, an increase in the size of the acicular crystals of lithium metasilicate to 1 μ was noted, as were an increase in the degree of crystallization and an increase in σ_f to 1680 and 1720 kg/cm^2 (Figs. 86c, d). An even greater increase in the amount of the crystalline phase and an even greater decrease in the amount of the glassy phase, accompanied by a slight decrease in the size of the crystals to 0.6 μ and the formation of a dense microcrystalline structure, took place after the temperature was increased to 700°C and the material held there for 1 h, which resulted in the σ_f increasing to 1970 kg/cm^2 (Fig. 86e). Finally, after the material was held for 2 h at the final crystallization temperature of 750°C, σ_f increased to 3200 kg/cm^2. The amount of the crystalline phase, consisting of lithium metasilicate crystals 0.2-0.4 μ in size and a small amount of β-quartz, increased to 90% (Fig. 86f).

For comparison purposes, some articles made of glass 2 were crystallized using procedure No. 8 without intermediate cooling (Fig. 85). Even in spite of the higher temperatures of final crystallization — 750, 780, 800, and 825°C — the σ_f of such samples did not exceed values of 2700-2970 kg/cm^2, as compared to 3200-5580 kg/cm^2 for samples which were subjected to the procedure involving intermediary cooling and a final crystallization temperature of 750°C. By introducing into procedure No. 8 intermediary cooling from 590°C to 300°C (procedure No. 8a in Fig. 85), the σ_f value at once increased to 3100 kg/cm^2. Apparently, one could obtain even higher strength values if the total time of the heat-treatment cycle were increased from 8 to 15-16 h.

The variation coefficient V characterizing the scatter of experimentally determined strength values fluctuated within a relatively narrow range (from 13 to 25%) for photosensitive glass-ceramics produced from nonhomogeneous photosensitive glass 1 and 2. This demonstrates the statistically uniform effect of defects

Table 66. Mechanical Flexure Strength of Photosensitive Glass–Ceramics Prepared from a Homogeneous Photosensitive Glass

Procedure No.	Heat-treatment procedure	Irradiation time, min	σ_f, kg/cm²	Average deviation, kg/cm²	Variation coeff. V, %	Crystalline phases
1	625°C for 15 min, cooled to 300°C; 825°C for 45 min	60	6590	755	16.3	Lithium metasilicate, β-quartz
2	625°C for 15 min, cooled to 370°C; 825°C for 15 min	90	1870	440	27.3	Lithium metasilicate, β-quartz
3	675°C for 15 min, cooled to 300°C; 825°C for 45 min	90 / 60 / 120	2265 / 2880 / 2400	322 / 321 / 298	21.3 / 14.5 / 15.7	Lithium metasilicate, β-quartz
4	500°C for 3 h, cooled to 250°C; 580°C for 2 h; 600°C for 1 h; 700°C for 1 h; 750°C for 2 h	60	3730	464	16.4	Lithium metasilicate, β-quartz
5	500°C for 2 h, cooled to 250°C; 825°C for 45 min	60	6800	631	14.2	Lithium metasilicate, β-quartz
6	500°C for 2 h, cooled to 250°C; 625°C for 15 min; 825°C for 45 min	60	6230	826	17.1	Lithium metasilicate, β-quartz
7	625°C for 15 min, taken up to 870°C	60	3380	476	20.1	β-quartz, lithium metasilicate, β-spodumene and solid solution of silica in lithium disilicate, α-quartz
8	625°C for 15 min, cooled to 300°C; taken up to 850°C	60	3250	171	17.4	β-quartz, lithium metasilicate, solid solution of silica in lithium disilicate, β-spodumene, α-quartz
9	625°C for 15 min, cooled to 300°C; taken up to 870°C	60	3920	757	23.6	β-quartz, lithium metasilicate, very small amount of β-spodumene and solid solution of silica in lithium disilicate, α-quartz

in the form of heterogeneities in photosensitive glasses melted in a batch-operated furnace on the strength of the photosensitive glass-ceramic articles produced.

It seemed to be of interest to verify the strengthening effect in photosensitive glass-ceramics produced from nonhomogeneous glasses using samples of photosensitive glass-ceramics prepared from the homogeneous photosensitive glass 3, which was melted in a potter's kiln with mechanical stirring of the melt (see page 162). The heat-treatment procedure and the irradiation used for the photosensitive glass, the σ_f values of the photosensitive glass-ceramic, and the identification of the crystalline phases, are shown in Table 66.

From the data of Table 66, it follows that intermediate cooling to 370°C (procedure No. 2, $\sigma_f = 1870$ kg/cm^2) is not sufficient for attaining the high strength which was obtained as a result of the crystallization according to procedure No. 1 — namely, 6590 kg/cm^2. Moreover, irradiation exposure of more than 60 min for a given glass decreases the σ_f values, which is in conformity with the data presented previously concerning the existence of an optimum irradiation exposure. A very important factor causing the strengthening, and simultaneous increase in deformation, of articles is the fact that following procedure No. 1, the material is held at the final temperature longer (45 min as compared to 15 min) than when procedure No. 2 is being followed. Procedure No. 4 is characterized by a long total time of the heat-treatment cycle, exceeding 18 h, by a moderate rate of initial heating (2.8 deg/min), by holding for a sufficient time within the temperature region of the precrystallization period (3 h at 500°C), by low intermediate cooling, and by further stepwise increase in the temperature to 580, 600, 700, and 750°C, with holding at each of these temperatures for 1-2 h. To this heat-treatment procedure there corresponds a high flexure strength, σ_f being 3730 kg/cm^2, with no deformation of the articles being observed. When procedure No. 6 was used, a sufficiently high σ_f — namely, 6230 kg/cm^2 — was obtained; however, the deformation was on the order of 17%, and for procedure No. 5, it was 27%. Most of the variation coefficient values V were within the range 14-20%, as compared to 13-25% for photosensitive glass-ceramics made of nonhomogeneous glass. In individual cases, this coefficient attained values of 27.3 or 23.6% (procedures Nos. 2 and 9 in Table 66). To these V values there correspond relative-

ly low σ_f values. The higher V values obtained for the homogeneous glass may not necessarily be associated with the increased degree of homogeneity, although this is not precluded. They may be
caused, as in case of photosensitive glass-ceramics made from
nonhomogeneous glass, by the effect of other factors, such as the
presence of surface defects and the corrosion by the surrounding
medium, in view of the fact that glass-crystalline materials, as
well as glass, show the presence of fatigue under the effect of mechanical loads and moisture in the atmosphere [529].

The effect of heat treatment on the mechanical strength of
glass-ceramics of the $Li_2O-MgO-Al_2O_3-SiO_2$ system was studied
by Sakka et al. [530]. Glass of the composition 4 Li_2O, 15 MgO,
23 Al_2O_3, and 62 SiO_2 was heated from room temperature to 1200°C
at a rate of 5 deg/min and held at that temperature for 2 h, and
was thus transformed into a glass-ceramic with the maximum
σ_f = 1550 kg/cm^2. At 850°C, β-eucryptite precipitated as the
primary phase, and at 1200°C, it was β-spodumene, the crystal
size of which decreased with increased temperature. Above
1000°C, a marked increase in the density of the samples was observed. Slow heating at a rate of 5 deg/min within the temperature range 800-900°C or increased holding at temperature resulted
in increased σ_f, which was caused by a decrease in the size of β-
spodumene grains and a denser microstructure [530].

Bondarev and Minakov [531, 532] studied the effect of crystallization temperature on the mechanical strength and structure
of glasses and glass-ceramics of the $SiO_2-Al_2O_3-Li_2O$ system
with silver additions and of the $SiO_2-Al_2O_3-CaO-Na_2O$ system
with fluorine additions. It was determined by electron microscopy
that in glasses of the former system, the catalytic crystallization
became stimulated without phase separation of the glass taking
place, whereas the glasses of the latter system separated into two
phases prior to crystallization. Upon heating the lithium aluminosilicate glass to 600°C, islets of acicular crystals of lithium metasilicate measuring from 1 to 5 μ in diameter developed, with the
flexure strength of the glass increasing from 340 to 650 kg/cm^2.
Upon heating the glass to 700°C, the Li_2SiO_3 needles became larger
and tridymite appeared; the degree of crystallization was 60%, and
the strength increased to 960 kg/cm^2. Taking the temperature up
to 830-850°C caused a sharp change in the structure — namely, recrystallization. The Li_2SiO_3 crystals disintegrated and, instead,

large columnar crystals of lithium disilicate $Li_2Si_2O_5$ appeared, the degree of crystallization increased, and σ_f increased to 1350 kg/cm^2. Upon raising the temperature to 900°C, the process of the formation of $Li_2Si_2O_5$ became completed, the degree of crystallization amounted to 90%, and σ_f attained a maximum value — namely, 1536 kg/cm^2. The structure of the glass-ceramic consisted of randomly oriented lithium disilicate crystals having a diameter of 0.5-1 μ and a length of 1-10 μ; between these crystals was a small amount of tridymite and the residual glassy phase.

A further increase of the temperature to 980°C was accompanied by softening, recrystallization, and a sharp deterioration in the properties of the glass-ceramic. The structure became friable and coarse-grained, and the strength decreased to 150 kg/cm^2.

After being prepared and after normal annealing, glass of the $SiO_2-Al_2O_3-CaO-Na_2O$ plus fluorine system was perfectly transparent, although separated into several noncrystalline phases. Its σ_f was 198 kg/cm^2. Upon being heated to 700°C, a small number of CaF_2 and NaF crystals up to 0.3 μ in size appeared, and the strength increased to 250 kg/cm^2. As the temperature was increased to 800°C, albite and anorthite crystals 1-2 μ in size appeared, the degree of crystallization amounted to 40%, and the strength of the glass-ceramic reached a value of 280 kg/cm^2. At 900°C, the degree of crystallization amounted to 70%, with the flexure strength being 630 kg/cm^2. After heating to 980-1000°C, total crystallization took place, accompanied by additional precipitation of small amounts of diopside, CaO · MgO · 2SiO$_2$, or enstatite, MgO · SiO$_2$. The size of these crystals ranged from one to several microns, with the strength of the glass-ceramic attaining a maximum value of 675 kg/cm^2. At 1100°C, the crystallized mass became fused and transformed into glass, while the strength decreased to 490 kg/cm^2. Figure 87 shows the strength of the glasses investigated and of the glass-ceramics made from them as a function of their crystallization temperature.

Chistoserdov and Soboleva [533] determined σ_f at various temperatures for photosensitive glass-ceramics based on the photosensitive glass of the following composition: 70-80 SiO_2, 4-10 Al_2O_3, 12-13 Li_2O, and 2-5 K_2O. Results, given in Fig. 88, show that at 800°C, the strength decreased by more than a factor of two. These authors also found that strength increases with increasing

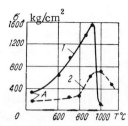

Fig. 87. Dependence of the strength of glass-ceramics on their crystallization temperature. T) Heat-treatment temperature; σ) strength. 1) For the SiO_2–Al_2O_3–Li_2O system; 2) for the SiO_2–Al_2O_3–CaO–Na_2O system. A) Original glass.

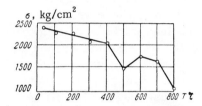

Fig. 88. Strength of lithium-containing glass-ceramics in the temperature range 20-800°C.

temperature for alkali-free cordierite glass-ceramics of the composition 40-70 SiO_2, 20-35 Al_2O_3, 10-25 MgO, and 5-20 TiO_2 for glasses crystallized using various procedures.

The behavior of lithium-containing materials during heating is explained by the authors [533] in the following manner. Crystallization of photosensitive glasses starts from the nuclei which are uniformly distributed throughout the bulk of the glass, while the glassy phase remains present in the external boundary of every microcrystal. Crystals growing on every nucleus take up a volume approximately 2-4% less than that occupied by the original glass. Because of the greater α, the volume of the crystals decreases more intensely during cooling than does the volume of the glass, as a result of which the thin layers of the glass present between the crystals are in a state of compression similar to that experienced by the external layers of tempered glass, and the entire system has considerable mechanical strength. During heating, the reverse process takes place and the strength decreases.

The increase in strength of cordierite materials with increasing temperature is explained either by saying that the growth of crystals proceeds not from the nucleus, but from the sides of the volumetric skeleton, within which there is a glassy phase, or by saying that the skeleton is permeated by a secondary skeleton of the residual glassy phase.

While investigating the dependence of the σ_f of phosphate-containing glass-ceramics on chemical and mineralogical composition, Partridge and McMillan [381] found that by adding Al_2O_3 to glass containing Li_2O and SiO_2, the formation of lithium alumino-silicate crystals resulted, which decreased the σ_f of the glass-ceramic. Corresponding to the maximum Al_2O_3 content was a minimum in the σ_f of the glass-ceramic. The high strength of these glass-ceramics, comparable to the strength of high-alumina ceramics, is explained by the authors [381] by the fine-crystalline interlaced microstructure. According to other investigators [534, 535], the strength of glass-ceramics is caused by the favorable combination between the strength of crystalline regions and the elasticity of amorphous portions. With the temperature increasing to 300-400°C, the σ_f of phosphate-containing glass-ceramics decreases, although upon further heating from 400 to 600°C, a slight recovery of σ_f takes place. Within the temperature range 20-700°C, these glass-ceramics retain a strength equal to the strength of high-alumina ceramics. The impact strength of phosphate-containing glass-ceramics is 2.5 times higher than that of high-alumina ceramics, and 8 times higher than that of Pyrex glass, which is explained by their fine-crystalline interlaced structure and a lower elastic modulus, allowing for the decrease in the deformation of the sample and in the stresses occurring in it during the absorption of the impact energy [381]. Phosphate-containing glass-ceramics of type A and B, in contrast to high-alumina ceramics, do not noticeably decrease their impact strength upon heating to 300°C.

The tensile strength of glass-ceramics of the $SiO_2-Al_2O_3-Li_2O-MgO$ system at the various stages of heat treatment was studied by Ownly et al. [536, 537], who found that there is an increase, and then a slight decrease, in the strength with increasing temperature and duration of heat treatment. A more significant effect on the strength of the glass-ceramic was shown by the initial period of heat treatment, corresponding to the formation of nuclei.

The strength and the elastic modulus of some two-phase glass-ceramics increased in proportion to the amount of the crystalline phase present, and attained, according to Binns' data [727], maximum values for identical thermal expansion of the glass and the crystalline phase.

b. Elastic Modulus

Young's modulus for conventional glasses ranges from 2100 to 9800 kg/mm^2 — more frequently, from 6000 to 8000 kg/mm^2 —

depending on the chemical composition and the heat treatment [538, 539]. The E of glass-ceramics and sintered ceramics depends primarily on the elastic modulus of the primary crystalline phase, ranging from 7000 kg/mm^2 for mullite or steatite to 37,100 kg/mm^2 for high-alumina ceramics [486]. The E of glass-ceramics is considerably higher than that of glasses of the same composition. Although glass-ceramics are lighter than aluminum, their rigidity is higher, i.e., they are less flexible than aluminum. Their E ranges between 8,760 and 14,000 kg/mm^2. The E values for glass-ceramics of the cordierite type range from 11,900 to 14,000 kg/mm^2, compared to 9,800 kg/mm^2 for glass of the same composition [486]. The elasticity of glass-ceramics of certain types is double that of window glass and is on the order of $^2/_3$ of the elasticity of high-carbon steel.

The E values for phosphate-containing glass-ceramics at room temperature range from 7,000 to 15,000 kg/mm^2, i.e., they are higher than the corresponding values for glasses and porcelain, but considerably lower than the values for high-alumina ceramics [381]. Glass-ceramics with a high quartz content have increased E values, and have a minimum on the curves showing the dependence of E on temperature within the region of the phase transformation of quartz, i.e., at 573°C. The presence of cristobalite caused the appearance of a minimum on these curves and a slight increase in E with increasing temperature to 300°C [381].

Kachan and Shalimo [540] studied the dependence of E of glasses and glass-ceramics of the BaO—CaO—Al$_2$O$_3$—SiO$_2$ system on the heating rate and on the final temperature of heat treatment, and found that there are changes in E in the temperature range 725-775°C which, in their opinion, are caused by phase separation in the glass and by the change in the phase composition of the glass-ceramics.

c. Hardness

The dense microcrystalline structure of glass-ceramics is responsible for the high hardness of the latter, approaching the hardness of tempered steels and exceeding the hardness of fused quartz, brass, cast iron, high-carbon stainless steel, granite, and glass [541-550]. Glass-ceramics have a high resistance to scratching, which has almost no effect on their strength. Pyroceram 9606 is 40% harder than borosilicate glass. It is very resistant to the abrasive action of sand and to erosion due to rain, and it can be ground and polished in the glassy and the crystallized states, making it possible to maintain rigid dimensional tolerances. The Vickers microhardness of Pyroceram 9606 indented with a diamond pyramid indenter at a 500-g load, is equal to 640 kg/mm^2, which is close to the hardness of tempered instrumental steel (550-580 kg/mm^2). For comparison purposes, the microhardness of sheet glass, as determined by us at a 200-g load, was 582-584 kg/mm^2, while that of continuously rolled glass was 607 kg/mm^2 [551]. Because of their high hardness, glass-ceramics have a high wear resistance [552].

Tashiro and Sakka [553] studied the Vickers diamond pyramid microhardness and σ_f of photosensitive glass of the composition 81 SiO$_2$, 12.5 Li$_2$O, 2.5 K$_2$O, 4 Al$_2$O$_3$, 0.03 CeO$_2$, and 0.027 Au, as dependent on the crystal size. Samples 2.5 × 5 × 50 mm in size were irradiated by the ultraviolet light emitted from a high-pressure, 500-W mercury lamp located 10 cm from the object. The duration of the exposure was from 2 to 1000 min. The heat treatment included heating at 510°C for 30 min for the formation of nuclei, increasing the temperature to 620°C and holding there for 60 min — which led to the crystallization from the glass matrix of approximately 40% Li$_2$SiO$_3$ — and heating the samples to 900°C and holding them there for 60 min so as to transform the glass into photosensitive glass-ceramic. The size of the Li$_2$Si$_2$O$_5$ and β-quartz crystals varied from 0.85 to 2.3 μ, depending on the duration of exposure. The microhardness and the σ_f values were measured on samples which were either subjected to a complete heat-treatment cycle, or only to heating to 620°C. Crystallization resulted in increased σ_f and microhardness of the photosensitive glass-ceramic. The relationship between the average size d of the grains of the crystals and the mechanical properties M (σ_f and microhardness) was expressed by the equation M = const d$^{-1/2}$ (Fig. 89). Partial crystallization of the glassy phase in samples heated to 620°C increased their σ_f. Glasses containing Au, Ag, Cu, or Pt as the catalysts also increased their microhardness after crystallization [554].

According to data of Hinz and Baiburt [345], the microhardness of samples containing cordierite and titanates of Mg and Al ranged from 800 to 850 kg/mm^2. Samples containing clinoenstatite and spinel or sappharine had the highest microhardness, 1400-1440

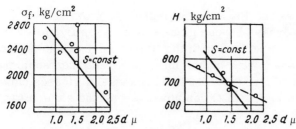

Fig. 89. Mechanical strength of a glass-ceramic as dependent on the size of the microcrystals. The glass had the following composition: $81SiO_2$, $12.5Li_2O$, $2.5K_2O$, $4Al_2O_3$, $0.03CeO_2$, and $0.027 Au$. Diameters of primary crystals (620°C) and secondary crystals (900°C), respectively, are as follows for the indicated durations of ultraviolet irradiation: 0 min − and 2.3 μ ; 2 min, 1.0 and 1.4 μ ; 30 min, 0.10 and 1.1 μ ; 180 min, 0.07 and 0.85 μ ; 600 min, 0.5 and 1.3 μ ; 1000 min, 1.0 and 1.4 μ.

Table 67. Microhardness of Crystallized Lithium Silicate Glasses

Heat-treatment conditions	Microhardness (kg/mm^2) at the Li_2O content (mol.%)								
	16.7	23.4	27.5	29.2	34.4	37.1	41.6	43.7	48.0
Original glass	540	470	455	455	470	460	410	390	375
480° C; 5; 20—24 h	—	495	495	465	480	635	740	—	765
620° C; 5; 20 h	—	670	—	—	660	—	—	—	—
480° C; 620—680°; for 20—24 h	—	710	645	635	560	620	765	—	—
800° C; 5; 20 h	—	680	—	—	565	—	—	—	—
480° C; 620—630; 960—1000°; for 18-24 h	—	465	435	435	—	505	360	—	—

kg/mm^2. According to these authors, the microhardness of glass-ceramics of the cordierite system depends to a larger degree on the precipitating crystalline phases than on the heterogeneity of the structure.

Nevertheless, Korelova et al. [555] showed that the scatter in the microhardness values of crystallized two-component lithium silicate glasses is associated with the heterogeneity of their microstructure. The compositions of the glasses they investigated, the heat-treatment procedures, and the respective microhardness values, are presented in Table 67 (from [555]), from which it can be seen that as the Li_2O content increases from 16.7 to 48.0 mol.%, the microhardness of these glasses decreases from 540 to 375 kg/mm^2. A comparison with the literature data shows that lithium silicate glasses have a higher microhardness than sodium or potassium silicate glasses. The microhardness of glasses containing from 23 to 34 mol.% Li_2O remained almost the same after it was treated at 480°C for 20-24 h.

Heating these glasses at 620 and 800°C for 5 and 20 h increased their microhardness values by 30-40% due to the precipitation of lithium disilicate crystals. After double heat treatment (480 and 620°C for 20 h each) of the glass containing 23.4 mol.% Li_2O, an even higher microhardness was observed, 700 kg/mm^2, which is explained in terms of the fine-crystalline structure of such samples. Increasing the temperature of heat treatment to 960°C resulted in a concomitant significant decrease in the microhardness and an increase in the brittleness of the crystallization products which, according to these authors, is associated with the crystallization at high temperatures of the residual glassy silica. The microhardness of glasses containing 37.1 and 41.6 mol.% Li_2O increased significantly after they were held at 480°C, which is explained in terms of their already crystallizing at this temperature. In addition to lithium disilicate, lithium metasilicate was also observed in the microstructure of these samples. Glasses with 41.6 mol.% Li_2O were characterized by an exceptionally thin crystalline structure and by the highest microhardness, 740-765 kg/mm^2. Crystals close in composition to lithium metasilicate had the same microhardness values. As a result of this investigation, it was determined that the microhardness of crystallized lithium silicate glasses depends not only on the chemical composition of the precipitating crystals, but also on their size, shape, and mutual wetting, as well as on the emergence or absence of internal cracks.

Using the infrared absorption spectra method, Avgustinik and Klanina [556] observed an increase in the microhardness of glass of the composition 15% Li_2O, 15% CaO, and 70% SiO_2 associated with the development of so-called prenucleation groups. Under favorable thermodynamic conditions, these prenucleation groups can be transformed into crystalline nuclei or seeds. The microhardness of transparent glass held during cooling from the melt at 1200, 1100, 900, and 800°C for 30 min at each of these temperatures increased from 70 to 89.2 kg/mm^2.

Phosphate-containing glass-ceramics are comparable in hardness to high-alumina ceramics. Here, glass-ceramics containing crystals of lithium aluminosilicates and metasilicates had a higher hardness and wear resistance than glass-ceramics in which crystalline quartz and lithium disilicate [381] were the primary crystalline phases. A glass-ceramic of type A had ten times greater wear resistance than stainless steel, while glass-ceramic B had an even better wear resistance. Phosphate-containing glass-ceramics are characterized by low coefficients of friction, with glass-ceramics containing large amounts of ZnO having the lowest values, which is explained [381] either by the improved physical and chemical properties of the surface, or by capability of the surface of being polished to a much higher degree.

4. THERMAL PROPERTIES

a. Linear Thermal Expansion Coefficient α

If the α values for glasses vary uniformly with their chemical composition, the α values for glass-ceramics and ceramics depend on the α values of the primary crystalline and the complementary glassy phases, respectively [486]. Here, the α of the glass-ceramic may differ sharply both from the α of the glass of the same composition and from the α of the ceramic having a similar chemical, but a different mineralogical, composition. Stookey [486] thinks that in this respect glass-ceramics are closer to ceramics than to glass. During their investigation of some lithium aluminosilicates, Avgustinik and Vasil'ev [335] determined that the α of the ceramic is determined by the relationship between the crystalline phase, having negative α values, and the glassy phase, with positive α values. This is also true for glass-ceramics which, however, have the advantage over ceramics in that the anisotropic crystals present in their microstructure, such as β-eucryptite crystals, due to their exceptional smallness, do not produce porosity, nor do they decrease mechanical strength upon heating due to the difference in expansion along the various crystallographic axes [486].

Glass-ceramics prepared from lithium aluminosilicate glasses and having β-spodumene, β-eucryptite, and β-quartz as the primary crystalline phases have significantly lower α values than parent glasses. However, upon crystallization of lithium aluminosilicate glasses, the compositions of which are presented in Table 20 and in Fig. 58, the α of the photosensitive glass-ceramics prepared does not decrease, but increases from 70-80 $\cdot$ 10^{-7} for the original glass to 100-120 $\cdot$ 10^{-7} for the resulting photosensitive glass-ceramics. This is explained by the fact that in photosensitive glass-ceramics of the lithium aluminosilicate system, the lithium disilicate predominates over β-quartz, lithium metasilicate, β-spodumene, or β-eucryptite. With increasing Al_2O_3 content at the expense of SiO_2, the amount of the β-spodumene precipitating increases and α decreases, which is also observed in photosensitive glasses, as well as in glasses close in composition to the latter and having up to 6% P_2O_5 present as the crystallization catalyst [557]. Nonetheless, an increase in the Al_2O_3 content in excess of 20%, although desirable for the precipitation of the maximum possible amount of β-spodumene and for an even greater decrease in α, causes these glasses to lose their photosensitivity, it worsens their technological properties, and it lowers the mechanical strength of the photosensitive glass-ceramic. Being able to lower the α of photosensitive glass-ceramics by increasing the Al_2O_3 content while at the same time maintaining satisfactory photosensitive and technological properties would be of great significance for improving the thermal stability of these glass-ceramics.

The α of glass-ceramics may vary within very wide ranges: from negative values — such as for Pyroceram 9607 and for glass-ceramics based on the lithium aluminosilicate glass "13," among others [168, 187, 558, 751, 752] — to 57 $\cdot$ 10^{-7} (for Pyroceram 9606) and higher. As was shown previously (see Tables 49 and 50), glass-ceramics have been prepared with α values of ~300 $\cdot$ 10^{-7}, which makes them suitable for sealing with many metals. Glass-ceramics with α close to zero are practically insensitive to thermal shock. Figure 90 shows the temperature dependence of linear expansion of Pyrocerams 9605-9608 [516].

The Czechoslovakian glass-ceramic known under the name "Kriston-100" is capable of sustaining a temperature drop of 700°C without breaking, and "Kriston-140" excels by a high wear resistance, having $\alpha_{0-100°} = 44 \cdot 10^{-7}$, which is lower than that of recrystallized basalt, and by a high degree of thermal stability [54].

It has been confirmed experimentally that the α of glass-ceramics depends on the mineralogical composition determined by

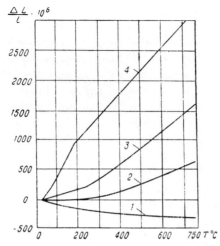

Fig. 90. Relative linear expansion of Pyrocerams as a function of temperature. T) Temperature; $\Delta L/L$) relative linear expansion. Curves 1, 2, 3, and 4 are for Pyrocerams 9607, 9608, 9605, and 9606, respectively.

the heat-treatment conditions. Glass-ceramics in the MgO—Al_2O_3—SiO_2 system, predominantly containing cordierite, possess low α values and good thermal stability. For glass-ceramics in the eucryptite—spodumene system, α depends to a large degree on the additives introduced. Thus, a partial substitution of Li_2O by ZnO and MgO (or a mixture of them) increased α [141]. Glass-ceramics containing B_2O_3 show the normal low thermal expansion behavior up to 560°C, after which a sharp increase in thermal expansion is noted which, at approximately 750°C, again reverts to a strong contraction, which is retained to the start of softening at a temperature higher than 1000°. No explanation has as yet been found for this phenomenon. Because of their low α values, these glass-ceramics had a very high thermal stability [141].

In phosphate-containing glass-ceramics, the α also varies within broad ranges. Glass-ceramics of types A and E are intended for forming seals with soft steel, whereas glass-ceramic C is intended for the production of airtight seals with copper [381]. Very low or negative values for α, say, $\alpha = -40 \cdot 10^{-7}$, were observed in the temperature range 20-500°C for glass-ceramics containing considerable amounts of crystals of lithium aluminosilicates, such as β-eucryptite. Expansion curves for glass-ceramics with a high cristobalite and quartz content showed deviations in the expansion behavior of these materials near 250 and 550-600°C, respectively, which is explained [381] by the phase transformations of the various modifications of silica. If crystals of lithium aluminosilicates with low α values and of lithium silicates with higher α values are also present in the microstructure of glass-ceramics of types B and D, then the resultant α of the glass-ceramic has average values. The amount of the glassy phase in these glass-ceramics is small (approximately 10%), which is the reason no temperature range of softening is observed near T_g, such as is characteristic for glasses. Above this temperature, the glass-ceramics soften very rapidly, due to the melting of the crystalline phases. Glass-ceramics with lower α values have higher softening temperatures [381].

Baum [559] studied glasses close in composition to stoichiometric β-eucryptite and produced from them glass-ceramics with very low α values, ranging from 0 to 10^{-7} at σ_f greater than 800 kg/cm^2. In spite of the large negative coefficient of anisotropic expansion for β-eucryptite, varying from $90 \cdot 10^{-7}$ to $-100 \cdot 10^{-7}$ within the temperature range 20-800°C along the various crystallographic axes, it was possible, by the addition of 4-5% B_2O_3, 4-12% MgO, and 4.0-4.6 TiO_2, to obtain glass-ceramics in the $Li_2O-Al_2O_3-SiO_2$ system in which the very small β-eucryptite crystals were separated from one another by a very thin glass film. Because of the decreased Li_2O content and the increased content of the glassy phase, the α of these glass-ceramics is close to zero. The content of the crystalline phase varies from 91 to 35%, and since the region of the theoretical content of β-eucryptite ranges from 100 to 60%, only the crystallization of that phase was observed, whereas, within the range 55-35%, only β-spodumene crystallized out. Adding B_2O_3 to the above had practically no effect on the α of the glass-ceramic; it did, however, lower its melting point. The optimum properties are possessed by glass-ceramics which contain more than 60% of β-eucryptite [559].

One of the primary shortcomings of existing photosensitive glass-ceramics based on photosensitive glasses of the lithium aluminosilicate system is their high linear expansion coefficient α and, through this, their inadequate thermal stability and mechanical strength, which may result in the cracking of such articles

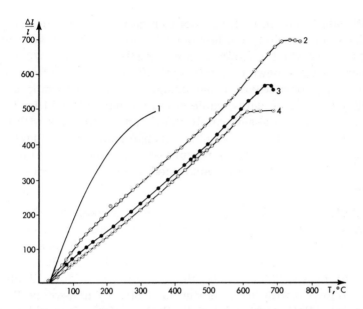

Fig. 91. Thermal expansion curves for photosensitive glass-ceramics based on the lithium—aluminosilicate system. 1) Without RO additions; 2) with addition of 5 mol.% MgO; 3) with addition of 5 mol.% ZnO; 4) with addition of 5 mol.% BeO.

during their exposure to multiple cyclic or abrupt changes to high temperatures, such as are encountered, for instance, during the metal-coating and tinplating processes, as well as during sealing of micromodular plates.

Besides the higher absolute values for α for the known photosensitive glass-ceramics of lithium aluminosilicate composition, the curves for its expansion, as measured on several different samples, are somewhat irregular, and have, as shown by Fig. 91 (curve 1), an inflection point within the temperature range 250-270°C corresponding to the structural phase transformations of α- and β-quartz, which may occur within the temperature range 219-274°C [765].

It was mentioned previously (see page 163) that, according to Stookey, quartz which is present in photosensitive glass-ceramics in amounts which are smaller than those of lithium disilicate or metasilicate is stable with respect to high temperatures, inasmuch as it does not change into other modifications, in contrast to ceramic products which contain larger amounts of quartz [276, 277]. However, as was shown by my investigations, the nonuniform expansion of photosensitive glass-ceramics in various temperature regions may have an unfavorable effect on thermal stability both of the photosensitive glass-ceramic itself and on its seals with various metals. The presence of phase transformations of quartz and their negative effect on the structure and on the electrical properties of glass-ceramics were confirmed by other investigators [381] (see page 327).

Cations of alkaline-earth MeO oxides weaken the effect of the Me ion on the Si—O bond in the —Si—O::: Me structural element. This leads to a lowering of the mobility of the alkali ions [766] which, in turn, results in a decrease in electrical conductivity and dielectric losses; thus, the chemical stability of alkali silicate glasses improve with the substitution of SiO_2 by RO, where RO is, for example, BeO, MgO, CaO, SrO, BaO, or ZnO. It would seem natural to expect the development of a similar effect in the glassy phase of a photosensitive glass-ceramic enriched with R_2O oxides if one of the RO oxides had been introduced into the composition of the initial photosensitive glass. The introduction of these oxides into the composition of a photosensitive glass-ceramic is also of value because they may act as agents retarding the formation or the phase transformations of cristobalite in glass-crystalline materials [767]. Based on this deduction, the oxides ZnO, MgO, and BeO were added in place of SiO_2 in amounts ranging from 1 to 10 mol.%, so as to lower the α, stabilize the thermal expansion curve, and improve the thermal, dielectric, and chemical properties of photosensitive glass-ceramics of the lithium aluminosilicate system.

As a result of the investigation performed, it was determined that there is an optimum amount of RO oxides which can be added; for instance, 5-6 mol.% ZnO, MgO, or BeO lowers the α of a typical photosensitive glass-ceramic from $148 \cdot 10^{-7}$ $(°C)^{-1}$ to $75\text{-}80 \cdot 10^{-7}$ $(°C)^{-1}$ within the temperature range 20-300°C, and thereby evens out its thermal expansion curve (Fig. 91, curves 2-4), which has a favorable effect on the thermal stability and mechanical strength of this material. An interesting characteristic of these photosensitive glass-ceramics is the fact that α values are lower than those of the corresponding original photosensitive glasses.

Table 68. Quantities Appearing in Equation (33)

Symbol	Definition	Pyroceram 9606	Ceramics with 99% Al_2O_3
S.	Rupture stress, kg/cm^2	1820	3150
α	Linear thermal expansion coefficient (°C)$^{-1}$	$5.7 \cdot 10^{-6}$	$7.3 \cdot 10^{-6}$
E	Elastic modulus, kg/cm^2	$121 \cdot 10^6$	$280 \cdot 10^6$
μ	Poisson's ratio	0.25	0.32
ΔT	Temperature drop, °C	396	210

b. Thermal Stability

The combination of a low α with high mechanical strength imparts a thermal stability to many of the glass-ceramics which is significantly higher than that of ceramic materials, and which is comparable to that of fused quartz [20, 21, 560-567]. For example, plates made of Pyroceram 9607 do not break upon rapid cooling from 900°C by immersion of the sample in water at 5°. Pyroceram 9606 is capable of sustaining twice the temperature drop that high-alumina ceramics can. Thin-walled tubes 1 mm in diameter and plates 6.3 mm thick made of Pyroceram 9608 can be quenched from 700°C in icy water without breaking [21]. The maximum operating temperature for parts not subjected to loads is 1000°C, and the temperature for parts subjected to loads is 850°C for 1000 h; the maximum softening temperature is 1350°C.

Glass-ceramics in the spodumene—eucryptite system with low positive or negative values of α can go through more than 70 cycles of heating to 800-850°C and cooling in water having a temperature of 5-6°C without changing their properties [558].

The high thermal stability of Pyroceram 9606 as compared to that of high-alumina ceramics is confirmed by calculating the temperature gradient between the opposite sides of plates made of these two materials and subjected to flexure loads while being used in cylinders of internal combustion engines or as nose cones and shields of guided missiles [568, 569]. The stresses at the surface of the plate caused by the constant drop in temperature, do not depend on the plate thickness, and are calculated according to the following formula [568]:

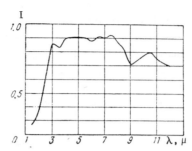

Fig. 92. Relative spectral radiation intensity of Pyroceram 9608. λ) Wavelength; I) radiation intensity. The thickness of the sample was 6.35 mm, and it was heated to 1000°K.

$$S = E \cdot a \frac{\Delta T}{2(1 - \mu)}, \qquad (33)$$

where the various quantities are defined in Table 68.

According to Eq. (33), a maximum temperature drop of 396°C is possible for Pyroceram 9606, while for ceramics with 99% Al_2O_3, it is equal to 210°C (Table 68).

The thermal stability of phosphate-containing glass-ceramics was tested by the rapid cooling in water at 10°C of rods 5 mm in diameter and 55 mm long which had been heated to various temperatures up to 700°C and held at the respective temperatures for 30 min. Thermal stability was characterized by the drop in temperature which resulted in a 10% decrease in the σ_f of the rods, as indicated by the appearance of minute cracks on their surface. Glass-ceramics having low α and high σ_f values had high thermal stability [381].

c. Heat Conductivity

Glass-ceramics are heat-insulating materials. Glass has a low heat conductivity, which increases with temperature, whereas nonporous ceramics have a heat conductivity which is higher than that of glass, and which decreases with increasing temperature. The heat conductivity of glass-ceramics is also greater than that of glasses, and it varies only slightly with temperature. Inasmuch as porosity decreases heat conductivity, then nonporous glass-ceramics should, according to Stookey [486], have a higher heat conductivity than porous ceramics of the same composition.

The heat conductivity of Pyrocerams of various types ranges over 0.047-0.010 kcal/cm-sec-deg, i.e., it is 3-4 times higher than that of borosilicate glass. The normal spectral radiation at 1000°K of Pyroceram 9608 in the form of a plate 6.35 mm thick is shown in Fig. 92 [570].

The heat conductivity of phosphate-containing glass-ceramics at 100°C is the same as that for normal glasses and less than that for high-alumina ceramics. With an increasing content of crystal-line lithium aluminosilicates in these glass-ceramics, their heat conductivity increases [381].

d. Heat Capacity

The specific heat of glass-ceramics at 25°C ranges over 0.185-0.190 cal/g-deg, with the average heat capacity within the temperature range 25-400°C being 0.185-0.230 cal/g-deg. The average heat capacity of phosphate-containing glass-ceramics with-in the same temperature range is the same as that of high-alumina ceramics and commercial glasses (Table 74).

5. ELECTRICAL PROPERTIES

Glass-ceramics are electrical insulators characterized by exceptionally low values of dielectric loss factor at high frequen-cies and high temperatures, a dielectric constant ε ranging from 5 to 10 at high frequencies, and a low scattering factor [571-574]. It was shown previously that it is possible to produce glass-ceramics with very high ε values, attaining several thousands of units (see Table 51). With regard to their electrical-insulating properties, glass-ceramics are comparable to the better ceramic dielectrics.

a. Electrical Resistivity

The present author, together with A. M. Gel'berger and A. A. Lychagova, investigated the specific bulk electrical resistivity ρ_b of photosensitive glass of the lithium aluminosilicate system, as well as of its crystallization products obtained by heat treatment at various temperatures. The ρ_b was measured with a MOM-4 megometer at sample temperatures no less than 100°C so as to avoid phenomena associated with the surface electrical conductivity.

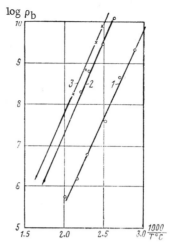

Fig. 93. Temperature dependence of electrical resistivity
of the original glass and of the photosensitive glass-ceramic.
T) Temperature; ρ_b) specific bulk resistivity. 1) Original
glass; 2) photosensitive glass-ceramic, heat treated at 650°C;
3) photosensitive glass heat treated at 750°C.

During the crystallization process of photosensitive glass, the
structure of the photosensitive glass-ceramic, the ratio between
the glassy and the crystalline phases, and the nature of the crystalline phases precipitating all change. In order to explain the dependence of electrical properties on the degree of crystallization and on the structure of the photosensitive glass-ceramic,
the heat-treatment procedure of the photosensitive glass was varied
from 450°C, which is the temperature at which nuclei being to form,
to 825°C, the temperature above which the softening and the deformation of the photosensitive glass-ceramic occur.

Figure 93 shows the temperature dependence of ρ_b for the
original photosensitive glass and for glass-ceramics crystallized
at 650 and 750°C. The crystallization of glass at 750°C is accompanied by an increase in ρ_b by two orders of magnitude, which
means that it is determined by the ratio between the crystalline and
the glassy phases. Figure 94 shows the temperature dependence of
ρ_b of glass crystallized following the different heat-treatment procedures represented in Fig. 95. Petrographic and x-ray studies
showed that samples differ from one another only in crystal size,

log ρh

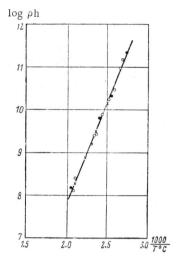

Fig. 94. Temperature dependence of the electrical resistivity of photosensitive glass-ceramics crystallized according to various heat-treatment procedures. T) Temperature; ρ_b) specific bulk resistivity. The heat-treatment procedures, given in more detail in Fig. 95, were:
●) (I) 470°C for 0.5 h, 750°C for 0.5 h; ×) (II), 450°C for
0.5 h, 550°C for 1 h, 750°C for 0.5 h; ○) (III), 450°C for
0.5 h, 550°C for 0.5 h, 750°C for 0.5 h; ⊗) (IV), 450°C
for 0.5 h, 600°C for 0.5 h, 750°C for 0.5 h.

which obviously does not show up in the electric resistivity values.
Figure 94 confirms the literature data, which state that the resistivity of partially crystallized material is above all determined by
the amount and resistivity of the residual glassy phase [575-578].

The original glass of the lithium aluminosilicate system is
basic, with a large amount of lithium ions present having the maximum mobility. It was shown by our calculations that the activation
energy for the electrical conductivity of a parent photosensitive
glass is equal to 0.845 eV. During the crystallization of this glass,
lithium metasilicate precipitates as the primary crystalline phase,
with its ions transferring into the crystalline phase, where they
are less mobile. The calculated activation energy for the electrical conductivity of a photosensitive glass-ceramic is 1.015 eV. Inasmuch as it is practically impossible to calculate the composition
and the amount of the residual glassy phase, one may only assume

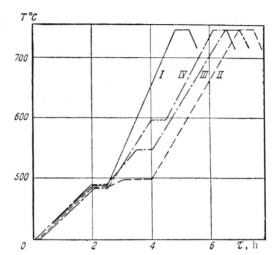

Fig. 95. Heat-treatment procedures for the crystallization of photosensitive glass. τ) Time; T) heating temperature.

that the electrical conductivity of a photosensitive glass-ceramic
is determined by the low-mobility potassium ions which remain in
the glassy phase in their entirety, this glassy phase thus being represented as potassium aluminosilicate glass.

The effect on ρ_b of the complete crystallization of lithium
aluminosilicate glasses with and without CaO, BaO, and F additions
was studied by Mazurin and Tsekhomskii [579], who determined
that for complete crystallization, ρ_b increases by several orders
of magnitude, while the activation energy is doubled. The introduction of the additives and change in the Li_2O content had only a
slight effect on the ρ_b value.

The ρ_b of phosphate-containing glass-ceramics at room temperature is comparable to the ρ_b of high-alumina ceramics and
glasses, and it decreases with increasing temperature. However,
up to 450°C, it is higher than for these other two types of materials.
It is interesting to note that the curve representing the dependence
of log ρ_b on 1/T for phosphate-containing glass-ceramic A consists of two straight-line segments joined at a point corresponding
to the transformation temperature of cristobalite, 230°C (see
Fig. 96); it is also seen that in the temperature region above 230°C,

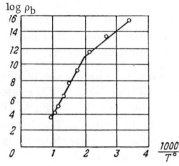

Fig. 96. Temperature dependence of electrical resistivity of type A phosphate-containing glass-ceramic. T) Temperature; ρ_b) specific bulk resistivity.

ρ_b decreases significantly faster with increasing temperature than is the case in the temperature region below 230°C. Partridge and McMillan [381] explain this in terms of the loosening of the structure of the glass-ceramic due to the transformation of cristobalite, the amount of which present in this glass-ceramic was approximately 47%. From this, they deduced quite conclusively that the primary carriers of electricity are the lithium ions which become dispersed in the glass-ceramic when it is being heated, not through the residual glassy phase, but through the loosened cristobalite. The surface resistivity of glass-ceramic A is higher than that of high-alumina ceramics all the way up to 700°C, and, at room temperature, after being exposed for 24 h to 70% relative humidity, its surface resistivity is higher than that of Pyrex glass or of sodium calcium borosilicate glass. Glass-ceramic A had twice the low current strength and resistance to high-voltage arc discharge as glazed electroporcelain has.

b. Dielectric Permeability ε and Dissipation Factor

Glass-ceramics are characterized by exceptional stability in ε with changes in temperature at frequencies near $8.5 \cdot 10^9$ Hz, and with values comparable to those for fused quartz. The ε of some glass-ceramics at 10^{10} Hz and 800°C differs from the ε at room temperature by only 0.3%. Pyroceram 9606 at 10^5 Hz has ε = 7.13, and is a good insulator at average frequencies and temperatures up to 350°C [21].

For a frequency of 10^{10} Hz, the dissipation factor of Pyroceram 9605 is equal to 0.0002 at room temperature and 0.015 at 500°C, which is only $\frac{2}{3}$ of the value of this coefficient for high-alumina ceramics at the same frequency.

Hirajama and Berg [580] studied the effect of TiO_2 on ε, $\tan\delta$, and ρ_b for glasses of the $TiO_2-Na_2O-SiO_2$ system, measuring ε over the frequency range $60-10^{10}$ Hz. Even at 10^{10} Hz, the ε of this glass was high, ranging from 8 to 13. The introduction of TiO_2 improved the electrical-insulating properties of these glasses. Crystallization of the glass resulted in increased ε at 10^{10} Hz, which was proportional to the growth in the density of crystallized samples. The behavior found is explained [580] in terms of the peculiar properties of the Ti ion, which has a high charge, a small radius, a relatively small mass, and has coordinating around itself a relatively large number (six) of oxygen ions.

The effect of heat treatment, chemical composition of the original glass of the $Li_2O-MgO-Al_2O_3-SiO_2$ system, and additions of the oxides Na_2O, K_2O, BeO, CaO, SrO, ZnO, CdO, and PbO on dielectric losses was studied by Sakka and Tashiro [581]. Glass of the composition 62 SiO_2, 15 MgO, 23 Al_2O_3, and 4-12 Li_2O was heated at a rate of 5 deg/min to 750-1200°C. After crystallization within the temperature region 750-950°C, an increase in $\tan\delta$ at 10^6 Hz was observed; further increase in the temperature resulted in a sharp decrease in $\tan\delta$, which is explained by the formation of β-eucryptite and β-spodumene. The basic components of the original glass did not have a marked effect on the change in $\tan\delta$. With decreasing Li_2O content, a sharp decrease in $\tan\delta$ was observed, which is associated with the formation of β-spodumene. Of the possible additives indicated above, PbO was the one that most effectively decreased $\tan\delta$ [581].

Determinations of ε and $\tan\delta$ for glass-ceramics of the cordierite system within the frequency range $4\cdot10^2$ to $3.7\cdot10^{10}$ Hz were performed by Mashkovich [582]. A decrease in $\tan\delta$ at 10^{10} Hz attested to an intensification of relaxation processes, since the dielectric losses of the samples with clearly expressed relaxation polarization sharply decreased during the transition from 10^7-10^{10} Hz. This author thinks that for the glass-ceramics investigated, the magnitude of $\tan\delta$ and the nature of its dependence on the frequency and temperature at superhigh frequencies are to a large degree determined by the extent and the closeness of low-frequency relaxation phenomena. No increase in tan δ was observed in optimally crystallized samples. Apparently because of the low amount of glassy phase, the start of the increase in tan δ, associated with absorption in the far infrared region, is displaced toward the side of the higher frequencies. The effect of reduction of TiO_2 on the dielectric properties of titanium-containing glass and glass-ceramic was also studied. It was determined that the introduction in glass of TiO_2 has practically no effect on tan δ, and that it only slightly increases ε. The reduction of glass during melting resulted in an insignificant increase in tan δ within the audio frequency region. At frequencies of 10^{10} Hz and above, tan δ and ε changed only slightly. The properties of the glass-ceramic proved to be much more sensitive to reduction of the original glass than did those of the glass itself. All samples of the glass-ceramic investigated showed a relaxation maximum of tan δ on the respective frequency dependence curves. With increasing degree of reduction of the glass-ceramic, the magnitude of tan δ at the maximum at a frequency of 10^{10} Hz increased. In samples with a minimum degree of reduction, the relaxation phenomena (maximum tan δ and a change in ε with frequency) developed to a much lesser degree. Electrical conductivity is not the reason for the observed effects. In the opinion of Mashkovich, the mechanism of dielectric loss in a heterogeneous system, i.e., in a glass-ceramic, is associated with interfacial polarization. The samples of the glass-ceramics investigated contained three phases: residual glass, cordierite, and magnesium aluminotitanate; the interfacial polarization was caused by boundary phenomena at the high-resistivity interphase surfaces between glass and cordierite and the titanium-containing crystals, the resistivity of which is influenced by the degree of reduction of the glass-ceramic. Based on the results obtained, Mashkovich concludes that the relaxation polarization is of ionic nature, associated with the defect state of the structure. It was not possible to establish the identity of the relaxation ion. Polycrystalline samples of cordierite prepared by sintering from the oxides or by crystallization from glass did not show a relaxation maximum within the frequency range investigated. It is possible that in the cordierite phase of the glass-ceramic samples, impurity ions could be present or that solid solutions could form, enhancing a further intensive development of relaxation polarization. It was proposed that the decisive role during relaxation is being played by the titanium-containing phase, since with increasing reduction, the intensity of the maximum on the curve showing the frequency dependence of tan δ increased. However, the absence of a frequency dependency of activation energy U, of natural frequency vibrations ν of the relaxation oscillator, and of the location of the maximum of tan δ work against this proposal. The author considers reduction to be only a factor increasing the general level of dielectric loss. The low value of ν (10^{10}-10^{11} Hz) in samples of the glass-ceramic investigated is explained in terms of the unusually weak bond between the relaxing ions and the lattice, or by relaxation, not of individual ions, but of a complex of ions.

X-ray diffraction analysis showed that the appearance of a relaxation maximum in the frequency dependence of tan δ is associated with the precipitation of cordierite during the crystallization of the glass-ceramic. According to the author, the presence of cordierite in the glass-ceramic is the reason the observed relaxation polarization takes place.

The same author [583] investigated the frequency and the temperature dependencies of tan δ and ε of glass-ceramics similar in composition to the mineral celsian (BaO · Al_2O_3 · $2SiO_2$) and containing TiO_2 as the catalyst. A decrease in tan δ was observed at a frequency of 10^{10} Hz, as was a decrease in ε with increasing crystallization temperature, i.e., depending on how much of the glass has been transformed into the optimally crystallized glass-ceramic, which is explained by a decrease in the amount of the residual glassy phase. At the same time, at audio frequencies of approximately 4 · 10^2 Hz, tan δ increased with the crystallization temperature to 1200°C, which, according to the author, is associated, just as in the case of glass-ceramics of the cordierite system, with interfacial polarization as a result of an intensification in the heterogeneous state of the structure. Within the transition region 1200-1250°C, a significant increase in ε and a sharp decrease in tan δ took place at 400 Hz. This is explained in terms of the "homogenization" of the structure, consisting in an increase in the size of the crystals and their mutual penetration, with a concomitant leveling off of the property gradients on the phase boundaries, a decrease in the total contact area, and interfacial polarization. Within the temperature range 1250-1300°C, ε and tan δ, for all practical purposes, remained the same. In contrast to glass-ceramics of the cordierite system, the celsian glass-ceramics do not show relaxation maxima on the curves of the frequency dependencies of $\tan\delta$. Both these and other glass-ceramics have large dielectric losses at audio frequencies, with the losses increasing at a greater rate with temperature than is the case for the original glasses. Glass-ceramics prepared from reduced celsian glass were characterized by a sharp increase in losses at low frequencies, and by a greater rate of losses decrease with increasing frequency.

Herczog [584] studied the dependence of ε on the size of the $BaTiO_3$ particles in glass-ceramics prepared on the basis of barium titanate and characterized by a high dielectric permeability [363, 364]. The largest values for ε were observed when the particle size was about $1\,\mu$; when the particle size was less than $0.2\,\mu$, the ε did not depend on the temperature, and the ferroelectric properties degenerated.

In order to produce glass-ceramics with high insulating properties, Pavlova and Chistoserdov [585] investigated the effect on $\tan\delta$ and ε of composition and heat-treatment procedures of alkali-free glass-ceramics in the $MgO-Al_2O_3-SiO_2-TiO_2$ and $BaO-B_2O_3-Al_2O_3-SiO_2$ systems. With increasing crystallization temperature in the frequency range 10^3-10^6 Hz, $\tan\delta$ of the glass-ceramic of the cordierite system increased. In a sample crystallized at 1200°C, a relaxation maximum was observed on the curve of the temperature dependence of $\tan\delta$, being displaced toward the side of higher temperatures with increasing frequencies. At a frequency of 10^{10} Hz at room temperature, $\tan\delta$ and ε decreased when the crystallization temperature increased to 1100-1200°C.

The minimum values for $\tan\delta$ were $(7-13)\cdot 10^{-4}$, while the minimum values for ε ranged from 5.6 to 5.9. Based on the data obtained on the changes in the frequency and temperature dependencies of $\tan\delta$ and ε of glass-ceramics of the cordierite system with TiO_2 additions, these authors concluded that it is primarily the crystalline phase, and not the residual glassy phase, that determines the electrical properties of these glass-ceramics. The appearance of a relaxation maximum on the curve of the temperature dependence of $\tan\delta$ is ascribed to the titanium-containing crystalline phase, inasmuch as the crystallized glasses of the ternary

Table 69. Tan δ and ε for Crystallization Products of Lithium Aluminosilicate Glass

Crystalliza-tion temp., °C	$\tan \delta \cdot 10^4$ at $\nu = 1 \times 10^6$ Hz	ε	Crystalliza-tion temp., °C	$\tan \delta \cdot 10^4$ at $\nu = 1 \times 10^6$ Hz	ε
Original glass	162	7.5	700	70	6.4
			725	67	6.5
450	133	7.5	750	64	6.6
500	—	7.6	775	72	6.5
500	140	7.6	800	82	6.7
600	134	7.6	825	90	6.8
620	125	7.3			
650	73	6.5			

Table 70. Tan δ and ε of Photosensitive Glass-Ceramics at Times Held at Crystallization Temperature

Time at temp., h	Zero	0.5	1.0	1.5	2.0	2.5	3.0
$\tan \delta \cdot 10^4$	64	64	68	68	71	72	75
ε		6.6	6.7	6.7	6.7	6.6	6.6	6.7

MgO—Al_2O_3—SiO_2 system did not show this maximum. Glass-ceramics of the BaO—B_2O_3—Al_2O_3—SiO_2 system had better insulating properties at elevated temperatures than glass-ceramics in the cordierite system, with the nature of the change in tan δ and ε here primarily depending on the residual glassy phase. The tan δ of alkali-free glass-ceramics investigated had both lower and higher values than the transition glasses, depending on the specific case.

Phosphate-containing glass-ceramics have low dielectric losses within a wide frequency range, from 1 kHz to 104 MHz. Their tan δ at high frequencies is comparable to tan δ of high-alumina ceramics. A change in frequency has no noticeable effect on the ε of these glass-ceramics. The presence of crystalline aluminosilicate resulted in increased ε [381].

In order to study the structural transformations during the crystallization of photosensitive glass, the present author, A. M. Gel'berger, and A. A. Lychagova jointly measured at room temperature and at a frequency of 10^6 Hz, tan δ and ε for crystallization products forming at various stages of heat treatment. The results of these measurements are presented in Table 69.

The results obtained indicate that a sharp change in tan δ is observed at 650°C, when crystallization starts throughout the bulk of the glass body. A further increase in the crystallization temperature to 750°C is accompanied by a slight decrease in tan δ, after which it again starts to increase. X-ray analysis showed that lithium metasilicate precipitates as the primary crystalline phase during all crystallization procedures followed. According to data from petrographic investigations, samples crystallized at temperatures 725-750°C have the most dense, most uniform, and fine-crystalline structure. As the crystallization temperature is further increased to 800-825°C, a worsening of dielectric properties is observed, which is in agrement with certain literature data [575, 576].

We also investigated the effect on the dielectric properties of photosensitive glass-ceramics of the period of time that the latter is held at the constant crystallization temperature of 750°C. The results (Table 70) show that an increase in the time at temperature not only improved the properties of the photosensitive glass-ceramic, but also resulted in a slight increase in ε.

Rindone [204] mentions that the crystallization process slows down as the amount of lithium present in the glass and crystallizing decreases. This is how the small change in tan δ can be explained for 0.5-1.5 h of holding at a temperature of 750°C.

The increase in the tan δ of glasses crystallized at 800-825°C at long periods of time is apparently caused by the change in the composition of the crystalline phase, i.e., by the appearance of β-quartz, as determined by x-ray analysis and by the enrichment of the residual glassy phase with alkalis. As a result of crystallization, ε is already reduced to unity at 650°C. With a further increase in the temperature and the change in the time at temperature, ε changes only slightly.

In order to explain the nature of dielectric losses in glass and in photosensitive glass-ceramics, we determined the tempera-

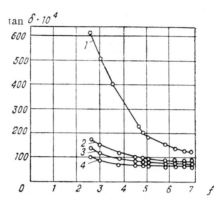

Fig. 97. Frequency dependency of the loss angle for a glass and for photosensitive glass-ceramics made from it. f) Frequency; δ) loss angle. 1) Glass; 2-4) photosensitive glass-ceramics heat treated at 825, 650, and 750°C, respectively.

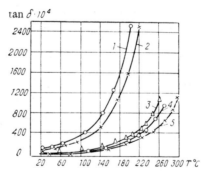

Fig. 98. Temperature dependency of the loss angle at various frequencies for a glass and for photosensitive glass-ceramics made from it. T) Temperature; δ) loss angle. 1,2) Glass at frequencies of $5 \cdot 10^6$ and $1 \cdot 10^6$ Hz, respectively; 3-5) photosensitive glass-ceramics at frequencies of $1 \cdot 10^5$, $5 \cdot 10^5$, and $1 \cdot 10^6$ Hz, respectively.

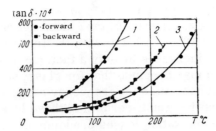

Fig. 99. Temperature dependency of the loss angle for
a glass and for photosensitive glass-ceramics crystallized from it at various temperatures. T) Temperature;
δ) loss angle. 1) Glass; 2,3) photosensitive glass-ceramics
heat treated at 650 and 750°C, respectively.

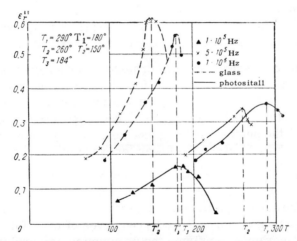

Fig. 100. Temperature dependency of relaxation losses for a glass
(dashed curve) and for photosensitive glass-ceramics made from it
(solid curves). T) Temperature; ε_r'') relaxation losses.

ture and the frequency characteristics of tan δ for glasses and
photosensitive glass-ceramics.

Figure 97 shows the room-temperature frequency dependence
of tan δ for a glass and photosensitive glass-ceramics. Within the
frequency range $1 \cdot 10^6$-$5 \cdot 10^7$ Hz, the losses for the glass hardly
change. With the frequency decreasing from $5 \cdot 10^5$ to $5 \cdot 10^2$ Hz,

tan δ for the glass is from four times larger than at 10^6 Hz. For the photosensitive glass-ceramic, tan δ does not change within the frequency range $5 \cdot 10^5$-$5 \cdot 10^7$ Hz; with the frequency decreasing to $4 \cdot 10^2$ Hz, tan δ increases by only a factor of two. From the results obtained, one may conclude that for glass, substantial conductivity losses are found within the frequency range $4 \cdot 10^2$-$5 \cdot 10^7$ Hz. For photosensitive glass-ceramics, these losses are apparently small, since relaxation losses predominate at room temperature at frequencies of the order of $4 \cdot 10^2$-$1 \cdot 10^6$ Hz.

To the dielectric losses of a relaxation character, there corresponds a shift in the curves of the temperature dependence of tan δ with decreasing frequency toward the lower temperature region. The curves showing the temperature dependence of relaxation losses are characterized by the presence of maxima. In order to confirm the relaxation character of the losses for photosensitive glass-ceramics, the respective curves were drawn, and calculations were made based on the previously described method [586].

Figure 98 shows the temperature dependency of tan δ within the temperature range 20-290°C for glass at frequencies of $5 \cdot 10^5$ and $1 \cdot 10^6$ Hz and for photosensitive glass-ceramic at frequencies $1 \cdot 10^5$, $5 \cdot 10^5$, and $1 \cdot 10^6$ Hz. With decreasing frequency, both the curves for the photosensitive glass-ceramic, and those for the glass are shifted toward the lower temperature region.

From Fig. 99 for data taken at a frequency of 10^6 Hz, one may note that tan δ for photosensitive glass-ceramics increases with temperature significantly slower than tan δ for glass. The shift in the temperature-dependence curves of tan δ for photosensitive glass-ceramics confirms the assumption concerning the relaxation character of the losses. In order to separate the relaxation losses, which also include the conductivity losses within this frequency range, we calculated the total losses observed as well as the conductivity losses. The difference between these two determined the losses caused by ionic relaxation. Figure 100 shows the temperature dependency of relaxation losses. The maximum of these curves is shifted toward the lower temperature region with decreasing frequency, as confirmed by the relaxation character of the losses.

The diffuse character of the maxima on the curve of the temperature dependency of relaxation losses for photosensitive glass-

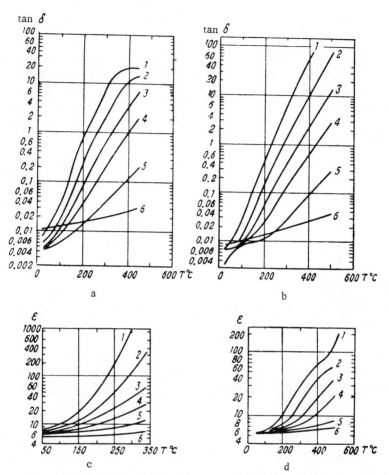

Fig. 101. Temperature dependency of the dielectric properties of Fotoform glass
B and C and of Fotoceram. T) Temperature; δ) angle of dielectric loss; ε) dielectric constant. a) Fotoform C; b) Fotoceram; c) Fotoform B; d) Fotoceram. Curves
1-6 correspond to frequencies of 10^2, 10^3, 10^4, 10^5, 10^7, and $8.5 \cdot 10^9$ Hz, respectively.

ceramics is characteristic of amorphous substances, and again indicates that the losses for photosensitive glass-ceramics are primarily determined by the residual glassy phase. In order to determine the nature of the relaxation elements, the activation energy of
the relaxation process and the natural frequency of vibration of the
relaxation oscillators were calculated. The activation energy of
the relaxation process was 0.380 eV for glass and ~0.593 eV for

photosensitive glass-ceramic, which is less than the activation energy of the conduction process.

From the activation energy values obtained for the relaxation process, the frequency of the natural vibrations of the relaxation oscillators at the resonance temperature was calculated. For glass, this frequency is $6.3 \cdot 10^{10}$ Hz at a temperature of 180°C, and for photosensitive glass-ceramic it is $7.9 \cdot 10^{11}$ Hz at a temperature of 260°C.

The magnitude of the activation energy of the relaxation process and the frequency of natural vibrations of the relaxation oscillators indicate the ionic character of these elements.

Thus, as a result, our study of the effect of crystallization on the electrical properties of photosensitive glass, it was determined that the electrical properties of the photosensitive glass-ceramic are significantly higher than those of the original glass. It was confirmed that electrical conductivity and dielectric loss are determined primarily by the composition and the amount of the glassy phase. The study of the frequency dependency of dielectric loss for glass and photosensitive glass-ceramic within the frequency range $4 \cdot 10^2$-$5 \cdot 10^7$ Hz and the separation of the maxima on the curves for the temperature dependency of dielectric loss indicate the relaxation character of this loss. The activation energy for the electrical conductivity and for the relaxation processes for glass and for photosensitive glass-ceramic were calculated, as was the natural frequency of vibration for the relaxation oscillators. The results indicated that the alkali-metal ions are the relaxation elements.

Figure 101 shows the temperature dependencies of tan δ and ε for Fotoform and Fotoceram [273].

Pavlova et al. [587] studied the effect of the chemical composition of the photosensitive glass of the Li_2O—Al_2O_3—SiO_2 system on tan δ and ε of photosensitive glass-ceramics. The Li_2O and the Al_2O_3 concentrations were varied at the expense of SiO_2. In addition, part of the SiO_2 was replaced by BaO, SrO, or CaO. It was shown that photosensitive glass-ceramics containing not more than 10% Al_2O_3 possessed higher electrical-insulating properties than the original glasses: tan δ at 1 MHz and 25°C was 2-3 times smaller, and ε was 1-1.7 times smaller. Increasing the Al_2O_3 content resulted in a sharp degradation of the insulating properties of photo-sensitive glass-ceramics, while increasing the Li_2O concentration from 10.5 to 16% at a constant Al_2O_3 content of 4% did not cause any such degradation. Introducing BaO, SrO, and CaO at the expense of SiO_2 increased the insulating properties of the photosensitive glass-ceramics: ρ_b at 150°C increased by 2-2.5 orders of magnitude, tan δ decreased by more than twice, and the beginning of its sharp increase with increasing temperature shifted toward the higher temperature region.

Based on the data obtained, the authors [587] think that the dielectric losses of photosensitive glass-ceramics of the lithium aluminosilicate system are determined by the composition and the structure of the precipitating crystalline phase and of the material as a whole, apparently also including its glassy phase, as we demonstrated in the work cited earlier.

While investigating the effect of oxides on the dielectric properties of photosensitive glass-ceramics, we determined that photosensitive glass-ceramics containing 5-6 mol.% ZnO, MgO, or BeO not only had a minimum α and a uniform behavior of the expansion curve (see Fig. 91), but also showed minimum values for tan δ, equal to $(50-60) \cdot 10^{-4}$ at 1 MHz and 20°C.

c. Electric Strength

Due to their dense microstructure and the absence of internal pores, glass-ceramics have a high electric strength at increased temperatures and high frequencies. The electric strength of phosphate-containing glass-ceramics at increased frequencies and at room temperature is higher than that for conventional ceramics and is comparable to the electric strength of glass [381].

6. CHEMICAL PROPERTIES

The stability against acids for the majority of glass-ceramics is approximately the same as that of borosilicate glass, while their stability with respect to bases is much higher. The chemical stability of Pyroceram 9608 with respect to strong acids and bases is somewhat less than that of borosilicate glass. Glass-ceramics do not oxidize even at elevated temperatures.

Löcsei [53] studied the dependence on the amount of glassy

Table 71. Corrosion Stability of the Glass-Ceramic Minelbite with Respect to Acids and Bases at Their Boiling Temperatures

Reagent	Concentration	Amount of material dissolved in		Dissolving rate, g/m^2-24 h, after etching for		
		first 24 h, g/m^2	second 24 h, g/m^2	4 h	24 h	48 h
HCl	10	1.94	0.10	3.6	0.7	0.02
	20	6.53	0.26	21.8	1.2	0.1
H_2SO_4	10	7.47	1.58	16.8	1.9	0.5
	20	4.50	1.34	8.4	2.9	0.5
HNO_3	10	12.34	4.58	19.7	6.5	2.2
	20	16.27	5.69	39.3	9.6	3.4
NaOH	10	13.97	3.22	36.7	4.1	0.2

phase and on crystal size of the stability against acids of glass-ceramics of the feldspar—diopside system catalyzed by the sulfides of heavy metals. The compositions of these glass-ceramics are shown on page 259. The chemical stability was determined with respect to HCl, H_2SO_4, and HNO_3 acids at 10% and 20% concentrations, as well as with respect to a 10% NaOH solution, by boiling in them samples with a surface area of 50-80 cm^2. A gradual increase in the stability to acids was observed, depending on how much of the glassy phase has been transformed into the chemically more stable crystalline phase. The glass-ceramics investigated were found to be most stable to HCl and H_2SO_4 solutions, and somewhat less stable to HNO_3 and NaOH solutions (see Table 71, taken from [53]).

The change in the chemical stability of minelbite as a function of the time spent in the acid is shown in Fig. 102, from which it can be seen that these glass-ceramics, which have an unusually high chemical stability, are even capable of increasing it with time, i.e., they become passivated. Thus, at the start of the test, the dissolving rate of the glass-ceramic was 0.85 g/m^2-h; however, the total amount of the material dissolved within 24 h was only 6.5 g/m^2. The weight losses gradually decreased, and asymptotically approached the minimum level, lying below 0.5 g/m^2-24 h, inde-

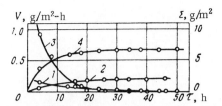

Fig. 102. Chemical stability of Minelbite to hydrochloric
acid. τ) Duration of etching; V) solution rate; Σ) total
amount of the material dissolved from the start of etching.
1,3) Solution rate; 2, 4) total amount of the dissolved material. 1,2) 10% acid concentration; 3,4) 20% acid concentration.

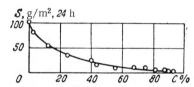

Fig. 103. Solubility S in 10% hydrochloric acid of partially crystallized glass as a function of the amount C of
the crystalline phase.

pendent of the type of reagent used. Based on the experimental results, the glass–ceramics tested reached the first class of chemical stability within 48 h with respect to all the reagents tested, except the 20% HNO_3 solution, for which 60 h were needed. The presence of the glass phase greatly lowered the chemical stability of
the glass–ceramic, as can be seen from Fig. 103, which shows the
solubility of the glass–ceramic in a 10% HCl as a function of the
amount of crystalline phase present. The same phenomenon was
previously observed by us with alumina ceramics, which decrease
their chemical stability relative to acids and bases with increasing
content of a glassy phase [588].

The chemical stability of glass–ceramics depends not only
on chemical composition, but also on microstructure. The dense,
nonporous microstructure of glass–ceramics makes it possible to
count on better chemical stability as compared to that of porous
ceramics, which have a more extensive surface and greater penetrability to liquids and vapors. Phosphate-containing glass–ceramics containing a high amount of cristobalite or quartz were more

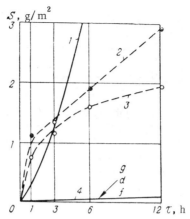

Fig. 104. Solubility of glass-ceramics and original glasses in a 5% HCl solution at 90°C. τ) Duration of etching; S) weight loss. 1,2,3) Glass of compositions g, d, and f, respectively, following the ternary phase diagram on Fig. 69; 4) glass-ceramics prepared from all these glasses.

stable to boiling water than glass-ceramics containing β-spodumene crystals in their microstructure. These glass-ceramics did not show traces of visible corrosion under the influence of atmosphere with a relative humidity of 95% when exposed at 65°C for 5000 h, whereas sodium calcium borosilicate glasses and Pyrex glass showed corroded surfaces when subjected to the same conditions [381].

Figure 104 shows the chemical stability of a glass-and glass-ceramics in the $Li_2O—Al_2O_3—SiO_2$ system with ZrO_2 and P_2O_5 additions [300].

Takizawa et al. [589, 590] investigated the solution of a glass-ceramic of the composition $Li_2O \cdot 2SiO_2$ in hydrofluoric acid which, at an initial concentration of 47%, was diluted with distilled water in the ratios 1:10 and 1:50. The etching time at 40°C was 10 min. Electron-microscope analysis showed that the glassy phase surrounding the crystals in the glass-ceramic dissolved faster in the HF, while the poorly soluble $Li_2O \cdot 2SiO_2$ crystals went into solution in the form of flakes at the instant the thickness of the dissolved layer of the glass became equal to the maximum crystal size. With increasing etching time, the glassy phase between the crystals dissolved to a greater and greater depth. The solution rate of the glass-ceramic increased in proportion to the acid concentration and depended on the solution rate in HF of the glassy phase, on the rate of flaking of the crystalline material, on the crystal size and their number per unit area, on the ratio between the crystalline and the glassy phases, and on the stresses at the interphase surfaces between the crystal and the glass. The curve showing the dependence of weight losses on the solution time had an S-shape, and its inflection point depended on the crystallization conditions and on the microstructure of the surface layer of the glass-ceramic. This point on the solution curve corresponded to the instant when the thickness of the dissolved layer became equal to the maximum crystal size in this layer.

The same authors [591] studied the chemical stability to acid and basic solutions of glass-ceramics and glasses of the composition $Li_2O \cdot Al_2O_3 \cdot 3SiO_2$ and of mica—spodumene composition. The solution in HF diluted in the ratio 1:50 was done at 42.3°C. The microstructure of the glass-ceramic in the mica—spodumene system consisted of mica and β-spodumene crystals, as well as of the glassy phase surrounding them; of these, the β-spodumene had the highest solubility in the HF. After the β-spodumene crystals dissolved, the mica crystals, which are more difficult to dissolve, went into solution in the form of small flakes, the appearance of which was not observed during the solution of the glass-ceramic of the $Li_2O \cdot Al_2O_3 \cdot 3SiO_2$ composition. The rate of solution of this glass-ceramic varied directly with time up to approximately 50 min from the instant it started to dissolve, after which the rate decreased with increasing time. The solution rate of the glass-ceramic of the mica—spodumene system increased with time at the start of the process, after which it became constant. The solution in H_2SO_4 with a concentration ranging from 0.5 N to 4 N was performed at 42.7°C and 78°C. The solution rate of the glass-ceramic $Li_2O \cdot Al_2O_3 \cdot 3SiO_2$ had a maximum near the 1 N concentration, with the shape of the curves for the solution process being different for different concentrations. An S-shaped curve corresponds to low H_2SO_4 concentrations, whereas, at higher concentrations, a monotonically increasing curve was obtained. The activation energy of the solution process for the glass-ceramic was 13.6 kcal per mole, as compared to 16 kcal/mole for the original glass. The dependence between the weight losses α and the solution time was

[591]: $\alpha^n = kT$, where n = 2 for mica—spodumene glass-ceramic, and n = 1 for glass of the mica—spodumene system, as well as for glass and glass-ceramic of the $Li_2O \cdot Al_2O_3 \cdot 3SiO_2$ composition. More complex dependencies were observed by dissolving the glass-ceramic $Li_2O \cdot Al_2O_3 \cdot 3SiO_2$ in a 4.4 N solution of NaOH at 88°C, due to the additional flakes going over into the solution. The activation energy for the solution process of this glass-ceramic in NaOH was 85.9 kcal/mole, while that of the mica—spodumene glass-ceramic was 37.6 kcal/mole. The solution rate of the $Li_2O \cdot Al_2O_3 \cdot 3SiO_2$ glass-ceramic varied in proportion to the logarithm of the basic-solution concentration, while for the mica—spodumene glass-ceramic, it varied in proportion to the solution concentration proper.

When kitchenware manufactured from the glass-ceramics described on page 272 have been used for a long time and have been cleaned a number of times by basic detergents, they acquire a degree of porosity, and unsightly stains form on their surface which are difficult to remove. Their appearance is caused by the penetration into the porous surface layers of certain components of the detergent solution. In order to eliminate the porosity, Calkins and Morrisey [592-594] proposed a method of improving the chemical stability of these glass-ceramics with respect to erosion by basic solutions. The proposed method was especially effective for the glass-ceramic whose composition is given on page 271 [462-464]. In this method, the heat treatment of the original glass in order to transform it into the glass-ceramic following the procedures presented on page 269 (Fig. 74) is done in a controlled reducing atmosphere containing not less than 25% by volume of water vapor or 1-10% by volume of excess of combustible components. After a temperature of 900-1000°C is reached, the products are held in an oxidizing atmosphere, which is maintained during the further heat treatment and cooling processes. The stability of the glass-ceramic relative to the formation of stains depends on the concentration of water vapor in the atmosphere; here, the highest stability was attained when that concentration was 18% by volume [592-594].

In addition to the works mentioned above, a very limited number of publications appeared in the literature dealing with the chemical stability of glass-ceramics [768-773]. There are no data in the literature on the chemical stability of photosensitive glass-

Table 72. Corrosion Resistance of Photosensitive Glass-Ceramics
Exposed for 24 h to Concentrated Solutions and Vapors
of Mineral Acids at Their Boiling Temperatures

Reagent	Concentration, %	Temperature, °C	Average corrosion rate, g/m^2 per 24 h	
			Liquid phase	Vapor phase
HNO_3	56.0	127.5	0.00008523	0.00004352
HCl	20.0	109	0.0001685	0.0002100
H_2SO_4	98.0	300	0.0001770	0.00006286

ceramics. In order to explore the possibility of employing photosensitive glass-ceramics for the manufacture of corrosion-resistant elements for pneumatic-jet instruments to be used in systems
regulating the feeding of very active liquid acids and gases, the
present author and L. I. Klimenkova first systematically investigated the stability of photosensitive glass-ceramic in concentrated
solutions and vapors of sulfuric, hydrochloric, and nitric acids
under high-temperature conditions and under prolonged exposure
to these very active reagents. All experiments dealing with the determination of the chemical stability of photosensitive glass-
ceramics were performed according to the same procedure, which
included the determination of the corrosion rate of the photosensitive glass-ceramic from the weight loss of the sample per unit surface. The samples tested were in the form of $55 \times 30 \times 1$ mm
plates, the total area being 14.5 dm^2. A 20% HCl (6 N) solution
was used as reagent, since this azeotropic mixture of water and
hydrogen chloride, boiling at 109°C, ensures a constant composition. Moreover, of the mineral acids (HCl, H_2SO_4, and HNO_3),
hydrochloric acid acts most aggressively toward glass, and it is
quite safe to handle. The tests for leaching of photosensitive glass-
ceramics in concentrated acids were performed at the following
boiling temperatures: in 20% HCl at 109°C, in 96% H_2SO_4 at 300°C,
and in 56% HNO_3 at 127.5°C.

The photosensitive glass-ceramic samples, which were first
weighed and degreased, were mounted in a special device, placed
in a vertical position in an apparatus made of quartz glass, and
then boiled using a cyclic testing procedure. The duration of each

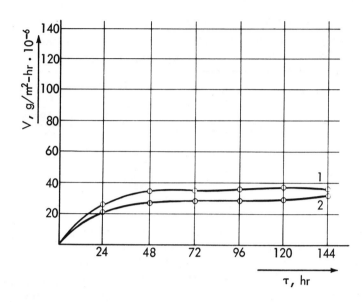

Fig. 105. Chemical stability of photosensitive glass-ceramic relative to the long-term action of 56% HNO₃ at 127.5°C. τ) Boiling time; v) corrosion rate. 1) in the solution; 2) in the vapor.

cycle was 24 h. Of importance during longer exposures are continuous circulation and stirring, which are done so as to ensure uniform and even boiling of the acid.

The cooled samples were washed in distilled water and then in ethyl alcohol, whereupon they were rubbed with batiste and calcined in a muffle furnace at 450°C to a uniform weight, so as to completely remove any moisture from the surface of the samples and from their thin surface layers. The total dehydration was completed after the samples were calcined for 2 h at a temperature of 420-450°C, when uniformity in the weight of the samples was achieved.

The results of the corrosion experiments on photosensitive glass-ceramics in solutions and vapors of concentrated hydrochloric, sulfuric, and nitric solutions at their boiling temperatures are presented in Table 72 and Figs. 105-107. Electron micrographs of the surface of photosensitive glass-ceramic samples which underwent corrosion in concentrated solutions of nitric and sulfuric acids are shown in Figs. 108 and 109.

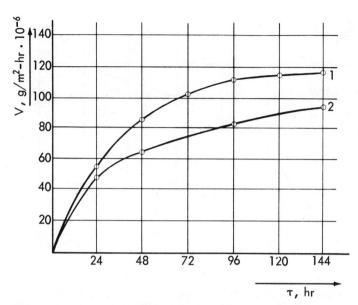

Fig. 106. Chemical stability of photosensitive glass-ceramic relative to the long-term action of 20% HCl at 109°C. τ) Boiling time; v) corrosion rate. 1) In the solution; 2) in the vapors.

As a result of the tests performed, the dependence of the corrosion on the duration of exposure to the above-mentioned reagents was determined, from which not only the degree of corrosion, but also the corrosion rate, can be characterized. The analysis of data presented in Table 72 shows that photosensitive glass-ceramic has a high chemical stability in solutions and vapors of hydrochloric, sulfuric, and nitric acids at elevated temperatures. With respect to chemical stability, photosensitive glass-ceramic is many times better than such acid-resistant materials as minelbite (see Table 71 [53]), and is more stable toward vapors of these acids than toward their aqueous solutions.

By examining the curves showing the dependence of the corrosion rate of photosensitive glass-ceramic samples on the duration of exposure to concentrated acids (Figs. 105-107), it can be seen that the corrosion process has a damping character, which is most clearly expressed in the case of nitric acid, and less clearly so in the case of H_2SO_4. Thus, for instance, for experiments in

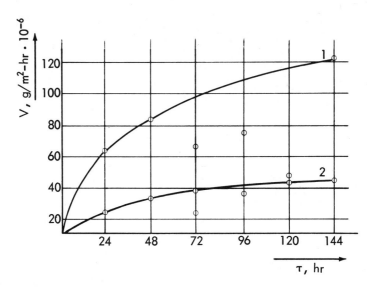

Fig. 107. Chemical stability of photosensitive glass-ceramic relative to the long-term action of 96% H_2SO_4 at 300°C. τ) Boiling time; v) corrosion rate. 1) In the solution; 2) in the vapor.

nitric acid, the largest weight losses occurred during the first 24 h of boiling, while after a 48-h exposure, the corrosion rate became practically constant. This is confirmed by electron-microscopy investigations of the microstructure of the samples, which showed that the most intensive corrosion of the surface occurred after the first 24 h of exposure of the photosensitive glass-ceramic in HNO_3 (Fig. 108a), with a somewhat less-intensive corrosion after a 48-h exposure (Fig. 108b). With boiling in HNO_3 increased to 72 and 96 h, the microstructure of the photosensitive glass-ceramic remains fine-crystalline and does not undergo substantial changes (Fig. 108c, d) and only after being exposed for 120–144 h does the microstructure start to break up slightly (Fig. 108e, f).

The damping character of the corrosion process of photosensitive glass-ceramic may be explained by the formation on its surface of a protective coating composed of the reaction products, which prevents the penetration of the reagent into deeper layers of the material, and thus hinders further corrosion.

A considerably more intensive corrosion of the surface took place when heating the plates of the photosensitive glass-ceramic in 96% H_2SO_4 at 300°C. In this case, the corrosion rate, although also slightly decreasing with time (Fig. 107), nevertheless continues to increase after a 120- to 144-h boiling in sulfuric acid. Electron micrographs of the surface of photosensitive glass-ceramic samples subjected to boiling in sulfuric acid (Fig. 109) also attest to a significantly higher degree of corrosion than for the action by nitric acid. By examining Fig. 109, it can be seen that with increasing time of action by sulfuric acid, the degree of corrosion of the photosensitive glass-ceramic surface increases, its microstructure becomes more and more loosened, and, after boiling in sulfuric acid for 5-6 days, microcracks appear on the surface (Fig. 109g, h). This may be explained not only by the high concentration of sulfuric acid (96%, as compared to 20% for HCl and 56% for HNO_3), but also by the high boiling temperature (300°C) in an extremely aggressive medium.

Electron micrographs of the corroded surface of photosensitive glass-ceramic in nitric acid (Fig. 108c, d), and especially in sulfuric acid (Fig. 109d, e, f), clearly show the presence of crater-shaped hillocks and depressions. The former are apparently due to the remains of the crystalline phase, which is most stable with respect to these acids (such as β-quartz or lithium disilicate), whereas the latter are due to traces of the glassy phase, which is least stable and dissolves in the acid, leaving behind the depression. Such a corrosion mechanism for photosensitive glass-ceramic, starting with the leaching away of the chemically least stable glassy phase surrounding the tiny crystal grains, agrees well with the literature data for glass-ceramics [589-591, 764].

Thus, as a result of the investigation performed relative to the chemical stability of photosensitive glass-ceramics to long-term action of concentrated mineral acids at their boiling temperatures, it was determined that this material has sufficiently high stability with respect to the given reagents for it to be recommended for use in high-flow apparatus, such as is intended for regulating the supply of liquid and gaseous aggressive media. The corrosion rate is at a maximum during the first few hours of exposure, after which it gradually slows down, finally reaching a practically constant value. This capability of photosensitive glass-ceramic to

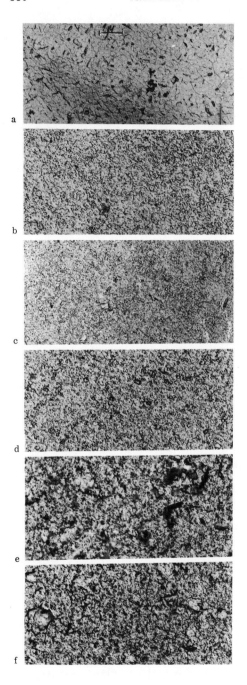

Fig. 108. Electron micrographs showing the corroded surfaces of photosensitive glass-ceramic samples subjected to the action of 56% HNO_3 solution at 127.5°C for: a) 24; b) 48; c) 72; d) 96; e) 120; f) 144 h.

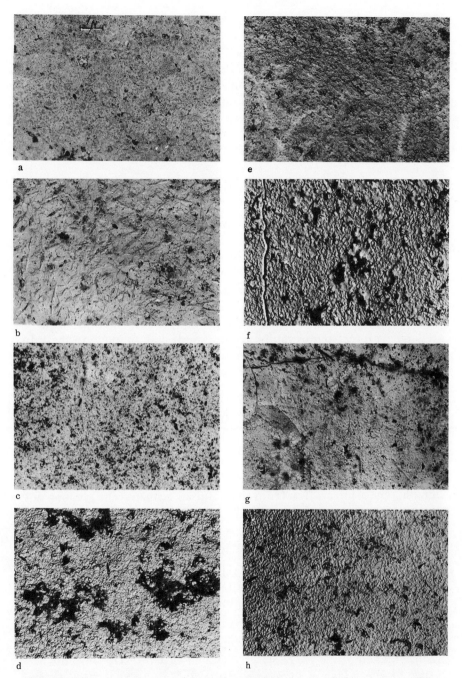

Fig. 109. Electron micrographs showing the corroded surfaces of photosensitive glass-ceramic samples subjected to the action of 96% H_2SO_4 solution at 300° for: a) 0; b) 24; c) 48; d) 72; e) 96; f) 120; g) 144; h) 168 h.

increase its chemical stability with time, i.e., to become passivated, is explained by the formation on its surface of a protective layer which prevents further corrosion. The corrosion of photosensitive glass-ceramic starts with the solution of the least stable residual glassy phase surrounding the very fine crystal grains. Photosensitive glass-ceramic proved to be most stable to 56% HNO_3, and somewhat less stable to 20% HCl and 96% H_2SO_4.

7. OPTICAL PROPERTIES. TRANSPARENT GLASS-CERAMICS

For the most part, glass-ceramics are nontransparent. However, a number of glass-ceramics containing not less than two crystalline phases have been prepared which are completely transparent, due to the absence of blisters and voids, and also due to the small crystal size and the absence of light scattering at the crystal boundaries, which requires good matching between the indices of refraction for the crystals and the glassy phase. In transparent glass-ceramics, the crystals are so small and so close in their indices of refraction that the material is as transparent as sheet glass, except that it has a slight colored tint.

The first transparent glass-ceramics were prepared from titanium-containing lithium aluminosilicate glasses, the compositions of which were presented earlier (compositions 1, 2, 5, and 7-13 in Table 34 [326, 327, 595]). If the heat-treatment temperature of these glasses does not exceed 900°C, then glass-ceramics are formed which are transparent with respect to visible wavelengths and which differ from the original transparent glasses only in having a lower α (less than $10 \cdot 10^{-7}$ as compared to $>30 \cdot 10^{-7}$ for glass), by the presence of β-eucryptite and β-spodumene, and by the absence of deformation at temperatures below 1200°C.

According to Herbert's [731] data, glass of the composition (in %) 70.9 SiO_2, 23.3 Al_2O_3, 5 Li_2O, 0.1 B_2O_3, and 0.8 TiO_2 may be transformed into a transparent glass-ceramic by crystallization at 925°C for 12 h.

Janakiramarao [714] prepared transparent glass-ceramics from glasses of the $K_2O-SiO_2-TiO_2$ and $Bi_2O_3-B_2O_3-PbO$ systems. Here, glass of the composition (in %): 30 SiO_2, 25 K_2O, and 45 TiO_2 with $\alpha = 110 \cdot 10^{-7}$ (°C)$^{-1}$ was transformed into transparent glass-ceramic with $\alpha = 94 \cdot 10^{-7}$, whereas glass of the composition

Table 73. Heat-Treatment Procedures of Glasses Used for the Preparation of Transparent Glass-Ceramics, Their Properties, and the Crystalline Phases

Comp. No.	Properties of glass			Heat treatment				Properties of glass-ceramics			Crystalline phase
	$\alpha \cdot 10^7$ 1/°C	density (g/cm³)	annealing temp., (°C)	preliminary		final		$\alpha \cdot 10^7$ 1/°C	density (g/cm³)	σ_f (kg/cm²)	
				T °C	τ h	T °C	τ h				
1	42.0	2.3429	678	800	2	880	2	−4.6	2.4703	—	β-Spodumene
2	59.9	2.4022	—	800	2	880	2	10.3	2.4660	—	β-Spodumene, Rutile
5	60.9	2.4247	—	700	2	800	2	5.2	2.4409	—	β-Spodumene
7	46.7	2.4500	688	700	2	800	2	1.1	2.5350	—	β-Spodumene
8	43.1	2.4138	676	800	2	880	2	−9.8	2.5439	—	The same
9	42.3	2.3828	671	800	1	880	4	−3.5	2.5137	683	The same
10	40.1	2.4430	672	800	1	880	4	−3.9	2.5495	760	The same
11	44.5	2.3964	680	800	1	880	4	−5.3	2.5054	822	—
12	42.5	4.3751	683	800	2	880	2	−3.8	2.4796	—	β-Spodumene
13	33.9	2.3973	689	815	2	870	6	8.7	2.5436	—	β-Eucryptite

35 SiO_2, 20 K_2O, and 45 TiO_2 with $\alpha = 94 \cdot 10^{-7}$ was transformed into semitransparent glass-ceramic with $\alpha = 92 \cdot 10^{-7}$ (°C)$^{-1}$. There are also transparent glass-ceramics in the $MgO-Al_2O_3-SiO_2$ [347] and $Li_2O-Ga_2O_3-SiO_2$ [189] systems.

Table 73, which is based on [326, 327], shows the heat-treatment procedures for glasses of the $Li_2O-Al_2O_3-SiO_2$ system with TiO_2 additions, the compositions of which are presented in Table 34; Table 73 also shows some properties of the transparent glass-ceramics which were prepared from the cited glasses.

The transformation of transparent glasses into transparent glass-ceramics cannot be observed visually; it is confirmed by a significant decrease in α and by the precipitation of crystalline phases, which can be observed by x-ray or infrared spectroscopic analyses.

When transparent glass-ceramics are heated to temperatures above 900°C, they lose their transparency, which may be caused by the increase in the size of their crystals or by the appearance of crystalline phases absent in the transparent glass-ceramic, i.e., by recrystallization.

In a number of works [159, 187], it was shown that precrystallization treatment has a favorable effect on the preparation of transparent glass-ceramics. Transparent glass-ceramics can be prepared within the temperature range corresponding to the precipitation of the primary crystalline phase. Podushko and Kozlova [187] determined that for each composition of the original glass of the $Li_2O-SiO_2-Al_2O_3-TiO_2$ system, there is an optimum temperature T_{opt} for preliminary heat treatment which raises to a maximum the temperature at which there is loss of transparency. Above this maximum temperature, there is a loss in transparency associated with the nucleation of a new crystalline phase due to the recrystallization of the phase responsible for the transparent state, or with the growth of a secondary crystalline phase.

Preliminary treatment at temperatures below T_{opt} lowers the temperature of the transparency loss, whereas, at temperatures higher than T_{opt}, not only is the temperature of the transparency loss lowered, but bulk cloudiness of the glass may result. At T_{opt}, the rate of nucleus formation is at a maximum, and it decreases with decreasing, as well as with increasing, temperature. With in-

creasing amount of catalyst present, the temperature of the transparency loss also increases, which is explained by the rise in the
amount of the nuclei present and, consequently, by a decrease in
the crystal size.

Baiburt and Gorbachev [737] investigated the absorption spectra in the ultraviolet region for a lithium aluminosilicate glass of
the spodumene type which produces a transparent glass-ceramic,
and they found a connection between the height of the absorption
maxima arising in the glass during its heat treatment at the precrystallization temperatures (600-700°C), and the degree of the
subsequent crystallization at higher temperatures (800°C and
higher). Based on the data obtained, the authors [737] recommend
that one estimate the potential crystallization of sitallizing glasses
from the height of their absorption spectra, these glasses having
been subjected to heat treatment within the precrystallization temperature range.

Florinskaya et al. [596] used infrared spectroscopy to observe the similarity between the phases in transparent and nontransparent glass-ceramics, and their work also indicates the dependence of transparency on crystal size.

By investigating transparent glass-ceramics of the lithium
aluminosilicate system by the combination scattering spectra method, it was shown that the crystals precipitated in it are not the
$nAl_2O_3 \cdot mSiO_2$ phase, but are rather a titanium-containing phase
the structure of which is similar to rutile [738].

Some authors associate the preparation of transparent glass-
ceramics with the structural peculiarities of the original glass.
Kondrat'ev [184] investigated a number of glasses in the Li_2O-
$Al_2O_3-SiO_2$ system with small TiO_2 additions, and he came to the
conclusion that one can obtain a transparent glass-ceramic only
if the following condition is observed:

$$\frac{[Al_2O_3] - [R_2O]}{[TiO_2]} < 1,$$

i.e., the TiO_2 concentration must exceed the concentration of the
octahedrally coordinated Al. In this case, at least a portion of the
Ti present must be in octahedral coordination in the amorphous
compounds $Al_2O_3 \cdot TiO_2$ (psuedo-brookite-structure type), contain-

Table 74. Properties of Glass-Ceramics,

Property	Pyroceram				Glass-ceramics catalyzed by phosphates				
	9605, non transparent	9606, non transparent	9607, non transparent	9608, non transparent	A	B	C	D	E
Density (g/cm^3) at 25°C	2.62	2.604—2,61	2.52	2.50—2.60	2.47	2.47	2.80	2.55	2.62
Water absorption (%)	0.00	0.00	0.00	0.00	—	—	—	—	—
Gas permeability	Impermeable to gas			—	—	—	—	—	—
Softening temperature (°C)	1350	1250—1350	—	1250	850—900	900	900	850	900
Specific capacity at 25°C, cgs units	0.185	0.185—0.190	—	1.190	—	—	—	—	—
Average heat capacity at 25-400°C, cgs units	0.23	0,230—0.232	—	0.235—0.240	0.24	0.28	—	0.27	0.25
Heat conductivity, cgs units: at 25°C	0,0100	0.0073—0.0087	—	0.0037—0.0047	—	—	—	—	—
at 100°C	—	—	—	—	0,0067	0.013	0.0052	0.0079	—
Linear thermal expansion coefficient, $\propto \times 10^{-7}$ (25-300°C)	14	57	—7	2—20	125—134	—	175	—	—
Thermal stability (temperature drop required for disintegration by immersion in cold water of samples 5 mm in diameter and 55 mm long)	—	—	—	—	160	—	130	285	—
Elastic modulus (kg/mm^2)	1386	12100—12460	—	8750	8900	10600	7500	7900	9700
Poisson's ratio	—	0.245	—	0.25	—	—	—	—	—
Tensile strength (yield point for metals) (kg/cm^2)	—	1400	—	1120—1610	—	—	—	—	—
Flexure strength (kg/cm^2)	2590	1400—2240	—	1138	>2800	2500	1800	1960	1950
Ratio between flexure strength* and density	14.1	12.3	—	—	—	—	—	—	—
Impact strength (kg/cm) at room temperature	—	—	—	—	7.5	3.9	—	—	—
at 300°C	—	—	—	—	6.6	4.0	—	—	—
Brinell hardness, 500-g loads	—	—	—	—	—	—	—	—	—
Rockwell C hardness	—	—	—	—	64	96	—	—	58
Knoop hardness: 50-g loads	1100	940	—	—	—	—	—	—	—
100-g loads	843	698—789	—	577—703	—	—	—	—	—
500-g loads	720	570- 619	—	588—708	—	—	—	—	—
Wear resistance during sandblast treatment relative to that of sheet glass (1.0)	27	20	—	—	—	—	—	—	—

Flexure strength was measured in lb/in^2.

Glasses, Ceramics, and Metals

Glass				Ceramic			Metal				
Fused quartz 7940	Vycor glass 7900	Lime glass 0080	Borosilicate glass 7740	Al₂O₃	Steatite, MgO·SiO₂	Forsterite, 2MgO·SiO₂	Aluminum, 99.0%, annealed	Aluminum, 75%, annealed	Gray iron	Stainless steel, annealed	Titanium
2.20	2.18	2.47	2.23	3.61—3.67	2.65—2.92	2.8	2.71	2.80	7.0—7.7	7.93	4.50
0.00	0.00	0.00	0.00	0.00	0.00—0.03	0.00—0.01	—	—	—	—	—
Impermeable to gas							—	—	—	—	—
1584	1500	696	820	1700—1745	1349	—					
0.176	0.178	0.200	0.186	0.181	—	—	0.23 (100°)	0.23 (100°)	0.131 (100°)	0.118 (100°)	0.053 (100°)
0.223	0.224	0.235	0.233	0.241	—	—					
0.0028	—	—	0.260—0.305	0.052—0.058	0.0062—0.0065	0.010	0.53	0.29	0.110	0.052	—
--	—	—									
5.5	4.45—8	92	17.8—32	73 (20—500°)	81.5—99 (20—500°)	99 (20—500°)	256	232	100 (25°)	95 (от 18 до 316°)	82
—	—	—									—
735	6710—6720	714	6650	2800	1050	—	700	728	812	2030	1113
0.17	0.17—0.18	0.24	0.20	0.32	—	—	0.33	0.33	0.17	—	—
—	350—630	—	420—700	1750—3500	910	700	910	2800	1400—4200	5600	2520
700	700	700	4500—7000	2800—3500	1400	1330	—	—	—	—	—
4.55	4.59	4.05	—	13.1—13.3	6.85	6.75	4.8	14.3	2.67—8.0	10.1	8.0
—	—	—	—	—	—	—	—	—	—	—	—
—	—	—	—	—	—	—	—	—	—	—	—
—	—	—	—	—	—	—	23	30	163—269	135—185	76
—	—	—	—	—	—	—	—	—			
644	630	520	—	1800	—	—	—	—	—	—	—
—	532	—	481	1880	—	—	—	—	—	—	—
—	477	—	442	1530—1553	—	—	—	—	180—300	147—201	100
3.60	3.53	1.23	—	—	—	—	—	—	—	—	—

Table 74 (Continued)

Property	Pyroceram				Glass-ceramics catalyzed by phosphates				
	9605, non transparent	9606, non transparent	9607, non transparent	9608, non transparent	A	B	C	D	E
Friction coefficient (polished surface):									
Static	—	—	—	—	0.185	—	0.086	0.157	—
Dynamic	—	—	—	—	0.157	—	0.071	0.143	—
Dielectric constant at a frequency of 10^6 Hz:									
$25°$	6.1	5.58—5.62	—	6.78	5.4	6.3	5.3	6.9	5.4
$300°$	6.3	5.60—5.80	—	—	—	—	—	—	—
$500°$	—	8.80	—	—	—	—	—	—	—
at a frequency of 10^8 Hz, $25°C$	—	—	—	—	5.3	6.6	5.4	—	5.4
at a frequency of 10^{10} Hz:									
$25°$	6.1	5.45—5.53	—	6.54	5.5	6.2	—	—	—
$300°$	6.1	5,51—5,53	—	6.65—6.68	—	—	—	—	—
$500°$	6.1	5.54—5,58	—	6.78	—	—	—	—	—
Scattering factor at a frequency of 10^6 Hz:									
$25°$	0.0017	0.0015—0.0024	—	—	—	—	—	—	—
$300°$	0.014	0.013—0.0154	—	—	—	—	—	—	—
$500°$	—	—	—	—	—	—	—	—	—
at a frequency of 10^{10} Hz:									
$25°$	0.0002	0.0003	—	0.0068	—	—	—	—	—
$300°$	0.0008	0.0006—0.00075	—	0.0115	—	—	—	—	—
$500°$	0.0025	0.0015—0.0018	—	0.040	—	—	—	—	—
Loss factor at a frequency of 10^6 Hz:									
$25°$	0.010	0.008—0.014	—	0.02	—	—	—	—	—
$300°$	0.078	0.075—0.086	—	—	—	—	—	—	—
$500°$	—	—	—	—	—	—	—	—	—
at a frequency of 10^{10} Hz:									
$25°$	0.001	0.002	—	0.015—0.045	—	—	—	—	—
$300°$	0.003	0.003—0.004	—	0.077	—	—	—	—	—
$500°$	0.015	0.008—0.010	—	0.27	—	—	—	—	—
Bulk electrical resistivity $\log_{10}$ (Q_V ohm · cm):									
at room temperature	—	—	—	—	16	15.5	13.6	13.6	—
$250°$	0.1	10	—	8.1	—	—	—	—	—
$300°$	—	—	—	—	10	9.3	6.4	7.5	—
$350°$	8.7	8.6	—	6.8	—	—	—	—	—
$700°$	—	—	—	—	5	4.2	3.9	4.4	—
Dielectric strength at room temperature (kV/mm) sample DiN	—	—	—	—	47	—	37.5	—	—

	Glass				Ceramic			Metal				
	Fused quartz 7940	Vycor glass 7900	Lime glass 0080	Borosilicate glass 7740	Al_2O_3	Steatite $MgO \cdot SiO_2$	Forsterite $2\,MgO \cdot SiO_2$	Aluminum, 99.0% annealed	Aluminum, 75% annealed	Gray iron	Stainless steel, annealed	Titanium
	—	—	—	—	—	—	—	—	—	—	—	—
	—	—	—	—	—	—	—	—	—	—	—	—
	3.78	3.8	7.2	4.6	8.81	5.9	6.3	—	—	—	—	—
	—	3.9	—	5.9	—	—	—	—	—	—	—	—
	—	—	—	—	9.03	—	—	—	—	—	—	—
	—	—	—	—	—	—	—	—	—	—	—	—
	3.78	3.8	6.71	4.5	8.79	5.8	5.8	—	—	—	—	—
	3.78	—	—	—	—	—	—	—	—	—	—	—
	3.78	—	—	—	9.03	—	—	—	—	—	—	—
	0.002–0.003	0.0005	0.009	0.0046	0.00035	0.0013	0.0003	—	—	—	—	—
	—	0.0042	—	0.0130	—	—	—	—	—	—	—	—
	—	—	—	—	0.012	—	—	—	—	—	—	—
	0.00017 0.00008	0.0009	0.017	0.0085	0.0015	0.0014	0.0010	—	—	—	—	—
	0.00009	—	—	—	0.0021	—	—	—	—	—	—	—
	0.0008	0.0019	0.065	0.0212	0.0031	0.0077	0.0019	—	—	—	—	—
	—	0.0164	—	0.0566	—	—	—	—	—	—	—	—
	—	—	—	—	0.108	—	—	—	—	—	—	—
	0.0007	0.0036	0.114	0.282	0.0082	0.0058	—	—	—	—	—	—
	0.0003	—	—	—	—	—	—	—	—	—	—	—
	0.0003	—	—	—	0.019	—	—	—	—	—	—	—
	12.0	9.7	6.4	8.1	14.00 (100°)	—	14 (20°)	14 (20°)	—	—	—	—
	9.7	8.1	5.1	8.6	12.95 (300°)	—	—	—	—	—	—	—
	—	—	—	—	—	—	—	—	—	—	—	—
	—	—	—	—	—	—	—	—	—	—	—	—

ing (TiO_6) and (AlO_6) nodes and (AlO_4) nodes joining them. In agreement with thermodynamic calculations, this compound is stable to 1500°C. This compound precipitates at low temperatures in the form of submicroscopic liquants, which also serve as the future nuclei for the start of crystallization. The first phase precipitating is aluminum titanate. If such glass is heat treated at temperatures which are not too high, then a transparent glass-ceramic is obtained.

Petrovskii et al. [191] believe that in order to produce a transparent glass-ceramic, the nature of the cation having the highest mobility is significant. In known transparent glass-ceramics, such cations are Li or Mg. Their presence in a glass is conducive to the formation of Al or Ga structural nodes, which covalently coordinate six bridging oxygen bonds. By confirming the fact that in glass of the $SiO_2—Al_2O_3—BeO$ system the Al is also present in a sixfold coordination, the authors [191] assume that by adding TiO_2 to this system, they should be able to produce a transparent glass-ceramic.

Maurer, in 1964, in his paper presented at the Fourth All-Union Conference on the Glassy State, stated that he associated the production of transparent glass-ceramics with the growth mechanism of the crystals. In his opinion, in most glass-ceramics, the growth of the crystals is determined by diffusion from the region around the nuclei. In connection with the formation of this region, the nuclei for the scattering of light become complex, i.e., they contain not only the crystalline nucleus, but also the diffusion region adjacent to it. Similar complex regions scatter light very poorly, which is the reason many partially crystallized glasses are transparent. The weak scattering intensity of similar materials is associated with the fact that during the crystal growth process, ions with a better polarizability than the average ion in the glass diffuse toward the crystal, and the polarization of glass decreases to the extent that it increases in the crystal. These diffusion regions scatter coherently, which results in a decrease in the intensity of the scattered light.

Some glass-ceramics of the Cer-Vit type [715] are capable of luminescing in ultraviolet light or when bombarded by electrons. They may be produced as transparent or as translucent materials,

and also in various colors. Other glass-ceramics of this type possess magnetic properties.

Table 74 summarizes the physical, mechanical, thermal, and
electrical properties of glass-ceramics, discussed above, based on
data by various authors [20, 21, 48, 57, 381, 481, 502, 571, 597].

Chapter VI

Areas of Application of Photosensitive Glasses, Glass-Ceramics, and Photosensitive Glass-Ceramics

1. PHOTOSENSITIVE GLASSES IN SCIENCE AND TECHNOLOGY AND IN CONSTRUCTION

Photosensitive glass may be produced in any shape, from very small jewelry, ornaments, and dinnerware, to large sheets of polished glass. In the same glass sample, one can produce indelible photographic images which do not become discolored with time, which can be of varying colors, and which can have a wide range of contrast, varying depths of penetration, and which are of different degrees of intensity. In the form of flat plates, this glass can be used in portrait and in scientific photography and in architecture for decorative walls and partitions, for finishing material, and for ornamental tile. It can also be used, for example, as decorative material for fresco painting, for jewelry, for colored windowpanes [58, 67, 598-601, 742].

Due to its fine-grained structure, good thermal conductivity, constancy of size, and clarity of image, one may use photosensitive glass for the manufacture of viewing screens for optical instruments characterized by their high resolution capability; one may use it in halftone printing, in photomicrography, as lantern slides, and for the manufacture of instrument dials, optical scales, measuring rules, pushbutton controls, and railroad and highway signs and signals. Photosensitive glasses may also be employed for the production of lighting fixtures, gratings, automobile lights, and so on.

Fig. 110. Articles made of the photosensitive glass Fotoform and of Fotoceram. a) Reticulated screens made from Fotolyte; b) "laces," obtained through chemical treatment of photosensitive glass; c) 1) plate made from black Fotoceram B with etched-through rectangular holes; 2) screen made from Fotoceram E with square holes; 3) spacer made from Fotoform B to be used in electronic tube; 4) mechanical part made of Fotoceram; 5) spacer made of Fotoceram; 6) casing made from Fotoceram to be used for digital computers, and having metal-coated through-holes; 7) a Fotoform B sample equipped with small holes for conductors; 8,9) Fotoform B samples; 10) transparent Fotoform B with a white, semitranslucent grid-line.

Completely new uses for glass have been developed for the photosensitive glass Fotoform, such as: precision dielectric spacers for photomultiplier tubes, optical coding disks, honeycombed constructions for light cells, brush holders for switches in numerical transformers of counters, potentiometer substrates for fixed and printed circuits, bases for electrical circuits with embedded contact, light collimators, as well as lamellar insulating and small complex mechanical parts (Figs. 110 and 111) [42, 274, 600-602].

Fig. 111. Precision articles of complex shape made of the photosensitive glass Fotoform and of Fotoceram.

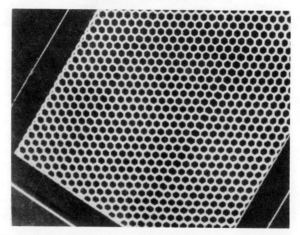

Fig. 112. High-strength honeycombed grating which can be made of the photosensitive glass Fotoform and of Fotoceram.

Two types of photosensitive glass have been employed in architecture: light-scattering Fotolyte in the form of sheets, into which a milk-white grid is imprinted, with the side of the square measuring 6.35 mm; and glass sheathing more than 600 m^2 of which has been used to face the northern facade of the UN General

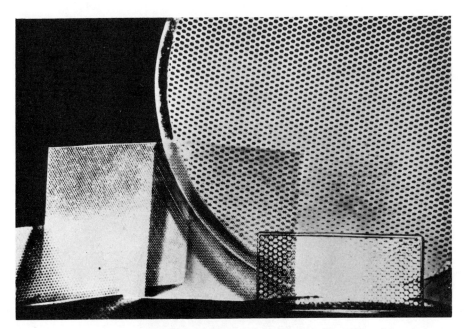

Fig. 113. Reticulated screens for half-tone printing which can be made of the photo-sensitive glass Fotoform or of Fotoceram.

Fig. 114. Gride made of Fotoform and having 40,000 through-holes of a high degree of tolerance per cm^2.

Assembly building in New York [36, 603]. The translucent and slightly cellular structure of Fotolyte sheets having a reddish external color produces a favorable aesthetic impression. Only direct light rays of maximum intensity are capable of being freely

transmitted through Fotolyte glass. The more the angle of inci-
dence of the light rays deviates from 0°, the more diffused they become in the glass which, in turn, eliminates the solar luster. One
can obtain a relief image of the intaglio shape in photosensitive
glass, with the convex and the concave portions in the image corresponding to the halftone portions of the negative with the lesser
and greater density, respectively. One can also obtain through-
holes whose depth is 10 times their width, which makes it possible
to fabricate sieves having holes whose wall thickness is $1/10$ their
height (Fig. 112). After such honeycombed constructions are transformed into photosensitive glass-ceramic, they are characterized
by a high mechanical strength, a high rigidity, and a relatively high
permeability, and may find applications in electronic devices and
chemical apparatus [271]. Photosensitive glasses are finding wider
and wider application in polygraphy (lie detectors), optics, chemo-
tronics, rocket technology, and microelectronics [728].

a. Fine-Structured Grids and Screens for Storage and Transmitter Tubes Used in Color Television

Corning Glass Works [604] fabricated reticulated screens
with a grid of 300-600 mesh from photosensitive glass (Fig. 113).
The screen, in the shape of a square 14.5 cm^2 in area, contains
more than 200,000 square holes of such a small size that human
hair does not go through them. These screens are employed in
cathode-ray tubes of television sets, where they provide a sharper
image. Rounded reticulated screens 38 mm in diameter and from
0.076 to 0.127 mm thick, depending on the width of the holes, which
varies from 0.022 to 0.0028 mm, have a transmission capability
ranging from 40 to 70%, respectively [605]. The number of holes
per cm^2 may range from 14,000 to 87,000. Fine-structured grids
(Fig. 114) contain from 40,000 to 97,200 holes per cm^2 [270, 606].
For storage cathode-ray tubes made from photosensitive glass
which is subsequently transformed into photosensitive glass-ceramic, storage targets in the form of disks 50.8 mm in diameter and
3-5 mm thick are used [607]. Every disk contains 500 holes with a
conicity of 10°. Targets made of photosensitive glass 150 μ thick
and containing 200 or 250 holes per 1 linear cm and coated with
MnO are being used in transmitter television tubes [608].

b. Masks for the Sputtering of Thin-Film Circuits and Shadow Masks for Color-Television Picture Tubes

Of great promise is the manufacture of masks of complex configuration and accurate dimensions from photosensitive glass or photosensitive glass-ceramic for use in thin-film electronics. Masks for the vacuum sputtering of thin-film circuits may have a thickness up to 0.1 mm and less, and a slit width or a hole diameter ranging from 100 to 20 μ, and they are capable of operating at temperatures of 400-450°C (for photosensitive glass) and 750-800°C (for photosensitive glass-ceramic) without buckling and sagging, which represents definite advantages over metallic masks in use at the present time. Due to their significantly lower linear thermal expansion coefficient as compared to metallic masks, masks made of photosensitive glass make it possible to attain a much higher degree of accuracy in the dimensions of the sputtered design and thereby to decrease the scatter in the electrical parameters of the circuit, which may easily be measured during the sputtering process.

Shadow masks made of photosensitive glass-ceramic 0.15-2.0 mm thick have found applications in color-television technology [609]. The mask made of photosensitive glass-ceramic is coated with the conducting material. When the mask is bombarded by electrons, secondary electrons form from the electron beam, the motion of which in the direction of the screen can be eliminated in the photosensitive glass-ceramic mask by using small-aperture holes and by cutting off of primary electrons which are moving in undesirable directions. In thicker photosensitive glass-ceramic masks, the field does not deflect in the direction of the electron beam, which increases the resolution of the assembly. The General Electric Company [609] developed a storage tube in which a photosensitive glass-ceramic mask containing 500 cells filled with metal was used as a two-way target. One side of the target is bombarded by accelerated electrons, while the other side is used for scanning and for the recording of the outgoing signal.

Photosensitive glass or photosensitive glass-ceramic may be employed for the elimination of secondary x-rays in x-ray diffractography. Previously, for this purpose, a collimating plate was installed between the objective and the photographic film, with the

plate being a composite made of lead and resin. Such plates, however, were found to be unsatisfactory. Instead of the plate and the
objective, one may employ photosensitive glass, and instead of the
x-ray source, one may employ an ultraviolet radiation source.
After irradiation and heat treatment, the irradiated portions are
etched away and the remaining parts are coated with lead and combined into a packet of several pieces, as a result of which the secondary x-ray image is eliminated and high resolution is obtained
[609].

The shadow mask for the color-television cathode-ray tubes,
measuring 53 cm together with the screen, contains 300,000 holes
0.25 mm in diameter and with a spacing of 0.7 mm [610].

c.   Plates for Pneumatic-Jet Technology
(Fluidics)

Photosensitive glass is used for the manufacture of the elements of pneumatic devices, such as jet boosters, which do not
contain moving parts and which are based on the aerodynamic interaction of air streams [611-614, 753]. Such pneumatic devices may
be manufactured in accord with principles similar to those used
for printed circuits in electronics. These are miniature devices
capable of operating at very high temperatures, are fast-acting,
operating at frequencies ranging from 5 to 20 kHz, and they may
be employed in pneumatic digital devices, such as are used both by
industry, as for the automatization of commercial processes, and
by the military, as for guiding rockets and ballistic missiles.
Based on these devices, one may construct analog and digital computers and carry out booster actions, as well as logical functions,
storage, etc., i.e., one may transform objects into guided systems.
The circuits, or flow patterns, of these devices are prepared on
the photosensitive glass Fotoform in the form of designs made of
canals and varying depressions (Fig. 115). During irradiation by
ultraviolet light using the contact printing method, molds fabricated by a special technique are used as masks. The exposed
plate is developed by heat treatment, whereupon it is etched down
to the required depth. By etching to a different depth, one may obtain a secondary circuit or flow pattern on the very same portion
of the photosensitive glass. The most critical and most difficult
part of such a device to build is its nozzle, on whose fineness and
accuracy in size the operating effectiveness of the entire element

Fig. 115. Complex circuits or flow patterns, engraved in
photosensitive glass for jet boosters for calculating and
guidance devices.

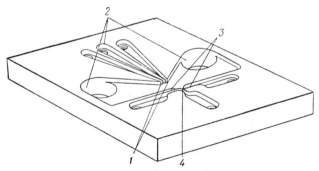

Fig. 116. Flat plate made of photosensitive glass in which a three-dimensional analog of the booster is engraved. Such plates may be sealed together, forming a completely assembled "solid" pneumatic circuit. 1)
Receivers; 2) inlet and outlet holes; 3) control nozzles; 4) power nozzle.

depends. Holes and canals up to 6.35 mm in width are produced in photosensitive glass by the photochemical method with an accuracy of ± 0.025 mm, and they have a degree of surface finish which entirely satisfies the requirements. The dimensions of the large holes and canals, attaining values of 25.4 mm, are maintained within an accuracy of ±0.5 mm. Attempts to produce nozzles 0.025 mm in diameter were unsuccessful. Only nozzles 0.14-0.50 mm in diameter, and, under special conditions, 0.050 mm in diameter, could be produced with sufficient reproducibility [615]. In spite of the extremely high solubility differential (1 : 20) of the photosensitive glass Fotoform used, the side walls of all nozzles, canals, and holes had a 3° taper, which imposed certain limitations on the size and the shape of the narrow wedge-shaped partitions produced between discrete elements. The reason for this is not only a slight underetching in hydrofluoric acid of the nonirradiated photosensitive glass, but also the difficulty with which fresh acid may reach all the areas to be etched uniformly, with the result that a constant rate of solution cannot be maintained and that uniform etching of the entire article is all but precluded. The etched glass plates are assembled in pairs or in even larger assemblies, forming a single flow mechanism in which canals can be produced which either flow into one another or proceed one on top of the other at various levels. The original glass may be subjected to irradiation and heat treatment more than once, thereby retaining photosensitivity in heat-treated, but nonirradiated, portions, which makes it possible to obtain the through-holes during the first cycle and the entire design pattern during the second cycle.

As can be seen from Fig. 116, the plates obtained in this fashion are individual circuits or flow patterns. In order to produce complex devices which include these individual circuits, these plates may be assembled by means of sintering through intermediary glass or cement into micromodular blocks, thus attaining the shape of a "multilayer cake." These blocks cannot be disassembled for repair purposes; they can, however, be washed out.

Discrete pneumatic-jet multivibrators and proportional boosters made from photosensitive glass are employed as elements of pneumatic and hydraulic guidance and control systems as well as for logical circuits [616]. Glassy pneumatic jet boosters have a number of advantages over analogous plastic or metallic elements; above all, they are stable when operating at temperatures up to 250°C and they resist the attack of various liquid and gaseous media. Glassy products may be transformed into photosensitive glass-ceramic products and are characterized by a mechanical strength higher by a factor of three, by their capability of operating at even higher temperatures (up to 500°C), and by increased radiation stability, although their dimensions are somewhat less accurate due to slight shrinkage during the crystallization process.

The sizes of jet elements vary from miniature (less than the smallest coins), such as are used in computers, to large sizes, such as are used for the production of very high-power guidance systems. Jet boosters fulfilling the same functions as electronic lamps and transistors are 10-100 times cheaper than the latter [612, 613].

2. PHOTOSENSITIVE, REVERSIBLY-DARKENING PHOTOCHROMIC GLASSES

Photochromic photosensitive glasses are silicate glasses containing small amounts of silver halide crystals precipitated in the glass during the cooling or the secondary heating processes. These glasses darken very fast under the effect of irradiation in the visible or near-visible spectral region and, after irradiation is stopped, i.e., in the darkness, they are capable of gradually restoring their transparency, the photochromic process in these glasses being based on the reversible decomposition of silver halide under the influence of activating radiation. The colloidal silver particles which form during this decomposition are the centers of coloration and produce a darkening of the glass. Some authors [617, 618] call glasses which exhibit a similar effect "phototropic." Photochromic glasses differ from the previously described Au- and Ag-containing photosensitive glasses with regard to the state of the silver prior to irradiation, as well as with regard to the nature and the stability of the vacancies arising in the glass while it is being irradiated. In conventional photosensitive glasses, the photoelectrons which have been trapped during irradiation by the structural defects are held so firmly that even heat treatment at elevated temperatures either does not liberate them, or liberates them, but nevertheless results in the irreversible precipitation of colloidal silver. In photochromic glasses, the vacancies which appear during the irradiation process at room temperature are entirely unstable, which is the reason colloidal silver does not form during the heat-treatment process, and in the dark, silver and the halogen are able to revert to their initial states, thereby again forming the silver halide.

Although the existence of the photochromism phenomenon has been known for a very long time [619, 620], and although there exist hundreds of organic and inorganic photochromic substances, nonetheless, many of these have an essential shortcoming — namely, the absence of reversibility, i.e., their properties deteriorate with repeated light—dark cycles. For glasses, the changes under the influence of ultraviolet light or other radiation of a high energy are slow and irreversible at room temperature. Cohen and Smith [621-622] produced photochromic silicate glasses sensitized with Ce and Eu additions. Although these glasses are capable of darkening and discoloring very rapidly, they do show fatigue, i.e., a weakening of the photochromic effect after repeated cycles.

Armistead and Stookey [623-628] developed photochromic glasses which changed their color in a reversible manner and whose properties make them useful candidates for practical applications. In contrast to the conventional photographic gelatin emulsion, photochromic glasses contain smaller crystals which, upon exposure to irradiation, produce a change in the color and darkening of glass. After the light source is removed, the color disappears and glass again becomes transparent. Multiple repeated effect of the darkening—restoring cycles, such as irradiation in open air for more than two years, or subjecting these glasses to 1000 of these cycles, does not degrade the properties of these photochromic glasses, i.e., does not produce the fatigue phenomenon, which makes them useful candidates for long-term applications [623, 729].

The reversibility of the process is explained [625] in terms of the distribution of very small amounts (0.05%) of minute silver halide crystals up to 40 Å in size in the solid, impenetrable, and chemically inert glass, as a result of which the diffusion of coloring centers is not possible, nor can they grow into stable silver particles and cause irreversible decomposition of silver halide by chemical interaction. According to electron-microscope analysis and small-angle x-ray scattering data, the concentration of silver halide crystals in photochromic glass is $8 \cdot 10^{15}$ per cm^3, with the diameter of the crystals being 50 Å and the distance between them 500 Å [623].

Table 75. Compositions of Some Photochromic Silver-Containing Glasses (Based on Chemical Analysis Data)

Component	Contents (in wt.%) of various compositions				
	1	2	3	4	5
SiO_2	60.1	60.3	59.6	59.8	62.8
Na_2O	10.1	10.0	10.0	10.0	10.9
Al_2O_3	9.5	9.5	9.5	9.5	10.0
B_2O_3	20.0	20.0	20.0	20.0	15.9
Ag	0.40	0.24	0.58	0.70	0.38
Br	0.17	0.28	—	0.09	—
Cl	0.10	—	0.31	0.16	1.7
F	0.84	0.80	0.94	0.85	2.5
CuO	—	—	—	—	0.016

a. Chemical Compositions and Production Technology of Photochromic Glasses

Quite a large range of glass compositions may serve as an appropriate medium for photochromic sensitizers, although the best are alkali borosilicate glasses containing 40-76 SiO_2, 4-26 Al_2O_3, 4-26 B_2O_3, one of the R_2O oxides, such as 2-8 Li_2O, not less than 0.2 Ag, and one of the halides present in an amount sufficient to ensure a stoichiometric reaction with Ag [617]. The total content of the fundamental components Ag and the halide, must be at least 85%. The concentration of the metallic silver in photochromic transparent glasses may reach 0.2-0.7%, whereas that in darkened glasses may reach 0.8-1.5% [623]. In order to intensify the sensitivity and the degree of photochromic darkening, one may add the following reducers in the amounts stated: 0.02-0.1 SnO, 0.002-0.02 FeO, 0.01-0.1 Cu_2O, or 0.1-1.0 Sb_2O_3 [617]. One may also add As_2O_3. In this case, the best results are obtained if the halide content is slightly higher than is necessary for a stoichiometric reaction with Ag. Glasses of the above-mentioned compositions darken under the influence of actinic blue and violet rays with a wavelength of 3000-5000 Å, and in this state they contain 0.005 vol.% of halide crystals. Transparent photochromic glasses, on the other hand, contain not more than 0.1 vol.% of AgCl, AgBr, or AgI crystals up to 0.1 μ in size.

Some typical compositions of photochromic glasses are presented in Table 75, based on [623].

Photochromic glasses are melted at 1400–1500°C for 4–8 h and they are shaped by conventional techniques. At increased silver halide concentrations, the glass becomes photochromic after normal annealing and cooling, while at lower concentrations, a secondary heating is required for a period ranging from several minutes to several hours within the annealing and the softening temperature region, which in turn results in the formation of nuclei, in the growth of colloidal droplets of fused silver halide, and in the nucleation of emulsion. The more the glass is cooled below the melting point of the halide, crystallization in the droplets proceeds at a greater rate. By employing different cooling procedures, it is possible to obtain the precipitation of submicrocrystalline particles ranging from $1\,\mu$ to several angstroms in diameter when their content ranges from several to almost 500 particles per million [625]. This makes it possible to control the photochromic properties of glasses and to decrease their transmission to 1% of the incident light. If the crystals attain sizes at which light is scattered — which may happen during too intensive a heat treatment or at a high silver halide concentration — then the glasses obtained are nontransparent. Although such glasses may also possess photochromic properties, there are nevertheless fewer applications for them than for transparent glasses, which contain silver halide crystals up to 600 Å in size.

b. Photochromic Properties and Spectral Sensitivity of Glasses, and the Mechanism of the Photochromic Process

By changing the composition of photochromic glasses as well as their heat-treatment procedures, one can, within wide ranges, regulate the rates and the temperature coefficients of the darkening and discoloration reactions, as well as light transmission, spectral sensitivity to radiation causing the darkening, and the density of the darkened glass [623]. In addition to the high degree of transparency, these glasses may have a reasonably high mechanical strength, a low α, a high ε, and other valuable properties. One of the photochromic glass samples tested had a transmission equal to 86% prior to irradiation; after being exposed to irradiation for 30 sec, its transmission decreased to 50%, and after an exposure

of 50 sec, it decreased to 28%. Fifty-two seconds after the ultraviolet light source was removed, the transmission increased to
74% [626]. The duration of the entire cycle until transparency of
glass was fully restored was 3 min. When another sample 4 mm
in diameter and 50 mm long was irradiated for 40 μsec, its transparency was decreased to 45-50%, and it was restored 2 min after
irradiation had ceased. When this sample was cooled below 0°, its
transparency decreased by 20% [627].

The spectral sensitivity of photochromic glasses encom-
passes a wide region, and, depending on the type of the sensitizing
additions present, it may range from the near-ultraviolet to the
visible spectrum up to 6500 Å. For glasses containing AgCl, rays
with wavelength λ = 3000-4000 Å are effective; for glasses containing AgCl and AgBr or only AgBr, rays with wavelength λ = 3000-
5500 Å are effective; and for glasses containing AgCl and AgI, rays
with λ = 3000-6500 Å are effective [623]. Glasses containing AgCl
are sensitive to ultraviolet light and they darken rapidly in the
open air under sunlight. When some of these glasses are exposed
to radiation of longer wavelength, such as to visible and near-
infrared irradiation, they are not darkened; on the contrary, they
are discolored, and this occurs more rapidly than in the dark. If
these glasses are irradiated only by ultraviolet light, they become
darkened to a higher degree than when irradiated with ultraviolet
and visible light simultaneously [623].

The duration of discoloration in the dark depends on the composition, the preceding heat treatment, and the temperature of the
glass. The rate of discoloration increases with temperature. When
cooled to liquid-nitrogen temperatures, discoloration does not occur. In order to decrease the optical density by a factor of two,
several seconds to several hours are needed.

In the opinion of Armistead and Stookey [623], the photochromic process is in many ways analogous to the photolytic dissociation
of silver halide into silver and the halogen in the conventional
photographic process and differs from it only by its reversibility.
The irreversible photographic process is represented in the following manner [623]:

$$n\,\mathrm{Ag\,Cl} \xrightarrow{\text{light}} n\,\mathrm{Ag^0} + n\,\mathrm{Cl^0}$$
$$\searrow (\mathrm{Ag^0})_n \nearrow$$

where $(Ag^0)_n$ represents the latent image made of silver particles. The reversible photochromic process may be described in the following manner:

$$AgCl \quad \underset{\text{light } I_2 \text{ or heating}}{\overset{\text{light } I_1}{\underset{\longleftarrow}{\longrightarrow}}} \quad Ag^0 + Cl^0,$$

or

$$Ag^+ + Cu^+ \quad \underset{\text{light or heating}}{\overset{\text{light}}{\underset{\longleftarrow}{\longrightarrow}}} \quad Ag^0 + Cu^{++}$$

According to these reactions, the Cl^- and Cu^+ ions give away an electron, which is captured by an Ag^+ ion. Silver atoms or their aggregates are the coloration centers. In glasses sensitized with copper, the Cu^{2+} ion intensifies light absorption just as well as silver [623].

Impenetrability, chemical inertness, and the hardness of this glass help preserve the reversibility in its photochromic properties, due to the prevention of reaction-product loss by diffusion, and due to insulation from atmospheric oxides and from moisture, which could cause similar reactions. The reaction products are metastable and may revert to their initial state. If the Ag^0 aggregate into colloidal particles at a high temperature, or if the Cl^0 diffuse out and are lost in the form of chlorine, or if they react with other ions, then the photochromic reaction becomes irreversible. This was confirmed experimentally when glass heated to 400°C was irradiated with ultraviolet light for a long time so as to provide for some diffusion of the ions and the atoms. In this glass, the formation of a permanent colored image was observed, consisting of colloidal particles of silver, and the reversible photochromic coloring which was obtained at room temperature first weakened with increasing irradiation time at 400°C and then completely disappeared [623].

c. Areas of Application for Photochromic Glasses

Photochromic glasses may be employed in optoelectronic storage devices equipped with self-erasing of information, as outgoing indicators for control systems in air transports, in measuring devices, as light modulators in new optical systems, and also in transmitting optical and other systems where the change in the quantity of light may be used for control or regulation purposes [627]. Photochromic glasses find applications in the manufacture of spectacles and goggles, windowpanes and automobile windshields, and in other areas where a dynamic, i.e., time-varying, control of sunlight as a function of its intensity is needed.

The windowpanes used in the UN building transmit 84% of the visible light in the absence of sunlight, while under the influence of sunlight, their transmission decreases to 50% after 30 sec, and to 28% after 52 sec [728]. Photochromic glass capable of darkening within microseconds under the influence of sunlight is being considered for use in illuminators of space vehicles [629]. The possibility is being studied of employing photochromic glasses for protection against the blinding flares of nuclear explosions, as chemical light switches, as well as for panels for the indication, micro-reduction, and processing of information [730].

3. PHOTOSENSITIVE GLASS-CERAMIC ARTICLES USED IN ELECTRONICS

a. Micromodular Boards

The first wide application of photosensitive glass-ceramics in mass production was in the manufacture of micromodular boards used in microminiature electronics [41, 42, 270, 272, 275, 482, 630-633, 731]. These boards, $8 \times 8 \times 0.25$ mm in size and equipped with depressions and through-holes, serve as substrate bases for electronic elements in micromodular blocks (Fig. 117), and can be produced from Fotoform glass by an automatized technique. They are every bit as good as known ceramics, both insofar as the accuracy and the quality of the article and the economic factors are concerned [271]. Boards made from Fotoceram and used for micromodules of the waffle type have the following electrical characteristics at 25°C: electrical resistivity of $6 \cdot 10^{15}$ Ω-cm, a power factor of 0.006 at 1 MHz, and a loss coefficient equal to 0.0034 [609]. The limiting operating temperature for these boards lies above 500°C. The primary area of application for microplates 0.25 mm thick is as bases for microresistors, diodes, transistors, and condensers in micromodular circuit devices [634].

Fig. 117. Microminiature boards made of photosensitive glass-ceramics
and used for micromodules.

Corning Glass Works [635] produced Fotoceram microminiature boards for condensers with a capacity of 1-10,000 nF at an
operating voltage of 300 V, capable of operating at temperatures
ranging from −55 to +125°, having reliability. They are intended
for use in delay lines with lumped constant parameters, in closed
assembly units, and in microminiature modular circuits, and they
allow the sealing of cables at elevated temperatures. The smallest element has a length of 7.1 mm and a width of 5.5 mm, and the
largest element is 20.6 mm long and 13.5 mm wide. The thickness
of these articles ranges from 1.5 to 2.3 mm.

b. Functional Boards for the Assembly of Basic Modular Blocks

Boards made of photosensitive glass-ceramic 32 × 15 × 14
mm in size are employed for the mounting of microminiature radio
components of high reliability [290].

The purpose of the functional or the supporting board made
of photosensitive glass-ceramic is to provide for the commutation
between microelements on 25 ceramic plates distributed over the
photosensitive glass-ceramic plate and constituting the basic modular block for electronic computers. After being assembled, the
block is covered with a metallic lid which is soldered onto the
sides of the supporting photosensitive glass-ceramic board.

Ramo-Woolridge [291] developed a new method for assembling aviation microminature electronic circuits based on photo-

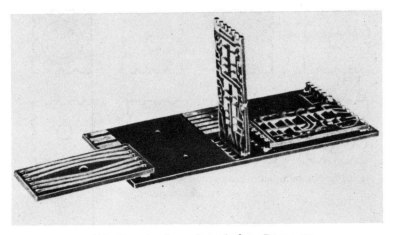

Fig. 118. Functional panels made from Fotoceram.

sensitive glass-ceramic panels having a thickness of 1.6 mm and a complex configuration, and found that they can be joined at any given side (Fig. 118). Using the photochemical etching method, holes can be etched into and through the panel which correspond in their shape to the microelements of the assembly (Fig. 119). The microelements assembled on one board — called the functional board — are interconnected by current lines embedded in deeper grooves which had been produced by etching. Each board may have different dimensions and a different hole distribution for various circuits. The boards are connected directly or through intermediate panels which, in turn, may include other microelements. The joining of the boards is done by simple interconnecting elements, which may be distributed along the lateral walls or inside the boards. The distance between the functional boards is equal to the thickness of the boards themselves, i.e., it measures 1.6 mm. Photosensitive glass-ceramic panels possess a high thermal conductivity, equal to 3.06 kcal/m-h-°C, as compared to 0.256 kcal per m-h-°C for laminated panels.

Sylvania Electric Products [636] employs both micromodular and functional boards made of photosensitive glass-ceramics in its micromodules (Fig. 120). Five microelements are distributed over a micromodular board 3.22 cm^2 in area and 0.25 mm thick. The material is capable of withstanding a heat-treatment temperature of 750°C and is reliable when the operating temperature is 500°C.

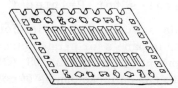

Fig. 119. Functional panel made of photosensitive glass-
ceramic equipped with holes for microelements.

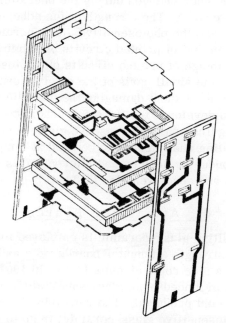

Fig. 120. Micromodular and functional boards made of
photosensitive glass-ceramic.

The functional boards which are used for the mounting of microplates, their hermetization, and their insulation from neighboring
circuits, have a constant wall thickness equal to 0.51 mm and a
variable height, which may be increased by the size of the module
spacing, i.e., by 0.025, 0.76, or 1.27 mm. The entire block is
mounted on the connecting panels made of photosensitive glass-
ceramic and equipped with holes for outlets. The length of the
panel may be varied, depending on the number of microplates and
functional boards in the assembled modular block.

c. Substrates for Printed Circuits

The Corning Glass Works plant in Bradford produces photo-sensitive glass-ceramic panels for printed circuits used in military electronic equipment [42, 268, 292, 293, 637-642, 732, 754]. One may produce patterns on these panels of complex designs with holes or canal-like depressions. The number of holes per cm^2 may reach 87,000. Printed circuits on photosensitive glass-ceramic substrates are capable of operating at 500°C, they do not experience buckling or other changes during the operation, and they can easily be metal-coated. The strength of the adhesion between the metallic coating and the photosensitive glass-ceramic is significantly higher than that of printed circuits on laminated plastics. The special advantage of printed circuits on photosensitive glass-ceramics is that the small parts of the circuits can be sealed and unsealed repeatedly without damaging the metallic coating. A new method has been developed for the electrochemical deposition of nickel conducting lines on photosensitive glass-ceramic substrates, allowing for sealing and intended to be used at temperatures up to 300°C in semiconductor devices and microcircuits in guidance systems of rockets and space vehicles [643-645].

d. Attenuator Boards

Photosensitive glass-ceramic is employed for the manufacture of high-strength attenuator boards used as bases for waveguides of various electronic circuits [646]. In 1962, in the US, attenuator boards produced from glass constituted, for the most, 10% of the entire amount produced. The remaining boards were produced from photosensitive glass-ceramic, in spite of their high cost. Photosensitive glass-ceramic attenuators are three times more reliable, they have a lower $\tan \delta$, and they show a more consistent dependence of the latter on temperature and frequency. The tensile strength of these boards is 210 kg/cm^2, and their flexure strength attains values up to 1750 kg/cm^2. Due to their higher mechanical strength, the attenuator boards made of photosensitive glass-ceramic were successfully tested under difficult operating conditions, in which glass was found to be of no use at all [646].

4. NOSE CONES AND/OR SHIELDS FOR GUIDED MISSILES

The first commercial application for Pyroceram 9606, which is characterized by an extremely uniform and insignificant change in electrical properties at decimeter wave frequencies and elevated temperatures, was in the production of nose cones and shields for guided missiles of various systems [454, 647-658]. The nose cone is in the form of a shell or casing which protects guidance devices from the corrosion of the surrounding medium (Fig. 121).

The material of which the shield is made must be able to transmit the decimeter waves well, it must have electrical properties which are not subject to change, it must have high heat resistance and thermal stability, and it must be capable of withstanding the effects of sudden aerodynamic loads, as well as the effects of vibration and the erosive effects of raindrops, which are moving at a very high velocity relative to the flying missile. Of importance are lightweight, moderate cost, and possibility of mass production. In order to preserve the exact electrical characteristics of the material, the wall thickness of the cones and/or shields with the sagittal (ogive) shape must be held within narrow ranges, which necessitates added mechanical treatment of the crystallized article which had been preshaped on a centrifugal casting machine. Due to the high hardness of the glass-ceramic, it takes four times as long to remove from it a 1.54-mm thick layer as it does to remove a layer of similar thickness from glass, which is why the cone is preground when still in the glassy state [454]. After crystallization, the inner and the outer surfaces of the article are ground further so as to achieve the desired contour, wall thickness, and length of the article. The base of the cone and/or shield which has been treated in this manner is then joined to a metallic ring by using a special binder, and the ring itself is attached to the main body of the guided missile by means of bolts or special hinges. It is desirable that the linear thermal coefficient of the material of the ring matches that of the glass-ceramic. If this condition cannot be fulfilled, then an elastic compound is used for the mounting.

Nose cones or shields made of glass-ceramics have substantial advantages over cones made from high-alumina ceramics or from glass-plastic materials, these advantages including light

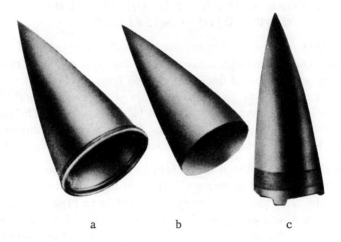

a   b   c

Fig. 121. Nose cones for guided missiles. a) Before crystallization; b)
After it; c) With ring shaped brackets.

weight, rapidity of shaping, and reproducibility of properties from
one article to another. A very important advantage is their exceptionally good dielectric properties, which vary only slightly within
a wide temperature range. For instance, at a frequency of 10^4
MHz, ε is equal to 5.45 at 25°C, 5.51 at 300°C, and 5.53 at 500°C
with the loss factor varying from 0.00033 to 0.0015 [454]. These
properties are almost constant to 980°C. Capable of maintaining
their properties at a maximum operating temperature of 850°C for
1000 h, glass-ceramic cones and/or shields are also capable of
withstanding short-term heating to 1200°C. At $\alpha = 57 \cdot 10^{-7}$, they
have 50% higher thermal stability than high-alumina ceramics.
Due to the good thermal emissivity, the heating temperature of the
glass-ceramic cone at a high missile speed and at an elevation of
30,500 m is 700°C as compared to 980°C for high-alumina ceramics.
With increasing velocity, this difference becomes even greater,
which significantly lessens this advantage of the high-alumina ceramics, the deformation temperature of which is 900°C higher. At
a lower flexure strength σ_f, equal to 1820 kg/cm^2, the glass-ceramic cones have a better strength-to-weight ratio than high-
alumina ceramics [454].

     Corning Glass Works is using Pyroceram for the production
of cones and/or shields for various guided missiles used by the

United States Navy and the United States Air Force [659, 660]. For instance, this firm is supplying the United States Navy with Pyroceram cones to be used for "Tartar" guided supersonic missiles of the ship-to-air type. Although good reproducibility of the properties and compatibility of rigidly limited parameters have already been achieved, work is going on to obtain even closer tolerances. In order to obtain uniform and exactly reproducible values for the ε of the glass-ceramic, a new glass-melting tank furnace has been constructed which is similar to those used in the production of highly homogeneous optical glass [661].

5. GLASS-CRYSTALLINE CEMENTS IN VACUUM TECHNOLOGY

Corning Glass Works [298, 605, 662, 663] developed crystallizing lead—boron—zinc solder glasses for the preparation of glass-crystalline cements, the compositions and the production technology of which were presented in Tables 46-48. Glass-crystalline cements are intended for sealing various glasses to each other, to a ceramic, or to a metal, and also for sealing metal to metal, including chrome—nickel stainless steels. They have the following advantages as compared to glass seals or solders: the possibility of soldering together glassy or other small parts with very different α at low stresses in the soldered junction, almost linear thermal expansion up to the softening point, good thermal stability, a higher mechanical strength and hardness than metal-soldered materials, and α ranges of $85-110 \cdot 10^{-7}$ or $162-198 \cdot 10^{-7}$ [28, 664, 665]. Besides many advantages, glass-crystalline cements also have some disadvantages. Sometimes, it is hard to obtain a sufficient flow of the initial glass necessary for attaining a satisfactory junction between the materials to be soldered together. Increasing the soldering temperature in order to increase the flow may result in rapid crystallization of the glass, which only has a narrow temperature range over which it can be sintered without crystallizing. Deviations in the properties of the cement depend to a greater degree than is the case for solder glasses on the glass composition, the conditions of melting and tempering, the degree of pulverization, the presence of contaminants, and the effect of moisture on the powdered glass [384].

Glass-crystalline cements based on lead-containing glasses are recommended for such uses as the production of multiple soldered junctions between glass and metal, for joining small parts of electron tubes, for hermetic sealing of windows into various vacuum and high-temperature apparatus, and for double glazing of windows [384]. The selection of a metal for obtaining a vacuum-tight seal is, to a considerable degree, a function of the hardening temperature of the glass-crystalline cement used. If this temperature is near 425°C, then Kovar can be used to form a seal with Pyroceram 9606; if this temperature is 750°C, then it is more expedient to use tungsten, which, within this temperature region, better matches the expansion curve of Pyroceram 9606 [21]. Cement which is intended for the production of vacuum-tight seals must have moderate flow properties in combination with good wettability to glassy or other parts to be sealed. Consequently, viscosity, thermal expansion, and thermal stability are the most important parameters, since they determine specific areas of application for glass-crystalline cements.

Cement No. 95, used for soldering with soft glasses and metals with α ranges of $80\text{-}100 \cdot 10^{-7}$ (see page 237 for the composition) is characterized by a high viscosity at high temperatures after soldering at 440°C as a result of which the soldered junction can be heated to 420°C without it being necessary to remove the parts [298]. Within the temperature region between the soldering and room temperatures, the glass-crystalline cement can be subjected to compressive stresses which cannot be sustained by conventional solder glasses since, within the softening temperature region, their compression is greater than that of the soldered parts. It is not recommended that cement No. 95 be used when the soldered area is to be coated with glaze which must be fired before the soldered parts can be put together. If it is nonetheless necessary that glaze be applied, then it is recommended that, in order to avoid its cracking or slipping off, it be applied in a thin layer first, heated for 5-10 min to 390°C, held there for 10 min, and then cooled at a maximum possible rate. It is not recommended that cement be used when there is a chance that it would be exposed to long-term action by nitric acid, NaOH, or boiling water [298, 605].

Glass-crystalline cement No. 45 serves well for the soldering of aluminosilicate glasses, Mo, and W, as well as for glass-ceramic vacuum envelopes capable of operating at the surrounding ambient temperature of 500°C [395, 397]. This cement is capable of producing a long-lasting vacuum-tight seal between Pyroceram 9606 and Mo or W at temperatures near 750°C. In order to protect the Mo and the W from oxidation and from the creation of diffusion layers of the silicides, various protective coatings were applied to them by electrodeposition and vacuum evaporation methods. After such treatment, W becomes more brittle than Mo. Thin coatings of Au and Pt were also tested as protective layers; it was found that with increasing thickness of these layers, the oxidation resistance of Mo and W at elevated temperatures increased. Coatings made of chromium oxide produced an analogous effect. The seals between Pyroceram 9606 articles 25 mm in diameter and aluminosilicate glasses were capable of withstanding multiple heating and cooling cycles without failure. A tungsten wire 0.75 mm in diameter could be soldered satisfactorily with Pyroceram 9606. The vacuum-tightness of such a soldered junction could be maintained over a wide temperature range.

In the German Democratic Republic [384], the glass-crystalline cement called Vitrokeram-cement found a fundamental application for the preparation of vacuum-tight seals between the cone and the tube of color-television cathode-ray tubes. After luminophore is applied to the base of the tube, the usual methods of sealing the bottom and the cone of the tube are not suitable because of the high temperatures employed, since luminophore loses its properties at the softening temperature of normal glasses. This is why soldering with Vitrokeram-cement was the only way to join the tube parts without having any harmful effects.

In Poland [666], low-melting crystallizing glasses whose composition includes the oxides SiO_2, B_2O_3, Al_2O_3, CaO, MgO, ZnO, PbO, BaO, K_2O, and Li_2O are used for the vacuum-tight joining of glassy parts of electron tubes, as well as of screens and cones of color-television cathode-ray tubes. The glasses developed have a very good wettability and spreadability at the soldering temperature, and they can be dissolved in hot concentrated nitric acid. The glass-crystalline soldered junction obtained after cooling has a high mechanical strength and is free of any significant mechanical stresses.

a. Properties of Glass-Crystalline Cements

Glass-crystalline cement No. 95 makes it possible to obtain vacuum-tight seals between the parts of color-television cathode-

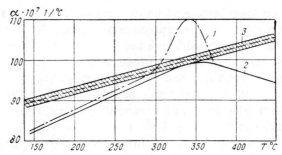

Fig. 122. Linear thermal expansion coefficients of Vitrokeram-cement and glass used for cathode-ray tubes as a function of temperature. 1) Vitrokeram-cement in the glassy state; 2) Vitrokeram cement in the crystallized state; 3) glass used for cathode-ray tubes.

Table 76. Electrical Properties of Glass-Crystalline Cement No. 95

Temp., °C	Tangent of dielectric loss angle			Dielectric constant		
	at frequency of (kHz)					
	0.1	1.0	100	0.1	1.0	100
25	0.0058	0.0064	0.0094	21.2	21.0	20.4
230	—	0.11	0.0057	—	23.4	22.2
373	—	—	0.15	—	—	—

Bulk electrical resistivity: at 250° C $\log_{10}$ = 8.550
350° C $\log_{10}$ = 7.030

ray tubes. This cement is stable with respect to the effects of moisture and the carbon dioxide of the atmosphere, and it is also stable toward the chemical reagents used for cleaning the tube. No changes were observed when the tube was held in a chamber with a relative humidity of 90% and a temperature of 50° [384].

Vacuum-Tightness of the Soldered Joint. The parts of a cathode-ray tube 1.48 m long soldered with glass-crystalline cement allowed less than 10^{-14} liter/sec of helium pass when tested in a closed chamber having a pressure of $2 \cdot 10^{-5}$ mm Hg.

Electrical Strength. The tubes sealed with glass-crystalline cement were capable of withstanding a voltage of 51 kV for 1 min.

Temperature Stability. When air is being pumped out, the tubes sealed with glass-crystalline cement must be able to withstand heating to 425°C for 1 h without destroying the vacuum.

Viscosity. This must be such that the glass-crystalline cement can be used for any given method of joining glass with glass, metal with metal, ceramic with ceramic, as well as for joining unlike materials. Glass-crystalline cement may be used for soldering chromic stainless steel, Pt, Te alloy No. 4, the alloy "Dumet," containing 50% Ni, the majority of glasses, forsterite, steatite, and other materials.

Table 76 presents the electrical properties for cement No. 95 [384]. The physical properties for this cement are: Young's modulus, 4700 kg/mm^2; shear strength, 1800 kg/cm^2; Poisson's ratio, 0.27; flexure strength at 25°C, 422 kg/cm^2, and at 425°C, 110 kg/cm^2; and density, 6.5 g/cm^3. As for the chemical properties, the solubility when immersed for 4 h in 10% H_2SO_4 is 0.1% by weight, and in 100% HF is 0.3% by weight.

Figure 122 shows the temperature dependence of α of Vitrokeram-cement in the glassy and the crystallized states, and of glass used for television cathode-ray tubes [384].

b. Direct Joining of Glass-Ceramics and Metals Without Employing Glass-Crystalline Cements

McMillan and Hodgson [667] described a method of directly joining glass-ceramics and various metals, such as copper and soft steel, or of directly joining Ni or Cr alloys and iron. The method basically consists of joining the metallic parts with the fused glass body while the article is being pressed and subsequently heated so as to transform glass into glass-ceramic. The glass may contain TiO_2, P_2O_5, Au, Ag, or Cu as crystallization catalysts. In order to oxidize certain Ni—Fe and Cu—Fe alloys, the metallic parts are subjected to preliminary heat treatment at 500-700°C, depending on the thickness of the parts. The part is then inserted in a steel or cast iron mold heated to 400-500°C, which facilitates the wetting of the metal by the fused glass. A gob of glass is fed into the mold, and pressing is done by the conventional technique; during the pressing process, the glass extruded by the plunger comes into contact with the metallic part and forms a strong joint with it. Thus, the shaping of the article and the joint formation occur simultaneously. The construction thus joined together is cooled in the mold until the glass becomes hardened, after which it is taken out of the mold and placed into a furnace for the purpose of heat treatment and so as to transform the metal—glass joint into a metal—glass-ceramic joint. The heating is done following typical sitallization procedures, with the article held at given temperatures, and with gradual increase in the temperature. Depending on the composition of the glass, the maximum crystallization temperature may be on the order of 700-900°C, and the necessary time at temperature 1 h.

The crystallized or glassy articles may also be joined directly by being heated to a temperature which is sufficient for welding but does not produce deformation [668]. For glassy articles which have holes or canals etched into them, their crystallization occurs at the same time that they are being joined.

6. GLASS-CERAMIC ENVELOPES FOR VACUUM ELECTRONIC APPARATUS OPERATING AT HIGH TEMPERATURES

In order to evaluate Pyroceram 9606 as a possible material for vacuum envelopes for electronic devices operating at high ambient temperatures, the degassing in vacuum and the gas permeability at elevated temperatures of the laboratory samples and of envelopes made from them were studied.

Figure 123, based on [397], shows the temperature dependency of helium permeability for Pyroceram 9606, for high-alumina ceramics (96% Al_2O_3), for borosilicate glass No. 7740, for aluminosilicate glass No. 1720, and for fused quartz. A somewhat steeper slope for the gas permeability curve of the glass-ceramic envelope as compared to the curve for the laboratory samples is explained by the authors of [397] by the influence of the solder glass used for hermetization. The air penetrability of these same materials is shown in Fig. 124, from which it can be seen that at temperatures above 800°C, Pyroceram 9606, alumina, and porcelain noticeably

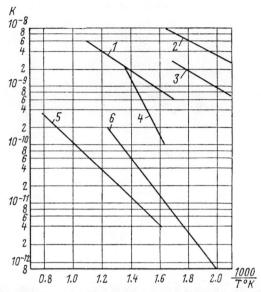

Fig. 123. Temperature dependency of permeability by helium for Pyroceram 9606 and other materials. T) Temperature; K) permeability coefficient at normal temperature and pressure. 1) Pyroceram 9606; 2) fused quartz; 3) glass No. 7740; 4) tube made of Pyroceram 9606; 5) ceramic (97% Al_2O_3); 6) glass No. 1720.

increased their air penetrability. It was determined by chemical analysis that the relative content by volume of chlorine, bromine, and iodine in the glass-ceramic was 5 ppm, that of fluorine was less than 20 ppm, and that of sulfur was 25 ppm. However, due to the protective outer layer which formed during the process of transforming glass into glass-ceramic, which prevents the penetration of gases into the inner layers of the material, the possible release of the halogens may be of the order of approximately $\frac{1}{300}$ of the above-given values [397]. The rate of degassing of the glass-ceramic with increasing temperature remains smaller than that for glass (Fig. 125). The assembled housings were sufficiently vacuum-tight within the temperature range 76-750°C, inasmuch as Pyroceram 9606, aided by the crystallizing solder glass, welds well with W or Mo wire, as well as with borosilicate and lead borosilicate glasses. Some parts made of Pyroceram 9606 and necessary for the assembling of vacuum envelopes are shown in Fig. 126.

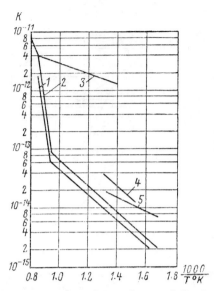

Fig. 124. Temperature dependency of permeability by air for Pyroceram 9606 and other materials. T) Temperature; K) permeability coefficient at normal temperature and pressure. 1) Pyroceram 9606; 2) ceramic (97% Al_2O_3); 3) porcelain; 4) tube made from Pyroceram 9606; 5) glass No. 7740.

The top part 1 and the bottom part 3 of the envelope are prepared by pressing and are equipped with grooves for the conductors 2 and the degassing tube 4. The latter consists of two parts: one, 6.35 mm long and 3.17 mm in diameter, is manufactured from glass-ceramic, and the other, which is longer but of the same diameter, is manufactured from aluminosilicate glass [397]. The wire conductors are also composite: through the weld region, the wire is made of tungsten, and beyond the housing it is made of nickel. The wires are 0.6 mm in diameter. The flanges of the housing and all other areas which have been welded or soldered are coated with crystallizing welding (solder) glass. After it is hermetically joined, the degassing tube is built up with an additional tube of aluminosilicate glass which has a larger diameter and contains barium—aluminum getters (Fig. 127). During degassing at 750°C, the getter becomes dispersed and serves as an indicator of the degree of vacuum during the tests. When electronic devices are in operation, the getter is placed inside the housing.

Table 77. Results of Tests of Pyroceram 9606 Envelopes for Vacuum Electronic Devices Operating at High Ambient Temperatures

Type of test	No. of samples	Duration of test, h	Testing conditions	Result
Storage	9	5000	High-frequency coil, observation with aid of getter	No damage
Salt spray	4	100	Military standard 202, method 101	No corrosion effects
Exposure to radioactive radiation	2	282	$7 \cdot 10^{18}$ neutrons/cm^2	Inleakage in one of them
Resistance to constant current	3	—	500°C, 250 V; electrode diameter 3.4 mm	125 megohms
Moisture stability	10	—	Military standard 202, method 106	9, normal; 1, vacuum upset
Thermal stability	14	3/80	Acetone from 23 to −76°C	No damage
Thermal cycling	13	3/4	Heating to 750°C at a rate of 40°/min; cooling from 750 to 200°C at a rate of 20° per min	No damage
Life at 500°C	5	1508	Held continuously at 500°C	3, normal; 2, broke up after 1409 h
Life at 400°C	5	5684	Held continuously at 500°C	No damage

Note: Permeability with respect to helium: At 500°C, equal to the permeability of glass No. 7740 at 300°C. Permeability with respect to air: $K = 4 \times 10^{-12}$ cm-mm/cm Hg at 500°C as compared to $K = 6 \times 10^{-14}$ cm-mm/cm Hg at 300°C for glass No. 7740.

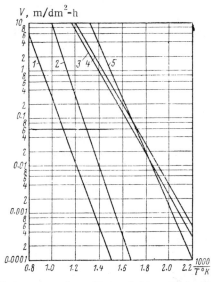

Fig. 125. Temperature dependency of degassing for Pyroceram 9606 and several glasses. T) Temperature; V) degassing rate. 1) Pyroceram; 2) glass No. 1720; 3) glass No. 7740; 4) glass No. 7720; 5) glass No. 9080.

The results of tests on vacuum glass-ceramic housings having seven outlets are presented in Table 77, as taken from [397].

From the data presented, it follows that Pyroceram 9606, which has a very low gas penetrability, as well as good mechanical, thermal, and electrical properties, is quite suitable for the manufacture of envelopes for vacuum electronic devices operating at high ambient temperatures. It produces vacuum-tight welds with the refractory metals W and Mo, although the latter leaves something to be desired with respect to its oxidation resistance. The glass-ceramic is stable with respect to action by gases and reagents, as well as to radioactive radiation at intensities up to 10^{18} neutrons/cm^2. Experimental glass-ceramic housings preserved satisfactory characteristics when held at 500°C for 1000 h, and at 400°C for 5684 h [397].

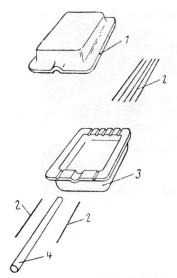

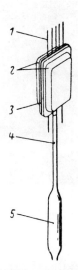

Fig. 126. Vacuum envelope parts made of Pyroceram 9606. 1) Upper part of the envelope; 2) wire conductors; 3) lower part of the envelope; 4) tube for degassing.

Fig. 127. Vacuum envelope made of Pyroceram 9606, ready for degassing. 1) Tungsten conductors; 2) envelope made of Pyroceram 9606; 3) high-temperature welding glass; 4) tube made of aluminosilicate glass; 5) getter.

7. GLASS-CERAMICS IN MACHINE BUILDING

a. Glass-Ceramic Ball Bearings

The high hardness, high refractoriness, good chemical stability, and low linear thermal expansion coefficient of the glass-ceramics, coupled with the ease with which they can be shaped, allow them to be used in the production of bearings (Fig. 128). The experiments performed showed that bearings made of Pyroceram 9606 are capable of operating at temperatures between 540 and 815°C without lubricants and at stresses which are 50% of those to which standard stainless steel bearings are subjected [21, 552, 568, 669-673]. The failure of glass-ceramic bearings in use takes place by gradual erosion, rather than by chewing action, which is an added advantage in cases when sudden jamming of equipment cannot be tolerated.

Fig. 128. Glass-ceramic bearings.

In order to evaluate the compatibility of glass-ceramics with other materials, the friction produced when sliding them over glass-ceramics and refractory metals at room temperature and at 540°C without the use of lubricants was studied. When the glass-ceramic was slid over another glass-ceramic, tremendous friction and wear took place, which could be reduced by the application of a lubricant. When glass-ceramic is slid over a metal, satisfactory results are obtained due to the transfer of the metal to the surface of the glass-ceramic, so that what we have here is basically slippage of metal over metal. The rolling friction under loads of 4.2 and 10 kg was studied by means of a contrivance consisting of a driving ball 12.7 mm in diameter mounted in a special holder, and of three driven balls 6.35 mm in diameter which were freely rolling in a cylindrical race equipped with a groove, whose degree of wear served as the criterion for the evaluation of the results. A force of 4.2 kg applied to the glass-ceramic is equivalent in stress to a load of 10 kg applied to steel and corresponds to a Hertz stress of 17,500 kg/cm^2 [552]. The best results, both at room temperature and at 370°C, were obtained on glass-ceramic—steel—glass-ceramic and steel—glass-ceramic—steel systems, and are comparable to those for the steel—steel-tool—steel system. The glass-ceramic—glass-ceramic—glass-ceramic system turned out to be unsatisfactory. Tests at 650°C relative to the compatibility between glass-ceramics and refractory alloys and carbides showed that the glass-ceramic—tungsten carbide alloy—glass-ceramic system is excellent and highly commendable. Carbides K161B and K162B are highly compatible with glass-ceramics, whereas the copper—nickel alloy Monel is not quite so compatible. The results of the tests are presented in Table 78, taken from [552].

Because they retain their high hardness, slip bearings made of glass-ceramics are capable of operating at 540-870°C under a load constituting 40% of the load of steel bearings which, within this temperature region, become deformed under the influence of the weight. Glass-ceramic bearings used in combination with tungsten carbide alloy C, Stellite 3, and titanium carbide operated satisfactorily without lubricants at 540-890°C under the conditions where conventional metallic bearings seized and wore off [552].

Table 79, based on [57], presents the results of friction coefficient determinations for glass-ceramic slip bearings with inner diameter of 12.7 mm, after working for 30 min without a lubricant at 540 rpm under a load of 12.5 kg with rollers made of different materials.

The glass-ceramics were tested in the same manner as the material intended for use in thrust bearings for axial fulcrums. Steel balls were rotated at a rate of 250 rpm at a temperature of 25°C with some lubricant present, on glass-ceramic plates and, for comparison purposes, on steel plates under various loads. Both the glass-ceramic and the steel plates were capable of enduring several hours of work under a load producing Hertz compression stresses of the order of 19,000-22,000 kg/cm^2, and broke up when these stresses attained a value of 26,6000 kg/cm^2, i.e., the value causing steel to flow [57].

The results of the experiments showed that antifriction bearings composed of glass-ceramic races, refractory steel balls, and separators made of some refractory alloy are capable of operating at elevated temperatures. Due to the maximum friction which develops in the bearing between the balls and the separator, the most difficult problem here is the selection of the proper material for the separator. Columbium and vanadium carbides, which have a melting point higher than 2760°C and whose hardness is close to that of tungsten carbide [57, 522], are recommended for use in the manufacture of balls and races of glass-ceramic bearings.

An important advantage of glass-ceramic bearings is their good chemical stability at elevated temperatures with respect to normal commercial reagents and the possibility of employing them

Table 78. Wear of Bearings Having Glass–Ceramic Parts

Materials			Load, kg	Wear of track, μ	Remarks
Driving ball	Driven ball	Race			
1. At room temperature, motor oil SAE 10 used as lubricant					
Glass–ceramic	Glass–ceramic	Glass–ceramic	4.2	13.7	Smooth tracks
Steel 52100	Glass–ceramic	Tool steel M–2	4.2	10.1	Smooth tracks
Glass–ceramic	Steel 52100	Glass–ceramic	4.2	<10	Indistinct tracks
Steel 52100	Steel 52100	Tool steel M–2	4.2	5.2	Smooth tracks
Glass–ceramic	Glass–ceramic	Glass–ceramic	10.0	44.8	Smooth tracks, high wear
Steel 52100	Steel 52100	Tool steel M–2	10.0	10.1	Smooth tracks
2. At 370°C, no lubricant used					
Glass–ceramic	Glass–ceramic	Glass–ceramic	4.2	40.5	Nonuniform wear, stopped after 1 min
Tool steel M–1	Glass–ceramic	Tool steel M–2	4.2	19.8	One driven ball was ruined after 15 min
Corundum	Corundum	Glass–ceramic	4.2	24.3	Nonuniform wear, rotated for 8 min
Tool steel M–1	Tool steel M–1	Tool steel M–1	4.2	31.3	Nonuniform wear, rotated for 30 min
3. At 370°C, triphenyl P–biphenyl silane used as lubricant					
Glass–ceramic	Glass–ceramic	Glass–ceramic	4.2	21.6	Smooth track
Tool steel M–1	Glass–ceramic	Tool steel M–2	4.2	17.8	Deep, smooth wear track
Glass–ceramic	Tool steel M–1	Glass–ceramic	4.2	9.4	Slight wear with cracking and spalling
Glass–ceramic	Glass–ceramic	Glass–ceramic	10.0	56.7	Nonuniform wear, rotated for 15 min
Tool steel M–1	Tool steel M–1	Tool steel M–2	10.0	10.8	Track smooth, low wear, rotated for 30 min
4. At 650°C, no lubricant used					
Glass–ceramic	Glass–ceramic	Glass–ceramic	4.2	High wear	Driven balls shattered after 4 min
Glass–ceramic	Stellite 3	Glass–ceramic	4.2	23	Glass–ceramic became metal–coated, with a dark smooth film forming on it
				—	

Glass-ceramic	K-Monel	Glass-ceramic	4.2	—	Skid marks; Monel is heavily damaged
Glass-ceramic	Tungsten carbide alloy A	Glass-ceramic	4.2	33.6	High wear, fairly smooth track, a small amount of material transferred to the glass-ceramic; tungsten carbide alloy was coated with a glassy oxide film
Glass-ceramic	Tungsten carbide alloy B	Glass-ceramic	4.2	12.0	A smooth, light, tan film on the track; no transfer of material observed; tungsten carbide alloy was coated with a glassy oxide film
Glass-ceramic	Tungsten carbide alloy B	Glass-ceramic	10.0	27.5	Smooth track on glass-ceramic; tungsten carbide alloy was coated with a glassy oxide film
Tungsten carbide alloy B	Tungsten carbide alloy B	Glass-ceramic	4.2	19.6	Track of driving ball had a slight depression and looked like it was worked; however, it was quite smooth
Glass-ceramic	Carbide K161B	Glass-ceramic	4.2	11.3	A smooth, light, tan film on track; no transfer of material; driven balls covered by a smooth glassy film
Glass-ceramic	Carbide K161B	Glass-ceramic	10.0	—	Glass-ceramic balls damaged; driven balls had quite a good shape; track split
Glass-ceramic	Carbide K162B	Glass-ceramic	4.2	18.9	Quite smooth track; several islands of built up material on glass-ceramic track
Glass-ceramic	Carboloy 608	Glass-ceramic	4.2	23.3	Results similar to those obtained with K162B

Table 79. Friction Coefficients for Glass-Ceramic Slip Bearings

Roller material	Temp., °C	Friction coeff.
Tool steel M-2	20—590	0.20—0.23
Stainless steel	20—870	0.20—0.25
Stellite	20—870	0.2—0.3
Tungsten carbide alloy C	20—980	0.5—0.6*
Inconel	20—980	Bearing seized

* During friction against such an alloy, alloy C sometimes jammed.

in production processes where corrosive liquids or vapors, together with high operating temperatures, present an exceptionally difficult problem with respect to the service life of the bearings and with respect to their shrinkage [481, 674]. Hot, active acids may even serve as lubricants for glass-ceramic bearings capable of operating in combination with glass-ceramic journals or metallic rollers and of withstanding normal operating loads under the conditions of the destructive action by the surrounding medium [675]. Such bearings are recommended for use in the chemical and food industry. Glass-ceramic bearings in combination with other materials were tested for immersion in concentrated solutions of NaCl, NaOH, HNO_3, and citric acid, as well as in 30% hydrogen peroxide and in fused lead at 370°C. The surface damage to the glass-ceramic was rather insignificant, the damage being less when glass-ceramic is slid over glass-ceramic than when glass-ceramic is slid over metal.

b. Glass-Ceramic Parts for Internal Combustion Engines

The good mechanical strength, high hardness, good chemical stability, and possibility of controlling α make glass-ceramics prospective materials for the manufacture of parts for Diesel and internal combustion engines, the design of which is complicated by the difference in the α values of the materials for the piston and the cylinder walls, as well as by the corrosive action of gas combustion products. One may use glass-ceramics for the manufacture

Table 80. Properties of Glass-Ceramic Coatings on Soft Steel

Properties	Normal corrosion resist. coatings	Glass-ceramic coatings	
		prior to heat treatment	after heat treatment
1. Abrasion resistance (weight loss per 15 min), mg	49-64	40-50	12-30
2. Thermal stability (temperature drop causing failure), °C	190-246	201-260	288-454
3. Maximum operating temperature, °C	260	400-700	650-815
4. Impact strength (impact load not causing rupture at 10,000 V), kg·cm	14-16	23-27	28-30
5. Corrosion resistance (weight loss per m² per year), mg/m²−year			
Vapor of boiling 20% HCl	4-30	5-30	5-45
5% NaOH at 65°C	9-25	10-35	12-65
Boiling distilled H₂O (liquid phase)	2-25	1-25	1-40

of, among other parts, pistons, fastened or freely mountable caps for aluminum pistons, exhaust-channel parts, and clutch couplings [568].

c. Heat-Resistant Glass-Ceramic Coatings for Metals

In order to protect various steels, alloys, and refractory metals from the effects of high temperatures, Little and Holl [676] developed heat-resistant glass-ceramic coatings of various compositions having good wettability with respect to the metals and having somewhat lower α values, which produces compressive stresses in the coating. The most appropriate materials for the application of glass-ceramic coatings, insofar as their α values are concerned, are soft and stainless steel, as well as Inconel alloy. The possibility of applying these coatings on refractory metals Mo, Ti, and W is being investigated; these metals, however, have high oxidation rates and low α values. In order to obtain a glass-ceramic coating, one must carefully control its application technology, including annealing, degreasing, and sandblast treatment of the metal so as to remove the oxide layer. Two types of crystallizing glasses are employed. One of them serves as the prime coating, which chemically interacts with the metal and provides for good adhesiveness, while the one creates an external layer which is stable to corrosion and is linked firmly to the prime coating. The first, or prime, layer is applied to the metal in the form of a water suspension of finely ground glass, which is then heated until the glass particles melt and adhere to the metal, thereby being transformed into a glassy prime coating which does not contain crystals. The second layer is applied in an analogous manner, whereupon both layers are transformed into a glass-ceramic coating by special heat treatment, with the coating containing several crystalline phases, the total crystal content being from 20 to 50%. By employing various compositions for the initial glasses, it is possible to produce coatings with specified physical and chemical properties. By employing glass-ceramic coatings instead of porcelain enamel, one can increase the operating temperature of steel normally coated with enamel from 260°C to 815-980°C. It is possible to obtain glass-ceramic coatings capable of withstanding heating to 1370°C and sharp temperature drops in excess of 650°C.

The properties of glass-ceramic coatings for metals are compared to those of conventional corrosion-resistant coatings in Table 80, based on [676].

It can be seen from this table that crystallization considerably increases the thermal stability, the impact strength, and the wear resistance of glass-ceramic coatings, which may be employed for the chemical and thermomechanical protection of metals from, for example, the corrosive action of sulfuric acid at 345°C, hydrochloric acid at 600°C, vigorous oxidizing agents at temperatures up to 260°C, Cl and CCl_4 at 315°C, fused metals Zn and Se at 600°C, abrasive slurry mixed with acids at 170°C [676].

8. GLASS-CERAMIC PIPING AND TUBING FOR THE CHEMICAL AND PETROLEUM REFINING INDUSTRIES

Glass-ceramic tubes 3-100 mm in diameter are recommended for use in heat exchangers with a large temperature drop intended for the passage of abrasive slurries and drosses. The high hardness, high strength, good thermal stability, and better thermal conductivity than glass makes it possible to use these tubes in high-temperature wear-resistant heat exchangers capable of withstanding high rates of heat transfer per unit area as well as considerable pressures [21, 27, 605, 677-679]. White, nontransparent glass-ceramic tubes have a thermal stability which is equal to that of

Fig. 129. Glass-ceramic piping.

Table 81. Dimensions of Glass-Ceramic Piping, Tubing, and
Flat Plates, and the Pressures to Which the Plates are Exposed

Type of article	Outer diam., mm	Thickness, mm	Length, mm	Pressure, kg/cm^2
Piping	6.35	1.17*	219	
	12.7	1.60*	219	
	19.04	1.52*	219	
	25.4	—	3048	
	50.8	4.37*	3048	
	76.2	5.46*	3048	
	101.6	6.74*	3048	
Tubing	3		219	
	6		219	
	12.7		219	
	19.1		219	
	25.4		219	
Sheets 305 mm wide		6.35	—	1565
		9.52	—	2345
		12.7	—	3125
		15.8	—	3900
		19.0	—	4690
		25.4	—	6250
		38.1	—	7325

* Wall thickness.

fused quartz. Thanks to their good chemical stability, glass-ceramics can be used for the manufacture of pipelines used in the chemical and petroleum industries for service in contact with corrosive liquids at high temperatures [25, 647, 648]. Table 81, based on [21], gives the dimensions of glass-ceramic piping, tubing, and flat plates, as well as the pressures which the plates have to endure.

Glass-ceramic piping (Fig. 129) was prepared by drawing from a production glass-melting tank furnace in continuous operation.

9. GLASS-CERAMICS FOR CONSTRUCTION AND CONSUMER GOODS

Glass-ceramics are very promising materials both for residential and commercial construction purposes, where they can be used in the form of large wall panels or partitions 3 × 10 m in size and as carriers of construction elements. Their strength, light weight, and fire-resistance ensure a wide use for glass-ceramics in construction in the form of facing material. The slag glass-ceramics developed in the USSR and elsewhere are recommended for use in the manufacture of attached self-supporting panels for the external walls of buildings, for partitions, slabs and blocks for internal wall tiling, the paving of roads and sidewalks, window cases, balcony enclosures, flights of stairs, corrugated roofing, sanitary and technical instruments, protective wear-resistant elements, and other construction parts [46, 432, 435, 680-683, 733, 734]. Sheetlike glass-ceramic panels may be reinforced with metal and coated with ceramic colorants from one or both sides. Colored glass-ceramics find applications in the manufacture of architectural panels, decorative tile for the lining of subway stations, large-size mosaics for plazas, colored road panels for sidewalks, and colored sculptures [441-445]. Glass-ceramic tile used for flooring in the hot shops of the Cherepovetskii Metallurgical Plant made it possible to reduce the temperature around the red-hot furnaces, thereby greatly improving the working conditions for the workers [684]. Foamed glass-ceramics have good heat-insulating properties and high strength, and can find wide applications as an inexpensive and highly effective material in the construction of installations in perennially frozen regions [685, 686]. Due to its buoyancy, foamed glass-ceramics are good structural material for pontoons, wharves, bridges, and ferries, as well as for underwater and above-water installations. In the warmer regions, slag glass-ceramics can be used for the building of mobile homes; in agricultural regions they can be used for the construction of granaries which can be kept free of rodents and insects; among their other uses are the construction of elevators and bunkers.

One of the very large areas of application for glass-ceramics is the manufacture of opaque, white, heat-resistant kitchenware, such as frying pans, pots, bowls, coffee pots, and plates possessing good thermal stability [43, 687-696, 755]. It was determined experimentally that glass-ceramics are capable of withstanding 6000 abrupt heat changes. This is equivalent to 20 years of service as a hot plate or heat-resistant dish [697]. Glass-ceramic plates 250 mm in diameter and glass-ceramic pots can be given a bluish color reminiscent of Chinese porcelain. Kitchenware made of glass-ceramics do not scratch easily, nor do they scorch; they can be taken from a stove in a red-hot state and plunged into icy water, or can be taken from a refrigerator and placed upon an open flame or on a heated range, without suffering any cracking or breaking. Glass-ceramic kitchenware under the trademark "Pyroceram" (Fig. 130) requires less heat for cooking and retains the heat longer than other types of kitchenware [695].

10. OTHER AREAS OF APPLICATION FOR GLASS-CERAMICS

Due to their favorable combination of properties, glass-ceramics can find uses in the most diverse applications. Their high hardness, coupled with high wear resistance, as well as their considerable impact strength and refractoriness make glass-ceramics very useful for the manufacture of thread guides in textile machines, beaters, pounders, lining in mills and grinders, abrasives for grinding purposes, impact-resistant settings for instruments in place of precious stones, halftone and hatched matrices for printing, spinnerets for drawing synthetic fibers, blades for air compressors and gas turbines, brake shoes, jet engine nozzles, and other structural parts of supersonic aircraft [29, 669, 698, 699]. Glass-ceramics whose α is close to zero are recommended for use in the manufacture of precision calipers and bases for special metal-cutting machines and other parts, the dimensions of which cannot be allowed to vary with temperature [57]. Glass-ceramics are being manufactured into laboratory ware, such as beakers,

Fig. 130. Glass-ceramic kitchenware.

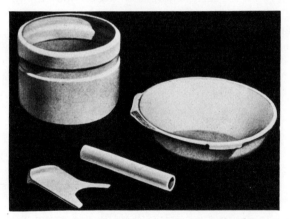

Fig. 131. Laboratory ware and other articles made of Pyroceram.

evaporating dishes, and other parts (Fig. 131). Glass-ceramics coated with an electrically conducting film may be used as electrical heaters, operating at a voltage of 110 V and emitting heat energy with an intensity of approximately 10 W/cm^2.

In electronics, glass-ceramics can be employed for the manufacture of windows for equipment operating at ultrahigh frequencies, parts for traveling and return-wave tubes, receiver-amplifier and mercury arc lamps, shells for discharge fuses, bases for at-

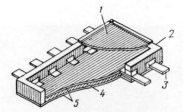

Fig. 132. Welded body with a glass-ceramic base used
for fixed circuits. 1) Lid; 2) body; 3) outlets; 4) glass-
ceramic base; 5) plates. All parts, except 4, are made
of Kovar, and the lid is welded to the body.

tenuators, resistors and microcircuits, flat bodies for fixed circuits (Fig. 132), and other articles [549, 700, 701].

Corning Glass Works [697, 702, 703] used Pyroceram in the
production of light, thin-walled, honeycombed structures of the
"Cercor" type, characterized by very low α values, equal to 10^{-7}
$(°C)^{-1}$, good thermal and corrosion stability, and a capability of
withstanding temperatures up to 1000°C and of continuously working at 700°C (Fig. 133). The low α values and the large surface
area of the materials of the "Cercor" type allow them to be used
as filler-catalysts in high-temperature heat exchangers, as heating and cooling elements, and as panels in architecture. Disks
508 mm in diameter and 95 mm thick have a compression strength
in the direction of the channels of approximately 140 kg/cm^2, the
density of the material is 486 kg/m^3, and its specific heat capacity
is 0.20. The surface area of the cells, distributed with a density
of three holes per cm^2, attains a value of 5000 m^2/m^3, with 75-80%
of this area taken up by the open space. The length of the cells is
equal to 2.4 mm, their height is 1.1 mm, and the average wall thickness is 0.13 mm.

Glass-ceramic with zero α within the temperature region
from -73 to $+66°C$ is used for the fabrication of mirrors for telescopes, since it has the capability of preserving the same curvature regardless of the changes in the temperature of the surrounding atmosphere [42].

Glass-ceramics based on the $CdO-In_2O_3-SiO_2$ and $CdO-$
$In_2O_3-B_2O_3$ systems, which are characterized by high absorption
of slow neutrons with an energy of 0.1 eV, high refractoriness, and

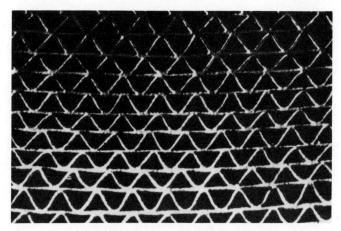

Fig. 133. Thin-walled honeycombed articles made of glass-ceramic.

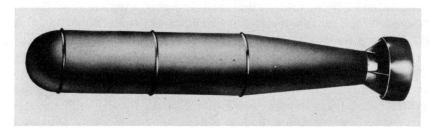

Fig. 134. Model for a deep-submersion capsule made of Pyroceram.

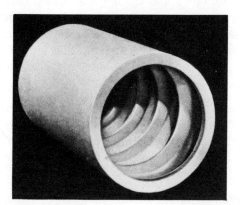

Fig. 135. Cylindrical corrugated section of deep-sea
capsule made of Pyroceram.

high α values — in excess of $100 \cdot 10^{-7}$ $(°C)^{-1}$ — and which are capable of being hermetically welded to steel, can be used for the manufacture of control rods in nuclear reactors [704]. The CdO, which is characterized by a high average capture cross section for thermal neutrons, must constitute not less than 50% in cadmium silicate, and not less than 30% in cadmium borate, initial glasses. These glass-ceramics are stable with regard to radiation effects and do not yield reaction products, which would have an adverse effect on the metallic housing within which the rods are enclosed. For some glass-ceramics, the coefficients for the absorption of neutrons with an energy of $\frac{1}{40}$ eV and their cadmium equivalents, i.e., the thickness of the metallic Cd layer having the same degree of absorption as a unit thickness of the glass-ceramic layer, were calculated. Glass-ceramics based on borate glasses had a neutron absorption coefficient equal to 26.1 cm^{-1} and a cadmium equivalent of 0.24. Glass-ceramics based on silicate glasses had a somewhat higher absorption coefficient, approximately 32.9 cm^{-1}, and a cadmium equivalent equal to 0.27. When comparing data, it must be stated that steel with 4% boron additions has an absorption coefficient of 13.5 cm^{-1} and a cadmium equivalent of 0.12. Thus, with respect to the absorption of thermal neutrons, glass-ceramics are twice as effective as steel with boron additions, making it possible to get the same degree of absorption at a lower section thickness, which is considerably more economical, both insofar as the weight and the cost of the construction are concerned. The glass-ceramics obtained had a flexure strength ranging from 1200 to 2400 kg/cm^2.

Corning Glass Works [710, 711, 756] is considering the use of Pyroceram for the production of the body for an unmanned deep-sea capsule intended for oceanographic investigations at depths down to 9200 m (Fig. 134). This deep-sea capsule, known as the "Benthos," has the shape of a torpedo, is 2.44 m long, has a diameter of 0.305 m, and can carry a net load of 45–68 kg. The body of the boat consists of four separate glass-ceramic sections (Fig. 135), plus a nosecap and a metallic section as the stabilizer. The sections are joined by metallic locking mechanisms. The selection of the proper glass-ceramic to be used as the body material is dictated by the high compression strength required, which is in excess of 21,000 kg/cm^2, and by the increase in the required strength with increasing depth of immersion. The low weight of the glass-ceramics provides for good buoyancy of the capsule even when it is immersed by 60% of its volume.

Glass or glass-ceramics may be used to manufacture the spherical buoys used for the experimental instrumental underwater platforms used by the United States Coast Guard and Geodetic Survey, which are anchored by chains at a depth of 30 m. These buoys have to withstand hydrostatic pressures of 190 kg/cm^2 for a period of six months. Model samples manufactured from glass-ceramics were tested at maximum compression stresses of the order of 25,000 kg/cm^2, which is considerably higher than what is required.

11. COST OF GLASS-CERAMICS

The economic advantages of glass-ceramics are determined by the low cost of the original nonstrategic raw materials and by the possibility of shaping glass articles from the glass melt by rapid conventional techniques. According to some data, glass-ceramics may cost from 30 cents per pound up, depending on the type, finishing, shape, and number of articles, as well as on other factors [705].

Tables 82-84 show the cost (ca. 1964) of piping, tubing, plates, and disks made of Pyroceram 9608, produced by Corning Glass Works [21].

According to Japanese data cited by Tamura [549], the cost of a production unit of a glass-ceramic of lithium aluminosilicate composition, for the production of which 1 kg of Li_2CO_3 was used, is approximately 1000 yen, whereas the cost of 1 kg of glass is 600 yen. The cost of glass-ceramics may be decreased if less expensive lithium materials, such as spodumene, petalite, and lepidolite, are used as raw materials. The cost of one ton of such raw material is approximately 50,000 yen, and the cost of 1 kg of the glass to be used for production of the glass-ceramic is less than 70 yen; it is thus cheaper than the cost of lead-containing electrovacuum glass.

The Soviet investigators Kitaigorodskii and Bondarev [46] performed preliminary calculations with respect to the technical and economical efficiency of structural materials made of glass-ceramics based on metallurgical slags; these calculations show that the production costs of a plant producing sheet glass-ceramic with a capacity of 5 million m^2 per year are estimated as 5,700,000 rubles, whereas the production costs of a plant producing ceramic tile and of the same capacity are 9,800,000 rubles. The cost of

Table 82. Cost of Piping and Tubing Made of Pyroceram 9608

Outer diam., mm	Wall thickness, mm	Length, mm	Unit price, US dollars	Outer diam., mm	Wall thickness, mm	Length, mm	Unit price, US dollars
				Piping			
3.0	0.60	1219	0.35	19.1	0.76	3048	7.05
6.0	1.00	1219	0.70	19.1	1.52	3048	10.15
6.4	1.19	1219	0.90	19.1	1.00	1219	4.05
8.0	1.00	1219	1.00	25.0	1.50	1219	5.15
9.0	1.00	1219	1.18				
10.0	1.00	1219	1.30	24.5	2.38	1219	12.70
12.7	1.60	1219	2.55	30.0	1.8	1219	7.35
15.0	1.20	1219	2.40	31.0	3.0	1016	10.25
15.9	2.16	1219	4.65				
				Tubing			
3.0	—	1219	0.50	6.4	—	1219	1.50
6.0	—	1219	1.10	12.7	—	1219	5.90

Table 83. Cost of Round Disks Made of Pyroceram 9608

Diameter, mm	Unit price in US dollars at thickness, mm						
	6.4	9.5	12.7	15.9	19.1	25.4	28.6
25.4	0.45	0.50	0.65	0.90	1.00	1.10	1.80
50.8	0.60	0.95	1.05	1.65	1.75	2.00	3.25
76.2	1.00	1.45	1.75	2.50	2.75	3.25	4.75
101.6	1.50	2.10	2.65	3.60	4.00	4.75	7.00
127.0	2.00	2.80	3.50	5.00	5.40	6.25	9.50
152.4	2.60	3.60	4.60	6.50	7.00	8.25	13.20
203.4	4.10	5.75	7.25	10.00	11.00	13.00	20.00
254.0	5.80	8.00	10.00	14.50	16.00	18.50	28.00

1 m^2 of glass-ceramic facing tile is half that of ceramic floor tile, and a glass-ceramic kitchen sink is six times less expensive than an enamel-coated cast-iron kitchen sink [685]. Glass-ceramic piping is considerably less expensive than metallic piping. Em-

Table 84. Cost of Square and Rectangular Plates Made of
Pyroceram 9608*

Area, dm^2	Unit price in US dollars at thickness, mm						
	6.4	9.5	12.7	15.9	19.1	25.4	28.6
0.26	0.20	0.25	0.30	0.35	0.45	0.55	0.75
0.58	0.45	0.50	0.65	0.80	1.00	1.15	1.70
1.03	0.75	0.90	1.10	1.40	1.70	2.10	3.05
1.61	1.20	1.40	1.75	2.20	2.65	3.25	4.75
2.32	1.70	2.00	2.50	3.15	3.85	4.70	6.80
3.16	2.30	2.75	3.50	4.30	5.20	6.40	9.25
4.13	3.00	3.60	4.45	5.65	6.80	8.30	12.10
5.23	3.80	4.55	5.60	7.15	8.60	10.55	15.30
6.45	4.70	5.60	6.95	8.80	10.65	13.00	18.90
7.74	5.65	6.70	8.30	10.60	12.75	15.60	22.70
11.61	8.50	10.60	12.45	15.80	19.10	23.40	34.00
15.48	11.30	13.40	16.60	21.00	25.50	31.20	45.40
23.23	17.00	20.00	25.00	31.60	33.30	48.80	68.00

* Maximum size of the plates is 254 × 914 mm.

ploying glass-ceramics in housing construction can result in considerable savings.

The processing of waste slages into glass-ceramics can represent a great benefit to the economy.

Literature Cited

1. M. Reaumur, Memoires de l'Academie des Sciences (1739), pp. 370-388.
2. H. Becker, Deutsches Reichspatent 287394.
3. H. Becker, H. Fehringer, and H. Johnke, Deutsches Reichspatent 332578.
4. H. Becker, Deutsches Reichspatent 410351.
5. H. Becker, Deutsches Reichspatent 430387.
6. B. Becker, Deutsches Reichspatent 630898.
7. B. Becker, Austrian Patent 180889 (1955).
8. H. Wagner, West German Patent 863176 (1953).
9. H. Wagner, West German Patent 910038 (1954).
10. H. Wagner, West German Patent 927978 (1955).
11. H. Wagner, West German Patent 952514 (1956).
12. C. Trenzen, Deutsches Reichspatent 569310.
13. C. Gehlhoff, Deutsches Reichspatent 443582 (1927).
14. I. I. Kitaigorodskii, Glass and Glass-Melting, Promstroiizdat, Moscow (1950), p. 32.
15. K. Sugiura, Japanese Patent 1121 (1951).
16. R. Sersale, Ric. Sci., 23(11): 1993-2008 (1953).
17. S. N. Lungu and D. Popescu-Has, Studii si Cercetari de Chimie, Academia, Republica Populara Romana, III (1955), p. 225.
18. F. Albrecht, Beispiele angewandter Forschung, Munchen (1955), pp. 19-22.
19. F. Albrecht, W. Appler, and Maucher, West German Patent 1007231 (1957).
20. S. D. Stookey, Pyroceram, Codes 9606, 9608, 1st Report, Corning Glass Works, Corning, New York (May 1957).
21. S. D. Stookey, Pyroceram, Codes 9606, 9608, 2nd Report, Corning Glass Works, Corning, New York (May 1957).
22. Glass Ind., 38(6): 331-332 (1957).
23. Ceram. Age., 69(6): 18-19 (1957).
24. Glass Ind., 18: 387-388 (1957).
25. Am. Ceram. Soc. Bull., 36(7): 278-280 (1957).
26. Ceramics, 9(103): 11-13 (1957).
27. Am. Glass Rev., 77(3): 29-30 (1957).
28. Ceram. Age, 70(6): 5 (1957).
29. Ceram. Ind., 69(1): 72-73 (1957).
30. Central Glass Ceram. Res. Inst. Bull (India), 4(3): 159 (1957).
31. Monthly Bull., p. 285 (1957).
32. R. H. Dalton, US Patent 2326012 (1943).
33. R. H. Dalton, US Patent 2422472 (1947).
34. S. D. Stookey, Canadian Patent 442273 (1947).

414 LITERATURE CITED

35. S. D. Stookey, Canadian Patent 444616 (1947).
36. Architectural Forum, 107(1): 160-162 (1957).
37. W. H. Armistead, Canadian Patent 442272 (1947).
38. S. D. Stookey, West German Patent 922734 (1955).
39. S. D. Stookey, Ind. Eng. Chem., 45(1): 115-118 (1953).
40. S. D. Stookey, Ind. Eng. Chem., 46(1): 174-176 (1954).
41. W. Hennig, Elektronische Rundschau, 6: 233-234 (1960).
42. Ceram. Age, 74(4): C6-C86 (1959).
43. S. D. Stookey, Chem. Eng. News, 39(25): 116-125 (1961).
44. B. Löcsei, Silikat Tech., 10(12): 589-596 (1959).
45. B. Löcsei, West German Patent 1085804 (1961).
46. I. I. Kitaigorodskii and K. T. Bondarev, "Glass-Ceramics — A New Universal Material," Pravda, March 22, 1963.
47. Steklo i Keram., No. 4, pp. 48-49 (1959).
48. A. I. Berezhnoi, Photosensitive Glasses and Glass-Crystalline Materials of the "Pyroceram" Type, VINITI, Akad. Nauk SSSR, Moscow (1960).
49. W. Hinz, Silikat Tech., 10: 119-122 (1959).
50. T. Sakaino, Kogyo Kagaku Zasshi, 63(7): 1104-1108 (1960).
51. S. N. Lungu and D. Popescu-Has, Ind. Usoara (Bucharest), 5: 63-65 (1958).
52. S. N. Lungu and D. Popescu-Has, Silicates Ind., 23(7-8): 391-395 (1958).
53. B. Löcsei, in: Symposium on Nucleation and Crystallization in Glasses and Melts, edited and published by the American Ceramic Society, Columbus, Ohio (1962), pp. 71-74.
54. J. Nebrensky and J. Voldan, Informativni prehled, Statni vys kymny ustav sklarksy, Nositel Radu Prace, Hradec Kralove (1961), Vol. 1.
55. The Glassy State, Trans. of the Third All-Union Conference, Leningrad, 1959, Izd. Akad. Nauk SSSR, Moscow-Leningrad (1960), pp. 528-529. [English translation: The Structure of Glass, Vol. 2, Consultants Bureau, New York (1960).]
56. The Glassy State, Vol. 1. Catalyzed Crystallization of Glass, Izd. Akad. Nauk SSSR, Moscow-Leningrad (1963). [English translation: The Structure of Glass, Vol. 3, Consultants Bureau, New York (1964).]
57. S. D. Stookey, Mech. Eng., 82(10): 65-68 (1960).
58. S. D. Stookey, J. Phot. Soc. Am., No. 14, pp. 399-401 (1948).
59. Chem. Eng. News, 25: 1822 (1947).
60. W. A. Weyl, Coloured Glasses, Society of Glass Technology, Sheffield, UK (1951), p. 10.
61. S. D. Stookey and F. W. Schuler, "Ultraviolet and x-ray irradiation effects on special photosensitive glasses," in: Fourth International Congress on Glass, Paris (1956), VII-5, pp. 2-7
62. X. Tazukado, Japanese Patent 9880 (1957).
63. V. A. Borgman, V. M. Petrov, and V. G. Chistoserdov, Zh. Fiz. Khim., 25(6): 1383-1385 (1961).
64. R. Zsigmondy, Dinglers Polyt. J., 306: 68-72, 91-95 (1874).
65. S. D. Stookey, J. Am. Ceram. Soc., 32(8): 246-249 (1949).
66. T. Sakaino, J. Ceram. Assoc. Japan, 69(783): 81-86 (1961).
67. S. D. Stookey, Ind. Eng. Chem., 41(4): 856-861 (1949).

68.   S. D. Stookey, West German Patent 809847 (1951).

69.   S. D. Stookey, Ind. Eng. Chem., 32: 246 (1949).

70.   S. D. Stookey, Ind. Eng. Chem., 51(7): 805-806 (1959).

71.   K. Barth, Silikat Tech., No. 3, pp. 101-105 (1960).

72.   V. A. Borgman and V. G. Chistoserdov, Opt. i Spektroskopiya, 13(3): 421-424 (1962).

73.   K. Riess, W. C. Bosch, and T. T. Reboul, Am. J. Phys., 16: 398-403 (1948).

74.   G. P. Rosenberg, Usp. Fiz. Nauk, 37(1): 116-117 (1949).

75.   S. D. Stookey, Colloid Chemistry, Theoretical and Applied, collected and edited by J. Alexander, New York (1950), pp. 697-706.

76.   R. D. Maurer, J. Appl. Phys., 29(1): 1-8 (1958).

77.   M. Tashiro and S. Sakka, J. Ceram. Assoc. Japan, 67: 263-269 (1959).

78.   W. A. Weyl, J. Soc. Glass Technol., 29(135): 291-389T (1945).

79.   A. E. Badger, W. A. Weyl, and H. Rudow, Glass Ind., 20(11): 407-414 (1939).

80.   H. Hünter, Elementa, 1: 17-22 (1959).

81.   K. T. Bondarev and F. Ya. Borodai, Steklo i Keram., No. 10, pp. 1-4 (1960).

82.   R. F. Tucker, Advances in Glass Technology, Technical Papers of the Sixth International Congress on Glass, Washington, D. C., July 8-14 (1962). Plenum Press, New York (1962), pp. 103-114.

83.   A. I. Berezhnoi and L. N. Il'chenko, Opt.-Mekh. Promyshlennost', No. 2, pp. 10-14 (1964).

84.   A. I. Berezhnoi and Yu. M. Polukhin, Opt.-Mekh. Promyshlennost', No. 8, pp. 33-36 (1964).

85.   W. W. Wargin and G. O. Karapetjan, Glastech. Ber., No. 11, pp. 443-450 (1959).

86.   G. O. Karapetyan, Opt. i Spektroskopiya, No. 3, p. 6 (1961).

87.   J. S. Stroud, J. Chem. Phys., 35(3): 844-850 (1961).

88.   J. S. Stroud, J. Chem. Phys., 37(4): 836-841 (1962).

89.   E. V. Gurkovskii, in: The Glassy State, Vol. 1, Catalyzed Crystallization of Glass, Izd. Akad. Nauk SSSR, Moscow-Leningrad (1963), pp. 151-155. [English translation: The Structure of Glass, Vol. 3, Consultants Bureau, New York (1964), pp. 163-165.]

90.   A. E. Badger and F. A. Hummel, Phys. Rev., 68: 231 (1945).

91.   V. A. Borgman and V. G Chistoserdov, Opt. i Spektroskopiya, 12(1):140-141 (1962)

92.   M. Tashiro, N. Soga, and S. Sakka, Bull. Inst. Chem. Res , Kyoto Univ., 37: 341 (1959).

93.   V. A. Borgman and V. G. Chistoserdov, The Glassy State, Vol. 1, Catalyzed Crystallization of Glass, Izd. Akad. Nauk SSSR, Moscow-Leningrad (1963), pp. 150-151. [English translation: The Structure of Glass, Vol. 3, Consultants Bureau, New York (1964), pp. 161-162.]

94.   V. A. Borgman, E. V. Gurkovskii, and V. G. Chistoserdov, Fourth All-Union Conference on the Glassy State, Abstracts of Papers, Izd. Khimiya, Moscow-Leningrad (1964), pp. 20-21. [For English translation, see The Structure of Glass, Vol. 7, Consultants Bureau, New York (1966).]

95.   P. Yokota, Advances in Glass Techology, Technical Papers of the Sixth International Congress on Glass, Washington, D. C., July 8-14, 1962, Plenum Press, New York (1962), pp. 424-428.

96.   A. I. Berezhnoi, L. N. Il'chenko, and V. V. Litarev, Bull. Izobretenii i Tovarnykh Znakov, No. 15 (1963).

97.   S. D. Stookey, in: Crystallization, Theory and Practice (A. Van Hook, ed.), Reinhold Publishing Corp, New York (1961), pp. 287-292.

98.   S. D. Stookey, in: Ceramic Fabrication Processes (W. D. Kingery, ed.), New York (1958), pp. 189-195.

99.   W. Ostwald, Z. Physik. Chem., 22: 289-330 (1897).

100.   G. Tamman, The States of Aggregation, D. Van Nostrand Co., New York (1925).

101.   "Nucleation phenomena," Ind. Eng. Chem., 44: 1269-1338 (1952).

102.   J. W. Gibbs, Collected Works, Vol. 1, Longmans, Green, and Co.., New York (1928), p. 94.

103.   J. J. Thompson, Application of Dynamics to Physics and Chemistry, Macmillan Co., London (1888), pp. 162-175.

104.   D. Turnbull, Trans. AIME, 175: 774-783 (1948).

105.   R. Becker and J. Doering, Ann. Physik, 24(5): 719-752 (1935).

106.   J. Frenkel, Kinetic Theory of Liquids, Dover Publications, New York.

107.   R. Becker, Ann. Physik, 32: 128-140 (1938).

108.   V. D. Kuznetsov, Crystals and Crystallization, Gostekhteorizdat (1950).

109.   W. A. Weyl, Sprechsaal Keramik-Glas-Email, 93(6): 128-136 (1960).

110.   W. A. Weyl and E. C. Marboe, Nucleation and Crystallization, Vol. 1, The Constitution of Glasses, a Dynamic Interpretation, Interscience Publishers, New York (1962), pp. 182-202.

111.   W. A. Weyl, Central Glass Ceram. Res. Inst. Bull.(India), 8(2): 57-72 (1961).

112.   W. A. Weyl, J. Phys. Chem., 19(2): 147-151 (1955).

113.   W. A. Weyl and E. C. Marboe, Glass Ind., 43(10): 549-559, 590 (1962); 41(11): 620-627, 658-659 (1960).

114.   W. A. Weyl and E. C. Marboe, Glass Ind., 41(12): 687-691, 694-695, 715 (1960); 42(1): 23-25, 28, 49; 42(2): 76-81, 106 (1961).

115.   A. Dietzel, Z. Elektrochem., 48(1): 9-23 (1942).

116.   W. B. Hillig, Symposium on Nucleation and Crystallization in Glasses and Melts, edited and published by the American Ceramic Society, Columbus, Ohio (1962), pp. 77-89.

117.   V. N. Filipovich, in: The Glassy State, Vol. 1, Catalyzed Crystallization of Glass, Izd. Akad. Nauk SSSR, Moscow-Leningrad (1963), pp. 9-23. [English translation: The Structure of Glass, Vol. 3, Consultants Bureau, New York (1964), pp. 9-20.]

118.   V. N. Filipovich, Fourth All-Union Conference on the Glassy State, Abstracts of Papers, Izd. Khimiya, Moscow-Leningrad (1964), p. 75. [For English translation of conference proceedings, see The Structure of Glass, Vols. 6 and 7, Consultants Bureau, New York (1966).]

119.   S. D. Stookey, Glastech. Ber., 5th International Congress on Glass, Verlag der deutschen Glastechn. Gesellschaft, Frankfurt-on-Main (1959), 32K(5): V/1–V/8.

120.   B. Vonnegut, Chem. Rev., 44: 277-289 (1949).

121.   D. Turnbull and J. C. Fisher, J. Chem. Phys., 17: 71-73 (1949).

122.   D. Turnbull, J. Chem. Phys., 20: 411-424 (1950).

123. S. D. Stookey, Sprechsaal Keramik-Glas-Email, 92(17):447 (1959).

124. F. Meyer, Beiträge zur angewandten Glasforschung, E. Schott Deutsches Verlag, Stuttgart (1959), pp. 121-132.

125. W. D. Kingery, Introduction to Ceramics, John Wiley and Sons, New York (1960), p. 314.

126. R. Roy, J. Am. Ceram. Soc., 43(12):670-671 (1960).

127. S. D. Stookey, DAS 1045056 (1958).

128. W. A. Weyl, Symposium on Nucleation and Crystallization in Glasses and Melts, edited and published by the American Ceramic Society, Columbus, Ohio (1962), pp. 37-38.

129. D. M. Roy, R. Roy, and E. F. Osborn, J. Am. Ceram. Soc., 33(3):85-90 (1960).

130. W. Vogel, in: Symposium on the Melting of Glass, Union Scientifique Continentale du Verre, Charleroi, Belgium (1958), pp. 741-770.

131. W. Vogel and K. Gerth, Silikat Tech., 9(12):539-543 (1958).

132. W. Vogel, Silikat Tech., 10:241-250 (1959).

133. B. E. Warren and A. G. Pincus, J. Am. Ceram. Soc., 23:301-304 (1940).

134. W. Hinz and P. O. Kunth, Glastech. Ber., 34(9):431-437 (1961).

135. E. M. Levin and G. W. Cleek, J. Am. Ceram. Soc., 41:175-179 (1958).

136. R. C. DeVries, R. Roy, and E. F. Osborn, Trans. Brit. Ceram. Soc., 53:525-540 (1954).

137. J. W. Greig, Am. J. Sci., 13(5):1-44, 133-154 (1927).

138. K. H. Kim and F. A. Hummel, J. Am. Ceram. Soc., 42:186-191 (1959).

139. R. C. DeVries, R. Roy, and E. F. Osborn, J. Am. Ceram. Soc., 38:158-171 (1955).

140. F. Massazza and E. Sirchia, Chim. Ind. (Milan), 40:376-380, 460-467 (1958).

141. W. Hinz and P. O. Kunth, Silikat Tech., 11:506-511 (1960).

142. F. A. Hummel, T. Y. Tien, and K. H. Kim, J. Am. Ceram. Soc., 43:192-197 (1960).

143. N. A. Toropov and F. Ya. Galakhov, Izv. Akad. Nauk SSSR, Otd. Khim. Nauk, pp. 158-161 (1956).

144. R. F. Geller and S. M. Lang, in: Phase Diagrams for Ceramists (E. M. Levin, H. F. McMurdie, and F. P. Hall, eds.), American Ceramic Society, Columbus, Ohio (1956), p. 67.

145. M. L. Keith, J. Am. Ceram. Soc., 37:490-496 (1954).

146. F. P. Glasser and E. F. Osborn, J. Am. Ceram. Soc., 41:358-367 (1958).

147. Ya. I. Ol'shanskii, Dokl. Akad. Nauk SSSR, 70:245-248 (1950).

148. B. P. Löcsei, DAS 1085804 (1960).

149. B. P. Löcsei, and K. Polinszky, Magy. Tech., 4:216-219 (1954).

150. B. P. Löcsei, Magy. Kem. Lapja, 9:254 (1954).

151. B. P. Löcsei, Epitöanyag, 10:408-414, 446-459 (1958).

152. B. P. Löcsei, Epitöanyag, 11:7, 247-256 (1959).

153. B. P. Löcsei, Acta Chem. Acad. Sci. Hung., 25(1):1-25 (1960).

154. Z. P. Ershova and Ya. I. Ol'shanskii, Geokhimiya, pp. 113, 214-221 (1957).

155. W. Hinz and P. O. Kunth, Am. Mineralogist, 45:1198-1210 (1960).

156. H. Schönborn, Silikat Tech., 10:390-400 (1959).

157. R. D. Maurer, in: Symposium on Nucleation and Crystallization in Glasses and Melts, edited and published by the American Ceramic Society, Columbus, Ohio (1962), pp. 5-9.

158. R. D. Maurer, J. Appl. Phys., 33(6): 2132-2139 (1962).

159. I. I. Kitaigorodskii and R. Ya. Khodakovskaya, in: The Glassy State, Vol. 1, Catalyzed Crystallization of Glass, Izd. Akad. Nauk SSSR, Moscow-Leningrad (1963), pp. 31-38. [English translation: The Structure of Glass, Vol. 3, Consultants Bureau, New York (1964), pp. 27-33.]

160. F. Ya. Galakhov, ibid., p. 38. [English translation: ibid., p. 34.]

161. N. M. Vaisfel'd and V. I. Shelyubskii, ibid., pp. 41-43. [English translation: ibid., pp. 37-41.]

162. V. N. Vertsner, Yu. M. Vorona, and Yu. M. Zhdanov, ibid., pp. 81-82. [English translation: ibid., pp. 83-85.]

163. V. N. Vertsner and L. V. Degteva, ibid., pp. 83-84. [English translation: ibid., pp. 86-89.]

164. D. A. Goganov, E. A. Porai-Koshits, and Yu. G. Sokolov, ibid., pp. 44-46. [English translation: ibid., pp. 45-46.]

165. N. S. Andreev, E. A. Goganov, E. A. Porai-Koshits, and Yu. G. Sokolov, ibid., pp. 46-53. [English translation: ibid., pp. 47-52.]

166. I. A. Bondar' and N. A. Toropov, ibid., pp. 39-41. [English translation: ibid., pp. 35-36.]

167. A. M. Kalinina, V. N. Filipovich, V. A. Kolesova, and I. A. Bondar', ibid., pp. 53-66. [English translation: ibid., pp. 53-64.]

168. I. M. Buzhinskii, E. I. Sabaeva, and A. N. Khomyakov, ibid., pp. 127-137. [English translation: ibid., pp. 133-145.]

169. N. A. Toropov and V. P. Barzakovskii, High-Temperature Chemistry of Silicate and Other Oxide Systems, Izd. Akad. Nauk SSSR, Moscow-Leningrad (1963), pp. 3-21. [English translation: Consultants Bureau, New York (1966).]

170. S. M. Ohlberg, H. R. Golob, and D. W. Strickler, in: Symposium on Nucleation and Crystallization in Glasses and Melts, edited and published by the American Ceramic Society, Columbus, Ohio (1962), pp. 55-62.

171. W. Vogel and K. Gerth, Glastech. Ber., 31: 15-28 (1958).

172. W. Vogel and K. Gerth, in: Symposium on Nucleation and Crystallization in Glasses and Melts, edited and published by the American Ceramic Society, Columbus, Ohio (1962), pp. 11-22.

173. T. Moriya, Bull. Tokyo Inst. Technol., Ser. B, 1 (1951).

174. G. W. Morey, J. Soc. Glass Technol., 35: 270-283 (1951).

175. W. Skatulla, W. Vogel, and H. Wessel, Silikat Tech., 9: 51-62 (1958).

176. N. S. Andreev and E. A. Porai-Koshits, Priroda, 182: 335-336 (1958).

177. N. S. Andreev and E. A. Porai-Koshits, Dokl. Akad. Nauk SSSR, 118: 735-737 (1958).

178. K. Kühne and W. Skatulla, Silikat Tech., 10: 105-119 (1959).

179. B. S. R. Sastry and F. A. Hummel, J. Am. Ceram. Soc., 42(2): 81-88 (1959).

180. M. Watanabe, H. Noake, and T. Aiba, J. Am. Ceram. Soc., 42(12): 593-599 (1959).

181. A. Dietzel, Glastech. Ber., 22(3/4): 41-50 (1948).

182. A. Dietzel, Kolloid-Z., 100(3) : 368-380 (1942).

183. S. Ya. Bobovich, in: The Glassy State, Vol. 1, Catalyzed Crystallization of Glass, Izd. Akad. Nauk SSSR, Moscow-Leningrad (1963), pp. 87-90. [English translation: The Structure of Glass, Vol. 3, Consultants Bureau, New York (1963), pp. 93-95.]

184. Yu. N. Kondrat'ev, Dokl. Akad. Nauk SSSR, 153(6) : 1370 (1963).

185. A. G. Alekseeva, V. N. Vertsner, and Yu. N. Kondrat'ev, Dokl. Akad. Nauk SSSR, 154(1) : 178-180 (1964).

186. R. L. Muller, Zh. Tekh. Fiz., 25(62) : 236 (1955).

187. E. V. Podushko and A. B. Kozlova, in: The Glassy State, Vol. 1, Catalyzed Crystallization of Glass, Izd. Akad. Nauk SSSR, Moscow-Leningrad (1963), pp. 74-81. [English translation: The Structure of Glass, Vol. 3, Consultants Bureau, New York (1963), pp. 77-82.]

188. L. A. Zhunina, V. N. Sharai, V. F. Tsitko, and N. N. Khripkova, ibid., pp. 178-180. [English translation: ibid., pp. 192-194.]

189. G. T. Petrovskii, E. N. Krestnikova, and I. I. Grebenshchikova, ibid., pp. 167-169. [English translation: ibid., pp. 177-179.]

190. G. T. Petrovskii and S. V. Nemilov, ibid., pp. 112-116. [English translation: ibid., pp. 118-121.]

191. G. T. Petrovskii, E. N. Krestnikova, I. I. Grebenshchikova, and M. V. Proskuryakov, Fourth All-Union Conference on the Glassy State, Abstracts of Papers, Khimiya, Moscow-Leningrad (1964), pp. 63-64. [For English translation, see The Structure of Glass, Vol. 7, Consultants Bureau, New York (1966).]

192. V. I. Shelyubskii and N. M. Vaisfel'd, Zh. Fiz. Khim., 35(11) : 2652-2654 (1961).

193. N. V. Solomin, V. I. Shelyubskii, and N. M. Vaisfel'd, Dokl. Akad. Nauk SSSR, 140 : 1087-1089 (1961).

194. S. M. Ohlberg, H. R. Golob, and C. M. Hollabaugh, J. Am. Ceram. Soc., 45(1) : 1-4 (1962).

195. G. E. Rindone and R. J. Ryder, Glass Ind., 38(1) : 29-31, 51 (1957).

196. M. G. Hawes, Glass Ind., 38(8) : 441-442, 445 (1957).

197. G. E. Rindone and J. L. Rhoads, J. Am. Ceram. Soc., 39 : 173-180 (1956).

198. R. J. Ryder and G. E. Rindone, J. Am. Ceram. Soc., 41(10) : 415-422 (1958).

199. M. D. Karkhanavala and W. A. Weyl, ONR Tech. Rept., Vol. 45, 6, 269108 NR. 032-264, College of Mineral Industries, Pennsylvania State University, State College, Pennsylvania (1952).

200. M. K. Murthy, J. Am. Ceram. Soc., 44(8) : 412-417 (1961).

201. R. J. Charles, J. Am. Ceram. Soc., 46(6) : 235-243 (1963).

202. W. Vogel and H. G. Byhan, Z. Chem., 3 : 154-156 (1963).

203. G. E. Rindone, J. Am. Ceram. Soc., 41(1) : 41 (1958).

204. G. E. Rindone, J. Am. Ceram. Soc., 45(1) : 7-12 (1962).

205. M. Tashiro, S. Sakka, and M. Wada, J. Ceram. Assoc. Japan, 68(10) : 223-231 (1960).

206. Platinum Metals Rev., 5(4) : 140 (1961).

207. G. E. Rindone, in: Symposium on Nucleation and Crystallization in Glasses and Melts, edited and published by the American Ceramic Society, Columbus, Ohio (1962), pp. 63-69.

208. C. L. Booth and G. E. Rindone, Am. Ceram. Soc. Bull., 42(4): 229 (1963).

209. E. M. Rabinovich, in: The Glassy State, Vol. 1, Catalyzed Crystallization of Glass, Izd. Akad. Nauk SSSR, Moscow-Leningrad (1963), pp. 24-31. [English translation: The Structure of Glass, Vol. 3, Consultants Bureau, New York (1964), pp. 21-26.]

210. I. I. Kitaigorodskii, E. M. Rabinovich, and V. I. Shelyubskii, Steklo i Keram., No. 12, pp. 1-9 (1963).

211. N. N. Sirota, in: Symposium on Crystallization and Phase Transitions, Izd. Akad. Nauk BelSSR, Minsk (1962), pp. 82-106.

212. P. D. Dankov, Dokl. Akad. Nauk SSSR, 23(6): 548-552 (1939).

213. P. D. Dankov, Zh. Fiz. Khim., 20(8): 853-867 (1946).

214. R. D. Maurer, J. Chem. Phys., 25: 1206-1209 (1956).

215. A. A. Shatalov, Properties and Transformations of Atomic, Molecular, and Colloidal Color Centers in Heated Alkali Halide Crystals, Dissertation, Veloruss. Gos. Univ. im. V. I. Lenin, published by the Inst. Kristallographii Akad. Nauk SSSR, Kiev (1959).

216. E. A. Kirillov, Fine Structure in the Absorption Spectrum of Photochemically Colored Silver Halide, Izd. Akad. Nauk SSSR, Moscow (1954).

217. I. M. Ratner, T. A. Koretskaya, and V. A. Kargin, Kolloid. Zh., 18(4): 468-469 (1956).

218. M. V. Savost'yanova and A. N. Toporets, Dokl. Akad. Nauk SSSR, 11(4) (1934).

219. A. A. Gorbachev, Yu. M. Polukhin, A. M. Ravich, and L. M. Yusim, in: The Glassy State, Vol. 1, Catalyzed Crystallization of Glass, Izd. Akad. Nauk SSSR, Moscow-Leningrad (1963), pp. 155-159. [English translation: The Structure of Glass, Vol. 3, Consultants Bureau, New York (1964), pp. 166-168.]

220. G. Mie, Ann. Physik, 25: 377 (1908).

221. E. A. Minor, Ann. Physik, No. 10, p. 581 (1903).

222. M. Otter, Z. Physik, 161(5): 539-549 (1961).

223. D. Mitchell and N. Mott, Problems in Modern Physics, No. 4, pp. 130-150 (1958).

224. Shifrin, Kolloidn. Zh., 13(4): 314 (1951).

225. N. F. Mott and R. W. Gurney, Electronic Processes in Ionic Crystals, Clarendon Press, Oxford (1950).

226. R. Yokota and K. Simidzu, Toshiba Rev., 16(7): 893-900 (1961).

227. R. Yokota, Japanese Patent 5021 (1962); Am. Ceram. Soc. Bull., 41(5): 356 (1962).

228. A. Ehringhaus and R. Wintgen, Z. Phys. Chem., 108: 301-314, 406-410 (1924).

229. M. Smoluchowski, Phys. Z., 17: 557-571, 585-599 (1916).

230. M. Smolochowski, Z. Phys. Chem., 92: 129-268 (1917).

231. T. Sakaino and T. Moriya, J. Ceram. Assoc. Japan, 70(2): 33-36 (1962).

232. M. Fanderlik, Silikaty, 7(1): 46-51 (1963).

233. R. D. Maurer, J. Chem. Phys., 31(2): 444-448 (1959).

234. N. H. Fletcher, J. Chem. Phys., 29: 572-576 (1958).

235. H. R. Lillie, Glass Technol., 1(3): 115-120 (1960).

236. R. H. Dalton, US Patent 2326012 (1943).

237. R. Haddan, British Patent 570111 (1945).

238. R. H. Dalton, US Patent 2422472 (1947).

239. S. D. Stookey, US Patent 2515938 (1950).

240. S. D. Stookey, British Patent 635649 (1947).

241. S. D. Stookey, West German Patent 816129 (1951).

242. S. D. Stookey, US Patent 2515939 (1950).

243. S. D. Stookey, US Patent 2515275 (1950).

244. S. D. Stookey, British Patent 654740 (1951).

245. S. D. Stookey, US Patent 2515940 (1950).

246. Corning Glass Works, Swiss Patent 283357 (1952).

247. S. D. Stookey, US Patent 2515941 (1950).

248. S. D. Stookey, British Patent 636152 (1950).

249. G. Miyake, Sh. Kuwayama, and M. Yagi, Japanese Patent 5023 (1962).

250. G. Miyake, Sh. Kuwayama, and M. Yagi, Japanese Patent 5022 (1962).

251. S. D. Stookey, US Patent 2515943 (1949).

252. Corning Glass Works, British Patent 668767 (1950).

253. F. Reinhart, Glas-Email-Keramo-Techn., 7(5): 153; 7(6): 208 (1956).

254. E. V. Gurkovskii, Legkaya promyshlennost', No. 7, pp. 36-37 (1952).

255. E. V. Gurkovskii, BNTI, VNII Steklovolokna, No. 2, p. 27 (1952).

256. E. V. Gurkovskii and N. L. Kaminskaya, Steklo i Keram., No. 6, pp. 33-34 (1962).

257. S. D. Stookey, US Patent 2515942 (1950).

258. W. H. Armistead, US Patent 2515936 (1950).

259. S. D. Stookey, US Patent 2651145 (1953).

260. S. D. Stookey, US Patent 2651146 (1953).

261. S. D. Stookey, West German Patent 844648 (1952).

262. Corning Glass Works, British Patent 699898 (1953).

263. S. D. Stookey, US Patent 2684911 (1954).

264. S. D. Stookey, West German Patent 922733 (1955).

265. S. D. Stookey, US Patent 2682134 (1954).

266. S. D. Stookey, US Patent 2911749 (1959).

267. S. D. Stookey, US Patent 2628160 (1953).

268. Electronics, 32(18): 70, 72-73 (1959).

269. F. W. Schuler, Chem. Eng. Progr., 52: 210-212 (1956).

270. W. Hennig, Glas-Instr.-Tech., 5(1): 3-5 (1961).

271. W. Hennig, Glas-Email-Keramo-Tech., 12(9): 219-321 (1961).

272. W. Hennig, VDI-Nachr., 16(28): 4 (1962).

273. N. Lazar, Prod. Eng., 28(11): 66-70 (1960).

274. Corning Glass Works, New Developments in Corning Fotoform Glass, Electrical Products Division, Corning, New York.

275. G. Herbert, Le Vide, 87(5/6): 268-285 (1960).

276. S. D. Stookey, West German Patent 962110 (1957).

277. S. D. Stookey, US Patent 2971853 (1961).

278. W. Hinz, Silikate, Einführung in Theorie und Praxis, VEB Verlag für Bauwesen, Berlin (1963), pp. 575-576.

279. H. Simpson, Glass Ind., No. 12, p. 701 (1959).

280. N. M. Vaisfel'd, A. A. Gorbachev, and L. M. Yusim, Dokl. Akad. Nauk SSSR, 152(4): 901-904 (1963).

281. V. G. Chistoserdov, N. A. Shmeleva, and A. I. Gerasimova, in: The Glassy State, Vol. 1, Catalyzed Crystallization of Glass, Izd. Akad. Nauk SSSR, Moscow-Leningrad (1963), pp. 159-161. [English translation: The Structure of Glass, Vol. 3, Consultants Bureau, New York (1964), pp. 172-174.]

282. N. A. Shmeleva and N. M. Ivanova, ibid., pp. 68-73. [English translation: ibid., pp. 69-76.]

283. N. Soga, S. Sakka, and M. Tashiro, "The chemically machinable photosensitive glasses of the $Li_2O-K_2O-ZnO-SiO_2$ system," in: Advances in Glass Technology, Part 2, Plenum Press, New York (1963), pp. 35-36.

284. S. D. Stookey, French Patent 1261198 (1961).

285. S. D. Stookey, Australian Patent 238920 (1959).

286. Corning Glass Works, British Patent 863570 (1961).

287. S. D. Stookey, Australian Patent 238921 (1959).

288. Corning Glass Works, British Patent 863569 (1961).

289. Glass Ind., 39(1): 52-53 (1958).

290. H. Bierman and R. Haavind, Electron. Design, 8(23): 61-97 (1960).

291. B. Miller, Aviation Week, 73(19): 97-103 (1960).

292. Ceram. Ind., No. 10, p. 51 (1961).

293. Ceram. Ind., No. 12, p. 40 (1961).

294. B. Ya. Kaznachei, Galvanoplastics in Industry, Gos. Izd. Mestnoi Promyshlennosti RSFSR (1955).

295. K. M. Gorbunova and A. K. Nikiforova, Physicochemical Bases for the Chemical Nickel-Plating Process, Izd. Akad. Nauk SSSR (1960).

296. A. Sedenka, J. Am. Ceram. Soc., 42(4): 139-141 (1959).

297. English Electric Co., Ltd., French Patent 1281747 (1961).

298. H. E. Simpson, Glass Ind., 39(1): 23-25, 49, 52 (1958).

299. Chem. Eng., 64(8): 178 (1957).

300. M. Tashiro and M. Wada, "Glass-ceramics catalyzed with zirconia," in: Advances in Glass Technology, Part 2, Plenum Press, New York (1963), pp. 18-19.

301. S. N. Lungu and D. Popescu-Has, J. Ceram. Assoc. Japan, 68: 18 (1960).

302. T. Moritani, T. Sakaino, H. Saino, and M. Endo, J. Ceram. Assoc. Japan, 68: 44 (1960).

303. T. Moritani, T. Sakaino, and N. Tanaka, Kogyo Kagaku Zasshi, 63: 1129 (1960).

304. Platinum Metals Rev., 5(4): 140 (1961).

305. M. Tashiro et al., Kogyo Kyokai Shi, 69(2): 391 (1958).

306. R. Yokota and S. Nakayama, Japanese Patent 19479 (1961).

307. J. Karwowska-Nowakowska, Szklo i Ceram., 8(6): 166-171 (1962).

308. J. Karwowska-Nowakowska and G. Mazur, Szklo i Ceram., 14(7): 188-189 (1963).

309. W. Sack, Beiträge zur angewandten Glasforschung, E. Schott Wiss. Verlagsgesellschaft, Stuttgart (1959), pp. 111-120.

310. J. Sawai, Glass Technol., 2(6): 245-247 (1961).

311. Bh. V. Janakiramarao, French Patent 1302830 (1962).

312. R. Hayami, H. Tanaka, and T. Ogura, Japanese Patent 926 (1963).

313. V. Nakayama and T. Asai, Toshiba Rev., 16(12): 1508-1513 (1961).

314. R. Hayami, T. Ogura, and H. Tanaka, Osaka Kogyu Gijutsu Shikensho Kiho, 12(4): 365-372 (1961).

315. F. Singer and S. Singer, Sprechsall Keramik-Glas-Email, 89:399-403, 430-432 (1956).

316. M. Mehmel, Glas-Email-Keramo-Tech., 10: 337-340 (1959).

317. F. H. Gillery and E. A. Bush, J. Am. Ceram. Soc., 42(4): 175-177 (1959).

318. W. R. Buessem, N. R. Thielke, and R. V. Sarakauskas, Ceram. Age, No. 11, pp. 38-40 (1952).

319. R. F. Geller and H. Insley, US Natl. Bur. Stand. J. Res., 9(1): 35-46 (1932).

320. S. D. Stookey, West German Patent 1045056 (1958).

321. S. D. Stookey, US Patent 2920971 (1960).

322. Corning Glass Works, British Patent 829447 (1960).

323. Corning Glass Works, French Patent 1283488 (1961).

324. D. S. Belyankin, V. V. Lapin, and N. A. Toropov, Physical-Chemical Systems of Silicate Technology, Promstroiizdat, Moscow (1954).

325. E. M. Levin, H. F. McMurdie, and F. P. Hall, Phase Diagrams for Ceramists, American Ceramic Society, Columbus, Ohio (1956).

326. Corning Glass Works, French Patent 1221174 (1960).

327. Corning Glass Works, British Patent 857367 (1960).

328. S. M. Brekhovskikh, Data presented at the Conference of Glass-Industry Workers, held in Vladimir in 1958, GOSINTI (1958), pp. 30-34.

329. T. Moriya, T. Sakaino, T. Saino, and K. Takizawa, J. Ceram. Assoc. Japan, 68(4): 772, 103-109 (1960).

330. Sh. Kuwayama, Japanese Patent 15320 (1962).

331. M. Karkhanavala and F. A. Hummel, J. Am. Ceram. Soc., 36(12): 393-397 (1953).

332. R. A. Hatch, Am. Mineralogist, 28: 471-496 (1943).

333. R. Roy, D. M. Roy, and E. F. Osborn, J. Am. Ceram. Soc., 33(5):152-159 (1950).

334. R. P. White and G. R. Rigby, Trans. Brit. Ceram. Soc., 53: 324-334 (1954).

335. A. I. Avgustinik and E. Ya. Vasil'ev, Zh. Prikl. Khim., 28(9): 939-943 (1955).

336. L. Cini, Sprechsaal Keramik-Glas-Email, 92: 312-314 (1959).

337. S. Urnes, Epitoanyäg, 14(8): 288-291 (1962).

338. V. N. Vertsner, N. E. Kind, E. M. Milyukov, and G. P. Tikhomirov, Dokl. Akad. Nauk SSSR, 154(3): 673-674 (1964).

339. N. E. Kind, in: The Glassy State, Vol. 1, Catalyzed Crystallization of Glass, Izd. Akad. Nauk SSSR, Moscow-Leningrad (1963), pp. 105-106. [English translation: The Structure of Glass, Vol. 3, Consultants Bureau, New York (1964), pp. 111-113.]

340. V. Blinov and R. Roy, Glass Ind., 43(9): 494 (1962).

341. I. I. Kitaigorodskii, L. S. Zevin, and M. V. Artamonova, in: The Glassy State, Vol. 1, Catalyzed Crystallization of Glass, Izd. Akad. Nauk SSSR, Moscow-Leningrad (1963), pp. 137-140. [English translation: The Structure of Glass, Vol. 3, Consultants Bureau, New York (1964), pp. 146-149.]

342. R. A. Eppler, J. Am. Ceram. Soc., 46(2): 97-101 (1963).

343. V. A. Kolesova, Opt.-Mekh. Promyshlennost', No. 1, pp. 9-12 (1964).

344. A. G. Siemens-Schuckert-Werke, British Patent 940706 (1963).
345. W. Hinz and L. Baiburt, Silikat Tech., 11(10): 455-459 (1960).
346. V. G. Chistoserdov, N. A. Shmeleva, and A. M. Serdyuk, in: The Glassy State, Vol. 1, Catalyzed Crystallization of Glass, Izd. Akad. Nauk SSSR, Moscow-Leningrad (1963), pp. 161-164. [English translation: The Structure of Glass, Vol. 3, Consultants Bureau, New York (1964), pp. 172-174.]
347. M. I. Kalinin and E. V. Podushko, ibid., pp. 164-166. [English translation: ibid., pp. 175-176.]
348. I. I. Kitaigorodskii, R. Ya. Kholakovskaya, and M. V. Artamonova, Dokl. Akad. Nauk SSSR, 155(2): 370-373 (1964).
349. Jenaer Glaswerk Schott Gen., French Patent 1250838 (1960).
350. Jenaer Glaswerk Schott Gen., French Patent 1267565 (1961).
351. W. Hinz and F. Wihsmann, Silikat Tech., 10(8): 408 (1959).
352. Compagnie Francaise Thomson-Houston, French Patent 1268125 (1961).
353. M. Tashiro, Japanese Patent 8313 (1961).
354. Corning Glass Works, British Patent 940403 (1963).
355. S. I. Sil'vestrovich and E. M. Rabinovich, Zh. Vses. Khim. Obshchestva im. D. I. Mendeleeva, 3(1): 57 (1958).
356. S. I. Sil'vestrovich and E. M. Rabinovich, Mosk. Khim.-Tekhnol. Inst., 37: 75-84 (1962).
357. N. J. Kreidl and R. A. Weidel, US Patent 3007804 (1964).
358. Corning Glass Works, French Patent 1171621 (1961).
359. H. Tanigawa and H. Tanaka, Japanese Patent 10172 (1962).
360. English Electric Co., Ltd., French Patent 1281746 (1961).
361. T. Moriya and Y. Idasegawa, Japanese Patent 18060 (1962).
362. H. Tanigawa and H. Tanaka, Osaka Kogyo Gijutsu Shikensho Kiho, 12(4): 358-364 (1961).
363. A. Herczog and S. D. Stookey, French Patent, 1272036 (1961).
364. Corning Glass Works, British Patent 905253 (1962).
365. M. Nagai and T. Moriya, Japanese Patent 3270 (1963).
366. I. D. Tykachinskii, F. G. Solinov, S. M Brekhovskikh, I. M. Buzhinskii, L. I. Demkina, G. V. Kataeva, E. M. Gorshkova, and V. V. Pyatnitskaya, Byul. Izobretenii, No. 21 (1959).
367. I. D. Tykachinskii et al., Steklo, Byul. Gos. NII Stekla, No. 5, p. 33 (1959).
368. Welwyn Electrical Laboratories, Ltd., French Patent 1148591 (1957).
369. Owens Illinois Glass Co., French Patent 1271391 (1960).
370. Y. Hasegawa and T. Moriya, Japanese Patent 3269 (1963).
371. K. Nagoaka, H. Tanaka, and M. Hara, Japanese Patent 924 (1963).
372. T. Moriya and M. Nagai, Japanese Patent 3272 (1963).
373. S. D. Stookey, West German Patent 1149866 (1959).
374. Corning Glass Works, British Patent 869315 (1961).
375. English Electric Co., Ltd., British Patent 924996 (1963).
376. K. Nagaoka and M. Hara, Osaka Kogyo Gijutsu Shikensho Kiho, 11(2): 115-121 (1960).
377. K. Nagaoka, H. Tanaka, and M. Hara, Japanese Patent 925 (1963).
378. K. Nagaoka, M. Hara, and H. Tanaka, Osaka Kogyo Gijutsu Shikensho Kiho, 13(2): 105-116 (1962).

379. K. Nagaoka, Japanese Patent 19480 (1961).
380. M. Tashiro, K. Takagi, and N. Wada, Japanese Patent 3912 (1963).
381. G. Partridge and W. McMillan, Glass Technol., 4(6) : 173-182 (1963).
382. Corning Glass Works, British Patent 863500 (1961).
383. Corning Glass Works, French Patent 1219093 (1959).
384. I. Bornemann, Nachrichtentechnik, No. 11, pp. 488-492 (1961).
385. F. W. Martin, Australian Patent 213411 (1961).
386. Corning Glass Works, British Patent 899901 (1962).
387. R. Yokota and S. Nakajama, Japanese Patent 6264 (1962).
388. P. P. Pirooz, US Patent 3088833 (1960).
389. P. P. Pirooz, US Patent 3088834 (1961).
390. P. P. Pirooz, US Patent 3088835 (1961).
391. C. L. Babcock, US Patent 3063198 (1962).
392. G. F. Berridge, British Patent 900912 (1962).
393. R. Bahr and E. Betzler, West German Patent 1082710 (1960).
394. W. Sack, West German Patent 1078294 (1960).
395. Glass Ind., 42(9) : 500-504, 536-540, 576-579; 42(10) : 599-601 (1961).
396. L. Harold and H. Putnam, Adhesives Age, 4(1) : 32-34 (1961).
397. C. F. Miller and R. W. Shepard, Vacuum, 11(2) : 58-63 (1961).
398. Corning Glass Works, British Patent 863891 (1961).
399. R. Bahr and E. Betzler, West German Patent 1031622 (1960).
400. Corning Glass Works, British Patent 851843 (1960).
401. W. Hinz and G. Solow, Silikat Tech., 3(8) : 272-277 (1962).
402. S. D. Stookey, US Patent 2933857 (1960).
403. Corning Glass Works, French Patent 1242292 (1960).
404. Corning Glass Works, British Patent 863776 (1961).
405. Corning Glass Works, French Patent 1272036 (1960).
406. R. C. Anderson and A. L. Friedberg, in: Symposium on Nucleation and Crystallization in Glasses and Melts, edited and published by the American Ceramic Society, Columbus, Ohio (1962), pp. 29-34.
407. Bh. V. Janakiramarao, US Patent 3031318 (1962).
408. Bh. V. Janakiramarao, French Patent 1302830 (1962).
409. S. N. Lungu and D. Popescu-Has, Epitöanyag, 1958, Mrcuis, 10, Evfolyam, 352 86-89.
410. D. Popescu-Has, Ind. Usoara (Bucharest), 7(3) : 103-107 (1960).
411. D. Popescu-Has and S. N. Lungu, French Patent 1159785 (1958).
412. Sklar Keram., No. 1, p. 31 (1958).
413. D. Popescu-Has and S. N. Lungu, British Patent 848447 (1960).
414. S. N. Lungu, D. Popescu-Has, N. Andreescu, and M. Martalogu, Culegere Articole Prima Consfatuire Tara Mater, Electroteh. Timisoara, Rumania (1960), pp. 143-150.
415. Mycalex Corporation of America, French Patent 1184685 (1959).
416. T. Moriya, T. Sakaino, H. Saino, and M. Endo, Yogyo Kyokai Shi, 68(2) : 78-79 (1960).
417. T. Moriya and T. Sakaino, Japanese Patent 14912 (1960).
418. F. P. H. Chen, J. Am. Ceram. Soc., 46(10) : 476-484 (1963).
419. H. D. Kivlighn, Australian Patent 240189 (1959).

420. Corning Glass Works, French Patent 1244101 (1960).

421. Corning Glass Works, British Patent 869328 (1961).

422. N. A. Toropov, in: The Glassy State, Vol. 1, Catalyzed Crystallization of Glass, Izd. Akad. Nauk SSSR, Moscow-Leningrad (1963), pp. 5-9. [English translation: The Structure of Glass, Vol. 3, Consultants Bureau, New York (1964), pp. 5-9.]

423. N. A. Toropov, Vestn. Akad. Nauk SSSR, No. 10, pp. 43-46 (1963).

424. V. N. Sharai, N. N. Ermolenko, and I. G. Lukinskaya, in: The Glassy State, Vol. 1, Catalyzed Crystallization of Glass, Izd. Akad. Nauk SSSR, Moscow-Leningrad (1963), pp. 169-172. [English translation: The Structure of Glass, Vol. 3, Consultants Bureau, New York (1964), pp. 180-182.]

425. V. S. Nikandrov, ibid., pp. 174-177. [English translation: ibid., pp. 188-191.]

426. L. A. Zhunina, V. Sharai, and E. Z. Novikova, Glass and Silicate Materials, Minsk (1962).

427. P. P. Budnikov, K. P. Azarov, and T. N. Keshishyan, Ukr. Khim. Zh., 29(11): 1215-1219 (1963).

428. B. Becker, West German Patent 971089 (1959).

429. E. Wolf, West German Patent 1065315 (1960).

430. J. Voldan, Advances in Glass Technology, Technical papers of the Sixth International Congress on Glass, Washington, D. C., July 8-14, 1962, Plenum Press, New York (1962), pp. 382-395.

431. I. I. Kitaigorodskii and K. T. Bondarev, Ekonomicheskaya Gazeta, 23 Oct. 1961.

432. I. I. Kitaigorodskii and K. T. Bondarev, Priroda, No. 9, pp. 111-114 (1962).

433. K. T. Bondarev, in: Symposium on the Problems of the Development of the Glass and Porcelain-Earthenware Industry, Akad. Nauk UkrSSR, Kiev (1962), pp. 47-54.

434. I. I. Kitaigorodskii, Stroit. Materialy, No. 5, pp. 1-2 (1963).

435. I. I. Kitaigorodskii, Zh. Vses. Khim. Obshchestva im. D. I. Mendeleeva, 8(2): 192-197 (1963).

436. I. I. Kitaigorodskii and M. D. Il'inichnina, in: The Glassy State, Vol. 1, Catalyzed Crystallization of Glass, Izd. Akad. Nauk SSSR, Moscow-Leningrad (1963), pp. 172-174. [English translation: The Structure of Glass, Vol. 3, Consultants Bureau, New York (1964), pp. 183-187.]

437. I. I. Kitaigorodskii, M. D. Beus, and M. V. Artamonova, Dokl. Akad. Nauk SSSR, 154(2): 427-429 (1964).

438. J. W. Morrisey, Australian Patent 239249 (1960).

439. J. W. Morrisey, French Patent 1264093 (1961).

440. Corning Glass Works, British Patent 874936 (1961).

441. I. I. Kitaigorodskii and P. I. Litvinov, Steklo. Inform. Byul. Vses. Nauchn.-Issled. Inst. Stekla, No. 1(110), pp. 3-10 (1961).

442. I. I. Kitaigorodskii, P. I. Litvinov, and A. I. Rymov, Steklo. Inform. Byul. Vses. Nauchn.-Issled. Inst. Stekla, No. 2(111), pp. 21-25 (1961).

443. I. I. Kitaigorodskii and P. I. Litvinov, Steklo. Inform. Byul. Vses. Nauchn.-Issled. Inst. Stekla, No. 3(112), pp. 1-5 (1961).

444. I. I. Kitaigorodskii, P. I. Litvinov, and N. M. Vaisfel'd, Steklo. Inform. Byul. Vses. Nauchn.-Issled. Inst. Stekla, No. 4(113), pp. 61-64 (1961).

445. I. I. Kitaigorodskii, P. I. Litvinov, and L. S. Zevin, Steklo. Inform. Byul. Vses. Nauchn.-Issled. Inst. Stekla, No. 1(114), pp. 1-5 (1962).

446. R. Hajami, T. Ogura, and H. Tanaka, Osaka Kogyo Gijutsu Shikensho Kiho, 11(4): 235-240, 241-245 (1960).

447. T. Moriya and M. Nakai, Japanese Patent 3271 (1963).

448. T. Moriya and T. Sakaino, Japanese Patent 15319 (1962).

449. T. Moriya and Y. Hasegawa, Japanese Patent 18061 (1962).

450. T. Moriya and Y. Hasegawa, Japanese Patent 18062 (1962).

451. T. Moriya and Y. Hasegawa, Japanese Patent 18063 (1962).

452. V. V. Vargin, in: The Glassy State, Vol. 1, Catalyzed Crystallization of Glass, Izd. Akad. Nauk SSSR, Moscow-Leningrad (1963), pp. 107-112. [English translation: The Structure of Glass, Vol. 3, Consultants Bureau, New York (1964), pp. 114-117.]

453. Westinghouse Electric Corp., British Patent 903706 (1962).

454. N. L. Baker, Missiles and Rockets, 4(2): 27-28, 30 (1958).

455. Chem. Week, 80(23): 64 (1957).

456. Ceram. Ind., Nov. 1957, p. 106.

457. C. Ch. Troebst, VDI Nachr., 12(2): 9 (1958).

458. Archit. Rec., 122(9): 266 (1957).

459. Automat. Ind., 117(15): 102 (1957).

460. Chem. Eng. News, 35(22): 24 (1957).

461. W. Sack, West German Patent 1082016 (1960).

462. R. O. Voss, US Patent 2960802 (1960).

463. R. O. Voss, Australian Patent 241955 (1960).

464. R. O. Voss, British Patent 896655 (1962).

465. C. B. King and S. D. Stookey, US Patent 2960801 (1960).

466. D. N. Brown and C. B. King, West German Patent 1096566 (1961).

467. Corning Glass Works, British Patent 858266 (1961).

468. D. N. Brown and C. B. King, US Patent 3113009 (1963).

469. Trans. Brit. Ceram. Soc., 63(4): 116A (1963).

470. Ceram. Age, 77(8): 28 (1961).

471. J. S. Olcott and S. D. Stookey, Australian Patent 237275 (1960).

472. J. S. Olcott and S. D. Stookey, US Patent 2998675 (1961).

473. J. S. Olcott and S. D. Stookey, French Patent 1260410 (1961).

474. Corning Glass Works, British Patent 885618 (1961).

475. Corning Glass Works, British Patent 885619 (1961).

476. S. D. Stookey, J. S. Olcott, H. M. Garfinkel, and D. L. Rothermel, Advances in Glass Technology, Technical papers of the Sixth International Congress on Glass, Washington, D. C., July 8-14, 1962, Plenum Press, New York (1962), pp. 397-411.

477. Sprechsaal Keramik-Glas-Email, 62(16): 447 (1962).

478. H. P. Hood and S. D. Stookey, US Patent 2779136 (1957).

479. Glass Ind., 43(10): 539-540 (1962).

480. M. Byer, Mater. Methods, 43(6): 134-137 (1956).

481. Engineering, 14: 41 (1959).

482. M. Batanabe and M. Fukase, Denki Tsushin Gakkai Dzassi, 43(9): 1022-1029 (1960).

483.   W. W. Shaver and S. D. Stookey, SAE J., 66(7): 29-30, 34-36 (1958).

484.   V. I. Shelyubskii and N. M. Vaisfel'd, Steklo i Keram., No. 5, pp. 23-24 (1960).

485.   S. D. Stookey, Glass Ind., 42(7): 381 (1961).

486.   S. D. Stookey, in: Symposium on Nucleation and Crystallization in Glasses
       and Melts, edited and published by the American Ceramic Society, Columbus,
       Ohio (1962), pp. 1-4.

487.   A. G. Alekseev and L. A. Fedorova, in: The Glassy State, Vol. 1, Catalyzed
       Crystallization of Glass, Izd. Akad. Nauk SSSR, Moscow-Leningrad (1963), pp.
       84-87. [English translation: The Structure of Glass, Vol. 3, Consultants
       Bureau, New York (1964), pp. 90-92.]

488.   J. P. Williams and G. B. Carrier, Glass Technol., 4(6): 183-190 (1963).

489.   A. I. Korelova, M. G. Degen, and O. S. Alekseeva, in: The Glassy State,
       Vol. 1, Catalyzed Crystallization of Glass, Izd. Akad. Nauk SSSR, Moscow-
       Leningrad (1963), pp. 66-68. [English translation: The Structure of Glass,
       Vol. 3, Consultants Bureau, New York (1964), pp. 65-68.]

490.   W. Klemm and H. Volkmann, Glastechn. Ber., 34(3): 152-159 (1961).

491.   S. M. Ohlberg and D. W. Strickler, Glass. Ind., 41(12): 681 (1960).

492.   S. D. Stookey, Res. Management, 1: 155 (1958).

493.   S. D. Stookey, Eng. Digest, 21(11): 85-86 (1960).

494.   H. Simpson, Glass Ind., 39(1): 17-26, 52-57 (1957).

495.   M. Fanderlik, Sklar Keram., 8(11): 334-335 (1958).

496.   Sprechsaal Keramik-Glas-Email, No. 24, p. 635 (1959); No.1, pp. 20-22 (1960).

497.   Sprechsaal Keramik-Glas-Email, No. 2, pp. 40-43 (1960) No. 5, p. 110 (1960).

498.   G. E. Rindone, Glass Ind., 41(12): 679 (1960).

499.   E. M. Rabinovich, Dokl. Akad. Nauk SSSR, 138(1):159-161 (1961).

500.   I. D. Tykachinskii and E. S. Sorkin, in: The Glassy State, Vol. 1, Catalyzed
       Crystallization of Glass, Izd. Akad. Nauk SSSR, Moscow-Leningrad (1963), pp.
       123-126. [English translation: The Structure of Glass, Vol. 3, Consultants
       Bureau, New York (1964), pp. 129-132.]

501.   E. S. Sorkin and N. M. Vaisfel'd, Dokl. Akad. Nauk SSSR, 151(3): 628-630
       (1963).

502.   W. Baum, Glastechn. Ber., 36(12): 468-481 (1963).

503.   G. Bayer, Tech. Rundschau, 51(7): 11-15 (1959).

504.   G. McLellan, SAE J., No. 6, p. 99 (1959).

505.   F. F. Fluss, Glass Instr. Techn., 2(12): 14-16 (1958).

506.   H. Tanaka and K. Nagasaka, Kinzoku (Metals), No. 30, pp. 12-16 (1960).

507.   D. S. Kessler, Cornell Eng., 27(1): 21-25 (1961).

508.   W. Espe, Werkstoffkunde der Hochvakuumtechnik, Vol. 2, Berlin (1960), pp.
       647-649.

509.   S. Hashi, J. Vacuum Soc. Japan, 4(9): 359-366 (1961).

510.   Mod. Machine, 54: 9-12 (1960).

511.   J. Lear, Glaswelt, No. 5, pp. 140-141 (1960).

512.   Die Umschau, No. 1, p. 19; No. 5, p. 153 (1960).

513.   Mater. Design Eng., 3(1): 14 (1960).

514.   D. Taylor, Petrol. Eng., 29(9): B-78, B-80, B-81 (1957).

515.   Suénosi, Érékuturonikusu, 4(4): 358-359 (1959).

516. Refractories J., 33:329-399 (1957).
517. Glas-Email-Keramo-Tech., No. 9, pp. 51-52 (1958).
518. Silicates Ind., No. 22, pp. 277-278 (1958).
519. P. Barta, Silikaty, No. 2, p. 296 (1958).
520. J. H. Stevels, Refractories J., 39(7):273 (1963).
521. Mech. Eng., No. 7, pp. 662-663 (1957).
522. M. Tashiro and N. Sakuchana, Kinzoku (Metals), 31(5):18-23 (1961).
523. M. Tashiro, Kagaku (Tokyo), 29(11):580-586 (1959).
524. Iron Age, 118(10):126-127 (1958).
525. Maschinenwelt und Elektrotechnik, No. 1, p. 34 (1960).
526. Angew. Chemie, Vol. 72(22) (1960).
527. W. D. Kingery (ed.), Ceramic Fabrication Processes, MIT Press, Cambridge, Massachusetts and John Wiley and Sons, New York (1958), p. 235.
528. E. A. Bush and F. A. Hummel, J. Am. Ceram. Soc., 42(8):388-391 (1959).
529. M. Watanabe, R. V. Caporali, and R. E. Mould, in: Symposium on Nucleation and Crystallization in Glasses and Melts, edited and published by the American Ceramic Society, Columbus, Ohio (1962), pp. 23-28.
530. S. Sakka, M. Wada, and M. Tashiro, Yogyo Kyokai Shi, 69(782):35-43 (1961).
531. K. T. Bondarev and V. A. Minakov, Opt.-Mekh. Promyshlennost', No. 9, pp. 26-30 (1962).
532. K. T. Bondarev and V. A. Minakov, in: The Glassy State, Vol. 3, Part 2, Mechanical Properties and Structure of Inorganic Glasses, Izd. Akad. Nauk SSSR, Moscow (1963), pp. 18-22.
533. V. G. Chistoserdov and I. A. Soboleva, Opt.-Mekh. Promyshlennost', No. 9, pp. 35-37 (1962).
534. A. R. Hippel, Science, 138(3537):91-114 (1962).
535. R. L. Thakur, Central Glass Ceram. Res. Inst. Bull. (India), 10(2):51-66, 1-2 (1963).
536. P. D. Ownly, D. E. Day, and R. E. Moore, Glass Ind., 44(7):353-379, 409 (1963).
537. Am. Ceram. Soc. Bull., 42(4):223-225, 227-229, 231 (1963).
538. I. I. Kitaigorodskii, T. N. Keshishyan, and A. I. Berezhnoi, Tr. Mosk. Khim.-Tekhnol. Inst., No. 21, pp. 39-44 (1956).
539. I. I. Kitaigorodskii, and A. I. Berezhnoi, Steklo i Keram., No. 6, pp. 7-12 (1956).
540. I. S. Kachan and Z. I. Shalimo, in: The Glassy State, Vol. 1, Catalyzed Crystallization of Glass, Izd. Akad. Nauk SSSR, Moscow-Leningrad (1963), pp. 182-184. [English translation: The Structure of Glass, Vol. 3, Consultants Bureau, New York (1964), pp. 198-199.]
541. P. Werner, Chem. Rundschau, 14(12):347-349 (1961).
542. T. Sauclifer, Ceram. Age, No. 2, pp. 15-16 (1959).
543. D. Johnston, Princeton Eng., 18(4):37-38 (1958).
544. Tsuken Geppo, 13(9):12-14 (1960).
545. F. A. West-Oram, Glastekn. Tidskr., 15(1):9-14, 21 (1960).
546. D. G. Holloway and P. A. P. Hastilow, Nature, 189(4762):385-386 (1961).
547. E. Umblia, Glastekn. Tidskr., 15(4):157-160 (1960).
548. A. Tosio, Yogyo Kyokai Shi, 68(776):291-297 (1960).
549. Tamura, Yogyo Kyokai Shi, 66(753):325-330 (1958).

550. J. Nowakowska, Szklo Ceram., 11(8): 230-231 (1960).
551. A. I. Berezhnoi, Izv. Vysshikh Uchebn. Zavedenii Khim. i Khim. Tekhnol., 2(1): 82-88 (1959).
552. W. Rosenberg, Machine Design, 31(17): 29-32 (1959).
553. M. Tashiro and S. Sakka, Yogyo Kyokai Shi, 68(6): 158 (1960).
554. L. Marchesini and A. Rapretti, Vetro Silicati, 5(28): 5-11 (1961).
555. A. I. Korelova, O. S. Alekseeva, and M. G. Degen, Opt.-Mekh. Promyshlennost', 29(9): 32-35 (1962).
556. A. I. Avgustinik and L. S. Klanina, Opt.-Mekh. Promyshlennost', 29(9): 30-31 (1962).
557. K. Nagaoka, M. Hara, and H. Tanaka, Osaka Kogyo Gijutsu Shikensho Kiho, No. 12, pp. 144-149; No. 2, pp. 15-161; No. 3, pp. 292-298 (1961).
558. V. G. Chistoserdov and V. I. Novgorodtseva, in: The Glassy State, Vol. 1, Catalyzed Crystallization of Glass, Izd. Akad. Nauk SSSR, Moscow-Leningrad (1963), pp. 145-148. [English translation: The Structure of Glass, Vol. 3, Consultants Bureau, New York (1964), pp. 154-156.]
559. W. Baum, Glastechn. Ber., 36(11): 444-453 (1963).
560. T. Sakaino, Kogyo Kazaku Zasshi, 63(7): 104-108 (1960).
561. P. P. Budnikov and A. M. Cherepadov, Zh. Prikl. Khim., No. 10, pp. 2093-2107 (1964).
562. O. Knapp, Epitöanyag, 12(9): 324-328 (1960).
563. S. Sakka and M. Tashiro, Yogyo Kyokai Shi, 69(783): 67-74 (1961).
564. S. Sakka and M. Tashiro, Yogyo Kyokai Shi, 69(784): 109-118 (1961).
565. B. Ziemba, Szklo Ceram., No. 12, p. 361 (1961).
566. B. Zemba, Investigation of Glasses and Glass-Ceramics in the Forsterite Region of the $MgO-Al_2O_3-SiO_2$ System, Dissertation, Mosk. Khim.-Tekhnol. Inst. im. D. I. Mendeleeva (1963).
567. B. Ziemba and E. Chlopicka, Szklo Ceram., 15(2): 36-38 (1964).
568. J. H. Munier, Prod. Eng., 29(11): 87-89 (1958).
569. Chem. Age, 78(1987): 214 (1957).
570. A. Weigandt and O. H. Olson, J. Am. Ceram. Soc., 44(12): 632 (1961).
571. Glass Technol., 1(1): 8-10 (1960).
572. H. Tanaka, Soda to enso, 12(11): 425-429 (1961).
573. B. V. J. Rao, Silikat Tech., 12(10): 434 (1961).
574. W. H. Barney, in: Fourth Conference on Electrical Insulation Materials and Applications, NEMA and AIEE, Washington (1962), pp. 82-85.
575. A. Ya. Kuznetsov, Zh. Fiz. Khim., 33(8): 1726-1729 (1959).
576. E. A. Antonova, Investigation of Electrical Properties of Glasses Containing Titanium Dioxide, Dissertation, Leningr. Teknol. Inst. im. Lensoveta, Leningrad (1955).
577. V. V. Bargin and E. A. Antonova, Tr. Leningr. Tekhnol. Inst. im. Lensoveta, No. 49, pp. 64-73 (1958)
578. O. V. Mazurin, Electrical Properties of Glass, Lengoskhimizdat, Leningrad (1962). [English translation: The Structure of Glass, Vol. 4, Consultants Bureau, New York (1965).]
579. O. V. Mazurin and V. A. Tsekhomskii, Tr. Leningr. Tekhnol. Inst. im Lensoveta, No. 59, pp. 36-39 (1961).

580. C. Hirajama and D. Berg, Phys. Chem. Glasses, 2(5): 145-151 (1961).

581. S. Sakka and M. Tashiro, Yogyo Kyokai Shi, 69(791): 393-400 (1961).

582. M. D. Mashkovich, Fiz. Tverd. Tela, 5(3): 843-850 (1963).

583. M. D. Mashkovich, Fiz. Tverd. Tela, 6(6): 1862-1865 (1964).

584. A. Herczog, J. Am. Ceram. Soc., 47(3): 107-115 (1964).

585. G. A. Pavlova and V. G. Chistoserdov, in: The Glassy State, Vol. 1,Catalyzed Crystallization of Glass, Izd. Akad. Nauk SSSR, Moscow-Leningrad (1963), pp. 184-190. [English translation: The Structure of Glass, Vol. 3, Consultants Bureau, New York (1964), pp. 200-204.]

586. L. Prod'homme, Verres Refractaires, No. 3 (1960).

587. G. A. Pavlova, M. M. Skornyakov, and V. G. Chistoserdov, in: The Glassy State, Vol. 1, Catalyzed Crystallization of Glass, Izd. Akad. Nauk SSSR, Moscow-Leningrad (1963), pp. 141-145. [English translation: The Structure of Glass, Vol. 3, Consultants Bureau, New York (1964), pp.150-153.]

588. N. M. Pavlushkin and A. I. Berezhnoi, Tr. Mosk. Khim.-Tekhnol. Inst. im. Mendeleeva, No. 18, pp. 175-178 (1954).

589. K. Takizawa, T. Sakaino, and T. Moriya, Bull. Tokyo Inst. Technol, No. 53, pp. 1-6 (1963).

590. K. Takizawa, T. Sakaino, and T. Moriya, Bull. Tokyo Inst. Technol, No. 53, pp. 7-37 (1963).

591. T. Moriya, T. Sakaino, and K. Takizawa, Bull. Tokyo Inst. Technol., No. 56, pp. 1-19 (1963).

592. F. A. Calkins and J. W. Morrisey, US Patent 3013362 (1961).

593. Corning Glass Works, French Patent 1283488 (1961).

594. Corning Glass Works, British Patent 905566 (1962).

595. S. D. Stookey, West German Patent 1090397 (1960).

596. V. A. Florinskaya, E. V. Podushko, I. N. Gonek, and E. F. Cherneva, in: The Glassy State, Vol. 1, Catalyzed Crystallization of Glass, Izd. Akad. Nauk SSSR, Moscow-Leningrad (1963), pp. 90-99. [English translation: The Structure of Glass, Vol. 3, Consultants Bureau, New York (1964), pp. 96-104.]

597. W. Baum, Glastechn. Ber., 36(2): 71 (1963).

598. Allgem. Glaserztg., No. 24, p. 444 (1961).

599. S. D. Stookey, Intern. Sci. Technol, No. 7, pp. 40-46 (1962).

600. F. S. Child, Glass Ind., 45(1): 13-16 (1964).

601. B. V. Rudoi, Znanie-sila, No. 1, pp. 54-55 (1964).

602. Am. Glass Rev., 80(6): 23 (1959).

603. Corning Glass Works, Glass and You, Corning, New York, 5, copyright 1947 (1953), p. 48.

604. Glass Ind., 35(12): 690 (1954).

605. H. E. Simpson, Glass Ind., 40(1): 12-20, 38, 40, 42 (1957).

606. R. Barta and J. Hlavac, Sklarstvi, Statni Nakladatelstvi Technicke Literatury, Prague (1963), pp. 164-169.

607. D. Davis, US Patent 3031597 (1962).

608. M. Watanabe and M. Hatakajama, J. Inst. Telev. Engrs. Japan, 17(5): 285-289 (1963).

609. Y. Yokoda, Electronics (Japan), 7(3): 317-321 (1962).

610. W. H. Jenkins, IEEE Trans. Components Parts, 10(1): 23-30 (1963).

611. R. E. Bowles, SAE J., 69(10) : 91-93 (1961).

612. G. T. Berezovets and I. V. Tatarko, Avtomatika i Telemekhanika, 24(3) : 414-424 (1963).

613. Avtomatika i Telemekhanika, 24(8) : 1155-1162 (1963).

614. Nat. Glass Budg., 78(6) : 17 (1962).

615. Metalwork Product, 107(7) : 69-70 (1963).

616. H. E. Simpson, Glass Ind., 45(2) : 3 (1964).

617. W. H. Armistead and S. D. Stookey, Belgian Patent 612171 (1962).

618. W. H. Armistead and S. D. Stookey, French Patent 1311557 (1962).

619. J. Phys. Chem., 66(12) (1962).

620. G. H. Brown and W. G. Shaw, Rev. Pure Appl. Chem., 11(1) (1961).

621. A. J. Cohen and H. L. Smith, Science, 137(3534) (1962).

622. New Scientist, 16(309) : 163 (1962).

623. W. H. Armistead and S. D. Stookey, Science, 144(3615) : 150-154 (1964).

624. Chem. Eng. News, 42(4) : T17 (1964).

625. Chem. Eng. News, 42(5) : T29 (1964).

626. Glass Ind., 45(2) : 88-89 (1964).

627. Electronics, 37(5) : 42-43 (1964).

628. Ceram. Ind., 82(3) : 32 (1964).

629. Missiles and Rockets, 3 June 1962, p. 23.

630. W. Hennig, Automatik, No. 6, pp. 1236-1239 (1961).

631. W. Hennig, Elektronik, 11(5) : 143-145 (1962).

632. W. Hennig, Sprechsaal Keramik-Glas-Email, No. 6, pp. 120-121 (1963).

633. M. Fanderlikch, Fotoplasticka skla Informativni prehled, No. 1, statni vyzkumny ustav, sklarsky v hradci Kralove (1963).

634. Nat. Glass Budg., 74(51) : 12 (1959).

635. Nat. Glass. Budg., 75(181) : 4 (1959).

636. G. J. Selvin, Proceedings, 1960 Electronic Components Conference, Washington, D.C., 10-12 May 1960, pp. 46-50.

637. H. E. Simpson, Glass Ind., 40(2) : 98, 100, 102 (1959).

638. Ceram. Age, 75(3) : 3-4, 42-48 (1960).

639. Electronics News, 5(192) : 4-6 (1960).

640. Electronics, 34 : 19, 20 (1961).

641. W. W. Shaver, Am. Glass Rev., 82(1) : 16-17, 47 (1961).

642. Electrotechn. Z., 13(7) : 173 (1961).

643. Ceram. Ind., 80(5) : 62-63 (1963).

644. Glass Ind., 44(11) : 642 (1963).

645. Ceram. Age, 80(2) : 56 (1964).

646. H. E. Simpson, Glass Ind., 43(3) : 131, 133 (1962).

647. Jet Propulsion, 27(6) : 690 (1957).

648. Iron Age, 179(23) : 58 (1957).

649. Glass Ind., 39(5) : 284 (1958).

650. Ceram. Age, 72(1) : 34 (1958).

651. D. Johnston, Princeton Eng., 18(4) : 37-38 (1958).

652. Glass Ind., 39(5) : 284 (1958).

653. N. Miller and W. Wheller, Ceram. Ind., 73(3) : 112-114, 132-138 (1959).

654. Ceram. Ind., No. 2, pp. 43-44 (1959).

655. Glass Ind., No. 6, pp. 309-312 (1959).

656. Glastekn. Tidskr., 14(5) : 126-127 (1959).

657. Ceram. Ind., No. 1, pp. 39-40 (1959).

658. Chem. Processing, 6(12) : 14-15 (1960).

659. Ceram. Ind., 71(2) : 5 (1959).

660. Am. Glass Rev., 79(13) : 42 (1959).

661. H. E. Simpson, Glass Ind., 44(3) : 133-138 (1963).

662. Am. Glass Rev., No. 8, p. 38 (1957).

663. P. Kleinteich, Glas-Instr.-Techn., 3(12) : 411-415 (1959).

664. Mater. Design Eng., 48(1) : 126-128 (1958).

665. Verres et Refractaires, 16(4) : 261 (1962).

666. P. Schleifer, Przegl. Elektron, 3(11) : 636-637, 639-640 (1962).

667. P. W. McMillan and B. P. Hodgson, Mater. Design Eng., 59(1) : 85-86 (1964).

668. M. Byer, US Patent 3040213 (1962).

669. Mater. Design Eng., 46(1) : 34-35, 142-143 (1957).

670. Machinery, 63(12) : 171 (1957).

671. Metals Rev., 30(12) (1957).

672. Mater. Design Eng., 3(11) : 705 (1960).

673. Steklo i Keram., No. 4, p. 45 (1960).

674. Am. Glass Rev., No. 12, p. 30 (1959).

675. Ceram. Ind., 72(5) : 82 (1959).

676. J. R. Little and D. H. Holl, Mater. Protection, 1(6) : 40-44 (1962).

677. Am. Glass Rev., 77(13) : 12, 29 (1958).

678. Am. Ceram. Soc. Bull., 37(5) : 245 (1958).

679. Am. Ceram. Soc. Bull., 37(1) : 75 (1958).

680. I. I. Kitaigorodskii and K. T. Bondarev, Ekonomicheskaya Gazeta, No. 12, p. 19 (23 Oct. 1961).

681. V. I. Vavilov, Ekonomicheskaya Gazeta, No. 19 (11 Dec. 1961).

682. Steklo i Keram., No. 5, pp. 1-2 (1963).

683. G. B. Blok, Znanie-sila, 38(1) : 4-5 (1963).

684. I. I. Kitaigorodskii, Izvestiya, No. 173 (14643), p. 3 (21 July 1964).

685. V. P. Belyaev, Pravda, No. 208 (16794) (26 July 1964).

686. I. I. Kitaigorodskii and T. L. Shirkevich, Steklo i Keram., No. 1, pp. 5-8 (1964).

687. Am. Ceram. Soc. Bull., 38(11) : 686 (1959).

688. Glas-Email-Keramo-Tech., No. 11, p. 450 (1959).

689. Am. Glass Rev., 80(3) : 10 (1959).

690. Sprechsaal Keramik-Glas-Email, 93 : 104 (1960).

691. Szklo i Ceram., 11(2) : 59 (1960).

692. Ceramics, 9 : 20-24 (1959).

693. Ceram. Ind., 72(4):114 (1959).

694. C. Green, New Scientist, 8(214) : 1708 (1960).

695. Ceramics, 13(163) : 25 (1962).

696. US Patent 1244146 (1960).

697.   Ceramics, 10(127): 20, 22, 24 (1959).

698.   Steel, 140: 22, 55 (1957).

699.   Electronic Ind. Teletech., 16: 5, 7 (1957).

700.   D. Preist and R. Talcott, Am. Ceram. Soc. Bull, 38(3): 99-105 (1959).

701.   Electronics, 36: 49, 71 (1963).

702.   Ceramics, 10(125): 12-13 (1959).

703.   Glass Ind., 39(11): 602 (1958).

704.   P. W. McMillan and B. P. Hodgson, Glass Technol., 5(4): 142-149 (1964).

705.   Iron Steel Eng., 34(6): 191 (1957).

706.   W. Tuszynski, B. Ziemba, and J. Jablokowski, Szklo i Ceram., 14(2): 45 (1963).

707.   B. Ziemba and E. Chlopicka, Szklo i Ceram., 15(2): 36-38 (1964).

708.   S. D. Stookey and R. D. Maurer, in: Progress in Ceramic Science (J. E. Burke, ed.), Pergamon Press, London-New York (1962), pp. 77-101.

709.   M. J. Jasumoto, Vacuum Soc. Japan, 7(3): 103-107 (1964).

710.   Ceramic News, 13: 9, 16 (1964).

711.   Am. Glass Rev., 85(3): 16 (1964).

712.   S. D. Stookey, US Patent 3157522 (1964).

713.   Bh. V. Janakiramrao, US Patent 3113877 (1963).

714.   Bh. V. Janakiramarao, Glass Technol., 5(2): 67-77 (1964).

715.   Ceramic News, 13(12): 7 (1964).

716.   P. W. McMillan and G. Partridge, British Patent 955653 (1964).

717.   P. W. McMillan and G. Partridge, British Patent 955701 (1964).

718.   S. G. Tresvyatskii, M. P. Parkhomenko, and A. D. Kondratenko, Izv. Akd. Nauk SSSR, Ser. Neorgan. Materialy, No. 4 (1963).

719.   M. P. Parkhomenko, Z. A. Yaremenko, and S. G. Tresvyatkii, Dopovidi Akad. Nauk UkrSSR, No. 5, 624-627 (1964).

720.   M. P. Parkhomenko, E. S. Lygovskaya, and S. G. Tresvyatkii, Dopovidi Akad. Nauk UkrSSR, No. 10, pp. 1359-1362 (1965).

721.   M. A. Parkhomenko, Investigations on the Preparation of Synthetic Micas and New Materials Based on Them. Dissertation, Inst. Probl. Materialoved. Akad. Nauk UkrSSR, Kiev (1965).

722.   P. G. Usov and G. N. Popova, in: Abstracts of Papers Presented at the Inter-University Scientific Technical Conference on Breakdown of Dielectrics and Semiconductors, Tomsk. Polytekh. Inst. im. Kirov, Tomsk (1963), p. 72.

723.   B. Ziemba and A. Chlopicka, Szklo i Ceram., No. 3, p. 69 (1965).

724.   G. B. Carrier, J. Am. Ceram. Soc., 47(8): 365-367 (1964).

725.   P. E. Doherty and R. R. Leombruno, J. Am. Ceram. Soc., 47(8): 368-370 (1964).

726.   B. Ziemba, Szklo i Ceram., No. 10, pp. 253-258 (1964).

727.   D. B. Binns, Sci. Ceram., Vol. 1, Academic Press, London-New York (1962), pp. 315-334.

728.   Ya. V. Marka, Nauka i Zhizn', No. 4, pp. 22-25 (1965).

729.   Plant Eng., 8(3): 150 (1964).

730.   Chem. Week, 94(7): 51-52 (1964).

731.   J. Herbert, Genie Chim., 90(5): 135-145 (1963).

732.   N. Lazar, Glaswelt, No. 5, pp. 130-133 (1963).

733.   J. Spitzner, Metallverarbeitung, No. 4, pp. 114-116 (1963).

734. W. Hinz and F. G. Wihsmann, Silikat Tech., 16(4):110-113 (1965).
735. V. N. Filipovich, in: Proceedings, Structural Transformations in Glasses at Elevated Temperatures, Izd. Nauka, Moscow-Leningrad (1965), pp. 30-43, 49-57.
736. W. Hinz and F. G. Wihsmann, Silikat. Tech., 16(4):110-113 (1965).
737. L. G. Baiburt and A. A. Gorbachev, Dokl. Akad. Nauk SSSR, 156(6):1420-1423 (1964).
738. A. G. Alekseev, V. V. Bargin, V. N. Vertsner, N. E. Kind, Yu. N. Kondrat'ev, E. V. Podushko, M. V. Serebryakova, G. P. Tikhomirov, N. A. Tudorovskaya, and V. A. Florinskaya, Catalyzed Controlled Crystallization of Glasses of the Lithium Aluminosilicate System, Part 1, Izd. Khimiya, Leningrad-Moscow (1964), p. 87.
739. M. Tashiro and M. Wada, in: Advances in Glass Technology, Part 2 (F. R. Matson and G. E. Rindone, eds.), Plenum Press, New York (1963), pp. 18-19.
740. N. M. Pavlushkin and S. A. Kamalyan, Tr. Mosk. Khim.-Tekhnol. Inst., No. 45, pp. 160-164 (1964).
741. M. Dobrzanski and W. Tuszynski, Szklo i Ceram., No. 10, pp. 259-260 (1964).
742. G. Slayter, US Patent 3151966 (1964).
743. Z. Karch, Szklo i Ceram., No. 3, pp. 78-80 (1965).
744. W. Kleber, Silikat Tech., 13(1):5-10 (1962).
745. W. Vogel, Silikat Tech., 16(5):152-158 (1965).
746. W. Vogel and K. Gerth, Z. Chemie, No. 2, pp. 261-274 (1962).
747. M. Goldstein, J. Am. Ceram. Soc., 48(3):126-130 (1965).
748. J. J. Hammel, in: Seventh International Congress on Glass, Brussels, 28 June to 3 July 1965, Commission International du Verre, (Gordon and Breach, eds.), New York (1965), p. 36.
749. W. Hinz, G. Solow, and G. Kranz, Silikat Tech., 16(7):210-215 (1965).
750. P. S. Hessinger and W. K. Haller, British Patent 973077 (1964).
751. P. W. McMillan, Glass-Ceramics, Academic Press, New York (1965).
752. B. Ziemba, Chimie Ind. (Paris), 94(2):133-136 (1965).
753. Mater. Design Eng., 61(5):156 (1965).
754. Ceramic Age, 81(5):53 (1965).
755. Am. Glass Rev., 83(11):8 (1963).
756. Mater. Design Eng., 61(5):144 (1965).
757. A. I. Berezhnoi and Yu. M. Polukhin, Neorgan. Materialy, Izv. Akad. Nauk SSSR, 3(6):986-992 (1967).
758. R. Kaiser, Z. Phys., 132:482 (1952).
759. M. Blau, Göttinger Nachr., Math., p. 401 (1933).
760. B. R. Gossik, J. Appl. Phys., 31:650 (1960).
761. W. Hampe, Z. Phys., 152:476 (1958).
762. L. I. Vidro, Yu. M. Khorol'skii, and L. A. Miroshenko, Steklo i Keram., No. 8, p. 22 (1960).
763. P. Ya. Bokin, A. I. Korelova, R. A. Govorova, O. S. Alekseeva, and G. A. Nikandrova, in: Structure of Glass, Izd. Akad. Nauk SSSR, Moscow-Leningrad (1965), pp. 126-134. [For English translation, see The Structure of Glass, Vol. 5, Consultants Bureau, New York (1965).]
764. M. Tashiro, Glass Ind., 47(8):428-435 (1966).

765.   V. V. Pollyak, I. D. Tykachinskii, and A. I. Berezhnoi, Handbook of Glass
        Production, Vol. 2, Gos. Izd. literatury po stroitel'stvu, arkhitekture i
        stroitel'nym materialam, Moscow (1963), p. 130.
766.   A. A. Appen, ibid., Vol. 1, pp. 18-19.
767.   J. F. Macdowell, British Patent 1005338 (1965).
768.   T. Moriya, T. Sakaino, and K. Takizawa, Kogyo Kagaku Zasshi, 66(5): 679-
        686, A-45 (1963).
769.   M. Tashiro, S. Sakka, and T. Yamamoto, Bull. Inst. Chem. Res. Kyoto Univ.,
        41(2-4): 197-206 (1963).
770.   K. N. Popov and V. S. Gorshkov, Sb. Trudov Vses. m.-i., In-ta Novykh
        Stroitel'nykh Materialov, No. 3(11), pp. 102-106 (1965).
771.   K. N. Popov and V. S. Gorshkov, Steklo i Keram., No. 10, pp. 22-26 (1965).
772.   A. S. Totesh, V. I. Aver'yanov, M. V. Strel'tsina, and G. P. Roskova, in:
        Structural Transformations in Glasses at High Temperatures, Izd. Akad. Nauk
        SSSR, Moscow-Leningrad (1965), pp. 177-178. [English translation: The
        Structure of Glass, Vol. 5, Consultants Bureau, New York (1965), pp. 150-159.]
773.   A. V. Goryainova, V. V. Degtyarev, and V. N. Maragaeva, Khim. i Neftyanoe
        Mashinostroenie, No. 8, pp. 26-29 (1965).

Index

A

Absorption spectra
dependence on particle size 103-116
differential 38
of photosensitive glasses 18-28, 35-49
98-110, 113
of transparent glass-ceramics 355
Activation energy
dielectric relaxation 337
diffusion 61
electrical conductivity 325-326
solution 344
Adhesion of plating 181, 184-190
Anisotropy effects on strength 293
Antimony oxide 131, 134, 138
Attenuator boards 382

B

Ball bearings, glass-ceramic 395-400
Barium titanate 220-222, 331
Basalt as a raw material 255
Batch constituents
for photosensitive glasses 138
purity of 227
raw materials 255-256
Beryllium oxide 202
Bibliography 413-436

C

Carbon
as a nucleation catalyst 214
black foaming agent 273
in copper containing slags 262
Cements, glass-ceramic 237, 385-389
Cercor 407
Cerium oxide
increasing solubility of Pd by 142

Cerium oxide (Continued)
photosensitive glasses using 11, 15, 30-
44, 128, 130, 136-140, 163
Cer-Vit 217, 287, 361
Chemical machining 6, 152-161
Chemically strengthened glass-ceramics
273-274
Chemical properties of glass-ceramics
260, 340-352, 402-404
degree of crystallinity and 340-341
kitchenware 344-345
microstructure and 343-345
Chemical stability 145, 400, 402-404
Chlorides, as specifying agents 130
Chromium oxide as nucleation catalyst 72,
254-256, 261-262
Clays as raw materials 256
Clustering 56-57, 60, 75, 90-91, 116-119
Coagulation 111-112
Coatings of glass-ceramics on metals 401-
402
Colloidal particles 10, 87, 94-124
in crystals 96, 107
of alkali in glass 117-119
Color
centers 42, 45-48
in glass-ceramics 262-266, 278
of photosensitive glasses 18, 28-31, 125-
127, 130-136, 143, 151
of transparent glass-ceramics 361
Construction panels 378, 404
Coordination number 80-82, 195-197
Copper
as a plating coating 191
as a poison for Ag, Au containing
glasses 130
in photosensitive glasses 13, 31-32, 125-
130

437

21817